# WRITING AND READING ACROSS THE CURRICULUM

## FIFTH EDITION

### LAURENCE BEHRENS
*University of California, Santa Barbara*

### LEONARD J. ROSEN
*The Expository Writing Program, Harvard University*

HarperCollins*CollegePublishers*

Other HarperCollins books by
Laurence Behrens and Leonard J. Rosen

*Writing Papers in College* (1986)
*Reading for College Writers* (1987)

——

*To Bonnie and Michael—*
*and to L.C.R., Jonathan, and Matthew*

——

*Acquisitions Editor:* Patricia Rossi
*Developmental Editor:* Randee Falk
*Project Coordination:* Nancy Benjamin
*Cover Design:* Sally Bindari, Designworks
*Production:* Willie Lane
*Compositor:* ComCom, Division of Haddon Craftsmen, Inc.
*Printer and Binder:* R. R. Donnelley & Sons Company
*Cover Printer:* The Lehigh Press, Inc.

*Writing and Reading Across the Curriculum*, Fifth Edition

**Library of Congress Cataloging-in-Publication Data**

Behrens, Laurence.
   Writing and reading across the curriculum / Laurence Behrens,
Leonard J. Rosen.—5th ed.
      p.   cm.
   Includes bibliographical references.
   ISBN 0-673-52272-5 (student edition)—ISBN 0-673-52273-3 (instructor's edition)
      1. College readers.   2. English language—Rhetoric.
3. Interdisciplinary approach in literature.   I. Rosen, Leonard J.
II. Title.
PE1417.B396 1994
808'.0427—dc20                                                     93-22929
                                                                          CIP

93  94  95  96  9  8  7  6  5  4  3  2  1

# BRIEF CONTENTS

# DETAILED CONTENTS

---

# 2

## THESIS, QUOTATIONS, INTRODUCTIONS, AND CONCLUSIONS    *36*

# 3

# CRITICAL READING AND CRITIQUE    65

# 4

# SYNTHESIS    86

5

## RESEARCH     *148*

---

PART II

# AN ANTHOLOGY OF READINGS     193

---

## 6

## ON BEING BLACK AND MIDDLE CLASS: A PRACTICE CHAPTER     195

*A black reporter explains how she "runs a gantlet between two worlds."*

*A speech by Muhammad Ali changes the way one black journalist thinks about himself, his work, and his relationship to whites.*

*An editor diagnoses five common attitudes that lead to "bicultural stress" in corporate America.*

*A journalist reports on a troubling development among black high school students: the academically talented are harassed for "acting white."*

---

### HISTORY

### 7

### THE CASE OF CHRISTOPHER COLUMBUS    235

PSYCHOLOGY

# 8

## OBEDIENCE TO AUTHORITY   *316*

POLITICAL SCIENCE

## 9

## AMERICA'S CRISIS OF CONFIDENCE

**FOLKLORE**

## 10

# FAIRY TALES: A CLOSER LOOK AT "CINDERELLA"
467

*A psychoanalytic reading of "Cinderella": "Every child believes at some period in his life . . . that because of his secret wishes, if not also his clandestine actions, he deserves to be degraded, banned from the presence of others, relegated to a netherworld of smut."*

*"Like the old conduct manuals for ladies, the moral of the tale warns against feminine excursions as well as ambition."*

*The well-known author of children's stories laments the "gutting" of older versions of "Cinderella" derived from oral tradition, which could legitimately instruct young children. Walt Disney's "heresy," by contrast, is coy and condescending.*

SOCIOLOGY AND MEDIA STUDIES

## 11

# GENDER STEREOTYPING AND THE MEDIA    *541*

*The renowned researchers on human sexuality trace patterns of gender role socialization from birth through adulthood.*

## BIOLOGY

# 12

## THE BRAVE NEW WORLD OF BIOTECHNOLOGY     *629*

*Tour the Central London Hatchery and Conditioning Centre, where human embryos are incubated and hatched, their intelligence and social class determined before "birth."*

*A professor of Public Health explains how genetic engineering works and reviews the current priorities of gene science.*

*Can we find an ethical approach to the new science that tampers with life's smallest components?*

*A skeptic raises some basic questions about how far (and whether) we should pursue human genetic engineering.*

*A biologist responds to Jeremy Rifkin.*

*A feminist charges that biotechnology represents "basically the same old patriarchal fears and dreams . . . the male insecurity before chaotic and unreliable Nature (so like women), the distrust of things that develop according to their own internal rhythms, the disdain for everything he has not personally manufactured. And it's the male envy of the female power to create life."*

*The celebrated opera singer explains her personal commitment to gene therapy: "We cannot let our fears destroy our hopes."*

**BUSINESS**

## 13

### BUSINESS ETHICS   *737*

# A NOTE TO THE INSTRUCTOR

*Writing and Reading Across the Curriculum,* Fifth Edition, is a combination rhetoric-reader designed to help bridge the gap between the composition course and courses in other disciplines. The rhetorical portion introduces key writing skills that will serve students well throughout their academic careers, whatever their majors. The readings are arranged in topical chapters focused on a variety of academic disciplines; individual selections represent the kinds of issues studied—and written about—in courses throughout the curriculum.

The close relationships among readings in a particular chapter allow students to view a given issue from a number of perspectives. For instance, in Chapter 7, students will read how a historian, a sixteenth-century missionary, a high school teacher, a Native American, and two fiction writers approach the subject of Christopher Columbus, and how these individuals present their particular assumptions and observations about the subject. In every chapter of the reader, students can practice the essential college-level skills introduced in the text:

- ◆ students will read and summarize articles;
- ◆ students will read articles critically and write critiques of them, identifying and discussing the authors' (and their own) assumptions;
- ◆ students will read several articles on a particular topic and synthesize them in both explanatory and argumentative essays.

## THE ORGANIZATION OF THIS BOOK

The fifth edition of *Writing and Reading Across the Curriculum* is divided into two parts. The first part introduces the skills of summary, critique, and synthesis. Students move step-by-step through the process of writing essays based on source material. The text explains and demonstrates how summaries, critiques, and syntheses can be generated from the kinds of readings students will encounter later in the book. The first part also offers a chapter on formulating thesis statements, quoting sources, and writing introductions and conclusions, as well as a new chapter on the research paper.

The second part of the text consists of eight chapters (leading off with a "practice chapter" on ethnic identity) on topics such as gender stereotypes in the media, biotechnology, and business ethics.

## A NOTE ON THE FIFTH EDITION

In preparing the current edition, as in preparing earlier editions, we have tried to retain the essential cross-curricular character of the text while providing ample new material to keep the book fresh and timely. Both Part I and Part II have been revised extensively.

Part I consists of five chapters, including a new chapter on conducting research and writing research papers. All of the readings in the chapters on summary, critique, and synthesis focus on the much-debated subject of bilingual education. Chapters 1 ("Summary and Paraphrase"), 3 ("Critical Reading and Critique"), and 4 ("Synthesis") have been rewritten and include new model student essays. Additionally, the chapter on summary includes new sections on summarizing figures, tables, and narratives. At the suggestion of several reviewers, we have moved the chapter dealing with thesis, introductions, and conclusions (Chapter 4 in the fourth edition) so that it now immediately follows the chapter on summary—thus allowing students to practice developing thesis statements, introductions, and conclusions as they work through the material on critique and synthesis. The material on "quoting sources" (Chapter 5 in the fourth edition) has been incorporated into the new Chapter 2 ("Thesis, Quotations, Introductions, and Conclusions"); and the material in the old Chapter 5 on "citing sources" has been incorporated into the new Chapter 5 on research papers.

To allow students to practice the skills they learn in the research chapter, we include, new to this edition, a set of Research Activities at the conclusion of every chapter in Part II, following the Synthesis Activities.

Also new to this edition is Chapter 6: "On Being Black and Middle Class: A Practice Chapter." This chapter—which serves as a kind of interchapter between Parts I and II—consists of six relatively short selections, followed by exercises with detailed guidance that allow students to practice the techniques of summary, critique, and synthesis that they have learned in Part I.

In the remainder of Part II, one chapter, "The Case of Christopher Columbus," is entirely new. Three chapters in the fourth edition have been reconceived, with a majority of new selections: "America's Crisis of Confidence" (formerly "Is America in Decline?"), "Gender Stereotyping and the Media" (formerly "Gender Identity: The Changing Rules of Dating and Marriage in American Life"), and "The Brave New World of Biotechnology" (formerly "The Brave New World of Genetic Engineering"). The remaining chapters that appeared in the fourth edition—"Obedience to Authority," "Fairy Tales: A Closer Look at Cinderella," and "Business Ethics"—also have been revised with new selections.

As in the fourth edition, we have included at least one work of imaginative literature in each chapter (except for the practice chapter) in Part II. And as before, we have increased the representation of women and non-Western writers.

While each chapter in Part II has been identified in the table of contents by a specific academic discipline, readers should note that selections in each chapter are drawn from across the curriculum and are not meant to represent only the named discipline. In this way, each chapter gives students experience reading and interpreting topic-related literature.

We encourage all users—students and teachers—of *Writing and Reading Across the Curriculum* to continue to send to the publisher their suggestions for improving the book and their evaluations of its effectiveness. In particular, we invite teachers to submit copies of especially successful student essays based on material in this text for possible inclusion in the Instructor's Edition for the next edition.

## ACKNOWLEDGMENTS

We would like to thank our colleagues whose evaluations and reviews helped us prepare this new edition of *Writing and Reading Across the Curriculum*. Specifically, we thank Nancy Westrich Baker, Southeast Missouri State University; Jo Ann Bomze, Beaver College; Keith Bromley, Front Range Community College; Anna Kirwan Carey, Clermont College; Robin Craig, University of California, Santa Barbara; Judith Salzinski Eastman, Orange Coast College; James W. Fulcher, Lincoln College; Krista May, Texas A & M University; Richard W. Moore, Delgado Community College; Meg Morgan, University of North Carolina, Charlotte; E. Suzanne Owens, Lorain County Community College; Donna Burns Phillips, Cleveland State University; Robert Romanelli, University of California, Santa Barbara; Robert L. Root, Jr., Central Michigan University; Albert C. Salzberg, Rhode Island College; Steven M. Strong, Massachusetts Institute of Technology; Chris Thaiss, George Mason University; Jacqueline Iossi Wheeler, Arizona State University; Thia Wolf, California State University, Chico; and Susan Wyche-Smith, Washington State University. Thanks to Peg Heffernan for explanations of statistical terminology. Thanks to the many students of our writing courses who field-tested much of the material here and let us know when we hadn't made things clear. Our special gratitude to Randee Falk, who solicited and painstakingly organized and analyzed reader response to the fourth edition and to the draft manuscript of this edition, and who provided us with enormously valuable guidance in the preparation of the final draft. Thanks to Nancy Benjamin, who ably coordinated the book's production. Finally, our heartfelt thanks for the counsel and support of our Director of Development, Betty Slack, and our English editor, Patricia Rossi.

Laurence Behrens
Leonard J. Rosen

# A NOTE TO THE STUDENT

Your psychology professor assigns you to write a critical report on a recently published book on human motivation. You are expected to consult additional sources, such as book reviews and related material on the subject.

Your professor is making a number of assumptions about your capabilities. Among them:

- ◆ that you can read and comprehend college-level material
- ◆ that you can synthesize separate pieces of related material
- ◆ that you can intelligently respond to such material

In fact, these same assumptions underlie practically all college writing assignments. Your professors will expect you to demonstrate that you can read and understand not only textbooks but also critical articles and books, primary sources, and other material related to a subject of study. For instance: In researching a paper on the Great Depression, you might read the historical survey you find in your history text, a speech by President Roosevelt reprinted in the *New York Times,* and a firsthand account of the people's suffering by someone who toured the country during the 1930s and witnessed harrowing scenes of poverty and despair. In a political science paper, you might discuss the concept of "executive privilege" in light of James Madison's Federalist Paper No. 51 on the proposed constitutional provision for division of powers among the three branches of government. In a sociology paper, you might undertake a critical analysis of your assigned text, which happens to be Marxist.

The subjects are different, of course, but the skills you need to work with them are the same. You must be able to read and comprehend. You must be able to perceive the relationships among several pieces of source material. And you must be able to apply your own critical judgments to these various materials.

*Writing and Reading Across the Curriculum* provides you with the opportunity to practice the three essential college-level skills we have just outlined and the forms of writing associated with them, namely:

- ◆ the *summary*
- ◆ the *critique*
- ◆ the *synthesis*

Each chapter of Part II of this text represents a subject from a particular area of the academic curriculum: history, psychology, political science, folklore, sociology and media studies, biology, and business. These chapters, dealing with such topics as "Obedience to Authority," "Gender Stereotyping and the Media," and "The Brave New World of Biotechnology," include the types of selections you will be asked to read in other courses.

Various sets of questions following the readings will allow you to practice typical college writing assignments. Review Questions help you recall key points of content in factual essays. Discussion and Writing Suggestions ask you for personal, sometimes imaginative responses to the readings. Synthesis Activities at the end of each chapter allow you to practice assignments of the type that are covered in detail in the first four chapters of this book. For instance, you may be asked to *describe* the Milgram experiment, and the reactions to it, or to *compare* and *contrast* a controlled experiment to a real-life (or fictional) situation. Finally, Research Activities ask you to go beyond the readings in this text in order to conduct your own independent research on these subjects.

Our selection of passages includes articles written by economists, sociologists, psychologists, lawyers, folklorists, diplomats, historians, and specialists from other fields. Our aim is that you become familiar with the various subjects and styles of academic writing and that you come to appreciate the interrelatedness of knowledge. Sociologists, historians, and novelists have different ways of contributing to our understanding of gender identity. Fairy tales can be studied by literary critics, folklorists, psychologists, and feminists. Don't assume that the novel you read in your literature course has nothing to do with an assigned article from your economics course. Human activity and human behavior are classified into separate subjects only for convenience.

We hope, therefore, that your writing course will serve as a kind of bridge to your other courses, and that as a result of this work you can become more skillful at perceiving relationships among diverse topics. Because it involves such critical and widely applicable skills, your writing course may well turn out to be one of the most valuable—and one of the most interesting—of your academic career.

Laurence Behrens
Leonard J. Rosen

# How to Write Summaries, Critiques, and Syntheses

# 1

# SUMMARY AND PARAPHRASE

## WHAT IS A SUMMARY?

The best way to demonstrate that you understand the information and the ideas in any piece of writing is to compose an accurate and clearly written summary of that piece. By a *summary* we mean a *brief restatement, in your own words, of the content of a passage* (a group of paragraphs, a chapter, an article, a book). This restatement should focus on the *central idea* of the passage. The briefest of all summaries (one or two sentences) will do no more than this. A longer, more complete summary will indicate, in condensed form, the main points in the passage that support or explain the central idea. It will reflect the order in which these points are presented and the emphasis given to them. It may even include some important examples from the passage. But it will not include minor details. It will not repeat points simply for the purpose of emphasis. And it will not contain any of your own opinions or conclusions. A good summary, therefore, has three central qualities: *brevity, completeness,* and *objectivity.*

## CAN A SUMMARY BE OBJECTIVE?

Of course, this last quality of objectivity might be difficult to achieve in a summary. By definition, writing a summary requires you to select some aspects of the original and to leave out others. Since deciding what to select and what to leave out calls for your own personal judgment, your summary is really a work of interpretation. And certainly your interpretation of a passage may differ from another person's. One factor affecting the nature and quality of your interpretation is your *prior knowledge* of the subject. If you're attempting to summarize an anthropological article, and you're a novice in the field, then your summary of the article might be quite different from that of your professor, who has spent twenty years studying this particular area and whose judgment about what is more significant and what is less significant is undoubtedly more reliable than your own. By the same token, your personal or professional *frame of reference* may also affect your interpretation. A union representative and a management representative attempting to summarize the latest management offer would probably come up with two very different accounts. Still, we believe that in most cases it's possible to produce a reasonably objective summary of a passage if you make a conscious, good-faith effort to be unbiased and not to allow your own feelings on the subject to distort your account of the text.

## USING THE SUMMARY

In some quarters, the summary has a bad reputation—and with reason. Summaries are often provided by writers as substitutes for analyses. As students, many of us have summarized books that we were supposed to *review* critically. All the same, the summary does have a place in respectable college work. First, writing a summary is an excellent way to understand what you read. This in itself is an important goal of academic study. If you don't understand your source material, chances are you won't be able to refer to it usefully in an essay or research paper. Summaries help you to understand what you read because they force you to put the text into your own words. Practice with writing summaries also develops your general writing habits, since a good summary, like any other piece of good writing, is clear, coherent, and accurate.

Second, summaries are useful to your readers. Let's say you're writing a paper about the McCarthy era in America, and in part of that paper you want to discuss Arthur Miller's *Crucible* as a dramatic treatment of the subject. A summary of the plot would be helpful to a reader who hasn't seen or read—or who doesn't remember—the play. (Of course, if the reader is your American literature professor, you can safely omit the plot summary.) Or perhaps you're writing a paper about nuclear arms control agreements. If your reader isn't familiar with the provisions of SALT I or SALT II, it would be a good idea to summarize these provisions at some early point in the paper. In many cases (a test, for instance), you can use a summary to demonstrate your knowledge of what your professor already knows; when writing a paper, you can use a summary to inform your professor about some relatively unfamiliar source.

Third, summaries are frequently required in college-level writing. For example, on a psychology midterm, you may be asked to explain Carl Jung's theory of the collective unconscious and to show how it differs from Freud's theory of the personal unconscious. The first part of this question requires you to *summarize* Jung's theory. You may have read about this theory in your textbook or in a supplementary article, or your instructor may have outlined it in his or her lecture. You can best demonstrate your understanding of Jung's theory by summarizing it. Then you'll proceed to contrast it with Freud's theory—which, of course, you must also summarize.

It may seem to you that being able to tell (or to retell) exactly what a passage says is a skill that ought to be taken for granted in anyone who can read at high school level. Unfortunately, this is not so: For all kinds of reasons, people don't always read carefully. In fact, it's probably safe to say that they usually don't. Either they read so inattentively that they skip over words, phrases, or even whole sentences or, if they do see the words in front of them, they see them without registering their significance.

When a reader fails to pick up the meaning and the implications of a sentence or two, there's usually no real harm done. (An exception: You could lose credit on an exam or paper because you failed to read or to realize the significance of a crucial direction by your instructor.) But over longer stretches—the paragraph, the section, the article, or the chapter—inattentive or haphazard reading creates problems, for you must try to perceive the shape of the argument, to grasp the central idea, to determine the main points that compose it, to relate the parts of the whole, and to note key examples. This kind of reading takes a lot more energy and determination than casual reading. But, in the long run, it's an energy-saving method because it enables you to retain the content of the material and to use that content as a basis for your own responses. In other words, it allows you to develop an accurate and coherent written discussion that goes beyond summary.

## HOW TO WRITE SUMMARIES

Every article you read will present a different challenge as you work to summarize it. As you'll discover, saying in a few words what has taken someone else a great many can be difficult. But like any other skill, the ability to summarize improves with practice. Here are a few pointers to get you started. These pointers are not meant to be ironclad rules; rather, they are designed to encourage habits of thinking that will allow you to vary your technique as the situation demands.

♦ *Read* the passage carefully. Determine its structure. Identify the author's purpose in writing. (This will help you distinguish between more important and less important information.)

♦ *Reread.* This time divide the passage into sections or stages of thought. The author's use of paragraphing will often be a useful guide. *Label*, on the passage itself, each section or stage of thought. *Underline* key ideas and terms.

♦ *Write one-sentence summaries*, on a separate sheet of paper, of each stage of thought.

♦ *Write a thesis: a one-sentence summary of the entire passage.* The thesis should express the central idea of the passage, as you have determined it from the preceding steps. You may find it useful to keep in mind the information contained in the lead sentence or paragraph of most newspaper stories—the *what, who, why, where, when,* and *how* of the matter. For persuasive passages, summarize in a sentence the author's conclusion. For descriptive passages, indicate the subject of the description and its key feature(s). *Note:* In some cases, a *suitable thesis may already be in the original passage.* If so, you may want to quote it directly in your summary.

♦ *Write the first draft of your summary* by (1) combining the thesis with your list of one-sentence summaries or (2) combining the thesis with one-sentence summaries *plus* significant details from the passage. In either case, eliminate repetition and less important information. Disregard minor details or generalize them (e.g., Reagan and Bush might be generalized as "recent presidents"). Use as few words as possible to convey the main ideas.

♦ *Check your summary against the original passage* and make whatever adjustments are necessary for accuracy and completeness.

♦ *Revise your summary,* inserting transitional words and phrases where necessary to ensure coherence. Check for style. *Avoid a series of short, choppy sentences.* Combine sentences for a smooth, logical flow of ideas. Check for grammatical correctness, punctuation, and spelling.

## DEMONSTRATION: SUMMARY

To demonstrate these pointers at work, let's go through the process of summarizing a passage of expository material. Read the following passage carefully.

# Bilingual Education: A War of Words

## RICHARD BERNSTEIN

In a well-worn classroom at the San Fernando Elementary School, 30    1
miles north of Los Angeles, Aracelis Tester, a second-grade teacher, is
reading "Cuidado, un Dinosaurio!"—"Watch Out, a Dinosaur!"—with
her diminutive pupils. This could just as well be Mexico City or San
Salvador, Grenada or Seville: a roomful of Hispanic children and a
Hispanic teacher speaking Spanish.

In downtown Los Angeles, at a school called the Wilton Place    2
Elementary, Chan Hee Hong, a first-grade teacher, is talking in Korean
with the children of recent immigrants about the wonderful world of
frogs. There are public schools in Oklahoma where Cherokee is the
language of instruction. In Astoria, Queens, Greek is taught in Public
School 122; Haitian Creole is a language of instruction in some 20 public
schools in Brooklyn and Queens; New York, in addition, offers schooling in Chinese, Korean, French, Italian, Russian, Vietnamese and Khmer.

In the San Fernando Elementary School, the teaching of non-Eng-    3
lish-speaking children in their native language enjoys a virtually religious status: it is seen as a kind of panacea for the generally poor
performance of Hispanic children in public schools. But at the Glenwood
Elementary School in the San Fernando Valley, a neighborhood of
neatly kept stucco homes festooned with bougainvillea, bilingual education is anathema. The Glenwood teachers often conduct classes in
Spanish, since they are given no choice by the Los Angeles School
District. The school, a political model for some, is notorious for others.
Hispanic demonstrators shouting "racist" and carrying signs printed
"KKK" have picketed outside the school, where teachers have been
outspoken in their view that teaching children in Spanish is a fraud, a
trick played by tendentious adult theoreticians on innocent children.
They say that bilingual education is a failure, a tactic that in the end will
harm the chances of generally poor, non-English-speaking children ever
having an equal share in the promise of American life.

The San Fernando school and the Glenwood school represent the    4
two poles of a debate, already 20 years old, that has lately become more
acrimonious than ever. This is a nation that has successfully absorbed
millions of immigrants without creating a huge bureaucracy or spending

tens of millions of dollars to teach them in the languages of their ancestors. But in the last few years, teaching children "Watch Out, a Dinosaur!" in Spanish and talking to them about frogs in Korean has become a matter of deep importance to an ever-growing minority.

Part of the reason for this is that in America today more people speak foreign languages than ever before. Neighborhoods like those in the San Fernando Valley, whose residents were largely white and English-speaking 10 to 20 years ago, today have a Hispanic population of at least 90 percent. In Los Angeles, school-district officials say that there are, besides Spanish and English, seven other major languages being spoken in their district—Korean, Cantonese, Armenian, Vietnamese, Filipino, Farsi and Cambodian.

Why aren't these students being taught only in the language of their newly adopted land? One reason is that organized minority groups are demanding they be educated in their native language, and they have won allies within the local education establishments of quite a few cities. For many of these minorities, the subject evokes deep emotions. Advocates of bilingual education believe that it represents the best chance for non-English-speaking children—who, not so coincidentally, often come from the lower-income groups—to enjoy the richness and opportunities of American life. "We have found a way to achieve educational parity and, by the way, to have people who are competent in two languages," said Raul Yzaguirre, the director of the National Council of La Raza in Washington, an umbrella group of several hundred Hispanic organizations. . . .

The forces in favor of bilingual education . . . gained an ally in the [Bush] White House,[1] [but] there are still plenty of people on the other side of the issue, people who are convinced that teaching children in their native languages is bad, both for them and the country. Bilingual education, they argue, is more likely to prepare minority children for careers in the local Taco Bell than for medical school or nuclear physics. "It doesn't work," said Sally Peterson, a teacher at the Glenwood School and the founder of Learning English Advocates Drive, or LEAD, a group of teachers and citizens that has quickly gathered adherents across the country. "It seemed to make a lot of sense and I bought it at the beginning, but after a year or so I saw that children were languishing in the program."

The other, more subterranean part of the argument is political. Ethnic pride is involved here on one side, a sense that what is sometimes called "white, Anglo" education is demeaning, psychologically harmful to minority groups. On the other side, there is a deep-seated worry that

_____
[1]The reference is to Rita Equivel, a proponent of bilingual education who headed federal programs in the Department of Education during the Bush administration.

more is involved than an educational program to help minority students. The country is becoming far more ethnically diverse. Immigration is no longer the European affair it was during the first half of this century. Hundreds of thousands of people each year come from the Caribbean Islands, from the Middle East and from a dozen countries in Asia. In other words, just at a time when a more powerful glue is needed to hold the various parts of the society together, some critics see an ethnic and cultural assertiveness pushing it apart.

Bilingual education is only one element in this picture, its opponents    9
believe, a reflection of intensifying demands within the schools for courses that represent the interests of particular ethnic constituencies. It's no longer enough for children to learn who George Washington was. They have to learn to feel good about their own heritage. The much-discussed "Curriculum of Inclusion," produced by a special minority task force in New York State last year, argued that "African-Americans, Asian-Americans, Puerto Ricans/Latinos and Native Americans have all been the victims of an intellectual and educational oppression that has characterized the culture and institutions of the United States and the European-American world for centuries."

The solution, the task force concluded, was a new curriculum that,    10
by concentrating on contributions by members of minority groups to the culture, would insure that minority children "have higher self-esteem and self-respect, while children from European cultures will have a less arrogant perspective of being part of the group that has 'done it all.'"

What's at stake, then, is nothing less than the cultural identity of the    11
country. Those who argue that bilingual education is a right make up a kind of informal coalition with those who are pressing for changes in the way the United States is perceived—no longer as a primarily European entity to which all others have to adapt, but as a diverse collection of ethnic groups, each of which deserves more or less equal status and respect.

"Rather than see the United States as a melting pot, we like to think    12
of it as a salad bowl, with equal recognition of everyone, and I think bilingual education is part of that," said Suzanne Ramos, a lawyer for the Mexican-American Legal Defense and Educational Fund, a group that has sued local school boards to force them to adopt native-language instruction for Hispanic youngsters. The fund's goal, she said, is to have Spanish-language instruction in conjunction with the teaching of English for Hispanic students through the 12th grade—in the fund's view, the best means of insuring that Hispanic culture is nurtured as part of the basic public-school routine.

"The disagreement is whether a child has a right to have his native    13
language developed—not just maintained but developed," said James J. Lyons, the executive director of the National Association for Bilingual

Education, a professional organization that drafted much of the Federal legislation on bilingual programs. "There is a racist xenophobia about Spanish in particular."

Those on the other side insist that diversity is all well and good; but 14 they argue that bilingual education could lead to an erosion of the national unity, a fragmentation of the nation into mutually hostile groups. Leading the fight is a group called U.S. English, whose major objectives are to promote opportunities for people to learn English and to get a constitutional amendment adopted that would make English the official language of Government. Founded by former Senator S. I. Hayakawa and including such eminent figures as Saul Bellow, Barry Goldwater and Eugene McCarthy on its board of advisers, U.S. English has seen its membership swell to 400,000 in just seven years of existence. "Language is so much a part of our lives that it can be a great tool either for unity or disunity," said Kathryn S. Bricker, the group's former executive director. "And we are getting close to the point where we have a challenge to the common language that we share. Just look at what's going on in Miami, where a candidate to be school superintendent wanted everybody to have to learn Spanish.

"We are basically at a crossroads," she added. "We can reaffirm our 15 need for a common language or we can slowly go down the road of division along language lines." . . .

In his autobiography, "A Margin of Hope," the critic Irving Howe, 16 speaking about the "ethnic" generation of the 1920's and 1930's, recalls his hunger for school as a child of Jewish immigrants growing up in the Bronx; for Howe, mastering the English language was a badge of Americanness. "The educational institutions of the city were still under the sway of a unified culture, that dominant 'Americanism' which some ethnic subcultures may have challenged a little, but which prudence and ambition persuaded them to submit to," he writes.

The question now is: What is the "dominant Americanism"? Can 17 there even be such a thing in a country committed to a kind of ethnic self-realization that did not exist when Howe was growing up? The answers will be hammered out in the years ahead in classrooms like Aracelis Tester's and Sally Peterson's, and they have to do with more than pedagogical philosophy. In the end, the way language is taught in this country will reflect where the country is going, its very identity.

## Reread, Underline, Divide into Stages of Thought

Let's consider our recommended steps for writing a summary.

As you reread the passage, consider its significance as a whole. What does it say? How is it organized? How does each part of the passage fit into the whole?

Many of the selections you read for your courses will have their main sections identified for you by subheadings. When a passage has no subheadings, as is the case with "Bilingual Education: A War of Words," you must read carefully enough that you can identify the author's main stages of thought.

How do you determine where one stage of thought ends and the next one begins? Assuming that what you have read is coherent and unified, this should not be difficult. (When a selection is unified, all of its parts pertain to the main subject; when a selection is coherent, the parts follow one another in logical order.) Look, particularly, for transitional sentences at the beginning of paragraphs. Such sentences generally work in one or both of the following ways: (1) they summarize what has come before; (2) they set the stage for what is to follow.

For example, look at the sentence that opens paragraph 4: "The San Fernando school and the Glenwood school represent the two poles of a debate, already 20 years old, that has lately become more acrimonious than ever." Notice how the first part of this sentence asks the reader to recall information from the previous three paragraphs. Holding in mind the two opposing views just presented, the reader is then cast forward into the coming paragraph with its discussion about the national debate on bilingual education. For a different (although common) transition, see paragraph 6, which begins with a question: "Why aren't these students being taught only in the language of their newly adopted land?" This question first requires the reader to recall the previous paragraph. Then the question helps the reader to anticipate what will immediately follow: an accounting of why bilingual education has gained support around the country.

Each section of an article will take several paragraphs to develop. Usually between paragraphs, and almost certainly between sections of an article, you will find transitions to help you understand. For articles that have no subheadings, try writing your own section headings in the margins as you take notes. Then proceed with your summary.

For review, the sections of Bernstein's article are as follows:

*Section 1:* Introduction—the national debate on how non-English-speaking students should be taught (paragraphs 1–5).

*Section 2:* Debate on the merits of bilingual education (paragraphs 6–7).

*Section 3:* Debate on the larger political and cultural issues related to bilingual education (paragraphs 8–10).

*Section 4:* Significance of the overall debate—key issue of how America will perceive itself (paragraphs 11–17).

Here is how the first of these sections might look after you had marked the main ideas, by underlining and by marginal notation:

> In a well-worn classroom at the San Fernando    1
> Elementary School, 30 miles north of Los An-

*Teachers teach-
ing in native
language*

geles, Aracelis Tester, a second-grade teacher, is reading "Cuidado, un Dinosaurio!"—
"Watch Out, a Dinosaur!"—with her diminutive pupils. This could just as well be Mexico
City or San Salvador, Grenada or Seville: a
roomful of Hispanic children and a Hispanic
teacher speaking Spanish.

In downtown Los Angeles, at a school    2
called the Wilton Place Elementary, Chan Hee
Hong, a first-grade teacher, is talking in Korean
with the children of recent immigrants about
the wonderful world of frogs. There are public
schools in Oklahoma where Cherokee is the
language of instruction. In Astoria, Queens,
Greek is taught in Public School 122; Haitian
Creole is a language of instruction in some 20
public schools in Brooklyn and Queens; New
York, in addition, offers schooling in Chinese,
Korean, French, Italian, Russian, Vietnamese
and Khmer.

*Key example of
debate in
S. California*

In the San Fernando Elementary School,    3
the teaching of non-English-speaking children
in their native language enjoys a virtually religious status; it is seen as a kind of panacea for
the generally poor performance of Hispanic
children in public schools. But at the Glenwood
Elementary School in the San Fernando Valley,
a neighborhood of neatly kept stucco homes
festooned with bougainvillea, bilingual education is anathema. The Glenwood teachers often
conduct classes in Spanish, since they are given
no choice by the Los Angeles School District.
The school, a political model for some, is notorious for others. Hispanic demonstrators shouting "racist" and carrying signs printed "KKK"
have picketed outside the school, where teachers have been outspoken in their view that
teaching children in Spanish is a fraud, a trick
played by tendentious adult theoreticians
on innocent children. They say that bilingual
education is a failure, a tactic that in the
end will harm the chances of generally poor,
non-English-speaking children ever having an
equal share in the promise of American life.

*Debate is 20 yrs. old & heated*

*Debate: important to growing minority*

*More than ever, America is multilingual*

The San Fernando school and the Glenwood school represent the two poles of a <u>debate,</u> already 20 years old, that has lately become more <u>acrimonious</u> than ever. This is a nation that has successfully absorbed millions of immigrants without creating a huge bureaucracy or spending tens of millions of dollars to teach them in the languages of their ancestors. But in the last few years, teaching children "Watch Out, a Dinosaur!" in Spanish and talking to them about frogs in Korean has become a matter of deep importance to an ever-growing minority.

Part of the reason for this is that in America today <u>more people speak foreign languages than ever before.</u> Neighborhoods like those in the San Fernando Valley, whose residents were largely white and English-speaking 10 to 20 years ago, today have a Hispanic population of at least 90 percent. In Los Angeles, school-district officials say that there are, besides Spanish and English, seven other major languages being spoken in their district—Korean, Cantonese, Armenian, Vietnamese, Filipino, Farsi and Cambodian.

4

5

## Write a One-Sentence Summary of Each Stage of Thought

The purpose of this step is to wean you from the language of the original passage, so that you are not tied to it when writing the summary. Student Brian Smith has written one-sentence summaries for each of these sections as follows:

*Section 1:*   Introduction—the national debate on how non-English-speaking students should be taught.

Over the past twenty years, there has been a bitter debate over the merits of bilingual education.

*Section 2:*   Debate on the merits of bilingual education.

Proponents and opponents of bilingual education strongly disagree over how much benefit students receive from such programs.

13

*Section 3:* Debate on the larger political and cultural issues related to bilingual education.

Underlying the educational arguments are powerful political arguments arising from the increasing diversity of America.

*Section 4:* Significance of the overall debate—key issue of how America will perceive itself.

The debate over bilingual education is a debate over the cultural identity of America.

## Write a Thesis: A One- or Two-Sentence Summary of the Entire Passage

The thesis is the most general statement of a summary (or any other type of academic writing—see Chapter 2). It is the statement that announces the paper's subject and the claim that you or—in the case of a summary—another author will be making about that subject. Every paragraph of a paper illuminates the thesis by providing supporting detail or explanation. The relationship of these paragraphs to the thesis is analogous to the relationship of the sentences within a paragraph to the topic sentence. Both the thesis and the topic sentence are general statements (the thesis being the more general) that are followed by systematically arranged details.

To ensure clarity for the reader, *the first sentence of your summary should begin with the author's thesis, regardless of where it appears in the article itself.* Authors may locate their thesis at the beginning of their work, in which case the thesis operates as a general principle from which details of the presentation follow. This is called a *deductive* organization: thesis first, supporting details second. Alternately, authors may locate their thesis at the end of their work, in which case they begin with specific details and build toward a more general conclusion, or thesis. This is called an *inductive* organization, an example of which you see in "Bilingual Education: A War of Words," where the thesis is stated last and is part of the conclusion. (By contrast, a conclusion in a deductively organized piece restates the thesis, which has already been presented at the beginning of the selection.)

Like any sentence, a thesis consists of a subject and an assertion about that subject. How can we go about fashioning an adequate thesis for "Bilingual Education: A War of Words"? Probably no two proposed thesis statements for this article would be worded exactly the same. But it is fair to say that any reasonable thesis will indicate that the subject is the debate over bilingual education and that the author asserts that this debate has large political and cultural significance. What issues, specifically, does Bernstein believe are raised by bilingual education? For a clue, look to his final sentence (his conclusion *and* his thesis, since this is an inductively organized piece): "The way language is taught in this country will reflect where the country is going, its very identity." Bernstein sees bilingual education as part of a larger debate about the role minorities will play in America's future identity. Mindful of Bernstein's subject and the assertion he makes about it, we can write a single statement *in our own words* and arrive at the following:

> The longstanding and increasingly bitter debate
> over bilingual education is part of a larger
> national debate over the role minorities will
> play in shaping America's identity.

To clarify for our reader the fact that this idea is Bernstein's, rather than ours, we'll qualify the thesis as follows:

> In "Bilingual Education: A War of Words," Richard
> Bernstein claims that the longstanding and
> increasingly bitter debate over bilingual
> education is part of a larger national debate
> over the role minorities will play in shaping
> America's identity.

The first sentence of a summary is crucially important, for it orients your readers by letting them know what to expect in the coming paragraph(s). Note that this sentence provides the reader with both a citation and thesis for the passage. The author and title reference also could be indicated in the summary's title, in which case it could be dropped from the thesis. And realize, lest you become too quickly frustrated, that writing an acceptable thesis for a summary takes time— in this case two drafts, roughly seven minutes of effort spent on one sentence and another few minutes of fine-tuning after a draft of the entire summary was completed. The first draft of the thesis was too cumbersome; the second draft was too vague; and the third draft needed minor refinements.

*Draft 1:* The debate over bilingual education is
part of a larger national debate ~~about the~~
~~extent to which the identity of ethnic~~
~~minorities will become a visible part of~~
~~the larger American identity.~~

(too long)

---

15

*Draft 2:* The debate over bilingual education is
part of a larger national debate ~~about the~~
~~direction in which America's cultural~~
~~identity will develop.~~

(*too vague*)

*and increasingly bitter*

*Draft 3:* The longstanding ∧ debate over bilingual
education is part of a larger national
debate over the role minorities will play
in shaping America's ~~future~~ identity.

*Final:* The longstanding and increasingly bitter
debate over bilingual education is part of a
larger national debate over the role
minorities will play in shaping America's
identity.

## Write the First Draft of the Summary

Let's consider two possible summaries of the example passage: (1) a short summary, combining a thesis with one-sentence section summaries, and (2) a longer summary, combining thesis, one-sentence section summaries, and some carefully chosen details. Again, realize that you are reading final versions; each of the summaries that follows is the result of at least two full drafts:

## Summary 1: Combine Thesis with One-Sentence Section Summaries

In "Bilingual Education: A War of Words," Richard
Bernstein claims that the longstanding and
increasingly bitter debate over bilingual
education is part of a larger national debate
over the role minorities will play in shaping
America's identity. Proponents and opponents of
bilingual education strongly disagree over how
much benefit students receive from such
programs. But underlying the educational
arguments in the debate over bilingual education
are powerful political arguments arising from the
increasing diversity of America. For Bernstein,

```
then, the bilingual education debate is a debate
over the cultural identity of America.
```

## Discussion

This passage consists essentially of Brian Smith's restatement of the author's thesis plus the four section summaries, altered or expanded a little for stylistic purposes. Notice that Brian has folded his summary of the article's first section into his thesis:

Summary of Section 1:

```
Over the past twenty years, there has been an
acrimonious debate over the merits of bilingual
education.
```

Thesis:

```
In "Bilingual Education: A War of Words," Richard
Bernstein claims that the longstanding and
increasingly bitter debate over bilingual
education is part of a larger national debate
over the role minorities will play in shaping
America's identity.
```

In summarizing section 1, Brian does not indicate Bernstein's interpretation of the debate's significance—something he is careful to do when incorporating that section summary into the thesis: The debate *is part of a larger national debate over the role minorities will play in shaping America's identity*. Notice as well that to the summary's first sentence Brian has added the article's author and title, information to help orient the reader. And for reasons of both content and style, Brian has condensed the section summary's "over the past twenty years" to the one-word adjective "longstanding." His original "acrimonious," revised to read "increasingly bitter," similarly becomes an adjective modifying "debate" and shows that the character of the debate has been changing.

Brian spent most of his energy folding the first section summary into the thesis. With this accomplished, he followed with the other section summaries and made minor stylistic adjustments.

## Summary 2: Combine Thesis Sentence, Section Summaries, and Carefully Chosen Details

The thesis and the one-sentence section summaries also can be used as the outline for a more detailed summary. Most of the details, however, won't be necessary in a summary. It isn't necessary even in a longer summary of this passage to discuss *particular* classrooms—for example, classes in which students are reading about dinosaurs in Spanish or frogs in Korean (paragraphs 1–4); it's sufficient to note that in schools where bilingual education is practiced students are taught in their native language. Nor is it necessary to quote extensively the various proponents and opponents of bilingual education that Bernstein cites—perhaps one or two *brief* quotations would do for your summary. Concentrate on a few carefully selected details that might be desirable for clarity. For example, you could mention New York State's "Curriculum of Inclusion" and its underlying principles (paragraphs 9–10); and you could mention the group U.S. English (paragraph 14), whose very existence and distinguished membership suggests the depth of the opposition's commitment to retaining English as the national language.

How do you know which details may be safely ignored and which ones may be advisable to include? The answer is that you won't always know. Developing good judgment in comprehending and summarizing texts is largely a matter of reading skill and prior knowledge (see pages 3–4). Consider the analogy of the seasoned mechanic who can pinpoint an engine problem by simply listening to a characteristic sound that to a less experienced person is just noise. Or consider the chess player who can plot three separate winning strategies from a board position that to a novice looks like a hopeless jumble. In the same way, the more practiced a reader you are, the more knowledgeable you become about the subject, the better able you will be to make critical distinctions between elements of greater and lesser importance. In the meantime, read as carefully as you can and use your own best judgment as to how to present your material.

Here's one version of a completed summary, with carefully chosen details:

*Thesis*

*Section 1*

> In "Bilingual Education: A War of
> Words," Richard Bernstein claims
> that the longstanding and
> increasingly bitter debate over
> bilingual education is part of a
> larger national debate over the
> role minorities will play in
> shaping America's identity.

*Summary of*
*¶s 1–5*

> Bilingual education programs have
> flourished because of the
> increasingly diverse ethnic makeup
> of American schools. But
> bilingual education is intensely

18

controversial. At one southern California high school, Hispanics picketed teachers who denounced bilingual education programs as "a fraud." (These teachers) had argued that such programs end up harming the very minority groups they are intended to help.

(Those favoring) bilingual education believe that teaching students in their native languages offers young people their best chance for success in American life. (Those opposed) insist that bilingual education fails to prepare students for today's competitive and advanced job markets.

(But) underlying the educational arguments in the debate over bilingual education are powerful political arguments arising from the increasing diversity of America. Most immigrants to this country are no longer from Europe, but from the Caribbean, from the Middle East, and from Asia. (Opponents) of bilingual education argue that now, more than ever, America needs the common bond of language to hold its increasingly diverse population together. (But advocates) see bilingual education

*Transitional words & phrases are circled*

*Section 2*

*Summary of ¶6*

*Summary of ¶7*

*Section 3*

*Transition & topic sentence*

*Summary of ¶8*

as a means of moving away from the
kind of "white Anglo" education
that has belittled the ethnic
identities of nonwhite
minorities. (Moreover,) advocates
of ethnic identity want to go
beyond bilingual education
programs to courses for all
children emphasizing the role of
America's ethnic minorities. (For
example,) New York's "Curriculum of
Inclusion" is designed to stress
minority involvement in important
historical developments.

For Bernstein, (then,) the
bilingual education debate is a
debate over the cultural identity
of America. (Those in favor) of
bilingual education and ethnic
identity see America as a "salad
bowl," rather than a "melting
pot." They want each ethnic group
to retain its own distinctive
qualities. (In contrast,) opponents
of bilingual education believe
that while diversity is valuable,
an overemphasis on ethnic identity
could lead to hostility between
ethnic groups and a breakdown of
national unity. (Indeed,) one
group, U.S. English, is lobbying
for a constitutional amendment
"that would make English the
official language of Government."

*Summary of Pts 9-10*

*Section 4*

*Transition &
summary of
Pt 11*

*Summary of
Pts 12-13*

*Summary of
Pts 14-15*

In the end, Bernstein believes, schools will encourage their students either to develop their "ethnic self-realization" or to be part of a "unified culture." These very different choices will determine America's future identity.

} Summary of ¶s 16-17

## Discussion

The final two of our suggested steps for writing summaries are (1) to check your summary against the original passage, making sure that you have included all the important ideas, and (2) to revise so that the summary reads smoothly and coherently.

The *structure* of Brian Smith's summary reflects what he understood was the four-part structure of the original passage. He devoted one paragraph of summary to each of Bernstein's four sections:

1. Paragraphs 1–5, the introduction
2. Paragraphs 6–7, the debate on the merits of bilingual education
3. Paragraphs 8–10, the political underpinnings of that debate
4. Paragraphs 11–17, the relationship between the debate and America's cultural identity

Within individual paragraphs of the summary, the structure generally reflects the sequence of ideas in the original. For example, paragraph 2 of the summary is two sentences; section two of Bernstein's article is two paragraphs. Brian wrote one sentence of summary for each paragraph.

The expanded summary communicates many more details than does the first summary. Both summaries begin with the same thesis. In the expanded summary, Brian Smith adds four sentences (in paragraph 1) to provide more background information on the bilingual debate. Recall that in the brief summary he collapsed that same background into a single sentence—the thesis. The first summary reduces the debate over bilingual education—paragraphs 6 and 7 of the article—to a single sentence ("Proponents and opponents of bilingual education strongly disagree over how much benefit students receive from such programs"). The expanded summary, however, offers two detailed sentences (paragraph 2), one devoted to the proponents in the debate and another to the opponents. In the expanded summary, Brian devotes a full paragraph (paragraph 3), not a single sentence, to the political underpinnings of the argument over bilingual education. In this instance, Brian retains the sentence from his original summary and adds details on the origin of America's recent immigrants, on U.S. English, and on New York's "Curriculum of Inclusion." He similarly devotes a whole paragraph (paragraph 4), as opposed to a single sentence, to Bernstein's final point about the relation between the bilingual debate and America's identity. Once again, Brian begins with a sentence from his original summary and then adds details.

How long should a summary be? This depends on the length of the original passage. A good rule of thumb is that a summary should be no longer than one-fourth of the original passage. Of course, if you were summarizing an entire chapter or even an entire book, it would have to be much shorter than that. The particular summary above is about one-fifth the length of the original passage. Although it shouldn't be very much longer, you have seen (page 16) that it could be quite a bit shorter.

The length of a summary, as well as the shape of the summary, also depends on its *purpose*. Let's suppose that you decided to use Bernstein's piece in a paper that dealt, primarily, with the evolution of America's cultural identity. You would likely be interested in summarizing the final section of the article, in which Bernstein introduces the "melting pot" and "salad bowl" as metaphors that can explain contrasting views of that identity. If, instead, you were writing a paper focused on the bilingual debate itself, you would likely be interested in summarizing the first three sections of Bernstein's article, which focus on the debate and its political underpinnings. Thus, depending on your purpose, you will summarize either *selected* portions of a source or an entire source, as we will see more fully in the chapter on synthesis.

## SUMMARIZING A NARRATIVE

A narrative is a story, a retelling of a person's experiences. That person and those experiences may be imaginary, as is the case with fiction, or they may be real, as in biography. Summarizing a narrative presents special challenges. You have seen that an author of an expository piece (such as Bernstein's "Bilingual Education: A War of Words") follows assertions with examples and statements of support. Narrative presentations are usually less direct. The author relates a story—event follows event—the point of which may never be stated directly. The charm, the force, and the very point of the narrative lies in the telling; and, generally, narratives do not exhibit the same logical development of expository writing. They do not, therefore, lend themselves to summary in quite the same way. Narratives do have a logic, but that logic may be emotional, imaginative, or plot-bound. The writer who summarizes a narrative is obliged to give an overview—a synopsis—of the story's events and an account of how these events affect the central character(s).

The following narrative appears in Rosalie Pedalino Porter's *Forked Tongue: The Politics of Bilingual Education*. Later, in Chapter 3, you will see a fuller version of this excerpt in which Porter argues against bilingual education. For the moment, read her account of growing up as a member of an ethnic minority. In Porter's narrative you will find the seeds of her present-day opposition to bilingual education.

# Perils in the Demand for Biculturalism

## ROSALIE PEDALINO PORTER

My family was poor, so the first necessity was for us to gain the economic means to survive. We children did not enjoy the middle-class luxury of a choice of schooling or careers. The thought of taking time to "get in touch with myself" did not exist. I was fortunate that my mother convinced my father to let me finish high school and not leave school at sixteen to work in his grocery store. Because I was the oldest of five children and a girl, I did not think to question my fate: I should help my mother after school every day, and when I reached the age of sixteen, I should leave high school and help in the store. In fact, my father would have preferred that we stay closely attached to the family and neither attend school nor learn English. Mandatory attendance at school saved us! For me, convention dictated that family bondage would not end until I married—and married within the ethnic group and preferably in the neighborhood, when I would then no longer be my father's but my husband's responsibility.

School, however, opened up my horizons, and the English language gave me the entry not only to the excitement of academic advancement but to friendships with children from very different families, other ethnic groups, and other religions. I began to want to learn, with a desire for a range of experiences, and, yes, a desire for material things and an interesting job.

Of course, my experience was not unusual. I wanted to be free from what seemed the restrictive customs and language of my family and community, free from the burden of being "different." The desire is common to young people of various ethnic groups, and it is not surprising, therefore, that this liberation is the enduring subject of a large body of literature and drama, in novels such as *The Fortunate Pilgrim, Call It Sleep,* and *Goodbye, Columbus* and films such as *West Side Story, Hester Street,* and *Crossing Delancey.*

It is daunting for anyone to cross the ethnic divide, but for women

Excerpt from *Forked Tongue: The Politics of Bilingual Education* by Rosalie Pedalino Porter. Copyright © 1990 by Basic Books, Inc. Reprinted by permission of Basic Books, a division of HarperCollins Publishers, Inc.

the voyage has been and continues to be even more difficult. To move out of poverty and beyond ethnicity requires individual motivation and strength of purpose *and* the reinforcement of outside help from the schools, job opportunities, and the presence of achievable role models.

I saw with renewed immediacy the clash of cultures and the hardship 5 it imposes on the young in the case of three refugee women from Afghanistan who were in the Newton North High School ESL program for two years. They had learned English fairly well and completed a good part of their high school graduation requirements. They longed to enroll in a local community college, but the families arranged marriages for all three, finding them Afghan husbands instead. The teacher who knew the students and their families and had been an advisor to the young women was deeply disappointed. It is often just not possible to effect such change in the first years of residence in a new country.

The language and culture shift in my own immigrant family took an 6 unusual twist. Oldest of the children in a family of three sons and two daughters, I have moved the farthest from my family geographically and in terms of assimilation into American middle-class life. My brothers and sister, who have all completed college degrees and achieved economic success, live near my mother and have, unlike me, married within the ethnic group and the religion of our upbringing. Yet I am the only one of us who has maintained and expanded her knowledge of Italian, which I speak and write fluently. None of the others is the least bit interested in the language, but they are still very close to the customs. Paradoxically, I am closer to our "roots," to our country of origin, because I travel to Italy frequently and have a husband and three sons who are all Italophiles. My sister and brothers, however, are more closely involved in Italian-American culture. We have each chosen the degree of ethnicity we wish to maintain. I am not convinced of the inevitability of guilt over some loss of ethnicity, the sort that Mario Puzo depicted in *The Fortunate Pilgrim*, when he wrote, "They spoke with guilty loyalty of customs they themselves had trampled into dust." It is not that I am without sentimental feelings, but I cannot honestly wish that I or my family had remained immersed in our original language and ethnicity. We are immeasurably richer for having that background and for having added to it some of the achievements that American life offers.

Certainly, Porter's experiences bear on her present-day opposition to bilingual and bicultural education. Porter believes that emphasizing a non-English-speaking student's native culture and native language "disables" the student, denying him or her "the knowledge and skills [necessary] to attain social and economic equality." If you were discussing her views on the subject in a paper, you might want to refer to her narrative. How would you do so? Bear in mind a few principles when summarizing a narrative, fictional or otherwise:

- Your summary will *not* be a narrative, but rather the synopsis of a narrative. Your summary will likely be a paragraph at most.
- You will want to name and describe the principal character(s) of the narrative and describe the narrative's main actions or events.
- You should seek to connect the narrative's characters and events: describe the significance of events for (or the impact of events on) the character.

To summarize events, reread the narrative and make a marginal note each time you see that an action advances the story from one moment to the next. The key here is to recall that narratives take place *in time*. In your summary, be sure to re-create for your reader a sense of time flowing. Name and describe the characters as well. (For our purposes, *character* refers to the person, real or fictional, about whom the narrative is written.) The trickiest part of the summary will be describing the connection between events and characters. Earlier (page 3) we made the point that summarizing any selection involves a degree of interpretation, and this is especially true of summarizing narratives. What, in the case of Porter, is the impact of the events described? An answer belongs in a summary of this piece, yet developing an answer is tricky. Five readers would interpret the narrative's significance in five distinct ways, would they not? Yes and no: yes, in the sense that these readers, given their separate experiences, will read differently; no, in the sense that readers should be able to distinguish between the impact of events as seen from a main character's (i.e., Porter's) point of view and the impact of these same events as seen from their (the readers') points of view. We should be able to agree that Porter was grateful for mandatory high school attendance. She felt liberated.

At times, you will have to infer from clues in a narrative the significance of events for a character; at other times, the writer will be more direct. In either case, remember that it is the narrative's main character, real or imaginary, whose perspective should be represented in the summary. Here is a one-paragraph summary of Porter's narrative. (The draft is the result of two prior drafts.)

In an excerpt from her book <u>Forked Tongue: The Politics of Bilingual Education</u>, Rosalie Pedalino Porter relates how attending school and learning English allowed her to see beyond the confines of her Italian-American community. Mandatory schooling moved Porter from a culturally closed environment to an open, heterogeneous one that motivated her to succeed, both intellectually and materially. Her transition into American culture

had its difficulties, though: Porter and women
like her were expected to marry young, within the
ethnic group, and remain close to home.  Her
desire, therefore, to move "beyond ethnicity"
into America's middle class resulted in a painful
clash of cultures.  But Porter was able to forge
a distinct and satisfying identity by developing
those parts of her Italian heritage that she
cherished and by adding "some of the achievements
that American life offers."

## SUMMARIZING FIGURES AND TABLES

In your reading in the sciences and social sciences, you will often find data and concepts presented in nontext forms—as figures and tables. Such visual devices offer a snapshot, a pictorial overview of material that is more quickly and clearly communicated in graphic form than as a series of (often complicated) sentences. The writer of a graph, which in an article or book is labeled as a numbered "figure," presents the quantitative results of research as points on a line or a bar, or as sections ("slices") of a pie. Pie charts show relative proportions, or percentages. Graphs, especially effective in showing patterns, relate one variable to another: for instance, income to years of education or a college student's grade point average to hours of studying.

In the following example, a graph relates enrollment in a bilingual program to test scores in mathematics for third-grade students with limited English proficiency (LEP). Over a five-year period, beginning in 1982–1983, a bilingual program was introduced in the Eastman Avenue School in Los Angeles. Study this graph (Figure 1.1) to distinguish the progress of students enrolled in the bilingual classes from those not enrolled.

Here is a summary of the information presented in this graph:

When taught in bilingual classrooms, third
graders with limited English proficiency (LEP) at
the Eastman Avenue School showed steady progress
on a statewide mathematics test.  In the
1980-1982 school years, before the beginning of
bilingual instruction, third-grade Eastman

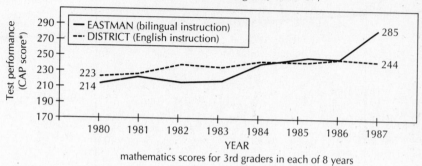

*California Assessment Program

**FIGURE 1.1** *Eastman Bilingual Project*

Source: *"Eastman School Outcomes: Math."* by James Crawford from *Bilingual Education: History, Politics, Theory, and Practice,* 2nd Edition. (Los Angeles: Bilingual Education Services, 1991.) Reprinted by permission.

students performed below the district average in mathematics. After two years of bilingual instruction (in the 1984-1985 academic year), LEP third graders taking the math test performed equally with their peers throughout the school district. After four years of bilingual instruction (kindergarten and grades 1-3), LEP third graders equaled or surpassed other district third graders in math.

In a second type of figure (see Figure 1.2, page 28), the writer presents a *conceptual overview.* Again the assumption is that a figure gives readers information more quickly and clearly than the same material in sentence form. In this next example, the author uses words, not numbers. Still, one variable is related to another: in this case, time (a three-year span) to the degree of instruction in a student's native language.

Here is a two-sentence summary of the "Transitional Bilingual Education Model":

The "Transitional Bilingual Education Model" for non-English-speaking students seeks a gradual

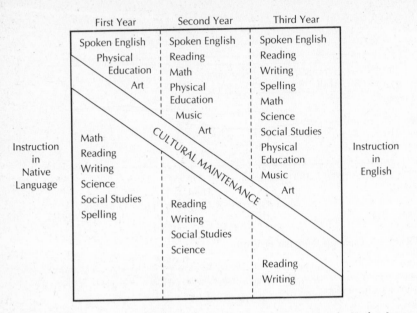

**FIGURE 1.2.** *Transitional Bilingual Education Model: Instruction in Native Language and in English.*

Source: From *Forked Tongue: The Politics of Bilingual Education* by Rosalie Pedalino Porter. Copyright © 1990 by Basic Books, Inc. Reprinted by permission of Basic Books, a division of HarperCollins Publishers, Inc.

transition from native-language instruction to English-based instruction. In this model, non-native speakers of English initially learn academic subjects in their native language, and only after increasing experience with English do they receive significant English-language instruction.

A *table* presents numerical data in rows and columns for quick reference. Tabular information can be incorporated into graphs, if the writer chooses. Graphs are preferable when the writer wants to emphasize a pattern or relationship; tables are used when the writer wants to emphasize numbers. The following example shows projections, through the year 2000, for numbers of minority students (the "N" column) with limited skills in English. The percentage ("%") column shows the percentage a particular language group represents of the total student population being studied.

**TABLE 1.1.** *Linguistic Minority Student Population with Limited English Proficiency, Aged 5–14 (in thousands)*

| | PROJECTIONS | | | | | |
| | 1980 | | 1990 | | 2000 | |
| LANGUAGE | N | % | N | % | N | % |
|---|---|---|---|---|---|---|
| Spanish | 1727.6 | 72.2 | 2092.7 | 74.8 | 2630.0 | 77.4 |
| Italian | 94.9 | 4.0 | 100.1 | 3.6 | 109.6 | 3.2 |
| French | 89.0 | 3.7 | 93.9 | 3.4 | 102.9 | 3.0 |
| German | 88.8 | 3.7 | 93.7 | 3.4 | 102.6 | 3.0 |
| Filipino | 33.2 | 1.4 | 35.0 | 1.2 | 38.3 | 1.1 |
| Chinese | 31.3 | 1.3 | 33.0 | 1.2 | 36.2 | 1.0 |
| Greek | 26.5 | 1.1 | 27.9 | 1.0 | 30.6 | 0.9 |
| Vietnamese | 24.9 | 1.0 | 26.2 | 0.9 | 28.7 | 0.8 |
| Navajo | 24.3 | 1.0 | 25.6 | 0.9 | 28.1 | 0.8 |
| Polish | 24.0 | 1.0 | 25.3 | 0.9 | 27.5 | 0.8 |
| Portuguese | 23.8 | 1.0 | 25.1 | 0.9 | 27.5 | 0.8 |
| Yiddish | 22.5 | 0.9 | 23.7 | 0.8 | 26.0 | 0.7 |
| Japanese | 13.3 | 0.6 | 14.0 | 0.5 | 15.3 | 0.4 |
| Korean | 12.2 | 0.5 | 12.8 | 0.4 | 14.1 | 0.4 |
| Not accounted for and other | 158.5 | 6.6 | 167.5 | 6.0 | 192.9 | 5.4 |
| Total | 2394.2 | | 2795.9 | | 3400.0 | |

Source: "Linguistic Minority Student Population with Limited English Proficiency" by Henry Treuba from *Raising Silent Voices.* Copyright © 1989 by Heinle & Heinle/Newbury House Publishers, Boston, MA. Reprinted by permission.

Here is a summary of the table "Linguistic Minority Student Population with Limited English Profiency, Aged 5–14."

By the year 2000, the number of five- to fourteen-year-old students in America with limited English proficiency (LEP) is projected to be 3.4 million, an increase of more than one million over twenty years. Among these students, native speakers of Spanish constitute the overwhelming majority. In 1980, they were a projected 1,727,600 (72.2 percent of all LEPs); in 1990 they were a projected 2,092,700 (74.8 percent); and in 2000 they were projected to number 2,630,000 (77.4 percent). Other LEP students (e.g., Korean, Navajo, and German) show a projected increase in numbers over the same period; yet these other

students constitute a decreasing percentage of
total LEP students, as compared to native
speakers of Spanish.

## PARAPHRASE

In certain cases, you may want to *paraphrase* rather than to summarize material. Writing a paraphrase is similar to writing a summary: it involves recasting a passage into your own words, and so it requires your complete understanding of the material. The difference is that whereas a summary is a shortened version of the original, the paraphrase is approximately the same length as the original.

Why write a paraphrase when you can quote the original? You may decide to offer a paraphrase of material written in language that is dense, abstract, archaic, or possibly confusing. For example, suppose you were writing a paper on some aspect of human progress and you came across the following passage by the Marquis de Condorcet, a French economist and politician, written in the late eighteenth century:

> If man can, with almost complete assurance, predict phenomena when he knows their laws, and if, even when he does not, he can still, with great expectation of success, forecast the future on the basis of his experience of the past, why, then, should it be regarded as a fantastic undertaking to sketch, with some pretense to truth, the future destiny of man on the basis of his history? The sole foundation for belief in the natural sciences is this idea, that the general laws directing the phenomena of the universe, known or unknown, are necessary and constant. Why should this principle be any less true for the development of the intellectual and moral faculties of man than for the other operations of nature?

You would like to introduce Condorcet's idea on predicting the future course of human history, but you don't want to slow down your narrative with this somewhat abstract quotation. You may decide to attempt a paraphrase, as follows:

The Marquis de Condorcet believed that if we can
predict such physical events as eclipses and
tides, and if we can use past events as a guide
to future ones, we should be able to forecast
human destiny on the basis of history. Physical
events, he maintained, are determined by natural

laws that are knowable and predictable.  Since humans are part of nature, why should their intellectual and moral development be any less predictable than other natural events?

Each sentence in the paraphrase corresponds to a sentence in the original. The paraphrase is somewhat shorter, owing to the differences of style between eighteenth- and twentieth-century prose (we tend to be more brisk and efficient, although not more eloquent). But the main difference is that we have replaced the language of the original with our own language. For example, we have paraphrased Condorcet's "the general laws directing the phenomena of the universe, known or unknown, are necessary and constant" with "Physical events, he maintained, are determined by natural laws that are knowable and predictable." To contemporary readers, "knowable and predictable" might be clearer than "necessary and constant" as a description of natural (i.e., physical) laws. Note that we added the specific examples of eclipses and tides to clarify what might have been a somewhat abstract idea. Note also that we included two attributions to Condorcet within the paraphrase to credit our source properly.

When you come across a passage that you don't understand, the temptation is strong to skip over it. Resist this temptation! Use paraphrase as a tool for explaining to yourself the main ideas of a difficult passage. By translating another writer's language into your own, you can clarify what you understand and what you don't. Thus, the paraphrase becomes a tool for learning the subject.

Some pointers for writing paraphrases:

♦ Make sure that you understand the source passage.
♦ Substitute your own words for those of the source passage; look for synonyms that carry the same meaning as the original words.
♦ Rearrange your own sentences so that they read smoothly. Sentence structure, even sentence order, in the paraphrase need not be based on that of the original. A good paraphrase, like a good summary, should stand by itself.

Let's consider some other examples. If you were investigating the debate on bilingual education, you would eventually want to examine the law mandating that students who are not proficient in English be taught in their native languages. Here is an excerpt from that law:

PUBLIC LAW 93–380, AUG. 21, 1974

BILINGUAL EDUCATIONAL PROGRAMS
Sec. 105. (a) (1) Title VII of the Elementary and Secondary Education Act of 1965 is amended to read as follows:

---

## "TITLE VII—BILINGUAL EDUCATION

### "SHORT TITLE

Sec. 701. This title may be cited as the "Bilingual Education Act".

### "POLICY; APPROPRIATIONS

"Sec. 702. (a) Recognizing—

"(1) that there are large numbers of children of limited English-speaking ability;

"(2) that many of such children have a cultural heritage which differs from that of English-speaking persons;

"(3) that a primary means by which a child learns is through the use of such child's language and cultural heritage;

"(4) that, therefore, large numbers of children of limited English-speaking ability have educational needs which can be met by the use of bilingual educational methods and techniques; and

"(5) that, in addition, children of limited English-speaking ability benefit through the fullest utilization of multiple language and cultural resources, the Congress declares it to be the policy of the United States, in order to establish equal educational opportunity for all children (A) to encourage the establishment and operation, where appropriate, of educational programs using bilingual educational practices, techniques, and methods, and (B) for that purpose, to provide financial assistance to local educational agencies, and to State educational agencies for certain purposes, in order to enable such local educational agencies to develop and carry out such programs in elementary and secondary schools, including activities at the preschool level, which are designed to meet the educational needs of such children; and to demonstrate effective ways of providing, for children of limited English-speaking ability, instruction designed to enable them, while using their native language, to achieve competence in the English language.

Like most legal passages, this is somewhat forbidding to laypeople: it consists of one sentence more than two hundred words long, with typically impenetrable legal phrasing. You decide, for clarity's sake, to paraphrase the law for your lay audience. First, of course, you must understand the meaning of the passage, perhaps no small task. But having read the material carefully, you might eventually draft a paraphrase like this one:

```
The federal guidelines for bilingual education

are presented in Public Law 93-380 (Aug. 21,

1974), an amendment to Title VII of the

Elementary and Secondary Education Act of 1965.

The "Bilingual Education Act" (the short title)

is premised on three assumptions: (1) that many

children have limited ability to speak English;
```

---

(2) that many come from ethnically diverse, non-English-speaking backgrounds; and (3) that native language and culture powerfully influence a child's learning. Based on these assumptions, Congress concluded that many children in the United States should be educated through programs in bilingual education. This approach makes full use of a student's native linguistic and cultural resources.

Accordingly, Congress declared that in the interests of establishing equal educational opportunities for all children, the government would encourage the creation of bilingual programs in preschools and in elementary and secondary schools. Congress would fund such programs at the state and local levels with the understanding that these programs would enable students, "while using their native language, to achieve competence in the English language."

In our paraphrase of Congress's one long sentence, we have written six sentences arranged in two paragraphs. Our paragraphs follow the logic and structure of the original, which is presented in two parts. The first part consists of the five "recognizing that" clauses. We have taken these clauses and paraphrased them in two sentences: one dealing with the assumptions underlying the law and the other addressing the conclusions Congress reached based on these assumptions. The second part of the original—and of the paraphrase—presents Congress's two declarations. Notice that we ended the paraphrase with a quotation. From earlier reading on the debate over bilingual education, we knew that a student's eventual proficiency in English (or lack thereof) has become a contentious issue. We therefore wanted to preserve in our paraphrase the exact language of the original. Although our paraphrase is somewhat briefer than the original, it follows the original's logic and structure. The paraphrase may not stand up in court, but it accurately conveys the sense of the law to the lay reader.

Finally, let's consider a passage written by a fine writer that may, nonetheless, best be conveyed in paraphrase. In "Identify All Carriers," an article on AIDS, editor and columnist William F. Buckley makes the following statement:

I have read and listened, and I think now that I can convincingly crystallize the thoughts chasing about in the minds of, first, those whose concern with AIDS victims is based primarily on a concern for them, and for the maintenance of the most rigid standards of civil liberties and personal privacy, and, second, those whose anxiety to protect the public impels them to give subordinate attention to the civil amenities of those who suffer from AIDS and primary attention to the safety of those who do not.

In style, Buckley's passage is more like Condorcet's than the legal extract: it is eloquent, balanced, and literate. Still, it is challenging. Here is another one hundred words–plus sentence, perhaps a bit too eloquent for some readers to grasp. For your paper on AIDS, you decide to paraphrase Buckley. You might draft something like this:

> Buckley finds two opposing sides in the AIDS debate: those concerned primarily with the civil liberties and the privacy of AIDS victims, and those concerned primarily with the safety of the public.

Our paraphrases have been somewhat shorter than the original, but this is not always the case. For example, suppose you wanted to paraphrase this statement by Sigmund Freud:

> We have found out that the distortion in dreams which hinders our understanding of them is due to the activities of a censorship, directed against the unacceptable, unconscious wish–impulses.

If you were to paraphrase this statement (the first sentence in the Tenth Lecture of his *General Introduction to Psychoanalysis*), you might come up with something like this:

> It is difficult to understand dreams because they contain distortions. Freud believed that these distortions arise from our internal censor, which attempts to suppress unconscious and forbidden desires.

Essentially, this paraphrase does little more than break up one sentence into two and somewhat rearrange the sentence structure for clarity.

Like summaries, then, *paraphrases* are useful devices, both in helping you to understand source material and in enabling you to convey the essence of this source material to your readers. When would you choose to write a summary instead of a paraphrase (or vice versa)? The answer to this question depends on your purpose in presenting your source material. As we've said, summaries are generally based on articles (or sections of articles) or books. Paraphrases are generally based on particularly difficult (or important) paragraphs or sentences. You would seldom paraphrase a long passage, or summarize a short one, unless there were particularly good reasons for doing so. (For example, a lawyer might want to paraphrase several pages of legal language so that his or her client, who is not a lawyer, could understand it.) The purpose of a summary is generally to save your reader time by presenting him or her with a brief and quickly readable version of a lengthy source. The purpose of a paraphrase is generally to clarify a short passage that might otherwise be unclear. Whether you summarize or paraphrase may also depend on the importance of your source. A particularly important source—if it is not too long—may rate a paraphrase. If it is less important, or peripheral to your central argument, you may choose to write a summary instead. And, of course, you may choose to summarize only part of your source—the part that is most relevant to the point you are making. In conclusion, then:

*Summarize:*
- ♦ To present main points of a lengthy passage (article or book)
- ♦ To condense peripheral points necessary to discussion

*Paraphrase:*
- ♦ To clarify a short passage
- ♦ To emphasize main points

At times, you will want to *quote* a source, instead of summarizing or paraphrasing it. You'll find a full discussion on quoting sources starting on page 43. In brief, though, you should quote sources when:

- ♦ Another writer's language is particularly memorable and will add interest and liveliness to your paper.
- ♦ Another writer's language is so clearly and economically stated that to make the same points in your own words would, by comparison, be ineffective.
- ♦ You want the solid reputation of a source to lend authority and credibility to your own writing.

# 2

## THESIS, QUOTATIONS, INTRODUCTIONS, AND CONCLUSIONS

### WRITING A THESIS

*A thesis statement is a one-sentence summary of a paper's content.* It is similar, actually, to a paper's conclusion but lacks the conclusion's concern for broad implications and significance. For a writer in the drafting stages, the thesis establishes a focus, a basis on which to include or exclude information. For the reader of a finished product, the thesis anticipates the author's discussion. *A thesis statement, therefore, is an essential tool for both writers and readers of academic material.*

This last sentence is our thesis for this section. Based on this thesis, we, as the authors, have limited the content of the section; and you, as the reader, will be able to form certain expectations about the discussion that follows. You can expect a definition of a thesis statement; an enumeration of the uses of a thesis statement; and a discussion focused on academic material. As writers, we will have met our obligations to you only if in subsequent paragraphs we satisfy these expectations.

### The Components of a Thesis

Like any other sentence, a thesis includes a subject and a predicate, which consists of an assertion about the subject. In the sentence "Lee and Grant were different kinds of generals," "Lee and Grant" is the subject and "were different kinds of generals" is the predicate. What distinguishes a thesis statement from any other sentence with a subject and predicate is the thesis statement's *level of generality and the care with which you word the assertion.* The subject of a thesis must present the right balance between the general and the specific to allow for a thorough discussion within the allotted length of the paper. The discussion might include definitions, details, comparisons, contrasts—whatever is needed to illuminate a subject and carry on an intelligent conversation. (If the sentence about Lee and Grant were a thesis, the reader would assume that the rest of the essay contained comparisons and contrasts between the two generals.)

Bear in mind when writing thesis statements that the more general your subject and the more complex your assertion, the longer your paper will be. For instance, you could not write an effective ten-page paper based on the following:

Democracy is the best system of government.

Consider the subject of this sentence, "democracy," and the assertion of its predicate, "is the best system of government." The subject is enormous in scope; it is a general category composed of hundreds of more specific subcategories, each of which would be appropriate for a paper ten pages in length. The predicate of our example is also a problem, for the claim that democracy is the best system of government would be simplistic unless accompanied by a thorough, systematic, critical evaluation of *every* form of government yet devised. A ten-page paper governed by such a thesis simply could not achieve the level of detail and sophistication expected of college students.

## Limiting the Scope of the Thesis

Before you can write an effective thesis and thus a controlled, effective paper, you need to limit your intended discussions by limiting your subject and your claims about it. Two strategies for achieving a thesis statement of manageable proportions are (1) to begin with a working thesis (this strategy assumes that you are familiar with your topic) and (2) to begin with a broad area of interest and narrow it (this strategy assumes that you are unfamiliar with your topic).

### Begin with a Working Thesis

Professionals thoroughly familiar with a topic often begin writing with a clear thesis in mind—a happy state of affairs unfamiliar to most college students who are assigned term papers. But professionals usually have an important advantage over students: experience. Because professionals know their material, are familiar with the ways of approaching it, are aware of the questions important to practitioners, and have devoted considerable time to study of the topic, they are naturally in a strong position to begin writing a paper. Not only do professionals have experience in their fields, but they also have a clear purpose in writing; they know their audience and are comfortable with the format of their papers.

Experience counts—there's no way around it. As a student, you are not yet an expert and therefore don't generally have the luxury of beginning your writing tasks with a definite thesis in mind. Once you choose and devote time to a major field of study, however, you will gain experience. In the meantime, you'll have to do more work than the professional to prepare yourself for writing a paper.

But let's assume that you *do* have an area of expertise, that you are in your own right a professional (albeit not in academic matters). We'll assume that you understand your nonacademic subject—say, backpacking—and have been given a clear purpose for writing: to discuss the relative merits of backpack designs. Your job is to write a recommendation for the owner of a sporting-goods chain, suggesting which line of backpacks the chain should carry. The owner lives in another city, so your remarks have to be written. Since you already know a good deal about backpacks, you may already have some well-developed ideas on the topic before you start doing additional research.

Yet even as an expert in your field, you will find that beginning the writing task is a challenge, for at this point it is unlikely that you will be able to conceive a thesis perfectly suited to the contents of your paper. After all, a thesis statement is a summary, and it is difficult to summarize a presentation yet to be written—especially if you plan to discover what you want to say during the process of writing. Even if you know your material well, the best you can do at the early stages is to formulate a *working thesis*—a hypothesis of sorts, a well-informed hunch about your topic and the claim to be made about it. Once you have completed a draft, you can evaluate the degree to which your working thesis accurately summarizes the content of your paper.[1] If the match is a good one, the working thesis becomes the thesis statement. If, however, sections of the paper drift from the focus set out in the working thesis, you'll need to revise the thesis and the paper itself to ensure that the presentation is unified. (You'll know that the match between the content and thesis is a good one when every paragraph directly refers to and develops some element of the thesis.)

### Begin with a Subject and Narrow It

Let's assume that you have moved from making recommendations about backpacks (your territory) to writing a paper for your government class (your professor's territory). Whereas you were once the professional who knew enough about your subject to begin writing with a working thesis, you are now the student, inexperienced and in need of a great deal of information before you can begin to think of thesis statements. It may be a comfort to know that your government professor would likely be in the same predicament if asked to recommend backpack designs. He would need to spend several weeks, at least, backpacking to become as experienced as you; and it is fair to say that you will need to spend several hours in the library before you are in a position to choose a topic suitable for an undergraduate paper.

Suppose you have been assigned a ten-page paper in Government 104, a

---

[1] Some writers work with an idea, committing it to paper only after it has been fully formed. Others begin with a vague notion and begin writing a first draft, trusting that as they write they'll discover what they wish to say. Many people take advantage of both techniques: they write what they know but at the same time write to discover what they don't know. As you'll see, we used both techniques in writing this section of the book.

course on social policy. Not only do you not have a thesis—you don't have a subject! Where will you begin? First, you need to select a broad area of interest and make yourself knowledgeable about its general features. What if no broad area of interest occurs to you? Don't despair—there's usually a way to make use of discussions you've read in a text or heard in a lecture. The trick is to find a topic that can become personally important, for whatever reason. (For a paper in your biology class, you might write on the digestive system because a relative has stomach troubles. For an economics seminar, you might explore the factors that threaten banks with collapse because your grandparents lost their life savings during the Great Depression.) Whatever the academic discipline, try to discover a topic that you'll enjoy exploring; that way, you'll be writing for yourself as much as for your professor. Some specific strategies to try if no topics occur to you: Review material covered during the semester, class by class if need be; review the semester's readings, actually skimming each assignment. Choose any subject that has held your interest, if even for a moment, and use that as your point of departure.

Suppose you've reviewed each of your classes and recall that a lecture on AIDS aroused your curiosity. Your broad subject of interest, then, will be AIDS. At this point, the goal of your research is to limit this subject to a manageable scope. Although your initial, broad subject will often be more specific than our example, "AIDS," we'll assume for the purposes of discussion the most general case (the subject in greatest need of limiting).

A subject can be limited in at least two ways. First, a general article like an encyclopedia entry may do the work for you by presenting the subject in the form of an outline, with each item in the outline representing a separate topic (which, for your purposes, may need further limiting). Second, you can limit a subject by asking several questions about it:

Who?

What aspects?

Where?

When?

How?

These questions will occur to you as you conduct your research and see the ways in which various authors have focused their discussions. Having read several sources and having decided that you'd like to use them, you might limit the subject "AIDS" by asking *who*—AIDS patients; and *which aspect*—civil rights of AIDS patients.

Certainly, "the civil rights of AIDS patients" offers a more specific focus than does "AIDS"; still, the revised focus is too broad for a ten-page paper in that a comprehensive discussion would obligate you to review numerous particular rights. So again you must try to limit your subject by posing a question. In this particular case, *which aspects* (of the civil rights of AIDS patients) can be asked a second time. Six aspects may come to mind:

♦ Rights in the workplace
♦ Rights to hospital care
♦ Rights to insurance benefits
♦ Rights to privacy
♦ Rights to fair housing
♦ Rights to education

Any *one* of these aspects could provide the focus of a ten-page paper, and you do yourself an important service by choosing one, perhaps two, of the aspects; to choose more would obligate you to too broad a discussion and you would frustrate yourself: Either the paper would have to be longer than ten pages or, assuming you kept to the page limit, the paper would be superficial in its treatment. In both instances, the paper would fail, given the constraints of the assignment. So it is far better that you limit your subject ahead of time, before you attempt to write about it. Let's assume that you settle on the following as an appropriately defined subject for a ten-page paper:

the rights of AIDS patients in the workplace

The process of narrowing an initial subject depends heavily on the reading you do. The more you read, the deeper your understanding of a topic. The deeper your understanding, the likelier it will be that you can divide a broad and complex topic into manageable—that is, researchable—categories. Identify these categories that compose the larger topic and pursue one of them. In the AIDS example, your reading in the literature suggested that the civil rights of AIDS patients was an issue at the center of recent national debate. So reading allowed you to narrow the subject "AIDS" by answering the initial questions— the *who* and *which aspects.* Once you narrowed your focus to "the civil rights of AIDS patients," you read further and quickly realized that civil rights in itself was a broad concern that also should be limited. In this way, reading provided an important stimulus as you worked to identify an appropriate subject for your paper.

### Make an Assertion

Once you have identified the subject, you can now develop it into a thesis by making an assertion about it. If you have spent enough time reading and gathering information, you will be knowledgeable enough to have something to say about the subject, based on a combination of your own thinking and the thinking of your sources. If you have trouble making an assertion, try writing your topic at the top of a page and then listing everything you now know and feel about it. Often from such a list you will discover an assertion that you then can use to fashion a working thesis. A good way to gauge the reasonableness of your claim is to see what other authors have asserted about the same topic. In fact, keep good notes on the views of others; the notes will prove a useful counterpoint to your own views as you write, and you may want to use them in your paper.

Next, make three assertions about your topic, in order of increasing complexity.

1. During the past few years, the rights of AIDS patients in the workplace have been debated by national columnists.
2. Several columnists have offered convincing reasons for protecting the rights of AIDS patients in the workplace.
3. The most sensible plan for protecting the rights of AIDS patients in the workplace has been offered by columnist Anthony Jones.

Keep in mind that these are *working thesis statements*. Because you haven't written a paper based on any of them, they remain *hypotheses* to be tested. After completing a first draft, you would compare the contents of the paper to the thesis and make adjustments as necessary for unity. The working thesis is an excellent tool for planning broad sections of the paper, but—again—don't let it prevent you from pursuing related discussions as they occur to you.

Notice how these three statements differ from one another in the forcefulness of their assertions. The third thesis is *strongly argumentative*. "Most sensible" implies that the writer will explain several plans for protecting the rights of AIDS patients in the workplace. Following the explanation would come a comparison of plans and then a judgment in favor of Anthony Jones. Like any working thesis, this one helps the writer plan the paper. Assuming the paper follows the three-part structure we've inferred, the working thesis would become the final thesis, on the basis of which a reader could anticipate sections of the essay to come.

The first of the three thesis statements, by contrast, is *explanatory*:

During the past few years, the rights of AIDS patients in the workplace have been debated by national columnists.

In developing a paper based on this thesis, the writer would assert only the existence of a debate, obligating himself merely to a summary of the various positions taken. Readers, then, would use this thesis as a tool for anticipating the contours of the paper to follow. Based on this particular thesis, a reader would *not* expect to find the author strongly endorsing the views of one or another columnist. The thesis does not require the author to defend a personal opinion.

The second thesis statement *does* entail a personal, intellectually assertive commitment to the material, although the assertion is not as forceful as the one found in statement 3:

Several columnists have offered convincing reasons for protecting the rights of AIDS patients in the workplace.

Here we have an *explanatory, mildly argumentative* thesis that enables the writer to express an opinion. We infer from the use of the word *convincing* that the writer will judge the various reasons for protecting the rights of AIDS patients; and, we can reasonably assume, the writer himself believes in protecting these rights. Note the contrast between this second thesis and the first one, where the writer committed himself to no involvement in the debate whatsoever. Still, the present thesis is not as ambitious as the third one, whose writer implicitly accepted the general argument for safeguarding rights (an acceptance he would need to justify) and then took the additional step of evaluating the merits of those arguments in relation to each other. (Recall that Anthony Jones's plan was the "most sensible.")

As you can see, for any subject you might care to explore in a paper, you can make any number of assertions—some relatively simple, some complex. It is on the basis of these assertions that you set yourself an agenda in writing a paper—and readers set for themselves expectations for reading. The more ambitious the thesis, the more complex will be the paper and the greater will be the readers' expectations.

## Using the Thesis

Different writing tasks require different thesis statements. The *explanatory thesis* is often developed in response to short-answer exam questions that call for information, not analysis (e.g., "List and explain proposed modifications to contemporary American democracy"). The *explanatory but mildly argumentative thesis* is appropriate for organizing reports (even lengthy ones), as well as essay questions that call for some analysis (e.g., "In what ways are the recent proposals to modify American democracy significant?"). The *strongly argumentative thesis* is used to organize papers and exam questions that call for information, analysis, *and* the writer's forcefully stated point of view (e.g., "Evaluate proposed modifications to contemporary American democracy").

The strongly argumentative thesis, of course, is the riskiest of the three, since you must unequivocally state your position and make it appear reasonable—which requires that you offer evidence and defend against logical objections. But such intellectual risks pay dividends, and if you become involved enough in your work to make challenging assertions, you will provoke challenging responses that enliven classroom discussions. One of the important objectives of a college education is to extend learning by stretching, or challenging, conventional beliefs. You breathe new life into this broad objective, and you enliven your own learning as well, every time you adopt a thesis that sets a challenging agenda both for you (as writer) and for your readers. Of course, once you set the challenge, you must be equal to the task. As a writer, you will need to discuss all the elements implied by your thesis.

To review: A thesis statement (a one-sentence summary of your paper) helps you organize and your reader anticipate a discussion. Thesis statements are distinguished by their carefully worded subjects and predicates, which should be just broad enough and complex enough to be developed within the length limitations of the assignment. Both novices and experts in a field typically begin the initial draft of a paper with a working thesis—a statement that provides writers with structure enough to get started but with latitude enough to discover what they want to say as they write. Once you have completed a first draft, you should test the "fit" of your thesis with the paper that follows. Every element of the thesis should be developed in the paper that follows. Discussions that drift from your thesis should be deleted, or the thesis changed to accommodate the new discussions.

# QUOTATIONS

A *quotation* records the exact language used by someone in speech or in writing. A *summary,* in contrast, is a brief restatement in your own words of what someone else has said or written. And a *paraphrase* is also a restatement, although one that is often as long as the original source. Any paper in which you draw upon sources will rely heavily on quotation, summary, and paraphrase. How do you choose among the three?

Remember that the papers you write should be your own—for the most part, your own language and certainly your own thesis, your own inferences, and your own conclusions. It follows that references to your source materials should be written primarily as summaries and paraphrases, both of which are built on restatement, not quotation. You will use summaries when you need a *brief* restatement, and paraphrases, which provide more explicit detail than summaries, when you need to follow the development of a source closely. When you quote too much, you risk losing ownership of your work: more easily than you might think, your voice can be drowned out by the voices of those you've quoted. So *use quotations sparingly,* as you would a pungent spice.

Nevertheless, *quoting just the right source at the right time can significantly improve your papers.* The trick is to know when and how to use quotations.

## Choosing Quotations

- ♦ Use quotations when another writer's language is particularly memorable and will add interest and liveliness to your paper.
- ♦ Use quotations when another writer's language is so clear and economical that to make the same point in your own words would, by comparison, be ineffective.
- ♦ Use quotations when you want the solid reputation of a source to lend authority and credibility to your own writing.

### Quoting Memorable Language

Assume you're writing a paper on Napoleon Bonaparte's relationship with the celebrated Josephine. Through research you learn that two days after their marriage Napoleon, given command of an army, left his bride for what was to be a brilliant military campaign in Italy. How did the young general respond to leaving his wife so soon after their wedding? You come across the following, written from the field of battle by Napoleon on April 3, 1796:

> I have received all your letters, but none has had such an impact on me as the last. Do you have any idea, darling, what you are doing, writing to me in those terms? Do you not think my situation cruel enough without intensifying my longing for you, overwhelming my soul? What a style! What emotions you evoke! Written in fire, they burn my poor heart![2]

A summary of this passage might read as follows:

> On April 3, 1796, Napoleon wrote to Josephine, expressing how sorely he missed her and how passionately he responded to her letters.

You might write the following as a paraphrase of the passage:

> On April 3, 1796, Napoleon wrote to Josephine that he had received her letters and that one among all others had had a special impact, overwhelming his soul with fiery emotions and longing.

How feeble this summary and paraphrase are when compared with the original! Use the vivid language that your sources give you. In this case, quote Napoleon in your paper to make your subject come alive with memorable detail:

> On April 3, 1796, a passionate, lovesick Napoleon responded to a letter from Josephine; she had written longingly to her husband, who, on a military campaign, acutely felt her absence. "Do you have any idea, darling, what you are doing, writing to me in those terms? . . . What emotions you evoke!" he said of her letters. "Written in fire, they burn my poor heart!"

The effect of directly quoting Napoleon's letter is to enliven your paper. A *direct* quotation is one in which you record precisely the language of another, as we did with the sentences from Napoleon's letter. In an *indirect* quotation, you report what someone has said, although you are not obligated to repeat the words exactly as spoken (or written):

> *Direct quotation:* Franklin D. Roosevelt said: "The only thing we have to fear is fear itself."

---

[2]Francis Mossiker, trans., *Napoleon and Josephine.* New York: Simon and Schuster, 1964.

---

*Indirect quotation:* Franklin D. Roosevelt said that we have nothing to fear but fear itself.

The language in a direct quotation, which is indicated by a pair of quotation marks (" "), must be faithful to the language of the original passage. When using an indirect quotation, you have the liberty of changing words (although not changing meaning). For both direct and indirect quotations, *you must credit your sources,* naming them either in (or close to) the sentence that includes the quotation or in a footnote.

### Quoting Clear and Concise Language

You should quote a source when its language is particularly clear and economical—when your language, by contrast, would be wordy. Read this passage from a text on biology:

The honeybee colony, which usually has a population of 30,000 to 40,000 workers, differs from that of the bumblebee and many other social bees or wasps in that it survives the winter. This means that the bees must stay warm despite the cold. Like other bees, the isolated honeybee cannot fly if the temperature falls below 10°C (50°F) and cannot walk if the temperature is below 7°C (45°F). Within the wintering hive, bees maintain their temperature by clustering together in a dense ball; the lower the temperature, the denser the cluster. The clustered bees produce heat by constant muscular movements of their wings, legs, and abdomens. In very cold weather, the bees on the outside of the cluster keep moving toward the center, while those in the core of the cluster move to the colder outside periphery. The entire cluster moves slowly about on the combs, eating the stored honey from the combs as it moves.[3]

A summary of this paragraph might read as follows:

Honeybees, unlike many other varieties of bee, are able to live through the winter by "clustering together in a dense ball" for body warmth.

A paraphrase of the same passage would be considerably more detailed:

Honeybees, unlike many other varieties of bee (such as bumblebees), are able to live through the winter. The 30,000 to 40,000 bees within a honeybee hive could not, individually, move about in cold winter temperatures. But when "clustering together in a dense ball," the bees generate heat by constantly moving their body parts. The cluster also moves slowly about the hive, eating honey stored in the combs. This nutrition, in addition to the heat generated by the cluster, enables the honeybee to survive the cold winter months.

---

[3]"Winter Organization" in Patricia Curtis, *Biology,* 2nd ed. New York: Worth, 1976, pp. 822–823.

---

In both the summary and the paraphrase we've quoted Curtis's "clustering together in a dense ball," a phrase that lies at the heart of her description of wintering honeybees. For us to describe this clustering in any language other than Curtis's would be pointless since her description is admirably brief and precise.

### Quoting Authoritative Language

You will also want to use quotations that lend authority to your work. When quoting an expert or some prominent political, artistic, or historical figure, you elevate your own work by placing it in esteemed company. Quote respected figures to establish background information in a paper, and your readers will tend to perceive that information as reliable. Quote the opinions of respected figures to endorse some statement that you've made, and your statement becomes more credible to your readers. For example, in an essay that you might write on the importance of reading well, you could make use of a passage from Thoreau's *Walden:*

> Reading well is hard work and requires great skill and training. It "is a noble exercise," writes Henry David Thoreau in *Walden,* "and one that will task the reader more than any exercise which the customs of the day esteem. It requires a training such as the athletes underwent. . . . Books must be read as deliberately and reservedly as they were written."

By quoting a famous philosopher and essayist on the subject of reading, you add legitimacy to your discussion. Not only do you regard reading to be a skill that is both difficult and important; so too does Henry David Thoreau, one of our most influential American thinkers. The quotation has elevated the level of your work.

You can also quote to advantage well-respected figures who've written or spoken about the subject of your paper. Here is a discussion of space flight. Author David Chandler refers to a physicist and an astronaut:

> A few scientists—notably James Van Allen, discoverer of the Earth's radiation belts—have decried the expense of the manned space program and called for an almost exclusive concentration on unmanned scientific exploration instead, saying this would be far more cost-effective.
>
> Other space scientists dispute that idea. Joseph Allen, physicist and former shuttle astronaut, says, "It seems to be argued that one takes away from the other. But before there was a manned space program, the funding on space science was zero. Now it's about $500 million a year."

Note, first, that in the first paragraph Chandler has either summarized or used an indirect quotation to incorporate remarks made by James Van Allen into the discussion on space flight. In the second paragraph, Chandler directly quotes his next source, Joseph Allen. Both quotations, indirect and direct, lend authority and legitimacy to the article, for both James Van Allen and Joseph Allen are experts on the subject of space flight. Note also that Chandler has provided brief but effective biographies of his sources, identifying both so that their qualifications to speak on the subject are known to all:

James Van Allen, *discoverer of the Earth's radiation belts* . . .

Joseph Allen, *physicist and former shuttle astronaut* . . .

The phrases in italics are called *appositives.* Their function is to rename the nouns they follow by providing explicit, identifying detail. Any information about a person that can be expressed in the following sentence pattern can be made into an appositive phrase:

James Van Allen is *the discoverer of the Earth's radiation belts.*

James Van Allen has decried the expense of the manned space program.

⇓

James Van Allen, *discoverer of the Earth's radiation belts,* has decried the expense of the manned space program.

Use appositives to identify authors whom you quote.

## Incorporating Quotations into Your Sentences

### *Quoting Only the Part of a Sentence or Paragraph That You Need*
As you've seen, a writer selects passages for quotation that are especially *vivid and memorable, concise, or authoritative.* Now we will put these principles into practice. Suppose that while conducting research on the topic of college sports you've come across the following, written by Robert Hutchins, former president of the University of Chicago:

If athleticism is bad for students, players, alumni and the public, it is even worse for the colleges and universities themselves. They want to be educational institutions, but they can't. The story of the famous halfback whose only regret, when he bade his coach farewell, was that he hadn't learned to read and write is probably exaggerated. But we must admit that pressure from trustees, graduates, "friends," presidents and even professors has tended to relax academic standards. These gentry often overlook the fact that a college should not be interested in a fullback who is a half-wit. Recruiting, subsidizing and the double educational standard cannot exist without the knowledge and the tacit approval, at least, of the colleges and universities themselves. Certain institutions encourage susceptible professors to be nice to athletes now admitted by paying them for serving as "faculty representatives" on the college athletic board.[4]

Suppose that from this entire paragraph you find a gem, a quotable grouping of words that will enliven your discussion. You may want to quote part of the following sentence:

These gentry often overlook the fact that a college should not be interested in a fullback who is a half-wit.

### Incorporating the Quotation into the Flow of Your Own Sentence
Once you've selected the passage you want to quote, work the material into your paper in as natural and fluid a manner as possible. Here's how we would quote Hutchins:

Robert Hutchins, a former president of the University of Chicago, asserts that "a college should not be interested in a fullback who is a half-wit."

Note that we've used an appositive to identify Hutchins. And we've used only the part of the paragraph—a single clause—that we thought memorable enough to quote directly.

### Avoiding Freestanding Quotations
A quoted sentence should never stand by itself—as in the following example:

Various people associated with the university admit that the pressures of athleticism have caused a relaxation of standards. "These gentry often overlook the fact that a college should not be interested in a fullback who is a half-wit." But this kind of thinking is bad for the university and even worse for the athletes.

Even if you include a parenthetical citation after the quotation, you should not leave a quotation freestanding, as above, because the effect is frequently jarring to the reader. Introduce the quotation by attributing the source in some other part of the sentence—beginning, middle, or end. Thus, you could write:

According to Robert Hutchins, "These gentry often overlook the fact that a college should not be interested in a fullback who is a half-wit."

A variation:

"These gentry," asserts Robert Hutchins, "often overlook the fact that a college should not be interested in a fullback who is a half-wit."

---

[4]Robert Hutchins, "Gate Receipts and Glory," *The Saturday Evening Post.* December 3, 1983.

Another alternative is to introduce a sentence-long quotation with a colon:

> But Robert Hutchins disagrees: "These gentry often overlook the fact that a college should not be interested in a fullback who is a half-wit."

Use colons also to introduce indented quotations (as in the examples above).

When attributing sources, try to vary the standard "states," "writes," "says," and so on. Other, stronger verbs you might consider: "asserts," "argues," "maintains," "insists," "asks," and even "wonders."

### Using Ellipsis Marks

Using quotations is made somewhat complicated when you want to quote the beginning and end of a passage but not its middle—as was the case when we quoted Henry David Thoreau. Here's part of the paragraph in *Walden* from which we quoted a few sentences:

> To read well, that is, to read true books in a true spirit, is a noble exercise, and one that will task the reader more than any exercise which the customs of the day esteem. It requires a training such as the athletes underwent, the steady intention almost of the whole life to this object. Books must be read as deliberately and reservedly as they were written.[5]

And here was how we used this material:

> Reading well is hard work and requires great skill and training. It "is a noble exercise," writes Henry David Thoreau in *Walden,* "and one that will task the reader more than any exercise which the customs of the day esteem. It requires a training such as the athletes underwent. . . . Books must be read as deliberately and reservedly as they were written."

*Whenever you quote a sentence but delete words from it, as we have done, indicate this deletion to the reader by placing an ellipsis mark, three spaced periods, in the sentence at the point of deletion.* The rationale for using an ellipsis mark is as follows: A direct quotation must be reproduced *exactly* as it was written or spoken. When writers delete or change any part of the quoted material, readers must be alerted so they don't think that the changes were part of the original. Ellipsis marks and brackets serve this purpose.

If you are deleting the middle of a single sentence, use an ellipsis in place of the deleted words:

> "To read well . . . is a noble exercise, and one that will task the reader more than any exercise which the customs of the day esteem."

If you are deleting the end of a quoted sentence, or if you are deleting entire

---

[5]Henry David Thoreau, "Reading" in *Walden.* New York: Signet Classic, 1960, p. 72.

---

sentences of a paragraph before continuing a quotation, add one additional period and place the ellipsis after the last word you are quoting, so that you have four in all:

"It requires a training such as the athletes underwent. . . . Books must be read as deliberately and reservedly as they were written."

If you begin your quotation of an author in the middle of a sentence, you need not indicate deleted words with an ellipsis. Be sure, however, that the syntax of the quotation fits smoothly with the syntax of your sentence:

Reading "is a noble exercise," writes Henry David Thoreau.

### Using Brackets

Use square brackets whenever you need to add or substitute words in a quoted sentence. The brackets indicate to the reader a word or phrase that does not appear in the original passage but that you have inserted to avoid confusion. For example, when a pronoun's antecedent would be unclear to readers, delete the pronoun from the sentence and substitute an identifying word or phrase in brackets. When you make such a substitution, no ellipsis marks are needed. Assume that you wish to quote the underlined sentence in the following passage:

Golden Press's *Walt Disney's Cinderella* set the new pattern for America's Cinderella. This book's text is coy and condescending. (Sample: "And her best friends of all were—guess who—the mice!") The illustrations are poor cartoons. And Cinderella herself is a disaster. She cowers as her sisters rip her homemade ball gown to shreds. (Not even homemade by Cinderella, but by the mice and birds.) She answers her stepmother with whines and pleadings. She is a sorry excuse for a heroine, pitiable and useless. She cannot perform even a simple action to save herself, though she is warned by her friends, the mice. She does not hear them because she is "off in a world of dreams." Cinderella begs, she whimpers, and at last has to be rescued by—guess who—the mice![6]

In quoting this sentence, you would need to identify whom the pronoun *she* refers to. You can do this inside the quotation by using brackets:

Jane Yolen believes that "[Cinderella] is a sorry excuse for a heroine, pitiable and useless."

If the pronoun begins the sentence to be quoted, as it does in this example, you can identify the pronoun outside of the quotation and simply begin quoting your source one word later:

---

[6]Jane Yolen, "America's 'Cinderella,' " APS Publications, Inc. in *Children's Literature in Education* 8, 1977, pp. 21–29.

Jane Yolen believes that Cinderella "is a sorry excuse for a heroine, pitiable and useless."

If the pronoun you want to identify occurs in the middle of the sentence to be quoted, then you'll need to use brackets. Newspaper reporters do this frequently when quoting sources, who in interviews might say something like the following:

After the fire they did not return to the station house for three hours.

If the reporter wants to use this sentence in an article, he or she needs to identify the pronoun:

An official from City Hall, speaking on the condition that he not be identified, said, "After the fire [the officers] did not return to the station house for three hours."

You also will need to add bracketed information to a quoted sentence when a reference essential to the sentence's meaning is implied but not stated directly. Read the following paragraphs from Robert Jastrow's "Toward an Intelligence Beyond Man's":

These are amiable qualities for the computer; it imitates life like an electronic monkey. As computers get more complex, the imitation gets better. Finally, the line between the original and the copy becomes blurred. In another 15 years or so—two more generations of computer evolution, in the jargon of the technologists—we will see the computer as an emergent form of life.

The proposition seems ridiculous because, for one thing, computers lack the drives and emotions of living creatures. But when drives are useful, they can be programmed into the computer's brain, just as nature programmed them into our ancestors' brains as a part of the equipment for survival. For example, computers, like people, work better and learn faster when they are motivated. Arthur Samuel made this discovery when he taught two IBM computers how to play checkers. They polished their game by playing each other, but they learned slowly. Finally, Dr. Samuel programmed in the will to win by forcing the computers to try harder—and to think out more moves in advance—when they were losing. Then the computers learned very quickly. One of them beat Samuel and went on to defeat a champion player who had not lost a game to a human opponent in eight years.[7]

If you wanted to quote only the underlined sentence, you would need to provide readers with a bracketed explanation; otherwise, the words "the proposition" would be unclear. Here is how you would manage the quotation:

[7]Excerpt from "Toward an Intelligence Beyond Man's" from *Time,* February 20, 1978. Copyright © 1978 Time Inc. Reprinted by permission.

According to Robert Jastrow, a physicist and former official at NASA's Goddard Institute, "The proposition [that computers will emerge as a form of life] seems ridiculous because, for one thing, computers lack the drives and emotions of living creatures."

Remember that when you quote the work of another, you are obligated to credit—or cite—the author's work properly; otherwise, you may be guilty of plagiarism. See pages 175–91 for guidance on citing sources.

## WRITING INTRODUCTIONS

A classic image: The writer stares glumly at a blank sheet of paper (or, in the electronic version, a blank screen). Usually, however, this is an image of a writer who hasn't yet begun to write. Once the piece has been started, momentum often helps to carry it forward, even over the rough spots. (These can always be fixed later.) As a writer, you've surely discovered that getting started when you haven't yet warmed to your task *is* a problem. What's the best way to approach your subject? With high seriousness, a light touch, an anecdote? How best to engage your reader?

Many writers avoid such agonizing choices by putting them off—productively. Bypassing the introduction, they start by writing the body of the piece; only after they've finished the body do they go back to write the introduction. There's a lot to be said for this approach. Because you have presumably spent more time thinking about the topic itself than about how you're going to introduce it, you are in a better position, at first, to begin directly with your presentation (once you've settled on a working thesis). And often, it's not until you've actually seen the piece on paper and read it over once or twice that a "natural" way of introducing it becomes apparent. Even if there is no natural way to begin, you are generally in better psychological shape to write the introduction after the major task of writing is behind you and you know exactly what you're leading up to.

Perhaps, however, you can't operate this way. After all, you have to start writing *somewhere,* and if you have evaded the problem by skipping the introduction, that blank page may loom just as large wherever you do choose to begin. If this is the case, then go ahead and write an introduction, knowing full well that it's probably going to be flat and awful. Set down any kind of pump-priming or throat-clearing verbiage that comes to mind, as long as you have a working thesis. Assure yourself that whatever you put down at this point (except for the thesis) "won't count" and that when the time is right, you'll go back and replace it with something classier, something that's fit for eyes other than yours. But in the meantime, you'll have gotten started.

The *purpose* of an introduction is to prepare the reader to enter the world of your essay. The introduction makes the connection between the more familiar world inhabited by the reader and the less familiar world of the writer's particular subject; it places a discussion in a context that the reader can understand.

There are many ways to provide such a context. We'll consider just a few of the most common.

## Quotation

Here is an introduction to a paper on democracy:

> "Two cheers for democracy" was E. M. Forster's not-quite-wholehearted judgment. Most Americans would not agree. To them, our democracy is one of the glories of civilization. To one American in particular, E. B. White, democracy is "the hole in the stuffed shirt through which the sawdust slowly trickles . . . the dent in the high hat . . . the recurrent suspicion that more than half of the people are right more than half of the time" (915). American democracy is based on the oldest continuously operating written constitution in the world—a most impressive fact and a testament to the farsightedness of the founding fathers. But just how farsighted can mere humans be? In *Future Shock,* Alvin Toffler quotes economist Kenneth Boulding on the incredible acceleration of social change in our time: "The world of today . . . is as different from the world in which I was born as that world was from Julius Caesar's" (13). As we move toward the twenty-first century, it seems legitimate to question the continued effectiveness of a governmental system that was devised in the eighteenth century; and it seems equally legitimate to consider alternatives.

The quotations by Forster and White help set the stage for the discussion of democracy by presenting the reader with some provocative and well-phrased remarks. Later in the paragraph, the quotation by Boulding more specifically prepares us for the theme of change that will be central to the essay as a whole.

## Historical Review

In many cases, the reader will be unprepared to follow the issue you discuss unless you provide some historical background. Consider the following introduction to an essay on the film-rating system:

> Sex and violence on the screen are not new issues. In the Roaring Twenties there was increasing pressure from civic and religious groups to ban depictions of "immorality" from the screen. Faced with the threat of federal censorship, the film producers decided to clean their own house. In 1930, the Motion Picture Producers and Distributors of America established the Production Code. At first, adherence to the Code was voluntary; but in 1934 Joseph Breen, newly appointed head of the MPPDA, gave the Code teeth. Henceforth all newly produced films had to be submitted for approval to the Production Code Administration, which had the power to award or withhold the Code seal. Without a Code seal, it was virtually impossible for a film to be shown anywhere in the United States, since exhibitors would not accept it. At about the same time, the

Catholic Legion of Decency was formed to advise the faithful which films were and were not objectionable. For several decades the Production Code Administration exercised powerful control over what was portrayed in American theatrical films. By the 1960s, however, changing standards of morality had considerably weakened the Code's grip. In 1968, the Production Code was replaced with a rating system designed to keep younger audiences away from films with high levels of sex or violence. Despite its imperfections, this rating system has proved more beneficial to American films than did the old censorship system.

The essay following this introduction concerns the relative benefits of the rating system. By providing some historical background on the rating system, the writer helps readers to understand his arguments. Notice the chronological development of details.

## Review of a Controversy

A particular type of historical review is the review of a controversy or debate. Consider the following introduction:

The *American Heritage Dictionary*'s definition of civil disobedience is rather simple: "the refusal to obey civil laws that are regarded as unjust, usually by employing methods of passive resistance." However, despite such famous (and beloved) examples of civil disobedience as the movements of Mahatma Gandhi in India and the Reverend Martin Luther King, Jr., in the United States, the question of whether or not civil disobedience should be considered an asset to society is hardly clear cut. For instance, Hannah Arendt, in her article "Civil Disobedience," holds that "to think of disobedient minorities as rebels and truants is against the letter and spirit of a constitution whose framers were especially sensitive to the dangers of unbridled majority rule." On the other hand, a noted lawyer, Lewis Van Dusen, Jr., in his article "Civil Disobedience: Destroyer of Democracy," states that "civil disobedience, whatever the ethical rationalization, is still an assault on our democratic society, an affront to our legal order and an attack on our constitutional government." These two views are clearly incompatible. I believe, though, that Van Dusen's is the more convincing. On balance, civil disobedience is dangerous to society.[8]

The negative aspects of civil disobedience, rather than Van Dusen's essay, are the topic of this essay. But to introduce this topic, the writer has provided quotations that represent opposing sides of the controversy over civil disobedience, as well as brief references to two controversial practitioners. By focusing at the outset on the particular rather than the abstract aspects of the subject, the writer hoped to secure the attention of her readers and to involve them in the controversy that forms the subject of her essay.

---

[8]Michele Jacques, "Civil Disobedience: Van Dusen vs. Arendt." [Unpublished paper. Used by permission.]

## From the General to the Specific

Another way of providing a transition from the reader's world to the less familiar world of the essay is to work from a general subject to a specific one. The following introduction to a discussion of the 1968 massacre at My Lai, Vietnam, begins with general statements and leads to the particular subject at hand:

> Though we prefer to think of man as basically good and reluctant to do evil, such is not the case. Many of the crimes inflicted on humankind can be dismissed as being committed by the degenerates of society at the prompting of the abnormal mind. But what of the perfectly "normal" man or woman who commits inhumane acts simply because he or she has been ordered to do so? It cannot be denied that such acts have occurred, either in everyday life or in war-time situations. Unfortunately, even normal, well-adjusted people can become cruel, inhumane, and destructive if placed in the hands of unscrupulous authority. Such was the case in the village of My Lai, Vietnam, on March 16, 1968, when a platoon of American soldiers commanded by Lt. William Calley massacred more than 100 civilians, including women and children.

## From the Specific to the General: Anecdote, Illustration

Consider the following paragraph:

> In late 1971 astronomer Carl Sagan and his colleagues were studying data transmitted from the planet Mars to the earth by the Mariner 9 spacecraft. Struck by the effects of the Martian dust storms on the temperature and on the amount of light reaching the surface, the scientists wondered about the effects on earth of the dust storms that would be created by nuclear explosions. Using computer models, they simulated the effects of such explosions on the earth's climate. The results astounded them. Apart from the known effects of nuclear blasts (fires and radiation), the earth, they discovered, would become enshrouded in a "nuclear winter." Following a nuclear exchange, plummeting temperatures and pervading darkness would destroy most of the Northern Hemisphere's crops and farm animals and would eventually render much of the planet's surface uninhabitable. The effects of nuclear war, apparently, would be more catastrophic than had previously been imagined. It has therefore become more urgent than ever for the nations of the world to take dramatic steps to reduce the threat of nuclear war.

The previous introduction went from the general (the question of whether or not man is basically good) to the specific (the massacre at My Lai); this one goes from the specific (scientists studying data) to the general (the urgency of reducing the nuclear threat). The anecdote is one of the most effective means at your disposal of capturing and holding your reader's attention. For decades, speakers have begun their general remarks with a funny, touching, or otherwise appropriate story; in fact, there are plenty of books that are nothing but collections of such stories, arranged by subject.

## Question

Frequently, you can provoke the reader's attention by posing a question or a series of questions:

> Are gender roles learned or inherited? Scientific research has established the existence of biological differences between the sexes, but the effect of biology's influence on gender roles cannot be distinguished from society's influence. According to Michael Lewis of the Institute for the Study of Exceptional Children, "As early as you can show me a sex difference, I can show you the culture at work." Social processes, as well as biological differences, are responsible for the separate roles of men and women.[9]

Opening your essay with a question can be provocative, since it places the reader in an active role: He or she begins by considering answers. *Are* gender roles learned? *Are* they inherited? In this active role, the reader is likely to continue reading with interest.

## Statement of Thesis

Perhaps the most direct method of introduction is to begin immediately with the thesis:

> Computers are a mixed blessing. The lives of Americans are becoming increasingly involved with machines that think for them. "We are at the dawn of the era of the smart machine," say the authors of a cover story on the subject in *Newsweek*, "that will change forever the way an entire nation works," beginning a revolution that will be to the brain what the industrial revolution was to the hand. Tiny silicon chips already process enough information to direct air travel, to instruct machines how to cut fabric—even to play chess with (and defeat) the masters. One can argue that development of computers for the household, as well as industry, will change for the better the quality of our lives: computers help us save energy, reduce the amount of drudgery that most of us endure around tax season, make access to libraries easier. Yet there is a certain danger involved with this proliferation of technology.

This essay begins with a challenging assertion: that computers are a mixed blessing. It is one that many readers are perhaps unprepared to consider, since they may have taken it for granted that computers are an unmixed blessing. The advantage of beginning with a provocative (thesis) statement is that it forces the reader to sit up and take notice—perhaps even to begin protesting. The paragraph goes on to concede some of the "blessings" of computerization but then

---

[9]Tammy Smith, "Are Sex Roles Learned or Inherited?" [Unpublished paper. Used by permission.]

concludes with the warning that there is "a certain danger" associated with the new technology—a danger, the curious or even indignant reader has a right to conclude, that will be more fully explained in the paragraphs to follow.

One final note about our model introductions: They may be longer than introductions you have been accustomed to writing. Many writers (and readers) prefer shorter, snappier introductions. This is largely a matter of personal or corporate style: there is no rule concerning the correct length of an introduction. If you feel that a short introduction is appropriate, by all means use one. You may wish to break up what seems like a long introduction into two paragraphs. (Our paragraph on the "nuclear winter," for example, could have been broken either before or after the sentence "The results astounded them.")

## WRITING CONCLUSIONS

One way to view the conclusion of your paper is as an introduction worked in reverse, a bridge from the world of your essay back to the world of your reader. A conclusion is the part of your paper in which you restate and (if necessary) expand on your thesis. Essential to any conclusion is the summary, which is not merely a repetition of the thesis but a restatement that takes advantage of the material you've presented. *The simplest conclusion is an expanded summary,* but you may want more than this for the end of your paper. Depending on your needs, you might offer a summary and then build onto it a discussion of the paper's significance or its implications for future study, for choices that individuals might make, for policy, and so on. You might also want to urge the reader to change an attitude or to modify behavior. Certainly, you are under no obligation to discuss the broader significance of your work (and a summary, alone, will satisfy the formal requirement that your paper have an ending); but the conclusions of better papers often reveal authors who are "thinking large" and want to connect the particular concerns of their papers with the broader concerns of society.

Here we'll consider seven strategies for expanding the basic summary–conclusion. But two words of advice are in order. First, no matter how clever or beautifully executed, a conclusion cannot salvage a poorly written paper. Second, by virtue of its placement, the conclusion carries rhetorical weight. It is the last statement a reader will encounter before turning from your work. Realizing this, writers who expand on the basic summary–conclusion often wish to give their final words a dramatic flourish, a heightened level of diction. Soaring rhetoric and drama in a conclusion are fine as long as they do not unbalance the paper and call attention to themselves. Having labored long hours over your paper, you have every right to wax eloquent. But keep a sense of proportion and timing. Make your points quickly and end crisply.

## Statement of the Subject's Significance

One of the more effective ways to conclude a paper is to discuss the larger significance of what you have written, providing readers with one more reason to regard your work as a serious effort. When using this strategy, you move from the specific concern of your paper to the broader concerns of the reader's world. Often, you will need to choose among a range of significances: A paper on the Wright brothers might end with a discussion of air travel as it affects economies, politics, or families; a paper on contraception might end with a discussion of its effect on sexual mores, population, or the church. But don't overwhelm your reader with the importance of your remarks. Keep your discussion well focused.

The following paragraphs conclude a paper on George H. Shull, a pioneer in the inbreeding and crossbreeding of corn:

> ... Thus, the hybrids developed and described by Shull 75 years ago have finally dominated U.S. corn production.
>
> The adoption of hybrid corn was steady and dramatic in the Corn Belt. From 1930 through 1979 the average yields of corn in the U.S. increased from 21.9 to 95.1 bushels per acre, and the additional value to the farmer is now several billion dollars per year.
>
> The success of hybrid corn has also stimulated the breeding of other crops, such as sorghum hybrids, a major feed grain crop in arid parts of the world. Sorghum yields have increased 300 percent since 1930. Approximately 20 percent of the land devoted to rice production in China is planted with hybrid seed, which is reported to yield 20 percent more than the best varieties. And many superior varieties of tomatoes, cucumbers, spinach, and other vegetables are hybrids. Today virtually all corn produced in the developed countries is from hybrid seed. From those blue bloods of the plant kingdom has come a model for feeding the world.[10]

The first sentence of this conclusion is a summary, and from it the reader can infer that the paper included a discussion of Shull's techniques for the hybrid breeding of corn. The summary is followed by a two-paragraph discussion on the significance of Shull's research for feeding the world.

## Calling for Further Research

In the scientific and social scientific communities, papers often end with a review of what has been presented (as, for instance, in an experiment) and the ways in which the subject under consideration needs to be further explored. If you raise questions that you call on others to answer, however, make sure

---

[10]From "Hybrid Vim and Vigor" by William L. Brown from pp. 77–78 in *Science 80–85*, November 1984. Copyright 1984 by the AAAS. Reprinted by permission.

you know that the research you are calling for hasn't already been conducted.

This next conclusion comes from a sociological report on the placement of elderly men and women in nursing homes.

Thus, our study shows a correlation between the placement of elderly citizens in nursing facilities and the significant decline of their motor and intellectual skills over the ten months following placement. What the research has not made clear is the extent to which this marked decline is due to physical as opposed to emotional causes. The elderly are referred to homes at that point in their lives when they grow less able to care for themselves—which suggests that the drop-off in skills may be due to physical causes. But the emotional stress of being placed in a home, away from family and in an environment that confirms the patient's view of himself as decrepit, may exacerbate—if not itself be a primary cause of—the patient's rapid loss of abilities. Further research is needed to clarify the relationship between depression and particular physical ailments as these affect the skills of the elderly in nursing facilities. There is little doubt that information yielded by such studies can enable health care professionals to deliver more effective services.

Notice how this call for further study locates the author in a large community of researchers on whom she depends for assistance in answering the questions that have come out of her own work. The author summarizes her findings (in the first sentence of the paragraph), states what her work has not shown, and then extends her invitation.

## Solution/Recommendation

The purpose of your paper might be to review a problem or controversy and to discuss contributing factors. In such a case, it would be appropriate, after summarizing your discussion, to offer a solution based on the knowledge you've gained while conducting research. If your solution is to be taken seriously, your knowledge must be amply demonstrated in the body of the paper.

. . . The major problem in college sports today is not commercialism—it is the exploitation of athletes and the proliferation of illicit practices which dilute educational standards.

Many universities are currently deriving substantial benefits from sports programs that depend on the labor of athletes drawn from the poorest sections of America's population. It is the responsibility of educators, civil rights leaders, and concerned citizens to see that these young people get a fair return for their labor both in terms of direct remuneration and in terms of career preparation for a life outside sports.

Minimally, scholarships in revenue-producing sports should be designed to extend until graduation, rather than covering only four years of athletic eligibility, and should include guarantees of tutoring, counseling, and proper medical care. At institutions where the profits are particularly large (such as Texas A & M, which can afford to pay its football coach $280,000 a year), scholarships should also provide salaries that extend beyond room, board, and tuition. The important thing is that the athlete be remunerated fairly and have the opportunity to gain skills from a university environment without undue competition from a physically and psychologically demanding full-time job. This may well require that scholarships be extended over five or six years, including summers.

Such a proposal, I suspect, will not be easy to implement. The current amateur system, despite its moral and educational flaws, enables universities to hire their athletic labor at minimal cost. But solving the fiscal crisis of the universities on the backs of America's poor and minorities is not, in the long run, a tenable solution. With the support of concerned educators, parents, and civil rights leaders, and with the help from organized labor, the college athlete, truly a sleeping giant, will someday speak out and demand what is rightly his—and hers—a fair share of the revenue created by their hard work.[11]

In this conclusion, the author summarizes his article in one sentence: "The major problem in college sports today is not commercialism—it is the exploitation of athletes and the proliferation of illicit practices which dilute educational standards." In paragraph 2, he continues with an analysis of the problem just stated and follows with a general recommendation—that "educators, civil rights leaders, and concerned citizens" be responsible for the welfare of college athletes. In paragraph 3, he makes a specific proposal, and in the final paragraph, he anticipates resistance to the proposal. He concludes by discounting this resistance and returning to the general point, that college athletes should receive a fair deal.

## Anecdote

An anecdote is a briefly told story or joke, the point of which in a conclusion is to shed light on your subject. The anecdote is more direct than an allusion. With an allusion, you merely refer to a story ("Too many people today live in Plato's cave . . ."); with the anecdote, you actually retell the story. The anecdote allows readers to discover for themselves the significance of a reference to another source—an effort most readers enjoy because they get to exercise their creativity.

The following anecdote concludes an article on homicide. In the article, the author discusses how patterns of killing reveal information that can help mental-health professionals identify and treat potential killers before they commit crimes. The author emphasizes both the difficulty and the desirability of approaching homicide as a threat to public health that, like disease, can be treated with preventive care.

[11]From Mark Naison, "Scenario for Scandal," *Commonweal* 109 (16), September 24, 1982. Reprinted by permission.

In his book, *The Exploits of the Incomparable Mulla Nasrudin,* Sufi writer Idries Shah, in a parable about fate, writes about the many culprits of murder:
"What is Fate?" Nasrudin was asked by a scholar.
"An endless succession of intertwined events, each influencing the other."
"That is hardly a satisfactory answer. I believe in cause and effect."
"Very well," said the Mulla, "look at that." He pointed to a procession passing in the street.
"That man is being taken to be hanged. Is that because someone gave him a silver piece and enabled him to buy the knife with which he committed the murder; or because someone saw him do it; or because nobody stopped him?"[12]

The writer chose to conclude the article with this anecdote. She could have developed an interpretation, but this would have spoiled the dramatic value for the reader. The purpose of using an anecdote is to make your point with subtlety, so resist the temptation to interpret. Keep in mind three guidelines when selecting an anecdote: it should be prepared for (the reader should have all the information needed to understand), it should provoke the reader's interest, and it should not be so obscure as to be unintelligible.

## Quotation

A favorite concluding device is the quotation—the words of a famous person or an authority in the field on which you are writing. The purpose of quoting another is to link your work to theirs, thereby gaining for your work authority and credibility. The first criterion for selecting a quotation is its suitability to your thesis. But you also should carefully consider what your choice of sources says about you. Suppose you are writing a paper on the American work ethic. If you could use a line by comedian David Letterman or one by the current secretary of labor to make the final point of your conclusion, which would you choose and why? One source may not be inherently more effective than the other, but the choice certainly sets a tone for the paper.

There is no doubt that machines will get smarter and smarter, even designing their own software and making new and better chips for new generations of computers. . . . More and more of their power will be devoted to making them easier to use—"friendly," in industry parlance—even for those not trained in computer science. And computer scientists expect that public ingenuity will come up with applications the most visionary researchers have not even considered. One day, a global network of smart machines will be exchanging rapid-fire bursts of information at unimaginable speeds. If they are used wisely, they could help mankind to educate its masses and crack new scientific frontiers. "For all

[12]From "The Murder Epidemic" by Nikki Meredith from pp. 42–48 in *Science 80–85,* December 1984. Copyright by AAAS. Reprinted by permission of the author.

of us, it will be fearful, terrifying, disruptive," says SRI's Peter Schwartz. "In the end there will be those whose lives will be diminished. But for the vast majority, their lives will be greatly enhanced." In any event, there is no turning back: if the smart machines have not taken over, they are fast making themselves indispensable—and in the end, that may amount to very much the same thing.[13]

Notice how the quotation is used to position the writer to make one final remark.

Particularly effective quotations may themselves be used to end an essay, as in the following example. Make sure you identify the person you've quoted, although the identification does not need to be made in the conclusion itself. For example, earlier in the paper from which the following conclusion was taken, Maureen Henderson was identified as an epidemiologist exploring the ways in which a change in diet can prevent the onset of certain cancers.

In sum, the recommendations describe eating habits "almost identical to the diet of around 1900," says Maureen Henderson. "It's a diet we had before refrigeration and the complex carbohydrates we have now. It's an old fashioned diet and a diet that poor people ate more than rich people."

Some cancer researchers wonder whether people will be willing to change their diets or take pills on the chance of preventing cancer, when one-third of the people in the country won't even stop smoking. Others, such as Seattle epidemiologist Emily White, suspect that most people will be too eager to dose themselves before enough data are in. "We're not here to convince the public to take anything," she says. "The public is too eager already. What we're saying is, 'Let us see if some of these things work.' We want to convince ourselves before we convince the public."[14]

There is a potential problem with using quotations: If you end with the words of another, you may leave the impression that someone else can make your case more eloquently than you can. The language of the quotation will put your own prose into relief. If your own prose suffers by comparison—if the quotations are the best part of your paper—you'd be wise to spend some time revising. The way to avoid this kind of problem is to make your own presentation strong.

## Question

Questions are useful for opening essays, and they are just as useful for closing them. Opening and closing questions function in different ways, however. The introductory question promises to be addressed in the paper that follows. But

[13]From "And Man Created the Chip," *Newsweek*, June 30, 1980. Copyright © 1980 by Newsweek, Inc. All rights reserved. Reprinted by permission.

[14]Reprinted by permission. From the September issue of *Science '84.* Copyright © 1984 by the American Association for the Advancement of Science.

the concluding question leaves issues unresolved, calling on the readers to assume an active role by offering their own solutions:

> How do we surmount the reaction that threatens to destroy the very gains we thought we had already won in the first stage of the women's movement? How do we surmount our own reaction, which shadows our feminism and our femininity (we blush even to use that word now)? How do we transcend the polarization between women and women and between women and men to achieve the new human wholeness that is the promise of feminism, and get on with solving the concrete, practical, everyday problems of living, working and loving as equal persons? This is the personal and political business of the second stage.[15]

Perhaps you will choose to raise a question in your conclusion and then answer it, based on the material you've provided in the paper. The answered question challenges a reader to agree or disagree with your response. This tactic also places the reader in an active role. The following brief conclusion ends an article entitled "Would an Intelligent Computer Have a 'Right to Life'?"

> So the answer to the question "Would an intelligent computer have the right to life?" is probably that it would, but only if it could discover reasons and conditions under which it would give up its life if called upon to do so—which would make computer intelligence as precious a thing as human intelligence.[16]

## Speculation

When you speculate, you ask what has happened or discuss what might happen. This kind of question stimulates the reader because its subject is the unknown.

The following paragraph concludes "The New Generation Gap" by Neil Howe and William Strauss. In this essay, Howe and Strauss discuss the differences among Americans of various ages, including the "GI Generation" (born between 1901 and 1924), the "Boomers" (born 1943–1961), the "Thirteeners" (born 1961–1981), and the "Millennials" (born 1981–2000):

> If, slowly but surely, Millennials receive the kind of family protection and public generosity that GIs enjoyed as children, then they could come of age early in the next century as a group much like the GIs of the 1920s and 1930s—as a stellar (if bland) generation of rationalists, team players, and can-do civic builders. Two decades from now Boomers entering old age may well see in their grown Millennial children an effective instrument for saving the world, while

---

[15]Betty Friedan, "Feminism's Next Step" in *The Second Stage*. New York: Summit Books, 1981.
[16]Robert E. Mueller and Eric T. Mueller, "Would an Intelligent Computer Have a 'Right to Life'?" *Creative Computing*, August 1983.

---

Thirteeners entering midlife will shower kindness on a younger generation that is getting a better deal out of life (though maybe a bit less fun) than they ever got at a like age. Study after story after column will laud these "best damn kids in the world" as heralding a resurgent American greatness. And, for a while at least, no one will talk about a generation gap.[17]

Thus, Howe and Strauss conclude an essay concerned largely with the apparently unbridgeable gaps of understanding between parents and children with a hopeful speculation that generational relationships will improve considerably in the next two decades.

---

[17]Excerpt from "The New Generation Gap" by Neil Howe and William Strauss. Originally appeared in *Atlantic,* December 1992. Reprinted by permission of Raphael Sagalyn, Inc.

# 3

# CRITICAL READING
# AND CRITIQUE

## CRITICAL READING

When writing papers in college, you are often called on to respond critically to source materials. Critical reading requires the abilities both to summarize and to evaluate a presentation. As you have seen, a *summary* is a brief restatement in your own words of the content of a passage. An *evaluation* is a more difficult matter. In your college work, you read to gain and *use* new information; but unless you are willing to accept every source as equally valid and equally useful, you must learn to distinguish critically among sources by evaluating them.

There is no ready-made formula for determining validity. Critical reading and its written analogue—the *critique*—require discernment, sensitivity, imagination, and, above all, a willingness to become involved in what you read. These skills cannot be taken for granted and must be developed through repeated practice. You must begin somewhere, though, and we recommend that you start by posing two broad categories of questions about passages, articles, and books that you read: (1) What is the author's purpose in writing? Does he or she succeed in this purpose? (2) To what extent do you agree with the author?

### Question Category 1: What Is the Author's Purpose in Writing? Does He or She Succeed in This Purpose?

All critical reading *begins with an accurate summary.* Before attempting an evaluation, you must be able to locate an author's thesis and identify the selection's content and structure. You must understand the author's *purpose.* Authors write to inform, to persuade, and to entertain. A given piece may be *primarily informative* (a summary of the reasons for the rapid spread of AIDS), *primarily persuasive* (an argument on why the government must do something about poverty), or *primarily entertaining* (a play about the frustrations of young lovers), or it may be all three (as in John Steinbeck's novel *The Grapes of Wrath,* about migrant workers during the Great Depression). Sometimes authors are not fully conscious of their purposes. Sometimes their purposes change as they write. But if the finished piece is coherent, it will have a primary reason for having been written, and it should be apparent that the author is attempting primarily to inform, persuade, or entertain you. To identify this primary reason, this purpose, is your first job as a critical reader. Your next job is to determine how successful the author has been.

## Informative Writing

A piece intended to inform will provide definitions, describe or report on a process, recount a story, give historical background, or provide facts and figures. An informational piece responds to questions like the following:

What (or who) is_____?

How does_____work?

What is the controversy or problem about?

What happened?

How and why did it happen?

What were the results?

What are the arguments for and against_____?

To the extent that an author answers these and related questions and the answers are a matter of verifiable record (you could check for accuracy if you had the time and inclination), the selection is informational. Having determined this, you can organize your response by considering three other criteria:

*Accuracy of information.* If you are going to use any of the information presented, you must be satisfied that it is trustworthy. One of your responsibilities as a critical reader is to find out if it is.

*Significance of information.* One useful question that you can put to a reading is, "So what?" In the case of selections that attempt to inform, you may reasonably wonder whether the information makes a difference. What can the person who is reading gain from this information? How is knowledge advanced by the publication of this material? Is the information of importance to you or to others? Why or why not? Elaborate.

*Fair interpretation of information.* At times you will read reports, the sole function of which is to relate raw data or information. In these cases, you will build your response on the two questions in question category 1. More frequently, once an author has presented information, he or she will attempt to evaluate or interpret it—which is only reasonable, since information that has not been evaluated or interpreted is of little use. One of your tasks as a critical reader is to make a distinction between the author's presentation of facts and figures and his or her attempts to evaluate them. You may find that the information is valuable but the interpretation is not. Perhaps the author's conclusions are not justified. Could you offer a contrary explanation for the same facts? Does more information need to be gathered before conclusions can be drawn? Why?

## Persuasive Writing

Writing is frequently intended to persuade—that is, to influence the reader's thinking. To make a persuasive case, the writer must begin with an assertion that is arguable, some statement about which reasonable people could disagree. Such an assertion, when it serves as the essential organizing principle of the article or book, is called a *thesis*. Examples:

> Because they do not speak English, many children in this affluent land are being denied their fundamental right to equal educational opportunity.

> Bilingual education, which has been stridently promoted by a small group of activists with their own agenda, is detrimental to the very students it is supposed to serve.

Thesis statements like this—and the subsidiary assertions used to help support them—represent conclusions that authors have drawn as a result of researching and thinking about the issue. You go through the same process yourself when you write persuasive papers or critiques. And just as you are entitled to critically evaluate the assertions of authors you read, so your professors—and other students—are entitled to evaluate *your* assertions, whether they are encountered as written arguments or as comments made in class discussion.

Keep in mind that writers organize arguments by arranging evidence to support one conclusion and oppose (or dismiss) another. You can assess the validity of the argument and the conclusion by determining whether the author has (1) clearly defined key terms, (2) used information fairly, (3) argued logically, and not fallaciously.

*Clearly defined terms.* The validity of an argument depends to some degree on how carefully key terms have been defined. Take the assertion, for example—made in the 1930s by the official motion-picture production code— that no film should be made that will "lower the moral standards of those who see it." What do the authors of this code mean by "lower the moral standards"? The validity of their argument depends on whether or not they and their readers agree on a definition of moral standards and on a definition of lowered moral standards. If an author writes, "The public safety demands that reasonable precautions be taken to protect the public against infection from HIV-positive persons," readers need to know what, exactly, is meant by "reasonable" before they can assess the validity of the argument. An author who writes, "Some cultures are better than others" must be careful to define just what she means by "better." (We may not agree with her definition, but at least it is now on the table, a subject for discussion.) In such cases, the success of the argument—its ability to persuade—hinges on the definition of a term. So, in responding to an argument, be sure you (and the author) are clear on what exactly is being argued. Only then can you respond to the logic of the argument, to the author's use of evidence, and to the author's conclusions.

***Fair use of information.*** Information is used as evidence in support of arguments. When presented with such evidence, bear several concerns in mind. The *first:* "Is the information accurate and up-to-date?" At least a portion of an argument is rendered invalid if the information used to support it is inaccurate or out-of-date. A *second* question: "Has the author cited *representative* information?" The evidence used in an argument must be presented in a spirit of fair play. An author is less than ethical who presents only evidence favoring his views when he is well aware that contrary evidence exists. For instance, it would be dishonest to argue that an economic recession is imminent and to cite as evidence only those indicators of economic well-being that have taken a decided turn for the worse while ignoring and failing to cite contrary (positive) evidence.

***Logical argumentation; avoiding logical fallacies.*** At some point, you will need to respond to the logic of the argument itself. To be convincing, an argument should be governed by principles of logic—clear and orderly thinking. This does *not* mean that an argument should not be biased. It may, in fact, be both valid and biased—that is, weighted toward one point of view and against others—as long as it is also logically sound.

Here are several examples of faulty thinking and logical fallacies to watch for:

EMOTIONALLY LOADED TERMS.    Writers sometimes will attempt to sway readers by using emotionally charged words: words with positive connotations to sway readers to their own point of view; words with negative connotations to sway readers away from the opposing point of view. For example, look again at the two assertions about bilingual education on page 67. In the first assertion (by Jeffrey W. Kobrick), the terms "fundamental right" and "equal . . . opportunity" carry positive connotations intended to sway the reader to the author's pro-bilingual education view. In the second assertion, the terms "stridently" and "small group of activists" carry negative connotations intended to influence the reader to reject the anti-bilingual arguments with which the author associates them. The fact that an author uses such emotionally loaded terms does not necessarily invalidate the argument. Emotional appeals are perfectly legitimate and time-honored modes of persuasion. But in academic writing, which is grounded in logical argumentation, they should not be the *only* means of persuasion. You should be sensitive to *how* emotionally loaded terms are being used. In particular, are they being used deceptively or to hide the essential facts?

AD HOMINEM ARGUMENT.    In an *ad hominem* argument, the writer rejects opposing views by attacking the person who holds them. By calling opponents names, an author avoids the issue:

I could more easily accept my opponent's plan to increase revenues by collecting on delinquent tax bills if he had paid more than a hundred dollars in state taxes in each of the past three years. But the fact is, he's a millionaire with a millionaire's tax shelters. This man hasn't paid a wooden nickel for the state services he and his family depend on. So I ask you: Is *he* the one to be talking about taxes to *us*?

It could well be that the opponent has paid virtually no state taxes for three years; but this fact has nothing to do with, and is a ploy to divert attention from, the merits of a specific proposal for increasing revenues. The proposal is lost in the attack against the man himself, an attack that violates the principles of logic. Writers (and speakers) must make their points by citing evidence in support of their views and by challenging contrary evidence.

**FAULTY CAUSE AND EFFECT.** The fact that one event precedes another in time does not mean that the first event has caused the second. An example: Fish begin dying by the thousands in a lake near your hometown. An environmental group immediately cites chemical dumping by several manufacturing plants as the cause. But other causes are possible: A disease might have affected the fish; the growth of algae might have contributed to the deaths; or acid rain might be a factor. The origins of an event are usually complex and are not always traceable to a single cause. So you must carefully examine cause-and-effect reasoning when you find a writer using it. This fallacy is also known as *post hoc, ergo propter hoc* ("after this, therefore because of this").

**EITHER/OR REASONING.** Either/or reasoning also results from an unwillingness to recognize complexity. If an author analyzes a problem and offers only two explanations, one of which he or she refutes, then you are entitled to object; for usually a third or fourth explanation (at the very least) would be possible. For whatever reason, the author has chosen to overlook these. As an example, suppose you are reading a selection on genetic engineering and the author builds an argument on the basis of the following:

Research in gene splicing is at a crossroads: Either scientists will be carefully monitored by civil authorities and their efforts limited to acceptable applications, such as disease control; or, lacking regulatory guidelines, scientists will set their own ethical standards and begin programs in embryonic manipulation that, however well intended, exceed the proper limits of human knowledge.

Certainly, other possibilities for genetic engineering exist beyond the two mentioned here. But the author limits debate by establishing an either/or choice. Such limitation is artificial and does not allow for complexity. As a critical reader, be on the alert for either/or reasoning.

**HASTY GENERALIZATION.** Writers are guilty of hasty generalization when they draw their conclusions from too little evidence or from unrepresentative evidence. To argue that scientists should not proceed with the human genome project because a recent editorial urged that the project be abandoned is to make a hasty generalization. This lone editorial may be unrepresentative of the views of most people—both scientists and laypeople—who have studied and written about the matter. To argue that one should never obey authority because the Milgram experiment shows the dangers of obeying authority is to ignore the fact that Milgram's experiment was concerned primarily with obedience to *immoral* authority. Thus, the experimental situation was unrepresentative of most routine demands for obedience—for example, to obey a parental rule or to comply with a summons for jury duty—and a conclusion about the malevolence of all authority would be a hasty generalization.

**FALSE ANALOGY.** Comparing one person, event, or issue to another may be illuminating, but it also may be confusing or misleading. The differences between the two may be more significant than the similarities, and the conclusions drawn from the one may not necessarily apply to the other. A writer who argues that it is reasonable to quarantine people with AIDS because quarantine has been effective in preventing the spread of smallpox is assuming an analogy between AIDS and smallpox that (because of the differences between the two diseases) is not valid.

**BEGGING THE QUESTION.** To beg the question is to assume as a proven fact the very thesis being argued. To assert, for example, that America is not in decline because it is as strong and prosperous as ever is not to prove anything: it is merely to repeat the claim in different words. This fallacy is also known as circular reasoning.

**NON SEQUITUR.** "Non sequitur" is Latin for "it does not follow"; the term is used to describe a conclusion that does not logically follow from a premise. "Since minorities have made such great strides in the last few decades," a writer may argue, "we no longer need affirmative action programs." Aside from the fact that the premise itself is arguable (*have* minorities made such great strides?), it does not follow that because minorities *may* have made great strides, there is no further need for affirmative action programs.

**OVERSIMPLIFICATION.** Be alert for writers who offer easy solutions to complicated problems. "America's economy will be strong again if we all 'buy American,' " a politician may argue. But the problems of America's economy are complex and cannot be solved by a slogan or a simple change in buying habits. Likewise, a writer who argues that we should ban genetic engineering assumes that simple solutions ("just say 'no' ") will be sufficient to deal with the complex moral dilemmas raised by this new technology.

## Writing That Entertains

Authors write not only to inform and persuade but also to entertain. One response to entertainment is a hearty laugh; but it is possible to entertain without laughter: A good book or play or poem may prompt you to ruminate, grow wistful, elated, angry. Laughter is only one of many possible reactions. You read a piece (or view a work) and react with sadness, surprise, exhilaration, disbelief, horror, boredom, whatever. As with a response to an informative piece or an argument, your response to an essay, poem, story, play, novel, or film should be precisely stated and carefully developed. Ask yourself some of the following questions (you won't have space to explore all of them, but try to consider some of the most important): Did I care for the portrayal of a certain character? Did that character seem too sentimentalized, for example, or heroic? Did his adversaries seem too villainous or stupid? Were the situations believable? Was the action interesting or merely formulaic? Was the theme developed subtly, powerfully, or did the work come across as preachy or shrill? Did the action at the end of the work follow plausibly from what had come before? Was the language fresh and incisive or stale and predictable? Explain as specifically as possible what elements of the work seemed effective or ineffective and why. Offer an overall assessment, elaborating on your views.

## Question Category 2: To What Extent Do You Agree with the Author?

When formulating a critical response to a source, try to distinguish your evaluation of the author's purpose and success at achieving that purpose from your agreement or disagreement with the author's views. The distinction allows you to respond to a piece of writing on its merits. As an unbiased, evenhanded critic, you evaluate an author's clarity of presentation, use of evidence, and adherence to principles of logic. To what extent has the author succeeded in achieving his or her purpose? Still withholding judgment, offer your assessment and give the author (in effect) a grade. Significantly, your assessment of the presentation may not coincide with your views of the author's conclusions: You may agree with an author entirely but feel that the presentation is superficial; you may find the author's logic and use of evidence to be rock solid, although you resist certain conclusions. A critical evaluation works well when it is conducted in two parts. Assuming that you have completed an evaluation of the author's purpose and design for achieving that purpose, turn to the author's main assertions—and respond. You'll want to keep two considerations in mind:

### Identify Points of Agreement and Disagreement

Be precise in identifying points of agreement and disagreement with an author. You should state as clearly as possible what *you* believe, and an effective way of doing this is to define your position in relation to that presented in the piece. Whether you agree enthusiastically, disagree, or agree with reservations, you can organize your reactions in two parts: first, summarize the author's position; second, state your own position and elaborate on your reasons for holding it. The elaboration, in effect, becomes an argument itself, and this is true regardless of the position you take. An opinion is effective when you support it by supplying evidence. Without such evidence, opinions cannot be authoritative. "I thought the article on inflation was lousy." Why? "I just thought so, that's all." This opinion is valueless because the criticism is imprecise: The critic has taken neither the time to read the article carefully nor the time to explore his own reactions carefully.

### Explore the Reasons for Agreement and Disagreement: Evaluate Assumptions

One way of elaborating your reactions to a reading is to explore the under-lying *reasons* for agreement and disagreement. Your reactions are based largely on assumptions that you hold and how these assumptions compare with the author's. An *assumption* is a fundamental statement about the world and its operations that you take to be true. A writer's assumptions may be explicitly stated; but just as often assumptions are implicit and you will have to "ferret them out," that is, to infer them. Consider an example:

> *In vitro* fertilization and embryo transfer are brought about outside the bodies of the couple through actions of third parties whose competence and technical activity determine the success of the procedure. Such fertilization entrusts the life and identity of the embryo into the power of doctors and biologists and establishes the domination of technology over the origin and destiny of the human person. Such a relationship of domination is in itself contrary to the dignity and equality that must be common to parents and children.[1]

This paragraph is quoted from the February 1987 Vatican document on artificial procreation. Cardinal Joseph Ratzinger, principal author of the document, makes an implicit assumption in this paragraph: that no good can come of the domi-nation of technology over conception. The use of technology to bring about conception is morally wrong. Yet there are thousands of childless couples, Roman Catholics included, who reject this assumption in favor of its opposite: that conception technology is an aid to the barren couple; far from creating a relationship of unequals, the technology brings children into the world who will be welcomed with joy and love.

Assumptions provide the foundation on which entire presentations are built. If you find an author's assumptions invalid, you'll likely disagree with conclusions that follow from these assumptions. The author of a book on developing nations may include a section outlining the resources and time that will be required to industrialize a particular country and so upgrade its general welfare. His assumption—that industrialization in that particular country will ensure or even have anything to do with what people themselves consider their general welfare—may or may not be valid. If you do not share the assumption, in your eyes the rationale for the entire book will be undermined.

Later in this text you will find a chapter on the changing attitudes toward Christopher Columbus. Read some of the assessments of Columbus written in the nineteenth century, and you will find that these writers (and doubtless the vast majority of their readers) shared the assumptions that Columbus was one of the great heroes of history and that his four voyages to the New World brought inestimable benefits to humankind. These assumptions, the truth of

---

[1]From the Vatican document *Instruction on Respect for Human Life in Its Origin and on the Dignity of Procreation*, given at Rome, from the Congregation for the Doctrine of the Faith, February 22, 1987, as presented in *Origins: N.C. Documentary Service* 16(40), March 19, 1987, p. 707.

which once was taken for granted, are certainly open to question, however—particularly by those indigenous American peoples who were "discovered" by Columbus and who were to be decimated and enslaved by those who followed him. In making your own critical analyses, then, you should strive to identify and examine *all* assumptions, especially those that are in harmony with what you believe (and so seem beyond examination!).

How do you determine the validity of assumptions once you have identified them? In the absence of more scientific criteria, validity may mean how well the author's assumptions stack up against your own experience, observations, and reading. A caution, however: The overall value of an article or book may depend only to a small degree on the validity of the author's assumptions. For instance, a sociologist may do a fine job of gathering statistical data about the incidence of crime in urban areas along the eastern seaboard. The sociologist also might be a Marxist, and you may disagree with her subsequent analysis of the data. Yet you may find the data extremely valuable for your own work.

## CRITIQUE

A *critique* is a *formalized, critical reading of a passage*. It is also a personal response; but writing a critique is considerably more rigorous than saying that a movie is "great," or a book is "fascinating," or "I didn't like it." These are all responses, and, as such, they're a valid, even essential, part of your understanding of what you see and read. But such responses don't help illuminate the subject for anyone—even you—if you haven't explained how you arrived at your conclusions.

Your task in writing a critique is to turn your critical reading of a passage into a systematic evaluation in order to deepen your reader's (and your own) understanding of that passage. Among other things, you're interested in determining what an author says, how well the points are made, what assumptions underlie the argument, what issues are overlooked, and what implications can be drawn from such an analysis. Critiques, positive or negative, should include a fair and accurate summary of the passage; they also should include a statement of your own assumptions. It is important to remember that you bring to bear an entire set of assumptions about the world. Stated or not, these assumptions underlie every evaluative comment you make; therefore, you have an obligation, both to the reader and to yourself, to clarify your standards. Not only do your readers stand to gain by your forthrightness, but you do as well: In the process of writing a critical assessment, you are forced to examine your own knowledge, beliefs, and assumptions. Ultimately, the critique is a way of learning about yourself.

### How to Write Critiques

You may find it useful to organize your critiques in five sections: introduction, summary, analysis of the presentation, your response to the presentation, and conclusion.

♦ *Introduction.* Introduce both the passage under analysis and the author. State the author's main argument and the point(s) you intend to make about it.

Provide background material to help your readers understand the relevance or appeal of the passage. This background material might include one or more of the following: an explanation of why the subject is of current interest; a reference to a possible controversy surrounding the subject of the passage or the passage itself; biographical information about the author; an account of the circumstances under which the passage was written; or a reference to the intended audience of the passage.

♦ *Summary.* Summarize the author's main points, making sure to state the author's purpose for writing.

♦ *Analysis of the presentation.* Evaluate the validity of the author's presentation, as distinct from your points of agreement or disagreement. Comment on the author's success in achieving his or her purpose by reviewing three or four specific points. You might base your review on one (or more) of the following criteria:

Is the information accurate?

Is the information significant?

Has the author defined terms clearly?

Has the author used and interpreted information fairly?

Has the author argued logically?

♦ *Your response to the presentation.* Now it is your turn to respond to the author's views. With which views do you agree? With which do you disagree? Discuss your reasons for agreement and disagreement, when possible tying these reasons to assumptions—both the author's and your own.

♦ *Conclusion.* State your conclusions about the overall validity of the piece—your assessment of the author's success at achieving his or her aims and your reactions to the author's views. Remind the reader of the weaknesses and strengths of the passage.

Two additional points about writing critiques:

♦ The preceding guidelines are meant to be just that: guidelines, not a rigid formula. Thousands of authors write critiques that do not follow the structure outlined here. Until you are more confident and practiced in writing critiques, however, we suggest you follow the guidelines. They are meant not to restrict you, but to provide you with a workable method of writing critical analyses that incorporates a logical sequence of development.

♦ Before writing a critique based on an essay in this text, read the discussion and writing questions following that essay. These questions will lead you to some of the more fruitful areas of inquiry. Beware of simply responding mechanically to them, however, or your essay could degenerate into a series of short, disjointed responses. You need to organize your reactions into a coherent whole: the critique should be informed by a consistent point of view.

## DEMONSTRATION: CRITIQUE

Read the following selection, "Perils in the Demand for Biculturalism," a passage from Rosalie Pedalino Porter's book *Forked Tongue: The Politics of Bilingual Education*. Porter's thesis, implied in her title, is certainly arguable, and it is based on assumptions that you should examine carefully. Use the points that we presented in the preceding discussion to stimulate your responses to Porter.

When reading an article you are likely to critique, have pencil in hand to keep notes. Marginal notations will help you write a summary (you would be interested in underlining the author's thesis, topic sentences, transitions, important examples); marginal notations in the form of questions and reactions can also help you organize a critical response.

After you have read Porter's essay, gather your notes and order them according to the five steps for writing critiques outlined above.

# Perils in the Demand for Biculturalism

## ROSALIE PEDALINO PORTER

*Rosalie Pedalino Porter is director of Bilingual and English-as-a-Second Language Programs in the Newton, Massachusetts, public schools and has lectured widely on the subject of bilingualism both in the United States and abroad.*

My family was poor, so the first necessity was for us to gain the economic means to survive. We children did not enjoy the middle-class luxury of a choice of schooling or careers. The thought of taking time to "get in touch with myself" did not exist. I was fortunate that my mother convinced my father to let me finish high school and not leave school at sixteen to work in his grocery store. Because I was the oldest of five children and a girl, I did not think to question my fate: I should help my mother after school every day, and when I reached the age of

From *Forked Tongue: The Politics of Bilingual Education* by Rosalie Pedalino Porter. Copyright © 1990 by Basic Books, Inc. Reprinted by permission of Basic Books, a division of HarperCollins Publishers, Inc.

sixteen, I should leave high school and help in the store. In fact, my father would have preferred that we stay closely attached to the family and neither attend school nor learn English. Mandatory attendance at school saved us! For me, convention dictated that family bondage would not end until I married—and married within the ethnic group and preferably in the neighborhood, when I would then no longer be my father's but my husband's responsibility.

School, however, opened up my horizons, and the English language gave me the entry not only to the excitement of academic advancement but to friendships with children from very different families, other ethnic groups, and other religions. I began to want to learn, with a desire for a range of experiences, and, yes, a desire for material things and an interesting job.

Of course, my experience was not unusual. I wanted to be free from what seemed the restrictive customs and language of my family and community, free from the burden of being "different." The desire is common to young people of various ethnic groups, and it is not surprising, therefore, that this liberation is the enduring subject of a large body of literature and drama, in novels such as *The Fortunate Pilgrim, Call It Sleep,* and *Goodbye, Columbus* and films such as *West Side Story, Hester Street,* and *Crossing Delancey.*

It is daunting for anyone to cross the ethnic divide, but for women the voyage has been and continues to be even more difficult. To move out of poverty and beyond ethnicity requires individual motivation and strength of purpose *and* the reinforcement of outside help from the schools, job opportunities, and the presence of achievable role models.

I saw with renewed immediacy the clash of cultures and the hardship it imposes on the young in the case of three refugee women from Afghanistan who were in the Newton North High School ESL program for two years. They had learned English fairly well and completed a good part of their high school graduation requirements. They longed to enroll in a local community college, but the families arranged marriages for all three, finding them Afghan husbands instead. The teacher who knew the students and their families and had been an advisor to the young women was deeply disappointed. It is often just not possible to effect such change in the first years of residence in a new country.

The language and culture shift in my own immigrant family took an unusual twist. Oldest of the children in a family of three sons and two daughters, I have moved the farthest from my family geographically and in terms of assimilation into American middle-class life. My brothers and sister, who have all completed college degrees and achieved economic success, live near my mother and have, unlike me, married within the ethnic group and the religion of our upbringing. Yet I am the only one of us who has maintained and expanded her knowledge of Italian, which

I speak and write fluently. None of the others is the least bit interested in the language, but they are still very close to the customs. Paradoxically, I am closer to our "roots," to our country of origin, because I travel to Italy frequently and have a husband and three sons who are all Italophiles. My sister and brothers, however, are more closely involved in Italian-American culture. We have each chosen the degree of ethnicity we wish to maintain. I am not convinced of the inevitability of guilt over some loss of ethnicity, the sort that Mario Puzo depicted in *The Fortunate Pilgrim*, when he wrote, "They spoke with guilty loyalty of customs they themselves had trampled into dust." It is not that I am without sentimental feelings, but I cannot honestly wish that I or my family had remained immersed in our original language and ethnicity. We are immeasurably richer for having that background and for having added to it some of the achievements that American life offers. . . .

The ethnic revival of the 1970s has prompted widespread recognition of the incredible diversity of the United States and has fostered a renewed interest in our various historical backgrounds—how we got here, what we have experienced, where we are today. Pushing cultural pluralism insensitively, as in the demand for "bicultural" education, disables the minority communities with the least power. The critical question for multicultural societies like our own is whether education policies that further the cultural identity of minority groups at the same time enable minority children to acquire the knowledge and skills to attain social and economic equality. As we have seen, school programs with extended use of the native language and enforced preservation of the home culture are, by definition, segregative in nature. James Lyons, counsel for the National Association for Bilingual Education, recognizes the legitimate concern that Transitional Bilingual Education tends to segregate pupils by language ability. He does not call this an invidious form of segregation, but he observes that it "creates a tension, because the ethic of American society is integration." Without sustained contact between majority and minority children, there will be isolation of the minority group, shamefully like the "separate but equal" policies that kept black children's schooling separate and unequal. 7

The demand for biculturalism, we must recognize, creates tensions for the individual members of language minority groups. Other nations have been sensitive to this conflict. In Sweden, the multilingual society that has enacted the most compassionate laws to protect minorities, the national government provides every group with the choice of being educated in its own language; supports retention and development of the values, religion, and customs of the original culture; and proposes that immigrants' cultures be regarded as beneficial influences on Sweden's social development. Sociolinguists like Barry McLaughlin and Christina Bratt Paulston, who generally favor bilingual education, are 8 skeptical of the Swedish policy. Although it appears decent and humane, McLaughlin points out, it is difficult to realize in practice, "especially when Swedes are asked to appreciate the 'beneficial influence' of customs and habits of poor, rural Mediterranean cultures that are quite at variance with those of affluent, urban Swedish society."

Paulston notes the difficulties that the demands of biculturalism **9** impose on young women from very traditional Turkish village backgrounds who are growing up in Sweden: "It is difficult to see how those girls can internalize both their fathers' value system of women and that of Swedish society. In fact, they can't, and that situation casts serious doubt on the many glib statements of biculturalism as one objective of bilingual education." This dilemma is unavoidable in countries where there are strikingly different cultures in contact and, perhaps, in conflict.

I do not believe that the bilingual child's best interests are necessar- **10** ily served by large-scale institutional support for different cultures. But is such a policy ultimately in the best interests of the nation? In the case of Sweden, Paulston quotes an official who sees this danger in the official policy: "How can one encourage cultural freedom of choice without society splitting into numerous groups, all of which compete with each other?" Paulston goes on to surmise that his question really concerns what is best for Sweden—not for individuals or ethnic groups, but for the country. She ends by saying, "It seems to me that the migrant children themselves have answered that question. By being allowed to assimilate and incorporate, they will with time become good Swedes, and Sweden herself will be infinitely the richer for enhanced cultural ties to the rest of Europe."

Retaining ethnic boundaries inevitably reinforces existing inequal- **11** ity. Cultural pluralism in America is uncomfortably linked to ethnic inequalities and exclusion or alienation of certain groups. In fact, it can be argued that groups on the margin of the country's economy have kept their ethnic distinctions because they have been isolated and excluded from the larger society. For these groups, however, the retention of ethnicity is not the crucial issue. As Irving Howe suggests, the central problems of our society have to do, not with ethnic groupings,

> but with economic policy, social rule, class relations . . . with vast inequities of wealth, with the shameful neglect of a growing class of subproletarians, with the readiness of policy-makers to tolerate high levels of unemployment. They have to do with 'the crises of the cities,' a polite phrase masking a terrible reality—the willingness of this country to dump millions of black (and white) poor into the decaying shells of once thriving cities. Toward problems of this kind and magnitude, what answers can ethnicity offer? Very weak ones, I fear.

Those of us who have experienced culture and language shift—and **12** we are many—have felt at different times both the sentimental longing for a seemingly simpler past of shared traditions, closer communities, and stable families and the sharp sense that our cultural symbols from the past cannot really shield us from the discontents of the modern world. Overcoming the discontents of minorities will not be achieved by having our schools emphasize biculturalism and resegregating children along language and ethnic lines, which are the realities in bilingual education classrooms. Biculturalism will not make up for the years of neglect of language-minority children when they were invisible in the mainstream classroom or out of school at an early age.

Now consider the following questions about Porter's argument:

♦ How does this passage tie in to the larger debate about bilingual education? Why is this subject important? What are Porter's qualifications for writing this piece?
♦ What are her main points? Why did she write this passage?
♦ Do Porter's arguments strike you as valid? Does she appear to have interpreted the evidence fairly, for example? Has she argued logically?
♦ To what extent do you agree with Porter? To what extent do you agree with her assumptions and her conclusions? Explain the reasons for your reactions.
♦ What are your overall conclusions about the strengths and weaknesses of Porter's arguments?

In the following critique, one student presents his responses to these questions:

## A Critique of Rosalie Pedalino Porter's "Perils in the Demand for Biculturalism"

In her essay "Perils in the Demand for Biculturalism," Rosalie Pedalino Porter, a director of bilingual and ESL programs, asks in effect: What's so great about ethnicity? Born into an immigrant Italian family, Porter draws on her own life to make the case against biculturalism. "I do not believe," she concludes, "that the bilingual child's best interests are necessarily served by large-scale institutional support for different cultures." In the course of her essay, Porter questions the value of traditional ethnicity and asserts that

1

biculturalism may prevent minority children from becoming successes like herself. Porter's own experiences undeniably lend credibility to her arguments; but ultimately, these arguments fail to convince the reader of the "perils" of biculturalism.

Porter begins by recalling that her own Italian father would have preferred that she and her sisters stay home--presumably until they were married off--neither attending school nor learning English. But school, she writes, "opened my horizons." She enjoyed learning and met people of many different backgrounds--things she would not have been able to do had her traditional father had his way. She explains, "I wanted to be free from what seemed the restrictive customs and language of my family and community." For some ethnic minorities, of course, liberation is not so easy. Porter tells of several young Afghan women who "longed" to go to college, but instead were forced by their families to marry. Returning to her own story, she notes that although she is more highly educated and fully assimilated than her siblings, she is in fact closer than they are to her "roots": she speaks Italian fluently and frequently travels to Italy. Her siblings, although living within more traditional Italian-American families, do neither. "We have each chosen the degree of ethnicity we wish to maintain," she declares. "I cannot honestly wish that I or my family had remained immersed in our original language and ethnicity."

In the second part of her essay, Porter                     3

turns from her own case to the general issue of
biculturalism, arguing that bicultural programs
hurt minority children because they are
"segregative," while "the ethic of American
society is integrative." She shows that experts
are skeptical of the success or value of
bicultural programs in Sweden and Switzerland.
How are children to successfully internalize the
value systems of two radically different
cultures? And don't countries that encourage
multiculturalism run the risk of fragmenting
their own societies? Porter acknowledges that in
our own country ethnic minorities often try to
hold on to their cultural ties because they have
been cut off from the mainstream culture. But
the problems of these minorities, she argues, are
less ethnic than economic, and "retention of
their ethnicity" will not solve these economic
problems. The desire for biculturalism, she
contends, is really a "sentimental longing for a
seemingly simpler past of shared traditions,
closer communities, and stable families."

Strongly influenced by her own experience,  4
Porter finds the traditional ethnic family
stifling, yet remains proud of her aesthetic and
linguistic connection to Italy. One problem with
Porter's position, however, lies in her
assumption that such an abstracted interest in
Italy (the interest of the Italophile, of the
language student, of the traveler) amounts to an
ethnic identity. Many members of minority
groups--perhaps even Porter's own siblings--might
find more "Italian" a lifestyle based on family
values and traditions: religion, mealtimes,

weddings, and other family gatherings. After
all, isn't Porter's Italophile status the kind of
thing that a Jewish, Swedish, or African-American
person could also attain?

This brings us to the main weakness of     5
Porter's case--her use of herself as a primary
example. Initially helpful to her credibility,
Porter's limited self-analysis now becomes a
double-edged sword to damage the logic of her
argument. Porter separates "good" from "bad"
ethnicity; and the result is an arbitrary and
illogical distinction. She describes how her
father would have rather kept her at home, but
she seems to take for granted the fact that once
in school she flourished. Psychologists point
out that a child's character is largely formed by
age six or seven--the years that a child spends
in the home. If Porter were well adjusted enough
emotionally and mentally to do well in school,
shouldn't she give her traditional family some of
the credit? Her father may have wanted to deny
her a higher education, but he must have done
something right to produce a woman so intelligent
and successful. And therefore wouldn't any
credit due to him also be due to the Italian
familial tradition that he so faithfully
represented? Porter has decided to attribute all
of her success to her participation in mainstream
American life--and, to a corresponding degree,
herself. Her natural egotism interferes with her
logic and damages her larger goal--to downplay
the value of the ethnic traditions that would be
diluted by assimilation.

In the second part of her argument, Porter     6

moves from an indictment of ethnicity (and praise for assimilation) to the charge that bilingual education programs segregate ethnic minorities from the majority and therefore harm the minority child. "Without sustained contact between majority and minority children," she argues, "there will be isolation of the minority group, shamefully like the 'separate but equal' policies that kept black children's schooling separate and unequal." But Porter's argument here against bilingual programs relies less on hard data than on assumptions about her audience's reaction to loaded language. When Porter calls bilingual education programs "by definition segregative in nature," she leaves it at that. Her reference to the "separate but unequal" policies of pre-civil rights America carries some weight, but she assumes that her audience will agree without question that "segregation" means bad. Her argument does not take into account the fact that from a minority standpoint, segregative situations can be equal--even superior--to integrative ones. Ready to debate Porter on this point would be proponents of women's schools, such as Oakland's Mills College, or all-African-American institutions, such as Howard University. Segregated education shelters minority students from ignorance and persecution, they would argue, allowing students to bond together for mutual support and allowing them to "bloom" unmolested.

Porter's related points about biculturalism are as sketchily argued. Citing the case of young Turkish girls in Sweden, she casts doubt on the ability of immigrants to "internalize"

7

differing value systems (such as cultural ideas
of women's roles) while neatly forgetting that
somehow she herself managed to overcome her own
Italian-American family's beliefs concerning the
place of women in the home. (Porter might
counter that America's opposition to
biculturalism is what prompted her to assimilate;
but many of us know immigrants and members of
ethnic minorities who are able to internalize the
cultural values of both their own and their
adopted country without either putting themselves
at a disadvantage or tearing the social fabric.)
This contradiction weakens her final paragraphs
and her case against the workability of a
bicultural and multicultural society.

    Certainly, when ethnic minorities fail to    **8**
assimilate, fail to come to terms with one
another or the majority culture, they may resort
to ethnic warfare. We have looked with horror at
the bloodshed in what used to be Yugoslavia. And,
recently, the violence in South-Central Los
Angeles reminded us that America itself is not
immune to such scourges. But in the face of such
an urgent necessity to deal with our racial and
ethnic differences, Rosalie Porter offers only a
traditional philosophy dating back to Horatio
Alger--faith in the individual to overcome all
odds in his or her rise to the top of the
ladder. The majority of immigrants in this land
do not aspire, like Porter, to become
professional educators and writers who regularly
travel as tourists to their native land. They
just want a basic opportunity; and biculturalism,

as an educational and social policy, provides
them with just that.  Porter hasn't convinced me
otherwise.

--Michael Arai

## Discussion

♦ In the first paragraph, the writer introduces his subject and describes Porter's purpose in writing the essay. The writer concludes the paragraph with his thesis: that Porter's narrative is effective, but that her argument ultimately fails to convince.

♦ In the second and third paragraphs, Arai objectively summarizes Porter's essay. Paragraph 3 deals with Porter's narrative section; paragraph 4 deals with her argument section. Again, the writer uses selected quotations to indicate Porter's key ideas.

♦ In the fourth paragraph, Arai questions the value of Porter's love of Italy as an indication of the degree to which she has retained her ethnicity. Because this is a relatively minor argument, it is not discussed at length.

♦ In the fifth paragraph, Arai takes up the "main weakness of Porter's case—her use of herself as a primary example." The writer points out that although Porter's use of her own example lends credibility to her argument, it also reveals how little credit she gives her family—and her family's ethnicity—for the very success that she attributes to her successful assimilation.

♦ In the sixth paragraph, Arai discusses Porter's use of the terms "segregative" and "integrative" and her allusions to the language of the civil rights years. He points out that not all minorities consider segregation a bad thing and integration a good thing.

♦ In the seventh paragraph, Arai points out that despite the "perils" of biculturalism, it is quite possible for ethnic minorities to internalize and to integrate successfully two differing cultural value systems—Porter herself did so.

♦ In the eighth and concluding paragraph, Arai concedes that ethnic differences can lead to horrors both abroad and at home; but he claims that Porter's solutions are too traditional and fail to take account of ethnic minorities who choose not to follow Porter's own path to assimilation.

# 4

# SYNTHESIS

## WHAT IS A SYNTHESIS?

A *synthesis* is a written discussion that draws on two or more sources. It follows that your ability to write syntheses depends on your ability to infer relationships among sources—essays, articles, fiction, and also nonwritten sources, such as lectures, interviews, observations. This process is nothing new for you, since you infer relationships all the time—say, between something you've read in the newspaper and something you've seen for yourself, or between the teaching styles of your favorite and least favorite instructors. In fact, if you've written research papers, you've already written syntheses. In an *academic* synthesis, you make explicit the relationships that you have inferred among separate sources.

The skills you've already learned and practiced from the previous three chapters will be vital in writing syntheses. Clearly, before you're in a position to draw relationships between two or more sources, you must understand what those sources say; in other words, you must be able to *summarize* these sources. It will frequently be helpful for your readers if you provide at least partial summaries of sources in your synthesis essays. At the same time, you must go beyond summary to make judgments—judgments based, of course, on your *critical reading* of your sources. You should already have drawn some conclusions about the quality and validity of these sources; and you should know how much you agree or disagree with the points made in your sources and the reasons for your agreement or disagreement.

Further, you must go beyond the critique of individual sources to determine the relationship among them. Is the information in source B, for example, an extended illustration of the generalizations in source A? Would it be useful to compare and contrast source C with source B? Having read and considered sources A, B, and C, can you infer something else—D (not a source, but your own idea)?

Because a synthesis is based on two or more sources, you will need to be selective when choosing information from each. It would be neither possible nor desirable, for instance, to discuss in a ten-page paper on the battle of Wounded Knee every point that the authors of two books make about their subject. What you as a writer must do is select the ideas and information from each source that best allow you to achieve your purpose.

## PURPOSE

Your purpose in reading source materials and then in drawing on them to write your own material is often reflected in the wording of an assignment. For instance, consider the following assignments on the Civil War:

*American History:* Evaluate your text author's treatment of the origins of the Civil War.

*Economics:* Argue the following proposition, in light of your readings: "The Civil War was fought not for reasons of moral principle but for reasons of economic necessity."

*Government:* Prepare a report on the effects of the Civil War on Southern politics at the state level between 1870 and 1917.

*Mass Communications:* Discuss how the use of photography during the Civil War may have affected the perceptions of the war by Northerners living in industrial cities.

*Literature:* Select two twentieth-century Southern writers whose work you believe was influenced by the divisive effects of the Civil War. Discuss the ways this influence is apparent in a novel or a group of short stories written by each author. The works should not be *about* the Civil War.

*Applied Technology:* Compare and contrast the technology of warfare available in the 1860s with the technology available a century earlier.

Each of these assignments creates for you a particular purpose for writing. Having located sources relevant to your topic, you would select, for possible use in a paper, only those parts that helped you in fulfilling this purpose. And how you used those parts, how you related them to other material from other sources, would also depend on your purpose. For instance, if you were working on the government assignment, you might possibly draw on the same source as another student working on the literature assignment by referring to Robert Penn Warren's novel *All the King's Men,* about Louisiana politics in the early part of the twentieth century. But because the purposes of these assignments are different, you and the other student would make different uses of this source. Those same parts or aspects of the novel that you find worthy of detailed analysis might be just mentioned in passing by the other student.

## USING YOUR SOURCES

Your purpose determines not only what parts of your sources you will use but also how you will relate them to one another. Since the very essence of synthesis is the combining of information and ideas, you must have some basis on which to combine them. *Some relationships among the material in your sources must make them worth synthesizing.* It follows that the better able you are to discover such relationships, the better able you will be to use your sources in writing syntheses. Notice that the mass communications assignment requires you to draw a *cause-and-effect* relationship between photographs of the war and Northerners' perceptions of the war. The applied technology assignment requires you to *compare and contrast* state-of-the-art weapons technology in the eighteenth and nineteenth centuries. The economics assignment requires you to *argue* a proposition. In each case, *your purpose will determine how you relate your source materials to one another.*

Consider some other examples. You may be asked on an exam question or in instructions for a paper to *describe* two or three approaches to prison reform during the past decade. You may be asked to *compare and contrast* one country's approach to imprisonment with another's. You may be asked to develop an *argument* of your own on this subject, based on your reading. Sometimes (when you are not given a specific assignment) you determine your own purpose: You are interested in exploring a particular subject; you are interested in making a case for one approach or another. In any event, your purpose shapes your essay. Your purpose determines which sources you research, which ones you use, which parts of them you use, at which points in your essay you use them, and in what manner you relate them to one another.

## HOW TO WRITE SYNTHESES

Although writing syntheses can't be reduced to a lockstep method, it should help you to follow these procedures:

♦ *Consider your purpose in writing.* What are you trying to accomplish in your essay? How will this purpose shape the way you approach your sources?

♦ *Select and carefully read your sources,* according to your purpose. Then reread the passages, mentally summarizing each. Identify those aspects or parts of your sources that will help you in fulfilling your purpose. When rereading, *label* or *underline* the passages for main ideas, key terms, and any details you want to use in the synthesis.

♦ *Formulate a thesis.* Your thesis is the main idea that you want to present in your synthesis. It should be expressed as a complete sentence. Sometimes the thesis is the first sentence, but more often it is *the final sentence of the first paragraph*. If you are writing *an inductively arranged* synthesis (see page 120), the thesis sentence may not appear until the final paragraphs. (See Chapter 2 for more information on writing an effective thesis.)

♦ *Decide how you will use your source material.* How will the information and the ideas in the passages help you to fulfill your purpose?

♦ *Develop an organizational plan,* according to your thesis. How will you arrange your material? It is not necessary to prepare a formal outline. But you should have some plan that will indicate the order in which you will present your material and that will indicate the relationships among your sources.

♦ *Write the first draft* of your synthesis, following your organizational plan. Be flexible with your plan, however. Frequently, you will use an outline to get started. As you write, you may discover new ideas and make room for them by adjusting the outline. When this happens, reread your work frequently, making sure that your thesis still accounts for what follows and that what follows still logically supports your thesis.

♦ *Document your sources.* You may do this by crediting them within the body of the synthesis or by footnoting them. (See Chapter 5 for more information on documenting sources.)

♦ *Revise* your synthesis, inserting transitional words and phrases where necessary. Make sure that the synthesis reads smoothly, logically, and clearly from beginning to end. Check for grammatical correctness, punctuation, spelling.

*Note:* The writing of syntheses is a recursive process, and you should accept a certain amount of backtracking and reformulating as inevitable. For instance, in developing an organizational plan (step 5) you may discover a gap in your presentation, which will send you scrambling for another source— back to step 2. You may find that steps 3 and 4, on formulating a thesis and making inferences among sources, occur simultaneously; indeed, inferences often are made before a thesis is formulated. Our recommendations for writing syntheses will give you a structure; they will get you started. But be flexible in your approach: expect discontinuity and, if possible, be comforted that through backtracking and reformulating you will eventually produce a coherent, well-crafted essay.

For clarity's sake, we'll consider two broad categories of essay (or synthesis) in the remainder of this chapter: the *explanatory* synthesis and the *argument* synthesis. We'll also consider techniques of developing your essays and, in particular, the techniques of *comparison-contrast*.

---

## THE EXPLANATORY SYNTHESIS

Many of the papers you write in college will be more or less explanatory in nature. An explanation helps readers to understand a topic. Writers explain when they divide a subject into its component parts and present them to the reader in a clear and orderly fashion. Explanations may entail descriptions that re-create in words some object, place, emotion, event, sequence of events, or state of affairs. As a student reporter, you may need to explain an event—to relate when, where, and how it took place. In a science lab, you would observe the conditions and results of an experiment and record them for review by others. In an education course, you might review research on a particular subject—say, the complexities underlying the debate over bilingual education—and then present the results of your research to your professor and the members of your class.

Your job in writing an explanatory paper—or in writing the explanatory portion of an argumentative paper—is not to argue a particular point, but rather *to present the facts in a reasonably objective manner*. Of course, explanatory papers, like other academic papers, should be based on a thesis. But the purpose of a thesis in an explanatory paper is less to advance a particular opinion than to provide a focus for the various facts contained in the paper. The following thesis might lead to an explanatory paper on bilingual education:

For the past twenty years, political differences
and debates over educational direction have kept
experts from agreeing on the usefulness of
bilingual education.

This statement obligates the writer to explain the twenty-year-old debate over bilingual education. Provided that the paper written to support this thesis drew on material clearly evident in source materials and did not seek to argue the writer's position, the paper would be explanatory. This thesis, like any thesis of an explanatory synthesis, gives shape and focus to materials already present in source materials.

Read the following four, relatively brief sources. (In writing a paper, you probably will use more and longer sources; but the same principles used here will apply.) Two of the authors you will read, Jeffrey W. Kobrick and Angelo Gonzalez, argue in favor of bilingual education; two others, Yolanda T. De Mola and Linda Chavez, argue against it. As you will see, these selections provide ample information to support the thesis above: you will discover that there is a debate over bilingual education; that the debate has lasted twenty years; that experts disagree on the soundness of bilingual education as educational policy; and that politics play a clear role in the debate.[1]

# The Compelling Case for Bilingual Education

JEFFREY W. KOBRICK (1972)

One reason schools are failing in their responsibility to [non-English-speaking students] is that they offer only one curriculum, only one way of doing things, designed to meet the needs of only one group of children. If a child does not fit the mold, so much the worse for him. It is the child who is different, hence deficient; it is the child who must change to meet the needs of the school.

During the first four years of life, a child acquires the sounds, the grammar, and the basic vocabulary of whatever language he hears around him. For many children this language is Spanish or Cree or Chinese or Greek. Seventy-three per cent of all Navajo children entering the first grade speak Navajo but little or no English. Yet when they arrive at school, they find not only that English is the language in which all subjects are taught but that English dominates the entire school life. Children cannot understand or make themselves understood even in the most basic situations. There are schools where a child cannot go to the bathroom without asking in English. One little boy, after being rebuffed repeatedly for failure to speak in English, finally said in Spanish: "If you don't let me go to the bathroom, maybe I piss on your feet."

---

[1]An overview: In 1968, President Johnson signed into law Title VII of the Elementary and Secondary Education Act. Known as the Bilingual Education Act, Title VII made federal money available for training and materials related to the instruction of poor children whose native language kept them from achieving in public school. The 1968 act did not specify how quickly (or whether) students should be mainstreamed into English classrooms or what the language of instruction should be (native or English). In 1970, reacting to pressure from language minority activists, the Office for Civil Rights notified school districts that to comply with civil rights law they must provide equal access to educational opportunity to all students, language minority students included. In 1974, Congress reapproved the Bilingual Education Act and expanded it to include any child (not just poor children) whose native language was not English. The 1974 version of the act mandated some native-language instruction. (See pages 31–32 for an excerpt from the 1974 act.) Congress reauthorized and amended the act in 1978, 1984, and 1988; in each instance, Congress debated the merits of and shifted funding priorities among the various forms of bilingual education. [James Crawford, *Bilingual Education: History, Politics, Theory, and Practice* (Trenton: Crane, 1989), pp. 31–49]

The effects of this treatment on a child are immediate and deep.   3
Language, and the culture it carries, is at the core of a youngster's
concept of himself. For a young child especially, as Theodore Andersson
and Mildred Boyer point out, "Language carries all the meanings and
overtones of home, family, and love; it is the instrument of his thinking
and feeling, his gateway to the world." We all love to be addressed, as
George Sánchez says, *en la lengua que mamamos* ("in the language we
suckled"). And so when a child enters a school that appears to reject the
only words he can use, "He is adversely affected in every aspect of his
being."

With English the sole medium of instruction, the child is asked to   4
carry an impossible burden at a time when he can barely understand or
speak, let alone read or write, the language. Children are immediately
retarded in their schoolwork. For many the situation becomes hopeless,
and they drop out of school. In other cases, believing the school system
offers no meaningful program, parents may fail to send their children to
school at all.

Schools seem unmoved by these results. At any rate, the possibility   5
of hiring some teachers who share a child's culture and could teach him
in a language he can understand does not occur to them. Since the
curriculum is in English, the child must sink or swim in English.

The injustice goes further: Having insisted that a child learn English,   6
schools make little or no constructive effort to help the child do so.
Instead schools assume, or expect, that any child in America will "pick
it up" without any help from the school. Alma Bagu tells this story about
a little Puerto Rican girl's day in school in New York:

> Sitting in a classroom and staring at words on a blackboard that were to me
> as foreign as Egyptian hieroglyphics is one of my early recollections of school.
> The teacher had come up to my desk and bent over, putting her face close to
> mine. "My name is Mrs. Newman," she said, as if the exaggerated mouthing
> of her words would make me understand their meaning. I nodded "yes"
> because I felt that was what she wanted me to do. But she just threw up her
> hands in despair and touched her fingers to her head to signify to the class I
> was dense. From that day on school became an ordeal I was forced to endure.

Like most of the people teaching Spanish-speaking or Indian chil-   7
dren, Mrs. Newman presumably did not know the child's language. Yet
she treated a five- or six-year-old as "dense" for the crime of not
knowing hers.

The variety and perversity of the abuses committed against chil-   8
dren are unending. In New York it is not unknown for teachers to lecture
Puerto Rican students on how rude it is to speak a "strange" language
in the presence of those who do not understand it. In the Southwest,
where it is widely believed that a child's native language itself "holds

him back," children are threatened, shamed, and punished for speaking the only language they know. Stan Steiner tells of children forced to kneel in the playground and beg forgiveness for speaking a Spanish word or having to write "I will not speak Spanish in school" 500 times on the blackboard. One teacher makes her children drop a penny in a bowl for every Spanish word they use. "It works!" she says. "They come from poor families, you know."

These are not the isolated acts of a few callous teachers. America's    9
intolerance of diversity is reflected in an ethnocentric educational system designed to "Americanize" foreigners or those who are seen as culturally different. America is the great melting pot, and, as one writer recently stated it, "If you don't want to melt, you had better get out of the pot." The ill-disguised contempt for a child's language is part of a broader distaste for the child himself and the culture he represents. Children who are culturally different are said to be culturally "deprived." Their language and culture are seen as "disadvantages." The children must be "reoriented," "remodeled," "retooled" if they are to succeed in school.

Messages are sent home insisting that parents speak English in the    10
home or warning of the perils of "all-starch diets" (which means rice and beans). Children are preached middle-class maxims about health and cleanliness. The master curriculum for California's migrant schools prescribes "English cultural games," "English culture, music, and song," "English concept of arithmetic"; nowhere is there mention of the Indo-Hispanic contributions to the history and culture of the Southwest. When Robert Kennedy visited an Indian school, the only book available on Indian history was about the rape of a white woman by Delawares. Even a child's *name* is not his own: Carlos becomes Charles; María, Mary.

Humiliated for their language and values, forced to endure the    11
teaching of a culture that is unrelated to the realities of their lives, it is no wonder that children withdraw mentally, then physically, from school. "School is the enemy," said a Ponca Indian testifying before Congress. "It strikes at the roots of existence of an Indian student."

Far from accomplishing its professed aim of integrating minorities    12
into the "mainstream," the monolingual, monocultural school system has succeeded only in denying whole generations of children an education and condemning them to lives of poverty and despair. There is no more tragic example of the fruits of such policies than that of the Cherokees.

In the nineteenth century, before they were "detribalized," the    13
Cherokees had their own highly regarded bilingual school system and bilingual newspaper. Ninety per cent were literate in their own language, and Oklahoma Cherokees had a higher English literacy level than

native English-speakers in either Texas or Arkansas. Today, after seventy years of white control, the Cherokee dropout rate in the public schools runs as high as 75 per cent. The median number of school years completed by the adult Cherokee is 5.5. Ninety per cent of the Cherokee families in Adair County, Oklahoma, are on welfare.

Obviously, no particular "program," not even a bilingual one, can  14
be expected to cure all this. The remark of the 1928 Meriam Report on Indian education holds true today: "The most fundamental need in Indian education is a change in point of view."

Bilingual-bicultural education is perhaps the greatest educational  15
priority today in bilingual communities. Its aim is to include children, not exclude them. It is neither a "remedial" program, nor does it seek to "compensate" children for their supposed "deficiencies." It views such children as *advantaged*, not disadvantaged, and seeks to develop bilingualism as a precious asset rather than to stigmatize it as a defect. The very fact of the adoption of a program recognizing a child's language and culture may help to change the way the school views the child. It may help to teach us that diversity is to be enjoyed and valued rather than feared or suspected.

There are also strong arguments supporting the pedagogical  16
soundness of bilingual education. Experts the world over stress the importance of allowing a child to begin his schooling in the language he understands best. Such a policy makes it more likely that a child's first experience with school will be a positive rather than a negative one. Moreover, as John Dewey and others have said, language is one of the principal tools through which children learn problem-solving skills in crucial early years. Policies that frustrate a child's native language development can cause permanent harm by literally jamming the only intellectual channel available to him when he arrives at school. Those who would concentrate on teaching a child English overlook the fact that it takes time for a child unfamiliar with the language to achieve a proficiency in it even approaching that of a child raised in an English-speaking home. In the meantime, struggling to understand other academic subjects, children fall hopelessly behind. In a bilingual program, by contrast, two languages are used as mediums of instruction; a child is thus enabled to study academic subjects in his own language at the same time he is learning English. Bilingual programs teach children to read their own language and to understand, speak, read, and write English (in that order). Language is oral. It is *"speech* before it is reading or writing." When a child enters school already speaking and understanding a language, he is ready to learn to read and write it. A program that prematurely forces English on a child can guarantee his eventual illiteracy in that language.

# Bilingual Education: The Key to Basic Skills

## ANGELO GONZALEZ (1985)

If we accept that a child cannot learn unless taught through the language    1
he speaks and understands; that a child who does not speak or understand English must fall behind when English is the dominant medium of
instruction; that one needs to learn English so as to be able to participate
in an English-speaking society; that self-esteem and motivation are
necessary for effective learning; that rejection of a child's native language and culture is detrimental to the learning process: then any
necessary effective educational program for limited or no English-speaking ability must incorporate the following:

♦ Language arts and comprehensive reading programs taught in the
  child's native language.
♦ Curriculum content areas taught in the native language to further
  comprehension and academic achievement.
♦ Intensive instruction in English.
♦ Use of materials sensitive to and reflecting the culture of children
  within the program.

### MOST IMPORTANT GOAL

The mastery of basic reading skills is the most important goal in primary    2
education since reading is the basis for much of all subsequent learning.
Ordinarily, these skills are learned at home. But where beginning reading is taught in English, only the English-speaking child profits from
these early acquired skills that are prerequisites to successful reading
development. Reading programs taught in English to children with
Spanish as a first language wastes their acquired linguistic attributes and
also impedes learning by forcing them to absorb skills of reading simultaneously with a new language.

Both local and national research data provide ample evidence for the    3
efficacy of well-implemented programs. The New York City Board of
Education Report on Bilingual Pupil Services for 1982–83 indicated that
in all areas of the curriculum—English, Spanish and mathematics—and
at all grade levels, students demonstrated statistically significant gains
in tests of reading in English and Spanish and in math. In all but two of
the programs reviewed, the attendance rates of students in the program,

ranging from 86 to 94 percent, were higher than those of the general school population. Similar higher attendance rates were found among students in high school bilingual programs.

At Yale University, Kenji Hakuta, a linguist, reported recently on a **4** study of working-class Hispanic students in the New Haven bilingual program. He found that children who were the most bilingual, that is, who developed English without the loss of Spanish, were brighter in both verbal and nonverbal tests. Over time, there was an increasing correlation between English and Spanish—a finding that clearly contradicts the charge that teaching in the home language is detrimental to English. Rather the two languages are interdependent within the bilingual child, reinforcing each another.

## ESSENTIAL CONTRIBUTION

As Jim Cummins of the Ontario Institute for Studies in Education has **5** argued, the use and development of the native language makes an essential contribution to the development of minority children's subject-matter knowledge and academic learning potential. In fact, at least three national data bases—the National Assessment of Educational Progress, National Center for Educational Statistics–High School and Beyond Studies, and the Survey of Income and Education—suggest that there are long-term positive effects among high school students who have participated in bilingual-education programs. These students are achieving higher scores on tests of verbal and mathematics skills.

These and similar findings buttress the argument stated persuasively **6** in the recent joint recommendation of the Academy for Educational Development and the Hazen Foundation, namely, that America needs to become a more multilingual nation and children who speak a non-English language are a national resource to be nurtured in school.

# The Language of Power

YOLANDA T. DE MOLA (1989)

One of the more unproductive discussions I have had in my life took **1** place in the lobby of a Madrid hotel in 1963. I was one of a group of Fulbright scholars, all teachers of Spanish from the United States, touring and studying in what was for some of us the land of our ancestors. A concierge remarked to me that there was no richer language in the world than his native Spanish. "Nowhere on earth can one find the nuances, the prolific lexicon of a Cervantes in his *Quixote*," he observed. Not so, I countered: "What you say may be true, but the blend of Latin and Anglo-Saxon has given English the largest vocabulary of any language in the world. In fact, the resonance, the vigor of English have caused it to replace French as the international language of diplomacy." Though I love both languages, as an American I felt compelled to uphold the primacy of English.

2  Today a somewhat more serious debate persists among educators, politicians and sociologists. It is a two-pronged polemic: Is bilingual education a help or a hindrance to Spanish-speaking children? Should English be made the official language of the United States? Both questions generate heated discussions and are no closer to resolution than when they were first raised some 20 years ago.

3  Alicia Coro, a native Cuban who has been director of Bilingual Education and Minority Affairs at the Department of Education in Washington, D.C., since September 1987, has a daughter who, in the early 1960's, was ready to start school. The child spoke no English whatsoever but did not have the option of enrolling in bilingual classes. Within a short time she was fluent in English. Today Mrs. Coro says: "If I had to make the decision now, I probably would not put her in a bilingual program." And she adds: "Some parents don't want their children in bilingual classes [because] they want them to progress in school and compete."

4  Perhaps today there are skilled bilingual teachers, but some 15 years ago I saw a man and a woman interviewed on television whose responses to the interviewer gave clear evidence that they were illiterate in two languages. At best, bilingual classes should be few and seen only as transitional rather than as a crutch to discourage maximum use of English. Far greater benefits might be reaped by the 1.5 million children with a limited knowledge of English if creative and intensive English programs were to be offered to them. Some 73 percent of the children whose English is limited are Hispanic. A much lower percentage of these, however, make the general academic progress that Asian children make who do not have the crutch of bilingual education.

5  In his provocative book *Hunger of Memory*, Richard Rodriguez writes: "Supporters of bilingual education today imply that students like me miss a great deal by not being taught in their family's language. What they seem not to recognize is that, as a socially disadvantaged child, I considered Spanish to be a private language. What I needed to learn in school was that I had the right and the obligation to speak the public language of *los gringos*. . . ."

"Without question, it would have pleased me to hear my teachers  6
address me in Spanish when I entered the classroom. But I would have
delayed having to learn the language of public society. I would have
evaded learning the great lesson of school, that I had a public identity."

It is regrettable that most children do not become fluent in the  7
language of their parents or grandparents as well as English. Ours is
probably the only world power whose citizens are not educated to be
bilingual. Nevertheless, if one is to live and work in the United States,
one must own the common language lest communication fail and we
become a babel of misunderstanding. It is difficult enough to live with
ethnic tensions without also losing the source of unity and comprehension—our public language. Perhaps it is the bridge that can enable us
to become in reality "one nation under God."

With many others whose first language was not English, I am  8
convinced today that its mastery is the fastest route out of the ghetto,
the best formula for professional and personal success. Language is
power and that power grows when one knows the dominant language
well. Self-confidence comes to the child who can express clearly and
accurately his or her thoughts and feelings. The danger of dropping out
of school is also diminished.

The longer I observe the process of integration (not assimilation) of  9
the Hispanic into our society, the more I am convinced that there are
those in government, industry and, yes, even the church who have a
vested interest in preventing the Hispanic from rising on the social and
corporate ladder. The role of Lord or Lady Bountiful can be very
congenial—the role of enabler perhaps less so. If signs in Spanish are
taken down, the Hispanic will be challenged to learn the name of the
product in English. An American living in Paris does not expect to see
signs for commodities in English.

Recently, after a meeting with bilingual teachers and principals of  10
District 10 in the Bronx, a member of a women's committee commented:
"Despite the public relations and budgeting additions, the [bilingual]
program is little more than a 'dumping ground' for kids with limited
English proficiency." Why is it that only 8 percent of the students in the
Bronx High School of Science, a school with rigorous entrance require-
ments, are Hispanic while Asians abound, in spite of their being numeri-
cally far fewer in New York City than the Latinos?

The movement to make English the official language of the United  11
States is in no way a put-down of other languages or cultures. But it is
the language used predominantly by the print and electronic media; it
is the tongue in which government at every level is conducted. To be
an effective citizen one ought to vote, and to do so intelligently one
must be well informed. Candidates, of course, present the issues and
outline their platforms in English.

Linda Chavez, former president of U.S. English as the Official Language of the Country, indicates that until that goal is achieved, legal empowerment for Hispanics is denied. She stresses that for social services, translators are always available for those (like the elderly) who do not yet use English well. In particular, Puerto Ricans who are citizens are not denied any rights because of their inability to speak English. Special interest groups who lobby for a bilingual nation (English and Spanish) fail to realize that such a posture is offensive to the millions whose second language is not Spanish. Let us indeed become a bilingual nation by learning well both English and the language of our ancestry or of our choice.

Many years ago my mother accompanied me, her oldest, to the first grade on the opening day of school. When she returned to the upper Manhattan school to take me home, the teacher said to her: "This child must be placed in kindergarten. All she can say in English is 'O.K.' " That was my earliest confrontation with the educational system. I do not recall having any problem picking up the dominant language easily and quickly. In time, English became my favorite subject; eventually it was my college major. My experience is not unique.

As long as we remain a polyglot society without one common linguistic system to unite us, fear of one another is perpetuated and ethnic prejudices endure.

## Why Bilingual Education Fails Hispanic Children

LINDA CHAVEZ (1991)

In Boston, half of all Hispanic junior high students enrolled in bilingual classes have been there for more than six years and still can't pass basic English-proficiency tests. In Los Angeles, some Hispanic youngsters in bilingual programs spend only 40 minutes a day receiving instruction in English.

These children are the victims of federal, state and local policies that promote teaching Hispanic children in their native language at the expense of teaching them English. Federal law requires that all non-English-speaking children be given special assistance so they don't fall behind in school. Most Asian and other non-Hispanic children receive such assistance through special courses that provide intensive English instruction so that they can quickly perform regular classroom work.

"Why Bilingual Education Fails Hispanic Children" by Linda Chavez as appeared in *McCall's*, March 1991, p. 60. Reprinted by permission of Linda Chavez.

Hispanic children, on the other hand, are more likely to be taught at least some of their lessons in their native language. Among Hispanic students with limited proficiency in English, 64 percent are taught reading in Spanish, and 72 percent receive oral-language development in Spanish.

Bilingual education theory ignores an important tenet of education: 3 Learning is directly related to what educators call "time on task." A student who spends five hours a week studying history, for example, will learn more history than she would if she spent only one hour a week doing the same thing. Anyone who has struggled to learn a foreign language knows that the only way to learn it is by intense exposure— literally immersing oneself in the language. By definition, children in bilingual classes spend fewer hours practicing English.

A school's first duty must be to help the child acquire the language 4 of the society in which he or she now lives. The first couple of years in a non-English-speaking child's education should be spent making sure the child develops full proficiency in English. That means intensive exposure to the sounds and sights of English. New teaching techniques such as structured immersion offer compassionate alternatives to other methods. In a structured-immersion classroom, the teacher teaches all subjects in English, starting with simple vocabulary and sentence structure. Children may ask questions in their native language, which the teacher understands, but the teacher responds in English. Only as a last resort does the teacher use the child's native language to communicate. The program has been very successful in teaching French to English-speaking Canadian children.

Hispanics are the fastest-growing minority group in the country. 5 They now number more than 20 million; one third of them are immigrants. If the children of these immigrants fail to master English, they will end up denied the American Dream their parents came seeking. No amount of ethnic pride can justify depriving children of the opportunity to succeed.

## Consider Your Purpose

Here, then, are four brief sources on the debate over bilingual education. When you read sources, pay attention to their date of publication. You can use this information to establish a time line or chronology if this is important to your topic. The publication date also can tell you whether a selection's information is current: if you are writing in a field in which knowledge changes rapidly, you will want the most current research. Dates of publication tell a story in the four pieces you've just read: Jeffrey W. Kobrick's "A Compelling Case for Bilingual Education" was written for *Saturday Review* in 1972, before reauthorization of the Bilingual Education Act in 1974 (see pages 31–32). Kobrick was one of the many public voices arguing for a change in the law to address the needs of non-English-speaking schoolchildren. Although the second article appeared thirteen years later, its author, Angelo Gonzalez, was still arguing for bilingual education as a "key to basic skills"—despite passage of the Bilingual Education Act. In 1989, Yolanda T. De Mola argued against programs in bilingual education in the journal *America*. And fully nineteen years after Kobrick's article appeared, Linda Chavez in 1991 explained her reasons for rejecting the theory underlying bilingual education. With justification, then, you could claim in your synthesis that the debate over bilingual education has continued for twenty years.

On what basis can you combine—or synthesize—these four articles? Before you can even begin to answer this question, you must consider your *purpose*. Consider that three researchers, working with three different purposes, could read these same articles and write very different papers, each of which would satisfy their reasons for writing. What you write depends significantly on your purpose for writing.

One purpose might be to determine the reasons why bilingual and bicultural education seem so much more important for recent immigrants (and American-born children of immigrants) than for immigrants at the turn of the century. These sources would help to explain this, but in themselves they are not sufficient. For a fuller explanation, you would need additional information, such as demographic data on who came to this country in the early 1900s (as opposed to who is coming now, why they are coming, and from where).

Your purpose might be more limited: to explain to your readers the debate over bilingual education. Certainly, these sources present sides in a single debate, the points of which you could define and discuss. One of these points might be the differing educational approaches to teaching non-native speakers of English. Each author devotes attention to educational matters. Kobrick explains important differences between one-language and two-language instruction for students who are not fluent in English (see his last paragraph). Gonzalez begins his essay with a series of assumptions about how students learn. De Mola suggests that educators offer "creative and intensive English programs" as an alternative to bilingual education. And Linda Chavez raises the educational issue of "time on task."

Another point in the debate involves politics. Kobrick writes of "America's intolerance of diversity." Gonzalez presents research on the effectiveness of bilingual education to make the point in his conclusion that "America needs to become a more multilingual nation." De Mola argues that to be an effective citizen one must vote and, therefore, speak English since candidates present their platforms in English. And Chavez warns that unless children master English, they will not become fully enfranchised citizens capable of realizing the American Dream. So aside from each author's concern with bilingual education as an *educational* issue, each is concerned with the *political* significance of bilingual education. Although De Mola questions the motives of some in business, government, and the church, virtually everyone wants the same end—the speediest route from exclusion to full participation for non-native speakers of English. A debate arises, however, when experts discuss how best to achieve this goal.

If your purpose were to present an overview of the debate, the simplest strategy would be to summarize your sources in whole or in part and then join these summaries in a logical manner. The simplest type of synthesis is little more than a *skillfully* connected series of summaries. We emphasize the word *skillfully*. With good reason, many professors do not accept as a synthesis a paper in which the writer summarizes one source, follows with the summary of another, and continues in this fashion until the paper's end. Such an approach involves little, if any, forging of relationships on the writer's part and no inclination to choose information selectively, according to a clearly defined purpose.

Resist the temptation to organize your synthesis by source—devoting, for instance, one paragraph of your paper to each of several sources. *You do not want to write a paper that says in effect: "I've read four sources. Here's a summary of each."* A much stronger approach is to organize your synthesis according to *ideas.* For instance, if your purpose were to present the debate over bilingual education, you could organize your paper in two parts and claim that the debate has an educational component and a political component. Your ability to understand that the debate in fact has two components, even (and especially) if none of your sources says so directly, shows a grasp of the topic not evident in a paper that uncritically stitches together a series of summaries. An acceptable explanatory synthesis requires that you see in your sources an interplay of ideas. You then relate those ideas in such a way that you choose from your sources selectively, in a manner that promotes your readers' understanding.

## Formulate a Thesis

The difference between your purpose and your thesis is a difference primarily of focus. Your purpose provides direction to your research and focus to your paper. Your thesis sharpens this focus by narrowing and formulating it in the words of a single declarative statement. (Refer to Chapter 2 for additional discussion on formulating thesis statements.)

Since your purpose in this case is simply to present the source material with little or no comment, your thesis would be the most obvious statement to be made about these passages. By "obvious" we mean a statement based on an idea that is clearly supported in all the passages.

Your first attempt at a thesis might yield something like this:

```
There is a debate over bilingual education.
```

One trouble with this thesis is that it fails to mention the time frame of the debate. Clearly, the fact that the debate has lasted two decades is significant. Additionally, the thesis is vague about what is being debated. The thesis could be revised this way:

```
During the past twenty years, the merits of
bilingual education have been debated.
```

---

102

This thesis is a little better, a little sharper. But the passive construction ("have been debated") leaves an important question unanswered: *Who* has been debating? If your sources were limited to the four presented above, the answer would be *experts,* since Kobrick, Gonzalez, De Mola, and Chavez are scholars—and in the last three cases have themselves come from homes where English was not the predominant language. Nor does the example thesis do much to reflect the contours of the debate. Of what elements does the debate consist? Based on a reading of the articles, you may conclude that the debate takes place, primarily, along two dimensions: political and educational. Two phrases come to mind: "political differences and debates over educational direction." Working these into the thesis, you would be moving toward a final draft: *For the past twenty years, political differences and debates over educational direction have kept experts from agreeing on the usefulness of bilingual education.*

## Decide How You Will Use Your Source Material

The easiest way to deal with sources is to summarize them. But because you are synthesizing ideas rather than sources, you will have to be more selective than if you were writing a simple summary. You don't have to treat *all* the ideas in your sources, just the ones related to your thesis. Some sources might be summarized in their entirety; others, only in part. Using the techniques of summary, determine section by section the main topics of each source, focusing on those topics related to your thesis. Write brief phrases in the margin, underline key phrases or sentences, or take notes on a separate sheet of paper.

## Develop an Organizational Plan

An organizational plan is your plan for presenting material to the reader. What material will you present? To find out, examine your thesis. Identify every element that will need explaining if, in your final draft, the thesis is to reflect the content of your paper. Critically review your thesis. Ask questions of it: Why? When? What's the definition? What are the parts? Who? What's the history? Questions like these, directed to every phrase of your thesis, should suggest to you the major sections of your paper. Expect to devote at least one paragraph of your paper to developing each section. Having identified likely sections, think through the possibilities of arrangement. Ask yourself: What information does the reader need to understand first? How do I build on this first section—what block of information will follow? Think of each section in relation to others until you have placed them all and have worked your way through to a plan for the whole paper.

Study your thesis, and let it help suggest an organization. Bear in mind that any one paper can be written—successfully—according to a variety of plans. Your job before beginning your first draft is to explore possibilities. Sketch a series of rough outlines: arrange and rearrange your paper's likely sections until you sketch a plan that both facilitates the reader's understanding and achieves your objectives as writer. Your final paper may well deviate from your final sketch, since in the act of writing you may discover the need to explore new material, to omit planned material, or to refocus your entire presentation. Just the same, a well-conceived organizational plan will encourage you to begin writing a draft.

Student Michael Arai worked with the material on bilingual education and arrived at this thesis:

> For the past twenty years, political differences
> and debates over educational direction have kept
> experts from agreeing on the usefulness of
> bilingual education.

Based on this thesis, Arai developed a five-part paper, including introduction and conclusion:

A. Introduction: brief background on bilingual education, with rationale for the program and an important date (1968)
B. The agreed-on goal for non-English-speaking students
C. Pro and con: educational direction and usefulness of bilingual education
D. Pro and con: political differences over bilingual education
E. Conclusion: what unites the country, if not language?

## Write the Topic Sentences

This is an optional step; but writing draft versions of topic sentences will get you started on each main section of your synthesis and will help give you the sense of direction you need to proceed. Here are some examples of topic sentences from the body of a synthesis, based on Michael Arai's thesis and organizational plan:

> Within the schools themselves, educators and
> experts share an agreed-on goal: the forging,
> through education, of non-English-speaking
> children into self-sufficient American citizens.

> Some argue that children should be plunged into
> English-speaking classes--the "immersion" method.

> Others argue that successful immersion
> experiences are rare and that bilingual education
> is an alternative to immersion.

Local and national research support the bilingual model.

Opponents charge that bilingual education programs have become dumping grounds for ethnic students.

Deep political differences underlie the opposing positions.

## Write Your Synthesis

Here is Michael Arai's completed synthesis, the product of two preliminary drafts. In the following example, thesis and topic sentences are highlighted. Modern Language Association (MLA) documentation style, explained in Chapter 5, is used throughout. Note that parenthetical references are to pages in *Writing and Reading Across the Curriculum*.

Bilingual Education: Still a Debate

Most Americans, harboring memories of high       1
school French or Spanish, respect the difficulty
of learning another language.  In 1968, U.S.
lawmakers recognized the difficulties of Hispanic
or Native American children who are forced to
pursue their studies wholly in English and passed
a law mandating the nationwide creation of
bilingual education programs.  Within these
special programs, non-English-speaking students
are taught academic subjects in their native
languages until (according to theory) they become
proficient in English.  For the past twenty
years, however, political differences and
debates over educational direction have kept
experts from agreeing on the usefulness of
bilingual education.
Within the schools themselves, educators and       2

experts share at least one agreed-on goal: the forging, through education, of non-English-speaking children into self-sufficient American citizens. All agree that this process will benefit both the children and the nation. Linda Chavez, of the Manhattan Institute for Policy Research and an opponent of bilingual education, writes that children with limited proficiency in English must gain proficiency or risk being excluded from the American Dream (100). Hispanic activist Angelo Gonzalez, writing from the opposing side, agrees: "One needs to learn English so as to be able to participate in an English-speaking society" (95).

But how should we teach the child English? 3 Some argue that children should be plunged into English-speaking classes--the "immersion" method. The necessity of learning English, they assert, outweighs the problems created by the students' partial confusion at being immersed in a curriculum of English-language lectures and textbooks. "A school's first duty," writes Chavez, "must be to help the child acquire the language of the society in which he or she now lives" (100). Yolanda De Mola of Fordham University, also an opponent of bilingual education, was held back a year in an American school to learn English and says she found herself better for the experience. She has no recollection of having had trouble learning English (99). De Mola claims that her experience was not unique. To support the point, she relates the story of a Cuban girl who quickly learned English in a non-bilingual program; she

also quotes writer Richard Rodriguez, who
considered Spanish "a private language" and went
to school to learn the "public language of <u>los
gringos</u>" (qtd. in De Mola 97).

But others argue that successful immersion          4
experiences are rare. Jeffrey Kobrick, an
attorney for the Harvard Center for Law and
Education, wrote in 1972: "With English the sole
medium of instruction, the child is asked to
carry an impossible burden at a time when he can
barely understand or speak, let alone read or
write, the language.. . . For many the situation
becomes hopeless, and they drop out of school"
(92). Kobrick believes that bilingual
education is the sensible alternative to
immersion: teaching a Hispanic student history
and math in Spanish, alongside a daily dose of
English instruction, will create a far more
positive experience for the student than
immersing that student in an English classroom
(94).

Local and national research appears to          5
support this view. Angelo Gonzalez cites a New
York City study that found bilingual education
students improving significantly in three areas:
English, Spanish, and math. These students had
attendance rates of 86 to 94 percent, higher than
that of their non-bilingual schoolmates.
Gonzalez also points to a Yale study
demonstrating links between students' abilities
in English and Spanish, which proves, he says,
that native-language instruction can be the
medium for achieving academically (96).

Recently, however, experts like De Mola and          6

Chavez have charged that most bilingual programs have simply become a dumping ground for ethnic students, a segregated outpost of mediocrity that simply does not get around to teaching students English. Chavez discusses a program in Los Angeles in which reading and oral-language classes in Spanish leave only forty minutes a day for instruction in English (99). In Boston, she points out, basic proficiency tests prove too difficult for half of all Hispanic junior-high students in the bilingual education program. And she suggests that the fact that 64 percent of Hispanic students learn reading skills in Spanish explains why they perform below Asian students, who are taught to read in English (99).

Experts have disagreed for so long, and with   7
such vigor, about the educational direction and usefulness of bilingual education that there is little wonder that deep political differences underlie the opposing positions. At issue is nothing less than two warring visions of our nation: America as the pot that "melts" different ethnic groups to forge a common, monolithic citizenry; and America as the land of diverse people united by a common love of democracy. The latter is Jeffrey Kobrick's America--a multicultural land. To Kobrick, the opposition to bilingual education suggests larger, uglier issues of intolerance and bigotry that have no place in this country. For De Mola, however, opposition is legitimate and warranted. She sees in the homogeneous America an ideal, especially in the realm of language. If we do not give

non-English-speaking students quick access to the
dominant culture's language, our conversations
may degenerate into a "babel of misunderstanding"
(98). That, she insists, is why we must teach
American youth the "source of unity and
comprehension--our public language. Perhaps it
is the bridge than can enable us to become in
reality 'one nation under God'" (98).

Bilingual education remains an issue deeply
divisive not only on educational grounds but on
political grounds. The debate treads upon our
hallowed, historical self-image of America as the
land of immigrants, public schools, and Horatio
Alger. But mostly, the debate forces us to ask
whether or not language itself truly unites a
nation--and if not language, what?

8

## Works Cited[2]

Chavez, Linda. "Why Bilingual Education Fails
     Hispanic Children." McCall's Mar. 1991: 60.
De Mola, Yolanda T. "The Language of Power."
     America 22 (Apr. 1989): 364-65.
Gonzalez, Angelo. "Bilingual Pro: The Key to
     Basic Skills." New York Times 10 Nov. 1985,
     sec. 2: 62.
Kobrick, Jeffrey W. "The Compelling Case for
     Bilingual Education." Saturday Review 29
     Apr. 1972: 54-58.

--Michael Arai

---

[2]These "Works Cited" entries refer to the pagination of articles in their original sources. In-text
citations in Michael Arai's paper refer to pages in *Writing and Reading Across the Curriculum*.

## Discussion

- Michael Arai devotes his first paragraph to a brief review that will orient readers who know little about bilingual education. He presents the government's rationale for mandating programs in bilingual education and notes the year in which the government acted to institute programs.
- Arai uses his thesis, the last sentence of his first paragraph, to telegraph sections of the paper to follow. Readers can anticipate a discussion of bilingual education's pedagogical soundness and philosophical assumptions.
- In paragraph 2, the first paragraph of the paper's body, Arai notes an agreed-on goal for both proponents and opponents of bilingual education. Proponents and opponents want what's best for the student: a mastery of English. Arai uses this common goal to set up the debate that follows.
- Paragraph 3 presents the position of those who believe that non-English-speaking students should be "immersed" in mainstream classrooms. Arai draws on three sources: Chavez, De Mola, and Rodriguez. Notice that at this point Arai does not present these writers' critiques of bilingual education.
- Paragraph 4 develops the proponent's position on bilingual education—presenting the proponent's reasoning in contrast to those who favor immersion. Arai relies on one source: Kobrick. In paragraph 5, Arai refers to research that corroborates Kobrick's support of bilingual education.
- In paragraph 6, Arai returns to the views of Chavez and De Mola, who favor immersion—this time presenting their critique of bilingual education. This paragraph concludes the first section of Arai's paper, the debate on the pedagogical soundness.
- In paragraph 7, Arai takes up the second main section of the paper, the deep political differences that separate proponents and opponents of bilingual education. Arai outlines their two views of America: as a melting pot, a land of ethnic homogeneity; and as an island of diversity and tolerance. Arai wants to establish that the longstanding debate about bilingual education has philosophical causes.
- In the final paragraph, Arai sums up, reminding the reader of the divisive nature of the debate and suggesting one reason why the debate has lasted so long: it "treads upon our hallowed, historical self-image." Arai ends with a speculation about what, if not language, unites a country. Note that in this presentation, Arai keeps his focus on the materials he has read, not on his personal views about bilingual education. He has written an *explanatory* synthesis.

# THE ARGUMENT SYNTHESIS

The explanatory synthesis, as we have seen, is fairly modest in purpose. It does not go much beyond what is obvious from a careful reading of the sources. Of course, since your reader is not always in a position to read your sources (carefully or not), this kind of synthesis, if well done, can be very informative. But the main characteristic of the explanatory synthesis is that it is designed more to *inform* than to *persuade*. As we have said, the thesis in the explanatory synthesis is less a device for arguing a particular point than a device for providing focus and direction to an objective presentation of facts or opinions. With an explanatory synthesis, you as a writer remain, for the most part, a detached observer. (The only exception, as we have seen in the previous model essay, is that writers may suggest their own opinions or offer a speculation at the conclusion of their work.)

This is not the case with the *argument synthesis,* the purpose of which is *to present your own point of view*—supported, of course, by relevant facts, drawn from sources, and presented in a logical manner. The reading you have done on bilingual education reveals heated disagreements among proponents and opponents. Even if you are just now learning of this debate, the issues are clear and contentious enough for you to adopt a point of view. You might contend that the thesis we developed for the explanatory synthesis *does* represent a particular point of view: "For the past twenty years, political differences and debates over educational direction have kept experts from agreeing on the usefulness of bilingual education." To an extent, this does represent a point of view, but note that the sources we provided do not allow any other point of view than this. Having read these sources, no one could disagree that the debate over bilingual education *has* lasted twenty years; that experts debate educational issues; and that experts also debate political issues.

By contrast, an argumentative thesis, unlike an explanatory one, *is debatable*. Writers working with the same source materials could conceive of and support other, opposite theses. So the theses for argument syntheses are propositions about which reasonable people could disagree. They are propositions about which (given the right arguments, as you formulate them) people could be persuaded to change their minds. This generally is not true of the kinds of theses that serve to unify explanatory syntheses.

Let's suppose, then, that you have researched material on bilingual education and wish to write a paper expressing your point of view. Let's suppose also that you have gathered not only the preceding four sources (used as the basis for the explanatory synthesis) but two additional ones as well.

# Bilingual Education and Politics

## JIM CUMMINS (1987)

Despite considerable recent research, confusion and disagreement persist among educators, politicians, and the general public, both about whether bilingual education programs actually succeed in promoting educational equity for language-minority students and whether such programs are consistent with U.S. social values. This debate must be considered in a political context for two reasons. First, research findings on bilingual education are abundant and clear; the common perception that research is largely unavailable and/or inadequate is a myth generated by strong vested interests. Second, the educational changes required to reverse the pattern of language-minority-group school failure are essentially *political* changes because they involve changes in power relations between dominant and dominated groups—specifically, in the ways that educators, as representatives of dominant-group institutions, relate to language-minority students and their communities.

Those against bilingual education maintain such programs are a threat to national unity and ineffective in teaching English to language-minority students, since the primary language, rather than English, is used for a considerable amount of instruction in the early grades. Many opponents of bilingual education argue that if children are deficient in English, they need instruction in English, not their native language. Unless minority students are immersed in English at school, the reasoning goes, they will not learn English, and thus will be unable to participate in the U.S. mainstream.

When we look at data on the academic achievement of language-minority students, a striking pattern emerges. The groups that tend to experience the most severe underachievement are those that have experienced subjugation and discrimination for several generations, namely, Latinos (with the exception of some groups of Cuban students), Native Americans, and African Americans. The same trend emerges in international studies.

The variation among groups, all of whom experience a home-school language shift, suggests that the language difference between home and school is not the crucial factor in explaining group underachievement. This conclusion, contrary to the usual rationale for bilingual programs, is strengthened by the fact that Latino students who speak English at home tend to perform just as poorly (when social class is taken into

"Bilingual Education and Politics" by Jim Cummins from *The Education Digest*, November 1987, pp. 30–33. Reprinted by permission.

account) as those who speak Spanish at home. This suggests that a rationale focusing on linguistic rather than social factors is oversimplified.

If the language difference between home and school is not the critical factor in explaining language-minority students' school failure (as both the "pro" and "anti" bilingual education groups have assumed), then what is? Several investigators have argued that status and power relations between majority and minority groups constitute the source of minority students' underachievement, with linguistic and other factors playing an important, but secondary or intervening, role.

School failure tends to occur among minority groups that have experienced persistent racism and who have been denied opportunities to validate their cultural and linguistic traditions. The dominated group, regarded as inherently inferior by the dominant group, is denied access to high-status positions, and language-minority students are disempowered in very much the same way that their communities are disempowered by institutions.

According to this analysis, reversing the pattern of language-minority students' school failure requires educators to redefine their roles in order to empower rather than disable students. Educators must become advocates for the promotion of language-minority students' linguistic talents. They must actively involve the parents in their children's education and institute assessment procedures that view the students' present academic performance as a function of the educational and social context in which the child has developed.

In short, reversing the pattern of language-minority students' underachievement involves much more than just some initial instruction in the students' first language or more effective teaching of English. Even though policy makers and educators see a linguistic problem involving only the learning of English, very clear data have been available for more than 20 years that social and historical causes—rather than linguistic causes—are central.

In-depth studies of bilingual programs that have explicitly attempted to develop full bilingualism among Latino students and to involve Latino parents in promoting their children's education report dramatic gains in students' academic performance. These studies demonstrate that bilingual programs *can* be highly effective in reversing language-minority students' academic failure.

These studies also refute the assumptions underlying the call for "English immersion" programs, since they show an *inverse* relationship between the amount of English in the program and students' achievement in English. This is precisely what is predicted by the "interdependence principle," which states that transfer of underlying academic skills across languages will occur provided there is sufficient environmental exposure to the second language and children are motivated to acquire that language. Thus, instruction in Spanish will develop not just Spanish academic skills, but also the underlying conceptual foundation for academic skills development in English.

## RESEARCH DATA

Virtually all the evaluation findings from bilingual education programs in North America, Europe, Africa, and Asia support the interdependence principle; they show either no relationship or an inverse relationship between exposure to the majority language in school and achievement in that language. Thus, it is difficult to understand the frequent claim that research data on bilingual education are lacking; rather, what has been lacking is a rational process of examining the research data in relation to the predictions derived from theory.   11

This conclusion is supported by preliminary results from a large-scale comparative evaluation of immersion and bilingual education programs involving about 4,000 students and being carried out for the U.S. Department of Education. The results support the interdependence principle and also suggest that the call for English immersion programs is more strongly based on political than on pedagogical considerations.   12

It is important to note that no claim is being made in this study regarding the general effectiveness of "bilingual education." The crucial element in reversing language-minority students' school failure is *not* the language of instruction but the extent to which educators work to reverse—rather than perpetuate—the subtle, and often not so subtle, institutionalized racism of the society as a whole. In other words, bilingual education becomes effective only when it becomes antiracist education. Strong promotion of students' primary language can be an important component in empowering language-minority students, but it is certainly not sufficient in itself. In addition, educators must develop a relationship of collaboration and partnership with language-minority communities and the pedagogy must permit students to become active generators of their own knowledge.   13

## "CONVENTIONAL WISDOMS"

It is perhaps naive to expect the policy debate on bilingual education to be any more rational than debates on other politically volatile issues. Nevertheless, it is sobering to realize the extent to which two patently inadequate "conventional wisdoms" have dominated the de-   14 bate for almost 15 years, even though each is clearly refuted by massive research and evidence. The usual rationale for bilingual programs is that children cannot learn in a language they do not understand and therefore some initial native language instruction is necessary to overcome the effects of a home-school language shift. This "linguistic mismatch" assumption is refuted by the success of many language-minority students under conditions of a home-school language shift.

## "INSUFFICIENT EXPOSURE"

The opposing conventional wisdom, however, fares no better. The "insufficient exposure" explanation of language minority students' difficulties in English academic skills assumes that there is a direct relationship between the amount of exposure to English and students' achievement in that language—an assumption refuted by virtually all evaluations of bilingual programs. As predicted by the interdependence principle, the data clearly show that instruction through the minority language entails no loss to the development of academic skills in the majority language. 15

In view of the overwhelming evidence against the "insufficient exposure" theory, what function do such arguments serve? Although spurious, they have served to emasculate many bilingual education programs, leading to implementation of relatively ineffective "quick-exit" models rather than the considerably more effective programs aimed at biliteracy. And because such quick-exit bilingual programs usually do not require or encourage any personal or institutional role redefinitions on the part of educators, institutionalized racism in the schools is preserved. In fact, it is probably preserved even more effectively because there is the appearance of change to meet "the needs" of language-minority students. 16

In this society, it is necessary to obscure contradictions between the rhetoric of quality and the reality of domination, and both quick-exit bilingual programs and immersion programs serve that function very well. It is for this reason that the two conventional wisdoms upon which these programs are based (the "linguistic mismatch" and "insufficient exposure" assumptions) have persisted and become almost immune from critical scrutiny despite their patent inadequacy. Effective, antiracist bilingual programs will continue to be vehemently resisted by the dominant group regardless of the research evidence in their favor. This resistance is entirely predictable because effective bilingual programs will threaten the power of the dominant group. 17

---

# Bilingual Miseducation

## ABIGAIL M. THERNSTROM (1990)

Are the students for whom [bilingual education] has been put in place  1
in fact benefiting? Has instruction in a native language given the students a leg up—as promised? Governor Mario Cuomo of New York has
declared bilingual education to be "extremely successful in helping
students to learn English." He sounds the right liberal notes, but is he
right?

Scholars and others who have posed this question have often met  2
with resistance from bilingual-education partisans, who have mounted
what Rosalie Pedalino Porter calls in a forthcoming study* a "shrill
campaign against any alternative programs." In 1978 the director of the
U.S. Office of Bilingual Education even maintained that bilingual education could not be evaluated. "It is a philosophy," he said. And so it was
and is. A sense of cultural sin, not educational failing, was the driving
force behind the original Act. And the conviction that an ethnocentric
society must mend its ways still informs much of the discussion of
bilingual programs.

Indeed, not everyone agrees even on the importance of learning  3
English. For instance, at a public meeting this past October, Adelaide
Sanford, a member of the New York State Board of Regents, reportedly
dismissed the importance of learning the nation's language. A lot of
people who speak English are not successful, she is said to have noted.

True enough, but is the converse of this proposition—the issue at  4
stake—true as well? Without English, the prospects for success are slim.
And on that score, the record of bilingual education—in its usual
"transitional" form—is not good.

In the first place, there is too often nothing transitional about  5
"transitional" bilingual education. A 1985 Massachusetts Board of Education study reported that substantial numbers of Hispanic children
remained in bilingual classrooms for six or more years. In general,
children are kept in the programs until they can perform successfully in
regular classes. For many children that day is long in coming. Since they
are not usually taught much English, they never learn it.

Furthermore, Christine Rossell, one of the country's leading experts  6
on bilingual education, has painstakingly tabulated the findings of studies that have evaluated bilingual and other methods of teaching limited-

---

*Forked Tongue: The Politics of Bilingual Education* (1990).

---

English-proficient children. Her conclusion: 71 percent of the studies show transitional bilingual education to be no different from or actually worse than doing nothing.

Similarly, in math achievement, 93 percent of the studies show bilingual programs to have either negative effects or no effects at all. As for social studies and other such subjects, too often the children in bilingual classes are not even exposed to the material that others get.    7

It is no secret to American businesses that the graduates of bilingual programs are inadequately educated. Striking evidence has recently been reported by Con Edison, New York. All applicants for entry-level jobs are required to pass an aptitude test in English. In 1988, 7,000 applicants, primarily from New York City schools, were tested and only 4,000 passed. The personnel manager checked the results and discovered, to her dismay, that not one product of the city's bilingual-education program was among those who had passed. The company also participated in a pilot program in a bilingual school in the Bronx. All the students with limited English from the program failed Con Edison's most basic test.    8

No wonder, then, that Motorola and other businesses are spending substantial sums to teach their employees to speak, read, and write English. By 1992 Motorola alone expects to have spent some $30 million on a program begun just three years ago. Many professional educators apparently do not realize it, but even low-level jobs require a reasonable command of English.    9

. . .

There are additional reasons for questioning the wisdom of continuing to offer "transitional" bilingual education. According to federal statistics, as many as 60 percent of the children to whom it is offered are not in need of a "transition" to English since English is already their best language. These children have been assigned to bilingual classes perhaps because someone in the household speaks Spanish or because they fall, say, below the 40th percentile on a standardized test. But of course lots of children who know *only* English do badly on such tests.    10

In addition, teachers are in short supply. In New York, advocates have charged that local school boards are simply refusing to fill bilingual-teaching positions. The teachers, they claim, are there for the asking. But the evidence suggests otherwise. Yes, teacher-certification requirements can be lowered or waived. Both are being done. And teachers can be recruited from other cities and other countries. That too is regularly tried. Los Angeles, for instance, frequently looks for bilingual teachers in New York. Many systems—including New York's—have sent emissaries to foreign ports to search for staff. And often they find them. But that process raises another question: are children being    11 properly served when their teachers may be unqualified and speak only the most halting English?

If teachers are recruited abroad, the books and workbooks they use 12 in class will often be imported as well. They will rely on the material with which they are comfortable—the material they know how to teach. In a class of Hispanic children, a Puerto Rican teacher will teach about Puerto Rico, using books from the island. The consequence is that the children are likely to learn almost nothing about American culture. And what happens to the two students in the room from the Dominican Republic and the three from El Salvador, the supposed reinforcement of whose cultural identity takes the form of lessons in Puerto Rican history and culture?

Beyond all this, the "transitional" bilingual programs are expen- 13 sive, as the New York State supervisor of bilingual education has admitted. U.S. English estimates that the revised New York plan will add $62 million per year to the state's current annual cost of $21.7 million—at a time of fiscal austerity. Nor is there anything distinc- tively expensive about providing such education in the Empire State. In Boston, in 1987–88, the per-pupil annual expenditure for students in the regular program was $4,340. The bilingual pupils cost $5,492.

Finally, bilingual classes amount to segregated education. Those 14 who monitor desegregation plans count ethnic and racial heads in a school and pretend that the presence of Hispanic and other language- minority children counts toward integration. Yet there is often little that is integrated about the education of these students. The students may dabble in paints and dribble a ball together but, for most of the day, a bilingual classroom is a school within a school—a world apart.

. . .

Children in bilingual programs are too often set up to fail. Not all 15 children in all programs, to be sure. There are important exceptions— classrooms in which good teachers ignore the rules, follow their in- stincts, and provide excellent education. These are teachers who would do well in any setting with any children. And there are school districts that have structured sensible programs to help children really in need— Rochester, New York, being one. But in too many schools, children with limited English start and end their academic life without the basic skills they need if they are ever to thrive.

The Hispanic children fare the worst. Cambodians and Vietnamese, 16 among others, are often luckier: the schools they attend frequently cannot find native-language teachers and are forced to offer English- based instruction. As a result, only Hispanic children "benefit" from the bilingual approach.

[Secretary of Education Lauro F.] Cavazos has recently reassured the 17 National Association of Bilingual Education (to much applause) that "the

118

sink-or-swim days of learning English are over" and must never come back. But no one is advocating their return—not even U.S. English. No one wants to go back to the days in which bewildered and often ridiculed immigrant children were left entirely to their own devices. Everyone agrees that children who speak little or no English can benefit from special language instruction. The question is the form that help should take.

This is an educational question. Bilingual education has been a part 18 of a political agenda, and the children whom the programs are supposed to serve have fallen through the cracks. Proponents often seem almost indifferent to the educational needs of these children. The proponents argue that building self-esteem is the first step to learning, and they define enhanced self-esteem as the feeling which comes from knowing one's own ethnic identity. It is a circular argument and it neglects the point that a sense of self-worth is most likely to result from concrete achievements. The child who stares blankly at one of the standard English achievement tests year after year can only feel defeat.

Such a child will learn English only if he is taught it. And there are 19 plenty of hand-holding ways to teach English. Berkeley, California, for instance, last year prevailed in a case in which the relatively heavy use of English in its bilingual program, and the choice it gave to parents to place their children in ESL classes instead, were both challenged. The school system convinced the federal district court that its English-based instruction had yielded good results.

Interviewed recently in the *New York Times*, a new arrival from the 20 Soviet Union voiced the frustration that all immigrants feel. "Without English," he said, "we cannot work, and without work, we are nowhere." But of course. It is time for educational "experts" to catch on to what most newcomers have always known.

Nor is it enough for children to master only the language of the 21 country in which they live; they also need to learn about its culture. It is exhilarating to walk into a school alive with a sense of the wider world. But it is dismaying to visit a classroom in which one feels in a foreign land. In transmitting national values that transcended ethnic lines, schools traditionally served an integrative function. They still can, and they still should.

## Consider Your Purpose

As with the explanatory synthesis, your purpose in writing an argument synthesis is crucial. What exactly you want to do will affect your thesis, the evidence you select to support your thesis, and the way you organize the evidence. Your purpose may be clear to you before you begin research, may emerge during the course of research, or may not emerge until after you have completed your research. (Of course, the sooner your purpose is clear to you, the fewer wasted motions you will make. On the other hand, the more you approach research as an exploratory process, the likelier that your conclusions will emerge from the sources themselves, rather than from preconceived ideas. For a discussion on the process of research, see Chapter 5.)

Let's say that, while reading your sources, you became increasingly convinced that in the bilingual education debate, educational issues have become subordinate to political issues. You find it curious, and irritating, that in discussing the topic writers seem to be working out some political agenda at the expense of children. Abigail M. Thernstrom, who defines the bilingual debate as an "educational question," believes that schools should teach national values. Jim Cummins, espousing the most radical position we have read on bilingual education, claims that these same national values are suspect in that they perpetuate racist attitudes. Thernstrom and Cummins hold sharply different views, and they both argue from deeply held political convictions.

Reading these articles, you ask: Is it possible to think about bilingual education *without* entering into an argument over politics? Your tentative answer to this question suggests a purpose for writing. You decide to write a paper in which you will argue that in the debate over bilingual education, political differences underlie—they *cause*—differences in educational policy. (You cannot be more specific and formulate a thesis until you have examined your sources more closely.)

## Formulate a Thesis

Your discussion is organized and tied together by your own thesis, which may have nothing to do with the thesis of any of your sources. For example, one of your sources may conclude that bilingual education is justified because it promotes a non-English-speaking minority student's sense of ethnic identity. But you may use that source to help demonstrate your point: that such justifications are based on politics, not on educational theory. You may use a source as a strawman, a weak argument that you set up and knock down again. Or the author of one of your sources may be so convincing to you that you adopt his or her thesis, or adopt it to some extent but not entirely. The point is that *the thesis is in your hands:* you must devise it yourself and use your sources in some way that will support that thesis.

You may not want to divulge your thesis until the very end of the paper, to draw the reader along toward your conclusion, allowing the thesis to flow naturally out of the argument and the evidence on which it is based. (If you do this, you are working *inductively.*) Or you may wish to be more direct and *begin* with your thesis, following the thesis statement with evidence to support it. (If you do this, you are working *deductively.*)

On closely studying your sources, you conclude that politics and education are not compatible. After a few tries, you arrive at the following tentative thesis:

The twenty-year debate over bilingual education will not be resolved until antagonists can find at least some area of agreement on the role and significance of ethnic minorities in American life.

## Decide How You Will Use Your Source Material

Your tentative thesis commits you (1) to explaining the opposing positions on bilingual education; (2) to arguing that a lack of one or two areas of agreement dooms efforts at teaching students with limited English proficiency; and (3) to argue that agreement must focus on the role and significance of ethnic minorities in America. The source materials provide plenty of examples that lay out the disagreements on educational and political grounds. Cummins and Gonzalez refer to research that supports the educational claims that bilingual education helps non-native speakers; Thernstrom, De Mola, and Chavez cite data and anecdotes to make the opposite point. The source materials also give ample opportunity to explore the political assumptions underlying the bilingual debate. Cummins is overtly political, and Thernstrom, who claims to be arguing an educational position, makes certain political assumptions as well. Chavez and De Mola also promote political agendas, and Bernstein (from Chapter 1, pages 7–10) directly addresses the political nature of the debate. These sources provide material to write the first part of the argument, an overview of the debate on bilingual education. In the second part of the synthesis, the writer will argue that a change of thinking is needed. The organizational plan of the synthesis, then, will be *problem-solution*.

## Develop an Organizational Plan

A writer faces a two-part challenge in constructing an effective problem-solution argument: to establish that a problem, in fact, exists and then to convince readers that a workable solution can be found. In effect, the problem-solution structure requires *two* arguments. Readers will not consider solutions to problems they do not believe exist. In the bilingual education example, the writer presents a comparative analysis of the debate over the issue. The purpose is to show that proponents and opponents operate with political assumptions so divergent that any resolution of the debate over bilingual education seems unlikely. And without resolution, students with limited English proficiency will suffer.

Having established the gravity of this problem, the writer is then in a position to ask: How can educators and politicians break the deadlock? Here, in the second part of the argument, is where a solution is proposed: that proponents and opponents of bilingual education must find "some area of agreement on the role and significance of ethnic minorities in American life." Notice that this statement, the thesis, is presented late in the paper—after the existence of the problem has been established.

## Write Your Synthesis

The second draft of a completed synthesis follows. Thesis and topic sentences are highlighted; Modern Language Association (MLA) documentation style, explained in Chapter 5, is used throughout. Note that with one exception (Treuba, in paragraph 8) page references are to pages in *Writing and Reading Across the Curriculum.*

The Disruptive Politics of Bilingual Education

Is America a melting pot or a salad   1
bowl?  How people answer that question should
indicate whether they support or oppose bilingual
education programs.  First established in 1968,
such programs mandate that students who are
non-native speakers of English be taught in their
own language until they become proficient in
English.  Proponents of bilingual education
believe that the programs provide a vital period
of transition for ethnic minority students, who
would otherwise fall behind in their academic
work and eventually drop out of school in
discouragement.  Opponents argue that the sooner
ethnic minority students "immerse" themselves in
English, the sooner they will master their
studies and integrate themselves into the
American mainstream.  Which side is right?  Are
bilingual programs effective or not?  The answer
is clear-cut, depending on your political point
of view--which is exactly the problem.  The
twenty-year debate over bilingual education will
not be resolved until antagonists can find at
least some area of agreement on the role and

significance of ethnic minorities in American
life.

The political undercurrent of the bilingual          2
education debate pits ethnic identity and
pride against cultural assimilation. Advocates
of bilingual education point out that ethnic
minority students have had to contend with Anglo
school systems that humiliate them for not being
proficient in English. According to Jeffrey
Kobrick, an attorney at the Harvard Center for
Law and Education, "the monolingual, monocultural
school system has succeeded only in denying whole
generations of children an education and
condemning them to lives of poverty and despair"
(93). Bilingual educational programs, on the
other hand, allow ethnic students to learn, while
affirming the value of their language and
culture. But opponents of bilingual education
argue that students can achieve the "American
Dream" only if they are fluent in English.
Bilingual classes, they charge, amount to
"segregated education" (Thernstrom 118). And
they assert that bilingualism "could lead to an
erosion of the national unity, a fragmentation of
the nation into mutually hostile groups"
(Bernstein 10).

The debate over bilingual education is          3
generally political, whether or not the
debaters admit it. Jim Cummins, an acknowledged
expert on the subject and the author of
Empowering Minority Students, freely admits it.
He contends that the debate must be considered
politically because there is no longer any
question of the educational value of bilingual

education.  Research findings regarding the effectiveness of bilingual education are extensive, he maintains, contrary to what opponents have argued (112).  Cummins believes that the academic failings of minority students often result from the "status and power relations between majority and minority groups."  Minority students are subjugated and disempowered, just as their communities have been subjugated and disempowered by American institutions (112). Without political change and without educators' refocusing their roles to "empower" their students, no improvement is possible.  However, he warns, the dominant group will continue to resist "effective, antiracist bilingual programs" as long as there is a perceived threat to its power (115).

Abigail Thernstrom, an opponent of bilingual     4
education and the author of a book on affirmative action and minority voting rights, insists that the issue is "an educational question" (119). She asks "Are the students for whom all this has been put in place in fact benefiting?"  (116).  And she charges that bilingual education "has been part of a political agenda, and the children whom the programs are supposed to serve have fallen through the cracks" (119).  Thernstrom is correct in making this point but, like Cummins, is advancing a political agenda.  She complains that one consequence of bilingual education is that children "are likely to learn almost nothing about American culture" (118).  And she concludes by declaring that "in transmitting national values that transcended ethnic lines, schools

124

traditionally served an integrative function. They still can, and they still should" (119). Both of these assertions are assimilationist arguments.

When the debate turns to data that one hopes might resolve some issues, political considerations again separate people into opposing camps. Antagonists interpret conflicting evidence depending on their views of what is most important for children of ethnic minorities: an educational system that reaffirms the value of their ethnicity or one that attempts to assimilate them into American culture as quickly as possible. For instance, despite Cummins's contention that "research findings on bilingual education are abundant and clear" (112), these findings do not seem clear to opponents of bilingualism. Angelo Gonzalez, executive director of a Hispanic advocacy and civic organization, cites "at least three national data bases" that support the effectiveness of bilingual education (96). But Thernstrom, Yolanda De Mola, and Linda Chavez have their own data and stories that cast doubt on such conclusions (Thernstrom 116-19; De Mola 97-98; Chavez 99-100).

For advocates of ethnic pride, building students' self-esteem and making them feel good about themselves is a primary consideration. Angelo Gonzalez, for example, believes schools must use "materials sensitive to and reflecting the culture of children within the program" (95). Jeffrey Kobrick believes that America is intolerant of diversity and that its "ethnocentric educational system [is] designed to 'Americanize' foreigners or those who are seen as culturally different" (92). To counteract such attitudes, and to force the schools to value diversity, he argues, bilingual, bicultural educational programs must have top priority in bilingual communities. Such programs seek "to develop bilingualism as a precious asset rather than to stigmatize it as a defect" (93-94). Only after making these points does Kobrick assert that "there are also [emphasis added] strong arguments supporting the pedagogical soundness of bilingual education" (94).

The assimilationists have their own priorities. Linda Chavez, a senior fellow at the Manhattan Institute for Policy Research, declares, "A school's first duty must be to help the child acquire the language of the society in which he or she now lives" (100). Students can start pursuing the American Dream by "immersing" themselves in English. Chavez claims that "no amount of ethnic pride can justify depriving children of the opportunity to succeed" (100). Like Chavez, Yolanda De Mola, a foreign study coordinator at Fordham University, believes that students have been victimized by bilingual education. She even charges that some people in government, industry, and church have a "vested interest" in preventing Hispanics from succeeding (98). Ethnic tensions in our "polyglot society" are bad enough, she argues. Without a common language to hold us together, communication fails and we become a "babel of misunderstanding" (98). De Mola cites the case of Richard Rodriguez, a

7

successful Hispanic writer who realized in high
school that in order to succeed in America, he
would have to learn the "public language" of
English:

> Without question, it would have pleased me
> to hear my teachers address me in Spanish
> when I entered the classroom. But I would
> have delayed having to learn the language of
> public society. I would have evaded learning
> the great lesson of school, that I had a
> public identity. (qtd. in De Mola 98)

So we return to our original question: Is
the nation a melting pot, in which different
nationalities are assimilated and blended into
nonhyphenated Americans? Or is it a salad bowl,
in which each nationality contributes to the
"salad," while retaining its distinctive
identity? Clearly, America is both a melting
pot and a salad bowl. Whether it's better to
emphasize one more than the other depends on
one's point of view and will change from
community to community. We should never expect
total agreement on this matter. In terms of
policy, this means that those who argue for
assimilation cannot win as totally and
convincingly as they would like. Language
difference is, and will increasingly become, a
fact that we must accept. The demographic trends
are clear: by the year 2000, nearly 3.5 million
students with limited English proficiency will be
attending our public schools (Trueba 139). We
must respond. We must insist that educators and

8

politicians at least try to subordinate their
political differences to the interests of the
children.

How will they do this, given their long 9
history of antagonism? We cannot look to their
present beliefs for hope of a resolution: their
two sets of assumptions are hopelessly at odds.
What is needed is some new, larger assumption, a
third way that to some extent incorporates both
positions and lays a new course. I suggest this:
that we come to understand America not as a
collection of self-serving tribes but as one nation
consisting of distinctive, flourishing communities.
Those who argue for assimilation cannot be so
arrogant as to insist that non-English-speaking
children surrender their culture and their language
to America. The America I want to believe in would
not ask for, nor would it accept, such a sacrifice.
We are not totalitarians who insist that everyone
must sound alike. Proponents of bilingual
education, at the same time, cannot be so arrogant
as to think that the interests of their special
group should be put above the nation's interest.

The solution I point to is a belief 10
incorporating something of value from both of
these positions: abelief that we must stand
together (although not necessarily with one
language) and simultaneously value and promote
our differences. Working with a new assumption,
proponents and opponents of bilingual education
might reach a consensus on goals. I do not, at the
moment, suggest particular policies. These grow
from a philosophy; and from the philosophy that I

suggest, actions, and very possibly consensus, could follow.

The risks of too heavy a reliance on tribal [11] identity are clear. We have only to look at the horror of Bosnia, in what used to be Yugoslavia, to recognize this. Also clear are the risks of absolutism, an insistence that all people must speak one language to be accepted as Americans. We must insist that antagonists in the bilingual debate find one area of agreement on the role and significance of ethnic minorities. Let this one area be a vision of an America secure enough to welcome and encourage diversity. We have seen, in the miniature battlefield of bilingual education, the failure of our present course. It is time to set a new direction.

## Works Cited[3]

Bernstein, Richard. "A War of Words." New York Times Magazine 14 Oct. 1990: 26+.

Chavez, Linda. "Why Bilingual Education Fails Hispanic Children." McCall's Mar. 1991: 60.

Cummins, Jim. "Bilingual Education and Politics." The Education Digest Nov. 1987: 30-33.

De Mola, Yolanda T. "The Language of Power." America 22 (Apr. 1989): 364-65.

Gonzalez, Angelo. "Bilingual Pro: The Key to

---

[3]These "Works Cited" entries, with the exception of Trueba, refer to pagination of articles in their original sources. In-text citations in Mark Tannaz's paper refer to pages in *Writing and Reading Across the Curriculum*.

Basic Skills." New York Times 10 Nov.

1985, sec. 2: 62.

Kobrick, Jeffrey W. "The Compelling Case for

Bilingual Education." Saturday Review 29

Apr. 1972: 54-58.

Thernstrom, Abigail M. "Bilingual Miseducation."

Commentary Feb. 1990: 44-48.

Trueba, Henry. Raising Silent Voices: Educating

the Linguistic Minorities for the 21st

Century. Cambridge: Newbury House, 1989.

--Mark Tannaz

## Discussion

◆ In the *introductory* paragraph, the writer opens with a question that invites the reader to respond, and so invites the reader into the essay. A definition of bilingual education follows, which leads to two sentences on the debate, which for the moment is limited to the merits of bilingual education. After a pair of questions to further draw the reader in, we have the central claim of the argument: "The twenty-year debate over bilingual education will not be resolved until antagonists can find at least some area of agreement on the role and significance of ethnic minorities in American life."

◆ The body of the essay consists of nine paragraphs. Six paragraphs (2–7) compare and contrast various views on bilingual education. This comparative analysis is developed point by point: Paragraph 2 explores the debate over ethnic identity versus cultural assimilation; paragraphs 3 and 4 work in tandem, with paragraph 3 summarizing the highly politicized (pro-bilingual education) views of Jim Cummins and paragraph 4 presenting the contrasting views of Abigail Thernstrom. In these three paragraphs, the writer is careful to point out the political content of the debate.

◆ Paragraph 5 explores a possible explanation for why the debate over bilingual education is so politicized—because the evidence for and against, based on educational merit, is contradictory. This paragraph is followed by a close look (in paragraphs 6 and 7) at how the educational arguments in the debate, whatever they may be, are subordinate to and grow from political arguments.

◆ Having spent six paragraphs establishing that a problem exists—a problem of political gridlock—the writer proposes a solution in paragraphs 8–11: "The solution I point to is a belief incorporating something of value from both of these positions: a belief that we must stand together (although not necessarily with one language) and simultaneously value and promote our differences." The writer, then, has given a problem-solution format to this synthesis.

Note that the *conclusions* drawn by the writer of this essay are not the only conclusions that could be drawn from the evidence of the sources provided. It is fair to say, however, that the sources themselves have been selected in such a way that they tend to point toward such conclusions. But what if a writer wishes to draw opposite conclusions? It is certainly possible to challenge the major assumption made in our model synthesis. For example, it could be argued, based on the same sources, that on the matter of bilingual education no discussion takes place without *some* political views coming into play. That is, one could argue that the position taken in the debate always involves personal politics: one is for assimilating minorities into mainstream American life or one is for maintaining ethnic identity. A critic of our example synthesis might argue that it shows naiveté and a misunderstanding of the issues to ask in the conclusion that educators and politicians lay aside political considerations and think of the children first—or that they readily abandon their own assumptions and embrace others. Obviously, everyone concerned is thinking of the children and wants them to succeed; the issue is *how* and whether it is ever possible to separate one's politics from one's views on the issue of bilingual education.

## TECHNIQUES FOR DEVELOPING YOUR PAPERS

Experienced writers seem to have an intuitive sense of how to present their ideas. Less experienced writers wonder what to say first, and, when they've decided on that, wonder what to say next. There is no single method of presentation. But the techniques of even the most experienced writers often boil down to a few tried and tested arrangements.

### Summary

The simplest—and least sophisticated—way of organizing an explanatory or an argument synthesis is to *summarize your most relevant sources, one after the other, but generally with the most important source(s) last.* The problem with this approach is that it reveals little or no independent thought on your part. Its main virtue is that it at least grounds your paper in relevant and specific evidence.

Summary can be useful—and sophisticated—if handled judiciously, selectively, and in combination with other techniques. At some point, you may need to summarize a crucial source in some detail. At another point, you may wish to summarize a key section or paragraph of a source in a single sentence. Try to anticipate what your reader needs to know at any given point of your paper in order to comprehend or appreciate fully the point you happen to be making. (See Chapter 1 for a discussion of summary.)

## Example or Illustration

At one or more points in your paper, you may wish to *refer to a particularly illuminating example or illustration from your source material.* You might paraphrase this example (i.e., recount it, in some detail, in your own words), summarize it, or quote it directly from your source. In all these cases, of course, you would properly credit your source. (See Chapter 5 on citation form.)

## Two (or More) Reasons

In his book *A Short Course in Writing,* Kenneth Bruffee presents some of the most effective ways of developing arguments. The first one is simply called *two reasons,* but it could just as well be called *three reasons* or whatever number of reasons the writer has. Here is this method in outline form:

> A. Introduction and thesis
> B. Two reasons the thesis is true
>   1. First reason
>   2. Second reason (the more important one)

You can advance as many reasons for the truth of the thesis as you think necessary; but save the most important reason(s) for the end, because the end of the paper—its climax—is what will remain most clearly in the reader's mind.

## Strawman

The next way of presenting an argument is called *strawman.* When you use the strawman technique, you present an argument *against* your thesis, but immediately afterward you show that this argument is weak or flawed. The advantage of this technique is that you demonstrate that you are aware of the other side of the argument and that you are prepared to answer it.

Here is how the strawman argument is organized:

> A. Introduction and thesis
> B. Main opposing argument
> C. Refutation of opposing argument
> D. Main positive argument

## Concession

Finally, one can use *concession* in an argument. Like strawman, you present the opposing viewpoint, but you do not proceed to demolish the opposition. Instead, you concede that the opposition does have a valid point but that even so the positive argument is the stronger one. Here is an outline for a concession argument:

A. Introduction and thesis
B. Important opposing argument
C. Concession that this argument has some validity
D. Positive argument(s)

Sometimes, when you are developing a *strawman* or *concession* argument, you may become convinced of the validity of the opposing point of view and change your own views. Don't be afraid of this happening. *Writing is a tool for learning.* To change your mind because of new evidence is a sign of flexibility and maturity, and your writing can only be the better for it.

## Comparison and Contrast

Comparison-and-contrast techniques enable you to examine two subjects (or sources) in terms of one another. When you compare, you consider *similarities.* When you contrast, you consider *differences.* By comparing and contrasting, you perform a multifaceted analysis that often suggests subtleties that otherwise might not have come to your attention.

To organize a comparison-and-contrast analysis, you must carefully read sources in order to discover *significant criteria for analysis.* A *criterion* is a specific point to which both of your authors refer and about which they may agree or disagree. (For example, in a comparative report on compact cars, criteria for *comparison* and *contrast* might be road handling, fuel economy, and comfort of ride.) The best criteria are those that allow you not only to account for obvious similarities and differences between sources but also to plumb deeper, to more subtle and significant similarities and differences.

There are two basic approaches to organizing a comparison-and-contrast analysis: organization by source and organization by criteria.

1. *Organizing by source.* You can organize a comparative analysis as two summaries of your sources, followed by a discussion in which you point out significant similarities and differences between passages. Having read the summaries and become familiar with the distinguishing features of each passage, your readers will most likely be able to appreciate the

more obvious similarities and differences. Follow up on these summaries by discussing both the obvious and subtle comparisons and contrasts, focusing on the most significant.

Organization by source is best saved for passages that are briefly summarized. If the summary of your source becomes too long, your audience might forget the remarks you made in the first summary while they read the second. A comparison-and-contrast synthesis organized by source might proceed like this:

   I. Introduce the essay; lead to thesis.
  II. Summarize passage A by discussing its significant features.
 III. Summarize passage B by discussing its significant features.
 IV. Write a paragraph (or two) in which you discuss the significant points of comparison and contrast between passages A and B.

End with a conclusion in which you summarize your points and, perhaps, raise and respond to pertinent questions.

2. *Organizing by criteria.* Instead of summarizing entire passages one at a time with the intention of comparing them later, you could discuss two passages simultaneously, examining the views of each author point by point (criterion by criterion), comparing and contrasting these views in the process. The criterion approach is best used when you have a number of points to discuss or when passages are long and/or complex. A synthesis organized by criteria might look like this:

   I. Introduce the essay; lead to thesis.
  II. Criterion 1
     A. Discuss what author A says about this point.
     B. Discuss what author B says about this point.
 III. Criterion 2
     A. Discuss what author A says about this point.
     B. Discuss what author B says about this point (be sure to arrange criteria with a clear method; knowing how the discussion of one criterion leads to the next will ensure smooth transitions throughout your paper).

And so on. Proceed criterion by criterion until you have completed your discussion. End with a conclusion in which you summarize your points and, perhaps, raise and respond to pertinent questions.

# A CASE FOR COMPARISON AND CONTRAST: SHOULD WE TEACH IMMIGRANTS IN THEIR OWN LANGUAGE?

We'll see how these principles can be applied to the following interviews with Ramón Santiago, former director of Georgetown University's Bilingual Service Center, and S. I. Hayakawa (1906–1992), a linguistics expert and former senator from California. In "Should We Teach Immigrants in Their Own Language?" the editors of *U.S. News & World Report* question these two experts on the merits of bilingual education.

## Yes

### INTERVIEW WITH RAMÓN SANTIAGO (1983)

**Q Mr. Santiago, why do you favor bilingual education—the teaching of academic subjects to immigrant children in their own language while simultaneously giving them English-language instruction?** 1

**A** Because bilingual education effectively meets the needs of linguistic-minority children. It respects what the children themselves bring to the classroom—their language and culture.

Bilingual-education programs funded by the federal government came into being in 1968 because non-English-speaking children were making little progress in school and were bored. Their dropout rate was tremendously high. In some ethnic groups, fewer than 20 percent of the students were getting through high school.

**Q What is the dropout rate now?** 2

**A** Participants in bilingual-education programs are four times as likely to finish high school, and the number entering college has increased.

Another gain from preserving native languages is that the United States now has more linguistic resources for its diplomatic dealings with other countries—Vietnam, El Salvador and the Middle East, for example.

**Q How many children are now studying in bilingual-education programs?** 3

**A** In grades one through 12, approximately 3.6 million children in this

Pro and Con, "Teach Immigrants in Their Own Language?" an interview with Ramón Santiago and S. I. Hayakawa from *U.S. News & World Report*, October 3, 1983. Copyright © 1983 by U.S. News & World Report. Reprinted by permission.

country don't speak English as a native language. But fewer than 10 percent of them—about 330,000—are in bilingual programs.

**Q Traditionally, immigrants have had to master English as the** 4 **first step toward receiving full political and economic benefits from American society. Doesn't bilingual education slow down this process?**

**A** No. Every immigrant who comes to the United States wants to be able to function in the language of the majority. That is the road to success, and, if anything, bilingual education accelerates this process.

There is a mistaken impression that whenever you teach in a language other than English, you're taking away time needed for English instruction. That is not necessarily true. If a child were taught English all day he'd go stir-crazy. You cannot expose a youngster to too much of a foreign language too soon.

Also, by teaching some subject matter in a child's native language, a child can build a basic store of facts. When he switches to classes in English, he will then have a fund of knowledge and be better able to concentrate on expressing himself in English.

**Q Opponents of bilingual education say that when a child does** 5 **not learn basic academic subjects in English, he is at a disadvantage in coping with American ways—**

**A** Some people assume that immersing a person in a language situation is like immersing him in a bath of water. Unfortunately, languages are not learned by osmosis that quickly. We have to keep in mind that a child cannot learn basic concepts of mathematics, science and other academic subjects in a language the child doesn't understand.

In bilingual education, you attempt to make a child as comfortable as possible by providing him with something he understands—instruction using his native language.

At the same time, you teach English as a second language. Gradually you alter the proportions until a child is getting zero instruction in his native language when he is ready for mainstreaming.

**Q Might not instruction in languages other than English tend to** 6 **overemphasize ethnic heritage and deepen the alienation of some groups from American society, perhaps even encouraging separatist movements or bilingual states?**

**A** In the first place, the melting-pot concept has been disavowed by many sociologists as not representative of U.S. society. Instead, the salad-bowl or mosaic concept is preferred. The U.S. is not any one thing, but a combination of many things.

If you try to de-emphasize the contribution made by people of different backgrounds, you do harm to the American fabric. This does not mean that each element of society has to have its own separate identity, government or schools. But groups should be allowed to keep their distinctiveness. Some people imply that diversity causes disunity. Yet the Civil War was fought between states that shared English as a native tongue. People can find many things to fight about other than language.

I often say that the U.S. could do without bilingual education if it were to do several things: Seal off the borders, take down the Statue of Liberty and enclose itself in a cocoon, ignoring the rest of the world.

**Q Some critics of bilingual education say that Hispanics resist assimilation into the mainstream more than other newcomers to the United States—** 7

A If they mean that Hispanics as a group have retained more of their language and culture, I would say more power to the Hispanics. When the Indo-Chinese came to the United States, they escaped from cities that were being bombed out of existence or they fled from repressive government. They pretty much burned their bridges behind them. Their choice in the U.S. is total assimilation or failure.

On the other hand, the two main segments of the Hispanic population, the Mexican Americans and the Puerto Ricans, are either American citizens from birth or migrants—they are not exiles.

Also, I don't believe that the U.S. in terms of pure self-interest would want the many Hispanics to lose their language and culture, because the United States is constantly trying to improve relations with Latin America and with countries that have Spanish language and culture.

Americanism is not expressed only in English. It's possible for linguistic minorities to be fully patriotic and American.

# No

INTERVIEW WITH S. I. HAYAKAWA (1983)

**Q Mr. Hayakawa, why do you oppose the type of bilingual education in which immigrants are taught academic subjects in their own language rather than in English?** 1

A Because the experience of many immigrants shows that the more quickly they are immersed in the use of the English language, whether at work or at school, the more quickly they learn English—and I believe it is vital that they do so. This is generally true for immigrants of practically any age, and it's especially true of small children.

**Q An exceptionally large number of Hispanics have come to the** 2

**U.S. in recent years. Isn't a special program such as bilingual education needed for them?**

A No. Just think of the enormous wave of immigration of Europeans between 1870 and the 1920s. They came in by the millions, and the U.S. population was smaller at the time.

No immigrant group, no matter how large, has ever made a claim for special treatment such as bilingual education. Even among the Spanish speaking, the rank and file do not seem to be making that demand now.

The push for bilingual education is coming mostly from political leaders, both Hispanic and non-Hispanic, who are courting the Hispanic vote, and from teachers who have a vested interest in continuing their jobs. Some politicians will do anything that a minority group—American Indians, Asians, blacks, Hispanics—asks of them, even at the cost of injustice to the majority.

**Q What evidence do you have that most Hispanics don't support the push for bilingual education?**  3

A In filling out questionnaires that I distributed to a million and a half of my constituents, including many Hispanics, a majority of the respondents indicated that they are in favor of a constitutional amendment which I proposed in the Senate making English the official language of the United States. They accept the idea of using Spanish as an instrument for learning English, but they do not accept the idea of full-time instruction using Spanish.

**Q Why is a constitutional amendment making English the official language needed?**  4

A Because political pressure groups can use a language difference as a basis for seeking more influence and power. This can be extremely divisive in any country. We know the long and difficult history of Belgium. We also see what's happening in Sri Lanka, where language differences have led to bloodshed.

Next door to us in Canada, politicians have taught the French-speaking Québécois not to use the English they already know. Bilingualism leads ultimately to a political hassle, driving out one language or the other.

**Q Are you saying there is danger of a separatist movement or bilingual states in the United States?**  5

A Yes, there's always such a danger. There could be a terrific temptation for those seeking power to rally millions of Spanish-speaking immigrants behind separatist movements.

**Q These are times when ethnic heritages are widely emphasized. Aren't immigrants who are thrust into English-speaking classes**  6

**forced to give up much of their own culture and that of their parents?**

**A** Well, that's what happened to me as a child of Japanese parents in Canada before coming to the U.S. But I was too busy acquiring the English-speaking culture, so I didn't miss Japanese culture, except that I did cherish what Japanese culture I acquired through my mother.

I got my degrees in the English language and then went into the study of Japanese. The first job for an American is to speak English, particularly if he or she intends to remain here.

**Q Hispanics say that the existing courses in English are not effective enough to eliminate the need for instruction of children in their native language—**    7

**A** I haven't had firsthand experience with this particular problem, but when you have a classroom in which, say, three quarters or more are English-speaking children and one quarter are Hispanics, Hispanic children learn English very fast.

**Q Under other circumstances, isn't it difficult for immigrant children to learn English quickly?**    8

**A** No. It depends very much upon the atmosphere created for them by the adults. For example, take the Vietnamese and the Korean children who are coming to the United States. How quickly they win spelling bees and become valedictorians for their high-school classes!

Once they get to this country, the parents say to them, "You've got to learn English, even if we can't learn it ourselves." Now, unless Hispanic parents are persuaded by their political leaders to hold out for bilingual education, Spanish-speaking children will be motivated by the same impulses as other immigrants.

**Q Those who favor bilingual education contend that forcing immigrants to learn English through the so-called sink-or-swim approach didn't benefit the mass of immigrants in the past as much as is generally thought—**    9

**A** The great thing about the United States is our ability to absorb foreign peoples and make them part of us. I am part of that process. My father came to San Francisco when he was 17 or 18 and washed dishes in somebody's kitchen. If somebody had said, "That young man will have a son, and that son is going to be a United States senator someday," people would have laughed.

The fact is that immigrants come here from every part of the world, and, in a generation or so, they become movie stars, politicians, businessmen, television personalities, and have all kinds of successful careers. But for these opportunities to open up, immigrants and their descendants must learn English as quickly as possible. That's the admission ticket into the culture.

## Organization of Comparison-Contrast by Source

Here is a comparison-and-contrast analysis of the two interviews, organized by *source:*

To Sink or Swim

What is the best way to teach non-English-    1
speaking students English?  Because large numbers
of immigrants come into the United States each
year, this has become an important--and hotly
debated--question.  In dual interviews, Ramón
Santiago, former director of the Georgetown
University Bilingual Service Center, and S. I.
Hayakawa, linguistics expert and former senator,
argue their positions on bilingual education.

Santiago believes in bilingual education, a    2
program in which non-English-speaking students
are taught at first in their own language and
then are gradually introduced to English.Santiago
says that bilingual education is necessary
because the approach retains and builds on what
students already have learned in their native
tongue.  He argues that the contrary approach--
immersion in an English-speaking classroom--is
ineffective and overwhelms immigrant students,
who cannot learn in a language they do not
understand.  The result of immersion, says
Santiago, is a high dropout rate.  Students who
participate in bilingual programs are four times
more likely to complete high school than are

students who do not begin their studies in their native language. On a more philosophical level, Santiago points out that nurturing different cultures and languages is a value inherent in the American ideal of the "salad bowl" or "mosaic": "Americanism is not expressed only in English," he says. "It's possible for linguistic minorities to be fully patriotic and American." Clearly, Santiago sees bilingual education as the fastest, most productive, and most humane means for giving non-English-speaking students a mastery of English.

S. I. Hayakawa disagrees--emphatically. 3 Claiming that success in America hinges on learning English, the former senator argues that the "first job for an American is to speak English." He believes that total immersion is the quickest method for teaching the language. Bilingual education, according to Hayakawa, is a political ruse designed to gain votes from minorities. The programs do a disservice to non-native speakers of English and may foster political discontent among different language groups. The aim of the non-English-speaking student should be to learn the majority language as quickly as possible: "That's the admission ticket into the culture."

Santiago and Hayakawa, both acknowledged 4 experts on language, could not disagree more. Both want to see non-English-speaking students learn quickly and use English as a means to advancement; but they disagree on the best strategy for achieving that end. On the issue of teaching methods for recent immigrants, Santiago believes that total immersion is useless, since students cannot learn in a language they do not understand. He claims that students find it overwhelming to learn a new language all at once and that they learn best in a bilingual classroom. Hayakawa, however, believes immersion into a language to be the fastest way to learn that language and thereby gain entry into the majority culture. These disagreements, perhaps, can be explained in terms of contrasting philosophical views of American culture. Santiago operates with the "salad bowl" metaphor, the belief that America is a rich nation precisely because of its distinctive ethnic groups. Hayakawa operates with a "melting pot" metaphor, the belief that in coming to America foreigners should relinquish what makes them separate (i.e., their language) in order to blend into the American mainstream. Both Santiago and Hayakawa want non-English-speaking students to learn the language and to advance. But how quickly and under what circumstances--these are points of profound disagreement.

--Mark Eaton

## Discussion

♦ The writer uses the first paragraph to introduce the subject and the individuals whose views will be analyzed.
♦ In paragraph 2, the writer summarizes Santiago's position.

♦ In paragraph 3, the writer summarizes Hayakawa's position. Notice the brief transition at the beginning of the paragraph.
♦ Paragraph 4 begins with a transitional sentence that links the preceding paragraphs and states the obvious disagreement. The second sentence summarizes the entire comparative analysis and thus operates as the thesis.

## Organization of Comparison-Contrast by Criteria

Here is a plan for a comparison-and-contrast synthesis, organized by *criteria*. The thesis is as follows:

While Santiago, an advocate for bilingual education, says that immigrants initially should be taught in their native language, Hayakawa believes that they should be immersed in English-speaking classrooms and that learning English should be their first priority.

A. Introduction: a scenario to introduce both the debate and Hayakawa and Santiago
B. The merits of bilingual education
  1. Santiago's position
  2. Hayakawa's position
C. The ways in which Americans perceive their culture
  1. Santiago's perception
  2. Hayakawa's perception
D. Significance and implications of the debate

Following is a comparison-and-contrast synthesis, written according to the preceding plan:

A Heated Debate Over Bilingual Education

Imagine an eight-year-old Hispanic immigrant     1
attending an American school for the first time.
She knows very little English, aside from some
basic terms taught to her by her Spanish-speaking

parents. Will she become more thoroughly accustomed to America and its culture if she is immersed in the English language in her classroom or if she gradually learns English and other subjects through bilingual education? This question has been pondered by teachers, politicians, and minority leaders since the late 1960s, when bilingual programs came into being. Two participants in this debate, Ramón Santiago and S. I. Hayakawa, present their different perspectives in the article "Should We Teach Immigrants in Their Own Language?" Both men recognize that speaking English is necessary to achieve success in the United States. But while Santiago, an advocate for bilingual education, says that immigrants initially should be taught in their native language, Hayakawa believes that they should be immersed in English-speaking classrooms and that learning English should be their first priority.

One element of the debate concerns whether 2 or not children actually benefit from bilingual education programs. Santiago says that teachers who respect native cultures encourage children to stay in school. He points out that in the late 1960s fewer than 20 percent of the students in some ethnic groups were graduating from high school. Today, however, students in bilingual education programs are four times more likely to get diplomas than those immigrant students who do not participate in bilingual programs. Santiago believes that a child's knowledge of basic academic subjects, learned in native tongue, gives him or her confidence in learning

English.  This confidence, he continues, is the primary motivation to complete high school and to continue education into the college years.  Hayakawa, however, points to some of the harmful effects of the bilingual programs that Santiago advocates.  The linguist and former senator says that politicians and bilingual teachers are the primary supporters of bilingual programs and that immigrant students do not benefit from them.  In fact, Hayakawa believes that teaching a child in a language other than English actually limits that child's ability to communicate in the majority culture and, thus, limits opportunities.  He adds that when students do learn in English at an early age, they do not lose their native cultural identity, as bilingual education advocates would indicate, but merely gain a new identity within the dominant American culture.  So while Santiago believes in gradually introducing English into the immigrant's education, Hayakawa emphasizes the immediate mastery of English as the best way to assimilate immigrant students into American culture.

The debate over bilingual education not only concerns the welfare of immigrant students, it also reflects fundamental notions of how Americans perceive their culture.  These different perceptions can be recognized in Santiago's and Hayakawa's definition of the American identity.  Hayakawa metaphorically defines America as a "melting pot."  This traditional notion likens our country to a cauldron where foreign cultures mix and homogenize.  Making English the official language

of the United States, says Hayakawa, would hasten
this homogenization process and thus would serve
to strengthen the country. Hayakawa suggests
that language differences alone can cause
disunity and that in order to eliminate the
possibility of separatism, we also must eliminate
bilingual education. Santiago, however, argues
that speaking English is not the only thing that
makes an American patriotic. The identity of the
United States, he says, is more like a "salad
bowl" than a melting pot. In the American
"salad," "groups should be allowed to keep their
distinctiveness" while at the same time
contributing to the character of the whole.
Hayakawa sees multilingual and multicultural
communities leading to disharmony. But Santiago
does not see tension as inevitable; furthermore,
he sees cultural and linguistic diversity as
national assets.

The debate over bilingual education is
likely to linger and will certainly continue to
raise difficult questions about the welfare of
immigrant students and the perceptions that
Americans have of their own culture. Is it to an
immigrant's advantage or disadvantage to
participate in bilingual programs? Will those
who participate stay in school longer? Will they
have higher earning power? Will holding onto
their cultural heritage enhance or limit their
opportunities? Ultimately, the success of
programs in bilingual education will be measured
by the achievements of the students themselves.

--Julie Yablonicky

## Discussion

- In the first paragraph, the writer uses an imaginary scenario to intro-duce—and make human—the debate over bilingual education. The writer then introduces two antagonists in that debate and indicates the key ways in which their views differ.
- In the second paragraph, the writer sets up her first criterion for compari-son and contrast: the merits of bilingual education, and then discusses the ways in which Santiago and Hayakawa differ. In the third paragraph, the writer sets up her second criterion: perceptions of American culture implied by the two sides in the debate over bilingual education. Once again, the writer discusses the ways in which Santiago and Hayakawa differ.
- The writer concludes with a paragraph of summary and comment in which she suggests that the debate over bilingual education will con-tinue. She poses a final series of questions about the progress of non-English-speaking students and suggests that the students themselves will answer many of the questions about the effectiveness of bilingual educa-tion.

Within any one essay, you are likely to adopt several techniques of devel-opment. We have reviewed here a few of the common techniques: summary, example, two (or more) reasons, strawman, concession, and comparison and contrast. Certainly, *critique* (see Chapter 3) would be another method of de-velopment. A critical evaluation does not need to exist in and of itself; often, a critique forms one part of a larger paper. The important point is that you be in control of your paper. Understand the main points you wish to make, under-stand the general sections, or stages, in which you intend to make them, and then use the various methods of development available to you.

## THE RESEARCH PAPER

The process of preparing and writing research papers is discussed in Chapter 5. Many of the principles of research-based writing, however, have already been treated in this chapter on synthesis. (In fact, the example syntheses in this chapter are short research papers.) Once you have researched your subject, your tasks in writing a research paper parallel those outlined on pages 88-89 on writing a synthesis: considering your purpose; reviewing your sources; formulat-ing a thesis; deciding how you will use your source material, developing an organizational plan; writing your first draft; documenting your sources; and revising your paper. And like explanatory and argument syntheses, research papers involve not only multiple sources but also elements of summary, para-phrase, quotation, and critique.

# 5

# RESEARCH

## GOING BEYOND THIS TEXT

In this chapter we'll discuss how you can use the skills you've learned in writing summaries, critiques, and syntheses to compose research papers and reports. A research paper is generally considered a major academic endeavor, and frequently it is. But even a paper based on only one or two sources outside the scope of assigned reading has been researched. Research requires you (1) to locate and take notes on relevant sources and organize your findings; (2) to summarize or paraphrase these sources; (3) to critically analyze them for their value and relevance to your subject; and (4) to synthesize information and ideas from several sources that best support your own critical viewpoint.

As you'll see, each chapter in Part II of *Writing and Reading Across the Curriculum* consists of a group of related readings on a particular subject— obedience to authority, gender roles, business ethics, and so on. The readings in a chapter will give you a basic understanding of the key issues associated with the subject. For a deeper understanding, however, you'll need to go beyond the relatively few readings included here. A paper based on even two or three additional sources will have a breadth missing from a paper that relies exclusively on the text readings.

Of course, you may be asked to prepare a research paper of some length. Each chapter in Part II concludes with a number of research activities on the subject just covered. In some cases, we suggest particular sources; in others, we provide only general directions. Your instructor may ask you to work on at least one of these assignments during the term. But whether you are preparing an in-depth research paper or just locating a few additional sources on your subject (or something in between), it's essential to know your way around a college library, to be able to locate quickly and efficiently the information you need. In this chapter, we'll give you some important research tips. For more comprehensive information (e.g., annotated lists of specialized reference tools), consult a text on research papers or the research section of your handbook.

# RESEARCH PAPERS IN THE ACADEMIC DISCIPLINES

Though most of your previous experience with research papers may have been in English classes, you should be prepared for instructors in other academic disciplines to assign papers with significant research components. Here, for example, is a sampling of research topics that have recently been assigned in a broad range of undergraduate courses:

*Anthropology:*   Identify, observe, and gather data pertaining to a particular subculture within the campus community; describe the internal dynamics of this group, and account for these dynamics in terms of theories of relevant anthropologists and sociologists.

*Art History:*   Discuss the main differences between Romanesque and Gothic sculpture, using the sculptures of Jeremiah (St. Pierre Cathedral) and St. Theodore (Chartres Cathedral) as major examples.

*Asian-American Studies:*   Address an important socio-psychological issue for Asian-American communities and/or individuals—for example, the effects of stereotypes, mental health problems, sex role relations, academic achievement, assertiveness, or interracial marriage. Review both the theoretical and research literature on the issue, conduct personal interviews, and draw conclusions from your data.

*Environmental Studies:*   Choose a problem or issue of the physical environment at any level from local to global. Use both field and library work to explore the situation. Include coverage of the following: (1) the history of the issue or problem; (2) the various interest groups involved, taking note of conflicts among them; (3) critical facts and theories from environmental science necessary to understand and evaluate the issue or problem; (4) impact and significance of management measures already taken or proposed; (5) your recommendations for management of the solution.

*Film Studies:*   Pick a particular period of British film and discuss major film trends or production problems within that period.

*History:*   Write a paper analyzing the history of a public policy (example: the U.S. Supreme Court's role in undermining the civil rights of African-Americans between 1870 and 1896), drawing your sources from the best, most current scholarly histories available.

*Physics:*   Research and write a paper on solar cell technology, covering the following areas: basic physical theory, history and development, structure and materials, types and characteristics, practical uses, state of the art, and future prospects.

**Political Science:**   Explain the contours of California's water policy in the last few decades and then, by focusing on one specific controversy, explain and analyze the way in which policy was adapted and why. Consider such questions as where does the water come from, how much, what quantity, who uses the water, who pays and how much, and should we develop more at all?

**Psychology:**   Explore some issue related to the testing of mental ability; for example, the effects of time limits upon test reliability.

**Religious Studies:**   Select a particular religious group or movement present in the nation for at least twenty years and show how its belief or practice has changed since members of the group have been in America or, if the group began in America, since its first generation.

**Sociology:**   Write on one of the following topics: (1) a critical comparison of two (or more) theories of deviance; (2) field or library research study of a specific deviant career: thieves, drug addicts, prostitutes, corrupt politicians, university administrators; (3) portrayals of deviance in popular culture—e.g., television "accounts" of terrorism, incest, spouse abuse; (4) old age as a form of deviance; (5) the relationship between homelessness and mental illness.

Some of these research papers allow students a considerable range of choice (within the general subject); others are highly specific in requiring students to address a particular issue. Most of these papers call for some library research; a few call for a combination of library and field research; others may be based entirely on field research.

## FINDING A SUBJECT

In your present writing course, finding a general subject shouldn't be a problem, since your research likely will concern one of the subjects covered in this text. And, as we've suggested, your instructor may assign you one of the research activities at the end of each chapter, for which some focus will be provided in our directions. Or your instructor may specify his or her own particular directions for your research activity. In other cases, you'll be asked simply to write a paper on some aspect of the subject.

Which aspect? Review the readings, the questions following the readings, and your responses to these questions. Something may immediately (or eventually) spring to mind. Perhaps while reading the selection from Betty Friedan's enormously influential *The Feminine Mystique,* you wonder how the book was received by critics and general readers when it first appeared in 1963 and launched the modern feminist revolution. Maybe while reading the selections on the Milgram experiment in the chapter on obedience to authority, you become curious about later experiments that also tested obedience to authority, or about a recent event that demonstrated the malign effects of obedience to unlawful or immoral authority. Consider the readings on bilingual education. What has been written on this subject since this book was published? To what extent have the terms of the debate changed? What programs on the federal, state, or local level have been instituted either to advance or to retard bilingual education?

## THE RESEARCH QUESTION

Research handbooks generally advise students to narrow their subjects as much as possible. A ten-page paper on the modern feminist movement would be unmanageable. You would have to do an enormous quantity of research (a preliminary computer search of this subject would yield several thousand items), and you couldn't hope to produce anything other than a superficial treatment of such a large subject. But a paper on the contemporary reception of *The Feminine Mystique* or on Betty Friedan's activities as a founder of the National Organization for Women should be quite manageable. It's difficult to say, however, how narrow is narrow enough. (A literary critic once produced a twenty-page article analyzing the first paragraph of Henry James's *The Ambassadors.*)

Perhaps more helpful as a guideline on focusing your research is to seek to answer a particular question, a *research question*. For example, how did the Bush administration respond to the demand for bilingual education? To what extent is America perceived by social critics to be in decline? Did Exxon behave responsibly in handling the *Valdez* oil spill? How has the debate over genetic engineering evolved during the past decade? To what extent do contemporary cigarette ads perpetuate sexist attitudes? Or how do contemporary cigarette ads differ in message and tone from cigarette ads in the 1950s? Focusing on questions like these and approaching your research as a way of answering such questions is probably the best way to narrow your subject and ensure focus in your paper. The essential answer to this research question eventually becomes your *thesis,* and in the paper you present evidence that systematically supports your thesis.

## PRELIMINARY RESEARCH

Once you have a research question, you want to see what references are available. You want to familiarize yourself quickly with the basic issues and to generate a preliminary list of sources. Here are some of the best ways to do this:

- ◆ Ask your professor for recommended sources on the subject.
- ◆ Ask your college librarian for useful reference tools in your subject area.
- ◆ If you're working on a subject from this text, use some of the sources we've mentioned in the research activities section.

- Read an encyclopedia article on the subject and use the bibliography following the article.
- Read the introduction to a recent book on the subject and review that book's bibliography.
- Consult the annual *Bibliographic Index* (see below for details).
- If you need help in narrowing a broad subject, consult one or more of the following:

   the subject heading in a computerized card catalog (the subject will be broken down into its components);

   the subject heading in a computerized periodical catalog, such as *Info-Trac*, or in a print catalog, such as the *Readers' Guide to Periodical Literature*;

   the *Library of Congress Subject Headings* catalog.

We'll consider a few of these suggestions in more detail.

## Consulting Knowledgeable People

When you think of research, you may immediately think of libraries and print material. But don't neglect a key reference source—other people. Your *professor* can probably suggest fruitful areas of research and some useful sources. Try to see your professor during office hours, however, rather than immediately before or after class, so that you'll have enough time for a productive discussion.

Once you get to the library, ask a *reference librarian* which reference sources (e.g., bibliographies, specialized encyclopedias, periodical indexes, statistical almanacs) you need for your particular area of research. Librarians won't do your research for you, but they'll be glad to show you how to research efficiently and systematically.

You can also obtain vital information from people when you interview them, ask them to fill out questionnaires or surveys, or have them participate in experiments. We'll cover this aspect of research in more detail below.

## Encyclopedias

Reading an encyclopedia entry about your subject will give you a basic understanding of the most significant facts and issues. Whether the subject is the life of Columbus or the mechanics of genetic engineering, the encyclopedia article—written by a specialist in the field—offers a broad overview that may serve as a launching point to more specialized research in a particular area. The article may illuminate areas or raise questions that you feel motivated to pursue further. Equally important, the encyclopedia article frequently concludes with an *annotated bibliography* describing important books and articles on the subject.

Encyclopedias have certain limitations. First, most professors don't accept encyclopedia articles as legitimate sources for academic papers. You should use encyclopedias primarily to familiarize yourself with (and to select a particular aspect of) the subject area and as a springboard for further research. Also, because new editions appear only once every five or ten years, the information they contain—including bibliographies—may not be current. The most recent editions of the *Encyclopaedia Britannica* and the *Encyclopedia Americana,* for instance, were published before any of the important new books on Columbus that appeared around the Columbus quincentennial of 1992.

Some of the most useful general encyclopedias include the following:

*American Academic Encyclopedia*

*Encyclopedia Americana*

*New Encyclopaedia Britannica*

Keep in mind that the library also contains a variety of more *specialized encyclopedias.* These encyclopedias restrict themselves to a particular disciplinary area, such as chemistry, law, or film, and are considerably more detailed in their treatment of a subject than general encyclopedias. Here are examples of specialized encyclopedias:

## Social Sciences

*Encyclopedia of Education*

*Encyclopedia of Psychology*

*Guide to American Law*

*International Encyclopedia of the Social Sciences*

## Humanities

*Encyclopedia of American History*

*Encyclopedia of Art*

*Encyclopedia of Religion and Ethics*

*International Encyclopedia of Film*

*The New College Encyclopedia of Music*

## Science and Technology

*Encyclopedia of Biological Sciences*

*Encyclopedia of Computer Science and Engineering*

*Encyclopedia of Physics*

*McGraw-Hill Encyclopedia of Environmental Science*

*Van Nostrand's Scientific Encyclopedia*

Business

*Encyclopedia of Banking and Finance*
*Encyclopedia of Economics*

## Overviews and Bibliographies in Recent Books

If your professor or one of your bibliographic sources directs you to an important recent book on the subject, skim the introductory (and possibly the concluding) material to the book, along with the table of contents, for an overview of the key issues. Look also for a bibliography. For example, Zvi Dor-Ner's 1991 book *Columbus and the Age of Discovery* includes a four-page annotated bibliography of important reference sources on Columbus and the age of exploration.

Keep in mind that authors are not necessarily objective about their subject, and some have particularly biased viewpoints that you may unwittingly carry over into your paper, treating them as objective truth.[1] However, you may still be able to get some useful information out of such sources. (For example, the selection by Kirkpatrick Sale in our Columbus chapter is considered by some historians to be biased against Columbus and his legacy. However, even Sale's critics concede that his descriptions of Columbus's four voyages are accurate and informative.) Alert yourself to authorial biases by looking up the reviews of your book in the *Book Review Digest* (described on page 156). Additionally, look up biographical information on the author (see Biographical Indexes, page 160), whose previous writings or professional associations may suggest a predictable set of attitudes on the subject of your book.

## Bibliographic Index

The *Bibliographic Index* is a series of annual volumes that enables you to locate bibliographies on a particular subject. The bibliographies it refers to generally appear at the end of book chapters or periodical articles, or they may themselves be book or pamphlet length. Browsing through the *Bibliographic Index* in a general subject area may give you ideas for further research in particular aspects of the subject, along, of course, with particular references.

---

[1]Bias is not necessarily bad. Authors, like all other people, have certain preferences and predilections that influence the way they view the world and the kinds of arguments they make. As long as they inform you of their biases, or as long as you are aware of them and take them into account, you can still use these sources judiciously. (You might gather valuable information from a book about the Watergate scandal, even if it were written by former president Richard Nixon or one of his top aides, as long as you make proper allowance for their understandable biases.) Bias becomes a potential problem only when it masquerades as objective truth or is accepted as such by the reader. For suggestions on identifying and assessing authorial bias, see the material on persuasive writing (pages 67–70) and evaluating assumptions (pages 72–73) in Chapter 3.

## Subject-Heading Guides

Seeing how a general subject (e.g., education) is broken down in other sources also could stimulate research in a particular area (e.g., bilingual primary education in California). As in the table of contents of a book, the general subject (the book title) is analyzed into its secondary subject headings (the chapter titles). To locate such sets of secondary subject headings, consult:

♦ an electronic card catalog
♦ an electronic or print periodical catalog (e.g., *InfoTrac, Readers' Guide, Social Science Index*)
♦ The *Library of Congress Subject Headings* catalog
♦ The *Propaedia* volume of the *New Encyclopaedia Britannica* (1988)

# FOCUSED RESEARCH

Once you've narrowed your scope to a particular subject and a particular research question (or set of research questions), you're ready to undertake more focused research. Your objective now is to learn as much as you can about your particular subject. Only in this way will you be qualified to make an informed response to your research question. This means you'll have to become something of an expert on the subject—or, if that's not possible, given time constraints, you can at least become someone whose critical viewpoint is based solidly on the available evidence. In the following pages we'll suggest how to find sources for this kind of focused research. In most cases, your research will be based on (1) *books;* (2) *articles;* and (3) specialized *reference* sources. In certain cases, your research may be based partially or even primarily on (4) *interviews* and *surveys.*

## Books

Books are often useful in providing both breadth and depth of coverage of a subject. Because they generally are published at least a year or two after the events treated, they also tend to provide the critical distance that is sometimes missing from articles. (Of course, books also may be shallow, inaccurate, outdated, or hopelessly biased; for help in making such determinations, see *Book Review Digest,* below.) You can locate relevant books through the card catalog, although in most libraries the card catalog has been converted to an electronic database retrievable on computer screens. In some cases, you may be able to obtain printouts of the data. Whether using a card or electronic catalog, you may search in three ways: (1) by *author,* (2) by *title,* and (3) by *subject.* Entries include the call number, the publication information, and, frequently, a summary of the book's contents. Larger libraries use the Library of Congress cataloging system for call numbers (example: E111/C6); smaller ones use the Dewey Decimal System (example: 970.015/C726).

### Book Review Digest

Perhaps the best way to determine the reliability and credibility of a book you may want to use is to look it up in the annual *Book Review Digest.* These volumes list (alphabetically by author) the most significant books published during the year, supply a brief description of each, and, most important, provide excerpts from (and references to) reviews. If a book receives bad reviews, you don't necessarily have to avoid it (the book still may have something useful to offer, and the review itself may be unreliable). But you should take any negative reaction into account when using that book as a source.

## Periodicals: General

### Magazines

Because many more periodical articles than books are published every year, you are likely (depending on the subject) to find more information in periodicals than in books. By their nature, periodical articles tend to be more current than books (the best way, for example, to find out about the federal government's current policy on AIDS is to look for articles in periodicals and newspapers). However, periodicals may have less critical distance than books, and they also may date more rapidly—to be superseded by more recent articles.

General periodicals (such as *Time, The New Republic,* and *The Nation*) are intended for nonspecialists. Their articles, which tend to be highly readable, may be written by staff writers, free-lancers, or specialists. But they usually do not provide citations or other indications of sources and so are of limited usefulness for scholarly research.

The most well known general index is the *Readers' Guide to Periodical Literature,* a print index of articles in several hundred general-interest magazines and a few more specialized magazines (such as *Business Week* and *Science Digest*). Articles in the *Readers' Guide* are indexed by author, title, and subject.

Another general reference for articles is the *Essay and General Literature Index,* which indexes articles contained in anthologies.

Electronic indexes are those that you access on the computer. They are generally of two types: *on-line* and *CD-ROM.* On-line databases generally originate off-campus from commercial information services. Such databases include MAGS and NEWS, which index magazine and newspaper articles, respectively, and DIALOG, which provides access to nearly two million records in hundreds of individual databases in fields such as psychology, sociology, and the humanities. A number of university libraries have their own database networks; ask the reference librarian if such a network is available at your library. (In some cases, you may be charged a fee for the use of on-line databases.)

You may also work from a CD-ROM, a compact disc that you insert in your own terminal. Many periodical indexes (such as the *Readers' Guide*) and newspaper indexes (such as the *New York Times* and the *Wall Street Journal*) are available on CD-ROM as well as in print. Also available is *InfoTrac,* which gives you access to several years' worth of general, business, government, and technical periodical articles. Often you can get "hard copies" of the electronic data from printers hooked up to the terminal.

### Newspapers

News stories, feature stories, and editorials (even letters to the editor) may be important sources of information. Your library certainly will have the *New York Times* index, and it may have indexes to other important newspapers, such as the *Washington Post,* the *Los Angeles Times,* the *Chicago Tribune,* the *Wall Street Journal,* and the *Christian Science Monitor.* Newspaper holdings will be on microfilm, and you will need a microprinter/viewer to get hard copies.

*Note:* Because of its method of cross-referencing, the *New York Times* index may at first be confusing to use. Suppose that you want to find *Times* stories on bilingual education during 1987. When you locate the "Bilingual education" entry, you won't find citations, but rather a *"See also* Education" reference that directs you to three dates (February 12, May 9, and October 22) under the heading of "Education." Under this major heading, references to 1987 stories on education are arranged in chronological order from January to December. When you look up the dates you were directed to, you'll see brief descriptions of the stories on bilingual education.

Some newspaper indexes also are available in electronic form, both on CD-ROM and in local and national on-line databases. The advantage of using databases (as opposed to print indexes) is that you can search several years' worth of different newspapers at the same time. Check with your reference librarian to see what is available on your campus.

## Periodicals: Specialized

### Articles

Many professors will expect at least some of your research to be based on articles in specialized periodicals. So instead of (or in addition to) relying on an article from *Psychology Today* for an account of the effects of crack cocaine on mental functioning, you might (also) rely on an article from the *Journal of Abnormal Psychology.* If you are writing a paper on the satirist Jonathan Swift, you may need to locate a relevant article in *Eighteenth-Century Studies.* Articles in such journals normally are written by specialists and professionals in the field, rather than by staff writers or free-lancers, and the authors will assume that their readers already understand the basic facts and issues concerning the subject.

To find articles in specialized periodicals, you'll use specialized indexes—that is, indexes for particular disciplines. You also may find it helpful to refer to *abstracts.* Like specialized indexes, abstracts list articles published in a particular discipline over a given period, but they also provide summaries of the articles listed. Abstracts tend to be more selective than indexes, since they consume more space (and involve considerably more work to compile); but, because they also describe the contents of the articles covered, they can save you a lot of time in determining which articles you should read and which ones you can safely skip.

Here are some of the more commonly used specialized periodical indexes and abstracts in the various disciplines:

## Social Science

*Abstracts in Anthropology*

*Education Index*

*Psychological Abstracts*

*Public Affairs Information Service (PAIS)*

*Social Science Index*

*Sociological Abstracts*

*Women's Studies Abstracts*

Social Science Databases:

ERIC (Educational Resources Information Center)

PAIS (Public Affairs Information Service)

PSYCHINFO (psychology)

Psychological Abstracts

Social SciSearch

Sociological Abstracts

## Humanities

*Abstracts of English Studies*

*America: History and Life*

*Art Index*

*Cambridge Bibliography of English Literature*

*Essay and General Literature Index*

*Film/Literature Index*

*Historical Abstracts*

*Humanities Index*

*International Index of Film Periodicals*

*MLA International Bibliography of Books and Articles on Modern Languages and Literatures*

*Music Index*

*Religion Index*

*Year's Work in English Studies*

Humanities Databases:

    Arts and Humanities Citation Index

    MLA Bibliography

    Philosopher's Index

    Historical Abstracts

## Science and Technology

*Applied Science and Technology Index*

*Biological Abstracts*

*Engineering Index*

*General Science Index*

*Index to Scientific and Technical Proceedings*

Science and Technology Databases:

    Agricola (agriculture)

    Biosis Previews (biology, botany)

    CA search (chemistry)

    Compendix (engineering)

    ORBIT (science and technology)

    SciSearch

## Business

*Business Index*

*Business Periodicals Index*

*Economic Titles/Abstracts*

*Wall Street Journal Index*

Business Databases:

    ABI/INFORM

    Econ Abstracts International

    Labor Statistics

    Standard and Poor's News

Finally, if you are interested in exploring the legal ramifications of a particular issue, check the *Index to Legal Periodicals*.

## Biographical Indexes

To look up information on particular people, you can use not only encyclopedias but an array of biographical sources. (You can also use biographical sources to alert yourself to potential biases on the part of your source authors.) A brief selection follows:

### Living Persons

*Contemporary Authors: A Biographical Guide to Current Authors and Their Works*
*Current Biography*
*International Who's Who*
*Who's Who in America*

### Persons No Longer Living

*Dictionary of American Biography*
*Dictionary of National Biography* (Great Britain)
*Dictionary of Scientific Biography*
*Who Was Who*

### Persons Living or Dead

*Biography Almanac*
*McGraw-Hill Encyclopedia of World Biography*
*Webster's Biographical Dictionary*

## Dictionaries

Use dictionaries to look up the meaning of general or specialized terms. Here are some of the most useful dictionaries:

### General

*Oxford English Dictionary*
*Webster's New Collegiate Dictionary*
*Webster's Third New International Dictionary of the English Language*

## Social Sciences

*Black's Law Dictionary*
*Dictionary of the Social Sciences*
*McGraw-Hill Dictionary of Modern Economics*

## Humanities

*Dictionary of American History*
*Dictionary of Films*
*Dictionary of Philosophy*
*Harvard Dictionary of Music*
*McGraw-Hill Dictionary of Art*

## Science and Technology

*Computer Dictionary and Handbook*
*Condensed Chemical Dictionary*
*Dictionary of Biology*
*Dorland's Medical Dictionary*

## Business

*Dictionary of Advertising Terms*
*Dictionary of Business and Economics*
*Mathematical Dictionary for Economics and Business Administration*
*McGraw-Hill Dictionary of Modern Economics: A Handbook of Terms and Organizations*

## Other Sources/Government Publications

You also may find useful information in other sources. For statistical and other basic reference information on a subject, consult a *handbook* (example: *Statistical Abstracts of the United States*). For current information on a subject as of a given year, consult an *almanac* (example: *World Almanac*). For annual updates of information, consult a *yearbook* (example: *The Statesman's Yearbook*). For maps and other geographic information, consult an *atlas* (example: *New York Times Atlas of the World*). (Often, simply browsing through the reference shelves for data on your general subject—such as biography, public affairs, or psychology—will reveal valuable sources of information.)

Many libraries keep pamphlets in a *vertical file* (i.e., a file cabinet). For example, a pamphlet on AIDS might be found in the vertical file, rather than in the library stacks. Such material is accessible through the *Vertical File Index* (a monthly subject and title index to pamphlet material).

Finally, note that the U.S. government regularly publishes large quantities of useful information. Some indexes to government publications are:

*American Statistics Index*

*Congressional Information Service*

*The Congressional Record*

*Information U.S.A.*

## Interviews and Surveys

Depending on the subject of your paper, some or all of your research may be conducted outside the library. You may pursue research in science labs, in courthouses, in city government files, in shopping malls (if you are observing, say, patterns of consumer behavior), in the quad in front of the humanities building, or in front of TV screens (if you are analyzing, say, situation comedies or commercials, or if you are drawing on documentaries or interviews—in which cases you should try to obtain transcripts or tape the programs).

You may want to *interview* your professors, your fellow students, or other individuals knowledgeable about your subject. Before interviewing your subject(s), become knowledgeable enough about the topic that you can ask intelligent questions. You also should prepare most of your questions beforehand. Ask "open-ended" questions designed to elicit meaningful responses, rather than "forced choice" questions that can be answered with a word or two, or "leading questions" that presume a particular answer. (Example: Instead of asking, "Do you think that men should be more sensitive to women's concerns for equality in the workplace?" ask, "To what extent do you see evidence that men are insufficiently sensitive to women's concerns for equality in the workplace?") Ask follow-up questions to elicit additional insights or details. If you record the interview (in addition to, or instead of, taking notes), get your subject's permission, preferably in writing.

*Surveys* or *questionnaires,* when well prepared, can produce valuable information about the ideas or preferences of a group of people. Before preparing your questions, determine your purpose in conducting the survey, exactly what kind of information you want to obtain, and whom you are going to ask for the information. Decide also whether you want to collect the questionnaires as soon as people have filled them out or whether you want the responses mailed back to you. (Obviously, in the latter case, you have to provide stamped, self-addressed envelopes and specify a deadline for return.) Keep in mind that the larger and the more representative your sample of people, the more reliable the survey. As with interviews, it's important to devise and word questions carefully, so that they (1) are understandable and (2) don't reflect your own biases. If you're surveying attitudes on capital punishment, for example, and you ask, "Do you believe that the state should endorse legalized murder?" you've loaded the question to influence people to answer in the negative, and thus you've destroyed the reliability of your survey.

Unlike interview questions, survey questions should be short answer or multiple choice; open-ended questions encourage responses that are difficult to quantify. (You may want to leave space, however, for "additional comments.") Conversely, "yes" or "no" responses or rankings on a 5-point scale are easy to quantify. For example, you might ask a random sample of students in your residence hall the extent to which they are concerned that genetic information about themselves might be made available to their insurance companies—on a scale of 1 (unconcerned) to 5 (extremely concerned). For surveys on certain subjects (and depending on the number of respondents), it may be useful to break out the responses by as many meaningful categories as possible—for example, gender, age, ethnicity, religion, education, geographic locality, profession, and income. Obtaining these kinds of statistical breakdowns, of course, means more work on the part of your respondents in filling out the surveys and more work for you in compiling the responses. If the survey is too long and involved, some subjects won't participate or won't return the questionnaires.

## FROM RESEARCH TO WORKING THESIS

The search strategy we've just described isn't necessarily a straight-line process. In other words, you won't always proceed from the kinds of things you do in "preliminary research" to the kinds of things you do in "focused research." You may not formulate a research question until you've done a good deal of focused research. And the fact that we've treated, say, biographical sources before, say, specialized periodical articles does not mean that you should read biographical material before you read articles. We've described the process as we have for convenience; and, *in general,* it is a good idea to proceed from more general sources to more particular ones. In practice, however, the research procedure often is considerably less systematic. You might begin, for example, by reading a few articles on the subject, continue by looking up a few books, and then looking up an encyclopedia article or two. Along the way, you might consult specialized dictionaries, book review indexes, and a guide to reference books in the area. Or, instead of proceeding in a straight line through the process, you might find yourself moving in circular patterns—backtracking to previous steps and following up leads you missed or ignored earlier. There's nothing wrong with such variations of the basic search strategy, as long as you keep in mind the kinds of resources that are available to you, and as long as you plan to look up as many of these resources as you can—given the constraints on your time.

One other thing you'll discover as you proceed: research is to some extent a self-generating process. That is, one source will lead you—through references in the text, citations, and bibliographic entries—to others. Your authors will refer to other studies on the subject; and, frequently, they'll indicate which ones they believe are the most important, and why. At some point, if your research has been systematic, you'll realize that you've already looked at most of the key work on the subject. This is the point at which you can be reasonably assured that the research stage of your paper is nearing its end.

As your work progresses, you may find that your preliminary research question undergoes a change. At first, you may have been primarily interested in the question of whether or not bilingual education is a good idea. During your research, you come across S. I. Hayakawa's controversial proposal that English be made the official language of the United States, and you decide to shift the direction of your research toward this particular debate. Or, having made an initial assessment that bilingual education is a good idea, you conclude the opposite. Be prepared for such shifts: they're a natural—and desirable—part of the research (and learning) process. They indicate that you haven't made up your mind in advance, that you're open to new evidence and ideas.

You're now ready to respond to your modified research question with a *working thesis*—a statement that controls and focuses your entire paper, points toward your conclusion, and is supported by your evidence. See our earlier discussion, in Chapter 2 (pages 36–43), on the process of devising and narrowing a thesis.

## THE WORKING BIBLIOGRAPHY

As you conduct your research, keep a working bibliography—that is, a set of bibliographic information on all the sources you're likely to use in preparing the paper. Compile full bibliographic information as you consider each source. It's better to spend time during the research process noting information on a source you don't eventually use than to go back to retrieve information—such as the publisher or the date—just as you're typing your final draft.

The most efficient way to compile bibliographic information is on 3" × 5" cards. You can easily add, delete, and rearrange cards as your research progresses. On each card record:

a. the author or editor (last name first)

b. the title (and subtitle) of the book or article

c. the publisher and place of publication (if a book) or the title of the periodical

d. the date of publication; if periodical, volume and issue number

e. the inclusive page numbers (if article)

You also may want to include on the bibliography card:

f. a brief description of the source (to help you recall it later in the research process)

g. the library call number (to help you relocate the source if you haven't checked it out)

h. a code number, which you can use as a shorthand reference to the source in your notecards

Your final bibliography, known as "Works Cited" in Modern Language Association (MLA) format and "References" in American Psychological Association (APA) format, consists of the sources you have actually summarized, paraphrased, or quoted in your paper. When you compile the bibliography, arrange the cards in alphabetical order and type the references one after another.

Here is an example of a working bibliography card for a book:

> (8)
>
> Sale, Kirkpatrick. *The Conquest of Paradise: Christopher Columbus and the Columbian Legacy.* New York: Knopf, 1990.
>
> Attacks Columbian legacy for genocide and ecocide. Good treatment of Columbus's voyages (Chaps. 6-8).

Here is an example of a working bibliography card for an article:

12) Axtell, James. "Europeans, Indians and the Age of Discovery in American History Textbooks." _American Historical Review_ 92.3 (1987): 621-32.

Finds treatments of subjects in title of article inadequate in most college-level American history texts. Specifies "errors," "half-truths" and "misleading assertions." Recommends changes in nine areas.

Some instructors may ask you to prepare—either in addition to or instead of a research paper—an _annotated bibliography_. This is a list of relevant works on a subject, with the contents of each briefly described or assessed. The bibliography cards shown provide examples of two entries in an annotated bibliography on the Columbian legacy. Annotations are different from _abstracts_ in that they do not claim to be comprehensive summaries; they indicate, rather, how the items may be useful to the prospective researcher.

## EVALUATING SOURCES

As you sift through what seems a formidable mountain of material, you'll need to work quickly and efficiently; you'll also need to do some selecting. This means, primarily, distinguishing the more important from the less important (and the unimportant) material. Some hints:

- _Skim_ the source: With a book, look over the table of contents, the introduction and conclusion, and the index; zero in on passages that your initial survey suggests are important. With an article, skim the introduction and the subheadings.
- Be on the alert for _references_ in your sources to other important sources, particularly to sources that several authors treat as important.
- Other things being equal, the more _recent_ the source, the better. Recent work often incorporates or refers to important earlier work.
- If you're considering making multiple references to a book, look up the _reviews_ in the _Book Review Digest_ or the _Book Review Index_. Also, check

the author's credentials in a source like *Contemporary Authors* or *Current Biography*.

♦ Draw on your *critical reading* skills to help you determine the reliability and value of a source (see Chapter 3).

## NOTE-TAKING

People have their favorite ways of notetaking: some use cards; others use legal pads or spiral notebooks; yet others type notes into a laptop computer, perhaps using a database program. We prefer 4" × 6" cards for notetaking. Such cards have some of the same advantages as 3" × 5" cards for working bibliographies: they can easily be added to, subtracted from, and rearranged to accommodate changing organizational plans. Also, discrete pieces of information from the same source can easily be arranged (and rearranged) into subtopics—a difficult task if you have three pages of notes on an entire article.

Whatever your preferred approach, we recommend including, along with the note itself,

a. a page reference

b. a topic or subtopic label, corresponding to your outline (see below)

c. a code number, corresponding to the number assigned the source in the working bibliography

Here is a sample notecard for an article by Charles Krauthammer entitled "Hail Columbus, Dead White Male" (*Time,* May 27, 1991):

Defenses of Columbus (III B)                                       ⑦
Defends Columbus against revisionist attacks.
Our civilization "turned out better" than that
of the Incas. "And mankind is the better for
it. Infinitely better. Reason enough to
honor Columbus and 1492" (74).

Here is a notecard for the specialized periodical article by Axtell (see bibliography card on page 166):

Problems with Textbooks (IIA)                                    (12)

American history textbooks do not give adequate coverage to the Age of Discovery. An average of only 4% of the textbook pages covering first-semester topics is devoted to the century that accounts for 30% of the time between Columbus and Reconstruction. "The challenge of explaining some of the most complex, important, and interesting events in human history – the discovery of a new continent, the religious upheavals of the sixteenth century, the forging of the Spanish empire, the Columbian biological exchange, the African diaspora – all in twenty or twenty-five pages is one that few, if any, textbook authors have met or are likely to meet" (623).

The notecard is headed by a topic label followed by the tentative location in the paper outline where the information will be used. The number in the upper right corner is coded to the corresponding bibliography card. The note itself in the first card uses *summary* ("Defends Columbus against revisionist attacks") and *quotation*. The note in the second card uses *summary* (sentence 1), *paraphrase* (sentence 2), and *quotation* (sentence 3). Summary was used to condense important ideas treated in several paragraphs in the sources; quotation, for particularly incisive language by the source authors. For general hints on when to use each of these three forms, see page 35.

## ARRANGING YOUR NOTES: THE OUTLINE

Recall that your research originally was stimulated by one or more *research questions,* to which you may have made a tentative response in your *working thesis* (see page 151). As you proceed with your research, patterns should begin to emerge that either substantiate, refute, or otherwise affect your working thesis. These patterns represent the relationships you discern among the various ideas and pieces of evidence that you investigate. They may be patterns of cause and effect, of chronology, of logical relationships, of comparison and contrast, of pro and con, of correspondence (or lack of correspondence) between theory and reality. Once these patterns begin to emerge, write them down as the components of a preliminary outline. This outline indicates the order in which you plan to support your original working thesis or a new thesis that you have developed during the course of research.

For example, on deciding to investigate the new genetic technologies, you devise a working thesis focused on the intensity of the debate over the applications of such technologies. Much of the debate, you discover, focuses on arguments about the morality of (1) testing for genetic abnormalities in the fetus, (2) using genetic information to screen prospective employees, and (3) disrupting the ecosystem by creating new organisms. Based on this discovery, you might create a brief outline, numbering each of these three main categories and using these numbers on your notecards to indicate how you have (at least provisionally) categorized each note. As you continue your research, you'll be able to expand or reduce the scope of your paper, modifying your outline as necessary. Your developing outline becomes a guide to continuing research.

Some people prefer not to develop an outline until they have more or less completed their research. At that point they will look over their notecards, consider the relationships among the various pieces of evidence, possibly arrange their cards into separate piles, and then develop an outline based on their perceptions and insights about the material. They will then rearrange (and code) the notecards to conform to their newly created outline.

In the past, instructors commonly required students to develop multileveled formal outlines (complete with Roman and Arabic numerals) before writing their first drafts. But many writers find it difficult to generate papers from such elaborate outlines, which sometimes restrict, rather than stimulate, thought. Now, many instructors recommend only that students prepare an *informal outline,* indicating just the main sections of the paper, and possibly one level below that. Thus, a paper on how the significance of Columbus's legacy has changed over the years may be informally outlined as follows:

```
Intro: Different views of Columbus, past and
     present;
     --thesis: view of Columbus varies with
     temper of times
Pre-20th-century assessments of Columbus and
     legacy
The debate over the quincentennial
     --positive views
     --negative views
Conclusion: How to assess Columbian heritage
```

Such an outline will help you organize your research and should not be unduly restrictive as a guide to writing.

The *formal outline* (a multileveled plan with Roman and Arabic numerals, capital and small lettered subheadings) may still be useful, not so much as an exact blueprint for composition—although some writers do find it useful for this purpose—but rather as a guide to revision. That is, after you have written your draft, outlining it may help you discern structural problems: illogical sequences of material; confusing relationships between ideas; poor unity or coherence; sections that are too abstract or underdeveloped. Many instructors also require that formal outlines accompany the finished research paper.

The formal outline should indicate the logical relationships in the evidence relating to your particular subject (see example below). But it also may reflect the general conventions of presenting academic ideas. Thus, after an *introduction*, papers in the social sciences often proceed with a description of the *methods* of collecting information, continue with a description of the *results* of the investigation, and end with a *conclusion*. Papers in the sciences often follow a similar pattern. Papers in the humanities generally are less standardized in form. In devising a logical organization for your paper, ask yourself how your reader might best be introduced to the subject, be guided through a discussion of the main issues, and be persuaded that your viewpoint is a sound one.

Formal outlines are generally of two types: *topic* and *sentence outlines.* In the topic outline, headings and subheadings are indicated by words or phrases—as in the informal outline above. In the sentence outline, each heading and subheading is indicated in a complete sentence. Both topic and sentence outlines generally are preceded by the topic sentence.

Here is an example of a sentence outline:

Thesis: How Columbus, his voyages, and his legacy are assessed varies, depending on the values of the times.

    I. Early 19th-century and late 20th-century assessments of Columbus are 180 degrees apart.

    A. 19th-century commentators idolize him.

    B. 20th-century commentators often demonize him.

    C. Shifting assessments are based less on hard facts about Columbus than on the values of the culture that assesses him.

    II. In the 16th and 17th centuries, Columbus was not yet being used for political purposes.

    A. In the early 16th century, his fame was eclipsed by that of others.

    1. Amerigo Vespucci and Vasco da Gama were
       considered more successful mariners.

    2. Cortés and Pizarro were more successful
       in bringing back wealth from the New
       World.

B. In the next century, historians and artists
   began writing of the achievements of
   Columbus, but without an overt political
   purpose.

    1. The first biography of Columbus was
       written by his son Fernando.

    2. Plays about Columbus were written by Lope
       de Vega and others.

C. An important exception was that in 1542 the
   monk Bartolomé de Las Casas attacked the
   Spanish legacy in the Americas--although he
   did not attack Columbus personally.

III. In the 18th and 19th centuries, Columbus and
   his legacy began to be used for political
   purposes.

A. During the late 18th century, Columbus's
   stature in America increased as part of the
   attempt to stir up anti-British sentiment.

    1. Columbus was opposed by kings, and he
       "discovered" a land to be free of royal
       authority.

    2. Columbus, the bold visionary who charted
       unknown territories, became symbolic of
       the American spirit.

B. During the 19th century, Columbus's
   reputation reached its peak.

    1. For some, Columbus represented
       geographical and industrial expansion,
       optimism, and faith in progress.

2. For others, Columbus's success was the archetypal rags-to-riches story at the heart of the American Dream.

3. After the Civil War, Catholics celebrated Columbus as an ethnic hero.

4. The 400th anniversary of Columbus's landfall both celebrated the past and expressed confidence in the future. Columbus became the symbol of American industrial success.

IV. By the quincentennial of Columbus's landfall, the negative assessments of Columbus were far more evident than positive assessments.

A. Historians and commentators charged that the consequences of Columbus's "discoveries" were imperialism, slavery, genocide, and ecocide.

B. The National Council of Churches published a resolution blasting the Columbian legacy.

C. Kirkpatrick Sale's The Conquest of Paradise also attacked Columbus.

D. Native Americans and others protested the quincentennial and planned counter-demonstrations.

V. Conclusion: How should we judge Columbus?

A. In many ways, Columbus was a man of his time and did not rise above his time.

B. In his imagination and boldness and in the impact of his discoveries, Columbus stands above others of his time.

C. When we assess Columbus and his legacy, we also assess our own self-confidence, our optimism, and our faith in progress.

---

# WRITING THE DRAFT

Your goal in drafting your paper is to support your thesis by clearly and logically presenting your evidence—evidence that you summarize, critique, and synthesize. (For a review of the techniques of summary, critique, and synthesis, see Chapters 1, 3, and 4.) In effect, you are creating and moderating a conversation among your sources that supports the conclusions you have drawn from your exploration and analysis of the material. The finished paper, however, should not merely represent an amalgam of your sources; it should present your own particular critical perspective on the subject. Your job is to select and arrange your material in such a way that your conclusions seem inevitable (or at least reasonable). You also must select and arrange your material in a way that is fair and logical; remember that your paper will be evaluated to some degree on whether it meets the standards of logical argumentation discussed on pages 68–70. Try not to be guilty of such logical fallacies as hasty generalization, false analogy, and either/or reasoning.

As we suggested in the section on introductions (pages 52–57), when writing the first draft it's sometimes best to skip the introduction (you'll come back to it later when you have a better idea of just what's being introduced) and to start with the main body of your discussion. What do you have to tell your audience about your subject? It may help to imagine yourself sitting opposite your audience in an informal setting like the student center, telling them what you've discovered in the course of your research, and why you think it's interesting and significant. The fact that you've accumulated a considerable body of evidence (in your notecards) to support your thesis should give you confidence in presenting your argument. Keep in mind, too, that there's no one right way to organize this argument; any number of ways will work, provided each makes logical sense. And if you're working on a computer, it is particularly easy to move whole paragraphs and sections from one place to another.

Begin the drafting process by looking at your notecards. Arrange the cards to correspond to your outline. Summarize, paraphrase, and quote from your notecards as you draft. (One timesaving technique for the first draft is to tape photocopied quotations in the appropriate places in your draft.) If necessary, review the material on explanatory and argument syntheses (pages 90–131). In particular, note the table "How to Write Syntheses" (inside back cover) and "Techniques for Developing Your Papers" (pages 131–47). When presenting your argument, consider such rhetorical strategies as strawman, concession, and comparison and contrast. The sample student papers in the synthesis chapter may serve as models for your own research paper.

As you work through your notecards, be selective. Don't provide more evidence or discussion than you need to prove your point. Resist the urge to use *all* of your material just to show how much research you've done. (One experienced teacher, Susan M. Hubbuch, scornfully refers to papers with too much information as "memory dumps"—consisting of nothing but "mindless regurgitation of everything you have read about a subject.") Also avoid going into extended discussions of what are essentially tangential issues. Keep focused on your research question and on providing support for your thesis.

At the same time, remember that you *are* working on a rough draft—one that will probably have all kinds of problems, from illogical organization to awkward sentence structure to a banal conclusion. Don't worry about it; you can deal with all such problems in subsequent drafts. The important thing now is get the words on paper (or on your disk).

## AVOIDING PLAGIARISM

Plagiarism generally is defined as the attempt to pass off the work of another as one's own. Whether born out of calculation or desperation, plagiarism is the least tolerated offense in the academic world. The fact that most plagiarism is unintentional—arising from ignorance of conventions rather than deceitfulness—makes no difference to many professors.

To avoid charges of plagiarism, follow two basic rules:

1. Cite (a) *all* quoted material and (b) *all* summarized and paraphrased material, unless the information is common knowledge (e.g., the Civil War was fought from 1861 to 1865).
2. Make sure that both the *wording* and the *sentence structure* of your summaries and paraphrases are substantially your own.

Following is a passage of text, followed by several student versions of the ideas represented. (The passage is from Richard Rovere's April 30, 1967, *New York Times Magazine* article, "The Most Gifted and Successful Demagogue This Country Has Ever Known.")

McCarthy never seemed to believe in himself or in anything he had said. He knew that Communists were not in charge of American foreign policy. He knew that they weren't running the United States Army. He knew that he had spent five years looking for Communists in the government and that—although some must certainly have been there, since Communists had turned up in practically every other major government in the world—he hadn't come up with even one.

One student version of this passage reads as follows:

```
McCarthy never believed in himself or in anything
he had said.  He knew that Communists were not in
charge of American foreign policy and weren't
running the United States Army.  He knew that he
```

```
had spent five years looking for Communists in
the government, and although there must certainly
have been some there, since Communists were in
practically every other major government in the
world, he hadn't come up with even one.
```

Clearly, this is intentional plagiarism. The student has copied the original passage almost word for word.

Here is another version of the same passage:

```
McCarthy knew that Communists were not running
foreign policy or the Army.  He also knew that
although there must have been some Communists in
the government, he hadn't found a single one,
even though he had spent five years looking.
```

This student has attempted to put the ideas into her own words, but both the wording and the sentence structure are still so heavily dependent on the original passage that even if it *were* cited, most professors would consider it plagiarism.

In the following version, the student sufficiently changes the wording and sentence structure, and properly credits the information to Rovere, so that there is no question of plagiarism:

```
According to Richard Rovere, McCarthy was cynical
enough to know that Communists were running
neither the government nor the Army.  He also
knew that he hadn't found a single Communist in
government, even though he had been looking for
five years (192).
```

Apart from questions of plagiarism, it's essential to quote accurately. You are not permitted to change any part of a quotation or to omit any part of it without using brackets or ellipses (see pages 49–52).

## CITING SOURCES

When you refer to or quote the work of another, you are obligated to credit or cite your source properly. These citations are generally of two types and work in tandem:

1. Those that indicate the source of quotations, paraphrases, and summarized information and ideas—these citations appear *in text,* within parentheses.
2. Those that appear in an alphabetical list of "Works Cited" or "References" following the paper.

If you are writing a paper in the humanities, you probably will be expected to use the Modern Language Association *(MLA)* format for citation. This format is fully described in the *MLA Handbook for Writers of Research Papers,* 3rd ed. (New York: Modern Language Association of America, 1988). A paper in the social sciences will probably use the American Psychological Association (APA) format. This format is fully described in the *Publication Manual of the American Psychological Association,* 3rd ed. (Washington, D.C.: American Psychological Association, 1983).

In the following section, we will focus on MLA and APA styles, the ones you are most likely to use in your academic work. Keep in mind, however, that instructors often have their own preferences. Some require the documentation style specified in the *Chicago Manual of Style,* 13th ed. (Chicago: University of Chicago Press, 1982). This style is similar to the APA style, except that publication dates are not placed within parentheses. Instructors in the sciences often follow the Council of Biology Editors (CBE) format. Or they may prefer a number format: each source listed on the bibliography page is assigned a number, and all text references to the source are followed by the appropriate number within parentheses. Some instructors like the old MLA style, which calls for footnotes and endnotes. Check with your instructor for the preferred documentation format if this is not specified in the assignment itself.

## In-Text Citation

The general rule for in-text citation is to include only enough information to alert the reader to the source of the reference and to the location within that source. Normally, this information includes the author's last name and page number (and, if you are using the APA system, the date). But if you have already named the author in the preceding text, just the page number is sufficient.

Here are sample in-text citations using the MLA and APA systems:

*MLA*

From the beginning, the AIDS antibody test has been "mired in controversy" (Bayer 101).

*APA*

From the beginning, the AIDS antibody test has been "mired in controversy" (Bayer, 1989, p. 101).

If you have already mentioned the author's name in the text, it is not necessary to repeat it in the citation:

*MLA*

According to Bayer, from the beginning, the AIDS antibody test has been "mired in controversy" (101).

*APA*

According to Bayer (1989), from the beginning, the AIDS antibody test has been "mired in controversy" (p. 101).

or:

According to Bayer, from the beginning, the AIDS antibody test has been "mired in controversy" (1989, p. 101).

When using the APA system, provide page numbers only for direct quotations, not for summaries or paraphrases. If you do not refer to a specific page, simply indicate the date:

Bayer (1989) reported that there are many precedents for the reporting of AIDS cases that do not unduly violate privacy.

In MLA format, you must supply page numbers for summaries and paraphrases, as well as for quotations:

According to Bayer, the AIDS antibody test has been controversial from the outset (101).

Notice that in the MLA system there is no punctuation between the author's name and the page number. In the APA system, there is a comma between the author's name and the page number, and the number itself is preceded by "p." or "pp." Notice also that in both systems the parenthetical reference is placed *before* the final punctuation of the sentence.

For block (indented) quotations, however, place the parenthetical citation *after* the period:

*MLA*

Robert Flaherty's refusal to portray primitive people's contact with civilization arose from an inner conflict:
> He had originally plunged with all his heart into the role of explorer and prospector; before Nanook, his own father was his hero. Yet as he entered the Eskimo world, he knew he did so as the advance guard of industrial civilization, the world of United States Steel and Sir William Mackenzie and

railroad and mining empires. The mixed feeling this gave him left his mark on all his films. (Barnouw 45)

*APA*

Robert Flaherty's refusal to portray primitive people's contact with civilization arose from an inner conflict:

He had originally plunged with all his heart into the role of explorer and prospector; before Nanook, his own father was his hero. Yet as he entered the Eskimo world, he knew he did so as the advance guard of industrial civilization, the world of United States Steel and Sir William Mackenzie and railroad and mining empires. The mixed feeling this gave him left his mark on all his films. (Barnouw, 1974, p. 45)

Again, were Barnouw's name mentioned in the sentence leading into the quotation, the parenthetical reference would be simply (45) for MLA style and (1974, p. 45) for APA style.

If the reference applies only to the first part of the sentence, the parenthetical reference is inserted at the appropriate point *within* the sentence:

*MLA*

While Baumrind argues that "the laboratory is not the place to study degree of obedience" (421), Milgram asserts that such arguments are groundless.

*APA*

While Baumrind (1963) argued that "the laboratory is not the place to study degree of obedience" (p. 421), Milgram asserted that such arguments are groundless.

There are times when you must modify the basic author/page number reference. Depending on the nature of your source(s), you may need to use one of the following citation formats:

### Quoted Material Appearing in Another Source

*MLA:* (qtd. in Milgram 211)

*APA:* (cited in Milgram, 1974, p. 211)

### An Anonymous Work

*MLA:* ("Obedience" 32)

*APA:* (Obedience, 1974, p. 32)

### Two Authors

*MLA:* (Woodward and Bernstein 208)

*APA:* (Woodward & Bernstein, 1974, p. 208).

### A Particular Work by an Author, When You List Two (or More) Works by That Author in the "Works Cited"

*MLA:* (Toffler, *Wave* 96–97)

*APA:* (Toffler, 1973, pp. 96–97)

### Two or More Sources as the Basis of your Statement (Arrange entries in alphabetic order of surname)

*MLA:* (Giannetti 189; Sklar 194)

*APA:* (Giannetti, 1972, p. 189; Sklar, 1974, p. 194)

### A Multivolume Work

*MLA:* (2:88)

*APA:* (Vol. 2, p. 88)

*MLA:* The location of a passage in a literary text, for example, Hardy's *The Return of the Native*: (224; ch. 7) [page 224 in the edition used by the writer; the chapter number, 7, is provided for the convenience of those referring to another edition]

*MLA:* The location of a passage in a play: (I:ii.308–22) [act:scene.line number(s)]

Occasionally, you may want to provide a footnote or an endnote as a *content* note—one that provides additional information bearing on or illuminating, but not directly related to, the discussion at hand. For example:

> ¹ Equally well known is Forster's distinction between story and plot: in the former, the emphasis is on sequence ("the king died and then the queen died"); in the latter, the emphasis is on causality ("the king died and then the queen died of grief").

Notice the format: Indent five spaces and type the note number, raised one-half line. Then space once more and begin the note. Subsequent lines of the note are flush with the left margin. If the note is at the bottom of the page (a footnote), quadruple-space between the text and the footnote, single-spacing the note itself. Content notes are numbered consecutively throughout the paper; do not begin renumbering on each page.

## Reference Page

In MLA format, your list of sources is called "Works Cited." In APA format, it is called "References." Entries in this listing should be double-spaced, with the second and subsequent lines of each entry indented—five spaces for MLA format; three spaces for APA. In both styles, two spaces follow the period.

The main difference between MLA and APA styles is that in MLA style the date of the publication follows the name of the publisher; in APA style, the date is placed within parentheses following the author's name. Other differences: In APA style, only the initial of the author's first name is indicated, and only the first word (and any proper noun) of the book or article title and subtitle is capitalized. However, all main words of journal/magazine titles are capitalized, just as in MLA style. For APA style, do *not* place quotation marks around journal/magazine article titles. However, do use "p." and "pp." to indicate page numbers of journal/magazine articles—except after volume and issue numbers. In both MLA and APA styles, publishers' names should be abbreviated; thus, "Random House" becomes "Random"; "William Morrow" becomes "Morrow."

Provided below are some of the most commonly used citations in both MLA and APA formats. For a more complete listing, consult the MLA *Handbook,* the APA *Manual,* or whichever style guide your instructor has specified.

## Books

### One Author

*MLA*

> Rose, Mike. <u>Lives on the Boundary</u>. New York:
>> Penguin, 1989.

*APA*

> Rose, M. (1989). <u>Lives on the boundary</u>. New
>> York: Penguin.

### Two or More Books by the Same Author

*MLA*

> Toffler, Alvin. <u>Future Shock</u>. New York: Random,
>> 1970.
> ---. <u>The Third Wave</u>. New York: Morrow, 1982.

*Note:* References are listed in alphabetical order of title.

*APA*

> Toffler, A. (1970). <u>Future shock</u>. New York:
> Random.
> Toffler, A. (1982). <u>The third wave</u>. New
> York: Morrow.

*Note:* References are listed in chronological order of publication.

### Two Authors

*MLA*

> Brockway, Wallace, and Herbert Weinstock. <u>Men of
> Music: Their Lives, Times, and Achievements</u>.
> New York: Simon and Schuster, 1939.

*APA*

> Brockway, W., & Weinstock, H. (1939). <u>Men of
> music: Their lives, times, and achievements</u>.
> New York: Simon and Schuster.

### Three Authors

*MLA*

> Young, Richard E., Alton L. Becker, and Kenneth
> L. Pike. <u>Rhetoric: Discovery and Change</u>.
> New York: Harcourt, 1970.

*APA*

> Young, R. E., Becker, A. L., & Pike, K. L.
> (1970). <u>Rhetoric: Discovery and change</u>. New
> York: Harcourt.

### More Than Three Authors

*MLA*

> Maimon, Elaine, et al. <u>Writing in the Arts and
> Sciences</u>. Boston: Little, Brown, 1982.

*APA*

> Maimon, E., Belcher, G. L., Hearn, G. W., Nodine,
>      B. N., & O'Connor, F. W.  (1982).  <u>Writing in
>      the arts and sciences</u>.  Boston: Little, Brown.

### Book with an Editor

*MLA*

> Weeks, Robert P., ed.  <u>Hemingway: A Collection of
>      Critical Essays</u>.  Englewood Cliffs, N.J.:
>      Prentice-Hall, 1962.

*APA*

> Weeks, R. P.  (Ed.).  (1962).  <u>Hemingway: A
>      collection of critical essays</u>.  Englewood
>      Cliffs, N.J.: Prentice-Hall.

### Later Edition

*MLA*

> Houp, Kenneth W., and Thomas E. Pearsall.
>      <u>Reporting Technical Information</u>.  3rd ed.
>      Beverly Hills: Glencoe, 1977.

*APA*

> Houp, K. W., & Pearsall, T. E. (1977).  <u>Reporting
>      technical information</u> (3rd ed.).  Beverly
>      Hills: Glencoe.

### Republished Book

*MLA*

> Lawrence, D. H.  <u>Sons and Lovers</u>.  1913.  New
>      York: Signet, 1960.

*APA*

> Lawrence, D. H.  (1960).  <u>Sons and lovers</u>.  New
>      York: Signet.  (Original work published 1913)

### One Volume of a Multivolume Work

*MLA*

Bailey, Thomas A.  <u>The American Spirit: United States History as Seen by Contemporaries</u>. 4th ed.  2 vols.  Lexington, Mass.: Heath, 1978.  Vol. 2.

*APA*

Bailey, T. A.  (1978).  <u>The American spirit: United States history as seen by contemporaries</u> (4th ed., Vol. 2).  2 vols. Lexington, MA: Heath.

### Separately Titled Volume of a Multivolume Work

*MLA*

Churchill, Winston.  <u>The Age of Revolution</u>. Vol. 3 of <u>A History of the English Speaking Peoples</u>.  New York: Dodd, 1957.

*APA*

Churchill, W.  (1957).  <u>A history of the English speaking peoples: Vol. 3.  The age of revolution</u>.  New York: Dodd.

### Translation

*MLA*

Chekhov, Anton.  <u>Chekhov: The Major Plays</u>. Trans. Ann Dunnigan.  New York: New American Library, 1974.

*APA*

Chekhov, A.  (1974).  <u>Chekhov: The major plays</u> (A. Dunnigan, Trans.).  New York: New American Library.

## Selection from an Anthology

*MLA*

> Russell, Bertrand. "Civil Disobedience and the
> Threat of Nuclear Warfare." <u>Civil</u>
> <u>Disobedience: Theory and Practice</u>.
> Ed. Hugo Adam Bedau. Indianapolis: Pegasus,
> 1969. 153-59.

*APA*

> Russell, B. (1969). Civil disobedience and the
> threat of nuclear warfare. In H. Bedau (Ed.),
> <u>Civil disobedience: Theory and practice</u>
> (pp. 153-159). Indianapolis: Pegasus.

## Reprinted Material in an Edited Collection

*MLA*

> McGinnis, Wayne D. "The Arbitrary Cycle of
> <u>Slaughterhouse-Five</u>: A Relation of Form
> to Theme." <u>Critique</u>: <u>Studies in Modern</u>
> <u>Fiction</u> 17, no. 1 (1975): 55-68. Rpt. in
> <u>Contemporary Literary Criticism</u>. Ed. Dedria
> Bryfonski and Phyllis Carmel Mendelson. Vol.
> 8. Detroit: Gale Research, 1978. 530-31.

*APA*

> McGinnis, W. D. (1975). The arbitrary cycle of
> <u>Slaughterhouse-five</u>: A relation of form to
> theme. In D. Bryfonski and P. C. Mendelson
> (Eds.), <u>Contemporary literary criticism</u>
> (Vol. 8, pp. 530-531). Detroit: Gale
> Research. Reprinted from <u>Critique: Studies in</u>

modern fiction, 1975 (Vol. 17, No. 1),
pp. 55-68.

## Government Publication

*MLA*

United States. Cong. House, Committee on the
Post Office and Civil Service, Subcommittee
on Postal Operations. Self-Policing of the
Movie and Publishing Industry. 86th Cong.,
2nd sess. Washington: GPO, 1961.

United States. Dept. of Health, Education and
Welfare. The Health Consequences of
Smoking. Washington: GPO, 1974.

*APA*

U.S. Cong. House Committee on the Post Office
and Civil Service, Subcommittee on Postal
Operations. (1961). Self-policing of the
movie and publishing industry. 86th Congress,
2nd session. Washington, DC: U.S. Government
Printing Office.

U.S. Dept. of Health, Education and Welfare.
(1974). The health consequences of
smoking. Washington, DC: U.S. Government
Printing Office.

## Signed Encyclopedia Article

*MLA*

Lack, David L. "Population." Encyclopaedia
Britannica: Macropaedia. 1974 ed.

*APA*

Lack, D. L. Population. Encyclopaedia
Britannica: Macropaedia. 1974 ed.

### *Unsigned Encyclopedia Article*

*MLA*

"Tidal Wave." <u>Encyclopedia Americana</u>. 1982 ed.

*APA*

Tidal wave. <u>Encyclopedia Americana</u>. 1982 ed.

## Periodicals

### *Continuous Pagination Throughout Annual Cycle*

*MLA*

Davis, Robert Gorham. "Literature's Gratifying
Dead End." <u>Hudson Review</u> 21 (1969): 774-78.

*APA*

Davis, R. G. (1969). Literature's gratifying
dead end. <u>Hudson Review</u>, <u>21</u>, 774-778.

### *Separate Pagination Each Issue*

*MLA*

Palmer, James W., and Michael M. Riley. "The
Lone Rider in Vienna: Myth and Meaning in
<u>The Third Man</u>." <u>Literature/Film Quarterly</u>
8. 1 (1980): 14-21.

*APA*

Palmer, J. W., & Riley, M. M. (1980). The lone
rider in Vienna: Myth and meaning in <u>The third
man</u>. <u>Literature/Film Quarterly</u>, <u>8</u>(1), 14-21.

### *Monthly Periodical*

*MLA*

Spinrad, Norman. "Home Computer Technology in
the 21st Century." <u>Popular Computing</u>. Sept.
1984: 77-82.

*APA*

> Spinrad, N. (1984, September). Home computer
> technology in the 21st century. <u>Popular
> Computing</u>, pp. 77-82.

### Signed Article in Weekly Periodical

*MLA*

> Hulbert, Ann. "Children as Parents." <u>The New
> Republic</u> 10 Sept. 1984: 15-23.

*APA*

> Hulbert, A. (1984, September 10). Children as
> parents. <u>The New Republic</u>, pp. 15-23.

### Unsigned Article in Weekly Periodical

*MLA*

> "Notes and Comment." <u>The New Yorker</u> 20 Feb.
> 1978: 29-32.

*APA*

> Notes and comment. (1978, February 20). <u>The New
> Yorker</u>, pp. 29-32.

### Signed Article in Daily Newspaper

*MLA*

> Surplee, Curt. "The Bard of Albany." <u>Washington
> Post</u> 28 Dec. 1983: B1, 9.

*APA*

> Surplee, C. (1983, December 28). The bard of
> Albany. <u>Washington Post</u>, section B, pp. 1, 9.

### Unsigned Article in Daily Newspaper

*MLA*

> "Report Says Crisis in Teaching Looms."
>     <u>Philadelphia Inquirer</u> 20 Aug. 1984: A3.

*APA*

> Report says crisis in teaching looms.  (1984,
>     August 20).  <u>Philadelphia Inquirer</u>, p. A3.

### Review

*MLA*

> Maddocks, Melvin.  Rev. of <u>Margaret Mead: A Life</u>,
>     by Jane Howard.  <u>Time</u> 27 Aug. 1984: 57.

*APA*

> Maddocks, M.  (1984, August 27).  [Review of
>     <u>Margaret Mead: A life</u>].  <u>Time</u>, p. 57.

## Other Sources

### Interview

*MLA*

> Emerson, Robert.  Personal interview.  10 Oct.
>     1989.

*APA*

> Emerson, R.  [Personal interview].  10 October
>     1989.

### Dissertation *(abstracted in* Dissertation Abstracts International*)*

*MLA*

> Gans, Eric L.  "The Discovery of Illusion:
>     Flaubert's Early Works, 1835-1837."  <u>DA</u> 27
>     (1967): 3046A. Johns Hopkins U.

*APA*

> Pendar, J. E.  (1982).  Undergraduate psychology majors: Factors influencing decisions about college, curriculum and career.  <u>Dissertation Abstracts International</u>, <u>42</u>, 4370A-4371A.

*Note:* If dissertation is available on microfilm, give University Microfilms number in parentheses at the conclusion of the reference.

### Lecture

*MLA*

> Osborne, Michael.  "The Great Man Theory: Caesar."  Lecture.  History 4A.  University of California, Santa Barbara, 5 Nov. 1992.

*APA*

> Baldwin, J.  (1993, January).  The self in social interactions.  Sociology 2 lecture, University of California, Santa Barbara.

### Paper Delivered at a Conference

*MLA*

> Worley, Joan.  "Texture: The Feel of Writing."  Conference on College Composition and Communication.  Cincinnati, 21 Mar. 1992.

*APA*

> Worley, J.  (1992, March).  Texture: The feel of writing.  Paper presented at the Conference on College Composition and Communication, Cincinnati, OH.

---

### Film

*MLA*

> Howard's End. Dir. James Ivory. With Emma
> Thompson and Anthony Hopkins. Merchant/
> Ivory and Film Four International, 1992.

*APA*

> Thomas, J. (Producer), & Cronenberg, D.
> (Director). (1991). Naked lunch [Film]. 20th
> Century Fox.

### TV Program

*MLA*

> Legacy of the Hollywood Blacklist. Videocassette.
> Dir. Judy Chaikin. Written and prod. Eve
> Goldberg and Judy Chaikin, One Step
> Productions. Public Affairs TV, KCET, Los
> Angeles, 1987. 57 min.

*APA*

> Chaikin, J. (Co-producer, director, &
> co-writer), & Goldberg, E. (Co-producer &
> co-writer), One Step Productions. (1987).
> Legacy of the Hollywood blacklist
> [videocassette]. Los Angeles, Public Affairs
> TV, KCET.

### Computer Software

*MLA*

> Microsoft Word. Computer software. Microsoft,
> 1984.

*APA*

> Microsoft word. (1984). [Computer
> software]. Bellevue, WA: Microsoft.

### Recording

*MLA*

```
Beatles.  "Eleanor Rigby."  The Beatles
     1962-1966. Capitol 4X2K 3403, 1973.
Schumann, Robert.  Symphonies Nos. 1 & 4.
     Cond. George Szell, Cleveland
     Orchestra.  Columbia, YT35502, 1978.
```

*APA*

```
Beatles.  (Singers) (1973).  Eleanor Rigby.  The
     Beatles 1962-1966. (Cassette Recording
     No. 4X2K 3403).  New York: Capitol.
Schumann, R.  (Composer).  (1978).  Symphonies
     nos. 1 & 4. (Cassette Recording
     No. YT35502).  New York: Columbia.
```

## SAMPLE RESEARCH PAPER

For an example of research paper format and documentation, see the student argument synthesis on pages 122–30. Although many research papers will be longer and draw on more sources than this example, the discussion and the text of "The Disruptive Politics of Bilingual Education" generally model both the finished product and the process by which a student goes from a research question (what issues underlie the bilingual education controversy?) to a systematic argument that supports a thesis ("The twenty-year-old debate over bilingual education will continue as long as these underlying political issues are unresolved").

# AN ANTHOLOGY
# OF READINGS

# 6

# ON BEING BLACK
# AND MIDDLE CLASS: A
# PRACTICE CHAPTER

## INTRODUCTION

This chapter will give you the opportunity to practice the skills of summary, critique, and synthesis that you learned in Part I of *Writing and Reading Across the Curriculum*. The selections in Chapter 6 are generally shorter than those in the rest of the book, and the writing instructions are considerably more detailed. Once you have successfully completed several of the assignments at the end of this chapter, you should be able to handle confidently the critical reading and writing tasks in the chapters that follow.

Your strategy with Chapter 6 should be to read the six articles that follow this introduction and then to work on the writing assignments specified by your instructor. You will find these assignments at the end of the chapter: three for summary; two for critique; and three for synthesis (explanatory, comparison and contrast, and argument). Note that the assignments in each category increase in complexity.

In succeeding chapters, each reading selection is followed by "Review Questions" and "Discussion and Writing Suggestions," and each chapter concludes with "Synthesis Activities" and "Research Activities." Such assignments are not included in this chapter because we want to focus your attention on practicing your skills in summary, critique, and synthesis.

## ON BEING BLACK AND MIDDLE CLASS

The subject matter in this chapter is thematically related to the subject of bilingual education, dealt with in the first four chapters. As we've seen, the larger political issue underlying the debate over bilingual education is ethnic identity, on the one hand, and cultural assimilation, on the other. Those who believe in the importance of reinforcing ethnic identity tend to favor bilingual education programs. Those who believe that ethnic minorities ought to be assimilated into the mainstream as much as possible tend to oppose bilingual education and to favor "immersion" programs. Our subject in this chapter (we borrow the title from Shelby Steele's essay) is "On Being Black and Middle Class." Underlying this subject is the same dilemma of ethnic identity versus cultural assimilation. The specific issue is the extent to which African-Americans ought to take pride in and hold on to their racial and cultural identity, and the extent to which they should try to blend in with the white majority culture, in the interest of assimilating into the American mainstream.

This is a particular problem for middle-class African-Americans. Most middle-class blacks are outnumbered by whites in their home, school, and work environments and are subject to great (generally unspoken) pressures to conform to the majority norms—in their dress, in their speech, in their socializing. But the frequent consequence of such conformity (sometimes scornfully dismissed as "acting white") is discomfort and guilt at abandoning one's racial and cultural heritage.

One of the most eloquent analysts of this dilemma was the civil rights leader and educator W. E. B. Du Bois (1868–1963) who wrote, in *The Souls of Black Folk* (1903), of the black American's "double consciousness":

> this sense of always looking at one's self through the eyes of others, of measuring one's soul by the tape of a world that looks on in amused contempt and pity. One ever feels his twoness,—an American, a Negro; two souls, two thoughts, two unreconciled strivings; two warring ideals in one dark body, whose dogged strength alone keeps it from being torn asunder.

More recently, the dilemma was dramatized by Bebe Moore Campbell in her article "Blacks Who Live in a White World":

> When Rodney Butler joined the Pittsburgh office of the Gulf Corp. . . . at 24, he became one of the few professional Blacks in the company. He hadn't been there long when a friend from the old days paid him a visit, bringing a touch of jitterbug to the conservative bulwark of billion dollar deals. "My man, Rod. S'happening, Bro." Several days later, an older Black manager took Butler aside. He didn't give him "five." Instead, he provided the corporate novitiate with advice on how to succeed in big business. "Trim your hair, stay married, go to lunch, and socialize with White managers, and stop running around with funny-looking Black People."
> Butler doesn't discard friends. But in the months that followed, he trimmed his hair, switched from round wire frames to a more conservative style of glasses, and purchased his first pair of wing tips. In his dark, three-piece suit, externally, he resembled the legions of other young corporate managers on the rise. Except, of course, for his color.

Some blacks, of course, refuse to forget their roots—and pay the consequence. Roger Wilkins, a civil rights activist in the 1960s and now a senior fellow at the Institute for Policy Studies, says, "There are people I knew in the sixties who think I'm crazy because I continue to work for black people. . . . One man said to my wife, 'By continuing the struggle, Roger's thrown away his opportunity to get rich.'" Some manage to straddle two worlds: one African-American guidance counselor tells students that although he speaks perfect English at school, he uses "Black talk" in his own neighborhood.

Others find themselves outsiders in both worlds. In her article "Between Two Worlds," freelance writer Martha Southgate tells of how she left her working-class black neighborhood in Cleveland to go to a predominantly white prep school. There, the images of "down coats, narrow-legged Levi cords and L. L. Bean boots . . . came to symbolize my discomfort with the place." She was unable to break into the inner circle of white girls, but she also found barriers to socializing with black kids: they "all seemed to be either impossible, unapproachable paragons of the Black bourgeoisie or tough, streetwise kinds who . . . exhibited a savvy I couldn't hope to achieve. . . . We were the same, but they frightened me and left me feeling as alienated and outside their world as the white kids did."

In the six articles that follow, we will explore further this dilemma of middle-class African-Americans, the psychological stresses that it creates, and some of the proposed solutions.

# The Middle-Class Black's Burden

## LEANITA MCCLAIN

*In this article, reporter and columnist Leanita McClain explains why she is "uncomfortably middle class." McClain worked for the* Chicago Tribune. *This essay first appeared in* Newsweek *in October 1980.*

I am a member of the black middle class who has had it with being    1
patted on the head by white hands and slapped in the face by black
hands for my success.

Here's a discovery that too many people still find startling: when    2
given equal opportunities at white-collar pencil pushing, blacks want the
same things from life that everyone else wants. These include the
proverbial dream house, two cars, an above-average school and a vaca-

"The Middle-Class Black's Burden" by Leanita McClain as appeared in *Newsweek*, October 13, 1980. Reprinted by permission of The Estate of Leanita McClain and Thomas Poulakidas.

tion for the kids at Disneyland. We may, in fact, want these things more than other Americans because most of us have been denied them so long.

Meanwhile, a considerable number of the folks we left behind in the "old country," commonly called the ghetto, and the militants we left behind in their antiquated ideology can't berate middle-class blacks enough for "forgetting where we came from." We have forsaken the revolution, we are told, we have sold out. We are Oreos, they say, black on the outside, white within.    3

The truth is, we have not forgotten; we would not dare. We are simply fighting on different fronts and are no less war weary, and possibly more heartbroken, for we know the black and white worlds can meld, that there can be a better world.    4

It is impossible for me to forget where I came from as long as I am prey to the jive hustler who does not hesitate to exploit my childhood friendship. I am reminded, too, when I go back to the old neighborhood in fear—and have my purse snatched—and when I sit down to a business lunch and have an old classmate wait on my table. I recall the girl I played dolls with who now rears five children on welfare, the boy from church who is in prison for murder, the pal found dead of a drug overdose in the alley where we once played tag.    5

## ATTACHÉ CASE

My life abounds in incongruities. Fresh from a vacation in Paris, I may, a week later, be on the milk-run Trailways bus in Deep South backcountry attending the funeral of an ancient uncle whose world stretched only 50 miles and who never learned to read. Sometimes when I wait at the bus stop with my attaché case, I meet my aunt getting off the bus with other cleaning ladies on their way to do my neighbors' floors.    6

But I am not ashamed. Black progress has surpassed our greatest expectations; we never even saw much hope for it, and the achievement has taken us by surprise.    7

In my heart, however, there is no safe distance from the wretched past of my ancestors or the purposeless present of some of my contemporaries; I fear such a fate can reclaim me. I am not comfortably middle class; I am uncomfortably middle class.    8

I have made it, but where? Racism still dogs my people. There are still communities in which crosses are burned on the lawns of black families who have the money and grit to move in.    9

What a hollow victory we have won when my sister, dressed in her designer everything, is driven to the rear door of the luxury high rise in which she lives because the cab driver, noting only her skin color,    10 assumes she is the maid, or the nanny, or the cook, but certainly not the lady of any house at this address.

I have heard the immigrants' bootstrap tales, the simplistic reproach 11 of "why can't you people be like us." I have fulfilled the entry requirements of the American middle class, yet I am left, at times, feeling unwelcome and stereotyped. I have overcome the problems of food, clothing and shelter, but I have not overcome my old nemesis, prejudice. Life is easier, being black is not.

I am burdened daily with showing whites that blacks are people. I 12 am, in the old vernacular, a credit to my race. I am my brothers' keeper, and my sisters', though many of them have abandoned me because they think that I have abandoned them.

I run a gantlet between two worlds, and I am cursed and blessed by 13 both. I travel, observe and take part in both; I can also be used by both. I am a rope in a tug of war. If I am a token in my downtown office, so am I at my cousin's church tea. I assuage white guilt. I disprove black inadequacy and prove to my parents' generation that their patience was indeed a virtue.

I have a foot in each world, but I cannot fool myself about either. 14 I can see the transparent deceptions of some whites and the bitter hopelessness of some blacks. I know how tenuous my grip on one way of life is, and how strangling the grip of the other way of life can be.

## NOVELTY

Many whites have lulled themselves into thinking that race relations are 15 just grand because they were the first on their block to discuss crab grass with the new black family. Yet too few blacks and whites in this country send their children to school together, entertain each other or call each other friend. Blacks and whites dining out together draw stares. Many of my co-workers see no black faces from the time the train pulls out Friday evening until they meet me at the coffee machine Monday morning. I remain a novelty.

Some of my "liberal" white acquaintances pat me on the head, 16 hinting that I am a freak, that my success is less a matter of talent than of luck and affirmative action. I may live among them, but it is difficult to live with them. How can they be sincere about respecting me, yet hold my fellows in contempt? And if I am silent when they attempt to sever me from my own, how can I live with myself?

Whites won't believe I remain culturally different; blacks won't 17 believe I remain culturally the same.

I need only look in a mirror to know my true allegiance, and I am 18 painfully aware that, even with my off-white trappings, I am prejudged by my color.

As for the envy of my own people, am I to give up my career, my [19] standard of living, to pacify them and set my conscience at ease? No. I have worked for these amenities and deserve them, though I can never enjoy them without feeling guilty.

These comforts do not make me less black, nor oblivious to the [20] woe in which many of my people are drowning. As long as we are denig-
rated as a group, no one of us has made it. Inasmuch as we all suffer for every one left behind, we all gain for every one who conquers the hurdle.

# I Have a Flag

## RICHARD A. CARTER

*In this article, journalist Richard Carter recounts a crucial moment in the formation of his racial identity, a moment that changed the course of his professional life. This article first appeared in* Essence *magazine in 1984.*

One of the most difficult things most of us men can do in the interest [1] of standing up for ourselves is to speak out on issues in which we really believe. But most of us never get the opportunity, as we go along doing our everyday things in our everyday way. This was especially true in the late 1950's, before Malcolm X, Muhammad Ali and Dr. Martin Luther King were so well known to us. Those of us who could manage it were employed, others of us treaded water, and still others went down and drowned in despair.

But life went on, and like many Black men, I thought *powerful* [2] thoughts, made *powerful* plans but was *powerless* to put them into practice. I sat there, on my journalism degree, in the U.S. Post Office—then a den of hopelessness for college-educated Negroes (as we were called then) unable to find work in their fields.

Oh, I tried to get a job, but establishment, i.e., white, newspapers [3] weren't hiring many Blacks 25 years ago, and Black papers, with few exceptions, couldn't provide the kind of security I needed with a wife and two children. So I played it safe.

And then, after four years of frustration, I heeded the advice of a [4] good friend, bit the bullet and took a part-time job with a Black weekly, continuing to work nights at the post office. This led, two years later, to my first big-league journalism job, with the town's morning daily.

*At last*, I thought, as do so many of us when we finally "make it." 5 I was so elated to have gotten over, I forgot what, besides ability, got me there. I forgot the kind of in-depth reporting on important issues I had done for that Black weekly, the visibility I had had in that Black community—and proceeded, for the next two years, to throw no stones and make no waves. I reported what was requested and wrote what was expected.

You could have colored me *bland*. 6

But all that changed on a night in June 1965 when, as the only Black 7 reporter on staff, I was dispatched to cover an impromptu visit to a new Muslim mosque by the newly crowned world heavyweight champion, Muhammad Ali. Almost as soon as I took my front-row seat, something began happening. It occurred to me, a northern-bred, college-educated "Negro," that this was the first time in my life I'd been part of such a large group of people of my own race. In Muhammad's Mosque No. 1 that night in Milwaukee, a largely white city with stringently segregated housing, it made me feel good. It made me feel like I truly belonged. It made me feel that, somehow, I'd been missing something. But there was more.

When Ali spoke, he said many of the things I'd been hearing 8 Malcolm X say. But now they made more sense to me. Ali recalled how, after winning a gold medal at the 1960 Olympic Games in Rome, he was unable to get a cup of coffee at a restaurant in his hometown of Louisville, Kentucky, while an African man was served without incident. "I asked him how *he* could be served when Louisville was *my* home," Ali went on. "And the man told me he was served because he has a flag." Ali paused for a few seconds and then shouted, of his new Islamic religion: "Now *I* have a flag!" The audience of some 300 answered: "That's right!"

As the responses escalated, things began to become clearer in my 9 mind. Although I certainly was no Muslim and always had accepted the benevolence of most whites toward Blacks—despite the evidence of my own eyes—I was agreeing with more and more of what I was hearing on that hot, steamy night. I now was a Black man conscious of the fact I was not alone in a white world but surrounded by and united with other Black people who, like me, were proud.

Ali's words "I have a flag!" settled in my mind, along with the pride 10 in being Black that for so long lay dormant beneath the surface of my consciousness—seeking an outlet but unsure when or how to get out. But then I knew I'd never again pass up an opportunity to tell others what I now knew: the truth as I saw it. I too now had a flag—not one of race or religion and not one of red, white and blue, but one of truth—of telling it like it is.

In the years since, I've found myself—despite leaving the day-to-day newspaper business for a corporate public-relations career three years after that night in 1965—speaking out in other ways about my new pride in being a Black man. Over time, some of my flag waving has cost me promotions I deserved. I decline to simply be part of the woodwork, and I demonstrate my ability to think through problems and come up with recommendations. So, I've gained respect—of the arm's-length variety. 11

And then, about six years ago, in that mystical way of fate, I once again found myself possessed of the means to wave my flag—I now write a weekly column for a newspaper chain in New York's Westchester County. Whether it's chiding white folks for seeking suntans "so they can look like us," or "repudiating" Walter Mondale for failing to consider a Black female running mate, or castigating Britain for granting citizenship to the white South African runner Zola Budd so she could compete in the recent Olympics or pointing out the professionalism of Black journalists—I'm in there, telling the truth as I see it. 12

But as anyone who writes for publication knows, *saying* it doesn't mean people are going to care about or believe it. The many hate letters I receive keep reminding me of this. Yet, every time I read one of them, I recall the night in Milwaukee nearly 20 years ago when I went from being a token Black man to an outspoken Black man—one who treads heavily and steps on a few toes along the way, who refuses to remain in the niche carved out for him by whites. A flag waver of truth. 13

# Crossover Dreams

## AUDREY EDWARDS

*In the following article, Audrey Edwards writes about blacks in corporate America. She analyzes the causes of "bicultural stress" in executive suites and prescribes some treatments. Edwards is the co-author with Craig Polite of* The Psychology of Black Success *(1987) and editor-at-large of* Essence, *where this article first appeared in March 1987.*

Making it in corporate America has not been without its costs—and    1
sometimes its losses—for Blacks. Remember Leanita McClain, the talented journalist who became the first Black member of the *Chicago
Tribune*'s elite editorial board by age 32, only to die by her own hand
a few months later? And then there was Janet Cooke, another Black
journalist, whose motto for success seemed to be "Make it by any
means necessary," even if that meant fabricating a story that was ultimately damaging to the entire Black community and ruined her own
career. Both women suffered from what Dr. Ella Bell, organizational
behaviorist at Yale University, has termed bicultural stress, the psychological schism created when Blacks, in seeking to assimilate, start
to lose their own identity because of the alien roles they adopt in
order to make it in the majority society. Since such role-playing usually requires that we negate much of who we are, this self-negation
leads to emotional conflict, and hence stress. W. E. B. Du Bois diag-
nosed this phenomenon nearly 100 years ago when he wrote about
there being two souls within Black folks—one white, one black—
warring with each other in a desperate need to be accepted in white
America.

Today that war still rages, though now more often in the halls of    2
corporate America, where Blacks have made the most recent advances
but have also undergone the most emotional contortions to accommodate themselves to what is still an alien environment. We've all heard
stories about the brother who is so Brooks Brothers–suited down that
he resembles a caricature of the man in the gray flannel suit; or the sister
who has taken up bridge playing to impress her boss, the local bridge
champion. What such behavior reveals is the belief among many Blacks
that in order to succeed in the corporation one must ape the majority
culture, all too often at the expense of the strengths inherent in our own
culture.

Such an attitude shouldn't be too surprising. For the last 10 to 15    3
years we've been bombarded with all manner of books and articles on
how to dress for success, how to conduct power lunches, how to play
the games Mother never taught you, how to network, find mentors,
identify your corporate culture, get on the fast track and win at office
politics. As we do with other aspects of American life, Black folks tend
to take such self-improvement advice more to heart than whites do.

"The message Blacks have been given is that we need to be reme-    4
diated, ameliorated or otherwise altered to make it," says Dr. Craig
Polite, a New York–based psychologist whose specialty is treating the
problems of the Black middle class. "Who you are isn't good enough,
and we get this message in a million different little ways—from the
media, from Black parents who are always telling their kids they have
to be a credit to the race, from the white boss who gives his favorite

Black employee the impression that 'You're an exceptional Black—
you're not like the rest of those people.' "

Inevitably, however, it turns out that all of us *are* just like the rest     5
of those people—Black. And despite whatever successes we achieve, or
don't achieve, our work and our workplace are still colored by race,
whether we like to admit it or not. For some, the admission is deadly.
A tragic case in point was Leanita McClain, who had traveled a great
psychic distance from her housing-project origins on Chicago's South
Side. Yet in the end she was consumed by despair over the hatred whites
exhibited during the Chicago mayoral race in which Harold Washington, the city's first Black candidate, was running. Shortly before her
suicide, McClain wrote an article published in *The Washington Post*
entitled "How Chicago Taught Me to Hate Whites." Her fundamental
dilemma was that her professional success as a journalist didn't translate
into success in her personal life, nor did her success make any difference
in the attitudes racist whites had toward Blacks in Chicago. The very
people McClain claimed to hate were the people she and her paper
served, and the same people, to some extent, who had helped make her
a star. "I have a foot in each world," McClain wrote in a *Newsweek*
magazine essay in 1980, "but I cannot fool myself about either. I can see
the transparent deceptions of some whites and the bitter hopelessness
of some Blacks. I know how tenuous my grip on one way of life is, and
how strangling the grip of the other way of life can be."

Apparently she was unable to reconcile the contradiction—or to     6
accept the fact that no matter how bright her star, to many whites in
Chicago she would always be just a nigger. Her poignant suicide note
and *The Washington Post* essay that brought her national notoriety are
included in a recently released book of her writings. *A Foot in Each
World: Articles and Essays by Leanita McClain*, edited by her former
husband, Clarence Page (Northwestern University Press, $8.95, paper-
back), gives insight into her inner conflict.

Janet Cooke's dilemma, on the other hand, was more clearly a case     7
of a Black woman deliberately making herself over in the image of
whites—or at least in the image she felt whites would find most
acceptable. Not only did her Pulitzer Prize–winning story turn out to
be a lie, but so also did her own credentials. It was not good enough to
have graduated from the University of Toledo (which she did) instead
of from Vassar (which she didn't, but said she did).

McClain and Cooke represent the most extreme cases of bicultural     8
stress in corporate America, which is why their stories continue to be
instructive morality tales about what can go wrong when Blacks either
try to be something they are not or lose touch with who they really are.

The sad truth is that lesser strains of bicultural stress break out among Blacks every day in the American corporation. Here are five of the most common Black corporate attitudes that can lead to a full-blown case of bicultural stress, along with some prescriptions for treatment.

STRESS ATTITUDE NUMBER 1: "I'M A _____ WHO 9 JUST HAPPENS TO BE BLACK." Fill in the blank with any modern-day profession, be it doctor, lawyer or corporate chief. The attitude is the same: Race is not an issue to this corporate Black. In fact, this particular corporate type spends most of the time trying to appear colorless and really wishes everybody else wouldn't focus on race at all. How many times has a Black working in the corporation been heard to say, "Why does Jones always give me the Black cases to handle? He should know by now that I'm a _____ who just happens to be Black." The implication here is that "being Black" is something one "just happens to be," like an accident or a sore that won't heal.

Blacks who think like this feel they fit in better and are less threaten- 10 ing if they come from a position of noncolor; that perhaps no one will notice their race if they downplay it. This type of person subconsciously views being Black as a negative, a liability, and Black assignments as carrying less value.

The trouble with this attitude is that whites in the corporation don't 11 respect it. Rather than fitting in, corporate Blacks who place no value on their own race are usually not highly valued by the whites they work for. Even if whites tend to view us negatively—and many in the corporation do—they view with outright disrespect Blacks who don't operate out of a strong sense of their own Blackness.

Ann Lemon, an account executive at the Kidder Peabody invest- 12 ment-banking firm in New York City, recalls that when she first started at the company, the account executives in the WASPish firm had cultivated relatively few Black clients. "They didn't really know how," she says, "but I knew there were a whole lot of Black people out there with money who needed to have it invested, so I worked on actively seeking Black clients in addition to white ones. They were a natural base." In her first year Lemon made over $138,000 in commissions, and she says that the whites at Kidder have now come to recognize the value of the Black market.

The truth is, no matter how colorless one tries to be, color is always 13 present, visible to all. It is healthier to make race work *for* you, as Lemon did, and that only happens when it is viewed as a source of strength.

STRESS ATTITUDE NUMBER 2: "TENNIS, ANYONE?" This is a 14 relatively new corporate attitude among some Blacks who believe they have to take up the leisure-time pursuits and affectations of white folks to succeed in the corporate world. These are the Blacks who believe all those stories about business being done socially, typically on the golf course or tennis courts. "How many people really seal deals on the tennis court?" Dr. Craig Polite asks. "What they seal is the social side of the business relationship. People with whom you're doing business need to feel comfortable with you, so social interaction is important. Playing golf or tennis can be relaxing and a good way to get to know someone outside of a strict corporate environment. But there's nothing holier about playing golf or tennis than playing basketball. A lot of Blacks really like playing golf, and that's fine. But don't contort yourself to take up a particular sport just because you think that's what whites are into. It's not like some kind of trick you can pull off and fool anybody with. There's no strength in pretense."

Polite suggests that Blacks who feel they need to establish social ties 15 with whites they work with find some natural common ground on which to do so. "Play to your strong suit," he advises. "Your boss or client may be into jazz as well as tennis, which is more likely to be an interest you share."

STRESS ATTITUDE NUMBER 3: "I'M MOVING ON UP AND 16 NOT LOOKING BACK." Everyone knows a story about the secretary who becomes an administrative assistant and then stops having lunch with the secretaries who were once her friends, or the administrative assistant who is promoted to manager and suddenly acts as if she doesn't remember what it was like to be an AA.

Like the corporate Black who thinks she has to develop a passion for 17 opera to make it socially in business, many Blacks who move into managerial ranks in the corporation feel they have to avoid Black subordinates. What's overlooked are the real strengths to be gained in maintaining old ties, especially Black ones in a white environment. It's surprising how much of the corporate grapevine "lower level" Blacks are privy to that managerial Blacks could benefit from.

Unfortunately, too many Black corporate managers learn the hard 18 way what can happen when they choose to distance themselves from other Blacks in the company. Amanda Davis (not her real name), an executive assistant to a vice president at a major West Coast department store, remembers one Black woman in her company who had become a department buyer and was in line for a vice-presidential position. "Whenever I tried to talk to this woman to get some advice on how I should be proceeding in my own career, she would never even give me the time of day," Davis says. "She never talked to any of us [other Blacks]. I think she thought that whites in the company frowned on Black executives talking to junior-level Blacks. Well, when it came time for her promotion, she didn't get it—they gave her a lateral move, and she was devastated. Now she's always up in my face complaining about what happened to her and trying to be friendly."

STRESS ATTITUDE NUMBER 4: "RIGHT, BOSS, ANYTHING YOU SAY, BOSS." Polite labels yes-man corporate Blacks as "social schizophrenics" who change with every situation. Like the colorless Black who feels that being neutral is the only safe position in the corporation, socially schizophrenic Blacks feel that the only safe opinion is a "yes" opinion, so they never develop any convictions about any-thing. "You lose power when you do that," says Polite. "You lose the gusto that's needed in decision making, and you also lose the regard of the whites you work with." Even if whites don't always agree with a Black person's opinion, for their own emotional well-being it's more important that Blacks *have* opinions *and* express them. **19**

STRESS ATTITUDE NUMBER 5: "THE RACE PROBLEM? WHAT RACE PROBLEM?" This is the attitude that is perhaps the most danger-ous, because corporate Blacks who feel there is no racism (at least not directed at them) tend to be those who have no sense of struggle or of history, and thus no sense of the present. Some of these corporate Blacks are under 30, too young to remember that there was a Civil Rights Movement and an affirmative-action mandate that helped get them into the halls of corporate power. They honestly believe they have made it up solely on their own merit and therefore owe allegiance to no one—least of all those other Blacks who haven't made it. **20**

But regarding one's emotional health, race isn't really the prob-lem—it is the attitudes we have about who we are and what is needed to survive and succeed. The ultimate success for Blacks in the corpora-tion lies in learning the skills the corporate arena has to offer, and then taking those skills and putting them to work on behalf of Black people through the creation of Black-owned businesses. This is not to say that Blacks should abandon the struggle to fully integrate the American corporation; it was the slave labor of our ancestors that made most of the corporations possible in the first place, so we do have a stake in claiming some of the territory. But our real survival and success as a people will depend on our forging our own business institutions. As Edward Gardner, president of Soft Sheen Products, said in a *Newsweek* story that reported on the danger of Black-owned hair-products compa-nies being taken over by white conglomerates: "They [Blacks] get the MBA and go right to work for the major corporations and forget about building their own businesses. If these young businessmen don't realize the importance of Black-owned enterprises, we will never break the cycle of poverty." Nor will we ever overcome the debilitating stress that **21** comes from trying to accommodate who we are with what we think whites think we should be.

# The Hidden Hurdle

SOPHFRONIA SCOTT GREGORY

*In the following article, a journalist reports on a troubling development among black high school students: the academically talented are being harassed by their less able peers for "acting white." This selection first appeared in* Time *in 1992.*

When it comes to achieving in school, Za'kettha Blaylock knows that 1
even dreaming of success can mean living a nightmare. She would, above all things, like to work hard, go to college and become a doctor. But to many other black 14-year-old girls in her corner of Oakland, these ideas are anathema. The telephone rings in her family's modest apartment, and the anonymous voice murmurs daggers. "We're gonna kill you," the caller says. Za'kettha knows the threat comes from a gang of black girls, one that specializes not in drugs or street fights but in terrorizing bright black students. "They think that just because you're smart," says the eighth-grader, "they can go around beating you up."

Of all the obstacles to success that inner-city black students face, the 2
most surprising—and discouraging—may be those erected by their own peers. Many children must also cope with broken families, inadequate schools and crumbling communities that do not value academic achievement as essential to survival and prosperity. But the ridicule of peers cuts most deeply of all. Students like Za'kettha find themselves reviled as "uppity," as trying to "act white," because many teenagers have come to equate black identity with alienation and indifference. "I used to go home and cry," says Tachelle Ross, 18, a senior at Oberlin High in Ohio. "They called me white. I don't know why. I'd say, 'I'm just as black as you are.' "

The phrase "acting white" has often been the insult of choice used 3
by blacks who stayed behind against those who moved forward. Once it was supposed to invoke the image of an African American who had turned his back on his people and community. But the phrase has taken

an ominous turn. Today it rejects all the iconography of white middle-class life: a good job, a nice home, conservative clothes and a college degree.

In the smaller world of high school, the undesirable traits are differ- 4 ent, but the attitude is the same. Promising black students are ridiculed for speaking standard English, showing an interest in ballet or theater, having white friends or joining activities other than sports. "They'll run up to you and grab your books and say, 'I'll tear this book up,'" says Shaquila Williams, 12, a sixth-grader at Webster Academy in East Oakland. "They'll try and stop you from doing your work." Honor students may be rebuked for even showing up for class on time.

The pattern of abuse is a distinctive variation on the nerd bashing 5 that almost all bright, ambitious students—no matter what their color—face at some point in their young lives. The anti-achievement ethic championed by some black youngsters declares formal education useless; those who disagree and study hard face isolation, scorn and violence. While educators have recognized the existence of an anti-achievement culture for at least a decade, it has only recently emerged as a dominant theme among the troubles facing urban schools.

The label "acting white" and the dismissal of white values are 6 bound up in questions of black identity. "If you see a black girl," explains Kareema Matthews, a street-smart 14-year-old from Harlem, "and she's black, not mixed or anything, and she wants to act like something she's not, in these days nobody considers that good. She's trying to be white. That's why nobody likes her. That's how it is now." But when asked what it is to be black, Kareema pauses. "I don't have the slightest idea."

The right attitude, according to the targets of ridicule, would be 7 shown by skipping class, talking slang and, as Tachelle says, "being cool, not combing your hair. Carrying yourself like you don't care." Social success depends partly on academic failure; safety and acceptance lie in rejecting the traditional paths to self-improvement. "Instead of trying to come up with the smart kids, they try to bring you down to their level," says eighth-grader Rachel Blates of Oakland. "They don't realize that if you don't have an education, you won't have anything—no job, no husband, no home."

It is a sad irony that achievement should have acquired such a 8 stigma within the black community. Hard work, scholarship and respect for family values have long been a cornerstone of black identity. In the years before the Civil War, many black slaves risked their lives learning how to read. In 1867, just four years after the Emancipation Proclamation, African Americans founded Morehouse and Howard universities. According to the Bureau of the Census, between Reconstruction and 1910, the literacy rate among Southern blacks climbed from 20% to

70%. "There has always been a strong pressure toward educational achievement," says Mae Kendall, director of elementary education for the Atlanta public schools. Kendall, who grew up in semirural Thomasville, Ga., recalls, "My mother was not a lettered woman by any means, but she said, with a good education, you could turn the world upside down. That was a strong common linkage among all black people, and it was instilled early on."

Some education experts associate the rise of the culture of anti-achievement with the advent of public school desegregation and the flight of the black middle class to the suburbs. That left fewer role models whose success reinforced the importance of education and more children from families who found little grounds for hope in schools that were decaying. 9

The civil-rights movement did produce pockets of progress: the number of black managers, professionals, and government officials rose 52% in the past decade. Black enrollment in colleges has climbed steeply. In 1990, 33% of all black high school graduates went on to college, in contrast to 23% in 1967. Since 1976, black Scholastic Aptitude Test scores have increased by a greater percentage than those of either whites or Asians. Still, blacks have higher truancy rates, and in spite of the gains, the test scores of African Americans remain the lowest among large ethnic groups. The high school dropout rate among young blacks averages 7.7%, nearly twice that of their white peers, at 3.9%. 10

As more black teachers and administrators reach positions of power in the public school system, the anti-achievement ethic presents a special challenge to them as educators. For years, the failure of black students to succeed in white-run schools was attributed in large part to institutional racism. But some black educators are reassessing the blame. "It's absolutely ridiculous for us to be talking about what's happening to black youngsters when you've got a 90% African-American staff teaching a 95% black student body," says Franklin Smith, who is superintendent of schools in Washington and black himself. "If you can't prove what you believe here in Washington, then you might as well forget it anywhere in this country." 11

The effort to reverse the pattern of black failure has prompted educators like Smith to try many experiments—Afrocentric curriculums, academic-achievement fairs and efforts to establish black all-male public schools that focus on building self-esteem. The reform movements seek to revive in black students the value system that prizes education as, among other things, a way out of poverty. "We dropped the ball," laments Trinette Chase, a Montgomery County, Md., mother. "Our generation failed to pass on the value of an education." 12

It is a truism to say the problem most often begins at home. When parents are not able to transmit the values of achievement, the ever 13 present peer group fills the vacuum. Moniqua Woods, 12, a student at the Webster Academy in Oakland, says it is easy to spot neglected children because they "come to school every day yawning and tired. You know they stayed out late that night." Concurs classmate Mark Martin, also 12: "Some of the kids' parents are on drugs. You go in their house, and you can smell it." Such a homelife can further strengthen the attitude that school does not matter, especially if the parents themselves are without a diploma.

Kiante Brown, 15, of Oakland, knows this all too well. His mother    14
is a recovering crack addict who, he says, pays little attention to his comings and goings, and he hasn't seen his father in two years. Kiante used to spend his afternoons selling drugs on street corners. What little education he has came in bits and pieces; he has missed so much school he'll have to repeat the eighth grade. "I didn't really drop out, but I haven't been going to school much," he says. "For a while my mom told me to get up and go to school, but she really doesn't say nothing about it anymore."

Teachers may try to move in where parents have retreated. But with    15
class sizes increasing and school violence growing, it is often all educators can do to maintain minimal order, much less give individual attention to any child. Some teachers admit that the insidious attitudes creep into the classroom. It becomes a self-fulfilling prophecy: when teachers have lower expectations for their black students, they give them less attention and do not push them as hard to do well. Such stereotypes have crossed racial barriers to the point where even black teachers may hold these same attitudes. "If teachers feel they cannot make any headway with a youngster," says Richard Mesa, superintendent of Oakland public schools, "they may write him off."

It is especially painful for teachers to watch their most talented    16
students sabotage their own learning in order to fit in with peers. "Some of them feign ignorance to be accepted," says Willie Hamilton, the principal of Oakland's Webster Academy. Seneca Valley's Martine Martin observed this self-destructive pattern when she formed a program for "at risk" black females at one of her previous schools. The group originally comprised girls who were pregnant or uninterested in learning. But then, little by little, Martin noticed honor students showing up in her program because they thought it was cool.

The environment outside the classroom also leaves its mark inside.    17
The persistence of recession has made it even more difficult to inspire black students to do well in school with the carrot of a job. "The lack of association between education and post-school employment has discouraged a lot of young people," says William Julius Wilson, professor of sociology and public policy at the University of Chicago. "They see that whether you graduate from high school or you drop out, you're still

going to be hanging around on a corner or the best job you're going to find is working at a McDonald's. After a time they develop a view that you're a chump if you study hard."

Many successful black role models feel the need to "give something **18** back," by reaching out to inner-city youths. But some are finding it hard to make the connection. Meeting with a group of young inmates from a correctional facility, Robert Johnson, founder and CEO of Black Entertainment Television, faced some hostile young men and responded in kind. "I told them they were playing themselves into the hands of people who don't care about them. That if they think the way to pull themselves up is to get into the drug trade, rob, shoot and steal they were going to lose."

But teenagers who have trouble identifying with Johnson choose **19** their role models accordingly. "There's a lot of violence and a lot of drugs where I grow up," says Harlem teenager Marcos Medrano, 15, whose role model is macho actor Steven Seagal. "I went to a party, and there was a shoot-out. You're constantly living in danger. Who you gonna look up to? Bill Cosby or somebody that comes out shooting a lot?"

Successful blacks can be intimidating for the young, especially if **20** they dress in suits and "sound white." Some suspect that the ease with which successful blacks move in a white world means that they have denied their heritage. "It's devastating for them because you begin to get this stereotype thinking that all blacks when they get to a certain level try to become white by assimilating themselves with whites," says Dorothy Young, principal of the Delano Elementary School on the west side of Chicago. "And that's not true. But once that seed is planted in any form, that seed is going to grow."

The need to define their identity may lead young blacks to reject the **21** values of achievement; but, according to Rutgers anthropologist Signithia Fordham, this does not mean they think being black is only about failure. "They may not be able to articulate fully what it means to be black, but they're more attuned to why it is they don't want to be white," she says of black students she researched. "They know they want very much to remain connected to the black community. They want to be successful on their own terms."

There are, of course, many schools that can point to their success **22** stories, to students who overcame all the private obstacles to graduation, often with the help of innovative programs. In Cleveland, the Scholarship-in-Escrow program was set up by local businessmen in 1987. To encourage students to work toward college, the program offers cash incentives—$40 for each A they earn, $20 for each B—which go into an escrow account for their tuition. Since its inception, SIE has paid $469,300 in earned funds for 2,199 graduates. "It's good to know that money is being put away for you," says Faith Bryant, an 11th-grader at John Adams High School. "I had always dreamed of being successful, but now I know I have a way to do it."

The hope for these students lies in their understanding that no 23 one group in society has a monopoly on success. "As long as you're able to term success as being black or white or red," says Oberlin's Sherman Jones, a placement specialist for the Jobs for Ohio's Graduates program, "as long as we put conditions and colors on success then it'll be difficult for our kids." Destroying such misconceptions is not easy, especially when they are old and deeply rooted. But given time, perhaps "acting white" can be a phrase retired to the history books as the emblem of a misguided attitude that vanished in the light of black achievement.

# The Finest Place to Be

## CHRISTOPHER B. DALY

*In the following article, a journalist writes of his travels to Martha's Vineyard, an island off Cape Cod, Massachusetts, to spend Labor Day weekend with black, middle-class vacationers who seek the island each year, in part, to get "a vacation from race." Daly covers New England for the* Washington Post. *This piece first appeared in* Boston Magazine *in 1993.*

**11:30 A.M.**

It's not even noon yet, and Debby Jackson can already tell that her 1 husband will be hurting later. She knows she'll have to have the Ben-Gay ready. Here he is, a 42-year-old man, an accomplished architect (in fact, *Spike Lee's* architect) and a respected man about town, and he's running around on that basketball court, with his shirt off, like a teenager. Well, let him play. There are worse ways to spend the Saturday of Labor Day weekend than here in Vineyard Haven on Martha's Vineyard, talking to the gorgeous actress Jasmine Guy, the star of TV's "A Different World"—which is just what Debby is doing.

Debby, a tough business executive in her own right who runs 2 Morgan Memorial Goodwill Industries, is explaining why she is sitting on the ground on this grassy slope surrounding this beat-up hoops court, with the missing net and the rusty fence. As she talks, more and more people arrive—lawyers, doctors, a pilot, business people—all black. Richard Taylor, the Rhodes Scholar–businessman who is serving as state transportation secretary [of Massachusetts], shows up, followed by lawyer Flash Wiley ("You put down that I'm the greatest over-45 basketball player in the world," the never-shy Wiley instructs.), Greg Moore, the [Boston] *Globe*'s deputy managing editor, and enough other brainpower to launch a medium-size company in about any field you would like to name.

Just a bunch of guys playing hoops, Debby says, only half seri-  3
ously. Actually, there is a bit more to it. Most of these guys have been playing in this game, on this court, on this weekend for about 20 years. Duane is captain of one team, the non-frats, who are in skins this day. Taylor, who played for Boston University, captains the other team, the frats.

Every summer, they renew the battle over the Soul Cup—an actual  4
silvery trophy, which at this moment is lying on its side in the muddy grass near the court, keeping some toddlers amused. And they play for other reasons, too. A friend of Debby's checks in and announces that she has fixed pigs' feet ("Come on, girl. *Pigs' feet?* You did not!"), but her husband can only eat them if he wins.

Talking to Debby, you get the feeling that for the men, this game  5
is some kind of guy thing—something to do with being able to shed that suit and tie, lace up the high-tops and come out and talk some trash. It's nice to hit the occasional jumper, but this game is not really about basketball.

It is now after noon, and there are hundreds of people here. On the  6
court, ten guys are huffing and puffing around (under the rules, each team may have only one player who's under 35), and at courtside a few dozen more—mostly younger guys—are looking on, seeing how it's done. They are seeing, among other things, how you can be a successful, prominent black man in America in the 1990s and still be a brother. Around them, on the hillside, dozens more have gathered—wives, kids, girlfriends. And there are plenty of people who are here just because they know that the Soul Cup game is *the* place to be on Labor Day weekend.

Debby explains that the captain of the winning team gets to keep  7
the cup all winter, to display at home or at the office. With it comes a year of bragging rights. Plus the champagne. According to tradition, the loser has to buy champagne for the winners and present it later that same day at the Inkwell, the beach in Oak Bluffs where most folks hang out. In fact, the loser has to pour the champagne into the Soul Cup and

then, *on his knees*, present it to the winner. Then the loser has to take 12 months of abuse and scorn.

"What this is really about," confides one spectator, "is not losing."  8

Of course, in a sense, there are no losers here. The overriding fact  9
about playing for the Soul Cup, or watching others play for the Soul Cup, or even just knowing about the Soul Cup, is that it is played for on Martha's Vineyard, a little island off our [Atlantic] coast that has become a very special place in the heart of black America. And of the six picture-postcard little towns on this beautiful island, none is more dear than Oak Bluffs.

Oak Bluffs is simply the finest place to be if you are a black person  10
with enough money to be taking a summer vacation in the first place. Long a tightly held secret among Boston's black establishment, Oak Bluffs became famous in the 1980s as a mecca for accomplished, established blacks. Beginning with a handful of families, the resort scene here gathered strength in the 1940s and 1950s with the arrival of [Member of Congress] Adam Clayton Powell and former Sen. Edward Brooke, then took off in the 1970s and 1980s, drawing nearly all of the Congressional Black Caucus, Washington Mayor Sharon Pratt Dixon and dozens and dozens of black writers, doctors, lawyers and other doers. Now, singles, couples, and whole families flock to the Vineyard from up and down the Eastern Seaboard and from as far away as California.

*California?*  11

Yes, people with the means to do whatever they want leave the  12
Golden State, with its miles of beaches, and fly clear across the country, only to drive from Logan [Airport] to Woods Hole, then wait for a ferry to carry them those last few miles across Vineyard Sound, just so they can spend a week or a month or a whole summer in a town whose most obvious assets are a carousel of antique Flying Horses, Mad Martha's ice cream shop, a narrow beach and large numbers of very straight white folks who flock to Oak Bluffs from across America to be part of the Methodist Camp Meeting. There must be a reason for such things, and there is: successful, well-to-do blacks feel that when they vacation in Oak Bluffs they are not only getting the sand, sky and surf but they are also getting a vacation from race. (So too, of course, are the white people who come here.)

Oak Bluffs is a rare and precious place because it is one of the few  13
places in America where blacks and whites meet in something approaching harmony. Having left their rules and roles behind on the mainland, people mingle, nod, even talk to each other. This place, more than

perhaps any other, is one that embodies the real promise of America. It is, right now, what the rest of the country could become—if we could ever get beyond skin color.

"When I hit the island," says Debby Jackson, "I just stop thinking 14 about race."


**2:00 P.M.**

Over at the Inkwell, the sandy, east-facing beach along Sea View 15 Avenue, Duane Jackson is on his knees. Dressed in lycra shorts, high tops and a windbreaker, Duane is once again the center of attention. Dozens of folks are gathered along the seawall and the sidewalk for the awarding of the Soul Cup. The cup has been filled with champagne, and Jackson presents it to Richard Taylor, who takes a drink, then passes it to teammate Flash Wiley. Duane gets up and slips into the crowd, just long enough to grab an open bottle of champagne, give it a good shake and fire a soaking spray at Taylor and all of his gloating teammates. Everyone hoots.

"For me, it's been part of my family," says Dick Francis, a member 16 of one of the old-line Boston families who have been coming here for generations. Francis is standing on the sidewalk here at the Inkwell. (It is a matter of etymological uncertainty where the beach got its name. Some say it derives from the beach's shape. Others say it is a reference to the color of its patrons. But if that is true, nobody seems to mind much. The name, which doesn't appear on any maps, is used fondly— it's another part of belonging.)

"My grandfather owned property here," Francis says, and now the 17 family has three houses. "I live in California now. People say, 'Do you miss Boston?' I say, 'No, but I damn sure miss the Vineyard'." In the 1950s, when Francis was young, he and the other boys would make money by diving for coins near the ferry dock. One summer he cleared $1,500. It sounds like a story from a simpler era, but his point is that the Vineyard hasn't changed that much. It is seen as a place that is safe, friendly and fun. It's the kind of place where you can tell a 10-year-old after breakfast to be home by supper-time and not worry half to death about what might happen in between.

Other blacks agree. Dave Grayer, a prominent Boston attorney, has 18 been coming to the Vineyard for decades. He and his wife, Penny (the sister of a former U.S. attorney), are building a house in Edgartown. Grayer, who lives in Andover [Massachusetts] and likes to ski, explains in an interview in his Boston office that he personally would just as soon go to Vermont, but there is no place where his whole family will feel so much at home as on the Vineyard. "It was the only place in the country where middle-class black people could feel comfortable."

For Grayer, a special appeal the Vineyard holds involves his older   19
daughter, Cara, who is 17. More and more often, wealthy black families are doing what wealthy white families have been doing for generations—sending their children to boarding schools. Cara Grayer attends a boarding school and likes it. But as often happens, she is one of very few blacks at her school. So, when summer rolls around, she naturally wants to meet young men, young black men. Her parents know this. So they figure, why not let her meet young black men on Martha's Vineyard, where they may know the young man's parents, or at least know that he comes from a decent background? Besides, many of the young men and women she will meet on the Vineyard she will meet again later at Howard or Harvard or at a charity ball or in a Cabinet meeting. (Well-to-do white readers know *exactly* what the Grayers are thinking.)

Henry Owens, another prominent Boston attorney, belongs to one   20
of the most established of Boston's black families, the Owenses of Cambridge. "As a black professional, Martha's Vineyard is the only place I can go to with people similarly situated. This is a place where you can go on vacation with other black professionals," says Owens, who has vacationed in St. Thomas, Bermuda and other places but comes back to the Vineyard. "My kids go out every night down there, and I don't have to worry about them."

What Grayer and Owens don't mention is that the Vineyard won't   21
hurt their practices, either. They will be shooting hoops, playing tennis, fishing and sharing cocktails with lots of other lawyers and a good fraction of all the black judges, magistrates, regulators and cabinet members in the state and federal governments.

Alfred Goldson, M.D., or "Doctor Al," as he is known, is a good   22
example of the way the Vineyard's appeal has spread beyond the old-line Boston families. Goldson is a professor and chairman of radiation oncology at Howard University Hospital in Washington. He is not from Boston, but he met his wife, the former Amy Lippman, on the Vineyard, got married there, and had his daughters baptized there. For him, the Vineyard is all about families.

"The backdrop is obviously nice. But it also has the backdrop of the   23
families. It's a great place for kids. You don't have to worry about crack and shootings and things like that," he says. "It's like a big camp for grown-ups, as well as kids. I can't think of any other place like it in America for blacks."

Goldson mentions Sag Harbor on New York's Long Island, one of   24
the few other resort towns anywhere in the country that is well known for welcoming blacks, but he says there is no comparison to the Vine-

yard. "Anybody can get in their car and drive to Sag Harbor. To get to Martha's Vineyard, you have to be organized. It eliminates day-trippers. In Sag Harbor, you get drug dealers and pimps. Also, Oak Bluffs is white and black. Sag Harbor is black only."

Indeed, the remarkable thing about Oak Bluffs is that blacks feel    25
comfortable here without being in the majority. Blacks own more and more businesses in town, including guest houses, a fitness club and the influential Cousen Rose art gallery, but the number still doesn't amount to more than a few handfuls. Even Oak Bluffs, the Vineyard town with the most black property-owners and visitors, is predominantly white. The point is, blacks and whites both feel comfortable. The strangest part may be that all this is happening only about 45 miles from Boston.

---

The Oak Bluffs Tennis Club, Inc.    26
Presents Its
33rd Annual Labor Day
Tennis Tournament 1992
Sponsored by Anheuser-Busch Companies
To Benefit the United Negro College Fund

---

**4:00 P.M.**

Larry Smith, the Tennis Club president and tournament director, is busy    27
this afternoon. He's got dozens of matches going, on eight courts, at two locations. Dressed in tennis togs, Smith, a Boston real estate developer and consultant, takes a minute to explain the history. Back in the old days of the 1950s, the tournament began as a friendly, mostly social event involving the property-owning black families of Oak Bluffs, most of whom came from Boston—including Ed Brooke, the former U.S. Senator and state Attorney General.

For years, in fact, they had a rule that said you could not enter the    28
Oak Bluffs Labor Day tennis tournament unless you owned property in town or could prove that you had played on the town courts at least three times during that summer. And for years the first prize was a dinky little trophy that somebody picked up in a five-and-dime store.

No more. During the 80s, things got more serious. The number of    29
players exploded, and the level of tennis soared. Smith, who was elected president nine years ago, describes himself as a transitional figure, spanning the gap between the old-timers and the "Buppies"— the Black Urban Professionals. "They came, they saw, they liked," Smith says of the Buppies. "Then they went on a buying binge a few

years ago." So now the tennis tournament is a big deal, with a corporate sponsor, lots of rules and lots of very good amateur tennis with players from all over the United States, all capped by a very social evening of awards.

On Saturday afternoon, dozens of folks are gathered around the 30 courts, which take up most of a triangle-shaped park several blocks back from the ocean. Some watch the tennis; more mingle, greeting friends and relations from distant cities. It's more like a giant family reunion than a tennis club. This is, after all, a public park, so anyone at all can just wander by, and the mood is very friendly.

On a bench, Duane and Debby sit watching the tennis matches, 31 accompanied by their golden retriever. Debby thumbs through a Gumps catalogue, while Duane explains, a bit apologetically, why he and Taylor, who were among the original urban pioneers, are pulling out of [Boston's] Roxbury [neighborhood]. He mentions their kids, who are 12 and 20 years old, and says they have spent every summer of their lives in Oak Bluffs, safe and happy, only to return to winters in Roxbury, which are not always safe or happy. The Jacksons are moving to Milton, but they're coming back to Oak Bluffs.[1]

Blacks have lived on Martha's Vineyard nearly as long as whites 32 have. The first blacks most likely came as slaves, and records indicate that at least a few blacks were living on the island by 1700. The Legislature did not abolish slavery in Massachusetts until 1783, and by the time of the first Federal Census, in 1790, only 39 blacks lived on the Vineyard, or 1 percent of the population. A century later, there were about 200 blacks on the Island, a figure that did not change much until the 1970s. In the past two decades, the black year-round population has grown to 332, or almost 3 percent of the Island's 11,639 residents.

A turning point came in 1900 with the arrival of the Rev. Oscar E. 33 Denniston, a black minister from Jamaica. Denniston began preaching to the Island blacks and built a church, giving the year-round population a leader and one of its first institutions, according to a history of Oak Bluffs written by Adelaide Cromwell, the former director of African-American Studies at Boston University, in the *Dukes County Intelligencer*, the journal of the Island's historical society.

After the turn of the century, whites began discovering the Island's 34 summer pleasures, and wealthy families began staying for weeks or

---

[1]Milton, Massachusetts, is a suburb of Boston.

months at a time. Some of them brought black servants with them. Among them was Sadie Shearer, who came to the Vineyard with her parents to operate a summer laundry service for white vacationers. Shearer saw a need for a guest house catering to blacks, so she closed the laundry and opened Shearer Cottage, which became the stopping-place for distinguished blacks visiting the Island. Guests included the composer Harry T. Burleigh, the singer Paul Robeson and the Rev. Adam Clayton Powell Sr. and his son Adam Jr.

The other major influence on black life on the Island was the arrival 35 in the early years of this century of about 40 black summer families from Boston. "This small and select group of successful Blacks knew each other in Boston and followed one another to the Island," Cromwell writes. "First they rented or boarded, but soon were buying homes, establishing the solid foundations for the black community in the High-lands of Oak Bluffs."

After World War II, more and more blacks bought summer places, 36 sometimes using a white "straw" to make the real estate transaction for them. Nowadays, for black celebrities like Spike Lee the concern about whether they would be able to buy property has been over-taken by worries about whether they will be allowed to enjoy their summer place in peace—free from gawkers, white or black.

Oak Bluffs has another distinction. It is the summer home not 37 only of the nation's black elite, but it also plays host to an annual "camp meeting" of Methodists from across the United States. They have been coming every summer (except one) since 1835, when nine tents were pitched for an open-air evangelical revival. By 1880, thou-sands were attending the summertime sessions of prayer, song and preaching, and the Martha's Vineyard Camp Meeting Association was organized. The association eventually bought quite a few acres of land and built a giant, open "tabernacle," topped by a lighted cross that can be seen for miles.

In time, the tents gave way to the ornate gingerbread cottages 38 that many people associate with Oak Bluffs. More than 300 of the cottages remain, and some are occupied each summer by the fourth or fifth generations in their families. The highlight of the summer comes in August on Illumination Night, when the cottagers light thou-sands of candle lanterns, sing hymns and visit each other's open houses.

It appears to be just a coincidence that Oak Bluffs is the summer 39 destination for these two groups, and there is some evidence that for many decades, the Camp-Meeting Association snubbed the Island's blacks in un-Christian ways. Nowadays, there seems to be a cordial co-existence.

**10 P.M.**

At Anthony's restaurant, the crowd is dressed. Inside, where they are      **40**
having the official awards ceremony for the tennis tournament, it's too
hot and the music is too loud for talking. But outside, in the cool evening
air, Kelly Wilson, a 33-year-old marketing executive with Prudential,
stops to explain why he made his way to the Vineyard from his home
in Ridgewood, N.J.

"Here, you're not that inhibited by the mainland cultural stereo-      **41**
types. Everyone's coming up here to enjoy themselves and have a good
time." He thinks the island's climate of racial tolerance comes from the
fact that nearly everyone—black and white—is a guest. "I was invited
by friends. They said, 'Where you been? Kelly, this is where you come
on Labor Day Weekend'," he says. "White or black, you got your old
money here. It's the old guard, in Boston and Martha's Vineyard."

A few minutes later, a member of that Old Guard steps out to get      **42**
some air. Jim Porter has been coming to the Vineyard for 54 summers,
since his father first visited from New York in 1938. Now Porter lives
here year-round. With a graduate degree from MIT, Porter runs an
environmental testing company he founded in 1979. This evening,
impeccably turned out in a double-breasted blazer, pink shirt and silk tie,
he is asked why this place is so special.

"For me, I think it has to do with trying to recapture my childhood,"      **43**
Porter says. Back then, he and his friends roamed the island, fishing and
crabbing. Now, he sees the children of his old friends spending their
summers in much the same way. In Porter's view, the racial climate
reflects the Vineyard's physical isolation. "It's a small island, so everybody *has* to get along."

There's another reason, too, one that hardly anybody likes to talk      **44**
about. The fact is, virtually everyone on Martha's Vineyard is well off,
and everyone knows it. The ferry imposes a kind of reverse "means test"
on everyone, so that if you don't have enough money to get to Woods
Hole, to get onto the ferry and to pay for your meals and lodging on
this pricey Island, you simply never show up on the Vineyard, no matter
what color you are.

As a result, everyone walks around secure in the knowledge that      **45**
everyone else could at least afford to get there and probably to spend
the night. So, you can feel pretty sure that anyone you bump into is
at least as well off as yourself. In this way, of course, Martha's Vineyard is not at all like America. But it provides a kind of social science
lab where you can carry out this kind of thought experiment: Do
Americans care more about class or race? Are we more comfortable
with people of our own race or income bracket? What do we mean by
"our own kind"? What would America be like if we eliminated poverty and racism?

**12:15 A.M.**

On Circuit Avenue, the main drag in Oak Bluffs, the sidewalks are in   46
gridlock and the street is just about impassable. Everywhere you look,
there are people clinging to these last precious hours of summer. The
most congested spot is outside The Atlantic Connection dance club, the
epicenter of the island social scene for young black singles and couples
who go out. It is so hot that people stand in a line more than 100 long
to get in. Just waiting in line is part of the scene, since this is the place
to see and be seen.

The dress is casual, ranging from shorts to blazers, but everyone   47
is definitely turned out. Carloads of whites, in Boston College sweat-
shirts or yachting togs, slow down to gawk, and black teenagers (too
young to meet the 21-year-old age minimum) cluster in knots on the
opposite side of the street, eating ice cream while they study their elders.

Two guys in their 20s pull to the curb in a black Porsche convertible   48
with Maryland plates. (In fact, it's a vanity plate that says "I KNOW.")
The car's sound system is pumping out rap. From the back seat emerges
a long-legged, pouting beauty. She wears a crimson satin jacket that
says "Harvard Lacrosse." To be so young and so cool and so assured,
to be in this place, at this time—it may not be heaven, but you can't
be sure.

# On Being Black and Middle Class

SHELBY STEELE

*Shelby Steele, a Professor of English at San Jose State University, is one of
today's most influential—and controversial—black writers. Several years
ago, Steele listened to one of those "hopeless debates" between blacks and
whites in which "public discussions of the race issue had become virtually
choreographed" according to pre-established and predictable positions. Tired
of his own "public/private racial split," Steele sat down to write an essay
about himself that was to become the kernel of his widely read book,* The
Content of Our Character: A New Vision of Race in America *(1990).
The essay, "Race-Holding," begins:*

I am a fortyish, middle-class, black American male with a teaching position
at a large state university in California. I have owned my own home for

more than ten years, as well as the two cars that are the minimal requirement for life in California. And I will confess to a moderate strain of yuppie hedonism. Year after year my two children are the sole representatives of their race in their classrooms, a fact they sometimes have difficulty remembering. We are the only black family in our suburban neighborhood, and even this claim to specialness is diminished by the fact that my wife is white. I think we are called an "integrated" family, though no one has ever used the term with me. For me to be among large numbers of blacks requires conscientiousness and a long car ride, and in truth, I have not been very conscientious lately. Though I was raised in an all-black community just south of Chicago, I only occasionally feel nostalgia for such places. Trips to the barbershop now and then usually satisfy this need, though recently, in the interest of convenience, I've taken to letting my wife cut my hair.

*Steele has published fiction, essays, and critical articles in a variety of magazines and academic journals. This article, which first appeared in* Commentary *in January 1988, later appeared in* The Content of Our Character.

Not long ago a friend of mine, black like myself, said to me that the term "black middle class" was actually a contradiction in terms. Race, he insisted, blurred class distinctions among blacks. If you were black, you were just black and that was that. When I argued, he let his eyes roll at my naiveté. Then he went on. For us, as black professionals, it was an exercise in self-flattery, a pathetic pretension, to give meaning to such a distinction. Worse, the very idea of class threatened the unity that was vital to the black community as a whole. After all, since when had white America taken note of anything but color when it came to blacks? He then reminded me of an old Malcolm X line that had been popular in the 60's. Question: What is a black man with a Ph.D.? Answer: A nigger.

For many years I had been on my friend's side of this argument. Much of my conscious thinking on the old conundrum of race and class was shaped during my high-school and college years in the race-charged 60's, when the fact of my race took on an almost religious significance. Progressively, from the mid-60's on, more and more aspects of my life found their explanation, their justification, and their motivation in race. My youthful concerns about career, romance, money, values, and even styles of dress became subject to consultation with various oracular sources of racial wisdom. And these ranged from a figure as ennobling as Martin Luther King, Jr. to the underworld elegance of dress I found in jazz clubs on the South Side of Chicago. Everywhere there were signals, and in those days I considered myself so blessed with clarity and direction that I pitied my white classmates who found more embarrassment than guidance in the fact of *their* race. In 1968, inflated by my new power, I took a mischievous delight in calling them culturally disadvantaged.

But now, hearing my friend's comment was like hearing a priest   3
from a church I'd grown disenchanted with. I understood him, but my
faith was weak. What had sustained me in the 60's sounded monotonous
and off-the-mark in the 80's. For me, race had lost much of its juju, its
singular capacity to conjure meaning. And today, when I honestly look
at my life and the lives of many other middle-class blacks I know, I can
see that race never fully explained our situation in American society.
Black though I may be, it is impossible for me to sit in my single-family
house with two cars in the driveway and a swing set in the back yard
and *not* see the role class has played in my life. And how can my friend,
similarly raised and similarly situated, not see it?

Yet despite my certainty I felt a sharp tug of guilt as I tried to   4
explain myself over my friend's skepticism. He is a man of many
comedic facial expressions and, as I spoke, his brow lifted in extreme
moral alarm as if I were uttering the unspeakable. His clear implication
was that I was being elitist and possibly (dare he suggest?) anti-black—
crimes for which there might well be no redemption. He pretended to
fear for me. I chuckled along with him, but inwardly I did wonder at
myself. Though I never doubted the validity of what I was saying, I felt
guilty saying it. Why?

After he left (to retrieve his daughter from a dance lesson) I realized   5
that the trap I felt myself in had a tiresome familiarity and, in a sort of
slow-motion epiphany, I began to see its outline. It was like the suddenly
sharp vision one has at the end of a burdensome marriage when
all the long-repressed incompatibilities come undeniably to light.

What became clear to me is that people like myself, my friend, and   6
middle-class blacks generally are caught in a very specific double bind
that keeps two equally powerful elements of our identity at odds with
each other. The middle-class values by which we were raised—the work
ethic, the importance of education, the value of property ownership, of
respectability, of "getting ahead," of stable family life, of initiative, of
self-reliance, etc.—are, in themselves, raceless and even assimilationist.
They urge us toward participation in the American mainstream, toward
integration, toward a strong identification with the society—and toward
the entire constellation of qualities that are implied in the word
individualism. These values are almost rules for how to prosper in a
democratic, free-enterprise society that admires and rewards individual
effort. They tell us to work hard for ourselves and our families and to
seek our opportunities whenever they appear, inside or outside the
confines of whatever ethnic group we may belong to.

But the particular pattern of racial identification that emerged in the   7

60's and that still prevails today urges middle-class blacks (and all blacks) in the opposite direction. This pattern asks us to see ourselves as an embattled minority, and it urges an adversarial stance toward the mainstream, an emphasis on ethnic consciousness over individualism. It is organized around an implied separatism.

The opposing thrust of these two parts of our identity results in the double bind of middle-class blacks. There is no forward movement on either plane that does not constitute backward movement on the other. This was the familiar trap I felt myself in while talking with my friend. As I spoke about class, his eyes reminded me that I was betraying race. Clearly, the two indispensable parts of my identity were a threat to one another. . . . **8**

The black middle class has always defined its class identity by means of positive images gleaned from middle- and upper-class white society, and by means of negative images of lower-class blacks. This habit goes back to the institution of slavery itself, when "house" slaves both mimicked the whites they served and held themselves above the "field" slaves. But in the 60's the old bourgeois impulse to dissociate from the lower classes (the "we-they" distinction) backfired when racial identity suddenly called for the celebration of this same black lower class. One of the qualities of a double bind is that one feels it more than sees it, and I distinctly remember the tension and strange sense of dishonesty I felt in those days as I moved back and forth like a bigamist between the demands of class and race. **9**

Though my father was born poor, he achieved middle-class standing through much hard work and sacrifice (one of his favorite words) and by identifying fully with solid middle-class values—mainly hard work, family life, property ownership, and education for his children (all four of whom have advanced degrees). In his mind these were not so much values as laws of nature. People who embodied them made up the positive images in his class polarity. The negative images came largely from the blacks he had left behind because they were "going nowhere." **10**

No one in my family remembers how it happened, but as time went on, the negative images congealed into an imaginary character named Sam who, from the extensive service we put him to, quickly grew to mythic proportions. In our family lore he was sometimes a trickster, sometimes a boob, but always possessed of a catalogue of sly faults that gave up graphic images of everything we should not be. On sacrifice: "Sam never thinks about tomorrow. He wants it now or he doesn't care about it." On work: "Sam doesn't favor it too much." On children: "Sam likes to have them but not to raise them." On money: "Sam drinks it up and pisses it out." On fidelity: "Sam has to have two or three women." **11**

On clothes: "Sam features loud clothes. He likes to see and be seen." And so on. Sam's persona amounted to a negative instruction manual in class identity.

I don't think that any of us believed Sam's faults were accurate representations of lower-class black life. He was an instrument of self-definition, not of sociological accuracy. It never occurred to us that he looked very much like the white racist stereotype of blacks, or that he might have been a manifestation of our own racial self-hatred. He simply gave us a counterpoint against which to express our aspirations. If self-hatred was a factor, it was not, for us, a matter of hating lower-class blacks but of hating what we did not want to be. 12

Still, hate or love aside, it is fundamentally true that my middle-class identity involved a dissociation from images of lower-class black life and a corresponding identification with values and patterns of responsibility that are common to the middle class everywhere. These values sent me a clear message: be both an individual and a responsible citizen, understand that the quality of your life will approximately reflect the quality of effort you put into it, know that individual responsibility is the basis of freedom and that the limitations imposed by fate (whether fair or unfair) are no excuse for passivity. 13

Whether I live up to these values or not, I know that my acceptance of them is the result of lifelong conditioning. I know also that I share this conditioning with middle-class people of all races and that I can no more easily be free of it than I can be free of my race. Whether all this got started because the black middle class modeled itself on the white middle class is no longer relevant. For the middle-class black, conditioned by these values from birth, the sense of meaning they provide is as immutable as the color of his skin. 14

I started the 60's in high school feeling that my class-conditioning was the surest way to overcome racial barriers. My racial identity was pretty much taken for granted. After all, it was obvious to the world that I was black. Yet I ended the 60's in graduate school a little embarrassed by my class background and with an almost desperate need to be "black." The tables had turned. I knew very clearly (though I struggled to repress it) that my aspirations and my sense of how to operate in the world came from my class background, yet "being black" required certain attitudes and stances that made me feel secretly a little duplicitous. The inner compatibility of class and race I had known in 1960 was gone. 15

For blacks, the decade between 1960 and 1969 saw racial identification undergo the same sort of transformation that national identity undergoes in times of war. It became more self-conscious, more nar- 16 rowly focused, more prescribed, less tolerant of opposition. It spawned an implicit party line, which tended to disallow competing forms of identity. Race-as-identity was lifted from the relative slumber it knew in the 50's and pressed into service in a social and political war against oppression. It was redefined along sharp adversarial lines and directed toward the goal of mobilizing the great mass of black Americans in this warlike effort. It was imbued with a strong moral authority, useful for denouncing those who opposed it and for celebrating those who honored it as a positive achievement rather than a mere birthright.

The form of racial identification that quickly evolved to meet this  17
challenge presented blacks as a racial monolith, a singular people with a common experience of oppression. Differences within the race, no matter how ineradicable, had to be minimized. Class distinctions were one of the first such differences to be sacrificed, since they not only threatened racial unity but also seemed to stand in contradiction to the principle of equality which was the announced goal of the movement for racial progress. The discomfort I felt in 1969, the vague but relentless sense of duplicity, was the result of a historical necessity that put my race and class at odds, that was asking me to cast aside the distinction of my class and identify with a monolithic view of my race.

If the form of this racial identity was the monolith, its substance was  18
victimization. The civil-rights movement and the more radical splinter groups of the late 60's were all dedicated to ending racial victimization, and the form of black identity that emerged to facilitate this goal made blackness and victimization virtually synonymous. Since it was our victimization more than any other variable that identified and unified us, moreover, it followed logically that the purest black was the poor black. It was images of him that clustered around the positive pole of the race polarity; all other blacks were, in effect, required to identify with him in order to confirm their own blackness.

Certainly there were more dimensions to the black experience than  19
victimization, but no other had the same capacity to fire the indignation needed for war. So, again out of historical necessity, victimization became the overriding focus of racial identity. But this only deepened the double bind for middle-class blacks like me. When it came to class we were accustomed to defining ourselves against lower-class blacks and identifying with at least the values of middle-class whites; when it came to race we were now being asked to identify with images of lower-class blacks and to see whites, middle-class or otherwise, as victimizers. Negative lining up with positive, we were called upon to reject what we had previously embraced and to embrace what we had previously rejected. To put it still more personally, the Sam figure I had been

raised to define myself against had now become the "real" black I was expected to identify with. . . .

The discomfort and vulnerability felt by middle-class blacks in the 60's, it could be argued, was a worthwhile price to pay considering the progress achieved during that time of racial confrontation. But what may have been tolerable then is intolerable now. Though changes in American society have made it an anachronism, the monolithic form of racial identification that came out of the 60's is still very much with us. It may be more loosely held, and its power to punish heretics has probably diminished, but it continues to catch middle-class blacks in a double bind, thus impeding not only their own advancement but even, I would contend, that of blacks as a group. 20

The victim-focused black identity encourages the individual to feel that his advancement depends almost entirely on that of the group. Thus he loses sight not only of his own possibilities but of the inextricable connection between individual effort and individual advancement. This is a profound encumbrance today, when there is more opportunity for blacks than ever before, for it reimposes limitations that can have the same oppressive effect as those the society has only recently begun to remove. 21

It was the emphasis on mass action in the 60's that made the victim-focused black identity a necessity. But in the 80's and beyond, when racial advancement will come only through a multitude of individual advancements, this form of identity inadvertently adds itself to the forces that hold us back. Hard work, education, individual initiative, stable family life, property ownership—these have always been the means by which ethnic groups have moved ahead in America. Regardless of past or present victimization, these "laws" of advancement apply absolutely to black Americans also. There is no getting around this. What we need is a form of racial identity that energizes the individual by putting him in touch with both his possibilities and his responsibilities. 22

It has always annoyed me to hear from the mouths of certain arbiters of blackness that middle-class blacks should "reach back" and pull up those blacks less fortunate than they—as though middle-class status were an unearned and essentially passive condition in which one needed a large measure of noblesse oblige to occupy one's time. My own image is of reaching back from a moving train to lift on board those who have no tickets. A noble enough sentiment—but might it not be wiser to show them the entire structure of principles, effort, and sacrifice that puts one in a position to buy a ticket any time one likes? This, I think, is something members of the black middle class can realistically 23 offer to other blacks. Their example is not only a testament to possibility but also a lesson in method. But they cannot lead by example until they are released from a black identity that regards that example as suspect, that sees them as "marginally" black, indeed that holds *them* back by catching them in a double bind.

To move beyond the victim-focused black identity we must learn to make a difficult but crucial distinction: between actual victimization, which we must resist with every resource, and identification with the victim's status. Until we do this we will continue to wrestle more with ourselves than with the new opportunities which so many paid so dearly to win.    **24**

---

**WRITING A SUMMARY:** Assignment 1—"The Hidden Hurdle," by Sophfronia Scott Gregory

Write a summary of "The Hidden Hurdle." In this selection, Gregory reports on the challenges faced by bright black students who want to excel at school and be accepted by their peers. As you begin to make notes toward writing a summary of Gregory's—or anyone's—article, put in mind some phrase that you think captures the gist of the author's work. You will extend the phrase later, into a thesis, but for the moment a few orienting words will do. So think of such a phrase describing "The Hidden Hurdle."

Next, identify sections of the article. You may have begun this task while reading the first time. Preparing your summary requires that you read at least once more. This time, you have the advantage of having read both the author's introduction and conclusion. Use these to help you identify the large blocks of information—the sections for which you will eventually write one- or two-sentence summaries. In Gregory's case, you might identify four sections: paragraphs 1–7, the introduction and statement of the problem; paragraphs 8–10, the irony of the problem when seen against the historical background of black achievement; paragraphs 11–22, efforts at and challenges of remedying the problem; and paragraph 23, the conclusion.

Following the boxed guidelines on page 6, write a one- or two-sentence summary of each section that you have identified. (In longer sections, especially in paragraphs 11–22, you might identify sub-sections and choose to write a one-sentence summary of each.) Next, recall the phrase with which you began thinking about Gregory's article. Review the section summaries you have just written and then extend your initial phrase into a thesis, which should function as a one-sentence summary of the entire article. Finally, place thesis and section summaries together, in a single paragraph. You will likely need to revise this rough summary for clarity and style.

---

**WRITING A SUMMARY:** Assignment 2—"I Have a Flag," by Richard G. Carter

Richard Carter's "I Have a Flag" is a narrative—a story. In Chapter 1, on summary, you saw that summarizing a narrative poses special challenges. First, your summary will be not a narrative but a paragraph-length synopsis. Second, you will want to describe the principal characters—in this case Carter, and likely a passing reference to Muhammad Ali—and the main actions or events of the narrative. Third, you will need to connect characters and events, describing the significant relationship between them.

How will you apply these guidelines to a summary of Carter? Begin rereading the piece and making "character" notes. Who is Carter? Jot down pertinent information. Your notes might include these labels: *black man, journalist, postal worker in dead-end job*. You would add other character notes to this list. What about the significant events in Carter's narrative? These, too, can be noted in the margins as you reread. Recall that your summary should present events in such a way that the reader is aware of time flowing—in Carter's case, some twenty-five years. Certainly, you will want to refer to the key event, the Ali speech, from which Carter takes his title.

The most challenging part of summarizing a narrative is the establishment of significant relationships between the character(s) and events. Why has this narrative been told? What is the meaning of these events for this character? Often, authors will leave it to you to make these relationships; but in the present selection, Carter is very explicit.

**WRITING A SUMMARY:** Assignment 3—"The Finest Place to Be," by Christopher B. Daly

Christopher B. Daly's "The Finest Place to Be" is an example of an article you could *not* usefully summarize by writing a one- or two-sentence summary of every section. Daly structures his piece chronologically, presenting readers with a window through which to view twelve hours in the life of middle-class blacks on the island of Martha's Vineyard. Implicitly, Daly is claiming that these twelve hours are representative and that by watching carefully, with him, we can learn something of the reasons that blacks are so fond of this vacation spot. While you might mention the structure of the piece, you should not reproduce that structure. As writer of the article, Daly has the space to unfold his main point slowly, and with subtlety. As writer of a summary, you have comparatively little space. Moreover, your purpose is to get right to the main point. Concentrate, therefore, on the cumulative point Daly is making (see especially paragraphs 13 and 45). Questions to consider as you prepare your summary:

♦ How much of the first-person accounts of the black professionals quoted in the article will you include in the summary?

- How much of the history of blacks on Martha's Vineyard will you include in the summary (see paragraphs 32–39)?
- To what extent will you dwell on the particular events of the day: the Soul Cup, the tennis match, the awards ceremony, the dance club?

---

## WRITING A CRITIQUE: Assignment 1—"Crossover Dreams," by Audrey Edwards

In Chapter 3, on critical reading and critique, you read the following:

> As an unbiased, evenhanded critic, you evaluate an author's clarity of presentation, use of evidence, and adherence to principles of logic. To what extent has the author succeeded in achieving his or her purpose? Still withholding judgment, you offer your assessment and give the author (in effect) a grade. Significantly, your assessment of the presentation may not coincide with your views of the author's conclusions.

"Crossover Dreams" provides an excellent opportunity to practice critique. As you read and reread the piece, consider the extent to which you agree with Edwards's main point: that bicultural stress challenges the psychological well-being of middle-class blacks and that five attitudes, not confronted, can induce such stress. To what extent do you agree with Edwards's conclusion (in paragraph 21) that "the ultimate success for Blacks in the corporation lies in learning the skills the corporate arena has to offer, and then taking those skills and putting them to work on behalf of Black people through the creation of Black-owned businesses"? You also might question Edwards's rationale for a black employee's continuing "the struggle to fully integrate the American corporation" (also paragraph 21). Remember that your agreement or disagreement with these views can stand separately from your estimate of the author's success in gathering and presenting information.

As you make notes for your critique, consult the guidelines on page 74. Above all, remember that a critique calls for you to know your own mind concerning what you have read. Read and respond; then explain that response to your audience. In preparing the summary portion of the critique, you may find it helpful to note that Edwards follows a problem-solution format.

---

## WRITING A CRITIQUE: Assignment 2—"The Middle-Class Black's Burden," by Leanita McClain

The title of Leanita McClain's essay, "The Middle-Class Black's Burden," implies a question: *What* is this burden? If you can read the article and answer this question, you will have taken an essential first step in writing a critique. Reread paragraphs 12–14 and paragraphs 16–19, and watch how eloquently McClain writes of the burden of belonging to two cultures, one black and the other white. In a word or phrase, name McClain's burden, and then develop this word or phrase into a sentence that begins this way: "According to Leanita McClain, middle-class blacks must bear the burden of _____ "

Having completed this sentence, you are in a good position to write a summary of the essay, which will form a key part of your critique. In planning your critique, identify three or four elements of McClain's essay (either points that she is making or the manner in which she is making them) that merit your reaction. You may want to evaluate her presentation for accuracy, fairness, and logic, and you may want to respond to her dilemma. In note form first, not as part of your first draft, list the elements on which you will concentrate and your reactions to each. Next, consult the guidelines for critique on page 74 and plan out your paper. Certainly, you will want to mention that McClain committed suicide (see Audrey Edwards, paragraphs 1 and 5–6). If you read the selections of this chapter in order, you did not discover this disturbing information until after your first reading of McClain. Did your subsequent awareness of the suicide alter your response to the article? Think of ways to explain and incorporate your reactions to the suicide into your critical response to her essay.

---

## WRITING A SYNTHESIS: Assignment 1—An Explanatory Essay

The writers in this chapter address the conflicts of race and class for black Americans. In a four-page synthesis in which you refer to four or more of these writers, *explain* the conflict's origins, its effects, and its possible solutions. Assume that your readers are your age and are interested in but unfamiliar with the conflict.

In responding to this assignment, and in preparing to write a synthesis, be sure of your purpose. As you reread this assignment, understand that it calls for an *explanation*. You may well have an opinion on the tensions between race and class among successful black Americans, but in this essay you should try to remain neutral. Your purpose as laid out in the assignment is to explain. When making notes and writing, think continually of an audience to whom you will provide information based mostly on your sources, the pertinent parts of which you will select and organize with care.

As you reread the assignment and consider your readers' level of knowledge about the topic, you might decide to define the conflict between race and class for black Americans. Think of the authors who can help you make this definition. Note that a structure for your synthesis is implied by the assignment. You are asked to explain origins, effects, and possible solutions. Aside from any definitions you offer, you will have at least three sections in your paper. Again, think of the sources that will help you to best develop each.

# WRITING A SYNTHESIS: Assignment 2—Comparison-and-Contrast Essay

In a four-page paper, compare and contrast the essays of Richard G. Carter and Leanita McClain. Whereas Carter seems to have managed the tensions of being middle-class and black, McClain found these tensions oppressive (she eventually committed suicide). How are we to understand Carter's and McClain's widely divergent reactions to being successful in a predominantly white culture? Answer this question by conducting a comparative analysis.

In a comparative analysis, your purpose is to make careful observations of two or more related people, places, events, or ideas and to discuss (1) how they differ and are the same and (2) how these similarities and differences are significant. Richard G. Carter's "I Have a Flag" and Leanita McClain's "The Middle-Class Black's Burden" present an opportunity to practice skills of comparison and contrast. Both authors are successful journalists who have written first-person accounts about the challenges of being middle-class blacks in a predominantly white culture. If many of the predicaments faced by Carter and McClain are the same, their strategies for coping with these predicaments, as well as their overall sense of well-being, differ considerably. What can you learn from conducting a comparative analysis of these selections?

In any essay of comparison and contrast, you work with *criteria,* categories by which you examine the objects under study. (See pages 131–45 for a discussion on conducting a comparative analysis and on organizing comparison-and-contrast essays.) For an analysis of Carter and McClain, you might consider using as one or more of your criteria any of the five attitudes that Audrey Edwards says lead to bicultural stress. (See "Crossover Dreams," pages 202–08.)

Remember that a comparative analysis should do more than simply announce similarities and differences. The successful essay should answer a question defined by you or, in this case, by an assignment: How are we to understand Carter's and McClain's widely divergent reactions to being successful in a predominantly white culture?

# WRITING A SYNTHESIS: Assignment 3—An Argumentative Essay

Use several of the articles in this chapter to help you argue for or against Shelby Steele's three-part thesis (1) that as a strategy for pressing home demands in the 1960s, blacks identified themselves as victims; (2) that the "victim-focused black identity" stands in contradiction to the values that make individual achievement possible, creating for the middle-class black a double bind; and (3) that blacks must reject victimization and aspire to the traditional middle-class values of "hard work, education, [and] individual initiative" that have enabled all peoples, regardless of circumstance, to advance in America.

Here is a summary of Shelby Steele's article "On Being Black and Middle Class":

> In his essay "On Being Black and Middle Class," Shelby Steele argues that a "Black-as-victim" identity developed during the racial unrest of the 1960s. This racial identity contradicted the values of individualism and active self-reliance that Steele had learned from his family and places Steele in a double bind: to be black he had to deny the individualist, self-reliant part of his character; to be a self-reliant individualist, he had to reject his racial identity (as this was defined in the 1960s). The legacy of this double bind lasted into Steele's adulthood. For a long time he believed that being a member of the "black middle class was actually a contradiction in terms."
>
> Steele suffered from his contradictory double identity. His black culture insisted that he adopt the identity of the group; and to an extent, Steele did. But he always felt uneasy about the part of his identity based on victimization. Victims were passive, but Steele all his life had been intellectually active; victims made excuses for what they could not accomplish, and Steele did not believe in excuses. He took personal responsibility for his successes and failures. The two components of his identity were at war with each other.
>
> Eventually, Steele rejected his double bind by rejecting the "monolithic" notion that all blacks are victims. This identity, he contends, impedes the progress of individual blacks and of blacks generally. What is needed is a new identity more accepting of middle-class values such as "hard work, education, individual initiative, stable family life, [and] property ownership—[which] have always been the means by which ethnic groups have moved ahead in America." Actual victimization of blacks must be fought; but the "victim-focused black identity" must be rejected and a new identity embraced if blacks are to achieve and prosper.

Use this summary to confirm your understanding of Steele's article. Then reexamine the essay question above and Steele's three-part thesis. Do you agree with the author in whole or in part? Determine your response, and your reasons for reacting as you do; then use the other readings in the chapter to bolster your response.

# 7

# THE CASE
# OF CHRISTOPHER COLUMBUS

In fourteen-hundred ninety-two,
Columbus crossed the ocean blue.
He found America and then
He sailed right back to Spain again.

But when the good news got around
That this great country had been found,
A lot of people came to stay—
And that is why we're here today!

Generations of American schoolchildren have been taught a version of Christopher Columbus more or less on the order of M. Lucille Ford's 1935 poem. For a good part of the five hundred years since 1492, Columbus (1451–1506) has been a hero of mythic proportions in American history. Interestingly, the "Admiral of the Ocean Sea" died a forgotten man: the continent he "discovered" was named for Amerigo Vespucci, a more skillful self-publicist; and his reputation was eclipsed by conquistadores like Cortés and Pizarro, who brought huge quantities of gold back to Spain and who conquered not merely a few small tribes in the West Indies, but the mighty Aztec and Inca empires. As a seaman, Columbus was less renowned than Vasco da Gama, who by rounding the southern tip of Africa actually did reach the Indies (which, to his dying day, Columbus believed he had found). And he was less acclaimed than Ferdinand Magellan, who in 1519 became the first person to circumnavigate the globe.

Columbus's reputation began to revive in the sixteenth century. In 1552 the historian Francisco Lopez de Gómara wrote, "The greatest event since the creation of the world (excluding the incarnation of Him who created it) is the discovery of the Indies." By the time of Washington's presidency, Columbus was a national hero: Kings College in New York was renamed Columbia, and in 1792 there was a three-hundredth anniversary celebration of Columbus's landfall. For the celebrators, as John Noble Wilford notes, "Columbus came to epitomize the explorer and discoverer, the man of vision and audacity, the hero who overcame opposition and adversity to change history." In the nineteenth century, Washington Irving's laudatory biography elevated Columbus even higher; and the four-hundredth anniversary in 1892 was the occasion for a yearlong celebration, which included the World's Columbian Exposition in Chicago. President Benjamin Harrison declared that "Columbus stood in his age as the pioneer of progress and enlightenment."

The five-hundredth anniversary celebrations in our own century were to be even grander than the quadricentennial. Coordinating the festivities was the Christopher Columbus Quincentenary Jubilee Commission. Its crown jewel: a re-creation of Columbus's original voyage with replicas of his three ships, the Niña, the Pinta, and the Santa María, making the voyage from Spain to San Salvador island in the Bahamas, with a subsequent tour of the Caribbean islands and various U.S. port cities. Major exhibitions were held at the Smithsonian Institution in Washington; PBS broadcast a seven-part series, "Columbus and the Age of Discovery"; and two major feature films about Columbus were launched, along with an opera by Philip Glass, and numerous smaller exhibitions.

But then, as Garry Wills noted, "a funny thing happened on the way to the quincentennial observation of America's 'discovery.' Columbus got mugged. This time the Indians were waiting for him." Native American activist Russell Means charged that Columbus "makes Hitler look like a juvenile delinquent." Revisionist historians (historians who reinterpret prevailing views of historical events and personages) also attacked the Columbus myth: Hans Koning wrote, "The year 1492 opened an era of genocide, cruelty, and slavery on a larger scale than had ever been seen before." Particularly objectionable to the Columbus critics was the supposition that Columbus had "discovered" a land where people were already living, a land he proceeded to appropriate for the King and Queen of Spain.

To writer Roberto Rodriguez, the Columbus celebrations are "a rewriting of history, an Orwellian attempt to deny the genocide, the theft of land, the destruction of civilizations and the enslavement of the indigenous peoples of the Americas." Native American groups organized their own activities in response to the official quincentenary activities, including a transatlantic voyage by Native Americans for the purpose of "discovering" Spain. In Denver (Colorado was the first state to make Columbus Day a national holiday) the Columbus Day parade was called off at the last moment to avoid a confrontation with more than five hundred supporters of Russell Means's American Indian Movement. The city of Berkeley officially renamed Columbus Day "Indigenous Peoples Day."

The director of the Jubilee Commission backtracked. The quincentenary was not a "celebration," he explained, but a "commemoration." And instead of speaking of Columbus's "discovery," "I refer to it as an 'encounter.'" To staunch defenders of Columbus, however, the revisionist views of their hero smacked of "political correctness" and distorted the historical record. Protested Karl E. Meyer, "Columbus, whatever his faults, was not Adolf Eichmann [the Nazi who devised the 'final solution' for exterminating Jews]. Despite their cruelties, Spanish colonizers were not simply war criminals." Michael Berliner, executive director of the Ayn Rand Institute, claimed, "Columbus should be honored, for in so doing we honor Western civilization. . . . Whatever the problems it brought, the vilified Western culture brought enormous, undreamed-of benefits, without which most of today's Indians would be infinitely poorer or not even alive. . . ."

The debate over Columbus and his legacy goes beyond the immediate issue of how people should respond to the five-hundredth anniversary of Columbus's landing in the Americas. First, it is a signal example of the larger debate over "political correctness." The general issue is whether historical events are to be interpreted according to the values of "dead, white European males"—or, to take a less inflammatory phrase, according to a "Eurocentric" standard (now considered by many as the "incorrect" standard)—or according to a standard by which Europeans and white Americans frequently are seen as oppressors and exploiters, guilty of racism, sexism, destruction of the environment, and, ultimately, genocide. As Garry Wills observed, "If any historical figure can appropriately be loaded up with all the heresies of our time—Eurocentrism, phallocentrism, imperialism, elitism and all-bad-things-generally-ism—Columbus is the man."

The Columbus debate also is significant because Columbus's voyage is a myth as well as a historical event; and the myth is pernicious and harmful if it reinforces in white Americans a racist interpretation of history or attitudes of arrogance and cultural superiority. The myth is particularly harmful if taught to schoolchildren, who accept it as truth, for it thereby is transmitted and perpetuated across generations.

In this chapter we will explore the dimensions of the Columbus debate, to which you will be invited to contribute your own views. We begin with a group of four nineteenth-century testimonials to Columbus by Washington Irving and others, which crystallize the popular, near-idolatrous view of the mariner. This is followed by two brief selections from American history textbooks written in the first half of our own century; these accounts of Columbus's voyages are typical of the way that the "discovery" of America has been taught to children. We follow with "Columbus in the Classroom," an attack on such adulatory accounts, written by Portland high school teacher Bill Bigelow. Next we present selections from two of the main primary sources on Columbus: his log describing his landfall on San Salvador island and a letter describing his discoveries to the treasurer of the King and Queen of Spain. This is followed by "The Destruction of the Indians," an outraged account of the Spanish experience in the Americas by one of the earliest Columbus revisionists, Bartolomé de Las Casas, a soldier-turned-monk and a younger contemporary of Columbus.

Las Casas is followed by a selection of contemporary arguments debating the Columbus legacy. First is the text of the National Council of Churches resolution, followed by a rebuttal by James Muldoon, "Should Christians Celebrate the Columbus Quincentennial?" Next: "What Columbus Discovered," an article by one of the major Columbus critics, Kirkpatrick Sale, followed by "Was America a Mistake?" by a defender of the Columbian legacy, historian Arthur Schlesinger. A Native American response is represented by Suzan Shown Harjo's "I Won't Be Celebrating Columbus Day." Renowned Peruvian novelist Mario Vargas Llosa explains, in "Questions of Conquest," the cultural reasons that the Inca Empire collapsed so rapidly and completely when faced by a mere handful of Spaniards. Finally, Vivian Twostar, the Native American heroine of Louise Erdrich and Michael Dorris's novel, *The Crown of Columbus,* attempts to discuss Columbus and his legacy with her students.

# PROLOGUE: THE VOYAGES OF CHRISTOPHER COLUMBUS

Columbus actually made four voyages to the New World, during which he acted as explorer, colonizer, and "Christ-bearer." Supremely self-confident, he was also arrogant, harsh in his treatment of subordinates, obsessed with his honor and good name, mystical (during his third voyage he became convinced that he had discovered the earthly paradise), and bitter toward those he believed had slighted or betrayed him. Columbus was a fine seaman but an incompetent administrator, a fact responsible for his downfall. He was born in Genoa, Italy, in 1451 (as Cristoforo Colombo), but after first going to sea at the age of fourteen, he never returned to his homeland, adopting the language of Spain and calling himself Cristóbal Colón (he never used the Latinized "Columbus").

Little is known of his early years, but he saw service as a pirate and a soldier during the 1470s, and in the following decade became an accomplished sailor. During this time also he became interested in searching for a westward route to the Indies (i.e., Asia, including China and Japan, as well as India). From 1250 to 1350, European trade with the Indies, facilitated by the Mongol Genghis Khan and by the Venetian Marco Polo, had become immensely profitable; but in 1368 the Chinese conquest of the Mongols closed the eastern trade route to the Indies. Finding a western route—across the Atlantic—became like a search for the holy grail. At that time, however, Portugal was the westernmost point of the known world, and although most educated people knew that the world was round, mariners were reluctant to venture further in exploration. An alternate route to the East appeared possible when the Portuguese captain Bartolomeu Dias rounded the tip of the Cape of Good Hope in southern Africa and from there could have sailed to India had not his terrified sailors forced him to turn back.

Armed with a plan to find a western route (his "Enterprise of the Indies"), Columbus for years attempted to obtain financial backing. He was turned down twice by the King of Portugal, and by two lesser nobles, one of whom, however, referred him to King Ferdinand V and Queen Isabella I of Spain. Columbus first

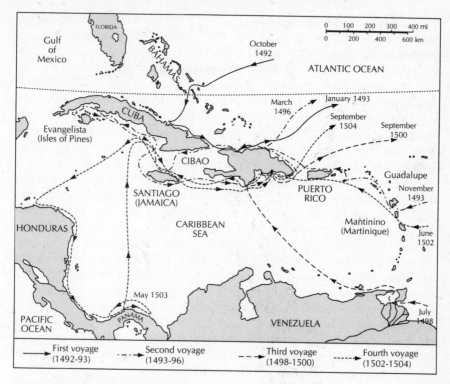

**The voyages of Christopher Columbus**

Map of "The Voyages of Christopher Columbus." Reproduced with permission from *Encyclopaedia Britannica*, 15th Edition, © 1988 by Encyclopaedia Britannica.

submitted his plan to the Spanish monarchs in 1486. They referred it to a commission, which after four years of consideration finally recommended against it. According to popular lore, the commissioners believed that Columbus was mad; in fact, they considered his plan poorly presented. The discouraged mariner soon afterward found an influential partner in shipowner Martín Alonso Pinzón, who shared his enthusiasm and, more important, had connections at court. When Columbus next presented his plan, he asked to be appointed grand admiral and viceroy of all lands he discovered and to be awarded 10 percent of all profits accruing from them. Appalled at his audacity, the monarchs at first turned him away; but on reconsideration, they agreed to all of Columbus's demands. (Isabella, contrary to myth, did not pawn her jewels to finance the venture.) Columbus's expedition, consisting of the famous three caravels—the Niña, the Pinta (commanded by Pinzón), and the Santa María (commanded by Columbus)—sailed from the port of Palos on August 3, 1492—the same day that the Jews were expelled from Spain.

The ships first headed south toward the Canary Islands off Africa, where they took on provisions, and then headed west. The trip was uneventful and the seas were calm; but by early October, the seamen were growing increasingly anxious and threatened to mutiny if they did not turn back. Columbus persuaded them to wait for a few more days, promising that if no land was seen by then, they could "cut off my head and you shall return." Fortunately for Columbus, on October 12 a lookout on the Pinta spotted land (Columbus later took credit for the sighting—and the reward), and that morning the ships landed on an island in the Bahamas that he named San Salvador. (Scholars dispute whether this island—called by the natives Guanahani—is the one now known as Samana Cay or the one known as Watling's Island.)

The natives Columbus and his sailors encountered were members of the Taino tribe. He was impressed with their physical beauty, peacefulness, and friendliness, and he cautioned his men to trade fairly with them. At the same time, he realized their potential as converts to Christianity and as laborers or slaves. Although San Salvador was pleasant enough, Columbus was more concerned to find the source of the gold that the natives wore as ornaments. He also knew that he had not yet reached the Indies, although he was convinced that Japan must be nearby. During the next few weeks, he sailed to other islands, encountering Haiti (which he called Española or Hispaniola) and Cuba (which he became persuaded was Japan). Finally, after the Santa María ran aground off the coast of Haiti on Christmas Day, 1492, Columbus established a colony of thirty-nine men that he called La Navidad (for Christmas), and sailed back to Spain on the Niña, carrying seven captive natives.

On his return, Columbus received a hero's welcome. His account of his journey, the captives he presented to the monarchs, and the samples of spices and minerals created a sensation. Ferdinand and Isabella addressed him as "Don Cristóbal Colón, Admiral of the Ocean Sea, Viceroy and Governor of the Islands that he hath discovered in the Indies." Columbus would never again experience such glory. His biographer Samuel Eliot Morison noted, "It would have been well for him had he then taken his profits and retired with honor, leaving to others the responsibility of colonization." But Columbus called nowhere home but the sea (as one of his critics observes, he was a "rootless man"), and he determined to continue his explorations.

On his second voyage, he traveled with seventeen ships and fifteen hundred crewmen. On landing, he discovered that the colony of La Navidad had been wiped out to the last man. He founded a new colony there, La Isabela (which was to become the first European city in the Americas), and later, another, Santo Tomás. He discovered more islands, including Puerto Rico and Jamaica. But the Indies eluded him. Frustrated, he forced his crewmen to swear, on pain of having their tongues pulled out should they ever recant, that Cuba was in fact the mainland. Meanwhile, Columbus was experiencing numerous difficulties in administering his colonies, both from recalcitrant colonists and increasingly rebellious natives. He put his younger brother Diego in charge of one of the colonies and dealt harshly with disobedience. He also captured sixteen hundred natives and sent five hundred back to Spain as slaves—an act that angered the monarchs, who considered the natives Spanish subjects and who were already displeased with Columbus for failing to return home immediately to give an account of conditions in the islands.

Columbus's final two voyages were even more disastrous than the second one. During his third voyage, he actually did reach the mainland when he landed off the coast of Venezuela, but believing he had found only another island (which he nevertheless thought might be the Garden of Eden), he soon set sail for what he thought was the mainland, Cuba. Conditions grew so bad on the colonies that Ferdinand and Isabella eventually sent a new administrator, Francisco de Bobadilla. After arriving in Santo Domingo in Española, Bobadilla made his own investigations and, following some heated jurisdictional disputes, had Columbus and his two brothers put in chains and sent back to Spain.

Shocked at this harsh treatment, the monarchs resolved to treat the aging mariner generously, but realized also that Columbus was unfit to govern the islands he had discovered. He was allowed to undertake a fourth voyage (this time with only four small ships) but was barred from landing at Española. (He was, in fact, refused admittance to the port of Santo Domingo by the new governor, Nicolás de Ovando.) Following a series of near mutinies and storms, Columbus's ship was grounded off the shore of Jamaica, where he was marooned for almost a year. Finally, in 1504, he was rescued by two of Ovando's caravels. After a brief stop in Española, he left the New World for the last time and returned to Spain a sick man. Shortly afterward, Queen Isabella died. Columbus petitioned the King to return his grants and titles, but Ferdinand, although sympathetic and willing to make some financial provisions for the old sailor, was unwilling to reappoint him as admiral or governor of the Indies. Humiliated, embittered, and crippled by arthritis, Columbus died in 1506 at the age of fifty-five. He was buried at the monastery of Santa María de las Cuevas in Seville. In 1542, his body was exhumed, transported to Española, and reburied in the cathedral of Santo Domingo.

# A Man of Great and Inventive Genius

## WASHINGTON IRVING AND OTHERS

*As his biographers take pains to emphasize, the renowned "Admiral of the Ocean Sea" died a forgotten and embittered man. Decades later, his reputation recovered; but Columbus's elevation to demigod did not begin until the early days of the American republic. Following the War of 1812 against England, Americans needed a hero of non-British descent to rouse patriotic spirit among European-Americans. Columbus, who was of Italian descent and sailed under a Spanish flag, filled the bill admirably. As Paul Gray noted, "Thus did the heyday of Columbus idolatry begin—in an early attempt to provide the nation with the icons of multicultural diversity." An early example of this idolatry was Washington Irving's biography* A History of the Life and Voyages of Christopher Columbus *(1828). Washington Irving (1783–1859) was an American author—and later in his life a diplomat, serving in Madrid—perhaps best known for his stories "Rip Van Winkle" and "The Legend of Sleepy Hollow." He also wrote a history of New York and a biography of George Washington.*

*Irving's biography of Columbus—idolatrous though it may seem to modern readers—is almost restrained in comparison to some of the century's later writings about the Admiral. The panegyrics of Alphonse de Lamartine, Chauncey M. Depew, and Henry William Elson are typical of the hyperbole used to characterize Columbus from the early nineteenth to the mid-twentieth century, particularly in speeches and textbooks. Alphonse de Lamartine (1790–1869) was a French poet, orator, and political leader (he once ran for the presidency of France), and was considered a leading figure of the French Romantic movement. Chauncey Depew (1834–1928) was an American lawyer, railroad executive, and politician, best known as an orator and after-dinner speaker. Henry William Elson authored the 1916 textbook* History of the United States of America.

## The Character of Columbus

### WASHINGTON IRVING

Columbus was a man of great and inventive genius. The operations of his mind were energetic, but irregular, bursting forth at times with that irresistible force which characterizes intellects of such an order. His ambition was lofty and noble, inspiring him with high thoughts, and an anxiety to distinguish himself by great achievements. He aimed at dignity and wealth in the same elevated spirit with which he sought renown; they were to rise from the territories he should discover, and be commensurate in importance. The vast gains that he anticipated from his discoveries he intended to appropriate to princely purposes; to institutions for the relief of the poor of his native city, to the foundation of churches, and above all to crusades for the recovery of the Holy Sepulchre.

He was tenacious of his rank and privileges, not from a mere vulgar love of titles, but because he prized them as testimonials and trophies of his illustrious deeds. Every question of compromise concerning them he repulsed with disdain. "These things," said he, nobly, "concern my honor." In his testament he enjoined on his son Diego, and whomsoever after him should inherit his estates, whatever other titles might be granted by the king, always to sign himself simply "The Admiral," by way of perpetuating in the family the source of its greatness.

His conduct was characterized by the grandeur of his views and the 3 magnanimity of his spirit. Instead of ravaging the newly found countries, like many of his contemporary discoverers, who were intent only on immediate gain, he regarded them with the eyes of a legislator; he sought to colonize and cultivate them, to civilize the natives, to subject everything to the control of law, order, and religion, and thus to found regular and prosperous empires. That he failed in this was the fault of the dissolute rabble which it was his misfortune to command, with whom all law was tyranny and all order oppression.

He was naturally irritable and impetuous, and keenly sensible to 4 injury and injustice; yet the quickness of his temper was counteracted by the benevolence and generosity of his heart. The magnanimity of his nature shone forth through all the troubles of his stormy career. Though continually outraged in his dignity, braved in his authority, foiled in his plans, and endangered in his person by the seditions of turbulent and worthless men, and that, too, at times when suffering under anguish of body and anxiety of mind enough to exasperate the most patient, yet he restrained his valiant and indignant spirit, and brought himself to forbear and reason, and even to supplicate. Nor should we fail to notice how free he was from all feeling of revenge, how ready to forgive and forget on the least signs of repentance and atonement. He has been extolled for his skill in controlling others, but far greater praise is due to him for the firmness he displayed in governing himself.

His piety was genuine and fervent; religion mingled with the whole 5 course of his thoughts and actions, and shone forth in his most private and unstudied writings. Whenever he made any great discovery, he devoutly returned thanks to God. The voice of prayer and the melody of praise rose from his ships on discovering the New World, and his first action on landing was to prostrate himself upon the earth, and offer up thanksgivings. Every evening, the *Salve Regina* and other vesper hymns were chanted by his crew, and masses were performed in the beautiful groves that bordered the wild shores of this heathen land. All his great enterprises were undertaken in the name of the Holy Trinity, and he partook of the Holy Sacrament previous to embarkation. He observed the festivals of the Church in the wildest situations. The Sabbath was to him a day of sacred rest, on which he would never sail from a port unless in case of extreme necessity. The religion thus deeply seated in his soul diffused a sober dignity and a benign composure over his whole deportment; his very language was pure and guarded, and free from all gross or irreverent expressions.

It cannot be denied, however, that his piety was mingled with 6 superstition and darkened by the bigotry of the age. He evidently concurred in the opinion that all the nations who did not acknowledge the Christian faith were destitute of natural rights; and that the sternest

measures might be used for their conversion, and the severest punish-
ments inflicted upon them, if obstinate in unbelief. In this spirit of
bigotry he considered himself justified in making captives of the Indians
and transporting them to Spain, to have them taught the doctrines of
Christianity, and in selling them for slaves if they pretended to resist his
invasions. In doing the latter he sinned against the natural goodness of
his heart, and against the feelings he had originally entertained and
expressed toward this gentle and hospitable people; but he was goaded
on by the mercenary impatience of the crown, and by the sneers of his
enemies at the unprofitable result of his enterprises. It is but justice to
his character to observe that the enslavement of the Indians thus taken
in battle was at first openly countenanced by the crown, and that, when
the question of right came to be discussed at the request of the queen,
several of the most distinguished jurists and theologians advocated the
practice; so that the question was finally settled in favor of the Indians
solely by the humanity of Isabella. As the venerable Bishop Las Casas
observes, where the most learned men have doubted, it is not surprising
that an unlearned mariner should err.

These remarks, in palliation of the conduct of Columbus, are re-    7
quired by candor. It is proper to show him in connection with the age
in which he lived, lest the errors of the times should be considered his
individual faults. It is not intended, however to justify him on a point
where it is inexcusable to err. Let it remain a blot on his illustrious name,
and let others derive a lesson from it.


## The Characteristics of Greatness in Columbus

ALPHONSE DE LAMARTINE

All the characteristics of a truly great man are united in Columbus.    8
Genius, patience, obscurity of origin, overcome by energy of will; mild
but persisting firmness, resignation toward heaven, struggle against the
world; long conception of the idea in solitude, heroic execution of it in
action; intrepidity and coolness in storms, fearlessness of death in civil
strife, confidence in the destiny—not of an individual, but of the human
race; a life risked without hesitation or retrospect in venturing into the
unknown and phantom-peopled ocean, 1,500 leagues across, and on
which the first step no more allowed of second thoughts than Caesar's
passage of the Rubicon; untiring study, knowledge as extensive as the
science of his day, skillful but honorable management of courts to
persuade them to truth; propriety of demeanor, nobleness, and dignity

in outward bearing, which afford proof of greatness of mind and attract eyes and hearts; language adapted to the grandeur of his thoughts; eloquence which could convince kings and quell the mutiny of crews; a natural poetry of style, which placed his narrative on a par with the wonders of his discoveries and the marvels of nature; an immense, ardent, and enduring love for the human race, piercing even into that distant future in which humanity forgets those that do it service; legislative wisdom and philosophic mildness in the government of his colonies; paternal compassion for those Indians, infants of humanity, whom he wished to give over to the guardianship—not to the tyranny and oppression—of the Old World; forgetfulness of injury and magnanimous forgiveness of his enemies; and lastly, piety, that virtue which includes and exalts all other virtues, when it exists as it did in the mind of Columbus—the constant presence of God in the soul, of justice in the conscience, of mercy in the heart, of gratitude in success, of resignation in reverses, of worship always and everywhere.

Such was the man. He contains several impersonations within himself. He was worthy to represent the ancient world before that unknown continent on which he was the first to set foot, and carry to these men of a new race all the virtues, without any of the vices, of the elder hemisphere. So great was his influence on the destiny of the earth, that none more than he ever deserved the name of a civilizer.   **9**

His influence in civilization was immeasurable. He completed the   **10** world. He realized the physical unity of the globe. He advanced, far beyond all that had been done before his time, the work of God—the spiritual unity of the human race. This work, in which Columbus had so largely assisted, was indeed too great to be worthily rewarded even by affixing his name to the fourth continent. America bears not that name, but the human race, drawn together and cemented by him, will spread his renown over the whole earth.

# Dreamer, Discoverer, Hero

## CHAUNCEY M. DEPEW

(From an oration delivered at the opening of the World's Fair, Chicago, October, 1892, the four hundredth anniversary of the discovery of America.)

Neither realism nor romance furnishes a more striking and picturesque   **11** figure than that of Christopher Columbus. The mystery about his origin heightens the charm of his story. That he came from among the toilers of his time is in harmony with the struggles of our period. The perils of the sea in his youth upon the rich argosies of Genoa, or in the service of the licensed rovers who made them their prey, had developed a skillful navigator and intrepid mariner. To secure the means to test the truth of his speculations this poor and unknown dreamer must win the support of kings and overcome the hostility of the Church. He never doubted his ability to do both. His unshakable faith that Christopher Columbus was commissioned from Heaven, both by his name and by divine command to carry "Christ across the sea" to new continents and pagan peoples, lifted him so far above the discouragements of an empty purse and a contemptuous court that he was proof against the rebuffs of fortune or of friends. To conquer the prejudices of the clergy, to win the approval and financial support of the State, to venture upon that unknown ocean which, according to the beliefs of the age, was peopled with demons and savage beasts of frightful shape, and from which there was no possibility of return, required the zeal of Peter the Hermit, the chivalric courage of the Cid, and the imagination of Dante . . .

All hail, Columbus, discoverer, dreamer, hero, and apostle! We 12 . . . recognize the horizon which bounded his vision and the infinite scope of his genius. The voice of gratitude and praise for all the blessings which have been showered upon mankind by adventure is limited to no language, but is uttered in every tongue. Neither marble nor brass can fitly form his statue. Continents are his monument, and unnumbered millions, past, present, and to come, who enjoy in their liberties and their happiness the fruits of his faith, will reverently guard and preserve, from century to century, his name and fame.

## A Commanding Genius

### HENRY WILLIAM ELSON

In the world of history we find here and there the name of some 13 commanding genius that stands out as a landmark, and shines with a luster that time has no power to dim. Such is the name of Christopher Columbus.

It will hardly be disputed, that among rulers and statesmen of all 14 time Julius Caesar must be placed at the head; that among military leaders the greatest the world has yet known was Napoleon Bonaparte;

and that in the still higher domain of literature William Shakespeare holds the foremost place. And it is no less true that the name of Columbus stands at the head of the list of navigators and discoverers. . . .

Columbus did a great work for mankind, and the world has rightly 15
chosen to give his name the highest place among the great names of that age of discovery. His greatness consisted, not in his conception of a new thought, for the thought was old, nor in doing for the world a work that no other could have done, but in his willingness to undertake to demonstrate the truth of his theory. He dared to do where others only talked and theorized. In this he stood far above every other man of his times. "He linked forever the two worlds." It is true he achieved more than he intended; but his intentions were great also, and he deserves the highest credit for carrying his vast plan into execution.

## Review Questions

1. Why was Columbus so concerned with wealth and rank, according to Irving?
2. How does Irving account for Columbus's failure as an administrator?
3. What does Irving consider the chief stain on Columbus's character?

## Discussion and Writing Suggestions

1. Irving praises Columbus for his virtues and condemns him for his faults, thus attempting to paint what he no doubt considers a balanced portrait of Columbus. To what extent do you think Irving has succeeded? Had you read Irving's account in a contemporary history text, would you consider it a fair portrait of Columbus? Why or why not? What particular statements might you question?
2. Based on your responses to the first question, what can you infer about the different standards by which early-nineteenth-century and late-twentieth-century Americans judged important figures like Columbus?
3. To what extent do you think that Lamartine, Depew, and Elson sincerely believed that the historical Christopher Columbus was accurately described in their fervent accolades? If you think they knew that there was a touch of exaggeration in their rhetorical portraits of the Admiral, what might be the motives of such romanticizing? By the same token, why not even hint (as Irving does) at any negative qualities of Columbus? What are the benefits and the dangers (for readers) of authors writing in such a manner about famous people of the past?
4. Using a model of an actual person (one you know personally or one you have

read about or seen on TV or in the movies), write a heroic portrait in the manner of Irving, Lamartine, Depew, and Elson writing of Columbus.

# Columbus and the Discovery of America: The Textbook Version

## WILLIAM M. DAVIDSON, HENRY NOBLE SHERWOOD

*The following selections are representative of the manner in which Columbus was treated in history textbooks in the early part of the twentieth century. Note particularly the language in which Columbus and his enterprise are described, as well as the language in which the native populations are described. The first selection is from William M. Davidson's* The History of the United States *(1902), a high school text. The second is from Henry Noble Sherwood's* Our Country's Beginnings *(1924), a grade school text.*

# Columbus and the Discovery of America

## WILLIAM M. DAVIDSON

### CHRISTOPHER COLUMBUS

In the affairs of men and of nations, it has usually happened, that when an emergency has arisen, the man has been found ready for the hour. At this time there appeared upon the scene the son of a Genoese wool-comber. The father had done valiant service for the king of Portugal as one of his able navigators. On his death he had bequeathed his charts and maps to his son who had inherited his passion for the sea. Christopher Columbus was the most conspicuous navigator of his age, and is clearly entitled to the distinction, The Great Navigator. He combined the learning of the scholar with a practical knowledge of the sea. This tall seaman of "grave and gentle manner, though noble and saddened look," was indeed an enthusiast of the most pronounced type, in whom the "passion for discovery rose to the dignity of an inspiration." For eighteen long, weary years he importuned monarchs and merchants,

From "Columbus Discovers America" in William Davidson, *History of the United States*, Scott, Foresman, 1902.

courts and bankers, for ships and men, that he might set out upon the western route to Asia. He sent his brother, Bartholomew, to England, but King Henry VII. gave a deaf ear to his appeal. France likewise lost her opportunity. King John II. of Portugal was encouraging his own seamen to make India by way of the Cape of Good Hope; he, therefore, could not be interested. The Italian merchants and bankers could not be induced to invest in the enterprise without its first having received the support of some powerful monarch.

Spain at this time was approaching the zenith of her power and was ready for new fields of conquest; still, she refused Columbus assistance. Discouraged, he was,

> The fountain of his spirit's prophecy
> Sinking away and wasting, drop by drop.
> In the ungrateful sands of skeptic ears.
> —*Lowell's "Columbus"*

But he was a man who knew no such word as fail. His whole life had been one of hardship. At the age of thirty his hair was white, made so by the suffering and hardships which he had endured. At last success crowned his efforts, and the jewels of the queen of Spain became security for the successful prosecution of his proposed enterprise. Thus, to Ferdinand and Isabella, king and queen of Castile, fell the honor of having first given encouragement and substantial aid to the discoverer of the New World.

## FIRST VOYAGE OF COLUMBUS

The three historic caravels with musical names were furnished him by Spain, but his task was still a difficult one. It was not easy to secure crews for these ships when the nature of the voyage became known. Only the boldest sea captains ventured out of sight of land. The vast majority of sailors in those days were timid, very ignorant, and superstitious. Noticing that a ship seemed to be sailing "down hill" as it went out into the ocean, they reasoned that should it go too far, it could never sail "up hill" on its return. Notwithstanding the long use of the mariner's compass, still by the ordinary ship's crew it was looked upon with superstitious awe.

By dint of much persuasion, promises of great reward and finally, by the use of force, crews were at last secured. They set sail amidst great rejoicing from Palos, Spain, on the third of August, 1492. First sailing south to the Canary Islands, they boldly took a westerly course . . .

## DISCOVERY OF THE NEW WORLD

At sunset on the evening of October 11, 1492, three Spanish caravels 5
were ploughing the waves of an unknown sea at a rapid rate. On board
all was expectancy and watchfulness, made so by the indomitable will
and the undiminished enthusiasm of the great navigator, who, ten weeks
before, had set sail from Palos, Spain, in search of a western passage to
the Golden Indies of the east. In spite of pleadings to return home, in
spite of mutiny and continuous discontent, in spite of threats to cast him
into the sea, he kept on his western course,—by his forbearance subdu-
ing his men, and by his courage and his hopefulness winning them to
his purpose and his plans. On that memorable night not an eye was
closed in sleep. It had been announced by the heroic admiral that he
thought it probable they would make land ere the morning. The greatest
animation prevailed throughout the fleet—the Pinta taking the lead, the
Santa Maria following, and the Nina in the rear.

To the admiral the moment was indeed a critical one. Should his 6
prediction fail him now, his last hope of controlling the turbulent crews
would be gone forever. Already the dusk of evening had settled upon
the sea when he took his station on top of the castle of the Santa Maria
and with eager eye scanned the western horizon. At ten o'clock at night
there burst upon his vision a gleam of light as if it were a torch in a
fisherman's canoe, dancing on the waves, or from a signal light in the
hands of some human being rushing from place to place upon the shore.
The first to behold that light, he alone of all on board attached any
importance to its transient gleams until, at two o'clock on the morning
of October 12, 1492, a gun from the Pinta was followed by the joyful
shout of "Land! Land!"—and Christopher Columbus became the discoverer of the western continent, and gave a new world to Castile and Leon,
"the like of which was never done by any man in ancient or in later
times."

When, on the morning of the discovery, Columbus landed on one 7
of the islands now known as the Bahamas, and, calling it San Salvador,
took possession in the name of Spain, the event marked the beginning
of a new era in the world's history.

From thence he sailed south to the coast of Cuba and Santo 8
Domingo, taking possession of those islands in the name of the king and
queen of Spain, Ferdinand and Isabella. Having lost his flagship, the
Santa Maria, in a storm, he sailed for home, taking with him several
natives, whom he called Indians, because he thought the island a part of
the East Indies. He also brought back with him many curiosities from
these new lands. His return to Spain was hailed with joy by the king and
queen, who bestowed great honors upon him.

## EFFECTS OF THE DISCOVERY

Perhaps no single event in history surpasses in importance this first 9
voyage of Columbus. It is true he did not discover the mainland of
North America, but he opened up the way, thereby making its discovery
an easy matter.

The return of Columbus set the world on fire. The printing press in 10
every city of Europe spread the news broadcast throughout the continent. "The revelation of the amazing fact that there were lands beyond
the great ocean, inhabited by strange races of human beings, roused to
passionate eagerness the thirst for fresh discoveries."

Three powerful motives urge man to action—the desire for 11
wealth, the desire for power, and the desire to spread his peculiar
religious tenets. These caused the voyage of Columbus, the success of
which threw open a vast field for the exploitation of each. The business world, the governing class, the church, responded with alacrity to
the call, and the sea of darkness was soon ablaze with the sail of the
adventurer and the explorer, to be followed later by the white sails of
commerce.

## LATER VOYAGES OF COLUMBUS

Columbus made three other voyages to the New World. In the au- 12
tumn of 1494 with a large expedition he set sail on his second voyage
for the purpose of taking possession of the new-found islands. He
explored the southern coast of Cuba; founded a colony on Santo
Domingo; and discovered the islands of Jamaica and Porto Rico. He
returned to Spain in 1496 to solicit reënforcements, provisions, and
funds.

On his third voyage, in 1498, he touched upon the continent of 13
South America, having reached the mainland at the mouth of the
Orinoco River. Notwithstanding that he believed the Orinoco to be a
continental river, he still held to the view that he was upon the eastern
coast of Asia. Proceeding thence to the colony which he had founded
in Santo Domingo he found he had been superseded in command by a
new governor who preferred charges of cruelty against Columbus and
sent him in chains to Spain. On his arrival there the charges against him
were investigated and he was released at once.

On his fourth and last voyage, made in 1502–1504, he explored the 14
coast of Central America, while still in quest of a "waterway to the far
east." No man ever held more tenaciously to an idea than did Columbus
to his belief in the direct western passage. Though he heard rumors of

an ocean lying beyond Central America, he still persisted that it must be the Indian Ocean.

He returned to Spain, and, it is said, died in poverty and distress in    15
1506, neglected by his king and his fellow-countrymen.


# Columbus and the Indians

### HENRY NOBLE SHERWOOD

When they landed Columbus, dressed in embroidered silk and scarlet    16
velvet, carried the royal flag of Spain in his hands. The captains of the
other two ships each had a white banner with a green cross on it. On
one side of the cross was the letter F; on the other side the letter I. Those
letters stood for the names of the king and queen of Spain. Over each
letter was the royal crown of each ruler. Before all the sailors Columbus
knelt down, kissed the soil and offered prayer. Then he declared that he
took the land for Spain. It was an island. Columbus named it San
Salvador, which means Holy Savior.

Neither Columbus nor his sailors had ever seen people like the    17
ones they found on this island. They were naked, and had paint
smeared on their faces. They had coarse, black, straight hair, and their
skins were the color of copper. Columbus, thinking that he had really
reached the Indies, called them Indians, by which name they have
been known ever since. The Indians thought Columbus and his men
had come down from Heaven. They did two things that seemed very
strange to Columbus and his men. They drew smoke into their
mouths from a hollow stick filled with dried leaves which were now
burning. They were smoking a plant which they called tobacco. It was
new to Columbus. He also saw them eating a new food. It was what
we call the potato. After his voyage the white people began to smoke
tobacco and eat potatoes.

When Columbus and the sailors went back to their ships, the Indians    18
followed. Some of them swam in the water; others went in boats which
they had hollowed out of logs. They wanted to trade their parrots,
cotton yarn and wooden spears for beads and little bells. The Indians
had very little gold.

Columbus and his companions visited the islands of Cuba and Hayti    19 before returning to Spain. For three months they searched for some indications that they had reached the spice lands. Once they thought they had found the palace of the Great Khan. Four men were chosen to journey into the jungle and carry greetings to this ruler of the East. Instead of a palace of marble and gold they found a cluster of rude huts. The naked savages greeted them kindly, kissed their hands and feet, and tried to follow them when they went away. Over five hundred wanted to go; they thought they would reach Heaven in this way. Three were allowed to accompany the four whites and when they reached the admiral's flagship he entertained them with great honor.

Wherever Columbus stopped on the islands he set up a wooden    20
cross "as a sign of Spanish dominion and in honor of the Christian faith."

It was difficult to carry on conversation with the Indians. Columbus    21
thought they told him about one island on which people with one eye lived; of another where the men had heads like dogs. These Indians cut off the heads of human beings and drank their blood. He learned of a third island whose people had no hair, and a fourth where they had long tails.

## Review Questions

1. What major areas of the New World did Columbus actually "discover" during his four voyages?
2. How are the Indians characterized in Sherwood's account?

## Discussion and Writing Suggestions

1. Textbooks serve the purpose not only of teaching schoolchildren the basic facts of history (i.e., those facts determined to be significant by the authors and by school and civic officials), but also of inculcating moral lessons, particularly about the heroes of American history. What lessons do you infer that schoolchildren were to draw from Davidson's and Sherwood's portraits of Columbus? Cite specific passages in your discussion.
2. Read a brief contemporary account of this portion of Columbus's life, perhaps in a college textbook or an encyclopedia, and compare it with the accounts by Davidson and Sherwood. In a short paper, discuss the differences you notice in (a) information covered, (b) characterization and other value judgments, (c) language, and (d) tone. In what ways might contemporary educators, historians, and students object to these earlier accounts of Columbus and his voyages?
3. How might the account by Sherwood and others of Columbus's encounter with the Indians have affected the attitudes of generations of students toward both European civilization and the culture and character of Native Americans?

4. Davidson writes, "Three powerful motives urge man to action—the desire for wealth, the desire for power, and the desire to spread his peculiar religious tenets." To what extent do you consider this a valid statement? Why?

# Columbus in the Classroom

## BILL BIGELOW

*In the following selection, Bill Bigelow, a history teacher at Jefferson High School in Portland, Oregon, reacts to and explains how he deals in his own classroom with the kind of uncritical treatments of American history typified in the previous examples. Bigelow has developed curricula on South Africa and on the history of work and workers in the United States. This essay originally appeared as the final chapter of Hans Koning's book* Columbus: His Enterprise: Exploding the Myth *(1976, 1991).*

Most of my students have trouble with the idea that a book—especially a *textbook*—can lie. When I tell them that I want them to argue with, not just read, the printed word they're not sure what I mean. That's why I start my U.S. history class by stealing a student's purse.

As the year opens, my students may not know when the Civil War was fought, what James Madison or Frederick Douglass did, or where the Underground Railroad went, but they do know that a brave fellow named Christopher Columbus discovered America. Okay, the Vikings may have actually *discovered* America, but students know it was Columbus who mapped it and *did* something with the place. Indeed, this bit of historical lore may be the only knowledge class members share in common.

What students don't know is that year after year their textbooks have, by omission or otherwise, been lying to them on a grand scale. Some students learned that Columbus sailed on three ships and that his sailors worried whether they would ever see land again. Others know from readings and teachers that when the Admiral landed he was greeted by naked, reddish skinned people whom he called Indians. And still others may know Columbus gave these people little trinkets and returned to Spain with a few of the Indians to show King Ferdinand and Queen Isabella.

All this is true. What is also true is that Columbus took hundreds

"Columbus in the Classroom" by Bill Bigelow from *Columbus: His Enterprise: Exploding the Myth* by Hans Koning. Copyright © 1991 by Bill Bigelow. Reprinted by permission of Monthly Review Foundation.

of Indians slaves and sent them back to Spain, where most of them were sold and subsequently died. What is also true is that in his quest for gold Columbus had the hands cut off any Indian who did not return with his or her three month quota. And what is also true is that on one island alone, Hispaniola, an entire race of people was wiped off the face of the earth in a mere forty years of Spanish administration.

So I begin by stealing a student's purse. I announce to the class that the purse is mine. Obviously, because look who has it. Most students are fair-minded. They saw me take the purse off the desk, so they protest: "That's not yours, it's Nikki's. You took it, we saw you." I brush these objections aside and reiterate that it is mine, and to prove it I'll show them all the things I have inside.                                                                          5

I unzip the bag and remove a brush or a comb, maybe a pair of dark glasses. A tube, or whatever it's called, of lipstick works best: "This is my lipstick," I say. "There, that proves it *is* my purse." They don't buy it and, in fact, are mildly outraged that I would pry into someone's possessions with such utter disregard for her privacy. (I've alerted the student to the demonstration before class, but no one else knows that.)                                                                          6

It's time to move on: "Okay, if it's Nikki's purse, how do you know? Why are you all so positive it's not my purse?" Different answers: We saw you take it; that's her lipstick, we know you don't wear lipstick; there is stuff in there with her name on it. To get the point across, I even offer to help in their effort to prove Nikki's possession: "If we had a test on the contents of the purse, who would do better, Nikki or me?" "Whose labor earned the money that bought the things in the purse, mine or Nikki's?" Obvious questions, obvious answers.                                                                          7

I make one last try to keep Nikki's purse: "What if I said I *discovered* this purse, then would it be mine?" A little laughter is my reward, but I don't get any takers; they still think the purse is rightfully Nikki's.                                                                          8

"So," I ask, "why do we say that Columbus discovered America?" Now they begin to see what I've been leading up to. I ask a series of rhetorical questions which implicitly make the link between Nikki's purse and the Indians' land: Were there people on the land before Columbus arrived? Who had been on the land longer, Columbus or the Indians? Who knew the land better? Who had put their labor into making the land produce? The students see where I'm going—it would be hard not to. "And yet," I continue, "what is the first thing that Columbus did when he arrived in the New World?" Right: he took possession of it. After all, he had discovered the place.                                                                          9

We talk about phrases other than "discovery" that textbooks could use to describe what Columbus did. Students start with the phrases they used to describe what I did to Nikki's purse: he stole it; he took it; he ripped it off. And others: he invaded it; he conquered it.                                                                          10

I want students to see that the word "discovery" is loaded. The                          11 word carries with it a perspective, a bias; it takes sides. "Discovery" is the phrase of the supposed discoverers. It's the conquerors, the invaders, masking their theft. And when the word gets repeated in textbooks those textbooks become, in the phrase of one historian, "the propaganda of the winners."

To prepare students to examine critically the textbooks of their past, 12 we begin with some alternative, and rather unsentimental, explorations of Columbus' "enterprise," as he called it. The Admiral-to-be was not sailing for mere adventure and to prove the world was round, as my fourth grade teacher had informed her class, but to secure the tremendous profits that were to be made by reaching the Indies. From the beginning, Columbus' quest was wealth, both for Spain and for himself personally. He demanded a 10 percent cut of everything shipped to Spain via the western route—and not just for himself but for all his heirs in perpetuity. And he insisted he be pronounced governor of any new lands he found, a title that carried with it dictatorial powers.

Mostly I want the class to think about the human beings Columbus 13 was to "discover"—and then destroy. I read from a letter Columbus wrote, dated March 14, 1493, following his return from the first voyage. He reports being enormously impressed by the indigenous people:

> As soon . . . as they see that they are safe and have laid aside all fear, they are very simple and honest and exceedingly liberal with all they have; none of them refusing anything he may possess when he is asked for it, but, on the contrary, inviting us to ask them. They exhibit great love toward all others in preference to themselves. They also give objects of great value for trifles, and content themselves with very little or nothing in return. . . . I did not find, as some of us had expected, any cannibals among them, but, on the contrary, men of great deference and kindness.[1]

But, on an ominous note, Columbus writes in his log, ". . . should 14 your Majesties command it, all the inhabitants could be taken away to Castile [Spain], or made slaves on the island. With fifty men we could subjugate them all and make them do whatever we want."[2]

---

[1] *The Annals of America, Volume 1: 1493–1754, Discovering a New World* (Chicago: Encyclopaedia Britannica, 1968), pp. 2, 4.

[2] Quoted in Hans Koning, *Columbus: His Enterprise*, p. 53. As Koning points out, none of the information included in his book is new. It is available in Columbus's own journals and letters and the writings of the Spanish priest Bartolomé de Las Casas. Even Columbus' adoring biographers admit the Admiral's outrages. For example, Pulitzer Prize winner Samuel Eliot Morison acknowledges that Columbus unleashed savage dogs on Indians, kidnapped Indian leaders, and encouraged his sailors to rape Indian women. At one point Morison writes, "The cruel policy initiated by Columbus and pursued by his successors resulted in complete genocide." See Samuel Eliot

I ask students if they remember from elementary school days what 15 it was Columbus brought back with him from his travels in the New World. Together students recall that he brought back parrots, plants, some gold, and a few of the people Columbus had taken to calling "Indians." This was Columbus' first expedition and it is also where most school textbook accounts of Columbus end—conveniently. Because the enterprise of Columbus was not to bring back exotic knickknacks, but riches, preferably gold. What about his second voyage?

I read to them a passage from this fine book, Hans Koning's 16 *Columbus: His Enterprise:*

> We are now in February 1495. Time was short for sending back a good "dividend" on the supply ships getting ready for the return to Spain. Columbus therefore turned to a massive slave raid as a means for filling up these ships. The brothers [Columbus and his brothers, Bartolomé and Diego] rounded up fifteen hundred Arawaks—men, women, and children—and imprisoned them in pens in Isabela, guarded by men and dogs. The ships had room for no more than five hundred, and thus only the best specimens were loaded aboard. The Admiral then told the Spaniards they could help themselves from the remainder to as many slaves as they wanted. Those whom no one chose were simply kicked out of their pens. Such had been the terror of these prisoners that (in the description by Michele de Cuneo, one of the colonists) "they rushed in all directions like lunatics, women dropping and abandoning infants in the rush, running for miles without stopping, fleeing across mountains and rivers."
>
> Of the five hundred slaves, three hundred arrived alive in Spain, where they were put up for sale in Seville by Don Juan de Fonseca, the archdeacon of the town. "As naked as the day they were born," the report of this excellent churchman says, *"but with no more embarrassment than animals . . ."*
>
> The slave trade immediately turned out to be "unprofitable, for the slaves mostly died." Columbus decided to concentrate on gold, although he writes, "Let us *in the name of the Holy Trinity* go on sending all the slaves that can be sold.[3]

Certainly Columbus' fame should not be limited to the discov- 17 ery of America: he also deserves credit for initiating the trans-Atlantic slave trade, albeit in the opposite direction than we're used to thinking of it.

Students and I role-play a scene from Columbus' second voyage. 18 Slavery is not producing the profits Columbus is seeking. He still believes there is gold in them thar hills and the Indians are selfishly holding

---

Morison, *Christopher Columbus, Mariner* (New York: New American Library, 1942), p. 99. But the sharpness of this judgment is buried in Morison's syrupy admiration for Columbus' courage and navigational skills.
[3]Koning, *Columbus,* p. 83; emphasis in original.

out on him. Students play Columbus; I play the Indians: "Chris, we don't have any gold, honest. Can we go back to living our lives now and you can go back to wherever you came from?" I call on several students to respond to the Indians' plea. Columbus thinks the Indians are lying. How can he get his gold? Student responses range from sympathetic to ruthless: Okay, we'll go home; *please* bring us your gold; we'll lock you up in prison if you don't bring us your gold; we'll torture you if you don't fork it over, etc. After I've pleaded for awhile and the students-as-Columbus have threatened, I read aloud another passage from Koning's book describing the system Columbus arrived at for extracting gold from the Indians:

> Every man and woman, every boy or girl of fourteen or older, in the province of Cibao (of the imaginary gold fields) had to collect gold for the Spaniards. As their measure, the Spaniards used . . . hawks' bells. . . . Every three months, every Indian had to bring to one of the forts a hawks' bell filled with gold dust. The chiefs had to bring in about ten times that amount. In the other provinces of Hispaniola, twenty-five pounds of spun cotton took the place of gold.
>
> Copper tokens were manufactured, and when an Indian had brought his or her tribute to an armed post, he or she received such a token, stamped with the month, to be hung around the neck. With that they were safe for another three months while collecting more gold.
>
> Whoever was caught without a token was killed by having his or her hands cut off. There are old Spanish prints . . . that show this being done: the Indians stumble away, staring *with surprise* at their arm stumps pulsing out blood.
>
> There were no gold fields, and thus, once the Indians had handed in whatever they still had in gold ornaments, their only hope was to work all day in the streams, washing out gold dust from the pebbles. It was an impossible task, but those Indians who tried to flee into the mountains were systematically hunted down with dogs and killed, to set an example for the others to keep trying. . . .
>
> Thus it was at this time that the mass suicides began: the Arawaks killed themselves with cassava poison.
>
> During those two years of the administration of the brothers Columbus, an estimated one half of the entire population of Hispaniola was killed or killed themselves. The estimates run from 125,000 to one-half million.[4]

It's important that students not be shielded from the horror of what "discovery" meant to its victims. The fuller they understand the consequences of Columbus' invasion of America, the better they'll be equipped to critically reexamine the innocent stories their textbooks have offered through the years. The goal is not to titillate or stun, but to force the question: Why wasn't I told this before?

Students' assignment is to find a textbook, preferably one they used

---

[4]Ibid., pp. 83–84.

in elementary school (but any textbook will suffice) and write a critique of the book's treatment of Columbus and the Indians. I distribute the following handout to students and review the questions aloud. I don't want them to merely answer the questions one by one, but to consider them as guidelines in completing their critiques:

—How factually accurate was the account?

—What was omitted—left out—that in your judgment would be important for a full understanding of Columbus? (For example, his treatment of the Indians; slave trading; his method of getting gold; the overall effect on the Indians.)

—What motives does the book give to Columbus? Compare those with his real motives.

—Who does the book get you to root for, and how do they accomplish that? (For example, is the book horrified at the treatment of Indians or thrilled that Columbus makes it to the New World?)

—What function do pictures play in the book? What do they communicate about Columbus and his "enterprise"?

—In your opinion, *why* does the book portray the Columbus/Indian encounter the way it does?

—Can you think of any groups in our society that might have an interest in people having an inaccurate view of history?

I tell students that this last question is tough but crucial. Is the continual distortion of Columbus simply an accident, repeated innocently over and over, or are there groups in our society that could benefit from everyone's having a false or limited understanding of the past? Whether or not students are able to answer the question effectively, it is still important that they struggle with it before our group discussion of their critiques.

The subtext of the assignment is to teach students that text material, indeed all written material, is to be read skeptically. I want students to explore the politics of print, that perspectives on history and social reality underlie the written word and that to read is not only to comprehend what is written, but also to question *why* it is written. My intention is not to encourage an "I-don't-believe-anything" cynicism,[5] but rather to equip students to bring the writer's assumptions and values to the surface so that they can decide what is useful and what is not in any particular work.

For practice, we look at some excerpts from a textbook that be-

---

[5]It's useful to keep in mind the distinction between cynicism and skepticism. As Norman Diamond writes, "In an important respect, the two are not even commensurable. Skepticism says, 'You'll have to show me, otherwise I'm dubious'; it is open to engagement and persuasion. . . . Cynicism is a removed perspective, a renunciation of any responsibility." See Norman Diamond, "Against Cynicism in Politics and Culture," in *Monthly Review* 28, no. 2 (June 1976): 40.

longed to my brother in the fourth grade in California, *The Story of American Freedom* (Macmillan, 1964). Students and I read aloud and analyze several paragraphs. The arrival of Columbus and crew is especially revealing—and obnoxious. As is true in every book on the "discovery" I've ever encountered, the reader watches events from the Spaniards' point of view. We are told how Columbus and his men "fell upon their knees and gave thanks to God," a passage included in virtually all elementary school accounts of Columbus. "He then took possession of it [the island] in the name of King Ferdinand and Queen Isabella of Spain."[6] No question is raised of what right Columbus had to assume control over a land which was obviously already occupied by people. The account is so adoring, so respectful of the Admiral, that students can't help but sense the book is offering approval for what is, quite simply, an act of naked imperialism.

The book keeps us close to God and church throughout its narrative. Upon returning from the New World, Columbus shows off his parrots and Indians (again no question of the propriety of the unequal relationship between "natives" and colonizers), and immediately following the show, "the king and queen lead the way to a near-by church. There a song of praise and thanksgiving is sung."[7] Intended or not, the function of linking church and Columbus is to remove him and his actions still further from question and critique. My job, on the other hand, is to encourage students to pry beneath every phrase and illustration; to begin to train readers who can both understand the word and challenge it.

I give students a week before I ask them to bring in their written critiques. In small groups, they share their papers with one another. I ask them to take notes toward what my co-teacher Linda Christensen and I call the "collective text": What themes seem to recur in the papers and what important differences emerge?

Here are some excerpts from papers written this year by students in the Literature and U.S. History course that Linda and I co-teach.

Maryanne wrote:

"In 1492 Columbus sailed the ocean blue." He ran into a land mass claiming it in the name of Spain. The next day Columbus went ashore. "Indians," almost naked, greeted Columbus who found them a simple folk who "invite you to share anything they possess." Columbus observed that "fifty Spaniards could subjugate this entire people." Then we are told, "By 1548 the Indians were almost all wiped out."—from a passage in *The Impact of Our Past.*

---

[6]Edna McGuire, *The Story of American Freedom* (New York: The Macmillan Company, 1964), p. 24.

[7]Ibid., p. 26.

That story is about as complete as swiss cheese. Columbus and the Span-iards killed off the "Indians," they didn't mystically disappear or die of dipth-eria.

Trey wrote his critique as a letter to Allyn and Bacon, publishers    **28**
of *The American Spirit:*

> . . . I'll just pick one topic to keep it simple. How about Columbus. No, you didn't lie, but saying, "Though they had a keen interest in the peoples of the Caribbean, Columbus and his crews were never able to live peacefully among them," makes it seem as if Columbus did no wrong. The reason for not being able to live peacefully is that he and his crew took slaves, and killed thousands of Indians for not bringing enough gold. . . .
>
> If I were to only know the information given in this book, I would have such a sheltered viewpoint that many of my friends would think I was stupid. Later in life people could capitalize on my ignorance by comparing Columbus's voyage with something similar, but in our time. I wouldn't believe the ugly truths brought up by the opposition because it is just like Columbus, and he did no harm, I've known that since the eighth grade.

Keely chose the same book, which happens to be the text adopted    **29**
by Portland Public Schools, where I teach:

> . . . I found that the facts left in were, in fact, facts. There was nothing made up. Only things left out. There was one sentence in the whole section where Indians were mentioned. And this was only to say why Columbus called them "Indians." Absolutely nothing was said about slaves or gold. . . .
>
> The book, as I said, doesn't mention the Indians really, so of course you're on Christopher's side. They say how he falls to his knees and thanks God for saving him and his crew and for making their voyage successful.

After students have read and discussed their papers in small groups    **30**
we ask them to reflect on the papers as a whole and write about our collective text: What did they discover about textbook treatments of Columbus? Here are some excerpts.

Matthew wrote:    **31**

> As people read their evaluations the same situations in these textbooks came out. Things were conveniently left out so that you sided with Columbus's quest to "boldly go where no man has gone before" . . . None of the harsh violent reality is confronted in these so-called true accounts.

Gina tried to account for why the books were so consistently rosy:    **32**

> It seemed to me as if the publishers had just printed up some "glory story" that was supposed to make us feel more patriotic about our country. In our group, we talked about the possibility of the government trying to protect young students from such violence. We soon decided that that was probably

one of the farthest things from their minds. They want us to look at our country as great, and powerful, and forever right. They want us to believe Columbus was a real hero. We're being fed lies. We don't question the facts, we just absorb information that is handed to us because we trust the role models that are handing it out.

Rebecca's collective text reflected the general tone of disillusion 33 with the official story of textbooks:

> Of course, the writers of the books probably think it's harmless enough—what does it matter who discovered America, really, and besides it makes them feel good about America. But the thought that I have been lied to all my life about this, and who knows what else, really makes me angry.

The reflections on the collective text became the basis for a class 34 discussion of these and other issues. Again and again, students blasted their textbooks for consistently making choices that left readers with inadequate, and ultimately untruthful, understandings. And while we didn't press to arrive at definitive explanations for the omissions and distortions, we did seek to underscore the contemporary abuses of historical ignorance. If the books wax romantic about Columbus planting the flag on island beaches and taking possession of land occupied by naked red-skinned Indians, what do young readers learn from this about today's world? That white people have a right to dominate peoples of color? That might—or wealth—makes right? That it's justified to take people's land if you are more "civilized" or have a "better" religion? Whatever the answers, the textbooks condition students to accept some form of inequality; nowhere do the books suggest that the Indians were, or even should have been, sovereign peoples with a right to control their own lands. And if Columbus' motives for exploration are mystified or ignored, then students are less apt to look beyond today's pious explanations for U.S. involvements in, say, Central America or the Middle East. As Bobby, approaching his registration day for the military draft, pointed out in class: "If people thought they were going off to war to fight for profits, maybe they wouldn't fight as well, or maybe they wouldn't go."

It's important to note that some students are left troubled from 35 these myth-popping discussions. One student wrote that she was "left not knowing who to believe." Josh was the most articulate in his skepticism. He had begun to "read" our class from the same critical distance from which we hoped students would approach textbooks:

> I still wonder. . . . If we can't believe what our first grade teachers told us, why should we believe you? If they lied to us, why wouldn't you? If one book is

wrong, why isn't another? What is your purpose in telling us about how awful Chris was? What interest do you have in telling us the truth? What is it you want from us?

What indeed? It was a wonderfully probing series of questions and    **36**
Linda and I responded by reading them (anonymously) to the entire class. We asked students to take a few minutes to write additional questions and comments on the Columbus activities or to try to imagine our response as teachers—what *was* the point of our lessons?

We hoped students would see that the intent of the unit was to    **37**
present a whole new way of reading, and ultimately of experiencing, the world. Textbooks fill students with information masquerading as final truth and then ask students to parrot back the information in end-of-the-chapter "checkups."

The Brazilian educator Paulo Freire calls it the "banking method":    **38**
students are treated as empty vessels waiting for deposits of wisdom from textbooks and teachers.[8] We wanted to assert to students that they shouldn't necessarily trust the "authorities," but instead need to be active participants in their own learning, peering between lines for unstated assumptions and unasked questions. Meaning is something *they* need to create, individually and collectively.

Josh asked what our "interest" was in this kind of education and it's    **39**
.a fair, even vital, question. Linda and I see teaching as political action: we want to equip students to build a truly democratic society. As Freire writes, to be an actor for social change one must "read the word and the world."[9] We hope that if a student is able to maintain a critical distance from the written word, then it's possible to maintain that same distance from one's society: to stand back, look hard and ask, "Why is it like this, how can I make it better?"

---

[8]See Paulo Freire, *Pedagogy of the Oppressed* (New York: Continuum, 1970). This banking method of education, Freire writes (p. 58), ". . . turns [students] into 'receptacles' to be 'filled' by the teacher. . . .

> Education thus becomes an act of depositing, in which the students are depositories and the teacher is the depositor. Instead of communicating, the teacher issues communiques and makes deposits which the students patiently receive, memorize, and repeat. This is the 'banking' concept of education, in which the scope of action allowed to the students extends only as far as receiving, filing, and storing the deposits. They do, it is true, have the opportunity to become collectors or cataloguers of the things they store. But in the last analysis, it is men [people] themselves who are filed away through the lack of creativity, transformation, and knowledge in this (at best) misguided system.

[9]Paulo Freire and Donaldo Macedo, *Literacy: Reading the Word and the World* (South Hadley, MA: Bergin and Garvey, 1987).

---

## Review Questions

1. What is the point of Bigelow's purse-snatching activity?
2. How does Koning's account of Columbus differ from the accounts in the textbooks read by Bigelow's students?
3. What, according to Bigelow, is his purpose in demanding that students question everything in their textbooks?

## Discussion and Writing Suggestions

1. According to Bigelow, "Textbooks fill students with information masquerading as final truth. . . ." To what extent does your own experience with textbooks, from the time you were in elementary school, support this conclusion? In what ways do you feel that important aspects of history or civics have been omitted or distorted from the "official version" presented in textbooks? Be specific about historical personages or events. To what extent do you feel—as did some of Bigelow's students—that you have been lied to? And if you have been lied to, then what *is* the truth, based on your own experience or additional reading?
2. Apply the questions Bigelow asks his students to consider (paragraph 20) to the first few selections in this chapter. In particular, try to answer the final two questions: *Why* are Columbus and the Indians portrayed as they are, and *who* stands to benefit from such portrayals? Why is it in the interest of certain people or certain social institutions to promote a false or sanitized version ("the official version") of history?
3. Bigelow writes that he wants to encourage skepticism in his students, but not cynicism. Some may claim, however, that students encouraged to be skeptical about *everything* they read may not develop sufficient patriotism for their country. To what extent do you feel that this is a problem? Does the urge to encourage skepticism—to "pry beneath every phrase"—run counter, for instance, to the sentiments expressed in the pledge of allegiance? Can one be a patriot and at the same time a skeptic—or is there an inherent conflict here? By the same token, does fostering distrust of all authority encourage anarchy (or at least disrespect for law)?
4. Write a critique of Bigelow's article. Take into account your responses to some of the questions above. (You may want to couch your critique in the form of an evaluation of Bigelow's teaching, assuming you are a student in his class.)

# I Take Possession for the King and Queen

## CHRISTOPHER COLUMBUS

*The most important primary source about Columbus's voyages is his daily log. Since the original log no longer survives, historians have come to rely on a transcription and an abstract prepared by Columbus's contemporary Bartolomé de Las Casas (see following selection). The first of the following passages, concerning the events of October 11–14, 1492, is a version of the log prepared by Columbus scholar Robert H. Fuson, professor emeritus of geography at the University of South Florida. Fuson has translated Las Casas's transcription and combined it with sections of the biography of Columbus written by his son Ferdinand. The second passage, a brief account of Columbus's entire first voyage, is a translation of Columbus's letter to Luis de Santángel, comptroller of the Treasury of the King and Queen of Spain.*

## The Log of Christopher Columbus

### THURSDAY, 11 OCTOBER 1492

I sailed to the WSW, and we took more water aboard than at any other time on the voyage. I saw several things that were indications of land. At one time a large flock of sea birds flew overhead, and a green reed was found floating near the ship. The crew of the *Pinta* spotted some of the same reeds and some other plants; they also saw what looked like a small board or plank. A stick was recovered that looks manmade, perhaps carved with an iron tool. Those on the *Niña* saw a little stick covered with barnacles. I am certain that many things were overlooked because of the heavy sea, but even these few made the crew breathe easier; in fact, the men have even become cheerful. I sailed 81 miles from sunset yesterday to sunset today. As is our custom, vespers were said in the late afternoon, and a special thanksgiving was offered to God for giving us renewed hope through the many signs of land He has provided.

1

Reprinted, with permission, from *The Log of Christopher Columbus*, by Robert H. Fuson. Copyright © 1987 by Robert H. Fuson. Published by International Marine, an imprint of TAB Books, a Division of McGraw-Hill Inc., Blue Ridge Summit, PA 17294-0850. (1-800-233-1128)

After sunset I ordered the pilot to return to my original westerly course, and I urged the crew to be ever-vigilant. I took the added precaution of doubling the number of lookouts, and I reminded the men that the first to sight land would be given a silk doublet as a personal token from me. Further, he would be given an annuity of 10,000 maravedíes from the Sovereigns.

2

About 10 o'clock at night, while standing on the sterncastle, I thought I saw a light to the west. It looked like a little wax candle bobbing up and down. It had the same appearance as a light or torch belonging to fishermen or travellers who alternately raised and lowered it, or perhaps were going from house to house. I am the first to admit that I was so eager to find land that I did not trust my own senses, so I called for Pedro Gutiérrez, the representative of the King's household, and asked him to watch for the light. After a few moments, he too saw it. I then summoned Rodrigo Sánchez of Segovia, the comptroller of the fleet, and asked him to watch for the light. He saw nothing, nor did any other member of the crew. It was such an uncertain thing that I did not feel it was adequate proof of land.

3

The moon, in its third quarter, rose in the east shortly before midnight. I estimate that we were making about 9 knots and had gone some 67½ miles between the beginning of night and 2 o'clock in the morning. Then, at two hours after midnight, the *Pinta* fired a cannon, my prearranged signal for the sighting of land.

4

I now believe that the light I saw earlier was a sign from God and that it was truly the first positive indication of land. When we caught up with the *Pinta*, which was always running ahead because she was a swift sailer, I learned that the first man to sight land was Rodrigo de Triana, a seaman from Lepe.

5

I hauled in all sails but the mainsail and lay-to till daylight. The land is about 6 miles to the west.

6

**FRIDAY, 12 OCTOBER 1492 (LOG ENTRY FOR 12 OCTOBER IS COMBINED WITH THAT OF 11 OCTOBER.)**

At dawn we saw naked people, and I went ashore in the ship's boat, armed, followed by Martín Alonso Pinzón, captain of the *Pinta*, and his brother, Vincente Yáñez Pinzón, captain of the *Niña*. I unfurled the royal

7

banner and the captains brought the flags which displayed a large green cross with the letters F and Y at the left and right side of the cross. Over each letter was the appropriate crown of that Sovereign. These flags were carried as a standard on all of the ships. After a prayer of thanksgiving I ordered the captains of the *Pinta* and *Niña*, together with Rodrigo de Escobedo (secretary of the fleet), and Rodrigo Sánchez of Segovia (comptroller of the fleet) to bear faith and witness that I was taking possession of this island for the King and Queen. I made all the necessary declarations and had these testimonies carefully written down by the secretary. In addition to those named above, the entire company of the fleet bore witness to this act. To this island I gave the name *San Salvador*,[1] in honor of our Blessed Lord.

No sooner had we concluded the formalities of taking possession of the island than people began to come to the beach, all as naked as their mothers bore them, and the women also, although I did not see more than one very young girl. All those that I saw were young people, none of whom was over 30 years old. They are very well-built people, with handsome bodies and very fine faces, though their appearance is marred somewhat by very broad heads and foreheads, more so than I have ever seen in any other race. Their eyes are large and very pretty, and their skin is the color of Canary Islanders or of sunburned peasants, not at all black, as would be expected because we are on an east-west line with Hierro in the Canaries. These are tall people and their legs, with no exceptions, are quite straight, and none of them has a paunch. They are, in fact, well proportioned. Their hair is not kinky, but straight, and coarse like horsehair. They wear it short over the eyebrows, but they have a long hank in the back that they never cut. Many of the natives paint their faces; others paint their whole bodies; some, only the eyes or nose. Some are painted black, some white, some red; others are of different colors.

The people here called this island *Guanahaní* in their language, and their speech is very fluent, although I do not understand any of it. They are friendly and well-dispositioned people who bare no arms except for small spears, and they have no iron. I showed one my sword, and through ignorance he grabbed it by the blade and cut himself. Their

8

9

---

[1]Samana Cay.

spears are made of wood, to which they attach a fish tooth at one end, or some other sharp thing.

I want the natives to develop a friendly attitude toward us because I    10
know that they are a people who can be made free and converted to our
Holy Faith more by love than by force. I therefore gave red caps to some
and glass beads to others. They hung the beads around their necks,
along with some other things of slight value that I gave them. And they
took great pleasure in this and became so friendly that it was a marvel.
They traded and gave everything they had with good will, but it seems
to me that they have very little and are poor in everything. I warned
my men to take nothing from the people without giving something in
exchange.

This afternoon the people of San Salvador came swimming to our ships    11
and in boats made from one log. They brought us parrots, balls of cotton
thread, spears, and many other things, including a kind of dry leaf[2] that
they hold in great esteem. For these items we swapped them little glass
beads and hawks' bells.

Many of the men I have seen have scars on their bodies, and when I    12
made signs to them to find out how this happened, they indicated that
people from other nearby islands come to San Salvador to capture
them; they defend themselves the best they can. I believe that people
from the mainland come here to take them as slaves. They ought to
make good and skilled servants, for they repeat very quickly whatever
we say to them. I think they can easily be made Christians, for they
seem to have no religion. If it pleases Our Lord, I will take six of them
to Your Highnesses when I depart, in order that they may learn our
language.

## SATURDAY, 13 OCTOBER 1492

After sunrise people from San Salvador again began to come to our    13
ships in boats fashioned in one piece from the trunks of trees. These
boats are wonderfully made, considering the country we are in, and
every bit as fine as those I have seen in Guinea. They come in all
sizes. Some can carry 40 or 50 men; some are so small that only one

---

[2]The "dry leaves" are not actually mentioned until the October 15 entry. At that time Columbus
tells us that these highly prized dry leaves were offered to him on 12 October. It is reasonable,
then, that the tobacco was part of "the many other things" cited in the Log entry.

---

man rides in it. The men move very swiftly over the water, rowing with a blade that looks like a baker's peel. They do not use oarlocks, but dip the peel in the water and push themselves forward. If a boat capsizes they all begin to swim, and they rock the boat until about half of the water is splashed out. Then they bail out the rest of the water with gourds that they carry for that purpose.

The people brought more balls of spun cotton, spears, and parrots. **14** Other than the parrots, I have seen no beast of any kind on this island.

I have been very attentive and have tried very hard to find out if **15** there is any gold here. I have seen a few natives who wear a little piece of gold hanging from a hole made in the nose. By signs, if I interpret them correctly, I have learned that by going to the south, or rounding the island to the south, I can find a king who possesses a lot of gold and has great containers of it. I have tried to find some natives who will take me to this great king, but none seems inclined to make the journey.

Tomorrow afternoon I intend to go to the SW. The natives have **16** indicated to me that not only is there land to the south and SW, but also to the NW. I shall go to the SW and look for gold and precious stones. Furthermore, if I understand correctly, it is from the NW that strangers come to fight and capture the people here.

This island is fairly large and very flat. It is green, with many trees and **17** several bodies of water. There is a very large lagoon[3] in the middle of the island and there are no mountains. It is a pleasure to gaze upon this place because it is all so green, and the weather is delightful. In fact, since we left the Canaries, God has not failed to provide one perfect day after the other.

I cannot get over the fact of how docile these people are. They have so **18** little to give but will give it all for whatever we give them, if only broken pieces of glass and crockery. One seaman gave three Portuguese *ceitis* (not even worth a penny!) for about 25 pounds of spun cotton. I probably should have forbidden this exchange, but I wanted to take the cotton to Your Highnesses, and it seems to be in abundance. I think the

---

[3]The Log states: ". . . *y muchas aguas y una laguna en medio muy grande.* . . ." The word is *laguna* (lagoon), not *lago* (lake). Columbus probably meant that the island had many small lakes and ponds (*muchas aguas*) and a saltwater lagoon in the middle ("halfway," "in between") on the coast he was on. This description fits Samana, not Watlings.

cotton is grown on San Salvador, but I cannot say for sure because I have not been here that long. Also, the gold they wear hanging from their noses comes from here, but in order not to lose time I want to go to see if I can find the island of Japan.

When night came, all of the people went ashore in their boats.  19

## SUNDAY, 14 OCTOBER 1492

At daybreak I ordered the small boats to be made ready, that is, put in  20
tow behind, and I went along the island to the NNE, to see the other part of the east and the villages. Soon I saw two or three of them, and the people came to the beach, shouting and praising God. Some brought us water; others, things to eat. Others, seeing that I did not care to go ashore, jumped into the sea and swam out to us. By the signs they made I think they were asking if we came from Heaven. One old man even climbed into the boat we were towing, and others shouted in loud voices to everyone on the beach, saying, "Come see the men from Heaven; bring them food and drink." Many men and women came, each one with something. They threw themselves on the sand and raised their hands to the sky, shouting for us to come ashore, while giving thanks to God. I kept going this morning despite the pleas of the people to come ashore, for I was alarmed at seeing that the entire island is surrounded by a large reef. Between the reef and the island it remained deep, and this port is large enough to hold all the ships of Christendom. There are a few shoal spots, to be sure, and the sea in it moves no more than water in a well. I found a very narrow entrance, which I entered with the ship's boat.

I kept moving in order to see all of this so that I can give an account  21
of everything to Your Highnesses. Also, I wanted to see if I could find a suitable place to build a fort. I saw a piece of land that looked like an island, even though it is not, with six houses on it. I believe that it could be cut through and made into an island in two days. I do not think this is necessary, however, for these people are very unskilled in arms. Your Highnesses will see this for yourselves when I bring to you the seven[4] that I have taken. After they learn our language I shall return them, unless Your Highnesses order that the entire population be taken to Castile, or held captive here. With 50 men you could subject everyone and make them do what you wished.

---

[4]The entry for 12 October said six. Columbus is inconsistent on this point.

## Columbus' Own Description of the New World

(From his letter to Luis de Santángel, comptroller of the Treasury of the King and Queen of Spain.)

Knowing of the pleasure you will receive in hearing of the great victory 22 which Our Lord has granted me in my voyage, I hasten to inform you, that after a passage of seventy-one days, I arrived at the Indies, with the fleet which the most illustrious King and Queen our sovereigns committed to my charge; where I discovered many islands inhabited by people without number, and of which I took possession for their Highnesses by proclamation with the royal banner displayed, no one offering any contradiction. The first which I discovered, I named *San Salvador*, in commemoration of our Holy Saviour, who has, in a wonderful manner, granted all our success. The Indians call it *Guanahani*. To the second, I gave the name of *Santa Maria de Concepcion*, to the third, that of *Fernandina*, to the fourth, that of *Isabela*, to the fifth, that of *Juana*,⁵ thus giving each island a new name. I coasted along the island of *Juana* to the West, and found it of such extent, that I took it for a continent, and imagined it must be the country of *Cathay*. Villages were seen near the sea-coast, but as I discovered no large cities, and could not obtain any communication with the inhabitants, who all fled at our approach, I continued on West, thinking I should not fail in the end to meet with great towns and cities, but having gone many leagues without such success, and finding that the coast carried me to the N., whither I disliked to proceed, on account of the impending winter, I resolved to return to the S., and accordingly put about and arrived at an excellent harbour in the island, where I dispatched two men into the country to ascertain whether the King, or any large cities were in the neighborhood. They travelled three days, and met with innumerable settlements of the natives, of a small size, but did not succeed in finding any sovereign of the territory, and so returned. I made out to learn from some Indians which I had before taken, that this was an island, and proceeded along the coast to the East, an hundred and seven leagues, till I reached the extremity. I then discovered another island E. of this eighteen leagues distant, which I named *Espanola*,⁶ and followed its northern coast as I did that of *Juana*, for the space of an hundred and seventy-eight leagues to the E. All these countries are of surpassing excellence, and in particular *Juana*, which contains abundance of fine harbours, excelling any in

⁵Cuba.
⁶Haiti.

Christendom, as also many large and beautiful rivers. The land is high and exhibits chains of tall mountains which seem to reach the skies, and surpass beyond comparison the isle of *Cetrefrey.* These display themselves in all manner of beautiful shapes. They are accessible in every part, and covered with a vast variety of lofty trees, which it appears to me, never lose their foliage, as we found them fair and verdant as in May in Spain. Some were covered with blossoms, some with fruit, and others in different stages, according to their nature. The nightingale and a thousand other sorts of birds were singing in the month of November wherever I went. There are palm-trees in these countries, of six or eight sorts, which are surprising to see, on account of their diversity from ours, but indeed, this is the case with respect to the other trees, as well as the fruits and weeds. Beautiful forests of pines are likewise found, and fields of vast extent. Here is also honey, and fruits of a thousand sorts, and birds of every variety. The lands contain mines of metals, and inhabitants without number. The island of *Espanola* is pre-eminent in beauty and excellence, offering to the sight the most enchanting view of mountains, plains, rich fields for cultivation, and pastures for flocks of all sorts, with situations for towns and settlements. Its harbours are of such excellence, that their description would not gain belief, and the like may be said of its abundance of large and fine rivers, the most of which abound in gold. The trees, fruits and plants of this island differ considerably from those of *Juana,* and the place contains a great deal of spicery and extensive mines of gold and other metals. . . .

I have already related that I proceeded along the coast of *Juana,* for an hundred and seven leagues from W. to E., from which, I dare affirm this island to be larger than England and Scotland together; for besides the extent of it which I coasted, there are two unexplored provinces to the W., in one of which, called *Cibau,* are people with tails. These districts cannot be less than fifty or sixty leagues in extent, according as I learn from my Indians, who are acquainted with these islands. The other island, called *Espanola,* is more extensive than the division of Spain from Corunna to Fontarabia, as I traversed one side of it for the distance of an hundred and thirty-eight leagues from W. to E. This is the most beautiful island, and although I have taken possession of them all in the name of their Highnesses, and every one remains in their power, and as much at their disposal as the kingdoms of Castile, and although they are all furnished with everything that can be desired, yet the preference must be given to *Espanola,* on account of the mines of gold which it possesses, and the facilities it offers for trade with the continent, and countries this side, and beyond that of the Great Can, which traffic will be great and profitable. I have accordingly taken possession of a place, which I named *Villa de Navidad,* and built there a fortress, which is at present complete, and furnished with a sufficiency of men for the enter-

23

prise; with these I have left arms, ammunition and provisions for more than a year, a boat, and expert men in all necessary arts. . . .

In conclusion, and to speak only of what I have performed; this  24 voyage, so hastily dispatched, will, as their Highnesses may see, enable any desirable quantity of gold to be obtained, by a very small assistance offered me on their part. At present there are within reach spices and cotton to as great an amount as they can desire, aloe in as great abundance, and an equal store of mastick, a production nowhere else found except in Greece and the island of Scio, where it is sold at such a price as the possessors choose. To these may be added slaves, as numerous as may be wished for. Besides I have as I think, discovered rhubarb and cinnamon, and expect countless other things of value will be found by the men whom I have left there, as I made it a point not to stay in any one place, while the wind enabled me to proceed upon the voyage, except at *Villa de Navidad*, where I left them, well established. I should have accomplished much more, had those in the other vessels done their duty. This is ever certain, that God grants to those that walk in his ways, the performance of things which seem impossible, and this enterprise might in a signal manner have been considered so, for although many have talked of these countries, yet it has been nothing more than conjecture. Our Saviour having vouchsafed his victory to our most illustrious King and Queen and their kingdoms, famous for so eminent a deed, all Christendom should rejoice, and give solemn thanks to the Holy Trinity for the addition of so many people to our holy faith, and also for the temporal profit accruing not only to Spain, but to all Christians.

*On board the Caravel, off the Azores, February 15th, 1493.*

## Review Questions

1. How does Columbus ensure that his taking possession of the lands he encounters would be considered legal?
2. From the first, Columbus's attitudes toward the natives of San Salvador was mixed. Explain.
3. What was Columbus seeking during his first voyage? To what extent was he successful?

## Discussion and Writing Suggestions

1. Based on Columbus's log, who deserved the credit and the reward for first sighting land? Why? Imagining that you are one of the contenders, write a paragraph or two justifying your claim.
2. Write (a) a newspaper article, datelined 1492 from Seville, reporting without

editorial comment on Columbus's first voyage; and (b) an editorial on this voyage, taking either a positive or a critical stance.

3. One of Columbus's primary motives in writing these accounts is to report on what he has encountered during his voyages. Another motive, no less important, is to present himself and his expedition in as favorable a light as he can. (He writes primarily to the monarchs of Spain and to Luis de Santángel, but he also addresses his contemporaries and future generations.) Citing particular passages, show how Columbus attempts to achieve this second objective. Using Bigelow's distinction, try to take a skeptical but not cynical stance.

4. Those who defend Columbus against accusations that he had no legal or moral right to take possession of territories on which people were already living claim that Columbus was merely acting in accordance with the custom of the time. In his drive to spread Christianity and to reap the riches of the lands he "discovered," he was nothing more than a particularly capable man of his age. They add that no one in Columbus's position—particularly one whose expeditions were dependent on royal patronage—could have acted any differently. (If he had, he probably would have been replaced.) To what extent does this defense seem reasonable? How blameworthy was Columbus for what happened during and after his voyages? Try to include both sides of the argument in your response.

# The Destruction of the Indians

## BARTOLOMÉ DE LAS CASAS

*Bartolomé de Las Casas (1472–1566), known as the "Apostle of the Indies," was a Spanish missionary and historian, the first priest to be ordained in the New World. As a young man in Seville, he observed the triumphant return of Columbus from his first voyage (later he was to transcribe and abstract Columbus's log). In 1502 he sailed to the Americas with Nicolás de Ovando, who was appointed by King Ferdinand to replace Columbus as governor of the new territories. In Hispaniola (now Haiti/Dominican Republic), he helped quash an Indian insurrection and was rewarded with a royal land grant including his own slaves—an encomienda. Over the years, however, Las Casas became increasingly outraged over the cruelty with which most of the Spaniards treated the Indians; and he determined to devote the rest of his life to denouncing the encomienda system and the Spanish conquest of the New World. In 1522, after retreating to a monastery, he began work on his History of the Indies. His Brief Report on the Destruction of the Indians (1542), translated into several languages, was used by Spain's enemies to*

From Bartolomé de Las Casas, *The Tears of the Indians*, Oriole Chapbooks, Oriole Editions, 1972.

*reinforce the "Black Legend" of Spanish brutality. Las Casas made several trips to the Spanish court to urge the abolition of the* encomienda *system, ultimately prevailing. He died at the age of ninety-two and was buried in a monastery in Madrid.*

*The following passage is the introductory section of* A Brief Report on the Destruction of the Indians, *also known as* The Tears of the Indians.

In the year 1492, the West-Indies were discovered, in the following year  1
they were inhabited by the Spaniards: a great company of the Spaniards going about 49 years ago. The first place they came to, was Hispaniola, being a most fertile Island, and for the bigness of it very famous, it being no less than six hundred miles in compass. Round about it lie an innumerable company of Islands, so thronged with Inhabitants, that there is not to be found a greater multitude of people in any part of the world. The Continent is distant from this about Two hundred miles, stretching it self out in length upon the sea side for above Ten thousand miles in length. This is already found out, and more is daily discovered. These Countries are inhabited by such a number of people, as if God had assembled and called together to this place, the greatest part of Mankind.

This infinite multitude of people was so created by God, as that  2
they were without fraud, without subtilty or malice, to their natural Governours most faithful and obedient. Towards the Spaniards whom they serve, patient, meek and peaceful, who laying all contentious and tumultuous thoughts aside, live without any hatred or desire of revenge; the people are most delicate and tender, enjoying such a feeble constitution of body as does not permit them to endure labour, so that the Children of Princes and great persons here, are not more nice and delicate than the Children of the meanest Country-man in that place. The Nation is very poor and indigent, possessing very little, and by reason that they gape not after temporal goods, neither proud nor ambitious. Their diet is such that the most holy Hermite cannot feed more sparingly in the wilderness. They go naked, only hiding the undecencies of nature, and a poor shag mantle about an ell or two long is their greatest and their warmest covering. They lie upon mats, only those who have larger fortunes, lie upon a kind of net which is tied at the four corners, and so fasten'd to the roof, which the Indians in their natural language call Hamecks. They are of a very apprehensive and docile wit, and capable of all good learning, and very apt to receive our Religion, which when they have but once tasted, they are carried on with a very ardent and zealous desire to make a further progress in it; so that I have heard divers Spaniards confess that they had nothing else to hinder them from enjoying Heaven, but their ignorance of the true God.

To these quiet Lambs, endued with such blessed qualities, came the 3
Spaniards like most cruel Tigers, Wolves, and Lions, enrag'd with a
sharp and tedious hunger; for these forty years past, minding nothing
else but the slaughter of these unfortunate wretches, whom with divers
kinds of torments neither seen nor heard before, they have so cruelly
and inhumanely butchered, that of three millions of people which Hispaniola itself did contain, there are left remaining alive scarce three
hundred persons. And for the Island of Cuba, which contains as much
ground in length, as from Valladolid to Rome; it lies wholly desert,
untill'd and ruin'd. The Islands of St. John and Jamaica lie waste and
desolate. The Lucayan Islands neighboring toward the North upon Cuba
and Hispaniola, being above Sixty or thereabouts with those Islands that
are vulgarly called the Islands of the Gyants, of which that which is least
fertile is more fruitful then the King of Spains Garden at Sevil, being
situated in a pure and temperate air, are now totally unpeopled and
destroyed; the inhabitants thereof amounting to above 500000 souls,
partly killed, and partly forced away to work in other places: so that
there going a ship to visit those parts and to glean the remainder of
those distressed wretches, there could be found no more than eleven
men. Other Islands there were near the Island of St. John more then
thirty in number, which were totally made desert. All which Islands,
though they amount to such a number containing in length of ground
the space of above Two thousand miles, lie now altogether solitary
without any people or Inhabitant.

Now to come to the Continent, we are confident, and dare affirm 4
upon our own knowledge, that there were ten Kingdomes of as large an
extent as the Kingdoms of Spain, joining to it both Arragon, and
Portugal, containing above a thousand miles every one of them in
compass, which the unhumane and abominable villanies of the Spaniards
have made a wilderness of, being now as it were stript of all their people,
and made bare of all their inhabitants, though it were a place formerly
possessed by vast and infinite numbers of men; And we dare confidently
aver, that for those Forty years, wherin the Spaniards exercised their
abominable cruelties, and detestable tyrannies in those parts, that there
have innocently perish'd above Twelve millions of souls, women and
children being numbred in this sad and fatal list; moreover I do verily
believe that I should speak within compass, should I say that above Fifty
millions were consumed in this Massacre.

As for those that came out of Spain, boasting themselves to be 5
Christians, they [had] two several ways to extirpate this Nation from the
face of the Earth, the first whereof was a bloody, unjust, and cruel war
which they made upon them: a second by cutting off all that so much
as sought to recover their liberty, as some of the stouter sort did intend.
And as for the Women and Children that were left alive, they laid so

heavy and grievous a yoke of servitude upon them that the condition of beasts was much more tolerable.

Upon these two heads all the other several torments and inhumanities which they used to the ruin of these poor Nations may be reduced. 6

That which led the Spaniards to these unsanctified impieties was the desire of Gold, to make themselves suddenly rich, for the obtaining of dignities & honours which were no way fit for them. In a word, their covetousness, their ambition, which could not be more in any people under heaven, the riches of the Country, and the patience of the people gave occasion to this their devilish barbarism. For the Spaniards so contemned them (I now speak what I have seen without the least untruth) that they used them not like beasts, for that would have been tolerable, but looked upon them as if they had been but the dung and filth of the earth, and so little they regarded the health of their souls, that they suffered this great multitude to die without the least light of Religion; neither is this less true then what I have said before, and that which those tyrants and hangmen themselves dare not deny, without speaking a notorious falsehood, that the Indians never gave them the least cause to offer them violence, but received them as Angels sent from heaven, till their excessive cruelties, the torments and slaughters of their Countrymen mov't them to take arms against the Spaniards. 7

## Review Questions

1. How does Las Casas characterize the natives of the West Indies?
2. According to Las Casas, what motivated the Spaniards to devastate the land and the peoples they encountered?

## Discussion and Writing Suggestions

1. How does Las Casas use language to sway his readers to his position? Cite words, phrases, and strategies of argument used with calculated emotional appeal.
2. Las Casas's work was written in the mid-sixteenth century and has been available in English since the mid-seventeenth century. Why do you think that authors such as Irving, Lamartine, Davidson, and Stewart failed to take it into sufficient account when they wrote about Columbus and the significance of his voyages?
3. To what extent do you believe what Las Casas writes? As far as you can tell, would he have a motive to lie or distort the facts (as Bigelow and others claim that the writers of textbooks have done)? Do you doubt the truth of anything he says? Explain.

# Resolution of the National Council of Churches

*In May 1990, the National Council of the Churches of Christ fanned the flames of controversy over the Columbus quincentennial by adopting a resolution sharply condemning Columbus's "invasion" and its heritage. "The official celebration that we are about to endure," charged Jim Wallis, editor of* Sojourners *magazine, "will be a liturgy of empire exercising the symbols of domination." The council pledged to put its resources behind a variety of efforts to "challenge the Columbus story, which functions as a creation story of this nation and which legitimates centuries of racial oppression." Included in these efforts were seminars, regional ecumenical conferences, meetings of indigenous Americans, and educational materials. During the conference at which the resolution was announced, some speakers noted the irony that many immigrants who had fled from oppression and genocide in Eastern Europe now embraced the Columbus myth, which appeared to sanction the genocide of Native Americans. Wallis argued that white Americans could not evade personal responsibility for racism, which is "America's original sin. . . . The idea of original sin is that you didn't do it . . . as free moral agents . . . but you are deeply affected and shaped and controlled by the original sin."*

*Note that the resolution draws on the work of Bartolomé de Las Casas, who more than four centuries earlier was the first cleric to denounce the heritage of Columbus.*

As U.S. Christians approach public observances marking the 500th   1
anniversary of Christopher Columbus's first landing in the Western hemisphere, we are called to review our full history, reflect upon it, and act as people of faith mindful of the significance of 1492. The people in our churches and communities now look at the significance of the event in different ways. What represented newness of freedom, hope and opportunity for some was the occasion for oppression, degradation and genocide for others. For the Church this is not a time for celebration but a time for a committed plan of action insuring that this "kairos" moment in history not continue to cosmetically coat the painful aspects of the American history of racism.

    1. In 1992, celebrations of the 500th anniversary of the arrival of   2
       Christopher Columbus in the "New World" will be held.[1] For the

---

"A Faithful Response To The 500th Anniversary Of The Arrival of Christopher Columbus" as adopted by the Governing Board May 17, 1990. A Resolution of the National Council of the Churches of Christ in the USA. Used by permission.

[1]A 30-member federal agency, the Christopher Columbus Quincentenary Jubilee Commission, was created by the U.S. Congress. Members appointed by President Reagan include James Baker,

descendants of the survivors of the subsequent invasion, genocide, slavery, "ecocide" and exploitation of the wealth of the land, a celebration is not an appropriate observation of this anniversary.

♦ For the indigenous people of the Caribbean islands, Christopher Columbus's invasion marked the beginning of slavery and their eventual genocide. 3

♦ For the indigenous people of Central America, the result was slavery, genocide and exploitation leading to the present struggle for liberation. 4

♦ For the indigenous people of South America, the result was slavery, genocide, and the exploitation of their mineral and natural resources, fostering the early accumulation of capital by the European countries. 5

♦ For the indigenous people of Mexico, the result was slavery, genocide, rape of mineral as well as natural resources and a decline of their civilization. 6

♦ For the peoples of modern Puerto Rico, Hawaii and the Philippines the result was the eventual grabbing of the land, genocide and the present economic captivity. 7

♦ For the indigenous peoples of North America, it brought slavery, genocide, and theft and exploitation of the land which has led to their descendants' impoverished lives.[2] 8

♦ For the peoples of the African Diaspora, the result was slavery, an evil and immoral system steeped in racism, economic exploitation, rape of mineral as well as human resources and national divisiveness along the lines of the colonizing nations. 9

♦ For the peoples from Asia brought to work the land, torn from their families and culture by false promises of economic prosperity, the result was labor camps, discrimination and today's victimization of the descendants facing anti-Asian racism. 10

♦ For the descendants of the European conquerors the subsequent legacy has been the perpetuation of paternalism and racism into our cultures and times.[3] 11

---

Robert Mosbacher, and John Goudie. Spain, Italy, and Portugal have designated observors to the U.S. Commission. A national program of commemorative activities are planned for 1991–1992. Twenty-two states have Quincentenary commissions. Among the projects: the Grand Columbus Regatta of tall ships to New York and Boston; commemorative coins; deployment of three space caravels. In Spain events will lead up to the 1992 World's Fair Expo with the theme of "The Age of Discovery."

[2] "Chief Seattle Speaks," December 1854.

[3] Zinn, Howard, *A People's History of the United States*, New York: Harper & Row, 1980. See also the Final Document of the European Ecumenical Assembly *Peace with Justice for the Whole Creation*, May 1989, Basel, Switzerland, issued by the Conference of European Churches and the Council

2. The Church, with few exceptions, accompanied and legitimized 12 this conquest and exploitation. Theological justifications for destroying native religious beliefs while forcing conversion to European forms of Christianity demanded a submission from the newly converted that facilitated their total conquest and exploitation.[4]

3. Therefore, it is appropriate for the church to reflect on its role in that 13 historical tragedy and, in pursuing a healing process, to move forward in our witness for justice and peace.[5]

Towards that end, we are called to: 14

a. reflect seriously on the complexities and complicities of the mis- 15 sionary efforts during this period of colonization and subjugation that resulted in the destruction of cultures and religions, the desecration of religious sites, and other crimes against the spirituality of indigenous peoples;[6]

b. review and reflect on the degree to which current missiologies 16 tend to promote lifestyles that perpetuate the exploitation of the descendants of the indigenous people, and that stand in the way of enabling their self-determination;

c. identify and celebrate the significant voices within the church that 17

---

of European Bishops' Conference (Doct.id.0116MPC/fm), 2 June 1989, which states that, "1992 will moreover mark the 500th anniversary of the beginning of a period of European expansion to the detriment of other peoples."

[4]Chief Seattle, *ibid.*

[5]See Basel Document, *ibid.*, where European churchpersons acknowledge having "failed to challenge with sufficient consistency political and economic systems which misuse power and wealth, exploit resources for their self-interest and perpetuate poverty and marginalisation. We consider it to be a scandal and a crime how human rights are violated. We commit ourselves to struggle against all violations of human rights and the social structures which favor them."

[6]"A Public Declaration to the Tribal Councils and Traditional Spiritual Leaders of the Indian and Eskimo Peoples of the Pacific Northwest," Bishop Thomas L. Blevins, Pacific Northwest Synod, Lutheran Church in America, and eight Bishops and leaders of other denominations, November, 1987. This statement speaks of "unconscious and insensitive" attitudes and actions by the church which reflect "the rampant racism and prejudice of the dominant culture with which we too willingly identified." In September 1987 Pope John Paul II spoke to Indian leaders of the Northwest Territories and assured them that the Roman Catholic Church "extols the equal human dignity of all peoples and defends their right to uphold their own cultural character, with its distinct traditions and customs." See King, Marsha, "Prejudice Recalled: Churches Pledge to Support Indian Spiritual Practices," *The Seattle Times*, November 22, 1987. See also 1969 Report from the Anglican Church of Canada which acknowledges the problems of Canadian Indians and the complicity of missionaries.

have consistently advocated the rights and dignities of indigenous peoples;

d. recognize that what some historians have termed a "discovery"   18
in reality was an invasion and colonization with legalized occupation, genocide, economic exploitation and a deep level of institutional racism and moral decadence;

e. reflect seriously on how the Church should and might accomplish   19
its task of witness and service to and with those of other faiths,
recognizing their integrity as children of God, and not contributing to new bondages.

4. *Therefore,*   20
the Governing Board of the National Council of the Churches of
Christ in the USA:

a. Declares 1992 to be a year of reflection and repentance, and calls   21
upon its member communions to enter into theological and mis-
sional reflection, study and prayer as a faithful observance of that
year;

b. Commits itself to be involved in activities that bring forward the   22
silenced interpretation of the 1492 event including:

♦ taking action to influence how governments or other institutions   23
plan to celebrate the "discovery" of America;

♦ using its TV, radio and print media resources to educate the   24
Church and its constituency about the factual histories of indigenous people, the colonization of their lands and the effects today
of colonization, including the loss of land, lives and cultures; and

♦ advocating the inclusion of the accurate factual history of indige-   25
nous people, including African Americans, in textbooks to be
used in public and parochial education systems in the United
States;[7] and

♦ cooperating with other hemispheric interfaith bodies in a gather-   26

---

[7]Bartolomé de Las Casas, *Historia de los indios* (ca 1550), *Tears of the Indians* (ca 1550), *In Defense of the Indians* (ca 1550).

DeLoria, Vine, Jr., *Custer Died for Your Sins,* 1970; *God is Red,* 1983.

Galeano, Eduardo, *Memory of Fire: Genesis,* NY: Pantheon, 1985.

Jackson, Helen Hunt, *A Century of Dishonor,* 1881.

Jennings, Francis, *The Invasion of America: Indians, Colonialism and the Cant of Conquest,* Chapel Hill, 1975.

Jordan, Winthrop, *White Over Black: American Attitudes Toward the Negro 1550–1812,* Baltimore: Penguin, 1968.

Limerick, Patricia Nelson, *The Legacy of Conquest: The Unbroken Past of the American West,* New York: W. W. Norton, 1987.

ing in the Caribbean islands to analyze the effects of the European invasion and colonization of the Americas from the perspective of their descendants;

c. Calls upon its member communions to join in affirming and implementing this resolution in dialogue with indigenous people of the Americas; 27

d. Requests that the Division of Church and Society (or its legal successor) in cooperation with the Division of Overseas Ministries (or its legal successor) develop programmatic materials for the speedy implementation of this resolution; 28

e. Requests appropriate units to explore convening a gathering of representatives of traditional tribes, urban Indian and tribal governments to discuss ways to strengthen Indian ministries; 29

f. Supports the endeavors of theological schools and seminaries to help open alternative understandings of 1492/1992; 30

g. Declares this resolution to be our humble and faithful first step contribution towards a deep understanding among peoples of our country. It is our hope that in a new spirit of reconciliation, we move forward together into a shared future as God's creatures honoring the plurality of our cultural heritage. 31

## Review Questions

1. Summarize the main objections of the authors of this resolution to the celebrations of Columbus.
2. Why does the church come in for its share of blame?
3. How do the authors of the resolution propose to deal with the quincentennial?

## Discussion and Writing Suggestions

1. Summarize this resolution, devoting no more than two sentences to each numbered section. Note the logic of the order of presentation.
2. To what extent do you agree with the ideas expressed in this resolution? For example, have the authors of the resolution focused only on the negative effects of Columbus and his followers, ignoring the positive effects? Or do words like *genocide* and *slavery* perfectly and justly describe the heritage of the European incursion to the Americas? Is it racist to celebrate Columbus Day? Write an editorial taking a position on the N.C.C. Resolution.
3. Devise an alternate scenario of the European encounter with Native Americans, a scenario of which the National Council of Churches would probably approve. Had this encounter actually taken place, would the United States exist? If so, how might it be different? How might your own life be different?

# Should Christians Celebrate the Columbus Quincentennial?

## JAMES MULDOON

*The N.C.C. Resolution drew considerable attention. Few articles on the Columbus quincentennial appearing after May 1990 failed to mention it as a significant contribution to the debate. But not everyone agreed with its wholesale attack on the European legacy in the Americas. Among those who dissented was James Muldoon, professor of history at Rutgers University. This article first appeared in* America *on October 27, 1990.*

On the eve of the quincentennial of Christopher Columbus's first voyage to the New World, the National Council of Churches (N.C.C.) passed a resolution condemning the forthcoming celebration of the event. At its May 1990 meeting the Governing Board of the N.C.C. adopted a resolution declaring: "For the descendants of the survivors of the subsequent invasion, genocide, slavery, 'ecocide' and exploitation of the wealth of the land, a celebration is not an appropriate observance of this anniversary."

The resolution goes on to condemn the importation of all these evils into the Caribbean Islands, Central and South America and, eventually, Hawaii and the Philippines. In addition, the resolution pointed to the evils inflicted on "the peoples of the African Diaspora" and "the peoples from Asia brought to work the land . . . by false promises of economic prosperity. . . ." For the former, the result was "slavery, an evil and immoral system steeped in racism, [and] economic exploitation" while for the latter it meant "labor camps, discrimination and . . . anti-Asian racism."

This is quite a burden for one man's shoulders to bear, but the resolution went on to spread the burden and guilt around. "The church, with few exceptions, accompanied and legitimized this conquest and exploitation. Theological justifications for destroying native religious beliefs, while forcing conversion to European forms of Christianity, demanded a submission from the newly converted that facilitated their total conquest and exploitation." So the N.C.C. goes from individual guilt in the past to collective guilt in the present. A nice leap of faith.

The N.C.C. resolution has received some criticism as being itself **4** racist. The Catholic News Service quoted Mario J. Paredes, director of the Northeast Hispanic Catholic Center in New York, who labeled the resolution "a racist depreciation of the heritages of most of today's American peoples, especially Hispanics." The fact that the resolution only once mentions the consequences of North American colonization, "slavery, genocide, and theft and exploitation of the land," suggests that Hispanic critics of the N.C.C. resolution have a point. The resolution was directed only at Columbus's voyages and, by implication, at the establishment of Spanish domination over much of the Americas. The English, French, Dutch, and even the Portuguese seem to have escaped this sweeping condemnation.

If Columbus was the first modern man, as some writers have said, **5** and if the modern world was the creation of the explorers, soldiers, government officials, settlers and others who followed them, then the N.C.C. resolution can be seen as a condemnation of the entire history of the modern world. At the very least, the resolution condemns one of the most significant consequences of Columbus's voyage, the creation of something like a world order, economic and cultural as well as political, under the control of Europeans.

For the N.C.C., Columbus's first voyage apparently had only disas- **6** trous consequences for the inhabitants of the world beyond Europe. The result was a "historical tragedy" for which the church ought "to repent of its complicity" and now pursue "a healing process, to move forward in our witness for justice and peace."

This resolution provides a large and inviting target for those who **7** might want to believe that one or two good things have happened in the world as the result of European expansion overseas. Some readers will even reject the N.C.C.'s words as pious rhetoric expressing a sense of humanitarian guilt in vaguely Marxist terminology. As such, the resolution has little relevance for Columbus or for the forthcoming celebration of the 500th anniversary of his first voyage.

But the N.C.C.'s resolution does deserve some serious attention **8** because of the way in which it distorts the historical record in order to justify its charge of collective guilt. It is one thing to condemn the consequences of Columbus's voyages. It is quite another to do so without serious consideration of the evidence.

The most interesting and unhistorical part of the N.C.C.'s text is **9** the patronizing manner in which all non-European, presumably non-Christian and non-white peoples, are treated. These people have no role to play in the N.C.C.'s history of European expansion except as passive victims of European aggression. These people did not even have any history before 1492 if the N.C.C. is to be believed. Apparently, outside of Europe in 1492, there were millions of people organized in numerous societies living lives of natural virtue. Only with the Europeans did "slavery, genocide and theft and exploitation of the land" appear in the various new worlds that Columbus and his successors encountered.

This is not only a strange argument for a religious body whose  10
theology accepts the concept of original sin affecting all history, it conflicts with what we know about those non-European societies. Slavery in particular would seem to be a universal institution, though not of the same kind and intensity everywhere. Indeed, the "African Diaspora" to which the resolution points was not in the beginning a displacement caused by Europeans. When Europeans reached the West Coast of Africa in the 15th century, they purchased slaves from already existing slave-trading networks. What is true is that the growth of a market for slaves in the New World led to an increase in the number of slaves for export and a redirection of the trade away from the Near East and toward the Americas. Even in the Caribbean Islands, contrary to the N.C.C.'s assertion that "Columbus's invasion marked the beginning of slavery," there was slavery before 1492. The peaceful people whom Columbus initially found there were on occasion enslaved by their more warlike neighbors.

The other evils that are said to characterize the modern world were  11
not solely European in origin either. The rulers of the Aztecs and the Incas, the Chinese Emperors and the chiefs of the Iroquois were quite capable of conquering, pillaging and enslaving their neighbors without any guidance from Europeans.

Furthermore, the inhabitants of all parts of the world were capable  12
of resisting European invaders in various ways. The Americas, for example, saw the gradual extension of European control, but it was not easy. What often made European conquest possible were the divisions among the local people that enabled the colonizers to throw support to one side or another, thus changing the local balance of power. From the indigenous population's point of view, the Europeans were no doubt seen as capable of themselves being manipulated to serve that local population's purposes.

In Mexico, for example, Cortez obtained the support of peoples  13
whom the Aztecs had subjugated and who no doubt saw in the Spaniards the means for reasserting their independence with the hope of subsequently overthrowing Cortez himself. Again, the inhabitants of the Americas did not need instruction from Machiavelli to understand power politics and the playing off of one power against another. The

fact that these people eventually fell under Spanish domination did not mean that they were simply passive victims at the mercy of the all-powerful invaders.

The main thrust of the N.C.C. resolution is not, however, to clarify the historical record. It is to encourage consideration of the moral and spiritual consequences of Columbus's discovery, or invasion as the resolution labels it, of the New World. In good preaching style, the resolution calls upon Christians to "reflect seriously on the complexities and complicities of the missionary efforts during this period of colonization and subjugation that resulted in the destruction of cultures and religions, the desecration of religious sites, and other crimes against the spirituality of indigenous peoples. . . ." **14**

Such reflection is, however, clearly missing in the council's own resolution. In the first place, not all indigenous cultures in the New World were simply destroyed as the survival of various Indian groups indicates. In addition, there was not a monolithic Catholic response to the spirituality of indigenous peoples as the resolution suggests. The attitude of missionaries varied in a number of ways, ranging from the destructiveness that the resolution mentions, to the Jesuit attempts to understand Confucianism and to find links between that tradition and Christianity. The attempts to develop a Chinese Rite or a Malabar Rite in India indicates the variety of Catholic approaches to non-Christian religions, a variety of which the resolution seems unaware. **15**

Not only does the N.C.C.'s resolution show little awareness of the historical situation about which it appears so anxious to feel guilty; the resolution also slights the fact that many of the issues of which it speaks were raised by Spanish writers within a generation of Columbus's death. There is a brief mention of "the significant voices within the church that have consistently advocated the rights and dignities of indigenous peoples," but that is an understatement. There were voices raised about the legitimacy of the Spanish conquest of the Americas not only in the church but in Spanish secular society as well. Furthermore, these voices paved the way for thinking about the possibility of a peaceful world order. Spanish theologians, philosophers and lawyers, often building on the criticisms of the conquest of the New World made by missionaries on the scene, sought to develop a basis upon which fruitful peaceful relations could exist between Christian societies and non-Christian ones. This collaborative work included passionate defenders of the Indian such as the Dominican Bartholomew de Las Casas, and theorists such as the Dominican Francis Vitoria, whose lectures at the University of Salamanca on the moral problems involved in the conquest of the New World influenced a generation of missionaries and imperial officials. On through the 17th century, Spanish thinkers were attempting to resolve these moral and legal problems. **16**

That we know much at all about the evils of the Spanish conquest    17
is due to the work of these writers who were anxious to publicize the
terrible effects that the Spanish colonization had on some aspects of life
in the Americas. The Black Legend that purports to tell of the evil deeds
of the Spanish in the New World, a staple of English and American
historical writing ever since Las Casas' writings became known to the
16th-century English, exists largely because some Spanish missionaries,
professors and bureaucrats were anxious to improve the situation in the
Americas by publicizing the evil consequences of thoughtless imperialism.

The reality of the conquest of the New World was a great deal more    18
complex, even paradoxical, than the N.C.C.'s resolution suggests. Las
Casas, after all, who was a companion of Columbus and a landowner
using forced Indian labor, turned priest and defender of the rights of the
Indians. He was also one of the original supporters of using African
slaves in place of the Indians as laborers. His rationale was that this
would save the lives of the Indians who were frail and dying in large
numbers. The Africans were less susceptible to the diseases that were
destroying the Indians, and consequently they were a more secure
supply of labor. Las Casas eventually repented of this policy, but it
shows the complexity of the issues that 16th-century Spanish rulers in
the Americas faced.

The major aim of the N.C.C. resolution is not, however, to debate    19
the historical realities of the late 15th and early 16th centuries, although
such a debate would help 20th-century critics of Columbus and his
successors to understand more clearly what actually happened, a necessary first step to making responsible judgments about the morality of
the explorers' behavior. Instead, the N.C.C., reasonably enough, is seeking to create a moral basis for relations between the major Western
industrialized nations and the third world, and between white, European
Governments and non-white, non-European minority groups within
their societies. These are clearly praiseworthy goals, but they cannot be
achieved by developing moral theories within a historical vacuum.

A good though neglected starting point for considering the moral    20
basis of international and intercultural relations would be the writings of
the Spanish moralists and jurists of the 16th and 17th centuries. These
scholars, after all, greatly influenced Western thought on human rights
issues. They raised the problems, asked the questions and proposed
solutions. In the late 20th century, we might well see the problems
differently, ask different questions and come to different solutions. Nevertheless, as the contemporary physical sciences continue to build upon
the work of those who initiated the scientific revolution in the 16th and

---

287

17th centuries, so too philosophers and theologians interested in dealing with the problems that Columbus and those who followed him created should return to a study of those thinkers who first raised the questions that the N.C.C.'s resolution seeks to address.

Should we, then, celebrate Columbus? Certainly. He was a brave 21 man whose actions made a major contribution to the formation of the modern world. Should we celebrate equally each and every consequence of Columbus's first voyage? Of course not, but then neither did many of his contemporaries. We praise the good and condemn the bad. To reject Columbus is in effect to reject the modern world. The tone of the N.C.C. resolution seems to suggest that nothing good has occurred in the past 500 years which, ironically enough, included among other events the Protestant Reformation. Surely the sponsors of the N.C.C. resolution could not really have intended to say that much.

## Review Questions

1. Why do some consider the N.C.C. Resolution racist?
2. Why does Muldoon consider the N.C.C.'s treatment of "non-European . . . non-Christian and non-white people" patronizing?
3. In what ways does the N.C.C. Resolution tend to oversimplify the issues, according to Muldoon?
4. According to Muldoon, what is the underlying purpose of the N.C.C. Resolution?

## Discussion and Writing Suggestions

1. Summarize Muldoon's arguments against the N.C.C. Resolution.
2. Muldoon notes that the N.C.C. Resolution "can be seen as a condemnation of the entire history of the modern world." He later asserts that "to reject Columbus is . . . to reject the modern world." To what extent do you agree with these statements?
3. Muldoon believes that "some readers will . . . reject the N.C.C.'s work as pious rhetoric expressing a sense of humanitarian guilt in vaguely Marxist terminology." If you have studied Marxism, explain how the resolution might be perceived as "vaguely Marxist." Do you perceive it as Marxist, vaguely or otherwise? Explain.
4. If Muldoon's assertions in paragraphs 9–13 are true, to what extent are the charges contained in the N.C.C. Resolution invalidated? Explain.
5. If you are more persuaded by the N.C.C. Resolution than by this article, write a critique of Muldoon. You may choose to put yourself in the position of a member of the governing board of N.C.C.

# What Columbus Discovered

## KIRKPATRICK SALE

*If the N.C.C. Resolution gave aid and comfort to the anti-Columbians, Kirkpatrick Sale provided the heavy artillery. His 1990 book* The Conquest of Paradise: Christopher Columbus and the Columbian Legacy *was a systematic debunking of the Columbus myth, perhaps the single most controversial work in the quincentennial debate.* The Conquest of Paradise *goes beyond a reassessment of Columbus to develop an extended critique of contemporary civilization. "I find it ironic that a man so rootless himself," said Sale in an interview, "should have helped create such a rootless society." A professional writer, Sale began his career as a journalist for the leftist* New Leader. *His books include* SDS *(a study of the revolutionary Students for a Democratic Society, which flourished in the 1960s),* Human Scale, *and* Dwellers in the Land *(concerned with "bioregionalism," a movement that urges humans to reverse their tendency to endless expansion and development). As Sale assesses his own work, "I write my books to help save society and the planet."* The Conquest of Paradise *continues that endeavor by holding up Columbus and his followers as models of civilization to avoid and by holding up the natives Columbus "discovered" as models to emulate. Even the Native Americans, Sale notes, would have been well advised to heed such models: "I make no plea for the innate superiority of the major nation groups like the Mayas and the Aztecs," he says, "but the smaller societies were genuinely benign, adjusted to each other and to nature. They could serve as a model for the possibility of a harmonious human life."*

*The following passage, a condensation of ideas developed at greater length in* The Conquest of Paradise, *originally appeared in* The Nation *on October 22, 1990.*

It is fitting that we begin with the night the New World first presented itself to the Old. It was October 11, and the moon was just a few days past full, the skies clear. Three small ships from the Spanish port of Palos, none of them bigger than a modern tennis court, were scudding before a brisk breeze of about ten knots, somewhere in the western part of the Ocean Sea. The mood of anticipation was high, even after thirty-two days at sea, for signs of land had come increasingly often in the previous few days.

Excerpt from "How Paradise Was Lost: What Columbus Discovered," by Kirkpatrick Sale from *The Nation*, October 22, 1990. This article is reprinted from *The Nation* magazine. © The Nation Company, Inc.

Around 10 o'clock the captain general of the little fleet, known to 2
his companions as Cristóbal Colón—"Columbus" was a latter-day La-
tinization that he himself never heard—thought he saw from his post
in the sterncastle a light on the western horizon. According to the ship's
log, "it was a thing so uncertain that he did not wish to affirm that it
was land," so he called the royal steward, who said he too saw the light,
and the royal inspector, who said he could see nothing. The captain
general kept staring. He thought he could see something out there, "like
a little wax candle that was lifting and rising," but no one on either of
the two other ships raised the call, so he merely told his crew to keep
"a good watch on the forecastle, and to look well for the land." And he
added that "to him who first said that he saw land he would then give
a doublet of silk," and this "besides the other rewards that the Sovereigns had promised, which were 10,000 maravedis as an annuity to
whoever should first sight it."

Sometime around 2 in the morning the lookout on the foremost 3
ship, Juan Rodríguez Bermejo, gave out the cry of "Tierra!" and the
watchcrew fired a cannon as a signal to the other ships that land was
ahead. And there, "at a distance of 2 leagues," was their long-awaited
goal in sight. Sails were lowered, and the fleet prudently lay-to until
daylight before making their landing.

Shortly after dawn the crew of the flagship broke out its official 4
banners and pennants, including the royal standard, in a display of
ceremonial grandeur. Soon, luckily for their theater, "they saw naked
people" on the sands. The captain general ordered the flagship's long-
boat lowered, stepped to its bow and then, with the two royal observers
to take notes, perhaps the official interpreter, and no doubt a few sailors
armed with swords and harquebuses to act as guards, he was rowed
ashore.

Ashore . . . to discover America. 5

Of course it was not America, not yet, and he did not discover it. 6
But those are minor matters. What counts, what is absolutely crucial,
is that with this act two vastly different cultures, which had evolved
on continents that had been drifting apart steadily for millions of
years, were suddenly joined. Everything of importance in the succeeding 500 years stems from that momentous event: the rise of Europe,
the triumph of capitalism, the creation of the nation-state, the dominance of science, the establishment of a global monoculture, the genocide of the indigenes, the slavery of people of color, the colonization
of the world, the destruction of primal environments, the eradication
and abuse of species and the impending catastrophe of ecocide for the
planet Earth.

Some say—it is highly doubtful, in fact—that Cristóbal Colón was 7
sailing for China. It is a shame that he didn't find it. This landfall would

then have been but a small episode in the dalliance of petty monarchs and their envoys.

Instead, it began the process by which the culture of Europe, aptly represented by this captain, implanted its diseased and dangerous seeds in the soils of the continents that represented the last best hope for humankind—and destroyed them. **8**

It is best to think of Colón as a man *without place*. He was a wanderer, always rootless and restless; without ever in his life a sense of family, no attachment to mother or father, very little to wife or mistress, caring for his son only as the bearer of his name; without ever a settled home, a place that he would stay in for more than a year or two at a time throughout his life; without even an established name, for it would change depending on the country he was in, until at the end it took the form of an indecipherable, cabalistic signature. **9**

He was a man whose strongest wish was always to go somewhere *else*. For much of his life he was consumed by the idea of sailing westward across the ocean, but once he had done it he was not content until he had done it again, and again, and yet again, going past this island and on to the next, never knowing a one of them past its superficialities, and then ever onward. **10**

He was a man who knew no singular and particular plot of the earth, nor was he ever concerned to know one, for his sense of himself was formed entirely by the sea, which offers no habitation for the human animal. The only place he could call his dwelling, such "home" as he ever was to know, was the wooden deck of an always moving ship, surrounded by the interminable gray waves of an ocean that forever changes. **11**

It is best to think of the cultures that Colón brought under European might as, until the conquest he initiated, *rooted in place*. There were differences among them, of course, and some of the statist ones of Mesoamerica were becoming less and less respectful of their ancient traditions intertwined with the sacralization of nature. But by and large they lived, as they had to live for long-term survival, with an exquisite sense of, and care for, the bioregions in which they were established, knowing the local soils and waters and flowers and animals with such intimacy that children were brought up knowing ten different words for different kinds of waterways, and elders could predict with exactitude when the roses or the buttercups would bloom. **12**

Take, for example, the Taino, our name for the people whom Colón first encountered in the "Islands of the Indies." They were a populous society that had been on those islands for some 1,500 years before the **13**

Europeans' arrival and that had developed lifeways precisely adapted to the environment. Their houses were large and spacious, perfect for the tropical climate, and made to be especially resistant to hurricanes, with circular walls of deep-set cane poles placed very close together, and conical roofs of branches and vines tightly woven on a frame of smaller poles. Their transportation was based primarily on canoes of all kinds and lengths—the word "canoe" comes from the Taino *canoa*—which they created from local silk-cotton trees by firing and carving and which were maneuvered, sometimes with as many as a hundred paddlers, with great dexterity and skill. Best of all, their agriculture was centered around fields of knee-high mounds called *conucos*, planted with *yuca* (sometimes called manioc), *batata* (sweet potatoes) and various squashes and beans grown all together in multicrop harmony. The root crops were excellent for discouraging erosion and producing minerals and potash, the leaf crops were effective in providing shade and moisture, and the mound configurations were largely resistant to erosion and flooding and adaptable to almost all topographical conditions, including steep hillsides. Not only was the system ecologically well balanced and protective but it was also marvelously productive, surpassing anything known in Europe at the time, and with labor that amounted to hardly more than two or three hours a week.

And with a similar genius, similarly rooted in the precise condi- 14 tions of place, the Taino had developed a social system that had refined the arts of civility and harmony to a degree that was remarkable (and remarked upon continually by the Europeans). So little a role did violence play in their life that they seem to have had a society without war (at least with no known war music or artifacts) and essentially even without individual violence (at least according to the reports of the Spanish who settled among them). So large a role did the social arts play that all those who first met them commented unfailingly on their friendliness, their warmth, their openness and especially their generosity. "In all the world," Colón was moved to say, "there is no better people nor better country. They love their neighbors as themselves, and they have the sweetest talk in the world, and are gentle and are always laughing."

As with the Taino, so with most other cultures of these two vast 15 continents: people who lived in harmony—with one another, with other species, with the land—for the greatest part of their long tenure. They knew, somehow across thousands of miles and despite great cultural differences, that they were living in a bountiful world with a multitude of treasures: buffalo herds that stretched from horizon to horizon, birds that darkened the sky in their flight, fish that were so numerous they could be caught by hand, forests in which grew every needed plant. They knew, too, that it was sacred.

Many of these aboriginal peoples had myths of Paradise. It was not, 16 however, of Paradise Lost, humans thrust out of an abundant land into a harsh and hostile world. It was a Paradise Found, the wonderful world they inhabited, having ascended from some darker depths, and it was precious and holy and to be protected. Creation myths, of course, have consequences.

Do not ask, by the way, what happened to those gentle Taino. The 17 story is too painful. Suffice it to say that on the large island that Colón thought so like Spain he named it Española there were probably close to 8 million people in 1492; twenty-two years later there were, by Spanish record, only about 28,000; by mid-century they were extinct.

Out of this history I would suggest some lessons for the present. 18 And the future, if there is to be one.

The only political vision that offers any hope of salvation is one 19 based on an understanding of, a rootedness in, a deep commitment to, and a resacralization of, *place*. Here is where any strategy of resistance to the industrial monolith and its merchants of death must begin; here is where any program of restoration and revitalization must be grounded. It is the only way we can effectively counterpose ourselves to the state and the ridiculous forms of acquiescence and co-optation that it calls politics. It is the only way we can build a politics that can spread the message that Western civilization itself, shot through with a denial of place and a utilitarian concept of nature, must be transformed. By making an awareness of, and attachment to, locality the centerpiece of our philosophy and practice, we can directly and decisively challenge that civilization and its monstrosities, can specifically and creatively offer an alternative.

Such a politics, based, as the original peoples of the Americas had 20 it, upon love of place, also implies the place of love. For ultimately love is the true cradle of politics, the love of the earth and its systems, the love of the particular bioregion we inhabit, the love of those who share it with us in our communities, and the love of that unnameable essence that binds us together with the earth, and provides the water for the roots we sink.

Juan Rodríguez Bermejo, lookout of the Pinta, did not collect the 21 10,000 maravedi reward or the silk doublet promised by the captain general. Although that amount represented only a little less than a seaman's annual wages, Colón, despite now being on his way to great wealth, kept all of it to himself, on the ground that, after all, he must have seen the lights of that landfall earlier in the evening, and wasn't there the royal steward who agreed with him? In 1493, upon his explicit petition, Ferdinand and Isabella dutifully assigned him this legacy, supposedly raising the money from a special tax on butcher shops in Seville, or possibly from a confiscation of valuables in the possession of suspect Jewish *conversos*.

Not so surprising that the enterprise of Europe's conquest of Para-    22 dise should have begun, as it was to continue, with deceit, robbery and ill-gotten gains. Surprising that we have heard so little about that all these centuries. We may redress that error now, in these months before the celebrations, and thus provide the opportunity for a serious and careful reassessment of what the Columbian legacy is for us today—a reassessment that just might allow us to look with new eyes at the discovery itself and the processes it unfolded so as to reflect, with the wisdom of hindsight, upon the values and attitudes inherent in that conquering culture and in the industrial civilization it has fostered.

## Review Questions

1. For Sale, why is the dispute over Columbus claiming the reward money for first sighting land particularly significant?
2. How, primarily, does Sale contrast Columbus with the native peoples he encountered?
3. What is the only pathway to our salvation, according to Sale?

## Discussion and Writing Suggestions

1. Columbus's landing, according to Sale, "began the process by which the culture of Europe, aptly represented by this captain, implanted its diseased and dangerous seeds in the soils of continents that represented the last best hope for humankind—and destroyed them." Respond to this statement.
2. Compare and contrast Sale's argument with the N.C.C. Resolution. Consider the points on which they focus, their language, their conclusions.
3. Sale concludes that by reassessing the Columbian legacy we reflect not only on the values of fifteenth-century European civilization, but also on "the industrial civilization it has fostered." To what extent is one justified in so linking the one civilization to the other? How is the guilt of an industrial civilization related to the guilt of the Spanish explorers?
4. Reread Columbus's log for October 11, 1492. Do you believe that Sale offers a fair interpretation of Columbus's thoughts and actions on that day? Explain.
5. In a paragraph or two, contrast paragraph 6 of Sale with a comparable paragraph in Lamartine, Depew, or Elson.
6. Toward the end of his article, Sale suggests that our only salvation is

one based on an understanding of, a rootedness in, a deep commitment to, and a resacralization of, *place*. Here is where any strategy of resistance to the industrial monolith and its merchants of death must begin; here is where any program of restoration and revitalization must be grounded. It is the only way we can effectively counterpose ourselves to the state and the ridiculous forms of acquiescence and co-optation that it calls politics.

Comment on this passage and on the two paragraphs that follow. To what extent do you think that Sale is justified in attacking the components of Western civilization? What does he mean by "industrial merchants of death" and "the ridiculous forms of acquiescence and co-optation that it calls politics"? What might the country be like if we were to follow his prescription?

7. Roberto Rodriguez, a Washington-based writer, has argued that the church's insistence on forcibly converting indigenous peoples to Christianity and

essentially attempting to culturally transform them into Europeans . . . taught the indigenous people to despise themselves. It taught them that Europe was the source of "civilization," and that all things European were good and all things non-European were bad. It also taught the indigenous people, and then the *mestizo* [a descendant of indigenous-Hispanic union], the concept of European racial superiority and the notion of racial purity.

Based on your own personal knowledge or reading, to what extent is Rodriguez's assertion valid?

# Was America a Mistake?

## ARTHUR SCHLESINGER

*The question of whether Columbus and his legacy was good or bad for the New World presumes that there was some alternative—either that Columbus or others never succeeded in finding America, or that when they did, they acted more humanely. In this passage, historian Arthur Schlesinger considers the likelihood of such alternatives and discusses the benefits of the European legacy. Schlesinger (b. 1917) was teaching at Harvard University when the newly inaugurated John F. Kennedy appointed him as special assistant to the president (a post he also held in the Johnson administration). Schlesinger has won two Pulitzer Prizes, the first at the age of twenty-eight for his* Age of Jackson *(1945); the second for* A Thousand Days *(1966), a history of the Kennedy administration. He has also written* The Age of Roosevelt *(1957– 1960),* The Imperial Presidency *(1973),* Robert Kennedy and His Times *(1978), and* The Cycles of American History *(1986).*

*The following passage is excerpted from an article that first appeared in*

Excerpt from "Was America a Mistake?" by Arthur Schlesinger, Jr. Originally published in September 1992 issue of *The Atlantic Monthly*. Reprinted by permission.

*The Atlantic (1992). Early in the article, Schlesinger surveys the objections to the Columbus celebrations, commenting, "Revisionism redresses the balance up to a point; but, driven by Western guilt, it may verge on masochism." Later, in accounting for the intense contemporary backlash against Columbus, he concludes:*

It reflects the revolt of the Third World against economic exploitation, against political control, against cultural despoliation, against personal and national humiliation, even at times, against modernity itself. It reflects the (belated) bad conscience of the West and the consequent re-examination of the Western impact on the rest of humanity.

Let us for a moment suppose that the Americas could have been indefinitely sealed off from Europe. Would the world be better off? Mario Vargas Llosa has asked, "What would America be like in the 1990s if the dominant cultures were those of the Aztecs and Incas?" The anthropologist Jorge Klor De Alva once speculated that it might be something like contemporary India—a mixture of religions, languages, and castes, somehow extracting coherence out of incoherence. But India had a century and a half of British imperialism, and therefore a legacy of parliamentary democracy. What would the destiny of the Americas have been without any European infusion? 1

One must hope that by the twentieth century the Aztecs and the Incas would have learned to read and write and would have abandoned their commitment to torture, obsidian knives, and blood-stained pyramids. But they would most likely have preserved their collectivist cultures and their conviction that the individual had no legitimacy outside the theocratic state, and the result would have been a repressive fundamentalism comparable perhaps to that of the Ayatollah Khomeini in Iran. Aztec and Inca traditions offer little hope for the status of women, for equality before the law, for religious tolerance, for civil liberties, for human rights, and for other purposes deriving uniquely from European culture. 2

But let us be realistic. The idea that the Americas could have survived in invincible isolation is fantasy. As a practical matter, America by the fifteenth century was fated to be found by a Europe bursting at the seams with its own dynamism, greed, and evangelical zeal. Columbus happened to make the decisive voyage, but he was not indispensable to that voyage's eventually being made. Europe's westward impulse had already embraced Madeira and the Canaries and the Azores. It would not, could not, halt there. If the "discoverer" was not to be Christopher Columbus, then it would have been Amerigo Ves- 3 pucci or John Cabot or some mute, inglorious mariner now lost to history. Had Columbus, like his brother Giovanni Pellegrino, died young, the quincentennial might have been delayed a few years, but would still be on its way.

Once the Europeans arrived, could they have pursued more-benign    4
policies? Obviously one wishes that in the treatment of natives the Spanish had followed Las Casas rather than Columbus. Perhaps more did so than we know; at least historians generally agree today that the Black Legend of Spanish Catholic villainy was an envenomed Protestant exaggeration. Las Casas, alas, had all too few equivalents in the British and French colonies. In general, the European record in dealing with the indigenous peoples of the Americas was miserable—and indefensible. But it is not clear that Europeans in those war-wracked and religiously fanatical centuries were any more humane in dealing with their enemies at home.

Obviously one also wishes that the Europeans had understood as    5
much about preserving the balance of nature as the Amerindians did, or as our ecologists do today. In their ignorance and arrogance the intruders did indeed bring about extreme ecological disruption. But the migration of peoples has gone on since the beginning of time and cannot be halted; and migrants inevitably bring with them their own habits, technologies, diets, animals, plants, diseases. Even the Amerindians were once migrants. Still, some anti-Columbus revisionists see "ecohubris" as Europe's peculiar sin and, in Kirkpatrick Sale's words, *"warring against species* as Europe's preoccupation as a culture."

Deeper questions are suggested: Does humanity have an obligation    6
to preserve every manifestation of life on the planet? Is every culture equally sacred, no matter how sadistic and horrible? And, assuming the answer is yes, is it possible to freeze history in place and immunize the world against what has heretofore seemed history's one constant—change?

The fact that we cannot stop change complicates one's response to    7
the idea that every culture and species is sacred. And to deny the right to change is to amputate the human spirit. What animated Columbus more than anything else, more than God or glory or gold, must surely have been those primal passions of curiosity and wonder, the response to the challenge of the unknown, the need to go where none had gone before. That everlasting quest for new frontiers continues today as earthlings burst terrestrial bonds and begin the endless voyage beyond planet and galaxy into the illimitable dark.

The fact that Heraclitus was right and nothing stands still does not    8
of course justify all the costs of change, especially unnecessary costs in

human suffering and destruction. If we are compelled to give this anniversary a balance sheet, those costs weigh heavily against Columbus and even more against those who followed him.

But there are benefits, too, and these require to be factored into the historical equation. The opening of the Americas ushered in a new era of human history. Not only did the gold and silver and furs of the New World stimulate economic growth, commercial integration, and intellectual analysis in the Old; even more, the age of exploration began to draw the world together into new potentialities of unity, and a new recognition of the varieties of human existence challenged the human intellect and the human imagination. 9

The era Columbus initiated has seen horror and sadism perhaps worse than the tortures and human sacrifices of the Aztecs. But out of anguish (out, too, of self-criticism and bad conscience) have evolved the great liberating ideas of individual dignity, political democracy, equality before the law, religious tolerance, cultural pluralism, artistic freedom—ideas that emerged uniquely from Europe but that empower people of every continent, color, and creed; ideas to which most of the world today aspires; ideas that offer a new and generous vision of our common life on this interdependent planet. The clash of cultures may yield in the end—not, certainly, to a single global culture (heaven forbid) but to a world in which many differentiated national cultures live side by side in reciprocal enrichment. This, too, is part of the legacy of Columbus. 10

## Review Questions

1. Why does Schlesinger believe it makes no sense to blame Columbus for the often bloody heritage of the Europeans in the Americas?
2. To what extent does Schlesinger condemn the Europeans for their actions in the New World?
3. Summarize the benefits of Europe's heritage in the Americas, according to Schlesinger.

## Discussion and Writing Suggestions

1. Respond to the suggestion that had it remained sealed off from Europe, America today "might be something like contemporary India—a mixture of religions, languages and castes. . . ." Do you agree? If so, would such a land be preferable to the contemporary United States? If not, what might it be like?
2. To what extent do you think that Schlesinger effectively counters the arguments of Sale and the authors of the N.C.C. Resolution? Has he persuaded you that, on balance, America is better off for Columbus and the European

heritage than it was before 1492—or than it would have been had no Europeans arrived on American shores? Explain. What are his most (and least) convincing arguments?

3. Putting yourself in the position of Sale, write an editorial responding to Schlesinger's article.
4. Michael Berliner, executive director of the Ayn Rand Institute, and, like Schlesinger, a defender of Western civilization in the Columbus debate, argues that life in the Americas in the pre-Columbian era was hardly ideal: "There was no wheel, no written language, little agriculture and scant permanent settlement; but there were endless, bloody wars. With rare exception, life was nasty, brutish, and short." He goes on to assert:

Some cultures are better than others. A free society is better than slavery; reason is better than brute force as a way to deal with other men; productivity is better than stagnation. In fact, Western civilization stands for man at his best. It stands for the values that sustain human life: reason, science, self-reliance, individualism, ambition, productive achievement. The values of Western civilization are values for all human beings; they cut across gender, ethnicity and geography. We should honor Western civilization not for the ethnocentric reason that some of us happen to have European ancestors but because it is the objectively superior culture. ("Man's Best Came With Columbus," Los Angeles Times, December 30, 1991)

In a critique, respond to Berliner's comments.

# I Won't Be Celebrating Columbus Day

## SUZAN SHOWN HARJO

*The following Native American perspective on Columbus appeared in a special issue of* Newsweek *on the quincentennial published in Fall/Winter 1991. Suzan Shown Harjo, who is Cheyenne and Muskogee, is the national coordinator of the 1992 Alliance, a coalition of Native groups.*

Columbus Day, never on Native America's list of favorite holidays,    1
became somewhat tolerable as its significance diminished to little more than a good shopping day. But this next long year of Columbus hoopla will be tough to take amid the spending sprees and horn blowing to tout a five-century feeding frenzy that has left Native people and this red quarter of Mother Earth in a state of emergency. For Native people, this

half millennium of land grabs and one-cent treaty sales has been no bargain.

An obscene amount of money will be lavished over the next year on parades, statues and festivals. The Christopher Columbus Quincentenary Jubilee Commission will spend megabucks to stage what it delicately calls "maritime activities" in Boston, San Francisco and other cities with no connection to the original rub-a-dub-dub lurch across the sea in search of India and gold. Funny hats will be worn and new myths born. Little kids will be told big lies in the name of education.

The pressure is on for Native people to be window dressing for Quincentennial events, to celebrate the evangelization of the Americas and to denounce the "Columbus-bashers." We will be asked to buy into the thinking that we cannot change history, and that genocide and ecocide are offset by the benefits of horses, cut-glass beads, pickup trucks and microwave ovens.

The participation of some Native people will be its own best evidence of the effectiveness of 500 years of colonization, and should surprise no one. But at the same time, neither should anyone be surprised by Native people who mark the occasion by splashing blood-red paint on a Columbus statue here or there. Columbus will be hanged in effigy as a symbol of the European invasion, and tried in planned tribunals.

It would be great to fast-forward to 1993, which the United Nations has declared the "Year of the Indigenous People." Perhaps then we can begin to tell our own stories outside the context of confrontation— begin to celebrate the miracle of survival of those remaining Native people, religions, cultures, languages, legal systems, medicine and values. In the meantime, it should be understood that, even in polite society, voices will be raised just to be heard at all over the din of the celebrators.

For what's left of 1991, Native people will continue marking the 500th anniversary of 1491, the good old days in our old countries. There was life here before 1492—although that period of our history is called "prehistory" in the European and American educational systems—and there is life after 1992.

We would like to turn our attention to making the next 500 years different from the past ones; to enter into a time of grace and healing. In order to do so, we must first involve ourselves in educating the colonizing nations, which are investing a lot not only in silly plans but in serious efforts to further revise history, to justify the bloodshed and destruction, to deny that genocide was committed here and to revive failed policies of assimilation as the answer to progress.

These societies must come to grips with the past, acknowledge responsibility for the present and do something about the future. It does no good to gloss over the history of the excesses of Western civilization, especially when those excesses are the root cause of deplorable conditions today. Both church and state would do well to commit some small pots of gold, gained in ways the world knows, to bringing some relief to the suffering and some measure of justice to all.

The United States could start by upholding its treaty promises—as it is bound to do by the Constitution that calls treaties the "Supreme law of the Land." Churches could start by dedicating money to the eradication of those diseases that Native people still die from in such disproportionately high numbers—hepatitis, influenza, pneumonia, tuberculosis.   9

Church and state could start defending our religious freedom and stop further destruction of our holy places. The general society could help more of our children grow into healthy adults just by eliminating dehumanizing images of Native people in popular culture. Stereotypes of us as sports mascots or names on leisure vans cannot be worth the low self-esteem they cause.   10

Native people are few in number—under 2 million in the United States, where there are, even with recent law changes, more dead Indians in museums and educational institutions than there are live ones today. Most of us are in economic survival mode on a daily basis, and many of us are bobbing about in the middle of the mainstream just treading water. This leaves precious few against great odds to do our part to change the world.   11

It is necessary and well past time for others to amplify our voices and find their own to tell their neighbors and institutions that 500 years of this history is more than enough and must come to an end.   12

This year, Native people will memorialize those who did not survive the invasion of 1492. It is fitting for others to join us at this time to begin an era of respect and rediscovery, to find a new world beyond 1992.   13

## Review Questions

1. Summarize Harjo's chief objections to celebrating Columbus Day and the quincentennial.
2. How does Harjo suggest that Western nations can partially atone for the plunder it has committed since Columbus?

## Discussion and Writing Suggestions

1. Compare and contrast Harjo's article with other anti-Columbian pieces, such as the N.C.C. Resolution and the articles by Bigelow, Las Casas, and Sale. Consider subject matter, language, and tone.
2. Some people, although sympathetic to the arguments made by Native Americans like Harjo, reject the idea of collective guilt, contending that individuals

born to one generation have no special responsibility to atone for the sins of past generations, of which they had no part. What is your position on this issue? If you are not Native American, to what extent do you feel a responsibility to help make amends for the injustices committed by others? How would you follow through on this responsibility?

3. Write a short paper indicating how you think Harjo might respond to the arguments of pro-Columbians, such as Muldoon and Schlesinger. You may want to design the paper as a critique written by Harjo.

# Questions of Conquest

## MARIO VARGAS LLOSA

*In the following selection, Mario Vargas Llosa focuses less on the Columbus debate itself than on the question of why a relatively small contingent of Spaniards was able so rapidly and decisively to defeat the huge Inca Empire. In responding to this question, the author casts doubt on sentimental views of Native American peoples sometimes advanced by opponents of Columbus, and he outlines a crucial structural difference between the two societies that accounted for the victory—for better or worse—of Western culture.*

*Mario Vargas Llosa is one of Peru's most eminent men of letters: a novelist, short-story writer, dramatist, and essayist. One critic (Suzanne Jill) has compared Vargas Llosa to Dickens and Balzac in his realism, and to Flaubert and Henry James in his technical skill, adding that he "has begun a complete inventory of the political, social, economic, and cultural reality of Peru." Vargas Llosa has been nominated several times for the Nobel Prize and, thanks to the political and social insight displayed in his novels, once was offered the post of prime minister of Peru, an honor he declined. More recently, he ran for president of Peru (but lost). Among his novels are* La casa verde *(1966,* The Green House*);* La tia el escribador *(1977,* Aunt Julia and the Scriptwriter*);* La guerra del fin del mundo *(1981,* The War of the End of the World*); and most recently,* In Praise of the Stepmother *(1991). This article originally appeared in* Harper's *(December 1990), and was reprinted in the present abridgment in* American Educator *(Spring 1992).*

In Madrid not long ago, a shadowy group calling itself the Association 1 of Indian Cultures held a press conference to announce that its members (it was not clear who these men and women might be) were preparing to undertake, in Spain and also throughout Latin America, a number of acts of "sabotage." It is, of course, a sad fact of life that in a number of Latin American countries—in Spain as well—the planting of bombs and the destruction of property continue to be perceived by some as a means of achieving justice, or self-determination, or, as in my country, Peru, the realization of a revolutionary utopia. But the Association of Indian Cultures did not seem interested in seizing the future. Their battle was with the past.

What are to be sabotaged by this group are the numerous quincen-  2
tennial ceremonies and festivities scheduled for 1992 to commemorate the epochal voyage nearly five hundred years ago of Columbus's three small caravels. The Association of Indian Cultures believes that the momentous events of 1492 should in no way be celebrated; and although I have yet to hear of other persons willing to make the point through subversion, I do know that the group will not lack for sympathizers.

The question most crucial to these individuals is the oldest one: Was  3
the discovery and conquest of America by Europeans the greatest feat of the Christian West or one of history's monumental crimes? It is a question they ask rhetorically and perhaps will answer with violence. This is not to say that to discuss what could have happened as opposed to what did happen is a useless undertaking: Historians and thinkers have pondered the question since the seventeenth century, producing wonderful books and speculations. But to me the debate serves no practical purpose, and I intend to stay out of it. What would America be like in the 1990s if the dominant cultures were those of the Aztecs and Incas? The only answer, ultimately, is that there is no way to know.

I have another question having to do with the conquest, and I  4
happen to think that an honest and thoughtful discussion of it is as timely and urgent as any others one could pose just now about Latin America. How was it possible that cultures as powerful and sophisticated as those of the ancient Mexicans and Peruvians—huge imperial cultures, as opposed to the scattered tribes of North America—so easily crumbled when encountered by infinitesimally small bands of Spanish adventurers? This question is itself centuries old, but not academic. In its answer may lie the basis for an understanding of the world the conquest engendered, a chronically "underdeveloped" world that has, for the most part, remained incapable of realizing its goals and visions. . . .[1]

---

[1]In the original article, Vargas Llosa also discusses a second question: "why have the postcolonial republics of the Americas—republics that might have been expected to have deeper and broader notions of liberty, equality, and fraternity—failed so miserably to improve the lives of their Indian citizens?"

The conquest of the Tawantinsuyu—the name given to the Inca 5
Empire in its totality—by a handful of Spaniards is a fact of history that
even now, after having digested and ruminated over all the explanations, we find hard to unravel. The first wave of conquistadores, Francisco Pizarro and his companions, was fewer than 200, not counting the
black slaves and the collaborating Indians. When the reinforcements
started to arrive, this first wave had already dealt a mortal blow and
taken over an empire that had ruled over at least twenty million people.
This was not a primitive society made up of barbaric tribes, like the ones
the Spaniards had found in the Caribbean or in Darién, but a civilization
that had reached a high level of social, military, agricultural, and handi-
craft development that in many ways Spain itself had not reached.

The most remarkable aspects of this civilization, however, were not 6
the paths that crossed the four *suyus*, or regions, of the vast territory,
the temples and fortresses, the irrigation systems, or the complex administrative organization, but something about which all the testimonies of
the chronicles agree. This civilization managed to eradicate hunger in
that immense region. It was able to distribute all that was produced in
such a way that all its subjects had enough to eat. Only a very small
number of empires throughout the whole world have succeeded in
achieving this feat. Are the conquistadores' firearms, horses, and armor
enough to explain the immediate collapse of this Inca civilization at the
first clash with the Spaniards? It is true the gunpowder, the bullets, and
the charging of beasts that were unknown to them paralyzed the Indians
with a religious terror and provoked in them the feeling that they were
fighting not against men but against gods who were invulnerable to the
arrows and slings with which they fought. Even so, the numerical
difference was such that the Quechua ocean would have had simply to
shake in order to drown the invader.

What prevented this from happening? What is the profound expla- 7
nation for that defeat from which the Inca population never recovered?
The answer may perhaps lie hidden in the moving account that appears
in the chronicles of what happened in the Cajamarca Square the day
Pizarro captured the last ruler of the empire, Inca Atahualpa. We must,
above all, read the accounts of those who were there, those who lived
through the event or had direct testimony of it.

At the precise moment the Inca emperor is captured, before the 8
battle begins, his armies give up the fight as if manacled by a magic
force. The slaughter is indescribable, but only from one of the two sides.
The Spaniards discharged their harquebuses, thrust their pikes and
swords, and charged their horses against a bewildered mass, which,
having witnessed the capture of their god and master, seemed unable to
defend itself or even to run away. In the space of a few minutes, the
army, which defeated Prince Huáscar, the emperor's half-brother, in a

battle for rule, and which dominated all the northern provinces of the empire, disintegrated like ice in warm water.

The vertical and totalitarian structure of the Tawantinsuyu was without doubt more harmful to its survival than all the conquistadores' firearms and iron weapons. As soon as the Inca, that figure who was the vortex toward which all the wills converged searching for inspiration and vitality, the axis around which the entire society was organized and upon which depended the life and death of every person, from the richest to the poorest, was captured, no one knew how to act. And so they did the only thing they could do with heroism, we must admit, but without breaking the 1,001 taboos and precepts that regulated their existence. They let themselves get killed. And that was the fate of dozens and perhaps hundreds of Indians stultified by the confusion and the loss of leadership they suffered when the Inca emperor, the life force of their universe, was captured right before their eyes. Those Indians who let themselves be knifed or blown up into pieces that somber afternoon in Cajamarca Square lacked the ability to make their own decisions either with the sanction of authority or indeed against it and were incapable of taking individual initiative, of acting with a certain degree of independence according to the changing circumstances. 9

Those 180 Spaniards who had placed the Indians in ambush and were now slaughtering them did possess this ability. It was this difference, more than the numerical one or the weapons, that created an immense inequality between those civilizations. The individual had no importance and virtually no existence in that pyramidal and theocratic society whose achievements had always been collective and anonymous—carrying the gigantic stones of the Machu Picchu citadel or of the Ollantay fortress up the steepest of peaks, directing water to all the slopes of the cordillera hills by building terraces that even today enable irrigation to take place in the most desolate places, and making paths to unite regions separated by infernal geographies. 10

A state religion that took away the individual's free will and crowned the authority's decision with the aura of a divine mandate turned the Tawantinsuyu into a beehive—laborious, efficient, stoic. But its immense power was, in fact, very fragile. It rested completely on the sovereign god's shoulders, the man whom the Indian had to serve and to whom he owed a total and selfless obedience. It was religion rather than force that preserved the people's metaphysical docility toward the Inca. It was an essentially political religion, which on the one hand turned the Indians into diligent servants and on the other was capable of receiving into its bosom as minor gods all the deities of the peoples that had been conquered, whose idols were moved to Cuzco and enthroned by the Inca himself. The Inca religion was less cruel than the 11

Aztec one, for it performed human sacrifices with a certain degree of moderation, if this can be said, making use only of the necessary cruelty to ensure hypnosis and fear of the subjects toward the divine power incarnated in the temporary power of the Inca.

We cannot call into question the organizing genius of the Inca. The **12** speed with which the empire, in the short period of a century, grew from its nucleus in Cuzco high in the Andes to become a civilization that embraced three quarters of South America is incredible. And this was the result not only of the Quechua's military efficiency but also of the Inca's ability to persuade the neighboring peoples and cultures to join the Tawantinsuyu. Once these other peoples and cultures became part of the empire, the bureaucratic mechanism was immediately set in motion, enrolling the new servants in that system that dissolves individual life into a series of tasks and gregarious duties carefully programmed and supervised by the gigantic network of administrators whom the Inca sent to the farthest borders. Either to prevent or to extinguish rebelliousness, there was a system called *mitimaes*, by which villages and people were removed en masse to faraway places where, feeling misplaced and lost, these exiles naturally assumed an attitude of passivity and absolute respect, which of course represented the Inca system's ideal citizen.

Such a civilization was capable of fighting against the natural ele- **13** ments and defeating them. It was capable of consuming rationally what it produced, heaping together reserves for future times of poverty or disaster. And it was also able to evolve slowly and with care in the field of knowledge, inventing only that which could support it and deterring all that which in some way or another could undermine its foundation— as, for example, writing or any other form of expression likely to develop individual pride or a rebellious imagination.

It was not capable, however, of facing the unexpected, that absolute **14** novelty presented by the balance of armored men on horseback who assaulted the Incas with weapons transgressing all the war-and-peace patterns known to them. When, after the initial confusion, attempts to resist started breaking out here and there, it was too late. The complicated machinery regulating the empire had entered a process of decomposition. Leaderless with the murder of Inca Huayana Capac's two sons, Huáscar and Atahualpa, the Inca system seems to fall into a monumental state of confusion and cosmic deviation, similar to the chaos that, according to the Cuzcan sages, the Amautas, had prevailed in the world before the Tawantinsuyu was founded by the mythical Manco Capac and Mama Ocllo.

While on the one hand caravans of Indians loaded with gold and **15** silver continued to offer treasures to the conquistadores to pay for the Inca's rescue, on the other hand a group of Quechua generals, attempting to organize a resistance, fired at the wrong target, for they were venting their fury on the Indian cultures that had begun to collaborate with the Spaniards because of all their grudges against their ancient masters. At any rate, Spain had already won the game. Rebellious outbreaks were always localized and counterchecked by the servile obedience that great sectors of the Inca system transferred automatically from the Incas to the new masters.

Those who destroyed the Inca Empire and created that country 16 called Peru, a country that four and a half centuries later has not yet managed to heal the bleeding wounds of its birth, were men whom we can hardly admire. They were, it is true, uncommonly courageous, but, contrary to what the edifying stories teach us, most of them lacked any idealism or higher purpose. They possessed only greed, hunger, and in the best of cases a certain vocation for adventure. The cruelty in which the Spaniards took pride, and the chronicles depict to the point of making us shiver, was inscribed in the ferocious customs of the times and was without doubt equivalent to that of the people they subdued and almost extinguished. Three centuries later, the Inca population had been reduced from twenty million to only six.

But these semiliterate, implacable, and greedy swordsmen, who 17 even before having completely conquered the Inca Empire were already savagely fighting among themselves or fighting the pacifiers sent against them by the faraway monarch to whom they had given a continent, represented a culture in which, we will never know whether for the benefit or the disgrace of mankind, something new and exotic had germinated in the history of man. In this culture, although injustice and abuse often favored by religion had proliferated, by the alliance of multiple factors—among them chance—a social space of human activities had evolved that was neither legislated nor controlled by those in power. This evolution would produce the most extraordinary economic, scientific, and technical development human civilization has ever known since the times of the cavemen with their clubs. Moreover, this new society would give way to the creation of the individual as the sovereign source of values by which society would be judged.

Those who, rightly, are shocked by the abuses and crimes of the 18 conquest must bear in mind that the first men to condemn them and ask that they be brought to an end were men, like Father Bartolomé de Las Casas, who came to America with the conquistadores and abandoned the ranks in order to collaborate with the vanquished, whose suffering they divulged with an indignation and virulence that still move us today.

Father Las Casas was the most active, although not the only one, of 19 those nonconformists who rebelled against the abuses inflicted upon the Indians. They fought against their fellow men and against the policies of their own country in the name of a moral principle that to them was higher than any principle of nation or state. This self-determination could not have been possible among the Incas or any of the other pre-Hispanic cultures. In these cultures, as in the other great civilizations of history foreign to the West, the individual could not morally question the social organism of which he was a part, because he existed only as an integral atom of that organism and because for him the dictates of the state could not be separated from morality. The first culture to interrogate and question itself, the first to break up the masses into individual beings who with time gradually gained the right to think and act for themselves, was to become, thanks to that unknown exercise, freedom, the most powerful civilization in our world.

It seems to me useless to ask oneself whether it was good that it [20] happened in this manner or whether it would have been better for humanity if the individual had never been born and the tradition of the antlike societies had continued forever. The pages of the chronicles of the conquest and discovery depict that crucial, bloody moment, full of phantasmagoria, when—disguised as a handful of invading treasure hunters, killing and destroying—the Judeo-Christian tradition, the Spanish language, Greece, Rome, the Renaissance, the notion of individual sovereignty, and the chance of living in freedom reached the shores of the Empire of the Sun. So it was that we as Peruvians were born. And, of course, the Bolivians, Chileans, Ecuadoreans, Colombians, and others.

## Review Questions

1. What is the main question with which Vargas Llosa is concerned in this article?
2. How does Vargas Llosa respond to this question?
3. What was the chief contribution of European civilization to the Americas, according to Vargas Llosa?

## Discussion and Writing Suggestions

1. What is the relationship of Vargas Llosa's article to the debate on Columbus represented in the earlier part of the chapter? To what extent do you see him as a proponent of one side or the other of this debate?
2. In analyzing the amazingly rapid collapse of the mighty Inca Empire, Vargas Llosa argues that it was the Incas' "beehive" social organization that prevented them from effectively fighting the Spaniards once their emperor had been captured. Might the author, however, be unduly downplaying the role of the superior Spanish weaponry? Can you think of other historical or contemporary examples in which a small number of well-armed men subdued a much larger, but less well-armed (or unarmed), body of people? In

light of your response, to what extent do you find Vargas Llosa's thesis plausible? Explain.

3. For Vargas Llosa, Columbus and his "three caravels" represented the notion of individual sovereignty and "the chance of living in freedom." This runs counter to the accusations of Las Casas, Sale, and the N.C.C. Resolution, who emphasize the negative heritage of Columbus. Comment on Vargas Llosa's interpretation, particularly in light of the other authors'.

# The Indians Encounter Columbus: "Another Set of Weirdos in an Unpredictable World"

## LOUISE ERDRICH AND MICHAEL DORRIS

*Over the centuries, numerous artists (and hacks) have created fictions based on the life of Columbus: poems, plays, novels, films. One of the earliest such works was Lope de Vega's play* The Discovery of the New World of Christopher Columbus *(1614). In Lope's work, upon setting foot on land, Columbus asks the ship's priest to "give me the cross." I shall place it here so that it will serve as a lantern to give the new world light." The year of the quincentennial saw the release of two feature films, which taken together illustrate our schizoid attitudes toward Columbus: one (according to the* Los Angeles Times*) takes "the heroic high road"; the other is "politically correct."*

*In between, we have an "infinite variety" of Columbus fictions: Walt Whitman's "Prayer of Columbus" has the explorer agonizing on his deathbed: "Is it the prophet's thought I speak, or am I raving? / What do I know of life? what of myself? shilling I know not even my own work, past or present. . . ."* I Discover Columbus, *a children's book by Robert Lawson (1941), is narrated by Columbus's parrot, who actually discovered the New World while Columbus himself lay seasick in his cabin. A play by Alice Sumner Varney has Columbus assuring the natives, "The Spanish people will be your friends," and then telling his brother, "I have never doubted. I have suffered long and been patient. To-day has come my reward; I know now that the world is round"—thus confirming a fact known to every educated person long before Columbus's three ships left Spain.*

*The following selection is excerpted from Louise Erdrich and Michael Dorris's 1991 novel* The Crown of Columbus. *In an interview for* Mother Jones, *Dorris characterized the heroine of* The Crown of Columbus, *Vivian Twostar, as "a forty-two-year-old, divorced, abrupt, mixed-blood woman [and "very pregnant anthropologist"] who is tired of being categorized by her ethnicity, but at the same time has been asked to write a puff piece for the alumni magazine about Columbus, because she happens to be part Indian." Twostar has found, "buried among forgotten papers in the basement of the Dartmouth Library, a document that may be the scholarly coup of the century—Columbus' legendary lost diary." In the following excerpt, Twostar conducts the final class session of her anthropology course in her home.*

*Erdrich's* Love Medicine *(1984) won the National Book Critics Circle award for fiction; she also has written poetry and two other best-selling novels. Michael Dorris won the same award in 1989; his other books include* The Broken Cord *and* A Yellow Raft in Blue Wlue Water.

Precisely at seven, punctual and cheerful, my students piled out of three cars, bearing their politically correct foods, including organic grapes and a meatless meatloaf made from crushed nuts. The class was the mix I regularly drew, including a few skeptical, sharp-eyed economics majors who had enrolled in order to fulfill a distribution requirement. Their contributions to the dinner were six kinds of chocolate cookies. Then there were the solemn five or six students who were truly interested in precontact civilizations, and finally, the one or two zealots who henceforth vowed to make Indian rights their life's cause.

One of my fanatics this term wouldn't last long—he was too sweet, too heart-on-his-sleeve, with the angel face and white-blond curls of Art Garfunkel and the conviction that he should attend a Lakota ceremonial gathering. He carried *Black Elk Speaks* against his heart. The Sioux would eat him for lunch. On the other hand, Kate, a no-nonsense redhead from Tulsa, intended to go to law school and specialize in water and mineral cases. She was the one I tried to hook and hold on to.

At the table Kate immediately fell into an intense conversation with Grandma, while the others clumped around the food. Black Elk looked bereft at the lack of traditional fare. He had clearly hoped for roots and berries.

My course was a survey of pre-1492 tribes but I always use the final class to introduce the impact of the Old World. Without writing systems, it was impossible for North American Indians to preserve precise accounts of their initial meetings with Europeans, and so I had to rely on hearsay, to read between the lines of the often pompous and fatuously self-serving Spanish or English accounts. Some of my hypotheses were pure logic: What would have been the reaction of people who were known to bathe several times a day when they found themselves closely quartered with a ship's crew who had not washed for months, for years, who did not even *believe* in washing? European chroniclers regularly assumed that the first Indians they met had bowed their heads and clapped their hands over their faces out of deep respect, but my guess was that they were holding their noses.

Bad news was another reason for waiting to discuss contact. I had 5 just spent ten weeks conducting a tour of ancient America's greatest hits: ingenious exchange systems, subtle and complicated religions, thriving agriculture, political equity between men and women. The students had been an appreciative audience, wowed by ethnoscience, impressed by traditional arts, fascinated by the richness and beauty I revealed. "Why didn't we know this?" they had asked time and again. "Where did it all go?"

Now I had to tell them. 6

After the food was gone I began by dealing out some "Discovery 7 of America" cartoons, culled from various magazines and newspapers. In every frame, Columbus is a naive innocent craftily observed by a couple of unseen, jaded Indians. Christopher is lost, confused, wrong-headed, and the Indians are wiseasses—not like in the old social studies books, where they fall all over themselves to worship the ships with the cloudlike sails.

"Do you have reservations?" a supercilious Native inquires of the 8 Discoverer in the first illustration.

"Contact was a different type of experience for Indians than it was 9 for Europeans," I said. "Over here you had hundreds of societies, millions of people, whose experience had told them that the world was a pretty diverse place. Walk for a day in any direction and what do you find? A tribe with a whole new set of gods, a language as distinct from your own as Tibetan is from Dutch—very little, in fact, that's even slightly familiar. The one common ground is how odd you and they appear to each other, so you figure, okay, different strokes for different folks, and let it go at that. There're too many of them, and no two tribes are the same. Forget sending out cultural missionaries, forget insisting that everybody agrees which end is up, except among your own group. So when Indians met the boys from France or Portugal or Spain for the first time, it was just, 'Great, another set of weirdos in an unpredictable world. No big deal.'"

"But they traded with them," Kate insisted. "They were interested." 10

"Naturally," I said. "Europeans had great stuff for sale. Do you know 11 how long it took an Arawak to fashion a nail out of shell? Then what do you do when it breaks? And mirrors! *You* try fixing your hair in a complicated do with nothing but a puddle of water to go by."

"You're saying technology," one of the budding economists noted. 12
"European inventions were attractive."

"It was a two-way street," I countered. "Indians gave as much as 13
they got, though they rarely received credit. What's a hamburger without fried *potatoes* and *tomato* ketchup?" His expression suggested that I
had just named his ideal food. I didn't let up.

"A third of the medicines we use today were developed over here 14
long before the fifteenth century. Not to mention the Iroquois concept
of representative government or the Equal Rights Amendment."

"If the Indians were so smart, why aren't we sitting here speaking 15
their language?" The salivating economist was not quite ready to concede. Thank God for a straight man.

"Languages," I corrected. "Thousands of them, which created a 16
certain problem with internal communication, for spreading the word
from tribe to tribe about what was going on. But really, it boiled down
to just a few things. Number one, Europeans were organized and self-
confident. After hundreds of years of fighting among themselves, they
had developed a whole system of weapons that were superior to anything the Indians—whose 'armies' rarely consisted of more than a bunch
of cousins out to raise hell—could throw back at them. Plus the fact that
European powers had not only the *will* to win but the belief that it was
their *right*. One god, one family from which all their languages originated, one creation story, one agenda: to rule the world. Never underes-
timate the power of chutzpah and positive thinking. They absolutely
believed that the earth was their oyster."

Black Elk was woebegone. He, dressed in his sandals and Nicaraguan 17
shirt, had resisted the charms of the Old World, so why did Indians
succumb?

"Why couldn't they fight back?" he said, chagrined. "Why did they 18
surrender their lands so easily?"

It was time to drop the real bomb. 19

"It wasn't the cavalry," I said. "It was germs. The assault began 20
invisibly, even accidentally, airborne, conveyed by touch, fleas, blood,
a handshake. The first European who stood on the North American
continent and coughed probably indirectly killed more Indians than
George Armstrong Custer ever imagined in his favorite wet dream. It's
estimated that more than a hundred million people lived in the Western
Hemisphere in 1491, and nineteen out of every last twenty of them died
from things like smallpox and measles and other infections imported
from overseas. They didn't know what hit them. There was no precedent, no medicine that worked. The world came to an end, almost. A few
people, by genetic chance, had a natural immunity, and they became the
ancestors of today's Indian people." . . .

## Discussion and Writing Suggestions

1. What does Twostar's description of her students in the opening three paragraphs (and elsewhere in the first section) of this excerpt tell you about her attitudes and values?

2. In straightforward prose, explain Twostar's reasons for why the "Indians" lost and the Spaniards won. How does Twostar's theory differ from Vargas Llosa's (previous selection)?

3. Create your own "fiction" about Columbus. Imagine some way of reinterpreting the Columbus story in dramatic, narrative, or poetic form (perhaps a music video?) for contemporary readers, viewers, or listeners. In 1992, for instance, actor-writer Tim Robbins created a radio play called *Mayhem*. This comic drama had two professors—one pro-Columbus, the other anti-Columbus—competing for points on a game show. The broadcast was occasionally interrupted by updates about the Persian Gulf War, and oblique parallels between that war and the Columbian invasion were drawn. Try something similarly outrageous—but something that exemplifies your own critical perspective on the subject.

## SYNTHESIS ACTIVITIES

1. Write a survey account of the Columbus controversy based on the passages in this chapter. Don't take sides, but do your best to give an objective account of the debate and the kind of arguments it has generated.

   You may wish to begin either with an anecdotal introduction—a story that exemplifies the extent to which the debate has gone—or a particularly arresting quotation. Then propound your thesis—not an argumentative statement, but a generalization that defines the precise nature of the debate. The account that follows might be organized along pro/con (or con/pro) lines or according to the kinds of topics about which the debate revolves. Cite as many sources as possible, although, of course, you will rely on some far more heavily than on others.

2. Take a position on the Columbus debate and defend it. You don't necessarily need to agree entirely with any of the pieces in this chapter (although that is a possibility), but you should draw on whatever sources are relevant to help you prove your thesis.

   The strawman or concession format might be effective for this paper. After presenting your thesis, outline the arguments made by people who take the opposite (or another) position. Then respond to those arguments. You may choose to concede that one or more of the counterarguments has some merit, or you may choose to refute all of them with your own arguments. Then argue your own position, drawing, when appropriate, on relevant passages from this chapter. Conclude with a "clincher" that reaffirms your position.

3. Select two or three of the articles opposing the Columbus legacy or the quincentennial (Bigelow, Las Casas, the N.C.C. Resolution, Sale, Harjo), *or* two or three of the articles defending that legacy (the testimonials and textbooks, Muldoon, Schlesinger) and *compare and contrast* their arguments. Devise categories for comparison and show the similarities and differences in their approaches and their arguments. Muldoon and Schlesinger, for example, defend the Columbus legacy against critics, but they conduct this defense in different ways. How? And how effective are their arguments?

4. Imagine that you are an administrator for a district school system. In light of the Columbus controversy, you have been assigned to draft a set of guidelines for the teaching of Columbus in the district's elementary and junior high schools. These guidelines will explain official policy in teaching children about Columbus and the significance of his voyages. They will also draw on arguments made on both sides of the controversy, as well as on historical facts on which both sides agree.

   Draft these guidelines. Suggested format: a prefatory section giving the rationale for the guidelines and a set of purposes governing the new policies, followed by the guidelines themselves with an explanation of each one (specifically citing sources). A conclusion is optional.

5. The average American—the legendary John Q. Public—is apt to be mystified, if not put off, by the Columbus debate. Columbus critic Hans Koning reported that one woman complained, "You are spoiling the pleasure of our children," to an American Indian demonstrating outside an exhibition called "First Encounters." Presumably, that woman might be expected to object just as strenuously were anyone to suggest that Thanksgiving also should not be celebrated because of white people's treatment of Native Americans.

   Assuming that you believe that the Columbus debate has been beneficial (regardless of your own particular position), explain what the benefits are, in a manner calculated to persuade John or Jennifer Q. Public. Argue in a way designed to persuade, not to antagonize. Draw on the selections in this chapter, as appropriate, but argue not for or against a particular position, but rather for the proposition that simply to have the debate has been a good thing for the country.

## RESEARCH ACTIVITIES

1. Conduct your own research into the manner in which Columbus and his voyages were viewed in generations past. Examine books, magazine and newspaper articles, poems, plays, and other sources. What personal qualities

are attributed to Columbus? What was the significance of his "discoveries," according to the authors? How is the reader invited to respond to what he or she reads? How is the reader invited to assess the native populations Columbus encountered?

2. Examine several grade school or junior high school American history textbooks for their treatment of an important event involving someone generally considered an American hero (e.g., George Washington, Benjamin Franklin, Thomas Jefferson, Andrew Jackson, Abraham Lincoln, General George Custer). See if you can locate at least one text written in the first half of the twentieth century. Apply to the passages you examine the questions Bill Bigelow asked his students to consider (paragraph 20). Develop your findings into a paper. To what extent have the historical figures been romanticized, heroicized? To what extent have unpleasant facts been ignored or distorted by euphemisms? To give your analysis some depth, you might consider comparing older treatments and more contemporary treatments.

3. Look into the role of the church during some particular period of the European invasion of America. To what extent is it true, as the N.C.C. Resolution charges, that "The Church, with few exceptions, accompanied and legitimized this conquest and exploitation"? What were some of the "exceptions"?

4. Research the controversy over the Columbus quincentennial of 1990–1992. At what point did significant objections to the celebrations begin? What form did they take? What was the outcome?

5. In 1988, after a long struggle, Japanese-American groups succeeded in pressuring the federal government to pay reparations to Japanese-Americans who were interned in camps following the attack on Pearl Harbor. Research the fate of Native Americans during a specified period since Columbus, and draw up a formal petition to the government for reparations. To narrow your subject, you may want to pursue in greater depth just one or two of the areas Suzan Shown Harjo mentions in her article.

6. The Columbus debate is only one of several debates involving "political correctness." Select and research another such debate (e.g., campus speech codes, bilingual education, readings for high school or college literature courses, environmentalism). Focus your discussion on what the "politically correct" position is—and on what it isn't (and why)—and on how the debate has progressed.

7. Research the response to one of the anti-Columbian books, such as Kirkpatrick Sale's *The Conquest of Paradise: Christopher Columbus and the Columbian Legacy* (1990) or Hans Koning's *Columbus: His Enterprise: Exploding the Myth* (1976, 1991). Look up the reviews in the *Book Review Digest* and the *Book Review Index,* consult the reviews themselves, and discuss the main types of reactions that the book generated. Of course, you should also read the book under discussion yourself, so that you are in a position to assess the validity of the critics' reactions.

# 8

# OBEDIENCE TO AUTHORITY

Would you obey an order to inflict pain on another person? Most of us, if confronted with this question, would probably be quick to answer: "Never!" Yet if the conclusions of researchers are to be trusted, it is not psychopaths who kill noncombatant civilians in wartime and torture victims in prisons around the world but ordinary people following orders. People obey: this is a basic, necessary fact of human society. As an author in this chapter has put it, "Obedience is as basic an element in the structure of social life as one can point to. Some system of authority is a requirement of all communal living."

The question, then, is not, "Should we obey the orders of an authority figure?" but rather, "To what *extent* should we obey?" Each generation seems to give new meaning to these questions. During the Vietnam War, a number of American soldiers followed a commander's orders and murdered civilians in the hamlet of My Lai. More recently, and less grotesquely, former White House aide Oliver North pleaded innocent to illegally funding the Contra (resistance) fighters in Nicaragua. North's attorneys claimed that he was following the orders of his superiors. And, although North was found guilty,[1] the judge who sentenced him to perform community service (there was no prison sentence) largely agreed with this defense when he called North a pawn in a larger game played by senior officials in the Reagan administration.

In less dramatic ways, conflicts over the extent to which we obey orders surface in everyday life. At one point or another, you may face a moral dilemma at work. Perhaps it will take this form: The boss tells you to overlook File X in preparing a report for a certain client. But you're sure that File X pertains directly to the report and contains information that will alarm the client. What should you do? The dilemmas of obedience also emerge on some campuses with the rite of fraternity hazing. Psychologists Janice Gibson and Mika Haritos-Fatouros

---

[1] In July 1990, North's conviction was overturned on appeal.

have recently made the startling observation that whether the obedience in question involves a pledge's joining a fraternity or a torturer's joining an elite military corps, the *process* by which one acquiesces to a superior's order (and thereby becomes a member of the group) is remarkably the same:

> There are several ways to teach people to do the unthinkable, and we have developed a model to explain how they are used. We have also found that college fraternities, although they are far removed from the grim world of torture and violent combat, use similar methods for initiating new members, to ensure their faithfulness to the fraternity's rules and values. However, this unthinking loyalty can sometimes lead to dangerous actions: Over the past 10 years, there have been countless injuries during fraternity initiations and 39 deaths. These training techniques are designed to instill unquestioning obedience in people, but they can easily be a guide for an intensive course in torture.
>
> 1) **Screening to find the best prospects:** normal, well-adjusted people with the physical, intellectual and, in some cases, political attributes necessary for the task.
> 2) **Techniques to increase binding among these prospects:** Initiation rites to isolate people from society and introduce them to a new social order, with different rules and values.
>    Elitist attitudes and "in-group" language, which highlight the differences between the group and the rest of society.
> 3) **Techniques to reduce the strain of obedience:** Blaming and dehumanizing the victims, so it is less disturbing to harm them.
>    Harrassment, the constant physical and psychological intimidation that prevents logical thinking and promotes the instinctive responses needed for acts of inhuman cruelty.
>    Rewards for obedience and punishments for not cooperating.
>    Social modeling by watching other group members commit violent acts and then receive rewards.
>    Systematic desensitization to repugnant acts by gradual exposure to them, so they appear routine and normal despite conflicts with previous moral standards.[2]

In this chapter, you will explore the dilemmas inherent in obeying the orders of an authority. First, in a brief essay adapted from a lecture, British novelist Doris Lessing helps set a context for the discussion by questioning the manner in which we call ourselves individualists yet fail to understand how groups define and exert influence over us. Psychologist Stanley Milgram then reports on a landmark study in which he set out to determine the extent to which ordinary individuals would obey the clearly immoral orders of an authority figure. The

---

[2]"The Education of a Torturer" by Janice T. Gibson and Mika Haritos-Fatouros from *Psychology Today*, November 1986. Reprinted with permission from *Psychology Today* Magazine. Copyright © 1986 Sussex Publishers, Inc.

results were shocking, not only to the psychiatrists who predicted that few people would follow such orders but also to many other social scientists and people—some of whom applauded Milgram for his fiendishly ingenious design, some of whom bitterly attacked him for unethical procedures. In three reviews following Milgram, we present arguments in that debate. Next, psychologists Janice T. Gibson and Mika Haritos-Fatouros explore the ways in which ordinary people—including high school and college students—can be taught to become agents of terror. Two essays and a short story conclude the chapter. In "Disobedience as a Psychological and Moral Problem," psychoanalyst and philosopher Erich Fromm discusses the comforts of obedient behavior; then psychologist Irving L. Janis outlines his theory of "groupthink," a pattern of conformist thinking that can lead to poor, sometimes disastrous, decisions. The chapter concludes with Shirley Jackson's "The Lottery," the story of a community's obedience to an age-old custom.

# Group Minds

## DORIS LESSING

*Doris Lessing sets a context for the discussion on obedience by illuminating a fundamental conflict: We in the Western world celebrate our individualism, but we're naive in understanding the ways that groups largely undercut our individuality. "We are group animals still," says Lessing, "and there is nothing wrong with that. But what is dangerous is . . . not understanding the social laws that govern groups and govern us." This chapter is largely devoted to an exploration of these tendencies. As you read selections by Milgram and the other authors here, bear in mind Lessing's troubling question: If we know that individuals will violate their own good common sense and moral codes in order to become accepted members of a group, why then can't we put this knowledge to use and teach people to be wary of group pressures?*

*Doris Lessing, the daughter of farmers, was born in Persia, now Iran, in 1919. She attended a Roman Catholic convent and a girls' high school in southern Rhodesia (now Zimbabwe). From 1959 through to the present, Lessing has written more than twenty works of fiction and has been called "the best woman novelist" of the postwar era. Her work has received a great deal of scholarly attention. She is, perhaps, best known for her* Five Short Novels *(1954),* The Golden Notebook *(1962), and* Briefing for a Descent into Hell *(1971).*

People living in the West, in societies that we describe as Western, or    1
as the free world, may be educated in many different ways, but they
will all emerge with an idea about themselves that goes something
like this: I am a citizen of a free society, and that means I am an
individual, making individual choices. My mind is my own, my opinions are chosen by me, I am free to do as I will, and at the worst the
pressures on me are economic, that is, I may be too poor to do as I
want.

This set of ideas may sound something like a caricature, but it is not    2
so far off how we see ourselves. It is a portrait that may not have been
acquired consciously, but is part of a general atmosphere or set of
assumptions that influence our ideas about ourselves.

People in the West therefore may go through their entire lives never    3
thinking to analyse this very flattering picture, and as a result are
helpless against all kinds of pressures on them to conform in many kinds
of ways.

The fact is that we all live our lives in groups—the family, work    4
groups, social, religious and political groups. Very few people indeed are
happy as solitaries, and they tend to be seen by their neighbours as
peculiar or selfish or worse. Most people cannot stand being alone for
long. They are always seeking groups to belong to, and if one group
dissolves, they look for another. We are group animals still, and there
is nothing wrong with that. But what is dangerous is not the belonging
to a group, or groups, but not understanding the social laws that govern
groups and govern us.

When we're in a group, we tend to think as that group does: we may    5
even have joined the group to find 'likeminded' people. But we also find
our thinking changing because we belong to a group. It is the hardest
thing in the world to maintain an individual dissident opinion, as a
member of a group.

It seems to me that this is something we have all experienced—    6
something we take for granted, may never have thought about it. But
a great deal of experiment has gone on among psychologists and
sociologists on this very theme. If I describe an experiment or two,
then anyone listening who may be a sociologist or psychologist will
groan, oh God not *again*—for they will have heard of these classic
experiments far too often. My guess is that the rest of the people will
never have heard of these experiments, never have had these ideas
presented to them. If my guess is true, then it aptly illustrates my
general thesis, and the general idea behind these talks, that we (the
human race) are now in possession of a great deal of hard information
about ourselves, but we do not use it to improve our institutions and
therefore our lives.

A typical test, or experiment, on this theme goes like this. A group **7** of people are taken into the researchers' confidence. A minority of one or two are left in the dark. Some situation demanding measurement or assessment is chosen. For instance, comparing lengths of wood that differ only a little from each other, but enough to be perceptible, or shapes that are almost the same size. The majority in the group— according to instruction—will assert stubbornly that these two shapes or lengths are the same length, or size, while the solitary individual, or the couple, who have not been so instructed will assert that the pieces of wood or whatever are different. But the majority will continue to insist—speaking metaphorically—that black is white, and after a period of exasperation, irritation, even anger, certainly incomprehension, the minority will fall into line. Not always, but nearly always. There are indeed glorious individualists who stubbornly insist on telling the truth as they see it, but most give in to the majority opinion, obey the atmosphere.

When put as badly, as unflatteringly, as this, reactions tend to be **8** incredulous: 'I certainly wouldn't give in, I speak my mind. . . .' But would you?

People who have experienced a lot of groups, who perhaps have **9** observed their own behaviour, may agree that the hardest thing in the world is to stand out against one's group, a group of one's peers. Many agree that among our most shameful memories is this, how often we said black was white because other people were saying it.

In other words, we know that this is true of human behaviour, but **10** how do we know it? It is one thing to admit it, in a vague uncomfortable sort of way (which probably includes the hope that one will never again be in such a testing situation) but quite another to make that cool step into a kind of objectivity, where one may say, 'Right, if that's what human beings are like, myself included, then let's admit it, examine and organize our attitudes accordingly.'

This mechanism, of obedience to the group, does not only mean **11** obedience or submission to a small group, or one that is sharply determined, like a religion or political party. It means, too, conforming to those large, vague, ill-defined collections of people who may never think of themselves as having a collective mind because they are aware of differences of opinion—but which, to people from outside, from another culture, seem very minor. The underlying assumptions and assertions that govern the group are never discussed, never challenged, probably never noticed, the main one being precisely this: that it *is* a group mind, intensely resistant to change, equipped with sacred assumptions about which there can be no discussion.

But suppose this kind of thing were taught in schools?    12

Let us just suppose it, for a moment. . . . But at once the nub of the    13
problem is laid bare.

Imagine us saying to children, 'In the last fifty or so years, the    14
human race has become aware of a great deal of information about its
mechanisms; how it behaves, how it must behave under certain circumstances. If this is to be useful, you must learn to contemplate these rules
calmly, dispassionately, disinterestedly, without emotion. It is information that will set people free from blind loyalties, obedience to slogans,
rhetoric, leaders, group emotions.' Well, there it is.

## Review Questions

1. What is the flattering portrait Lessing paints of people living in the West?
2. Lessing believes that individuals in the West are "helpless against all kinds of
   pressures on them to conform in many kinds of ways." Why?
3. Lessing refers to a class of experiments on obedience. Summarize the "typical" experiment.

## Discussion and Writing Suggestions

1. Lessing writes that "what is dangerous is not the belonging to a group, or
   groups, but not understanding the social laws that govern groups and govern
   us." What is the danger Lessing is speaking of here?
2. Lessing states that "we (the human race) are now in possession of a great
   deal of hard information about ourselves, but we do not use it to improve our
   institutions and therefore our lives." First, do you agree with Lessing? Can you
   cite other examples (aside from information on obedience to authority) in
   which we do not use knowledge to better humankind?
3. Explore some of the difficulties in applying this "hard information" about
   humankind that Lessing speaks of. Assume she's correct in claiming that we
   don't incorporate our knowledge of human nature into the running of our
   institutions. Why don't we? What are the difficulties of *acting* on information?
4. Lessing speaks of "people who remember how they acted in school" and
   of their guilt in recalling how they succumbed to group pressures. Can you
   recall such an event? What feelings do you have about it now?

# The Perils of Obedience

## STANLEY MILGRAM

*In 1963, a Yale psychologist conducted one of the classic studies on obedience that Doris Lessing refers to in "Group Minds." Stanley Milgram designed an experiment that forced participants either to violate their conscience by obeying the immoral demands of an authority figure or to refuse those demands. Surprisingly, Milgram found that few participants could resist the authority's orders, even when the participants knew that following these orders would result in another person's pain. Were the participants in these experiments incipient mass murderers? No, said Milgram. They were "ordinary people, simply doing their jobs." The implications of Milgram's conclusions are immense.*

*Consider: Where does evil reside? What sort of people were responsible for the Holocaust, and for the long list of other atrocities that seem to blight the human record in every generation? Is it a lunatic fringe, a few sick but powerful people who are responsible for atrocities? If so, then we decent folk needn't ever look inside ourselves to understand evil since (by our definition) evil lurks out there, in "those sick ones." Milgram's study suggested otherwise: that under a special set of circumstances the obedience we naturally show authority figures can transform us into agents of terror.*

*The article that follows is one of the longest in this text, and it may help you to know in advance the author's organization. In paragraphs 1–11, Milgram discusses the larger significance and the history of dilemmas involving obedience to authority; he then summarizes his basic experimental design and follows with a report of one experiment. Milgram organizes the remainder of his article into sections, which he has subtitled "An Unexpected Outcome," "Peculiar Reactions," "The Etiquette of Submission," and "Duty without Conflict." He begins his conclusion in paragraph 108. If you find the article too long to complete in a single sitting, then plan to read sections at a time, taking notes on each until you're done. Anticipate the three articles immediately following Milgram's: they are reviews of his work and largely concern the ethics of his experimental design. Consider these ethics as you read so that you, in turn, can respond to Milgram's critics.*

*Stanley Milgram (1933–1984) taught and conducted research at Yale and Harvard universities and at the Graduate Center, City University of New York. He was named Guggenheim Fellow in 1972–1973 and a year later was nominated for the National Book Award for* Obedience to Authority. *His other books include* Television and Antisocial Behavior *(1973), The*

City and the Self *(1974),* Human Aggression *(1976), and* The Individual in a Social World *(1977).*

Obedience is as basic an element in the structure of social life as one can point to. Some system of authority is a requirement of all communal living, and it is only the person dwelling in isolation who is not forced to respond, with defiance or submission, to the commands of others. For many people, obedience is a deeply ingrained behavior tendency, indeed a potent impulse overriding training in ethics, sympathy, and moral conduct.

The dilemma inherent in submission to authority is ancient, as old as the story of Abraham, and the question of whether one should obey when commands conflict with conscience has been argued by Plato, dramatized in *Antigone,* and treated to philosophic analysis in almost every historical epoch. Conservative philosophers argue that the very fabric of society is threatened by disobedience, while humanists stress the primacy of the individual conscience.

The legal and philosophic aspects of obedience are of enormous import, but they say very little about how most people behave in concrete situations. I set up a simple experiment at Yale University to test how much pain an ordinary citizen would inflict on another person simply because he was ordered to by an experimental scientist. Stark authority was pitted against the subjects' strongest moral imperatives against hurting others, and, with the subjects' ears ringing with the screams of the victims, authority won more often than not. The extreme willingness of adults to go to almost any lengths on the command of an authority constitutes the chief finding of the study and the fact most urgently demanding explanation.

In the basic experimental design, two people come to a psychology laboratory to take part in a study of memory and learning. One of them is designated as a "teacher" and the other a "learner." The experimenter explains that the study is concerned with the effects of punishment on learning. The learner is conducted into a room, seated in a kind of miniature electric chair; his arms are strapped to prevent excessive movement, and an electrode is attached to his wrist. He is told that he will be read lists of simple word pairs, and that he will then be tested on his ability to remember the second word of a pair when he hears the first one again. Whenever he makes an error, he will receive electric shocks of increasing intensity.

The real focus of the experiment is the teacher. After watching the learner being strapped into place, he is seated before an impressive shock generator. The instrument panel consists of thirty lever switches set in a horizontal line. Each switch is clearly labeled with a voltage designation ranging from 15 to 450 volts. The following designations are clearly indicated for groups of four switches, going from left to right: Slight Shock, Moderate Shock, Strong Shock, Very Strong Shock, Intense Shock, Extreme Intensity Shock, Danger: Severe Shock. (Two switches after this last designation are simply marked XXX.)

When a switch is depressed, a pilot light corresponding to each switch is illuminated in bright red; an electric buzzing is heard; a blue light, labeled "voltage energizer," flashes; the dial on the voltage meter swings to the right; and various relay clicks sound off.    6

The upper left-hand corner of the generator is labeled SHOCK GENERA-    7
TOR, TYPE ZLB, DYSON INSTRUMENT COMPANY, WALTHAM, MASS. OUTPUT 15
VOLTS—450 VOLTS.

Each subject is given a sample 45-volt shock from the generator    8
before his run as teacher, and the jolt strengthens his belief in the authenticity of the machine.

The teacher is a genuinely naïve subject who has come to the    9
laboratory for the experiment. The learner, or victim, is actually an actor who receives no shock at all. The point of the experiment is to see how far a person will proceed in a concrete and measurable situation in which he is ordered to inflict increasing pain on a protesting victim.

Conflict arises when the man receiving the shock begins to show    10
that he is experiencing discomfort. At 75 volts, he grunts; at 120 volts, he complains loudly; at 150, he demands to be released from the experiment. As the voltage increases, his protests become more vehement and emotional. At 285 volts, his response can be described only as an agonized scream. Soon thereafter, he makes no sound at all.

For the teacher, the situation quickly becomes one of gripping    11
tension. It is not a game for him; conflict is intense and obvious. The manifest suffering of the learner presses him to quit; but each time he hesitates to administer a shock, the experimenter orders him to continue. To extricate himself from this plight, the subject must make a clear break with authority.[1]

The subject, Gretchen Brandt,[2] is an attractive thirty-one-year-old    12
medical technician who works at the Yale Medical School. She had emigrated from Germany five years before.

On several occasions when the learner complains, she turns to the    13
experimenter coolly and inquires, "Shall I continue?" She promptly returns to her task when the experimenter asks her to do so. At the administration of 210 volts, she turns to the experimenter, remarking firmly, "Well, I'm sorry, I don't think we should continue."

---

[1]The ethical problems of carrying out an experiment of this sort are too complex to be dealt with here, but they receive extended treatment in the book from which this article is adapted.

[2]Names of subjects described in this piece have been changed.

EXPERIMENTER: The experiment requires that you go on until he has learned 14
all the word pairs correctly.

BRANDT: He has a heart condition, I'm sorry. He told you that before. 15

EXPERIMENTER: The shocks may be painful but they are not dangerous. 16

BRANDT: Well, I'm sorry, I think when shocks continue like this, they *are* 17
dangerous. You ask him if he wants to get out. It's his free will.

EXPERIMENTER: It is absolutely essential that we continue. . . . 18

BRANDT: I'd like you to ask him. We came here of our free will. If he wants 19
to continue I'll go ahead. He told you he had a heart condition. I'm sorry.
I don't want to be responsible for anything happening to him. I wouldn't
like it for me either.

EXPERIMENTER: You have no other choice. 20

BRANDT: I think we are here on our own free will. I don't want to be 21
responsible if anything happens to him. Please understand that.

She refuses to go further and the experiment is terminated. 22

The woman is firm and resolute throughout. She indicates in the 23
interview that she was in no way tense or nervous, and this corresponds
to her controlled appearance during the experiment. She feels that the
last shock she administered to the learner was extremely painful and
reiterates that she "did not want to be responsible for any harm to him."

The woman's straightforward, courteous behavior in the experi- 24
ment, lack of tension, and total control of her own action seem to make
disobedience a simple and rational deed. Her behavior is the very
embodiment of what I envisioned would be true for almost all subjects.


## AN UNEXPECTED OUTCOME

Before the experiments, I sought predictions about the outcome from 25
various kinds of people—psychiatrists, college sophomores, middle-
class adults, graduate students and faculty in the behavioral sciences.
With remarkable similarity, they predicted that virtually all subjects
would refuse to obey the experimenter. The psychiatrists, specifically,
predicted that most subjects would not go beyond 150 volts, when the
victim makes his first explicit demand to be freed. They expected that
only 4 percent would reach 300 volts, and that only a pathological
fringe of about one in a thousand would administer the highest shock
on the board.

These predictions were unequivocally wrong. Of the forty subjects 26
in the first experiment, twenty-five obeyed the orders of the experimenter to the end, punishing the victim until they reached the most
potent shock available on the generator. After 450 volts were administered three times, the experimenter called a halt to the session. Many
obedient subjects then heaved sighs of relief, mopped their brows,

rubbed their fingers over their eyes, or nervously fumbled cigarettes. Others displayed only minimal signs of tension from beginning to end.

When the very first experiments were carried out, Yale undergraduates were used as subjects, and about 60 percent of them were fully obedient. A colleague of mine immediately dismissed these findings as having no relevance to "ordinary" people, asserting that Yale undergraduates are a highly aggressive, competitive bunch who step on each other's necks on the slightest provocation. He assured me that when "ordinary" people were tested, the results would be quite different. As we moved from the pilot studies to the regular experimental series, people drawn from every stratum of New Haven life came to be employed in the experiment: professionals, white-collar workers, unemployed persons, and industrial workers. *The experiment's total outcome was the same as we had observed among the students.*   27

Moreover, when the experiments were repeated in Princeton, Munich, Rome, South Africa, and Australia, the level of obedience was invariably somewhat *higher* than found in the investigation reported in this article. Thus one scientist in Munich found 85 percent of his subjects to be obedient.   28

Fred Prozi's reactions, if more dramatic than most, illuminate the conflicts experienced by others in less visible form. About fifty years old and unemployed at the time of the experiment, he has a good-natured, if slightly dissolute, appearance, and he strikes people as a rather ordinary fellow. He begins the session calmly but becomes tense as it proceeds. After delivering the 180-volt shock, he pivots around in his chair and, shaking his head, addresses the experimenter in agitated tones:   29

PROZI: I can't stand it. I'm not going to kill that man in there. You hear him hollering?   30

EXPERIMENTER: As I told you before, the shocks may be painful, but . . .   31

PROZI: But he's hollering. He can't stand it. What's going to happen to him?   32

EXPERIMENTER *(his voice is patient, matter-of-fact)*: The experiment requires that you continue, Teacher.   33

PROZI: Aaah, but, unh, I'm not going to get that man sick in there—know what I mean?   34

EXPERIMENTER: Whether the learner likes it or not, we must go on, through all the word pairs.   35

PROZI: I refuse to take the responsibility. He's in there hollering!   36

EXPERIMENTER: It's absolutely essential that you continue, Prozi.   37

PROZI *(indicating the unused questions)*: There's too many left here, I mean, Jeez, if he gets them wrong, there's too many of them left. I mean, who's going to take the responsibility if anything happens to that gentleman?   38

EXPERIMENTER: I'm responsible for anything that happens to him. Continue, please. **39**

PROZI: All right. *(Consults list of words.)* The next one's "Slow—walk, truck, dance, music." Answer, please. *(A buzzing sound indicates the learner has signaled his answer.)* Wrong. A hundred and ninety-five volts. "Dance." *(Zzumph!)* **40**

LEARNER *(yelling)*: Let me out of here! My heart's bothering me! *(Teacher looks at experimenter.)* **41**

EXPERIMENTER: Continue, please. **42**

LEARNER *(screaming)*: Let me out of here! You have no right to keep me here! Let me out of here, my heart's bothering me, let me out! **43**

PROZI *(shakes head, pats the table nervously)*: You see, he's hollering. Hear that? Gee, I don't know. **44**

EXPERIMENTER: The experiment requires . . . **45**

PROZI *(interrupting)*: I know it does, sir, but I mean—hunh! He don't know what he's getting in for. He's up to 195 volts! *(Experiment continues, through 210 volts, 225 volts, 240 volts, 255 volts, 270 volts, at which point Prozi, with evident relief, runs out of word-pair questions.)* **46**

EXPERIMENTER: You'll have to go back to the beginning of that page and go through them again until he's learned them all correctly. **47**

PROZI: Aw, no. I'm not going to kill that man. You mean I've got to keep going up with the scale? No sir. He's hollering in there. I'm not going to give him 450 volts. **48**

EXPERIMENTER: The experiment requires that you go on. **49**

LEARNER: Ohhh. I absolutely refuse to answer anymore. *(Shouting urgently now.)* Let me out of here! You can't hold me here! Get me out. Get-me-out-of-here! **50**

EXPERIMENTER: Continue. The next word is "Green," please. **51**

PROZI: "Green—grass, hat, ink, apple." *(Nothing happens. No answering buzz. Just gloomy silence.)* **52**

PROZI: I don't think he is going to answer. **53**

EXPERIMENTER: If the learner doesn't answer in a reasonable time, about four or five seconds, consider the answer wrong. And follow the same procedures you have been doing for wrong answers. Say, "Wrong," tell him the number of volts, give him the punishment, read him the correct answer. Continue, please. **54**

PROZI: "Green—grass, hat, ink, apple." Answer, please. *(More silence. Subject just sits there.)* **55**

EXPERIMENTER: Go on with the procedure, please. **56**

PROZI: Three hundred and fifteen volts. The answer is "ink." *(Zzumph!)* **57**

LEARNER: Ohh. Ooohh. **58**

PROZI *(relieved to hear response)*: Next one . . . **59**

LEARNER: I absolutely refuse to answer. **60**

PROZI: You got to. You get a shock if you don't answer. *(Experiment continues* **61** *with learner refusing to answer, and, finally, failing even to grunt or groan. At 375 volts, the subject stands up.)*

PROZI: I think something's happened to that fellow in there. I don't get no answer. He was hollering at less voltage. Can't you check in and see if he's all right, please? **62**

EXPERIMENTER *(with same detached calm)*: Not once we've started. Please continue, Teacher. **63**

PROZI *(sits down, sighs deeply)*: "Cool—day, shade, water, paint." Answer, please. Are you all right in there? Are you all right? **64**

EXPERIMENTER: Please continue, Teacher. Continue, please. *(Subject pushes lever. Zzumph!)* **65**

PROZI *(swiveling around in his chair)*: Something's happened to that man in there. *(Swiveling back.)* Next one. "Low—dollar, necklace, moon, paint." *(Turning around again.)* Something's happened to that man in there. You better check in on him, sir. He won't answer or nothing. **66**

EXPERIMENTER: Continue. Go on, please. **67**

PROZI: You accept all responsibility? **68**

EXPERIMENTER: The responsibility is mine. Correct. Please go on. *(Subject returns to his list, starts running through words as rapidly as he can read them, works through to 450 volts.)* **69**

PROZI: That's that. **70**

EXPERIMENTER: Continue using the 450 switch for each wrong answer. Continue, please. **71**

PROZI: But I don't get anything! **72**

EXPERIMENTER: Please continue. The next word is "white." **73**

PROZI: Don't you think you should look in on him, please? **74**

EXPERIMENTER: Not once we've started the experiment. **75**

PROZI: What if he's dead in there? *(Gestures toward the room with the electric chair.)* I mean, he told me he can't stand the shock, sir. I don't mean to be rude, but I think you should look in on him. All you have to do is look in on him. All you have to do is look in the door. I don't get no answer, no noise. Something might have happened to the gentleman in there, sir. **76**

EXPERIMENTER: We must continue. Go on, please. **77**

PROZI: You mean keep giving him what? Four-hundred-fifty volts, what he's got now? **78**

EXPERIMENTER: That's correct. Continue. The next word is "white." **79**

PROZI *(now at a furious pace)*: "White—cloud, horse, rock, house." Answer, please. The answer is "horse." Four hundred and fifty volts. *(Zzumph!)* Next word, "Bag—paint, music, clown, girl." The answer is "paint." Four hundred and fifty volts. *(Zzumph!)* Next word is "Short—sentence, movie . . ." **80**

EXPERIMENTER: Excuse me, Teacher. We'll have to discontinue the experiment. **81**

## PECULIAR REACTIONS

Morris Braverman, another subject, is a thirty-nine-year-old social [82] worker. He looks older than his years because of his bald head and serious demeanor. His brow is furrowed, as if all the world's burdens were carried on his face. He appears intelligent and concerned.

When the learner refuses to answer and the experimenter instructs [83] Braverman to treat the absence of an answer as equivalent to a wrong answer, he takes his instruction to heart. Before administering 300 volts he asserts officiously to the victim, "Mr. Wallace, your silence has to be considered as a wrong answer." Then he administers the shock. He offers halfheartedly to change places with the learner, then asks the experimenter, "Do I have to follow these instructions literally?" He is satisfied with the experimenter's answer that he does. His very refined and authoritative manner of speaking is increasingly broken up by wheezing laughter.

The experimenter's notes on Mr. Braverman at the last few shocks [84] are:

> *Almost breaking up now each time gives shock. Rubbing face to hide laughter. Squinting, trying to hide face with hand, still laughing. Cannot control his laughter at this point no matter what he does. Clenching fist, pushing it onto table.*

In an interview after the session, Mr. Braverman summarizes the [85] experiment with impressive fluency and intelligence. He feels the experiment may have been designed also to "test the effects on the teacher of being in an essentially sadistic role, as well as the reactions of a student to a learning situation that was authoritative and punitive." When asked how painful the last few shocks administered to the learner were, he indicates that the most extreme category on the scale is not adequate (it read EXTREMELY PAINFUL) and places his mark at the edge of the scale with an arrow carrying it beyond the scale.

It is almost impossible to convey the greatly relaxed, sedate quality [86] of his conversation in the interview. In the most relaxed terms, he speaks about his severe inner tension.

EXPERIMENTER: At what point were you most tense or nervous? [87]
MR. BRAVERMAN: Well, when he first began to cry out in pain, and I realized [88] this was hurting him. This got worse when he just blocked and refused to answer. There was I. I'm a nice person, I think, hurting somebody, and caught up in what seemed a mad situation . . . and in the interest of science, one goes through with it.

When the interviewer pursues the general question of tension, Mr. [89] Braverman spontaneously mentions his laughter.

---

"My reactions were awfully peculiar. I don't know if you were 90 watching me, but my reactions were giggly, and trying to stifle laughter. This isn't the way I usually am. This was a sheer reaction to a totally impossible situation. And my reaction was to the situation of having to hurt somebody. And being totally helpless and caught up in a set of circumstances where I just couldn't deviate and I couldn't try to help. This is what got me."

Mr. Braverman, like all subjects, was told the actual nature and 91 purpose of the experiment, and a year later he affirmed in a questionnaire that he had learned something of personal importance: "What appalled me was that I could possess this capacity for obedience and compliance to a central idea, i.e., the value of a memory experiment, even after it became clear that continued adherence to this value was at the expense of violation of another value, i.e., don't hurt someone who is helpless and not hurting you. As my wife said, 'You can call yourself Eichmann.'[3] I hope I deal more effectively with any future conflicts of values I encounter."

## THE ETIQUETTE OF SUBMISSION

One theoretical interpretation of this behavior holds that all people 92 harbor deeply aggressive instincts continually pressing for expression, and that the experiment provides institutional justification for the release of these impulses. According to this view, if a person is placed in a situation in which he has complete power over another individual, whom he may punish as much as he likes, all that is sadistic and bestial in man comes to the fore. The impulse to shock the victim is seen to flow from the potent aggressive tendencies, which are part of the motivational life of the individual, and the experiment, because it provides social legitimacy, simply opens the door to their expression.

It becomes vital, therefore, to compare the subject's performance 93 when he is under orders and when he is allowed to choose the shock level.

The procedure was identical to our standard experiment, except that 94 the teacher was told that he was free to select any shock level on any

---

[3] *Adolf Eichmann* (1906–1962), the Nazi official responsible for implementing Hitler's "Final Solution" to exterminate the Jews, escaped to Argentina after World War II. In 1960, Israeli agents captured Eichmann and brought him to Israel, where he was tried as a war criminal and sentenced to death. At his trial, Eichmann maintained that he was merely following orders in arranging the murders of his victims.

of the trials. (The experimenter took pains to point out that the teacher could use the highest levels on the generator, the lowest, any in between, or any combination of levels.) Each subject proceeded for thirty critical trials. The learner's protests were coordinated to standard shock levels, his first grunt coming at 75 volts, his first vehement protest at 150 volts.

The average shock used during the thirty critical trials was less than 60 volts—lower than the point at which the victim showed the first signs of discomfort. Three of the forty subjects did not go beyond the very lowest level on the board, twenty-eight went no higher than 75 volts, and thirty-eight did not go beyond the first loud protest at 150 volts. Two subjects provided the exception, administering up to 325 and 450 volts, but the overall result was that the great majority of people delivered very low, usually painless, shocks when the choice was explicitly up to them. **95**

This condition of the experiment undermines another commonly offered explanation of the subjects' behavior—that those who shocked the victim at the most severe levels came only from the sadistic fringe of society. If one considers that almost two-thirds of the participants fall into the category of "obedient" subjects, and that they represented ordinary people drawn from working, managerial, and professional classes, the argument becomes very shaky. Indeed, it is highly reminiscent of the issue that arose in connection with Hannah Arendt's 1963 book, *Eichmann in Jerusalem.* Arendt contended that the prosecution's effort to depict Eichmann as a sadistic monster was fundamentally wrong, that he came closer to being an uninspired bureaucrat who simply sat at his desk and did his job. For asserting her views, Arendt became the object of considerable scorn, even calumny. Somehow, it was felt that the monstrous deeds carried out by Eichmann required a brutal, twisted personality, evil incarnate. After witnessing hundreds of ordinary persons submit to the authority in our own experiments, I must conclude that Arendt's conception of the banality of evil comes closer to the truth than one might dare imagine. The ordinary person who shocked the victim did so out of a sense of obligation—an impression of his duties as a subject—and not from any peculiarly aggressive tendencies. **96**

This is, perhaps, the most fundamental lesson of our study: ordinary people, simply doing their jobs, and without any particular hostility on their part, can become agents in a terrible destructive process. Moreover, even when the destructive effects of their work become patently clear, and they are asked to carry out actions incompatible with fundamental standards of morality, relatively few people have the resources needed to resist authority. **97**

Many of the people were in some sense against what they did to **98**

331

the learner, and many protested even while they obeyed. Some were totally convinced of the wrongness of their actions but could not bring themselves to make an open break with authority. They often derived satisfaction from their thoughts and felt that—within themselves, at least—they had been on the side of the angels. They tried to reduce strain by obeying the experimenter but "only slightly," encouraging the learner, touching the generator switches gingerly. When interviewed, such a subject would stress that he had "asserted my humanity" by administering the briefest shock possible. Handling the conflict in this manner was easier than defiance.

The situation is constructed so that there is no way the subject can 99 stop shocking the learner without violating the experimenter's definitions of his own competence. The subject fears that he will appear arrogant, untoward, and rude if he breaks off. Although these inhibiting emotions appear small in scope alongside the violence being done to the learner, they suffuse the mind and feelings of the subject, who is miserable at the prospect of having to repudiate the authority to his face. (When the experiment was altered so that the experimenter gave his instructions by telephone instead of in person, only a third as many people were fully obedient through 450 volts.) It is a curious thing that a measure of compassion on the part of the subject—an unwillingness to "hurt" the experimenter's feelings—is part of those binding forces inhibiting his disobedience. The withdrawal of such deference may be as painful to the subject as to the authority he defies.

## DUTY WITHOUT CONFLICT

The subjects do not derive satisfaction from inflicting pain, but they 100 often like the feeling they get from pleasing the experimenter. They are proud of doing a good job, obeying the experimenter under difficult circumstances. While the subjects administered only mild shocks on their own initiative, one experimental variation showed that, under orders, 30 percent of them were willing to deliver 450 volts even when they had to forcibly push the learner's hand down on the electrode.

Bruno Batta is a thirty-seven-year-old welder who took part in the 101 variation requiring the use of force. He was born in New Haven, his parents in Italy. He has a rough-hewn face that conveys a conspicuous lack of alertness. He has some difficulty in mastering the experimental procedure and needs to be corrected by the experimenter several times. He shows appreciation for the help and willingness to do what is required. After the 150-volt level, Batta has to force the learner's hand down on the shock plate, since the learner himself refuses to touch it.

When the learner first complains, Mr. Batta pays no attention to 102
him. His face remains impassive, as if to dissociate himself from the
learner's disruptive behavior. When the experimenter instructs him to
force the learner's hand down, he adopts a rigid, mechanical procedure.
He tests the generator switch. When it fails to function, he immediately
forces the learner's hand onto the shock plate. All the while he maintains
the same rigid mask. The learner, seated alongside him, begs him to stop,
but with robotic impassivity he continues the procedure.

What is extraordinary is his apparent total indifference to the 103
learner; he hardly takes cognizance of him as a human being. Meanwhile,
he relates to the experimenter in a submissive and courteous fashion.

At the 330-volt level, the learner refuses not only to touch the shock 104
plate but also to provide any answers. Annoyed, Batta turns to him, and
chastises him: "You better answer and get it over with. We can't stay
here all night." These are the only words he directs to the learner in the
course of an hour. Never again does he speak to him. The scene is brutal
and depressing, his hard, impassive face showing total indifference as he
subdues the screaming learner and gives him shocks. He seems to derive
no pleasure from the act itself, only quiet satisfaction at doing his job
properly.

When he administers 450 volts, he turns to the experimenter and 105
asks, "Where do we go from here, Professor?" His tone is deferential and
expresses his willingness to be a cooperative subject, in contrast to the
learner's obstinacy.

At the end of the session he tells the experimenter how honored he 106
has been to help him, and in a moment of contrition, remarks, "Sir, sorry
it couldn't have been a full experiment."

He has done his honest best. It is only the deficient behavior of the 107
learner that has denied the experimenter full satisfaction.

The essence of obedience is that a person comes to view himself as 108
the instrument for carrying out another person's wishes, and he therefore no longer regards himself as responsible for his actions. Once this
critical shift of viewpoint has occurred, all of the essential features of
obedience follow. The most far-reaching consequence is that the person
feels responsible *to* the authority directing him but feels no responsibility *for* the content of the actions that the authority prescribes. Morality
does not disappear—it acquires a radically different focus: the subordinate person feels shame or pride depending on how adequately he has
performed the actions called for by authority.

Language provides numerous terms to pinpoint this type of moral- 109
ity: *loyalty, duty, discipline* all are terms heavily saturated with moral
meaning and refer to the degree to which a person fulfills his obligations
to authority. They refer not to the "goodness" of the person per se but
to the adequacy with which a subordinate fulfills his socially defined

role. The most frequent defense of the individual who has performed a heinous act under command of authority is that he has simply done his duty. In asserting this defense, the individual is not introducing an alibi concocted for the moment but is reporting honestly on the psychological attitude induced by submission to authority.

For a person to feel responsible for his actions, he must sense that 110 the behavior has flowed from "the self." In the situation we have studied, subjects have precisely the opposite view of their actions—namely, they see them as originating in the motives of some other person. Subjects in the experiment frequently said, "If it were up to me, I would not have administered shocks to the learner."

Once authority has been isolated as the cause of the subject's 111 behavior, it is legitimate to inquire into the necessary elements of authority and how it must be perceived in order to gain his compliance. We conducted some investigations into the kinds of changes that would cause the experimenter to lose his power and to be disobeyed by the subject. Some of the variations revealed that:

- ◆ *The experimenter's physical presence has a marked impact on his* 112 *authority.* As cited earlier, obedience dropped off sharply when orders were given by telephone. The experimenter could often induce a disobedient subject to go on by returning to the laboratory.
- ◆ *Conflicting authority severely paralyzes action.* When two experi- 113 menters of equal status, both seated at the command desk, gave incompatible orders, no shocks were delivered past the point of their disagreement.
- ◆ *The rebellious action of others severely undermines authority.* In one 114 variation, three teachers (two actors and a real subject) adminis- tered a test and shocks. When the two actors disobeyed the experimenter and refused to go beyond a certain shock level, thirty-six of forty subjects joined their disobedient peers and refused as well.

Although the experimenter's authority was fragile in some respects, 115 it is also true that he had almost none of the tools used in ordinary command structures. For example, the experimenter did not threaten the subjects with punishment—such as loss of income, community ostra- cism, or jail—for failure to obey. Neither could he offer incentives. Indeed, we should expect the experimenter's authority to be much less than that of someone like a general, since the experimenter has no power to enforce his imperatives, and since participation in a psychological experiment scarcely evokes the sense of urgency and dedication found in warfare. Despite these limitations, he still managed to command a dismaying degree of obedience.

I will cite one final variation of the experiment that depicts a 116 dilemma that is more common in everyday life. The subject was not ordered to pull the lever that shocked the victim, but merely to perform a subsidiary task (administering the word-pair test) while another person administered the shock. In this situation, thirty-seven of forty adults continued to the highest level on the shock generator. Predictably, they excused their behavior by saying that the responsibility belonged to the man who actually pulled the switch. This may illustrate a dangerously typical arrangement in a complex society: it is easy to ignore responsibility when one is only an intermediate link in a chain of action.

The problem of obedience is not wholly psychological. The form 117 and shape of society and the way it is developing have much to do with it. There was a time, perhaps, when people were able to give a fully human response to any situation because they were fully absorbed in it as human beings. But as soon as there was a division of labor things changed. Beyond a certain point, the breaking up of society into people carrying out narrow and very special jobs takes away from the human quality of work and life. A person does not get to see the whole situation but only a small part of it, and is thus unable to act without some kind of overall direction. He yields to authority but in doing so is alienated from his own actions.

Even Eichmann was sickened when he toured the concentration 118 camps, but he had only to sit at a desk and shuffle papers. At the same time the man in the camp who actually dropped Cyclon-b into the gas chambers was able to justify *his* behavior on the ground that he was only following orders from above. Thus there is a fragmentation of the total human act; no one is confronted with the consequences of his decision to carry out the evil act. The person who assumes responsibility has evaporated. Perhaps this is the most common characteristic of socially organized evil in modern society.

## Review Questions

1. Milgram states that obedience is a basic element in the structure of social life. How so?
2. What is the dilemma inherent in obedience to authority?
3. Summarize the obedience experiments.
4. What predictions did experts and laypeople make about the experiments before they were conducted? How did these predictions compare with the experimental results?
5. What are Milgram's views regarding the two assumptions bearing on his experiment that (1) people are naturally aggressive and (2) a lunatic, sadistic fringe is responsible for shocking learners to the maximum limit?
6. How do Milgram's findings corroborate Hannah Arendt's thesis about the "banality of evil"?

7. What, according to Milgram, is the "essence of obedience"?
8. How did being an intermediate link in a chain of action affect a subject's willingness to continue with the experiment?
9. In the article's final two paragraphs, Milgram speaks of a "fragmentation of the total human act." To what is he referring?

## Discussion and Writing Suggestions

1. "Conservative philosophers argue that the very fabric of society is threatened by disobedience, while humanists stress the primacy of the individual conscience." Develop the arguments of both the conservative and the humanist regarding obedience to authority. Be prepared to debate the ethics of obedience by defending one position or the other.
2. Would you have been glad to have participated in the Milgram experiments? Why or why not?
3. The ethics of Milgram's experimental design came under sharp attack. Diana Baumrind's review of the experiment typifies the criticism; but before you read her work, try to anticipate the objections she raises.
4. Given the general outcome of the experiments, why do you suppose Milgram gives as his first example of a subject's response the German émigré's refusal to continue the electrical shocks?
5. Does the outcome of the experiment upset you in any way? Do you feel the experiment teaches us anything new about human nature?
6. Comment on Milgram's skill as a writer of description. How effectively does he portray his subjects when introducing them? When re-creating their tension in the experiment?
7. Mrs. Braverman said to her husband: "You can call yourself Eichmann." Do you agree with Mrs. Braverman? Explain.
8. Reread paragraphs 29 through 81, the transcript of the experiment in which Mr. Prozi participated. Appreciating that Prozi was debriefed, that is, was assured that no harm came to the learner, imagine what Prozi might have been thinking as he drove home after the experiment. Develop your thoughts into a monologue, written in the first person, with Prozi at the wheel of his car.

## REVIEWS OF STANLEY MILGRAM'S *OBEDIENCE TO AUTHORITY*

*Many of Milgram's colleagues saluted him for providing that "hard information" about human nature that Doris Lessing speaks of. Others attacked him for violating the rights of his subjects. Still others faulted his experimental design and claimed he could not, with any validity, speculate on life outside the laboratory based on the behavior of his subjects within.*

*We reproduce something of this debate in the pieces that follow. First, psychologist Richard Herrnstein praises Milgram, acknowledging the subjects' discomfort but arguing that the discomfort of a few is a price worth paying for educating the many. Psychologist Diana Baumrind then excoriates Milgram for "entrapping" his subjects and potentially harming their "self-image or ability to trust adult authorities in the future." In a footnote, we summarize Milgram's response to Baumrind's critique. In a third review, Philip Meyer draws a parallel between Milgram's own behavior as a scientist who was willing (for a "higher" cause) to see his subjects squirm and the behavior of the subjects themselves, who continued to shock innocent victims despite their protests.*

*As you read, note the ways each writer lays out basic principles on which the critique will rest before building on those principles with arguments for or against Milgram. A critique, as you learned in Chapter 3, should proceed methodically. The writer should summarize the author's work under review and then examine significant points of that work according to clearly stated principles, or assumptions. To save space, we've deleted the summary of Milgram's experiment in each critique. You can assume that Herrnstein, Baumrind, and Meyer all adequately began their critiques with a neutral, brief recounting of the experiment. As for their providing other elements of an effective critique—we leave it to you to make this determination.*

# Review of Stanley Milgram's Experiments on Obedience

## RICHARD HERRNSTEIN

*Richard Herrnstein (b. 1930), a research psychologist at Harvard University, has written numerous books, including* I.Q. in the Meritocracy. *He is a regular contributor of articles to professional journals and is currently editor of the* Psychological Bulletin.

. . . No doubt about it, these experiments were a surprise, and a nasty    1
surprise at that. The essence of a major discovery is its capacity to cause
a large shift in our beliefs about some part of the world. Milgram's data
show us something about the human world that we had failed to grasp
before. They show us, not precisely that people are callous, but that they

---

can slip into a frame of mind in which their actions are not entirely their own. Psychologically, it is not they alone who are flipping the switches, but also the institutional authority—the austere scientist in the laboratory coat. The authority is taken to have the right to do what he is doing, by virtue of knowledge or status. Permutations of the basic procedure made it clear that the subjects' obedience depended on a sense of passivity, and that disobedience resulted if the subject was made to feel as if he were acting on his own initiative. Ordinary people will, in fact, not easily engage in brutality on their own. But they will apparently do so if someone else is in charge.

The experiments prove decisively that ordinary people can turn    2
into lethal instruments in the hands of an unscrupulous authority. The subjects who obeyed did not appear to be in any way atypical; they were not stupid, maladjusted, psychopathic, or immoral in usual terms. They simply did not apply the usual standards of humanity to their own conduct. Or, rather, the usual standards gave way to a more pressing imperative, the command of authority. The brutality latent in these ordinary people—in all of us—may have little to do with aggression or hostility. In fact hostility was here the humane impulse, for when it turned on the pseudo-experimenter it was a source of disobedience. In Milgram's procedure, and in the many natural settings it more or less mimics, brutality is the awful corollary of things we rightly prize in human society, like good citizenship or personal loyalty.

Milgram's work is said by some to show how close our society has    3
come to Nazi Germany. But does it really? In Italy, Australia, South Africa, and contemporary Germany, subjects in comparable experiments have been *more*, not less, obedient. No experiment any place has yet produced a negative result to boast about. In the totalitarian countries— from Spain to China—experiments like Milgram's have not been done for they would be considered subversive, as they would indeed be. But just picture how people would behave in Spain or Albania or China, where obedience is taken far more seriously than in permissive, turbulent America. Ironically, we live in a society where disobedience, not obedience, is in vogue, contrary to the fashionable rhetoric of journalists and social commentators. Still, Milgram's American subjects mostly obeyed, and would probably do so even today, ten tumultuous years later.

The parallels to Nazi Germany, then, really say something about the    4
quality of the authority rather than the obedience to it. A degree of obedience is the given in human society; enough of it to turn dangerous if the wrong people wield it. The political problem is how to decide who shall be the authority, for it is futile if not dangerous to hope for a society of disobeyers. Consider a contemporary case in point. Federal

Judge Gesell recently accused some lawyers of a "Nuremberg mentality." They had defended their client, Egil Krogh, on the grounds that he was obeying the orders of the President, his Commander-in-Chief, when he lied under oath.[1] The judge's view was that Krogh may indeed have been obeying orders, but he should have disobeyed. At other times, people honor their loyal and obedient citizens instead of imprisoning them, and I suspect that Judge Gesell is no different. The judge saw it the way he did because a bitter alienation of many people from our government has fostered the illusion that obedience to authority is itself malevolent.

The illusion is palpably false, though the authority may, alas, be    5
malevolent. There is a crucial dilemma here, one that will plague any political scheme that values both social order and individual autonomy. But the horns of the dilemma have never been so clear as they are in the light of Milgram's experiments. On one side, we find that even permissive, individualistic America creates people who can become agents of terror. As the weapons of terror become more powerful and more remote from their victims, the dangers of obedience grow. We know that bombardiers in military aircraft suffer little of the conflict and anxiety shown by Milgram's subjects, for they inflict punishment at an even greater distance and they serve an authority with greater license. That horn of the dilemma is much in the news these days. But the other horn is the penalty if we set too high a value on individual conscience and autonomy. The alternative to authority and obedience is anarchy, and history teaches that that is the surest way to chaos and, ultimately, tyranny.

Though he recognizes the alternatives, Milgram's sympathies are    6
libertarian. He wants a more defiant citizenry, a higher percentage of disobeyers to authority. I have no doubt that it would be easy to make people more likely to say no to authority, simply by reducing the penalties for doing so. But the evidence does not suggest that people use only benevolence or moral sensitivity as the criteria for rejecting authority. Think of some real examples. Would it be greed or a higher virtue that would be the main reason for defaulting on taxes if the penalties were reduced? What deserter from the army would fail to claim it was conscience, not cowardice, once conscientious desertion became permissible? Milgram, and no doubt others, would probably answer that reducing the penalties is not enough—that people need to be taught

---

[1] Egil Krogh headed Richard Nixon's Special Investigative Unit known as the "Plumbers." He was indicted for burglarizing the office of Dr. Fielding, psychiatrist to Daniel Ellsberg. High officials in the Nixon administration wanted to gather and leak to the press embarrassing information on Ellsberg, who had released the *Pentagon Papers* to the *New York Times*. Krogh maintained at his trial that orders to commit the burglary had originated in the White House.

virtue, not just relieved of the hazards of vice. That is fine, but it does not seem like cynicism to insist that the burden of proof falls on those who think they know a way to make people better than they have ever been. I find no proof in this book, or in the contemporary literature of civil disobedience. Milgram's work, brilliant as it is, resolves no dilemmas.

Psychology does not often spawn a finding that is neither trivial, obvious, nor false. Milgram's is the rare exception. The research is well conceived and done with care and skill, even elegance. It was both unexpected and timely, which are virtues that add up to far more than the sum of the parts. Why, then, has the work produced the poles of response? It won Milgram professional recognition and numerous honors, and it was also attacked again and again in the technical literature. The book was reviewed on the front page of the *New York Times Book Review*, an uncommon distinction for an academic work in social science, but the review was a hatchet job by a professor of literature whose distaste for social science was the main message.

Many people, besides the *Times* reviewer, do not like social science. There are so many of them that I can even sort them into categories: those who dislike it because they believe it tells us nothing they did not know and those who dislike it because it tells us something they did not want to hear. Milgram's work arouses those in the latter category, who typically insist that they belong in the former category. It is one thing to contemplate the banality of evil in the abstract, but something else to learn that the spore will germinate in New Haven [at Yale University] at the prompting of a man in a laboratory coat. The gross discrepancy between what people predicted for the experiment and what others did as subjects is the tangible proof of the findings' power to inform us about ourselves—about our capacity for cruelty and our ignorance of the capacity. Those who continue to insist that the experiment teaches nothing may be relying on ignorance to solve the awful dilemma of authority. It will resolve nothing, of course, but it is no surprise that Milgram's news has driven some heads into the sand.

But that is not the only problem with Milgram's work. Some people, often social scientists themselves, object to the element of deception, especially when it is calculated to produce acute discomfort. This seems to me a valid concern, a secondary dilemma arising from the fact of the research itself rather than from its findings. To learn how people behave under duress or danger, the researcher dissembles, for he cannot subject people to real-life hazards. If there is to be experimentation on people in social settings, there is therefore likely to be deception and manipulation. It is an unpleasant prospect, and easy to reject. But, then, consider Milgram's experiments. Deception and manipulation led to a remarkable

7

8

9

addition to our knowledge of the perils of authority. Knowledge like that comes hard and slow. Can we afford to prohibit further discoveries of that caliber and relevance?

Some people answer the question with a dogmatic yes, setting the 10 highest priority on individual privacy at the risk of continuing ignorance. That happens not to be my view. I value privacy but worry about ignorance. A small, temporary loss of a few people's comfort and privacy seems a bearable price for a large reduction in ignorance, but I can see, as can Milgram, how delicate a judgment this implies. Even so, I hope there are other experiments like Milgram's coming along— experiments that will teach us about ourselves, with no more than the minimum necessary deception and discomfort, elegantly and economically conducted. It should not be easy to do experiments like Milgram's—for they should not be done casually—but it should be possible, and, needless to say, the experimenter should not be held in contempt if the outcome is unexpected or uncomfortable. The goal of science is *news*, not *good* news.

## Review Questions

1. Why does Herrnstein call "palpably false" the sentiment that any kind of obedience to authority is malevolent?
2. What is the "crucial dilemma" that Herrnstein discusses?
3. What does Herrnstein see as the alternative to obedience to authority? What is his view of the alternative?
4. How does Herrnstein account for the varying critical reception of Milgram's work?
5. What is Herrnstein's view of the deception practiced in the experiment?

## Discussion and Writing Suggestions

1. Herrnstein says that it is possible that the "perfectionist dogma" of human society—that we are, basically, decent, caring, and humane people—may be giving way to humbler expectations. Is Milgram's work, after all, a surprise? If so, what are your assumptions about human nature? If not, what are you conceding about our behavior? How do your views on the future of the race depend on your answers?
2. "In Milgram's procedure, and in the many natural settings it more or less mimics, brutality is the awful corollary of things we rightly prize in human society, like good citizenship or personal loyalty." What does Herrnstein mean?
3. Is it possible to set too high a value on individual conscience and autonomy? What are the dangers of refusing to compromise one's autonomy?

**4.** Herrnstein says that "Milgram's work, brilliant as it is, resolves no dilemmas" about the nature of authority. In an essay, discuss the dilemmas that
need resolving (see Review Question 2). What solution would you propose?

# Review of Stanley Milgram's Experiments on Obedience

## DIANA BAUMRIND

*Diana Baumrind is a psychologist who, when writing this review, worked at
the Institute of Human Development, University of California, Berkeley. The
review appeared in* American Psychologist *shortly after Milgram published
the results of his first experiments in 1963.*

. . . The dependent, obedient attitude assumed by most subjects in the      1
experimental setting is appropriate to that situation. The "game" is
defined by the experimenter and he makes the rules. By volunteering,
the subject agrees implicitly to assume a posture of trust and obedience. While the experimental conditions leave him exposed, the subject has the right to assume that his security and self-esteem will be
protected.

There are other professional situations in which one member—the      2
patient or client—expects help and protection from the other—the
physician or psychologist. But the interpersonal relationship between
experimenter and subject additionally has unique features which are
likely to provoke initial anxiety in the subject. The laboratory is unfamiliar as a setting and the rules of behavior ambiguous compared to a
clinician's office. Because of the anxiety and passivity generated by the
setting, the subject is more prone to behave in an obedient, suggestible
manner in the laboratory than elsewhere. Therefore, the laboratory is
not the place to study degree of obedience or suggestibility, as a
function of a particular experimental condition, since the base line for
these phenomena as found in the laboratory is probably much higher
than in most other settings. Thus experiments in which the relationship
to the experimenter as an authority is used as an independent condition

are imperfectly designed for the same reason that they are prone to injure the subjects involved. They disregard the special quality of trust and obedience with which the subject appropriately regards the experimenter.

Other phenomena which present ethical decisions, unlike those mentioned above, *can* be reproduced successfully in the laboratory. Failure experience, conformity to peer judgment, and isolation are among such phenomena. In these cases we can expect the experimenter to take whatever measures are necessary to prevent the subject from leaving the laboratory more humiliated, insecure, alienated, or hostile than when he arrived. To guarantee that an especially sensitive subject leaves a stressful experimental experience in the proper state sometimes requires special clinical training. But usually an attitude of compassion, respect, gratitude, and common sense will suffice, and no amount of clinical training will substitute. The subject has the right to expect that the psychologist with whom he is interacting has some concern for his welfare, and the personal attributes and professional skill to express his good will effectively.

Unfortunately, the subject is not always treated with the respect he deserves. It has become more commonplace in sociopsychological laboratory studies to manipulate, embarrass, and discomfort subjects. At times the insult to the subject's sensibilities extends to the journal reader when the results are reported. Milgram's (1963) study is a case in point. The following is Milgram's abstract of his experiment:

> This article describes a procedure for the study of destructive obedience in the laboratory. It consists of ordering a naive S to administer increasingly more severe punishment to a victim in the context of a learning experiment.[1] Punishment is administered by means of a shock generator with 30 graded switches ranging from Slight Shock to Danger: Severe Shock. The victim is a confederate of E. The primary dependent variable is the maximum shock the S is willing to administer before he refuses to continue further.[2] 26 Ss obeyed the experimental commands fully, and administered the highest shock on the generator. 14 Ss broke off the experiment at some point after the victim protested and refused to provide further answers. The procedure created extreme levels of nervous tension in some Ss. Profuse sweating, trembling, and stuttering were typical expressions of this emotional disturbance. One unexpected sign of tension—yet to be explained—was the regular occurrence of nervous laughter, which in some Ss developed into uncontrollable seizures. The variety of interesting behavioral dynamics observed in the experiment, the reality of the situation for the S, and the possibility of parametric variation[3]

---

[1]In psychological experiments, S is an abbreviation for *subject*; E is an abbreviation for *experimenter*.
[2]In the context of a psychological experiment, a *dependent variable* is a behavior that is expected to change as a result of changes in the experimental procedure.

within the framework of the procedure point to the fruitfulness of further study [p. 371].

The detached, objective manner in which Milgram reports the    5
emotional disturbance suffered by his subjects contrasts sharply with his graphic account of that disturbance. Following are two other quotes describing the effects on his subjects of the experimental conditions:

> I observed a mature and initially poised businessman enter the laboratory smiling and confident. Within 20 minutes he was reduced to a twitching, stuttering wreck, who was rapidly approaching a point of nervous collapse. He constantly pulled on his earlobe, and twisted his hands. At one point he pushed his fist into his forehead and muttered: "Oh God, let's stop it." And yet he continued to respond to every word of the experimenter, and obeyed to the end [p. 377].
>
> In a large number of cases the degree of tension reached extremes that are rarely seen in sociopsychological laboratory studies. Subjects were observed to sweat, tremble, stutter, bite their lips, groan, and dig their fingernails into their flesh. These were characteristic rather than exceptional responses to the experiment.
>
> One sign of tension was the regular occurrence of nervous laughing fits. Fourteen of the 40 subjects showed definite signs of nervous laughter and smiling. The laughter seemed entirely out of place, even bizarre. Full-blown, uncontrollable seizures were observed for 3 subjects. On one occasion we observed a seizure so violently convulsive that it was necessary to call a halt to the experiment . . . [p. 375].

Milgram does state that,

> After the interview, procedures were undertaken to assure that the subject would leave the laboratory in a state of well being. A friendly reconciliation was arranged between the subject and the victim, and an effort was made to reduce any tensions that arose as a result of the experiment [p. 374].

It would be interesting to know what sort of procedures could dissipate the type of emotional disturbance just described. In view of the effects on subjects, traumatic to a degree which Milgram himself considers nearly unprecedented in sociopsychological experiments, his casual as-

---

[3]*Parametric variation* is a statistical term that describes the degree to which information based on data for one experiment can be applied to data for a slightly different experiment.

surance that these tensions were dissipated before the subject left the laboratory is unconvincing.

What could be the rational basis for such a posture of indiffer-  6 ence? Perhaps Milgram supplies the answer himself when he partially explains the subject's destructive obedience as follows, "Thus they assume that the discomfort caused the victim is momentary, while the scientific gains resulting from the experiment are enduring [p. 378]." Indeed such a rationale might suffice to justify the means used to achieve his end if that end were of inestimable value to humanity or were not itself transformed by the means by which it was attained.

The behavioral psychologist is not in as good a position to objec-  7 tify his faith in the significance of his work as medical colleagues at points of breakthrough. His experimental situations are not sufficiently accurate models of real-life experience; his sampling techniques are seldom of a scope which would justify the meaning with which he would like to endow his results; and these results are hard to reproduce by colleagues with opposing theoretical views. Unlike the Sabin vac- cine,[4] for example, the concrete benefit to humanity of his particular piece of work, no matter how competently handled, cannot justify the risk that real harm will be done to the subject. I am not speaking of physical discomfort, inconvenience, or experimental deception per se, but of permanent harm, however slight. I do regard the emotional disturbance described by Milgram as potentially harmful because it could easily effect an alteration in the subject's self-image or ability to trust adult authorities in the future. It is potentially harmful to a subject to commit, in the course of an experiment, acts which he himself considers unworthy, particularly when he has been entrapped into com- mitting such acts by an individual he has reason to trust. The subject's personal responsibility for his actions is not erased because the experi- menter reveals to him the means which he used to stimulate these actions. The subject realizes that he would have hurt the victim if the current were on. The realization that he also made a fool of himself by accepting the experimental set results in additional loss of self-esteem. Moreover, the subject finds it difficult to express his anger outwardly after the experimenter in a self-acceptant but friendly manner reveals the hoax.

A fairly intense corrective interpersonal experience is indicated  8 wherein the subject admits and accepts his responsibility for his own actions, and at the same time gives vent to his hurt and anger at being

---

[4]The Sabin vaccine provides immunization against polio.

fooled. Perhaps an experience as distressing as the one described by Milgram can be integrated by the subject, provided that careful thought is given to the matter. The propriety of such experimentation is still in question even if such a reparational experience were forthcoming. Without it I would expect a naive, sensitive subject to remain deeply hurt and anxious for some time, and a sophisticated, cynical subject to become even more alienated and distrustful.

In addition the experimental procedure used by Milgram does not   **9** appear suited to the objectives of the study because it does not take into account the special quality of the set which the subject has in the experimental situation. Milgram is concerned with a very important problem, namely, the social consequences of destructive obedience. He says,

> Gas chambers were built, death camps were guarded, daily quotas of corpses were produced with the same efficiency as the manufacture of appliances. These inhumane policies may have originated in the mind of a single person, but they could only be carried out on a massive scale if a very large number of persons obeyed orders [p. 371].

But the parallel between authority-subordinate relationships in Hitler's Germany and in Milgram's laboratory is unclear. In the former situation the SS man or member of the German Officer Corps, when obeying orders to slaughter, had no reason to think of his superior officer as benignly disposed towards himself or their victims. The victims were perceived as subhuman and not worthy of consideration. The subordinate officer was an agent in a great cause. He did not need to feel guilt or conflict because within his frame of reference he was acting rightly.

It is obvious from Milgram's own descriptions that most of his   **10** subjects were concerned about their victims and did trust the experimenter, and that their distressful conflict was generated in part by the consequences of these two disparate but appropriate attitudes. Their distress may have resulted from shock at what the experimenter was doing to them as well as from what they thought they were doing to their victims. In any case there is not a convincing parallel between the phenomena studied by Milgram and destructive obedience as that concept would apply to the subordinate-authority relationship demonstrated in Hitler Germany. If the experiments were conducted "outside of New Haven and without any visible ties to the university," I would still question their validity on similar although not identical grounds. In addition, I would question the representativeness of a sample of subjects who would voluntarily participate within a noninstitutional setting.

In summary, the experimental objectives of the psychologist are   **11** seldom incompatible with the subject's ongoing state of well being, provided that the experimenter is willing to take the subject's motives and interests into consideration when planning his methods and correctives. Section 4b in *Ethical Standards of Psychologists* (APA, undated) reads in part:

> Only when a problem is significant and can be investigated in no other way is the psychologist justified in exposing human subjects to emotional stress or other possible harm. In conducting such research, the psychologist must seriously consider the possibility of harmful aftereffects, and should be prepared to remove them as soon as permitted by the design of the experiment. Where the danger of serious aftereffects exists, research should be conducted only when the subjects or their responsible a-gents are fully informed of this possibility and volunteer nevertheless [p. 12].

From the subject's point of view procedures which involve loss of dignity, self-esteem, and trust in rational authority are probably most harmful in the long run and require the most thoughtfully planned reparations, if engaged in at all. The public image of psychology as a profession is highly related to our own actions, and some of these actions are changeworthy. It is important that as research psychologists we protect our ethical sensibilities rather than adapt our personal standards to include as appropriate the kind of indignities to which Milgram's subjects were exposed. I would not like to see experiments such as Milgram's proceed unless the subjects were fully informed of the dangers of serious aftereffects and his correctives were clearly shown to be effective in restoring their state of well being.[5]

---

[5]Stanley Milgram replied to Baumrind's critique in a lengthy critique of his own. [From Stanley Milgram, "Issues in the Study of Obedience: A Reply to Baumrind," *American Psychologist* 19, 1964, pp. 848–851] Following are his principal points:

♦ Milgram believed that the experimental findings were in large part responsible for Baumrind's criticism. He writes:

Is not Baumrind's criticism based as much on the unanticipated findings as on the method? The findings were that some subjects performed in what appeared to be a shockingly immoral way. If, instead, every one of the subjects had broken off at "slight shock," or at the first sign of the learner's discomfort, the results would have been pleasant, and reassuring, and who would protest?

♦ Milgram objected to Baumrind's assertion that those who participated in the experiment would have trouble justifying their behavior. Milgram conducted follow-up question-naires. The results, summarized in Table 1, indicate that 84 percent of the subjects claimed they were pleased to have been a part of the experiment.

## REFERENCES

American Psychological Association. Ethical standards of psychologists: A summary of ethical principles. Washington, D.C.: APA, undated.

Milgram, S. Behavioral study of obedience. *J. Abnorm. Soc. Psychol.* 67, 1963, pp. 371–378.

## Review Questions

1. Why might a subject volunteer for an experiment? Why do subjects typically assume a dependent, obedient attitude?
2. Why is a laboratory not a suitable setting for a study of obedience?
3. For what reasons does Baumrind feel that the Milgram experiment was potentially harmful?
4. For what reasons does Baumrind question the relationship between Milgram's findings and the obedient behavior of subordinates in Nazi Germany?

**TABLE 1**  *Excerpt from Questionnaire Used in a Follow-up Study of the Obedience Research*

| NOW THAT I HAVE READ THE REPORT, AND ALL THINGS CONSIDERED . . . | DEFIANT | OBEDIENT | ALL |
|---|---|---|---|
| 1. I am very glad to have been in the experiment | 40.0% | 47.8% | 43.5% |
| 2. I am glad to have been in the experiment | 43.8% | 35.7% | 40.2% |
| 3. I am neither sorry nor glad to have been in the experiment | 15.3% | 14.8% | 15.1% |
| 4. I am sorry to have been in the experiment | 0.8% | 0.7% | 0.8% |
| 5. I am very sorry to have been in the experiment | 0.0% | 1.0% | 0.5% |

Note—Ninety-two percent of the subjects returned the questionnaire. The characteristics of the nonrespondents were checked against the respondents. They differed from the respondents only with regard to age; younger people were overrepresented in the nonresponding group.

♦ Baumrind objected that studies of obedience cannot meaningfully be carried out in a laboratory setting, since the obedience occurred in a context where it was appropriate. Milgram's response: "I reject Baumrind's argument that the observed obedience does not count because it occurred where it is appropriate. That is precisely why it *does* count. A soldier's obedience is no less meaningful because it occurs in a pertinent military context."

♦ Milgram concludes his critique in this way: "If there is a moral to be learned from the obedience study, it is that every man must be responsible for his own actions. This author accepts full responsibility for the design and execution of the study. Some people may feel it should not have been done. I disagree and accept the burden of their judgment."

## Discussion and Writing Suggestions

1. Baumrind contends that the Milgram experiment is imperfectly designed for two reasons: (1) The laboratory is not the place to test obedience; (2) Milgram disregarded the trust that subjects usually show an experimenter. Do you agree with Baumrind's objections? Do you find them equally valid?

2. Baumrind states that the ethical procedures of the experiment keep it from having significant value. In this respect, she directly disagrees with Richard Herrnstein (pp. 337–41), who justifies the experimental procedures by claiming that the momentary discomfort of a few subjects is worth adding to human knowledge. With whom do you agree?

3. Do you agree with Baumrind that the subjects were "entrapped" into committing unworthy acts?

4. Assume the identity of a participant in Milgram's experiment who obeyed the experimenter by shocking the learner with the maximum voltage. You have just returned from the lab, and your spouse asks you about your day. Write the conversation between you and your spouse.

# Review of Stanley Milgram's Experiments on Obedience

## PHILIP MEYER

> *Philip Edward Meyer (b. 1930) began his career as a journalist for the* Topeka Daily Capital *in 1954, working subsequently for the* Miami Herald *(1958–1962) and as correspondent in Washington for Knight-Ridder newspapers (1962–1978). In 1966, Meyer was named a Nieman Fellow at Harvard University and a year later shared a Pulitzer Prize for his reporting of the Detroit riots. He is a co-author of* Precision Journalism *(1979),* To Keep the Republic *(1975), and* Editors, Publishers and Newspaper Ethics *(1983). The present selection appeared in a piece in* Esquire *(February 1970), "If Hitler Asked You to Electrocute a Stranger, Would You? (Probably)."*

. . . The first question [concerning Milgram's work] is this: Should we    1
really be surprised and alarmed that people obey? Wouldn't it be even more alarming if they all refused to obey? Without obedience to a relevant ruling authority there could not be a civil society. And without a civil society, as Thomas Hobbes pointed out in the seventeenth century, we would live in a condition of war, "of every man against every other man," and life would be "solitary, poor, nasty, brutish and short."

---

In the middle of one of Stanley Milgram's lectures at C.U.N.Y. **2** recently, some mini-skirted undergraduates started whispering and giggling in the back of the room. He told them to cut it out. Since he was the relevant authority in that time and that place, they obeyed, and most people in the room were glad that they obeyed.

This was not, of course, a conflict situation. Nothing in the coeds' **3** social upbringing made it a matter of conscience for them to whisper and giggle. But a case can be made that in a conflict situation it is all the more important to obey. Take the case of war, for example. Would we really want a situation in which every participant in a war, direct or indirect—from front-line soldiers to the people who sell coffee and cigarettes to employees at the Concertina barbed-wire factory in Kansas—stops and consults his conscience before each action? It is asking for an awful lot of mental strain and anguish from an awful lot of people. The value of having civil order is that one can do his duty, or whatever interests him, or whatever seems to benefit him at the moment, and leave the agonizing to others. When Francis Gary Powers was being tried by a Soviet military tribunal after his U-2 spy plane was shot down, the presiding judge asked if he had thought about the possibility that his flight might have provoked a war. Powers replied with Hobbesian clarity: "The people who sent me should think of these things. My job was to carry out orders. I do not think it was my responsibility to make such decisions."

It was not his responsibility. And it is quite possible that if everyone **4** felt responsible for each of the ultimate consequences of his own tiny contributions to complex chains of events, then society simply would not work. Milgram, fully conscious of the moral and social implications of his research, believes that people should feel responsible for their actions. If someone else had invented the experiment, and if he had been the naïve subject, he feels certain that he would have been among the disobedient minority.

"There is no very good solution to this," he admits, thoughtfully. **5** "To simply and categorically say that you won't obey authority may resolve your personal conflict, but it creates more problems for society which may be more serious in the long run. But I have no doubt that to disobey is the proper thing to do in this [the laboratory] situation. It is the only reasonable value judgment to make."

The conflict between the need to obey the relevant ruling authority **6** and the need to follow your conscience becomes sharpest if you insist on living by an ethical system based on a rigid code—a code that seeks to answer all questions in advance of their being raised. Code ethics cannot solve the obedience problem. Stanley Milgram seems to be a situation ethicist, and situation ethics does offer a way out: When you feel conflict, you examine the situation and then make a choice among the competing evils. You may act with a presumption in favor of obedience, but reserve the possibility that you will disobey whenever obedience demands a flagrant and outrageous affront to conscience. This, by the way, is the philosophical position of many who resist the draft. In World War II, they would have fought. Vietnam is a different, an outrageously different, situation.

Life can be difficult for the situation ethicist, because he does not see the world in straight lines, while the social system too often assumes such a God-given, squared-off structure. If your moral code includes an injunction against all war, you may be deferred as a conscientious objector. If you merely oppose this particular war, you may not be deferred.  **7**

Stanley Milgram has his problems, too. He believes that in the laboratory situation, he would not have shocked Mr. Wallace.[1] His professional critics reply that in his real-life situation he has done the equivalent. He has placed innocent and naïve subjects under great emotional strain and pressure in selfish obedience to his quest for knowledge. When you raise this issue with Milgram, he has an answer ready. There is, he explains patiently, a critical difference between his naïve subjects and the man in the electric chair. The man in the electric chair (in the mind of the naïve subject) is helpless, strapped in. But the naïve subject is free to go at any time.  **8**

Immediately after he offers this distinction, Milgram anticipates the objection.  **9**

"It's quite true," he says, "that this is almost a philosophic position, because we have learned that some people are psychologically incapable of disengaging themselves. But that doesn't relieve them of the moral responsibility."  **10**

The parallel is exquisite. "The tension problem was unexpected," says Milgram in his defense. But he went on anyway. The naïve subjects didn't expect the screaming protests from the strapped-in learner. But they went on.  **11**

"I had to make a judgment," says Milgram. "I had to ask myself, was this harming the person or not? My judgment is that it was not. Even in the extreme cases, I wouldn't say that permanent damage results."  **12**

Sound familiar? "The shocks may be painful," the experimenter kept saying, "but they're not dangerous."  **13**

After the series of experiments was completed, Milgram sent a report of the results to his subjects and a questionnaire, asking whether they were glad or sorry to have been in the experiment. Eighty-three and seven-tenths percent said they were glad and only 1.3 percent were  **14**

---

[1]*Mr. Wallace* was the name of the learner (i.e., the experimenter's confederate) in a number of the obedience experiments.

sorry; 15 percent were neither sorry nor glad. However, Milgram could not be sure at the time of the experiment that only 1.3 percent would be sorry.

Kurt Vonnegut, Jr., put one paragraph in the preface to *Mother Night*, in 1966, which pretty much says it for the people with their fingers on the shock-generator switches, for you and me, and maybe even for Milgram. "If I'd been born in Germany," Vonnegut said, "I suppose I would have *been* a Nazi, bopping Jews and gypsies and Poles around, leaving boots sticking out of snowbanks, warming myself with my sweetly virtuous insides. So it goes." 15

Just so. One thing that happened to Milgram back in New Haven during the days of the experiment was that he kept running into people he'd watched from behind the one-way glass. It gave him a funny feeling, seeing those people going about their everyday business in New Haven and knowing what they would do to Mr. Wallace if ordered to. Now that his research results are in and you've thought about it, you can get this funny feeling too. You don't need one-way glass. A glance in your own mirror may serve just as well. 16

## Review Questions

1. What was Francis Gary Powers's response to a Soviet judge's question about the possibility of his U-2 flight's having provoked a war?
2. What are code ethics? Why can they not solve the obedience problem?

## Discussion and Writing Suggestions

1. Meyer opens his discussion with a question: "Should we really be surprised and alarmed that people obey?" What's your answer?
2. Do you agree with Meyer (paragraph 3) that "it is asking for an awful lot of mental strain and anguish from an awful lot of people" to have everyone associated with the military stop and examine their consciences before following orders?
3. "It is quite possible that if everyone felt responsible for each of the ultimate consequences of his own tiny contributions to complex chains of events, then society simply would not work." Your comments?
4. In paragraphs 8–13, Meyer draws a parallel relationship that can be expressed as follows: The subject exists in a relationship with the learner (in the experiment) in the same way that Milgram exists in a relationship with the subject. Explain this proposed parallel relationship and comment on its validity.
5. "You don't need one-way glass. A glance in your own mirror may serve just as well." Use Meyer's final lines as a point of departure for a dialogue

between you and the image of yourself in the mirror. Would you or wouldn't you shock the innocent victim? Assume in the dialogue that the image in the mirror takes one position and you take the other. See what develops—in four or five pages.

# The Education of a Torturer

JANICE T. GIBSON
MIKA HARITOS-FATOUROS

*This article provides an example of the way knowledge is constructed in the social sciences. In 1963, Stanley Milgram published the results of his experiments and speculated on the psychological mechanisms that allow people to obey the orders of a malevolent authority. In 1986, two other psychologists examined these proposed psychological mechanisms and applied them to a related, although somewhat different, set of behaviors: prolonged, systematic torture. Gibson and Haritos-Fatouros were interested in the process by which individuals are taught to become torturers. Were the same psychological mechanisms at work in real-life torturers as in the subjects who shocked learners in Milgram's experiments? No, conclude the researchers, who then altered and extended Milgram's theories to account for new facts. Although twenty-three years separated the work of Milgram (now deceased) and Gibson and Haritos-Fatouros, the three scholars have participated in a written conversation through which they've constructed and extended knowledge. It seems likely, in the years to come, that other researchers will conduct their own studies and take up the conversation again.*

*In one crucial and chilling respect, Gibson and Haritos-Fatouros agree with Milgram: It is ordinary people, not psychopaths, who become the Eichmanns of history. You may be fascinated to learn that the authors include college students as perfectly suitable candidates for becoming torturers. In fact, they say, any one of us could systematically inflict pain on another, given the right (i.e., a particularly brutalizing) set of circumstances. Chilling as well is the observation that college fraternities draft and indoctrinate pledges in much the same way that the Greek military did torturers. (See the quotation from Gibson and Haritos-Fatouros in this chapter's introductory essay, page 317.)*

*Janice T. Gibson teaches educational and developmental psychology at the*

University of Pittsburgh. Mika Haritos-Fatouros is dean of the School of Philosophy and teaches clinical psychology at the University of the Thessaloniki in Greece.

Torture—for whatever purpose and in whatever name—requires a  **1**
torturer, an individual responsible for planning and causing pain to others. "A man's hands are shackled behind him, his eyes blindfolded," wrote Argentine journalist Jacobo Timerman about his torture by Argentine army extremists. "No one says a word. Blows are showered. . . . [He is] stripped, doused with water, tied. . . . And the application of electric shocks begins. It's impossible to shout—you howl." The governments of at least 90 countries use similar methods to torture people all over the world, Amnesty International reports.

What kind of person can behave so monstrously to another human  **2**
being? A sadist or a sexual deviant? Someone with an authoritarian upbringing or who was abused by parents? A disturbed personality affected somehow by hereditary characteristics?

On the contrary, the Nazis who tortured and killed millions during  **3**
World War II "weren't sadists or killers by nature," Hannah Arendt reported in her book *Eichmann in Jerusalem*. Many studies of Nazi behavior concluded that monstrous acts, despite their horrors, were often simply a matter of faithful bureaucrats slavishly following orders.

In a 1976 study, University of Florida psychologist Molly Harrower  **4**
asked 15 Rorschach experts to examine inkblot test reports from Adolf Eichmann, Rudolf Hess, Hermann Goering and five other Nazi war criminals, made just before their trials at Nuremberg. She also sent the specialists Rorschach reports from eight Americans, some with well-adjusted personalities and some who were severely disturbed, without revealing the individuals' identities. The experts were unable to distinguish the Nazis from the Americans and judged an equal number of both to be well-adjusted. The horror that emerges is the likelihood that torturers are not freaks; they are ordinary people.

Obedience to what we call the "authority of violence" often plays  **5**
an important role in pushing ordinary people to commit cruel, violent and even fatal acts. During wartime, for example, soldiers will follow orders to kill unarmed civilians. Here, we will look at the way obedience and other factors combine to produce willing torturers.

Twenty-five years ago, the late psychologist Stanley Milgram  **6**
demonstrated convincingly that people unlikely to be cruel in everyday life will administer pain if they are told to by someone in authority. In a famous experiment, Milgram had men wearing laboratory coats direct average American adults to inflict a series of electric shocks on other people. No real shocks were given and the "victims" were acting, but the people didn't know this. They were told that the purpose of the

study was to measure the effects of punishment on learning. Obediently, 65 percent of them used what they thought were dangerously high levels of shocks when the experimenter told them to. While they were less likely to administer these supposed shocks as they were moved closer to their victims, almost one-third of them continued to shock when they were close enough to touch.

This readiness to torture is not limited to Americans. Following Milgram's lead, other researchers found that people of all ages, from a wide range of countries, were willing to shock others even when they had nothing to gain by complying with the command or nothing to lose by refusing it. So long as someone else, an authority figure, was responsible for the final outcome of the experiment, almost no one absolutely refused to administer shocks. Each study also found, as Milgram had, that some people would give shocks even when the decision was left up to them.

Milgram proposed that the reasons people obey or disobey authority fall into three categories. The first is personal history: family or school backgrounds that encourage obedience or defiance. The second, which he called "binding," is made up of ongoing experiences that make people feel comfortable when they obey authority. Strain, the third category, consists of bad feelings from unpleasant experiences connected with obedience. Milgram argued that when the binding factors are more powerful than the strain of cooperating, people will do as they are told. When the strain is greater, they are more likely to disobey.

This may explain short-term obedience in the laboratory, but it doesn't explain prolonged patterns of torture during wartime or under some political regimes. Repeatedly, torturers in Argentina and elsewhere performed acts that most of us consider repugnant, and in time this should have placed enough strain on them to prevent their obedience. It didn't. Nor does Milgram's theory explain undirected cruel or violent acts, which occur even when no authority orders them. For this, we have developed a more comprehensive learning model; for torture, we discovered, can be taught.

We studied the procedures used to train Greek military police as torturers during that country's military regime from 1967 through 1974. We examined the official testimonies of 21 former soldiers in the ESA (Army Police Corps) given at their 1975 criminal trials in Athens; in addition, Haritos-Fatouros conducted in-depth interviews with 16 of them after their trials. In many cases, these men had been convicted and had completed prison sentences. They were all leading normal lives when interviewed. One was a university graduate, five were graduates of higher technical institutes, nine had completed at least their second year of high school and only one had no more than a primary school education.

All of these men had been drafted, first into regular military service   11
and then into specialized units that required servicemen to torture
prisoners. We found no record of delinquent or disturbed behavior
before their military service. However, we did find several features of
the soldiers' training that helped to turn them into willing and able
torturers.

The initial screening for torturers was primarily based on physical   12
strength and "appropriate" political beliefs, which simply meant that the
recruits and their families were anticommunists. This ensured that the
men had hostile attitudes toward potential victims from the very beginning.

Once they were actually serving as military police, the men were   13
also screened for other attributes. According to former torturer Michae-
lis Petrou, "The most important criterion was that you had to keep your
mouth shut. Second, you had to show aggression. Third, you had to be
intelligent and strong. Fourth, you had to be 'their man,' which meant
that you would report on the others serving with you, that [the officers]
could trust you and that you would follow their orders blindly."

Binding the recruits to the authority of ESA began in basic training,   14
with physically brutal initiation rites. Recruits themselves were cursed,
punched, kicked and flogged. They were forced to run until they collapsed and prevented from relieving themselves for long stretches of
time. They were required to swear allegiance to a symbol of authority
used by the regime (a poster of a soldier superimposed on a large
phoenix rising from its own ashes), and they had to promise on their
knees to obey their commander-in-chief and the military revolution.

While being harassed and beaten by their officers, servicemen were   15
repeatedly told how fortunate they were to have joined the ESA, the
strongest and most important support of the regime. They were told
that an ESA serviceman's action is never questioned: "You can even flog
a major." In-group language helped the men to develop elitist attitudes.
Servicemen used nicknames for one another and, later, they used them
for victims and for the different methods of torture. "Tea party" meant
the beating of a prisoner by a group of military police using their fists,
and "tea party with toast" meant more severe group beatings using
clubs. Gradually, the recruits came to speak of all people who were not
in their group, parents and families included, as belonging to the "outside world."

The strain of obedience on the recruits was reduced in several ways.   16
During basic training, they were given daily "national ethical education"
lectures that included indoctrination against communism and enemies of
the state. During more advanced training, the recruits were constantly
reminded that the prisoners were "worms," and that they had to "crush"
them. One man reported that when he was torturing prisoners later, he

caught himself repeating phrases like "bloody communists!" that he had heard in the lectures.

The military police used a carrot-and-stick method to further dimin- 17
ish the recruits' uneasiness about torture. There were many rewards, such as relaxed military rules after training was completed, and torturers often weren't punished for leaving camp without permission. They were allowed to wear civilian clothes, to keep their hair long and to drive military police cars for their personal use. Torturers were frequently given a leave of absence after they forced a confession from a prisoner. They had many economic benefits as well, including free bus rides and restaurant meals and job placement when military service was over. These were the carrots.

The sticks consisted of the constant harassment, threats and punish- 18
ment for disobedience. The men were threatened and intimidated, first by their trainers, then later by senior servicemen. "An officer used to tell us that if a warder helps a prisoner, he will take the prisoner's place and the whole platoon will flog him," one man recalled. Soldiers spied on one another, and even the most successful torturers said that they were constantly afraid.

"You will learn to love pain," one officer promised a recruit. Sensi- 19
tivity to torture was blunted in several steps. First, the men had to endure it themselves, as if torture were a normal act. The beatings and other torments inflicted on them continued and became worse. Next, the servicemen chosen for the Persecution Section, the unit that tortured political prisoners, were brought into contact with the prisoners by carrying food to their cells. The new men watched veteran soldiers torture prisoners, while they stood guard. Occasionally, the veterans would order them to give the prisoners "some blows."

At the next step, the men were required to participate in group 20
beatings. Later, they were told to use a variety of torture methods on the prisoners. The final step, the appointment to prison warder or chief torturer, was announced suddenly by the commander-in-chief, leaving the men no time to reflect on their new duties.

The Greek example illustrates how the ability to torture can be 21
taught. Training that increases binding and reduces strain can cause decent people to commit acts, often over long periods of time, that otherwise would be unthinkable for them. Similar techniques can be found in military training all over the world, when the intent is to teach soldiers to kill or perform some other repellent act. We conducted extensive interviews with soldiers and ex-soldiers in the U.S. Marines and the Green Berets, and we found that all the steps in our training model were part and parcel of elite American military training. Soldiers are screened for intellectual and physical ability, achievement and mental health. Binding begins in basic training, with initiation rites that isolate

trainees from society, introduce them to new rules and values and leave them little time for clear thinking after exhausting physical exercise and scant sleep. Harassment plays an important role, and soldiers are severely punished for disobedience, with demerits, verbal abuse, hours of calisthenics and loss of eating, sleeping and other privileges.

Military training gradually desensitizes soldiers to violence and    22
reduces the strain normally created by repugnant acts. Their revulsion is diminished by screaming chants and songs about violence and killing during marches and runs. The enemy is given derogatory names and portrayed as less than human; this makes it easier to kill them. Completing the toughest possible training and being rewarded by "making it" in an elite corps bring the soldiers confidence and pride, and those who accomplish this feel they can do anything. "Although I tried to avoid killing, I learned to have confidence in myself and was never afraid," said a former Green Beret who served in Vietnam. "It was part of the job. . . . Anyone who goes through that kind of training could do it."

The effectiveness of these techniques, as several researchers have    23
shown, is not limited to the army. History teacher Ronald Jones started what he called the Third Wave movement as a classroom experiment to show his high school students how people might have become Nazis in World War II. Jones began the Third Wave demonstration by requiring students to stand at attention in a unique new posture and follow strict new rules. He required students to stand beside their desks when asking or answering questions and to begin each statement by saying, "Mr. Jones." The students obeyed. He then required them to shout slogans, "Strength through discipline!" and "Strength through community!" Jones created a salute for class members that he called the Third Wave: the right hand raised to the shoulder with fingers curled. The salute had no meaning, but it served as a symbol of group belonging and a way of isolating members from outsiders.

The organization expanded quickly from 20 original members to    24
100. The teacher issued membership cards and assigned students to report members who didn't comply with the new rules. Dutifully, 20 students pointed accusing fingers at their classmates.

Then Jones announced that the Third Wave was a "nationwide    25
movement to find students willing to fight for political change," and he organized a rally, which drew a crowd of 200 students. At the rally, after getting students to salute and shout slogans on command, Jones explained the true reasons behind the Third Wave demonstration. Like the Nazis before them, Jones pointed out, "You bargained your freedom for the comfort of discipline."

The students, at an age when group belonging was very important    26
to them, made good candidates for training. Jones didn't teach his

students to commit atrocities, and the Third Wave lasted for only five days; in that time, however, Jones created an obedient group that resembled in many ways the Nazi youth groups of World War II (see "The Third Wave: Nazism in a High School," *Psychology Today*, July 1976).

Psychologists Craig Haney, W. Curtis Banks and Philip Zimbardo went even further in a remarkable simulation of prison life done at Stanford University. With no special training and in only six days' time, they changed typical university students into controlling, abusive guards and servile prisoners.                                27

The students who agreed to participate were chosen randomly to be guards or prisoners. The mock guards were given uniforms and nightsticks and told to act as guards. Prisoners were treated as dangerous criminals: Local police rounded them up, fingerprinted and booked them and brought them to a simulated cellblock in the basement of the university psychology department. Uniformed guards made them remove their clothing, deloused them, gave them prison uniforms and put them in cells.                                28

The two groups of students, originally found to be very similar in most respects, showed striking changes within one week. Prisoners became passive, dependent and helpless. In contrast, guards expressed feelings of power, status and group belonging. They were aggressive and abusive within the prison, insulting and bullying the prisoners. Some guards reported later that they had enjoyed their power, while others said they had not thought they were capable of behaving as they had. They were surprised and dismayed at what they had done: "It was degrading. . . . To me, those things are sick. But they [the prisoners] did everything I said. They abused each other because I requested them to. No one questioned my authority at all."[1]                                29

The guards' behavior was similar in two important ways to that of the Greek torturers. First, they dehumanized their victims. Second, like the torturers, the guards were abusive only when they were within the prison walls. They could act reasonably outside the prisons because the two prison influences of binding and reduced strain were absent.                                30

All these changes at Stanford occurred with no special training, but the techniques we have outlined were still present. Even without training, the student guards "knew" from television and movies that they were supposed to punish prisoners; they "knew" they were supposed to feel superior; and they "knew" they were supposed to blame their victims. Their own behavior and that of their peers gradually numbed                                31

---

[1] For the authors' discussion on the relationship between torture and hazing rituals at college fraternities, see the introduction to this chapter, page 317.

their sensitivity to what they were doing, and they were rewarded by the power they had over their prisoners.

There is no evidence that such short-term experiments produce 32 lasting effects: None were reported from either the Third Wave demonstration or the Stanford University simulation. The Stanford study, however, was cut short when depression, crying and psychosomatic illnesses began to appear among the students. And studies of Vietnam veterans have revealed that committing abhorrent acts, even under the extreme conditions of war, can lead to long-term problems. In one study of 130 Vietnam veterans who came to a therapist for help, almost 30 percent of them were concerned about violent acts they had committed while in the service. The veterans reported feelings of anxiety, guilt, depression and an inability to carry on intimate relationships. In a similar fashion, after the fall of the Greek dictatorship in 1974, former torturers began to report nightmares, irritability and episodes of depression.

"Torturing became a job," said former Greek torturer Petrou. "If the 33 officers ordered you to beat, you beat. If they ordered you to stop, you stopped. You never thought you could do otherwise." His comments bear a disturbing resemblance to the feelings expressed by a Stanford guard: "When I was doing it, I didn't feel regret. . . . I didn't feel guilt. Only afterwards, when I began to reflect . . . did it begin to dawn on me that this was a part of me I hadn't known before."

We do not believe that torture came naturally to any of these young 34 men. Haritos-Fatouros found no evidence of sadistic, abusive or authoritarian behavior in the Greek soldiers' histories prior to their training. This, together with our study of Marine training and the Stanford and Third Wave studies, leads to the conclusion that torturers have normal personalities. Any of us, in a similar situation, might be capable of the same cruelty. One probably cannot train a deranged sadist to be an effective torturer or killer. He must be in complete control of himself while on the job.

## Review Questions

1. What was Molly Harrower's Rorschach-test experiment? What conclusions did she reach?
2. What explanation did Milgram propose as the reason people obey or disobey authority? How do the authors modify this explanation?
3. What attributes did the Greek military look for in drafting potential torturers?
4. What was the Third Wave? What did its creator intend to demonstrate?
5. What did the Stanford "prison" experiment demonstrate?

## Discussion and Writing Suggestions

1. See page 317 in the introductory essay to this chapter. Reread the indented quotation in that essay, describing the process by which one can be taught to torture. In this piece, Janice T. Gibson and Mika Haritos-Fatouros draw a parallel between the drafting and indoctrination of torturers and the "rushing" and hazing of college students who wish to join fraternities. Based on your understanding of college fraternities and their initiation rites, comment on the parallel that Gibson and Haritos-Fatouros have observed.

2. What is your response to the observation that all the steps in the "training model [that the authors developed to explain the 'education' of torturers] were part and parcel of elite American military training"?

3. Gibson and Haritos-Fatouros conclude that "torturers have normal personalities. Any of us, in a similar situation, might be capable of the same cruelty." Your response?

4. How do you account for the behavior of students in the Stanford experiment, who were so quick to learn their roles as guards and prisoners?

5. What parallel is there between techniques used by the Greek military and techniques used by our own military academies such as West Point, the Air Force Academy, and the Naval Academy? Can these techniques be used for good purposes?

# Disobedience as a Psychological and Moral Problem

## ERICH FROMM

*Erich Fromm (1900–1980) was one of this century's distinguished writers and thinkers. Psychoanalyst and philosopher, historian and sociologist, he ranged widely in his interests and defied easy characterization. Fromm studied the works of Freud and Marx closely, and published on them both, but he was not aligned strictly with either. In much of his voluminous writing, he struggled to articulate a view that could help bridge ideological and personal conflicts and bring dignity to those who struggled with isolation in the industrial world. Author of more than thirty books and contributor to numerous edited collections and journals, Fromm is best known for* Escape from Freedom *(1941),* The Art of Loving *(1956), and* To Have or To Be? *(1976).*

*In the essay that follows, first published in 1963, Fromm discusses the seductive comforts of obedience; and he makes distinctions among varieties of obedience, some of which he believes are destructive, and others, life affirming. His thoughts on nuclear annihilation may seem dated in these days of post—cold war cooperation, but it is worth remembering that Fromm wrote his essay just after the Cuban missile crisis, when fears of a third world war ran high. (We might note that despite the welcomed reductions of nuclear stockpiles, the United States and Russia still possess, and retain battle plans for, thousands of warheads.) On the major points of his essay, concerning the psychological and moral problems of obedience, Fromm remains as pertinent today as when he wrote thirty years ago.*

For centuries kings, priests, feudal lords, industrial bosses and parents have insisted that *obedience is a virtue* and that *disobedience is a vice.* In order to introduce another point of view, let us set against this position the following statement: *human history began with an act of disobedience, and it is not unlikely that it will be terminated by an act of obedience.* 1

Human history was ushered in by an act of disobedience according to the Hebrew and Greek myths. Adam and Eve, living in the Garden of Eden, were part of nature; they were in harmony with it, yet did not transcend it. They were in nature as the fetus is in the womb of the mother. They were human, and at the same time not yet human. All this changed when they disobeyed an order. By breaking the ties with earth and mother, by cutting the umbilical cord, man emerged from a pre-human harmony and was able to take the first step into independence and freedom. The act of disobedience set Adam and Eve free and opened their eyes. They recognized each other as strangers and the world outside them as strange and even hostile. Their act of disobedience broke the primary bond with nature and made them individuals. "Original sin," far from corrupting man, set him free; it was the beginning of history. Man had to leave the Garden of Eden in order to learn to rely on his own powers and to become fully human. 2

The prophets, in their messianic concept, confirmed the idea that man had been right in disobeying; that he had not been corrupted by his "sin," but freed from the fetters of pre-human harmony. For the prophets, *history* is the place where man becomes human; during its unfolding he develops his powers of reason and of love until he creates a new harmony between himself, his fellow man and nature. This new harmony is described as "the end of days," that period of history in which there is peace between man and man, and between man and nature. It is a "new" paradise created by man himself, and one which he alone could create because he was forced to leave the "old" paradise as a result of his disobedience. 3

Just as the Hebrew myth of Adam and Eve, so the Greek myth of 4

Prometheus sees all of human civilization based on an act of disobedience. Prometheus, in stealing the fire from the gods, lays the foundation for the evolution of man. There would be no human history were it not for Prometheus' "crime." He, like Adam and Eve, is punished for his disobedience. But he does not repent and ask for forgiveness. On the contrary, he proudly says: "I would rather be chained to this rock than be the obedient servant of the gods."

Man has continued to evolve by acts of disobedience. Not only was   5
his spiritual development possible only because there were men who dared to say no to the powers that be in the name of their conscience or their faith, but also his intellectual development was dependent on the capacity for being disobedient—disobedient to authorities who tried to muzzle new thoughts and to the authority of long-established opinions which declared a change to be nonsense.

If the capacity for disobedience constituted the beginning of human   6
history, obedience might very well, as I have said, cause the end of human history. I am not speaking symbolically or poetically. There is the possibility, or even the probability, that the human race will destroy civilization and even all life upon earth within the next five to ten years. There is no rationality or sense in it. But the fact is that, while we are living technically in the Atomic Age, the majority of men—including most of those who are in power—still live emotionally in the Stone Age; that while our mathematics, astronomy, and the natural sciences are of the twentieth century, most of our ideas about politics, the state, and society lag far behind the age of science. If mankind commits suicide it will be because people will obey those who command them to push the deadly buttons; because they will obey the archaic passions of fear, hate, and greed; because they will obey obsolete clichés of State sovereignty and national honor. The Soviet leaders talk much about revolutions, and we in the "free world" talk much about freedom. Yet they and we discourage disobedience—in the Soviet Union explicitly and by force, in the free world implicitly and by the more subtle methods of persuasion.

But I do not mean to say that all disobedience is a virtue and all   7
obedience a vice. Such a view would ignore the dialectical relationship between obedience and disobedience. Whenever the principles which are obeyed and those which are disobeyed are irreconcilable, an act of obedience to one principle is necessarily an act of disobedience to its counterpart, and vice versa. Antigone is the classic example of this dichotomy. By obeying the inhuman laws of the State, Antigone necessarily would disobey the laws of humanity. By obeying the latter, she must disobey the former. All martyrs of religious faiths, of freedom and of science have had to disobey those who wanted to muzzle them in order to obey their own consciences, the laws of humanity and of

reason. If a man can only obey and not disobey, he is a slave; if he can only disobey and not obey, he is a rebel (not a revolutionary); he acts out of anger, disappointment, resentment, yet not in the name of a conviction or a principle.

However, in order to prevent a confusion of terms an important  8
qualification must be made. Obedience to a person, institution or power (heteronomous obedience) is submission; it implies the abdication of my autonomy and the acceptance of a foreign will or judgment in place of my own. Obedience to my own reason or conviction (autonomous obedience) is not an act of submission but one of affirmation. My conviction and my judgment, if authentically mine, are part of me. If I follow them rather than the judgment of others, I am being myself; hence the word *obey* can be applied only in a metaphorical sense and with a meaning which is fundamentally different from the one in the case of "heteronomous obedience."

But this distinction still needs two further qualifications, one with  9
regard to the concept of conscience and the other with regard to the concept of authority.

The word *conscience* is used to express two phenomena which are  10
quite distinct from each other. One is the "authoritarian conscience" which is the internalized voice of an authority whom we are eager to please and afraid of displeasing. This authoritarian conscience is what most people experience when they obey their conscience. It is also the conscience which Freud speaks of, and which he called "Super-Ego." This Super-Ego represents the internalized commands and prohibitions of father, accepted by the son out of fear. Different from the authoritarian conscience is the "humanistic conscience"; this is the voice present in every human being and independent from external sanctions and rewards. Humanistic conscience is based on the fact that as human beings we have an intuitive knowledge of what is human and inhuman, what is conducive of life and what is destructive of life. This conscience serves our functioning as human beings. It is the voice which calls us back to ourselves, to our humanity.

Authoritarian conscience (Super-Ego) is still obedience to a power  11
outside of myself, even though this power has been internalized. Consciously I believe that I am following *my* conscience; in effect, however, I have swallowed the principles of *power*; just because of the illusion that humanistic conscience and Super-Ego are identical, internalized authority is so much more effective than the authority which is clearly experienced as not being part of me. Obedience to the "authoritarian conscience," like all obedience to outside thoughts and power, tends to debilitate "humanistic conscience," the ability to be and to judge oneself.

The statement, on the other hand, that obedience to another person  12
is *ipso facto* submission needs also to be qualified by distinguishing

"irrational" from "rational" authority. An example of rational authority is to be found in the relationship between student and teacher; one of irrational authority in the relationship between slave and master. Both relationships are based on the fact that the authority of the person in command is accepted. Dynamically, however, they are of a different nature. The interests of the teacher and the student, in the ideal case, lie in the same direction. The teacher is satisfied if he succeeds in furthering the student; if he has failed to do so, the failure is his and the student's. The slave owner, on the other hand, wants to exploit the slave as much as possible. The more he gets out of him the more satisfied he is. At the same time, the slave tries to defend as best he can his claims for a minimum of happiness. The interests of slave and master are antagonistic, because what is advantageous to the one is detrimental to the other. The superiority of the one over the other has a different function in each case; in the first it is the condition for the furtherance of the person subjected to the authority, and in the second it is the condition for his exploitation. Another distinction runs parallel to this: rational authority is rational because the authority, whether it is held by a teacher or a captain of a ship giving orders in an emergency, acts in the name of reason which, being universal, I can accept without submitting. Irrational authority has to use force or suggestion, because no one would let himself be exploited if he were free to prevent it.

Why is man so prone to obey and why is it so difficult for him to disobey? As long as I am obedient to the power of the State, the Church, or public opinion, I feel safe and protected. In fact it makes little difference what power it is that I am obedient to. It is always an institution, or men, who use force in one form or another and who fraudulently claim omniscience and omnipotence. My obedience makes me part of the power I worship, and hence I feel strong. I can make no error, since it decides for me; I cannot be alone, because it watches over me; I cannot commit a sin, because it does not let me do so, and even if I do sin, the punishment is only the way of returning to the almighty power. 13

In order to disobey, one must have the courage to be alone, to err and to sin. But courage is not enough. The capacity for courage depends on a person's state of development. Only if a person has emerged from mother's lap and father's commands, only if he has emerged as a fully developed individual and thus has acquired the capacity to think and feel for himself, only then can he have the courage to say "no" to power, to disobey. 14

A person can become free through acts of disobedience by learning to say no to power. But not only is the capacity for disobedience the condition for freedom; freedom is also the condition for disobedience. If I am afraid of freedom, I cannot dare to say "no," I cannot have the 15 courage to be disobedient. Indeed, freedom and the capacity for disobedience are inseparable; hence any social, political, and religious system which proclaims freedom, yet stamps out disobedience, cannot speak the truth.

There is another reason why it is so difficult to dare to disobey, to say "no" to power. During most of human history obedience has been identified with virtue and disobedience with sin. The reason is simple: thus far throughout most of history a minority has ruled over the majority. This rule was made necessary by the fact that there was only enough of the good things of life for the few, and only the crumbs remained for the many. If the few wanted to enjoy the good things and, beyond that, to have the many serve them and work for them, one condition was necessary: the many had to learn obedience. To be sure, obedience can be established by sheer force. But this method has many disadvantages. It constitutes a constant threat that one day the many might have the means to overthrow the few by force; furthermore there are many kinds of work which cannot be done properly if nothing but fear is behind the obedience. Hence the obedience which is only rooted in the fear of force must be transformed into one rooted in man's heart. Man must want and even need to obey, instead of only fearing to disobey. If this is to be achieved, power must assume the qualities of the All Good, of the All Wise; it must become All Knowing. If this happens, power can proclaim that disobedience is sin and obedience virtue; and once this has been proclaimed, the many can accept obedience because it is good and detest disobedience because it is bad, rather than to detest themselves for being cowards. From Luther to the nineteenth century one was concerned with overt and explicit authorities. Luther, the pope, the princes, wanted to uphold it; the middle class, the workers, the philosophers, tried to uproot it. The fight against authority in the State as well as in the family was often the very basis for the development of an independent and daring person. The fight against authority was inseparable from the intellectual mood which characterized the philosophers of the enlightenment and the scientists. This "critical mood" was one of faith in reason, and at the same time of doubt in everything which is said or thought, inasmuch as it is based on tradition, superstition, custom, power. The principles *sapere aude* and *de omnibus est dubitandum*—"dare to be wise" and "of all one must doubt"—were characteristic of the attitude which permitted and furthered the capacity to say "no."

The case of Adolf Eichmann is symbolic of our situation and has a significance far beyond the one which his accusers in the courtroom in Jerusalem were concerned with. Eichmann is a symbol of the organization man, of the alienated bureaucrat for whom men, women and children have become numbers. He is a symbol of all of us. We can see ourselves in Eichmann. But the most frightening thing about him is that after the entire story was told in terms of his own admissions, he was able in perfect good faith to plead his innocence. It is clear that if he were once more in the same situation he would do it again. And so would we—and so do we.

The organization man has lost the capacity to disobey, he is not  18
even aware of the fact that he obeys. At this point in history the capacity to doubt, to criticize and to disobey may be all that stands between a future for mankind and the end of civilization.

## Review Questions

1. What does Fromm mean when he writes that disobedience is "the first step into independence and freedom"?
2. Fromm writes that history began with an act of disobedience and will likely end with an act of obedience. What does he mean?
3. What is the difference between "heteronomous obedience" and "autonomous obedience"?
4. How does Fromm distinguish between "authoritarian conscience" and "humanistic conscience"?
5. When is obedience to another person *not* submission?
6. What are the psychological comforts of obedience, and why would authorities rather have people obey out of love than out of fear?

## Discussion and Writing Suggestions

1. Fromm suggests that scientifically we live in the twentieth century but that politically and emotionally we live in the Stone Age. As you observe events in the world, both near and far, would you agree? Why?
2. Fromm writes: "If a man can only obey and not disobey, he is a slave; if he can only disobey and not obey, he is a rebel (not a revolutionary)." Explain Fromm's meaning here. Explain, as well, the implication that to be fully human one must have the freedom to both obey and disobey.
3. Fromm writes that "obedience makes me part of the power I worship, and hence I feel strong." Does this statement ring true for you? Discuss, in writing, an occasion in which you felt powerful because you obeyed a group norm.
4. In paragraph 16, Fromm equates obedience with cowardice. Can you identify a situation in which you were obedient but, now that you reflect on it, also were cowardly? That is, can you recall a time when you caved in to a group but now wish you hadn't? Explain.
5. Fromm says that we can see ourselves in Adolf Eichmann—that as an organization man he "has lost the capacity to disobey, he is not even aware of the fact that he obeys." To what extent do you recognize yourself in this portrait?

# Groupthink

## IRVING L. JANIS

*Irving Lester Janis (b. 1918) has led a distinguished career as a professor of psychology 1947–1985 and a professor emeritus since 1985 at Yale University. He is the author of numerous articles for scholarly journals and magazines, as well as the recipient of international prizes and fellowships, largely for his work in the psychology of decision making. His books include* Communication and Persuasion *(1953),* Psychological Stress *(1958),* Stress and Frustration *(1971),* Victims of Groupthink *(1972), and* Groupthink *(1983).*

The idea of "groupthink" occurred to me while reading Arthur M. Schlesinger's chapters on the Bay of Pigs in *A Thousand Days*. At first I was puzzled: How could bright men like John F. Kennedy and his advisers be taken in by such a stupid, patchwork plan as the one presented to them by the C.I.A. representatives? I began wondering if some psychological contagion of complacency might have interfered with their mental alertness.

I kept thinking about this notion until one day I found myself talking about it in a seminar I was conducting at Yale on the psychology of small groups. I suggested that the poor decision-making performance of those high officials might be akin to the lapses in judgment of ordinary citizens who become more concerned with retaining the approval of the fellow members of their work group than with coming up with good solutions to the tasks at hand.

When I re-read Schlesinger's account I was struck by many further observations that fit into exactly the pattern of concurrence-seeking that has impressed me in my research on other face-to-face groups when a "we" feeling of solidarity is running high. I concluded that a group process was subtly at work in Kennedy's team which prevented the members from debating the real issues posed by the C.I.A.'s plan and from carefully appraising its serious risks.

By now I was sufficiently fascinated by what I called the "groupthink" hypothesis to start looking into similar historic fiascoes. I selected for intensive analysis three that were made during the administrations of three other American presidents: Franklin D. Roosevelt (failure to be prepared for Pearl Harbor), Harry S Truman (the invasion of North Korea) and Lyndon B. Johnson (escalation of the Vietnam war). Each decision was a group product, issuing from a series of meetings held by a small and cohesive group of government officials and advisers. In each case I found the same kind of detrimental group process that was at work in the Bay of Pigs decision. In my earlier research with ordinary citizens I had been impressed by the effects—both unfavorable and favorable—of the social pressures that develop in cohesive groups: in infantry platoons, air crews, therapy groups, seminars and self-study or encounter groups. Members tend to evolve informal objectives to preserve friendly intra-group relations, and this becomes part of the hidden agenda at their meetings. When conducting research on groups of heavy smokers, for example, at a clinic established to help people stop smoking, I noticed a seemingly irrational tendency for the members to exert pressure on each other to increase their smoking as the time for the final meeting approached. This appeared to be a collusive effort to display mutual dependence and resistance to the termination of the sessions.

Sometimes, even long before the final separation, pressures toward uniformity subverted the fundamental purpose. At the second meeting of one group of smokers, consisting of 12 middle-class American men and women, two of the most dominant members took the position that heavy smoking was an almost incurable addiction. Most of the others soon agreed that nobody could be expected to cut down drastically. One man took issue with this consensus, arguing that he had stopped smoking since joining the group and that everyone else could do the same. His declaration was followed by an angry discussion. Most of the others ganged up against the man who was deviating from the consensus.

At the next meeting the deviant announced that he had made an important decision. "When I joined," he said, "I agreed to follow the two main rules required by the clinic—to make a conscientious effort to stop smoking, and to attend every meeting. But I have learned that you can only follow one of the rules, not both. I will continue to attend every meeting but I have gone back to smoking two packs a day and I won't make any effort to stop again until after the last meeting." Whereupon the other members applauded, welcoming him back to the fold.

No one mentioned that the whole point of the meetings was to help each person to cut down as rapidly as possible. As a psychological consultant to the group, I tried to call this to the members' attention and so did my collaborator, Dr. Michael Kahn. But the members ignored our comments and reiterated their consensus that heavy smoking was an addiction from which no one would be cured except by cutting down gradually over a long period of time.

This episode—an extreme form of groupthink—was only one manifestation of a general pattern that the group displayed. At every meeting the members were amiable, reasserted their warm feelings of solidarity and sought concurrence on every important topic, with no reappearance of the unpleasant bickering that would spoil the cozy atmosphere. This tendency could be maintained, however, only at the expense of ignoring realistic challenges—like those posed by the psychologists.

The term "groupthink" is of the same order as the words in the "newspeak" vocabulary that George Orwell uses in *1984*—a vocabulary with terms such as "doublethink" and "crimethink." By putting "groupthink" with those Orwellian words, I realize that it takes on an invidious connotation. This is intentional: groupthink refers to a deterioration of mental efficiency, reality testing and moral judgment that results from in-group pressures.    9

When I investigated the Bay of Pigs invasion and other fiascoes, I found that there were at least six major defects in decision-making which contributed to failures to solve problems adequately.    10

First, the group's discussions were limited to a few alternatives (often only two) without a survey of the full range of alternatives. Second, the members failed to re-examine their initial decision from the standpoint of non-obvious drawbacks that had not been originally considered. Third, they neglected courses of action initially evaluated as unsatisfactory; they almost never discussed whether they had overlooked any non-obvious gains.    11

Fourth, members made little or no attempt to obtain information from experts who could supply sound estimates of losses and gains to be expected from alternative courses. Fifth, selective bias was shown in the way the members reacted to information and judgments from experts, the media and outside critics; they were only interested in facts and opinions that supported their preferred policy. Finally, they spent little time deliberating how the policy might be hindered by bureaucratic inertia, sabotaged by political opponents or derailed by the accidents that happen to the best of well-laid plans. Consequently, they failed to work out contingency plans to cope with foreseeable setbacks that could endanger their success.    12

I was surprised by the extent to which the groups involved in these fiascoes adhered to group norms and pressures toward uniformity, even when their policy was working badly and had unintended consequences that disturbed the conscience of the members. Members consider loyalty to the group the highest form of morality. That loyalty requires each member to avoid raising controversial issues, questioning weak arguments or calling a halt to soft-headed thinking.    13

Paradoxically, soft-headed groups are likely to be extremely hardhearted toward out-groups and enemies. In dealing with a rival nation, policy-makers constituting an amiable group find it relatively easy to    14 authorize dehumanizing solutions such as large-scale bombings. An affable group of government officials is unlikely to pursue the difficult issues that arise when alternatives to a harsh military solution come up for discussion. Nor are they inclined to raise ethical issues that imply that this "fine group of ours, with its humanitarianism and its high-minded principles, could adopt a course that is inhumane and immoral."

15   The greater the threat to the self-esteem of the members of a cohesive group, the greater will be their inclination to resort to concurrence-seeking at the expense of critical thinking. Symptoms of groupthink will therefore be found most often when a decision poses a moral dilemma, especially if the most advantageous course requires the policymakers to violate their own standards of humanitarian behavior. Each member is likely to become more dependent than ever on the in-group for maintaining his self-image as a decent human being and will therefore be more strongly motivated to maintain group unity by striving for concurrence.

16   Although it is risky to make huge inferential leaps from theory to practice, we should not be inhibited from drawing tentative inferences from these fiascoes. Perhaps the worst mistakes can be prevented if we take steps to avoid the circumstances in which groupthink is most likely to flourish. But all the prescriptive hypotheses that follow must be validated by systematic research before they can be applied with any confidence.

17   The leader of a policy-forming group should, for example, assign the role of critical evaluator to each member, encouraging the group to give high priority to airing objections and doubts. He should also be impartial at the outset, instead of stating his own preferences and expectations. He should limit his briefings to unbiased statements about the scope of the problem and the limitations of available resources.

18   The organization should routinely establish several independent planning and evaluation groups to work on the same policy question, each carrying out its deliberations under a different leader.

19   One or more qualified colleagues within the organization who are not core members of the policy-making group should be invited to each meeting and encouraged to challenge the views of the core members.

20   At every meeting, at least one member should be assigned the role of devil's advocate, to function like a good lawyer in challenging the testimony of those who advocate the majority position.

21   Whenever the policy issue involves relations with a rival nation, a sizable block of time should be spent surveying all warning signals from the rivals and constructing alternative scenarios.

22   After reaching a preliminary consensus the policy-making group

should hold a "second chance" meeting at which all the members are expected to express their residual doubts and to rethink the entire issue. They might take as their model a statement made by Alfred P. Sloan, a former chairman of General Motors, at a meeting of policymakers:

"Gentlemen, I take it we are all in complete agreement on the   23
decision here. Then I propose we postpone further discussion until our next meeting to give ourselves time to develop disagreement and perhaps gain some understanding of what the decision is all about."

It might not be a bad idea for the second-chance meeting to take   24
place in a relaxed atmosphere far from the executive suite, perhaps over drinks. According to a report by Herodotus dating from about 450 B.C., whenever the ancient Persians made a decision following sober deliberations, they would always reconsider the matter under the influence of wine. Tacitus claimed that during Roman times the Germans also had a custom of arriving at each decision twice—once sober, once drunk.

Some institutionalized form of allowing second thoughts to be   25
freely expressed might be remarkably effective for breaking down a false sense of unanimity and related illusions, without endangering anyone's reputation or liver.

## Review Questions

1. Define groupthink.
2. Why are dissenting opinions crucial to the health of the decision-making process?
3. What Orwellian connotations are associated with the term "groupthink"?
4. Summarize the six major defects in group decision making that characterize groupthink.
5. According to Janis, what is the relationship between concurrence-seeking behavior and self-esteem?

## Discussion and Writing Suggestions

1. For various reasons, groups tend toward uniformity. Discuss how this tendency can be both a strength and a weakness.
2. Why would one's reliance on a group consensus increase when a decision made by the group violates conventional morality? (See paragraph 15.) Describe an instance in which you observed such reliance taking place.
3. Reread paragraph 23, the statement attributed to a former chairman of General Motors. In what ways is the statement paradoxical? At what point in a group's deliberations should "agreement" be considered a legitimate end to discussion?

**4.** Describe an experience in which you participated that demonstrates the dynamics of groupthink. Organize your description around the six points that Janis claims characterize the phenomenon. (See paragraphs 10–12.)

# The Lottery

## SHIRLEY JACKSON

On the morning of June 28, 1948, I walked down to the post office in our little Vermont town to pick up the mail. I was quite casual about it, as I recall—I opened the box, took out a couple of bills and a letter or two, talked to the postmaster for a few minutes, and left, never supposing that it was the last time for months that I was to pick up the mail without an active feeling of panic. By the next week I had had to change my mailbox to the largest one in the post office, and casual conversation with the postmaster was out of the question, because he wasn't speaking to me. June 28, 1948, was the day *The New Yorker* came out with a story of mine in it. It was not my first published story, nor my last, but I have been assured over and over that if it had been the only story I ever wrote or published, there would be people who would not forget my name.[1]

*So begins Shirley Jackson's "biography" of her short story "The Lottery." The* New Yorker *published the story the summer of 1948 and some months later, having been besieged with letters, acknowledged that the piece had generated "more mail than any . . . fiction they had ever published"—the great majority of it negative. In 1960, Jackson wrote that "millions of people, and my mother, had taken a pronounced dislike to me" for having written the story—which, over the years, proved to be Jackson's most widely anthologized one. If you've read "The Lottery," you will have some idea of why it was so controversial. If you haven't, we don't want to spoil the effect by discussing what happens.*

*Shirley Jackson, short-story writer and novelist, was born in San Francisco in 1919 and was raised in California and New York. She began her college education at the University of Rochester and completed it at Syracuse University. She married Stanley Edgar Hyman (writer and teacher) and with him had four children. In her brief career, Jackson wrote six novels and two works of nonfiction. She won the Edgar Allen Poe Award (1961) as well as a Syracuse University Arents Pioneer Medal for Outstanding Achievement (1965).*

The morning of June 27th was clear and sunny, with the fresh warmth of a full-summer day; the flowers were blossoming profusely and the grass was richly green. The people of the village began to gather in the square, between the post office and the bank, around ten o'clock; in some towns there were so many people that the lottery took two days and had to be started on June 26th, but in this village, where there were only about three hundred people, the whole lottery took less than two hours, so it could begin at ten o'clock in the morning and still be through in time to allow the villagers to get home for noon dinner.

The children assembled first, of course. School was recently over for the summer, and the feeling of liberty sat uneasily on most of them; they tended to gather together quietly for a while before they broke into boisterous play, and their talk was still of the classroom and the teacher, of books and reprimands. Bobby Martin had already stuffed his pockets full of stones, and the other boys soon followed his example, selecting the smoothest and roundest stones; Bobby and Harry Jones and Dickie Delacroix—the villagers pronounced this name "Dellacroy"—eventually made a great pile of stones in one corner of the square and guarded it against the raids of the other boys. The girls stood aside, talking among themselves, looking over their shoulders at the boys, and the very small children rolled in the dust or clung to the hands of their older brothers or sisters.

Soon the men began to gather, surveying their own children, speaking of planting and rain, tractors and taxes. They stood together, away from the pile of stones in the corner, and their jokes were quiet and they smiled rather than laughed. The women, wearing faded house dresses and sweaters, came shortly after their menfolk. They greeted one another and exchanged bits of gossip as they went to join their husbands. Soon the women, standing by their husbands, began to call to their children, and the children came reluctantly, having to be called four or five times. Bobby Martin ducked under his mother's grasping hand and ran, laughing, back to the pile of stones. His father spoke up sharply, and Bobby came quickly and took his place between his father and his oldest brother.

The lottery was conducted—as were the square dances, the teenage club, the Halloween program—by Mr. Summers, who had time and energy to devote to civic activities. He was a round-faced, jovial man and he ran the coal business, and people were sorry for him, because he had no children and his wife was a scold. When he arrived in the square, carrying the black wooden box, there was a murmur of conversation among the villagers, and he waved and called, "Little late today, folks." The postmaster, Mr. Graves, followed him, carrying a three-legged stool, and the stool was put in the center of the square and Mr. Summers set the black box down on it. The villagers kept their distance, leaving a space between themselves and the stool, and when Mr. Summers said, "Some of you fellows want to give me a hand?" there was a hesitation before two men, Mr. Martin and his oldest son, Baxter, came forward to hold the box steady on the stool while Mr. Summers stirred up the papers inside it.

The original paraphernalia for the lottery had been lost long ago, 5 and the black box now resting on the stool had been put into use even before Old Man Warner, the oldest man in town, was born. Mr. Summers spoke frequently to the villagers about making a new box, but no one liked to upset even as much tradition as was represented by the black box. There was a story that the present box had been made with some pieces of the box that had preceded it, the one that had been constructed when the first people settled down to make a village here. Every year, after the lottery, Mr. Summers began talking again about a new box, but every year the subject was allowed to fade off without anything's being done. The black box grew shabbier each year; by now it was no longer completely black but splintered badly along one side to show the original wood color, and in some places faded or stained.

Mr. Martin and his oldest son, Baxter, held the black box securely 6 on the stool until Mr. Summers had stirred the papers thoroughly with his hand. Because so much of the ritual had been forgotten or discarded, Mr. Summers had been successful in having slips of paper substituted for the chips of wood that had been used for generations. Chips of wood, Mr. Summers had argued, had been all very well when the village was tiny, but now that the population was more than three hundred and likely to keep on growing, it was necessary to use something that would fit more easily into the black box. The night before the lottery, Mr. Summers and Mr. Graves made up the slips of paper and put them in the box, and it was then taken to the safe of Mr. Summers' coal company and locked up until Mr. Summers was ready to take it to the square next morning. The rest of the year, the box was put away, sometimes one place, sometimes another; it had spent one year in Mr. Graves's barn and another year underfoot in the post office, and sometimes it was set on a shelf in the Martin grocery and left there.

There was a great deal of fussing to be done before Mr. Summers 7 declared the lottery open. There were the lists to make up—of heads of families, heads of households in each family, members of each household in each family. There was the proper swearing-in of Mr. Summers by the postmaster, as the official of the lottery; at one time, some people remembered, there had been a recital of some sort, performed by the official of the lottery, a perfunctory, tuneless chant that had been rattled off duly each year; some people believed that the official of the lottery used to stand just so when he said or sang it, others believed that he was supposed to walk among the people, but years and years ago this part of the ritual had been allowed to lapse. There had been, also, a ritual salute, which the official of the lottery had had to use in addressing each person who came up to draw from the box, but this also had changed with time, until now it was felt necessary only for the official to speak to each person approaching. Mr. Summers was very good at all this; in his clean white shirt and blue jeans, with one hand resting carelessly on the black box, he seemed very proper and important as he talked interminably to Mr. Graves and the Martins.

Just as Mr. Summers finally left off talking and turned to the assem- **8** bled villagers, Mrs. Hutchinson came hurriedly along the path to the square, her sweater thrown over her shoulders, and slid into place in the back of the crowd. "Clean forgot what day it was," she said to Mrs. Delacroix, who stood next to her, and they both laughed softly. "Thought my old man was out back stacking wood," Mrs. Hutchinson went on, "and then I looked out the window and the kids was gone, and then I remembered it was the twenty-seventh and came a-running." She dried her hands on her apron, and Mrs. Delacroix said, "You're in time, though. They're still talking away up there."

Mrs. Hutchinson craned her neck to see through the crowd and **9** found her husband and children standing near the front. She tapped Mrs. Delacroix on the arm as a farewell and began to make her way through the crowd. The people separated good-humoredly to let her through; two or three people said, in voices just loud enough to be heard across the crowd, "Here comes your Missus, Hutchinson," and "Bill, she made it after all." Mrs. Hutchinson reached her husband, and Mr. Summers, who had been waiting, said cheerfully, "Thought we were going to have to get on without you, Tessie." Mrs. Hutchinson said, grinning, "Wouldn't have me leave m'dishes in the sink, now, would you, Joe?," and soft laughter ran through the crowd as the people stirred back into position after Mrs. Hutchinson's arrival.

"Well, now," Mr. Summers said soberly, "guess we better get **10** started, get this over with, so's we can go back to work. Anybody ain't here?"

"Dunbar," several people said. "Dunbar, Dunbar." **11**

Mr. Summers consulted his list. "Clyde Dunbar," he said. "That's **12** right. He's broke his leg, hasn't he? Who's drawing for him?"

"Me, I guess," a woman said, and Mr. Summers turned to look at **13** her. "Wife draws for her husband," Mr. Summers said. "Don't you have a grown boy to do it for you, Janey?" Although Mr. Summers and everyone else in the village knew the answer perfectly well, it was the business of the official of the lottery to ask such questions formally. Mr. Summers waited with an expression of polite interest while Mrs. Dunbar answered.

"Horace's not but sixteen yet," Mrs. Dunbar said regretfully. "Guess I gotta fill in for the old man this year." 14

"Right," Mr. Summers said. He made a note on the list he was holding. Then he asked, "Watson boy drawing this year?" 15

A tall boy in the crowd raised his hand. "Here," he said. "I'm drawing for m'mother and me." He blinked his eyes nervously and ducked his head as several voices in the crowd said things like "Good fellow, Jack," and "Glad to see your mother's got a man to do it." 16

"Well," Mr. Summers said, "guess that's everyone. Old Man Warner make it?" 17

"Here," a voice said, and Mr. Summers nodded. 18

A sudden hush fell on the crowd as Mr. Summers cleared his throat and looked at the list. "All ready?" he called. "Now, I'll read the names—heads of families first—and the men come up and take a paper out of the box. Keep the paper folded in your hand without looking at it until everyone has had a turn. Everything clear?" 19

The people had done it so many times that they only half listened to the directions; most of them were quiet, wetting their lips, not looking around. Then Mr. Summers raised one hand high and said, "Adams." A man disengaged himself from the crowd and came forward. "Hi, Steve," Mr. Summers said, and Mr. Adams said, "Hi, Joe." They grinned at one another humorlessly and nervously. Then Mr. Adams reached into the black box and took out a folded paper. He held it firmly by one corner as he turned and went hastily back to his place in the crowd, where he stood a little apart from his family, not looking down at his hand. 20

"Allen," Mr. Summers said. "Anderson. . . . Bentham." 21

"Seems like there's no time at all between lotteries any more," Mrs. Delacroix said to Mrs. Graves in the back row. "Seems like we got through with the last one only last week." 22

"Time sure goes fast," Mrs. Graves said. 23

"Clark. . . . Delacroix." 24

"There goes my old man," Mrs. Delacroix said. She held her breath while her husband went forward. 25

"Dunbar," Mr. Summers said, and Mrs. Dunbar went steadily to the box while one of the women said, "Go on, Janey," and another said, "There she goes." 26

"We're next," Mrs. Graves said. She watched while Mr. Graves came around from the side of the box, greeted Mr. Summers gravely, and selected a slip of paper from the box. By now, all through the crowd 27 there were men holding the small folded papers in their large hands, turning them over and over nervously. Mrs. Dunbar and her two sons stood together, Mrs. Dunbar holding the slip of paper.

"Harburt. . . . Hutchinson." 28

"Get up there, Bill," Mrs. Hutchinson said, and the people near her 29 laughed.

"Jones." 30

"They do say," Mr. Adams said to Old Man Warner, who stood 31 next to him, "that over in the north village they're talking of giving up the lottery."

Old Man Warner snorted. "Pack of crazy fools," he said. "Listening 32 to the young folks, nothing's good enough for *them*. Next thing you know, they'll be wanting to go back to living in caves, nobody work any more, live *that* way for a while. Used to be a saying about 'Lottery in June, corn be heavy soon.' First thing you know, we'd all be eating stewed chickweed and acorns. There's *always* been a lottery," he added petulantly. "Bad enough to see young Joe Summers up there joking with everybody."

"Some places have already quit lotteries," Mrs. Adams said. 33

"Nothing but trouble in *that*," Old Man Warner said stoutly. "Pack 34 of young fools."

"Martin." And Bobby Martin watched his father go forward. "Over- 35 dyke. . . . Percy."

"I wish they'd hurry," Mrs. Dunbar said to her older son. "I wish 36 they'd hurry."

"They're almost through," her son said. 37

"You get ready to run tell Dad," Mrs. Dunbar said. 38

Mr. Summers called his own name and then stepped forward pre- 39 cisely and selected a slip from the box. Then he called, "Warner."

"Seventy-seventh year I been in the lottery," Old Man Warner said 40 as he went through the crowd. "Seventy-seventh time."

"Watson." The tall boy came awkwardly through the crowd. Some- 41 one said, "Don't be nervous, Jack," and Mr. Summers said, "Take your time, son."

"Zanini." 42

After that, there was a long pause, a breathless pause, until Mr. 43 Summers, holding his slip of paper in the air, said, "All right, fellows." For a minute, no one moved, and then all the slips of paper were opened. Suddenly, all the women began to speak at once, saying, "Who is it?," "Who's got it?," "Is it the Dunbars?," "Is it the Watsons?" Then the voices began to say, "It's Hutchinson. It's Bill," "Bill Hutchinson's got it."

"Go tell your father," Mrs. Dunbar said to her older son. 44

People began to look around to see the Hutchinsons. Bill Hutchinson was standing quiet, staring down at the paper in his hand. Suddenly, Tessie Hutchinson shouted to Mr. Summers, "You didn't give him time enough to take any paper he wanted. I saw you. It wasn't fair!"  **45**

"Be a good sport, Tessie," Mrs. Delacroix called, and Mrs. Graves said, "All of us took the same chance."  **46**

"Shut up, Tessie," Bill Hutchinson said.  **47**

"Well, everyone," Mr. Summers said, "that was done pretty fast, and now we've got to be hurrying a little more to get done in time." He consulted his next list. "Bill," he said, "you draw for the Hutchinson family. You got any other households in the Hutchinsons?"  **48**

"There's Don and Eva," Mrs. Hutchinson yelled. "Make *them* take their chance!"  **49**

"Daughters draw with their husbands' families, Tessie," Mr. Summers said gently. "You know that as well as anyone else."  **50**

"It wasn't *fair*," Tessie said.  **51**

"I guess not, Joe," Bill Hutchinson said regretfully. "My daughter draws with her husband's family, that's only fair. And I've got no other family except the kids."  **52**

"Then, as far as drawing for families is concerned, it's you," Mr. Summers said in explanation, "and as far as drawing for households is concerned, that's you, too. Right?"  **53**

"Right," Bill Hutchinson said.  **54**

"How many kids, Bill?" Mr. Summers asked formally.  **55**

"Three," Bill Hutchinson said. "There's Bill, Jr., and Nancy, and little Dave. And Tessie and me."  **56**

"All right, then," Mr. Summers said. "Harry, you got their tickets back?"  **57**

Mr. Graves nodded and held up the slips of paper. "Put them in the box, then," Mr. Summers directed. "Take Bill's and put it in."  **58**

"I think we ought to start over," Mrs. Hutchinson said, as quietly as she could. "I tell you it wasn't *fair*. You didn't give him time enough to choose. *Every*body saw that."  **59**

Mr. Graves had selected the five slips and put them in the box, and he dropped all the papers but those onto the ground, where the breeze caught them and lifted them off.  **60**

"Listen, everybody," Mrs. Hutchinson was saying to the people around her.  **61**

"Ready, Bill?" Mr. Summers asked, and Bill Hutchinson, with one quick glance around at his wife and children, nodded.  **62**

"Remember," Mr. Summers said, "take the slips and keep them folded until each person has taken one. Harry, you help little Dave." Mr. Graves took the hand of the little boy, who came willingly with him up to the box. "Take a paper out of the box, Davy," Mr. Summers said.  **63**

Davy put his hand into the box and laughed. "Take just *one* paper," Mr. Summers said. "Harry, you hold it for him." Mr. Graves took the child's hand and removed the folded paper from the tight fist and held it while little Dave stood next to him and looked up at him wonderingly.

"Nancy next," Mr. Summers said. Nancy was twelve, and her school 64 friends breathed heavily as she went forward, switching her skirt, and took a slip daintily from the box. "Bill, Jr.," Mr. Summers said, and Billy, his face red and his feet overlarge, nearly knocked the box over as he got a paper out. "Tessie," Mr. Summers said. She hesitated for a minute, looking around defiantly, and then set her lips and went up to the box. She snatched a paper out and held it behind her.

"Bill," Mr. Summers said, and Bill Hutchinson reached into the box 65 and felt around, bringing his hand out at last with the slip of paper in it.

The crowd was quiet. A girl whispered, "I hope it's not Nancy," and 66 the sound of the whisper reached the edges of the crowd.

"It's not the way it used to be," Old Man Warner said clearly. 67 "People ain't the way they used to be."

"All right," Mr. Summers said. "Open the papers. Harry, you open 68 little Dave's."

Mr. Graves opened the slip of paper and there was a general sigh 69 through the crowd as he held it up and everyone could see that it was blank. Nancy and Bill, Jr., opened theirs at the same time, and both beamed and laughed, turning around to the crowd and holding their slips of paper above their heads.

"Tessie," Mr. Summers said. There was a pause, and then Mr. 70 Summers looked at Bill Hutchinson, and Bill unfolded his paper and showed it. It was blank.

"It's Tessie," Mr. Summers said, and his voice was hushed. "Show 71 us her paper, Bill."

Bill Hutchinson went over to his wife and forced the slip of paper 72 out of her hand. It had a black spot on it, the black spot Mr. Summers had made the night before with the heavy pencil in the coal-company office. Bill Hutchinson held it up, and there was a stir in the crowd.

"All right, folks," Mr. Summers said. "Let's finish quickly." 73

Although the villagers had forgotten the ritual and lost the original 74 black box, they still remembered to use stones. The pile of stones the boys had made earlier was ready; there were stones on the ground with the blowing scraps of paper that had come out of the box. Mrs. Delacroix selected a stone so large she had to pick it up with both hands and turned to Mrs. Dunbar. "Come on," she said. "Hurry up."

Mrs. Dunbar had small stones in both hands, and she said, gasping 75 for breath, "I can't run at all. You'll have to go ahead and I'll catch up with you."

The children had stones already, and someone gave little Davy    76
Hutchinson a few pebbles.

Tessie Hutchinson was in the center of a cleared space by now, and    77
she held her hands out desperately as the villagers moved in on her. "It
isn't fair," she said. A stone hit her on the side of the head.

Old Man Warner was saying, "Come on, come on, everyone." Steve    78
Adams was in the front of the crowd of villagers, with Mrs. Graves
beside him.

"It isn't fair, it isn't right," Mrs. Hutchinson screamed, and then they    79
were upon her.


## Discussion and Writing Suggestions

1. Many readers believed that the events depicted in "The Lottery" actually
   happened. A sampling of the letters that Jackson received in response to the
   story:

   (Kansas) Will you please tell me the locale and the year of the custom?
   (Oregon) Where in heaven's name does there exist such barbarity as
   described in the story?
   (New York) Do such tribunal rituals still exist and if so where?
   (New York) To a reader who has only a fleeting knowledge of traditional rites in various parts of the country (I presume the plot was laid
   in the United States) I found the cruelty of the ceremony outrageous,
   if not unbelievable. It may be just a custom or ritual which I am not
   familiar with.
   (New York) Would you please explain whether such improbable rituals
   occur in our Middle Western states, and what their origin and purpose
   are?
   (Nevada) Although we recognize the story to be fiction is it possible
   that it is based on fact?

   What is your response to comments such as these that suggest surprise,
   certainly, but also acceptance of the violence committed in the story?
2. One reader of the "The Lottery," from Missouri, wrote to the New Yorker and
   accused it of "publishing a story that reached a new low in human viciousness." Do you feel that Jackson has reached this "new low"? Explain your
   answer.
3. Several more letter writers attempted to get at the meaning of the story:

   (Illinois) If it is simply a fictitious example of man's innate cruelty, it isn't
   a very good one. Man, stupid and cruel as he is, has always had sense
   enough to imagine or invent a charge against the objects of his persecution: the Christian martyrs, the New England witches, the Jews and

Negroes. But nobody had anything against Mrs. Hutchinson, and they only wanted to get through quickly so they could go home for lunch.

(California) I missed something here. Perhaps there was some facet of the victim's character which made her unpopular with the other villagers. I expected the people to evince a feeling of dread and terror, or else sadistic pleasure, but perhaps they were laconic, unemotional New Englanders.

(Indiana) When I first read the story in my issue, I felt that there was no moral significance present, that the story was just terrifying, and that was all. However, there has to be a reason why it is so alarming to so many people. I feel that the only solution, the only reason it bothered so many people is that it shows the power of society over the individual. We saw the ease with which society can crush any single one of us. At the same time, we saw that society need have no rational reason for crushing the one, or the few, or sometimes the many.

Take any one of these readings of the story and respond to it by writing a brief essay or, perhaps, a letter.

4. What does the story suggest to you about authority and obedience to authority? Who—or what—holds authority in the village? Why do people continue with the annual killing, despite the fact that "some places have already quit lotteries"?

---

## SYNTHESIS ACTIVITIES

1. Assume for the moment you agree with Doris Lessing: Children need to be taught how to disobey so they can recognize and avoid situations that give rise to harmful obedience. If you were the curriculum coordinator for your local school system, how would you teach children to disobey? What would be your curriculum? What homework would you assign? What class projects? What field trips? One complicated part of your job would be to train children who understand the difference between *responsible* disobedience and anarchy. What is the difference?

   Take up these questions in an essay that draws on both your experiences as a student and your understanding of the selections in this chapter. Points that you might want to consider in developing the essay: defining overly obedient children; appropriate classroom behavior for responsibly disobedient children (as opposed to inappropriate behavior); reading lists (would "The Lottery" be included?); homework assignments; field trips; class projects.

2. The creator of the Third Wave (in "Education of a Torturer") explained to students in a rally that like the Nazis they "bargained [their] freedom for the

comfort of discipline." Doris Lessing makes much the same point (in paragraph 7) when she refers to experiments in which people will say, in effect, that black is white in order to be accepted as a member of a group. What, in your view, are the "comforts" of discipline? Why is an obedient attitude more psychologically comforting than a disobedient one?

Draw from sources in the chapter as you consider this question. As you develop an answer, you might first want to investigate the reasons people are insecure. You could then discuss the psychological mechanisms involved in obeying figures of authority and finally explore the features of obedience that make for security. You might want to refer to the tight-knit village in "The Lottery." See also Fromm's essay, paragraphs 13–16.

3. A certain amount of obedience is a given in society, observe Stanley Milgram and others (see Herrnstein and Meyer). Social order, civilization itself, would not be possible unless individuals were willing to surrender a portion of their autonomy to the state. Allowing that we all are obedient (we must be), define the point at which obedience to a figure of authority becomes dangerous.

As you develop your definition, consider the ways you might use the work of authors in this chapter and their definitions of acceptable and unacceptable levels of obedience. Do you agree with the ways in which others have drawn the line between reasonable and dangerous obedience? What examples from current stories in the news or from your own experience can you draw on to test various definitions?

4. In paragraphs 6 and 7 of his review, Philip Meyer draws a distinction between situation ethics and code ethics, an important distinction that helps explain why one person will obey orders blindly, whereas another will obey only so long as the dictates of his or her conscience are not violated.

In an essay, distinguish between situation and code ethics, in your own words, and then apply that distinction as a way of explaining various examples of obedience and disobedience discussed in this chapter. Your essay will take the form of an "application of principles." A standard structure would have you define your principles and then test their explanatory power by applying them to various scenarios. Conclude by evaluating the strengths and limitations of your principles.

5. Describe a situation in which you were faced with a moral dilemma of whether or not to obey a figure of authority. After describing the situation and the action you took (or didn't take), discuss your behavior in light of any two readings in this chapter. You might consider a straightforward, four-part structure for your essay: (1) your description; (2) your discussion, in light of source A; (3) your discussion, in light of source B; and (4) your conclusion— an overall appraisal of your behavior.

6. At one point in his essay (paragraph 16), Erich Fromm equates obedience with cowardice. Earlier in the chapter, Doris Lessing (paragraph 7) observes that "among our most shameful memories is this, how often we said black was white because other people were saying it." Ronald Jones (paragraph 23 of Gibson and Haritos-Fatouros) tells his history students that they had

"bargained [their] freedom for the comfort of discipline." Using the work of these three authors as a point of departure, reconsider an act of obedience or disobedience in your own life. Describe pertinent circumstances for your reader. Based on what you have learned in this chapter, reassess your behavior. Would you behave similarly if given a second chance in the same situation?

7. Reread "The Lottery" and analyze the patterns of and reasons for obedience in the story. Base your analysis on three sources in this chapter: Erich Fromm's essay, especially paragraphs 13–16 on the psychological comforts of obedience; Doris Lessing's speech on the dangers of "not understanding the social laws that govern groups"; and Irving Janis's theory of groupthink.

---

## RESEARCH ACTIVITIES

1. When Milgram's results were first published in book form in 1974, they generated heated controversy. The three reactions reprinted here (by Herrnstein, Baumrind, and Meyer) represent only a very small portion of that controversy. Research other reactions to the Milgram experiments and discuss your findings. Begin with the reviews listed and excerpted in the *Book Review Digest*; also use the *Social Science Index,* the *Readers' Guide to Periodical Literature,* and newspaper indexes to locate articles, editorials, and letters to the editor on the experiments. (Note that editorials and letters are not always indexed. Letters appear within two to four weeks of the weekly magazine articles to which they refer, and within one to two weeks of newspaper articles.) What were the chief types of reactions? To what extent were the reactions favorable?

2. Milgram begins his article "Obedience to Authority" with a reference to Nazi Germany. The purpose of his experiment, in fact, was to help throw light on how the Nazi atrocities could have happened. Research the Nuremberg war crimes tribunals following World War II. Drawing specifically on the statements of those who testified at Nuremberg, as well as those who have written about it, show how Milgram's experiments do help explain the Holocaust and other Nazi crimes. In addition to relevant articles, see Telford Taylor's *Nuremberg and Vietnam: An American Tragedy* (1970); Hannah Arendt's *Eichmann in Jerusalem: A Report on the Banality of Evil* (1963); Richard A. Falk, Gabriel Kolko, and Robert J. Lifton (eds), *Crimes of War* (1971).

3. Obtain a copy of the transcript of the trial of Adolf Eichmann—the Nazi official who carried out Hitler's "final solution" for the extermination of the Jews. Read also Hannah Arendt's *Eichmann in Jerusalem: A Report on the Banality of Evil,* along with the reviews of this book. Write a critique both of Arendt's book and of the reviews it received.

4. The My Lai massacre in Vietnam in 1969 was a particularly egregious case

of overobedience to military authority in wartime. Show the connections between this event and Milgram's experiments. Note that Milgram himself treated the My Lai massacre in the epilogue to his *Obedience to Authority: An Experimental View* (1974).

5. Investigate the court-martial of Lt. William Calley, convicted for his role in the My Lai massacre. Discuss the question of whether or not President Nixon was justified in commuting his sentence. Examine in detail the dilemmas the jury must have faced when presented with Calley's defense that he was only following orders.

6. Research the Watergate break-in of 1972 and the subsequent coverup by Richard Nixon and members of his administration, as an example of overobedience to authority. Focus on one particular aspect of Watergate (e.g., the role of the counsel to the president, John Dean, or why the crisis was allowed to proceed to the point where it actually toppled a presidency). In addition to relevant articles, see Robert Woodward and Carl Bernstein, *All the President's Men* (1974); Leon Jaworski, *The Right and the Power: The Prosecution of Watergate* (1976); *RN: The Memoirs of Richard Nixon* (1978); John Dean, *Blind Ambition* (1976); John Sirica, *To Set the Record Straight: The Break-in, the Tapes, the Conspirators, the Pardon* (1979); Sam Ervin, *The Whole Truth: The Watergate Conspiracy* (1980); John Ehrlichman, *Witness to Power: The Nixon Years* (1982).

7. Business disasters frequently result from groupthink. In his article "Following the Leader" (*Science '85*, October 1985), Daniel Goleman, a psychologist and editor, discusses a notorious check-kiting scheme that eventually cost the brokerage firm of E. F. Hutton millions of dollars. Many people could have "blown the whistle" on this scam, but no one did. Research another financial scandal (consider, e.g., the savings and loan debacles of the late 1980s or the downfall of Wall Street financial wizards such as Michael Milken, and detail the groupthink elements of the case. Or you may wish to consider in this light such marketing disasters as the Edsel automobile and new formula Coke.

8. At the outset of his article, Stanley Milgram refers to imaginative works revolving around the issue of obedience to authority: the story of Abraham and Isaac, three of Plato's dialogues, "Apology," "Crito," and "Phaedo," and the story of Antigone (dramatized by both the fifth-century B.C. Athenian Sophocles and the twentieth-century Frenchman Jean Anouilh). In this chapter, we have reprinted Shirley Jackson's "The Lottery," which also can be read as a story about obedience to authority. And many other fictional works deal with obedience to authority—for example, Herman Wouk's novel *The Caine Mutiny* (and his subsequent play *The Caine Mutiny Court Martial*). Check with your instructor, with a librarian, and with such sources as the *Short Story Index* to locate other imaginative works on this theme. Write a paper discussing the various ways in which the subject has been treated in fiction and drama. To ensure coherence, draw comparisons and contrasts among works showing the connections and the variations on the theme of obedience to authority.

# 9

## AMERICA'S CRISIS OF CONFIDENCE

> I want to speak to you tonight about a subject even
> more serious than energy or inflation. I want to talk to
> you right now about a fundamental threat to American
> democracy. . . . The threat is nearly invisible in ordinary
> ways. It is a crisis of confidence. It is a crisis that strikes
> at the very heart and soul and spirit of our national
> will.
> —Jimmy Carter

The year was 1979, and America was caught in the grip of an energy crisis caused by a steep and sudden increase in the cost of petroleum shipped by member nations of the Organization of Petroleum Exporting Countries (OPEC). President Carter retreated to Camp David for ten days, summoning advisers to assist him in creating a unified, strategic response to an emergency that had deepened inflation and unemployment and had angry Americans waiting for hours in gasoline lines. The sense of anticipation was high when the president addressed the nation on the evening of July 15 with a speech entitled "Energy and National Goals." What America heard that night, later dubbed the "malaise" speech (although Carter himself never used the word), was part lecture, part sermon, part lament, part exhortation. We suffer from "a crisis of confidence," he said. "We can see this crisis in the growing doubt about the meaning of our own lives and in the loss of a unity of purpose for our nation." Americans listened—and then rejected Carter's dour assessment in favor of the more optimistic view that America's spirit was far from exhausted. Whatever malaise existed, they believed, was limited to the Carter administration.

Fourteen years and nearly $4 trillion in debt later, the word *malaise* has crept back into the national vocabulary. We have grown accustomed to the recent wringing of hands over America's lost preeminence in the world. *We are losing our place,* goes the refrain. *We owe too much debt, individually and as a nation. Americans consume; we don't produce; we don't save; we don't reinvest sufficiently in rebuilding our industries or highways. The Japanese own Rockefeller Center. They build better cars than we do and better electronics. Our cities are decaying; crack cocaine use is on the rise; one-fifth of our children live in poverty; our system of public education is among the worst of the industrialized world. What has happened to our standards of excellence, to the belief that "made in America" meant "well-built"?*

Running like a fault line below these anxieties lies the uneasy recognition that America's spirit indeed is suffering. Without the Soviet Union to serve as an international enemy, we have turned inward and met another enemy. Our nation was once "proud of hard work, strong families, close-knit communities and our faith in God," said President Carter, and now "too many of us . . . tend to worship self-indulgence and consumption." Was Jimmy Carter right—albeit before his fellow citizens could listen? If he was, and we can acknowledge some truth to his moralizing, what is it about life in the 1990s that underlies this worrisome recognition? Fifty years ago, no one spoke of malaise. To the contrary, after World War II the United States was the preeminent world power, its wealth and influence unchallenged. In 1945, the United States, to paraphrase Shakespeare, bestrode the world like a colossus. While other industrialized nations lay in ruins, the American homeland was virtually untouched by the war. During the following two decades, America's position in the world was like Rome's in the time of Christ or like Britain's in the nineteenth century. But that preeminence would eventually be challenged, based as it was on a skewed and temporary set of circumstances. Beginning in the 1960s, America reentered the "roller coaster" of history, according to novelist Walker Percy. The country's luck turned, and suddenly it was no longer immune to the "ordinary catastrophes" that befell other nations. The Vietnam War, assassinations, years of civil unrest, and the trauma of Watergate all damaged our national psyche. But these traumas, debilitating as they were, did little to shake the bedrock belief that ambitious individuals still could succeed through hard work and talent. If the country was off course, at least disciplined, visionary *individuals* could flourish. But these days, even that confidence is shaken.

And yet no one can deny the advantages of living in the United States. Certainly, there is much to celebrate in our nation's achievements and in our national character. Immigrants continue flocking to our shores for a chance to live out an American Dream that they insist (and frequently prove) is alive and well. Much of the world continues to find inspiration in the durable American model of government, in its reverence for personal and political freedoms—the same freedoms that impelled hundreds of thousands to bring down the Soviet Union and totalitarian regimes throughout Eastern Europe. America *won* the cold war. Other nations (such as Kuwait) look to us for protection, counsel— and support. The American economy, for all its problems, remains a behemoth: powerful, permitting great wealth and a standard of living that is among the highest in the world.

If all this is so, then—to pose a question the editors of *Forbes* recently put to eleven distinguished writers—"why do we feel so bad?" This question, as well as the erosion of confidence that it suggests, provides the focus of this chapter. We begin with a selection entitled "An American Morality Tale," by political economist and Secretary of Labor Robert Reich. If America has lost its way, then we might profit by examining the values we used to hold dear, values that Reich ably summarizes in his story of George. It is to these same values that Jimmy Carter appeals in his 1979 "malaise" speech, which we have excerpted so that you can judge for yourself how accurately the president identified America's crisis of confidence before the public was prepared to listen. Three examinations of the state of our country follow. Anthropologist Katherine S. Newman examines the lives of the downwardly mobile in "American Nightmares." For a surprising number of once-comfortable middle-class people, life in the United States has turned grim. Charles Derber follows with his provocative thesis that America has become a "wilding society" in which people think only of themselves, even if self-interest means doing violence to others. Then, suggesting the degree to which dwellers of the inner city have surrendered hope that police and politicians can eradicate openly defiant drug users, P. J. O'Rourke describes an evening spent with a vigilante group, the Guardian Angels, as they raid a crack house.

Three commentators and a president then share their views on America's crisis of confidence. Natwar M. Gandhi, an immigrant, explains why the world continues to look on America as a "triumphant nation," despite its problems. James Q. Wilson writes on the price Americans pay for prosperity, freedom, and democracy, while Gertrude Himmelfarb examines the consequences of living in a society that we have "de-moralized." Next, President Bill Clinton in his inaugural address rejects pessimism and challenges Americans to renew their faith in their country. "There is nothing wrong with America that cannot be cured by what is right with America," he says. The chapter concludes with two imaginative pieces: a dark, sardonic vision of America by Jerry Sterner, from his play *Other People's Money;* and a poem of hope about the survival of Americans— and of all humanity—composed by Maya Angelou for the inauguration of Bill Clinton on January 20, 1993.

# An American Morality Tale

## ROBERT REICH

*As we begin our exploration of America's crisis of confidence, we can antici-
pate the remarks of authors who will refer directly or indirectly to "core"
American values. It is worthwhile to examine these attitudes, as political
economist Robert Reich does in the selection that follows. Reich's story of
"George" constitutes one version of the American myth. As you'll see, commentators will often judge the behavior of present-day Americans against
elements of the myth, whether or not they invoke the myth directly. George's
story will provide a point of reference, a touchstone, as you read the rest of
the chapter.*

*Reich interprets the story for us by examining the "parables" embedded
within it. "These are [parables] of aspiration," says Reich, that "summon us
to duty and destiny." As you read, consider the extent to which America does
have a destiny. You might also consider the values that Reich will call "core"
American values. Are these your values? Those of your neighbors, business
leaders, political representatives? Your response to these questions will prepare
you for the remaining selections in the chapter.*

*Born in 1946 and reared in Fairfield County, Connecticut, Robert Reich
graduated from Dartmouth College in 1968 and attended Oxford University
(with Bill Clinton) on a Rhodes scholarship. He went on to attend Yale
University law school and served four years directing policy planning at the
Federal Trade Commission in Washington. A former professor of public
policy at Harvard University's John F. Kennedy School of Government, Reich
now serves as secretary of labor in the Clinton administration. Before this
appointment, he contributed regularly to* The New Republic *as well as to
other national magazines and journals. He is the author or co-author of
several books, including* The Next American Frontier *(1983),* Minding
America's Business *(1982), and* The Work of Nations *(1991). The present
selection appears in Reich's* Tales of a New America *(1987).*

You've heard the story a hundred times, with different names, different    1
details. George was a good man, the son of immigrants who had made
their way to Marysville. They came with no money, with nothing but
grim determination and hard-won freedom. Dad worked all his life in the
mill; he was union, hard, and proud. George was quick by nature,
dogged by necessity. He studied hard at school, and after school worked

long and well at anything that would bring in a few dollars. George was good at sports, but he had little time for games. He had few close friends, and yet he was fair and decent with everyone, and quietly kind to anybody in real trouble. He never picked a fight in his life. But in eighth grade, when the town bully Albert Wade was slapping around the smallest kid in the class, George stepped between them without saying a word. He let Wade throw the first punch, then put him away with one straight left, turned around, and walked away.

George finished high school in 1943, and joined the army the day  2
he graduated. Four months later he was in Europe. On the sixth day of the Normandy invasion his squad was on patrol, passing through a French orchard when a German machine-gun nest opened up from behind a stone wall, picking off the squad one by one. George broke from cover and, dodging from tree to tree, raced toward the Nazis as bullets chewed the bark and ground around him. He took out the nest with a grenade and his rifle, and he saved his buddies, but he never wore the medals they gave him and he never talked about it much. After the war he came back to Marysville and married Kate, his childhood sweetheart. He raised three kids, and he started a little construction business, which his hard work and integrity gradually made into a big construction business. By and by, George made a lot of money. But his family continued to live modestly, and he gave generously to the local boys' club and an orphanage he founded. He was generous with his time, too, and headed the community chest. Still he kept pretty much to himself until Albert Wade inherited his father's bank, the only bank in town. Wade risked his depositors' money on shaky loans to his cronies, bought and bullied his way into power with Marysville's political leaders. When he was elected mayor the election smelled bad to everyone, but only George openly accused Wade of corruption. For six months Wade's bank refused every mortgage on houses built by George's company, and George risked everything in the showdown. But in that tense town meeting, one of the city councilmen Wade had paid off could no longer hide his shame under George's steady gaze and simple question from the back of the room. He spilled how Wade had rigged the election. Albert Wade went from city hall to county jail, and George went back to his family, his work, and his quiet service to Marysville.

George's story is an American morality tale. It is a national parable,  3
retold time and again in many different versions, about how we should live our lives in this country. George is the American Everyman. He's Gary Cooper in *High Noon*. He's Jimmy Stewart in *It's a Wonderful Life*. He's the American private eye, the frontier hero, the kid who makes good. He's George Washington and Abe Lincoln. He appears in countless political speeches, in newspaper stories, on the evening news, in American ballads, and sermons.

Everyone has a favorite variation, but the basic theme is the same    4
and speaks to the essence of our national self-image: Ours is a nation of
humble, immigrant origins, built out of nothing and into greatness
through hard work; generous to those in need, those who cannot make
it on their own; a loner among nations, suspicious of foreign entanglements, but willing to stand up against tyranny; and forever vigilant
against corruption and special privilege.

The American morality tale defines our understanding of who we    5
are, and of what we want for ourselves and one another. It is the tacit
subtext of our daily conversations about American life. It permeates *both*
American conservatism and American liberalism. And—the essential
point—it is a fundamentally noble, essentially life-affirming story. Much
is made of the American political distinctiveness of a Constitution
inspired by theory rather than by tradition. But there is a subtler yet
equally profound *cultural* distinctiveness as well, a national sense of
identity rooted not in history but in self-told mythology. Political
scientist Carl Friedrich captured the distinction in 1935: "To be an
American is an ideal, while to be a Frenchman is a fact."

This basic mythology, however integral to the American identity,    6
is so vague as to admit of many interpretations, to present itself in
multiple manifestations over time. At different times in our history,
different aspects of the parable have come to the fore while others
receded. Some variants of the myth are more faithful to its essence than
others; some variants are more supple accommodations to current
American reality than others. Our history is punctuated with wrenching
national contests between competing versions of the ideal; both world
wars, for example, forced us to decide whether we must love peace more
or justice more. Indeed, these episodes of editing our common mythology, as painful as they may be, are themselves affirmations of the
American distinctiveness.

. . .

George's story embodies four basic American morality tales, our    7
core cultural parables. They are rooted in the central experiences of
American history: the flight from older cultures, the rejection of central
authority and aristocratic privilege, the lure of the unspoiled frontier, the
struggle for harmony and justice.

1. THE MOB AT THE GATES. The first mythic story is about tyranny    8
and barbarism that lurk "out there." It depicts America as a beacon
light of virtue in a world of darkness, a small island of freedom and
democracy in a perilous sea. We are uniquely blessed, the proper
model for other peoples' aspirations, the hope of the world's poor and
oppressed. The parable gives voice to a corresponding fear: we must
beware, lest the forces of darkness overwhelm us. Our liberties are

fragile; our openness renders us vulnerable to exploitation or infection from beyond.

Hence our endless efforts to isolate ourselves from the rest of the globe, to contain evil forces beyond our borders, and to convey our lessons with missionary zeal to benighted outsiders. George fought the "good war" against the Nazis; Daniel Boone, a somewhat less savory campaign against Indians; Davy Crockett, Mexicans. The American amalgam of fear and aggressiveness toward "them out there" appears in countless fantasies of space explorers who triumph over alien creatures from beyond. It is found in Whig histories of the United States, and in the anti-immigration harangues of the late nineteenth and early twentieth centuries. We heeded George Washington's warning to maintain our independence from the monarchical powers of Europe, and then proceeded for more than a century to conquer, purchase, or otherwise control vast territories to our west and south.

In this century Woodrow Wilson grimly rallied Americans to "defeat once and for all . . . the sinister forces" that rendered peace impossible; Franklin Roosevelt warned of "rotten apple" nations that spread their rot to others; Dean Acheson adopted the same metaphor to describe the Communist threat to Greece and Turkey immediately after Hitler's war; to Eisenhower, South Vietnam was the first in a series of dominoes that might fall to communism; to John F. Kennedy it was "the finger in the dike," holding back the Soviet surge. The underlying lesson: We must maintain vigilance, lest dark forces overrun us.

2. THE TRIUMPHANT INDIVIDUAL. This is the story of the little guy who works hard, takes risks, believes in himself, and eventually earns wealth, fame, and honor. It's the parable of the self-made man (or, more recently, woman) who bucks the odds, spurns the naysayers, and shows what can be done with enough drive and guts. He's a loner and a maverick, true to himself, plain speaking, self-reliant, uncompromising in his ideals. He gets the job done.

Determination and integrity earned George his triumph. Benjamin Franklin employed a carefully conceived system of self-control (Franklin's *Autobiography* is but the first of a long line of American manuals on how to become rich through self-denial and diligence). The theme recurs in the tale of Abe Lincoln, log splitter from Illinois who goes to the White House; in the hundred or so novellas of Horatio Alger, whose heroes all rise promptly and predictably from rags to riches (not only through pluck; luck plays a part too); and in the manifold stories of American detectives and cowboys—mavericks all—who reluctantly get involved in a dangerous quest and end up with the girl, the money, and the glory. It appears in the American morality tales of the underdog who eventually makes it, showing up the bosses and bullies who tried to put him down; think of *Rocky* or *Iacocca*. Regardless of the precise form, the moral is the same: With enough guts and gumption, anyone can make it on their own in America.

3. THE BENEVOLENT COMMUNITY. The third parable is about the American community. It is the story of neighbors and friends rolling up their sleeves and pitching in to help one another, of self-sacrifice, community pride, and patriotism. It is about Americans' essential generosity and compassion toward those in need. 13

The story is rooted in America's religious traditions, and its earliest formulations are found in sermons like John Winthrop's "A Model of Christian Charity," delivered on board ship in Salem Harbor just before the Puritans landed in 1630. He described the enterprise on which they were embarking in the terms of Matthew's version of the Sermon on the Mount: The new settlers would be "as a City on a Hill" whose members would "delight in each other" and be "of the same body." America began as a nation of religious communities, centered in the church and pledged to piety and charity—Shakers, Amish, Mennonite, New England Congregationalist. Biblical language and symbols continued to propel American social movements committed to enlarging membership in the benevolent community—the drive for emancipation of the slaves, women's suffrage, civil rights. "I have a dream that every valley shall be exalted, every hill and mountain shall be made low," said Martin Luther King. 14

The story extends beyond religion to embrace social solidarity and civic virtue. It summons images of New England villagers who meet to debate their future; of frontier settlers who help build one another's barns and gather for quilting bees; of neighbors who volunteer as fire fighters and librarians, whose generosity erects the local hospital and propels high school achievers to college; of small towns that send their boys off to fight wars for the good of all. The story celebrates America's tradition of civic improvement, philanthropy, and local boosterism. 15

It also tells of national effort on behalf of those in need. The theme permeated Roosevelt's New Deal, Truman's Fair Deal, Johnson's Great Society: America is a single, national community, bound by a common ideal of equal opportunity, and generosity toward the less fortunate. E Pluribus Unum. 16

Our popular culture has echoed these sentiments. Three hundred years after John Winthrop's sermon they could be found in Robert Sherwood's plays, the novels of John Steinbeck and William Saroyan, Aaron Copland's music and Frank Capra's films. The last scene in *It's a Wonderful Life* conveys the lesson: Jimmy Stewart learns that he can count on his neighbors' generosity and goodness, just as they had 17 always counted on him. They are bound together in common cause. The principle: We must nurture and preserve genuine community.

4. THE ROT AT THE TOP. The fourth parable is about the malevolence 18 of powerful elites, be they wealthy aristocrats, rapacious business leaders, or imperious government officials. The American parable differs subtly but profoundly from a superficially similar European mythology: The struggle is only occasionally and incidentally a matter of money or class. There are no workers pitted against capitalists at the heart of this American story. It is, rather, a tale of corruption, decadence, and irresponsibility among the powerful, of conspiracy against the broader public.

This morality tale has repeatedly provoked innovation and reform. 19 Experience with the arbitrary authority of the English Crown produced in the Founding Fathers an acute sensitivity to the possibilities of abuse of power. The result was a government premised on the Enlightenment idea that power must be constrained and limited through checks and balances, and be kept firmly tied to the consent of the governed. A century later America responded to mounting concentrations of private economic power through antitrust laws, designed to diffuse such power, and later by government support for other groups—labor unions, farmers, and retailers—capable of exercising countervailing power. The nation dealt with concentrations of governmental power through civil service rules that limited favoritism, and through electoral reforms and limitations on campaign contributions, to render politicians more accountable to the public. Government power also was held in check by periodic efforts to extend power to the states and cities, to open government decision making to greater public observation and scrutiny, to reduce the power of senior legislators, and to limit the ability of the president to take action without congressional approval. Since the beginning, in sum, Americans have been suspicious of elites and anxious to circumscribe their power.

At their worst, suspicions about the Rot at the Top have expressed 20 themselves in conspiracy theories. America has harbored a long and infamous line of rabble-rousers, from the pre–Civil War Know-Nothings and Anti-Masonic movements, through the populist agitators of the late nineteenth century, the Ku Klux Klan, Senator Joseph McCarthy, and Lyndon LaRouche. They have fomented against bankers, Catholics, big corporations, blacks, Jews, foreigners, either or both major political parties, and other unnamed "interests." In this version of the story, the Rot at the Top is in a great conspiracy with the Mob at the Gates to keep down the common man and allow evil forces to overrun us.

Our popular culture revels in tales of corruption in high places. At 21 the turn of the century, muckrakers like Upton Sinclair and Ida Tarbell uncovered sordid tales of corporate malfeasance; their modern heirs (revealing CIA depredations, White House scandals, and corporate transgressions) are called investigative reporters. The theme recurs in real or invented stories of honest undercover agents—Sam Spade, Serpico, Jack Nicholson in *Chinatown*—who trace the rot back to the most powerful members of the community. It's embodied by the great bullies of American fiction: Judge Thatcher of *Huckleberry Finn*, Broderick Crawford as the Huey Long–like character in *All the King's Men*, Lionel Barrymore's demonic Mr. Potter in *It's a Wonderful Life.* And in the tales of humble folk, like the Joad family of *The Grapes of Wrath*, who struggle valiantly against avaricious bankers and landowners. The moral is clear: Power corrupts, privilege perverts.

These are stories of aspiration. They summon us to duty and des-  22
tiny. Importantly, the American ideal can never really be fulfilled. The goals it mandates are at once too vast and too vague for objective achievement. To pursue them is its own accomplishment. The striving gives meaning to our collective life; the aspiration bestows on us a national identity. In this respect, America may be unique; probably no other culture so clearly defines itself by its morality tales. As a nation of immigrants without a deep common history, we are bound together by a common hope.

## Review Questions

1. What distinctive themes emerge in the morality tale about George? How do these themes speak to "the essence of our national self-image"?
2. Summarize the four "core" parables embodied in George's story.
3. Reich states that the American ideal can never be fulfilled. Why?

## Discussion and Writing Suggestions

1. Write a morality tale—a myth that you think embodies life on your college or university campus. Now compare *your* morality tale to Reich's.
2. Reich quotes political scientist Carl Friedrich as follows: "To be an American is an ideal. . . ." What does Friedrich mean, in the context of Reich's morality tale about George?
3. Cite examples from your own experience, from books you've read, or from movies you've seen that illustrate one or more of the core parables that Reich discusses. Develop your response into an essay.
4. At one point Reich states: "As a nation of immigrants without a deep common history, we are bound together by a common hope." What does Reich mean?

---

# Energy and National Goals

## JIMMY CARTER

*James Earl Carter, Jr. (b. 1924) was thirty-ninth president of the United States, 1977–1981. Carter ascended to the presidency from humble beginnings as a peanut farmer in Plains, Georgia. After two years of college, he attended the U.S. Naval Academy, after which he was assigned as a nuclear engineering specialist to a submarine program. On the death of his father, he returned to Plains and, building the family business, moved into a career in state politics, eventually achieving the governorship in 1970. During his term, the Watergate scandal broke and Richard Nixon resigned in disgrace from office. Carter declared as a candidate for the presidency and defeated Gerald Ford in 1976.*

*As president, Carter is remembered for his emphasis on human rights and for brokering a peace between Egypt and Israel. A hostage crisis in Iran, along with high unemployment and inflation at home, led to his reelection defeat to Ronald Reagan. As an ex-president, however, Carter has gained enormous respect. He remains a highly regarded statesman who has the ear of leaders worldwide and who has traveled to Central America as an observer of elections (to verify their honesty); he also has worked with international experts on problems as various as starvation, immunization, and human rights; and he has helped in this country to build housing for the poor. Since 1975, Carter has published more than a dozen books, including his presidential papers. Two books,* Why Not the Best *(1975) and (with wife Rosalynn Carter)* Everything to Gain *(1987), earned especially high praise. In reviewing* Turning Point *(1992), Carter's recollections of his first political campaign (as a candidate for the Georgia state senate), Robert Dallek for the* Los Angeles Times *wrote that "no Chief Executive in his presidential and post-presidential careers has been a greater moral conscience of the nation than [Carter]."*

*The following speech was delivered to the American people on the evening of July 15, 1979. For background on this speech, see the general introduction to the chapter on page 386.*

I want to speak to you tonight about a subject even more serious than    1
energy or inflation. I want to talk to you right now about a fundamental
threat to American democracy.

I do not mean our political and civil liberties. They will endure. And    2
I do not refer to the outward strength of America—the nation that is
at peace tonight everywhere in the world with unmatched economic
power and military might. The threat is nearly invisible in ordinary
ways. It is a crisis of confidence. It is a crisis that strikes at the very heart
and soul and spirit of our national will.

We can see this crisis in the growing doubt about the meaning of 3
our own lives and in the loss of a unity of purpose for our nation.

The erosion of our confidence in the future is threatening to destroy 4
the social and the political fabric of America. The confidence that we
have always had as a people is not simply some romantic dream or a
proverb in a dusty book that we read just on the Fourth of July. It is the
idea which founded our nation and which has guided our development
as a people. Confidence in the future has supported everything else—
public institutions and private enterprise, our own families and the very
Constitution of the United States. Confidence has defined our course
and has served as a link between generations.

We've always believed in something called progress. We've always 5
had a faith that the days of our children would be better than our own.

Our people are losing that faith. Not only in Government itself, but 6
in their ability as citizens to serve as the ultimate rulers and shapers of
our democracy. As a people, we know our past and we are proud of it.
Our progress has been part of the living history of America, even the
world. We always believed that we were part of a great movement of
humanity itself called democracy, involved in the search for freedom.
And that belief has always strengthened us in our purpose. But just as
we are losing our confidence in the future, we are also beginning to close
the door on our past.

In a nation that was proud of hard work, strong families, close-knit 7
communities and our faith in God, too many of us now tend to worship
self-indulgence and consumption. Human identity is no longer defined
by what one does but by what one owns.

But we've discovered that owning things and consuming things 8
does not satisfy our longing for meaning.

We have learned that piling up material goods cannot fill the empti- 9
ness of lives which have no confidence or purpose. The symptoms of
this crisis of the American spirit are all around us. For the first time in
the history of our country a majority of our people believe that the next
five years will be worse than that past five years. Two-thirds of our
people do not even vote. The productivity of American workers is
actually dropping and the willingness of Americans to save for the
future has fallen below that of all other people in the Western world.

As you know there is a growing disrespect for Government and for 10
churches and for schools, the news media and other institutions. This is
not a message of happiness or reassurance but it is the truth. And it is
a warning. These changes did not happen overnight. They've come
upon us gradually over the last generation. Years that were filled with
shocks and tragedy.

We were sure that ours was a nation of the ballot, not of the bullet, 11
until the murders of John Kennedy and Robert Kennedy and Martin

Luther King Jr. We were taught that our armies were always invincible and our causes were always just only to suffer the agony of Vietnam. We respected the Presidency as a place of honor until the shock of Watergate. We remember when the phrase "sound as a dollar" was an expression of absolute dependability until 10 years of inflation began to shrink our dollar and our savings. We believed that our nation's resources were limitless until 1973, when we had to face a growing dependence on foreign oil.

These wounds are still very deep. They have never been healed. 12

Looking for a way out of this crisis, our people have turned to the 13 Federal Government and found it isolated from the mainstream of our nation's life. Washington, D.C., has become an island. The gap between our citizens and our Government has never been so wide. The people are looking for honest answers, not easy answers, clear leadership, not false claims and evasiveness and politics as usual. What you see too often in Washington and elsewhere around the country is a system of government that seems incapable of action.

You see a Congress twisted and pulled in every direction by hun- 14 dreds of well-financed and powerful special interests. You see every extreme position defended to the last vote, almost to the last breath, by one unyielding group or another.

You often see a balance and a fair approach that demands sacrifice, 15 a little sacrifice from everyone abandoned like an orphan without support and without friends.

Often you see paralysis and stagnation and drift. You don't like it. 16
And neither do I. 17
What can we do? First of all, we must face the truth and then we 18 can change our course. We simply must have faith in each other. Faith in our ability to govern ourselves and faith in the future of this nation. Restoring that faith and that confidence to America is now the most important task we face.

It is a true challenge of this generation of Americans. One of the 19 visitors to Camp David last week put it this way: We've got to stop crying and start sweating; stop talking and start walking; stop cursing and start praying. The strength we need will not come from the White House but from every house in America.

We know the strength of America. We are strong. We can regain 20 our unity. We can regain our confidence. We are the heirs of generations who survived threats much more powerful and awesome than those that challenge us now.

Our fathers and mothers were strong men and women who shaped 21 the new society during the Great Depression, who fought world wars and who carved out a new charter of peace for the world. We ourselves are the same Americans who just 10 years ago put a man on the moon.

We are the generation that dedicated our society to the pursuit of human rights and equality.

And we are the generation that will win the war on the energy   22 problem, and in that process rebuild the unity and confidence of America. We are at a turning point in our history. There are two paths to choose. One is the path I've warned about tonight—the path that leads to fragmentation and self-interest. Down that road lies a mistaken idea of freedom.

The right to grasp for ourselves some advantage over others. That   23 path would be one of constant conflict between narrow interests ending in chaos and immobility. It is a certain route to failure.

All the traditions of our past, all the lessons of our heritage, all the   24 promises of our future point to another path: the path of common purpose and the restoration of American values. That path leads to true freedom for our nation and ourselves.

## Review Questions

1. President Carter says that Americans (in 1979) were losing confidence in the future. Of what attitudes did this confidence consist?
2. To what traditional values does Carter exhort Americans to remember and rededicate themselves? What values have taken the place of these traditional ones?
3. How does the crisis of confidence affect Americans' belief in their government?
4. What events in our nation's history have helped to shake Americans' confidence in their country?
5. Carter claims that Americans can choose one of two paths concerning their future and national character. What are these paths?

## Discussion and Writing Suggestions

1. Carter offered his assessment of the nation's crisis of confidence in 1979. In your view, to what extent do his words apply today? Do Americans now suffer a crisis of confidence? Do you? Do you believe that your life will be better than that of your parents? (To paraphrase Carter, do you believe that the next five years will be better or worse than the last five years?) In responding, identify particular sentences from the speech and develop your answer from these sentences.
2. Carter believed that the American spirit was ailing, and he spoke (in paragraphs 8–9) of a "longing for meaning." What does he mean?
3. How have you responded on a personal, emotional level to this speech? When this speech was delivered, many Americans felt themselves being lectured to. Can you explain this response?

**4.** Presidents are expected to address economic, political, and military matters. Does a president have an obligation to address the nation's spiritual concerns as well?

# American Nightmares

## KATHERINE S. NEWMAN

*In Reich's "An American Morality Tale," you read a fable of achievement that in part defines our culture. Stories like George's confirm our faith that individuals who are industrious usually find their way up the ladder of success. Anthropologist Katherine S. Newman tells a much different story— of movement in the opposite direction:*

> Hundreds of thousands of middle-class families plunge down America's social ladder every year. They lose their jobs, their income drops drastically, and they confront prolonged economic hardship, often for the first time. In the face of this downward mobility, people long accustomed to feeling secure and in control find themselves suddenly powerless and unable to direct their lives.

*"American Nightmares" forms the first chapter of Newman's* Falling from Grace: The Experience of Downward Mobility in the American Middle Class. *Newman based her analysis of downward mobility on 150 in-depth interviews. As you read this selection, you might pause to consider your level of confidence in the American Dream. For instance, you might reflect on what your being in college has to do with an expectation that you'll get (and keep) a good job and succeed in the world of commerce. Does losing a job and sliding down the ladder of success seem remotely possible to you? Read on. For a disturbingly high number of people, downward mobility is a grim fact of life.*

*Katherine S. Newman teaches at Columbia University, where she is associate professor of anthropology and a fellow of the Center for American Culture Studies.*

David Patterson was a practical man. All his life—from his youth in a      1
run-down working-class district of Philadelphia to his adulthood in the
affluent suburbs of New York—he had made rational decisions about
the future. David had a talent for music, but he studied business. He had
a flare for advertising, but he pursued a job in the computer industry. He

From *Falling from Grace: The Experience of Downward Mobility in the American Middle Class* by Katherine S. Newman. Copyright © 1988 by Katherine S. Newman. Reprinted with permission of The Free Press, a Division of Macmillan, Inc.

wore his rationality proudly. Having steered clear of personal indulgence, he had a lot to show for his efforts: a beautiful home, two luxury cars, a country club membership, a rewarding executive job, and a comfortable, stable family. The Philadelphia slums seemed a million miles away and a million years ago.

When David's boss left frantic messages with the secretary, asking    2
him to stay late one Friday afternoon, his stomach began to flutter. Only the previous week David had pored over the company's financial statements. Things weren't looking too good, but it never occurred to him that the crisis would reach his level. He was, after all, the director of an entire division, a position he had been promoted to only two years before. But when David saw the pained look on the boss' face, he knew his head had found its way to the chopping block.

He was given four weeks of severance pay, the use of the company    3
telephone credit card, and a desk in a remote part of the building for the month. Despite these assurances, the credit card was canceled a week later. The company made good on the severance pay agreement, but David was made to feel increasingly uncomfortable about the desk. So he cleared out and went home.

Wasting no time, he set to work on the want ads every morning.    4
He called all his friends in the business to let them know he was looking, and he sent his resume out to the "headhunters"—the executive search firms that match openings to people. David was sure, in the beginning, that it wouldn't be long before a new position opened up. He had some savings put aside to cushion the family in the meanwhile. He was not worried. By the third month of looking, he was a bit nervous. Six fruitless months down the line he was in a full-fledged panic. Nothing was coming through. The message machine he had bought the day after losing his job was perpetually blank.

After nine months, David and his wife Julia were at a crossroads.    5
Their savings eroded, they could not keep up the mortgage payments on their four-bedroom neocolonial house. Julia had gone back to work after a two-year hiatus, but her earnings were a fraction of what David's had been. His unemployment compensation together with her paycheck never amounted to more than 25 percent of the income they had had in the old days. The house, their pride and joy and the repository of virtually all their savings, went up for sale. They reasoned that if the house sold, at least they could salvage some cash to support the family while David continued to look for a job. But their asking price was too high to attract many qualified buyers. Finally it was sold for a song.

Broke and distressed beyond imagining, the family found a small    6
apartment in a modest section of a nearby town. David continued to look for an executive job, but the massive downturn of the mid-1980s in the computer industry virtually ensured that his search would bear no

fruit. From Silicon Valley to Boston's Route 128, the shakeout in his field was stranding hundreds of equally well-qualified men. David could not get past the personnel offices of firms in other industries. He was not given the chance to show how flexible he could be, how transferable his managerial experience was to firms outside the computer field.

After a while David stopped calling his friends, and they ceased                 7
trying to contact him. Having always been sociable people, David and Julia found it hard to cope with the isolation. But with no good news to share, they didn't really feel like seeing old acquaintances. Friendship in their social circles revolved around outings to fancy restaurants, dances at the country club, and the occasional Broadway show or symphony in New York City. The Pattersons' budget simply could not sustain these luxuries anymore. For a time their friends were understanding, inviting them to dinner parties in their homes instead of excursions to places the Pattersons could not afford. But eventually the unspoken rules of reciprocity put an end to that. The Pattersons couldn't issue return invitations, and the potluck dinners of their youth were not a viable alternative.

David and Julia were almost relieved by the ensuing isolation. It had           8
been a strain to put on a calm countenance when, in fact, they felt that life was falling apart. At the same time, however, they interpreted the sounds of silence as abandonment. When friends ceased to call, David was convinced this meant that they no longer cared what happened to him. At least they should try to help him, he thought.

Like many other executive families, they were newcomers to subur-           9
ban New York. Only two years before, David's firm had transferred him from its California branch to its New York headquarters. The move east held the promise of a more important executive job for David and a taste of real affluence. The transition had not been easy, since the social barriers of suburban society were hard to penetrate. Making new friends was no small accomplishment, and after two years there were only a few they could count as close. But they weren't the kind of old friends one could lean on in a crisis, and this surely was a crisis.

Their two teenage children were equally disoriented. Like most kids,       10
they had opposed moving away from the place where they had grown up. They made no secret of their fury at being disrupted in the middle of high school, exiled to a new state where they knew no one. The girl had become rather withdrawn. The boy had worked hard to make new friends, leaning on his father's prestige as a company executive as an avenue into the status-conscious cliques of the local high school. When the son first arrived, as David put it, "No one would even talk to him. He was looked upon as a transient. Everyone else in his school had been in the same area since grammar school." The son's efforts to break into the networks met with only mild success, and even then, it took nearly

the entire two years before he felt on solid social ground. He had finally reached a comfortable plateau when David lost his job. The whole family was thrown into turmoil, and the prospect of moving surfaced once again.

This was too much. David's teenagers unleashed their fury: How 11 could he do this to them? The whole move to New York had been his idea in the first place. Now he was going to drag them through another upheaval! How dare he interfere with their lives so drastically once again? How were they supposed to explain to their friends that their father-the-executive was unemployed? Conformity was the watchword in their friendship circles. Not only did they have to look right and act right, they had to come from acceptable backgrounds. An unemployed father hardly fit the bill. In fact, it threatened their standing altogether because it made it impossible for them to buy the clothes and cars that were commonplace in their social set.

David was accustomed to the normal tensions of life with teenagers. 12 But in his shaken condition, he felt guilty. In retrospect, he agreed with his kids that the move to New York had been ill advised. But it wasn't as if he had had any warning of the debacle when they left the familiar comforts of California. He was simply doing what any intelligent man in his position would do: pursue every opportunity for upward mobility, even if the family is disrupted in the process.

Harder to contend with was the strain on his wife. Julia had long 13 dabbled as a receptionist in art galleries, but her work had been more of a hobby and occasional supplement to the family budget than a main-stay. It had not been easy for her to pick up where she left off when the family moved to New York. Eventually, she found a part-time reception-ist position, but her wages could not begin to cover the family's ex-penses. The move had bequeathed the Pattersons a staggering mortgage for a house twice as expensive as their old one. They could manage the bills as long as David was employed. But with his job gone, Julia's earnings could not stretch far enough. In one fell swoop, Julia found herself the major breadwinner in the family. Though she tried to find a job that would pay more, she had never thought of her work as a "career." She lacked the experience and stable employment history needed to land a better position.

It was the uncertainty of the situation that Julia found hardest to 14 bear. She just could not tell when it would end or where they might land. It was difficult enough to batten down the hatches, cut purchases, and figure out a way to keep the credit cards from sliding too far into arrears. The family did not venture into the shopping malls any more, although this had once been a major form of weekend recreation. If she could figure out when things were going to bottom out, at least she would know what standard of living they had to adapt to. But, lacking any concrete sense of destination, Julia did not know how to begin the adjustment. Adjust to what?

Little help was forthcoming from the suburban matrons in the 15 neighborhood, who—it appears—had never faced anything even remotely resembling this crisis. Where Julia expected to find sympathy and even offers of assistance, she found disbelief and not a little finger pointing. David could sense the damage this was doing:

> Since becoming unemployed there's really nothing, especially for my wife— no place where a woman can talk about things. There are no real relationships. She's hurt. People say to her, "With all the companies on Long Island, your husband can't find a job? Is he really trying? Maybe he likes not working." This really hurts her and it hurts me. People don't understand that you can send out 150 letters to headhunters and get 10 replies. Maybe one or two will turn into something, but there are a hundred qualified people going after each job. The computer industry is contracting all over the place and as it contracts, my wife contracts emotionally.

Secretly David worried whether Julia didn't share just a bit of her 16 friends' attitudes. He could see the despair on her face when he would come home with no news to report. But on too many occasions, it seemed that her rage over the unfairness of his plight was mixed with doubt. She would bombard him with questions: Did you follow up on this lead? Did you call your cousin Harry about another? What did the headhunter tell you about that job downtown? David had few satisfying answers and after a while he began to resent the questions. Couldn't Julia see he was doing his best? It got to the point where he preferred taking a train into the city to look for work to riding with her in the car. Two hours together in the car with nothing but a bleak future to talk about was sometimes more than he could face.

The whole situation left David at a loss. No one was playing by the 17 rules. He had credentials; he had experience; he was in a high-tech field that was touted as the wave of the future. Every time he turned on the news he would hear commentators lament the closing of the steel plants, the auto plants, and the coal mines. This was to be expected in an era when the United States no longer seemed able to compete in the world of heavy industry. But computers? They were supposed to be our salvation, and as a man who always kept one eye on the future, David had aggressively and successfully pursued a career in the field. How could he have gotten into such a quagmire?

The truth is, the computer industry was taking a bath in the 18 mid-1980s. Thousands of employees had been turned out from Atari, Honeywell, Apple. Even IBM, the giant of the industry, had had to tighten its belt. David's entire division had been closed down: fifty people axed in one stroke. The industry shakeout was headline news in the *Wall Street Journal* and on the business pages of the major dailies. But it was only slowly seeping into general public consciousness, where computers still hold a special place as the glamour industry for the twenty-first century. The news had clearly failed to reach the Pattersons' friends. They were dumbfounded by David's disaster. High tech was the answer to the country's economic ills; computers were booming. How could David be having so much trouble finding a job? And what was the *real* reason he had lost his old one?

David could recite the litany of problems in the computer business   19 so familiar to insiders. He could understand completely why his division, located at the market research end of the company, had been targeted as "nonessential" to its survival. In the beginning he told himself that his personal situation could be explained logically. Market forces had put pressure on the company, and it responded, as any rational actor in a competitive capitalist economy would, by cost cutting, aiming first at those activities that were most remote from the nuts and bolts of production and sales. Indeed, had David been at the helm, he argued, he would have made the same decision. For David Patterson is no rebel. He is a true believer in the American way of doing business. Up until now, it had satisfied his every ambition. Hence there was no reason to question its fundamental premise: In economics, as in life, the strong survive and the weak fall by the wayside.

But after months of insecurity, depression, and shaking fear, the   20 economic causes of his personal problems began to fade from view. All David could think about was, What is wrong with me? Why doesn't anyone call me? What have I done wrong? He would spend hours bent over his desk, rubbing his forehead, puffing on his pipe, examining his innermost character, wondering whether this or that personality flaw was holding him back. Could people tell that he was anxious? Were people avoiding him on the street because they couldn't stand to come face to face with desperation? Was he offending potential employers, coming on too strong? With failure closing in from all directions the answer came back "It must be me." The ups and downs of the computer industry and the national economy were forgotten. David's character took center stage as the villain in his own downfall.

. . .

David Patterson has joined the ranks of a little-known group in   21 America, a lost tribe: the downwardly mobile. They are men and women who once had secure jobs, comfortable homes, and reason to believe that the future would be one of continued prosperity for themselves and their children. Longtime members of the American middle class, they suddenly find everything they have worked to achieve—careers, lifestyles, and peace of mind—slipping through their fingers. And despite sustained efforts to reverse the slide, many discover there is little they can do to block their descent.

The lack of attention downward mobility receives—from policy-    22
makers, scholars, and the public—has little to do with its actual incidence. Its low visibility is hardly a product of size: About one in five
American men skid down the occupational hierarchy in their working
lives. In recessions and depressions, their numbers grow at a particularly
rapid rate. But downward mobility is not simply an episodic or unusual
phenomenon in this country. It is a regular feature of the economic
landscape that has been with us for many years.

Yet we hear very little about the downwardly mobile. Magazine    23
covers and television programs focus attention on upward mobility, the
emergence of the Yuppies, the exploits of the rich and famous, and in
less dramatic terms, the expectation of ordinary Americans that from
one year to the next, their lives will keep getting better. But many
middle-class families are headed in the opposite direction—falling on
hard times—and relatively little systematic attention is paid to their
experience.

In the public mind, downward mobility is easily confused with    24
poverty, and the downwardly mobile are mistaken for those who live
below the poverty line. But the two groups are quite different. More
than seven million American families are officially classified as poor, and
they have been the subject of countless studies. The poor *can* experience
downward mobility—they can lose their hold on a meager, but stable
existence and become homeless, for example—but many are at the
bottom of the class hierarchy and some have been there for generations.

The experience of the downwardly mobile middle class is quite    25
different. They once "had it made" in American society, filling slots from
affluent blue-collar jobs to professional and managerial occupations.
They have job skills, education, and decades of steady work experience.
Many are, or were, homeowners. Their marriages were (at least initially)
intact. As a group they savored the American dream. They found a place
higher up the ladder in this society and then, inexplicably, found their
grip loosening and their status sliding.

Some downwardly mobile middle-class families end up in poverty,    26
but many do not. Usually they come to rest at a standard of living above
the poverty level but far below the affluence they enjoyed in the past.
They must therefore contend not only with financial hardship but with
the psychological, social, and practical consequences of "falling from
grace," of losing their "proper place" in the world.

Besides confusing the downwardly mobile with the poor, Ameri-    27
cans tend to overlook these refugees from the middle class because their
experience flies in the face of everything American culture stands for.
From our earliest beginnings, we have cultivated a national faith in
progress and achievement. The emphasis on success has always made it
difficult for Americans to acknowledge defeat: No one ever talks about

the Pilgrims who gave up and headed back to England. Our optimistic heritage stands in the way of recognizing how frequently economic failure occurs.

When academics study occupational mobility, most of the energy goes into trying to account for upward mobility. It is true that the majority of adults enjoy an upward trajectory in income and occupational status over the course of their working lives. Yet, despite the fact that a large number have the opposite experience, downward mobility is relegated to footnotes or to a few lines in statistical tables. Rarely is it treated as a topic in its own right. **28**

When the media, in times of economic hardship, do touch on the problem, they show sympathy for the victims but express bewilderment at their fate. The downwardly mobile are often portrayed as the exceptions that prove the rule. Occasional reminders of what can go wrong seem to strengthen the nation's assumptions about what constitutes the normal and positive course of events. Downward mobility appears, therefore, as an aberration. **29**

What is worse, America's Puritan heritage, as embodied in the work ethic, sustains a steadfast belief in the ability of individuals to control the circumstances of their lives. When life does not proceed according to plan, Americans tend to assume that the fault lies within. We are far more likely to "blame the victim" than to assume that systemic economic conditions beyond the influence of any individual are responsible. This tendency is so pervasive that at times even the victims blame the victims, searching within to find the character flaw that has visited downward mobility upon them. Even they assume that occupational dislocation is somehow uniquely their problem. But the fact is, downward mobility has always been with us and exists in larger numbers than most of us realize. **30**

American culture is rich in rituals and symbols that celebrate worldly success. The extravagant bar mitzvah, the debutante ball, the society wedding, and the lavish golden anniversary celebration all signal the value that Americans attach to economic achievement. Our symbolic vocabulary for failure is, by comparison, stunted. Downward mobility has virtually no ritual face. It is not captured in myths or ceremonies that might help individuals in its grip to make the transition from a higher to a lower social status—there is no equivalent to Horatio Alger stories for the downwardly mobile. **31**

The fact that downward mobility happens so often, yet has not been institutionalized through social convention or public ritual, points to something very significant about the problem. Downward mobility is a hidden dimension of our society's experience because it simply does not fit into our cultural universe. The downwardly mobile therefore become an invisible minority—their presence among us unacknowledged. **32**

This impoverishes public discourse about the problem. Even more important, it has a savage impact on the downwardly mobile themselves. Lacking social and cultural support, the downwardly mobile are stuck in a transitional state, a psychological no-man's-land. They straddle an "old" identity as members of the middle class and a "new" identity as working poor or unemployed. They are in suspended animation. The chaotic feeling of displacement creates confusion that can only be resolved through reintegration in a new capacity. Yet the downwardly mobile are unable to find a "new place" that satisfies their expectations. Hence they are left hanging, with one foot in the world of the professions, the corporate empire, the realm of the economically secure, and another in the troubled world of the financially distressed, the dispossessed, and the realm of low-level occupations. **33**

Hanging between two worlds is a distressing state of existence, for the downwardly mobile individual has to juggle two incompatible senses of personhood. On the one hand, he or she is a well-educated, skilled professional, accustomed to power, to deference, to middle-class norms of consumption. Yet behind the facade of the split-level executive home, the wallpaper is peeling, appliances are breaking down, clothes and shoes are wearing thin, and adults are venturing out to work at low-level white- or blue-collar jobs which afford no authority, no autonomy, no sense of self-importance. **34**

Which self is the real and which the artificial for the downwardly mobile? Some cling to the old persona for years. When asked, they claim their previous occupations as engineers, vice presidents of marketing, or sales managers. But even after hundreds of interviews fail to rescue them from a bottom-level job, after the family home has been sold to pay off debts, after the sense of self-assurance fades to be replaced by self-recrimination, the torture of two selves endures. For the kids' sake, for the wife's sake, or simply for the sake of one's own sanity, it is hard to ditch yesterday's honored identity in order to make room for today's poor substitute. And one never knows, perhaps tomorrow's mail will bring news of a job interview, a passport back to the only occupational reality that makes sense. **35**

Without any guidelines on how to shed the old self, without any instruction or training for the new, the downwardly mobile remain in a social and cultural vacuum. And society looks the other way because, frankly, it is embarrassing to see someone in such a state, and it's disturbing to treat the situation as anything other than an aberration. Any closer scrutiny makes us squirm, for it jeopardizes our own comfort. **36**

This is not to say that there is no template for failure in American culture. Indeed, there have been periods when images of downward mobility were fresh in America's mind. The massive wave of farm foreclosures in the 1930s had a quality of collective public mourning: **37** groups of worn and dejected faces surrounding the old homestead or the last tractor. John Steinbeck's *Grapes of Wrath* memorialized the plight of the dispossessed Dust Bowl refugees. We remember the fate of the Joad family, ejected from their land by the nameless, faceless, hated bankers. The devastation of the Great Depression lingers in our historical consciousness. When the 1980s saw the United States facing the worst rate of farm foreclosures since the depression, the specter of the 1930s was a constant subtext. The beleaguered Midwest, America's breadbasket, recalled an old calamity suffered by others in other times. The words "not since the 1930s" were repeated again and again as if to assure today's farmers that they are not the first to see their livelihoods destroyed.

Despite the cold comfort of history's example, farm foreclosures are not rituals: They do not happen regularly enough to have acquired the character of a culturally recognized transition from one status to another. They are catastrophes, extraordinary events. They remind us of the calamities that can befall the nation, but they cannot structure the experience of individuals whose descent down the status ladder takes place in ordinary times. **38**

The absence of socially validated pathways for dealing with economic decline has important consequences for the downwardly mobile. They often mourn in isolation and fail to reach any sense of closure in their quest for a new identity. Their disorientation suggests how critical culture is in "explaining" to individuals the meaning of their fate. **39**

To a certain extent, the experience of downward mobility in middle-class America is the same for all of its victims. Catastrophic losses create a common feeling of failure, loss of control, and social disorientation. Most people who experience downward mobility long for the "golden days" to return; some genuinely believe they will. Those who have sunk far below their original social status simply don't know where they belong in the world. This is the core of what it means to "fall from grace": to lose your place in the social landscape, to feel that you have no coherent identity, and finally to feel, if not helpless, then at least stymied about how to rectify the situation. **40**

## Review Questions

1. How did the layoff of David Patterson affect his relationship with friends and family?
2. What is "downward mobility"? How often does it occur in the United States?
3. What are the differences between the downwardly mobile and the impoverished?
4. What factors cause downward mobility to become a "hidden dimension of our society's experience"?

## Discussion and Writing Suggestions

1. Discuss the possible reasons Newman titled this first chapter of her book "American Nightmares."

2. Newman observes that David Patterson became the villain in his own downfall. After months of trying to find new work, he began to ask, "What is wrong with me?" Patterson was caught in the grip of economic forces over which he had no control. Have you seen others lose their livelihoods under similar circumstances? How did they respond? Discuss the ways in which their responses did or did not parallel Patterson's.

3. As an anthropologist, Katherine Newman is interested in the ritualized behaviors and myths that help to define cultures. In the preface to her book, she writes that "downward mobility is a subject crying out for anthropological analysis. It is an experience as foreign to many in the United States as the lives of exotic peoples in New Guinea." Review this first chapter of *Falling from Grace* and highlight those passages that suggest to you an anthropological point of view. For instance, you might look for evidence of a cultural analysis that relies on myths and on group identities and interactions.

4. "Falling from grace" is a particularly evocative phrase that Newman uses both for the title of her book and in the selection you've read. Usually, "falling from grace" denotes the biblical story of Adam and Eve's banishment from the Garden of Eden. Why do you suppose Newman appropriates the phrase for use in this book? Develop your answer into an essay.

5. To what extent do David Patterson's experiences undermine for you the common and widely shared assumption that in America an individual's effort and ingenuity can overcome all obstacles?

# The Good Man Fills His Own Stomach

## CHARLES DERBER

*What does a vicious attack on a jogger in Central Park by underclass teenagers have in common with the murder of a pregnant woman by her middle-class husband? Wilding. In the selection that follows, Charles Derber advances the provocative thesis that America has become a society in which people have perverted the American Dream, using it as a pretext for acting selfishly and, in extreme cases, committing heinous crimes. Derber's argument represents an extreme form of the spiritual crisis that Jimmy Carter addressed in the "malaise" speech of 1979. Derber, like Carter before him, claims that*

*America has lost its moral bearings. He feels the very survival of our society is threatened, as is clear from the quotation with which he begins his article.*

*Charles Derber (b. 1944), professor of sociology at Boston College, studied political science at Yale University and earned his Ph.D. in sociology from the University of Chicago. He has written widely on the subjects of political sociology, social change, and American culture; his many publications include* The Pursuit of Attention *(1983),* Power in the Highest Degree *(1990),* The Nuclear Seduction *(1990), and* Money, Murder and the American Dream *(1992), in which the present selection appears.*

The readings of history and anthropology . . . give us no reason to
believe that societies have built-in self-preservative systems.
—Margaret Mead

On April 19, 1989, in New York City, a group of teenagers ages fourteen to sixteen, went into Central Park. It was a clear night and not too cold, at least not too cold to discourage hardy joggers from getting their exercise. The teenagers dispersed into small bands and began targeting victims for some mischief. One group of six youths came upon a young woman jogging alone past a grove of sycamore trees. They cornered her in a gully and began to have some "fun."

That fun would capture headlines around the world. Using rocks, knives, and a metal pipe, they attacked her. Some pinned her down, while others beat and raped her. One defendant, Kharey Wise, aged seventeen, told police that he held the jogger's legs while a friend repeatedly cut her with a knife. They then smashed her with a rock and punched her face, Wise said, until she "stopped moving." After half an hour, she had lost three-quarters of her blood and was unconscious. The group left her for dead.[1]

What most captured public attention were the spirits of the assaulters during and after their crime. According to fifteen-year-old Kevin Richardson, one of the participants, "Everyone laughed and was leaping around." One youth was quoted by police as saying, "It was fun . . . something to do." Asked if they "felt pretty good about what they had done," Richardson said "Yes." Police reported a sense of "smugness" and "no remorse" among the youths.[2]

From this event, a new word was born: "wilding." According to press reports, it was the term the youths themselves used to describe their behavior—and it seemed appropriate. The savagery of the crime, which

---

[1]"Move to Kill Victim Described by Defendant in Jogger Rape," *New York Times,* November 2, 1989, p. 1.
[2]"Testimony Has Youths Joyous After Assault," *New York Times,* November 4, 1989, p. 1.

left the victim brain-damaged and in a coma for weeks, evoked the image of a predatory lion in the bush mangling its helpless prey. Equally "wild" was the blasé mood of the attackers. It had been no big deal, a source perhaps of temporary gratification and amusement. They were "mindless marauders seeking a thrill," said Judge Thomas B. Galligan of Manhattan, who sentenced three of the teenagers to a maximum term of five to ten years, charging them with turning Central Park into a "torture chamber." These were youths who seemed stripped of the emotional veneer of civilized humans, creatures of a wilderness where anything goes.[3]

The story of wilding quickly became tied to the race and class of the [5] predators and their prey. The youths were black and from the "inner city," although from stable working families. The victim was white, with degrees from Wellesley and Yale, a wealthy twenty-eight-year-old investment banker at Salomon Brothers, one of the great houses of Wall Street.

To white middle-class Americans, wilding symbolized something [6] real and terrifying about life in the United States at the turn of the decade. Things were falling apart, at least in the heart of America's major cities. Most suburbanites did not feel their own neighborhoods had become wild, but they could not imagine walking into Central Park at night. Drugs, crime, and unemployment had made the inner city wild. The fear of wilding became fear of the Other: those locked outside of the American Dream. They had not yet invaded the world most Americans felt part of, but they menaced it. The Central Park attack made the threat real—and it unleashed fear among the general population and a backlash of rage among politicians and other public figures. Mayor Koch called for the death penalty. Donald Trump took out ads in four newspapers, writing "I want to hate these murderers . . . I want them to be afraid." Trump told *Newsweek* that he "had gotten hundreds and hundreds of letters of support."[4]

Six months later, a second remarkably vicious crime grabbed people's attention all over the country. On October 23, 1989, Charles and [7] Carol Stuart left a birthing class at Boston's Brigham and Women's Hospital, walked to their car parked in the adjoining Mission Hill neighborhood, and got in. Within minutes, Carol Stuart, eight months pregnant, was dead, shot point blank in the head. Her husband, a stunned nation would learn from police accounts two months later, was her assassin. He had allegedly killed her to collect hundreds of thousands of dollars in life insurance money and open a restaurant. Opening a restaurant, Americans everywhere learned, had long been Chuck Stuart's American Dream.

---

[3]"Three Youths Jailed in Rape of Jogger," *Boston Globe*, September 12, 1990, p. 9.
[4]"The Central Park Rape Sparks a War of Words," *Newsweek*, May 15, 1989, p. 40.

White middle Americans instinctively believed Stuart's story when he told police that a black gunman shot him and his wife, leaving Carol Stuart dead and Stuart himself with a severe bullet wound in the abdomen. When Stuart's brother Matthew went to the police to tell them of Chuck's involvement, and Charles Stuart subsequently apparently committed suicide by jumping off the Tobin Bridge into the river bearing his name, some of the threads connecting his crime to the horrible rape in Central Park began to emerge. Stuart had duped a whole nation by playing on the fear of the wild Other. Aware of the vivid images of gangs of black youths rampaging through dark city streets, Stuart brilliantly concocted a story that would resonate with white Americans' deepest anxieties. Dr. Alvin Poussaint, Harvard professor and advisor to Bill Cosby, said, "Stuart had all the ingredients. . . . he gave blacks a killer image and put himself in the role of a model, an ideal Camelot type that white people could identify with."[5]

Chuck Stuart's crime became a national obsession. A twenty-one-year-old Oklahoman visiting Boston told a *Boston Globe* reporter, "You wouldn't believe the attention this is getting back home. It's all anyone can talk about. I've taken more pictures of this fur shop and Stuart's house than any of the stuff you're supposed to take pictures of in Boston."[6] The quiet Stuart block in Reading had become what the *Globe* called a "macabre mecca," with hundreds of cars, full of the curious and the perplexed, parked or passing by. One reason may have been that white middle Americans everywhere had an uncomfortable sense that, as the decade of the nineties emerged, the Stuart case was telling them something about themselves. Stuart, after all, was living the American Dream and reaping its benefits—a tall, dark, athletic man making over one hundred thousand dollars a year selling fur coats, married to a lovely, adoring wife, and living the good life in suburban Reading complete with swimming pool—a large step upward from his roots in working-class Revere. Had the American Dream itself, by the late 1980s, become the progenitor of a kind of wilding? Was it possible that not only the inner cities of America but its comfortable suburbs were becoming wild places? Could "white wilding" be as serious a problem as the "black wilding" publicized in the mass media? Was, indeed, America at the turn of the decade becoming a "wilding" society?

To answer these questions we have to look far beyond such exceptional events as the Central Park rape or the Stuart murder. We shall see that there are many less extreme forms of wilding, including a wide range of antisocial acts that are neither criminal nor physically violent.

---

[5] Quoted in the *Boston Globe*, January 11, 1990, p. 24.
[6] Cited in article by Renee Graham, "Fur Store, Quiet Street are Now Macabre Meccas," *Boston Globe*, January 16, 1990, p. 20.

---

Wilding includes the ordinary as well as the extraordinary, may be profit-oriented or pleasure-seeking, and can infect corporations and governments as well as individuals of every race, class, and gender.

## THE MOUNTAIN PEOPLE: A WILDING CULTURE

Between 1964 and 1967, anthropologist Colin Turnbull lived among the people of Uganda known as the Ik, an unfortunate people expelled by an uncaring government from their traditional hunting lands to extremely barren mountainous areas. In 1972, Turnbull published a haunting book about his experiences which left no doubt that a whole society can embrace "wilding" as a way of life.[7]     **11**

When Turnbull first came to the Ik, he met Atum, a sprightly, little     **12**
old barefoot man with a sweet smile, who helped guide Turnbull to remote Ik villages. Atum warned Turnbull right away that everyone would ask for food. While many would indeed be hungry, he said, most could fend for themselves, and their pleas should not be trusted; Turnbull, Atum stressed, should on no account give them anything. But before he left that day, Atum mentioned that his own wife was severely ill and desperately needed food and medicine. On reaching his village, Atum told Turnbull his wife was too sick to come out. Later, Turnbull heard exchanges between Atum and his sick wife, and moans of her suffering. The moans were wrenching, and when Atum pleaded for help, Turnbull gave him food and some aspirin.

Some weeks later, Atum had stepped up his requests for food and     **13**
medicine, saying his wife was getting sicker. Turnbull was now seriously concerned, urging Atum to get her to a hospital. Atum refused, saying "she wasn't *that* sick." Shortly thereafter, Atum's brother-in-law came to Turnbull and told him that Atum was selling the medicine that Turnbull had been giving him for his wife. Turnbull, not terribly surprised, said that "that was too bad for his wife." Whereupon the brother-in-law, enjoying the joke enormously, told him that Atum's wife "had been dead for weeks," and that Atum had buried her inside the compound so you wouldn't know." No wonder Atum had not wanted his wife to go to the hospital, Turnbull thought to himself: "She was worth far more to him dead than alive."[8]

Startling to Turnbull was not only the immense glee the brother-in-     **14**
law seemed to take in the "joke" inflicted on his dying sister, but the utter lack of embarrassment shown by Atum when confronted with his lie. Atum shrugged it off, showing no remorse whatsoever, saying he

---

[7] Colin Turnbull, *The Mountain People* (New York: Simon and Schuster, 1987).
[8] Ibid. p. 86.

had simply forgotten to tell Turnbull. That his little business enterprise may have led to his wife's death was the last thing on Atum's mind. This was one of the first of many events that made Turnbull wonder whether there was any limit to what an Ik would do to get food and money.

Some time later, Turnbull came across Lomeja, an Ik man he had met  15 much earlier. Lomeja had been shot during an attack by neighboring tribesmen and was lying in a pool of his own blood, apparently dying from two bullet wounds in the stomach. Still alive and conscious, Lomeja looked up at Turnbull and asked for some tea. Shaken, Turnbull returned to his Land Rover and filled a big, new yellow enamel mug. When he returned, Lomeja's wife was bending over her husband. She was trying to "fold him up" in the dead position although he was not yet dead, and started shrieking at Turnbull to leave Lomeja alone because he was already dead. Lomeja found the strength to resist his wife's premature efforts to bury him and was trying to push her aside. Turnbull managed to get the cup of tea to Lomeja, who was still strong enough to reach out for it and sip it. Suddenly Turnbull heard a loud giggle and saw Lomeja's sister, Kimat. Attracted by all the yelling, she had "seen that lovely new, bright yellow enamel mug of hot, sweet tea, had snatched it from her brother's face and made off with it, proud and joyful. She not only had the tea, she also had the mug. She drank as she ran, laughing and delighted at herself."[9]

Turnbull came to describe the Ik as "the loveless people." Each Ik  16 valued only his or her own survival—and regarded everyone else as a competitor for food. Ik life had become a grim process of trying to find enough food to stay alive each day. The hunt consumed all of their resources, leaving virtually no reserve for feelings of any kind, nor for any moral scruples that might interfere with filling their stomachs. As Margaret Mead wrote, the Ik had become "a people who have become monstrous beyond belief." The scientist Ashley Montagu wrote that the Ik are "a people who are dying because they have abandoned their own humanity."

Ik families elevated wilding to a high art. Turnbull met Adupa, a  17 young girl of perhaps six, who was so malnourished that her stomach was grossly distended and her legs and arms spindly. Her parents had decided she had become a liability and threw her out of their hut. Since she was too weak now to go out on long scavenging ventures, as did the other children, she would wander as far as her strength would allow, pick up scraps of bone or half-eaten berries, and then come back to her parents' place, waiting to be brought back in. Days later, her parents, tiring of her crying, finally brought her in and promised to feed her.

---

[9]Ibid. p. 153.

Adupa was happy and stopped crying. The parents went out and "closed the asak behind them, so tight that weak little Adupa could never have moved it if she had tried."[10] Adupa waited for them to come back with the food they had promised. But they did not return until a whole week had passed, when they knew Adupa would be dead. Adupa's parents took her rotting remains, Turnbull writes, and threw them out, "as one does the riper garbage, a good distance away."[11] There was no burial—and no tears.

Both morality and personality among the Ik were dedicated to the **18** single all-consuming passion for self-preservation. There was simply "not room in the life of these people," Turnbull observes dryly, "for such luxuries as family and sentiment and love." Nor for any morality beyond "marangik," the new Ik concept of goodness, which means filling one's own stomach.

## AMERICA AS A WILDING SOCIETY

Long before the rape in Central Park or the Stuart murder, Ashley **19** Montagu, commenting on Turnbull's work, wrote that "the parallel with our own society is deadly." In 1972, when Turnbull published his book, wilding had not become part of the American vocabulary, nor did Americans yet face declining living standards, let alone the starvation of the Iks. Americans were obviously not killing their parents or children for money, but they dedicated themselves to self-interested pursuits with a passion not unlike that of the Ik. In America, a land of plenty, there was the luxury of a rhetoric of morality and feelings of empathy and love. But was not the American Dream a paean to individualistic enterprise, and could not such enterprise be conceived in some of the same unsentimental metaphors used by Turnbull about the Ik: The Ik community "reveals itself for what it is, a conglomeration of individuals of all ages, each going his own way in search of food and water, like a plague of locusts spread over the land."[12]

In what may be the most penetrating film on American life as the **20** 1990s dawned, Woody Allen's *Crimes and Misdemeanors* hints that wilding is becoming part and parcel of the American Dream. The movie's protagonist is Judah, a doctor who has it all. A brilliant opthalmologist, Judah is at the top of his profession and married to a beautiful and loving wife. He has a six-figure income, a gorgeous house on four acres, and is a pillar of the community, known for his philanthropic

---

[10]Ibid. p. 132.

[11]Ibid.

[12]Ibid. p. 137.

works. He is cultured as well as rich. "You can call Judah to find out which is the best restaurant in Paris or in Athens, or the best hotel in Moscow, or the best recording of a particular Mozart symphony," says a community leader toasting Judah. Judah is living the American Dream.

Judah's affair with his mistress Delores exposes the shadowy side of  21 the modern American success story. When Delores learns that Judah is not serious about leaving his marriage, she threatens to tell his wife about the affair and to reveal to the world that Judah has dipped into his philanthropy trusts to cover his own cash-flow problems. Judah believes his life is about to go up in smoke. At his wit's end, he calls his brother, Jack, the black sheep of the family who has shady friends from the underworld. Jack assures Judah that Delores can be "handled." "We're talking about a human being," Judah haltingly protests. "She's not an insect. You can't just step on her." He says, "I can't do it. I can't think that way." But shortly thereafter, Judah calls Jack back and tells him to go ahead. Judah pays for the murder and his brother sees that it is carried out. Judah, a man who exemplifies success in the late 1980s, has become a killer.

For a while, Judah is "plagued by deep-seated guilt" and because of his  22 religious upbringing is tortured by the notion that he "has violated God's order." But after many sleepless nights, one morning he "wakes up, the sun is shining, his family is around him," and "the guilt has lifted." Yes, "every once in a while," he has a "twinge" of conscience, but "with time it all fades." Judah accepts that in the real world, we must all "rationalize" and "deny," to live with inevitable moral compromises. The important thing now is that "he is scot free," that "he is not punished," indeed, "he prospers." He can, with a quiet conscience, put this behind him and go back to his life. The difference between Judah, who symbolizes the American Dream, and Jack, representing its dirty underside, has blurred. The viewer leaves wondering whether Judah or Jack is the greater wilder, which leads inexorably to the larger question of what has happened to the American Dream at the end of the twentieth century?

A spate of books about the Reagan era suggest a corruption of the  23 American Dream in our time.[13] Most Americans do not become killers to make it up the ladder or hold on to what they have, but the traditional restraints on naked self-aggrandizement seem weaker—and the insatiability greater. Donald Trump is only the most visible of the American heroes defining life as "The Art of the Deal," the title of Trump's best-selling autobiography. Trump feels no moral contradiction about building the most luxurious condos in history in a city teeming with homeless. Trump writes triumphantly about the Trump Tower in Man-

---

[13]For an excellent book on the subject see: John Taylor, *Circus of Ambition: The Culture of Wealth and Power in the Eighties* (New York: Warner Books, 1989).

hattan: "We positioned ourselves as the only place for a certain kind of very wealthy person to live—the hottest ticket in town. We were selling fantasy."[14] Trump is a living advertisement for Ronald Reagan's manifesto in his inaugural address, "We are too great a nation to limit ourselves to small dreams."

In 1835, Alexis de Tocqueville wrote that in America "no natural boundary seems to be set to the efforts of man." But in the 1980s, John Taylor writes, a new version of the American Dream emerged, both more expansive and more morally perverted than its predecessors. America entered a new Gilded Age, where the celebration and "lure of wealth has overpowered conventional restraints."[15] Laurence Shames writes that the name of the American game has become simply *more.*[16] 24

In the 1980s, yuppies, with their "vaunting ambition and outsized expectations," came to symbolize this new chapter of the American Dream. Youthful commodity traders fresh out of business school engaged in feeding frenzies in the exchanges, pursuing quick fortunes "as if they'd invented the habit of more, when in fact they'd only inherited it the way a fetus picks up an addiction in the womb. The craving was there in the national bloodstream."[17] Many of these young entrepreneurs would turn to inside trading—and more serious crime—when their risky ventures went bad. The notorious Billionaire Boys' Club, made famous in the movie *Wall Street*, would show that respectable young men consumed by the dream could become killers. 25

Shames notes there has always been a tenuous connection between the American Dream and civilized behavior: "Grabs at personal prosperity" can "come precisely at the expense of those civilized and civilizing privileges" that prosperity is for.[18] The peculiar feature of the dream emerging in the 1980s was its instability, each success and gorging creating a more acute sense of starvation. Such inability to satisfy chronic gnawing hunger is fertile breeding ground for a culture of wilding. 26

The new outsized dream could engulf the entire personality. The horrifying combination of narcissism and sociopathy, so marked among the Ik, became the focal point of discussion among psychologists speculating about Charles Stuart. In the 1970s, culture watchers like Christopher Lasch had already identified narcissism (a distorted love of self masking inner self-contempt and emptiness) as a mushrooming psychic cancer, the most widespread personality disorder in late twentieth- 27

---

[14]Donald Trump, *The Art of the Deal* (New York: Warner Books, 1987).

[15]Taylor, *Circus of Ambition,* p. 8.

[16]Laurence Shames, *The Hunger for More* (New York: Times Books, 1989).

[17]Ibid. p. 27.

[18]Ibid. p. 40.

century America. In the Reagan-Bush era, narcissism became mixed with a deadly brew of sociopathic indifference, cloaked as a virtue in the official rhetoric of entrepreneurship, individual initiative, and self-reliance. The psychological and ideological preconditions of a wilding society were beginning to converge: tortured personalities driven by pounding needs for attention, power, and status in a holy "money culture" embracing the unrestrained pursuit of wealth and self-aggrandizement. Me, Me, Me, hollered the relentless voices from inside; look after Number One, echoed the reassuring voices from high places. The new operational credo: Anything Goes.

## Review Questions

1. How was the term "wilding" coined?
2. How was wilding initially tied to issues of race and class, and how did those connections need to be expanded, in Derber's view?
3. How is the logic of wilding connected to the American Dream?
4. Who are the Ik, and what have they to do with wilding?
5. In what ways did the social and ideological climate of the 1970s and 1980s converge to create the wilding of the 1990s?

## Discussion and Writing Suggestions

1. What are the differences between ambition, a virtue to most Americans, and wilding? Put another way, at what point does pursuit of the American Dream turn pathological?
2. Reread the epigraph by Margaret Mead, which Derber uses to set a context for his essay. Why has Derber chosen this particular sentence?
3. Derber points to Woody Allen's *Crimes and Misdemeanors* as a representation of what has become of the "American Dream at the end of the twentieth century." If you have seen the film, discuss the ways in which the dream has been exploded and replaced by naked and perverse self-interest.
4. In one or two paragraphs, describe some incident you have witnessed or heard about that might be described as wilding. Using what you have learned from Derber, write a brief essay in which you analyze that incident.
5. To what extent do you, like Derber, see a relation between Ik culture and American culture?

# Slamming and Jamming

## P. J. O'ROURKE

*As executive editor and then editor-in-chief of the* National Lampoon *for nine years (1973–1981), P. J. O'Rourke (b. 1947) is no stranger to irrever-*

*ence. In his work he takes a biting and often humorous look at his subjects, which in the case of his best-selling* Parliament of Whores *(from which this selection is taken) is the federal government. Convinced that Washington's programs on preventing poverty and urban drug use do not work and in fact lead to despair among the very people intended as beneficiaries, O'Rourke searches for approaches that do have a chance of succeeding. He finds the Guardian Angels and accompanies them one night on a "slamming and jamming" patrol through two of New York's tougher neighborhoods—to visit a crack house.*

*The account you will read is vivid, and you will be drawn in by O'Rourke's description of a world most likely foreign to you. By all means, read for the immediate effect; when you are finished, consider the author's implicit message about our government's inability to address the fundamental problem of drugs. Do we live in a society in which people must look to vigilantes, and not to city hall or Washington, for protection? You might recall, as you read, the series of Charles Bronson* Death Wish *movies that glorified vigilantism. During the 1980s, audiences across the country cheered a hero who took the law into his own hands.*

I called Curtis Sliwa, founder of the Guardian Angels. The Guardian [1] Angels are, like Batman, Miss Marple and the Baker Street Irregulars, unarmed amateur fighters of crime. Such groups are ubiquitous in popular fiction but never exist in real life. Unarmed amateur crime fighting would be useless in a lawful society and suicidal in a lawless one. In America, however, we have managed to produce a combination of vandalized wealth and spoiled want, police legalism and ACLU firepower that makes something as fundamentally absurd as the Guardian Angels not only possible but a godsend.

And it says a lot about the nature of American poverty that I went [2] to see it with a group of young men trained in the martial arts and operating under military-style discipline instead of with a social worker.

Correct choice, incidentally. We got out of the subway in the Mott [3] Haven section of New York's South Bronx just as some fellow down the block was shot stepping into his Cadillac. He was carrying a gun. Obviously his assailant was, too. And so were all the witnesses on the street. *"Everybody* had a gun," a cop said later, stringing yellow "crime scene" tape around the Coup de Ville.

Mott Haven was once a district of substantial apartment houses, [4] comfortable if not luxurious, the tract homes of their day. These sheltered the Jewish middle classes on their way from the Lower East Side to White Plains. Now the buildings are in various stages of decomposition, ranging from neglected paint to flattened rubble. Abandoned buildings are office space for the local criminals, who deal almost entirely in drugs. (There's not much felonious creativity in a modern slum.) Scattered among the remaining turn-of-the-century structures and the empty lots piled with trash are various housing projects with large, ill-lighted areas of "public" space, dead to all traffic and commercial activity. Squalor and overcrowding are often spoken of as almost a single phenomenon, but in New York's poor neighborhoods the lower the population density, the greater the filth and crime.

The Guardian Angels walked through this neighborhood in single    5
file looking for muggers and drug users. The Angels got handshakes, thumbs-up signals and loud shouts of encouragement from the old people. Women flirted with them. Little kids wanted to know how old they had to be to join. But the young men looked away or yelled—from a distance—"*maricon*" or "Charlie's Angels." It was interesting, the percentage of these young men who were visibly drunk at nine in the evening—100. But it was also interesting to look through lighted windows here, in the streets Tom Wolfe picked to terrify his Mercedes-driving anti-hero in *The Bonfire of the Vanities,* and see freshly painted walls and bright curtains, pictures of Christ and the Madonna (the one who *didn't* get her video banned from MTV), cooing women with crying babies, families clearing away supper plates and kids eating ice cream in front of the TV—interesting to see how much tame and ordinary life goes on in the notorious South Bronx.

We walked on through the odd landscape, with its equal parts of the    6
depraved, the deserted and the normal, down to one more decayed apartment house with the Bruckner Elevated Expressway nearly running through its back hall. The Guardian Angels had helped squatters here resist an eviction order. The building was clean but an utter wreck, and the squatters' small-time attempts at big-time repairs hadn't helped. The people in the building to whom I talked—an earnest sculptor, a couple belonging to some Muslim-type religious group and a neo-hippie—had a complicated tale of woe.

The building's landlord had offered tenants cheap apartments in    7
return for help repairing the building, a so-called sweat-equity deal. But the leases the tenants signed weren't legally binding because the corporation that actually owned the building hadn't paid property taxes in ten years. Then the city took over. New York has so many laws about rent control, occupancy permits, real estate transfers, co-op conversions and so forth that a special housing court is needed to sort it all out. A housing-court judge appointed an administrator to run the building. The

tenants went to another city agency, the Department of Housing, Preservation and Development, which promised them that in return for an enormous amount of bureaucratic frog-walking, they'd be able to buy the building themselves. But while the tenants tried to repair the building they thought they were buying, the court-appointed administrator went into cahoots with a real estate speculator who obtained the building's mortgage, paid off the back taxes and got the tenants (now squatters) evicted by the same housing-court judge who'd appointed the administrator.

If you've ever been to New York and wondered how a city where 8
a decent apartment is almost impossible to find got mile after mile of abandoned, semi-abandoned and eminently abandonable apartment buildings, this is one of the ways it's done.

Mott Haven is by no means the worst section of the South Bronx. 9
That's probably Hunt's Point, where we went next.

Riding with the DC police, I'd been in neighborhoods where there 10
was a lot of drug use and even in neighborhoods where drug use was the dominant factor, more important in shaping the environment than weather or wealth. But there are parts of Hunt's Point where the actual numerical majority of the residents are drugged to the eyes. Hunt's Point doesn't look much worse than other lousy neighborhoods, but the people do—dirty, skinny, disordered base-heads yelling at each other and us and people who aren't there. American slums are usually stylish places, their residents far up the fashion scale of evolution from the sack-assed, Brooks Brothered princes of Wall Street. But in the crack neighborhoods people are still wearing whatever they happened to have on at the moment the crack craze hit.

Here the women, too, jeered the Guardian Angels, and when our 11
group had passed one gaggle of druggies on the corner of Hunt's Point Avenue and Lafayette, bottles and brick-halves were thrown at our backs. The Guardian Angels held their pace and disdained to duck or look over their shoulders as stuff smashed onto the sidewalk around them.

Farther down Hunt's Point Avenue the Angels' patrol leader, José 12
Miller ("GI Joe"), went up to an old car hood leaning against a burned-out building and pulled it away to reveal a scarecrow-shaped addict piping down. José smashed the pipe. On the next block the Angels took drugs away from several large guys in an alley. The largest of the guys feigned a threatening gesture at the Angels, then rounded on his fellows shouting, "Just walk away! Just walk away! They got . . ." He pointed at the Guardian Angels. "They got . . . They got . . ." He couldn't seem to think what it was the Angels had that justified his backing down. "Just walk away!" he yelled and walked away.

Around the corner on Casanova Street, near the Spofford Juvenile  13
Detention Center, a woman on a porch stoop said crack addicts were
smoking in the empty building next door. The Guardian Angels ran into
the building with no caution and not enough flashlights, leaping across
abysmal pits left by missing steps in the stairwells and pounding down
wrecked hallways through smashed doorframes into black, stinking
rooms full of burned mattresses and human shit. But the addicts had fled.

The building hadn't been derelict long. You could tell because only  14
half the copper plumbing had been ripped out to sell for scrap. I found
someone's photo album lying in the muddy courtyard. Snapshots of
weddings and christenings and first communions had been carefully
arranged beneath sheets of clear plastic and then just left in the dirt. It
was the kind of orphaned possession you might find in the wake of a
tornado or after a war.

José wanted to show me a couple of wood-frame houses on Casa-  15
nova that the Angels had raided repeatedly. But when we got there, the
houses were gone. The night-shift workers at a freight depot across the
street said somebody had taken a bulldozer from a road repair site last
weekend and crushed the homes. "We're beginning to have an effect,"
said José. Maybe. Or maybe not. In the gutter in front of the razed crack
houses was a brand-new Porsche 928 flipped on its back and wadded like
Kleenex.

. . .

That night the Guardian Angels invited me to come with them back  16
to Hunt's Point. Michael Dixon ("Recon"), an Angel who specializes in
dirtying himself like a dope user and scouting vile locales, had discovered a gruesome nest of drug behavior—a crack house, shooting gallery, dope bazaar and place to get a cheap blowjob all in one. And the
Angels were going to raid it.

At first I assumed this would be a privatized version of the police  17
raid I'd gone on in Washington. But the Guardian Angels said no, that
wasn't the point. The Angels weren't going to arrest anyone, because
a citizen's arrest means—just as a cop's arrest does—days spent in
court, only to see some scumbag released on probation. And the Angels
weren't trying to convince any individual person to stop taking drugs.
"There's plenty of education—everybody knows drugs are bad," one of
the Angels said. What Sliwa and his men intended to do was wreck this
crack house—break everything breakable, rough up the patrons and
take their drugs and money away. The Guardian Angels call it slamming
and jamming. The purpose is to show the flag of decency, to destroy the
permissive atmosphere of the inner city and to provide, by main
strength of hand, the social opprobrium missing in the slums. The
Guardian Angels are trying to enforce the kind of propriety, the mores,
that were usual in American society, at every income level, twenty-five

years ago. They're trying to make the South Bronx as dull and bland and conventional as my mother's old neighborhood. But modern society has become so lawless and screwy that the Guardian Angels have had to start a street gang to teach people decorum.

Twenty-seven Guardian Angels went on the raid, most of them in   **18** a U-Haul-style moving truck and the rest in a van and a car. The Angels arrived in the Bronx about sunset and gathered in an Amtrak rail yard, where Curtis Sliwa scratched battle plans on the pavement with a rock. The crack den was in the basement of a large, empty building on the block where we'd had bottles and bricks thrown at us. The only way inside was across a board over a four-foot ditch and through a hole in the basement wall.

The Guardian Angels were divided into three squads. The first   **19** squad was to rush through the hole and grab all the dopies and immobilize them, that is, throw them against walls. The second squad was to come in behind the first, pass through the melee in the basement and fan out through the upper floors to clear the rest of the building. The third squad would secure a defense perimeter.

Speed was important. Crack houses are defended by armed enforc-   **20** ers, but the enforcers, to avoid being caught by police, stay several blocks away. Lookouts with walkie-talkies would send the alarm, and the enforcers would get there, the Angels told me, in about ten minutes. "I want this operation completed in six to eight minutes," Sliwa told the Angels.

I went into the building between the first and second squads.   **21** Electricity had been pirated from somewhere for a couple of bulbs, and a sofa, half-burned and half-moldering, had been dragged off the street. On one damp-stained, scaly wall a skull and crossbones had been spray-painted above the words NO CREDIT. There were humps of garbage and rags, piles of busted cement and broken pipes and earth and muck everywhere in a retching funk of shit and drug-addict body odor. About a dozen crack-heads were down there, the men shrieking for mercy and the women just shrieking while they tried to pull their clothes back on over skaggy, mottled flanks. "My shoes! Let me get my shoes!" one woman yelled, and I thought this was an odd, feminine-vanity sort of concern to be having at the moment until I looked at the basement floor. There were hypodermic needles lying like spilled pretzel sticks all around the thin rubber soles of my Topsiders.

The Guardian Angels were shoving drug addicts and hollering   **22** horrible imprecations at them, then dragging them outside and making them kneel on the sidewalk. There the crack-heads had their pockets emptied; their drugs, pipes, needles and paraphernalia given the bootheel and their money torn up in front of their faces.

I was down in the terrible basement taking notes. The raid seemed     23
to be a success as far as I could tell. But outside things were going awry.

When the second squad came through the basement, they found the     24
stairs to the rest of the building had been blocked with rubble. They ran
back out, hoisted themselves past the bricked-up first floor and went in
the second-story windows. Meanwhile, the perimeter squad had, as
Sliwa described it later, "gotten greedy." Seeing how some of the
bystanders were obvious druggies, the Angels began grabbing people
out of the gathering crowd and tossing them in with the kneeling
crack-heads. The crowd grew and turned uglier, throwing things and
pushing its way in on the defense perimeter.

After the second squad finished its sweep through the upper floors     25
of the crack house—which were empty—they found themselves cut off
from their fellows. They jumped down into the angry crowd, and
putting their backs together, began to fight.

Sliwa gave the signal for retreat—a long blast on a whistle. When     26
the remaining Angels in the basement and I ran out through the hole in
the wall, all hell had broken loose. Bottles and beer cans and chunks of
masonry were coming down like animated polka dots out of the pink
evening sky. The enforcers had arrived from their outposts and were
firing shots from a nearby roof. The fuddled crack addicts were tossed
aside, and the first squad sprinted for the Guardian Angel vehicles while
the perimeter squad fell in behind them. I had just dived into the van
when something huge and heavy hit its roof. The van, truck and car took
off with the street crowd running down on us. The three Guardian
Angel drivers, winching on the steering-wheel rims as hard as they
could, squealed around the block and into the backside of this same
crowd, where the second squad of Angels was surrounded.

We were in the lead in the van and came through the drug mob at     27
about twenty-five miles an hour, grazing several people and sending
dozens leaping out of the way. In front of us two guys with complicated
haircuts were pulling open their sports-team jackets and reaching into
their waistbands, but the van's driver chased them up on the sidewalk
before they could get their pistols free. The moving truck was right
behind us, and as it came through, the members of the second squad
jumped into the back. Just as the last Guardian Angel was being pulled
onboard, his legs still dangling over the tailgate, some lunatic ran out
of the crowd swinging an ax. The lunatic took aim at the Angel's foot
but hooked his swing and only connected with the flat of the ax head.
The two Guardian Angels bringing up the rear in the car smashed the
lunatic's knees between their bumper and the back of the truck. Then we
got the hell out of there.

The Guardian Angels were lucky. Only four of them were injured     28

---

and only one seriously—John Rodrigues ("Hot Rod"), a young Angel on his first patrol. John's face was badly cut by somebody using a gin bottle as a shillelagh, but what was bothering John most was what his mother was going to say. The mob of drug lovers was not so lucky. I looked out the van's back window and saw a score of people staggering around in the middle of Hunt's Point Avenue holding parts of their bodies, such as groins and faces.

The Guardian Angels went back to the relative calm and safety of 29 Mott Haven to get some sodas and first aid. At 138th Street and Cypress Avenue the block association was holding a street festival with a salsa band, and all the respectable citizens were out on the sidewalks with their children, eating cuchifritos and doing dance steps.

"This neighborhood used to be just like Hunt's Point," an Angel 30 who'd grown up in Mott Haven told me.

"Before you guys started patrolling it?" I said. 31

"It's not because of us," said the Guardian Angel with remarkable 32 modesty, considering the amount of adrenaline still in the air. "It's because of the support that the people here give to getting the scum out of their neighborhood."

And when the officers of the block association saw Curtis Sliwa, 33 they insisted he come up to the bandstand and give a speech. Curtis tried to demur. He doesn't speak Spanish, and most of these people don't speak English. But that didn't matter to the crowd. The Guardian Angels had a real poverty program, one that could actually mitigate some of the horrible effects of privation. The people of Mott Haven didn't need to understand Curtis Sliwa's exact words, any more than they needed to understand every aspect of federal social legislation. They could see the results of government policy, and they could see the results of the Guardian Angels. They could tell what works.

## Discussion and Writing Suggestions

1. O'Rourke writes, "It says a lot about the nature of American poverty that I went to see [that poverty] with a group of young men trained in the martial arts and operating under military-style discipline instead of with a social worker." What, in your view, does this say?
2. Select one paragraph of O'Rourke's description of Mott Haven or Hunt's Point, in the South Bronx. In two paragraphs, analyze O'Rourke's language. How does he use description to create a vivid picture of the life he sees? What is that picture, and what is your impression of it?
3. A definition of *vigilantism:* the acts of one citizen, or a group of citizens banding together, to fight crime without police involvement. Police forces frown on vigilantism. Are the Guardian Angels vigilantes? What message is communicated by their presence in New York's South Bronx and in other urban neighborhoods? Are the Guardian Angels truly guardians? Are they

"angels"? Is their existence necessary, in your view? What larger issues do the Guardian Angels raise about people's confidence in law and order?

4. What attitude does O'Rourke take regarding the Guardian Angels? Look for evidence of this attitude in his description of the members and of their raid on the crack house.

5. The Guardian Angels have a "real" poverty program (paragraph 33), says O'Rourke—as opposed to what? What's the implication, and do you agree with it?

# Still the Promised Land

## NATWAR M. GANDHI

*Natwar M. Gandhi, an immigrant from India and a tax policy analyst in Washington, D.C., disagrees with the gloomy assessments of America. Gandhi sees America as a promised land—especially for immigrants, despite "the crime, the drugs, the social promiscuity and the homelessness."*

Recently, *The Atlantic* carried excerpts from the diaries of George F. Kennan, diplomat, historian and a major architect of postwar American foreign policy, in which Kennan views "the United States of these last few years of the 20th century as essentially a tragic country."  1

This is a serious indictment, and one that all concerned Americans should take note of. Kennan, the last of America's wise old men, possesses one of the finest intellects in America today. He does find some solace in America's magnificent natural resources and some of its people, but too much of his diaries contain, by his own admission, "bleakness of impressions of my own country."  2

Nearly 30 years ago, Edmund Wilson, the great literary critic and another Princetonian, had similar observations. As he was approaching old age, Wilson wrote, "I have finally come to feel that this country, whether or not I live in it, is no longer, any place for me. . . . When, for example, I look through *Life* magazine, I feel that I do not belong to the country depicted there, that I do not even live in that country."  3

These statements are neither the rhetorical outbursts of frustrated old men nor the diatribes of modern-day revolutionaries. They are the thoughtful comments of two of America's most distinguished public men after long lives of study and contemplation.  4

Millions of immigrants like me, however, would find these comments a bit incomprehensible. As immigrants, we made a deliberate choice to come to America. Personally, I find these comments hard to believe and yet disturbing because I greatly admire both Kennan and Wilson. To me these men represent all that is best in American thought. I always listen to what they have to say and nearly always find merit in their words. Yet I believe that their harsh judgments on America are unwarranted.

Why would such thoughtful people give up on America? I believe it is a matter of perspective. Wilson and Kennan belong to what Wilson himself calls a "pocket of the past." They represent the old professional class, which provided America its dedicated doctors, diplomats, lawyers, professors, clergymen and writers. They have a vision of America that is not easily reconciled with what one reads in daily newspapers or sees on television.

They are deeply patriotic men. Their idea of patriotism, as once expressed by Albert Camus, is the devotion to the ideal of what their country might be. And this is the problem.

They compare American reality with the America of their dreams and bemoan the gap. They lament what has not been done and miss what has. Mesmerized by a dream, they cannot be happy with reality. Their concept of America is Utopian.

What matters, however, is not that America falls short of its promise, but that it continually strives toward that promise. That is the American genius. There is something to be said for the American belief, some would call it naiveté, that if you keep trying, things will get better.

I can say that even in the short two decades that I have been here America has indeed changed for the better. Take, for example, the progress made on the issue of race relations, which seemed to tear the country apart during the '60s. Who would have thought then in the midst of all the acrimonious debate, the agitated demonstrations and the exploding cities that within just two decades Jesse Jackson would carry Virginia and be a credible candidate for the Democratic nomination for president? Or that thousands of blacks would be elected officials throughout the country, particularly in the South?

America never ceases to evolve. It is an ever-improving, ever-improvising process. Mostly, it is muddling through. Things are never really neat and orderly, but always changing.

No other country changes as fast and as much as America. Even the complexion of its own people changes. The French and the Japanese essentially have remained French and Japanese throughout their histories. So have the Indians and Chinese. Not so with Americans. They let people of all kinds and colors come to their shores. Just imagine: In a

mere half-century, America will no longer be a country of white majority.

And the melting pot not only remakes the immigrant, it also re-   13
shapes the country. New generations of immigrants bring vitality. The
fresh new stream keeps the old water from stagnating. That is America's
unique strength. No other country attracts the best and the brightest
from all over the world. What's more, even the wretched, tired and
poor—those who come risking their lives—gratefully repay this country with their hard work and dedication.

Currently the Asians are remaking the country much the same way   14
that the Europeans once did. I look to them and their offspring—those
who populate spelling bees and win Westinghouse science scholarships—when I envision America's future greatness.

In their zeal to reshape their lives in this land of opportunity, these   15
immigrants are reshaping American destiny far beyond the comprehension of most Americans. They have come here endowed with cultural
heritages and traditions that date back thousands of years. These Asians
may come empty-handed, but not empty-headed. They value entrepreneurship, hard work, family solidarity and community—traits we
particularly need in these troubled times when, we are told, America is
in decline.

Despite all of its ills—the crime, the drugs, the social promiscuity   16
and the homelessness—I do not see contemporary America as a tragic
country. On the contrary, I see it as a triumphant nation that has
provided an unprecedentedly high standard of living and freedom of
expression to the majority of its heterogeneous people.

No other country has done it on the vast American scale. It has   17
made the "good life" possible even for the common man. It gives him
a chance to make something of his life by liberating him from the
crushing burden of poverty plaguing most of the world. Any country
that can do that within just 200 years of its formation should not be
called tragic.

Most Americans take their good fortune for granted. I don't. I know   18
better. I am from the old world, where they still see America as the
promised land.


## Review Questions

1. According to Gandhi, Kennan and Wilson, two "deeply patriotic men," are
   pessimistic about America. Why?
2. Why does Gandhi have a difficult time accepting the negative assessments
   of Kennan and Wilson?
3. The racial complexion of America is changing, says Gandhi. How so?

4. "Most Americans take their good fortune for granted." Gandhi does not. Why?

## Discussion and Writing Suggestions

1. According to Albert Camus, patriotism "is the devotion to the ideal of what [a] country might be." What do you believe America "might be," even with its problems?
2. "Some would call it naiveté, [but Americans believe] that if you keep trying, things will get better." Do you agree with this statement? Do you find evidence that Americans are trying to improve? What in your view needs improving?
3. "The fresh new stream [of immigrants] keeps the old water from stagnating." What does Gandhi mean here? What is your reaction?
4. Gandhi sees triumph, not tragedy, in American life. Kennan and Wilson see tragedy. How do you reconcile these vastly different points of view? With whom do you agree?
5. In paragraph 10, Gandhi discusses strides made in race relations in this country. Given the Los Angeles riots of 1992, can you agree with Gandhi? What, in your view, is the state of race relations in this country? How does your view square with what you regard to be the "promise" of America?

# The Contradictions of an Advanced Capitalist State

## JAMES Q. WILSON

*The editors of* Forbes *called on James Q. Wilson (b. 1931), along with ten other distinguished writers and academics, to answer this question: If things are so good, why do we feel so bad? Bringing a political perspective to bear on the issue, Wilson argues that life in a society such as ours is bound to be messy—that, in fact, there is no system of government that does a better job in assuring its citizens prosperity, freedom, and democracy. Wilson acknowledges America's problems. As a political scientist whose main work has been in the areas of crime and police, he is supremely aware of the problems that beset our country—in urban centers especially. Still, says Wilson, Americans should "cheer up" and stop being so grumpy. Perhaps you will agree.*

*Wilson earned his Ph.D. from the University of Chicago in 1959. He teaches at the Graduate School of Management at the University of California and has written numerous books and articles, including* Varieties of Police Behavior

"The Contradictions of an Advanced Capitalist State" by James Q. Wilson from *Forbes*, September 14, 1992, pp. 110–118.

*(1968),* American Government: Institutions and Policies *(1980), and (with Robert J. Herrnstein)* Crime and Human Nature *'1985). He has chaired the National Advisory Council for Drug Abuse Prevention and has served as a member of the U.S. Attorney's Task Force on Violent Crime.*

Karl Marx thought that the contradictions of capitalism were the inevi-   1
tability of declining profits and exhausted markets. He got it only
slightly wrong: Those turned out to be the problems of *communist*
states. The problems of advanced capitalist, democratic societies are not
economic at all, they are political and cultural.

The U.S. has pursued happiness with greater determination and   2
more abundant success than any other nation in history. For 45 years it
waged, with steady resolve and remarkable forbearance, a Cold War that
preserved the security of the Western world without sacrificing its
liberty in the process. So remarkable has been our achievement that
millions of people from every corner of the globe have come here to be
part of America. And what have they found? A nation of grumpy
citizens, convinced that their country, or at least its government, has
gone to hell in a hand basket.

More Americans today than at any time since the late 1950s say   3
that they distrust the people who manage their affairs: Around 75%
believe that they have little or no confidence in the government.

Part of this grumpiness reflects the recent recession. As we recover   4
from those bad times, we will recover a bit from our bad mood. But only
a bit. The decline in popular confidence did not begin with the recession,
or the Bush Administration, or Watergate or Vietnam; it began in the
early 1960s and has been going, with only occasional and modest
upticks, ever since. Whatever irritates us, it has been irritating us for a
long time.

Politicians can take some solace in the fact that the decline in   5
confidence has not been limited to government but has affected virtually
every major institution in our society, especially corporations and labor
unions. But it is little solace: We don't vote for corporate officials; we
do vote for governmental ones.

Before trying to explain why the public is so grumpy now, I think   6
it worth asking why they were so euphoric before. Maybe low public
confidence in government is the norm and the high confidence that
existed in the 1950s was the aberration. It's not hard to imagine why
we felt so good then. We had just waged, with great success, an
immensely popular war for a manifestly good cause; at the end of the
war we were indisputably Top Nation, with a currency that was the
world's standard, a productive capacity that was unrivaled, export markets that took everything we produced and begged for more and a
monopoly on the atom bomb.

My guess is that Americans have usually been suspicious of their 7
politicians and that the Eisenhower-era euphoria was unusual, perhaps
unprecedented. I'd like to believe that because I find it troubling that
Americans might normally be so silly as to think they could always trust
officials in Washington to do the right thing.

But even if we discount the slide on the grounds that we were 8
overdue for a return to normalcy, there are features of the current anger
that strike me as more troublesome than anything we can attribute to
the post-Ike hangover.

One is the condition of our inner cities. It is not just that they are 9
centers of unemployment, high crime rates, school dropouts and drug
abuse; that has, alas, always been the case. Today, however, the problems seem more pervasive, more widespread and more threatening than
in the past. Once there were bad neighborhoods to be avoided; elsewhere, life was, if not prosperous, at least orderly. Today the signs of
decay seem omnipresent—panhandlers and graffiti are everywhere,
senseless shootings can occur anywhere and drug use has penetrated
even the best schools.

To cope with these problems in the past we have relied on the 10
schools and the police. But today that reliance seems misplaced; the
schools don't teach students, the police can't maintain order.

Indeed, the government as a whole seems to be out of control. It has 11
a huge peacetime deficit at which politicians feebly gesture; the number
of interest groups besieging Congress has risen tenfold since 1960; we
are entertained by the prospect of legislators easily writing bad checks
when many ordinary folk find it impossible to write good ones; everybody knows that the nation faces serious problems, but the only issue
on which Congress has been able to break out of its policy gridlock has
been doling out favors to the savings and loan industry; the presidential
race confronts us with the wearying spectacle of candidates exchanging
personal barbs and policy bromides.

While I think there is some exaggeration in most of these com- 12
plaints, there is much truth in all of them. To this extent the public's
grouchiness is well founded. Why do these problems exist?

There are three reasons: prosperity, freedom and democracy. 13

*Prosperity.* For a century or more, dangerous drugs have been consumed. 14
Middle-class people used opium, jazz musicians used heroin, stockbro-
kers sniffed cocaine. But starting in the 1960s, these drugs moved out
of the elite markets and entered the mass market. The reason was that
the nation had become prosperous enough so that ordinary people
could afford them. The discovery of crack cocaine in the early 1980s
brought that drug within the reach of almost everyone. Everybody
knows that drug addicts often steal to support their habits. What most

people don't know is that today many addicts do not have to steal to do this; they can get by on the strength of part-time jobs, family support and public aid.

The inner city has always been a haven for criminals who could take advantage of its anonymity, disorder and low-cost housing. So long as they had to search out their victims on foot, the victims were neighbors. The availability of cheap automobiles put everyone within reach of burglars and robbers. As these offenders began to share in the general prosperity, they were able to replace fists with guns and cheap Saturday-night specials with modern semiautomatic weapons. 15

We have always had youth gangs in our cities, but even as late as the 1950s they were armed, if at all, with knives. When I was growing up in southern California, a dangerous gang was one whose members had made zip guns out of lengths of tubing taped to crude wooden stocks and loaded, one round per gun, with .22-caliber bullets. Today many gangs can afford Uzis, MAC-10s and 9mm pistols. 16

All of these changes should have been anticipated because there is no way to confine prosperity to law-abiding people only. The extraordinary standard of living that makes Americans the envy of much of the world extends to the criminal as well as the noncriminal; the rising tide has, indeed, lifted all boats, including those carrying pirates. 17

What frustrates many Americans, I think, is that their hard-earned prosperity was supposed to produce widespread decency. They had been taught to believe that if you went to school, worked hard, saved your money, bought a home and raised a family, you would enjoy the good life. About this they were right. But they also thought that if most people acted this way their communities would improve. About this they were not right. What produced the good life for individuals did not produce it for cities. 18

The reason is that prosperity enabled people to move to the kinds of towns Americans have always wanted to live in—small, quiet and nice. As the middle class moved out to the suburbs they took with them the system of informal social controls that had once helped maintain order in the central cities. As employers noticed that their best workers were now living outside these cities, they began moving their offices, stores and factories to the periphery. 19

Prosperity not only enhanced the purchasing power of urban criminals, it deprived them of the legitimate jobs that had once existed as alternatives to crime and it emancipated them from the network of block clubs, PTAS and watchful neighbors that are the crucial partners of the police. 20

As we Americans got better off individually, our cities got worse off collectively. This was probably inevitable. But it left us feeling angry and cheated. 21

*Freedom.* Freedom in the last 30 years has undergone an extraordinary 22 expansion in at least two ways. The powers exercised by the institutions of social control have been constrained and people, especially young people, have embraced an ethos that values self-expression over self-control. The constraints can be found in laws, court rulings and interest-group pressure; the ethos is expressed in the unprecedented grip that the youth culture has on popular music and entertainment.

One should not exaggerate these constraints. The police, for exam- 23 ple, must now follow much more elaborate procedures in stopping, arresting and questioning suspects. This is burdensome, but it is not clear that it has materially reduced their ability to solve crimes or arrest criminals. Most homicides, robberies and burglaries are solved because there is eyewitness testimony or physical evidence; confessions are not typically the critical determinant of a successful prosecution. An important exception involves consensual crimes, such as drug dealing. Lacking a victim or a witness, many prosecutions depend on undercover drug purchases or overheard conversations, and what can be purchased or overheard is now far more tightly regulated.

These constraints have become particularly restrictive with respect 24 to the police's ability to maintain order. Gangs, vagrants, panhandlers, rowdy teenagers and graffiti painters were once held in check by curb-side justice: threats, rousts and occasional beatings. Today the threats are emptier, the rousts rarer, the beatings forbidden. In many places vagrancy and public drunkenness have been decriminalized. In cities where the police kicked or arrested graffiti painters they now must organize graffiti paint-out campaigns.

Many of the same restraints have reduced the authority of the 25 schools. Disorderly pupils can still be expelled, but now with much greater difficulty than once was the case. The pressure to pass students without demanding much of them has intensified. As the freedom of students has grown, that of teachers has shrunk. The immense bureaucratic burdens on classroom teachers have deprived them of both time and power, with the result that they have both less time in which to teach and less authority with which to make teaching possible.

The expansion in personal freedom has been accompanied by a deep 26 distrust of custodial institutions. The mentally ill were deinstitutional-ized in the belief that they would fare better in community mental health clinics than in remote asylums, but there weren't enough clinics to treat the patients, the patients were not compelled to enter the clinics and their families were unequipped to deal with them. The mentally ill and the drug dependent now constitute a majority, it is estimated, of homeless adults on the streets.

*Democracy.* Americans have two chief complaints about our govern-  27
ment. One is that it seems unable or unwilling to cope adequately with
the costs of prosperity and the darker side of freedom. The other is that
it has not managed to extend that prosperity and freedom to everyone.
These two views are not in principle incompatible, but many Americans
suspect that in practice they are. That is one reason, I think, that race
relations are, at least rhetorically, so bad. Whites think the government
is too tolerant of crime, gangs, drug abuse and disorderly behavior;
blacks think it is too preoccupied with law and order and not concerned
enough with ending racism and widening opportunities. Public reaction
to the Los Angeles riots expressed that tension.

But even if that tension did not exist, it is not clear that democracy,  28
American style, could effectively meet popular expectations. Those
expectations are that government should be nonintrusive and have a
balanced budget; spend more money on education, health care, crime
control and environmental protection; strike the right balance between
liberty and order; and solve the problems of racism, drug abuse, school
failures and senseless violence.

I am not making this up. Every poll that I know of taken over the  29
last few decades shows that large majorities think that the federal
government taxes too heavily and spends too little, that deficit financing
is wrong, and that Washington should solve problems that no state or
local government has been able to solve.

If people are asked how the government can reconcile more spend-  30
ing, lower taxes and a balanced budget, the answer they give is clear:
Eliminate waste, fraud and mismanagement. That no amount of waste
reduction, fraud detection and bureaucratic reorganization can possibly
achieve this reconciliation seems beside the point.

Now, a strong, decisive government might cut through the rhetoric  31
and actually make the "tough choices" of which Americans are so fond
(provided, of course, that the tough choices gore someone else's ox). But
democracy, American style, does not lend itself to making tough
choices. The reason is simple: the Constitution of the United States.

That Constitution was written not to make governing easy but to  32
make it hard; not to facilitate choices but to impede them; not to
empower leaders but to frustrate them. The constitutions, written and
unwritten, of European democracies are very different: They were designed to allow the government to govern, subject only to the periodic
checks of a popular election. Here, popular participation is encouraged;
there, it is discouraged. Here, the courts can overturn presidential and
congressional actions; there, they cannot. Here, many officials have the
power to say "no" and none has the power to say "yes" and make it
stick; there, a prime minister can say "yes" and make it stick.

European democracies are designed to be run by leaders like Ross  33

Perot. Of course, abroad no one like Ross Perot would have a chance of becoming a leader, because the system for picking officials is designed to insure that only insiders and never outsiders have a chance at grabbing the golden ring. Candidates for office in England and Europe are chosen by party managers, guaranteeing that only people acceptable to the managers can be nominated. Candidates in the U.S. are picked by people attending caucuses, voting in primaries and signing petitions, creating the possibility for candidates detested by party managers to become party nominees.

This system for making policy and choosing candidates creates quite [34] predictable results, and among them are the very things that so many Americans find distasteful about politics.

Politicians, knowing that party leaders are powerless, run personal [35] campaigns stressing media images and relying on personal attacks. Knowing that money is essential to politics and that party leaders don't have much, candidates raise funds from individuals and interest groups. Aware that a primary campaign is the most important campaign, incumbents look for ways to discourage challengers from appearing.

Once in office, politicians know that it is their personal visibility and [36] not their party's slogans that affect their chances of staying in office. Accordingly, they organize the Congress so that all members will have large staffs, all members will be able to introduce high-profile bills (even if many are doomed to defeat) and as many members as possible will have a chance to chair a committee or subcommittee. When a bill is passed, it is in everyone's interest to insure that it contains something for every important constituency; if the result is confusion or contradiction, the bureaucracy can be left with the task of sorting things out. When the bureaucracy can't sort it out—when it can't both build highways and make it easy for people to go to court to block highway construction—Congress and the White House can blame the mess on "the bureaucrats" and promise that heads will be knocked and names taken.

In making policy in a highly participatory system, officials will have [37] no incentive to say that the government shouldn't tackle a problem or doesn't know how to solve it and every incentive to claim that government must "do something" and that they know just what to do. As a result, we have crime bills that don't reduce crime, drug abuse bills that don't curb drug abuse, education bills that don't improve learning and disability insurance that can't define "disability." The more such things are done, the more interest groups will have an incentive to organize lobbying efforts and open offices in Washington. The more such offices are opened, the more pressure there will be for more bills and the smaller the chances that any given bill will make much sense.

What Americans don't see is a constitutional system at work in an [38] era of big government and mass participation; what they do see are the things that they don't like about politics.

They see interminable, expensive, attack-based campaigns. They   39
don't see the fact that campaigns would be very short (about two months), much less expensive and (perhaps) less attack-based if we didn't have primary elections or caucuses, if party managers picked candidates and if candidates had to run defending a party record.

They see special-interest groups proliferating. They don't see that   40
these organizations are simply the most visible form of popular participation in government, participation that cannot be extended to individuals without also extending it to groups, and they don't see that having many interests is a *result*, not the cause, of big government.

They see American politicians accused of lying, corruption and   41
self-dealing. They don't see the lying, corruption and self-dealing in parliamentary regimes, and they don't see it because there are not in those places the checks and balances and incessant rivalries of American-style democracy that provide politicians with an incentive to expose such misconduct.

They see a government that cannot solve the critical problems of   42
our time. They don't see that no other free government has solved those critical problems, either. European democracies run big deficits (often they are, relative to GNP, bigger than ours), are equally baffled by youth disorders and drug abuse and have made even less progress in combatting racism.

What, a citizen may ask, do we get out of all of this confusion,   43
pettiness, incompetence and gridlock?

Prosperity, freedom and democracy.   44

Cheer up, Americans. You are right to be grumpy, but there is no   45
system for governing a large, free and complex society such as ours that is likely to do much better or make you less grumpy. If you don't believe it, travel.

On your travels you will meet countless people who want to know   46
how to immigrate to the U.S. You will discover that our standard of living, in purchasing power equivalents, is the highest in the world. You will discover that among the larger democracies, our tax rates are the lowest in the world. You can talk to conservative leaders in England, Germany and Sweden who will speak enviously of a nation, America, that has managed to keep the economic burden of social welfare programs so small. (Relatively small, anyway.) American environmental regulations, though sometimes poorly designed and badly administered, set the standard for most of the world.

If you get arrested abroad, you will appreciate the constraints on the   47

American police. The Swiss and the Swedes may strike you as civilized people, and they are, but I would not advise you to provoke the police in Geneva or Stockholm.

If it irritates you that members of Congress pay themselves so much **48** and have such large staffs, try getting your problems solved by a member of the British House of Commons or the French Chamber of Deputies. You will discover that those skilled debaters and bright intellects can't really do very much for you. As individuals, they don't have much power. And not having much power, it stands to reason that they won't be able to vote themselves big salaries or large staffs. If you don't want your legislators to have many perks, strip them of their power—which necessarily includes the power to help you.

And when you get home, look up the public opinion polls that **49** compare how Americans feel about their country and its institutions with how many Europeans feel about theirs. By then you may not be surprised to learn that Americans have much more confidence in their institutions, public and private, than Germans, Frenchmen or Spaniards have in theirs. And you may not be surprised to learn that by majorities of roughly two-to-one Americans are more inclined than many Europeans to say that they are very proud to be citizens of their country and willing, if necessary, to fight for it.

## Review Questions

1. According to Wilson, "what produced a good life for individuals did not produce it for cities." Why not?
2. What problems have followed from laws that have increasingly restrained police and teachers from dealing roughly with disorderly people?
3. In what ways does the Constitution incline the federal government *not* to make tough choices?
4. What is the "contradiction" to which Wilson refers in the title of his article? (See also Discussion and Writing Suggestion 1, below.)
5. Wilson says that Americans should "cheer up." Why?

## Discussion and Writing Suggestions

1. To answer Review Question 4, you will need to read carefully, for nowhere does the author directly state: "This is the contradiction of advanced capitalism." To answer the question, you will need to develop a structural sense of the article—a sense of where the main message lies and how Wilson sets it up. As you search for the "contradiction," keep a record of your search, and then compare that record with those of your classmates.
2. Wilson suggests that we "cheer up." Does his argument, extended, become an argument for complacency? That is, if our present messy system is as good as we're likely to get, should we consider *not* expending the effort to reform

the system, even if it produces "confusion, pettiness, incompetence, and gridlock"?

3. In his final five paragraphs, Wilson sets the current grumpiness of Americans in an international, political context. What is your response to these paragraphs? Do they, as Wilson surely intended, cheer you up at all?

4. To what extent have you observed, like Wilson, the negative effects of taking authority away from teachers and police (see paragraphs 22–25)? Presumably, the authority has been restricted in order to protect the rights of the people with whom teachers and police come into contact. Do you feel that our society has adequately balanced the rights of the individual, on the one hand, and the need to maintain public order, on the other? Develop your response to these questions in a brief essay.

5. Write an account that illustrates your experience with the "confusion, pettiness, incompetence, [or] gridlock" that Wilson claims is inherent in our system of government.

6. Do you detect Wilson relying on stereotypes at any point in his argument? If so, identify these and comment.

7. Reread paragraphs 14–21. What is your reaction to Wilson's discussion of prosperity?


# A De-moralized Society?

## GERTRUDE HIMMELFARB

*The editors of* Forbes *called on Gertrude Himmelfarb, along with ten other distinguished writers and academics, to answer this question: If things are so good, why do we feel so bad? A historian, Himmelfarb sets key issues of this chapter in relation to another era: Victorian England and nineteenth-century America, where moral concerns were a matter of both public debate and government policy. Things today appear bad, says Himmelfarb, because they are bad—morally, that is. Our nation has lost its moral bearing (a lament you will recall Jimmy Carter making). If that bearing is to be corrected, who will set the course? That is, if you agree with Himmelfarb (as many do), to whom can we look to set a moral agenda for America? How can we be sure that this agenda would not abrogate the rights of those who might disagree? How would we teach, and enforce, such an agenda? The questions are many, and they are difficult. (Note that Himmelfarb does not suggest an agenda.)*

*Gertrude Himmelfarb (b. 1922) attended the Jewish Theological Seminary and earned her Ph.D. in history from the University of Chicago in 1950.*

Excerpts from "A De-moralized Society" by Gertrude Himmelfarb from *Forbes*, September 14, 1992, pp. 120–128.

*Aside from her distinguished career as a professor of history at the Graduate School of the City College of New York, Himmelfarb has been a council member of the National Endowment for the Humanities, has served on the council of scholars at the Library of Congress, and is a member of learned societies in England and America. She has won numerous awards and honors, including a Woodrow Wilson Center fellowship and the distinction of delivering the Jefferson Lecture in 1991. Himmelfarb has written seven major books, including* Victorian Minds *(1968),* The Idea of Poverty *(1984), and* The New History and the Old *(1987). She also contributes to scholarly journals and to mainstream publications, such as* Forbes.

Why, we are asked, if things are so good, do we think that they are so 1
bad? The short answer is that we think they are bad because they *are* bad. Indeed, they may be worse than we think.

We think, for example, and quite rightly, that unemployment is bad. 2
But unemployment, and the state of the economy in general, is only part of the problem, and, perhaps, the least part of it. Most of the unemployed will find employment. They will also find themselves saddled with a host of other problems that may be less immediately, personally urgent, but that are no less serious and troubling because they are more permanent and intractable.

I am not talking about the "malaise" that was bandied about in the 3
Carter Administration, a bit of psychobabble referring to an emotional, inchoate species of discontent—"alienation," "anomie" or whatever other modish term was current at the time. I am talking of the justified discontent of the responsible citizen who discovers that economic and material goods are no compensation for social and moral ills.

A hundred and fifty years ago, while his contemporaries were 4
debating "the standard of living question"—whether the standard of living of the working class had improved or declined in those early decades of industrialism—Thomas Carlyle reformulated the issue to read, "the condition of England question." That question, he insisted, could not be resolved by citing "figures of arithmetic" about wages and prices, earnings and expenditures. What was important was the "condition" and "disposition" of the poor: their beliefs and feelings, their sense of right and wrong, the attitudes and habits that would dispose them either to a "wholesome composure, frugality and prosperity," or to an "acrid unrest, recklessness, gin-drinking and gradual ruin."

We do not use such language today, to our great loss. We are more 5
comfortable adding up "figures of arithmetic" than analyzing or judging "conditions" and "dispositions." Those figures provide fodder for "pessimists" and "optimists" alike, the former concluding that recessions are an inevitable feature of the economy and that the living standards of the poor, if not of the rich, are in a permanent state of decline; the latter that

the present recession is temporary and that in the long run the poor as well as the rich will benefit from a productive, expanding economy. But if the debate were enlarged to include the question of condition and disposition, some of us might find ourselves in the awkward position of being economic optimists and at the same time moral pessimists. Indeed, we might be all the more pessimistic because we would be deprived of the comforting view that a sound economy is necessarily conducive to a sound society. We might even be inclined to reverse that formula, to entertain the possibility that a sound society is the precondition for a sound economy.

In fact there are "figures of arithmetic" bearing upon moral and **6** social issues as well as economic and material ones. Victorians called these "social statistics"—statistics relating to religion, education, literacy, pauperism, crime, vagrancy, drunkenness, illegitimacy. These statistics were meant to elucidate the "condition of England question": the moral, spiritual, cultural and intellectual state of the poor in particular and of the country as a whole. We no longer use the term, but we too have social statistics, in a quantity and degree of precision that would have been the envy of the Victorians.

Our social statistics are far more depressing than those produced by **7** the supposedly "dismal science" of economics. There are, to be sure, some brave souls, inveterate optimists, who try to put the best gloss on them. But they are hard put to counteract the overwhelming evidence on the negative side.

It is not much consolation to be informed that the high rate of **8** divorce is partly compensated for by a moderate rate of remarriage, since no degree of remarriage nullifies the fact of divorce, which itself testifies to an unstable marital and family life. Nor is it reassuring to be told that a greater proportion of Americans enjoy a higher education than do most other nationalities, if that higher education is higher in name alone—indeed if it is intellectually lower than ever before, and lower than that of other nationalities. Nor that elementary school children today have computer skills that their college-educated parents lack, if they have to use those skills to correct primitive spelling mistakes or to be instructed in the multiplication tables. Nor that more cassettes and CDs are sold than ever before, if more of them spew out hard rock music or soft (or hard) pornographic rap. Nor that heroin addiction may be decreasing, if crack-cocaine addiction is increasing. Nor that the white illegitimacy rate is considerably lower than the black illegitimacy rate, if both rates are rapidly increasing. Nor that middle-class blacks are faring better, materially and socially, than ever before, if a considerable and growing black "underclass" is faring so much worse that it is becoming a permanent "outcaste" class.

For a long time Americans found it hard to face up to such depress- **9** ing facts, even when they appeared in the hard guise of statistics. Instead we expended much ingenuity in "decoding" these statistics—qualifying, modifying, interpreting, explaining them, in the hope that we could explain them away. We could not confront them candidly because it was, and is, part of the liberal ethos—the prevailing American ethos— that such disagreeable things should not, and therefore could not, be happening. They violate the idea of progress that is so much a part of that ethos: the idea that material and moral progress are the necessary by-products of a free society, an expanding economy, a mobile social structure, a diverse and highly accessible system of public education and an even more diverse and accessible popular culture.

Those statistics also go against the grain of our ethos in being so **10** "moralistic." While it is generally assumed that moral progress goes hand in hand with material progress, this assumption is rarely made explicit, because moral concepts, still more moral judgments, are understood to be somehow undemocratic and unseemly. We pride ourselves on being liberated from such retrograde Victorian notions. And they were, indeed, an important part of the Victorian ethos. In 19th-century America, as in England, morality was not only a natural part of social discourse; it was a conscious part of social policy, the test of any legislative or administrative reform being its effect upon the character as well as material welfare of those affected.

Today we have so completely rejected that Victorian ethos that we **11** deliberately, systematically, divorce morality from social policy. In the current climate of moral relativism and skepticism, it is thought improper to impose any moral conditions or requirements upon the beneficiaries of the public largesse—not only upon welfare recipients but upon artists and other free spirits seeking grants from the National Endowment for the Arts. Such conditions are regarded as infringements of freedom (even, some have argued, of the First Amendment), as an arrogant usurpation of authority (who are we to decide what is moral and what is not?) and as an intolerable imposition of bourgeois, patriarchal, archaic "values."

We are now confronting the consequences of this policy of moral **12** "neutrality." Having made the most valiant attempt to "objectify" the problems of poverty, criminality, illiteracy, illegitimacy and the like,* we are discovering that the economic and social aspects of these problems are inseparable from the moral and psychological ones. And hav-

---

*The National Center on Health Statistics informs us that "illegitimacy" is no longer acceptable, being derogatory and old-fashioned. The preferred term is "nonmarital childbearing."

ing made the most determined effort to devise remedies that are "value-free," we find that these policies imperil the material, as well as the moral, well-being of their intended beneficiaries—and not only of individuals but of society as a whole. We have, in short, so succeeded in "de-moralizing," as the Victorians would say, social policy—divorcing it from any moral criteria, requirements, even expectations—that we have "demoralized," in the more familiar sense, society itself.

This is our present "malaise." There is nothing sentimental or utopian about it; it is not the product of an exacerbated sensibility, or romantic aspiration, or yearning for personal "fulfillment." Nor is there anything fanciful about our fears and grievances; indeed, there is something fanciful in the attempts to deny them. We have, in fact, as individuals and as a society, good reason for alarm. **13**

It is this "condition" of society, this "disposition" of the people, as Carlyle would have said, that liberal intellectuals cannot credit or appreciate. They can sympathize with the sentimental idea of "malaise," but not with the realistic one. They do not understand the anxieties of those who believe that the "social order" (the very term seems to them archaic) is in an acute state of disorder, that the "moral order" (another archaic term) is de-moralized, or that the "legal order" has abdicated responsibility for law and order. They are contemptuous of "philistines," as they see them, who are less than respectful of an "art community" that flaunts its contempt for ordinary people while demanding to be subsidized by them. They have no misgivings about a "sexual revolution" that has legitimized every form of sexual behavior and has made all "lifestyles" equal before the law, before society, even, some claim, before God. They have, in short, divorced themselves not only from conventional morality but also from all those conventional people who still adhere to that morality. **14**

. . .

This is the challenge that confronts us. Families, churches, communities cannot operate in isolation, cannot long maintain values at odds with those endorsed by the state and popularized by the culture. The task is critical and difficult. It is to restore a polity that reflects and supports the values implicit in the very idea of a social, a legal and a moral "order"—a federalist polity, in which local and state governments assume responsibility for some of the controversial issues that confront us. . . . **15**

Even a modest restoration would be significant—a return not, as some fear, to a long-since-discarded puritanism but only to the *status quo ante*—*ante* the excesses and excrescences of the most recent decades. Only then can we hope to overcome our present state of "acrid unrest, **16** recklessness, gin-drinking, and gradual ruin," and attain that "whole-some composure, frugality, and prosperity" that Carlyle understood to be the disposition of a healthy society.

## Review Questions

1. Himmelfarb believes that over the last few decades America has become a "de-moralized" society. What does she mean?
2. In paragraphs 3 and 13–14, Himmelfarb draws a distinction between "justified discontent" and the term "malaise," which was current during the Carter years (see the "malaise" speech, page 396). What is this distinction?
3. Why have liberals had a hard time accepting the truth of depressing social statistics?
4. How public a part of the social and legal fabric was morality in Victorian England and in nineteenth-century America?
5. Reread paragraphs 9–11 and 14, and summarize the liberal position on morality. What are the consequences of this position?

## Discussion and Writing Suggestions

1. Himmelfarb suggests that a sound economy may not, in itself, ensure a moral society. (See paragraphs 5 and 9.) What is your view on the relationship between economic and moral well-being?
2. Reread paragraphs 7 and 8, and explain their rhetorical force. How does Himmelfarb use paragraph 7 to set up the paragraph that follows? How is paragraph 8 structured? Examine its sentence patterns; look—here and in the previous paragraph—for a topic sentence. Do these paragraphs persuade you that America's social statistics are depressing?
3. In paragraph 3, Himmelfarb makes a disparaging reference to "psychobabble" in the Carter administration. Himmelfarb is revealing a point of view here. What is this point of view? If you have read Carter's "malaise" speech, would you characterize it as Himmelfarb has?
4. In your view, does government—federal, state, or local—have a role to play in setting a moral tone for this country? Should government (including public education) be morally neutral—that is, no attempt to teach values? Develop your answer into a brief essay.
5. In paragraph 14, you read that Himmelfarb believes our social, moral, and legal order to be in severe disrepair. Do you agree?
6. In her conclusion, Himmelfarb calls for a restoration of "values implicit in the very idea of a social, a legal and a moral 'order' " (paragraph 15). What might these values be? That is, if one wants to live in a culture (a moral, legal, and social universe), what values must one endorse?
7. Study Himmelfarb's use of Victorian England in this article. Why does she refer to the Victorians as often as she does? How apt are the references? How does she use them in her argument?
8. Accept Himmelfarb's position for a moment. If morality is to become an

important part of public and legal discourse again (and there is some evidence that it has—witness the talk of "family values" in the 1992 presidential campaign), then who is to decide which values should be endorsed and which ones suppressed? By what process would these decisions be made?

9. Himmelfarb does not set a specific moral agenda for America in this selection, although she argues that one is needed. Speculate on why she chose not to explain her solutions to the problems she raises.

## Bill Clinton's Inaugural Address

*Bill Clinton, born in Hope, Arkansas, on August 19, 1946, took the oath of office as president of the United States on January 20, 1993. Considered a long shot within his own party, then-Governor Clinton (of Arkansas) began his campaign for the democratic nomination and the right to oppose George Bush by talking about the need for change. Indeed, change became the watchword of the campaign as Clinton gained momentum and finally won the nomination, arguing that recent Republican stewardship of government had generated a false prosperity built on huge deficits. Clinton tapped into the electorate's anger that the country, facing troubled times, was ill served by politicians more concerned with reelection than with reinvigorating the economy. In his inaugural address, Clinton argues that Americans should reject cynicism and embrace the belief that a people united can make the country flourish.*

*Any inaugural is an attempt to set an agenda and a mood for the country. As you read this speech, you might identify and reflect on Clinton's agenda and the mood he would set. Doubtless, you will find in the speech an optimism not generally shared by other writers in this chapter. But Clinton is optimistic. Widely admired as a policy expert, he is better versed than most on the problems besetting this country; but he refuses to see America as defeated. As he says in his address, "There is nothing wrong with America that cannot be cured by what is right with America."*

My fellow citizens, today we celebrate the mystery of American renewal. 1

This ceremony is held in the depth of winter. But, by the words we speak and the faces we show the world, we force the spring. A spring reborn in the world's oldest democracy, that brings forth the vision and courage to reinvent America. 2

When our founders boldly declared America's independence to the world and our purposes to the Almighty, they knew that America, to endure, would have to change. 3

Not change for change's sake, but change to preserve America's ideals—life, liberty, the pursuit of happiness. Though we march to the music of our time, our mission is timeless. 4

Each generation of Americans must define what it means to be an   5
American.

On behalf of our nation, I salute my predecessor, President Bush for   6
his half-century of service to America.

And I thank the millions of men and women whose steadfastness   7
and sacrifice triumphed over depression, fascism and communism.

Today, a generation raised in the shadows of the Cold War assumes   8
new responsibilities in a world warmed by the sunshine of freedom but
threatened still by ancient hatreds and new plagues.

Raised in unrivaled prosperity, we inherit an economy that is still   9
the world's strongest but is weakened by business failures, stagnant
wages, increasing inequality, and deep divisions among our people.

When George Washington first took the oath I have just sworn to   10
uphold, news traveled slowly across the land by horseback and across
the ocean by boat. Now, the sights and sounds of this ceremony are
broadcast instantaneously to billions around the world.

Communications and commerce are global; investment is mobile;   11
technology is almost magical; and ambition for a better life is now
universal. We earn our livelihood in peaceful competition with people
all across the earth.

Profound and powerful forces are shaking and remaking our world,   12
and the urgent question of our time is whether we can make change our
friend and not our enemy.

This new world has already enriched the lives of millions of Ameri-   13
cans who are able to compete and win in it. But when most people are
working harder for less; when others cannot work at all; when the cost
of health care devastates families and threatens to bankrupt many of our
enterprises, great and small; when fear of crime robs law-abiding citizens
of their freedom; and when millions of poor children cannot even
imagine the lives we are calling them to lead—we have not made
change our friend.

We know we have to face hard truths and take strong steps. But we   14
have not done so. Instead, we have drifted, and that drifting has eroded
our resources, fractured our economy, and shaken our confidence.

Though our challenges are fearsome, so are our strengths. And   15
Americans have ever been a restless, questing, hopeful people. We must
bring to our task today the vision and will of those who came before
us.

From our revolution, to the Civil War, to the Great Depression, to   16
the civil rights movement, our people have always mustered the determination to construct from these crises the pillars of our history.

Thomas Jefferson believed that to preserve the very foundations of   17 our nation, we would need dramatic change from time to time. Well, my fellow citizens, this is our time. Let us embrace it.

Our democracy must be not only the envy of the world but the engine of our own renewal. There is nothing wrong with America that cannot be cured by what is right with America. **18**

And so today, we pledge an end to the era of deadlock and drift—a new season of American renewal has begun. **19**

To renew America, we must be bold. **20**

We must do what no generation has had to do before. We must invest more in our own people, in their jobs, in their future, and at the same time cut our massive debt. And we must do so in a world in which we must compete for every opportunity. **21**

It will not be easy; it will require sacrifice. But it can be done, and done fairly, not choosing sacrifice for its own sake, but for our own sake. We must provide for our nation the way a family provides for its children. **22**

Our founders saw themselves in the light of posterity. We can do no less. Anyone who has ever watched a child's eyes wander into sleep knows what posterity is. Posterity is the world to come—the world for whom we hold our ideals, from whom we have borrowed our planet, and to whom we bear sacred responsibility. **23**

We must do what America does best: Offer more opportunity to all and demand responsibility from all. **24**

It is time to break the bad habit of expecting something for nothing, from our government or from each other. Let us all take more responsibility, not only for ourselves and our families but for our communities and our country. **25**

To renew America, we must revitalize our democracy. **26**

This beautiful capital, like every capital since the dawn of civilization, is often a place of intrigue and calculation. Powerful people maneuver for position and worry endlessly about who is in and who is out, who is up and who is down, forgetting those people whose toil and sweat sends us here and pays our way. **27**

Americans deserve better, and in this city today, there are people who want to do better. And so I say to all of us here, let us resolve to reform our politics, so that power and privilege no longer shout down the voice of the people. Let us put aside personal advantage so that we can feel the pain and see the promise of America. **28**

Let us resolve to make our government a place for what Franklin Roosevelt called "bold, persistent experimentation," a government for our tomorrows, not our yesterdays. **29**

Let us give this capital back to the people to whom it belongs. **30**

To renew America, we must meet challenges abroad as well as at    31
home. There is no longer division between what is foreign and what is
domestic—the world economy, the world environment, the world
AIDS crisis, the world arms race—they affect us all.

Today, as an old order passes, the new world is more free but less    32
stable. Communism's collapse has called forth old animosities and new
dangers. Clearly, America must continue to lead the world we did so
much to make.

While America rebuilds at home, we will not shrink from the chal-    33
lenges, nor fail to seize the opportunities, of this new world. Together
with our friends and allies, we will work to shape change, lest it engulf
us.

When our vital interests are challenged, or the will and conscience    34
of the international community is defied, we will act—with peaceful
diplomacy whenever possible, with force when necessary. The brave
Americans serving our nation today in the Persian Gulf, in Somalia, and
wherever else they stand are testament to our resolve.

But our greatest strength is the power of our ideas, which are still    35
new in many lands. Across the world, we see them embraced—and we
rejoice. Our hopes, our hearts, our hands, are with those on every
continent who are building democracy and freedom. Their cause is
America's cause.

The American people have summoned the change we celebrate    36
today. You have raised your voices in an unmistakable chorus. You have
cast your votes in historic numbers. And you have changed the face of
Congress, the presidency and the political process itself. Yes, you, my
fellow Americans have forced the spring. Now, we must do the work
the season demands.

To that work I now turn, with all the authority of my office. I ask    37
the Congress to join with me. But no president, no Congress, no
government, can undertake this mission alone. My fellow Americans,
you, too, must play your part in our renewal. I challenge a new generation of young Americans to a season of service—to act on your idealism
by helping troubled children, keeping company with those in need,
reconnecting our torn communities. There is so much to be done—
enough, indeed, for millions of others who are still young in spirit to
give of themselves in service, too. In serving, we recognize a simple but
powerful truth—we need each other. And we must care for one another.

Today, we do more than celebrate America; we rededicate ourselves    38
to the very idea of America. An idea born in revolution and renewed
through two centuries of challenge. An idea tempered by the knowledge
that, but for fate, we—the fortunate and the unfortunate—might have

been each other. An idea ennobled by the faith that our nation can summon from its myriad diversity the deepest measure of unity. An idea infused with the conviction that America's long heroic journey must go forever upward.

And so, my fellow Americans, at the edge of the 21st century, **39** let us begin with energy and hope, with faith and discipline, and let us work until our work is done. The scripture says, "And let us not be weary in well-doing, for in due season, we shall reap, if we faint not."

From this joyful mountaintop of celebration, we hear a call to service **40** in the valley. We have heard the trumpets. We have changed the guard. And now, each in our way, and with God's help, we must answer the call.

Thank you and God bless you all. **41**

## Discussion and Writing Suggestions

1. Presidents use their inaugural addresses to sound the themes and to set the moods of their administrations. What are the themes and the mood of the Clinton inaugural address?

2. What is your response to this speech on reading it—or on hearing it, if you watched the inaugural ceremonies? Are you (were you) moved? Does the speech help you to feel more hopeful about your personal future? About America's future? In developing your answer, refer to the lines that helped form your impressions.

3. Clinton speaks of the "vision and courage to reinvent America." What is it about America that needs reinventing? Why does the effort take vision and courage? And how does what is "re" or "newly" invented preserve honored traditions and values in American democracy? That is, in the reinvention, what remains the same about America?

4. Examine how Clinton uses the word *change* in his inaugural address. What does he mean by the word? In what ways does Clinton suggest that change is part of the American tradition?

5. To what extent does Clinton acknowledge the problems of America, the same problems that writers like Carter, O'Rourke, Derber, Newman, Sterner, and Himmelfarb have referred to? What is Clinton's response to these problems? (See especially paragraphs 13–17.)

6. "We must provide for our nation the way a family provides for its children." How does, or should, a family provide for its children? How does this relate to the way we should "provide for our nation"? Does Clinton's analogy work for you? Explain.

7. "Spring" is an important image in this speech (see paragraphs 2, 36, 37, and 39). What does Clinton mean by his references to "spring" and "season"? Columnist and presidential observer Gary Wills commented that the image of "forcing the spring" is not consistent with the long-lasting changes that

Clinton wants to make, since "forced" flowers (grown out of season, in artificial conditions) are notoriously short lived. Your comment?

8. In paragraph 5, Clinton writes: "Each generation of Americans must define what it means to be an American." For you, what does it mean to be an American? How do you define this personally? (If you have not, why?)

9. Clinton speaks several times of sacrifice and service. How personally do you take this challenge? To what extent do you feel that it is each American's role to serve and to sacrifice for the good of the country?

# Other People's Money

JERRY STERNER

*Jerry Sterner's* Other People's Money *is a play about a hostile takeover: a business maneuver in which a person or company, called a "raider," forces the sale of another company against that (second) company's wishes. Andrew Jorgenson (Jorgy) is president of New England Wire & Cable, an eighty-one-year-old Rhode Island firm begun by Jorgenson's father. Although the production of cable and wire is no longer profitable, the company owns subsidiaries that do make money. Overall, New England's financial picture is good, so good in fact that its stock is rising. But in Manhattan, Lawrence (Larry the Liquidator) Garfinkle studies a computer analysis that gives him tips on companies ripe for raiding. Garfinkle loves money, especially other people's money. Seeing a profit to be made in New England Wire & Cable, he buys up as much stock as he can in order to gain control of the company. His plan is to close the unprofitable manufacturing division that Jorgenson oversees and that employs more than a hundred people in the local community. Andrew Jorgenson is a patriarchal figure who runs his company according to a system of values much respected in American lore: he is committed to community, trust, hard work, and building a product people can believe in. In contrast, Lawrence Garfinkle represents a newer breed of business executive, someone who makes money not by building but by seizing. He has no qualms about putting an entire division of New England Wire & Cable out of work—an entire community out of business—if this will increase the value of his own considerable holdings in the company.*

*But for Garfinkle to seize control of New England Wire & Cable, he must control 51 percent of the stock, and this he cannot do without first appealing to the stockholders at the company's annual meeting. Jorgenson also will make an appeal at this meeting. Both men want the stockholders to vote for different slates of candidates who will sit on the company's board of directors. Garfin-*

*kle's board members, if elected, will immediately close the money-losing division of New England Wire & Cable; Jorgenson's board members, if elected, will vote to keep the company open. First Jorgenson—the tall, white-haired patriarch—speaks. Then the microphone goes to Garfinkle, the slick corporate raider. In their speeches, these men present their opposing philosophies of a business' obligations to its employees and to its shareholders. One character in the play calls the takeover bid an "important story that needs to be told. It goes way beyond numbers. It's about loyalty, tradition, friendship and, of course, money."*

*The excerpt from the play begins just before the annual meeting of New England Wire & Cable, with an exchange between Kate Sullivan, attorney for Jorgenson, and Garfinkle (who, it should be added, loves donuts). Other players: Bea Sullivan, Kate's mother and a longtime assistant to Jorgenson; and William Coles, president of New England Wire & Cable, who in an earlier scene sold Garfinkle the right to vote his (Coles's) stock if Garfinkle needed it to seize control of the company. Mention is made of Ossie, an old-time friend of Jorgenson who vowed to remain a loyal shareholder.*

*Before becoming a successful playwright, Jerry Sterner devoted himself to business, eventually becoming president of a large real estate company based in Brooklyn, New York. He resigned that job in 1983 to follow his artistic impulses and write plays. His first play closed after a single performance. His next,* Other People's Money, *became a long-running sellout at an off-Broadway theater in 1989 and, subsequently, a movie starring Danny DeVito and Gregory Peck (available for rent at many video stores). Sterner attributes the inspiration for his play to the time he sold his stock in a manufacturing company to a corporate raider. The raider seized the Michigan company, shut it down, and left a community unemployed. Troubled by the development, Sterner later wrote* Other People's Money.

*Lights up on* Kate *Cross Stage.*

KATE: You bring out the best in me. 1

GARFINKLE: I know I do. Katie, me girl. 2

KATE: The Irish in me. 3

GARFINKLE: . . . Same thing. 4

KATE: What's the matter? Are you becoming melancholy on me? 5

GARFINKLE: Melancholy? Why would you say that? Just 'cause the Governor calls every hour . . . the unions are picketing my house . . . prayer meetings daily chant for my demise— 6

KATE: *(Moving toward him.)* You're in the wrong profession. You should head the U.N. Nobody can bring people together like you . . . not even a chuckle? You must really be in bad shape. Feeling unloved? 7

GARFINKLE: Unappreciated. I'm doing the right thing. I'm taking unproductive assets and making them productive. Just following the law of free enterprise economics. 8

KATE: What law is that?  9

GARFINKLE: Survival of the fittest.  10

KATE: The Charles Darwin of Wall Street  11

GARFINKLE: *(Laughing.)* . . . I like that. The Charles Darwin of Wall Street.  12

KATE: Maybe they don't see it that way. Maybe they don't see it as  13
survival of the fittest. Maybe they see it as survival of the fattest.

GARFINKLE: Aw, Katie, why are you so hard on me?  14

KATE: 'Cause you're not nice.  15

GARFINKLE: Since when do you have to be nice to be right?  16

KATE: You're not right. You're "What's happening." One day we'll smarten  17
up and pass some laws and put you out of business. Ten years from now
they'll be studying you at the Wharton School. They'll call it the "Garfinkle Era" and rinse out their mouths when they leave the room.

GARFINKLE: That's how you talk about family?  18

KATE: Family?  19

GARFINKLE: Immediate family. For every deal I find, you guys bring me ten.  20
We happen to be in bed together, lady. Calling it family, that's being
nice. Look at me, Kate.

KATE: I'm going to put you away, Garfinkle.  21

GARFINKLE: I'm not going away. They can pass all the laws they want—all  22
they do is change the rules—they can't stop the game. I don't go away.
I adapt. Look at me, Kate. Look at you. God damn it! We're the same!

KATE: We are not the same. We are not the same! We sit on opposite sides  23
here. I like where I sit. You sit in shit.

GARFINKLE: You sit with me.  24

KATE: You sit alone.  25

GARFINKLE: Alone? Get off it, will you? We've come from "Ask not what  26
your country can do for you" to "What's in it for me?" to "What's in it
for me—today!" all in one short generation. That's why those stockholders all love me and that's why you guys all work for me. Nobody's
putting a gun to anyone's head. Everybody's got their hand out.

KATE: Not everybody. Not me. Not them.  27

GARFINKLE: Forget them. It's about you and me, now, Kate. I'm the last  28
thought you have when you fall asleep at night and the first when you
wake in the morning. I make those juices flow and you know it.

KATE: Garfinkle, if you knew what you do to me you wouldn't brag about  29
it.

GARFINKLE: Bullshit. And you know what makes the two of us so special?  30
What sets us apart? We care more about the game than we do the
players. That's not bad. That's smart.

KATE: That's grotesque. Garfinkle, you don't know me at all. You're not  31
capable of knowing me. You can't see beyond your appetite.

GARFINKLE: Then what the fuck are you doing here!? You can't stay away.  32
You don't want to stay away. Come—play with me. Be a player—not

a technician. Feel the power. This is where you belong, Kate. With me. I know you. I know who you are. I like who you are. I want you, Kate.

*He reaches for her. She pulls away.*

KATE: I'm going to nail you, Garfinkle. I'm going to send you back to Wall     33
Street with donuts up your ass and everyone's going to know how some broad wet behind the ears did you. And whatever happens from this day forward, whatever successes I achieve, none—none will be sweeter than this one!

*She exits. Garfinkle, a beat after the exit, yells to her.*

GARFINKLE: You're so perfect for me! *(Turns, begins to exit.)* To be continued.     34
In Grimetown.[1]

*He exits. Lights up on Jorgenson alone in his office. Bea enters.*

BEA: Hey, good lookin', whatcha got cookin'. How's about cookin' some-     35
thing up with me?

*He smiles weakly.*

You okay?

JORGENSON: Just going over in my head what I want to say.     36

BEA: They're putting speakers out in the hallways. The auditorium won't     37
fit everyone. I feel like we're Harry and Bess on election night.

JORGENSON: Harry was a better man than me. Went to sleep election night.     38
I haven't slept good for days.

BEA: Talk to me.     39

JORGENSON: I'm scared, Bea. I'm scared time has passed us by. I'm scared I     40
don't know this new environment. I'm scared what I do know doesn't count for anything any more.

BEA: *(Moves behind him. Rubs his neck.)* I'm not scared. I'm proud. I'm proud     41
of the business we built. Most of all I'm proud of you. And if what we are counts for nothing anymore, that won't be our failing—it'll be theirs.

*He smiles. Squeezes her hand.*

It'll be all right. Just go out and tell the truth. Go out and give them hell, Harry.

*They remain frozen. Garfinkle enters. Looks at them.*

GARFINKLE: The truth? Why don't you tell the truth, lady? The truth is     42
Harry Truman is dead.

---

[1]That is, in Rhode Island, at the annual meeting of New England Wire & Cable. [Behrens and Rosen]

*Lights dim on* Bea *and* Jorgenson *though they continue visible.* Garfinkle *moves to his darkened office.* Bea *moves Downstage Center to a podium. We're at the Annual Meeting. Scene is played as if audience were the stockholders.*

BEA: That concludes the formal aspect of our Annual Meeting. The one    43
remaining item of business is the election of directors. Is there anyone
entitled to vote who does not have a ballot? Please raise your hand. *(She
looks about at the audience.)* Will the inspector of elections distribute the
ballots? Please keep your hand raised so you can receive your ballot.
Thank you.

Jorgenson *rises from his office and moves to lectern.*

JORGENSON: It's nice to see so many familiar faces . . . so many old friends    44
. . . many of you I haven't seen for years. Thank you for coming and
welcome to the 73rd Annual Meeting of New England Wire and
Cable—the 38th of which I am addressing you as your Chief Executive.

Bill Coles, our able President, has told you about our year; what we
accomplished—where we need to make further improvements—what
our business goals are for next year and the years beyond.

I'd like to talk to you about something else. On this, our 73rd year,
I'd like to share with you some of my thoughts concerning the vote you
are about to make in the company you own.

We've had some very good years. We've had some difficult ones as
well. Though the last decade has been troubling for us it's been devastating for our industry. Ten short years ago we were the twelfth largest
manufacturer of wire and cable in the country, the fourth largest in New
England. We're now the third largest in the country and the largest in
New England.

We might not have flourished—but we survived. And we're stronger
for it. I'm proud of what we accomplished.

So, we're at that point where this proud company, which has survived
the death of its founder, numerous recessions, a major depression and
two world wars, is in imminent danger of self-destructing this day in the
town of its birth.

And there is the instrument of our destruction. I want you to see him
in all his glory. Larry the Liquidator—the entrepreneur in post-industrial
America—playing God with other people's money.

Garfinkle *waves to stockholders. Sits once again.*

At least the robber barons of old left something tangible in their wake.
A coal mine. A railroad. Banks. This man leaves nothing. He creates
nothing. He builds nothing. He runs nothing. In his wake lies nothing but
a blizzard of paper to cover the pain.

If he said, "I could run this business better." Well, that's something
worth talking about. He's not saying that. He's saying, "I am going to

kill you because at this particular moment in time you're worth more dead than alive."

Well, maybe that's true. But it is also true that one day this industry will turn. One day when the dollar is weaker or the yen stronger or when we finally begin to rebuild the roads, the bridges, the infrastructure of our country demand will skyrocket. And when those things happen we will be here—stronger for our ordeal—stronger for having survived. And the price of our stock will make his offer pale by comparison.

God save us if you vote to take his paltry few dollars and run. God save this country if *(Pointing to* Garfinkle. *)* "that" is truly the wave of the future. We will then have become a nation that makes nothing but hamburgers, creates nothing but lawyers, and sells nothing but tax shelters.

And if we have come to the point in this country where we kill something because at the moment it's worth more dead than alive, then turn around and take a good look at your neighbor. You won't kill him because it's called "murder" and it's illegal. This, too, is murder, on a mass scale, only on Wall Street they call it "maximizing shareholder values" and they call it legal and they substitute dollar bills where a conscience should be.

Damn it. A business is more than the price of its stock. It is the place where we make our living, meet our friends and dream our dreams. It is, in every sense, the very fabric that binds our society together.

So let us, right now, at this meeting, say to every Garfinkle in this land, that here we build things—we don't destroy them.

Here, we care for more than the price of our stock.

Here . . . we care about people!

Jorgenson *moves from lectern back to table.* Bea, Coles, *and* Kate *stand and applaud.* Garfinkle *follows* Jorgenson *back and as the applause dies, says to* Bea, Coles *and* Jorgenson *respectively:*

GARFINKLE: Amen . . . And Amen . . . And Amen. Say "Amen," someone, please! *(Moves to lectern in and says in a hushed tone.)* You'll excuse me. I'm not familiar with local custom . . . The way I was brought up you always said "Amen" after you heard a prayer. You hear someone praying, after he finishes, you say "Amen" and drink a little wine.

'Cause that's what you just heard—a prayer. The way I was brought up we called the particular prayer "the prayer for the dead." You just heard the prayer for the dead, and, fellow stuckholders, you didn't say "Amen" and you didn't even get to sip the wine.

What—You don't think this company is dead? Steel—you remember steel, don't you? Steel used to be an industry. Now heavy metal is a rock group.

This company is dead. Don't blame me. I didn't kill it. It was dead when I got here. It is too late for prayers, for even if the prayers were answered and a miracle occurred and the yen did this and the dollar did that and the infrastructure did the other thing, we would still be dead. Know why? Fiber-optics. New technologies. Obsolescence.

We're dead, all right. We're just not broke. And you know the surest way to go broke? Keep getting an increasing share of a shrinking market. Down the tubes. Slow but sure. You know, at one time there must have been dozens of companies making buggy whips. And I'll bet you anything the last one around was the one that made the best goddamned buggy whip you ever saw. How would you have liked to have been a stuckholder of that company?

You invested in a business. And that business is dead. Let's have the intelligence, let's have the decency, to sign the death certificate, collect the insurance and invest the money in something with a future.

Aha—But we can't, goes the prayer—we can't because we have a responsibility—a responsibility to our employees, our community . . . What will happen to them? I got two words for that—"Who cares?" Care about them? They didn't care about you. They sucked you dry. You have no responsibility to them.

For the last ten years this company has bled your money. Did this Community care? Did they ever say, "I know things are tough. We'll lower your taxes, reduce water and sewer?" Check it out. We're paying twice what we paid ten years ago. And the mayor is making twice what he made ten years ago. And our devoted employees, after taking no increases for three years, are still making twice what they made ten years ago. And our stock is one-sixth what it was ten years ago.

Who cares? I'll tell you—me! I'm not your best friend—I'm your only friend. I care about you in the only way that matters in business. I don't make anything? I'm making you money. And, lest we forget, that's the only reason any of you became stuckholders in the first place. To make money. You don't care if they manufacture wire and cable, fry chicken, or grow tangerines. You want to make money. I'm making you money. I'm the only friend you got.

Take that money. Invest it somewhere else. Maybe—maybe you'll get lucky and it will be used productively—and if it is—you'll create more jobs and provide a service for the economy and—God forbid—even make a few bucks for yourself. Let the Government and the Mayor and the unions worry about what you paid them to worry about. And if anyone asks, tell them you gave at the plant.

And it pleases me that I'm called "Larry the Liquidator." You know why, fellow stuckholders? Because at my funeral you'll leave with a smile on your face . . . and a few bucks in your pocket. Now, that's a funeral worth having.

(*Breathing heavily,* Garfinkle *pauses a beat and sits.*)

---

BEA: . . . Will the inspector of elections please collect the ballots.  46

*The lights dim. Players are now in shadows. Coles rises, moves slowly Center Stage.*

COLES: That's what happened. That's it. All of it.  47

BEA: Is there anyone entitled to vote who has not turned in a ballot?  48

COLES: It's happening everywhere. No one is immune.  49

BEA: To retain the present Board: 1,741,416.  50

COLES: I think the old man gave the speech of his life. I can't think how he  51
could have said it better.

BEA: For the opposition slate: 2,219,901.  52

COLES: What do we do? Pass another law. There's already a law against  53
murder. All he did was supply the weapon.

BEA: Not voting: 176,111.  54

COLES: Garfinkle won in a landslide. Didn't even need my votes. Cost me  55
the second half million, but I feel good about that. I feel better about
getting the first half million. I feel best it cost him money he didn't have
to spend. That's the only kind of lasting satisfaction you get when you
deal with people like him.

BEA: Mr. Garfinkle, your slate is elected.  56

COLES: He had the nerve to ask me to stay on while he dismembered the  57
company. Even offered me a raise. I said "no," of course. There's a point
at which we all draw the line.

JORGENSON: *(In his office.)* We can't leave now. I have to tell the men.  58

BEA: They know.  59

JORGENSON: . . . Already?  60

BEA: Let's go home. There'll be time tomorrow.  61

JORGENSON: Even . . . Ossie voted for him.  62

*He exits. She remains.*

COLES: He didn't take it well. From me . . . I think he expected it. Ossie  63
. . . kind of threw him. With all his money you'd think he would have
left. Gone somewhere nice . . . somewhere warm. He didn't. Stayed right
here. Died almost two years later. Left more than thirty million.

BEA: Jorgy, you only made one mistake in your life. You lived two years  64
too long.

COLES: Bea became executor of his estate. Bought the land the plant used  65
to sit on. Put up a kind of . . . Employee Retraining Center—Actually
placed a few people . . . about a hundred of the twelve hundred or so
that worked there when the plant closed. It wasn't easy retraining
middle-aged men who are used to working with their hands. Some went
to work for McDonald's . . . or as night watchmen.

Me? I didn't do too badly. I moved back to Florida. Run a mid-sized
division for a nationally known food processor. I won't ever run the
company . . . but I'm financially secure. And you can't beat the weather.

---

*Lights up on* Garfinkle.

GARFINKLE: I'm sorry, Kate. I'm surprised myself. See, you do bring out the **66** best in me . . . Come—Ride back to New York with me . . . You worried it wouldn't look right? Don't. It's the perfect ending . . . Come.

*She enters the playing area. Stops. Looks at him. He extends his arms to her, beckoning.*

Come.

*She doesn't move.*

I got donuts in the car.

COLES: Kate and Garfinkle? Well, three months later, which is as soon as she **67** could work things out at Morgan, Stanley, she went to work for him.

*Kate moves next to a seated Garfinkle in his office.*

She was very good. Three months after that she became his partner . . .

*Her arm moves to the back of Garfinkle's chair.*

. . . then his wife.

*Her arm is around his shoulder. Garfinkle beams. Bea exits.*

They have two kids. Set of twins. Call them their "little bull and little bear." Friend of mine saw them the other day . . . *(Moves to exit.)* Said he never saw them happier. *(Exits.)*

CURTAIN

## Discussion and Writing Suggestions

1. What value systems underlie the two positions in this debate? What does Jorgenson believe about America and the way it works such that he could make the speech he does? What does Lawrence Garfinkle believe?
2. Garfinkle to Kate: "We've come from 'Ask not what your country can do for you' to 'What's in it for me?' to 'What's in it for me—today!' in one short generation." Is Garfinkle accurate in his assessment? Comment.
3. Assume that you own stock in New England Wire & Cable and that you will cast your vote for Garfinkle or Jorgenson. (Recall that you are voting for a slate of candidates that will control a board that, in turn, controls the company. Larry the Liquidator wants you to vote for his slate, which if elected will immediately close New England Wire & Cable; Andrew Jorgenson wants you to vote for his slate, which will vote to keep the company open.) In deciding which of the speeches is more compelling, list the advantages and disadvantages of each position. Cast your vote. Then in one or two paragraphs, express any reservations you have about your vote.
4. Should a business be concerned with more than its immediate profitability, as Jorgenson argues? If so, with what else should it be concerned?

5. Why might a stockholder be sympathetic to Jorgenson's position and yet still vote with Garfinkle? Put another way: What tension might exist between a person's ideals and his or her pocketbook?
6. Adopt a pro or con response to the following statement and write an argument: Lawrence Garfinkle may be causing pain and suffering to the people of New England Wire & Cable, but ultimately his takeover bid advances the cause of American business.

# On the Pulse of Morning

## MAYA ANGELOU

*Maya Angelou (b. 1928) is a distinguished poet, author, playwright, and performer. She has written critically acclaimed volumes of poetry, screenplays, television plays, and autobiographical works—the best known of which is* I Know Why the Caged Bird Sings *(1970). As a performer, Angelou traveled with the twenty-two-nation tour of Gershwin's opera* Porgy and Bess *(1954–1955); as an academic, she has taught at the University of Ghana, University of California, and University of Kansas; she currently holds an endowed chair in American studies at Wake Forest University. On January 20, 1993, Angelou became the first poet in thirty years to read at a presidential inauguration (the last was Robert Frost at John F. Kennedy's swearing-in). For that occasion, Angelou composed "On the Pulse of Morning"; on her choice as inaugural poet, Angelou remarked that she thought it "fitting that [the president would ask] a woman, and a black woman, to write a poem about the tenor of the times. It is probably fitting that a black woman try to speak to the alienation, the abandonment and to the hope of healing" the recent problems of Americans. Given the occasion of its writing and delivery, "On the Pulse of Morning" is certainly a poem about America and the very crisis of confidence taken up by the various writers in this chapter. It is also a poem about the survival of our species and of our planet. As you read, you might ask: Who is the speaker of this poem (as distinct from Angelou, the poet)? What does this speaker know of America's problems and its promise? Of its history and its future? How does the speaker challenge us to change?*

A Rock, a River, a Tree
    Hosts to species long since departed,
    Marked the mastodon.

The dinosaur, who left dry tokens
Of their sojourn here                                                                    5
On our planet floor.
Any broad alarm of their hastening doom
Is lost in the gloom of dust and ages.

But today, the Rock cries out to us, clearly, forcefully,
Come, you may stand upon my                                              10
Back and face your distant destiny,
But seek no haven in my shadow.
I will give you no hiding place down here.

You, created only a little lower than
The angels, have crouched too long in                                  15
The bruising darkness,
Have lain too long
Face down in ignorance.
Your mouths spilling words
Armed for slaughter.                                                                20
The Rock cries out to us today, you may stand upon me,
But do not hide your face.

Across the wall of the world,
A River sings a beautiful song,
It says, come, rest here by my side.                                      25

Each of you a bordered country,
Delicate and strangely made, proud,
Yet thrusting perpetually under siege.
Your armed struggles for profit
Have left collars of waste upon                                            30
My shore, currents of debris upon my breast.
Yet, today I call you to my riverside,
If you will study war no more. Come,
Clad in peace and I will sing the songs
The Creator gave to me when I and the                              35
Tree and the Rock were one.
Before cynicism was a bloody sear across your
Brow and when you yet knew you still
Knew nothing.
The River sang and sings on.                                               40

There is a true yearning to respond to
The singing River and the wise Rock.

So say the Asian, the Hispanic, the Jew
The African, the Native American, the Sioux,
The Catholic, the Muslim, the French, the Greek          45
The Irish, the Rabbi, the Priest, the Sheikh,
The Gay, the Straight, the Preacher,
The privileged, the homeless, the Teacher.
They all hear
The speaking of the Tree.          50

They hear the first and last of every Tree
   Speaks to humankind today. Come to me, here beside the River.
   Plant yourself beside the River.

Each of you, descendant of some passed
   On traveller, has been paid for.          55
   You, who gave me my first name, you
   Pawnee, Apache, Seneca, you
   Cherokee Nation, who rested with me, then
   Forced on bloody feet, left me to the employment of
   Other seekers—desperate for gain,          60
   Starving for gold.
   You, the Turk, the Arab, the Swede, the German, the Eskimo,
      the Scot . . .
   You the Ashanti, the Yoruba, the Kru, bought
   Sold, stolen, arriving on a nightmare
   Praying for a dream.          65
   Here, root yourselves beside me.
   I am that Tree planted by the River,
   Which will not be moved.
   I, the Rock, I the River, I the Tree
   I am yours—your Passages have been paid.          70
   Lift up your faces, you have a piercing need
   For this bright morning dawning for you.
   History, despite its wrenching pain,
   Cannot be unlived, and if faced
   With courage, need not be lived again.          75

Lift up your eyes upon
   This day breaking for you.
   Give birth again
   To the dream.

Women, children, men,          80
   Take it into the palms of your hands.

Mold it into the shape of your most
Private need. Sculpt it into
The image of your most public self.
Lift up your hearts                                         85
Each new hour holds new chances
For new beginnings.
Do not be wedded forever
To fear, yoked eternally
To brutishness.                                            90

The horizon leans forward,
Offering you space to place new steps of change.
Here, on the pulse of this fine day
You may have the courage
To look up and out and upon me, the                        95
Rock, the River, the Tree, your country.
No less to Midas than the mendicant.
No less to you now than the mastodon then.

Here on the pulse of this new day
You may have the grace to look up and out            100
And into your sister's eyes and into
Your brother's face, your country
And say simply
Very simply
With hope                                                 105
Good morning.

## Discussion and Writing Suggestions

1. Angelou read her poem immediately after Bill Clinton delivered his inaugural address. In what ways is this a poem about and for America? About all people, regardless of nationality? In developing your answer, see especially lines 76–79: "Lift up your eyes upon / This day breaking for you. / Give birth again / To the dream." Why reference to *the dream?* Which dream? Refer to other lines, as needed.

2. Locate the one or two lines of this poem that drew a particularly strong response from you. Copy that line at the top of a page and then, for five minutes, explore your response in writing. Begin by stating your reaction to the quoted line(s). Continue by attempting to explain your reaction.

3. In a word or a phrase, identify the mood of Angelou's "On the Pulse of Morning." Then reread the poem and explain, by referring to specific lines, how Angelou creates this mood.

4. Three elements of the natural landscape dominate this poem: the rock, the river, and the tree. Referring to specific lines, show how and where these

elements are developed. Where does each "speak" to the reader? What does each say—what challenge does each make? In what ways might the three also be considered as part of one whole (see line 69)?

5. Examine the structure of this poem. Determine in which lines the rock, the river, and the tree each "speak." How are these speeches prepared for? That is, who is speaking to us when the rock, the river, and the tree are not? Who is this narrator? What is the narrator's knowledge? What is the narrator's relationship with the reader?

6. Why does Angelou begin with images of the mastodon and the dinosaur? What is the relation of "their sojourn here" to our sojourn? (See also line 98, where the narrator refers a final time to the mastodon.)

7. The narrator says: "The horizon leans forward, / Offering you space to place new steps of change" (lines 91–92). What change is being urged by the narrator?

8. Examine the poem's title and reread lines 76–77, 93, 99, and 106. What is the effect of Angelou's choosing "morning" as the time of day presented in the poem? What might be the "pulse" of morning? Generally, what does this language suggest for you?

9. What is the effect of Angelou's cataloging different people in lines 41–50? Of her naming four Indian nations in lines 57–58? Of her naming African tribes in line 63? Generally, what evidence do you see of Angelou's urging unity out of separateness?

---

## SYNTHESIS ACTIVITIES

1. Writers like Robert Reich and Natwar M. Gandhi believe that the American Dream is a dream about reaching—that it is a dream that may never be realized, per se, but is always in the making and being strived for. Develop a synthesis in which you respond to this question: When, in your view, does the reaching of Americans keep them hopeful; and when does the reaching give rise to despair?

   In developing an essay in response to this question, first develop *your own* response. Once you have a point of view firmly in mind, consider how the writers in this chapter can help you to make your point. Consider, for instance, that themes of cynicism and hope converge in Maya Angelou's "On the Pulse of Morning," where in lines 33–38 she writes: "Come, / Clad in peace and I will sing the songs / The Creator gave to me when I and the / Tree and the Rock were one. / Before cynicism was a bloody sear across your / Brow. . . ." You might use Angelou's poem as a starting point in discussing the relationship between cynicism and hope, as these are expressed in the chapter's readings. You might want to address some (but not all) of these questions: What is the cynicism that Angelou's narrator speaks of? How have you seen this cynicism reflected in the readings of this chapter and in your own experience? How does the poem's narrator respond to this cynicism? How does Bill Clinton respond? How did Carter anticipate the cynicism? To what extent does the hopefulness of Gandhi, Clinton, and Angelou offset for you the brooding of writers like Derber, O'Rourke, Himmelfarb, and Sterner? To what extent does Reich help to set a larger context for the expressions of cynicism and hope in this chapter?

2. Jimmy Carter asserted in 1979 that Americans were suffering from a crisis of confidence. Certainly, the thesis of this chapter is that such a crisis exists today. Develop an explanatory synthesis in which, drawing on the work of Katherine S. Newman, Charles Derber, and P. J. O'Rourke, you illustrate Carter's main point.

3. In an extended discussion, set the hopeful views of Bill Clinton, Maya Angelou, and Natwar M. Gandhi against the views of others who believe that America is suffering a crisis of confidence. Your comparative analysis should lead to a conclusion in which you state your opinion. Which set of views are you more inclined to accept? Why?

4. In his speech "Energy and National Goals," Jimmy Carter appeals to values and attitudes that Robert Reich explores in his story of George. In a synthesis that draws on these two sources, on Natwar M. Gandhi's "Still the Promised Land," on Gertrude Himmelfarb's essay, and on Bill Clinton's inaugural address, identify the core American values and then comment on the extent to which you see them in evidence today.

5. Had you been a shareholder of New England Wire & Cable, which way would you have voted at the annual meeting? Using any three articles in this chapter as evidence, and building on your critique of the speeches by Garfinkle and Jorgenson, argue that one of the speeches in *Other People's Money* is more persuasive than the other. (If you are interested in writing this essay, you should probably read the entire play by Jerry Sterner or rent and view the movie, which is based on the play.)

6. Katherine S. Newman discusses the despair that strikes those in the middle class when they lose their jobs. P. J. O'Rourke hints at the despair of communities who find themselves cheering for vigilante groups because their neighborhoods are not being protected by police. We see here examples of middle-class and underclass hopelessness. What, in Clinton's inaugural address and in Clinton's policies as president, do you see as a response to this hopelessness? Do you sense that attitudes about America's future are changing? Develop your answer into an argument.

7. Carter, Derber, and Himmelfarb discuss what they term the moral crisis of our society. In an explanatory essay that draws on these three sources, describe the crisis and its origins.

8. What connections can you forge between life for the inhabitants of Mott Haven (P. J. O'Rourke), life for David Patterson (Katherine S. Newman), and life for Lawrence Garfinkle on Wall Street (*Other People's Money*)? In forging possible relationships, you might draw on the work of Jimmy Carter, Charles Derber, and Gertrude Himmelfarb.

9. Prepare a three-part synthesis based on a comparison and contrast of Bill

Clinton's inaugural address and Maya Angelou's poem, "On the Pulse of Morning." (1) Compare and contrast the *imagery* of Clinton's inaugural address with the imagery of Angelou's poem. Citing specific lines, discuss how each writer uses images to make an impression on the listener/reader. (2) Next, compare and contrast the *themes* of the inaugural address and those of the poem, answering this question: To what extent does the word *change* play an important role in each? (3) Finally, discuss the ways in which the content of each presentation is related to imagery of each presentation. What conclusions about the relationship of language and content can you draw from your three related analyses of the inaugural address and the poem?

10. For students who have visited other countries or foreign-born nationals studying in the United States: Having lived and/or traveled in two or more countries, you are in a unique position to make observations about American culture in that you can compare this culture with others. In an essay that explores the question of America's crisis of confidence, draw on your international experiences. (Or interview someone who has lived abroad and answer these same questions.) What have your travels led you to observe about American values, ideals, or productivity? Based on your experiences, comment on the views expressed by some of the authors in this chapter.

## RESEARCH ACTIVITIES

1. You have likely heard the phrase "rags to riches." There are many rags-to-riches stories in literature, "Cinderella" being one. In America, the most famous and often-referred-to variety was written by Horatio Alger, Jr. (1834–1899). So commonplace was his theme of poor but honest and hardworking lad (it was always a boy) makes good that Alger is remembered more for his idealization of the American Dream than for the literary merits of his books. Read any of the novels. (A few of the titles: *Julius the Street Boy, Ragged Dick, Tom the Bootblack, Tony the Hero.*) Read also, any commentaries on Alger that you can find. Then write a paper in which you provide a biography of the author, a discussion of the themes in the novel you have read, and a discussion of Alger's significance as an American writer.

2. Numerous books have been published on America's prospects for the 1990s and beyond. Read any one of these, along with all the reviews you can find, and write a paper in which you evaluate the book (with the help of other reviewers). Several suggestions: Jack Nelson-Pallmeyer, *Brave New World Order* (1992); Daniel F. Burton, Jr., ed., *Vision for the 1990s;* Robert L. Bartley, *The Seven Fat Years* (1992); Richard M. Nixon, *Seize the Moment* (1992); Lester Thurow, *Head to Head* (1992); James Fallows, *More Like Us* (1989); and Isabell V. Sawhil, ed., *Challenge to Leadership* (1988).

3. Read the seventy-fifth-anniversary issue of *Forbes* (September 14, 1992), in

which the editors put the following question to eleven distinguished writers and scholars: "Why, if things are so good, do we feel so bad?" You can find two responses to this question in this chapter—see Wilson and Himmelfarb. Read the other responses and then write a paper in which you synthesize the views offered with your own response to the editors' question.

4. Locate a copy of the book *Where We Stand: Can America Make It in the Global Race for Wealth, Health, and Happiness?* by Peter Rutten, Albert F. Bayers III, and the World Rank Research Team (1992). In this book, jammed with fascinating statistics, the authors compare the performance of the world's nations along dozens of dimensions. One comparative statistic: the United States incarcerates a higher percentage of its citizens—426 people per 100,000—than any other industrial nation. (South Africa follows with 333 per 100,000.) Skim the book. Find a category of comparison, on any topic, that intrigues you. Then launch a research project, gathering as much information on the topic as you can.

5. Research the condition of America's infrastructure: its roads, bridges, railways, sewer and water lines, and computer links. For each, determine the current state of repair or disrepair, the extent of any work needed, and the likely cost of development. If you develop strong views during your research, present your findings as an argument. Otherwise, prepare an explanatory synthesis.

6. In an article appearing in this chapter, Gertrude Himmelfarb draws several comparisons between the morality-neutral Americans of today and the morality-conscious Victorians and nineteenth-century Americans. Today, government officials avoid making judgments about morally correct behavior; Victorians and their American counterparts did not hesitate to make such judgments as a matter of public conversation and public policy. Investigate the pervasiveness of moral instruction and legislation in Victorian England or in nineteenth-century America. Then answer this question: To what extent are Americans today in need of moral guidance? Explain your answer in the context of what you have discovered about nineteenth-century attitudes, both British and American.

7. Most observers agree that the Watergate scandal, which led to the resignation of President Nixon, traumatized the nation. In a research paper, investigate the impact of this scandal on the national psyche. Both immediately after Nixon was forced from office and now—twenty years later—what has been the reactions of Americans? What effect, if any, has the burglary had on the confidence that citizens have in their country? At least part of your paper will need to recount the events leading to the burglary, the main participants, the congressional investigation, and Nixon's resignation. (These events are matters of public record and will be summarized in any encyclopedia. As part of your common knowledge, the circumstances of the burglary and the hearings would not need to be cited—unless, of course, you quoted sources directly.)

# 10

# FAIRY TALES: A CLOSER LOOK AT "CINDERELLA"

"Once upon a time . . . ." Millions of children around the world have listened to these (or similar) words. And, once upon a time, such words were magic archways into a world of entertainment and fantasy for children and their parents. But in our own century, fairy tales have come under the scrutiny of anthropologists, linguists, educators, psychologists, and psychiatrists, as well as literary critics, who have come to see them as a kind of social genetic code—a means by which cultural values are transmitted from one generation to the next. Some people, of course, may scoff at the idea that charming tales like "Cinderella" or "Snow White" are anything other than charming tales, at the idea that fairy tales may really be ways of inculcating young and impressionable children with culturally approved values. But even if they are not aware of it, adults and children use fairy tales in complex and subtle ways. We can, perhaps, best illustrate this by examining variants of a single tale—"Cinderella."

"Cinderella" appears to be the best-known fairy tale in the world. In 1892, Marian Roalfe Cox published 345 variants of the story, the first systematic study of a single folktale. In her collection, Cox gathered stories from throughout Europe in which elements or motifs of "Cinderella" appeared, often mixed with motifs of other tales. All told, more than 700 variants exist throughout the world—in Europe, Africa, Asia, and North and South America. Scholars debate the extent to which such a wide distribution is explained by population migrations or by some universal quality of imagination that would allow people at different times and places to create essentially the same story. But for whatever reason, folklorists agree that "Cinderella" has appealed to storytellers and listeners everywhere.

The great body of folk literature, including fairy tales, comes to us from an oral tradition. Written literature, produced by a particular author, is preserved through the generations just as the author recorded it. By contrast, oral literature changes with every telling: The childhood game comes to mind in which one child whispers a sentence into the ear of another; by the time the second child repeats the sentence to a third, and the third to a fourth (and so on), the sentence has changed considerably. And so it is with oral literature, with the qualification that these stories are also changed quite consciously when a teller wishes to add or delete material.

The modern student of folk literature finds her- or himself in the position of *reading* as opposed to hearing a tale. The texts we read tend to be of two types, which are at times difficult to distinguish. We might read a faithful transcription of an oral tale or a tale of *literary* origin—a tale that was originally written (as a short story would be), not spoken, but that nonetheless may contain elements of an oral account. In this chapter, we include tales of both oral and literary origin. Jakob and Wilhelm Grimm published their transcription of "Cinderella" in 1812. The version by Charles Perrault (1697) is difficult to classify as the transcription of an oral source, since he may have heard the story originally but appears (according to Bruno Bettelheim) to have "freed it of all content he considered vulgar, and refined its other features to make the product suitable to be told at court." Of unquestionable literary origin are the Walt Disney version of the story, based on Perrault's text; Anne Sexton's poem; and Tanith Lee's "When the Clock Strikes," a version in which the Cinderella figure is a witch bent on avenging the murder of her royal family. We include, as well, three transcriptions from oral sources: a Chinese version of the tale; an African version, originally told in the Hausa language; and an Algonquin (Native American) version.

Preceding these variants of "Cinderella," we present a general reading on fairy-tale literature by Stith Thompson. Following the eight variants, we present three selections that respond directly to the tale. We hear from Bruno Bettelheim, who, following psychoanalytic theory, finds in "Cinderella" a "Story of Sibling Rivalry and Oedipal Conflicts." Madonna Kolbenschlag then offers a feminist reading of the tale, followed by Jane Yolen's lament on the "gutting" of a story that once was richly magical and instructive.

A note on terminology: "Cinderella," "Jack and the Beanstalk," "Little Red Riding Hood," and the like are commonly referred to as fairy tales, although, strictly speaking, they are not. True fairy tales concern a "class of supernatural beings of diminutive size, who in popular belief are said to possess magical powers and to have great influence for good or evil over the affairs of humans" (*Oxford English Dictionary*). "Cinderella" and the others just mentioned concern no beings of diminutive size, although extraordinary, magical events do occur in the story. Folklorists would be more apt to call these stories "wonder tales." We retain the traditional "fairy tale," though, with the proviso that in popular usage the term is misapplied. You may notice that the authors in this chapter use the terms "folktale" and "fairy tale" interchangeably. The expression "folktale" refers to *any* story conceived orally and passed on in an oral tradition. Thus, "folktale" is a generic term that incorporates both fairy tales and wonder tales.

# Universality of the Folktale

## STITH THOMPSON

*Folklorists travel around the world, to cities and rural areas alike, recording the facts, traditions, and beliefs that characterize ethnic groups. Some folklorists record and compile jokes; others do the same with insults or songs. Still others, like Stith Thompson, devote their professional careers to studying tales. And, as it turns out, there are many aspects of stories and storytelling worth examining. Among them: the art of narrative—how tellers captivate their audiences; the social and religious significance of tale telling; the many types of tales that are told; the many variants, worldwide, of single tales (like "Cinderella"). In a preface to one of his own books, Thompson raises the broad questions and the underlying assumptions that govern the folklorist's study of tales. We begin this chapter with Thompson's overview to set a context for the variants of "Cinderella" that you will read.*

*Note the ways that Thompson's approach to fairy tales differs from yours. Whether or not you're conscious of having an approach, you do have one: Perhaps you regard stories like "Cinderella" as entertainment. Fine—this is a legitimate point of view, but it's only one of several ways of regarding folktales. Stith Thompson claims that there's much to learn in studying tales. He assumes, as you might not, that tales should be objects of study as well as entertainment.*

*Stith Thompson (1885–1976) led a distinguished life as an American educator, folklorist, editor, and author. Between 1921 and 1955, he was a professor of folklore and English, and later dean of the Graduate School and Distinguished Service Professor at Indiana University, Bloomington. Five institutions have awarded Thompson honorary doctorates for his work in folklore studies. He has published numerous books on the subject, including* European Tales Among North American Indians *(1919),* The Types of the Folktales *(1928), and* Tales of the North American Indian *(1929). He is best known for his six-volume* Motif Index of Folk Literature *(1932–1937; 1955–1958, 2nd ed.).*

The teller of stories has everywhere and always found eager listeners. 1 Whether his tale is the mere report of a recent happening, a legend of long ago, or an elaborately contrived fiction, men and women have hung upon his words and satisfied their yearnings for information or amusement, for incitement to heroic deeds, for religious edification, or for release from the overpowering monotony of their lives. In villages of central Africa, in outrigger boats on the Pacific, in the Australian bush, and within the shadow of Hawaiian volcanoes, tales of the present and of the mysterious past, of animals and gods and heroes, and of men and women like themselves, hold listeners in their spell or enrich the conversation of daily life. So it is also in Eskimo igloos under the light of seal-oil lamps, in the tropical jungles of Brazil, and by the totem poles of the British Columbian coast. In Japan too, and China and India, the priest and the scholar, the peasant and the artisan all join in their love of a good story and their honor for the man who tells it well.

When we confine our view to our own occidental world, we see that   **2** for at least three or four thousand years, and doubtless for ages before, the art of the story-teller has been cultivated in every rank of society. Odysseus entertains the court of Alcinous with the marvels of his adventures. Centuries later we find the long-haired page reading nightly from interminable chivalric romances to entertain his lady while her lord is absent on his crusade. Medieval priests illustrate sermons by anecdotes old and new, and only sometimes edifying. The old peasant, now as always, whiles away the winter evening with tales of wonder and adventure and the marvelous workings of fate. Nurses tell children of Goldilocks or the House that Jack Built. Poets write epics and novelists novels. Even now the cinemas and theaters bring their stories direct to the ear and eye through the voices and gestures of actors. And in the smoking-rooms of sleeping cars and steamships and at the banquet table the oral anecdote flourishes in a new age.

In the present work we are confining our interest to a relatively   **3** narrow scope, the traditional prose tale—the story which has been handed down from generation to generation either in writing or by word of mouth. Such tales are, of course, only one of the many kinds of story material, for, in addition to them, narrative comes to us in verse as ballads and epics, and in prose as histories, novels, dramas, and short stories. We shall have little to do with the songs of bards, with the ballads of the people, or with poetic narrative in general, though stories themselves refuse to be confined exclusively to either prose or verse forms. But even with verse and all other forms of prose narrative put aside, we shall find that in treating the traditional prose tale—the folktale—our quest will be ambitious enough and will take us to all parts of the earth and to the very beginnings of history.

Although the term "folktale" is often used in English to refer to the   **4** "household tale" or "fairy tale" (the German *Märchen*), such as "Cinderella" or "Snow White," it is also legitimately employed in a much broader sense to include all forms of prose narrative, written or oral, which have come to be handed down through the years. In this usage the important fact is the traditional nature of the material. In contrast to the modern story writer's striving after originality of plot and treatment, the teller of a folktale is proud of his ability to hand on that which he has received. He usually desires to impress his readers or hearers with the fact that he is bringing them something that has the stamp of good authority, that the tale was heard from some great story-teller or from some aged person who remembered it from old days.

So it was until at least the end of the Middle Ages with writers like 5 Chaucer, who carefully quoted authorities for their plots—and sometimes even invented originals so as to dispel the suspicion that some new and unwarranted story was being foisted on the public. Though the individual genius of such writers appears clearly enough, they always depended on authority, not only for their basic theological opinions but also for the plots of their stories. A study of the sources of Chaucer or Boccaccio takes one directly into the stream of traditional narrative.

The great written collections of stories characteristic of India, the 6 Near East, the classical world, and Medieval Europe are almost entirely traditional. They copy and recopy. A tale which gains favor in one collection is taken over into others, sometimes intact and sometimes with changes of plot or characterization. The history of such a story, passing it may be from India to Persia and Arabia and Italy and France and finally to England, copied and changed from manuscript to manuscript, is often exceedingly complex. For it goes through the hands of both skilled and bungling narrators and improves or deteriorates at nearly every retelling. However well or poorly such a story may be written down, it always attempts to preserve a tradition, an old tale with the authority of antiquity to give it interest and importance.

If use of the term "folktale" to include such literary narratives seems 7 somewhat broad, it can be justified on practical grounds if on no other, for it is impossible to make a complete separation of the written and the oral traditions. Often, indeed, their interrelation is so close and so inextricable as to present one of the most baffling problems the folklore scholar encounters. They differ somewhat in their behavior, it is true, but they are alike in their disregard of originality of plot and of pride of authorship.

Nor is complete separation of these two kinds of narrative tradition 8 by any means necessary for their understanding. The study of the oral tale . . . will be valid so long as we realize that stories have frequently been taken down from the lips of unlettered taletellers and have entered the great literary collections. In contrary fashion, fables of Aesop, anecdotes from Homer, and saints' legends, not to speak of fairy tales read from Perrault or Grimm, have entered the oral stream and all their association with the written or printed page has been forgotten. Frequently a story is taken from the people, recorded in a literary document, carried across continents or preserved through centuries, and then retold to a humble entertainer who adds it to his repertory.

It is clear then that the oral story need not always have been oral. 9
But when it once habituates itself to being passed on by word of mouth it undergoes the same treatment as all other tales at the command of the raconteur. It becomes something to tell to an audience, or at least to a listener, not something to read. Its effects are no longer produced indirectly by association with words written or printed on a page, but directly through facial expression and gesture and repetition and recurrent patterns that generations have tested and found effective.

This oral art of taletelling is far older than history, and it is not 10
bounded by one continent or one civilization. Stories may differ in subject from place to place, the conditions and purposes of taletelling may change as we move from land to land or from century to century, and yet everywhere it ministers to the same basic social and individual needs. The call for entertainment to fill in the hours of leisure has found most peoples very limited in their resources, and except where modern urban civilization has penetrated deeply they have found the telling of stories one of the most satisfying of pastimes. Curiosity about the past has always brought eager listeners to tales of the long ago which supply the simple man with all he knows of the history of his folk. Legends grow with the telling, and often a great heroic past evolves to gratify vanity and tribal pride. Religion also has played a mighty role everywhere in the encouragement of the narrative art, for the religious mind has tried to understand beginnings and for ages has told stories of ancient days and sacred beings. Often whole cosmologies have unfolded themselves in these legends, and hierarchies of gods and heroes.

World-wide also are many of the structural forms which oral narra- 11
tive has assumed. The hero tale, the explanatory legend, the animal anecdote—certainly these at least are present everywhere. Other fictional patterns are limited to particular areas of culture and act by their presence or absence as an effective index of the limit of the area concerned. The study of such limitations has not proceeded far, but it constitutes an interesting problem for the student of these oral narrative forms.

Even more tangible evidence of the ubiquity and antiquity of the 12
folktale is the great similarity in the content of stories of the most varied peoples. The same tale types and narrative motifs are found scattered over the world in most puzzling fashion. A recognition of these resemblances and an attempt to account for them brings the scholar closer to an understanding of the nature of human culture. He must continually ask himself, "Why do some peoples borrow tales and some lend? How does the tale serve the needs of the social group?" When he adds to his

task an appreciation of the aesthetic and practical urge toward story-telling, and some knowledge of the forms and devices, stylistic and histrionic, that belong to this ancient and widely practiced art, he finds that he must bring to his work more talents than one man can easily possess. Literary critics, anthropologists, historians, psychologists, and aestheticians are all needed if we are to hope to know why folktales are made, how they are invented, what art is used in their telling, how they grow and change and occasionally die.

## Review Questions

1. According to Thompson, what are the reasons people consistently venerate a good storyteller?
2. What does Thompson state as features that distinguish a "folktale" from modern types of fiction?
3. How does religion help encourage the existence of folktale art?
4. What is a strong piece of evidence for the great antiquity and universality of folktales?

## Discussion and Writing Suggestions

1. Based on Thompson's explanation of the qualities of oral folktales, what do you feel is gained by the increasing replacement of this form of art and entertainment by TV?
2. What do you suppose underlies the apparent human need to tell stories, given that storytelling is practiced in every culture known?
3. Interview older members of your family, asking them about stories they were told as children. As best you can, record a story. Then examine your work. How does it differ from the version you heard? Write an account of your impressions on the differences between an oral and written rendering of a story. Alternately, you might record a story and then speculate on what the story might mean in the experiences of the family member who told it to you.

# Eight Variants of "Cinderella"

*It comes as a surprise to many that there exist Chinese, French, German, African, and Native American versions of the popular "Cinderella," along with 700 other versions worldwide. Which is the real "Cinderella"? The question is misleading in that each version is "real" for a particular group of people in a particular place and time. Certainly, you can judge among versions and select the most appealing. You can also draw comparisons. Indeed, the grouping of the stories that we present here invites comparisons. A few of the categories you might wish to consider as you read:*

- ◆ *Cinderella's innocence or guilt, concerning the treatment she receives at the hands of her stepsisters*
- ◆ *Cinderella's passive (or active) nature*
- ◆ *Sibling rivalry—the relationship of Cinderella to her sisters*
- ◆ *The father's role*
- ◆ *The rule that Cinderella must return from the ball by midnight*
- ◆ *Levels of violence*
- ◆ *Presence or absence of the fairy godmother*
- ◆ *Cinderella's relationship with the prince*
- ◆ *Characterization of the prince*
- ◆ *The presence of Cinderella's dead mother*
- ◆ *The function of magic*
- ◆ *The ending*

# Cinderella

## CHARLES PERRAULT

*Charles Perrault (1628–1703) was born in Paris of a prosperous family. He practiced law for a short time and then devoted his attentions to a job in government, in which capacity he was instrumental in promoting the advancement of the arts and sciences and in securing pensions for writers, both French and foreign. Perrault is best known as a writer for his* Contes de ma mère l'oie *(Mother Goose Tales), a collection of fairy tales taken from popular folklore. He is widely suspected of having changed these stories in an effort to make them more acceptable to his audience—members of the French court.*

Once there was a nobleman who took as his second wife the proudest and haughtiest woman imaginable. She had two daughters of the same character, who took after their mother in everything. On his side, the husband had a daughter who was sweetness itself; she inherited this from her mother, who had been the most kindly of women.

No sooner was the wedding over than the stepmother showed her ill-nature. She could not bear the good qualities of the young girl, for they made her own daughters seem even less likable. She gave her the roughest work of the house to do. It was she who washed the dishes and the stairs, who cleaned out Madam's room and the rooms of the two Misses. She slept right at the top of the house, in an attic, on a lumpy mattress, while her sisters slept in panelled rooms where they had the most modern beds and mirrors in which they could see themselves from top to toe. The poor girl bore everything in patience and did not dare to complain to her father. He would only have scolded her, for he was entirely under his wife's thumb.

When she had finished her work, she used to go into the chimney-corner and sit down among the cinders, for which reason she was usually known in the house as Cinderbottom. Her younger stepsister, who was not so rude as the other, called her Cinderella. However, Cinderella, in spite of her ragged clothes, was still fifty times as beautiful as her sisters, superbly dressed though they were. 3

One day the King's son gave a ball, to which everyone of good family was invited. Our two young ladies received invitations, for they cut quite a figure in the country. So there they were, both feeling very pleased and very busy choosing the clothes and the hair-styles which would suit them best. More work for Cinderella, for it was she who ironed her sisters' underwear and goffered their linen cuffs. Their only talk was of what they would wear. 4

"I," said the elder, "shall wear my red velvet dress and my collar of English lace." 5

"I," said the younger, "shall wear just my ordinary skirt; but, to make up, I shall put on my gold-embroidered cape and my diamond clasp, which is quite out of the common." 6

The right hairdresser was sent for to supply double-frilled coifs, and patches were bought from the right patch-maker. They called Cinderella to ask her opinion, for she had excellent taste. She made useful suggestions and even offered to do their hair for them. They accepted willingly. 7

While she was doing it, they said to her: 8

"Cinderella, how would you like to go to the ball?" 9

"Oh dear, you are making fun of me. It wouldn't do for me." 10

"You are quite right. It would be a joke. People would laugh if they saw a Cinderbottom at the ball." 11

Anyone else would have done their hair in knots for them, but she had a sweet nature, and she finished it perfectly. For two days they were so excited that they ate almost nothing. They broke a good dozen laces trying to tighten their stays to make their waists slimmer, and they were never away from their mirrors. 12

At last the great day arrived. They set off, and Cinderella watched them until they were out of sight. When she could no longer see them, she began to cry. Her godmother, seeing her all in tears, asked what was the matter. 13

"If only I could . . . If only I could . . ." She was weeping so much that she could not go on. 14

Her godmother, who was a fairy, said to her: "If only you could go to the ball, is that it?" 15

"Alas, yes," said Cinderella with a sigh.   16

"Well," said the godmother, "be a good girl and I'll get you there."   17

She took her into her room and said: "Go into the garden and get   18
me a pumpkin."

Cinderella hurried out and cut the best she could find and took it to   19
her godmother, but she could not understand how this pumpkin would
get her to the ball. Her godmother hollowed it out, leaving only the
rind, and then tapped it with her wand and immediately it turned into
a magnificent gilded coach.

Then she went to look in her mouse-trap and found six mice all alive   20
in it. She told Cinderella to raise the door of the trap a little, and as each
mouse came out she gave it a tap with her wand and immediately it
turned into a fine horse. That made a team of six horses, each of fine
mouse-coloured grey.

While she was wondering how she would make a coachman, Cin-   21
derella said to her:

"I will go and see whether there is a rat in the rat-trap, we could   22
make a coachman of him."

"You are right," said the godmother. "Run and see."   23

Cinderella brought her the rat-trap, in which there were three big   24
rats. The fairy picked out one of them because of his splendid whiskers
and, when she had touched him, he turned into a fat coachman, with the
finest moustaches in the district.

Then she said: "Go into the garden and you will find six lizards   25
behind the watering-can. Bring them to me."

As soon as Cinderella had brought them, her godmother changed   26
them into six footmen, who got up behind the coach with their striped
liveries, and stood in position there as though they had been doing it
all their lives.

Then the fairy said to Cinderella:   27

"Well, that's to go to the ball in. Aren't you pleased?"   28

"Yes. But am I to go like this, with my ugly clothes?"   29

Her godmother simply touched her with her wand and her clothes   30
were changed in an instant into a dress of gold and silver cloth, all
sparkling with precious stones. Then she gave her a pair of glass slippers,
most beautifully made.

So equipped, Cinderella got into the coach; but her godmother   31
warned her above all not to be out after midnight, telling her that, if she
stayed at the ball a moment later, her coach would turn back into a
pumpkin, her horses into mice, her footmen into lizards, and her fine
clothes would become rags again.

She promised her godmother that she would leave the ball before   32
midnight without fail, and she set out, beside herself with joy.

The King's son, on being told that a great princess whom no one   33 knew had arrived, ran out to welcome her. He handed her down from the coach and led her into the hall where his guests were. A sudden silence fell; the dancing stopped, the violins ceased to play, the whole company stood fascinated by the beauty of the unknown princess. Only a low murmur was heard: "Ah, how lovely she is!" The King himself, old as he was, could not take his eyes off her and kept whispering to the Queen that it was a long time since he had seen such a beautiful and charming person. All the ladies were absorbed in noting her clothes and the way her hair was dressed, so as to order the same things for themselves the next morning, provided that fine enough materials could be found, and skillful enough craftsmen.

The King's son placed her in the seat of honour, and later led her **34** out to dance. She danced with such grace that she won still more admiration. An excellent supper was served, but the young Prince was too much occupied in gazing at her to eat anything. She went and sat next to her sisters and treated them with great courtesy, offering them oranges and lemons which the Prince had given her. They were astonished, for they did not recognize her.

While they were chatting together, Cinderella heard the clock strike **35** a quarter to twelve. She curtsied low to the company and left as quickly as she could.

As soon as she reached home, she went to her godmother and, **36** having thanked her, said that she would very much like to go again to the ball on the next night—for the Prince had begged her to come back. She was in the middle of telling her godmother about all the things that had happened, when the two sisters came knocking at the door. Cinderella went to open it.

"How late you are!" she said, rubbing her eyes and yawning and **37** stretching as though she had just woken up (though since they had last seen each other she had felt very far from sleepy).

"If you had been at the ball," said one of the sisters, "you would not **38** have felt like yawning. There was a beautiful princess there, really ravishingly beautiful. She was most attentive to us. She gave us oranges and lemons."

Cinderella could have hugged herself. She asked them the name of **39** the princess, but they replied that no one knew her, that the King's son was much troubled about it, and that he would give anything in the world to know who she was. Cinderella smiled and said to them:

"So she was very beautiful? Well, well, how lucky you are! Couldn't **40** I see her? Please, Miss Javotte, do lend me that yellow dress which you wear about the house."

"Really," said Miss Javotte, "what an idea! Lend one's dress like that **41** to a filthy Cinderbottom! I should have to be out of my mind."

Cinderella was expecting this refusal and she was very glad when **42**

---

it came, for she would have been in an awkward position if her sister had really lent her her frock.

On the next day the two sisters went to the ball, and Cinderella too, **43** but even more splendidly dressed than the first time. The King's son was constantly at her side and wooed her the whole evening. The young girl was enjoying herself so much that she forgot her godmother's warning. She heard the clock striking the first stroke of midnight when she thought that it was still hardly eleven. She rose and slipped away as lightly as a roe-deer. The Prince followed her, but he could not catch her up. One of her glass slippers fell off, and the Prince picked it up with great care.

Cinderella reached home quite out of breath, with no coach, no **44** footmen, and wearing her old clothes. Nothing remained of all her finery, except one of her little slippers, the fellow to the one which she had dropped. The guards at the palace gate were asked if they had not seen a princess go out. They answered that they had seen no one go out except a very poorly dressed girl, who looked more like a peasant than a young lady.

When the two sisters returned from the ball, Cinderella asked them **45** if they had enjoyed themselves again, and if the beautiful lady had been there. They said that she had, but that she had run away when it struck midnight, and so swiftly that she had lost one of her glass slippers, a lovely little thing. The Prince had picked it up and had done nothing but gaze at it for the rest of the ball, and undoubtedly he was very much in love with the beautiful person to whom it belonged.

They were right, for a few days later the King's son had it pro- **46** claimed to the sound of trumpets that he would marry the girl whose foot exactly fitted the slipper. They began by trying it on the various princesses, then on the duchesses and on all the ladies of the Court, but with no success. It was brought to the two sisters, who did everything possible to force their feet into the slipper, but they could not manage it. Cinderella, who was looking on, recognized her own slipper, and said laughing:

"Let me see if it would fit me!" **47**

Her sisters began to laugh and mock at her. But the gentleman who **48** was trying on the slipper looked closely at Cinderella and, seeing that she was very beautiful, said that her request was perfectly reasonable and that he had instructions to try it on every girl. He made Cinderella sit down and, raising the slipper to her foot, he found that it slid on without difficulty and fitted like a glove.

Great was the amazement of the two sisters, but it became greater **49** still when Cinderella drew from her pocket the second little slipper and put it on her other foot. Thereupon the fairy godmother came in and, touching Cinderella's clothes with her wand, made them even more magnificent than on the previous days.

Then the two sisters recognized her as the lovely princess whom  50
they had met at the ball. They flung themselves at her feet and begged her forgiveness for all the unkind things which they had done to her. Cinderella raised them up and kissed them, saying that she forgave them with all her heart and asking them to love her always. She was taken to the young Prince in the fine clothes which she was wearing. He thought her more beautiful than ever and a few days later he married her. Cinderella, who was as kind as she was beautiful, invited her two sisters to live in the palace and married them, on the same day, to two great noblemen of the Court.

# Ashputtle

## JAKOB AND WILHELM GRIMM

*Jakob Grimm (1785–1863) and Wilhelm Grimm (1786–1859) are best known today for the 200 folktales they collected from oral sources and reworked in* Kinder- und Hausmärchen *(popularly known as Grimm's Fairy Tales), which has been translated into seventy languages. The techniques Jakob and Wilhelm Grimm used to collect and comment on these tales became a model for other collectors, providing a basis for the science of folklore. Although the Grimm brothers argued for preserving the tales exactly as heard from oral sources, scholars have determined that they sought to "improve" the tales by making them more readable. The result, highly pleasing to lay audiences the world over, nonetheless represents a literary reworking of the original oral sources.*

A rich man's wife fell sick and, feeling that her end was near, she called  1
her only daughter to her bedside and said: "Dear child, be good and say your prayers; God will help you, and I shall look down on you from heaven and always be with you." With that she closed her eyes and died. Every day the little girl went out to her mother's grave and wept, and she went on being good and saying her prayers. When winter came, the snow spread a white cloth over the grave, and when spring took it off, the man remarried.

Excerpts from Grimm's Tales for Young and Old by Jakob and Wilhelm Grimm, translated by Ralph Manheim, translation copyright © 1977 by Ralph Manheim. Reprinted by permission of Doubleday, a division of Bantam, Doubleday, Dell Publishing Group, Inc.

His new wife brought two daughters into the house. Their faces **2** were beautiful and lily-white, but their hearts were ugly and black. That was the beginning of a bad time for the poor stepchild. "Why should this silly goose sit in the parlor with us?" they said. "People who want to eat bread must earn it. Get into the kitchen where you belong!" They took away her fine clothes and gave her an old gray dress and wooden shoes to wear. "Look at the haughty princess in her finery!" they cried and, laughing, led her to the kitchen. From then on she had to do all the work, getting up before daybreak, carrying water, lighting fires, cooking and washing. In addition the sisters did everything they could to plague her. They jeered at her and poured peas and lentils into the ashes, so that she had to sit there picking them out. At night, when she was tired out with work, she had no bed to sleep in but had to lie in the ashes by the hearth. And they took to calling her Ashputtle because she always looked dusty and dirty.

One day when her father was going to the fair, he asked his two **3** stepdaughters what he should bring them. "Beautiful dresses," said one. "Diamonds and pearls," said the other. "And you, Ashputtle. What would you like?" "Father," she said, "break off the first branch that brushes against your hat on your way home, and bring it to me." So he brought beautiful dresses, diamonds and pearls for his two step- daughters, and on the way home, as he was riding through a copse, a hazel branch brushed against him and knocked off his hat. So he broke off the branch and took it home with him. When he got home, he gave the stepdaughters what they had asked for, and gave Ashputtle the branch. After thanking him, she went to her mother's grave and planted the hazel sprig over it and cried so hard that her tears fell on the sprig and watered it. It grew and became a beautiful tree. Three times a day Ashputtle went and sat under it and wept and prayed. Each time a little white bird came and perched on the tree, and when Ashputtle made a wish the little bird threw down what she had wished for.

Now it so happened that the king arranged for a celebration. It was **4** to go on for three days and all the beautiful girls in the kingdom were invited, in order that his son might choose a bride. When the two stepsisters heard they had been asked, they were delighted. They called Ashputtle and said: "Comb our hair, brush our shoes, and fasten our buckles. We're going to the wedding at the king's palace." Ashputtle obeyed, but she wept, for she too would have liked to go dancing, and she begged her stepmother to let her go. "You little sloven!" said the stepmother. "How can you go to a wedding when you're all dusty and dirty? How can you go dancing when you have neither dress nor shoes?" But when Ashputtle begged and begged, the stepmother finally said: "Here, I've dumped a bowlful of lentils in the ashes. If you can pick

---

them out in two hours, you may go." The girl went out the back door to the garden and cried out: "O tame little doves, O turtledoves, and all the birds under heaven, come and help me put

> the good ones in the pot,
> the bad ones in your crop."

Two little white doves came flying through the kitchen window, and then came the turtledoves, and finally all the birds under heaven came flapping and fluttering and settled down by the ashes. The doves nodded their little heads and started in, peck peck peck peck, and all the others started in, peck peck peck peck, and they sorted out all the good lentils and put them in the bowl. Hardly an hour had passed before they finished and flew away. Then the girl brought the bowl to her stepmother, and she was happy, for she thought she'd be allowed to go to the wedding. But the stepmother said: "No, Ashputtle. You have nothing to wear and you don't know how to dance; the people would only laugh at you." When Ashputtle began to cry, the stepmother said: "If you can pick two bowlfuls of lentils out of the ashes in an hour, you may come." And she thought: "She'll never be able to do it." When she had dumped the two bowlfuls of lentils in the ashes, Ashputtle went out the back door to the garden and cried out: "O tame little doves, O turtledoves, and all the birds under heaven, come and help me put

> the good ones in the pot,
> the bad ones in your crop."

Two little white doves came flying through the kitchen window, and then came the turtledoves, and finally all the birds under heaven came flapping and fluttering and settled down by the ashes. The doves nodded their little heads and started in, peck peck peck peck, and all the others started in, peck peck peck peck, and they sorted out all the good lentils and put them in the bowls. Before half an hour had passed, they had finished and they all flew away. Then the girl brought the bowls to her stepmother, and she was happy, for she thought she'd be allowed to go to the wedding. But her stepmother said: "It's no use. You can't come, because you have nothing to wear and you don't know how to dance. We'd only be ashamed of you." Then she turned her back and hurried away with her two proud daughters.

When they had all gone out, Ashputtle went to her mother's grave. 5 She stood under the hazel tree and cried:

> "Shake your branches, little tree,
> Throw gold and silver down on me."

---

481

Whereupon the bird tossed down a gold and silver dress and slippers embroidered with silk and silver. Ashputtle slipped into the dress as fast as she could and went to the wedding. Her sisters and stepmother didn't recognize her. She was so beautiful in her golden dress that they thought she must be the daughter of some foreign king. They never dreamed it could be Ashputtle, for they thought she was sitting at home in her filthy rags, picking lentils out of the ashes. The king's son came up to her, took her by the hand and danced with her. He wouldn't dance with anyone else and he never let go her hand. When someone else asked for a dance, he said: "She is my partner."

She danced until evening, and then she wanted to go home. The king's son said: "I'll go with you, I'll see you home," for he wanted to find out whom the beautiful girl belonged to. But she got away from him and slipped into the dovecote. The king's son waited until her father arrived, and told him the strange girl had slipped into the dovecote. The old man thought: "Could it be Ashputtle?" and he sent for an ax and a pick and broke into the dovecote, but there was no one inside. When they went indoors, Ashputtle was lying in the ashes in her filthy clothes and a dim oil lamp was burning on the chimney piece, for Ashputtle had slipped out the back end of the dovecote and run to the hazel tree. There she had taken off her fine clothes and put them on the grave, and the bird had taken them away. Then she had put her gray dress on again, crept into the kitchen and lain down in the ashes.

Next day when the festivities started in again and her parents and stepsisters had gone, Ashputtle went to the hazel tree and said:

> "Shake your branches, little tree,
> Throw gold and silver down on me."

Whereupon the bird threw down a dress that was even more dazzling than the first one. And when she appeared at the wedding, everyone marveled at her beauty. The king's son was waiting for her. He took her by the hand and danced with no one but her. When others came and asked her for a dance, he said: "She is my partner." When evening came, she said she was going home. The king's son followed her, wishing to see which house she went into, but she ran away and disappeared into the garden behind the house, where there was a big beautiful tree with the most wonderful pears growing on it. She climbed among the branches as nimbly as a squirrel and the king's son didn't know what had become of her. He waited until her father arrived and said to him: "The strange girl has got away from me and I think she has climbed up in the pear tree." Her father thought: "Could it be Ashputtle?" He sent for an ax and chopped the tree down, but there was no one in it. When they went into the kitchen, Ashputtle was lying there in the ashes as usual, for she had jumped down on the other side of the tree, brought her fine clothes back to the bird in the hazel tree, and put on her filthy gray dress.

On the third day, after her parents and sisters had gone, Ashputtle **8** went back to her mother's grave and said to the tree:

> "Shake your branches, little tree,
> Throw gold and silver down on me."

Whereupon the bird threw down a dress that was more radiant than either of the others, and the slippers were all gold. When she appeared at the wedding, the people were too amazed to speak. The king's son danced with no one but her, and when someone else asked her for a dance, he said: "She is my partner."

When evening came, Ashputtle wanted to go home, and the king's **9** son said he'd go with her, but she slipped away so quickly that he couldn't follow. But he had thought up a trick. He had arranged to have the whole staircase brushed with pitch, and as she was running down it the pitch pulled her left slipper off. The king's son picked it up, and it was tiny and delicate and all gold. Next morning he went to the father and said: "No girl shall be my wife but the one this golden shoe fits." The sisters were overjoyed, for they had beautiful feet. The eldest took the shoe to her room to try it on and her mother went with her. But the shoe was too small and she couldn't get her big toe in. So her mother handed her a knife and said: "Cut your toe off. Once you're queen you won't have to walk any more." The girl cut her toe off, forced her foot into the shoe, gritted her teeth against the pain, and went out to the king's son. He accepted her as his bride-to-be, lifted her up on his horse, and rode away with her. But they had to pass the grave. The two doves were sitting in the hazel tree and they cried out:

> "Roocoo, roocoo,
> There's blood in the shoe.
> The foot's too long, the foot's too wide,
> That's not the proper bride."

He looked down at her foot and saw the blood spurting. At that he turned his horse around and took the false bride home again. "No," he said, "this isn't the right girl; let her sister try the shoe on." The sister went to her room and managed to get her toes into the shoe, but her heel was too big. So her mother handed her a knife and said: "Cut off a chunk of your heel. Once you're queen you won't have to walk any more." The girl cut off a chunk of her heel, forced her foot into the shoe, gritted her teeth against the pain, and went out to the king's son. He accepted her as his bride-to-be, lifted her up on his horse, and rode away with her. As they passed the hazel tree, the two doves were sitting there, and they cried out:

"Roocoo, roocoo,
There's blood in the shoe.
The foot's too long, the foot's too wide,
That's not the proper bride."

He looked down at her foot and saw that blood was spurting from her shoe and staining her white stocking all red. He turned his horse around and took the false bride home again. "This isn't the right girl, either," he said. "Haven't you got another daughter?" "No," said the man, "there's only a puny little kitchen drudge that my dead wife left me. She couldn't possibly be the bride." "Send her up," said the king's son, but the mother said: "Oh no, she's much too dirty to be seen." But he insisted and they had to call her. First she washed her face and hands, and when they were clean, she went upstairs and curtseyed to the king's son. He handed her the golden slipper and sat down on a footstool, took her foot out of her heavy wooden shoe, and put it into the slipper. It fitted perfectly. And when she stood up and the king's son looked into her face, he recognized the beautiful girl he had danced with and cried out: "This is my true bride!" The stepmother and the two sisters went pale with fear and rage. But he lifted Ashputtle up on his horse and rode away with her. As they passed the hazel tree, the two white doves called out:

"Roocoo, roocoo,
No blood in the shoe.
Her foot is neither long nor wide,
This one is the proper bride."

Then they flew down and alighted on Ashputtle's shoulders, one on the right and one on the left, and there they sat.

On the day of Ashputtle's wedding, the two stepsisters came and 10 tried to ingratiate themselves and share in her happiness. On the way to church the elder was on the right side of the bridal couple and the younger on the left. The doves came along and pecked out one of the elder sister's eyes and one of the younger sister's eyes. Afterward, on the way out, the elder was on the left side and the younger on the right, and the doves pecked out both the remaining eyes. So both sisters were punished with blindness to the end of their days for being so wicked and false.

# When the Clock Strikes

## TANITH LEE

*Tanith Lee has written what might be called an inversion of "Cinderella" wherein the heroine is a witch. You will find all elements of the traditional tale here, and Lee's rendering is unmistakably "Cinderella." But with devious consistency, Lee turns both the magic and the unrighted wrong that lie at the heart of the tale to a dark purpose: revenge. Tanith Lee is a prolific writer of stories for young adults and of adult fantasy and science fiction. Born in 1947 in London, Lee had her first story published when she was twenty-four and has written more than two dozen stories and plays since.*

Yes, the great ballroom is filled only with dust now. The slender columns of white marble and the slender columns of rose-red marble are woven together by cobwebs. The vivid frescoes, on which the Duke's treasury spent so much, are dimmed by the dust; the faces of the painted goddesses look grey. And the velvet curtains—touch them, they will crumble. Two hundred years now, since anyone danced in this place on the sea-green floor in the candle-gleam. Two hundred years since the wonderful clock struck for the very last time.

1

I thought you might care to examine the clock. It was considered exceptional in its day. The pedestal is ebony and the face fine porcelain. And these figures, which are of silver, would pass slowly about the circlet of the face. Each figure represents, you understand, an hour. And as the appropriate hours came level with this golden bell, they would strike it the correct number of times. All the figures are unique, as you see. Beginning at the first hour, they are, in this order, a girl-child, a dwarf, a maiden, a youth, a lady and a knight. And here, notice, the figures grow older as the day declines: a queen and king for the seventh and eighth hours, and after these, an abbess and a magician and next to last, a hag. But the very last is strangest of all. The twelfth figure; do you recognize him? It is Death. Yes, a most curious clock. It was reckoned a marvelous thing then. But it has not struck for two hundred years. Possibly you have been told the story? No? Oh, but I am certain that you have heard it, in another form, perhaps.

2

However, as you have some while to wait for your carriage, I will recount the tale, if you wish.

3

I will start with what was said of the clock. In those years, this city was prosperous, a stronghold—not as you see it today. Much was made

4

in the city that was ornamental and unusual. But the clock, on which the twelfth hour was Death, caused something of a stir. It was thought unlucky, foolhardy, to have such a clock. It began to be murmured, jokingly by some, by others in earnest, that one night when the clock struck the twelfth hour, Death would truly strike with it.

Now life has always been a chancy business, and it was more so then. The Great Plague had come but twenty years before and was not yet forgotten. Besides, in the Duke's court there was much intrigue, while enemies might be supposed to plot beyond the city walls, as happens even in our present age. But there was another thing.  5

It was rumored that the Duke had obtained both his title and the city treacherously. Rumor declared that he had systematically destroyed those who had stood in line before him, the members of the princely house that formerly ruled here. He had accomplished the task slyly, hiring assassins talented with poisons and daggers. But rumor also declared that the Duke had not been sufficiently thorough. For though he had meant to rid himself of all that rival house, a single descendant remained, so obscure he had not traced her—for it was a woman.  6

Of course, such matters were not spoken of openly. Like the prophecy of the clock, it was a subject for the dark.  7

Nevertheless, I will tell you at once, there was such a descendant he had missed in his bloody work. And she was a woman. Royal and proud she was, and seething with bitter spite and a hunger for vengeance, and as bloody as the Duke, had he known it, in her own way.  8

For her safety and disguise, she had long ago wed a wealthy merchant in the city, and presently bore the man a daughter. The merchant, a dealer in silks, was respected, a good fellow but not wise. He rejoiced in his handsome and aristocratic wife. He never dreamed what she might be about when he was not with her. In fact, she had sworn allegiance to Satanas. In the dead of night she would go up into an old tower adjoining the merchant's house, and there she would say portions of the Black Mass, offer sacrifice, and thereafter practise witchcraft against the Duke. This witchery took a common form, the creation of a wax image and the maiming of the image that, by sympathy, the injuries inflicted on the wax be passed on to the living body of the victim. The woman was capable in what she did. The Duke fell sick. He lost the use of his limbs and was racked by excruciating pains from which he could get no relief. Thinking himself on the brink of death, the Duke named his sixteen-year-old son his heir. This son was dear to the Duke, as everyone knew, and be sure the woman knew it too. She intended sorcerously to murder the young man in his turn, preferably in his father's sight. Thus, she let the Duke linger in his agony, and commenced planning the fate of the prince.  9

Now all this while she had not been toiling alone. She had one  10 helper. It was her own daughter, a maid of fourteen, that she had recruited to her service nearly as soon as the infant could walk. At six or seven, the child had been lisping the satanic rite along with her mother. At fourteen, you may imagine, the girl was well versed in the Black Arts, though she did not have her mother's natural genius for them.

Perhaps you would like me to describe the daughter at this point. 11 It has a bearing on the story, for the girl was astonishingly beautiful. Her hair was the rich dark red of antique burnished copper, her eyes were the hue of the reddish-golden amber that traders bring from the East. When she walked, you would say she was dancing. But when she danced, a gate seemed to open in the world, and bright fire spangled inside it, but she was the fire.

The girl and her mother were close as gloves in a box. Their games 12 in the old tower bound them closer. No doubt the woman believed herself clever to have got such a helpmate, but it proved her undoing.

It was in this manner. The silk merchant, who had never suspected 13 his wife for an instant of anything, began to mistrust the daughter. She was not like other girls. Despite her great beauty, she professed no interest in marriage, and none in clothes or jewels. She preferred to read in the garden at the foot of the tower. Her mother had taught the girl her letters, though the merchant himself could read but poorly. And often the father peered at the books his daughter read, unable to make head or tail of them, yet somehow not liking them. One night very late, the silk merchant came home from a guild dinner in the city, and he saw a slim pale shadow gliding up the steps of the old tower, and he knew it for his child. On impulse, he followed her, but quietly. He had not considered any evil so far, and did not want to alarm her. At an angle of the stair, the lighted room above, he paused to spy and listen. He had something of a shock when he heard his wife's voice rise up in glad welcome. But what came next drained the blood from his heart. He crept away and went to his cellar for wine to stay himself. After the third glass he ran for neighbours and for the watch.

The woman and her daughter heard the shouts below and saw the 14 torches in the garden. It was no use dissembling. The tower was littered with evidence of vile deeds, besides what the woman kept in a chest beneath her unknowing husband's bed. She understood it was all up with her, and she understood too how witchcraft was punished hereabouts. She snatched a knife from the altar.

The girl shrieked when she realized what her mother was at. The 15 woman caught the girl by her red hair and shook her.

"Listen to me, my daughter," she cried, "and listen carefully, for the 16 minutes are short. If you do as I tell you, you can escape their wrath and only I need die. And if you live I am satisfied, for you can carry on my labor after me. My vengeance I shall leave you, and my witchcraft to exact it by. Indeed, I promise you stronger powers than mine. I will beg my lord Satanas for it and he will not deny me, for he is just, in his fashion, and I have served him well. Now, will you attend?"

"I will," said the girl.     17

So the woman advised her, and swore her to the fellowship of Hell.     18
And then the woman forced the knife into her own heart and dropped dead on the floor of the tower.

When the men burst in with their swords and staves and their     19
torches and their madness, the girl was ready for them.

She stood blank-faced, blank-eyed, with her arms hanging at her     20
sides. When one touched her, she dropped down at his feet.

"Surely she is innocent," this man said. She was lovely enough that     21
it was hard to accuse her. Then her father went to her and took her hand and lifted her. At that the girl opened her eyes and she said, as if terrified: "How did I come here? I was in my chamber and sleeping—"

"The woman has bewitched her," her father said.     22

He desired very much that this be so. And when the girl clung to     23
his hand and wept, he was certain of it. They showed her the body with the knife in it. The girl screamed and seemed to lose her senses totally.

She was put to bed. In the morning, a priest came and questioned     24
her. She answered steadfastly. She remembered nothing, not even of the great books she had been observed reading. When they told her what was in them, she screamed again and apparently would have thrown herself from the narrow window, only the priest stopped her.

Finally, they brought her the holy cross in order that she might kiss     25
it and prove herself blameless.

Then she knelt, and whispered softly, that nobody should hear but     26
one—"Lord Satanas, protect thy handmaid." And either that gentleman has more power than he is credited with or else the symbols of God are only as holy as the men who deal in them, for she embraced the cross and it left her unscathed.

At that, the whole household thanked God. The whole household     27
saving, of course, the woman's daughter. She had another to thank.

The woman's body was burnt, and the ashes put into unconsecrated     28
ground beyond the city gates. Though they had discovered her to be a witch, they had not discovered the direction her witchcraft had selected. Nor did they find the wax image with its limbs all twisted and stuck through with needles. The girl had taken that up and concealed it. The Duke continued in his distress, but he did not die. Sometimes, in the dead of night, the girl would unearth the image from under a loose brick by the hearth, and gloat over it, but she did nothing else. Not yet. She was fourteen and the cloud of her mother's acts still hovered over her. She knew what she must do next.

---

The period of mourning ended.                                                    29

"Daughter," said the silk merchant to her, "why do you not remove     30
your black? The woman was malign and led you into wickedness. How
long will you mourn her, who deserves no mourning?"

"Oh my father," she said, "never think I regret my wretched mother.    31
It is my own unwitting sin I mourn." And she grasped his hand and
spilled her tears on it. "I would rather live in a convent," said she, "than
mingle with proper folk. And I would seek a convent too, if it were not
that I cannot bear to be parted from you."

Do you suppose she smiled secretly as she said this? One might      32
suppose it. Presently she donned a robe of sackcloth and poured ashes
over her red-copper hair. "It is my penance," she said, "I am glad to
atone for my sins."

People forgot her beauty. She was at pains to obscure it. She slunk    33
about like an aged woman, a rag pulled over her head, dirt smeared on
her cheeks and brow. She elected to sleep in a cold cramped attic and
sat all day by a smoky hearth in the kitchens. When someone came to
her and begged her to wash her face and put on suitable clothes and sit
in the rooms of the house, she smiled modestly, drawing the rag or a
piece of hair over her face. "I swear," she said, "I am glad to be humble
before God and men."

They reckoned her pious and they reckoned her simple. Two       34
years passed. They mislaid her beauty altogether, and reckoned her
ugly. They found it hard to call to mind who she was exactly, as
she sat in the ashes, or shuffled unattended about the streets like a
crone.

At the end of the second year, the silk merchant married again. It     35
was inevitable, for he was not a man who liked to live alone.

On this occasion, his choice was a harmless widow. She already      36
had two daughters, pretty in an unremarkable style. Perhaps the merchant hoped they would comfort him for what had gone before, this
normal cheery wife and the two sweet, rather silly daughters, whose
chief interests were clothes and weddings. Perhaps he hoped also that
his deranged daughter might be drawn out by company. But that
hope foundered. Not that the new mother did not try to be pleasant
to the girl. And the new sisters, their hearts grieved by her condition,
went to great lengths to enlist her friendship. They begged her to
come from the kitchens or the attic. Failing in that, they sometimes
ventured to join her, their fine silk dresses trailing on the greasy floor.
They combed her hair, exclaiming, when some of the ash and dirt
were removed, on its color. But no sooner had they turned away, than
the girl gathered up handfuls of soot and ash and rubbed them into
her hair again. Now and then, the sisters attempted to interest their
bizarre relative in a bracelet or a gown or a current song. They spoke

to her of the young men they had seen at the suppers or the balls which were then given regularly by the rich families of the city. The girl ignored it all. If she ever said anything it was to do with penance and humility. At last, as must happen, the sisters wearied of her, and left her alone. They had no cares and did not want to share in hers. They came to resent her moping greyness, as indeed the merchant's second wife had already done.

"Can you do nothing with the girl?" she demanded of her husband. **37** "People will say that I and my daughters are responsible for her condition and that I ill-treat the maid from jealousy of her dead mother."

"Now how could anyone say that?" protested the merchant, "when **38** you are famous as the epitome of generosity and kindness."

Another year passed, and saw no huge difference in the household. **39** A difference there was, but not visible. **40**

The girl who slouched in the corner of the hearth was seventeen. **41** Under the filth and grime she was, impossibly, more beautiful, although no one could see it.

And there was one other invisible item—her power (which all this **42** time she had nurtured, saying her prayers to Satanas in the black of midnight), her power was rising like a dark moon in her soul.

Three days after her seventeenth birthday, the girl straggled about **43** the streets as she frequently did. A few noted her and muttered it was the merchant's ugly simple daughter and paid no more attention. Most did not know her at all. She had made herself appear one with the scores of impoverished flotsam which constantly roamed the city, beggars and starvelings. Just outside the city gates, these persons congregated in large numbers, slumped around fires of burning refuse or else wandering to and fro in search of edible seeds, scraps, the miracle of a dropped coin. Here the girl now came, and began to wander about as they did. Dusk gathered and the shadows thickened. The girl sank to her knees in a patch of earth as if she had found something. Two or three of the beggars sneaked over to see if it were worth snatching from her—but the girl was only scrabbling in the empty soil. The beggars, making signs to each other that she was touched by God—mad—left her alone. But, very far from mad, the girl presently dug up a stoppered clay urn. In this urn were the ashes and charred bones of her mother. She had got a clue as to the location of the urn by devious questioning here and there. Her occult power had helped her to be sure of it.

In the twilight, padding along through the narrow streets and alleys **44** of the city, the girl brought the urn homewards. In the garden at the foot of the old tower, gloom-wrapped, unwitnessed, she unstoppered the urn and buried the ashes freshly. She muttered certain unholy magics over the grave. Then she snapped off the sprig of a young hazel tree, and planted it in the newly turned ground.

I hazard you have begun to recognize the story by now. I see you 45
suppose I tell it wrongly. Believe me, this is the truth of the matter. But
if you would rather I left off the tale . . . No doubt your carriage will
soon be here—No? Very well. I shall continue.

I think I should speak of the Duke's son at this juncture. The prince 46
was nineteen, able, intelligent, and of noble bearing. He was of that
rather swarthy type of looks one finds here in the north, but tall and slim
and clear-eyed. There is an ancient square where you may see a statue
of him, but much eroded by two centuries, and the elements. After the
city was sacked, no care was lavished on it.

The Duke treasured his son. He had constant delight in the sight of 47
the young man and what he said and did. It was the only happiness the
invalid had.

Then, one night, the Duke screamed out in his bed. Servants came 48
running with candles. The Duke moaned that a sword was transfixing
his heart, an inch at a time. The prince hurried into the chamber, but in
that instant the Duke spasmed horribly and died. No mark was on his
body. There had never been a mark to show what ailed him.

The prince wept. They were genuine tears. He had nothing to 49
reproach his father with, everything to thank him for. Nevertheless, they
brought the young man the seal ring of the city, and he put it on.

It was winter, a cold blue-white weather with snow in the streets 50
and countryside and a hard wizened sun that drove thin sharp blades
of light through the sky, but gave no warmth. The Duke's funeral
cortege passed slowly across the snow, the broad open chariots
draped with black and silver, the black-plumed horses, the chanting
priests with their glittering robes, their jeweled crucifixes and golden
censers. Crowds lined the roadways to watch the spectacle. Among
the beggar women stood a girl. No one noticed her. They did not
glimpse the expression she veiled in her ragged scarf. She gazed at the
bier pitilessly. As the young prince rode by in his sables, the seal ring
on his hand, the eyes of the girl burned through her ashy hair, like a
red fox through grasses.

The Duke was buried in the mausoleum you can visit to this day, 51
on the east side of the city. Several months elapsed. The prince put his
grief from him, and took up the business of the city competently. Wise
and courteous he was, but he rarely smiled. At nineteen his spirit seemed
worn. You might think he guessed the destiny that hung over him.

The winter was a hard one, too. The snow had come, and having 52
come was loath to withdraw. When at last the spring returned, flushing
the hills with color, it was no longer sensible to be sad.

The prince's name day fell about this time. A great banquet was 53
planned, a ball. There had been neither in the palace for nigh on three
years, not since the Duke's fatal illness first claimed him. Now the

royal doors were to be thrown open to all men of influence and their families. The prince was liberal, charming and clever even in this. Aristocrat and rich trader were to mingle in the beautiful dining room, and in this very chamber, among the frescoes, the marbles and the candelabra. Even a merchant's daughter, if the merchant were notable in the city, would get to dance on the sea-green floor, under the white eye of the fearful clock.

The clock. There was some renewed controversy about the clock. 54 They did not dare speak to the young prince. He was a skeptic, as his father had been. But had not a death already occurred? Was the clock not a flying in the jaws of fate? For those disturbed by it, there was a dim writing in their minds, in the dust of the street or the pattern of blossoms. *When the clock strikes*—But people do not positively heed these warnings. Man is afraid of his fears. He ignores the shadow of the wolf thrown on the paving before him, saying: It is only a shadow.

The silk merchant received his invitation to the palace, and to be 55 sure, thought nothing of the clock. His house had been thrown into uproar. The most luscious silks of his workshop were carried into the house and laid before the wife and her two daughters, who chirruped and squealed with excitement. The merchant stood smugly by, above it all yet pleased at being appreciated. "Oh, father!" cried the two sisters, "may I have this one with the gold piping?" "Oh, father, this one with the design of pineapples?" Later, a jeweler arrived and set out his trays. The merchant was generous. He wanted his women to look their best. It might be the night of their lives. Yet all the while, at the back of his mind, a little dark spot, itching, aching. He tried to ignore the spot, not scratch at it. His true daughter, the mad one. Nobody bothered to tell her about the invitation to the palace. They knew how she would react, mumbling in her hair about her sin and her penance, paddling her hands in the greasy ash to smear her face. Even the servants avoided her, as if she were just the cat seated by the fire. Less than the cat, for the cat saw to the mice—Just a block of stone. And yet, how fair she might have looked, decked in the pick of the merchant's wares, jewels at her throat. The prince himself could not have been unaware of her. And though marriage was impossible, other less holy, though equally honorable contracts, might have been arranged to the benefit of all concerned. The merchant sighed. He had scratched the darkness after all. He attempted to comfort himself by watching the two sisters exult over their apparel. He refused to admit that the finery would somehow make them seem but more ordinary than they were by contrast.

The evening of the banquet arrived. The family set off. Most of the 56 servants sidled after. The prince had distributed largesse in the city; oxen roasted in the squares and the wine was free by royal order.

The house grew somber. In the deserted kitchen the fire went out. 57

By the heart, a segment of gloom rose up.    58

The girl glanced around her, and she laughed softly and shook out    59
her filthy hair. Of course, she knew as much as anyone, and more than
most. This was to be her night, too.

A few minutes later she was in the garden beneath the old tower,    60
standing over the young hazel tree which thrust up from the earth. It
had become strong, the tree, despite the harsh winter. Now the girl
nodded to it. She chanted under her breath. At length a pale light began
to glow, far down near where the roots of the tree held to the ground.
Out of the pale glow flew a thin black bird, which perched on the girl's
shoulder. Together, the girl and the bird passed into the old tower. High
up, a fire blazed that no one had lit. A tub steamed with scented water
that no one had drawn. Shapes that were not real and barely seen flitted
about. Rare perfumes, the rustle of garments, the glint of gems as yet
invisible filled and did not fill the restless air.

. Need I describe further? No. You will have seen paintings which    61
depict the attendance upon a witch of her familiar demons. Now one
bathes her, another anoints her, another brings clothes and ornaments.
Perhaps you do not credit such things in any case. Never mind that. I
will tell you what happened in the courtyard before the palace.

Many carriages and chariots had driven through the square, avoid-    62
ing the roasting oxen, the barrels of wine, the cheering drunken citizens,
and so through the gates into the courtyard. Just before ten o'clock (the
hour, if you recall the clock, of the magician) a solitary carriage drove
through the square and into the court. The people in the square gawked
at the carriage and pressed forward to see who would step out of it, this
latecomer. It was a remarkable vehicle that looked to be fashioned of
solid gold, all but the domed roof that was transparent flashing crystal.
Six black horses drew it. The coachman and postillions were clad in
crimson, and strangely masked as curious beasts and reptiles. One of
these beast-men now hopped down and opened the door of the carriage.
Out came a woman's figure in a cloak of white fur, and glided up the
palace stair and in at the doors.

There was dancing in the ballroom. The whole chamber was bright    63
and clamorous with music and the voices of men and women. There,
between those two pillars, the prince sat in his chair, dark, courteous,
seldom smiling. Here the musicians played, the deep-throated viol, the
lively mandolin. And there the dancers moved up and down on the
sea-green floor. But the music and the dancers had just paused. The
figures on the clock were themselves in motion. The hour of the magician was about to strike.

As it struck, through the doorway came the figure in the fur cloak.    64
And, as if they must, every eye turned to her.

For an instant she stood there, all white, as though she had brought    65

493

the winter snow back with her. And then she loosed the cloak from her shoulders, it slipped away, and she was all fire.

She wore a gown of apricot brocade embroidered thickly with gold. 66 Her sleeves and the bodice of her gown were slashed over ivory satin sewn with large rosy pearls. Pearls, too, were wound in her hair that was the shade of antique burnished copper. She was so beautiful that when the clock was still, nobody spoke. She was so beautiful it was hard to look at her for very long.

The prince got up from his chair. He did not know he had. Now he 67 started out across the floor, between the dancers, who parted silently to let him through. He went toward the girl in the doorway as if she drew him by a chain.

The prince had hardly ever acted without considering first what he 68 did. Now he did not consider. He bowed to the girl.

"Madam," he said. "You are welcome. Madam," he said. "Tell me 69 who you are."

She smiled. 70

"My rank," she said. "Would you know that, my lord? It is similar 71 to yours, or would be were I now mistress in my dead mother's palace. But, unfortunately, an unscrupulous man caused the downfall of our house."

"Misfortune indeed," said the prince. "Tell me your name. Let me 72 right the wrong done you."

"You shall," said the girl. "Trust me, you shall. For my name, I would 73 rather keep it secret for the present. But you may call me, if you will, a pet name I have given myself—Ashella."

"Ashella. . . . But I see no ash about you," said the prince, dazzled 74 by her gleam, laughing a little, stiffly, for laughter was not his habit.

"Ash and cinders from a cold and bitter hearth," said she. But she 75 smiled again. "Now everyone is staring at us, my lord, and the musicians are impatient to begin again. Out of all these ladies, can it be you will lead me in the dance?"

"As long as you will dance," he said. "You shall dance with me." 76

And that is how it was. 77

There were many dances, slow and fast, whirling measures and 78 gentle ones. And here and there, the prince and the maiden were parted. Always then he looked eagerly after her, sparing no regard for the other girls whose hands lay in his. It was not like him, he was usually so careful. But the other young men who danced on that floor, who clasped her fingers or her narrow waist in the dance, also gazed after her when she was gone. She danced, as she appeared, like fire. Though if you had asked those young men whether they would rather tie her to themselves, as the prince did, they would have been at a loss. For it is not easy to keep pace with fire.

The hour of the hag struck on the clock.   79

The prince grew weary of dancing with the girl and losing her in   80
the dance to others and refinding her and losing her again.

Behind the curtains there is a tall window in the east wall that opens   81
on the terrace above the garden. He drew her out there, into the spring
night. He gave an order, and small tables were brought with delicacies
and sweets and wine. He sat by her, watching every gesture she made,
as if he would paint her portrait afterward.

In the ballroom, here, under the clock, the people murmured. But it   82
was not quite the murmur you would expect, the scandalous murmur
about a woman come from nowhere that the prince had made so much
of. At the periphery of the ballroom, the silk merchant sat, pale as a
ghost, thinking of a ghost, the living ghost of his true daughter. No one
else recognized her. Only he. Some trick of the heart had enabled him
to know her. He said nothing of it. As the step-sisters and wife gossiped
with other wives and sisters, an awful foreboding weighed him down,
sent him cold and dumb.

And now it is almost midnight, the moment when the page of the   83
night turns over into day. Almost midnight, the hour when the figure
of Death strikes the golden bell of the clock. And what will happen
when the clock strikes? Your face announces that you know. Be patient;
let us see if you do.

"I am being foolish," said the prince to Ashella on the terrace. "But   84
perhaps I am entitled to foolish, just once in my life. What are you
saying?" For the girl was speaking low beside him, and he could not
catch her words.

"I am saying a spell to bind you to me," she said.   85

"But I am already bound."   86

"Be bound then. Never go free."   87

"I do not wish it," he said. He kissed her hands and he said, "I do   88
not know you, but I will wed you. Is that proof your spell has worked?
I will wed you, and get back for you the rights you have lost."

"If it were only so simple," said Ashella, smiling, smiling. "But the   89
debt is too cruel. Justice requires a harsher payment."

And then, in the ballroom, Death struck the first note on the golden   90
bell.

The girl smiled and she said,   91

"I curse you in my mother's name."   92

The second stroke.   93

"I curse you in my own name."   94

The third stroke.   95

"And in the name of those that your father slew."   96

The fourth stroke.   97

"And in the name of my Master, who rules the world." 98

As the fifth, the sixth, the seventh strokes pealed out, the prince 99
stood nonplussed. At the eighth and the ninth strokes, the strength of
the malediction seemed to curdle his blood. He shivered and his brain
writhed. At the tenth stroke, he saw a change in the loveliness before
him. She grew thinner, taller. At the eleventh stroke, he beheld a thing
in a ragged black cowl and robe. It grinned at him. It was all grin below
a triangle of sockets of nose and eyes. At the twelfth stroke, the prince
saw Death and knew him.

In the ballroom, a hideous grinding noise, as the gears of the clock 100
failed. Followed by a hollow booming, as the mechanism stopped entirely.

The conjuration of Death vanished from the terrace. 101

Only one thing was left behind. A woman's shoe. A shoe no woman 102
could ever have danced in. It was made of glass.

Did you intend to protest about the shoe? Shall I finish the story, 103
or would you rather I did not? It is not the ending you are familiar with.
Yes, I perceive you understand that, now.

I will go quickly, then, for your carriage must soon be here. And 104
there is not a great deal more to relate.

The prince lost his mind. Partly from what he had seen, partly from 105
the spells the young witch had netted him in. He could think of nothing
but the girl who had named herself Ashella. He raved that Death had
borne her away but he would recover her from Death. She had left the
glass shoe as token of her love. He must discover her with the aid of
the shoe. Whomsoever the shoe fitted would be Ashella. For there was
this added complication, that Death might hide her actual appearance.
None had seen the girl before. She had disappeared like smoke. The one
infallible test was the shoe. That was why she had left it for him.

His ministers would have reasoned with the prince, but he was past 106
reason. His intellect had collapsed as totally as only a profound intellect
can. A lunatic, he rode about the city. He struck out at those who argued
with him. On a particular occasion, drawing a dagger, he killed, not
apparently noticing what he did. His demand was explicit. Every
woman, young or old, maid or married, must come forth from her home,
must put her foot into the shoe of glass. They came. They had not
choice. Some approached in terror, some weeping. Even the aged beggar
women obliged, and they cackled, enjoying the sight of royalty gone
mad. One alone did not come.

Now it is not illogical that out of the hundreds of women whose feet 107
were put into the shoe, a single woman might have been found that the
shoe fitted. But this did not happen. Nor did the situation alter, despite
a lurid fable that some, tickled by the idea of wedding the prince, cut off

their toes that the shoe might fit them. And if they did, it was to no avail, for still the shoe did not.

Is it really surprising? The shoe was sorcerous. It constantly changed 108 itself, its shape, its size, in order that no foot, save one, could ever be got into it.

Summer spread across the land. The city took on its golden summer 109 glaze, its fetid summer smell.

What had been a whisper of intrigue, swelled into a steady distant 110 thunder. Plots were being hatched.

One day, the silk merchant was brought, trembling and grey of face, 111 to the prince. The merchant's dumbness had broken. He had unburdened himself of his fear at confession, but the priest had not proved honest. In the dawn, men had knocked on the door of the merchant's house. Now he stumbled to the chair of the prince.

Both looked twice their years, but, if anything, the prince looked the 112 elder. He did not lift his eyes. Over and over in his hands he turned the glass shoe.

The merchant, stumbling too in his speech, told the tale of his first 113 wife and his daughter. He told everything, leaving out no detail. He did not even omit the end: that since the night of the banquet the girl had been absent from his house, taking nothing with her—save a young hazel from the garden beneath the tower.

The prince leapt from his chair. 114

His clothes were filthy and unkempt. His face was smeared with 115 sweat and dust . . . it resembled, momentarily, another face.

Without guard or attendant, the prince ran through the city toward 116 the merchant's house, and on the road, the intriguers waylaid and slew him. As he fell, the glass shoe dropped from his hands, and shattered in a thousand fragments.

There is little else worth mentioning. 117

Those who usurped the city were villains and not merely that, but 118 fools. Within a year, external enemies were at the gates. A year more, and the city had been sacked, half burnt out, ruined. The manner in which you find it now, is somewhat better than it was then. And it is not now anything for a man to be proud of. As you were quick to note, many here earn a miserable existence by conducting visitors about the streets, the palace, showing them the dregs of the city's past.

Which was not a request, in fact, for you to give me money. Throw 119 some from your carriage window if your conscience bothers you. My own wants are few.

No, I have no further news of the girl, Ashella, the witch. A devotee 120 of Satanas, she has doubtless worked plentiful woe in the world. And a witch is long-lived. Even so, she will die eventually. None escapes Death. Then you may pity her, if you like. Those who serve the gentleman below—who can guess what their final lot will be? But I am very sorry the story did not please you. It is not, maybe, a happy choice before a journey.

And there is your carriage at last. 121

What? Ah, no, I shall stay here in the ballroom where you came on 122 me. I have often paused here through the years. It is the clock. It has a certain—what shall I call it—power, to draw me back.

I am not trying to unnerve you. Why should you suppose that? 123 Because of my knowledge of the city, of the story? You think that I am implying that I myself am Death? Now you laugh. Yes, it is absurd. Observe the twelfth figure on the clock. Is he not as you have always heard Death described? And am I in the least like that twelfth figure?

Although, of course, the story was not as you have heard it, either. 124


# A Chinese "Cinderella"

## TUAN CH'ÊNG-SHIH

*"The earliest datable version of the Cinderella story anywhere in the world occurs in a Chinese book written about 850–860 A.D." Thus begins Arthur Waley's essay on the Chinese "Cinderella" in the March 1947 edition of Folk-Lore. The recorder of the tale is a man named Tuan Ch'êng-shih, whose father was an important official in Szechwan and who himself held a high post in the office arranging the ceremonies associated with imperial ancestor worship.*

Among the people of the south there is a tradition that before the Ch'in 1 and Han dynasties there was a cave-master called Wu. The aborigines called the place the Wu cave. He married two wives. One wife died. She had a daughter called Yeh-hsien, who from childhood was intelligent and good at making pottery on the wheel. Her father loved her. After some years the father died, and she was ill-treated by her step-mother, who always made her collect firewood in dangerous places and draw water from deep pools. She once got a fish about two inches long, with red fins and golden eyes. She put it into a bowl of water. It grew bigger every day, and after she had changed the bowl several times she could find no bowl big enough for it, so she threw it into the back pond.

"The Chinese Cinderella Story" by Tuan Ch'êng-Shih, translated by Arthur Waley. Folk-Lore 58, March 1947, pp. 226–238. Reprinted by permission of the Folklore Society.

Whatever food was left over from meals she put into the water to feed it. When she came to the pond, the fish always exposed its head and pillowed it on the bank; but when anyone else came, it did not come out. The step-mother knew about this, but when she watched for it, it did not once appear. So she tricked the girl, saying, "Haven't you worked hard! I am going to give you a new dress." She then made the girl change out of her tattered clothing. Afterwards she sent her to get water from another spring and reckoning that it was several hundred leagues, the step-mother at her leisure put on her daughter's clothes, hid a sharp blade up her sleeve, and went to the pond. She called to the fish. The fish at once put its head out, and she chopped it off and killed it. The fish was now more than ten feet long. She served it up and it tasted twice as good as an ordinary fish. She hid the bones under the dung-hill. Next day, when the girl came to the pond, no fish appeared. She howled with grief in the open countryside, and suddenly there appeared a man with his hair loose over his shoulders and coarse clothes. He came down from the sky. He consoled her, saying, "Don't howl! Your step-mother has killed the fish and its bones are under the dung. You go back, take the fish's bones and hide them in your room. Whatever you want, you have only to pray to them for it. It is bound to be granted." The girl followed his advice, and was able to provide herself with gold, pearls, dresses and food whenever she wanted them.

When the time came for the cave-festival, the step-mother went, leaving the girl to keep watch over the fruit-trees in the garden. She waited till the step-mother was some way off, and then went herself, wearing a cloak of stuff spun from kingfisher feathers and shoes of gold. Her step-sister recognized her and said to the step-mother, "That's very like my sister." The step-mother suspected the same thing. The girl was aware of this and went away in such a hurry that she lost one shoe. It was picked up by one of the people of the cave. When the step-mother got home, she found the girl asleep, with her arms around one of the trees in the garden, and thought no more about it.

This cave was near to an island in the sea. On this island was a kingdom called T'o-han. Its soldiers had subdued twenty or thirty other islands and it had a coast-line of several thousand leagues. The cave-man sold the shoe in T'o-han, and the ruler of T'o-han got it. He told those about him to put it on; but it was an inch too small even for the one among them that had the smallest foot. He ordered all the women in his kingdom to try it on, but there was not one that it fitted. It was light as down and made no noise even when treading on stone. The king of T'o-han thought the cave-man had got it unlawfully. He put him in prison and tortured him, but did not end by finding out where it had come from. So he threw it down at the wayside. Then they went everywhere[1] through all the people's houses and arrested them. If there was a woman's shoe, they arrested them and told the king of T'o-han. He thought it strange, searched the inner-rooms and found Yeh-hsien. He made her put on the shoe, and it was true.

Yeh-hsien then came forward, wearing her cloak spun from halcyon feathers and her shoes. She was as beautiful as a heavenly being. She now began to render service to the king, and he took the fish-bones and Yeh-hsien, and brought them back to his country.                              4

The step-mother and step-sister were shortly afterwards struck by flying stones, and died. The cave people were sorry for them and buried them in a stone-pit, which was called the Tomb of the Distressed Women. The men of the cave made mating-offerings there; any girl they prayed for there, they got. The king of T'o-han, when he got back to his kingdom, made Yeh-hsien his chief wife. The first year the king was very greedy and by his prayers to the fish-bones got treasures and jade without limit. Next year, there was no response, so the king buried the fish-bones on the sea-shore. He covered them with a hundred bushels of pearls and bordered them with gold. Later there was a mutiny of some soldiers who had been conscripted and their general opened (the hiding-place) in order to make better provision for his army. One night they (the bones) were washed away by the tide.                              5

This story was told me by Li Shih-yüan, who has been in the service of my family a long while. He was himself originally a man from the caves of Yung-chou and remembers many strange things of the South.                              6

# The Maiden, the Frog, and the Chief's Son (An African "Cinderella")

*The version of the tale that follows was recorded in the (West African) Hausa language and published, originally, in 1911 by Frank Edgar. The tale remained unavailable to nonspeakers of Hausa until 1965, when Neil Skinner (of UCLA) completed an English translation.*

There was once a man had two wives, and they each had a daughter. And the one wife, together with her daughter, he couldn't abide; but the other, with her daughter, he dearly loved.                              1

---

[1]Something here seems to have gone slightly wrong with the text. [Waley]
Excerpt from "Cinderella in Africa" by William Bascom from *Cinderella: A Folklore Casebook* edited by Alan Dundes. Reprinted by permission of Garland Publishing, Inc.

Well, the day came when the wife that he disliked fell ill, and it so          2
happened that her illness proved fatal, and she died. And her daughter
was taken over by the other wife, the one he loved; and she moved into
that wife's hut. And there she dwelt, having no mother of her own, just
her father. And every day the woman would push her out, to go off to
the bush to gather wood. When she returned, she had to pound up the
*fura.* Then she had the *tuwo* to pound, and, after that, to stir. And then
they wouldn't even let her eat the *tuwo.* All they gave her to eat were
the burnt bits at the bottom of the pot. And day after day she continued
thus.

Now she had an elder brother, and he invited her to come and eat          3
regularly at his home—to which she agreed. But still when she had been
to the bush, and returned home, and wanted a drink of water, they
wouldn't let her have one. Nor would they give her proper food—only
the coarsest of the grindings and the scrapings from the pot. These she
would take, and going with them to a borrow-pit, throw them in. And
the frogs would come out and start eating the scrapings. Then, having
eaten them up, they would go back into the water; and she too would
return home.

And so things went on day after day, until the day of the Festival          4
arrived. And on this day, when she went along with the scrapings and
coarse grindings, she found a frog squatting there; and realised that he
was waiting for her! She got there and threw in the bits of food.
Whereupon the frog said, "Maiden, you've always been very kind to us,
and now we—but just you come along tomorrow morning. That's the
morning of the Festival. Come along then, and we'll be kind to you, in
our turn." "Fine" she said, and went off home.

Next morning was the Festival, and she was going off to the          5
borrow-pit, just as the frog had told her. But as she was going, her
half-sister's mother said to her, "Hey—come here, you good-for-nothing girl! You haven't stirred the *tuwo,* or pounded the *fura,* or fetched
the wood or the water." So the girl returned. And the frog spent the
whole day waiting for her. But she, having returned to the compound,
set off to fetch wood. Then she fetched water, and set about pounding
the *tuwo,* and stirred it till it was done and then took it off the fire. And
presently she was told to take the scrapings. She did so and went off to
the borrow-pit, where she found the frog. "Tut tut, girl!" said he, "I've
been waiting for you here since morning, and you never came." "Old
fellow" she said, "You see, I'm a slave." "How come?" he asked. "Simple"
she said, "My mother died—died leaving me her only daughter. I have
an elder brother, but he is married and has a compound of his own. And
my father put me in the care of his other wife. And indeed he had never
loved my mother. So I was moved into the hut of his other wife. And,
as I told you, slavery is my lot. Every morning I have to go off to the

bush to get wood. When I get back from that I have to pound the *fura*, and then I pound the *tuwo*, and then start stirring it. And even when I have finished stirring the *tuwo*, I'm not given it to eat—just the scrapings." Says the frog, "Girl, give us your hand." And she held it out to him, and they both leaped into the water.

Then he went and picked her up and swallowed her. (And he vomited her up.) "Good people" said he, "Look and tell me, is she straight or crooked?" And they looked and answered, "She is bent to the left." So he picked her up and swallowed her again and then brought her up, and again asked them the same question. "She's quite straight now" they said. "Good" said he.   6

Next he vomited up cloths for her, and bangles, and rings, and a pair of shoes, one of silver, one of gold. "And now" said he, "Off you go to the dancing." So all these things were given to her, and he said to her "When you get there, and when the dancing is nearly over and the dancers dispersing, you're to leave your golden shoe, the right one, there." And the girl replied to the frog, "Very well, old fellow, I understand," and off she went.   7

Meanwhile the chief's son had caused the young men and girls to dance for his pleasure, and when she reached the space where they were dancing he saw her. "Well!" said the chief's son, *"There's* a maiden for you, if you like. Don't you let her go and join in the dancing—I don't care whose home she comes from. Bring her here!" So the servants of the chief's son went over and came back with her to where he was. He told her to sit down on the couch, and she took her seat there accordingly.   8

They chatted together for some time, till the dancers began to disperse. Then she said to the chief's son, "I must be going home." "Oh, are you off?" said he. "Yes," said she and rose to her feet. "I'll accompany you on your way for a little" said the chief's son, and he did so. But she had left her right shoe behind. Presently she said, "Chief's son, you must go back now," and he did so. And afterwards she too turned and made her way back.   9

And there she found the frog by the edge of the water waiting for her. He took her hand and the two of them jumped into the water. Then he picked her up and swallowed her, and again vomited her up; and there she was, just as she had been before, a sorry sight. And taking her ragged things she went off home.   10

When she got there, she said, "Fellow-wife of my mother, I'm not feeling very well." And the other said, "Rascally slut! You have been up to no good—refusing to come home, refusing to fetch water or wood, refusing to pound the *fura* or make the *tuwo*. Very well then! No food for you today!" And so the girl set off to her elder brother's compound, and there ate her food, and so returned home again.   11

---

But meanwhile the chief's son had picked up the shoe and said to his father, "Dad, I have seen a girl who wears a pair of shoes, one of gold, one of silver. Look, here's the golden one—she forgot it and left it behind. She's the girl I want to marry. So let all the girls of this town, young and old, be gathered together, and let this shoe be given to them to put on." "Very well" said the chief. 12

And so it was proclaimed, and all the girls, young and old, were collected and gathered together. And the chief's son went and sat there beside the shoe. Each girl came, and each tried on the shoe, but it fitted none of them, none of the girls of the town; until only the girl who had left it was left. Then someone said "Just a minute! There's that girl in so-and-so's compound, whose mother died." "Yes, that's right," said another, "Someone go and fetch her." And someone went and fetched her. 13

But the minute she arrived to try it on, the shoe itself of its own accord, ran across and made her foot get into it. Then said the chief's son, "Right, here's my wife." 14

At this, the other woman—the girl's father's other wife—said, "But the shoe belongs to my daughter; it was she who forgot it at the place of the dancing, not this good-for-nothing slut." But the chief's son insisted that, since he had seen the shoe fit the other girl, as far as he was concerned, she was the one to be taken to his compound in marriage. And so they took her there, and there she spent one night. 15

Next morning she went out of her hut and round behind it, and there saw the frog. She knelt respectfully and said, "Welcome, old fellow, welcome" and greeted him. Says he, "Tonight we shall be along to bring some things for you." "Thank you" said she, and he departed. 16

Well, that night, the frog rallied all the other frogs, and all his friends, both great and small came along. And he, their leader, said to them, "See here—my daughter is being married. So I want every one of you to make a contribution." And each of them went and fetched what he could afford, whereupon their leader thanked them all, and then vomited up a silver bed, a brass bed, a copper bed, and an iron bed. And went on vomiting up things for her—such as woollen blankets, and rugs, and satins, and velvets. 17

"Now" said he to the girl, "If your heart is ever troubled, just lie down on this brass bed" and he went on, "And when the chief's son's other wives come to greet you, give them two calabashes of cola-nuts and ten thousand cowrie shells; then, when his concubines come to greet you, give them one calabash of cola-nuts and five thousand cowries." "Very well" said she. Then he said, "And when the concubines come to receive corn for making *tuwo*, say to them, 'There's a hide-bag full, help yourselves'." "Very well" she said. "And" he went on, "If your father's wife comes along with her daughter and asks you what it is like living 18 in the chief's compound, say 'Living in the chief's compound is a wearisome business—for they measure out corn there with the shell of a Bambara groundnut'."

So there she dwelt, until one day her father's favourite wife brought 19 her daughter along at night, took her into the chief's compound, and brought the other girl out and took her to her own compound. There she said. "Oh! I forgot to get you to tell her all about married life in the chief's compound." "Oh, it's a wearisome business" answered our girl. "How so?" asked the older woman, surprised. "Well, they use the shell of a Bambara groundnut for measuring out corn. Then, if the chief's other wives come to greet you, you answer them with the 'Pf' of contempt. If the concubines come to greet you, you clear your throat, hawk, and spit. And if your husband comes into your hut, you yell at him." "I see" said the other—and her daughter stayed behind the chief's son's compound.

Next morning when it was light, the wives came to greet her—and 20 she said "Pf" to them. The concubines came to greet her, and she spat at them. Then when night fell, the chief's son made his way to her hut, and she yelled at him. And he was amazed and went aside, and for two days pondered the matter.

Then he had his wives and concubines collected and said to them, 21 "Look, now—I've called you to ask you. They haven't brought me the same girl. How did that one treat all of you?" "Hm—how indeed!" they all exclaimed. "Each morning, when we wives went to greet her, she would give us cola-nuts, two calabashes full, and cowries, ten thousand of them to buy tobacco flowers. And when the concubines went to greet her, she would give them a calabash of cola-nuts, and five thousand cowries to buy tobacco flowers with; and in the evening, for corn for *tuwo*, it would be a whole hide-bag full." "You see?" said he, "As for me, whenever I came to enter her hut, I found her respectfully kneeling. And she wouldn't get up from there, until I had entered and sat down on the bed."

"Hey," he called out, "Boys, come over here!" And when they came, 22 he went into her hut and took a sword, and chopped her up into little pieces, and had them collect them and wrap them up in clothing; and then taken back to her home.

And when they got there, they found his true wife lying in the 23 fireplace, and picking her up they took her back to her husband.

And next morning when it was light, she picked up a little gourd 24 water-bottle and going around behind her hut, there saw the frog. "Welcome, welcome, old fellow," said she, and went on. "Old fellow, what I should like is to have a well built; and then you, all of you, can come and live in it and be close to me." "All right" said the frog, "You tell your husband." And she did so.

And he had a well dug for her, close to her hut. And the frogs came 25 and entered the well and there they lived. That's all. *Kungurus kan kusu.*

## Oochigeaskw—The Rough-Faced Girl (A Native American "Cinderella")

*The following version of the tale was told, originally, in the Algonquin language. Native Americans who spoke Algonquian lived in the Eastern Woodlands of what is now the United States and in the northern, semiarctic areas of present-day Canada.*

There was once a large village of the MicMac Indians of the Eastern 1 Algonquins, built beside a lake. At the far end of the settlement stood a lodge, and in it lived a being who was always invisible. He had a sister who looked after him, and everyone knew that any girl who could see him might marry him. For that reason there were very few girls who did not try, but it was very long before anyone succeeded.

This is the way in which the test of sight was carried out: at 2 evening-time, when the Invisible One was due to be returning home, his sister would walk with any girl who might come down to the lakeshore. She, of course, could see her brother, since he was always visible to her. As soon as she saw him, she would say to the girls:

"Do you see my brother?" 3

"Yes," they would generally reply—though some of them did say 4 "No."

To those who said that they could indeed see him, the sister would 5 say:

"Of what is his shoulder strap made?" Some people say that she 6 would enquire:

"What is his moose-runner's haul?" or "With what does he draw his 7 sled?"

And they would answer: 8

"A strip of rawhide" or "a green flexible branch," or something of 9 that kind.

Then she, knowing that they had not told the truth, would say: 10

"Very well, let us return to the wigwam!" 11

When they had gone in, she would tell them not to sit in a certain    12
place, because it belonged to the Invisible One. Then, after they had
helped to cook the supper, they would wait with great curiosity, to see
him eat. They could be sure that he was a real person, for when he took
off his moccasins they became visible, and his sister hung them up. But
beyond this they saw nothing of him, not even when they stayed in the
place all the night, as many of them did.

Now there lived in the village an old man who was a widower, and    13
his three daughters. The youngest girl was very small, weak and often
ill: and yet her sisters, especially the elder, treated her cruelly. The
second daughter was kinder, and sometimes took her side: but the
wicked sister would burn her hands and feet with hot cinders, and she
was covered with scars from this treatment. She was so marked that
people called her *Oochigeaskw*, the Rough-Faced-Girl.

When her father came home and asked why she had such burns, the    14
bad sister would at once say that it was her own fault, for she had
disobeyed orders and gone near the fire and fallen into it.

These two elder sisters decided one day to try their luck at seeing    15
the Invisible One. So they dressed themselves in their finest clothes, and
tried to look their prettiest. They found the Invisible One's sister and
took the usual walk by the water.

When he came, and when they were asked if they could see him,    16
they answered: "Of course." And when asked about the shoulder strap
or sled cord, they answered: "A piece of rawhide."

But of course they were lying like the others, and they got nothing    17
for their pains.

The next afternoon, when the father returned home, he brought    18
with him many of the pretty little shells from which wampum was made,
and they set to work to string them.

That day, poor Little Oochigeaskw, who had always gone barefoot,    19
got a pair of her father's moccasins, old ones, and put them into water
to soften them so that she could wear them. Then she begged her sisters
for a few wampum shells. The elder called her a "little pest", but the
younger one gave her some. Now, with no other clothes than her usual
rags, the poor little thing went into the woods and got herself some
sheets of birch bark, from which she made a dress, and put marks on it
for decoration, in the style of long ago. She made a petticoat and a loose
gown, a cap, leggings and a handkerchief. She put on her father's large
old moccasins, which were far too big for her, and went forth to try her
luck. She would try, she thought, to discover whether she could see the
Invisible One.

She did not begin very well. As she set off, her sisters shouted and    20 hooted, hissed and yelled, and tried to make her stay. And the loafers around the village, seeing the strange little creature, called out "Shame!"

The poor little girl in her strange clothes, with her face all scarred, was an awful sight, but she was kindly received by the sister of the Invisible One. And this was, of course, because this noble lady understood far more about things than simply the mere outside which all the rest of the world knows. As the brown of the evening sky turned to black, the lady took her down to the lake. 21

"Do you see him?" the Invisible One's sister asked. 22

"I do, indeed—and he is wonderful!" said Oochigeaskw. 23

The sister asked: 24

"And what is his sled-string?" 25

The little girl said: 26

"It is the Rainbow." 27

"And, my sister, what is his bow-string?" 28

"It is The Spirit's Road—the Milky Way." 29

"So you *have* seen him," said his sister. She took the girl home with her and bathed her. As she did so, all the scars disappeared from her body. Her hair grew again, as it was combed, long, like a blackbird's wing. Her eyes were now like stars: in all the world there was no other such beauty. Then, from her treasures, the lady gave her a wedding garment, and adorned her. 30

Then she told Oochigeaskw to take the *wife's* seat in the wigwam: the one next to where the Invisible One sat, beside the entrance. And when he came in, terrible and beautiful, he smiled and said: 31

"So we are found out!" 32

"Yes," said his sister. And so Oochigeaskw became his wife. 33

# Walt Disney's "Cinderella"

## ADAPTED BY CAMPBELL GRANT

*Walter Elias Disney (1901–1966), winner of twenty-nine Academy Awards, is world famous for his cartoon animations. After achieving recognition with cartoon shorts populated by such immortals as Mickey Mouse and Donald Duck, he produced the full-length animated film version of* Snow White and the Seven Dwarfs *in 1936. He followed with other animations, including*

*"Cinderella" (1949), which he adapted from Perrault's version of the tale. A Little Golden Book, the text of which appears here, was then adapted from the film by Campbell Grant.*

Once upon a time in a far-away land lived a sweet and pretty girl named Cinderella. She made her home with her mean old stepmother and her two stepsisters, and they made her do all the work in the house. 1

Cinderella cooked and baked. She cleaned and scrubbed. She had no time left for parties and fun. 2

But one day an invitation came from the palace of the king. 3

A great ball was to be given for the prince of the land. And every young girl in the kingdom was invited. 4

"How nice!" thought Cinderella. "I am invited, too." 5

But her mean stepsisters never thought of her. They thought only of themselves, of course. They had all sorts of jobs for Cinderella to do. 6

"Wash this slip. Press this dress. Curl my hair. Find my fan." 7

They both kept shouting, as fast as they could speak. 8

"But I must get ready myself. I'm going, too," said Cinderella. 9

"You!" they hooted. "The Prince's ball for you?" 10

And they kept her busy all day long. She worked in the morning, while her stepsisters slept. She worked all afternoon, while they bathed and dressed. And in the evening she had to help them put on the finishing touches for the ball. She had not one minute to think of herself. 11

Soon the coach was ready at the door. The ugly stepsisters were powdered, pressed, and curled. But there stood Cinderella in her workaday rags. 12

"Why, Cinderella!" said the stepsisters. "You're not dressed for the ball." 13

"No," said Cinderella. "I guess I cannot go." 14

Poor Cinderella sat weeping in the garden. 15

Suddenly a little old woman with a sweet, kind face stood before her. It was her fairy godmother. 16

"Hurry, child!" she said. "You are going to the ball!" 17

Cinderella could hardly believe her eyes! The fairy godmother turned a fat pumpkin into a splendid coach. 18

Next her pet mice became horses, and her dog a fine footman. The barn horse was turned into a coachman. 19

"There, my dear," said the fairy godmother. "Now into the coach with you, and off to the ball you go." 20

"But my dress—" said Cinderella. 21

"Lovely, my dear," the fairy godmother began. Then she really looked at Cinderella's rags. 22

"Oh, good heavens," she said. "You can never go in that." She waved her magic wand. 23

"Salaga doola,
Menchicka boola,
Bibbidy bobbidy boo!" she said.

There stood Cinderella in the loveliest ball dress that ever was. And    24
on her feet were tiny glass slippers!

"Oh," cried Cinderella. "How can I ever thank you?"    25

"Just have a wonderful time at the ball, my dear," said her fairy    26
godmother. "But remember, this magic lasts only until midnight. At the
stroke of midnight, the spell will be broken. And everything will be as
it was before."

"I will remember," said Cinderella. "It is more than I ever dreamed    27
of."

Then into the magic coach she stepped, and was whirled away to    28
the ball.

And such a ball! The king's palace was ablaze with lights. There was    29
music and laughter. And every lady in the land was dressed in her
beautiful best.

But Cinderella was the loveliest of them all. The prince never left    30
her side, all evening long. They danced every dance. They had supper
side by side. And they happily smiled into each other's eyes.

But all at once the clock began to strike midnight, Bong Bong    31
Bong—

"Oh!" cried Cinderella. "I almost forgot!"    32

And without a word, away she ran, out of the ballroom and down    33
the palace stairs. She lost one glass slipper. But she could not stop.

Into her magic coach she stepped, and away it rolled. But as the    34
clock stopped striking, the coach disappeared. And no one knew where
she had gone.

Next morning all the kingdom was filled with the news. The Grand    35
Duke was going from house to house, with a small glass slipper in his
hand. For the prince had said he would marry no one but the girl who
could wear that tiny shoe.

Every girl in the land tried hard to put it on. The ugly stepsisters    36
tried hardest of all. But not a one could wear the glass shoe.

And where was Cinderella? Locked in her room. For the mean    37
old stepmother was taking no chances of letting her try on the slipper.
Poor Cinderella! It looked as if the Grand Duke would surely pass
her by.

But her little friends the mice got the stepmother's key. And they    38
pushed it under Cinderella's door. So down the long stairs she came, as
the Duke was just about to leave.

"Please!" cried Cinderella. "Please let me try."    39

And of course the slipper fitted, since it was her very own.    40

That was all the Duke needed. Now his long search was done. And    41

so Cinderella became the prince's bride, and lived happily ever after—
and the little pet mice lived in the palace and were happy ever after, too.

# Cinderella

## ANNE SEXTON

*Anne Sexton (1928–1974) has been acclaimed as one of America's outstand-
ing contemporary poets. In 1967, she won the Pulitzer Prize for poetry for*
Live or Die. *She published four other collections of her work, including*
Transformations, *in which she recast, with a modern twist, popular European fairy tales such as "Cinderella." Sexton's poetry has appeared in* The
New Yorker, Harper's, *the* Atlantic, *and* Saturday Review. *She received
a Robert Frost Fellowship (1959), a scholarship from Radcliffe College's New
Institute for Independent Study (1961–1963), a grant from the Ford Foundation (1964), and a Guggenheim Award (1969). In her book* All My Pretty
Ones *Sexton quoted Franz Kafka: "The books we need are the kind that act
upon us like a misfortune, that make us suffer like the death of someone we
love more than ourselves. A book should serve as the axe for the frozen sea
within us." Asked in an interview (by Patricia Marx) about this quotation,
Sexton responded: "I think [poetry] should be a shock to the senses. It should
almost hurt."*

You always read about it:
the plumber with twelve children
who wins the Irish Sweepstakes.
From toilets to riches.
That story.                                                              5

Or the nursemaid,
some luscious sweet from Denmark
who captures the oldest son's heart.
From diapers to Dior.
That story.                                                             10

Or a milkman who serves the wealthy,
eggs, cream, butter, yogurt, milk,

the white truck like an ambulance
who goes into real estate
and makes a pile.
From homogenized to martinis at lunch.                        15

Or the charwoman
who is on the bus when it cracks up
and collects enough from the insurance.
From mops to Bonwit Teller.
That story.                                                   20

Once
the wife of a rich man was on her deathbed
and she said to her daughter Cinderella:
Be devout. Be good. Then I will smile                         25
down from heaven in the seam of a cloud.
The man took another wife who had
two daughters, pretty enough
but with hearts like blackjacks.
Cinderella was their maid.                                    30
She slept on the sooty hearth each night
and walked around looking like Al Jolson.
Her father brought presents home from town,
jewels and gowns for the other women
but the twig of a tree for Cinderella.                        35
She planted that twig on her mother's grave
and it grew to a tree where a white dove sat.
Whenever she wished for anything the dove
would drop it like an egg upon the ground.
The bird is important, my dears, so heed him.                 40

Next came the ball, as you all know.
It was a marriage market.
The prince was looking for a wife.
All but Cinderella were preparing
and gussying up for the big event.                            45
Cinderella begged to go too.
Her stepmother threw a dish of lentils
into the cinders and said: Pick them
up in an hour and you shall go.
The white dove brought all his friends;                       50
all the warm wings of the fatherland came,
and picked up the lentils in a jiffy.

---

No, Cinderella, said the stepmother,
you have no clothes and cannot dance.
That's the way with stepmothers.                                    55

Cinderella went to the tree at the grave
and cried forth like a gospel singer:
Mama! Mama! My turtledove,
send me to the prince's ball!
The bird dropped down a golden dress                                 60
and delicate little gold slippers.
Rather a large package for a simple bird.
So she went. Which is no surprise.

Her stepmother and sisters didn't
recognize her without her cinder face                                65
and the prince took her hand on the spot
and danced with no other the whole day.

As nightfall came she thought she'd better
get home. The prince walked her home
and she disappeared into the pigeon house                           70
and although the prince took an axe and broke
it open she was gone. Back to her cinders.
These events repeated themselves for three days.
However on the third day the prince
covered the palace steps with cobbler's wax                         75
and Cinderella's gold shoe stuck upon it.
Now he would find whom the shoe fit
and find his strange dancing girl for keeps.
He went to their house and the two sisters
were delighted because they had lovely feet.                        80
The eldest went into a room to try the slipper on
but her big toe got in the way so she simply
sliced it off and put on the slipper.
The prince rode away with her until the white dove
told him to look at the blood pouring forth.                        85
That is the way with amputations.
They don't just heal up like a wish.
The other sister cut off her heel
but the blood told as blood will.
The prince was getting tired.                                       90
He began to feel like a shoe salesman.
But he gave it one last try.

This time Cinderella fit into the shoe
like a love letter into its envelope.

At the wedding ceremony                                                    95
the two sisters came to curry favor
and the white dove pecked their eyes out.
Two hollow spots were left
like soup spoons.

Cinderella and the prince                                                  100
lived, they say, happily ever after,
like two dolls in a museum case
never bothered by diapers or dust,
never arguing over the timing of an egg,
never telling the same story twice,                                        105
never getting a middle-aged spread,
their darling smiles pasted on for eternity.

Regular Bobbsey Twins.
That story.


# "Cinderella": A Story of Sibling Rivalry and Oedipal Conflicts

## BRUNO BETTELHEIM

*Having read several variants of "Cinderella," you may have wondered what it is about this story that's prompted people in different parts of the world, at different times, to show interest in a child who's been debased but then rises above her misfortune. Why are people so fascinated with "Cinderella"?*

*Depending on the people you ask and their perspectives, you'll find this question answered in various ways. As a Freudian psychologist, Bruno Bettelheim believes that the mind is a repository of both conscious and unconscious elements. By definition, we aren't aware of what goes on in our unconscious; nonetheless, what happens there exerts a powerful influence on what we believe and on how we act. This division of the mind into conscious* and unconscious parts is true for children no less than for adults. Based on these beliefs about the mind, Bettelheim analyzes "Cinderella" first by pointing to what he calls the story's essential theme: sibling rivalry, or Cinderella's mistreatment at the hands of her stepsisters. Competition among brothers and sisters presents a profound and largely unconscious problem to children, says Bettelheim. By hearing "Cinderella," a story that speaks directly to their unconscious, children are given tools that can help them resolve conflicts. Cinderella resolves her difficulties; children hearing the story can resolve theirs as well: This is the unconscious message of the tale.

Do you accept this argument? To do so, you'd have to agree with the author's reading of "Cinderella's" hidden meanings; and you'd have to agree with his assumptions concerning the conscious and unconscious mind and the ways in which the unconscious will seize upon the content of a story in order to resolve conflicts. Even if you don't accept Bettelheim's analysis, his essay makes fascinating reading. First, it is internally consistent—that is, he begins with a set of principles and then builds logically upon them, as any good writer will. Second, his analysis demonstrates how a scholarly point of view—a coherent set of assumptions about the way the world (in this case, the mind) works—creates boundaries for a discussion. Change the assumptions (as Kolbenschlag and Yolen will in the articles that conclude the chapter) and you'll change the analyses that follow from them.

Bettelheim's essay is long and somewhat difficult. While he uses no subheadings, he has divided his work into four sections: paragraphs 2–10 are devoted to sibling rivalry; paragraphs 11–19, to an analysis of "Cinderella's" hidden meanings; paragraphs 20–24, to the psychological makeup of children at the end of their Oedipal period; and paragraphs 25–27, to the reasons why "Cinderella," in particular, appeals to children in the Oedipal period.

Bruno Bettelheim, a distinguished psychologist and educator, was born in 1903 in Vienna. He was naturalized as an American citizen in 1939 and served as a professor of psychology at Rockford College and the University of Chicago. Awarded the honor of fellow by several prestigious professional associations, Bettelheim was a prolific writer and contributed articles to numerous popular and professional publications. His list of books includes Love Is Not Enough: The Treatment of Emotionally Disturbed Children (1950), The Informed Heart (1960), Surviving, and The Uses of Enchantment, from which this selection has been excerpted. Bettelheim died in 1990.

By all accounts, "Cinderella" is the best-known fairy tale, and probably 1 also the best-liked. It is quite an old story; when first written down in China during the ninth century A.D., it already had a history. The unrivaled tiny foot size as a mark of extraordinary virtue, distinction, and beauty, and the slipper made of precious material are facets which point to an Eastern, if not necessarily Chinese, origin.[1] The modern hearer does not connect sexual attractiveness and beauty in general with extreme smallness of the foot, as the ancient Chinese did, in accordance with their practice of binding women's feet.

"Cinderella," as we know it, is experienced as a story about the   **2** agonies and hopes which form the essential content of sibling rivalry; and about the degraded heroine winning out over her siblings who abused her. Long before Perrault gave "Cinderella" the form in which it is now widely known, "having to live among the ashes" was a symbol of being debased in comparison to one's siblings, irrespective of sex. In Germany, for example, there were stories in which such an ash-boy later becomes king, which parallels Cinderella's fate. "Aschenputtel" is the title of the Brothers Grimm's version of the tale. The term originally designated a lowly, dirty kitchenmaid who must tend to the fireplace ashes.

There are many examples in the German language of how being   **3** forced to dwell among the ashes was a symbol not just of degradation, but also of sibling rivalry, and of the sibling who finally surpasses the brother or brothers who have debased him. Martin Luther in his *Table Talks* speaks about Cain as the God-forsaken evildoer who is powerful, while pious Abel is forced to be his ash-brother *(Asche-brüdel)*, a mere nothing, subject to Cain; in one of Luther's sermons he says that Esau was forced into the role of Jacob's ash-brother. Cain and Abel, Jacob and Esau are Biblical examples of one brother being suppressed or destroyed by the other.

The fairy tale replaces sibling relations with relations between step-   **4** siblings—perhaps a device to explain and make acceptable an animosity which one wishes would not exist among true siblings. Although sibling rivalry is universal and "natural" in the sense that it is the negative consequence of being a sibling, this same relation also generates equally as much positive feeling between siblings, highlighted in fairy tales such as "Brother and Sister."

No other fairy tale renders so well as the "Cinderella" stories the   **5** inner experiences of the young child in the throes of sibling rivalry, when he feels hopelessly outclassed by his brothers and sisters. Cinderella is pushed down and degraded by her stepsisters; her interests are sacrificed to theirs by her (step)mother; she is expected to do the dirtiest work and although she performs it well, she receives no credit for it; only more is demanded of her. This is how the child feels when devastated by the miseries of sibling rivalry. Exaggerated though Cinderella's tribulations and degradations may seem to the adult, the child carried

---

[1]Artistically made slippers of precious material were reported in Egypt from the third century on. The Roman emperor Diocletian in a decree of A.D. 301 set maximum prices for different kinds of footwear, including slippers made of fine Babylonian leather, dyed purple or scarlet, and gilded slippers for women. [Bettelheim]

away by sibling rivalry feels, "That's me; that's how they mistreat me, or would want to; that's how little they think of me." And there are moments—often long time periods—when for inner reasons a child feels this way even when his position among his siblings may seem to give him no cause for it.

When a story corresponds to how the child feels deep down—as no realistic narrative is likely to do—it attains an emotional quality of "truth" for the child. The events of "Cinderella" offer him vivid images that give body to his overwhelming but nevertheless often vague and nondescript emotions; so these episodes seem more convincing to him than his life experiences. 6

The term "sibling rivalry" refers to a most complex constellation of feelings and their causes. With extremely rare exceptions, the emotions aroused in the person subject to sibling rivalry are far out of proportion to what his real situation with his sisters and brothers would justify, seen objectively. While all children at times suffer greatly from sibling rivalry, parents seldom sacrifice one of their children to the others, nor do they condone the other children's persecuting one of them. Difficult as objective judgments are for the young child—nearly impossible when his emotions are aroused—even he in his more rational moments "knows" that he is not treated as badly as Cinderella. But the child often feels mistreated, despite all his "knowledge" to the contrary. That is why he believes in the inherent truth of "Cinderella," and then he also comes to believe in her eventual deliverance and victory. From her triumph he gains the exaggerated hopes for his future which he needs to counteract the extreme misery he experiences when ravaged by sibling rivalry. 7

Despite the name "sibling rivalry," this miserable passion has only incidentally to do with a child's actual brothers and sisters. The real source of it is the child's feelings about his parents. When a child's older brother or sister is more competent than he, this arouses only temporary feelings of jealousy. Another child being given special attention becomes an insult only if the child fears that, in contrast, he is thought little of by his parents, or feels rejected by them. It is because of such an anxiety that one or all of a child's sisters or brothers may become a thorn in his flesh. Fearing that in comparison to them he cannot win his parents' love and esteem is what inflames sibling rivalry. This is indicated in stories by the fact that it matters little whether the siblings actually possess greater competence. The Biblical story of Joseph tells that it is jealousy of parental affection lavished on him which accounts for the destructive behavior of his brothers. Unlike Cinderella's, Joseph's parent does not participate in degrading him, and, on the contrary, prefers him to his other children. But Joseph, like Cinderella, is turned into a slave, and, like her, he miraculously escapes and ends by surpassing his siblings. 8

Telling a child who is devastated by sibling rivalry that he will grow    9
up to do as well as his brothers and sisters offers little relief from his
present feelings of dejection. Much as he would like to trust our assurances, most of the time he cannot. A child can see things only with
subjective eyes, and comparing himself on this basis to his siblings, he
has no confidence that he, on his own, will someday be able to fare as
well as they. If he could believe more in himself, he would not feel
destroyed by his siblings no matter what they might do to him, since
then he could trust that time would bring about a desired reversal of
fortune. But since the child cannot, on his own, look forward with
confidence to some future day when things will turn out all right for him,
he can gain relief only through fantasies of glory—a domination over
his siblings—which he hopes will become reality through some fortunate event.

Whatever our position within the family, at certain times in our lives    10
we are beset by sibling rivalry in some form or other. Even an only child
feels that other children have some great advantages over him, and this
makes him intensely jealous. Further, he may suffer from the anxious
thought that if he did have a sibling, his parents would prefer this other
child to him. "Cinderella" is a fairy tale which makes nearly as strong an
appeal to boys as to girls, since children of both sexes suffer equally
from sibling rivalry, and have the same desire to be rescued from their
lowly position and surpass those who seem superior to them.

On the surface, "Cinderella" is as deceptively simple as the story of    11
Little Red Riding Hood, with which it shares greatest popularity. "Cinderella" tells about the agonies of sibling rivalry, of wishes coming true,
of the humble being elevated, of true merit being recognized even when
hidden under rags, of virtue rewarded and evil punished—a straightforward story. But under this overt content is concealed a welter of
complex and largely unconscious material, which details of the story
allude to just enough to set our unconscious associations going. This
makes a contrast between surface simplicity and underlying complexity
which arouses deep interest in the story and explains its appeal to the
millions over centuries. To begin gaining an understanding of these
hidden meanings, we have to penetrate behind the obvious sources of
sibling rivalry discussed so far.

As mentioned before, if the child could only believe that it is the    12
infirmities of his age which account for his lowly position, he would
not have to suffer so wretchedly from sibling rivalry, because he could
trust the future to right matters. When he thinks that his degradation
is deserved, he feels his plight is utterly hopeless. Djuna Barnes's per-
ceptive statement about fairy tales—that the child knows something
about them which he cannot tell (such as that he likes the idea of Little
Red Riding Hood and the wolf being in bed together)—could be

extended by dividing fairy tales into two groups: one group where the child responds only unconsciously to the inherent truth of the story and thus cannot tell about it; and another large number of tales where the child preconsciously or even consciously knows what the "truth" of the story consists of and thus could tell about it, but does not want to let on that he knows. Some aspects of "Cinderella" fall into the latter category. Many children believe that Cinderella probably deserves her fate at the beginning of the story, as they feel they would, too; but they don't want anyone to know it. Despite this, she is worthy at the end to be exalted, as the child hopes he will be too, irrespective of his earlier shortcomings.

Every child believes at some period of his life—and this is not only at rare moments—that because of his secret wishes, if not also his clandestine actions, he deserves to be degraded, banned from the presence of others, relegated to a netherworld of smut. He fears this may be so, irrespective of how fortunate his situation may be in reality. He hates and fears those others—such as his siblings—whom he believes to be entirely free of similar evilness, and he fears that they or his parents will discover what he is really like, and then demean him as Cinderella was by her family. Because he wants others—most of all, his parents—to believe in his innocence, he is delighted that "everybody" believes in Cinderella's. This is one of the great attractions of this fairy tale. Since people give credence to Cinderella's goodness, they will also believe in his, so the child hopes. And "Cinderella" nourishes this hope, which is one reason it is such a delightful story.  **13**

Another aspect which holds large appeal for the child is the vileness of the stepmother and stepsisters. Whatever the shortcomings of a child may be in his own eyes, these pale into insignificance when compared to the stepsisters' and stepmother's falsehood and nastiness. Further, what these stepsisters do to Cinderella justifies whatever nasty thoughts one may have about one's siblings: they are so vile that anything one may wish would happen to them is more than justified. Compared to their behavior, Cinderella is indeed innocent. So the child, on hearing her story, feels he need not feel guilty about his angry thoughts.  **14**

On a very different level—and reality considerations coexist easily with fantastic exaggerations in the child's mind—as badly as one's parents or siblings seem to treat one, and much as one thinks one suffers because of it, all this is nothing compared to Cinderella's fate. Her story reminds the child at the same time how lucky he is, and how much worse things could be. (Any anxiety about the latter possibility is relieved, as always in fairy tales, by the happy ending.)  **15**

The behavior of a five-and-a-half-year-old girl, as reported by her father, may illustrate how easily a child may feel that she is a "Cinderella." This little girl had a younger sister of whom she was very jealous.  **16**

The girl was very fond of "Cinderella," since the story offered her material with which to act out her feelings, and because without the story's imagery she would have been hard pressed to comprehend and express them. This little girl had used to dress very neatly and liked pretty clothes, but she became unkempt and dirty. One day when she was asked to fetch some salt, she said as she was doing so, "Why do you treat me like Cinderella?"

Almost speechless, her mother asked her, "Why do you think I treat 17 you like Cinderella?"

"Because you make me do all the hardest work in the house!" was 18 the little girl's answer. Having thus drawn her parents into her fantasies, she acted them out more openly, pretending to sweep up all the dirt, etc. She went even further, playing that she prepared her little sister for the ball. But she went the "Cinderella" story one better, based on her unconscious understanding of the contradictory emotions fused into the "Cinderella" role, because at another moment she told her mother and sister, "You shouldn't be jealous of me just because I am the most beautiful in the family."

This shows that behind the surface humility of Cinderella lies the 19 conviction of her superiority to mother and sisters, as if she would think: "You can make me do all the dirty work, and I pretend that I am dirty, but within me I know that you treat me this way because you are jealous of me because I am so much better than you." This conviction is supported by the story's ending, which assures every "Cinderella" that eventually she will be discovered by her prince.

Why does the child believe deep within himself that Cinderella 20 deserves her dejected state? This question takes us back to the child's state of mind at the end of the oedipal period.[2] Before he is caught in oedipal entanglements, the child is convinced that he is lovable, and loved, if all is well within his family relationships. Psychoanalysis describes this stage of complete satisfaction with oneself as "primary narcissism." During this period the child feels certain that he is the center of the universe, so there is no reason to be jealous of anybody.

The oedipal disappointments which come at the end of this develop- 21 mental stage cast deep shadows of doubt on the child's sense of his worthiness. He feels that if he were really as deserving of love as he had thought, then his parents would never be critical of him or disappoint him. The only explanation for parental criticism the child can think of is that there must be some serious flaw in him which accounts for what he experiences as rejection. If his desires remain unsatisfied and his

---

[2]*Oedipal:* Freud's theory of the Oedipus complex held that at an early stage of development a child wishes to replace the parent of the same sex in order to achieve the exclusive love of the parent of the opposite sex.

parents disappoint him, there must be something wrong with him or his desires, or both. He cannot yet accept that reasons other than those residing within him could have an impact on his fate. In this oedipal jealousy, wanting to get rid of the parent of the same sex had seemed the most natural thing in the world, but now the child realizes that he cannot have his own way, and that maybe this is so because the desire was wrong. He is no longer so sure that he is preferred to his siblings, and he begins to suspect that this may be due to the fact that *they* are free of any bad thoughts or wrongdoing such as his.

All this happens as the child is gradually subjected to ever more    22
critical attitudes as he is being socialized. He is asked to behave in ways which run counter to his natural desires, and he resents this. Still he must obey, which makes him very angry. This anger is directed against those who make demands, most likely his parents; and this is another reason to wish to get rid of them, and still another reason to feel guilty about such wishes. This is why the child also feels that he deserves to be chastised for his feelings, a punishment he believes he can escape only if nobody learns what he is thinking when he is angry. The feeling of being unworthy to be loved by his parents at a time when his desire for their love is very strong leads to the fear of rejection, even when in reality there is none. This rejection fear compounds the anxiety that others are preferred and also maybe preferable—the root of sibling rivalry.

Some of the child's pervasive feelings of worthlessness have their    23
origin in his experiences during and around toilet training and all other aspects of his education to become clean, neat, and orderly. Much has been said about how children are made to feel dirty and bad because they are not as clean as their parents want or require them to be. As clean as a child may learn to be, he knows that he would much prefer to give free rein to his tendency to be messy, disorderly, and dirty.

At the end of the oedipal period, guilt about desires to be dirty and    24
disorderly becomes compounded by oedipal guilt, because of the child's desire to replace the parent of the same sex in the love of the other parent. The wish to be the love, if not also the sexual partner, of the parent of the other sex, which at the beginning of the oedipal development seemed natural and "innocent," at the end of the period is repressed as bad. But while this wish as such is repressed, guilt about it and about sexual feelings in general is not, and this makes the child feel dirty and worthless.

Here again, lack of objective knowledge leads the child to think that    25
he is the only bad one in all these respects—the only child who has such desires. It makes every child identify with Cinderella, who is relegated to sit among the cinders. Since the child has such "dirty" wishes, that is where he also belongs, and where he would end up if his parents knew

of his desires. This is why every child needs to believe that even if he were thus degraded, eventually he would be rescued from such degradation and experience the most wonderful exaltation—as Cinderella does.

For the child to deal with his feelings of dejection and worthlessness 26 aroused during this time, he desperately needs to gain some grasp on what these feelings of guilt and anxiety are all about. Further, he needs assurance on a conscious and an unconscious level that he will be able to extricate himself from these predicaments. One of the greatest merits of "Cinderella" is that, irrespective of the magic help Cinderella receives, the child understands that essentially it is through her own efforts, and because of the person she is, that Cinderella is able to transcend magnificently her degraded state, despite what appear as insurmountable obstacles. It gives the child confidence that the same will be true for him, because the story relates so well to what has caused both his conscious and his unconscious guilt.

Overtly "Cinderella" tells about sibling rivalry in its most extreme 27 form: the jealousy and enmity of the stepsisters, and Cinderella's sufferings because of it. The many other psychological issues touched upon in the story are so covertly alluded to that the child does not become consciously aware of them. In his unconscious, however, the child responds to these significant details which refer to matters and experiences from which he consciously has separated himself, but which nevertheless continue to create vast problems for him.

## Review Questions

1. What does living among ashes symbolize, according to Bettelheim?
2. What explanation does Bettelheim give for Cinderella's having stepsisters, not sisters?
3. In what ways are a child's emotions aroused by sibling rivalry?
4. To a child, what is the meaning of Cinderella's triumph?
5. Why is the fantasy solution to sibling rivalry offered by "Cinderella" appropriate for children?
6. Why is Cinderella's goodness important?
7. Why are the stepsisters and stepmother so vile, according to Bettelheim?
8. In paragraphs 20–26, Bettelheim offers a complex explanation of oedipal conflicts and their relation to sibling rivalry and the child's need to be debased, even while feeling superior. Summarize these seven paragraphs, and compare your summary with those of your classmates. Have you agreed on the essential information in this passage?

## Discussion and Writing Suggestions

1. One identifying feature of psychoanalysis is the assumption of complex unconscious and subconscious mechanisms in human personality that ex-

plain behavior. In this essay, Bettelheim discusses the interior world of a child in ways that the child could never articulate. The features of this world include the following:

All children experience sibling rivalry.

The real source of sibling rivalry is the child's parents.

Sibling rivalry is a miserable passion and a devastating experience.

Children have a desire to be rescued from sibling rivalry (as opposed to rescuing themselves, perhaps).

Children experience an Oedipal stage, in which they wish to do away with the parent of the same sex and be intimate with the parent of the opposite sex.

"Every child believes at some point in his life . . . that because of his secret wishes, if not also his clandestine actions, he deserves to be degraded, banned from the presence of others, relegated to a netherworld of smut."

To what extent do you agree with these statements? Take one of these statements and respond to it in a four- or five-paragraph essay.

2. A critic of Bettelheim's position, Jack Zipes argues that Bettelheim distorts fairy-tale literature by insisting that the tales have therapeutic value and speak to children almost as a psychoanalyst might. Ultimately, claims Zipes, Bettelheim's analysis corrupts the story of "Cinderella" and closes down possibilities for interpretation. What is your view of Bettelheim's psychoanalytic approach to fairy tales?

# A Feminist's View of "Cinderella"

## MADONNA KOLBENSCHLAG

*Madonna Kolbenschlag approaches "Cinderella" from a feminist's point of view. Feminist criticism, as it is applied across the curriculum, attempts to clarify the relations of women and men in a broad array of human activities: for instance, in literary works, the structure of family life, and economic and political affairs. The object of analysis in the case of "Cinderella" is a story, and Kolbenschlag brings a unique set of questions to bear: In the world of "Cinderella," what is the relationship between men and women? Among* women themselves? How is power divided in this world? How is a woman's achievement defined as opposed to a man's? What would children reading this story learn about gender identity? Feminists themselves might disagree in answering these questions; but the fact that these and not Bettelheim's questions are guiding the analysis ensures that Kolbenschlag's treatment of "Cinderella" and what we can learn from it will differ significantly from Bettelheim's.

Note that the essay begins with epigraphs, or brief statements, from other writers meant to suggest something of the content of what follows. Authors place epigraphs to set a context for you, and the author who places two or more before a piece is implicitly suggesting that you make comparisons among them.

You'll encounter two particularly difficult sentences: the last sentence of the essay, in which the author equates the behavior of women in "Cinderella" to the behavior of women in our own society, where power is largely held by men. And there's another difficult sentence in paragraph 5: "The personality of the heroine is one that, above all, accepts abasement as a prelude to and precondition of affiliation." Read these sentences in the context of the entire essay. Try getting the gist of Kolbenschlag's main point and then try seeing how these sentences fit in.

Madonna Kolbenschlag is the author of Kiss Sleeping Beauty Good-Bye: Breaking the Spell of Feminine Myths and Models (1979), in which the following selection appears.

Overtly the story helps the child to accept sibling rivalry as a rather common fact of life and promises that he need not fear being destroyed by it; on the contrary, if these siblings were not so nasty to him, he could never triumph to the same degree at the end. . . . There are also obvious moral lessons: that surface appearances tell nothing about the inner worth of a person; that if one is true to oneself, one wins over those who pretend to be what they are not; and that virtue will be rewarded, evil punished.

Openly stated, but not as readily recognized, are the lessons that to develop one's personality to the fullest, one must be able to do hard work and be able to separate good from evil, as in the sorting of the lentils. Even out of lowly matter like ashes things of great value can be gained, if one knows how to do it.

—Bruno Bettelheim, The Uses of Enchantment

The literature on female socialization reminds one of the familiar image of Cinderella's stepsisters industriously lopping off their toes and heels so as to fit into the glass slipper (key to the somewhat enigmatic heart of the prince)—when of course it was never intended for them anyway.

> • —Judith Long Laws, "Woman as Object."

The important factor to us is Cinderella's conditioning. It is decidedly not to go on dutifully sweeping the floor and carrying the wood. She is conditioned to get the hell out of those chores. There is, the American legend tells her, a good-looking man with dough, who will put an end to the onerous tedium of making a living. If he doesn't come along (the consumer must consequently suppose), she isn't just lacking in good fortune, she is being cheated out of her true deserts. Better, says our story, go out and make the guy. In other words, we have turned the legend backwards and our Cinderella now operates as her sisters did. . . .

The goal of security, seen in terms of things alone and achieved in those terms during the least secure period in human history, has predictably ruined Cinderella; she has the prince, the coach, the horses—but her soul's a pumpkin and her mind's a rat-warren. She desperately needs help.

> —Philip Wylie, *Generation of Vipers*

*Cinderella*, the best-known and probably best-liked fairy tale, is above    1
all a success story. The rags-to-riches theme perhaps explains its equal popularity among boys as well as girls. It is a very old fairy tale, having at least 345 documented variants and numerous unrecorded versions. The iconic focus of the tale on the lost slipper and Cinderella's "perfect fit" suggests that the story may have originated in the Orient where the erotic significance of tiny feet has been a popular myth since ancient times.

The basic motifs of the story are well-known: an ill-treated heroine,    2
who is forced to live by the hearth; the twig she plants on her mother's grave that blossoms into a magic tree; the tasks demanded of the heroine; the magic animals that help her perform the tasks and provide her costume for the ball; the meeting at the ball; the heroine's flight from the ball; the lost slipper; the shoe test; the sisters' mutilation of their feet; the discovery of the true bride and the happy marriage. The variants retain the basic motifs; while differing considerably in detail, they range more widely in their origins than any other fairy tale: Asiatic, Celtic, European, Middle-Eastern and American Indian versions numbered among them.

The Horatio Alger quality of the story helps to explain its special    3
popularity in mercantile and capitalistic societies. As a parable of social mobility it was seized upon by the writers of the new "literature of

aspiration" in the seventeenth and eighteenth centuries as a basic plot for a new kind of private fantasy—the novel. Our literary world has not been the same since *Pamela* and all her orphaned, governess sisters.[1] Most Anglo-American novels, early and late, are written in the shadow of *Pamela* and the Cinderella myth. Even Franklin's *Autobiography*, the seminal work in the success genre, owes much to the myth. The primary "moral" of the fairy tale—that good fortune can be merited—is the very essence of the Protestant Ethic.

At the personal and psychological level, Cinderella evokes intense **4** identification. It is a tale of sibling rivalry (and subliminally, of sex-role stereotyping)—a moral fable about socialization. Very few themes could be closer to the inner experience of the child, an emerging self enmeshed in a family network. As Bettelheim observes, it is deceptively simple in the associations it evokes:

> *Cinderella* tells about the agonies of sibling rivalry, of wishes coming true, of the humble being elevated, of true merit being recognized even when hidden under rags, of virtue rewarded and evil punished—a straightforward story. But under this overt content is concealed a welter of complex and largely unconscious material. . . .

The personality of the heroine is one that, above all, accepts *abase-* **5** *ment* as a prelude to and precondition of *affiliation*. That abasement is characteristically expressed by Cinderella's servitude to menial tasks, work that diminishes her. This willing acceptance of a condition of worthlessness and her expectation of rescue (as a reward for her virtuous suffering) is a recognizable paradigm of traditional feminine socialization. Cinderella is deliberately and systematically excluded from meaningful achievements. Her stepmother assigns her to meaningless tasks; her father fails her as a helpful mentor. Her sisters, inferior in quality of soul, are preferred before her.

But Cinderella does not become a teenage runaway, nor does she **6** wreak any kind of Gothic sabotage on the family. Like many of the Jews who went to the gas chambers in World War II, she has internalized the consciousness of the victim. She really believes she belongs where she is. The paradox of this acceptance of a condition of worthlessness in the self, along with a conviction of the ultimate worthiness and heroism of one's role, is part of the terrible appeal of the fairy tale. For women, especially, it is both mirror and model. Perrault's version of the tale ends with a pointed poetic moral:

---

[1]*Pamela* by Samuel Richardson (1689–1761) is a sentimental romance set in early-eighteenth-century England in which a virtuous servant girl, Pamela Andrews, holds off the lascivious advances of her master until, struck by her goodness, he proposes marriage.

'Tis that little gift called grace,
Weaves a spell round form and face . . .
And if you would learn the way
How to get that gift today—

How to point the golden dart
That shall pierce the Prince's heart—
Ladies, you have but to be
Just as kind and sweet as she!

Cinderella's place by the hearth and her identification with ashes 7
suggests several associations. At the most obvious level, her place by
the chimney is an emblem of her degradation. But it is also symbolic of
her affinity with the virtues of the hearth: innocence, purity, nurturance,
empathy, docility. Cinderella has a vestal quality that relieves her of any
obligation to struggle and strive to better her world. She must appren-
tice herself to this time of preparation for her "real" life with the
expected One.

Like most fairy tales, *Cinderella* dramatizes the passage to maturity. 8
Her sojourn among the ashes is a period of grieving, a transition to a
new self. On the explicit level of the story, Cinderella is literally grieving
for her dead mother. Grimm's version of the tale preserves the sense of
process, of growth that is symbolized in the narrative. Instead of a fairy
godmother—*deus ex machina*[2]—Cinderella receives a branch of a hazel
bush from her father. She plants the twig over her mother's grave
and cultivates it with her prayers and tears. This is her contact with her
past, her roots, her essential self. Before one can be transformed one
must grieve for the lost as well as the possible selves, as yet un-
fulfilled—Kierkegaard's existential anguish.[3]

The mother is also identified in several variants with helpful ani- 9
mals, a calf, a cow, or a goat—all milk-giving creatures. In Grimm's
version the magic helpers are birds that live in the magic tree. The
animals assist her in the performance of the cruel and meaningless tasks
her stepmother assigns. The magic trees and helpful animals are em-
blems of the faith and trust that is demanded of Cinderella, the belief that
something good can be gained from whatever one does. There is a
subliminal value implied here, that work is seldom to be enjoyed for its
own sake, but only to be endured for some greater end. It is essentially
a "predestined" view of work as incapable of redemption. Service at the
hearth is not intrinsically worthwhile, but acquires its value through the

---

[2]*"deus ex machina"*: literally, "God out of the machine"; a sudden and unexpected (and often
unconvincing) solution to a major problem faced by a character or group of characters toward
the end of a literary or dramatic work.

[3][Soren] Kierkegaard: Danish existentialist philosopher (1813–1855).

virtue it extracts from the heroine. Significantly, when the heroine is released from her servitude, the structure of belief—the myth—collapses. Cinderella's father destroys the pear tree and the pigeon house.

The Perrault version places great emphasis on the "Midnight" 10 prohibition given to Cinderella. A traditional connotation would, of course, associate it with the paternal mandate of obedience, and a threat: if the heroine does not return to domesticity and docility at regular intervals she may lose her "virtue" and no longer merit her expected one. Like the old conduct manuals for ladies, the moral of the tale warns against feminine excursions as well as ambition. Too much time spent "abroad" may result in indiscreet sex or unseemly hubris, or both. "No excelling" and "no excess."

As a dynamic metaphor of the feminine condition, it illuminates the 11 double life that many women experience: the attraction of work and achievement, perhaps "celebrity," outside the home, and the emotional pull of the relationships and security within the home. For most women diurnal life is not a seamless robe. There are sharp divisions between creative work and compulsive activity, between assertiveness and passivity, between social life and domestic drudgery, between public routines and private joys. Women are, in the contemporary world, acutely aware of the need for integration. "Midnight" strikes with a terrible insistence, a cruel regularity in their lives.

Cinderella's threefold escape from the ball (Perrault's version) is of 12 course designed to make her more desirable to the Prince. Or is it a reflection of her own ambivalence? (In Grimm's version, she is under no prohibition, she leaves of her own accord.) Bettelheim offers two interesting interpretations:

1. She wants to be "chosen" for herself, in her natural state, rather than because of a splendid appearance wrought by magic.
2. Her withdrawals show that, in contrast to her sisters, she is not "aggressive" in her sexuality but waits patiently "to be chosen."

The latter interpretation is underscored by the "perfect fit" of Cin- 13 derella's foot in the slipper, and by the sisters' frantic efforts to mutilate their own feet in order to diminish their size (symbolic of their aggressive, masculine traits). Here we see the two sides of the "formula female." On the surface, perfectly conformed to the feminine stereotype; within, massive lacerations of the spirit. The slipper is indeed the ultimate symbol of "that which is most desirable in a woman," with all of its stereotypical seductiveness and destructiveness.

The slipper, the central icon in the story, is a symbol of sexual 14 bondage and imprisonment in a stereotype. Historically, the virulence of its significance is born out in the twisted horrors of Chinese foot-binding practices. On another level, the slipper is a symbol of power—with all of its accompanying restrictions and demands for conformity. When the Prince offers Cinderella the lost slipper (originally a gift of the magic bird), he makes his kingdom hers.

We know little of Cinderella's subsequent role. In Grimm's version 15 she is revenged by the birds which pluck out the eyes of the envious sisters. But Perrault's version celebrates Cinderella's kindness and forgiveness. Her sisters come to live in the palace and marry two worthy lords. In the Norse variant of the tale, Aslaug, the heroine, marries a Viking hero, bears several sons, and wields a good deal of power in Teutonic style. (She is the daughter of Sigurd and Brynhild.) But in most tales Cinderella disappears into the vague region known as the "happily ever after." She changes her name, no doubt, and—like so many women—is never heard of again.

There are moments when all of us can find ourselves in the Cinder- 16 ella tale: as bitchy, envious, desperate sibling-peers; or victim-souls like Cinderella, passive, waiting patiently to be rescued; or nasty, domineering "stepmothers," fulfilling ourselves by means of manipulative affiliations—all of them addicted to needing approval. And then we know that for the Prince we should read "Patriarchy."[4]

At Madonna Kolbenschlag's request, neither Review Questions nor Discussion and Writing Suggestions are provided.

# America's "Cinderella"

## JANE YOLEN

*As a writer of children's stories, Jane Yolen is used to making decisions about ways in which stories develop: who wins, who loses (if anyone), what's learned, what traits of character endure, how relations among characters resolve themselves—these are just a few of the decisions a writer makes in shaping a story. So it's no surprise to find Yolen interested in decisions that other writers have made regarding "Cinderella." The tale has changed in the telling—Yolen is well aware of the many variants and in her article traces the changes "Cinderella" has undergone in becoming an American tale.*

*As you read, note Yolen's analysis of the "Cinderella" texts. Like Bettel-*

---

[4]"Patriarchy": A social system in which authority is vested in the male.
"America's Cinderella" from pp. 21–29 *Children's Literature in Education*, Vol. 8, 1977, by Jane Yolen. Reprinted by permission of Curtis Brown, Ltd. Copyright © 1977 by Jane Yolen.

*heim and Kolbenschlag, she weaves quotations from the story into her article. This is standard procedure when writing an essay—a procedure you yourself should adopt when pulling together sources in a paper. Regardless of what point you're making (and the points made by Bettelheim, Kolbenschlag, and Yolen are certainly diverse), you will want to allude to the work of other writers into your own work, to suit your own purposes.*

*A noted author of children's books, Jane Yolen (b. 1939) began her career in the editorial departments of* Saturday Review, Gold Medal Books, Ruttledge Books, *and* Alfred A. Knopf. *Since 1965, she has been a full-time professional writer, publishing more than seventy books for children as well as books for adults (about writing for children). According to one reviewer, she "is uncommonly skilled at using elements from other storytellers and folklorists, transforming them into new and different tales."*

It is part of the American creed, recited subvocally along with the pledge of allegiance in each classroom, that even a poor boy can grow up to become president. The unliberated corollary is that even a poor girl can grow up and become the president's wife. This rags-to-riches formula was immortalized in American children's fiction by the Horatio Alger stories of the 1860s and by the Pluck and Luck nickel novels of the 1920s. [1]

It is little wonder, then, that Cinderella should be a perennial favorite in the American folktale pantheon. [2]

Yet how ironic that this formula should be the terms on which "Cinderella" is acceptable to most Americans. "Cinderella" is *not* a story of rags to riches, but rather riches recovered; *not* poor girl into princess but rather rich girl (or princess) rescued from improper or wicked enslavement; *not* suffering Griselda[1] enduring but shrewd and practical girl persevering and winning a share of the power. It is really a story that is about "the stripping away of the disguise that conceals the soul from the eyes of others. . . ." [3]

We Americans have it wrong. "Rumpelstiltskin," in which a miller tells a whopping lie and his docile daughter acquiesces in it to become queen, would be more to the point. [4]

But we have been initially seduced by the Perrault cinder-girl, who was, after all, the transfigured folk creature of a French literary courtier. Perrault's "Cendrillon" demonstrated the well-bred seventeenth-century female traits of gentility, grace, and selflessness, even to the point of graciously forgiving her wicked stepsisters and finding them noble husbands. [5]

---

[1]In Chaucer's "Clerk's Tale" (from *The Canterbury Tales*) Griselda endures a series of humiliating tests of her love for and fidelity to her husband. She has become a symbol of the patient and enduring wife.

The American "Cinderella" is partially Perrault's. The rest is a spun-sugar caricature of her hardier European and Oriental forbears, who made their own way in the world, tricking the stepsisters with double-talk, artfully disguising themselves, or figuring out a way to win the king's son. The final bit of icing on the American Cinderella was concocted by that master candy-maker, Walt Disney, in the 1950s. Since then, America's Cinderella has been a coy, helpless dreamer, a "nice" girl who awaits her rescue with patience and a song. This Cinderella of the mass market books finds her way into a majority of American homes while the classic heroines sit unread in old volumes on library shelves.

Poor Cinderella. She has been unjustly distorted by storytellers, misunderstood by educators, and wrongly accused by feminists. Even as late as 1975, in the well-received volume *Womenfolk and Fairy Tales*, Rosemary Minard writes that Cinderella "would still be scrubbing floors if it were not for her fairy godmother." And Ms. Minard includes her in a sweeping condemnation of folk heroines as "insipid beauties waiting passively for Prince Charming."

Like many dialecticians, Ms. Minard reads the fairy tales incorrectly. Believing—rightly—that the fairy tales, as all stories for children, acculturate young readers and listeners, she has nevertheless gotten her target wrong. Cinderella is not to blame. Not the real, the true Cinderella. She does not recognize the old Ash-girl for the tough, resilient heroine. The wrong Cinderella has gone to the American ball.

The story of Cinderella has endured for over a thousand years, surfacing in a literary source first in ninth-century China. It has been found from the Orient to the interior of South America and over five hundred variants have been located by folklorists in Europe alone. This best-beloved tale has been brought to life over and over and no one can say for sure where the oral tradition began. The European story was included by Charles Perrault in his 1697 collection *Histoires ou Contes du temps passé* as "Cendrillon." But even before that, the Italian Straparola had a similar story in a collection. Since there had been twelve editions of the Straparola book printed in French before 1694, the chances are strong that Perrault had read the tale *"Peau d'Ane"* (Donkey Skin).

Joseph Jacobs, the indefatigable Victorian collector, once said of a Cinderella story he printed that it was "an English version of an Italian adaption of a Spanish translation of a Latin version of a Hebrew translation of an Arabic translation of an Indian original." Perhaps it was not a totally accurate statement of that particular variant, but Jacobs was making a point about the perils of folktale-telling: each teller brings to a tale something of his/her own cultural orientation. Thus in China, where the "lotus foot," or tiny foot, was such a sign of a woman's worth that the custom of foot-binding developed, the Cinderella tale lays emphasis on an impossibly small slipper as a clue to the heroine's

6

7

8

9

10

identity. In seventeenth-century France, Perrault's creation sighs along with her stepsisters over the magnificent "gold flowered mantua" and the "diamond stomacher." In the Walt Disney American version, both movie and book form, Cinderella shares with the little animals a quality of "lovableness," thus changing the intent of the tale and denying the heroine her birthright of shrewdness, inventiveness, and grace under pressure.

Notice, though, that many innovations—the Chinese slipper, the    11
Perrault godmother with her midnight injunction and her ability to change pumpkin into coach—become incorporated in later versions. Even a slip of the English translator's tongue (*de vair*, fur, into *de verre*, glass) becomes immortalized. Such cross fertilization of folklore is phenomenal. And the staying power, across countries and centuries, of some of these inventions is notable. Yet glass slipper and godmother and pumpkin coach are not the common incidents by which a "Cinderella" tale is recognized even though they have become basic ingredients in the American story. Rather, the common incidents recognized by folklorists are these: an ill-treated though rich and worthy heroine in Cinders-disguise; the aid of a magical gift or advice by a beast/bird/ mother substitute; the dance/festival/church scene where the heroine comes in radiant display; recognition through a token. So "Cinderella" and her true sister tales, "Cap o'Rushes"[2] with its King Lear judgment[3] and "Catskin" wherein the father unnaturally desires his daughter, are counted.

Andrew Lang's judgement that "a naked shoeless race could not    12
have invented Cinderella," then, proves false. Variants have been found among the fur-wearing folk of Alaska and the native tribes in South Africa where shoes were not commonly worn.

"Cinderella" speaks to all of us in whatever skin we inhabit: the child    13
mistreated, a princess or highborn lady in disguise bearing her trials with patience and fortitude. She makes intelligent decisions for she knows that wishing solves nothing without the concomitant action. We have each of us been that child. It is the longing of any youngster sent supperless to bed or given less than a full share at Christmas. It is the adolescent dream.

To make Cinderella less than she is, then, is a heresy of the worst    14

---

[2]"*Cap o'Rushes*": One of the 700 variants of "Cinderella" in which the heroine is debased by having to wear a cap (and in other variants, a coat) made of rushes.
[3]"*King Lear judgment*": The story of King Lear has been identified as a variant of "Cinderella." In this variant, the King's one faithful daughter is cast out of the home because she claims to love her father according to her bond (but certainly not more than she would love her husband). The King's other daughters, eager to receive a large inheritance, profess false love and then plot against their father to secure their interests. The evil sisters are defeated and the father and faithful daughter, reunited. Before his death, Lear acknowledges his error.

kind. It cheapens our most cherished dreams, and it makes a mockery of the true magic inside us all—the ability to change our own lives, the ability to control our own destinies.

Cinderella first came to America in the nursery tales the settlers **15** remembered from their own homes and told their children. Versions of these tales can still be found. Folklorist Richard Chase, for example, discovered "Rush Cape," an exact parallel of "Cap o'Rushes" with an Appalachian dialect in Tennessee, Kentucky, and South Carolina among others.

But when the story reached print, developed, was made literary, **16** things began to happen to the hardy Cinderella. She suffered a sea change, a sea change aggravated by social conditions.

In the 1870s, for example, in the prestigious magazine for children **17** *St. Nicholas*, there are a number of retellings or adaptations of "Cinderella." The retellings which merely translate European variants contain the hardy heroine. But when a new version is presented, a helpless Cinderella is born. G. B. Bartlett's "Giant Picture-Book," which was considered "a curious novelty [that] can be produced . . . by children for the amusement of their friends . . ." presents a weepy, prostrate young blonde (the instructions here are quite specific) who must be "aroused from her sad revery" by a godmother. Yet in the truer Cinderella stories, the heroine is not this catatonic. For example, in the Grimm "Cinder-Maid," though she weeps, she continues to perform the proper rites and rituals at her mother's grave, instructing the birds who roost there to:

> Make me a lady fair to see,
> Dress me as splendid as can be.

And in "The Dirty Shepherdess," a "Cap o'Rushes" variant from **18** France, ". . . she dried her eyes, and made a bundle of her jewels and her best dresses and hurriedly left the castle where she was born." In the *St. Nicholas* "Giant Picture-Book" she has none of this strength of purpose. Rather, she is manipulated by the godmother until the moment she stands before the prince where she speaks "meekly" and "with downcast eyes and extended hand."

*St. Nicholas* was not meant for the mass market. It had, in Selma **19** Lanes' words, "a patrician call to a highly literate readership." But nevertheless, Bartlett's play instructions indicate how even in the more literary reaches of children's books a change was taking place.

However, to truly mark this change in the American "Cinderella," **20** one must turn specifically to the mass-market books, merchandised products that masquerade as literature but make as little lasting literary impression as a lollipop. They, after all, serve the majority the way the storytellers of the village used to serve. They find their way into millions of homes.

Mass-market books are almost as old as colonial America. The **21** chapbooks of the eighteenth and nineteenth century, crudely printed tiny paperbacks, were the source of most children's reading in the early days of our country. Originally these were books imported from Europe. But slowly American publishing grew. In the latter part of the nineteenth century one firm stood out—McLoughlin Bros. They brought bright colors to the pages of children's books. In a series selling for twenty-five cents per book, *Aunt Kate's Series*, bowdlerized folk tales emerged. "Cinderella" was there, along with "Red Riding Hood," "Puss in Boots," and others. Endings were changed, innards cleaned up, and good triumphed with very loud huzzahs. Cinderella is the weepy, sentimentalized pretty girl incapable of helping herself. In contrast, one only has to look at the girl in "Cap o'Rushes" who comes to a great house and asks "Do you want a maid?" and when refused, goes on to say " . . . I ask no wages and do any sort of work." And she does. In the end, when the master's young son is dying of love for the mysterious lady, she uses her wits to work her way out of the kitchen. Even in Perrault's "Cinderella," when the fairy godmother runs out of ideas for enchantment and "was at a loss for a coachman, I'll go and see, says Cinderella, if there be never a rat in the rat-trap, we'll make a coachman of him. You are in the right, said her godmother, go and see."

Hardy, helpful, inventive, that was the Cinderella of the old tales **22** but not of the mass market in the nineteenth century. Today's massmarket books are worse. These are the books sold in supermarket and candystore, even lining the shelves of many of the best bookstores. There are pop-up Cinderellas, coloring-book Cinderellas, scratch-and-sniff Cinderellas, all inexpensive and available. The point in these books is not the story but the *gimmick*. These are books which must "interest 300,000 children, selling their initial print order in one season and continuing strong for at least two years after that." Compare that with the usual trade publishing house print order of a juvenile book—10,000 copies which an editor hopes to sell out in a lifetime of that title.

All the folk tales have been gutted. But none so changed, I believe, **23** as "Cinderella." For the sake of Happy Ever After, the mass-market books have brought forward a good, malleable, forgiving little girl and put her in Cinderella's slippers. However, in most of the Cinderella tales there is no forgiveness in the heroine's heart. No mercy. Just justice. In "Rushen Coatie" and "The Cinder-Maid," the elder sisters hack off their toes and heels in order to fit the shoe. Cinderella never stops them, never implies that she has the matching slipper. In fact, her tattletale birds warn the prince in "Rushen Coatie":

Hacked Heels and Pinched Toes
Behind the young prince rides,
But Pretty Feet and Little Feet
Behind the cauldron bides.

Even more graphically, they call out in "Cinder-Maid":

Turn and peep, turn and peep,
There's blood within the shoe;
A bit is cut from off the heel
And a bit from off the toe.

Cinderella never says a word of comfort. And in the least bowdlerized of the German and Nordic tales, [when] the two sisters come to the wedding "the elder was at the right side and the younger at the left, and the pigeons pecked out one eye from each of them. Afterwards, as they came back, the elder was on the left, and the younger at the right, and then the pigeons pecked out the other eye from each. And thus, for their wickedness and falsehood, they were punished with blindness all their days." That's a far cry from Perrault's heroine who "gave her sisters lodgings in the palace, and married them the same day to two great lords of the court." And further still from Nola Langner's Scholastic paperback "Cinderella":

[The sisters] began to cry.
They begged Cinderella to forgive them for being so mean to her.
Cinderella told them they were forgiven.
"I am sure you will never be mean to me again," she said.
"Oh, never," said the older sister.
"Never, ever," said the younger sister.

Missing, too, from the mass-market books is the shrewd, even witty 24
Cinderella. In a Wonder Book entitled "Bedtime Stories," a 1940s adaptation from Perrault, we find a Cinderella who talks to her stepsisters, "in a shy little voice." Even Perrault's heroine bantered with her stepsisters, asking them leading questions about the ball while secretly and deliciously knowing the answers. In the Wonder Book, however, the true wonder is that Cinderella ever gets to be princess. Even face-to-face with the prince, she is unrecognized until she dons her magic ball gown. Only when her clothes are transformed does the Prince know his true love.

In 1949, Walt Disney's film *Cinderella* burst onto the American scene. The story in the mass market has not been the same since.
The film came out of the studio at a particularly trying time for 25

Disney. He had been deserted by the intellectuals who had been champions of this art for some years. Because of World War II, the public was more interested in war films than cartoons. But when *Cinderella*, lighter than light, was released it brought back to Disney—and his studio—all of his lost fame and fortune. The film was one of the most profitable of all time for the studio, grossing $4.247 million dollars in the first release alone. The success of the movie opened the floodgates of "Disney Cinderella" books.

Golden Press's *Walt Disney's Cinderella* set the new pattern for **26** America's Cinderella. This book's text is coy and condescending. (Sample: "And her best friends of all were—guess who—the mice!") The illustrations are poor cartoons. And Cinderella herself is a disaster. She cowers as her sisters rip her homemade ball gown to shreds. (Not even homemade by Cinderella, but by the mice and birds.) She answers her stepmother with whines and pleadings. She is a sorry excuse for a heroine, pitiable and useless. She cannot perform even a simple action to save herself, though she is warned by her friends, the mice. She does not hear them because she is "off in a world of dreams." Cinderella begs, she whimpers, and at last has to be rescued by—guess who—the mice!

There is also an easy-reading version published by Random House, **27** *Walt Disney's Cinderella*. This Cinderella commits the further heresy of cursing her luck. "How I did wish to go to the ball," she says. "But it is no use. Wishes never come true."

But in the fairy tales wishes have a habit of happening—*wishes* **28** *accompanied by the proper action*, bad wishes as well as good. That is the beauty of the old stories and their wisdom as well.

Take away the proper course of action, take away Cinderella's **29** ability to think for herself and act for herself, and you are left with a tale of wishes-come-true-regardless. But that is not the way of the fairy tale. As P. L. Travers so wisely puts it, "If that were so, wouldn't we all be married to princes?"

The mass-market American "Cinderellas" have presented the ma- **30** jority of American children with the wrong dream. They offer the passive princess, the "insipid beauty waiting . . . for Prince Charming" that Rosemary Minard objects to, and thus acculturate millions of girls and boys. But it is the wrong Cinderella and the magic of the old tales has been falsified, the true meaning lost, perhaps forever.

## Review Questions

1. Why does Yolen find it ironic that Americans regard "Cinderella" as the classic rags-to-riches story?
2. According to Yolen, why have feminists misdirected their attack on "Cinderella"?

**3.** What does Yolen find objectionable in Walt Disney's *Cinderella?*

**4.** In what ways have we each been Cinderella, according to Yolen?

## Discussion and Writing Suggestions

**1.** Yolen contends that "fairy tales, as all stories for children, acculturate young readers and listeners." How are children acculturated by tales like "Cinderella"?

**2.** Yolen believes that Walt Disney's *Cinderella* is a "heresy of the worst kind." Respond to this comment in a brief essay. (Review Yolen's reasons for stating this view and then agree and/or disagree.)

**3.** "All the folk tales have been gutted," says Yolen. Having read the different versions of Cinderella, would you agree—at least with respect to this one tale? Explain your answer.

---

## SYNTHESIS ACTIVITIES

**1.** In 1910, Antti Aarne published one of the early classifications of folktale types as an aid to scholars who were collecting tales and needed an efficient means for telling where, and with what changes, similar tales had appeared. In 1927, folklorist Stith Thompson, translating and enlarging Aarne's study, produced a work that is now a standard reference for folklorists the world over. We present the authors' description of type 510 and its two forms 510A ("Cinderella") and 510B. Use this description as a basis on which to compare and contrast any three versions of "Cinderella."

**510.** *Cinderella and Cap o' Rushes.*

I.   *The Persecuted Heroine.* (a) The heroine is abused by her stepmother and stepsisters, or (b) flees in disguise from her father who wants to marry her, or (c) is cast out by him because she has said that she loved him like salt, or (d) is to be killed by a servant.

II.  *Magic Help.* While she is acting as servant (at home or among strangers) she is advised, provided for, and fed (a) by her dead mother, (b) by a tree on the mother's grave, or (c) a supernatural being, (d) by birds, or (e) by a goat, a sheep, or a cow. When the goat is killed, there springs up from her remains a magic tree.

III. *Meeting with Prince.* (a) She dances in beautiful clothing several times with a prince who seeks in vain to keep her, or she is seen by him in church. (b) She gives hints of the abuse she has endured, as servant girl, or (c) she is seen in her beautiful clothing in her room or in the church.

IV.  *Proof of Identity.* (a) She is discovered through the slipper-test, or (b) through a ring which she throws into the prince's drink or bakes in his bread. (c) She alone is able to pluck the gold apple desired by the knight.

V.   *Marriage with the Prince.*

---

VI.     *Value of Salt.* Her father is served unsalted food and thus learns the meaning of her earlier answer.

Two forms of the type follow.

**A.** *Cinderella.* The two stepsisters. The stepdaughter at the grave of her own mother, who helps her (milks the cow, shakes the appletree, helps the old man). Three-fold visit to church (dance). Slipper test.

**B.** *The Dress of Gold, of Silver, and of Stars. (Cap o' Rushes).* Present of the father who wants to marry his own daughter. The maiden as servant of the prince, who throws various objects at her. The threefold visit to the church and the forgotten shoe. Marriage.

**2.** Speculate on the reasons folktales are made and told. As you develop a theory, rely first on your own hunches regarding the origins and functions of folktale literature. You might want to recall your experiences as a child listening to tales so that you can discuss their effects on you. Rely as well on the variants of "Cinderella," which you should regard as primary sources (just as scholars do). And make use of the critical pieces you've read—Thompson, Bettelheim, Kolbenschlag, and Yolen—selecting pertinent points from each that will help clarify your points. *Remember:* Your own speculation should dominate the paper. Use sources to help you make *your* points.

**3.** At the conclusion of his article, Stith Thompson writes:

> Literary critics, anthropologists, historians, psychologists, and aestheticians are all needed if we are to hope to know why folktales are made, how they are invented, what art is used in their telling, how they grow and change and occasionally die.

What is your opinion of the critical work you've read on "Cinderella"? Writing from various perspectives, authors in this chapter have analyzed the tale. To what extent have the analyses illuminated "Cinderella" for you? (Have the analyses in any way "ruined" your ability to enjoy "Cinderella"?) To what extent do you find the analyses off the mark? Are the attempts at analysis inappropriate for a children's story? In your view, what place do literary critics, anthropologists, historians, and psychologists have in discussing folktales?

In developing a response to these questions, you might begin with Thompson's quotation and then follow directly with a statement of your thesis. In one part of your paper, you will want to critique the work of Bettelheim, Kolbenschlag, and/or Yolen as a way of demonstrating which analyses of folktales (if any) seem worthwhile to you. In another section of the paper (or perhaps woven into the critiques), you'll want to refer directly to the variants of "Cinderella." For the sake of convenience, you may want to refer to a single variant. If so, state as much to the reader and explain your choice of variant.

4. Review the variants of "Cinderella" and select two you would read to your child. In an essay, justify your decision. Which of the older European variants do you prefer: Grimm? Perrault? How do the recent versions by Sexton, Lee, and Disney affect you? And what of the Chinese, African, and Algonquin versions—are they recognizably "Cinderella"?

You might justify the variants you've selected by defining your criteria for selection and then analyzing the stories separately. (Perhaps you will want to use Aarne and Thompson's classification—see Synthesis Activity 1.) You might want to justify your choices negatively—that is, by defining your criteria and then *eliminating* certain variants because they don't meet the criteria. In concluding the paper, you might explain how the variants you've selected work as a pair. How do they complement each other? (Or, perhaps, they *don't* complement each other and this is why you've selected them.)

5. Try writing a version of "Cinderella" and setting it on a college campus. For your version of the story to be an authentic variant, you'll need to retain certain defining features, or motifs. See Aarne and Thompson—Synthesis Activity 1. As you consider the possibilities for your story, recall Thompson's point that the teller of a folktale borrows heavily on earlier versions; the virtue of telling is not in rendering a new story but in retelling an old one and *adapting* it to local conditions and needs. Unless you plan to write a commentary "Cinderella," as Sexton's poem is, you should retain the basic motifs of the old story and add details that will appeal to your particular audience: your classmates.

6. In her 1981 book *The Cinderella Complex*, Colette Dowling wrote:

> It is the thesis of this book that personal, psychological dependency—the deep wish to be taken care of by others—is the chief force holding women down today. I call this "The Cinderella Complex"—a network of largely repressed attitudes and fears that keeps women in a kind of half-light, retreating from the full use of their minds and creativity. Like Cinderella, women today are still waiting for something external to transform their lives.

In an essay, respond to Dowling's thesis. First, apply her thesis to a few of the variants of "Cinderella." Does the thesis hold in each case? Next, respond to her view that "the chief force holding women down today" is psychological dependency, or the need for "something external" (i.e., a Prince) to transform their lives. In your experience, have you observed a Cinderella complex at work? (You might want to discuss the views of Jane Yolen, who in her article—paragraphs 7, 8, and 31—responds directly to a feminist's criticisms of "Cinderella.")

7. Discuss the process by which Cinderella falls in love in these tales. The paper that you write will be an extended comparison and contrast in which you observe this process at work in the variants and then discuss similarities and differences. (In structuring your paper, you'll need to make some choices: Which variants will you discuss and in what order?) At the conclusion of your

extended comparison and contrast, try to answer the "so what" question. That is, pull your observations together and make a statement about Cinderella's falling in love. What is the significance of what you've learned? Share this significance with your readers.

8. Write an essay in which you attempt to define a feminist perspective on "Cinderella," as this is expressed by Kolbenschlag and Sexton. Once you have defined this perspective, compare and contrast it with other perspectives in the chapter. To what extent do the feminist items here differ significantly from the nonfeminist analyses or tales?

## RESEARCH ACTIVITIES

1. Research the fairy-tale literature of your ancestors, both the tales and any critical commentary that you can find on them. Once you have read the material, talk with older members of your family to hear any tales they have to tell. (Seek, especially, oral versions of stories you have already read.) In a paper, discuss the role that fairy-tale literature has played, and continues to play, in your family.

2. Locate the book *Morphology of the Folktale* (1958), by Russian folklorist Vladimir Propp. Use the information you find there to analyze the elements of any three fairy tales of your choosing. In a paper, report on your analysis and evaluate the usefulness of Propp's system of classifying the key elements of fairy-tale literature.

3. Bruno Bettelheim's *Uses of Enchantment* (1976) generated a great deal of reaction on its publication. Read Bettelheim and locate as many reviews of it as possible. Based on your own reactions and on your reading of the reviews, write an evaluation in which you address Bettelheim's key assumption that fairy-tale literature provides important insights into the psychological life of children.

4. Locate and study multiple versions of any fairy tale other than "Cinderella." ("Little Red Riding Hood" would be a likely candidate.) Having read the versions, identify—and write your paper on—what you feel are the defining elements that make the tales variants of a single story. See if you can find the tale listed as a "type" in Aarne and Thompson, *The Types of Folk-Tales.* If you wish, argue that one version of the tale is preferable to others.

5. Various critics, such as Madonna Kolbenschlag (who has an essay in this chapter) and Jack Zipes, author of *Breaking the Magic Spell* (1979), have taken the approach that fairy tales are far from innocuous children's stories; rather, they inculcate the unsuspecting with the value systems of the dominant culture. Write a paper in which you evaluate an interpretation of fairy-tale literature. In your paper, explicitly address the assumption that fairy tales are not morally or politically neutral but, rather, imply a distinct set of values.

6. Write a children's story. Decide on the age group that you will address, and

then go to a local public library and find several books directed to the same audience. (1) Analyze these books and write a brief paper in which you identify the story elements that seem especially important for your intended audience. (2) Then attempt your own story. (3) When you have finished, answer this question: What values are implicit in your story? What will children who read or hear the story learn about themselves and their world? Plan to submit your brief analytical paper, your story, and your final comment.

7. Videotape, and then study, several hours of Saturday morning cartoons. Then locate and read a collection of Grimm's fairy tales. In a comparative analysis, examine the cartoons and the fairy tales along any four or five dimensions that you think are important. The point of your comparisons and contrasts will be to determine how well the two types of presentations stack up against each other. Which do you find more entertaining? Illuminating? Ambitious? Useful? (These criteria are suggestions only. You should generate your own criteria as part of your research.)

8. Arrange to read to your favorite young person a series of fairy tales. Based on your understanding of the selections in this chapter, develop a list of questions concerning the importance or usefulness of fairy-tale literature to children. Read to your young friend on several occasions and, if possible, talk about the stories after you read them (or while you are reading). Then write a paper on your experience, answering as many of your initial questions as possible. (Be sure in your paper to provide a profile of the child with whom you worked; to review your selection of stories; and to list the questions you wanted to explore.)

# *11*

# GENDER STEREOTYPING
# AND THE MEDIA

In her classic study *Male and Female* (1949), anthropologist Margaret Mead writes that every known culture claims there are differences between men and women, but that once these differences are examined they are found to be social—*not* biological—in origin. Mead observes that no culture has "said, articulately, that there is no difference between men and women."[1] Cultures the world over believe in gender differences, but what these differences are, exactly, can't be pinpointed precisely because they are arbitrary.

In American life, gender differences are not easily defined. There is the traditionalist view that men should dominate the world of commerce while women rear children and order home life. Many embrace the feminist view, shaped by a sustained and widely welcomed revolt against male privilege, that seeks fundamental changes in the equations of power and domestic responsibilities between the sexes. And then there is what may be called an ambivalent view, in which men and women find themselves caught between old definitions of gender and appealing new freedoms. Women may enjoy being the primary (or at least an equal) wage earner in a household but may feel torn at leaving a two-year-old in day care for forty hours each week. Men may appreciate the freedom of being more intuitive than analytical in their approach to problems, yet they wouldn't dream of letting down their "analytical guard" at the office.

Gender identities are in flux. Both the women's and men's liberation movements reject traditional masculine and feminine traits and advocate instead "an androgynous human mean" in which men and women exhibit the same traits without fear of violating gender norms. Human sexuality researchers Masters and Johnson observe that social scientists who once regarded male and female personality traits as existing on a single scale (feminine to masculine) now view these traits as "separate characteristics that coexist to some degree in every

---

[1]From *Male and Female* by Margaret Mead. Copyright 1949, 1976, 1977 by Margaret Mead.

---

541

individual." We see in some quarters of American life an apparent step toward androgyny. But the picture is confused: on the one hand, we receive signals that it is permissible, even desirable, for men to be both sensitive yet strong, for women to be assertive yet nurturing; on the other hand, we live in a media culture that bombards us with traditional images of gender. Think of the Marlboro Man or the woman (inevitably a woman) who sells soap or paper towels on television. At the same time that liberationists (male and female) urge us to adopt an androgynous ideal, the media broadcasts its own potent message: that traditional gender roles are the most attractive and the most powerful roles available to us. At the same time that state legislatures act to protect the rights of gays and lesbians, movies depict gays and lesbians as self-loathing psychopaths. These are confused times, therefore, when mixed messages dominate the news and the media.

Whatever definitions of masculine and feminine one adopts, social and psychological consequences follow—and these consequences provide the organizing theme for the first part of this chapter. To begin, Masters and Johnson review the social patterns, from birth through adulthood, that largely determine our gender identities. The next pair of readings concern the consequences of having learned too well the traditional roles of the American male and female. In an excerpt from *The Feminine Mystique,* Betty Friedan investigates "the problem that has no name," the emptiness felt by many housewives in the 1950s and early 1960s—an era of gender traditionalism in American life. Women had achieved the supposed ideal of husband, suburban home, and children, yet they wanted more. Next, Warren Farrell tells the story of a high-powered lawyer, Ralph, who worked diligently to achieve traditional white-collar (male) success only to discover that he had made himself, his wife, and children unhappy in the process. These selections suggest a need for new gender roles that encourage greater independence among women and a more nurturing attitude in men. Over the past thirty years, feminists (and, more recently, men's liberationists) have fought for these new roles. Yet according to sources cited by Susan Faludi in "Blame It on Feminism," feminism has led to a whole new set of psychological (and, in some cases, physical) difficulties for women. Faludi rejects this suggestion, however, and believes that such objections constitute a "backlash" against feminism rooted in a fear that equal treatment for women threatens the status quo.

The second part of this chapter consists of discussions on gender portrayals in the media. You may be surprised to discover that despite changing attitudes in the broader culture, images of men and women, of heterosexuals and homosexuals, remain remarkably consistent—and conservative. Katha Pollitt begins the discussion with her "Smurfette Principle," claiming that makers of America's "preschool culture" present our children with gender roles as traditional and stereotyped as any broadcast during the 1950s, when Betty Friedan began writing *The Feminine Mystique.* Ian Harris follows with an argument against the disservice done to men by the stereotyped depictions of male, white-collar success on television. In a sociological analysis reprinted from the journal *Sex*

*Roles,* researcher R. Stephen Craig analyzes the gender content of television commercials. Then journalist Matthew Gilbert and gay activist and critic Vito Russo explore images of homosexuality in the movies. The chapter concludes with a brief and humorous short story by Sandra Cisneros, "The Marlboro Man."

Without question, gender portrayals in the media influence the ways that we, and others, see us. If Margaret Mead is right and gender identity is culturally constructed, then we can begin to understand the importance of gender portrayals on television, in the movies, and in magazines. Questions you might consider as you read the selections in this chapter: How have *you* learned to be the man or woman you are? Who, or what, has been a gender influence in your life? To what extent has the media played a role? Are you content with your gender identity? Are there ways in which you would change your behavior, or your values, if you did not encounter resistance in the culture in which you live?

# Gender Roles

## WILLIAM H. MASTERS
## VIRGINIA E. JOHNSON
## ROBERT C. KOLODNY

*In this selection, noted researchers Masters, Johnson, and Kolodny discuss the ways in which we learn sex-appropriate behaviors. As social scientists, the authors describe (but do not judge) the behavior of groups and the ways in which group expectations can affect individuals. Notice how the authors consciously build on the work of other researchers as they explore the patterns and pressures of gender-role socialization. The discussion that follows appeared originally as a chapter of a textbook on human sexuality.*

*William Masters and Virginia Johnson are credited with being the first to conduct physiological and anatomical studies of human sexual behavior, on the basis of which they published two pioneering works:* Human Sexual Response *(1966) and* Human Sexual Inadequacy *(1970). As a faculty member at the Washington University School of Medicine in St. Louis, Masters (b. 1915) began studying human sexual activity in 1954. Psychologist Virginia Johnson (b. 1925) joined the laboratory research team three years later. Together, they have collaborated on more than two hundred publications and have received numerous awards.*

"Gender Roles" by William Masters, Virginia Johnson, and Robert Kolodny from pp. 274–287 in *Human Sexuality,* third edition. Copyright © 1988 by William H. Masters, Virginia E. Johnson, and Robert C. Kolodny. Reprinted by permission of HarperCollins Publishers.

On a television soap opera, a self-confident, smooth-talking business-man seduces a beautiful but not too bright female secretary. A children's book describes a warm, caring, stay-at-home mother while depicting father as an adventuresome traveler. A newspaper advertisement for cigarettes shows a husky young man enthusiastically dousing a shapely, squealing, female companion with water, her wet T-shirt clinging to her bust—the headlined caption reads "Refresh Yourself." Each of these messages tells us something about stereotypes and sexism.

In the past 25 years, there has been considerable scientific interest in studying differences and similarities between the sexes, for a number of reasons. First, various beliefs about sex differences in traits, talents, and temperaments have greatly influenced social, political, and economic systems throughout history. Second, recent trends have threatened age-old distinctions between the sexes. In 1987, for instance, more than half of American women worked outside the home. Unisex fashions in hairstyles, clothing, and jewelry are now popular. Even anatomic status is not fixed in a day where change-of-sex surgery is possible. Third, the women's movement has brought increasing attention to areas of sex discrimination and sexism and has demanded sexuality equality.

As a result of these trends, old attitudes toward sex differences, childrearing practices, masculinity and feminity, and what society de-fines as "appropriate" gender-role behavior have undergone considera-ble change. Many of today's young adults have been raised in families where a progressive attitude toward gender roles has been taught or where parents struggled to break away from stereotyped thinking. Thus, there is a continuum of types of socialization today that ranges from old, traditional patterns to modern versions. This essay will examine these issues and trends as they influence the experience of being male or female.

## MASCULINITY AND FEMININITY

Before you read any further, you might take a few minutes to write out a list of the traits you would use to describe a typical American man and woman. If your descriptions are similar to most other people's, you probably listed characteristics like strong, courageous, self-reliant, com-petitive, objective, and aggressive for a typical man, while describing a typical woman in terms like intuitive, gentle, dependent, emotional, sensitive, talkative, and loving.

Most people not only believe that men and women differ but share similar beliefs about the ways in which they differ (Broverman et al., 1972). Beliefs of this sort, held by many people and based on oversimpli-fied evidence or uncritical judgment, are called *stereotypes*. Stereotypes can be harmful because they lead to erroneous judgments and generalizations and can thus affect how people treat one another.

Because many stereotypes about sexuality are based on assumptions about the nature of masculinity and femininity, it is difficult to offer a concise definition of these two terms. In one usage, a "masculine" man or a "feminine" woman is a person who is sexually attractive to members of the opposite sex. Advertisements for clothing and cosmetics constantly remind us of this fact. In another sense, masculinity or femininity refers to the degree a person matches cultural expectations of how males and females should behave or look. In the not too distant past, some segments of our society were upset when long hair became fashionable among young men or when women applied for admission to West Point because these patterns did not "fit" prevailing expectations about differences between the sexes. In still another meaning, masculinity and femininity refer to traits measured by standardized psychological tests that compare one person's responses to those of large groups of men and women.

According to traditional assumptions, it is highly desirable for males to be masculine and females to be feminine. If behavior matches cultural expectations, it helps to preserve social equilibrium and allows for a certain amount of stability in the details of everyday living. Conformity to cultural norms presumably indicates "adjustment" and "health," while straying too far from expected behavior patterns indicates abnormality or even disease. Finally, "masculine" men and "feminine" women are relatively predictable and behave in ways that are fairly consistent and complementary. Fortunately (or unfortunately, depending on your viewpoint), it now appears that masculinity and femininity are unlikely to tell us much about your personality, sexual preferences, or lifestyle, and old stereotypes are now giving way to more useful and dynamic scientific views.

The traditional approach to studying masculinity and femininity looked at these traits as opposites. According to this view, if you possess "feminine" characteristics you cannot have "masculine" characteristics and vice versa (Spence and Helmreich, 1978). It was assumed that people who scored high on certain traits judged as masculine (e.g., independence, competitiveness) would also have a general lack of femininity. As a result, most psychological tests designed to measure masculinity and femininity were set up as a single masculinity-femininity scale (Kaplan and Sedney, 1980). Furthermore, men and women whose masculinity or femininity scores differed substantially from group averages were judged to be less emotionally healthy and less socially adjusted than others with "proper" scores.

Recent research findings have changed this approach. Instead of viewing masculinity and femininity as opposites, various behavioral scientists now look at them as separate characteristics that coexist to some degree in every individual (Bem, 1972; Spence and Helmreich, 1978; Cook, 1985). Thus, a woman who is competitive can be quite feminine in other areas; a man who is tender and loving may also be very masculine. As we discuss the ways in which gender roles are learned and the impact they have on our lives, it will be helpful to keep this viewpoint in mind.

## PATTERNS OF GENDER-ROLE SOCIALIZATION

Even before a baby is born, parents are likely to have different attitudes about the sex of their child. In most societies, male children are clearly preferred over female children (Markle, 1974; Coombs, 1977), and having a son is more often seen as a mark of status and achievement than having a daughter (Westoff and Rindfuss, 1974). This preference probably stems from the belief that men are stronger, smarter, braver, and more productive than women and that "it's a man's world" (certainly true in the past)—meaning that there are more and better educational, occupational, political, and economic opportunities open to males than to females.   10

Parents often try to guess the sex of their unborn child and may construct elaborate plans and ambitions for the child's life. If the child is thought to be a boy, the parents are likely to think of him as sports-oriented, achievement-oriented, tough, and independent. If the child is thought to be a girl, parents are more apt to envision beauty, grace, sensitivity, artistic talents, and marriage. These different attitudes are nicely shown in lyrics from the Broadway musical *Carousel* as a father-to-be dreams about his unborn child:   11

I'll teach him to wrassle, and dive through a wave,
When we go in the morning's for our swim.
His mother can teach him the way to behave,
But she won't make a sissy out o'him. . . .
He'll be tall and as tough as a tree, will Bill!
Like a tree he'll grow, with his head held high
And his feet planted firm on the ground,
And you won't see nobody dare to try
To boss him or toss him around! . . .

Wait a minute! Could it be—
What the hell! What if he is a girl? . . .

She mightn't be so bad at that,
A kid with ribbons in her hair!
A kind o' neat and petite

Little tin-type of her mother! What a pair!
My little girl, pink and white
As peaches and cream is she.
My little girl is half again as bright
As girls are meant to be!
Dozens of boys pursue her,
Many a likely lad does
What he can to woo her.
From her faithful Dad.[1]

This sort of prenatal thinking is one form of stereotyping, as is 12
guessing that the baby will be a boy because "he" kicks a lot inside the
uterus. It is not surprising then to find that the earliest interactions
between parents and their newborn child are influenced in subtle ways
by cultural expectations.

## Birth and Infancy

At the moment of birth, the announcement of the baby's sex ("It's a 13
boy" or "It's a girl") sets in motion a whole chain of events such as
assigning a pink or blue identification bracelet, choosing a name, selecting a wardrobe, and decorating the baby's room, each of which involves
making distinctions between males and females.[2]

As friends, relatives, and parents discuss the newborn's appearance, 14
gender stereotypes are everywhere: "Look at his size—he'll be a football player, I bet." "She has beautiful eyes—she's a real doll." "See how
intelligent he looks!" "She's got great legs already! You'll have to work
to keep the boys away." Informal banter about the child's future is also
likely to be gender-linked: if friends remark, "You better start saving for
the wedding," you can bet they are not talking about a baby boy.

Parents of newborn infants describe daughters as softer, smaller, 15
finer-featured, and less active than sons, although no objective differences in appearance or activity level were noted by physicians (Rubin,
Provenzano, and Luria, 1974). In early infancy, boys receive more physical contact from their mothers than girls do, while girls are talked to and
looked at more than boys (Lewis, 1972)—a difference in treatment

---

[1]"Soliloquy," written by Richard Rodgers and Oscar Hammerstein II. Copyright 1945 by William-
son Music, Co. Copyright renewed. International copyright secured. Used by permission. All
rights reserved.

[2]In the song, "A Boy Named Sue," written by S. Silverstein and recorded by Johnny Cash, the
father reversed usual gender distinctions in name selection in order to achieve the paradoxical
effect of improving his son's masculinity. By giving him the name Sue, the father forced the boy
to fight frequently to defend himself from ridicule, thus becoming "tough."

which tends to reinforce a female's verbal activities and a male's physical activity. Walum (1977) reports an exploratory study in which two groups of young mothers were given the same six-month-old infant dressed either in blue overalls and called Adam or wearing a pink frilly dress and called Beth: the results showed that "Beth" was smiled at more, given a doll to play with more often, and viewed as "sweet" compared with "Adam." Another recent study confirms that both mothers and fathers behave differently toward unfamiliar infants on the basis of perceived sex, although the parents were unaware of this differential treatment (Culp, Cook, and Housley, 1983).

Parents respond differently to infant boys and girls in other ways. **16** They react more quickly to the cries of a baby girl than a baby boy (Frieze et al., 1978) and are more likely to allow a baby boy to explore, to move farther away, or to be alone, thus fostering independence. In contrast, the baby girl seems to be unintentionally programmed in the direction of dependency and passivity (Weitzman, 1975; Long Laws, 1979).

Gender differences in socializing children occur for reasons that are **17** not fully understood at present. Certainly, cultural influences are important, but biological factors may also be involved. For example, boys' higher rates of metabolism, greater caloric intake, and higher rates of activity may prepare them for earlier independence, or parental encouragement of independence may reflect cultural expectations (Walum, 1977). Furthermore, the different prenatal hormone exposures of males and females may possibly account for behavioral differences in infancy. Often, parents are unaware of how their actions with their children are different depending on the child's sex. Nevertheless, differential socialization seems to occur even in parents who are philosophically committed to the idea of avoiding gender stereotypes (Scanzoni and Fox, 1980).

## Early Childhood (Ages Two to Five)

By age two, a child can determine in a fairly reliable way the gender of **18** other people and can sort clothing into different boxes for boys and girls (Thompson, 1975). However, two-year-olds do not usually apply correct gender labels to their own photographs with any consistency—this ability usually appears around $2\frac{1}{2}$ years. As already mentioned, core gender identity, the personal sense of being male or female, seems to solidify by age three. This process is probably assisted by the acquisition of verbal skills, which allow children to identify themselves in a new dimension and to test their abilities of gender usage by applying pronouns such as "he" or "she" to other people.

At age two or three, children begin to develop awareness of gender **19** roles, the outward expression of maleness or femaleness, in their families and in the world around them. It might seem that the child forms very sketchy impressions at first—"Mommies don't smoke pipes" or "Daddies don't wear lipstick"—but the toddler's understanding is greater than his or her ability to verbally express it. It is likely that impressions of what is masculine or feminine form across a broad spectrum of behaviors.

The serious business of young childhood is play, so by examining the objects used in play activities we may be able to learn something about gender-role socialization. Walk through the toy department of a large store and you will quickly see the principle of differential socialization at work. Boys' toys are action-oriented (guns, trucks, spaceships, sports equipment) while girls' toys reflect quieter play, often with a domestic theme (dolls, tea sets, "pretend" makeup kits, or miniature vacuum cleaners, ovens, or refrigerators). Where a particular toy is marketed to both girls and boys, the version for girls is usually feminized in certain ways. For instance, a boys' bicycle is described as "rugged, fast, and durable." The girls' model of the same bike has floral designs on the seat and pretty pink tassels on the hand-grips and is described as "petite and safe." A detailed analysis of the content of 96 children's rooms showed that boys were given more toy cars and trucks, sports equipment, and military toys, while girls received many more dolls, doll houses, and domestic toys (Rheingold and Cook, 1975). Although many boys today play with "E.T." or "Rambo" dolls or other action-oriented figures, most parents of boys are likely to become concerned if their sons develop a preference for frilly, "feminine" dolls (Collins, 1984).

Picture books are another important source for learning gender roles. As Weitzman (1975) observes, "Through books, children learn about the world outside their immediate environment: they learn what is expected of children of their age" (p. 110). Although in recent years some changes have occurred, an analysis of award-winning books for preschoolers showed marked evidence of gender-role bias (Weitzman et al., 1972). First, males were shown much more frequently than females (there were 261 males and 23 females pictured, a ratio of 11 to 1). Second, most males were portrayed as active and independent, while most females were presented in passive roles. Third, adult women shown in these books were consistently identified as mothers or wives, while adult men were engaged in a wide variety of occupations and professions. It is no wonder that girls get a strong message that "success" for them is measured in terms of marriage and motherhood. Fortunately, this imbalance is beginning to change today, with many recent books aimed at preschoolers showing women in a more favorable light.

Television is also a powerful force in the gender-role socialization 22
of young children because it provides a window to the rest of the world.
The fictionalized world of Saturday morning children's cartoons is filled
with gender stereotypes: the heroes are almost all males, and females are
shown as companions or as "victims" needing to be rescued from the
forces of evil. Even award-winning children's shows such as Sesame
Street have been criticized because women were seldom shown employed outside the home and male figures predominated (Vogel, Broverman, and Gardner, 1970). Advertisements geared at preschoolers perpe-
trate the same patterns: boys are shown as tough, action-oriented
people, while girls are portrayed as more domestic, quieter, and refined.

## The School-Age Child

By the time children enter elementary school, gender-role expectations 23
are applied with some unevenness. A seven-year-old girl who likes
sports and climbs trees is generally regarded as "cute" and is affection-
ately, even proudly, called a tomboy. A seven-year-old boy who prefers
playing with dolls and jumping rope to throwing a football is labeled
a "sissy" and may be the source of great parental consternation. Although child psychiatrists regard tomboyishness in girls as a "normal
passing phase" (Green, 1974), "effeminate" boys are thought by many
researchers to require treatment to prevent them from becoming homosexual or having later sexual problems (Lebovitz, 1972; Green, 1974,
1987; Newman, 1976; Rekers et al., 1978).

Different patterns of gender-linked play continue during the school 24
years and are now reinforced firmly by peer group interactions. School-
yard and neighborhood play is noticed by other boys and girls, and
children whose play preferences do not match everyone else's are
thought to be "weird" and are often the butt of jokes. Since there is a
powerful motivation to be like everyone else in order to have friendship
and group acceptance, this teasing can have a negative influence on a
child's sense of self-esteem.

At this age, boys are generally expected to show masculinity by 25
demonstrating physical competence and competitive spirit in sports
activities, which become the primary focus of boyhood play. They are
rewarded for bravery and stamina and criticized for showing fear or
frustration ("Big boys don't cry"). Girls, on the other hand, although
physically more mature than boys at corresponding ages in childhood,
have traditionally been steered away from highly competitive sports
and sheltered from too much exertion. (Today, this pattern is changing
considerably as girls are encouraged to enter competitive swimming,
gymnastics, soccer, and Little League baseball just as much as they are

encouraged to take ballet or music lessons.) Girls are expected to stay clean and be neat, to avoid fighting, and to avoid dangerous activities ("Be a lady"). Young girls often seem to be programmed to cry to show hurt or frustration and find that crying (at least in the presence of adults) often elicits comforting. Thus, males are encouraged to solve problems in an active, independent way, whereas females are more likely to be shown that *their* best way of solving problems is to act helpless and to rely on someone else to take care of them.

Even for the children of relatively "liberated" parents, sexism some- 26 times inadvertently looms:

> Take my friend Irene, a vice-president of a Fortune 500 company, who at a recent dinner party bemoaned the stiff resistance of male executives to women in senior management. Not ten minutes later, she proudly regaled us with tales of her eight-year-old son who struts around the house shouting, "Boys are the best, boys are the best."
>
> In Irene's mind, 40- or 50-year-old executives practice sexist oppression. But when her Jonathan shuts girls out, he is cute, natural ("It's the age," she told me), and turning out to be a "real boy." (Rommel, 1984, p. 32)

There are also, of course, instances where parents react differently 27 to a child's seemingly sexist behavior. In one case, a mother who encountered her eight-year-old son telling his friends that girls are poor athletes took her son on successive weekends to watch the UCLA women's basketball team and to a women's weightlifting contest. The boy apparently gained a different perspective on female athletic capacity, because he was seen soon thereafter playing softball with a nine-year-old girl from down the street.

While these sorts of situations are of concern to some parents who 28 want to raise their children in a nonsexist fashion, other well-meaning parents feel that since many young girls "shut boys out" and believe that "girls are best," this is not really sexist at all. They point out that while these responses aren't appropriate for adults, such attitudes foster self-esteem in children.

Much of the child's time is spent in school, where gender-role 29 stereotypes still exist in many classrooms. History lessons portray a view of the world as male-dominated; in the few instances when women are mentioned, they are usually in a subservient or domestic role (recall how Betsy Ross served the cause of the American Revolution by sewing). Girls are usually assigned different classroom "chores" than boys are (for example, boys might be asked to carry a stack of books, while girls are asked to "straighten up the room"), and teachers often assign activities to boys and girls based on their presumptions about gender-role preferences. In one school, third grade girls were asked to draw a mural while the boys were asked to build a fort. A girl who said she would rather work on the fort was told by her teacher, "That's not a job for young ladies."

School-age children are also exposed to obvious gender-role 30 stereotypes on television. From commercials children learn that most women are housewives concerned about important decisions like which detergent to use, which soap does not leave a bathtub ring, and which brand of toilet paper is softest. Men, on the other hand, are concerned about health issues ("Four out of five doctors recommend . . ."), economics, automobiles, or recreation (most beer commercials play upon themes of masculinity, for example). With a few notable exceptions, the lawyers, doctors, and detectives on TV are all men, and women—even when cast in adventurous occupations—are shown as emotional, romantic sex objects who cannot make up their minds. It is no wonder that stereotypes about masculinity and femininity continue: children are exposed to them so widely that they come to believe they are true. Supporting this observation, McGhee and Frueh (1980) found that children who watched television more than 25 hours per week had more stereotyped gender-role perceptions than age-matched children who watched less than 10 hours of television weekly.

## Adolescence

Adhering to gender-appropriate roles is even more important during 31 adolescence than at younger ages. What was earlier seen as rehearsal or play is now perceived as the real thing. The rules are more complicated, the penalties for being "different" are harsher, and future success seems to hinge on the outcome.

Adolescent boys have three basic rules to follow in relation to 32 gender roles. First, succeed at athletics. Second, become interested in girls and sex. Third, do not show signs of "feminine" interests or traits. Teenage boys who disregard these rules too obviously are likely to be ridiculed and ostracized, while those who follow them closely are far more likely to be popular and accepted.

The traditional prohibition of feminine traits in male adolescents 33 probably relates to two separate factors. The first is the view of masculinity and femininity as complete opposites that was discussed earlier in the chapter. For a teenage boy to "fit" the male stereotype, he must be achievement-oriented, competitive, independent, self-confident, and so on. If the opposite traits emerge, his masculinity is subject to question. Second, a teenage boy who shows "feminine" interests or traits is often regarded suspiciously as a potential homosexual. In a variation on this theme, in schools where home economics courses were opened to male enrollment, some parents have voiced concern that it would "rob" boys of their masculinity and lead to "sexual deviance" (Spence and Helmreich, 1978). However, in communities where boys take home economics and girls take shop courses, it is remarkable that an easy equilibrium has been reached, with no one "harmed" psychologically by the experience.

The adolescent girl is confronted by a different set of gender-role **34** expectations and different socialization pressures. In keeping with the traditional expectation that a female's ultimate goals are marriage and motherhood rather than career and independence, the prime objective seems to be heterosexual attractiveness and popularity. As a result, the adolescent girl's school experience may push her toward learning domestic or secretarial skills instead of orienting her toward a profession, and the message she gets—from peers and parents—is that academic achievement may lessen her femininity (Weitzman, 1975; Frieze et al., 1978; Long Laws, 1979). However, it appears that this pattern is now undergoing considerable change. As it has become more culturally "permissible" for women to enter professions such as medicine and law or to enter the business world at the management level, more and more teenage females have become comfortable with maintaining a high level of academic success.

For many women, the high value that society places on both **35** achievement and popularity poses a problem. One factor that seems to influence female nonachievement is fear of success, that is, being anxious about social rejection and loss of perceived femininity if success is achieved (Horner, 1972; Schaffer, 1981). This fear is not entirely irrational, as studies show that in adulthood, men often seem to be threatened by a woman who is more successful than they are, resulting in lower rates of marriage for high-achieving women (Frieze et al., 1978). Interestingly, a recent report noted that females who are masculine sex-typed have lower fear of success scores than those who are feminine sex-typed (Forbes and King, 1983).

Female adolescents also get mixed messages about the relationship **36** between femininity and sexuality. While the traditional message about sexual behavior has been "nice girls don't" or should feel guilty if they do, the primary allure of femininity is sexual, and the "proof" of femininity is sexual desirability. But if femininity is to be valued, why not be sexually active? The dilemma lies partly in the cultural double standard that sanctions varied male sexual experience but regards the female with more than one partner as promiscuous.

To be certain, the traditional gender-role stereotypes related to **37** sexual behavior have been set aside by many adolescents. Teenage girls are much more apt to ask boys out today than they were 20 years ago and often take the initiative in sexual activity. This is seen as a major relief by some adolescent males, who feel freed from the burden of having to be the sexual expert, but is frightening to others who feel more comfortable with traditional sexual scripts. As one 17-year-old boy put it, "I don't like the feeling of not being in control. What am I supposed to do if a girl wants to make love and I'm not in the mood?" (Authors' files).

In many ways, the old "quarterback-cheerleader" idea of masculine and feminine gender roles during adolescence has broadened into newer, more complex, and less clearly defined patterns. Athletic, educational, and career aspirations have become less compartmentalized, styles of dress have been altered, and many colleges that were previously restricted to one sex have now become coeducational. Nevertheless, it is important to realize that the influence of traditional gender-role attitudes continues to affect today's adolescents, showing that the present is still very much the product of the past.  **38**

## Adulthood

Before proceeding any further with our overview of gender-role socialization, two points must be made. First, our discussion has deliberately highlighted common denominators of this process while ignoring many sources of variability. To believe that children in Beverly Hills, Detroit, and rural Vermont are exposed to identical messages about gender roles is obviously incorrect. Differences in religion, socioeconomic status, family philosophies, and ethnic heritage all influence the socialization process: for instance, researchers have found that gender-role distinctions are sharper in the lower class than in the middle or upper classes (Reiss, 1980). Second, to think that gender roles are entirely shaped in childhood or adolescence implies that adults cannot change. In recent years, however, many young adults have moved away from the traditional gender-role distinctions with which they were brought up and have chosen alternative patterns with which they can live more comfortably. How this trend will ultimately affect future generations is not known.  **39**

Despite differences in upbringing and changing attitudes, our culture's gender-role stereotypes usually come into full bloom in the adult years, although the patterns change a little. For men, although heterosexual experience and attractiveness continue as important proofs of masculinity, strength and physical competence (as in hunting, fighting, or sports) are no longer as important as they once were. Occupational achievement, measured by job status and financial success, has become the yardstick of contemporary masculinity for middle- and upper-class America.  **40**

For women, marriage and motherhood remain the central goals of  **41** our cultural expectations, although this stereotype is now beginning to change significantly. As more and more women join the work force, as more and more women are divorced, as more and more people choose childless marriages, the notion that femininity and achievement are antithetical is slowly beginning to crumble away.

Marriage is a fascinating social institution in which gender roles play out in some unexpected ways. Tavris and Offir (1977) observe: **42**

> The irony is that marriage, which many men consider a trap, does them a world of good, while the relentless pressure on them to be breadwinners causes undue strain and conflict. Exactly the reverse is true for women. Marriage, which they yearn for from childhood, may prove hazardous to their health, while the optional opportunities of work help keep them sane and satisfied. (p. 220)

Married men are physically and mentally healthier than single men (Weissman, 1980; Gurman and Klein, 1980; Scanzoni and Fox, 1980), but married women have higher rates of mental and physical problems than single women (Knupfer, Clark, and Room, 1966). Gove (1979) suggests several aspects of gender roles and marriage that conspire to cause such problems:

1. Women usually have their "wife-mother" role as their only source of gratification, whereas most men have two sources of gratification—worker and household head.
2. Many women find raising children and household work to be frustrating, and many others are unhappy with the low status of their "wife-mother" role.
3. The relatively unstructured and invisible role of the housewife is a breeding ground for worry and boredom.
4. Even when a married woman works outside the home, she is generally expected to do most of the housework (and thus is under greater strain than the husband) and typically has a low-status, lower-paying job and must contend with sex discrimination at work.
5. The expectations confronting married women are diffuse and unclear; uncertainty and lack of control over the future often conspire to create problems and low self-esteem. (pp. 39–40)

Fortunately, there are some positive indications that change is not just on the horizon but is actually here in our midst today. Dual-career families are becoming common, and more and more men are willingly participating in ordinary household tasks that were previously regarded as strictly "women's work." A small but growing number of men are staying home to be househusbands while their wives pursue outside careers (Beer, 1983). **43**

Adult gender roles hinge on areas other than marriage, of course. It **44** is fascinating to see how the same status inconsistency found in many marriages also applies to situations outside the home. In the business world, very few companies have substantial numbers of women as executives (and the secretarial pool is unlikely to have many men). Although a young man who is successful in business is pegged as a "boy wonder," a young woman who achieves corporate success is sometimes accused of having "slept her way to the top." Medical schools and law schools only began to admit sizable numbers of women in the last decade, and even then it took some prodding from the federal government. Furthermore, changes in admissions policies do not necessarily reflect an open-armed embrace. As one woman attending medical school put it:

> From the beginning, I could notice great astonishment that I was attractive *and* bright. My teachers seemed to think that only ugly women have brains. Then there was a constant sense of being singled out for "cruel and unusual punishment." From the anatomy labs to the hospital wards, the female medical students were gleefully given the dirtiest assignments and made the butt of jokes. I never did understand why a woman physician examining a penis is so different from a male physician doing a pelvic exam, but this seemed to be a constant source of humor. (Authors' files)

Complicating matters even more, and showing how widespread 45 sexism remains in our society, is the indisputable fact that many women who enter even the most prestigious professions are also subjected to sexual harassment. For instance, a recent report found that 25 percent of female students and faculty at Harvard Medical School had encountered varying forms of sexual harassment ranging from leering, sexually oriented remarks to instances of unwanted touching and requests for sexual favors (*American Medical News,* Nov. 11, 1983, p. 1). At Atlanta's old-line law firm of King & Spaulding, where a former female associate had filed a sex discrimination lawsuit to protest against being denied partnership, a summer outing for law students working at the firm featured a bathing suit contest for women at which one male partner proclaimed, "She has the body we'd like to see more of" (*Wall Street Journal,* Dec. 20, 1983, p. 1).

Not only do women have difficulty gaining access to nontraditional 46 occupations, they also are frequently penalized by lower salaries than those for men and face more obstacles to advancing on the job. Furthermore, when women are successful in their achievements at work, the results are more likely to be attributed to luck than to skill, dedication, or effort (Walum, 1977; Heilman, 1980). Another form of prejudice that women often have to overcome is shown in a recent research study that had 360 college students—half of them male, half of them female— evaluate academic articles that were presented as written by either "John

T. McKay" or "Joan T. McKay." Although the same articles were used for the evaluations, with only the first name of the author varying, the articles supposedly written by a male were more favorably evaluated by both sexes than the articles supposedly written by a female (Paludi and Bauer, 1983).

Clearly, sex discrimination is a problem of today's world that will  47 not disappear overnight (Heilman, 1980). However, there are certainly signs of changing times as women now enter "male" occupations like welding and making telephone repairs and as men increasingly infiltrate traditionally "female" occupations. With Sandra Day O'Connor now serving as the first woman on the U.S. Supreme Court, with a woman having run for vice-president of the United States in 1984, and with women increasingly gaining access to high-visibility and high-status occupations, the impression that times are changing becomes even more pronounced.

## WORKS CITED

Beer, W. R. *Househusbands: Men and Housework in American Families.* New York: Praeger, 1983.

Bem, S. L. "Psychology Looks at Sex Roles: Where Have All the Androgynous People Gone?" Paper presented at the UCLA Symposium on Women. Los Angeles: May 1972.

———. "The Measurement of Psychological Androgyny." *Journal of Consulting and Clinical Psychology* 42(2):155–62, 1974.

———. "Sex Role Adaptability: One Consequence of Psychological Androgyny." *Journal of Personality and Social Psychology* 31(4):634–43, 1975.

Broverman, I. K., et al. "Sex-Role Stereotypes: A Current Appraisal." *Journal of Social Issues* 28(2):59–78, 1972.

Collins, G. "New Studies of 'Girl Toys' and 'Boy Toys.'" *New York Times*, 13 February 1984.

Cook, E. P. *Psychological Androgyny.* New York: Pergamon Press, 1985.

Coombs, L. C. "Preferences for Sex of Children Among U.S. Couples." *Family Planning Perspectives* 9:259–65, 1977.

Culp, R. E.; Cook, A. S.; and Housley, P. C. "A Comparison of Observed and Reported Adult-Infant Interactions: Effect of Perceived Sex." *Sex Roles* 9:475–79, 1983.

Forbes, G. B., and King, S. "Fear of Success and Sex-Role: There Are Reliable Relationships." *Psychological Reports* 53:735–38, 1983.

Frieze, I. H., et al. *Women and Sex Roles: A Social Psychological Perspective.* New York: Norton, 1978.

Gove, W. R. "Sex Differences in the Epidemiology of Mental Disorder: Evidence and Explanations." In Gomberg, E. S., and Franks, V. (eds.), *Gender and Disordered Behavior*, pp. 23–68. New York: Brunner/Mazel, 1979.

Green, R. *Sexual Identity Conflict in Children and Adults.* New York: Basic Books, 1974.

Gurman, A. S., and Klein, M. "Marital and Family Conflicts." In Brodsky, A. M., and Hare-Mustin, R. (eds.), *Women and Psychotherapy*, pp. 159–88. New York: Guilford Press, 1980.

Heilman, M. E. "Sex Discrimination." In Wolman, B. E., and Money, J. (eds.), *Handbook of Human Sexuality*, pp. 227–49. Englewood Cliffs, N.J.: Prentice-Hall, 1980.

Horner, M. "Toward an Understanding of Achievement Related Conflicts in Women." *Journal of Social Issues* 28:157–75, 1972.

Kaplan, A., and Sedney, M. A. *Psychology and Sex Roles: An Androgynous Perspective.* Boston: Little, Brown, 1980.

Knupfer, F.; Clark, W.; and Room, R. "The Mental Health of the Unmarried." *American Journal of Psychiatry* 122:841–51, 1966.

Lebovitz, P. S. "Feminine Behavior in Boys: Aspects of Its Outcome." *American Journal of Psychiatry* 128:1283–89, 1972.

Lewis, M. "State as an Infant-Environment Interaction: An Analysis of Mother-Infant Interaction as a Function of Sex." *Merrill-Palmer Quarterly* 18:95–121, 1972.

McGhee, P. E., and Frueh, T. "Television Viewing and the Learning of Sex-role Stereotypes." *Sex Roles* 6:179–88, 1980.

Markle, G. E. "Sex Ratio at Birth: Values, Variance and Some Determinants." *Demography* 11:131–42, 1974.

Newman, L. E. "Treatment for the Parents of Feminine Boys." *American Journal of Psychiatry* 133:683–87, 1976.

Paludi, M. A., and Bauer, W. D. "Goldberg Revisited: What's in an Author's Name?" *Sex Roles* 9:387–90, 1983.

Reiss, I. L. *Family Systems in America.* 3rd ed. New York: Holt, Rinehart and Winston, 1980.

Rekers, G. A., et al. "Sex-Role Stereotype and Professional Intervention for Childhood Gender Disturbance." *Professional Psychology* 9:127–36, 1978.

Rommel, E. "Grade School Blues." *Ms.*, pp. 32–35, January 1984.

Rubin, J.; Provenzano, F.; and Luria, Z. "The Eye of the Beholder: Parents' Views on Sex of Newborns." *American Journal of Orthopsychiatry* 44:512–19, 1974.

Scanzoni, J., and Fox, G. L. "Sex Roles, Family and Society: The Seventies and Beyond." *Journal of Marriage and the Family* 42:743–58, 1980.

Schaffer, K. *Sex Roles and Human Behavior.* Cambridge, Mass.: Winthrop, 1981.

Spence, J. T., and Helmreich, R. L. *Masculinity & Femininity: Their Psychological Dimensions, Correlates, and Antecedents.* Austin: University of Texas Press, 1978.

Tavris, C., and Offir, C. *The Longest War: Sex Differences in Perspective.* New York: Harcourt Brace Jovanovich, 1977.

Vogel, S.; Broverman, I.; and Gardner, J. *Sesame Street and Sex-Role Stereotypes.* Pittsburgh: Know, 1970.

Walum, L. R. *The Dynamics of Sex and Gender: A Sociological Perspective.* Chicago: Rand McNally College Publishing Co., 1977.

Weissman, M. "Depression." In Brodsky, A. M., and Hare-Mustin, R. (eds.), *Women and Psychotherapy*, pp. 97–112. New York: Guilford Press, 1980.

Weitzman, L. J. "Sex-Role Socialization." In Freeman, J. (ed.), *Women: A Feminist Perspective.* Palo Alto, Calif.: Mayfield, 1975.

Weitzman, L. J., et al. "Sex Role Socialization in Picture Books for Pre-School Children." *American Journal of Sociology* 77:1125–50, 1972.

## Review Questions

1. Traditionally, what have been the stereotyped gender roles for American men and women?
2. How have assumptions underlying psychological tests for gender-role characteristics changed in recent years?
3. Based on this article, summarize the pattern of gender-role socialization of either a boy or girl, from birth through adulthood.
4. What evidence of sex discrimination do the authors find in contemporary American culture?

## Discussion and Writing Suggestions

1. The authors begin their discussion with examples of gender-role stereotyping in popular culture (see paragraph 1). Conduct your own informal survey of popular culture: Locate three illustrations of gender-role stereotyping in a medium of your choice—television, newspapers, billboards, movies, books. Describe the stereotyping that you find, compare and contrast stereotypes, and draw conclusions.
2. Reread the authors' section on gender-role socialization in adolescence. How accurate is their description of the pressures adolescents face in becoming "masculine" young men and "feminine" young women?
3. Locate and read any one of the articles that the authors cite in their own discussion. Summarize the article (odds are, the author will have done this for you) and share your impressions with the class.

# The Problem That Has No Name

## BETTY FRIEDAN

*Betty Naomi Friedan (b. 1921) a feminist organizer and writer, has lectured at more than fifty universities, institutes, and professional organizations and has written numerous feminist-oriented articles for national magazines. She is also the author of two important books on gender issues, the groundbreaking* The Feminine Mystique *(1963), in which the following selection appears, and* The Second Stage *(1981). In "The Problem That Has No Name," Friedan explores the psychological costs to women of letting themselves be defined completely as wives and mothers.*

*Friedan's exploration of gender serves a double purpose in this chapter: both as an important historical document (The Feminine Mystique was a catalyst for the women's movement) and as a standard against which to measure any changes in the ways men and women define themselves today. As you read from this essay, which opens Friedan's book, you might reflect on the extent to which women's lives have changed in the last thirty years. Several writers in this chapter will suggest that in essential respects, the roles that our culture assigns to men and women have not changed.*

The problem lay buried, unspoken, for many years in the minds of American women. It was a strange stirring, a sense of dissatisfaction, a yearning that women suffered in the middle of the twentieth century in the United States. Each suburban wife struggled with it alone. As she made the beds, shopped for groceries, matched slipcover material, ate peanut butter sandwiches with her children, chauffeured Cub Scouts and Brownies, lay beside her husband at night—she was afraid to ask even of herself the silent question—"Is this all?" 1

For over fifteen years there was no word of this yearning in the millions of words written about women, for women, in all the columns, books and articles by experts telling women their role was to seek fulfillment as wives and mothers. Over and over women heard in voices of tradition and of Freudian sophistication that they could desire no greater destiny than to glory in their own femininity. Experts told them how to catch a man and keep him, how to breastfeed children and handle their toilet training, how to cope with sibling rivalry and adolescent rebellion; how to buy a dishwasher, bake bread, cook gourmet snails, and build a swimming pool with their own hands; how to dress, look, and act more feminine and make marriage more exciting; how to keep their husbands from dying young and their sons from growing into delinquents. They were taught to pity the neurotic, unfeminine, unhappy women who wanted to be poets or physicists or presidents. They learned that truly feminine women do not want careers, higher education, political rights—the independence and the opportunities that the old-fashioned feminists fought for. Some women, in their forties and fifties, still remembered painfully giving up those dreams, but most of the younger women no longer even thought about them. A thousand expert voices applauded their femininity, their adjustment, their new maturity. All they had to do was devote their lives from earliest girlhood to finding a husband and bearing children. 2

By the end of the nineteen-fifties, the average marriage age of women in America dropped to 20, and was still dropping, into the teens. Fourteen million girls were engaged by 17. The proportion of women attending college in comparison with men dropped from 47 per cent in 1920 to 35 per cent in 1958. A century earlier, women had fought for 3 higher education; now girls went to college to get a husband. By the mid-fifties, 60 per cent dropped out of college to marry, or because they were afraid too much education would be a marriage bar. Colleges built dormitories for "married students," but the students were almost always the husbands. A new degree was instituted for the wives—"Ph.T." (Putting Husband Through).

Then American girls began getting married in high school. And the women's magazines, deploring the unhappy statistics about these young marriages, urged that courses on marriage, and marriage counselors, be installed in the high schools. Girls started going steady at twelve and thirteen, in junior high. Manufacturers put out brassieres with false bosoms of foam rubber for little girls of ten. And an advertisement for a child's dress, sizes 3–6x, in the *New York Times* in the fall of 1960, said: "She Too Can Join the Man-Trap Set."

By the end of the fifties, the United States birthrate was overtaking India's. The birth-control movement, renamed Planned Parenthood, was asked to find a method whereby women who had been advised that a third or fourth baby would be born dead or defective might have it anyhow. Statisticians were especially astounded at the fantastic increase in the number of babies among college women. Where once they had two children, now they had four, five, six. Women who had once wanted careers were now making careers out of having babies. So rejoiced *Life* magazine in a 1956 paean to the movement of American women back to the home.

In a New York hospital, a woman had a nervous breakdown when she found she could not breastfeed her baby. In other hospitals, women dying of cancer refused a drug which research had proved might save their lives: its side effects were said to be unfeminine. "If I have only one life, let me live it as a blonde," a larger-than-life-sized picture of a pretty, vacuous woman proclaimed from newspaper, magazine, and drugstore ads. And across America, three out of every ten women dyed their hair blonde. They ate a chalk called Metrecal, instead of food, to shrink to the size of the thin young models. Department-store buyers reported that American women, since 1939, had become three and four sizes smaller. "Women are out to fit the clothes, instead of vice-versa," one buyer said.

Interior decorators were designing kitchens with mosaic murals and original paintings, for kitchens were once again the center of women's lives. Home sewing became a million-dollar industry. Many women no longer left their homes, except to shop, chauffeur their children, or attend a social engagement with their husbands. Girls were growing up in America without ever having jobs outside the home. In the late fifties, a sociological phenomenon was suddenly remarked: a third of American women now worked, but most were no longer young and very few were pursuing careers. They were married women who held part-time jobs, selling or secretarial, to put their husbands through school, their sons through college, or to help pay the mortgage. Or they were widows supporting families. Fewer and fewer women were entering professional work. The shortages in the nursing, social work, and teaching professions caused crises in almost every American city. Concerned over the Soviet Union's lead in the space race, scientists noted that America's greatest source of unused brain-power was women. But girls would not study physics: it was "unfeminine." A girl refused a science fellowship at Johns Hopkins to take a job in a real-estate office. All she wanted, she said, was what every other American girl wanted—to get married, have four children and live in a nice house in a nice suburb.

The suburban housewife—she was the dream image of the young    8
American women and the envy, it was said, of women all over the world. The American housewife—freed by science and labor-saving appliances from the drudgery, the dangers of childbirth and the illnesses of her grandmother. She was healthy, beautiful, educated, concerned only about her husband, her children, her home. She had found true feminine fulfillment. As a housewife and mother, she was respected as a full and equal partner to man in his world. She was free to choose automobiles, clothes, appliances, supermarkets; she had everything that women ever dreamed of.

In the fifteen years after World War II, this mystique of feminine    9
fulfillment became the cherished and self-perpetuating core of contemporary American culture. Millions of women lived their lives in the image of those pretty pictures of the American suburban housewife, kissing their husbands goodbye in front of the picture window, depositing their stationwagonsful of children at school, and smiling as they ran the new electric waxer over the spotless kitchen floor. They baked their own bread, sewed their own and their children's clothes, kept their new washing machines and dryers running all day. They changed the sheets on the beds twice a week instead of once, took the rug-hooking class in adult education, and pitied their poor frustrated mothers, who had dreamed of having a career. Their only dream was to be perfect wives and mothers; their highest ambition to have five children and a beautiful house, their only fight to get and keep their husbands. They had no thought for the unfeminine problems of the world outside the home; they wanted the men to make the major decisions. They gloried in their role as women, and wrote proudly on the census blank: "Occupation: housewife."

For over fifteen years, the words written for women, and the words    10
women used when they talked to each other, while their husbands sat on the other side of the room and talked shop or politics or septic tanks, were about problems with their children, or how to keep their husbands

happy, or improve their children's school, or cook chicken or make slipcovers. Nobody argued whether women were inferior or superior to men; they were simply different. Words like "emancipation" and "career" sounded strange and embarrassing; no one had used them for years. When a Frenchwoman named Simone de Beauvoir wrote a book called *The Second Sex*, an American critic commented that she obviously "didn't know what life was all about," and besides, she was talking about French women. The "woman problem" in America no longer existed.

If a woman had a problem in the 1950's and 1960's, she knew that    11
something must be wrong with her marriage, or with herself. Other women were satisfied with their lives, she thought. What kind of a woman was she if she did not feel this mysterious fulfillment waxing the kitchen floor? She was so ashamed to admit her dissatisfaction that she never knew how many other women shared it. If she tried to tell her husband, he didn't understand what she was talking about. She did not really understand it herself. For over fifteen years women in America found it harder to talk about this problem than about sex. Even the psychoanalysts had no name for it. When a woman went to a psychiatrist for help, as many women did, she would say, "I'm so ashamed," or "I must be hopelessly neurotic." "I don't know what's wrong with women today," a suburban psychiatrist said uneasily. "I only know something is wrong because most of my patients happen to be women. And their problem isn't sexual." Most women with this problem did not go to see a psychoanalyst, however. "There's nothing wrong really," they kept telling themselves. "There isn't any problem."

But on an April morning in 1959, I heard a mother of four, having    12
coffee with four other mothers in a suburban development fifteen miles from New York, say in a tone of quiet desperation, "the problem." And the others knew, without words, that she was not talking about a problem with her husband, or her children, or her home. Suddenly they realized they all shared the same problem, the problem that has no name. They began, hesitantly, to talk about it. Later, after they had picked up their children at nursery school and taken them home to nap, two of the women cried, in sheer relief, just to know they were not alone.

Gradually I came to realize that the problem that has no name was    13
shared by countless women in America. As a magazine writer I often interviewed women about problems with their children, or their marriages, or their houses, or their communities. But after a while I began to recognize the telltale signs of this other problem. I saw the same signs in suburban ranch houses and split-levels on Long Island and in New Jersey and Westchester County; in colonial houses in a small Massachusetts town; on patios in Memphis; in suburban and city apartments; in living rooms in the Midwest. Sometimes I sensed the problem, not as

a reporter, but as a suburban housewife, for during this time I was also bringing up my own three children in Rockland County, New York. I heard echoes of the problem in college dormitories and semiprivate maternity wards, at PTA meetings and luncheons of the League of Women Voters, at suburban cocktail parties, in station wagons waiting for trains, and in snatches of conversation overheard at Schrafft's. The groping words I heard from other women, on quiet afternoons when children were at school or on quiet evenings when husbands worked late, I think I understood first as a woman long before I understood their larger social and psychological implications.

Just what was this problem that has no name? What were the words **14** women used when they tried to express it? Sometimes a woman would say "I feel empty somehow . . . incomplete." Or she would say, "I feel as if I don't exist." Sometimes she blotted out the feeling with a tranquilizer. Sometimes she thought the problem was with her husband, or her children, or that what she really needed was to redecorate her house, or move to a better neighborhood, or have an affair, or another baby. Sometimes, she went to a doctor with symptoms she could hardly describe: "A tired feeling . . . I get so angry with the children it scares me . . . I feel like crying without any reason." (A Cleveland doctor called it "the housewife's syndrome.") A number of women told me about great bleeding blisters that break out on their hands and arms. "I call it the housewife's blight," said a family doctor in Pennsylvania. "I see it so often lately in these young women with four, five and six children who bury themselves in their dishpans. But it isn't caused by detergent and it isn't cured by cortisone."

Sometimes a woman would tell me that the feeling gets so strong **15** she runs out of the house and walks through the streets. Or she stays inside her house and cries. Or her children tell her a joke, and she doesn't laugh because she doesn't hear it. I talked to women who had spent years on the analyst's couch, working out their "adjustment to the feminine role," their blocks to "fulfillment as a wife and mother." But the desperate tone in these women's voices, and the look in their eyes, was the same as the tone and the look of other women, who were sure they had no problem, even though they did have a strange feeling of desperation.

A mother of four who left college at nineteen to get married told **16** me:

> I've tried everything women are supposed to do—hobbies, gardening, pickling, canning, being very social with my neighbors, joining committees, running PTA teas. I can do it all, and I like it, but it doesn't leave you anything to think about—any feeling of who you are. I never had any career ambitions. All I wanted was to get married and have four children. I love the kids and Bob and my home. There's no problem you can even put a name to. But I'm

desperate. I begin to feel I have no personality. I'm a server of food and a putter-on of pants and a bedmaker, somebody who can be called on when you want something. But who am I?

A twenty-three-year-old mother in blue jeans said: 17

I ask myself why I'm so dissatisfied. I've got my health, fine children, a lovely new home, enough money. My husband has a real future as an electronics engineer. He doesn't have any of these feelings. He says maybe I need a vacation, let's go to New York for a weekend. But that isn't it. I always had this idea we should do everything together. I can't sit down and read a book alone. If the children are napping and I have one hour to myself I just walk through the house waiting for them to wake up. I don't make a move until I know where the rest of the crowd is going. It's as if ever since you were a little girl, there's always been somebody or something that will take care of your life: your parents, or college, or falling in love, or having a child, or moving to a new house. Then you wake up one morning and there's nothing to look forward to.

A young wife in a Long Island development said: 18

I seem to sleep so much. I don't know why I should be so tired. This house isn't nearly so hard to clean as the cold-water flat we had when I was working. The children are at school all day. It's not the work. I just don't feel alive.

. . .

Are the women who finished college, the women who once had 19 dreams beyond housewifery, the ones who suffer the most? According to the experts they are, but listen to these four women:

My days are all busy, and dull, too. All I ever do is mess around. I get up at eight—I make breakfast, so I do the dishes, have lunch, do some more dishes and some laundry and cleaning in the afternoon. Then it's supper dishes and I get to sit down a few minutes before the children have to be sent to bed. . . . That's all there is to my day. It's just like any other wife's day. Humdrum. The biggest time, I am chasing kids.

Ye Gods, what do I do with my time? Well, I get up at six. I get my son dressed and then give him breakfast. After that I wash dishes and bathe and feed the baby. Then I get lunch and while the children nap, I sew or mend or iron and do all the other things I can't get done before noon. Then I cook supper for the family and my husband watches TV while I do the dishes. After I get the children to bed, I set my hair and then I go to bed.

The problem is always being the children's mommy, or the minister's wife and never being myself.

A film made of any typical morning in my house would look like an old Marx Brothers' comedy. I wash the dishes, rush the older children off to school, dash out in the yard to cultivate the chrysanthemums, run back in to make a phone call about a committee meeting, help the youngest child build a blockhouse, spend fifteen minutes skimming the newspapers so I can be well-informed, then scamper down to the washing machines where my thrice-weekly laundry includes enough clothes to keep a primitive village going for an entire year. By noon I'm ready for a padded cell. Very little of what I've done has been really necessary or important. Outside pressures lash me through the day. Yet I look upon myself as one of the more relaxed housewives in the neighborhood. Many of my friends are even more frantic. In the past sixty years we have come full circle and the American housewife is once again trapped in a squirrel cage. If the cage is now a modern plate-glass-and-broadloom ranch house or a convenient modern apartment, the situation is no less painful than when her grandmother sat over an embroidery hoop in her gilt-and-plush parlor and muttered angrily about women's rights.

The first two women never went to college. They live in develop-     20
ments in Levittown, New Jersey, and Tacoma, Washington, and were interviewed by a team of sociologists studying workingmen's wives. The third, a minister's wife, wrote on the fifteenth reunion questionnaire of her college that she never had any career ambitions, but wishes now she had. The fourth, who has a Ph.D. in anthropology, is today a Nebraska housewife with three children. Their words seem to indicate that housewives of all educational levels suffer the same feeling of desperation.

## Review Questions

1. In paragraph 9, Friedan refers to the "mystique of feminine fulfillment." What is the feminine mystique?
2. What is "the problem that has no name"?
3. How is this problem related to the mystique of feminine fulfillment?
4. Reread the paragraphs (16–19) in which Friedan uses first-person narratives. What is her purpose in using them?

## Discussion and Writing Suggestions

1. To what extent do you sense today, thirty years after publication of *The Feminine Mystique*, that women—and men—ask themselves the question "Is this all?" When Friedan wrote her book, "this" referred to an emptiness and lack of meaning. To what might "this" refer today?
2. Reread the first-person testimonies of women who are suffering from the problem that has no name. (See paragraphs 16–19.) Select one of these testimonies and write a two-paragraph personal response. You might consider these questions: How does the woman speaking make you feel? Have you ever felt her frustration? Has anyone close to you felt it?
3. At the time of its publication and for years after, *The Feminine Mystique* had

an explosive effect on American culture. What about the passage you have read might have touched a cultural nerve?

4. One criticism of Friedan is that her thesis was true mainly of white suburban housewives, but not of working-class women—both white and of color. Based on your reading of this excerpt, how fair do you think this criticism is?

# Ralph's Story

## WARREN FARRELL

*Psychologist Warren Farrell recounts the story of a man who, at his wife's insistence, attends a men's group and discovers that the masculine role he has played so adroitly (as a high-powered lawyer) has left him a stranger to himself, his wife, and his children. Farrell lets Ralph speak in his own words in a chilling tale of self-discovery. Ralph's narrative raises important questions about the price we pay for rigidly adhering to gender-based codes of success. As you read Ralph's story, you might consider the reasons men so often define themselves through their work.*

*Warren Farrell, active in the men's movement for more than twenty years, is the author of* The Liberated Man *(1974) and* Why Men Are the Way They Are: The Male-Female Dynamic *(1986), from which the present selection was taken.*

Ralph was a forty-one-year-old man in our men's group. He was mar-  1
ried, the father of two children. He had been in the group for three months, and had hardly said a word. One evening he looked up and said, "I think I'd like to speak up tonight. I'm afraid I joined this group only because my wife forced me to. She got involved in one of these women's movement operations and started changing. She called it 'growing.' About three months ago she said, 'Ralph, I'm tired of having to choose between a relationship with you and a relationship with myself.' Pretty fancy rhetoric, I thought. Then she added, 'There's a men's group forming that's meeting next Tuesday. Why don't you get involved?'

"Well, I kind of laughed her off. But a week later she started again.  2
'The group's meeting next Tuesday. As far as I'm concerned, if you're not doing some changing in *three* months, that's the end.'

" 'The end! For the sake of a *men's group?*' I asked.  3

" 'It's symbolic, Ralph,' she said.  4

---

"So I figured I'd join this symbol and see what you fags were talking    5
about! But the problem was, you didn't fit my image, and I began
identifying with some of the things you were saying. Well, anyway, last
night Ginny reminded me the three months were up tomorrow. So I
think I'd like to speak up tonight."

We laughed at Ralph's motivation, but encouraged him to continue.    6

"Well, what struck me was how each of you chose different careers,    7
but you all worried about succeeding. Even you, Jim—even though
you're unemployed and have a laid-back facade. That started me thinking about my career.

"All my life I wanted to play baseball. As a pro. When I was a    8
sophomore in high school I was pretty hot stuff, and my uncle came and
scouted me. Later he said, 'Ralph, you're good. Damn good. And you
might make it to the pros if you really work at it. But only the best make
good money for a long time. If you really want to be good to yourself,
make use of your intelligence, get yourself a good job—one you can
depend on for life.'

"I was surprised when my folks agreed with him. Especially Dad.    9
Dad always called me 'Ralph, who pitched the no-hitter.' Dad stopped
calling me that after that conversation. Maybe that turned the tide for
me." Ralph hesitated, as if he were piecing something together, but he
quickly withdrew from his introspection.

"Anyway, I was proud of myself for making the transition like a    10
man. I'd always liked reading and learning, but just hadn't focused much
on it. But I figured just for a couple of years I'd 'play the system': borrow
friends' old term papers, take a look at old exams, focus my reading on
the questions different teachers tended to ask, and so on. I never cheated.
I just figured I'd 'play the system' for a couple of years, raise my grades,
then when I got into college, I could really learn—I could do what I
wanted after that.

"Well, 'playing the system' worked. I got into a top-notch univer-    11
sity. But it soon became apparent that a lot of people graduated from
good universities—if I wanted to really stand out it would help to 'play
the system' for just a few more years, get into a good grad school or
law school, and then, once I did that, I could do with my life what I
wanted after that.

"I decided on law school—but to become a social-work lawyer, so    12
I could make a real contribution to people who most needed it. But
about my second or third year of law school—when my colleagues saw
I was taking what they called this 'missionary law' seriously, they
explained that if I really wanted to be effective as a social-work lawyer,
I'd better get some experience first in the hard-knocks, reality-based field
of corporate law rather than ease into the namby-pamby area of social-
work law right away—if I didn't I wouldn't get the respect to be

effective. Frankly, that made sense. So I joined a top corporate law firm in New York. I knew I could work there for a couple of years, and then really do what I wanted with my life after that.

"After a couple of years in the firm, I was doing well. But the whole    13
atmosphere of the corporate legal community made it clear that if I dropped out after two years it would be seen as a sign that I just couldn't hack the pressure. If I continued for just a couple more years, and became a junior partner—junior partners were the ones marked with potential—then I could really do what I wanted with my life after that.

"Well, it took me seven years to get the junior partnership offered    14
to me—with politics and everything. But I got it. By that time I had lost some of the desire to be a social-work lawyer—it was considered a clear step backward. In other ways I maintained that ideal—it seemed more meaningful than kowtowing to rich money. But I also knew the switch would mean forfeiting a lot of income. My wife Ginny and I had just bought a new home—which we pretty much had to do with two kids—and I knew they'd be going to college. . . . Ginny's income was only part-time now, and she was aching to travel a bit.

"By that time, I also realized that while junior partners had potential,    15
the people with the real ins in the legal community were not the junior partners, but the senior partners. I figured I had a pretty big investment in the corporate law area now—if I just stuck it out for a couple more years, I could get a senior partnership, get a little money saved for the kids' education and travel, and *then* I could really do with my life what I wanted. . . .

"It took me eight more years to get the senior partnership. I can    16
remember my boss calling me into the office and saying, 'Ralph, we're offering you a senior partnership.' I acted real calm, but my heart was jumping toward the phone in anticipation of telling Ginny. Which I did. I told Ginny I had a surprise. I'd tell her when I got home. I asked her to get dressed real special. I refused to leak what it was about. I made reservations in her favorite restaurant, bought some roses and her favorite champagne.

"I came home real early so we'd have time to sip it together; I    17
opened the door and said, 'Guess what?' Ginny was looking beautiful. She said, 'What is it, Ralph?' I said 'I got the senior partnership!' She said, 'Oh, fine, that's great,' but there was a look of distance in her eyes. A real superficial enthusiasm, you know what I mean?"

We nodded.    18

"So I said, 'What do you mean "Oh, fine"—I've been working since    19
the day we met to get this promotion for us, and you say "Oh, fine"?'

" 'Every time you get a promotion, Ralph,' Ginny announced, 'you    20
spend less time with me. I guess I just wish you'd have more time for me. More time to love me.'

" 'Why do you think I've been working my ass off all these years  21
if it isn't to show you how much I love you?' I said.

" 'Ralph, that's not what I mean by love. Just look at the kids, Ralph.'  22

"Well, I did look at the kids. Randy is seventeen. And Ralph, Jr., is  23
fifteen. Randy just got admitted to college—a thousand miles from here.
Each year I keep promising myself that 'next year' I'll really get to know
who they are. 'Next year . . .' 'Next year.' But next year he'll be in
college. And I don't even know who he is. And I don't know whether
I'm his dad or his piggy bank.

"I don't know where to begin with Randy, but a few weeks ago I  24
tried to change things a bit with Ralph, Jr. He was watching TV. I asked
him if he wouldn't mind turning it off so we could talk. He was a little
reluctant, but he eventually started telling me some of what was happening at school. We talked baseball, and I told him about some of my days
pitching. He said I'd already told him. He told me about some of his
activities, and I spotted a couple of areas where I thought his values
were going to hurt him. So I told him. We got into a big argument. He
said I wasn't talking with him, I was lecturing him . . . 'spying' on him.

"We've hardly talked since. I can see what I did wrong—boasting  25
and lecturing—but I'm afraid if I try again, he'll be afraid to say much
now, and we'll just sit there awkwardly. And if he mentions those
values, what do I say? I want to be honest, but I don't want to lecture.
I don't even know where to begin."

Ralph withdrew from the group. He had struck so many chords it  26
took us more than ten minutes to notice that he was fighting back tears.
Finally one of the men picked up on it and asked, "Ralph, is there
anything else you're holding back?" Ralph said there wasn't, but his
assurance rang false. We prodded.

"I guess maybe I am holding something back," he said hesitantly. "I  27
feel like I spent forty years of my life working as hard as I can to become
somebody I don't even like."

When I heard that sentence fifteen years ago, I was twenty-seven.  28
It's been perhaps the most important sentence I've heard in my life: "I
feel like I've spent forty years of my life working as hard as I can to become
somebody I don't even like." Even as I heard it, the ways it was threatening
to be true in my own life flashed through my mind.

Ralph continued: "I was mentioning some of my doubts to a few of  29
my associates at work. They listened attentively for a couple of minutes,
then one made a joke, and another excused himself. Finally I mentioned
this men's group—which I never should have done—and they just
laughed me out of the office. I've been the butt of jokes ever since: 'How
are the U.S. Navel Gazers doing, Ralph boy?'

"Suddenly I realized. Ginny has a whole network of lady friends she  30 can talk with about all this. Yet the men I've worked with for seventeen years, sixty hours a week, hardly know me. Nor do they want to."

Ralph withdrew again. But this time he seemed to be taking in what 31 he had just said as if he were putting together his life as he was speaking. Then his face grew sad. A few of us who might otherwise have said something held back.

"I guess I could handle all this," Ralph volunteered, fighting back the 32 tears again, "but I think, for all practical purposes, I've lost Ginny in the process. And maybe I could handle that, too. But the only other people I love in this world are Randy and Ralph, Jr. And when I'm really honest with myself—I mean *really* honest—I think for all practical purposes I've lost them too—."

We started to interrupt, but Ralph stopped us, tears silently escaping 33 his eyes. "What really gets me . . . what really gets me *angry* is that I did everything I was supposed to do for forty years, did it better than almost any other man I know, and I lost everyone I love in the process, including myself. I don't mean to be philosophical, but the more I did to stand out, the more I became the same. Just one more carbon copy. Oh, I got to a high level, okay. A high-level mediocre.

"In some ways, I feel I could handle all that, too. But look at 34 me—paid more than any two of you guys put together, supposedly one of the top decision-makers in the country, and when it comes to my own home, my own life, I don't even know how to begin."

Ralph cried. For the first time in twenty-two years. 35

## Review Questions

1. Of what problem does Ralph become aware as a consequence of having joined a men's group?
2. In paragraphs 8–16, Ralph recounts a pattern of forgoing what he really wants to do for the sake of success. He calls this "playing the system." Summarize the sacrifices Ralph made in order to succeed.
3. Ralph's definition of love turned out to differ from his wife's definition. How so?

## Discussion and Writing Suggestions

1. In paragraphs 2 and 3, Ralph relates how his wife insisted he join a men's group. He seems to have been astonished that his wife felt so adamant about his joining that she would end the marriage if he didn't. How does Ralph's astonishment suggest the existence of the very problem he has come to recognize as a member of the group?
2. Ralph makes a stunning confession in paragraph 27: "I feel like I spent forty

years of my life working as hard as I can to become somebody I don't even like." In an informally written two paragraphs, perhaps a journal entry, respond to this statement.

3. Ralph suggests that women have a network of friends with whom they can talk about difficult personal matters but that men do not. Is this true in your experience? In reflecting on this question, consider your closest friends, same sex and opposite sex. What forms the bonds of friendship with each? In what ways do these bonds differ?

4. Do you know any Ralphs, men who have fulfilled the male stereotype: who have succeeded professionally but who have paid a terrible price emotionally? What price did these men pay? Do they themselves acknowledge any loss? In a few paragraphs, tell their story. If you wish, write from their point of view—that is, make this account a first-person narrative.

5. In your estimate, is Ralph a better man for having vented his feelings in the men's group? In Ralph's estimate, do you think he sees himself as better, or potentially better?

# Blame It on Feminism

## SUSAN FALUDI

*Writing nearly thirty years after the publication of* The Feminine Mystique, *Susan Faludi explores a growing tendency among people in business, the government, and the media to target feminism as the cause of women's unhappiness today. Anti-feminists argue that revised gender roles have created as many problems for women (including psychological and physical stress) as they have resolved. But Faludi rejects these arguments and counters that significant problems for women persist and that traditionalists, who are threatened by hard-won feminist gains, wish to make "a preemptive strike that stops women long before they reach" their goal of full equality with men.*

*Susan Faludi is a Pulitzer Prize—winning journalist and writer for the* Wall Street Journal. *"Blame It on Feminism" is excerpted from her widely admired* Backlash: The Undeclared War Against American Women *(1991).*

To be a woman in America at the close of the 20th century—what good fortune. That's what we keep hearing, anyway. The barricades have fallen, politicians assure us. Women have "made it," Madison Avenue cheers. Women's fight for equality has "largely been won," *Time*                                                    1 magazine announces. Enroll at any university, join any law firm, apply for credit at any bank. Women have so many opportunities now, corporate leaders say, that we don't really need equal opportunity policies. Women are so equal now, lawmakers say, that we no longer need an Equal Rights Amendment. Women have "so much," former President Ronald Reagan says, that the White House no longer needs to appoint them to higher office. Even American Express ads are saluting a woman's freedom to charge it. At last, women have received their full citizenship papers.

And yet . . .                                                                                    2

Behind this celebration of the American woman's victory, behind   3
the news, cheerfully and endlessly repeated, that the struggle for women's rights is won, another message flashes. You may be free and equal now, it says to women, but you have never been more miserable.

This bulletin of despair is posted everywhere—at the newsstand, on   4
the TV set, at the movies, in advertisements and doctors' offices and academic journals. Professional women are suffering "burnout" and succumbing to an "infertility epidemic." Single women are grieving from a "man shortage." The New York Times reports: Childless women are "depressed and confused" and their ranks are swelling. Newsweek says: Unwed women are "hysterical" and crumbling under a "profound crisis of confidence." The health advice manuals inform: High-powered career women are stricken with unprecedented outbreaks of "stress-induced disorders," hair loss, bad nerves, alcoholism, and even heart attacks. The psychology books advise: Independent women's loneliness represents "a major mental health problem today." Even founding feminist Betty Friedan has been spreading the word: she warns that women now suffer from a new identity crisis and "new 'problems that have no name.' "

How can American women be in so much trouble at the same time   5
that they are supposed to be so blessed? If the status of women has never been higher, why is their emotional state so low? If women got what they asked for, what could possibly be the matter now?

The prevailing wisdom of the past decade has supported one, and   6
only one, answer to this riddle: it must be all that equality that's causing all that pain. Women are unhappy precisely because they are free. Women are enslaved by their own liberation. They have grabbed at the gold ring of independence, only to miss the one ring that really matters. They have gained control of their fertility, only to destroy it. They have pursued their own professional dreams—and lost out on the greatest female adventure. The women's movement, as we are told time and again, has proved women's own worst enemy.

"In dispensing its spoils, women's liberation has given my genera-   7
tion high incomes, our own cigarette, the option of single parenthood, rape crisis centers, personal lines of credit, free love, and female

gynecologists," Mona Charen, a young law student, writes in the *National Review*, in an article titled "The Feminist Mistake." "In return it has effectively robbed us of one thing upon which the happiness of most women rests—men." The *National Review* is a conservative publication, but such charges against the women's movement are not confined to its pages. "Our generation was the human sacrifice" to the women's movement, *Los Angeles Times* feature writer Elizabeth Mehren contends in a *Time* cover story. Baby-boom women like her, she says, have been duped by feminism: "We believed the rhetoric." In *Newsweek*, writer Kay Ebeling dubs feminism "the Great Experiment That Failed" and asserts "women in my generation, its perpetrators, are the casualties." Even the beauty magazines are saying it: *Harper's Bazaar* accuses the women's movement of having "lost us [women] ground instead of gaining it."

In the last decade, publications from the *New York Times* to *Vanity Fair* to the *Nation* have issued a steady stream of indictments against the women's movement, with such headlines as WHEN FEMINISM FAILED or THE AWFUL TRUTH ABOUT WOMEN'S LIB. They hold the campaign for women's equality responsible for nearly every woe besetting women, from mental depression to meager savings accounts, from teenage suicides to eating disorders to bad complexions. The "Today" show says women's liberation is to blame for bag ladies. A guest columnist in the *Baltimore Sun* even proposes that feminists produced the rise in slasher movies. By making the "violence" of abortion more acceptable, the author reasons, women's rights activists made it all right to show graphic murders on screen.

At the same time, other outlets of popular culture have been forging the same connection: in Hollywood films, of which *Fatal Attraction* is only the most famous, emancipated women with condominiums of their own slink wild-eyed between bare walls, paying for their liberty with an empty bed, a barren womb. "My biological clock is ticking so loud it keeps me awake at night," Sally Field cries in the film *Surrender*, as, in an all too common transformation in the cinema of the '80s, an actress who once played scrappy working heroines is now showcased groveling for a groom. In prime-time television shows, from "thirtysomething" to "Family Man," single, professional, and feminist women are humiliated, turned into harpies, or hit by nervous breakdowns; the wise ones recant their independent ways by the closing sequence. In popular novels, from Gail Parent's *A Sign of the Eighties* to Stephen King's *Misery*, unwed women shrink to sniveling spinsters or inflate to fire-breathing she-devils; renouncing all aspirations but marriage, they beg for wedding bands from strangers or swing sledgehammers at reluctant bachelors. We "blew it by waiting," a typically remorseful careerist sobs in Freda Bright's *Singular Women;* she and her sister professionals are "condemned to be childless forever." Even Erica Jong's high-flying independent heroine literally crashes by the end of the decade, as the author supplants *Fear of Flying*'s saucy Isadora Wing, a symbol of female sexual emancipation in the '70s, with an embittered careerist-turned-recovering-"co-dependent" in *Any Woman's Blues*—a book that is intended, as the narrator bluntly states, "to demonstrate what a deadend the so-called sexual revolution had become, and how desperate so-called free women were in the last few years of our decadent epoch."

Popular psychology manuals peddle the same diagnosis for contem- 10 porary female distress. "Feminism, having promised her a stronger sense of her own identity, has given her little more than an identity *crisis*," the best-selling advice manual *Being a Woman* asserts. The authors of the era's self-help classic *Smart Women/Foolish Choices* proclaim that women's distress was "an unfortunate consequence of feminism," because "it created a myth among women that the apex of self-realization could be achieved only through autonomy, independence, and career."

In the Reagan and Bush years, government officials have needed no 11 prompting to endorse this thesis. Reagan spokeswoman Faith Whittlesey declared feminism a "straitjacket" for women, in the White House's only policy speech on the status of the American female population— entitled "Radical Feminism in Retreat." Law enforcement officers and judges, too, have pointed a damning finger at feminism, claiming that they can chart a path from rising female independence to rising female pathology. As a California sheriff explained it to the press, "Women are enjoying a lot more freedom now, and as a result, they are committing more crimes." The U.S. Attorney General's Commission on Pornography even proposed that women's professional advancement might be responsible for rising rape rates. With more women in college and at work now, the commission members reasoned in their report, women just have more opportunities to be raped.

Some academics have signed on to the consensus, too—and they 12 are the "experts" who have enjoyed the highest profiles on the media circuit. On network news and talk shows, they have advised millions of women that feminism has condemned them to "a lesser life." Legal scholars have railed against "the equality trap." Sociologists have claimed that "feminist-inspired" legislative reforms have stripped women of special "protections." Economists have argued that well-paid working women have created "a less stable American family." And demographers, with greatest fanfare, have legitimated the prevailing wisdom with so-called neutral data on sex ratios and fertility trends; they say they actually have the numbers to prove that equality doesn't mix with marriage and motherhood.

Finally, some "liberated" women themselves have joined the lamen- 13 tations. In confessional accounts, works that invariably receive a hearty greeting from the publishing industry, "recovering Superwomen" tell all.

In *The Cost of Loving: Women and the New Fear of Intimacy*, Megan Marshall, a Harvard-pedigreed writer, asserts that the feminist "Myth of Independence" has turned her generation into unloved and unhappy fast-trackers, "dehumanized" by careers and "uncertain of their gender identity." Other diaries of mad Superwomen charge that "the hard-core feminist viewpoint," as one of them puts it, has relegated educated executive achievers to solitary nights of frozen dinners and closet drinking. The triumph of equality, they report, has merely given women hives, stomach cramps, eye-twitching disorders, even comas.

But what "equality" are all these authorities talking about?　　　14

If American women are so equal, why do they represent two-thirds　15
of all poor adults? Why are nearly 75 percent of full-time working women making less than $20,000 a year, nearly double the male rate? Why are they still far more likely than men to live in poor housing and receive no health insurance, and twice as likely to draw no pension? Why does the average working woman's salary still lag as far behind the average man's as it did twenty years ago? Why does the average female college graduate today earn less than a man with no more than a high school diploma (just as she did in the '50s)—and why does the average female high school graduate today earn less than a male high school dropout? Why do American women, in fact, face one of the worst gender-based pay gaps in the developed world?

If women have "made it," then why are nearly 80 percent of　16
working women still stuck in traditional "female" jobs—as secretaries, administrative "support" workers and salesclerks? And, conversely, why are they less than 8 percent of all federal and state judges, less than 6 percent of all law partners, and less than one half of 1 percent of top corporate managers? Why are there only three female state governors, two female U.S. senators, and two Fortune 500 chief executives? Why are only nineteen of the four thousand corporate officers and directors women—and why do more than half the boards of Fortune companies still lack even one female member?

If women "have it all," then why don't they have the most basic　17
requirements to achieve equality in the work force? Unlike virtually all other industrialized nations, the U.S. government still has no family-leave and child care programs—and more than 99 percent of American private employers don't offer child care either. Though business leaders say they are aware of and deplore sex discrimination, corporate America has yet to make an honest effort toward eradicating it. In a 1990 national poll of chief executives at Fortune 1000 companies, more than 80 percent acknowledged that discrimination impedes female employees' progress—yet, less than 1 percent of these same companies regarded *remedying* sex discrimination as a goal that their personnel departments should pursue. In fact, when the companies' human resource officers

were asked to rate their department's priorities, women's advancement ranked last.

If women are so "free," why are their reproductive freedoms in greater jeopardy today than a decade earlier? Why do women who want to postpone childbearing now have fewer options than ten years ago? The availability of different forms of contraception has declined, research for new birth control has virtually halted, new laws restricting abortion—or even *information* about abortion—for young and poor women have been passed, and the U.S. Supreme Court has shown little ardor in defending the right it granted in 1973.    18

Nor is women's struggle for equal education over; as a 1989 study found, three-fourths of all high schools still violate the federal law banning sex discrimination in education. In colleges, undergraduate women receive only 70 percent of the aid undergraduate men get in grants and work-study jobs—and women's sports programs receive a pittance compared with men's A review of state equal-education laws in the late '80s found that only thirteen states had adopted the minimum provisions required by the federal Title IX law—and only seven states had anti-discrimination regulations that covered all education levels.    19

Nor do women enjoy equality in their own homes, where they still shoulder 70 percent of the household duties—and the only major change in the last fifteen years is that now middle-class men *think* they do more around the house. (In fact, a national poll finds the ranks of women saying their husbands share equally in child care shrunk to 31 percent in 1987 from 40 percent three years earlier.) Furthermore, in thirty states, it is still generally legal for husbands to rape their wives; and only ten states have laws mandating arrest for domestic violence— even though battering was the leading cause of injury of women in the late '80s. Women who have no other option but to flee find that isn't much of an alternative either. Federal funding for battered women's shelters has been withheld and one third of the 1 million battered women who seek emergency shelter each year can find none. Blows from men contributed far more to the rising numbers of "bag ladies" than the ill effects of feminism. In the '80s, almost half of all homeless women (the fastest growing segment of the homeless) were refugees of domestic violence.    20

The word may be that women have been "liberated," but women themselves seem to feel otherwise. Repeatedly in national surveys, majorities of women say they are still far from equality. Nearly 70 percent of women polled by the *New York Times* in 1989 said the movement for women's rights had only just begun. Most women in the 1990 Virginia Slims opinion poll agreed with the statement that conditions for their sex in American society had improved "a little, not a lot." In poll after poll in the decade, overwhelming majorities of    21 women said they needed equal pay and equal job opportunities, they needed an Equal Rights Amendment, they needed the right to an abortion without government interference, they needed a federal law guaranteeing maternity leave, they needed decent child care services. They have none of these. So how exactly have we "won" the war for women's rights?

Seen against this background, the much ballyhooed claim that feminism is responsible for making women miserable becomes absurd—and irrelevant. As we shall see in the chapters to follow, the afflictions ascribed to feminism are all myths. From "the man shortage" to "the infertility epidemic" to "female burnout" to "toxic day care," these so-called female crises have had their origins not in the actual conditions of women's lives but rather in a closed system that starts and ends in the media, popular culture, and advertising—an endless feedback loop that perpetuates and exaggerates its own false images of womanhood.    22

Women themselves don't single out the women's movement as the source of their misery. To the contrary, in national surveys 75 to 95 percent of women credit the feminist campaign with *improving* their lives, and a similar proportion say that the women's movement should keep pushing for change. Less than 8 percent think the women's movement might have actually made their lot worse.    23

What actually is troubling the American female population, then? If the many ponderers of the Woman Question really wanted to know, they might have asked their subjects. In public opinion surveys, women consistently rank their own *inequality*, at work and at home, among their most urgent concerns. Over and over, women complain to pollsters about a lack of economic, not marital, opportunities; they protest that working men, not working women, fail to spend time in the nursery and the kitchen. The Roper Organization's survey analysts find that men's opposition to equality is "a major cause of resentment and stress" and "a major irritant for most women today." It is justice for their gender, not wedding rings and bassinets, that women believe to be in desperately short supply. When the *New York Times* polled women in 1989 about "the most important problem facing women today," job discrimination was the overwhelming winner; none of the crises the media and popular culture had so assiduously promoted even made the charts. In the 1990 Virginia Slims poll, women were most upset by their lack of money, followed by the refusal of their men to shoulder child care and domestic duties. By contrast, when the women were asked where the quest for a husband or the desire to hold a "less pressured" job or to stay at home ranked on their list of concerns, they placed them at the bottom.    24

As the last decade ran its course, women's unhappiness with in-    25
equality only mounted. In national polls, the ranks of women protesting discriminatory treatment in business, political, and personal life
climbed sharply. The proportion of women complaining of unequal
employment opportunities jumped more than ten points from the '70s,
and the number of women complaining of unequal barriers to job
advancement climbed even higher. By the end of the decade, 80 percent to 95 percent of women said they suffered from job discrimination and unequal pay. Sex discrimination charges filed with the Equal
Employment Opportunity Commission rose nearly 25 percent in the
Reagan years, and charges of general harassment directed at working
women more than doubled. In the decade, complaints of sexual harassment nearly doubled. At home, a much increased proportion of
women complained to pollsters of male mistreatment, unequal relationships, and male efforts to, in the words of the Virginia Slims poll,
"keep women down." The share of women in the Roper surveys who
agreed that men were "basically kind, gentle, and thoughtful" fell from
almost 70 percent in 1970 to 50 percent by 1990. And outside their
homes, women felt more threatened, too: in the 1990 Virginia Slims
poll, 72 percent of women said they felt "more afraid and uneasy on
the streets today" than they did a few years ago. Lest this be attributed only to a general rise in criminal activity, by contrast only 49
percent of men felt this way.

While the women's movement has certainly made women more    26
cognizant of their own inequality, the rising chorus of female protest
shouldn't be written off as feminist-induced "oversensitivity." The
monitors that serve to track slippage in women's status have been
working overtime since the early '80s. Government and private surveys are showing that women's already vast representation in the
lowliest occupations is rising, their tiny presence in higher-paying
trade and craft jobs stalled or backsliding, their minuscule representation in upper management posts stagnant or falling, and their pay
dropping in the very occupations where they have made the most
"progress." The status of women lowest on the income ladder has
plunged most perilously; government budget cuts in the first four
years of the Reagan administration alone pushed nearly 2 million fe-
male-headed families and nearly 5 million women below the poverty
line. And the prime target of government rollbacks has been one sex
only: one-third of the Reagan budget cuts, for example, came out of
programs that predominantly serve women—even more extraordinary when one considers that all these programs combined represent
only 10 percent of the federal budget.

The alarms aren't just going off in the work force. In national    27
politics, the already small numbers of women in both elective posts and

political appointments fell during the '80s. In private life, the average amount that a divorced man paid in child support fell by about 25 percent from the late '70s to the mid-'80s (to a mere $140 a month). Domestic-violence shelters recorded a more than 100 percent increase in the numbers of women taking refuge in their quarters between 1983 and 1987. And government records chronicled a spectacular rise in sexual violence against women. Reported rapes more than doubled from the early '70s—at nearly twice the rate of all other violent crimes and four times the overall crime rate in the United States. While the homicide rate declined, sex-related murders rose 160 percent between 1976 and 1984. And these murders weren't simply the random, impersonal by-product of a violent society; at least one-third of the women were killed by their husbands or boyfriends, and the majority of that group were murdered just after declaring their independence in the most intimate manner—by filing for divorce and leaving home.

28     By the end of the decade, women were starting to tell pollsters that they feared their sex's social status was once again beginning to slip. They believed they were facing an "erosion of respect," as the 1990 Virginia Slims poll summed up the sentiment. After years in which an increasing percentage of women had said their status had improved from a decade earlier, the proportion suddenly shrunk by 5 percent in the last half of the '80s, the Roper Organization reported. And it fell most sharply among women in their thirties—the age group most targeted by the media and advertisers—dropping about ten percentage points between 1985 and 1990.

29     Some women began to piece the picture together. In the 1989 *New York Times* poll, more than half of black women and one-fourth of white women put it into words. They told pollsters they believed men were now trying to retract the gains women had made in the last twenty years. "I wanted more autonomy," was how one woman, a thirty-seven-year-old nurse, put it. And her estranged husband "wanted to take it away."

30     The truth is that the last decade has seen a powerful counterassault on women's rights, a backlash, an attempt to retract the handful of small and hard-won victories that the feminist movement did manage to win for women. This counterassault is largely insidious: in a kind of pop-culture version of the Big Lie, it stands the truth boldly on its head and proclaims that the very steps that have elevated women's position have actually led to their downfall.

. . .

31     To blame feminism for women's "lesser life" is to miss entirely the point of feminism, which is to win women a wider range of experience. Feminism remains a pretty simple concept, despite repeated—and enormously effective—efforts to dress it up in greasepaint and turn its

proponents into gargoyles. As Rebecca West wrote sardonically in 1913, "I myself have never been able to find out precisely what feminism is: I only know that people call me a feminist whenever I express sentiments that differentiate me from a doormat."

The meaning of the word "feminist" has not really changed since it 32 first appeared in a book review in the *Athenaeum* of April 27, 1895, describing a woman who "has in her the capacity of fighting her way back to independence." It is the basic proposition that, as Nora put it in Ibsen's *A Doll's House* a century ago, "Before everything else I'm a human being." It is the simply worded sign hoisted by a little girl in the 1970 Women's Strike for Equality: I AM NOT A BARBIE DOLL. Feminism asks the world to recognize at long last that women aren't decorative ornaments, worthy vessels, members of a "special-interest group." They are half (in fact, now more than half) of the national population, and just as deserving of rights and opportunities, just as capable of participating in the world's events, as the other half. Feminism's agenda is basic: It asks that women not be forced to "choose" between public justice and private happiness. It asks that women be free to define themselves— instead of having their identity defined for them, time and again, by their culture and their men.

The fact that these are still such incendiary notions should tell us 33 that American women have a way to go before they enter the promised land of equality.

## Review Questions

1. According to "prevailing wisdom," why are women today unhappy?
2. According to Faludi, why are women unhappy?
3. What groups have targeted the women's movement with criticism?
4. In what ways are women not equal with men, according to Faludi?
5. What is "the backlash"?

## Writing and Discussion Suggestions

1. If you read the opening to *The Feminine Mystique*, you know that Betty Friedan addresses a "problem that has no name." Similarly, Faludi begins her book with an essay about a problem among women. Think about the two essays in light of each other; compare the problems being addressed by the two authors and answer these questions: Do both sets of problems seem equally compelling to you? Has Faludi convinced you that a latter-day problem exists?
2. Faludi's central argument is that the continued inequality of women, *not* the supposed equality won in the last three decades, is responsible for many problems among women today. How do you respond to this claim?

3. Have you observed a backlash against feminism—in your family, your place of employment, your school?

4. Reread Faludi's definition of feminism in paragraphs 31 and 32. Look particularly at what Faludi terms feminism's "basic" agenda: "that women not be forced to 'choose' between public justice and private happiness." What is your response to feminism, as Faludi defines it? Given her definitions, would you call yourself a feminist? Explain.

# The Smurfette Principle

## KATHA POLLITT

*Children learn sex-appropriate behavior well before entering school. For instance, a child learns about the division of labor in the home. Perhaps Daddy, not Mommy, leaves the house for work each morning; or if both parents leave, perhaps one and not the other habitually prepares meals and washes clothes. Children learn about sex roles from other sources, too: notably movies, television, and books. In the essay that follows, Katha Pollitt gives a playful name (borrowed from a children's television show) to a troubling fixture of America's "preschool culture." Pollitt is a poet and essayist. This selection first appeared in the "Hers" column in the* New York Times Magazine *in 1991.*

This Christmas, I finally caved in: I gave my 3-year-old daughter,   1
Sophie, her very own cassette of "The Little Mermaid." Now, she, too, can sit transfixed by Ariel, the perky teen-ager with the curvy tail who trades her voice for a pair of shapely legs and a shot at marriage to a prince. ("On land it's much preferred for ladies not to say a word," sings the cynical sea witch, "and she who holds her tongue will get her man." Since she's the villain, we're not meant to notice that events prove her correct.)

    Usually when parents give a child some item they find repellent,   2
they plead helplessness before a juvenile filibuster. But "The Little Mermaid" was my idea. Ariel may look a lot like Barbie, and her adventure may be limited to romance and over with the wedding bells, but unlike, say, Cinderella or Sleeping Beauty, she's active, brave and determined, the heroine of her own life. She even rescues the prince. And that makes her a rare fish, indeed, in the world of preschool culture.

Take a look at the kids' section of your local video store. You'll find     3
that features starring boys, and usually aimed at them, account for 9 out
of 10 offerings. Clicking the television dial one recent week—admit-
tedly not an encyclopedic study—I came across not a single network
cartoon or puppet show starring a female. (Nickelodeon, the children's
cable channel, has one of each.) Except for the crudity of the animation
and the general air of witlessness and hype, I might as well have been
back in my own 1950's childhood, nibbling Frosted Flakes in front of
Daffy Duck, Bugs Bunny, Porky Pig and the rest of the all-male Warner
Brothers lineup.

Contemporary shows are either essentially all-male, like "Garfield,"     4
or are organized on what I call the Smurfette principle: a group of male
buddies will be accented by a lone female, stereotypically defined. In the
worst cartoons—the ones that blend seamlessly into the animated
cereal commercials—the female is usually a little-sister type, a bunny in
a pink dress and hair ribbons who tags along with the adventurous bears
and badgers. But the Smurfette principle rules the more carefully made
shows, too. Thus, Kanga, the only female in "Winnie-the-Pooh," is a
mother. Piggy, of "Muppet Babies," is a pint-size version of Miss Piggy,
the camp glamour queen of the Muppet movies. April, of the wildly
popular "Teen-Age Mutant Ninja Turtles," functions as a girl Friday to
a quartet of male superheroes. The message is clear. Boys are the norm,
girls the variation; boys are central, girls peripheral; boys are individuals,
girls types. Boys define the group, its story and its code of values. Girls
exist only in relation to boys.

Well, commercial television—what did I expect? The surprise is that     5
public television, for all its superior intelligence, charm and commitment
to worthy values, shortchanges preschool girls, too. Mister Rogers lives
in a neighborhood populated mostly by middle-aged men like himself.
"Shining Time Station" features a cartoon in which the male characters are
train engines and the female characters are passenger cars. And then
there's "Sesame Street." True, the human characters are neatly divided
between the genders (and among the races, too, which is another rarity).
The film clips, moreover, are just about the only place on television in
which you regularly see girls having fun together: practicing double
Dutch, having a sleep-over. But the Muppets are the real stars of "Sesame
Street," and the important ones—the ones with real personalities, who
sing on the musical videos, whom kids identify with and cherish in dozens
of licensed products—are *all* male. I know one little girl who was so
outraged and heartbroken when she realized that even Big Bird—her last
hope—was a boy that she hasn't watched the show since.

Well, there's always the library. Some of the best children's books     6
ever written have been about girls—Madeline, Frances the badger. It's
even possible to find stories with funny, feminist messages, like "The

Paperbag Princess." (She rescues the prince from a dragon, but he's so ungrateful that she decides not to marry him, after all.) But books about girls are a subset in a field that includes a much larger subset of books about boys (12 of the 14 storybooks singled out for praise in last year's Christmas roundup in *Newsweek*, for instance) and books in which the sex of the child is theoretically unimportant—in which case it usually "happens to be" male. Dr. Seuss's books are less about individual characters than about language and imaginative freedom—but, somehow or other, only boys get to go on beyond Zebra or see marvels on Mulberry Street. Frog and Toad, Lowly Worm, Lyle the Crocodile, all *could* have been female. But they're not.

Do kids pick up on the sexism in children's culture? You bet.    7
Preschoolers are like medieval philosophers: the text—a book, a movie, a TV show—is more authoritative than the evidence of their own eyes. "Let's play weddings," says my little niece. We grownups roll our eyes, but face it: it's still the one scenario in which the girl is the central figure. "Women are *nurses*," my friend Anna, a doctor, was informed by her then 4-year-old, Molly. Even my Sophie is beginning to notice the back-seat role played by girls in some of her favorite books. "Who's that?" she asks every time we reread "The Cat in the Hat." It's Sally, the timid little sister of the resourceful boy narrator. She wants Sally to matter, I think, and since Sally is really just a name and a hair ribbon, we have to say her name again and again.

The sexism in preschool culture deforms both boys and girls. Little    8
girls learn to split their consciousness, filtering their dreams and ambitions through boy characters while admiring the clothes of the princess. The more privileged and daring can dream of becoming exceptional women in a man's world—Smurfettes. The others are being taught to accept the more usual fate, which is to be a passenger car drawn through life by a masculine train engine. Boys, who are rarely confronted with stories in which males play only minor roles, learn a simpler lesson: girls just don't matter much.

How can it be that 25 years of feminist social change have made so    9
little impression on preschool culture? Molly, now 6 and well aware that women can be doctors, has one theory: children's entertainment is mostly made by men. That's true, as it happens, and I'm sure it explains a lot. It's also true that, as a society, we don't seem to care much what goes on with kids, as long as they are reasonably quiet. Marshmallow cereal, junky toys, endless hours in front of the tube—a society that accepts all that is not going to get in a lather about a little gender stereotyping. It's easier to focus on the bright side. I had "Cinderella," Sophie has "The Little Mermaid"—that's progress, isn't it?

"We're working on it," Dulcy Singer, the executive producer of    10
"Sesame Street," told me when I raised the sensitive question of those

all-male Muppets. After all, the show has only been on the air for a quarter of a century; these things take time. The trouble is, our preschoolers don't have time. My funny, clever, bold, adventurous daughter is forming her gender ideas right now. I do what I can to counteract the messages she gets from her entertainment, and so does her father—Sophie watches very little television. But I can see we have our work cut out for us. It sure would help if the bunnies took off their hair ribbons, and if half of the monsters were fuzzy, blue—and female.

## Review Questions

1. What is the Smurfette principle?
2. What are the gender messages communicated in children's television?
3. To what extent do children's programs on public television exhibit the same gender problems as shows on the commercial channels?
4. To what extent do children's books exhibit these problems?
5. What is the result of gender stereotyping in the culture of children?

## Discussion and Writing Suggestions

1. In watching contemporary cartoons, Pollitt says that she "might as well have been back in [her] own 1950's childhood." She had expected the content of preschool culture to reflect the changes of the last twenty-five years—but it has not. She is surprised. Are you?
2. Pollitt believes that sexism "deforms" young girls and boys. To what extent do you agree? Write a brief essay in which you develop your response.
3. Pollitt places the sexism of preschool culture in a larger context of indifference. As long as children remain well behaved, this logic goes, it doesn't much matter what children eat, watch, or play with. Do you agree that such logic underlies American pre-school culture?

# Media Myths and the Reality of Men's Work

## IAN HARRIS

*Ian Harris discusses the ways in which traditional views of male gender identity continue to dominate the media. Specifically, he challenges the myth of male success so prevalent in advertisements: of the wealthy white-collar male whose expendable income allows him to live luxuriously. Most men, working jobs that barely, if at all, resemble the ones presented in the media,*

Excerpt from "Media Myths and the Reality of Men's Work" by Ian Harris from *Media&Values*, Number 48, 1989, pp. 12–13. Copyright © 1989 by the Center for Media and Values. Reprinted by permission.

*earn far too little to enjoy the benefits supposedly due every successful male. The media's portrayal of white-collar success damages fixed-wage American men by creating expectations that can never be satisfied.*

*Ian Harris teaches at the University of Wisconsin, Milwaukee, where he chairs the department of Educational Policy and Community Studies. "Media Myths and the Reality of Men's Work" first appeared in* Media & Values *(Fall 1989).*

The dominant image of the American male portrayed on television, in 1 film and in magazines depicts a white-collar gentleman living in the suburbs in affluent circumstances. These individuals own American Express credit cards and buy the latest model cars. From Ozzie and Harriet to Bill Cosby, these images occupy a powerful place in the American psyche and set standards for male behavior. They run the media and the large corporations. They speak to us through radios and television. They teach our children. They are not only standard bearers but also the image makers who provide a model for male expectations.

While entertainment programs often create the stereotype of the 2 violent adventurer, advertising campaigns used to promote American products create the deceptive view that the majority of men enjoy the privileges of white-collar professional status. But these images are a myth. In reality, . . . few achieve the success portrayed by media images.

Of those men fortunate enough to be employed at all, most work 3 in jobs where they cannot live out the media's version of "the American dream." According to 1981 U.S. government statistics, individuals who fit the category "Males in Professional White Collar Occupations" account for only 15 percent of all employed men, or eight percent of the total male population. Yet certainly they are not the only men satisfied with their professional lives. The non-professional technical occupations, representing an additional 27 percent of employed men, include engineers, skilled craftsmen and other technicians who experience relatively high status and success. Some males in blue-collar jobs and service and farm occupations also earn good salaries and, by their own accounts, feel successful in their work and in their lives. Yet men in all classes are affected by white-collar professional images broadcast through the media and rarely supplemented by images of men in other job categories and occupations. The restriction of work images to wealthy white-collar professionals has severe consequences. Raised in a society that honors the Horatio Alger myth, most men believe that a man who works hard will get ahead. Male sex role standards describe a life where American men are supposed to be good fathers, contribute to their communities and occupy positions of power and wealth. The reality of most men's lives, however, is very different from those media-promoted financial and professional success images.

## MOST MEN'S LIVES

With 71 percent of U.S. men making less than $25,000 annually in 1984,   4
relatively few male workers and their families can approach the standards of consumerism portrayed by television and advertising. The
media myth that most men enjoy or have access to the material benefits
of the successful white-collar professional is a hoax. Most men will never
get status jobs. The vast majority of men either work in occupations
other than white collar, are institutionalized, unemployed or have
dropped out of the active work force. However, their stories are not told
in the media and their plight is ignored.

The 45 percent of working men in blue-collar jobs "man" the   5
factories and other skilled or unskilled trades. Although often taking
great pride in their work, many of them labor in positions that offer little
or no opportunities for advancement and that may be dull, repetitive
and dangerous. Their lives are marked by economic stress, they usually
have little or no control over their working conditions and are increasingly threatened by company shifts to cheaper overseas labor and other
contractions of the global work force.

Although always the unsung heroes of the U.S. economy, their   6
current media invisibility is something of a change. From 1950 to 1978,
this group of men enjoyed some economic security, and media images
of the happy, beer-drinking blue-collar worker abounded in the broad
range of ads and commercials and such TV programs as *The Life of
Riley*.

Although these men are excluded from the mediated version of the   7
American dream, it is incorrect to assume that men who do achieve
some measure of white-collar success necessarily lead more fulfilling
lives. The majority of white-collar men spend their lives battling within
highly competitive organizations that are so stressful that working
within them predisposes them to cancer, heart attack and other stress-
related diseases.

Displaced from the labor statistics as they are from society, under-   8
class men lead desperate lives. Seventy percent of these hard-pressed
males belong to minority groups. As the migrant workers, prisoners,
welfare recipients, homeless street people and patients in mental hospitals, the underclass appears in entertainment programming mainly as
criminals. They are seen as a threat to society, but the portraits drawn
of them seldom probe the violent worlds that shaped them and their
constant fights—often unsuccessful—to survive.

Underclass men do not have regular work. Their hustles for survival   9
include part-time work at low wages, robbery, pimping, drug pushing
and other illegal activities. Many end up in prison when they break the
law to earn their livelihoods. In fact, prison becomes a sort of brutal
haven to escape the viciousness of the street. For the thousands of men

of this class, life has no future, few possessions and little purpose. Many are filled with anger at a system that denies them access to the cultural norms of success.

Whether employed or unemployed, whether blue or white collar, **10** men in the United States share a common alienation regarding the conditions of their employment. This alienation is rooted in the realization that a man's work (or lack of work) is at odds with his personal goals.

Unfortunately, male socialization does not help men cope with the **11** realities of the modern workplace. Indeed, male training is designed to create good workers, not full human beings. To cope with deep-felt insecurities, men learn to put up a facade that they are competent and in charge of their destiny. The intense competitiveness of the workplace causes men to be distrustful of their peers, preventing real communication and empathy with others.

These problems in men's lives have become issues for the men's **12** movement. They are also media issues to the degree that the movement seeks to shatter media myths that set sex-role expectations. The mostly white, middle-class leaders of the movement are shaped by the media they see and hear. They are largely ignorant of the problems of most men in the United States, in part because the media seldom, if ever, realistically present underclass and working-class existence.

The media and society as a whole need to bury the popular myth **13** that male success consists of making money. Instead of glorifying male violence, they should portray the pain that causes it. Let's create a new American myth where men are concerned human beings promoting a better life for all creatures on this planet. Liberation is a long and difficult struggle that requires the economic transformation of society as well as the alteration of personal relationships. The media has played its role in creating the problem. It must also be a part of the solution.

## Review Questions

1. What is the dominant image of the American male, as portrayed by television advertisers, and why is this image a myth?
2. According to Harris, under what conditions do most American men work?
3. What are the "rewards" of white-collar life in the actual working world?
4. Who are men of the "underclass," and how do televised images of success exclude them?
5. How have images of men in television advertisements affected the men's movement?
6. Why should the media help to shape a new definition of men?

## Discussion and Writing Suggestions

1. Watch an hour of prime-time television and note the portrayal of men in the advertisements. Based on your notes, write a one-paragraph profile of the American male as he is depicted in these ads.

2. If you are male, think of, and in one paragraph describe, a television advertisement that helped you to define, however slightly, masculinity. If you are female, identify an advertisement that has helped you to define what is attractive in a male. How have your experiences compared with these impressions gained from advertisements?

3. Recast the preceding question to focus on women in advertisements. If you are female, describe an advertisement that helped you to define femininity. If you are male, describe an advertisement that helped you to define what is attractive in a female.

4. Reread paragraph 10, in which Harris claims that the majority of men, regardless of employment profile, are alienated by their work. Do you agree? Harris claims that this alienation is rooted in a split between "a man's work" and his "personal goals." What might these goals be? Do they differ, necessarily, from a woman's personal goals?

5. In paragraph 13, Harris calls for the creation of a "new American myth," as far as men are concerned, and says that the media should help to promote this myth. In a one-page letter in which you assume the identity of an advertising executive, respond to this suggestion.

# A Gender Analysis of TV Commercials

## R. STEPHEN CRAIG

*Portrayals of masculine and feminine behavior on television have been the subject of sociological research for forty years. A 1954 study of television drama showed that women did not appear on-screen as often as men (32 percent vs. 68 percent) and that when women did appear, they did so in such conventional roles as homemaker. In 1972 the National Organization for Women (NOW) conducted a "content analysis" of television commercials to study the ways that women were being portrayed. The analysis required the videotaping and study of 1,241 commercials. Judges counted and recorded (they "coded," in sociological parlance) the number of times woman were depicted in various occupations, and they concluded that advertisers were*

"The Effect of Television" by R. Stephen Craig from *Sex Roles: A Journal of Research 26*, pp. 197–211. Copyright © 1992 by Plenum Publishing Company. Reprinted by permission of Plenum Publishing Company.

*presenting women primarily as homemakers and as sexual objects. Five years later, a landmark study undertaken by the U.S. Commission on Civil Rights reached much the same conclusion. Between 1977 and the present, repeated content analyses of television programming and commercials have shown a remarkable consistency of stereotyped role portrayals.*

*Content analysis continues to be a favored method of inquiry among sociologists interested in studying gender. The present study, conducted by R. Stephen Craig at the University of Maine, uses this method to determine whether advertisers plan the gender content of commercials according to the time of day in which the commercials are aired. Originally titled "The Effect of Television Day Part on Gender Portrayal in Television Commercials: A Content Analysis," this article is representative of much sociological research. The author begins with a review of the literature on content analysis, notes where prior studies are incomplete, and offers a rationale for his own study. He then organizes the remainder of his presentation into standard social science format:* method, results, *and* discussion.

*Remember as you read that Craig is writing for fellow sociologists (the article was published originally in the journal* Sex Roles*), and this article is typical of those that appear in professional journals. He relies heavily on the passive voice and, in his* results *section, refers to various statistical tests (chi-squares, probabilities, alpha means) that will likely perplex you. Don't be overwhelmed. Read the article to understand the writer's research questions, his general method, and his conclusions. That is, read the article in this order:* introduction *(which is not labeled as such),* method, *and* discussion. *These nontechnical parts of the presentation will give you a feel for the questions about gender that Craig is investigating and about his strategies for conducting this investigation. Once you are sure of this much, turn to the article's* results *section and give yourself permission (as a nonspecialist) not to understand the statistics. Concentrate, instead, on the ways in which Craig supports his conclusions and on how this support differs, say, from the ways in which Ian Harris or Katha Pollitt support their arguments. (If you wanted to challenge Craig's position, you would need to study statistics and methods of sociological research, which you would do as a sociology major.) For the moment, focus on the ways in which questions that other authors in this chapter have investigated are treated in a distinctive way by a sociologist.*

[ABSTRACT:] Gender portrayals in 2,209 network television commercials were content analyzed. To compare differences between three day parts, the sample was chosen from three time periods: daytime, when the audience is mostly women; evening prime time, when the sex of the audience is more evenly distributed; and weekend afternoon sportscasts, when men are a large percentage of the audience. The results indicate large and consistent differences in the way men and women are portrayed in these three day parts, with almost all comparisons reaching significance at the .05 level. Although ads in all day parts tended to portray men in stereotypical roles of authority and dominance, those on weekends tended to emphasize escape from home and family. The findings of earlier studies which did not consider day part differences may now have to be reevaluated.

Since 1972, at least 18 gender-oriented content analyses of U.S. television commercials and another seven using non-U.S. advertising have been reported in academic sources. Growing from the concerns of the women's movement about negative stereotyping in advertising, these studies have consistently supported the contention that TV ads generally portray women in the traditional stereotypical roles of subservience allocated them by a patriarchal society.   2

Many of these studies have been summarized by Bretl & Cantor (1988). Additional research, such as Courtney & Whipple (1983), Gunter (1986), Kear (1985), Macklin & Kolbe (1984), Seggar, Hafen, & Hannonen-Gladden (1981), Skelly & Lundstrom (1981), and Steeves (1987) has examined gender portrayals in other media texts.   3

Understandably, almost all of this earlier research has focused on images of women. Portrayals of men, when they have been studied at all, have often been seen as unproblematic and even as the laudatory standard by which female portrayals could be measured. With the exception of a single study by Meyers (1980), no major content analysis has been conducted primarily to investigate stereotyped presentations of men in television commercials.   4

Furthermore, past research has all but ignored the heavy reliance advertisers place on audience demographics in their design and placement of commercials. Instead, previous studies have tended to treat gender portrayals in television advertising as fixed and homogeneous. Consequently, previous researchers have generally selected commercial samples from only one or two day parts in which women are the primary audience, or have mixed their sample from several day parts with little or no distinction made between them. The result has been a failure to adequately consider whether and how gender portrayals in ads aimed at men differ from those in ads aimed at women.   5

Scheibe & Condry (1984, p. 32) did examine commercials by program type, including a limited comparison of those shown during soap operas with those shown during sports programs. Their research found major gender differences in the values promoted in commercials. For example, ads aimed at women stressed beauty and youth while those aimed at men valorized ambition and physical strength (pp. 42–43).   6

While content analysis is limited in the information it can provide about television gender representations, it can and should provide the essential starting point for further critical analysis. Fiske & Hartley (1978, p. 21) point out that content analysis, although not concerned with questions of quality, response, or interpretation, does serve the   7 important function of establishing exactly "what is there" to be studied. By ignoring the importance of demographic targeting and day part placement of ads, previous research has given an incomplete picture of "what is there."

This content analysis comparing 2,209 TV commercials attempts **8** to remedy the shortcomings of earlier work. By so doing, it will provide a foundation for further critical analysis of gender and television commercials. First, it considers the traditional stereotypes of both women and men seen in television advertising to be problematic, and attempts to fill in the gaps of past research by focusing on images of men as well as women. Second, it recognizes that television commercials are not homogeneous nor randomly scattered throughout the broadcast day, but vary greatly in form and content with the age, sex, and social situation of the audience the advertiser intends to reach. For this reason, it uses the advertising industry's concept of "day part" as the major independent variable,[1] and concentrates on differences between ads seen during the daytime, when women make up most of the audience, and those seen on weekends, when men viewers predominate.

## METHOD[2]

Three videotape recorders were used to simultaneously record selected **9** hours of programming on the local affiliates of the three major networks during the period January 6–14, 1990. To examine gender differences in commercials aired at different times, three day parts[3] were separately sampled. The daytime day part (in this sample, Monday–Friday, 2–4 P.M.) consisted exclusively of soap operas and was chosen for its high percentage of women viewers. The weekend day part (two consecutive Saturday and Sunday afternoons during sports telecasts) was selected

---

[1]A social scientist designs an experiment to see what factors affect human behavior. In this design, the researcher works with variables. An *independent* variable is the part of the experiment that the researcher manipulates to see its effect on behavior. In Craig's experiment, the major independent variable is "day part" and all the commercials will be assigned a level of this variable: daytime, weekend, or evening. [Behrens and Rosen]

[2]A more detailed explanation of the method and results of this study can be found in Craig (1991). [Craig]

[3]The term "day part" is commonly used in the industry to describe a period of the day (such as the "prime time" day part) when advertisers consider the audience to be relatively stable demographically. Television audience research services such as Nielsen and Arbitron typically report ratings estimates for a large number of day parts. The term is used in this study to underscore the importance of demographic targeting in the advertising industry. In order to facilitate sampling, the hours represented by the "day parts" used in this study do not precisely correspond with those reported by the ratings services. [Craig]

for its high percentage of men viewers. Evening "prime time" (Monday–Friday, 9–11 P.M.) was chosen as a basis for comparison with past studies and the other day parts. All programming and commercials on all three network affiliates were recorded simultaneously, resulting in a total of 30 hours of daytime (e.g. 2 hours per day × 3 stations × 5 days), 30 hours of prime time, and 39.5 hours of weekend television.

Each tape was reviewed and each cluster of commercials (i.e. each    10
group of ads between two program segments) was cataloged and given a serial number. Clusters containing only promotional announcements, public service announcements, and/or advertisements clearly originating at the local station were disregarded. A total of 664 commercial clusters were thus obtained, with each cluster containing one to seven different ads for a total of 2,209 separate commercials. The day part in which each ad had originally aired was noted for later analysis; then the 664 commercial clusters were edited onto new video tapes in random order to reduce the possibility of coder bias. All program material, public service announcements, billboards, promotional announcements, and advertisements clearly originating at the local station were deleted. This procedure yielded a series of video tapes containing only the network commercials, randomized by cluster, with all clues removed as to their original program context and time of broadcast. Coders were also kept uninformed of the study's focus on day part differences.

All network commercials recorded during the sample period were    11
included in the initial database, regardless of the number of times they appeared or the ages of the characters. Animated characters were also included and were coded based on the gender and age they appeared to represent. Repeats were coded since the aim of the study is to examine exposure to stereotypes rather than to specific commercials. Each commercial appearance must therefore be considered a separate exposure (Verna, 1975, p. 303).

## Categories

Coding categories were based on those which had proven effective in    12
other recent content analyses, especially those of Bretl & Cantor (1988) and Harris & Stobart (1986). Modifications and additions to these earlier categories were made as considered appropriate to reflect the hypotheses of the present study.

**Characters**    To get an overall view of the treatment of gender, each    13
commercial was classified as to the apparent age and gender of all characters who appeared. The categories were "all male adult"; "all female adult"; "all adults, mixed gender"; "male adults with children or teens (no

women)"; "female adults with children or teens (no men)"; and "mixture of ages and genders." For this and all other codings, children and teens were defined as characters who appear to be under 18 years old.

**Primary Visual Character**     Bretl & Cantor (1988) defined "primary    14
character" as "the character with the greatest amount of on-screen time" (p. 599). However, pretesting indicated a substantial number of commercials with only brief glimpses of many characters. Following the strategy of Dominick & Rauch (1972), a time-limit was imposed, so that for this study, the definition used was "the one visual character who appears on the screen longest, but for no less than five seconds." Coders were instructed to indicate whether the primary visual character was an adult male, an adult female, a child or a teen, or whether no character meeting the established criteria appeared.

**Role**     Harris & Stobart's (1986) categories were adopted with slight    15
rewording (e.g. "spouse" became "spouse/partner") and the addition of the category "child/teen." The other categories were "celebrity," "homemaker," "interviewer/demonstrator," "parent/child care," "professional," "sex object/model," "spouse/partner," "worker," and "other."

**Product**     Several studies (e.g. Dominick & Rauch, 1972; Culley &    16
Bennett, 1976; Marecek et al., 1978; Scheibe & Condry, 1984; Bretl & Cantor, 1988) have examined differences in the sex of characters associated with various products. Harris and Stobart (1986) used the following categories: "services," "body," "home," "food," and "auto." Because of the special interest in male-oriented weekend ads, the present study added the categories "business products" and "alcohol."

**Setting**     The setting categories used by Bretl and Cantor (1988) were    17
adopted, except that instead of using their "unknown" category the present study used "other/unclear." The other categories were "kitchen," "bathroom," "other room of home," "outdoors at home," "outdoors away from home," "restaurant/bar," "business," and "school."

**Primary Narrator**     Bretl & Cantor (1988, p. 605) list ten previous    18
studies which investigated the sex of off-screen announcers or "narrators." The present study defined the primary narrator as "the voice, not attributable to any on-screen character, which is heard for the longest time." Voices which only sang were not considered narrators.

**Statistical Analysis**     One subsample of 30 commercials was selected    19
for a reliability check and coded by all three coders. Inter-coder reliability was calculated using Krippendorff's alpha statistic (1980, Chapter 12)

for three coders, with the results ranging from a low of .62 for "Primary Character Role" to a high of 1.00 for "Product Category." The mean alpha for the six reported codings was .82.[4]

Statistical analysis was completed using the "Tables" subprogram of the MS-DOS version of the computer program SYSTAT, and the Pearson chi-square calculation was used to test for significant differences. For analyses of three-way interactions, loglinear modeling was conducted as suggested by Fienberg (1980) using the Tables "Model" command and the Pearson chi-square of the model is reported (Wilkinson, 1989, Chapter 28).[5]   20

Initially, all 2,209 commercials were coded and analyzed. However, Bretl and Cantor (1988) compared results from earlier studies, and most of these findings were based on commercials in which only adult primary characters appear. To better allow comparisons to these studies, the sample was modified by dropping all commercials that were coded as having no adult primary visual character (i.e. those coded as "child or teen" or "none or unclear"), yielding a new sample of 1,431 commercials which had either adult male or adult female primary visual characters.   21

## RESULTS

### Analysis of Age and Gender of All Characters

To get an overall view of the treatment of gender, each commercial was categorized as to the mixture of age and gender of all characters, regardless of their importance to the ad or their time on the screen. The results are shown in Table I.   22

Significant differences in the age and gender of characters among the day parts were found. Although approximately equal percentages of ads during the evening hours portrayed either all adult male (18%) or all adult female characters (19%), commercials with all adult male characters   23

---

[4]Researchers must tell the reader how likely it is that any commercial assigned to a category by one group would be similarly assigned by another group. Craig therefore conducted a reliability check. He took 30 of the commercials to be studied, analyzed (by means of a technique called "Krippendorff's alpha statistic") how the commercials were coded, and found that his coders were 100% successful in agreeing on the product category. Coders were less successful, though, in agreeing on the primary character's role, agreeing approximately 62% of the time. [Behrens and Rosen]

[5]Here Craig is telling us how he examined the commercials—with the Pearson chi-square technique, which reveals that there is a different number of types of commercials in certain parts of the day than would be expected to occur by chance. Craig uses the "loglinear modeling technique" to examine the interactions of day part and the various categories used to code commercials. [Behrens and Rosen]

**TABLE I.** *Percentages of Commercials with Characters of Various Sex and Age Categories in Three Day Parts[a]*

| | | PERCENT | | |
| CATEGORY | N | DAYTIME (N = 888) | EVENING (N = 445) | WEEKEND (N = 623) |
| --- | --- | --- | --- | --- |
| All male adult | 406 | 14 | 18 | 33 |
| All female adults | 291 | 20 | 19 | 5 |
| All adults, mixed gender | 651 | 32 | 32 | 37 |
| All children or teens | 69 | 6 | 2 | 1 |
| Male adults w/children/teens (no adult women) | 54 | 2 | 2 | 4 |
| Female adults w/children/teens (no adult men) | 144 | 11 | 8 | 3 |
| Mixture of ages and genders | 341 | 16 | 20 | 18 |

[a] All numbers except N represent column percentages. $\chi^2$ (12, N = 1956) = 196.1, p < .001. Figures do not include commercials without any visual characters.[6]

were more than twice as likely to be found during weekend (33%) as daytime (14%) telecasts. Conversely, commercials with only adult female characters made up only five percent of the weekend sample, but 20% of that during the daytime hours. Commercials showing only adult men with children were relatively rare in all three day parts; however, those featuring only adult women with children made up 11% of the daytime and 8% of the evening sample. Commercials with only children or teen characters made up 6% of the daytime but only 1% of the weekend ads.

## Sex and Age of the Primary Visual Character

A more detailed analysis was made of the primary visual character in each commercial. Coders were instructed to indicate whether the primary visual character was an adult male, an adult female, a child or a teen, or if no character meeting the established criteria appeared.    24

---

[6] Researchers are expected to report all relevant values discovered through statistical analysis so that another researcher can review and make his or her own judgment about the work. In this table, Craig is presenting these values. "N" stands for the number of commercials studied. "chi²" is the symbol for the chi-square technique (see note 5), which yielded the value of 196.1. The number 12 represents the "degrees of freedom," a number approximately equal to the number of categories into which the data are placed. The level of significance, or "p," is .001—which means that the probability is less than 1 in 1,000 that the researcher's results occurred by chance. [Behrens and Rosen]

**TABLE II.** *Percentages of Adult Primary Visual Characters by Sex Appearing in Commercials in Three Day Parts*[a]

| | | PERCENT | | |
| | | DAYTIME | EVENING | WEEKEND |
| CATEGORY | N | (N = 668) | (N = 300) | (N = 463) |
| --- | --- | --- | --- | --- |
| Adult male | 792 | 40 | 52 | 80 |
| Adult female | 639 | 60 | 48 | 20 |

[a]All numbers except N represent column percentages. $\chi^2$ (2, N = 1431) = 185.1, p < .001.

Twenty-seven percent of the overall sample had no identifiable primary visual character category, but an absence of codable primary visual characters was much more prevalent in weekend (33%) and evening (32%) commercials than in daytime ads (20%). Children or teens were primary visual characters in only a small percentage of the commercials sampled, but were much more likely to be found in daytime (11%) than in evening (7%) or weekend ads (5%).

In examining ads with only adult primary characters, men and women were found to appear in about equal proportions (52% and 48%) in commercials aired during the evening hours, but the findings for the other two day parts are significantly different (see Table II). During the daytime hours, only 40% of the adult primary visual characters were men, but during the weekend period, 80% were.

## The Role Played by the Primary Visual Character

Results also indicate large differences in the roles played by primary visual characters in different day parts (see Table III). Primary characters in weekend commercials were more likely to portray celebrities, professionals and workers than those in daytime commercials, but were much less likely to portray children/teens, home-makers, parents, or spouse/partners. Primary visual characters were about equally likely to portray "sex object/models" in all three day parts.

Further analysis indicated that male primary characters were proportionately more likely than females to be portrayed as celebrities and professionals in every day part, while women were proportionately more likely to be portrayed as interviewer/demonstrators, parent/spouses, or sex object/models in every day part. In the daytime and evening, women were proportionately more likely to be portrayed as homemakers and proportionately less likely to be portrayed as workers; during the weekend, men and women primary characters were portrayed in about equal proportions in these two categories. However,

597

**TABLE III.** *Percentage of Commercials with Primary Visual Characters in Various Role Categories During Three Day Parts[a]*

| CATEGORY | N | PERCENT | | |
| | | DAYTIME (N = 971) | EVENING (N = 498) | WEEKEND (N = 740) |
|---|---|---|---|---|
| Celebrity | 241 | 8 | 12 | 14 |
| Child/teen | 161 | 10 | 7 | 4 |
| Homemaker | 65 | 5 | 2 | 1 |
| Interviewer/demonstrator | 164 | 10 | 7 | 4 |
| Parent | 125 | 7 | 6 | 4 |
| Professional | 212 | 7 | 10 | 12 |
| Sex object/model | 126 | 6 | 5 | 6 |
| Spouse/partner | 153 | 9 | 7 | 4 |
| Worker | 95 | 3 | 2 | 7 |
| Other role | 266 | 14 | 9 | 11 |
| No primary visual char. | 601 | 20 | 32 | 33 |

[a]All numbers except N represent column percentages. $\chi^2$ (20, N = 2209) = 180.1, p < .001.

women were proportionately more likely to appear as sex object/models during the weekend than during the day. Men were proportionately more likely to be coded as having some "other role" in all three day parts.

Analysis also revealed that in the evening, 12% of the male and 32% of the female primary visual characters were portrayed as spouses or parents. Further, a greater proportion of women primary characters portrayed spouses or parents in the evening (32%) than in daytime (28%) or on weekends (21%). Male primary characters were much more likely to portray spouses or parents during the day (17%) than during the evening (12%) or on the weekend (9%).

## Analysis of Products Advertised

The analysis also revealed major differences in the products advertised in different day parts. While virtually all the daytime ads fell into either the "body," "food," or "home" categories, only 30% of the weekend ads did so. On weekends, 29% of the ads were for "automotive," and 27% were for "business products" or "services" (the category "business products" was used in only nine cases and so was combined with "services"). In the daytime period, 44% of the ads fell into the "body" category, while only 15% of the weekend ads did so. Almost no ads for "alcohol" were found in the daytime or evening sample, but 10% of those in the weekend sample fell into that category.

Further analysis revealed that portrayals by the adult primary characters varied widely with the sex of the character, the day part, and the product category. Forty-four percent of daytime male primary characters appeared in food commercials, compared to only 20% of the daytime female characters. However, on weekends, men and women primary characters appeared in food ads with about proportionately equal likelihood. Men were most likely to be primary characters in food or body commercials during daytime and prime time, but equally likely to be primary characters in automotive, body, or business product/services ads on weekends. Women were proportionately more likely than men to be portrayed in a body ad in either daytime or prime time but less likely on weekends. On weekends, men were proportionately more likely than women to be the primary character in an alcohol ad, but proportionately less likely than women to be the primary character in an automotive or business product/services commercial.

## Analysis of Primary Setting

Table IV details differences in the commercials' primary location or setting in the three day parts. The results indicate significant differences among the settings of the commercials appearing in the three day parts. Of the categories depicting a specific location, most daytime commercials were set in the kitchen, "other room," or "outdoors away from home." A major percentage of both evening and weekend ads were set "outdoors away from home." 31

Additional analysis broke these settings down by both day part and sex for those commercials with adult primary visual characters. Sex differences related to setting were small in the evening day part, and did 32

**TABLE IV.** *Percentages of Primary Settings of Commercials Aired During Three Day Parts[a]*

| | | PERCENT | | |
| --- | --- | --- | --- | --- |
| CATEGORY | N | DAYTIME (N = 971) | EVENING (N = 498) | WEEKEND (N = 740) |
| Kitchen of home | 175 | 13 | 8 | 1 |
| Bathroom of home | 56 | 4 | 2 | 1 |
| Other room of home | 322 | 20 | 14 | 8 |
| Outdoors at home | 111 | 5 | 4 | 6 |
| Outdoors away from home | 624 | 15 | 31 | 44 |
| Restaurant/bar | 75 | 4 | 2 | 4 |
| Business | 149 | 6 | 8 | 7 |
| School | 21 | 1 | 1 | 1 |
| Other/unclear | 676 | 33 | 30 | 28 |

[a]All numbers except N represent column percentages. $\chi^2$ (16, N = 2209) = 271.0, p < .001.

not reach significance at the .05 level. Daytime differences were significant, however. In that day part, women primary characters were proportionately more likely than men primary characters to appear in ads in all three "indoors at home" categories. Daytime men were proportionately more likely to appear in ads set in the two outdoors categories as well as at business locations. Men and women primary characters appeared with about proportionately equal frequency in a restaurant or bar during the daytime.

Weekend differences also appear to be large, but the chi-square test is suspect due to a low frequency in more than one fifth of the cells.[7] These low frequencies are due to the near absence of any weekend commercials with settings of kitchen, bathroom, or school. However, results from the populous cells are still of interest. In the weekend day part, men were proportionately more likely than women to be portrayed outdoors away from home, but women were proportionately more likely than men (12% vs. 4%) to be the primary visual character in restaurant/bar settings, and both men and women appeared in business locations with proportionately equal frequency.  33

## Analysis of Primary Narrator

Male narrators were found to clearly form a large majority in all day parts; however, significant differences in the proportion of male and female narrators among the day parts were found. While male narrators were heard on virtually all weekend ads with narrators (97%), a somewhat smaller percentage (91%) were found in the evening ads. For the daytime commercials, the percentage dropped even further (to 86%), but the narrators were still overwhelmingly male. Of the overall sample, 332 commercials did not have narrators, but even on this measure, there were day part differences. Twenty percent of all daytime commercials had no narrators, a much larger proportion than either the evening (12%) or weekends (11%).  34

Although the small number of women narrators in the sample makes further detailed analysis tenuous, the data does suggest that when women were heard as narrators it was overwhelmingly for products classified as "body." Sixty percent of the women narrators heard during the daytime and 62% of those heard in the evening were in commercials for "body" products.  35

---

[7]Every statistical technique has a number of rules associated with its use. One of the rules of the chi-square test is that every category must have at least 5 members. If this rule is not followed, the results are distorted, probably in the researcher's favor. Craig is informing his readers that this problem occurred in his analysis. [Behrens and Rosen]

## DISCUSSION

The results of this study support the hypothesis that television commer- **36** cials targeted to one sex tend to portray gender differently than ads targeted to the other sex. Large and consistent differences were found in the way men and women were portrayed in daytime ads aired during soap operas and the way they were portrayed in commercials during weekend sports broadcasts. This means that the strategy of day part targeting goes beyond the relatively simple practice of matching a particular product with a particular broadcast time—detergent ads dur- ing soap operas or beer ads on weekends; it also means matching a particular image of gender with a particular audience.

Advertisers wish to make commercials a pleasurable experience for **37** the intended audience. They construct the ads in ways that reinforce the image of gender most familiar to and comfortable for their target audience. Daytime ads, generally aimed at women homemakers, focus on the traditional stereotypical images associated with the American housewife. Products and settings were found to be those identified with home and family life, and generally involved cooking, cleaning, child care, or maintaining an attractive physical appearance. Men are por- trayed as the primary characters in less than half these commercials, but when they do appear, it is generally in a position of authority and patriarchal dominance, such as celebrity spokesman, husband, or profes- sional. The daytime men are almost always seen in ads for either "food" or "body" rather than other product categories, reinforcing the image that the housewife's primary role is in meeting the needs of the male.

Commercials aimed at the weekend audience are quite different in **38** both content and style. Products and settings were found to be generally associated with life away from the home and family, and the commer- cials frequently exclude women and children altogether. The ads and the sports programming in which they appear stress traditional stereotypes of masculinity such as the importance of physical strength and rugged- ness, independence, aggressiveness, competitiveness, and daring. If fam- ily scenes are portrayed at all, they are only to remind men of their traditional responsibility as breadwinner or protector. The large percent- age of weekend ads for alcoholic beverages (and their near-absence from the other two day parts) typifies the exploitation of male fantasy and escapism prevalent in the weekend day part. Automobile and truck ads also capitalize on these attitudes in such a way that the motor vehicle becomes the promised extension of either male strength, or sexuality, or both.

The women who appeared in weekend ads were almost never **39** portrayed without men and seldom as the commercial's primary charac- ter. They were generally seen in roles subservient to men (e.g. hotel receptionist, secretary, or stewardess), or as sex objects or models in which their only function seemed to be to lend an aspect of eroticism to the ad.

These findings are of special interest when compared with those for **40** the prime time evening day part—the time period which has been the focus of many past studies. The evening audience is much more heterogeneous than that of either daytime or weekend day parts, and one would intuitively expect that advertisers would select this time to air ads for products aimed at a more general audience. While this may have been true in past years, prime time has now become one of the few day parts when today's advertisers can reach what Nielsen calls "working women."[8] With more women working outside the home and thus away from the television set during the traditional woman-oriented daytime hours, prime time has become an increasingly important day part for advertisers seeking to sell those products, such as cosmetics, more heavily used by "working women."

It was not surprising to find, therefore, that gender portrayals during **41** prime time are different from those of either daytime or weekends. During prime time, women were more likely to be portrayed in positions of authority and in settings away from home than they were in daytime. Men, on the other hand, were more likely to be portrayed as a parent or spouse and in settings at home than they were on weekends. In short, prime time commercials represent a more sophisticated and balanced portrayal of gender than either daytime or weekend ads. While this is doubtless a reflection of the more general nature of the audience advertisers are seeking to reach in prime time, it may also be that advertisers believe the "working woman" target audience is less than willing to accept the gender portrayals commonly seen in the other two day parts.

Perhaps the most surprising outcome of the study is the magnitude **42** of the day part differences found. In all but one comparison, differences were significant at the .05 level and in the majority of comparisons, $p$ was less than .001.[9] Large differences suggest that the television day part cannot be ignored as a variable in studying gender portrayals. Unfortunately, most past research has done just that. The results from

---

[8]That is, "women who work outside the home 30 or more hours per week" (Nielsen, 1988, p. A). Evidently the sexism implied by this term is not a concern to the Nielsen company. To avoid confusion in this paper, the term "working women" (in quotation marks) will be used as Nielsen does, to mean women who work away from home. Of course, women who are homemakers and parents work at home whether or not they also work outside the home.

[9]Craig is reporting the level of significance, or "p" level, which defines the likelihood of the experiment's outcome being a product of chance. A level of significance .05 means that there is less than a 5 in 100 chance that Craig's results occurred by chance. A level of .001 means that there is less than a 1 in 1,000 chance that his results occurred by chance. [Behrens and Rosen]

studies such as those by Marecek et al. (1978) and Scheibe (1979), which indiscriminately mixed commercials from various day parts, must now be reevaluated. Likewise, the findings of the many studies which drew their sample only from prime time (e.g. Dominick & Rauch, 1972; Lovdal, 1989; Silverstein & Silverstein, 1974) must now be viewed with these results in mind.

This study was meant to quantify the images of men in network television commercials as a basis for further study. The limits of content analysis are well known, but the results do suggest several areas for further study. More close textual analysis needs to be conducted to examine the way commercials aimed at men work, and a Freudian analysis of beer, automotive, and business ads might be extremely revealing. The application of some of the newer concepts emerging from men's studies scholars could also be usefully applied. For example, Wenner & Gantz (1989) have analyzed the role sports television plays in the lives of men and Duroche (1990) has discussed the relationship between the social construction of masculinity and male perception. Works such as these may help explain how men read television commercials.

Gender images in television commercials provide an especially intriguing field of study. The ads are carefully crafted bundles of images, frequently designed to associate the product with feelings of pleasure stemming from deep-seated fantasies and anxieties. Advertisers seem quite willing to manipulate these fantasies and exploit our anxieties, especially those concerning our gender identities, to sell products. What's more, they seem to have no compunction about capitalizing on dehumanizing gender stereotypes to seek these ends. At the same time, many businesses rely on the consumer's adherence to these stereotypes to sell their products. The entire manufacturing and marketing strategy behind many products such as convenience foods, cosmetics, beer, and cars is tied to the exploitation of gender-specific behaviors. Thus, the reinforcement of traditional gender stereotypes has an important economic motivation for business and this is seen nowhere better than in the portrayals used in television commercials.

## REFERENCES

Bretl, D. J. & Cantor, J. (1988). The portrayal of men and women in U.S. television commercials: A recent content analysis and trends over 15 years. *Sex Roles, 18(9/10),* 595–609.

Courtney, A. & Whipple, T. (1983). *Sex stereotyping in advertising.* Lexington, MA: Lexington Books.

Craig, R. (1991). *A content analysis comparing gender images in network television commercials aired in daytime evening and weekend telecasts.* Orono: University of

Maine, Department of Journalism and Mass Communication. (ERIC Document Reproduction Service No. ED 329 217).

Culley, J. D. & Bennett, R. (1976). Selling women, selling blacks. *Journal of Communication, 26*(4), 160–174.

Dominick, J. & Rauch, G. (1972). The image of women in network TV commercials. *Journal of Broadcasting, 16*(3), 259–265.

Duroche, L. (1990). Male perception as social construct. In J. Hearn & D. Morgan (Eds.), *Men, Masculinities and Social Theory* (pp. 170–185). London: Unwin Hyman.

Fienberg, S. E. (1980). *The analysis of cross-classified categorical data* (2nd ed.). Cambridge, MA: MIT.

Fiske, J. & Hartley, J. (1978). *Reading television.* New York: Methuen.

Gunter, B. (1986). *Television and sex role stereotyping.* London: John Libbey.

Harris, P. & Stobart, J. (1986). Sex-role stereotyping in British television advertisements at different times of the day: An extension and refinement of Manstead and McCulloch (1981). *British Journal of Social Psychology, 25,* 155–164.

Kear, L. (1985, September). *Television and sex roles: A selected annotated bibliography.* Unpublished Manuscript. (ERIC Document Reproduction Service No. ED 262 444).

Krippendorff, K. (1980). *Content analysis: An introduction to its methodology.* Beverly Hills, CA: Sage.

Lovdal, L. T. (1989). Sex role messages in television commercials: An update. *Sex Roles, 21(11/12),* 715–724.

Macklin, M. C. & Kolbe, R. H. (1984). Sex role stereotyping in children's advertising: Current and past trends. *Journal of Advertising, 13,* 34–42.

Marecek, J., Piliavin, J. A., Fitzsimmons, E., Krogh, E. C., Leader, E., & Trudell, B. (1978). Women as TV experts: The voice of authority. *Journal of Communication, 28*(1), 159–168.

Meyers, R. (1980, November). *An examination of the male sex role model in prime time television commercials.* Paper presented at the meeting of the Speech Communication Association, New York, NY. (ERIC Document Reproduction Service No. ED 208 437).

Nielsen Media Research (1988, November). *Nielsen Television Index national audience demographics report,* Vol. 1. Northbrook, IL: Nielsen Media Research.

Scheibe, C. (1979). Sex roles in TV commercials. *Journal of Advertising Research, 19*(1), 23–27.

Scheibe, C. L. & Condry, J. C. (1984, August). Character portrayals and social values in TV commercials. Paper presented at the meeting of the American Psychological Association, Toronto, Ontario (ERIC Document Reproduction Service No. ED 264 827).

Seggar, J., Hafen, J. & Hannonen-Gladden, H. (1981). Television's portrayals of minorities and women in drama and comedy drama 1971–80. *Journal of Broadcasting, 25*(3), 277–288.

Silverstein, A. J., & Silverstein, R. (1974). The portrayal of women in television advertising. *Federal Communications Bar Journal, 27*(1), 71–98.

Skelly, G. & Lundstrom, W. (1981). Male sex roles in magazine advertising, 1959–1979. *Journal of Communication, 31*(4), 52–57.

Steeves, H. (1987). Feminist theories and media studies. *Critical Studies in Mass Communication 4*(2), 95–135.

---

Verna, M. E. (1975). The female image in children's TV commercials. *Journal of Broadcasting, 19*(3), 301–309.

Wenner, L. A., & Gantz, W. (1989). The audience experience with sports on television. In L. A. Wenner (Ed.), *Media, Sports, and Society*, pp. 241–269. Newbury Park, CA: Sage.

Wilkinson, L. (1989). *SYSTAT: The system for statistics.* Evanston, IL: SYSTAT, Inc.

## Review Questions

1. Why, in Craig's view, is his content analysis of television commercials needed?
2. What is the relationship of "demographic targeting" to "day part"?
3. In paragraphs 10–11, Craig explains how he prepared videotapes for analysis by coders. Why did Craig not inform coders about the day part differences he was intending to study?
4. What hypothesis did Craig's research support?
5. What are the differences between commercials on prime time and those in either the daytime or on the weekend?

## Discussion and Writing Suggestions

1. In her essay on the portrayal of gender in television shows for children, Katha Pollitt conducted an informal content analysis of several programs. In this article, Craig's content analysis is highly rigorous—different in tone and method, although reaching much the same conclusion (albeit for commercials, not children's shows): gender portrayals on television are stereotyped. Given the similarity of Pollitt's and Craig's conclusions, why is it important—if it is important—that Craig performed the rigorous analysis he did?
2. Use Craig's categories for coding gender portrayals (paragraphs 12–18) to analyze three television commercials, aired in three different day parts. Compare your results to Craig's.
3. What were your reactions to Craig's conclusions? Were you at all surprised? Why do you think that the portrayal of the sexes on television commercials has not reflected shifting gender roles in American culture? Or do you think that the commercials *are* accurate in their portrayals? (If you do, what, then, of the supposed role changes taking place in American culture? Are these changes real?)
4. Throughout his article, and especially in the first section, Craig repeatedly refers to the work of others who have researched portrayals of gender on television commercials. Why?
5. Think of examples that *disprove* the following statement: "The entire manufacturing and marketing strategy behind many products such as convenience foods, cosmetics, beer, and cars is tied to the exploitation of gender-specific behaviors." Do examples that disprove Craig's contention occur to you?

Reflect on the ease or difficulty of arriving at these examples. In a paragraph or two, recount your efforts.

# Homosexuality in the Movies: Beyond Villains and Buffoons

MATTHEW GILBERT
VITO RUSSO

*In the following selection, Matthew Gilbert, staff writer for the Boston Globe, surveys portrayals of homosexuality in the movies and on television. As you will see, Hollywood's presentation of homosexuals as villains or as buffoons has remained consistent over the years (in much the same way that portrayals of men as dominant and women as submissive and housebound have remained consistent). Mainstream U.S. film companies have not often varied their representation of gays and lesbians as self-loathing deviants; sympathetic treatments most often are found in European films or in the work of independent producers and directors.*

*As you read, contrast Gilbert's easy, reportorial style (he writes for a general audience) with the presentation of R. Stephen Craig, who writes for sociologists. Recall that in the preceding article Craig relied on statistical analyses to support his arguments about gender portrayals on television commercials. As a reporter, Gilbert establishes authority for his work on entirely different grounds—with sources in the gay community, whom he quotes liberally.*

*Following Gilbert's article, gay activist and film critic Vito Russo analyzes the unstated homosexual content of several movies.*

Political correctness is rapping on everyone's door, and Hollywood is no exception. Kevin Costner's revision of American frontier myths, "Dances with Wolves," is the most dynamic case of a minority—the Sioux Indians—winning in-depth treatment on film. Also faring well are black directors such as Spike Lee and John Singleton, who are remaking black screen characters from waxen stereotypes into breathing human beings.

This month, the question of gay and lesbian representation in Hollywood films has taken the spotlight. Last week, groups including Queer Nation and Out in Film continued to voice outrage over the Michael Douglas–Sharon Stone thriller "Basic Instinct," in which three lesbian

"Beyond Villains and Buffoons" by Matthew Gilbert from the *Boston Globe*, March 22, 1992. Reprinted by permission.

and bisexual characters are suspected ice-pick killers. In a clever move, a San Francisco-based protest group named itself after the guilty character and lobbied hard to deflate the plot for potential audiences, to harm box-office returns. The movie, of course, has also gained free publicity from the protests. As Columbia Pictures producer Harry Gittes points out, "The gay community is seizing upon an opportunity, which is fair play in the world of PR. But it's a PR victory for 'Basic Instinct,' too."

Simultaneously, Queer Nation, Out in Film and other activist groups are planning an action at this year's Academy Awards on March 30, both as guests arrive outside the Dorothy Chandler Pavilion in Los Angeles, and later during the show, near the presentation of a major prize. "It's all for more parity of gay and lesbian images in movies," says Scott Robbe of Out in Film. "Generally, we only see ourselves depicted as villains and buffoons." 3

What is the correct homosexual screen image? The Academy Awards and "Basic Instinct" turmoil arrives amid dissension within gay and lesbian communities over homosexual portrayals in a number of 1991 Oscar-nominated films. In "Prince of Tides," George Carlin plays Nick Nolte's slightly mincing New York roommate. Closeted Tommy Lee Jones, wacked-out Joe Pesci and jailed hooker Kevin Bacon are part of the murder conspiracy in "JFK." The serial killer played by Ted Levine in "The Silence of the Lambs," while not identified as gay, is a cross-dresser with stereotypically gay affect—makeup, a lisp, a poodle named Precious. Also, in "Fried Green Tomatoes" two women, Mary Stuart Masterson and Mary Louise Parker, live together romantically during the 1930s. While the film doesn't call their relationship lesbian, the bond between the boozing, pants-wearing Masterson and the demure Parker is more clearly portrayed as lesbian in the novel "Fried Green Tomatoes at the Whistle Stop Cafe" by Fannie Flagg. 4

The Gay and Lesbian Alliance Against Defamation (GLAAD) gave "Fried Green Tomatoes" a Media Award for its positive portrayal, yet many have knocked the film's lesbianism for daring not to speak its name in fear of box-office repercussions. George Mansour, curator of the Boston Gay and Lesbian Film Festival and independent film buyer and consultant, says "Fried Green Tomatoes" is more offensive than "Basic Instinct." "I'd rather have three gay psychopaths than two closeted lesbians. At least gays are being portrayed openly. It's almost as bad to pretend to people, so they will accept us when we don't say what we are." 5

Even minor characters such as George Carlin in "Prince of Tides," or Nathan Lane in "Frankie and Johnnie," spark disagreement. The Carlin character was "a mistake," says David Ehrenstein, film critic for *The Advocate*, the country's largest-circulation gay and lesbian magazine. And Mansour found him "kind of condescending. Do we really want to 6 only see these lovable, 'La Cage aux Folles,' patronizing gay characters?" Rick Wilson of Queer Nation in New York says that "people were laughing at Carlin, and not with him." At the same time, Michael Bronski, film critic for *Gay Community News* and author of "Culture Clash: The Making of Gay Sensibility," believes Carlin's character was handled properly. "I thought he was fine—attractive, cute, funny, perfectly positive and nice. I loved the fact that he comes on to Nick Nolte in a way that wasn't lecherous."

## MISSING IN ACTION

Beyond the fray, however, there is agreement on the fundamental 7
shortage of gay characters in the history of Hollywood films. Even the most vehement critics of "Basic Instinct" say that the movie's lesbian portrayal would be less harmful, and less worthy of comment, were it one of many. While the *Advocate*'s Ehrenstein condemns "Basic Instinct" as "a good look at the mentality of straight studio executives" and "pathological mysogyny," he says that it would be more tolerable if there were some balance—"if this weren't the only thing we were getting." Mansour, too, says that "more is better." (The filmmakers of "Basic Instinct" declined to comment for this story.)

Gay and, in particular, lesbian invisibility in Hollywood movies is 8
as old as the medium itself. There are famous cases of homosexual themes being dropped from plays and novels as they became film scripts, particularly during the early 1930s through the 1950s, when the Motion Picture Production Code forbade screen depictions of homosexuality. The first time Lillian Hellman's play "The Children's Hour" came to Hollywood, in 1936, the tale of two teachers accused of lesbianism became the story of a heterosexual triangle called "These Three." Even the famous screen version of "A Streetcar Named Desire," starring Marlon Brando and Vivien Leigh, omitted a more pointed reference to the homosexuality of Leigh's dead husband.

In the post-code years, homosexual characters and themes continue 9
to be excised. When Steven Spielberg adapted Alice Walker's novel "The Color Purple" in 1985, he left out the lesbian sexual affair of Whoopi Goldberg's character, Celie. More recently, says Jehan Agrama of GLAAD in LA, lesbian themes were dropped from Steve Martin's "LA Story," Blake Edwards' "Switch" and Winona Ryder's "Welcome Home, Roxy Carmichael," which she says was originally intended as a lesbian coming-out story. There are countless such examples in "The Celluloid Closet," the definitive source of film homosexuality by the late Vito Russo.

As a result of the invisibility, ambiguous characters such as those in 10

"Fried Green Tomatoes," and heterosexual characters such as Susan Sarandon and Geena Davis in "Thelma and Louise," can become homosexual icons, Mansour says. "There are so few portrayed, gay audiences have to invent their heroes. Just the idea of two women being together and empowering each other is enough. That's where you start getting into the idea of gay sensibility." Mansour often includes such sensibility films, like Blake Edwards' "The Wild Rovers," in the Boston Gay and Lesbian Film Festival. This summer, the festival will include Rouben Mamoulian's "Queen Christina" from 1933, in which Greta Garbo appears as a heterosexual but in male attire.

## VILLAINS, VICTIMS, CLOWNS

Because of the low quantity of homosexual portrayals, there is intense    11
scrutiny of the quality of those that make it to the screen. The gay and lesbian spokespeople interviewed for this story point out that the bulk of gay and lesbian characters in Hollywood films are little more than stereotypes, what Robbe calls "villains and buffoons."

Frequently, homosexual characters are the murdering bad guys,    12
from Will Paton in "No Way Out" and Al Pacino in "Cruising" to Elizabeth Ashley in "Windows" and Michael Caine and Christopher Reeve in "Deathtrap." Just as often, they are filled with self-loathing and doom, suffering for their homosexuality, from Marlon Brando in "Reflections in a Golden Eye" and Rod Steiger in "The Sergeant" to Sandy Dennis in "The Fox." Homosexuals also find themselves the occasion for comic relief, generally in supporting roles as with Martin Short in "Father of the Bride" but also in cameos, as in "Bird on a Wire" and "Crocodile Dundee II."

There are, of course, gay villains in real life. And, as producer Gittes    13
says, "movies treat *everything* in stereotype. You can't single out gays, because Hollywood stereotypes everybody in order to be more middle of the road, and more commercial." But *Gay Community News'* Michael Bronski points out that there is a critical distinction "between those gay characters who are intrinsically bad because they're homosexual and those who are bad and then happen to be homosexual." He says that the gay and lesbian political agenda may have shifted in the past decade. "We've learned there's a difference between simply looking for positive images, which are important, and looking for complexity. Just having a bad homosexual in a movie isn't enough to complain about. In 'JFK,' all the gay characters were complex. It was a movie in which they weren't trying to kill the president because they were gay."

In "Basic Instinct," says Donald Suggs of GLAAD in New York, the    14
characters' villainy largely arises from their sexual orientations. And by

making all the lesbian and bisexual characters in "Basic Instinct" murderers, "you're implying that it's a pathology," he says. "There's never been a lesbian protagonist of a Hollywood film portrayed in an accurate and balanced manner. The history of lesbians in movies is suicidal maniacs and psycho killers."

Indeed, it is difficult to point to a Hollywood movie hero who happens to be gay or lesbian. The place to look is not Hollywood, the *Advocate*'s David Ehrenstein points out, but in independent and European releases. "While Hollywood is making a fool of itself, there is a growing legion of independent filmmakers whose movie characters are very imaginative and honest," he says, mentioning last year's "My Own Private Idaho" by Gus Van Sant and "Poison" by Todd Haynes. "Desert Hearts," "Parting Glances" and "My Beautiful Laundrette" are other examples. "Hollywood," he says, "is way behind." 15

Television, it seems, is also ahead of Hollywood. Gay and lesbian portrayals are increasingly prevalent on the small screen, where there have been recurring homosexual or bisexual characters on shows such as "Roseanne," "LA Law," "Hill Street Blues" and "thirtysomething." One of the main characters in "Melrose Place," the forthcoming spinoff of "Beverly Hills 90210," will be gay. Series such as "Murphy Brown," "Northern Exposure," "The Simpsons" and "Quantum Leap" have built episodes around homosexual themes and characters, as have TV movies such as "Doing Time on Maple Drive," "Consenting Adult," "My Two Loves" and "An Early Frost." And talk shows consistently focus on issues of homosexuality. 16

While advertisers are often shaky about buying time during homosexual-themed shows, the queasiness has not stopped the television powers that be. "Supposedly there is an advertising problem," says Agrama of GLAAD. "But I don't see the ratings of 'Roseanne' plummeting from having a gay character" (played by Martin Mull). And if advertisers do withdraw from homosexuality, TV's weekly format allows all to be forgiven by the next episode. In film, of course, it's once and forever. 17

Television's willingness to treat homosexuality may be a personnel matter, says Paul Monette, author and scriptwriter (he co-wrote the "thirtysomething" with an HIV-related plot). "In TV, there really are people who have power that can't be taken away. Every one in film is a paranoid lunatic because there are so few jobs. . . . I'm not saying I love TV, but there are people behind it who aren't out to hold up some distance from reality and be glamorous." Monette is not optimistic about the future of gays and lesbians in Hollywood movies. "I think we are wrong to expect Hollywood to be anything more than the province of hustlers and hucksters. These are the descendants of the people who put the Elephant Man on stage. I have no expectations." 18

## HOLLYWOOD'S BAD RAP

It is unclear why Hollywood hands down so few images of homosexu- 19
als. Some say individuals, homosexual or heterosexual, fear becoming
branded as "the gay one" by committing themselves to such projects.
Actors such as Marlon Brando and Shirley MacLaine may have played
homosexuals onscreen and not been pigeonholed, but their star power
is much larger than their roles. "They are people with already big
reputations, who can overcome the stigma," says Patrick McGilligan,
author of "George Cukor: A Double Life." "Most actors justifiably
might fear being cut off from other heterosexual roles."[1]

Some suggest that closeted homosexuals in Hollywood may be 20
responsible. "Only when gays and lesbians are able to be out in the
movie industry will we begin to see some change," says Bronski.
"There's such an enforced closetry in the industry, AIDS being just one
more added on, that there isn't anyone willing to go to bat and fight for
a movie. . . . We always talk about Hollywood as an industry, and we
lose track that, on some level, these are all personal decisions for people.
Roseanne made a personal decision to put a gay character on her show."

McGilligan says its no different for homosexuals in Hollywood 21
today than it was for George Cukor before his death in 1983. "Even
though the progressive wing of America is represented in Hollywood,
there has always been a powerful right wing there. Even back in the '30s
and '40s, there was personal blacklisting by Hollywood producers of
people's lifestyles. And people are afraid of that right wing, especially
at the box office. It's all about survival at the box office. There are few
message pictures, and few real-life or humanistic scenarios in movies,
because there's a tremendous fear of being targeted. It's not just among
gay people."

Producer Harry Gittes agrees that money is what matters in Holly- 22
wood. "If 'Longtime Companion' had made $80 million, they'd come up
with 10 more of them. Period.[2] Things in Hollywood are about survival.
It's the '90s. Hollywood doesn't owe a debt to anyone but itself right
now, to stay healthy and robust. It's a difficult time to be different here.
The old-boy network is trying to protect only itself."

Meanwhile, in order to educate Hollywood about gay and lesbian 23
issues, GLAAD has begun sensitivity training sessions with a number of
studios, including Touchstone, Columbia and Universal. Among other

---

[1]George Cukor (1899–1983) was a major Hollywood director known for films with strong
women characters. He is best known for: *Little Women* (1933), *The Philadelphia Story* (1940),
*Gaslight* (1944), *Adam's Rib* (1949), *A Star Is Born* (1954), and *My Fair Lady* (1964). [Behrens and
Rosen]
[2]*Longtime Companion* is a movie sympathetic to a group of characters, many of whom develop
AIDS. [Behrens and Rosen]

things, GLAAD helps them with larger issues—how to attract scripts with homosexual themes, for instance—as well as with finer points of language and character nuance. "It's definitely having an effect," says GLAAD's Agrama. "People are on the whole conscientious. When we talk to them, they see the difference. There is in Hollywood the decision to do something about it."

## THE POWER OF FILM

Criticism of Hollywood's ways is, of course, nothing new. At its root,   24
political correctness is an American tradition, one that has led to protests of movies as far back as the racially controversial "Birth of a Nation" in 1915. As Tri-Star's formal statement about "Basic Instinct" reads, "Freedom of expression covers filmmakers and moviegoers as well as protesters."

Movies have always held a huge symbolic import. Film is a powerful   25
medium that feeds our dreams and seeps into the depths of our consciousness. It may even affect our behavior. This is what GLAAD's Jehan Agrama has in mind when she says that Hollywood's portrayal of homosexuality as bad or silly has "an impact not only on the self-esteem of gays and lesbians, but on violence and hate crimes" against them.

> *Vito Russo (1946–1990) was an accomplished writer and lecturer best known for his* Celluloid Closet *(1981), from which the following analyses of horror films and "buddy" films are drawn. Russo's award-winning book, considered a standard reference on the history of homosexuality in the movies, first took shape as a lecture that he delivered beginning in the 1970s. Russo co-founded GLAAD (Gay and Lesbian Alliance Against Defamation) and wrote for national publications such as the* Village Voice, Rolling Stone, *and* Esquire. *Vito Russo died of AIDS in 1990.*

Nobody likes a sissy. That includes dykes, faggots and feminists of both   26
sexes. Even in a time of sexual revolution, when traditional roles are being examined and challenged every day, there is something about a man who acts like a woman that people find fundamentally distasteful. A 1979 *New York Times* feature on how some noted feminists were raising their male children revealed that most wanted their sons to grow up to be feminists—but real men, not sissies.

This chapter is concerned primarily with the genesis of the sissy and   27

---

not the tomboy because homosexual behavior onscreen, as almost every other defined "type" of behavior, has been cast in male terms. Homosexuality in the movies, whether overtly sexual or not, has always been seen in terms of what is or is not masculine. The defensive phrase "Who's a sissy?" has been as much a part of the American lexicon as "So's your old lady." After all, it is supposed to be an insult to call a man effeminate, for it means he is like a woman and therefore not as valuable as a "real" man. The popular definition of gayness is rooted in sexism. Weakness in men rather than strength in women has consistently been seen as the connection between sex role behavior and deviant sexuality. And while sissy men have always signaled a rank betrayal of the myth of male superiority, tomboy women have seemed to reinforce that myth and have often been indulged in acting it out.

In celebrating maleness, the rendering invisible of all else has caused lesbianism to disappear behind a male vision of sex in general. The stigma of tomboy has been less than that of sissy because lesbianism is never allowed to become a threatening reality any more than female sexuality of other kinds. Queen Victoria, informed that a certain woman was a lesbian, asked what a lesbian might be. When the term had been explained, she flatly refused to believe that such creatures existed. Early laws against homosexuality referred only to acts between men. In England the penalty for male homosexual acts was reduced from death to imprisonment in 1861, but the new law made no mention of lesbianism. Nor did the target of the pioneering German gay liberation movement, Paragraph 175, which outlawed homosexual acts between men but omitted any mention of lesbians. [28]

The German movement, begun in 1897, was eliminated by the Nazis in the early 1930s. The trial and jailing of Oscar Wilde in England had already silenced leading literary figures who had vocally supported homosexual rights, and such movements as existed had little effect in the United States. The first American gay liberation group, the Society for Human Rights, chartered in 1924 by the State of Illinois, was disbanded after less than a year when its members were arrested by Chicago police. An organized gay visibility did not re-emerge in America until after World War II. In many ways, Queen Victoria spoke for everyone. In the popular mind, no such creatures existed except in a national fear of effeminacy, a word listed in Roget's Thesaurus as a synonym for weakness. [29]

A nation of immigrants recently mesmerized by the flicker of the nickelodeon seized the larger-than-life images of the silent screen to play out its own dream of itself, and there was little room for weakness in the telling. Suspicions of inadequacy, however, were rife. The predominantly masculine character of the earliest cinema reflected an America that saw itself as a recently conquered wilderness. Actually there was not much wilderness left in the early twentieth century, but the movies [30] endlessly recreated the struggles, the heroism and the romance of our pioneer spirit. There were western movies but no easterns; our European origins were considered tame and unworthy of the growing American legend. Men of action and strength were the embodiment of our culture, and a vast mythology was created to keep the dream in constant repair. Real men were strong, silent and ostentatiously unemotional. They acted quickly and never intellectualized. In short, they did not behave like women.

Unspeakable in the culture, the true nature of homosexuality 31 haunted only the dim recesses of our celluloid consciousness. The idea that there was such a thing as a real man made the creation of the sissy inevitable. Men who were perceived to be "like women" were simply mama's boys, reflections of an overabundance of female influence. It became the theme of scores of silent films to save the weakling youth and restore his manhood. Although at first there was no equation between sissyhood and actual homosexuality, the danger of gayness as the consequence of such behavior lurked always in the background.

. . .

The line between the effeminate and the real man was drawn rou- 32 tinely in every genre of American film, but comedies more often allowed the explicit leap to the homosexual possibilities inherent in such definitions. Indeed, the relationship between sissyhood and real homosexuality was born in the "anything can happen" jests of silent comedy. The outrageous nature of such films left a lot of room for nonsensical possibilities, and occasionally real sexuality of a "different" nature would intrude as one of them, though it was never taken seriously as a realistic option.

In the films of Buster Keaton, Charlie Chaplin and especially Harold 33 Lloyd, combat with the bully and the winning of the girl were as much tributes to the spirit of America as the conquest of the land itself. And in the end, the dreams they evoked were equally transparent. All films reflected and reinforced such an impossibly pure masculine drive and image that the pressure to be a real man was absolute and unyielding. Even Carole Lombard admitted that, in bed, Clark Gable was no Clark Gable, but that didn't stop men from trying. Gable was a purveyor of the dream onscreen and off, at first refusing to cry as Rhett Butler in *Gone With the Wind* because it might tarnish his masculine screen image, and later referring to Montgomery Clift, his co-star in *The Misfits*, as "that fag."

Crucially at issue always was the connection between feminine 34 behavior and inferiority. The conclusive message was that quiet souls could be real men—but not if they displayed qualities that properly belonged to women.

. . .

## HORROR FILMS

Gays as predatory, twilight creatures were a matter of style and personal    35
interpretation in the horror films of the 1930s. The equation of horror
with the sins of the flesh is easily seen in monster movies of the period.
Creatures like the Frankenstein monster and Dracula were almost always
linked with the baser instincts of human beings; Frankenstein especially
is a film character created outside every boundary the film calls normal.

Gays were often created as monsters. In her review of John Flynn's    36
*The Sergeant* (1968), Pauline Kael points out that Rod Steiger's gay
soldier isn't *just* homosexual—he's psychopathic—and part of that has
to do with his appearing in "normal" surroundings. "Why," she asked,
"are all the other soldiers so incredibly, so antiseptically straight that it
really begins to look as if you *did* have to be crazy to be a homosexual?
In this army situation, there is nothing in the atmosphere that links up
with the Sergeant's homosexuality . . . and homosexuality is, to all
appearances, unknown and without cause [so that] it does begin to seem
as if only a monster could have such aberrant impulses."

The essence of homosexuality as a predatory weakness permeates    37
the depiction of gay characters in horror films. In *Dracula's Daughter*
(1936), Countess Alesca (Gloria Holden) has a special attraction
to women, a preference that was even highlighted in some of the original ads for the film. ("Save the women of London from Dracula's
Daughter!") Roger Vadim's *Blood and Roses* (1960) and Joseph Larraz'
*Vampyres* (1974) both deal with lesbian vampires. Homosexual parallels in *Frankenstein* (1931) and *The Bride of Frankenstein* (1935) arose
from a vision both films had of the monster as an antisocial figure in
the same way that gay people were "things" that should not have happened.

In both films the homosexuality of director James Whale may have    38
been a force in the vision. Director Robert Aldrich recalls that "Jimmy
Whale was the first guy who was blackballed because he refused to stay
in the closet. Mitchell Leisen and all those other guys played it straight,
and they were onboard, but Whale said, 'fuck it, I'm a great director and
I don't have to put up with this bullshit'—and he *was* a great director,
not just a company director. And he was just unemployed after that—
never worked again." According to Aldrich, an obviously lesbian director like Dorothy Arzner got away with her lifestyle because she was
officially closeted and because "it made her one of the boys." But a man
who, like Whale, openly admitted his love relationship with another
man, in this case producer David Lewis, did not stand a chance. Although James Whale worked again briefly in 1943, he fell into obscurity
soon after. In 1961 he was found dead at the bottom of his swimming
pool, and there has never been a full investigation of the circumstances
surrounding the event.

Whale's Frankenstein monster was the creation that would eventu- **39** ally destroy its creator, just as Whale's own "aberration" would eventually destroy his career. The monster in *Frankenstein* bears the brunt of society's reaction to his existence, and in the sequel, *The Bride of Frankenstein*, the monster himself is painfully aware of his own unnaturalness. In a graveyard scene, character actor Ernest Thesiger, a friend of Whale and a man who played the effete sissy with as much verve and wit as Franklin Pangborn or Grady Sutton, listens as the monster confesses his knowledge of his own creation. In *Frankenstein*, it is the monster who limits Henry Frankenstein's contact with the normal world. The old baron, Frankenstein's father, continually beseeches his son to "leave this madness," to come home and marry the young Elizabeth. Finally, the father, Elizabeth and Henry's best friend go to the castle and force him, for his health and sanity, to leave his creation, to be free from his "obsession." Later the monster fulfills Mary Shelley's prophecy by joining his creator on his wedding night, carrying off Elizabeth and thereby preventing the consummation of the impending marriage. The monster is then hunted by the townspeople in the same way that groups of men in silent comedies had once run effeminate men off piers and out of town. Their outrage echoes again and again in film. "What is this creature? I abhor it!"

In *The Bride of Frankenstein*, it is the odd, sissified Dr. Praetorius **40** (Ernest Thesiger) who comes to entice Henry Frankenstein from his bridal bed in the middle of the night. Praetorius too has created life, and Henry's curiosity again overcomes his "good" instincts and proves his downfall. Praetorius proclaims himself to be in love with evil and professes to detest goodness. No accident, then, that the monster, seeing the unnaturalness and folly of his own existence, takes the evil Praetorius with him when he pulls the lever to destroy himself and his bride, crying out to Henry and Elizabeth, "Go! *You* live. We belong dead."

One may see Whale's horror films, including *The Old Dark House* **41** (1932), in which all the characters can be read as gay, as either revisionist thinking (and therefore dangerous and false) or as crackpot theory (and therefore harmless and irrelevant). But one may no longer ignore the implications of the homosexual artist's being tied to a heterosexual dream. Of gay filmmaker F. W. Murnau, Natalie Edwards wrote for the Toronto Film Society, "His homosexuality had been cruelly subverted during his German period due to incredibly strict German laws, and it may well be that it was partly as a result of this forced restriction that his films of that period so often contained horror, dread, fantasy and perversion." Once homosexuality had become literally speakable in the early 1960s, gays dropped like flies, usually by their own hand, while continuing to perform their classically comic function in lesser and more ambiguous roles. In twenty-two of twenty-eight films dealing with gay subjects from 1962 to 1978, major gay characters onscreen ended in suicide or violent death.

Probably the "gayest" film yet made by a major studio and an **42** excellent spoof of gay/horror conventions is *The Rocky Horror Picture Show*, a cult rock musical that Twentieth Century-Fox has never given a proper release in the United States. Since 1976 the film has been playing midnight shows in cities throughout the country. A truly subversive and anarchistic film on the subjects of sexuality, movies, sex roles and the homosexual as monster, *Rocky Horror* features two innocents (Susan Sarandon and Barry Bostwick) whose car runs out of gas not far from a haunted mansion that appears to be a parody of the creepy mansion in James Whale's *The Old Dark House*. In it they discover Dr. Frank N Furter (Tim Curry), the apotheosis of deviant sexuality, who introduces himself by singing a sizzling "I'm a Sweet Transvestite from Transsexual, Transylvania." Frank N Furter is an androgyne who comes from outer space, from a galaxy called Transsexual and a planet called Transylvania. When the timid couple arrive, he is in the process of showing off his latest creation, a hunky blond named Rocky, who is straight off the slab and wears nothing but tight gold lamé trunks. Pointing to Rocky, Frank N Furter sings a lusty "In Just Seven Days, I Can Make You a Man," then proceeds to introduce Brad and Janet to the joys of the unmentionable.

As both catalogue and spoof of old monster movies and science **43** fiction films, *Rocky Horror* becomes almost dizzying in its references, but its most expert satire is of the age-old fear with which straight society encounters deviant sexuality. This is established at the beginning of the film (Janet says, "Brad, there's something *unhealthy* about this place") and is followed through to the very end, when Frank N Furter is destroyed "for the good of society," having been carried by Rocky, in the manner of King Kong, to the top of the RKO-Radio Pictures tower. Nevertheless he returns to life to perform, with the entire cast, an underwater ballet version of the film's message, "Don't Just Dream It, Be It," and the song becomes an anthem of hope for an androgynous world. Tim Curry's performance, especially in his rendition of "Sweet Transvestite," is the essence of what every parent in America fears will happen if our sexual standards are relaxed. It becomes the living horror of making deviant sexuality visible and tangible in the only kind of setting in which it could possibly work, an old dark house populated by lesbians, transvestites, acid freaks and goons who sing rock and roll as they seduce the innocent youth of America. Hollywood didn't know what to do with *The Rocky Horror Picture Show* when it had been completed, but despite its shabby treatment, it has grossed a fortune as a popular cult film, and it continues to play throughout the country to audiences made up largely of young people who dress for the showings like the characters in the film.

. . .

## "BUDDY" FILMS

Most buddy films involve a group of men going off to fight a war or to **44** conquer a wilderness—men's work, in which a female presence is superfluous but tolerated. In *Test Pilot* (1938), Clark Gable and Spencer Tracy play a pair of buddies who blow each other a ritualistic kiss each time they leave on a mission—for good luck. In William A. Wellman's *Wings* (1927), Richard Arlen and Charles "Buddy" Rogers have a more meaningful relationship with each other than either of them has with Jobyna Ralston or Clara Bow, both token love interests whom male adolescents all over America correctly identified as "the boring parts" of the movie. In fact Arlen and Rogers have the only real love scene in *Wings*, and Rogers learns the true meaning of love through his relationship with his buddy, just as in Howard Hawks' *Only Angels Have Wings* (1939) Cary Grant and Richard Barthelmess find satisfaction only in each other, despite the intrusive presence of Jean Arthur and Rita Hayworth. In *The Big Sky* (1952), it is with profound hesitation and to the ultimate detriment of the film that Kirk Douglas sends Dewey Martin back to his girl after the exciting comradeship they have shared in the great outdoors.

Joan Mellon, in her study of masculinity in the movies, *Big Bad* **45** *Wolves*, says that the less violent men were in their film personas, the more likely they were to be interested in heterosexual love. Just the opposite has been true for homoeroticism. The perception of homosexual feelings as a brutal, furtive and dangerous force saw it flourish in films of male bonding and violence. Gentle men in the movies—Jimmy Stewart in any "Smalltown, U.S.A." picture or Spencer Tracy in *Father of the Bride*, for example—would never, even subtextually, approach such relationships or feelings. The concept of the gentle man who chooses to love other men does not exist in American film except as slapstick comedy. Stan Laurel and Oliver Hardy had the perfect sissy-buddy relationship throughout their long career, and it is naive now, looking at their films, to assume that they were not aware of and did not consciously use this aspect of their screen relationship to enrich their comedy.

In a film such as *Liberty* (1929), directed by Leo McCarey, the **46** homosexuality emerged in traditionally comic ways, chiefly as farcical misunderstanding. Stan and Ollie have just escaped from prison, and in their haste they have put on each other's trousers. The running joke throughout the first half of the film is that each time they attempt to exchange trousers—in the back seat of a car, behind some crates in an alley, at a construction site—they are discovered by someone who thinks that they have been playing with each other. The French film critic André S. Labarthe maintained that *Liberty* "offers, to anyone who can read, the unequivocal sign of unnatural love." Yet this is the same, safe comic device that was used in Harold Lloyd films, when he found himself holding the hand of another man that he had thought belonged to a woman. But Laurel and Hardy, perhaps because of their adolescent behavior in general, often took such mistakes further than other comics did in their display of natural affection for each other. Their brand of unconscious affection was missing from the often brutal antics of Bud Abbott and Lou Costello or Dean Martin and Jerry Lewis (who were sometimes really cruel to each other).

In the films of Laurel and Hardy, their relationship was given a sweet **47** and very real loving dimension. The two often wound up in bed together, and their wives were almost always portrayed as obstacles to their friendship. In a classic example of this, one with unmistakably gay overtones, they play a married couple complete with newborn baby in *Their First Mistake* (1932), a Hal Roach film directed by George Marshall. Ollie's wife (Mae Busch) complains that he sees too much of Stan and not enough of her, and the two friends discuss the situation.

> *Stan:* Well, what's the matter with her, anyway?
> *Ollie:* Oh, I don't know. She says I think more of you than I do of her.
> *Stan:* Well, you do, don't you?
> *Ollie:* We won't go into *that.*
> *Stan:* You know what the trouble is?
> *Ollie:* What?
> *Stan:* You need a baby in your house.
> *Ollie:* Well, what's that got to do with it?
> *Stan:* Well, if you had a baby . . . it would keep your wife's mind occupied . . . you could go out nights with me . . . and she'd never think anything about it.

So they go out and adopt a baby. When they return home with it, **48** they discover that Ollie's wife is suing him for divorce for "alienation of affections," having named Stan Laurel as "the other woman." The remainder of the film is a beautifully timed and performed domestic scene, with Stan and Ollie in bed and the baby between them. The scene climaxes when Stan reaches into his pajama top—as if reaching for a breast to feed the baby—and comes up with the baby's bottle, which he has been keeping warm.

All this is charming, sometimes very funny and certainly of no great **49** consequence. Yet when one suggests that there may be clues to homosexual behavior in the ways that Laurel and Hardy related to one another, it is as though one were attacking America itself. Charles Barr, in his study *Laurel and Hardy*, says that "there is something rather absurd about discussing this [the homosexual nature of *Their First Mistake*] seriously at all." In the often infantile, "presexual" nursery world in which Stan and Ollie lived, Barr argues, such behavior would be "natural."

It is fast becoming evident, however, that there is no such thing as 50 a "presexual" age. Notice, too, that it is the "naturalness" of Laurel and Hardy's behavior that Barr and other critics choose to defend, not the sexuality. The homosexuality is unmistakably there; it remains only for people to say that *in this case* such behavior would be natural to fend off charges of unnaturalness in beloved film figures. And so it is indeed an attack on America itself to suggest that homosexuality is present in the Laurel and Hardy routines. In pointing these things out, one attacks the American illusion—the illusion that there is in fact such a thing as a real man and that to become one is as easy as changing one's name from Marion Morrison to John Wayne. The fact is that comedy has been able to comment on sexual roles more readily than drama could do only because people may dismiss it as impossible farce.

. . .

When buddy films returned in the late Sixties, the presence on- 51 screen of homosexual characters was a perfect way of saying, Oh, no, this isn't what we mean at all. Homosexuals drew suspicion away from the buddies—it was yardstick time again. In John Schlesinger's *Midnight Cowboy* (1969), the relationship between Joe Buck (Jon Voight) and Ratso Rizzo (Dustin Hoffman) is lily pure. Their contempt for faggots and faggot behavior is well established in the course of their growing buddyhood and justified by the behavior of the "real" homosexuals in the film. When Joe Buck hustles a desperate-looking student (Bob Balaban) in the balcony of a Times Square movie house, we are being shown how pathetic such creatures are. The student, who has no money, ends up vomiting in the men's toilet in self-disgust and fear of retaliation.

When Joe hustles another pitiable spectre of the night, an aging, 52 guilt-ridden Catholic (Barnard Hughes), the incident ends in violence and more self-hatred. As Joe is beating him, the old man mutters to himself, "I deserve this. I brought this about myself, I know I did. Oh! How I loathe life!" Joe's naivete and wholesomeness is contrasted with his seedy surroundings, and the film makes it clear who are the villains and who the innocent victim. The audience's sympathy is all for the virginal young man innocently drawn into the big-city web as he tries to raise the money to take his dying friend to Florida.

In an August 1979 interview in *Playgirl* magazine, Dustin Hoffman 53 told how he thought the characters of Joe and Ratso would both hate blacks, being white trash from Texas and Italian white trash from the Bronx. In a restaurant scene, Hoffman suggested to Schlesinger, a black guy should come in and the two move away muttering "scum bags" or "niggers." Schlesinger replied, "My God, we're trying to get people to like Joe and Ratso. We'll lose every liberal in the audience." Instead, Ratso is vocally bigoted against gays in that scene, muttering "faggot" when a Times Square queen walks in.

Ratso delivers a devastating criticism when he attacks Joe's cowboy 54 outfit and calls into question the innocence of this ultimate masculine ideal, one that had dominated the American screen in its formative years. "If you wanna know the truth," he shouts, "that stuff is strictly for faggots! That's faggot stuff." Wounded and confused, Joe shoots back in defense, "John Wayne! You're gonna tell me that John Wayne's a fag?"

This defines the fear. If there is no real difference between the cowboy 55 hero and the faggot on Forty-second Street, then what remains of American masculinity? This scene comes closest to saying that the costume is only an image, as much a lie as all the other ways in which we force the movies to serve our dreams of an America that never really existed. To preserve a shred of "real" manhood becomes the goal of buddy characters, both in spite of their true feelings and because of them.

## Review Questions

1. Why did gay and lesbian activists target for protest the 1992 movie *Basic Instinct?* What larger issues, beyond this particular movie, concerned the protesters?

2. Characterize the controversy among the gay and lesbian communities concerning portrayals of homosexuality in the movies.

3. According to Gilbert, why do the portrayals of gays and lesbians on-screen receive such careful scrutiny?

4. In what ways is television "ahead" of the film industry in presenting homosexuality?

5. According to Vito Russo, why was there little room for portrayals of "weak" men in early movies?

6. What, according to Russo, is the homosexual content of *Frankenstein?*

## Discussion and Writing Suggestions

1. Gilbert closes his article by quoting a spokesperson for GLAAD, who suggests that "Hollywood's portrayal of homosexuality as bad or silly has 'an impact not only on the self-esteem of gays and lesbians, but on violence and hate crimes against them." What is this impact, both on gays and lesbians and on the general public?

2. Vito Russo attributes a particularly memorable line to Carol Lombard, a famous actress: "Even Carol Lombard admitted that, in bed, Clark Gable was no Clark Gable. . . ." What does Lombard mean? What are the implications of this remark for all moviegoers—regardless of sexual orientation?

3. What is your response to Vito Russo's analysis of the various films discussed here? Respond to his analysis of one film, particularly. Do you agree that the homosexual content that Russo sees is, in fact, present?

4. Russo writes of Joe Buck's fear, in *Midnight Cowboy*, of John Wayne's being gay. "This defines the fear," writes Russo. "If there is no real difference between the cowboy hero and the faggot on Forty-second Street, then what remains of American masculinity? This scene comes closest to saying that the costume is only an image, as much a lie as all the other ways in which we force the movies to serve our dreams of an America that never really existed." In one or two paragraphs, comment on Russo's claim.

5. Rent and watch any of the movies referred to in the discussions by Gilbert or Russo. In three or four paragraphs, describe the gay and lesbian content of these films and the filmmaker's attitude toward gay and lesbian characters.

6. Examine Gilbert's opening and closing paragraphs, in which he frames his discussion of homosexuality in the movies in the context of political correctness. What is the logic of this framing? How does it work?

# The Marlboro Man

## SANDRA CISNEROS

> *An award-winning poet and writer of short fiction, Sandra Cisneros has most recently completed* Woman Hollering Creek *(1991), a collection of stories in which "The Marlboro Man" appears. A reviewer in the* New York Times *called Cisneros's writing radiant and filled with characters who cling to their Hispanic heritage like an "anchor." Cisneros's previous books include* Bad Boys *(poems, 1980),* The House on Mango Street *(1983), and* My Wicked, Wicked Ways *(1987).*

**Durango was his name. Not his *real* name. I don't remember his real name, but it'll come to me. I've got it in my phone book at home. My girlfriend Romelia used to live with him. You *know* her, in fact. The real pretty one with big lips who came over to our table at the Beauregards' once when the Number Two Dinners were playing.** 1

The one with the ponytail?

**No. Her friend. Anyway, she lived with him for a year even though he was *way* too old for her.** 2

For real? But I thought the Marlboro Man was gay.

**He *was?* Romelia never told me *that.*** 3

Yeah. In fact, I'm positive. I remember because I had a bad-ass crush on him, and one day I see a commercial for *60 Minutes,* right?

SPECIAL. TONIGHT! THE MARLBORO MAN. I remember saying to myself, Hot damn, I can't miss that.

**Maybe Romelia *did* insinuate, but I didn't pick up on it.** 4

What's his name? That guy from *60 Minutes.*

**Andy Rooney?** 5

*Not* Andy Rooney, *girl*friend! The other guy. The one that looks sad all the time.

**Dan Rather.** 6

Yeah, him. Dan Rather interviewed him on *60 Minutes.* You know, "Whatever happened to the Marlboro Man" and all that shit. Dan Rather interviewed him. The Marlboro Man was working as an AIDS clinic volunteer and he died from it even.

**No, he didn't. He died from cancer. Too many cigarettes, I guess.** 7

Are we talking about the same Marlboro Man?

**He and Romelia lived on this fabulous piece of real estate in the** 8 **hill country, outside Fredericksburg. Beautiful house on a bluff, next to some cattle ranches. You'd think you were miles from civilization, deer and wild turkey and roadrunners and hawks and all that, but it was only a ten-minute drive to town. They had a big Fourth of July party there once and invited everybody who was anybody. Willie Nelson, Esteban Jordán, Augie Meyers, all that crowd.**

No kidding.

**He had this habit of taking off all his clothes in public. I ran into** 9 **them once at the Liberty, and he was dressed up in this luscious suit. Very *GQ,* know what I mean? *Très élégant.* Well, I waved to Romelia, meaning to go over to the bar later and say hi. But by the time I got to my pecan pie, he was already marching out the door wearing nothing but a cocktail napkin. I swear, he was *some*thing.**

GOD! Don't kill me. I used to dream he'd be the father of my children.

**Well, yeah. That is if we're talking about the same Marlboro Man.** 10 **There've been lots of Marlboro Men. Just like there've been lots of Lassies, and lots of Shamu the Whale, and lots of Ralph the Swimming Pig. Well, what did you think, girlfriend? *All* those billboards. *All* those years!**

Did he have a mustache?

**Yeah.**                                                                                              11

And did he play bit parts in Clint Eastwood westerns?

**I think so. At least he played in some Wells Fargo things that I**   12
**know of.**

And was he originally from northern California, used to have a little
brother who was borderline mentally retarded, did some porno flicks
before Marlboro discovered him?

**Well, all I know is he was called Durango. And he owned a ranch**   13
**out in the hill country that once belonged to Lady Bird Johnson.**
**And he and some friends of the Texas Tornadoes lost a lot of**
**money investing in some recording studio that was supposed to**
**have thirty-six tracks instead of the usual sixteen, or whatever.**
**And he gave Romelia hell, always chasing any young *thang* that**
**wore a skirt and . . .**

But Dan Rather said he was the *original* Marlboro Man.

**The original, huh? . . . Well, maybe the one I'm talking about who**   14
**lived with Romelia wasn't the *real* Marlboro Man. . . . But he *was***
**old.**

## Discussion and Writing Suggestions

1. What is your image of the Marlboro Man? Find an advertisement for the
   cigarette, in a magazine or newspaper, and discuss the setting in which the
   character is presented. What associations do you have with this setting?
2. Why are the two girls conversing in this story surprised that the Marlboro
   Man might be gay? (See paragraphs 2–6.) If this were true, would you be
   surprised? Why?
3. There is confusion in the story about how many Marlboro Men there actually
   are. The possibility that there is more than one (the story suggests that one
   died from AIDS and another from cancer) upsets the two girls. Why?
4. In paragraph 12, the narrator suggests that the Marlboro Man "did some
   porno flicks." How does this possibility contradict the image that advertisers
   were so careful to develop?
5. "The Marlboro Man" is structured as a conversation—which puts the reader
   in the position of overhearing, or eavesdropping. How does this strategy
   work to draw you into the story?
6. Reread paragraphs 52–55 in Vito Russo (the preceding selection). How do
   Russo's comments about the cowboy image bear on Cisneros's story?

## SYNTHESIS ACTIVITIES

1. In a five-page argument, forge a relationship between the personal narratives in Betty Friedan's *The Feminine Mystique* and Warren Farrell's "Ralph's Story." What have these stories to do with one another? And what have these stories to do with relationships that you have observed in your own life?

2. How do you explain the persistence of traditional gender portrayals in America's preschool culture (see Katha Pollitt) and television commercials (see R. Stephen Craig)? To what extent are these portrayals an example of the backlash that Susan Faludi discusses in "Blame It on Feminism"? Write a paper in which you refer to these three sources and discuss the extent to which you feel a backlash against feminism is at work in our culture.

3. Should our culture maintain more or less distinct gender identities? Develop an essay in response to this question. You might want to address one or more of the following questions: Are distinctions between male and female behaviors useful economically? Psychologically? Sociologically? When do we learn gender-appropriate behaviors? Who teaches these behaviors? Possible sources: include Friedan, Farrell, Pollitt, and Masters/Johnson/Kolodny.

4. How prevalent is gender stereotyping in the media? Using the selections by Ian Harris, R. Stephen Craig, Matthew Gilbert and Vito Russo, and Katha Pollitt as starting points, choose one medium—television ads, television dramas (e.g., cartoons, sitcoms, game shows), movies, magazines, radio, newspapers, billboards—and explain the ways in which males and females are portrayed in stereotypical roles.

5. Examine four selections in this chapter—Masters/Johnson/Kolodny, Craig, Gilbert, and Pollitt—in terms of the ways in which the writers establish the authority to speak knowledgeably about the topics that concern them. That is, in a synthesis discuss the ways in which these writers support their arguments. To what do Masters/Johnson/Kolodny refer in order to appear to readers as credible authorities who can write on gender-role socialization? Similarly, how does Craig establish authority for—how does he *support*—his arguments about gender portrayals on television commercials? Katha Pollitt reaches much the same conclusion as Craig (albeit about children's programming), although her method for establishing the authority of her essay differs significantly from Craig's. And, as a journalist, Matthew Gilbert establishes his authority to report on his topic not by an appeal to his own experience but by virtue of some other appeal. Organize your observations into a synthesis.

6. Pollitt, Craig, and Gilbert clearly establish that stereotypical portrayals of gender in the media have not changed in decades, despite changing attitudes in the broader culture about the roles of men and women and about gay and lesbian relationships. In a synthesis that draws on sources in this

chapter, speculate on the reasons that gender portrayals have remained so consistent over the years.

7. In Sandra Cisneros's "The Marlboro Man," two girls try sorting out the Marlboro Man in fact from the Marlboro Man in myth—and they don't get very far. The conversation is reminiscent of a line in Vito Russo, that, according to Carol Lombard, "in bed, Clark Gable was no Clark Gable." When real men give physical form to myths of masculinity, the men themselves can hardly live up to the masculine ideal. Why, then, do you suppose that our popular culture continues churning out images of the manly man? Respond to this question by drawing on the above-mentioned sources and on other selections in the chapter.

8. Write an explanatory essay about a day of your life—assuming you were a member of the opposite sex. Work in pairs on this assignment, one man and one woman to a pair. Exchange descriptions and then verbally critique one another's work. How accurate has your partner been in depicting life as a woman or a man? As part of your paper, describe as well the discussion you and your partner have had over your day-in-the-life description.

You face challenges in completing this assignment: to imagine the *physical, emotional, psychological,* or *sexual* consequences of living as a member of the opposite sex. If you plan to take up more than one of these challenges in your description, you should do so in distinct stages, in an order that seems sensible to you.

Feel free to use the first person "I" in narrating your description—in which case the writing would read as a journal entry or letter. Alternately, you might feel more comfortable describing your "new" gender self from a distance—in which case you would use the third person "he" or "she."

9. Reflect on the household of your childhood and define the gender-role identities of your parent(s) or guardian(s). Once you've completed these definitions, comment on them, based on your reading in this chapter.

If a single individual raised you, consider how that person took to himself or herself both masculine and feminine roles. If two people raised you, examine the gender dynamics: Who worked outside the home? Who stayed in with the kids, mostly? What interests aside from work and family did your parents pursue, individually and together? What were the topics of conversation and how did these topics reveal (in retrospect) gender-role typing?

10. A variation on question 9. Consider a recent dating relationship of yours. As best you can, define the gender roles of you and your friend and then comment on these roles, based on your reading in this chapter.

11. Masters/Johnson/Kolodny discuss the social pressures brought to bear on individuals throughout their younger lives to conform to gender-specific identities. Use the observations of these authors to help recall your own gender-role socialization. How did you learn—through what process did you learn—to become the man or woman that you are?

At the beginning or end of your paper, you'll need to describe your present gender identity. (What sort of male or female do you see yourself as being—how traditionally assertive, intuitive, emotional, etc.?) Your tracing of your gender-role socialization (the part of the paper in which you identify and discuss stages of gender development) will either extend away from or build toward your characterization of your (present) gender identity.

## RESEARCH ACTIVITIES

1. Conduct your own survey of television commercials or prime-time shows to determine the extent to which advertisers and producers continue to depict men, women, and children in stereotyped roles. Although your analysis will not be as rigorous as a formal, sociological study, you nonetheless might profit from examining such studies found in issues of these journals: *Journal of Communication, Sex Roles, Journal of Broadcasting*, and *Journalism Quarterly*. If possible, begin with the much-cited 1977 study published by the U.S. Commission on Civil Rights: "Window Dressing on the Set: Women and Minorities in Television."

   Those who investigate gender-role portrayals on television devise a rating scheme according to which they "code" or analyze these portrayals. You should do the same. Two items on your rating scheme might be (1) the number of men or women in an ad or show and (2) the professions of male and female actors. You would add other items to your scheme. Once you determine what you wish to study (ads or shows) and how often, conduct your study and write a report consisting of four parts: (1) a discussion of what you expected to find, based on readings in this chapter; (2) an account of your method, including a copy of your rating scheme; (3) a summary of your results; and (4) a discussion of your results in the context of any two or three selections in this chapter.

2. Research the literature of the men's movement and write a paper in which you (1) explain to readers what important themes have emerged from the movement over the past ten years and (2) take a stand with respect to one or more of these themes. Following are several sources you might want to consult: *Utne Reader* (May/June 1991); *Men's Studies Review; Fire in the Belly: On Being a Man,* by Sam Keen (1991); *Iron John,* by Robert Bly (1991); *The Liberated Man* (1975) and *Why Men Are the Way They Are* (1986), by Warren Farrell; and *How Men Feel,* by Anthony Astrachan (1986).

3. Culturally accepted definitions of masculinity change from culture to culture and, over time, within individual cultures. Investigate what it has meant to "be a man" in American culture over the past 250 years. Write a paper showing the changing definitions, and explain the reasons for those changes. Following are several sources you might want to consult: *The Making of Masculinities,* by Harry Brod, ed. (1987); *The Changing Definition of Masculinity,* by Clyde W. Franklin II (1984); *A Man's Place,* by Joe L. Dubbert (1979); and *Be a Man!* by Peter N. Stearns (1979).

4. In her *Future of Marriage* (1972 and 1982, revised ed.), Jessie Bernard argues that every marriage in fact consists of two marriages—one perceived by the wife and one by the husband. Bernard generated controversy by claiming that marriage was more beneficial to men than to women: "There is a very considerable research literature . . . which shows that: more wives than husbands report marital frustration and dissatisfaction; more report negative feelings; more wives than husbands report marital problems; more wives than husbands consider their marriages unhappy, have considered separation or divorce, have regretted their marriages; and fewer report positive companionship" (26–27, 1982 ed.). Research the literature on the relative happiness of American men and women, both married and unmarried, and write a paper in which you summarize and explain the significance of your findings.

5. Many men and women advocate an *androgynous* identity (*androgyny,* from the Greek for *male* and *female*). Androgynous men and women, abandoning traditional gender roles, draw on the full range of human emotional response—without fear of being labeled inappropriately masculine or feminine. Androgynous men feel free to express intimacy; androgynous women show aggression or leadership skills without contradicting their identities as women. Many people aspire to an androgynous, as opposed to a masculine or feminine, identity. Research the general topic of androgyny and define for yourself a specific question you would like to answer. In a paper, explore the ways in which modern social, political, or economic conventions might change if more people in our culture adopted an androgynous identity.

6. Betty Friedan's *The Feminine Mystique* (1963) is universally cited as a key work in modern feminist literature. Read Friedan's book and as many reviews of it as you can find. Seek out both contemporary reviews (i.e., written at or shortly after publication) and later reviews, which have the advantage of perspective that earlier reviews do not. Write a paper on the history of the book's reception and, in the context of this history, write your own review of *The Feminine Mystique.*

7. Make a study of children's toys or books. To what extent do manufacturers and publishers reflect in their products the changing gender roles of men and women in contemporary America? After your study of the toys or books, find the *Social Science Index* in your library and look for studies on these topics as they relate to sex-role stereotyping. In a paper, synthesize your own observations of children's toys or books with the studies and articles that you find.

8. Advertisers are adept at making a given product appeal to men or women, depending on market analysis. The same cigarette, for instance, can be marketed to one sex or the other for reasons having nothing to do with the cigarette itself. Investigate the ways in which advertisers entice women and men to buy perfume and cologne. How does gender stereotyping play a role in these advertisements? Once you have completed your study, locate articles on the topic in popular magazines and journals. In a research paper, synthesize your own observations of these advertisements with your conclusion about the literature you have read.

# 12

# THE BRAVE NEW WORLD
# OF BIOTECHNOLOGY

As recently as fifty years ago, the world was plagued by devastating food
shortages and by numerous physical and mental diseases. Hundreds of millions
of people suffered blighted lives and early deaths. Today, all that has changed.
Using our gene splicing techniques, we can dramatically increase agricultural
yields and protect our crops from frost and other blights. And since we know
exactly what sequence of genetic information is necessary to produce perfect
people, we can make sure that all humans are born without defect by examining
their genetic makeup while they are still fetuses and correcting any abnormalities we find.

This is a paragraph from an imaginary textbook of the future. It paints a rosy picture
of what the most avid proponents of biotechnology view as our future prospects.
Of course, the future may not be so bright. Some believe that one of our genetic
legacies to the future may be an enhanced ability to fight biological wars. And as
for "perfect" people—just what would we mean by "imperfect"? (A fetus carrying
a gene for schizophrenia? A fetus with only one arm? A fetus likely to have lower
than average intelligence?) And who is to determine what is "perfect"?

The moral dilemmas now enveloping biotechnology would not be so hotly
debated if the technology itself were not so remarkable—and effective. Thanks
to its successes so far—in making possible, for instance, the cheap and plentiful
production of such disease-fighting agents as insulin and interferon—numerous
people have been able to live longer and healthier lives. Its promise in improved
agricultural production is exciting. And even without considering the practical
consequences, we have the prospect of a new world of knowledge about life
itself and the essential components of our own humanity, our own individuality,
as revealed in our distinctive genetic codes.

The authors would like to thank Louise Clarke, professor of biochemistry and genetics at the
University of California, Santa Barbara, for her assistance in clarifying certain technical concepts
used in this chapter.

What is biotechnology? Specifically, it is "the use of microorganisms, plant cells, animal cells or other parts of cells—such as enzymes—to make products or carry out processes" (Monsanto Co. pamphlet). In the public mind, however, the term has a looser meaning (one that we will adopt in this chapter): the use of technology in the pursuit and application of genetic knowledge. Probably the most well-known component of biotechnology is *genetic engineering.* (Others we'll discuss below include genetic testing and the Human Genome Project.) The foundation of genetic engineering was laid in 1953 when James Watson, an American, and Francis Crick, a Briton, published a landmark article in the scientific journal *Nature,* revealing for the first time the double-helix structure of the DNA molecule—the basis of all life. Genes—sequences of nucleic acids—are formed out of DNA. The particular and distinctive sequence of nucleic acids in the gene (part of the organism's "genetic code") determines its function and characteristics. Genes carry information not only about physical characteristics but also about how the organism will progress through its life cycle; and, just as important, they are the basis of the hereditary information that is transmitted from one generation to another.

Genetic engineering is essentially a kind of crossbreeding at the genetic level. It is sometimes called "gene splicing" because the process involves isolating and removing a gene with a certain desired function (e.g., that of generating a particular antibody) from the cell of one organism and then "splicing" it into the genetic material (lacking this desired function) of a second organism. The spliced DNA is then reinserted into the cell of the second organism. When the "engineered" cell divides, the new cells contain the desired genetic information, and so the physical characteristics of the host organism will change, according to its new genetic instructions.

Gene splicing experiments began in the early 1970s, at first involving DNA exchanges between unicellular organisms, such as viruses and bacteria. But recipients of "foreign" DNA soon included more complex organisms, such as fruit flies and frogs (although no humans, at this stage). During this early period of experimentation, some began to worry about the possibility of a genetic disaster. What if some newly engineered microbes escaped from the lab and caused an epidemic of a new and unknown disease, for which there was no known cure? What if the delicate ecological balance of nature or the course of evolution were drastically affected? (Fears of DNA experimentation gone haywire were expertly—and thrillingly—exploited by Michael Crichton's book (and Steven Speilberg's movie) *Jurassic Park,* in which a new race of rampaging dinosaurs is cloned from ancient DNA, and spliced with frog DNA.) Some proposed an outright ban on genetic engineering experiments. At an international conference in Asilomar, California, in 1975, scientists agreed on a set of guidelines to govern future research.

In time, these early fears turned out to be groundless, and the restrictions were eased or lifted. Meantime, considerable strides were made in genetic engineering, with new applications discovered in agriculture, pollution control, and the fight against a host of diseases. Genetic engineering became big business, as many scientists abandoned the academy to found and work for firms with names like Genentech and Genex.

But reservations persist. Some are uncomfortable with the fact of genetic engineering itself, considering it an unwarranted intrusion by human beings into the fragile structure of Nature, with too little knowledge or care about the consequences. Others have no philosophical objections to genetic engineering but worry about its effects on the environment and on humans. For some, however, gene splicing is not the only troublesome aspect of biotechnology. Another is the *genetic testing* of human cells to determine the existence of genetic abnormalities. Based on the results of such testing, prospective parents may choose to abort fetuses; employers may deny employment and insurers may refuse to issue policies to people they consider bad risks. Still another area of concern is the *Human Genome Project,* a massive scientific undertaking begun in the late 1980s (and directed by James Watson) to determine the complete genetic makeup of human chromosomes. Some believe that the knowledge gained from this project could lead to eugenics programs. Armed with the knowledge of what each gene does and where it is located, scientists (it is feared) would be able to manipulate human cells to create humans with qualities considered desirable, while eliminating qualities considered undesirable. For many, such possibilities bring to mind the notorious Nazi eugenics programs aimed at exalting an Aryan "master race" and exterminating "inferior" races.

For most, perhaps, the problem is not so much biotechnology itself as its possible abuses. As *Time* writer Philip Elmer-Dewitt notes, "To unlock the secrets hidden in the chromosomes of human cells is to open up a host of thorny legal, ethical, philosophical and religious issues, from invasion of privacy to the question of who should play God with men's genes." Some of these thorny issues are explored in the following pages. Our first passage is the opening chapter of Aldous Huxley's dystopian novel *Brave New World,* which for more than sixty years has served as an unforgettable warning of the dark side of scientific "progress." Here we see human ova fertilized outside the womb and conditioned before birth so that they eventually will serve as productive and contented citizens in a stable society. A more positive (non-fictional) view of biotechnology follows in Ann C. Vickery's "Gene Science," which explains the mechanics of genetic engineering and the current priorities of gene science. Following, Dennis Chamberland's "Genetic Engineering: Promise and Threat" surveys the chief advantages and ethical dilemmas of this new technology. Next we hear from perhaps the chief opponent of genetic engineering—activist Jeremy Rifkin, who has successfully blocked a number of bioengineering programs. Following, biologist Stephen Jay Gould launches a blistering attack on Rifkin's book *Algeny.* In "Killing Us Softly: Toward a Feminist Analysis of Genetic Engineering," Linda Bullard argues that biotechnology is inherently a eugenics program (devoted to the creation of "good" genes and the elimination of "bad" ones) promoted by a patriarchal male power structure. A countervailing positive (and personal) view of gene therapy is next offered by former opera singer Beverly Sills Greenough. The final set of articles deal with the Human Genome Project and the potential abuse of genetic information and genetic testing. In "The Gene Hunt," *Time* staff writer Leon Jaroff explains what is involved in the Human Genome Project and discusses its potential benefits. In "The Human Genome Project: A Personal View," James D. Watson, co-discoverer of DNA's helical structure, defends the genome project from adversaries and skeptics and argues its potential role in helping us to understand and combat diseases. In "Achilles Helix," Robert Wright, focusing on what he calls "homemade eugenics," discusses the kind of dilemmas we are likely to face when Huxley's *Brave New World* becomes a near reality. Finally, in "The Genetic Labyrinth," Daniel J. Kevles and Leroy Hood focus on the misuse of genetic information by insurers and employers.

# Brave New World

## ALDOUS HUXLEY

*The title of Aldous Huxley's novel* Brave New World *derives from a line in Shakespeare's final comedy,* The Tempest. *Miranda is a young woman who has grown up on an enchanted island; her father is the only other human she has known. When she suddenly encounters people from the outside world (including a handsome young prince), she remarks, "O brave [wondrous] new world that has such people in it!" Shakespeare used the line ironically (the world of* The Tempest *is filled with knaves and fools); and almost three hundred years later, Huxley employed not only the language but also the irony in labeling his nightmare society of A.F. 632 (After [Henry] Ford).*

*In comparison with other dystopias, like George Orwell's* 1984, *Huxley's brave new world of creature comforts seems, at first glance, a paradise. People are given whatever they need to keep happy: unlimited sex, tranquilizers, and soothing experiences. No one goes hungry; no one suffers either physical or spiritual pain. But the cost of such comfort is an almost total loss of individuality, creativity, and freedom. Uniformity and stability are exalted above all other virtues. The population is divided into castes, determined from before birth, with the more intelligent Alphas and Betas governing and managing the society, while the less intelligent Deltas, Gammas, and Epsilons work at the menial tasks. Epsilons are not unhappy with their lot in life because they have been conditioned to be content; and, in fact, they are incapable of conceiving anything better. Love, art, and science are suppressed for all castes because they lead to instability, and instability threatens happiness. Idle reflection is discouraged for the same reason; and, to avoid the effects of any intense emotions, positive or negative, the inhabitants of brave new world are given regular doses of the powerful tranquilizer "soma."*

*Huxley's brave new world, then, is a projection into the future of tendencies he saw in his own world that he thought were disturbing or dangerous. In the context of our present chapter on biotechnology, we are most interested in Huxley's portrait of a "hatchery," where fertilized human ova—removed from the womb—are programmed before "birth" to produce an assortment of the kind of people who will be most desirable to society. In the following passage, the first chapter of* Brave New World *(1932), we are taken on a tour through the Central London Hatchery and Conditioning Centre, where we follow an egg from fertilization through conditioning. To many people today, Huxley's dramatic portrait of the manipulation of human germ cells is uncomfortably close to what modern genetic engineers are beginning, with ever greater facility, to make possible: the substitution of "more desirable" for "less desirable" genes in order to create "better" people.*

*Born in Surrey, England, Aldous Huxley (1894–1963), grandson of naturalist T. H. Huxley, intended to pursue a medical career; but after being stricken with a corneal disease that left him almost blind, he turned to literature. Among his works are* Crome Yellow *(1921),* Antic Hay *(1923),* Point Counterpoint *(1928), and* Eyeless in Gaza *(1936). Huxley moved to the United States in 1936, settling in California. In the latter part of his life, he tended toward the mystical and experimented with naturally occurring hallucinogenic drugs—the subject of his* Doors of Perception *(1954).*

A squat grey building of only thirty-four stories. Over the main entrance the words, CENTRAL LONDON HATCHERY AND CONDITIONING CENTRE, and, in a shield, the World State's motto, COMMUNITY, IDENTITY, STABILITY.     1

The enormous room on the ground floor faced towards the north.     2
Cold for all the summer beyond the panes, for all the tropical heat of the room itself, a harsh thin light glared through the windows, hungrily seeking some draped lay figure, some pallid shape of academic gooseflesh, but finding only the glass and nickel and bleakly shining porcelain of a laboratory. Wintriness responded to wintriness. The overalls of the workers were white, their hands gloved with a pale corpse-coloured rubber. The light was frozen, dead, a ghost. Only from the yellow barrels of the microscopes did it borrow a certain rich and living substance, lying along the polished tubes like butter, streak after luscious streak in long recession down the work tables.

"And this," said the Director opening the door, "is the Fertilizing Room." 3

Bent over their instruments, three hundred Fertilizers were plunged, 4 as the Director of Hatcheries and Conditioning entered the room, in the scarcely breathing silence, the absent-minded, soliloquizing hum or whistle, of absorbed concentration. A troop of newly arrived students, very young, pink and callow, followed nervously, rather abjectly, at the Director's heels. Each of them carried a notebook, in which, whenever the great man spoke, he desperately scribbled. Straight from the horse's mouth. It was a rare privilege. The D.H.C. for Central London always made a point of personally conducting his new students round the various departments.

"Just to give you a general idea," he would explain to them. For of 5 course some sort of general idea they must have, if they were to do their work intelligently—though as little of one, if they were to be good and happy members of society, as possible. For particulars, as every one knows, make for virtue and happiness; generalities are intellectually necessary evils. Not philosophers but fret-sawyers and stamp collectors compose the backbone of society.

"To-morrow," he would add, smiling at them with a slightly menac- 6 ing geniality, "you'll be settling down to serious work. You won't have time for generalities. Meanwhile . . ."

Meanwhile, it was a privilege. Straight from the horse's mouth into 7 the notebook. The boys scribbled like mad.

Tall and rather thin but upright, the Director advanced into the 8 room. He had a long chin and big, rather prominent teeth, just covered, when he was not talking, by his full, floridly curved lips. Old, young? Thirty? Fifty? Fifty-five? It was hard to say. And anyhow the question didn't arise; in this year of stability, A.F. 632, it didn't occur to you to ask it.

"I shall begin at the beginning," said the D.H.C. and the more 9 zealous students recorded his intention in their notebooks: *Begin at the beginning.* "These," he waved his hand, "are the incubators." And open- ing an insulated door he showed them racks upon racks of numbered test-tubes. "The week's supply of ova. Kept," he explained, "at blood heat; whereas the male gametes," and here he opened another door, "they have to be kept at thirty-five instead of thirty-seven. Full blood heat sterilizes." Rams wrapped in theremogene beget no lambs.

Still leaning against the incubators he gave them, while the pencils 10 scurried illegibly across the pages, a brief description of the modern fertilizing process; spoke first, of course, of its surgical introduction— "the operation undergone voluntarily for the good of Society, not to mention the fact that it carries a bonus amounting to six months' salary";

continued with some account of the technique for preserving the excised ovary alive and actively developing; passed on to a consideration of optimum temperature, salinity, viscosity; referred to the liquor in which the detached and ripened eggs were kept; and, leading his charges to the work tables, actually showed them how this liquor was drawn off from the test-tubes; how it was let out drop by drop onto the specially warmed slides of the microscopes; how the eggs which it contained were inspected for abnormalities, counted and transferred to a porous receptacle; how (and he now took them to watch the operation) this receptacle was immersed in a warm bouillon containing free-swimming spermatozoa—at a minimum concentration of one hundred thousand per cubic centimetre, he insisted; and how, after ten minutes, the container was lifted out of the liquor and its contents re-examined; how, if any of the eggs remained unfertilized, it was again immersed, and, if necessary, yet again; how the fertilized ova went back to the incubators; where the Alphas and Betas remained until definitely bottled; while the Gammas, Deltas and Epsilons were brought out again, after only thirty-six hours, to undergo Bokanovsky's Process.

"Bokanovsky's Process," repeated the Director, and the students    11
underlined the words in their little notebooks.

One egg, one embryo, one adult—normality. But a bokanovskified    12
egg will bud, will proliferate, will divide. From eight to ninety-six buds, and every bud will grow into a perfectly formed embryo, and every embryo into a full-sized adult. Making ninety-six human beings grow where only one grew before. Progress.

"Essentially," the D.H.C. concluded, "bokanovskification consists of    13
a series of arrests of development. We check the normal growth and, paradoxically enough, the egg responds by budding."

*Responds by budding.* The pencils were busy.    14

He pointed. On a very slowly moving band a rack-full of test-tubes    15
was entering a large metal box, another rack-full was emerging. Machinery faintly purred. It took eight minutes for the tubes to go through, he told them. Eight minutes of hard X-rays being about as much as an egg can stand. A few died; of the rest, the least susceptible divided into two; most put out four buds; some eight; all were returned to the incubators, where the buds began to develop; then, after two days, were suddenly chilled, chilled and checked. Two, four, eight, the buds in their turn budded; and having budded were dosed almost to death with alcohol; consequently burgeoned again and having budded—bud out of bud out of bud—were thereafter—further arrest being generally fatal—left to develop in peace. By which time the original egg was in a fair way to becoming anything from eight to ninety-six embryos—a prodigious improvement, you will agree, on nature. Identical twins—but not in

piddling twos and threes as in the old viviparous days, when an egg would sometimes accidentally divide; actually by dozens, by scores at a time.

"Scores," the Director repeated and flung out his arms, as though he were distributing largesse. "Scores." 16

But one of the students was fool enough to ask where the advantage lay. 17

"My good boy!" The Director wheeled sharply round on him. "Can't you see? Can't you *see?*" He raised a hand; his expression was solemn. "Bokanovsky's Process is one of the major instruments of social stability!" 18

*Major instruments of social stability.* 19

Standard men and women; in uniform batches. The whole of a small factory staffed with the products of a single bokanovskified egg. 20

"Ninety-six identical twins working ninety-six identical machines!" The voice was almost tremulous with enthusiasm. "You really know where you are. For the first time in history." He quoted the planetary motto. "Community, Identity, Stability." Grand words. "If we could bokanovskify indefinitely the whole problem would be solved." 21

Solved by standard Gammas, unvarying Deltas, uniform Epsilons. Millions of identical twins. The principle of mass production at last applied to biology. 22

"But, alas," the Director shook his head, "we *can't* bokanovskify indefinitely." 23

Ninety-six seemed to be the limit; seventy-two a good average. From the same ovary and with gametes of the same male to manufacture as many batches of identical twins as possible—that was the best (sadly a second best) that they could do. And even that was difficult. 24

"For in nature it takes thirty years for two hundred eggs to reach maturity. But our business is to stabilize the population at this moment, here and now. Dribbling out twins over a quarter of a century—what would be the use of that?" 25

Obviously, no use at all. But Podsnap's Technique had immensely accelerated the process of ripening. They could make sure of at least a hundred and fifty mature eggs within two years. Fertilize and bokanovskify—in other words, multiply by seventy-two—and you get an average of nearly eleven thousand brothers and sisters in a hundred and fifty batches of identical twins, all within two years of the same age. 26

"And in exceptional cases we can make one ovary yield us over fifteen thousand adult individuals." 27

Beckoning to a fair-haired, ruddy young man who happened to be passing at the moment, "Mr. Foster," he called. The ruddy young man approached. "Can you tell us the record for a single ovary, Mr. Foster?" 28

"Sixteen thousand and twelve in this Centre," Mr. Foster replied 29 without hesitation. He spoke very quickly, had a vivacious blue eye, and took an evident pleasure in quoting figures. "Sixteen thousand and twelve; in one hundred and eighty-nine batches of identicals. But of course they've done much better," he rattled on, "in some of the tropical Centres. Singapore had often produced over sixteen thousand five hundred; and Mombasa has actually touched the seventeen thousand mark. But then they have unfair advantages. You should see the way a negro ovary responds to pituitary! It's quite astonishing, when you're used to working with European material. Still," he added, with a laugh (but the light of combat was in his eyes and the lift of his chin was challenging), "still, we mean to beat them if we can. I'm working on a wonderful Delta-Minus ovary at this moment. Only just eighteen months old. Over twelve thousand seven hundred children already, either decanted or in embryo. And still going strong. We'll beat them yet."

"That's the spirit I like!" cried the Director, and clapped Mr. Foster on the shoulder. "Come along with us and give these boys the benefit of your expert knowledge." 30

Mr. Foster smiled modestly. "With pleasure." They went. 31

In the Bottling Room all was harmonious bustle and ordered activity. Flaps of fresh sow's peritoneum ready cut to the proper size came shooting up in little lifts from the Organ Store in the subbasement. Whizz and then, click! the lift-hatches flew open; the bottle-liner had only to reach out a hand, take the flap, insert, smooth-down, and before the lined bottle had had time to travel out of reach along the endless band, whizz, click! another flap of peritoneum had shot up from the depths, ready to be slipped into yet another bottle, the next of that slow interminable procession on the band. 32

Next to the Liners stood the Matriculators. The procession advanced; one by one the eggs were transferred from their test-tubes to the larger containers; deftly the peritoneal lining was slit, the morula dropped into place, the saline solution poured in . . . and already the bottle had passed, and it was the turn of the labellers. Heredity, date of fertilization, membership of Bokanovsky Group—details were transferred from test-tube to bottle. No longer anonymous, but named, identified, the procession marched slowly on; on through an opening in the wall, slowly on into the Social Predestination Room. 33

"Eighty-eight cubic metres of card-index," said Mr. Foster with relish, as they entered. 34

"Containing *all* the relevant information," added the Director. 35

"Brought up to date every morning." 36

"And co-ordinated every afternoon." 37

"On the basis of which they make their calculations." 38

"So many individuals, of such and such quality," said Mr. Foster. 39

"Distributed in such and such quantities." 40

"The optimum Decanting Rate at any given moment." 41

"Unforeseen wastages promptly made good." 42

"Promptly," repeated Mr. Foster. "If you knew the amount of over- 43
time I had to put in after the last Japanese earthquake!" He laughed
good-humouredly and shook his head.

"The Predestinators send in their figures to the Fertilizers." 44

"Who give them the embryos they ask for." 45

"And the bottles come in here to be predestinated in detail." 46

"After which they are sent down to the Embryo Store." 47

"Where we now proceed ourselves." 48

And opening a door Mr. Foster led the way down a staircase into 49
the basement.

The temperature was still tropical. They descended into a thickening 50
twilight. Two doors and a passage with a double turn insured the cellar
against any possible infiltration of the day.

"Embryos are like photograph film," said Mr. Foster waggishly, as 51
he pushed open the second door. "They can only stand red light."

And in effect the sultry darkness into which the students now 52
followed him was visible and crimson, like the darkness of closed eyes
on a summer's afternoon. The bulging flanks of row on receding row and
tier above tier of bottles glinted with innumerable rubies, and among the
rubies moved the dim red spectres of men and women with purple eyes
and all the symptoms of lupus. The hum and rattle of machinery faintly
stirred the air.

"Give them a few figures, Mr. Foster," said the Director, who was 53
tired of talking.

Mr. Foster was only too happy to give them a few figures. 54

Two hundred and twenty metres long, two hundred wide, ten high. 55
He pointed upwards. Like chickens drinking, the students lifted their
eyes towards the distant ceiling.

Three tiers of racks: ground floor level, first gallery, second gallery. 56

The spidery steel-work of gallery above gallery faded away in all 57
directions into the dark. Near them three red ghosts were busily unload-
ing demijohns from a moving staircase.

The escalator from the Social Predestination Room. 58

Each bottle could be placed on one of fifteen racks, each rack, though 59
you couldn't see it, was a conveyor travelling at the rate of thirty-three
and a third centimetres an hour. Two hundred and sixty-seven days at
eight metres a day. Two thousand one hundred and thirty-six metres in
all. One circuit of the cellar at ground level, one on the first gallery, half
on the second, and on the two hundred and sixty-seventh morning,
daylight in the Decanting Room. Independent existence—so called.

"But in the interval," Mr. Foster concluded, "we've managed to do 60 a lot to them. Oh, a very great deal." His laugh was knowing and triumphant.

"That's the spirit I like," said the Director once more. "Let's walk round. You tell them everything, Mr. Foster." 61

Mr. Foster duly told them. 62

Told them of the growing embryo on its bed of peritoneum. Made 63 them taste the rich blood surrogate on which it fed. Explained why it had to be stimulated with placentin and thyroxin. Told them of the *corpus luteum* extract. Showed them the jets through which at every twelfth metre from zero to 2040 it was automatically injected. Spoke of those gradually increasing doses of pituitary administered during the final ninety-six metres of their course. Described the artificial maternal circulation installed on every bottle at Metre 112; showed them the reservoir of blood-surrogate, the centrifugal pump that kept the liquid moving over the placenta and drove it through the synthetic lung and waste-product filter. Referred to the embryo's troublesome tendency to anæmia, to the massive doses of hog's stomach extract and fetal foal's liver with which, in consequence, it had to be supplied.

Showed them, the simple mechanism by means of which, during the 64 last two metres out of every eight, all the embryos were simultaneously shaken into familiarity with movement. Hinted at the gravity of the so-called "trauma of decanting," and enumerated the precautions taken to minimize, by a suitable training of the bottled embryo, that dangerous shock. Told them of the tests for sex carried out in the neighbourhood of metre 200. Explained the system of labelling—a T for the males, a circle for the females and for those who were destined to become freemartins a question mark, black on a white ground.

"For of course," said Mr. Foster, "in the vast majority of cases, 65 fertility is merely a nuisance. One fertile ovary in twelve hundred—that would really be quite sufficient for our purposes. But we want to have a good choice. And of course one must always leave an enormous margin of safety. So we allow as many as thirty per cent of the female embryos to develop normally. The others get a dose of male sex-hormone every twenty-four metres for the rest of the course. Result: they're decanted as freemartins—structurally quite normal ("except," he had to admit, "that they *do* have just the slightest tendency to grow beards), but sterile. Guaranteed sterile. Which brings us at last," continued Mr. Foster, "out of the realm of mere slavish imitation of nature into the much more interesting world of human invention."

He rubbed his hands. For of course, they didn't content themselves 66 with merely hatching out embryos: any cow could do that.

"We also predestine and condition. We decant our babies as social- 67 ized human beings, as Alphas or Epsilons, as future sewage workers or future . . ." He was going to say "future World controllers," but correcting himself, said "future Directors of Hatcheries," instead.

The D.H.C. acknowledged the compliment with a smile. 68

They were passing Metre 320 on rack 11. A young Beta-Minus 69 mechanic was busy with screwdriver and spanner on the blood-surrogate pump of a passing bottle. The hum of the electric motor deepened by fractions of a tone as he turned the nuts. Down, down . . . A final twist, a glance at the revolution counter, and he was done. He moved two paces down the line and began the same process on the next pump.

"Reducing the number of revolutions per minute," Mr. Foster ex- 70 plained. "The surrogate goes round slower; therefore passes through the lung at longer intervals; therefore gives the embryo less oxygen. Nothing like oxygen-shortage for keeping an embryo below par." Again he rubbed his hands.

"But why do you want to keep the embryo below par?" asked an 71 ingenuous student.

"Ass!" said the Director, breaking a long silence. "Hasn't it occurred 72 to you that an Epsilon embryo must have an Epsilon environment as well as an Epsilon heredity?"

It evidently hadn't occurred to him. He was covered with confusion. 73

"The lower the caste," said Mr. Foster, "the shorter the oxygen." 74 The first organ affected was the brain. After that the skeleton. At seventy per cent of normal oxygen you got dwarfs. At less than seventy eyeless monsters.

"Who are no use at all," concluded Mr. Foster. 75

Whereas (his voice became confidential and eager), if they could 76 discover a technique for shortening the period of maturation what a triumph, what a benefaction to Society!

"Consider the horse." 77

They considered it. 78

Mature at six; the elephant at ten. While at thirteen a man is not yet 79 sexually mature; and is only full-grown at twenty. Hence, of course, that fruit of delayed development, the human intelligence.

"But in Epsilons," said Mr. Foster very justly, "we don't need human 80 intelligence."

Didn't need and didn't get it. But though the Epsilon mind was 81 mature at ten, the Epsilon body was not fit to work till eighteen. Long years of superfluous and wasted immaturity. If the physical development could be speeded up till it was as quick, say, as a cow's what an enormous saving to the Community!

"Enormous!" murmured the students. Mr. Foster's enthusiasm was 82 infectious.

He became rather technical; spoke of the abnormal endocrine co- 83 ordination which made men grow so slowly; postulated a germinal mutation to account for it. Could the effects of this germinal mutation be undone? Could the individual Epsilon embryo be made a revert, by a suitable technique, to the normality of dogs and cows? That was the problem. And it was all but solved.

Pilkington, at Mombasa, had produced individuals who were sexu- 84 ally mature at four and full-grown at six and a half. A scientific triumph. But socially useless. Six-year-old men and women were too stupid to do even Epsilon work. And the process was an all-or-nothing one; either you failed to modify at all, or else you modified the whole way. They were still trying to find the ideal compromise between adults of twenty and adults of six. So far without success. Mr. Foster sighed and shook his head.

Their wanderings through the crimson twilight had brought them 85 to the neighbourhood of Metre 170 on Rack 9. From this point onwards Rack 9 was enclosed and the bottles performed the remainder of their journey in a kind of tunnel, interrupted here and there by openings two or three metres wide.

"Heat conditioning," said Mr. Foster. 86

Hot tunnels alternated with cool tunnels. Coolness was wedded to 87 discomfort in the form of hard X-rays. By the time they were decanted the embryos had a horror of cold. They were predestined to emigrate to the tropics, to be miners and acetate silk spinners and steel workers. Later on their minds would be made to endorse the judgment of their bodies. "We condition them to thrive on heat," concluded Mr. Foster. "Our colleagues upstairs will teach them to love it."

"And that," put in the Director sententiously, "that is the secret of 88 happiness and virtue—liking what you've *got* to do. All conditioning aims at that: making people like their unescapable social destiny."

In a gap between two tunnels, a nurse was delicately probing with 89 a long fine syringe into the gelatinous contents of a passing bottle. The students and their guides stood watching her for a few moments in silence.

"Well, Lenina," said Mr. Foster, when at last she withdrew the 90 syringe and straightened herself up.

The girl turned with a start. One could see that, for all the lupus and 91 the purple eyes, she was uncommonly pretty.

"Henry!" Her smile flashed redly at him—a row of coral teeth. 92

"Charming, charming," murmured the Director and, giving her two 93 or three little pats, received in exchange a rather deferential smile for himself.

"What are you giving them?" asked Mr. Foster, making his tone 94 very professional.

"Oh, the usual typhoid and sleeping sickness."                                      95

"Tropical workers start being inoculated at Metre 150," Mr. Foster    96
explained to the students. "The embryos still have gills. We immunize
the fish against the future man's diseases." Then, turning back to Lenina,
"Ten to five on the roof this afternoon," he said, "as usual."

"Charming," said the Director once more, and, with a final pat,     97
moved away after the others.

On Rack 10 rows of next generation's chemical workers were being     98
trained in the toleration of lead, caustic soda, tar, chlorine. The first of
a batch of two hundred and fifty embryonic rocket-plane engineers was
just passing the eleven hundred metre mark on Rack 3. A special
mechanism kept their containers in constant rotation. "To improve their
sense of balance," Mr. Foster explained. "Doing repairs on the outside
of a rocket in mid-air is a ticklish job. We slacken off the circulation when
they're right way up, so that they're half starved, and double the flow
of surrogate when they're upside down. They learn to associate topsy-
turvydom with well-being; in fact, they're only truly happy when
they're standing on their heads.

"And now," Mr. Foster went on, "I'd like to show you some very     99
interesting conditioning for Alpha Plus Intellectuals. We have a big
batch of them on Rack 5. First Gallery level," he called to two boys who
had started to go down to the ground floor.

"They're round about Metre 900," he explained. "You can't really    100
do any useful intellectual conditioning till the fetuses have lost their tails.
Follow me."

But the Director had looked at his watch. "Ten to three," he said.   101
"No time for the intellectual embryos, I'm afraid. We must go up to the
Nurseries before the children have finished their afternoon sleep."

Mr. Foster was disappointed. "At least one glance at the Decanting   102
Room," he pleaded.

"Very well then." The Director smiled indulgently. "Just one     103
glance."

## Review Questions

1. What is the Bokanovsky Process? Why is it central to Huxley's "brave new
   world"?
2. How does Huxley comment sardonically on the racism of the Hatchery's
   personnel—and of Europeans, in general?
3. What is the difference—and the social significance of the difference—among Alphas, Betas, Deltas, Gammas, and Epsilons?
4. What technological problems concerning the maturation process have the
   scientists of brave new world still not solved?

## Discussion and Writing Suggestions

1. How does the language of the first two paragraphs reveal Huxley's tone, that is, his attitude toward his subject? For example, what is the function of the word "only" in the opening sentence: "A squat grey building of only thirty-four stories"? Or the adjectives describing the building?

2. What does the narrator mean when he says (paragraph 5) that "particulars, as every one knows, make for virtue and happiness; generalities are intellectually necessary evils. Not philosophers but fret-sawyers [operators of fret-saws, long, narrow, fine-toothed hand saws used for ornamental detail work] and stamp collectors compose the backbone of society"? To what extent do you believe that such an ethic operates in our own society? Give examples of the relatively low value placed on "philosophers" and the relatively high value placed on "fret-sawyers."

3. Throughout this chapter, Huxley makes an implied contrast between the brisk, technological efficiency of the Hatchery and the ethical nature of what takes place within its walls. What aspects of our own civilization show similar contrasts? (Example: We are now able to build more technologically sophisticated weapons of destruction than ever before in history.) Explore this subject in an essay, devoting a paragraph or so to each aspect of our civilization that you consider.

4. In the Hatchery, bottled, fertilized eggs pass into the "Social Predestination Room." In that room, their future lives will be determined. Is there an equivalent of the Social Predestination Room in our own society? (In other words, are there times and places when and where our future lives are determined?) If so, describe its features, devoting a paragraph to each of these features.

5. Foster explains how the undecanted embryos are conditioned to adapt to certain environments—for instance, conditioned to like heat so that, years later, they will feel comfortable working in the tropics or working as miners; or they may be conditioned to improve their sense of balance, so that they will be able to repair rockets in midair. What evidence do you see in our own society that people are or will be subject to conditioning to "like their unescapable social destiny"? Consider, for example, the influence of the conditioning exerted by parents, siblings, teachers, friends, or various social institutions. If you have lived or traveled abroad, what evidence do you see that conditioning in the United States is different from that in other countries? Explore this subject in a multiparagraph essay.

6. As we noted in the headnote, Huxley's Brave New World (like much science fiction) is a projection into the future of contemporary aspects of culture that the author finds disturbing or dangerous. Select some present aspect of our culture that *you* find disturbing or dangerous and—in the form of a short story, or chapter from a novel, or section from a screenplay—dramatize your vision of what *could* happen.

# Gene Science

## ANN C. VICKERY

*Many of the public policy dilemmas of our modern world—the use of nuclear weapons, for example, or the debate about when to "pull the plug" on persons near death—have arisen as a direct result of recent and often spectacular scientific breakthroughs. This is clearly true of genetic engineering, now considered one of the most revolutionary scientific achievements of the century. Much of our chapter will deal with various aspects of the public policy debate surrounding genetic engineering. But we thought it would be illuminating to precede these discussions with a scientific description of just what is entailed in this process.*

*In the following selection, reprinted from* Van Nostrand's Scientific Encyclopedia, *the author surveys the field of gene science, describing the current concerns of the field and some of its major achievements, as well as the procedures involved in genetic recombination. Although this article was intended primarily for an audience with some degree of scientific background, it is not overly technical and should present few difficulties for the general reader.*

*Ann C. Vickery is a professor in the College of Public Health at the University of South Florida.*

### GENE SCIENCE

In the field of biology, the study and manipulation of *genes* has received    1
the major emphasis throughout the 1980s. This intense interest and activity stems from a discovery made during the early 1970s that certain classes of enzymes have the ability to "cut and splice" hereditary material of living organisms in a precise, unprecedented manner. These *restriction* enzymes can be used to cut the long DNA molecules of living matter into what may be termed *manageable fragments*. Thus, for the first time in the long history of gene and hereditary research, it is possible to study genes in the laboratory by cutting them apart and reassembling (splicing) them in different ways. For lack of a better analogy, these recombinant procedures provide a "hands on" approach to genes, in contrast with depending largely upon theoretical abstractions. This burgeoning technology is *genetic recombination*, frequently referred to as *recombinant DNA*.

Excerpt from "Gene Science" from *Van Nostrand's Scientific Encyclopedia*, 7th Edition, edited by Douglas M. Considine, P.E. Copyright © 1989 by Van Nostrand Reinhold. Reprinted by permission of Van Nostrand Reinhold.

Throughout the 1980s, there have been advancements in labora-  2
tory procedures and research instrumentation to assist thousands of
scientists and technicians (affiliated with government, university, and
private facilities worldwide) who are engaged in gene research. Information on gene research from these large numbers of researchers has
flooded the literature. By the mid-1980s, the means for storing and
interpreting raw gene data became (and continues to be) one of the
major concerns in the field. Although instruments and computers have
alleviated the data problem on a small scale, a point was reached just
a few years ago where much greater sophistication was needed for
utilizing gene information in an orderly and prompt manner. The data
problem lies in two principal areas: (1) storage and retrievability of
gene data, which accumulate daily at a tremendous rate; and (2) sim-
plification and at least partial automation of laboratory work involved
in generating new information.

As early as 1982, two major gene databases were established—the  3
European database at Heidelberg (Germany) in connection with the
European Molecular Biology Laboratory (EMBL); and the U.S. National
Laboratories database, known as *GenBank*, at Los Alamos, New Mexico.[1] These are central repositories for information, not only regarding
human DNA, but also the DNA of bacteria, viruses, laboratory animals,
and agricultural plants among others. As of early 1987, the EMBL
contained more than 8 million bases; GenBank had over 12 million
bases, with an estimated rate of addition of 4 million bases per year.
GenBank thus is in the process of extending its service, including the
establishment of the Human Genome Information Resource, which features the most advanced state-of-the-art data handling equipment.

These repositories resemble what biologists have been doing for  4
decades (and continue to do) in terms of storing *natural* plant genetic materials in what are called *germ plasm banks.* In these banks, the emphasis has been on plant species that may be nearing extinction, but
whose properties may at some time contribute to creating improved crops . . . through natural hybridization techniques.

The most ambitious project in gene science, getting underway in the  5
late 1980s, is that of mapping and sequencing the complete *human
genome.*[2] The work proposed and the funding requirements predicted
are reminiscent of the post-Sputnik days of the space program. The

---

[1]Currently, the output of the Los Alamos flow-sorting and processing facilities is transferred to
the American Type Culture Collection in Rockville, Maryland. This facility is funded by the
National Institutes of Health. Samples are frozen in liquid nitrogen. It is estimated that over 300
laboratories use this service.

[2]A genome consists of all the genes carried by a single gamete, . . . , by the single representative
of all the chromosome pairs; sometimes used for the total chromosome content of any nucleus.

human genome is made up of an estimated 300,000 genes (an individual's set of chromosomes). To map and sequence 3 billion DNA base pairs[3] partitioned among 23 pairs of chromosomes represents a super-monumental task, one that has been roughly estimated to require a minimum of 10 years at a minimum cost of $50 million per year. Early time and cost predictions of projects like this are almost invariably low.

## Priorities in Gene Science

With funding and people power limitations, it follows that there are **6** differences of opinion as to where the effort during the next decade or two should be concentrated. What are the incentives for greatly accelerated gene research?

1. One very obvious benefit is that of finding ways to correct (and **7** prevent) inborn errors that are responsible for a host of genetic diseases in humans. An abridged list would include the Down, Ehlers-Danlos, Fanconi, Hunter, Hurler, Klinefelter, Marfan, Lesch-Nyhan, and Scheie syndromes, among others, as well as cystic fibrosis, phenylketonuria, alkaptonuria, osteogenesis imperfecta, the Tay-Sachs, Gaucher's, and Niemann-Pick diseases, plus many of the more common disorders that are suspected to be directly or indirectly related to gene structures—diabetes mellitus, goiter, gout, immunodeficiency diseases, muscular dystrophies, porphyrias, sickle cell anemia, renal tubular acidosis, Alzheimer's disease, and, of course, tumor proliferation (cancer). Much research, with some notable successes, has been proceeding along these lines.

2. Another benefit of gene research that can yield worldwide advan- **8** tages, particularly in terms of diet and alleviating famine, is the alteration of gene structures in plant crops to make them more resistant to environmental factors (frequently present in third world countries), such as greater resistance to insects, nematodes, bacteria, viruses, etc.; reduced requirements for nutrients from the soil; and increased endurance in extremes of climate, among other

---

[3]A base pair consists of two bases, a purine and a pyrimidine, which pair together in the genetic code of DNA and RNA. Cytosine pairs with guanine in both; adenine pairs with thymine in DNA and with uracil in RNA.

factors. Activity thus far in this area has been limited mainly to universities and private institutions that specialize in agricultural science.

3. Less active thus far, but promising, has been gene research on behalf    9
of improving industrial processes. For well over a century, industrial fermentation processes have depended upon natural microorganisms, which have both positive and negative attributes. Gene restructuring provides an opportunity for customizing such organisms to processing and product requirements.

In the United States, organizations supporting and/or conducting    10
gene research include the Department of Energy, the National Institutes of Health, the Howard Hughes Medical Institute, the National Science Foundation, and the National Academy of Sciences, among others. Similar sponsorship is found in a number of other countries, notably in Europe and Japan. As of 1988, there essentially are two schools of thought concerning public funding of gene research—those authorities who prefer to focus efforts on specific genetic diseases and others who support a massive effort to fully map the human genome as previously mentioned. The Japanese are planning to build a super-sequencer for DNA analysis capable of analyzing 1 million bases per day. Sequencing is a way of finding the exact order of the bases within a mapped gene. . . .

## RECOMBINANT DNA

### Mutations

New organisms in nature are normally created by very slow processes.    11
A change in the base sequence of the DNA constituting a gene results in an inherited alteration in the code and is called a *gene mutation.* Mutations are genetic changes which occur suddenly and are thereafter heritable.

Mutations arise through three general mechanisms: (1) chemical    12
modification of preformed DNA, such as breakage and aberrant reunion of molecules or the changes elicited by ultraviolet light, for example; (2) errors in incorporation of the purine and pyrimidine bases, or additions and subtractions of bases, during DNA replication; and (3) unequal exchange between two identical or similar DNA molecules

("unequal crossing over") during recombination. These chemical changes normally occur with low frequency (spontaneous mutations), but the frequency can be increased by means of various chemical and physical treatments (induced mutations). Even when so induced, the frequency of bacterial mutants for a particular trait, for example, is low, e.g., one mutant in $10^4$ to $10^{10}$ bacteria. Thus, any biological evolutionary alterations brought about by the mechanism of mutation represent a very slow pathway. Such procedures do not comprise effective tools for what has been referred to as *genetic engineering* (genetic manipulation) wherein gene structures can be willfully directed under laboratory conditions.

## Gene Splicing

In the early 1970s, an interesting observation of great significance to biologists, biochemists, molecular biologists, and related scientists was made, as previously mentioned: the discovery of certain enzymes that have the ability of cutting and splicing hereditary material. The cut pieces are approximately the order of a gene in length. Also, some of these enzymes have the further ability of cutting a few bases further down than the others, so that what sometimes are known as "sticky ends" are produced. Thus, any species of DNA, if cut by the same enzyme, will possess the same type of sticky ends, and fragments of differing DNAs, through a form of biological "scissors and paste" process, can cause the lower part of one DNA molecule to stick well onto the upper part of another molecule. The result is a hybrid molecule. Theoretically, the technique can cross the boundaries of species by selecting DNA material from fully different sources. The ability to cut and recombine is the basis for the term *recombinant DNA*. 13

A useful modification of the basic clip-and-paste process involves inserting the DNA fragments into a DNA molecule which has the power of self-replication. Many bacteria contain small circular cytoplasmic DNA molecules called *plasmids*, which are capable of self-replication inside the bacterial cell. The characteristics of rapid bacterial growth and multiplication allow quantity replication of the recombinant plasmids in short periods of time. This technique thus offers an obvious advantage over the slow and laborious chemical methods. . . . 14

The advantages of recombinant techniques for increasing knowledge of the genetic construction of any organism are immediately recognized. A number of practical findings from such investigations can be envisaged, such as incorporation of nitrogen-fixing genes in agricultural plants to eliminate the need for nitrogen fertilizers; the bacterial 15 manufacture of large quantities of polypeptide hormones, such as insulin; the bacterial production of vaccines and enzymes as well as the treatment of genetic diseases. Possible production of fermentation products (alcohol, methane, etc.) as fossil fuel substitutes may be aided by this technique.

It should be stressed that recombinant DNA methodology is *not* a way of constructing new forms of life in vitro. Even the simplest **16**

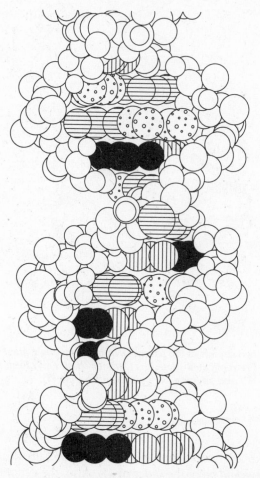

*Consisting of two helically intertwined strands, the DNA molecule is composed of deoxyribose and phosphate. As shown here, at periodic intervals the sugar-phosphate backbones are joined together by the complementary purine and pyrimidine bases. A single base linked to a deoxyribose-phosphate moiety constitutes a deoxyribonucleotide. Legend: Solid black circles = Thymine; Vertical bars = Adenine; Horizontal bars = Guanine; Dotted circles = Cytosine.*

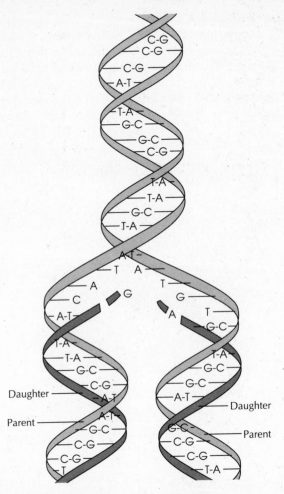

*For replication, the two strands of the parent DNA molecule (light gray) separate as the base pairs detach. The replicated (daughter) strands (dark gray) form as guanine (G) pairs with cytosine (C) and adenine (A) pairs with thymine (T).*

organisms are extremely complex and the maximum alteration of the simplest genome would be of the order of 1%. Also, the genomes of the simplest organisms are highly ordered and the random insertion of a few genes from an unrelated organism is unlikely to create a whole new organism.

In the initial stages of recombinant DNA research, there was considerable concern regarding possible serious consequences of producing biologically hazardous DNA molecules. Both self-policing and govern-

17

mental guidelines, which are under continuous review, were established and continue in most countries where recombinant DNA research is being conducted. The concept of *biological containment* was developed. By this means, safety factors may be built into the genetic structure of the organism to be studied. For example, as bases for recombinant experiments, EK2 derivatives of *E. coli* cells have been used. These are 100 million times less able to survive in nature outside an artificial laboratory environment and thus present no biohazards to the community. These mutant cell lines are usually constructed by causing a deletion of a portion of DNA in a gene responsible for critical cell characteristics, such as ability to metabolize a certain substrate or to construct a rigid cell wall. Alternatively, defective mutant genes may be inserted into the genome replacing normal genes responsible for properties critical to the survival of the cell.

## Review Questions

1. Explain the process of genetic recombination.
2. Describe the main areas of research in gene science.
3. What are the essential similarities and differences between "mutations" and "gene splicing"?
4. What kind of measures have scientists taken to avoid unwanted consequences from recombinant DNA research?

## Discussion and Writing Suggestions

1. Write a brief (one paragraph) summary of this article.
2. Vickery discusses three sets of "priorities in gene science." To what extent do you agree with these priorities? Do one or more of the priorities seem troubling to you? If so, explain why. Of the "two schools of thought concerning public funding of gene research" (paragraph 10), which would you prefer scientists focus on (assuming there is insufficient public funding for both)? Why?
3. Describe (if possible, in scientific report format) an experiment that you conducted in high school, or that you are conducting now in chemistry, physics, biology, or environmental science. Write in language that your non-scientific readers will be able to follow.

# Genetic Engineering: Promise and Threat

## DENNIS CHAMBERLAND

*During the last few centuries, religion has often been at odds with science. In the seventeenth century, Galileo was condemned by the Catholic church for his belief in a heliocentric solar system, since such a belief denied the prevailing interpretation of Scripture. In the nineteenth century, Darwin's theory of evolution was attacked by the church for the same reason. More recently, religious attacks on scientific developments have been issued as much for ethical as for doctrinal reasons. In the early 1980s a group of Catholic bishops wrote a "pastoral letter" opposing the use of nuclear weapons. And such new technological developments as artificial insemination and in vitro fertilization of human ova have generated concern and opposition not only from the clergy but also from lay people of all faiths. It is therefore not surprising that religious voices are among those most strongly objecting to—or cautioning about—genetic engineering.*

*In the following article, Dennis Chamberland, a science writer and nuclear engineer, explains what genetic engineering is, summarizes its relatively brief history, and discusses both the benefits and the dangers of this new technology. "Genetic Engineering: Promise and Threat" first appeared in* Christianity Today, *and, accordingly, the article is written from a Christian perspective. Certainly, this fact should not invalidate the article for non-Christians. Chamberland is concerned primarily with the ethical aspects of genetic engineering, and these ethical concerns go beyond particular religious issues. The question is, Now that we have (or are rapidly developing) the technology, what should we do with it? Few would argue, for example, that advances in genetic engineering should not be used to help cure or prevent diseases. But other applications (some of which will be explored in later articles in this chapter) are more questionable. Is it legitimate, for instance, to test a fetus for genetic defects, a test that may result in termination of the pregnancy? Chamberland does not attempt to answer such questions but rather tries to lay out the issues for his audience by explaining what genetic engineers can do now and what they may be able to do in the future.*

Sometimes uneasy allies, both science and religion seek to improve the lot of mankind. Nevertheless, their conflicting values have often forced them into a showdown.  1

Now the social and ethical stakes are as high as they have ever been. With even the slightest advances in genetic engineering, such afflictions  2

"Genetic Engineering: Promise and Threat" by Dennis Chamberland. *Christianity Today,* February 7, 1986. Reprinted by permission of the author.

as cancer, viral diseases, and even certain aspects of the aging process may become curses of the past. Science is carefully unraveling DNA's double helix, probing and mapping the stuff of life. Yet genetic engineering's place in society and its boundaries are ill defined. And the religious community has yet to establish a firm equilibrium with the new, powerful science that has dared to tamper with life's smallest material components.

The genetic engineering debate may well be irreconcilable at the most elemental levels of logic as scientists and moral theologians address each other from different dimensions. But one thing is certain: The ultimate outcome will determine the future shape of humanity.    3

## THE NEW FRONTIER

Biotechnology swept upon us quickly. Most of the advances in genetic engineering have come about within five years; the last decade nearly encompasses its entire history. In a few short years we have moved from obscure x-ray photographs of bacterial DNA (deoxyribonucleic acid) to methods of precisely trimming, clipping, and changing infinitesimal parts of the genetic code itself.    4

Already gone is the simplistic notion that the expression of genetic information of all life is the same. Now we know that the mechanism of mammalian and bacterial gene expression differs in radically different ways—which suggests an overt complexity and redundancy of higher life we had never dreamed of before. From the four chemical codes of life common to every life form on earth, we have learned how we can change the process that defines our existence.    5

On April 25, 1953, James Watson and Francis Crick published a paper that described for the first time the shape of the DNA molecule. For their insight, they won the Nobel prize. They had successfully initiated a biological revolution by describing the smallest units of life.    6

Watson and Crick had described the DNA molecule as large (for a molecule) and coiled in the shape of a spiral staircase, or double helix. This smallest denominator of life was linked together by only four chemical building blocks whose varied sequence provided a coded blueprint for all life forms on earth from bacteria to humankind. Their discovery, which enabled us to visualize growth and reproduction as a common link between all life, would enable us to change life at its most basic levels.    7

This understanding of the elemental life processes led to the ultimate development of four methods of altering the normal functions of    8 cell replication. This is accomplished by directly changing or interfering with its DNA.

Experiments with human life began in 1970. A physician attempted to introduce the gene for production of the enzyme arginase into patients whose bodies were incapable of normally producing the chemical. Otherwise doomed to death, the patients were injected with a virus capable of producing the enzyme. Some evidence had suggested the virus would invade the patients' DNA, be destroyed by the patients' immune system, and leave behind the necessary gene to produce arginase. The experiment's designer, biochemist-physician Stanford Rogers, was wrong. Though his effort was designed to save lives, his failure brought an avalanche of criticism, and he lost much of his research funding.   9

A more elaborate experiment was attempted on July 10, 1980, by a team directed by Dr. Martin Cline, then head of hematology and oncology at UCLA, and an Israeli medical group including Dr. Eliezer Rachmilewitz at Jerusalem's Hadassah Hospital.   10

Rachmilewitz's patients were born with a rare but fatal blood disease called beta zero thalassemia. Cline's treatment consisted of injecting their bone marrow with a purified gene, cloned by recombinant DNA technology, to correct the defect. Cline's efforts also failed. The subsequent storm of protest forced him to step down from his job. He too lost a great deal of his research funding.   11

The scientific community was ruling the new science with an unforgiving hand. For the moment, genetic engineering seemed too risky to apply to humans, and only indirectly would we benefit from the new biotechnology. But by the early 1980s, the bacterial production of cheap interferon and human insulin was being carried on by the new genetic engineering companies. By advances in such areas as agriculture and the production of medical products, the last few years have shown the incredible potential of this new technology of life.   12

## THE SIMPLE AND THE COMPLEX

The DNA contained in every human cell is compacted and coiled in 23 pairs of tight bundles called chromosomes. If all the DNA in a single cell were uncoiled, it would stretch out about three meters. And in these three meters of human DNA there are about 5,000,000 genes, of which at least 100,000 define the human form. In every molecule of DNA there is the blueprint for eyes, brain, liver, heart, and bones.   13

Directly altering an organism by changing its genetic code requires that the gene (or set of instructions) along the DNA coil be modified and   14 that this same set of instructions be changed in every cell of the organism. With single-cell organisms, such as bacteria, that is not too hard to accomplish. But the human organism is 100 trillion times as complicated.

Changing a multicellular organism was first accomplished in 1982  15
when the Carnegie Institute implanted a foreign gene in a fruit fly. The change was functional and was passed along to subsequent generations. In the Carnegie experiment, red-eye genes were passed to brown-eye flies.

Genetic researchers who first contemplated the problem of directly  16
altering the coding sequence of DNA were faced with problems that were simultaneously simple and complex. The simple part was the exchange of molecules in the DNA to bring about the desired modifications. The complex task would be to locate the right gene and to alter only that part of the code. Although the basic idea was simple, they would be working at the molecular level, beyond the range of any microscope.

The most likely candidate for the pioneer work was a single-cell  17
bacterium. The organism enlisted early was the most common bacterium in the human intestinal tract: *Escherichia coli.*

*E. coli* is easy to care for and maintain. And it holds the distinction  18
of being the single most carefully studied organism in history. For this reason, *E. coli* has been used not only for the majority of the early DNA studies, but its genetically altered forms have been patented as life forms invented by human beings.

Methods of mapping the DNA sequence were developed by clip-  19
ping off the ends of an uncoiled DNA strand and analyzing and identifying the individual molecules as they were encountered on the strand.

After a gene was mapped, changes were induced in the DNA,  20
altering the sequence by introducing mutagenic chemicals—compounds that increase the frequency of genetic mutations by "scrambling" the DNA sequence. Researchers observed the effects on the microorganism, remapped the gene, thereby learning the functions of specific parts of the DNA code.

Recombinant DNA technology, the most refined process of genetic  21
engineering, came in 1974 when genetic researchers discovered they could clip off a known sequence of the DNA and replace it with DNA from other sources. This form of gene splicing quickly became the most important genetic engineering tool. Science was learning enough to make changes at will without relying on the slower random mutational techniques.

Ultimately, geneticists at CalTech invented two machines that were  22
quantum leaps in genetic engineering research. One machine automatically identified the sequence of cellular amino acids, spelling out the

DNA code of the particular gene. Another machine assembled artificial genes piece by piece.

With these advances it became necessary for the scientific commu- 23 nity to keep track of the avalanche of mapped genes. In 1982, the Los Alamos National Laboratory set up GenBank, a computerized data base of millions of nucleic acid sequences. That data base soon contained information on hundreds of living species—including parts of man's genetic constitution. One day, reconstructing these genetic constitutions may consist of connecting a laboratory computer to this massive data base, which in turn would spell out the genetic make-up of interest.

It is only a matter of time until the entire human DNA sequence is 24 catalogued and computerized. With this information, the science of genetic engineering may be able to manipulate the human life form in ways we have not yet even imagined.

## HEALTH CARE AND BIG BUSINESS

Genetic engineering established a powerful foothold when the U.S. 25 Supreme Court gave Dr. Ananda Chakrabarty the right to patent a life form he had engineered, a microorganism that would metabolize petroleum and help clean up oil spills.

The result of the Court's decision was to open the field to commer- 26 cial enterprise. With big money riding on the right processes, a handful of genetic engineering companies went public and became multimillion-dollar enterprises virtually overnight. Firms with futuristic names—Genentech, Cetus, Lenex, Hybratech, Petrogen—started the race to invent new life forms.

The companies signed nearly every genetic scientist and researcher 27 in the field, creating great concern over this historically unique, apparent conflict of interest between industry and pure science.

Three important medical products came from this new industry in 28 quick succession:

*Human interferon,* a possible solution to such afflictions as cancer and 29 viral diseases, used to cost a quarter of a million dollars per thousandth of a gram. With newly engineered bacteria that produce human interferon as a metabolic by-product, we can now produce the same amount of interferon for about a nickel.

*Human growth hormone,* for children whose pituitary glands could 30 not produce enough to help them reach a normal height (hypopituitarism), was formerly produced by extracting the hormone from cadavers. An average child required pituitaries from over 500 cadavers over a 10-year period. Thus they were faced with a life of stunted growth unless they could afford $50,000 to $100,000 worth of treatment.

Genentech of San Francisco changed the genetic constitution of *E. coli*, and now human growth hormone is churned out at affordable prices.

*Human insulin,* now manufactured by genetically altered bacteria for tens of thousands of diabetics, replaces the beef- and pork-based product against which many patients build up antibodies. In October 1982, the Eli Lilly Company was given permission by the Food and Drug Administration to begin marketing human insulin.  31

But the genetic engineering industry was not focusing on making medical breakthroughs alone. Industrial microorganisms have been "invented" to mine precious metals from ore through extracellular secretions and leaching. A potato was given the blight-resistant genes of a tomato to become a "pomato." A sunflower was given the genes of a bean to produce protein. One strain of bacteria was engineered to convert ethylene to ethylene glycol (a constituent of antifreeze), another to change subterranean oil to make it easier to remove. And the University of California at Berkeley recently engineered a strain of bacteria that would protect plants from frost, sparking a controversy over introducing the plant into the environment. In November 1985, the EPA finally okayed its release in a California strawberry field.  32

On the horizon are genetic wonders that used to be mere science fiction. For example, aging is reflected in the behavior of DNA. In pioneering work, Ronald Hart and Richard Setlow tied the biological clock directly to the repair processes in older cells. And in 1979, Dr. Joan Smith-Sonneborn significantly extended the life span of single-cell paramecium by manipulating specific DNA repair processes.  33

In order to organize the search for cures for the 3,500 known human genetic disorders, the Human Genetic Mutant Cell Repository was established in Camden, New Jersey. Here frozen cell cultures from afflicted individuals are stored for reference.  34

And serious thought has been given to storing biological materials from organisms soon to be extinct, from smallpox to mammals, birds, and plants, in frozen storage for future, possible genetic reconstruction of entire organisms.  35

By 1985, the business of genetic engineering was a billion-dollar industry and growing. Already, medicine, agriculture, and energy were becoming dependent on its products, and the emerging possible future uses were astonishing.  36

**BENEFIT AND PERIL**

The first decade of genetic engineering has passed with little threat to the environment or the public. The somber warnings and tight regulations issued by the National Institutes of Health (NIH) from 1974–76 have been relaxed and their initial fears determined to be unfounded.  37

The NIH, initially worried about the inadvertent design of a deadly microorganism, strictly regulated the genetic engineering business in its infancy. The industry, however, successfully demonstrated that their organisms were usually so task-specific that they could survive only in carefully controlled conditions. One strain of *E. coli*, called K-12, which is used widely in genetic research, has been so extensively modified that it is virtually impossible for the organism to survive outside a carefully controlled laboratory environment. **38**

To date, the genetic engineering industry has shown itself to be the harbinger only of good, making medicines and food better and cheaper. We have been left in awe at both the reality and the possibilities. **39**

Yet, like any other human enterprise, genetic engineering has a possibility for malevolence equal to its potential for good. For example, since some genetic diseases strike only members of certain races (sickle cell anemia afflicts only blacks, and Tay-Sachs disease strikes only Jews), it is conceivable that we could copy nature and create an organism to carry out a horrible genocide. If biological warfare is terrible, its genetic equivalent would be unspeakable. **40**

Aside from examples of potential abuse, deeply troubling questions remain over the direction civil genetic engineering may take. **41**

Already, in its first years of existence, genetic screening has been used by a multinational corporation in what amounts to high-tech racism. **42**

One multinational corporation defended its use of genetic screening for sickle cell anemia among black job applicants to prevent susceptible workers from exposure to toxic substances. But such genetic screening could become the ultimate invasion of privacy. **43**

On the visible horizon, genetic engineering could be used in conjunction with gametic engineering, the laboratory manipulation of human germ cells, to create a human being in any desired image. In this seriously discussed (but not yet possible) procedure, a human's genes would be altered to order. The new genetic information would be passed to a human egg cell *in vitro*, where a new human would be nourished through the gestation period under theoretically perfect conditions. This procedure could hypothetically produce "super humans" resistant or immune to physical disease, and endowed in advance with superior intelligence. **44**

Part of this procedure is now possible. The more difficult procedures will probably be in reach within our lifetimes. **45**

Dr. Landrum Shettles, a reproductive biologist, has reported nourishing a normally developed, cloned human egg cell to the stage of intrauterine impregnation. Said Shettles, the remaining obstacles to the cloning of human beings are social, not scientific. **46**

The first animal cloned, a frog, was produced by biologists Thomas **47**

Briggs and Thomas King in 1952. Nearly three decades later, the first mammals were cloned, mice produced by biologists Karl Illmensee and Peter Hoppe. Yet many still believe that cloning by the transplanting of nuclei of adult mammalian cells, as Shettles claimed, is still impossible. The debate continues.

Genetic prejudice is already being expressed. The famous Nobel 48 Sperm Bank, formally called the Repository for Germinal Choice, in Escondido, California, contains sperm donated by some Nobel laureates for insemination of "acceptable" candidates. The only laureate-donor to identify himself thus far has been Stanford physicist William Shockley, who stirred controversy by claiming that blacks are inherently inferior to whites.

The sperm bank's clients have already produced children. Los An- 49 geles psychologist Afton Blake bore the second child from the bank. One of Blake's reasons for using the bank's services was the genetic legacy she wanted to pass on to her children and subsequent generations.

## MORAL IMPERATIVES

The scientific community has historically shown itself to be vigorously 50 self-regulated. Its moral standards are nearly always surprisingly conservative. Renegades and apostates are usually criticized and denounced, their research funds cut quickly. It is hard to find many examples of scientists continually abusing their positions.

Remarks made by Robert Sinsheimer of the California Institute of 51 Technology to the Genetics Society of America illustrate this notion: "To impose any limit upon freedom of inquiry is especially bitter for the scientist whose life is one of inquiry; but science has become too potent. . . . Rights are not found in nature. Rights are conferred within a human society and for each there is expected a corresponding responsibility. . . . Science is the major organ of inquiry for a society—and perhaps a society, like an organism, must follow a developmental program in which the genetic information is revealed in an orderly sequence."

From a Christian perspective, the real dangers of genetic engineer- 52 ing do not seem to emanate from the scientific community, but from the same places as other causes of social concern.

The abuse of genetic engineering will come from two familiar 53 directions: (1) ill-defined or nonexistent norms of acceptable social direction and (2) disguised social principles of accomplishing one goal by way of another.

Thus, genetic engineering stands in the same place as the other 54 powerful technologies of history, from nuclear weapons to wonder drugs: controlled completely by the hand of mankind and the conventional or surreptitious operational rules of society. Whatever good or evil shall come from it will be determined through the underlying social motivations and allowances for excess over which Christians may exercise influence.

The Christian response must be controlled by accurate and thorough knowledge of the field and a sober realization that the morality of many of the issues will not be clear-cut or obvious. Most important, we must understand our value systems and decide that what we can do is not necessarily what we should do. 55

The Christian input will be only one of many. It must be coordinated if the counsel of all those with moral concerns is to be effective. 56

The opinions of the poorly informed and emotional have already been discounted. The President's Commission for the Study of Ethical Problems in Medicine and Biomedical and Behavioral Research (1982) stated, "Genetic engineering has become a target for simplistic slogans that try to capture vague fears." 57

The concepts that underlie genetic engineering are far from simple. They are some of the most profound and powerful ideas ever. The promise of genetic engineering lies in the miracles that we have already created and will soon invent from the living code. But the nightmare is real and, ironically, is expressed in the words attributed to DNA codiscoverer Sir Francis Crick by journalist David Rorvik: 58

"No newborn infant should be declared human until it has passed certain tests regarding its genetic endowment. . . . If it fails these tests, it forfeits the right to live." 59

The evil we face, therefore, is not from the tools of life but from the minds that made them. There is only one certainty: The river that is the knowledge of life has been crossed, and we cannot go back again. 60

## Review Questions

1. What was Watson and Crick's contribution to the study of genetics?
2. What is *E. coli*? Why is it well suited for experiments in genetic engineering?
3. What does Chamberland cite as some of the products of the partnership between science and business in the area of genetic engineering?
4. What are some of the possible abuses of genetic engineering, according to Chamberland?
5. What are Chamberland's conclusions as to the "threat" of genetic engineering?

## Discussion and Writing Suggestions

1. Chamberland begins his essay by discussing the conflicts between religion and science—in particular, the science of genetic engineering. In what other areas have there been conflicts of values between religion and science? From what different value systems do these conflicts originate? How (if at all) have they been resolved? How has the rapid evolution of science and technology aggravated the problem?

2. To those not scientifically inclined, paragraphs 13–24, detailing the structure of DNA and recent scientific advances in "mapping" genetic sequences may present some difficulty. To ensure that you understand the basic ideas in this section, summarize these paragraphs in 200 to 350 words.

3. To what extent are you concerned about the abuse of genetic engineering technology? What guidelines do you suggest for its future development? What limits, if any, should be placed on existing or future technology? Do you recommend restrictions on commercial development of new genetically engineered substances? Explore these questions in a multiparagraph essay, using some of the above questions as your subtopics.

4. In a sidebar (entitled "Catching Up With the Revolution") to Chamberland's article, Lewis Smedes, a professor of theology and ethics at Fuller Theological Seminary, wrote as follows:

Technological events are getting ahead of our ability to cope with them in traditional moral categories. That is reason enough for a Christian moralist to view the revolution in biotechnology with unease.

Rather than apply moral standards to genetic engineering in general, we must examine the moral implications of each discrete stage in the specific applications of biotechnology to human beings. We will need to give careful thought to such questions as these:

1. Is it permissible to alter humanness at its core, to tamper with our essential humanity? Many people agree that it is right to tamper with some aspects of our humanness, as we do in giving people mechanical hearts. But is there a core of humanity that makes us the special godlike creatures we are—a core that should not be monkeyed with? If so, moralists and theologians must try to specify more exactly what is uniquely human about us.

2. Is it permissible for some people to alter other people's humanity? It is misleading to talk about *humanity* re-creating itself. Some persons are recreating other persons. The questions are these: Who sets the norms for what other people ought to be? And who has the wisdom and the right to use such power over the destiny of other people?

3. Is it socially responsible to give almost free rein to a biotech industry whose bottom line is profit? While some see the National Institutes of Health's relaxation as a signal that the dangers are small, NIH's relaxation may actually be a sign that public guardians are easily seduced by scientific authorities. Laissez-faire human technology needs to be watched carefully.

We need to remember that every good gift from above, including biotechnology, is likely to be turned against us by arrogant people who believe in the irresistible goodness of what they are doing.[1]

Select one of these sets of questions and, in a multiparagraph essay, discuss the issues Smedes raises.

5. Write a future newspaper or magazine report detailing some new development, either promising or threatening, in genetic technology.

6. Write a scenario for a science fiction movie about some genetic engineering experiment or development that has gotten out of control.

# A Heretic's View on the New Bioethics

JEREMY RIFKIN

*From its beginnings in the early 1970s, genetic engineering has been surrounded in controversy. Initial fears focused on the nightmare scenario of newly engineered microorganisms escaping from the lab and causing uncontrollable damage to other organisms and the environment. Some scientists proposed a moratorium on gene splicing experiments; and in 1975, during a landmark international conference at Asilomar, California, scientists agreed to strict guidelines to govern all future research. A year later, the city council of Cambridge, Massachusetts, enacted a three-month moratorium on certain high-risk DNA experiments conducted at nearby Harvard University.*

*During the past decade, the science-fiction scenarios have subsided, but the controversy over genetic engineering continues—focusing now on the ethical aspects of manipulating the genetic code for our own utilitarian and commercial purposes. Repeatedly, critics associate bioengineering with eugenics, the infamous pseudoscience practiced by the Nazis in their efforts to perpetuate the "Aryan" races and to exterminate "inferior" races. Then, as now, critics have wondered, Who should determine what is "superior" (or normal) and what is "inferior" (or defective)?*

*For some years, the most vocal critic of biotechnology has been Jeremy Rifkin. A philosopher and environmental activist involved in science and technology issues, Rifkin, through his publications, his lectures, his congressional testimony, and his Foundation on Economic Trends, has been tireless in attacking both the practices and the underlying premises of genetic engineer-*

[1]"Catching Up with the Revolution," by Lewis Smedes. *Christianity Today*, February 7, 1986. Reprinted by permission of the author.
From "The New Cosmic Mirror" in *Algeny* by Jeremy Rifkin. Reprinted by permission of William Morris Agency, Inc. on behalf of the Author. Copyright © 1983 by Jeremy Rifkin.

*ing. He has also been successful in halting or delaying the testing of several newly developed microorganisms with agricultural applications—for example, a new bacteria developed by Advanced Genetics Sciences to prevent frost damage to crops and a reengineered virus developed by Biologics Corporation to check an epidemic of pseudorabies, a disease fatal to pigs.*

*Born in 1945, Rifkin attended the Wharton School of Business and then earned a degree in law and diplomacy from Tufts. As a graduate student, he was an activist against the Vietnam War; he began focusing his attention on bioengineering after the Asilomar Conference. Rifkin's first book on biotechnology was* Who Should Play God? *(1977), coauthored with Ted Howard. This was followed by* Entropy *(1980), which sold more than 750,000 copies worldwide. In an article in the* New York Times Magazine, *"Jeremy Rifkin Just Says No" (October 16, 1988), he was quoted as follows:*

> No parliament ever debated the old technologies—the Industrial Revolution, the petrochemical revolution, the computer revolution. . . . The biotech revolution will have a more intimate effect on our lives than anything else in history. We can't afford the luxury of a small elite making public policy. . . . The rule of thumb [should be] to intervene in nature in the most prudent and conservative fashion rather than the most disruptive and radical fashion. (43)

*Following are two passages that reveal Rifkin's attitude toward genetic research—and beyond that, toward the ethical dimensions of scientific inquiry. The first passage is from his 1985 book* Algeny *(the title is a wordplay on* alchemy*); the second is from a 1985 interview with Andrew Revkin, a senior writer for* Science Digest.

Darwin's world was populated by machine-like automata. Nature was conceived as an aggregate of standardized, interchangeable parts assembled into various functional combinations. If one were to ascribe any overall purpose to the entire operation, it would probably be that of increased production and greater efficiency with no particular end in mind. [1]

The new temporal theory of evolution replaces the idea of life as mere machinery with the idea of life as mere information. By resolving structure into function and reducing function to information flows, the new cosmology all but eliminates any remaining sense of species identification. Living things are no longer perceived as carrots and peas, foxes and hens, but as bundles of information. All living things are drained of their aliveness and turned into abstract messages. Life becomes a code to be deciphered. There is no longer any question of sacredness or inviolability. How could there be when there are no longer any recognizable boundaries to respect? Under the new temporal theory, structure is abandoned. Nothing exists at the moment. Everything is pure activity, [2] pure process. How can any living thing be deemed sacred when it is just a pattern of information?

By eliminating structural boundaries and reducing all living things to information exchanges and flows, the new cosmology provides the proper degree of desacralization for the bioengineering of life. After all, in order to justify the engineering of living material across biological boundaries, it is first necessary to desacralize the whole idea of an organism as an identifiable, discrete structure with a permanent set of attributes. In the age of biotechnology, separate species with separate names gradually give way to systems of information that can be reprogrammed into an infinite number of biological combinations. It is much easier for the human mind to accept the idea of engineering a system of information than it is for it to accept the idea of engineering a dog. It is easier still, once one has fully internalized the notion that there is really no such thing as a dog in the traditional sense. In the coming age it will be much more accurate to describe a dog as a very specific pattern of information unfolding over a specific period of time.

Life as information flow represents the final desacralization of nature. Conveniently, humanity has eliminated the idea of fixed biological borders and reduced matter to energy and energy to information in its cosmological thinking right at the very time that bioengineers are preparing to cut across species boundaries in the living world.

## THE NEW ETHICS

Civilization is experiencing the euphoric first moments of the next age of history. The media are already treating us to glimpses of a future where the engineering of life by design will be standard operating procedure. Even as the corporate laboratories begin to dribble out the first products of bioengineering, a subtle shift in the ethical impulse of society is becoming perceptible to the naked eye. As we begin to reprogram life, our moral code is being similarly reprogrammed to reflect this profound change in the way humanity goes about organizing the world. A new ethics is being engineered, and its operating assumptions comport nicely with the activity taking place in the biology laboratories.

Eugenics is the inseparable ethical wing of the age of biotechnology. First coined by Charles Darwin's cousin Sir Francis Galton, eugenics is generally categorized in two ways, negative and positive. Negative eugenics involves the systematic elimination of so-called biologically undesirable characteristics. Positive eugenics is concerned with the use of genetic manipulation to "improve" the characteristics of an organism or species.

Eugenics is not a new phenomenon. At the turn of the century the    7
United States sported a massive eugenics movement. Politicians, celebrities, academicians, and prominent business leaders joined together in support of a eugenics program for the country. The frenzy over eugenics reached a fever pitch, with many states passing sterilization statutes and the U.S. Congress passing a new immigration law in the 1920s based on eugenics considerations. As a consequence of the new legislation, thousands of American citizens were sterilized so they could not pass on their "inferior" traits, and the federal government locked its doors to certain immigrant groups deemed biologically unfit by then-existing eugenics standards.

While the Americans flirted with eugenics for the first thirty years    8
of the twentieth century, their escapades were of minor historical account when compared with the eugenics program orchestrated by the Nazis in the 1930s and '40s. Millions of Jews and other religious and ethnic groups were gassed in the German crematoriums to advance the Third Reich's dream of eliminating all but the "Aryan" race from the globe. The Nazis also embarked on a "positive" eugenics program in which thousands of S.S. officers and German women were carefully selected for their "superior" genes and mated under the auspices of the state. Impregnated women were cared for in state facilities, and their offspring were donated to the Third Reich as the vanguard of the new super race that would rule the world for the next millennium.

Eugenics lay dormant for nearly a quarter of a century after World    9
War II. Then the spectacular breakthroughs in molecular biology in the 1960s raised the specter of a eugenics revival once again. By the mid-1970s, many scientists were beginning to worry out loud that the potential for genetic engineering might lead to a return to the kind of eugenics hysteria that had swept over America and Europe earlier in the century. Speaking at a National Academy of Science forum on recombinant DNA, Ethan Signer, a biologist at M.I.T., warned his colleagues that

> this research is going to bring us one more step closer to genetic engineering of people. That's where they figure out how to have us produce children with ideal characteristics. . . . The last time around, the ideal children had blond hair, blue eyes and Aryan genes.

The concern over a re-emergence of eugenics is well founded but    10
misplaced. While professional ethicists watch out the front door for telltale signs of a resurrection of the Nazi nightmare, eugenics doctrine has quietly slipped in the back door and is already stealthily at work reorganizing the ethical priorities of the human household. Virtually overnight, eugenics doctrine has gained an impressive if not an impregnable foothold in the popular culture.

Its successful implantation into the psychic life of civilization is **11** attributable to its going largely unrecognized in its new guise. The new eugenics is commercial, not social. In place of the shrill eugenic cries for racial purity, the new commercial eugenics talks in pragmatic terms of increased economic efficiency, better performance standards, and improvement in the quality of life. The old eugenics was steeped in political ideology and motivated by fear and hate. The new eugenics is grounded in economic considerations and stimulated by utilitarianism and financial gain.

Like the ethics of the Darwinian era, the new commercial eugenics **12** associates the idea of "doing good" with the idea of "increasing efficiency." The difference is that increasing efficiency in the age of biotechnology is achieved by way of engineering living organisms. Therefore, "good" is defined as the engineering of life to improve its performance. In contrast, not to improve the performance of a living organism whenever technically possible is considered tantamount to committing a sin.

For example, consider the hypothetical case of a prospective **13** mother faced with the choice of programming the genetic characteristics of her child at conception. Let's assume the mother chooses not to have the fertilized egg programmed. The fetus develops naturally, the baby is born, the child grows up, and in her early teenage years discovers that she has a rare genetic disease that will lead to a premature and painful death. The mother could have avoided the calamity by having that defective genetic trait eliminated from the fertilized egg, but she chose not to. In the age of biotechnology, her choice not to intervene might well constitute a crime for which she might be punished. At the least, her refusal to allow the fetus to be programmed would be considered a morally reprehensible and irresponsible decision unbefitting a mother, whose duty it is always to provide as best she can for her child's future well-being.

Proponents of human genetic engineering contend that it would be **14** irresponsible not to use this powerful new technology to eliminate serious "genetic disorders." The problem with this argument, says *The New York Times* in an editorial entitled "Whether to Make Perfect Humans," is that "there is no discernible line to be drawn between making inheritable repairs of genetic defects, and improving the species." The *Times* rightly points out that once scientists are able to repair genetic defects, "it will become much harder to argue against adding genes that confer desired qualities, like better health, looks or brains."

Once we decide to begin the process of human genetic engineering, **15** there is really no logical place to stop. If diabetes, sickle cell anemia, and cancer are to be cured by altering the genetic makeup of an individual, why not proceed to other "disorders": myopia, color blindness, left-handedness? Indeed, what is to preclude a society from deciding that a certain skin color is a disorder?

As knowledge about genes increases, the bioengineers will inevita- **16** bly gain new insights into the functioning of more complex characteristics, such as those associated with behavior and thoughts. Many scientists are already contending that schizophrenia and other "abnormal" psychological states result from genetic disorders or defects. Others now argue that "antisocial" behavior, such as criminality and social protest, are also examples of malfunctioning genetic information. One prominent neurophysiologist has gone so far as to say, "There can be no twisted thought without a twisted molecule." Many sociobiologists contend that virtually all human activity is in some way determined by our genetic makeup, and that if we wish to change this situation, we must change our genes.

Whenever we begin to discuss the idea of genetic defects, there is **17** no way to limit the discussion to one or two or even a dozen so-called disorders, because of a hidden assumption that lies behind the very notion of "defective." Ethicist Daniel Callahan penetrates to the core of the problem when he observes that "behind the human horror at genetic defectiveness lurks . . . an image of the perfect human being. The very language of 'defect,' 'abnormality,' 'disease,' and 'risk,' presupposes such an image, a kind of proto-type of perfection."

The idea of engineering the human species is very similar to the **18** idea of engineering a piece of machinery. An engineer is constantly in search of new ways to improve the performance of a machine. As soon as one set of imperfections is eliminated, the engineer immediately turns his attention to the next set of imperfections, always with the idea in mind of creating a perfect piece of machinery. Engineering is a process of continual improvement in the performance of a piece of machinery, and the idea of setting arbitrary limits to how much "improvement" is acceptable is alien to the entire engineering conception.

The question, then, is whether or not humanity should "begin" the **19** process of engineering future generations of human beings by technological design in the laboratory. What is the price we pay for embarking on a course whose final goal is the "perfection" of the human species? How important is it that we eliminate all the imperfections, all the defects? What price are we willing to pay to extend our lives, to ensure our own health, to do away with all the inconveniences, the irritations, the nuisances, the infirmities, the suffering, that are so much a part of the human experience? Are we so enamored with the idea of physical perpetuation at all costs that we are even willing to subject the human species to rigid architectural design?

With human genetic engineering, we get something and we give **20** up something. In return for securing our own physical well-being we are forced to accept the idea of reducing the human species to a technologically designed product. Genetic engineering poses the most fundamental of questions. Is guaranteeing our health worth trading away our humanity?

People are forever devising new ways of organizing the environment in order to secure their future. Ethics, in turn, serves to legitimize the drive for self-perpetuation. Any organizing activity that a society deems to be helpful in securing its future is automatically blessed, and any activity that undermines the mode of organization a society uses to secure its future is automatically damned. The age of bioengineering brooks no exception. In the years to come a multitude of new bioengineering products will be forthcoming. Every one of the breakthroughs in bioengineering will be of benefit to someone, under some circumstance, somewhere in society. Each will in some way appear to advance the future security of an individual, a group, or society as a whole. Eliminating a defective gene trait so that a child won't die prematurely; engineering a new cereal crop that can feed an expanding population; developing a new biological source of energy that can fill the vacuum as the oil spigot runs dry. Every one of these advances provides a modicum of security against the vagaries of the future. To forbid their development and reject their application will be considered ethically irresponsible and inexcusable. 21

Bioengineering is coming to us not as a threat but as a promise; not as a punishment but as a gift. We have already come to the conclusion that bioengineering is a boon for humanity. The thought of engineering living organisms no longer conjures up sinister images. What we see before our eyes are not monstrosities but useful products. We no longer feel dread but only elated expectation at the great possibilities that lie in store for each of us. 22

How could engineering life be considered bad when it produces such great benefits? Engineering living tissue is no longer a question of great ethical import. The human psyche has been won over to eugenics with little need for discussion or debate. We have already been convinced of the good that can come from engineering life by learning of the helpful products it is likely to spawn. 23

As in the past, humanity's incessant need to control the future in order to secure its own well-being is already dictating the ethics of the age of biotechnology. Engineering life to improve humanity's own prospects for survival will be ennobled as the highest expression of ethical behavior. Any resistance to the new technology will be castigated as inhuman, irresponsible, morally reprehensible, and criminally culpable. 24

## "SCIENCE DIGEST" INTERVIEW

*"A public nuisance." "A scourge on science." These are just two of the labels that normally staid scientists have applied to genetic-engineering foe Jeremy Rifkin. If he is any of these things, he is also a force to be reckoned with. Recently, a federal court, ruling on a lawsuit brought by Rifkin, stopped what would have been the first field test of a genetically modified organism. Since then, as head of the privately funded Foundation on Economic Trends, Rifkin has filed additional suits, including one against the U.S. Department of Agriculture. He contends that the USDA is violating the "ethical canons of civilization" by transferring genes between mammalian species.*

*Science Digest senior writer Andrew Revkin talked with Rifkin in his Washington office to see what gives this perennial gadfly his punch.*

SCIENCE DIGEST: When you speak in public, you take a very pragmatic view  1
of biotechnology. You're careful to describe the potential payoffs. You mainly discuss questions of implementation—how will we control what is done or who will decide on it.

But in your books and legal maneuvers you attack science and call  2
for an outright ban on genetic engineering. Will the real Jeremy Rifkin please stand up?

JEREMY RIFKIN: I'm often criticized as being opposed to progress and science  3
and freedom of inquiry when in fact I'm not. My whole life has been about that. What my critics are really livid about is my view on the nature of knowledge, how we pursue it, what our goals are.

There's a scholarly tradition which is part of the science of the  4
modern world. Francis Bacon summed it up by saying, "Knowledge is power, power is control, control is security." It's very easy to develop this sort of isolation science, where you sever relationships, and you try to manipulate and control from a distance.

It's much more intellectually expansive to develop a wholly different  5
perspective on science. There is a small group in my generation that is starting to talk about a new formula: "Knowledge is empathy with the environment, empathy allows us to establish a new type of security by becoming a member in good standing in the community of life."

SD: Most of the scientists I've met have a remarkably empathetic view of  6
the world. That's what drove them into science—their curiosity about things around them, their interest in the interplay between organisms and their environment. Do you really think that empathetic science isn't already out there?

Interview with Jeremy Rifkin from *Science Digest*, May 1985. Reprinted by permission of Jeremy Rifkin, The Foundation of Economic Trends, Washington, DC.

JR: I think it's there, but it is the minority report. Look at the major actors 7
in molecular biology. You can't find more than a handful that aren't on
corporate boards and aren't involved in the engineering part of it. If
you're saying there are still some pure-research scientists around, you're
right, but if you're saying they are the majority, you're wrong. And if
you're saying they are the trend, you're wrong. The trend is that science
is becoming increasingly reduced to technology.

SD: Your lawsuits are directed at basic research as well as at applied 8
research. The main fear I have seen in the scientific establishment is that
this will impede pure science along with commercial biotechnology.

JR: If they're only interested in research to observe how something works 9
so that we can better respect and empathize with normal working
relationships in nature, fine. If these people are there, I would ask them
to speak up. I've never seen one article from these people. I do assume
they exist; I'm not that cynical. But they don't speak up. Let them be a
third force.

SD: I think the majority of scientists out there are aware of these things and 10
are very involved in the idea of discussing them.

JR: I have not seen this nurturing, supportive effort toward a rational 11
dialogue. I have seen a few individual scientists who are willing to do it,
but by and large the others have squawked, kicked, yelled and screamed
all the way. I have been subjected to all sorts of attacks. They never deal
with the issues. It's always "Rifkin this" and "Rifkin that." There was no
discussion of this until I raised my litigation, and then they went crazy.
Now, a year and a half after the litigation, they're all saying we have to
regulate.

SD: Isn't genetic engineering just another technology, one that can be 12
either misused or used properly?

JR: That is wrong. In fact, it's ridiculous. There is no neutral technology. 13
This is the myth of the modern age. Let's take nuclear power. You're
saying, well, it can be used for good or bad. What I'm saying is, look at
the inherent power in the technology and ask, is the power inordinate?
Did we learn truth by splitting the atom? No. We got a new form of
power. I would agree with Amory Lovins, who said nuclear power, even
for domestic purposes, is like using a chain saw to cut butter. The
inherent power of the technology was so inordinate that its mere use—
regardless of the intentions of those using it—was irresponsible. The
power was out of balance with our indebted relationship to all other
things. . . .

With genetic engineering, I would say the same thing. There are 14
tremendous benefits to genetic engineering. The question is not the
benefits versus the harm; I *assume* that the intentions are to make a better
world. The question is whether the power inherent in the process is

appropriate; should we human beings have the authority to determine what are good or bad genes. Who sets up the criteria?

SD: If you could fashion the world according to Jeremy Rifkin, what would it be like? **15**

JR: We have seen our mandate as manipulating, controlling, rearranging, becoming the co-creator of life. I think that is a misguided notion. We are one of many creatures on a planet that is a single organism. It's not just an environmental platitude to say this. We rely in every aspect of our life on a whole set of relationships that we live within. I would like us to ask, "How can we become good stewards?" I think the Iroquois Indians had a very interesting idea. Whenever they looked at a new policy option, they went into council, and the elders had to speculate on how this decision would affect their people, seven generations removed. They used the greatest gift the human species has—our consciousness—and they used it in the most civilized way possible. We need that continuity today. We don't have it. We think in terms of two-year reelections. **16**

SD: Given our systems of government and regulation, how would we get from here to there? **17**

JR: You cannot legislate what I'm talking about into existence; you cannot command it into existence. The only way this can happen is by a change in consciousness. I don't know why it isn't possible to develop an empathetic stewardship approach. I don't think you can do it in a generation; it's too big. **18**

SD: In the world according to Jeremy Rifkin, what would a university be like? Would there be a biology department and, if so, what kind? **19**

JR: Sure there would. There is a whole alternative biology to the one the established order sets up. A whole new approach to science—using a rigorous methodology for empathetic pursuit of knowledge. We tend to think there is only one way. Let's look at some of the fields where genetics is involved—medicine, for example. **20**

SD: A quick example from medicine. The clotting factor for hemophiliacs. It costs tens of thousands of dollars to maintain a hemophiliac. Suppose we could engineer the clotting factor for a few dollars per person? **21**

JR: Back in 1831 or 1832, we discovered chloroform in the West. Centuries earlier, the Chinese discovered acupuncture. Why did we never discover acupuncture? Why did China never discover chloroform? The cultural orientation in each of those civilizations set up the context for the whole range of discoveries they might find. Let's get to the clotting. Is it possible that we could have come up with some other completely different medical approach to clotting that would not have relied on the same technology we are using today? **22**

SD: That seems doubtful. **23**

JR: It depends on one's faith. You might, you might not. Acupuncture    24
stunned us because we would never have imagined it.

SD: Most of the potential of gene therapy is in treating specific defects that    25
might cause death or disability. Are you saying we shouldn't go ahead
with this?

JR: What is a defect? Why would we ever say no to any genetic change    26
in somatic or germ-line cells that could in some way lessen the possibility
of death? Once you begin the process, is a cleft palate a defect? Wouldn't
everyone want that out of their baby? How about a clubfoot? Acne?
Once you start the process, whenever a monogenic "disorder" is
mapped, programmed and can be altered, what parent, what society
would not want to eliminate it?

What happens if a child comes down with a genetic disease at 15 and    27
dies, and the parents could have intervened and eliminated that monogenic disease in the embryo? Wouldn't they be considered unethical,
perhaps even legally culpable?

In the end that is a eugenic civilization. Eugenics is the philosophy    28
of using genetic manipulation to create a better organism. Genetic engineering is inseparable from eugenics. You have these professional ethicists who keep looking out the front door for Hitler or Dr. Strangelove
or some kind of forced cabal that's going to move us into a brave new
world. But the new eugenics came in the back door. It's called commercial
eugenics. . . .

SD: You conclude *Algeny* by saying that it is "by giving something back,    29
by leaving something behind, by going without that we live on." I guess
what you're saying is that we will have to do something that is absolutely against human nature, to put knowledge—in this case, about
bioengineering—back where we found it.

JR: No. It means we have to change our approach to knowledge. There's    30
a difference between a respectful, mutual give-and-take and outright
exploitation.

SD: Isn't there a danger here of a broader rejection of science?    31

JR: There is always that danger. But I would say that today's scientists are    32
rejecting science; they're turning it into technology. The people who
have squelched science are not Jeremy Rifkin—I know I'm the archetypal
Luddite now for Western society. It's not me. Science is being destroyed
by our culture's determination to reduce everything to utilitarianism, to
reduce all science to what will work, to commercial application. If you
want to look at what's destroyed true inquiry, it's our own desire to use
our knowledge for power over nature, to control every last aspect of this
Earthly existence.

If there is an evil party here, please don't believe it's the scientists.    33
Scientists are just a reflection of the assumptions of the culture. What I
am critiquing here is the human race. We all want healthier babies. We

all want more efficient plants and animals. We all want a better GNP. The problem in this society and in all societies I know of today is that knowledge is important only to the extent that it allows us to control and manipulate. We want predictability, order, foresight, planning—and genetics is the ultimate planning.

SD: Aren't you just coming to the conclusion that such desires are part of the human condition? 34

JR: Yes. But I think it's possible for a change in the human condition. The Bomb has changed a lot. The small change since World War II has been profound. My parents' generation always believed more power is more security. There is a willingness on the part of every generation since the Bomb to begin entertaining at some small level the idea that more power is *less* security. 35

SD: In dealing with this type of issue, why should people listen to the arguments of a political activist with no extensive training in science? 36

JR: They don't have to if they don't want to. I'm not qualified; I'm a human being. One reason people in the establishment are frightened and upset about me is they're worried about their own legitimacy and credentials. Everything we do intimately affects everything else, but we become so narrowly confined in our own fields that we don't develop the other aspects of our knowledge that are essential to be able to place our specific specialty into some context. Many scientists are saying, "Well, this is really for the experts—the question of engineering life." They're wrong. This is a question for the human species to deal with: Do we embark on a journey where we increasingly become the engineers and the architects of life? If we can't engage the entire human race in this set of discussions, then there's never going to be another discussion worthy of public comment. 37

## Review Questions

1. What does Rifkin mean by the "desacralization" of life to mere information?
2. What is eugenics? What is the legacy of eugenics in the first part of this century? Why are current advances in genetic engineering associated with eugenics? What is the difference between the old eugenics and the new, according to Rifkin?
3. In his interview, what distinction does Rifkin make between the kind of science he opposes and the kind he favors?

## Discussion and Writing Suggestions

1. Does Rifkin seem justified in his charge that modern scientists have succeeded in reducing life to mere patterns of [genetic] information? Has genet-

ics succeeded in "desacralizing life"? While formulating your response, consider some of the cases in Vickery and Chamberland.

2. To what extent do you share Rifkin's antipathy toward genetic engineering? Do you agree, for instance, with the *New York Times* article he quotes, which argues that "once scientists are able to repair genetic defects, 'it will become much harder to argue against adding genes that confer desired qualities, like better health, looks, or brains' "?

3. In a multiparagraph essay, explore the connections you detect between Rifkin's reservations about genetic engineering and Huxley's imaginary portrait of a "brave new world."

4. Rifkin asks (in paragraph 19 from *Algeny*): "How important is it that we eliminate all the imperfections, all the defects? What price are we willing to pay to extend our lives, to ensure our own health, to do away with all the inconveniences, the irritations, the nuisances, the infirmities, the suffering, that are so much a part of the human experience?" Respond to these questions. To what extent do you agree with the premise that we may guarantee our health at the cost of our humanity? To what extent do you agree with the premise that we should accept some imperfections, just as we accept our humanity?

5. In the final section of this passage from *Algeny*, Rifkin argues that once we decide that bioengineering is a "boon for humanity," we will find all the rationalizations we need to support this questionable technology, and we will reject all arguments against it. Can you think of other areas—on the political, the social, or even the personal level—in which we are so anxious to gain something we have already determined is desirable that we will rationalize any actions we think necessary to achieve our goal, while rejecting any objections or reservations?

   For example, suppose that the American people, as well as high government officials, are fed up with a third world dictator who delights in provoking the United States; should we take steps to "eliminate" the problem? Or suppose that we're so frustrated by some social problem—drugs or AIDS—that we're willing to consider suspending civil liberties to deal with it. Both in these cases and in the case of genetic engineering, what are the negatives that we would prefer not to think about? Do you think the analogy—between such cases and genetic engineering—holds up? Explore these questions in a multiparagraph essay.

6. Do you sense a difference between the Jeremy Rifkin who wrote the passage from *Algeny* and the Rifkin who is interviewed for *Science Digest?* If so, try to identify the difference and account for it.

7. In paragraphs 22–24 of the *Science Digest* interview, Rifkin appears to be arguing for an alternative approach to medicine. To what extent do you find his approach desirable? Plausible?

8. In paragraph 32 of the interview, Rifkin asserts:

   Science is being destroyed by our culture's determination to reduce everything to utilitarianism, to reduce all science to what will work, to commercial application. If you want to look at what's destroyed true inquiry, it's our own desire to use our knowledge for power over nature, to control every last aspect of this Earthly existence.

By "science" Rifkin appears to mean the systematic pursuit of knowledge, in the form of general laws, through the testing of hypotheses. (Such fields of knowledge include genetics and nuclear physics.) He distinguishes this from utilitarian applications of science, such as we find in technology. (These applications include genetic engineering and nuclear reactors.) Comment on this idea in a multiparagraph essay. Draw on examples from your own prior knowledge.

**9.** Write a critique of Rifkin's article, drawing on your responses to some of the above questions.

# On the Origin of Specious Critics

## STEPHEN JAY GOULD

*Rifkin's attacks on bioengineering have not gone unanswered. Many scientists have pointed to Rifkin's lack of scientific credentials. (Rifkin has at least partially turned this charge against his attackers, asserting that scientists often consider themselves an elite community, immune to criticism from laypeople, who have as much stake as scientists in the effects of technological advances.) Rifkin's strategies, as well as his ideas, have also been attacked. An article about him in* Forbes *(a business magazine) was entitled "Ministry of Fear." David Baltimore, a Nobel laureate from MIT, who once refused to share a speaker's platform with Rifkin, argues that "he has poisoned the whole atmosphere around which biotechnology has developed, rather than allowing it to be developed in a rational and thoughtful manner." Baltimore claimed that Rifkin's successful effort to ban the Monsanto Company's "Frostban" microbe was ridiculous, since the organism found in Frostban also appears in nature. In fact, so notorious has Rifkin become, to such an extent has he "radicalized" the debate over genetic engineering, that more moderate critics, who have (according to some scientists) more legitimate reservations about bioengineering, are afraid to speak out, for fear of being associated with Rifkin.*

*Perhaps the most influential of Rifkin's critics has been Stephen Jay Gould. Born in New York City in 1941, Gould teaches biology and geology at Harvard University. He has written both scholarly papers on paleontology (the study of prehistoric forms of life through the fossil record) and popular*

"On the Origin of Specious Critics" by Stephen Jay Gould from pp. 34–42 in *Discover*, January 1985. Reprinted by permission of the author.

*essays that have helped make science understandable to nonscientists. Gould is particularly concerned with the misuse of science for political and social purposes—or "scientific racism." As he wrote in* The Mismeasure of Man *(1982), "Few tragedies can be more extensive than the stunting of life, few injustices deeper than the denial of an opportunity to strive or even to hope, by a limit imposed from without but falsely identified as lying within." Gould's frequently prize-winning essays, written originally for the magazine* Natural History, *have been collected into several volumes, including* Ever Since Darwin *(1977),* The Panda's Thumb *(1980),* Hen's Teeth and Horse's Toes *(1983), and* The Flamingo's Smile *(1985). His style has been characterized by one reviewer as "full of fun, totally without pretentiousness, and absolutely clear."*

*As you read the following article, consider not only what Gould says but the systematic method by which he makes his points. Gould's review, whether or not you agree with it, may be seen as a model critique.*

Evolution has a definite geometry well portrayed by our ancient meta- 1
phor, the tree of life. Lineages split and diverge like the branches of a tree. A species, once distinct, is permanently on its own; the branches of life do not coalesce. Extinction is truly forever, persistence a personal odyssey. But art does not always imitate nature. Biotechnology, or genetic engineering, has aroused fear and opposition because it threat- ens to annul this fundamental property of life—to place genes of one species into the program of another, thereby combining what nature has kept separate from time immemorial. Two concerns—one immediate and practical, the other distant and deep—have motivated the opposi- tion.

Some critics fear that certain conjunctions might have potent and 2
unanticipated effects—creating a resistant agent of disease or simply a new creature so hardy and fecund that, like Kurt Vonnegut's *ice-nine*, it spreads to engulf the earth in a geological millisecond. I am not per- suaded by these excursions into science fiction, but the distant and deeper issue does merit discussion: What are the consequences, ethical, aesthetic, and practical, of altering life's fundamental geometry and permitting one species to design new creatures at will, combining bits and pieces of lineages distinct for billions of years?

Jeremy Rifkin has been the most vocal opponent of genetic engi- 3
neering in recent months. He has won court cases and aroused fury in the halls of science with his testimony about immediate dangers. How- ever, his major statement, a book titled *Algeny* (for the modern al- chemy of genes), concentrates almost entirely on the deep and distant issue. His activities based on immediate fears have been widely re-

ported and rebutted. But *Algeny*, although it was published more than a year ago, has not been adequately analyzed or dissected. Its status as prophecy or pretension, philosophy or pamphleteering, must be assessed, for *Algeny* touts itself as the manifesto of a movement to save nature and simple decency from the hands of impatient and rapacious science.

I will state my conclusion—bald and harsh—at the outset: I regard *Algeny* as a cleverly constructed tract of anti-intellectual propaganda masquerading as scholarship. Among books promoted as serious intellectual statements by important thinkers, I don't think I have ever read a shoddier work. Damned shame, too, because the deep issue is troubling and I do not disagree with Rifkin's basic plea for respecting the integrity of evolutionary lineages. But devious means compromise good ends, and we shall have to save Rifkin's humane conclusion from his own questionable tactics. 4

The basic argument of *Algeny* rests upon a parody of an important theme advanced by contemporary historians of science against the myth of objectivity and inexorable scientific progress: science is socially embedded; its theories are not simple deductions from observed facts of nature, but a complex mixture of social ideology (often unconsciously expressed) and empirical constraint. This theme is liberating for science; it embodies the human side of our enterprise and depicts us as passionate creatures struggling with limited tools to understand a complex reality, not as robots programmed to convert objective information into immutable truth. But in Rifkin's hands the theme becomes a caricature. Rifkin ignores the complex interplay of social bias with *facts* of nature and promotes a crude socioeconomic determinism that views our historical succession of biological worldviews—from creationism to Darwinism to the new paradigm now supposedly under construction—as so many simple reflections of social ideology. 5

From this socioeconomic determinism, Rifkin constructs his specific brief: Darwinian evolutionism, he asserts, was the creation of industrial capitalism, the age of pyrotechnology. Arising in this context as a simple reflection of social ideology, it never had any sound basis in reason or evidence. It is now dying because the age of pyrotechnology is yielding to an era of biotechnology—and biotech demands a new view of life. Darwinism translated the industrial machine into nature; biotech models nature as a computer and substitutes information for material parts. 6

Darwinism spawned (or reflected) evil in its support for exploitation of man and nature, but at least it respected the integrity of species (while 7 driving some to extinction) because it lacked the technology to change them by mixture and instant transmutation. But the new paradigm dissolves species into strings of information that can be reshuffled at will.

The new temporal theory of evolution replaces the idea of life as **8** mere machinery with the idea of life as mere information. All living things are drained of their aliveness and turned into abstract messages. There is no longer any question of sacredness or inviolability. How could there be when there are no longer any recognizable boundaries to respect? In the age of biotechnology, separate species with separate names gradually give way to systems of information that can be reprogrammed into an infinite number of biological combinations.

But what can we do if we wish to save nature as we know it—a **9** system divided into packages of porcupines and primroses, cabbages and kings? We can seek no help from science, Rifkin claims, for science is a monolith masquerading as objective knowledge, but really reflecting the dominant ideology of a new technological age. We can only make an ethical decision to "re-sacralize" nature by respecting the inviolability of its species. We must, for the first time in history, decide *not* to institute a possible technology, despite its immediately attractive benefits in such areas as medicine and agriculture.

I have devoted my own career to evolutionary biology, and I have **10** been among the strongest critics of strict Darwinism. Yet Rifkin's assertions bear no relationship to what I have observed and practiced for 25 years. Evolutionary theory has never been healthier or more exciting. We are experiencing a ferment of new ideas and theories, but they are revising and extending Darwin, not burying him. How can Rifkin construct a world so different from the one I inhabit and know so well? Either I am blind or he is wrong—and I think I can show, by analyzing his slipshod scholarship and basic misunderstanding of science, that his world is an invention constructed to validate his own private hopes. I shall summarize my critique in five charges:

1. Rifkin does not understand Darwinism, and his arguments re- **11** fute an absurd caricature, not the theory itself. He trots out all the standard mischaracterizations, usually confined nowadays to creationist tracts. Just three examples: "According to Darwin," Rifkin writes, "everything evolved by chance." Since the complexity of cellular life cannot arise by accident, Darwinism is absurd: "According to the odds, the one-cell organism is so complex that the likelihood of its coming together by sheer accident and chance is computed to be around $1/10^{78436}$." But Darwin himself, and Darwinians ever since, always stressed, as a cardinal premise, that natural selection is not a theory of randomness. Chance may describe the origin of new variation by mutation, but natural selection, the agent of change, is a conventional

deterministic process that builds adaptation by preserving favorable variants.

Rifkin then dismisses Darwinism as a tautology; fitness is defined by   **12** survival, and the catch phrase "survival of the fittest" reduces to "survival of those that survive"—and therefore has no meaning. Darwin resolved this issue, as Darwinians have ever since, by defining fitness as predictable advantage before the fact, not as recorded survival afterward (as we may predict the biomechanical improvements that might help zebras outrun or outmaneuver lions; survival then becomes a testable consequence).

Rifkin regards Darwinism as absurd because "natural selection   **13** makes no room for long-range considerations. Every new trait has to be immediately useful or it is discarded." How, therefore, can natural selection explain the origin of a bird's wing, since the intermediate forms cannot fly: What good is five per cent of a wing? The British biologist St. George Jackson Mivart developed this critique in 1871 as the argument about "incipient stages of useful structures." Darwin met the challenge by adding a chapter to the sixth edition of the *Origin of Species*. One need not agree with Darwin's resolution, but one does have a responsibility to acknowledge it. Darwin argued that intermediate stages performed different functions; feathers of an incipient wing may act as excellent organs of thermoregulation—a particular problem in the smallest of dinosaurs, which evolved into birds.

Rifkin displays equally little comprehension of basic arguments   **14** about evolutionary geometry. He thinks that *Archaeopteryx* has been refuted as an intermediate link between reptiles and birds because some true birds have been found in rocks of the same age. But evolution is a branching bush, not a ladder. Ancestors survive after descendants branch off. Dogs evolved from wolves, but wolves (though threatened) are hanging tough. And a species of *Australopithecus* lived side by side with its descendant *Homo* for more than a million years in Africa.

Rifkin doesn't grasp the current critiques of strict Darwinism any   **15** better. He caricatures my own theory of punctuated equilibrium [that evolution moves in fits and starts rather than by slow, steady change] as a sudden response to ecological catastrophe: "The idea is that these catastrophic events spawned monstrous genetic mutations within existing species, most of which were lethal. A few of the mutations, however, managed to survive and become the precursors of a new species." But punctuated equilibrium, as Niles Eldredge and I have always emphasized, is about ordinary speciation (taking tens of thousands of years) and its abrupt appearance at low scales of geological resolution, not about ecological catastrophe and sudden genetic change.

---

Rifkin, it appears, understands neither the fundamentals of Darwin- **16** ism, its current critiques, nor even the basic topology of the evolutionary tree.

2. Rifkin shows no understanding of the norms and procedures of **17** science: he displays little comprehension of what science is and how scientists work. He consistently misses the essential distinction between fact (claims about the world's empirical content) and theory (ideas that explain and interpret facts)—using arguments against one to refute the other. Against Darwinism (a theory of evolutionary mechanisms) he cites the British physiologist Gerald Kerkut's *Implications of Evolution*, a book written to refute the factual claim that all living creatures have a common ancestry, and to argue instead that life may have arisen several times from chemical precursors—an issue not addressed by Darwinism. (Creationist lawyers challenged me with the same misunderstanding during my cross-examination at the Arkansas "equal time" trial three years ago, in which the creationists unsuccessfully fought for compulsory presentation of their views in science classrooms.) Rifkin then suggests that the entire field of evolution may be a pseudo science because the great French zoologist Pierre-Paul Grassé is so critical of Darwinism (the theory of natural selection might be wrong, but Grassé has devoted his entire life to study the fact of evolution).

Science is a pluralistic enterprise, validly pursued in many modes. **18** But Rifkin ignores its richness by stating that direct manipulation by repeatable experiment is the only acceptable method for reaching a scientific conclusion. Since evolution treats historically unique events that occurred millions of years ago, it cannot be a science. Rifkin doesn't seem to realize that he is throwing out half of science—nearly all of geology and most of astronomy, for instance—with his evolutionary bath water. Historical science is a valid pursuit, but it uses methods different from the controlled experiment of Rifkin's all-encompassing caricature—search for an underlying pattern among unique events, and retrodiction (predicting the yet undiscovered results of past events), for example.

3. Rifkin does not respect the procedures of fair argument. He uses **19** every debater's trick in the book to mischaracterize and trivialize his opposition, and to place his own dubious claims in a rosy light. Just four examples:

*The synecdoche* (trying to dismiss a general notion by citing a single **20** poor illustration). He suggests that science knows nothing about the evolutionary tree of horses, and has sold the public a bill of goods (the great horse caper, he calls it), because one exhibit, set up at the American Museum of Natural History in 1905, arranged fossil horses in order of size, not genealogy. Right, Jeremy, that was a lousy exhibit, but you might read George Gaylord Simpson's book *Horses* to see what we do know.

*The half quote* (stopping in the middle so that an opponent appears to agree with you, or seems merely ridiculous). Rifkin quotes me on the argument about incipient stages of useful structures discussed a few paragraphs ago: "Harvard's Stephen Jay Gould posed the dilemma when he observed, 'What good is half a jaw or half a wing?' " Sure, I posed the dilemma, but then followed it with an entire essay supporting Darwin's resolution based on different function in intermediate stages. Rifkin might have mentioned it and not adduced me in his support. Rifkin then quotes a famous line from Darwin as if it represented the great man's admission of impotence: "Darwin himself couldn't believe it, even though it was his own theory that advanced the proposition. He wrote: 'To suppose that the eye, with all of its inimitable contrivances . . . could have been formed by natural selection, seems, I freely confess, absurd in the highest possible degree.' " But Rifkin might have mentioned that Darwin follows this statement with one of his most brilliant sections—a documentation of nature's graded intermediates between simple pinhole eyes and the complexity of our own, and an argument that the power of new theories resides largely in their ability to resolve previous absurdities.

*Refuting what your opponents never claimed.* In the 1950s, Stanley Miller performed a famous experiment that synthesized amino acids from hypothetical components of the earth's original atmosphere. Rifkin describes it with glaring hype: "With great fanfare, the world was informed that scientists had finally succeeded in forming life from nonlife, the dream of magicians, sorcerers, and alchemists from time immemorial." He then points out, quite correctly, that the experiment did no such thing, and that the distance from amino acid to life is immense. But Miller never claimed that he had made life. The experiment stands in all our text books as a demonstration that some simple components of living systems can be made from inorganic chemicals. I was taught this 25 years ago; I have lectured about it for 15 years. I have never in all my professional life heard a scientist say that Miller or anyone else has made life from nonlife.

*Refuting what your opponents refuted long ago.* Rifkin devotes a whole section to ridiculing evolution because its supporters once advanced the "biogenetic law" that embryos repeat the adult stages of their ancestry—now conclusively refuted. But Darwinian evolutionists did the refuting more than 50 years ago (good science is self-correcting).

4. Rifkin ignores the most elementary procedures of fair scholarship. His book, brought forth as a major conceptual statement about the nature of science and the history of biology, displays painful ignorance

of its subject. His quotations are primarily from old and discredited secondary sources (including some creationist propaganda tracts). I see no evidence that he has ever read much of Darwin in the original. He obviously knows nothing about (or chooses not to mention) all the major works of Darwinian scholarship written by modern historians. His continual barrage of misquotes and half quotes records this partial citation from excerpts in hostile secondary sources.

His prose is often purple in the worst journalistic tradition. When 25 invented claims are buttressed by such breathless description, the effect can be quite amusing. He mentions the geneticist T. H. Morgan's invocation of the tautology argument discussed previously in this essay: "Not until Morgan began to suspect that natural selection was a victim of circular reasoning did anyone in the scientific community even question what was regarded by all as a profound truth. . . . Morgan's observation shocked the scientific establishment." Now, I ask, how does he know this? He cites no evidence of any shock, even of any contemporary comment. He quotes Morgan himself only from secondary sources. In fact, everything about the statement is wrong, just plain wrong. The tautology argument dates from the 1870s. Morgan didn't invent it (and Darwin, in my opinion, ably refuted it when Morgan was a baby). Morgan, moreover, was no noble knight sallying forth against a monolithic Darwinian establishment. When he wrote his critique in the 1920s, natural selection was a distinctly unpopular theory among evolutionists (the tide didn't turn in Darwin's favor until the late 1930s). Morgan, if anything, *was* the establishment, and his critique, so far as I know, didn't shock a soul or elicit any extensive commentary.

5. *Algeny* is full of ludicrous, simple errors. I particularly enjoyed 26 Rifkin's account of Darwin in the Galapagos. After describing the "great masses" of vultures, condors, vampire bats, jaguars, and snakes that Darwin saw on these islands, Rifkin writes: "It was a savage, primeval scene, menacing in every detail. Everywhere there was bloodletting, and the ferocious, unremittent battle for survival. The air was dank and foul, and the thick stench of volcanic ash veiled the islands with a kind of ghoulish drape." Well, I guess Rifkin has never been there; and he obviously didn't bother to read anything about these fascinating islands. Except for snakes, none of those animals live on the Galapagos. In fact, the Galapagos house no terrestrial predators at all; as a result, the animals have no fear of human beings and do not flee when approached. The Galapagos are unusual, as Darwin noted, precisely because they are not scenes of Hobbes's *bellum omnium contra omnes* (the war of all against all). And, by the way, no thick stench or ghoulish drape either; the volcanic terrains are beautiful, calm, and peaceful—not in eruption when Darwin visited, not now either.

Jeremy Rifkin, in short, has argued himself, inextricably, into a 27 corner. He has driven off his natural allies by silly, at times dishonest, argument and nasty caricature. He has saddled his legitimate concern with an extremism that would outlaw both humane and fascinating scientific research. His legitimate brief speaks for the integrity of organisms and species. It would be a bleak world indeed that treated living things as no more than separable sequences of information, available for disarticulation and recombination in any order that pleased human whim. But I do not see why we should reject all of genetic engineering because its technology might, one day, permit such a perversion of decency in the hands of some latter-day Hitler—you may as well outlaw printing because the same machine that composes Shakespeare can also set *Mein Kampf*. The domino theory does not apply to all human achievements. If we could, by transplanting a bacterial gene, confer disease or cold resistance upon an important crop plant, should we not do so in a world where people suffer so terribly from malnutrition? Must such an event imply that, tomorrow, corn and wheat, sea horses and orchids will be thrown into a gigantic vat, torn apart into genetic units, and reassembled into rows of identical human servants? Eternal vigilance, to recombine some phrases, is the price of technological achievement.

28 The debate about genetic engineering has often been portrayed, falsely, as one of many battles between the political left and right— leftists in opposition, rightists plowing ahead. It is not so simple; it rarely is. Used humanely for the benefit of ordinary people, not the profits of a few entrepreneurs, this technology need not be feared by the left. I, for one, would rather campaign for proper use, not abolition. If Rifkin's argument embodies any antithesis, it is not left versus right, but romanticism, in its most dangerous anti-intellectual form, versus respect for knowledge and its humane employment. In both its content and presentation, *Algeny* belongs in the sordid company of anti-science. Few campaigns are more dangerous than emotional calls for proscription rather than thought.

29 I have been so harsh because I believe that Rifkin has seriously harmed a cause that is very dear to me and to nearly all my scientific colleagues. Rifkin has placed all of us beyond the pale of decency by arguing that scientific paradigms are simple expressions of socioeconomic bias, that biotech implies (and will impose) a new view of organisms as strings of separable information (not wholes of necessary integrity), and that all scientists will eventually go along with this heartless idea. Well, Mr. Rifkin, who then will be for you? Where will you find your allies in the good fight for respect of evolutionary lineages? You have rejected us, reviled us, but we are with you. We are taxonomists, ecologists, and evolutionists—most of us Darwinians. We have devoted our lives to the study of species in their natural habitats.

We have struggled to understand—and we greatly admire—the remarkable construction and operation of organisms, the product of complex evolutionary histories, cascades of astounding improbability stretching back for millions of years. We know these organisms, and we love them—as they are. We would not dissolve this handiwork of four billion years to satisfy the hubris of one species. We respect the integrity of nature, Mr. Rifkin. But your arguments lack integrity. This we deplore.

## Review Questions

1. At what point near the beginning does Gould summarize his overall critical reaction to *Algeny?*
2. What are Gould's chief objections to Rifkin's *Algeny?*
3. Does Gould reject all the arguments made by Rifkin in *Algeny?* Explain.

## Discussion and Writing Suggestions

1. Determine the organization of Gould's critique. Compare this organization with the paradigm for critique discussed in Chapter 3.
2. Based on your reading of the passage from *Algeny* and the interview with Rifkin, do you believe that Gould has been fair in his criticism? Has he summarized Rifkin's views accurately, for instance? Are his criticisms reasonable? Logical?
3. Gould spends most of the final paragraph directly addressing Rifkin. Why do you think he does this? Is his technique effective? Why or why not?
4. In your personal (if not your academic) life, do you recall being guilty of any of the types of unfair argument cited by Gould in paragraphs 20–23? For example, have you ever tried "to dismiss a general notion by citing a single poor illustration"? Recount several such incidents. (If you have never been guilty of a single one of these practices, explain how someone you know—your mother or father, perhaps, or your teacher—has been.)
5. As we mentioned in the headnote, Gould's style has been characterized as "full of fun, totally without pretentiousness, and absolutely clear." Based on his critique of *Algeny,* to what extent do you agree with this characterization? Cite specific examples.
6. Write a critique of a text you have read recently (it may be another essay in this book), imitating Gould's approach in his *Algeny* critique. State your conclusion near the outset and categorize your negative or positive reactions into several types, providing examples from the text to support these reactions.
7. Write a critique of Gould's essay, drawing on your responses to some of the questions above.

# Killing Us Softly: Toward a Feminist Analysis of Genetic Engineering

## LINDA BULLARD

*As its subtitle indicates, the following article takes a feminist position on the debate over genetic engineering. Feminist viewpoints are as various as the authors (not necessarily women) who present them. Generally, however, feminist critics analyze the ways in which women have suffered discrimination and mistreatment by men—or by male-dominated views of the world—and they seek a new social order in which domination is replaced by cooperation. In "Killing Us Softly," Linda Bullard argues that genetic engineering should be opposed by feminists because it represents a patriarchal quest for control over nature and people. Bullard's article first appeared in* Made to Order: The Myth of Reproductive and Genetic Progress *(1987), edited by Patricia Stallone and Deborah Lynn Steinberg.*

If the present trend continues, genetic engineering will very soon permeate every facet of human activity, having profound social, political, legal, and economic ramifications. Reproduction technologies represent one of the more visible manifestations of the new industry. Perhaps more subtle, but not less dramatic, will be applications in agriculture, pharmaceuticals, animal husbandry, energy production, pollution control, and the military, to cite only a few. The US Patent Office has received to date more than 5500 applications for patenting biotechnology products, and issued 850 such patents last year (Moore, 1986). It is estimated that by the year 2010, 70 percent of the US Gross National Product will be linked to biotechnology (*Chemical Reporter*, 1984). That means Big Business, and the Big Businessmen are well aware of it. When the first biotechnology company, Genentech, made its initial public offering on the stockmarket in 1980, it set the Wall Street record for fastest increase in price per share (from $35 to $89 in 20 minutes). The next year Cetus set another Wall Street record for the largest amount of money raised in an initial public offering (Yoxen, 1984). Here are some of the kinds of things they're investing in.

Currently about 83 percent of all capital investment in biotechnology is in the field of human health-related products (Office of Technology Assessment, 1984). Many drugs and vaccines will be produced by

1

2

living factories, drugs such as insulin, growth hormone, and interferon, which are already on the market. In one of these living factory experiments, biologists at Monsanto have transplanted a human gene into a pink petunia with the aim of getting it to secrete a female reproductive hormone (Hotz and Cook, 1985). One hundred therapeutic and diagnostic products of biotechnology are awaiting regulatory approval by the US Food and Drug Administration. These are tending to move through the approval process in only a fraction of the time required for conventionally produced pharmaceuticals, on the justification that they resemble substances which the human body itself produces (Moore, 1986).

In the area of animal husbandry, the US Department of Agriculture is currently conducting experiments to engineer new super-breeds of livestock by transplanting the gene for human growth hormone into the animals. By so doing they hope to be able to produce cows the size of elephants and pigs the size of cows, which grow to maturity in half the time it now takes. This has already been successful with mice, and so there is now a variety of mice in our world which expresses the human trait for growth hormone (Fox, 1986). In West Germany a pig has been developed which has no eyes, so that it is not distracted from eating. 3

Gene technology contains the seeds of a new even greener Green Revolution in agriculture. Plants are now being engineered which can make their own fertilizer (nitrogen-fixation) and insecticide, and which are resistant to herbicides (Doyle, 1985). A bacterium has been invented which can even lower the temperature at which plants suffer frost damage thus extending the geographic range and growing season for many crops (Mathiessen and Kohn, 1985). It is also anticipated that agricultural products will soon be put to more and more industrial uses, particularly straw and cereals for energy production (Rexen and Munck, 1984). 4

In the area of information technology, computers of the new Age may have their chips replaced by proteins called "biochips." Part of the Pentagon's Star Wars budget is devoted to research on this kind of "molecular computer." 5

In the field of environmental engineering, microorganisms have already been created which can eat up oil spills and consume wood pulp, as well as mine copper (Lappé, 1984). 6

We won't need passports anymore, because "DNA fingerprinting" will provide irrefutable proof of each person's identity. This technique has already been used by police in England and is being hailed by forensic experts. In addition, genetic screening has already been used for hiring purposes and may be used by insurance companies in the future to take the gamble out of health and life insurance (Henifin and Hubbard, 1983). 7

And last but not least, we must not forget that gene technology 8 opens up marvelous new possibilities in the field of weaponry. In fact, genetic engineering itself is in a very real sense the direct descendent of the Bomb. When we entered the Atomic Age with the bombing of Hiroshima and Nagasaki in 1945 scientists and some government officials realized that radiation could have harmful effects on human gene mutation. This sparked a renewed interest in genetics research, and the Atomic Energy Commission began to pour funds into this field. One of their grants went to James Watson and Francis Crick, who, in 1953, unraveled the molecular structure of DNA, the key to genetic engineering.

Biological weapons (BW), however, date back much earlier than the atomic bomb. For example, the spread of the "Black Death" to Europe in the fourteenth century resulted from the use of biological warfare by the Mongols, who catapulted plague diseased corpses over the walls of Caffa. Another famous instance of biological weapons use occurred during an American Indian uprising in 1763 when the British gave the Indians blankets which were contaminated with smallpox. The Japanese also used biological agents, including plague, anthrax, and paratyphoid, in at least 11 Chinese cities during World War II. Furthermore, they carried out an extensive research program using 3000 prisoners of war as subjects. Interestingly, the United States blocked prosecution of the Japanese for these war crimes in exchange for the data they had collected (Geissler, 1986). . . . 9

The Biological Weapons Convention (BWC) was concluded in 1972, *before* the discovery of recombinant DNA, cloning, and the other major techniques of genetic engineering; had it been delayed only slightly, it probably would not have been concluded at all. Despite the existence of this treaty, there are clear indications that a dangerous new spiral of the arms race has already begun using the technology of genetic engineering. 10

The first and most striking indication is how much money is being spent by the military on biological weapons and genetic engineering research. . . . The second indication . . . is the marked shift in what Defense Department and administration officials have been doing and saying in public. . . . Two recent reports from the Pentagon to the US Congress make the reevaluation of the military significance of biological weapons abundantly clear. In August of 1986 the Deputy Assistant Secretary of Defense for Negotiations Policy, Douglas Feith, told the US House of Representatives, "The technology that makes possible so-called 'designer drugs' also makes possible designer BW." He referred to these weapons as "easy, fast, clean, and versatile." In speaking to a *Washington Post* reporter, he said: "It is now clear, using the newest technology, that BW can be highly militarily significant. We have changed our opinion about the military utility of BW. . . . 11

It certainly cannot be denied that genetic engineering promises 12 some wondrous benefits to humankind. So why should we reject all of it? Isn't that just throwing the baby out with the bath water? Can't we just try to prevent the abuses but take all the goodies? My view is that like a broken hologram in which each shard reflects the entire original image, reproduction technologies and biological weapons express the totality of what's wrong with genetic engineering in general.

One irony of the whole thing is that in a way we got what we were 13 asking for. As ecofeminists we asked for the soft energy path and renewable resources and "organic" farming and protection of the environment. Now the gene technology industry is selling itself to us in the costume of environmentalism. You don't want poisonous chemical pesticides and fertilizers? Then we'll give you designer crops which have disease and pest resistance built into their genetic structure and photosynthesize at twice the speed. You don't like experimentation on live animals? Then we'll use cell cultures instead. You are pro-choice? Then we'll give you lots of choices—eight different ways to make a baby, any kind of baby you want.

You don't like starvation in the Third World, and birth defects and 14 disease, and environmental degradation and failing economies? Then we'll solve it all for you with genetic engineering—because at last we have found what we were looking for: the means to control, quite simply, everything—from the inside out. Now, finally, we can make living things as efficient and predictable and perfect as machines. We'll take care of everything—just don't ask any questions.

If something about all this somehow doesn't sound all that new, it's 15 because it's not. It's basically the same old patriarchal fears and dreams. It's the male insecurity before chaotic and unreliable Nature (so like women), the distrust of things that develop according to their own internal rhythms, the disdain for everything he has not personally manufactured. And it's the male envy of the female power to create life. Man's drive has been especially strong ever since he succeeded in fulfilling the first half of the fantasy a few years ago by figuring out how to destroy all life. But the Bomb turned out not to be so much fun after all, because he never gets to use it. Genetic engineering promises to be much more fun because everyone wants it. It's the Soft Bomb.

The male *drives* which produced both nuclear and gene technology 16 are certainly all too familiar to us. But the capacity to *realize* the nightmare, by means of the tools of genetic engineering, is something new and plunges us into a qualitatively different and more frightening situation.

For genetic engineering is not just another one of the new technolo- 17 gies like computers, and it is more than a set of products which happen to be alive. It is the method put forward by those currently in power for organizing the entire Age of Biology. Its prime objectives are efficiency, speed, and control, and its great underlying myth is that it is possible to continually accelerate the production of living utilities without ever running out. Nature is just too slow to supply our current growth-oriented economies, and genetic engineering is a way of speeding her up. Genetic engineering is the most important and disturbing technological change in recorded history. It is the perfect technological fix, the absolute final solution, the ultimate expression of the patriarchal worldview. As such, it is totally contrary to the underlying principles of the feminist vision.

I have no quarrel with entering the Age of Biology—that is to say, leaving the Industrial Era, the Age of Pyrotechnology, and moving into economies based on renewable resources. This is what environmentalists have been demanding for several decades, and anyway it is inevitable, since we will eventually run out of the fossil fuels on which the present world economy is based. However, we must not be fooled into thinking that a transition to renewable resources means a victory for ecology. Feminist analysis can be very helpful in sorting out this confusion and offering an alternative approach to organizing the Age of Biology, one based on empathy and sustainability of natural systems, rather than control and short-term profit. 18

The most important point which I want to make here is that genetic engineering *as a whole* is a women's issue. We must not allow ourselves to be "ghettoized" into a struggle against only that which affects us most immediately—reproduction technologies: we must place this concern in the broader context of the entire technology. We must point out that there will be a very heavy price exacted for the marvelous short-term benefits which are being held out to us in this softening-up phase. This price will include erosion of the genetic diversity of the planet, further concentration of power and capital, wiping out the small farmer, reinforcing the dependency of Third World countries, and contamination of the environment through the introduction of thousands of living products which can never be recalled. 19

Like nuclear power, genetic engineering is not a neutral technology. It is by its very nature too powerful for our present state of social and scientific development, no matter whose hands are controlling it. Just as we would say, especially after Chernobyl, that a nuclear power plant is just as dangerous in a socialist nation as it is in a capitalist one, so I would say the same thing for genetic engineering. It is *inherently* Eugenic in that it always requires someone to decide what is a good and a bad gene. 20

The genetic engineers, like their predecessors since the Enlightenment (who were also terribly insecure), are pursuing science and knowledge as a means for gaining power, and power is defined as the ability 21 to control, and control for them is the way to have security. Feminists, on the other hand, must continue to redefine security—as we have done in the peace movement. We must show that true security results from the pursuit of knowledge, not for power over Nature and other people, but rather for better understanding how to participate in the web of life over the long term without rupturing its delicate threads. . . .

In the coming years we are going to witness a historic public debate about which of the two competing approaches we should choose for our journey into the Age of Biology—the path of genetic engineering or the path of deep ecology. Our opponents are already gearing up for a massive and precisely calculated propaganda campaign to win hearts and minds over this issue. . . . 22

Challenging the dominant worldview and power structures on a fundamental level is nothing new for feminists. We have been doing it in a relatively organized way for more than 100 years. We need only look to our own history for the lessons to inform our development of a strategy against this latest onslaught of the patriarchy, genetic engineering. . . . 23

In addition, I think we might do well to consider a method of decision making employed by people native to the northeastern part of what is now the United States. Whenever they were faced with a major and difficult problem, these Iroquois Indians would come together in a Tribal Council and ask themselves a single question: What will be the effect of the action which we take today on the seventh generation of our children? And they wouldn't take a decision until they could answer that question. 24

I don't think we can answer that question today for gene technology—we simply don't have a predictive ecology methodology which enables us, and until we can answer it, I don't think it's an acceptable or necessary risk. 25

## REFERENCES

*Chemical Reporter.* 1984, July 6. **8** (14).

Doyle, Jack. 1985. *Altered Harvest: Agriculture, Genetics and the Fate of the World's Food Supply.* Viking, New York.

Fox, Michael W. 1986. *Agricide, the Hidden Crisis that Affects Us All.* Schocken Books, New York.

Geissler, Erhard, ed. 1986. *Biological and Toxin Weapons Today.* Oxford University Press, Oxford.

Girard, Rowland. 1985. *Le Fruit de vos Ventrails.* Editions Suger, Jean-Jaques Pauvert. Paris.

Henifin, Mary Sue and Ruth Hubbard. 1983, November/December. Genetic Screening in the Workplace. *geneWatch.*

Hilts, Philip J. 1986, August 17. Biological weapons reweighed, defense official cites strides in technology. *Washington Post.*

Hotz, Robert Lee and Robert Cook. 1985. The Eighth Day. Special series in *The Atlanta Journal* and *The Atlanta Constitution.*

Lappé, Marc. 1984. *Broken Code, the Exploitation of DNA.* Sierra Club Books, San Francisco.

Mathiessen, Constance and Howard Kohn. 1985, May/June. Ice minus and beyond. *Science for the People* **3.**

Moore, John. 1986, June 21. Genes for sale. *National Journal.* 1528.

Office of Technology Assessment. 1984, January. *Commercial Biotechnology: An International Analysis.* US Government Printing Office, (no. OTA-BA-218). US.

Rexen, F. and L. Munck. 1984. *Cereal Crops for Industrial Use in Europe.* Carlsberg Research Laboratora, Copenhagen.

Richards, Bill and Tim Carrington. 1986, September 19. Controversy grows over Pentagon's work on biological agents. *Wall Street Journal.*

Wright, Susan and Robert L. Sinsheimer. 1983, November 22. Recombinant DNA and biological warfare. *Bulletin of the Atomic Scientists.*

Yoxen, Edward. 1984. *The Gene Business: Who Should Control Biotechnology.* Harper and Row, New York.

## Review Questions

1. In what main areas does Bullard see genetic engineering permeating "every facet of human activity"?
2. Why does Bullard consider it ironic that genetic engineering may have been offered by scientists as "what [feminists] were asking for"?
3. What are Bullard's general and specific objections to genetic engineering?

## Discussion and Writing Suggestions

1. For Bullard, genetic engineering is the result of "the old patriarchal fears and dreams" in which science and knowledge are pursued "as a means for gaining power, and power is defined as the ability to control, and control for [genetic engineers] is the way to have security." To what extent do you agree with this viewpoint? Explain, as specifically as possible.
2. Bullard argues that genetic engineering "is *inherently* Eugenic in that it always requires someone to decide what is a good and a bad gene." Is this a fair statement? Why or why not?
3. To what extent has Bullard persuaded you that genetic engineering is not "an acceptable or necessary risk" and that the path of "deep ecology" is to be preferred to biotechnology? Write your response in the form of a critique.

# Why I Support Gene Therapy

## BEVERLY SILLS GREENOUGH

*Beverly Sills Greenough, more widely known as Beverly Sills, is one of the most celebrated opera singers of our time. Born in 1929 in Brooklyn, New York, she made her operatic debut at the age of 17 and has sung for such companies as the New York City Opera, La Scala, and the Metropolitan Opera. From 1979 to 1989 she served as director of the New York City Opera. Even before she ended her singing career in 1980 (she still serves as a managing director of the Metropolitan Opera), Greenough was active in public health issues, and (as she notes in the following piece) now serves as national chair of the March of Dimes Birth Defects Foundation. This article first appeared as a "My Turn" column in* Newsweek *on April 5, 1993.*

Some people recoil when they hear the phrase "gene therapy." It conjures frightening images of scientists trying to play God. But the words actually hold great promise for doctors fighting to conquer crippling and lethal diseases.

Genes, units of DNA housed in human chromosomes, are the keys to heredity. They hold the codes that control individual characteristics like our eye color and blood type. Genes can also determine our long-term health. Persons with damaged or missing genes are vulnerable to a wide range of serious illnesses. Through gene therapy, scientists have begun to restore or replace faulty or missing genes with healthy ones.

Obviously, all of this isn't as simple as it sounds. Before researchers can replace a damaged gene, they have to locate it and determine its function. Thirty years ago, scientists knew the location of fewer than 100 of the estimated 100,000 genes that humans carry. By 1990, the number had risen to 1,850. That same year researchers began a massive effort to map the rest. The Human Genome Project, funded by the Department of Energy and the National Institutes of Health, is the largest biological research effort ever undertaken. The work is painstaking. It could take 15 to 20 years to complete a genetic blueprint of the human body.

But there have already been breakthroughs. One involves a 4-year-

Excerpt from "Breaking the Genetic Code" by Beverly Sills Greenough as appeared originally in *Newsweek*, April 5, 1993. Reprinted by permission of Beverly Sills Greenough.

old girl who, because of a missing gene, had been ill from birth with an inherited deficiency of her immune system. Like the "bubble boy" in Texas who suffered from a similar ailment, any minor infection could have been life threatening. The condition made both the girl and her family virtual prisoners. Her mother and siblings seldom left home for fear they might bring back a potentially lethal infection.

In September 1990, doctors removed some of the girl's white blood 5 cells, treated them with copies of the missing gene and reintroduced them into her body. Within a year, the child's immune system began to respond. She was well enough to take dancing lessons, swim, even go to a shopping mall. While the results are not conclusive, her prognosis is very promising. More than a happy ending for one little girl, the case marked the beginning of a new medical era. She was the world's first recipient of gene therapy.

Scientists have identified genes responsible for cystic fibrosis, Du- 6 chenne muscular dystrophy, Marfan syndrome, fragile X syndrome and certain cancers. The next step is the development of successful techniques to deliver corrected versions of genes to the cells of patients suffering from such disorders. Alzheimer's, diabetes and some forms of heart disease may be conquered by this technology.

Why should I care about all of this? One reason is that I am national 7 chairman of the March of Dimes Birth Defects Foundation. We know that a large number of birth defects have a genetic origin. That's why the foundation devotes a sizable amount of its annual research budget to grants for the study of gene therapy.

There's a personal side for me as well. 8

My daughter was born profoundly deaf. And my son, soon after 9 birth, was found to be autistic, epileptic *and* deaf. Unless you've been there, you cannot imagine how all this feels. Yet, during my pregnancies, I had the very best of prenatal care. I didn't smoke, drink or use any sort of drugs. It didn't matter.

## PUBLIC IGNORANCE

We still do not know all of the reasons why babies are born sick or with 10 major disabilities. But we *do* know some. One baby, maybe more, out of one hundred is born with a serious *genetic* problem. Gene therapy offers a very real possibility of correcting many of these disorders. It could transform—indeed, it already has—lives that are doomed to the pain and anguish of chronic illness.

But scientific advances can also generate misunderstanding and fear. 11 The Salk polio vaccine, so closely identified with the March of Dimes, was one of the most important medical gains of our time. It was safe. It worked. But because earlier vaccines used "live" viruses that caused fatalities, researchers had to overcome public apprehension. (The Salk vaccine used a benign, "dead" virus).

Some critics are concerned that gene therapy will be abused to 12 create "super" humans. Others are disturbed about possible disclosures of personally sensitive medical history. Still, the public seems to be giving this new technology the benefit of the doubt. A recent survey conducted for the foundation revealed that 89 percent of Americans support gene therapy and favor continued research. Curiously, this same poll showed widespread public ignorance about this form of treatment. So the need for public education on a broad scale is self-evident. There is much yet for both scientists and lay people to learn.

The main thing is this: we *cannot* let our fears destroy our hopes. We 13 cannot let myth and misinterpretation prevent us from seeking treatment for the thousands who suffer from genetic diseases. Let's continue to resolve the issues while moving onward to intensify the research effort.

From my own viewpoint, if gene therapy can spare *one* mother the 14 anguish of knowing that her newborn will suffer throughout its whole life—if it can help sick little girls get well enough to dance—can we afford *not* to make the effort?

## Review Questions

1. According to Greenough, how do doctors use gene therapy to correct immune system deficiencies?
2. How does Greenough acknowledge and respond to the views of critics of gene therapy?

## Discussion and Writing Suggestions

1. Greenough clearly favors the use and continued development of gene therapy. To what extent do you think that her arguments sufficiently rebut the anti-gene therapy arguments of other writers in this chapter, such as Rifkin, Bullard, and (later) Wright?
2. At the end of paragraph 9, Greenough notes that she "had the very best of prenatal care. I didn't smoke, drink, or use any sort of drugs." Why do you think she points out these facts? What kind of arguments might they be intended to rebut?
3. Analyze the structure and development of Greenough's argument. (Notice, for example, her introduction and conclusion.) Explain how this structure works in creating and reinforcing the logical and emotional force of her argument.

# The Gene Hunt

## LEON JAROFF

*One of the most monumental scientific undertakings of our time is the Human Genome Project launched in 1988. A genome is the complete set of genes in the chromosomes of an organism (humans have forty-six chromosomes in the nucleus of each cell); and the purpose of the Human Genome Project is to identify, locate, and sequence all of the genes in human chromosomes. As a diagram caption in the following article explains, "Encoded in the genome, the DNA in the . . . 46 chromosomes, are instructions that affect not only structure, size, coloring and other physical attributes, but also intelligence, susceptibility to disease, life-span and even some aspects of behavior. The ultimate goal of the Human Genome Project is to read and understand those instructions." Among the instructions that scientists are most eager to understand are those that determine human diseases, many of which are genetic in origin. Scientists hope to develop the capability to treat and even to prevent such diseases.*

*In the following article, which first appeared in* Time *in March 1988, staff writer Leon Jaroff explains what is involved in the Human Genome Project and discusses its potential benefits. In subsequent articles in this chapter, other writers discuss some of the potential problems arising from the Human Genome Project and from our increased knowledge of genes.*

Know then thyself . . . the glory, jest, and riddle of the world.
—Alexander Pope

In an obscure corner of the National Institutes of Health (NIH), molecular biologist Norton Zinder strode to a 30-ft.-long oval conference table, sat down and rapped his gavel for order. A hush settled over the Human Genome Advisory Committee, an unlikely assemblage of computer experts, biologists, ethicists, industry scientists and engineers. "Today we begin," chairman Zinder declared. "We are initiating an unending study of human biology. Whatever it's going to be, it will be an adventure, a priceless endeavor. And when it's done, someone else will sit down and say, 'It's time to begin.' " 1

With these words, spoken in January, Zinder formally launched a monumental effort that could rival in scope both the Manhattan Project, which created the A-bomb, and the Apollo moon-landing program— and may exceed them in importance. The goal: to map the human 2 genome and spell out for the world the entire message hidden in its chemical code.

Genome? The word evokes a blank stare from most Americans, 3 whose taxes will largely support the project's estimated $3 billion cost. Explains biochemist Robert Sinsheimer of the University of California at Santa Barbara: "The human genome is the complete set of instructions for making a human being." Those instructions are tucked into the nucleus of each of the human body's 100 trillion cells* and written in the language of deoxyribonucleic acid, the fabled DNA molecule.

In the 35 years since James Watson and Francis Crick first discerned 4 the complex structure of DNA, scientists have managed to decipher only a tiny fraction of the human genome. But they have high hopes that with new, automated techniques and a huge coordinated effort, the genome project can reach its goal in 15 years.

The achievement of that goal would launch a new era in medicine. 5 James Wyngaarden, director of the NIH, which will oversee the project, predicts that it will make "major contributions to understanding growth, development and human health, and open new avenues for therapy." Full translation of the genetic message would enable medical researchers to identify the causes of thousands of still mysterious inherited disorders, both physical and behavioral.

With this insight, scientists could more accurately predict an indi- 6 vidual's vulnerability to such obviously genetic diseases as cystic fibrosis and could eventually develop new drugs to treat or even prevent them. The same would be true for more common disorders like heart disease and cancer, which at the very least have large genetic components. Better knowledge of the genome could speed development of gene therapy—the actual alteration of instructions in the human genome to eliminate genetic defects.

The NIH and the Food and Drug Administration have already taken 7 a dramatic step toward gene therapy. In January [1988] they gave approval to Dr. W. French Anderson and Dr. Steven Rosenberg, both at the NIH, to transplant a bacterial gene into cancer patients. While this gene is intended only to make it easier for doctors to monitor an experimental cancer treatment and will not benefit the patients, its successful implantation should help pave the way for actual gene therapy.

The very thought of being able to read the entire genetic message, 8 and perhaps alter it, is alarming to those who fear the knowledge could create many moral and ethical problems. Does genetic testing constitute

---

*Except red blood cells, which have no nucleus.

an invasion of privacy, for example, and could it lead to more abortions and to discrimination against the "genetically unfit"? Should someone destined to be stricken with a deadly genetic disease be told about his fate, especially if no cure is yet available? Does it demean humans to have the very essence of their lives reduced to strings of letters in a computer data bank? Should gene therapy be used only for treating disease, or also for "improving" a person's genetic legacy?

Although scientists share many of these concerns, the concept of     9
deciphering the human genome sends most of them into paroxysms of rapture. "It's the Holy Grail of biology," says Harvard biologist and Nobel laureate Walter Gilbert. "This information will usher in the Golden Age of molecular medicine," says Mark Pearson, Du Pont's director of molecular biology. Predicts George Cahill, a vice president at the Howard Hughes Medical Institute: "It's going to tell us everything. Evolution, disease, everything will be based on what's in that magnificent tape called DNA."

That kind of enthusiasm is infectious. In an era of budgetary re-     10
straint, Washington has been unblinkingly generous toward the genome project, especially since last April [1987], when an array of scientists testified on the subject at a congressional committee hearing. There, Nobel laureate Watson of DNA fame, since picked by the NIH to head the effort, mesmerized listeners with his plea for support: "I see an extraordinary potential for human betterment ahead of us. We can have at our disposal the ultimate tool for understanding ourselves at the molecular level . . . The time to act is now."

Congress rose to the challenge. It promptly allocated more than $31     11
million for genome research to the NIH and to the Department of Energy and the National Library of Medicine, which are also involved in the quest. The combined appropriations rose to $53 million for fiscal 1989.

Even more will be needed when the effort is in full swing, involving     12
hundreds of scientists, dozens of Government, university and private laboratories, and several computer and data centers. With contributions from other Government agencies and private organizations like the Hughes institute, the total annual cost of the project will probably rise to $200 million, which over 15 years will account for the $3 billion price tag.

The staggering expense and sheer size of the genome project were     13
what bothered scientists most when the idea was first broached in 1985 by Sinsheimer, then chancellor of the University of California at Santa Cruz. "I thought Bob Sinsheimer was crazy," recalls Leroy Hood, a biologist at the California Institute of Technology. "It seemed to me to be a very big science project with marginal value to the science community."

Nobel laureate David Baltimore, director of M.I.T.'s Whitehead     14

# MAPPING CHROMOSOMES

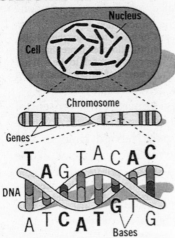

chromosome, there is a corresponding gene on the other member of the chromosome pair.* One of the two genes came from the person's mother, and the other came from the father. The two genes may be the same or different, but they both affect the same characteristic.

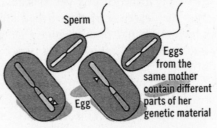

Eggs from the same mother contain different parts of her genetic material

When **sperm** and **egg** cells are formed, they contain only one member of each chromosome pair. Before the chromosome pairs separate, they exchange pieces. In the process, some genes that were together on one chromosome wind up on different chromosomes and thus go into different sperm or egg cells. The closer two genes are to each other on a chromosome, the more likely they are to stay linked and be inherited together.

The **nucleus** of human cells contains a complete blueprint for a man or woman. That information resides on 46 **chromosomes** made primarily of long chains of **DNA**, the master chemical that controls the development and functioning of organisms. The crucial components of DNA are four nitrogenous **bases**: adenine, thymine, cytosine and guanine (**A, T, C** and **G**). The sequence of these bases determines the order in which amino acids are linked together to form proteins. A segment of the DNA chain that contains the instructions for a complete protein is called a **gene**.

During cell division, the DNA arranges itself into **23 pairs of complementary chromosomes**, each containing thousands of genes. The chromosomes in each pair have slight differences from each other that can be used as signposts or **markers** to help find genes. For every gene on a

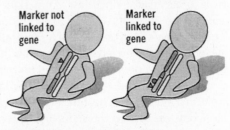

Marker not linked to gene

Marker linked to gene

That fact enables biologists to construct **maps of chromosomes**. To do so, the researchers must extract and analyze DNA from cells. They use a large set of chemicals known as restriction enzymes to chop up the DNA chain into much shorter pieces. Differences between these pieces are called restriction-fragment-length polymorphisms, or RFLPs (pronounced *rif*-lips). Gene mappers have identified a whole catalog of RFLPs, each with its own characteristic sequence of bases. By studying how frequently certain RFLPs are inherited

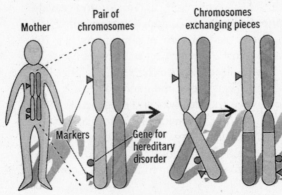

Mother — Pair of chromosomes — Chromosomes exchanging pieces

Markers — Gene for hereditary disorder

* An exception is a man's pair of sex chromosomes, which are called X and Y. A gene on the X chromosome does not necessarily have a complementary gene on the Y.

together in several generations of large families, and thus how close to one another the RFLPs are on the DNA chain, researchers can determine their approximate location on a chromosome.

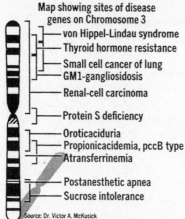

**Map showing sites of disease genes on Chromosome 3**

- von Hippel-Lindau syndrome
- Thyroid hormone resistance
- Small cell cancer of lung
- GM1-gangliosidosis
- Renal-cell carcinoma
- Protein S deficiency
- Oroticaciduria
- Propionicacidemia, pccB type
- Atransferrinemia
- Postanesthetic apnea
- Sucrose intolerance

Source: Dr. Victor A. McKusick

RFLPs form a valuable series of markers along the chromosomes and make it possible, in many cases, to track down the location of the genetic defect that causes a disease. DNA from many patients must be analyzed for the presence of telltale RFLPs. If a particular RFLP is always found in people with a certain disease, then the gene that causes the condition is likely to be close to that RFLP on its chromosome.

# SEQUENCING GENES

**1** Through a process known as gene cloning, thousands of copies of the **DNA** being studied are made and a **radioactive label** is attached to one end of a single stand.

**2** The DNA is separated into four test tubes. To each tube is added a **chemical** that destroys one of the four bases and thus can break the chain wherever that base occurs. The reactions are stopped before all the possible breakpoints are split, yielding fragments of different lengths.

**3** The DNA is removed from each tube and applied to a slab of gel. An electric field is used to move the DNA through the gel. Smaller pieces move faster than larger pieces. After a time, the radioactive labels show up as distinctive bands that are visible in the gel. The pattern of the bands reveals the order of the bases in the original DNA chain.

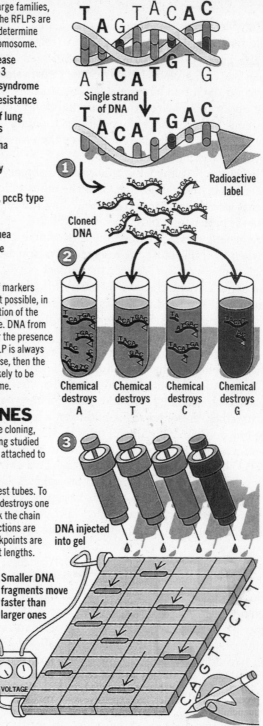

Single strand of DNA

① Radioactive label

Cloned DNA

②

Chemical destroys A | Chemical destroys T | Chemical destroys C | Chemical destroys G

③

DNA injected into gel

Smaller DNA fragments move faster than larger ones

VOLTAGE

Institute, was one of the many who feared that such a megaproject would have much the same impact on biology that the shuttle had on the U.S. space program: soaking up so much money and talent that smaller but vital projects would dry up. Others stressed that the technology to do the job in a reasonable time was not available. But by 1986 some opponents realized they were fighting a losing battle. "The idea is gaining momentum. I shiver at the thought," said Baltimore then. Now, however, he approves of the way the project has evolved and has thrown his weight behind it.

What really turned the tide was a February 1988 report by the   15
prestigious National Research Council enthusiastically endorsing a project that would first map and interpret important regions of the genome, then—as better technology became available—proceed to reading the entire genetic message. Most of the remaining critics were silenced last fall when the NIH chose the respected Watson as project director. Still, some scientists remain wary of the project. Says David Botstein, a vice president at Genentech and a member of the Human Genome Advisory Committee: "We need to test its progress, regulate its growth and slap it down if it becomes a monster. Jim Watson understands the dangers as well as any of us."

The concern, as well as the cost, reflects the complexity of the   16
human genome and the magnitude of the effort required to understand it. DNA is found in the human-cell nucleus in the form of 46 separate threads, each coiled into a packet called a chromosome. Unraveled and tied together, these threads would form a fragile string more than 5 ft. long but only 50 trillionths of an inch across.

And what a wondrous string it is. As Watson and Crick discovered   17
in 1953, DNA consists of a double helix, resembling a twisted ladder with sidepieces made of sugar and phosphates and closely spaced connecting rungs. Each rung is called a base pair because it consists of a pair of complementary chemicals called nitrogenous bases, attached end to end, either adenine (A) joined to thymine (T) or cytosine (C) attached to guanine (G).

Fundamental to the genius of DNA is the fact that A and T are   18
mutually attractive, as are C and G. Consequently, when DNA separates during cell division, coming apart at the middle of each rung like a zipper opening, an exposed T half-rung on one side of the ladder will always attract an A floating freely in the cell. The corresponding A half-rung on the other section of the ladder will attract a floating T, and so on, until two double helixes, each identical to the original DNA molecule, are formed.

Even more remarkable, each of the four bases represents a letter in   19
the genetic code. The three-letter "words" they spell, reading in sequence along either side of the ladder, are instructions to the cell on how

to assemble amino acids into the proteins essential to the structure and life of its host. Each complete DNA "sentence" is a gene, a discrete segment of the DNA string responsible for ordering the production of a specific protein.

Reading these genetic words and deciphering their meaning is apparently a snap for the clever machinery of a cell. But for mere scientists it is a formidable and time-consuming task. For instance, a snippet of DNA might read ACGGTAGAT, a message that researchers can decipher rather easily. It codes for a sequence of three of the 20 varieties of amino acids that constitute the building blocks of proteins. But the entire genome of even the simplest organism dwarfs that snippet. The genetic blueprint of the lowly E. coli bacterium, for one, is more than 4.5 million base pairs long. For a microscopic yeast plant, the length is 15 million units. And in a human being, the genetic message is some 3 billion letters long. **20**

Like cartographers mapping the ancient world, scientists over the past three decades have been laboriously charting human DNA. Of the estimated 100,000-odd genes that populate the genome, just 4,550 have been identified. And only 1,500 of those have been roughly located on the various chromosomes. The message of the genes has been equally difficult to come by. Most genes consist of between 10,000 and 150,000 code letters, and only a few genes have been completely deciphered. Long segments of the genome, like the vast uncharted regions of early maps, remain terra incognita. **21**

To complicate matters, between the segments of DNA that represent genes are endless stretches of code letters that seem to spell out only genetic gibberish. Geneticists once thought most of the unintelligible stuff was "junk DNA"—useless sequences of code letters that accidentally developed during evolution and were not discarded. That concept has changed. "My feeling is there's a lot of very useful information buried in the sequence," says Nobel laureate Paul Berg of Stanford University. "Some of it we will know how to interpret; some we know is going to be gibberish." **22**

In fact, some of the nongene regions on the genome have already been identified as instructions necessary for DNA to replicate itself during cell division. Their message is obviously detailed and complex. Explains George Bell, head of genome studies at Los Alamos National Laboratory: "It's as if you had a rope that was maybe 2 in. in diameter and 32,000 miles long, all neatly arranged inside a structure the size of a superdome. When the appropriate signal comes, you have to unwind the rope, which consists of two strands, and copy each strand so you end up with two new ropes that again have to fold up. The machinery to do that cannot be trivial." **23**

One of the most formidable tasks faced by geneticists is to learn the 24 nature of that machinery and other genetic instructions buried in the lengthy, still undeciphered base sequences. To do so fully requires achievement of the project's most challenging goal: the "sequencing" of the entire human genome. In other words, the identification and listing in order of all the genome's 3 billion base pairs.

That effort, says Caltech research fellow Richard Wilson, "is analo- 25 gous to going around and shaking hands with everyone on earth." The resulting string of code letters, according to the 1988 National Research Council report urging adoption of the genome project, would fill a million-page book. Even then, much of the message would be obscure. To decipher it, researchers would need more powerful computer systems to roam the length of the genome, seeking out meaningful patterns and relationships.

It was from the patterns and relationships of pea plants that a 26 concept of heredity first arose in the mind of Gregor Mendel, an Austrian monk. In 1865, after studying the flower colors and other characteristics of many generations of pea plants, Mendel formulated the laws of heredity and suggested the existence of packets of genetic information, which became known as genes. Soon afterward, chromosomes were observed in the nuclei of dividing cells, and scientists later discovered a chromosomal difference between the sexes. One chromosome, which they named Y, was found in human males' cells, together with another, called X. Females' cells, on the other hand, had two copies of X.

But it was not until 1911 that a gene, only a theoretical entity at the 27 time, was correctly assigned to a particular chromosome. After studying the pedigrees of several large families with many color-blind members (males are primarily affected), Columbia University scientist E. B. Wilson applied Mendelian logic and proved that the trait was carried on the X chromosome. In the same manner over the next few decades, several genes responsible for such gender-linked diseases as hemophilia were assigned to the X chromosome and a few others attributed to the Y.

Scientists remained uncertain about the exact number of human 28 chromosomes until 1956, when improved photomicrographs of dividing cells clearly established that there were 46. This revelation led directly to identification of the cause of Down syndrome (a single extra copy of chromosome 21) and other disorders that result from distinctly visible errors in the number or shape of certain chromosomes.

But greater challenges lay ahead. How could a particular gene be 29 assigned to any of the nonsex chromosomes? Scientists cleverly tackled that problem by fusing human cells with mouse cells, then growing hybrid mouse-human cells in the laboratory. As the hybrid cells divided again and again, they gradually shed their human chromosomes until only one—or simply a fragment of one—was left in the nucleus of each cell.

By identifying the kind of human protein each of these hybrid cells    30
produced, the researchers could deduce that the gene responsible for that protein resided in the surviving chromosome. Using this method, they assigned hundreds of genes to specific chromosomes.

Finding the location of a gene on a chromosome is even more    31
complicated. But over the past several years, scientists have managed to draw rough maps of all the chromosomes. They determine the approximate site of the genes, including many associated with hereditary diseases, by studying patterns of inheritance in families and chopping up their DNA strands for analysis. With this technique, they have tracked down the gene for cystic fibrosis in the midsection of chromosome 7, the gene for a rare form of colon cancer midway along the long arm of chromosome 5, and the one for familial Alzheimer's disease on the long arm of chromosome 21.

One of the more dramatic hunts for a disease gene was led by    32
Nancy Wexler, a neuropsychologist at Columbia University and president of the Hereditary Disease Foundation. Wexler was highly motivated; her mother died of Huntington's disease, a debilitating and painful disorder that usually strikes adults between the ages of 35 and 45 and is invariably fatal. This meant that Wexler had a 50% chance of inheriting the gene from her mother and contracting the disease.

In a search coordinated by Wexler's foundation, geneticist James    33
Gusella of Massachusetts General Hospital discovered a particular piece of DNA, called a genetic marker, that seemed to be present in people suffering from Huntington's disease. His evidence suggested that the marker must be near the Huntington's disease gene on the same chromosome, but he needed a larger sample to confirm his findings. This was provided by Wexler, who had previously traveled to Venezuela to chart the family tree of a clan of some 5,000 people, all of them descendants of a woman who died of Huntington's disease a century ago. Working with DNA samples from affected family members, Gusella and Wexler in 1983 concluded that they had indeed found a Huntington's marker, which was located near one end of chromosome 4.

That paved the way for a Huntington's gene test, which is now    34
available. The actual gene has not yet been isolated and since there is no cure at present, many people at risk for Huntington's are reluctant to take it. "Before the test," Wexler says, "you can always say, 'Well, it can't happen to me.' After the test, if it is positive, you can't say that anymore." Has Wexler, 43, taken the test? "People need to have some privacy," she answers.

Tracking down the location of a gene requires tedious analysis. But    35 it is sheer adventure when compared with the task of determining the sequence of base pairs in a DNA chain. Small groups of scientists, working literally by hand, have spent years simply trying to sequence a single gene. This hands-on method of sequencing costs as much as a dollar per base pair, and deciphering the entire genome by this method might take centuries.

The solution is automation. "It will improve accuracy," says Stan-    36
ford's Paul Berg. "It will remove boredom; it will accomplish what we want in the end." The drive for automation has already begun; a machine designed by Caltech biologist Leroy Hood can now sequence 16,000 base pairs a day. But Hood, a member of the Genome Advisory Committee, is hardly satisfied. "Before we can seriously take on the genome initiative," he says, "we will want to do 100,000 to a million a day." The cost, he hopes, will eventually drop to a penny per base pair.

Hood is not alone in his quest for automation. That is also the goal    37
of Columbia University biochemist Charles Cantor, recently appointed by the Energy Department to head one of its two genome centers. "It's largely an engineering project," Cantor explains, intended to produce tools for faster, less expensive sequencing and to develop data bases and computer programs to scan the data. Not to be outdone, Japan has set up a consortium of four high-tech companies to establish an automated assembly line, complete with robots, that researchers hope will be capable of sequencing 100,000 base pairs a day within three years.

Is there a better way? In San Francisco in January, Energy Depart-    38
ment scientists displayed a photograph of a DNA strand magnified a million times by a scanning tunneling microscope. It was the first direct image of the molecule. If sharper images can be made, the scientists suggested, it may be possible to read the genetic code directly. But that day seems very far off.

One of the early benefits of the genome project will be the identifi-    39
cation of more and more of the defective genes responsible for the thousands of known inherited diseases and development of tests to detect them. Like those already used to find Huntington's and sickle-cell markers, for example, these tests will allow doctors to predict with near certainty that some patients will fall victim to specific genetic diseases and that others are vulnerable and could be stricken.

University of Utah geneticist Mark Skolnick is convinced that map-    40
ping the genome will radically change the way medicine is practiced. "Right now," he says, "we wait for someone to get sick so we can cut them and drug them. It's pretty old stuff. Once you can make a profile of a person's genetic predisposition to disease, medicine will finally become predictive and preventive."

Eventually, says Mark Guyer of the NIH's Human Genome Office,    41

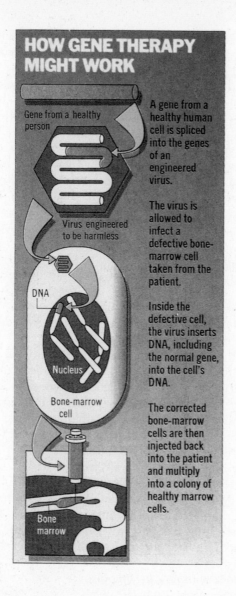

**HOW GENE THERAPY MIGHT WORK**

Gene from a healthy person

Virus engineered to be harmless

DNA

Nucleus

Bone-marrow cell

Bone marrow

A gene from a healthy human cell is spliced into the genes of an engineered virus.

The virus is allowed to infect a defective bone-marrow cell taken from the patient.

Inside the defective cell, the virus inserts DNA, including the normal gene, into the cell's DNA.

The corrected bone-marrow cells are then injected back into the patient and multiply into a colony of healthy marrow cells.

people might have access to a computer readout of their own genome, with an interpretation of their genetic strengths and weaknesses. At the very least, this would enable them to adopt an appropriate life-style, choosing the proper diet, environment and—if necessary—drugs to minimize the effects of genetic disorders.

The ever improving ability to read base-pair sequences of genes will enable researchers to speed the discovery of new proteins, assess their role in the life processes, and use them—as the interferons and interleu-

42

kins are already used—for fighting disease. It will also help them pinpoint missing proteins, such as insulin, that can correct genetic diseases.

Mapping and sequencing the genes should accelerate progress in another highly touted and controversial discipline: gene therapy. Using this technique, scientists hope someday to cure genetic diseases by actually inserting good genes into their patients' cells. One proposed form of gene therapy would be used to fight beta-thalassemia major, a blood disease characterized by severe anemia and caused by the inability of hemoglobin to function properly. That inability results from the lack of a protein in the hemoglobin, a deficiency that in turn is caused by a defective gene in bone-marrow cells. **43**

To effect a cure, doctors would remove bone-marrow cells from a patient and expose them to a retrovirus* engineered to carry correctly functioning versions of the patient's faulty gene. When the retrovirus invaded a marrow cell, it would insert itself into the cellular DNA, as retroviruses are wont to do, carrying the good gene with it. Reimplanted in the marrow, the altered marrow cells would take hold and multiply, churning out the previously lacking protein and curing the thalassemia patient. **44**

Easier said than done. Scientists have had trouble getting such implanted genes to "turn on" in their new environment, and they worry about unforeseen consequences if the gene is inserted in the wrong place in a chromosome. Should the gene be slipped into the middle of another vital gene, for example, it might disrupt the functioning of that gene, with disastrous consequences. Also, says M.I.T. biologist Richard Mulligan, there are limitations to the viral insertion of genes. "Most genes," he explains, "are too big to fit into a retrovirus." **45**

Undaunted, researchers are refining their techniques in experiments with mice, and Mulligan believes that the first human-gene-therapy experiments could occur in the next three years. Looking further ahead, other scientists are experimenting with a kind of genetic microsurgery that bypasses the retrovirus, mechanically inserting genes directly into the cell nucleus. **46**

Not only those with rare genetic disorders could benefit from the new technology. Says John Brunzell, a University of Washington medicine professor: "Ten years ago, it was thought that only 10% of premature coronary heart disease came from inherited abnormalities. Now that proportion is approaching 80% to 90%." **47**

Harvard geneticist Philip Leder cites many common diseases— hyper-tension, allergies, diabetes, heart disease, mental illness and some **48**

---

*A virus consisting largely of RNA, a single-stranded chain of bases similar to the DNA double helix.

(perhaps all) cancers—that have a genetic component. Unlike Hunting-ton's and Tay-Sachs diseases, which are caused by a single defective gene, many of these disorders have their roots in several errant genes and would require genetic therapy far more sophisticated than any now even being contemplated. Still, says Leder, "in the end, genetic mapping is going to have its greatest impact on these major diseases."

Of all the enthusiasm that the genome project has generated among scientists and their supporters in Washington, however, none matches that of James Watson as he gears up for the monumental task ahead. "It excites me enormously," he says, and he remains confident that it can be accomplished despite the naysayers both within and outside the scientific community. "How can we not do it?" he demands. "We used to think our fate was in our stars. Now we know, in large measure, our fate is in our genes."  **49**

## Review Questions

1. Cite the main potential benefits of the Human Genome Project, as foreseen by its supporters.
2. What are genetic markers? How do they function in helping to locate genes?
3. Indicate some of the difficulties facing scientists attempting to map the human genome.
4. What was Gregor Mendel's role in the science of genetics?
5. Why will the Human Genome Project lead to a new era of preventative medicine, according to its proponents?

## Discussion and Writing Suggestions

1. Do you find this article primarily positive, primarily negative, or generally balanced in its treatment of the Human Genome Project? Explain the reasons for your conclusion, citing particular passages.
2. In paragraph 8, Jaroff indicates some of the fears expressed by many people about the consequences of the Human Genome Project. He does not, however, elaborate on these concerns. (They will be treated more fully in the subsequent articles by Wright and by Kevles and Hood). To what extent do you share these fears? For example, to what extent do you sense parallels to Huxley's brave new world in the concerns sketched by Jaroff? Explain.
3. One of the arguments against the Human Genome Project was that the enormous costs involved would dry up funding for other worthy scientific projects (see paragraph 14). As a parallel example, some people, although sympathetic to persons with AIDS, have come to resent the intense media focus and the ever-increasing funding for AIDS research, fearing that less money will be available for research into cancer and heart disease, which,

they argue, kill more people each year than AIDS. To what extent do you believe that some of the $3 billion estimated funding for the Human Genome Project should be devoted to other types of scientific research? Explain.

**4.** Based on your reading of Jeremy Rifkin ("A Heretic's View on the New Bioethics"), how do you think he would respond to this article? How would you respond to *his* response?

# The Human Genome Project: A Personal View*

## JAMES D. WATSON

*The previous article concluded with an (understandably) enthusiastic endorsement of the Human Genome Project by its director, James D. Watson. In the following article, Watson offers a "personal" perspective on this project and its meaning for him. One of the most influential scientists of modern times, Watson, together with Francis Crick, discovered the double-helix structure of the DNA molecule, a discovery that won them the 1962 Nobel Prize and that has been the basis of almost all subsequent genetic research. Born in 1928, Watson earned his doctorate in biology from Indiana University. In 1951, while conducting research at the Cavendish Laboratory at Cambridge University, Watson met Francis Crick, and the two began their epoch-making studies into the molecular basis of heredity. Watson and Crick's paper, announcing their discovery, was published in the journal* Nature *in 1953.*

*Watson taught at Harvard University from 1955 to 1976, and starting in 1968 served as director of the Cold Spring Harbor Biological Laboratories, working primarily on cancer research. In 1989 Watson was appointed director of the National Institutes of Health's (NIH) Human Genome Project. Watson's books include* The Double Helix *(1968), an account of the discovery of DNA structure;* The Molecular Biology of the Gene *(1965); and* Recombinant DNA *(1985; with John Tooze and David T. Kurtz). This article first appeared in an anthology,* The Code of Codes: Scientific and Social Issues in the Human Genome Project *(1992), edited by Daniel J. Kevles and Leroy Hood.*

When I was going into science, people were concerned with questions    1
of where we came from. Some people gave mystical answers—for

---

Excerpt from "Personal View of the Project" * For permission to photocopy this selection, please contact Harvard University Press. Reprinted by permission of the publishers from *The Code of Codes: Scientific and Social Issues in the Human Genome Project* by Daniel J. Kevles and Leroy Hood, Cambridge, Mass.: Harvard University Press, Copyright © 1992 by Daniel J. Kevles and Leroy Hood.

example, "the truth came from revelation." But as a college kid I was influenced by Linus Pauling, who said, "We came from chemistry." I have spent my career trying to get a chemical explanation for life, the explanation of why we are human beings and not monkeys. The reason, of course, is our DNA. If you can study life from the level of DNA, you have a real explanation for its processes. So of course I think that the human genome project is a glorious goal.

People ask why *I* want to get the human genome. Some suggest that   2
the reason is that it would be a wonderful end to my career—start out with the double helix and end up with the human genome. That *is* a good story. It seems almost a miracle to me that fifty years ago we could have been so ignorant of the nature of the genetic material and now can imagine that we will have the complete genetic blueprint of man. Just getting the complete description of a bacterium—say, the five million bases of *E. coli*—would make an extraordinary moment in history. There is a greater degree of urgency among older scientists than among younger ones to do the human genome now. The younger scientists can work on their grants until they are bored and still get the genome before they die. But to me it is crucial that we get the human genome now rather than twenty years from now, because I might be dead then and I don't want to miss out on learning how life works.

Still, I sometimes find myself moved to wonder, Is it ethical for me   3
to do my job? A kind of backlash against the human genome project has cropped up from some scientists—good ones as well as not so good ones. What seems to have outraged many people was that, in 1990, against the proposed increase of 3.6 percent in the president's budget for all NIH funds, the human genome project was proposed for an increase of 86 percent—from roughly $60 million to $108 million. Feeling dispossessed, some scientific groups have begun to behave like postal workers' unions. The biological chemists, the molecular biologists, and the cell biologists have hired a lobbyist, a former congressman from Maine, to get the overall NIH appropriation increased. If such moves succeed, then maybe we won't have this terrible situation of really good scientists claiming that they are not getting funded because all the money is going to the human genome project.

In the meantime, hate letters have made the rounds, including the   4
rounds of Congress, contending that the project is "bad science"—not only bad, but sort of wicked. The letters say that the project is wasting money at a time when resources for research are greatly threatened: If good people are failing to get grants, why go ahead with a program that is just going to spend billions of dollars sequencing junk? In 1990, someone in my office tried to get a distinguished biologist to help peer-review a big grant application. The biologist said, "No, not the human genome!" as though he were talking about syphilis.

The biologist sent me a FAX asking me to explain why he should not oppose the human genome program. I called him up and said that, though I couldn't prove it, Congress actually seemed to *like* the human genome program because it promised to find out something about disease. Congress was excited that maybe we scientists were worried about disease instead of just about getting grants. The primary mission of the National Institutes of Health is to improve American health, to give us healthier lives, not to give jobs to scientists. I think that the scientific community, if it wants to be ethically responsible to society, has to ask whether we are spending research money in a way that offers the best go at diseases.

The fact is that understanding how DNA operates provides an enormous advantage over working only with proteins or fats or carbohydrates. The best illustration of this advantage has been tumor viruses. If we had not been able to study cancer at the level of the change in DNA that starts it, the disease would still be a hopeless field. Every time a new enzyme was discovered, hope would rise that it was the cause of cancer. Cancer used to be considered a graveyard for biochemists, even good ones, many of whom wanted to cap their careers by solving cancer but failed. Not until the genetic foundation for cancer was identified could you really begin to say what goes wrong to make this terrible human affliction.

A similar example is Alzheimer's disease. Are we going to find out what Alzheimer's is and why it causes brain failure without getting the genes that we know predispose certain people to the disease? Maybe we will, but I would not bet on it. But if we can get the gene or genes implicated in the disease, I am confident that we will save hundreds of millions of dollars, if not billions, that would have been spent on worthless research.

Every year, Congress passes a bill for even more money to study Alzheimer's. Congress is voting for good goals, but we do not really know how to use the money. It is not as if all the federal budget for health and all the basic research grants add up to good research. All the study sections in the National Institutes of Health do not receive applications of equal value; they often endorse research projects or programs because they address important problems. The programs themselves are not terrible, but they often have a low probability of paying off. I am sure that half the NIH budget is spent on good intentions rather than on a realistically high probability that a research program will have a direct impact on one of the major human diseases.

The pressure is enormous to do something about mental disease because it can be terrible, as anyone knows who has a friend or family member suffering from it. We do spend a vast amount of money studying mental diseases, yet the effort yields very little. Manic-depressive disease leads to great moments of mania—perhaps the successful careers of a number of scientists can be attributed to it—but it also leads to depression, tragedy, and suicides. Lithium relieves some of the symptoms, but a drug is not the complete answer, as any psychiatrist will tell you. It is pretty clear that manic depression has a genetic cause. Several scientists thought they had located the gene on a chromosome. But then it got lost, and so long as it is lost, we are lost.

It is also pretty clear that alcoholism bears some relationship to 10 genes. This view comes from studies on identical twins adopted and raised by different families. There *are* alcoholic families. It is not likely that their members are morally weak; they just cannot tolerate alcohol chemically. But no one has found the gene or genes for susceptibility to alcoholism, and the chance of finding the genetic sources are probably low until a much more sophisticated human genetic community exists—plus the money to get the pedigrees and all the genetic markers.

Some diseases are not going to be easy to crack. For a long time, 11 people have been trying to discover the cause of schizophrenia by looking for chemical differences in the urine or the blood, a research strategy that has not been successful. It is not going to be easy to find the genes behind schizophrenia either, because reliable pedigree data[1] are difficult to compile and the condition is hard to diagnose. Thus both directions offer low probabilities, but it is still better to waste your money doing genetics because genetics lies at the heart of so much. Of course scientists should find out what the brain is. I believe in neurobiology and have tried to help raise money to support the field. But I do not believe that its current approaches will necessarily lead to the real, deep cause of manic-depressive disease.

In 1989 Congressman Joe Early said to me, "I'm tired of putting 12 fingers in dikes!" In combating disease, genetics helps enormously if it is a bad gene that contributes to the cause. Ignoring genes is like trying to solve a murder without finding the murderer. All we have are victims. With time, if we find the genes for Alzheimer's disease and for manic depression, then less money will be wasted on research that goes nowhere. Congressmen can only feel good if they are spending money on good things, so we have to convince them that the best use for their money is DNA research.

The human genome project is really trying to push a little more 13 money toward DNA-based research. Since we can now produce good genetic maps that allow us to locate culprit chromosomes and then actually find the genes for disease (as Francis Collins found the gene for cystic fibrosis), genetics should be a very high priority on the agenda of

---

[1]*pedigree data:* data that establish the genetic lineage of a particular trait or defect; the process involves gathering genetic information about the parents, grandparents, and so on.

NIH research. We are extremely lucky that when James Wyngaarden was director of NIH, he saw to the establishment of what is now a permanent division within NIH called the Center for Human Genome Research. I doubt that I convinced the biologist who sent me the FAX, but I may eventually, since he is very bright. I want to convince as many people as I can of the merits of the human genome project, but not to cap my career and have something that sounds good in my obituary. I can make best use of my time by trying to mobilize the country to do something about diseases that have hit my family and many others. I am sort of a concerned parent for whom things have not gone completely right. So, I am trying to enlist a group of people who will help us get these genes, and do what I think Congress wants us to do.

The ultimate objective of the human genome program is to learn the  **14** nucleotide sequence of human DNA. We want the program completed in roughly fifteen years. By completed we do not mean every last nucleotide sequence. If we get 98 percent of the regions that are functional, that will probably be the end of it. We will not worry about spending infinite amounts of money trying to sequence things we know probably contain little information. We could define the end of it to be the identification of all the human genes—that is, we will be done when we have located the coding sequences and can declare that human beings on the average contain, say, 248,000 genes, with variations such that some individuals, for example, have a gene present in four copies and some in three, and that for some the gene is nonessential. It has recently been learned that only a third of yeast genes are essential. Knock out two-thirds of them and the yeast still multiply. Studying things that are not essential will keep the people in the yeast world going for a long time. I think we can safely say the project will be over when we can identify the genes.

We probably will be unable to identify the genes until we get most  **15** of the DNA sequenced, because we will not know where they are. It would be nice if the whole program could be done by copy DNA (cDNA)—that is, by purely functional DNA[2]—so that we would not have to sequence all the junk, but we will never know whether we have all the cDNAs. This is not to say we should not do cDNA; we will actually fund grants for people trying to find better techniques for getting rare cDNA in tissue-specific places. But I think that we have got to sequence the whole thing.

In the first five years, we will push to achieve three major objectives.  **16** First, we will try to get good genetic maps, so that each chromosome

---

[2]*cDNA:* Watson considers "functional DNA" only that kind of DNA that copies the messenger RNA molecules that contain instructions for synthesizing proteins.

has enough genetic markers[3] on it actually to locate a gene if a pedigree is available. Currently, we have only about 150 markers that are sufficiently informative for assigning the location of genes. We have started a crash program to persuade people to make a lot of markers and to put them into a public repository made available to the whole world. We want to change the current practice among researchers of not sharing their markers because they want to be the first to find a gene and encourage everyone to make markers available to everyone.

The second objective is to make overlapping fragments of DNA   **17** available so that anyone looking for a gene in a particular piece of a certain chromosome will be able to get it by paying some nominal sum. The fragment will not be totally free, but it will certainly be there for anyone who seriously wants it. Techniques for doing this seem to be available now; it should not require more than $10 million to stockpile overlapping fragments of a given chromosome. To put this figure into perspective, Francis Collins has said that finding the cystic fibrosis gene was expensive—between $10 million and $50 million. If all the markers had been available, it would have cost only $5 million. I think we can establish an overlapping fragment library for the entire human genome for a couple of hundred million dollars, which will certainly reduce the costs of subsequent disease hunts. We will end up with a map of overlapping fragments, each one identified by three or four DNA sequences along it called sequence tag sites. With PCR,[4] researchers will be able to pull out all the human DNA that may be wanted.

The third major objective is to support scientists trying to do   **18** megabase[5] sequencing in one place in a reasonable period of time. An example of this type of project is a proposal from Walter Gilbert to sequence a mycoplasma, which is really a small (800 kilobases) bacterium. Gilbert's proposal, whether he lives up to it or not, is to do a million bases a year within two years. We want to encourage people to do sequencing of megabases with the aim of reducing the cost—so that within a couple of years it will fall to about a dollar a base pair, and then perhaps even to fifty cents. We will not accept a grant application from someone who proposes to sequence some DNA the old fashioned way, with graduate students or postdoctoral fellows, at the current cost—five to ten dollars a base pair—just out of curiosity about it. . . .

The NIH genome project will also try to get some real data on   **19**

---

[3]*genetic marker:* genetic "signposts"—differences in a complementary pair of chromosomes—that help locate particular genes; see diagram "Mapping Chromosomes" in Jaroff, pages 698–99.

[4]*PCR:* polymerase chain reaction: a powerful technique for amplifying a gene sequence, for obtaining a large amount of DNA from a small amount; somewhat analogous to cloning, PCR has also been used in paternity suits to establish parentage.

[5]*megabase:* one million base pairs.

model organisms. I will be happy if we get ten quite different bacteria sequenced up through yeast. We are now supporting a joint program between the Medical Research Council, in England, and the Laboratory of Molecular Biology in Cambridge, and the group in St. Louis that has developed yeast artificial chromosomes to sequence the genome of a roundworm. The roundworm community is eager to do it because they've already got the overlapping DNA fragments. We hope to get the sequence out in ten years. It's about the equivalent of an average human chromosome—about a hundred megabases—but with less repetitive DNA, and so probably with fewer problems. There is also an effort to sequence a plant genome, arabadopsis, which we hope will be led by the National Science Foundation with help from other agencies, including ourselves. This is roughly seventy megabases, and the project should be a real boon to botany. Except for perhaps one bacterium, none of this probably would ever have been funded in the absence of the human genome program.

Among the reasons for wanting to find bacterial genes is to help find [20] the human ones. People ask, How are you going to identify a gene if it is interspersed with so much junk and you lack a cDNA? How are you going to know you have it? That is obviously going to be hard in some cases, but if you have obtained the corresponding bacterial gene without many repetitive sequences and if you are clever, you ought to be able to spot the differences. I can imagine that typical work for undergraduates will be to find the gene once all the sequence has been obtained. Professors could tell their students: If you can identify a gene, we will let you go on to graduate school and do real science.

The human genome project is sufficiently justifiable so that if no [21] other country wants to help fund it, the United States should do the whole thing. We are rich enough to do it. But I doubt that we will be allowed to do it alone, because others are going to worry that it might actually be commercially interesting, and they will worry that we will be disinclined to distribute the data very fast if we have paid for it ourselves. It is my hope that we can spread out the cost of sequencing and data distribution over many countries. As soon as a gene has been identified, it should be thrown into an international data base.

But there are problems that I don't see how to get around. If a [22] stretch of DNA is sequenced in an academic laboratory, a university lawyer will say, "That looks like a serotonin receptor. Patent it!" Mutant forms of the cystic fibrosis gene have been patented by the universities of Toronto and Michigan. They will get some royalties and maybe build better student unions with the revenues. I am at a loss to know how to put valuable DNA sequences in the public domain fast when a lot of people want to keep them private. I just hope that other major nations come in. The Japanese will not let anyone who doesn't pay for it see their work. I figure that strategy might work. People might actually pay for sequence information if that is the only way to get to see it. So I have to seem a bad guy and say: I *will* withhold information that we generate if other countries refuse to join in an open sharing arrangement. But, in truth, it would be very distasteful to me to get into a situation where we were withholding the data for reasons of national advantage.

The acquisition of human DNA information has already begun to pose serious ethical problems. I think that somehow we have to get it into the laws that anyone's DNA—the message it gives—is confidential and that the only one who has a right to look at it is the person herself or himself. Still, the ethics get complicated if you can spot a gene in a newborn child that produces a disease for which no treatment exists. Sometimes these defects will be hard to spot, but sometimes, as in muscular dystrophy, they can be very easy to detect. As we begin to get data of this kind, people are going to get nervous and some are going to be violent opponents of the project unless they can feel that they or their friends will not be discriminated against on the basis of their DNA. If someone can go look at your DNA and see that you have a deletion on one of your anti-oncogenes and that you will be more liable to die of cancer at an early age, then you might be discriminated against in, say, employment or insurance coverage.   23

Laws are needed to prevent genetic discrimination and to protect rights that should not be signed away too easily. If you are poor, it will be highly tempting to say, "Yes, look at my DNA because I want the job in the asbestos factory." If you have no money, a job in an asbestos factory is better than no job. Issues like these demand a lot of discussion, at least so that DNA-related laws are not enacted prematurely. For that reason, we are putting more than 3 percent of the genome project money into an ethics program; and we will put more into it if we find that it needs more.   24

We have faced up to this challenge already with DNA fingerprints. The National Center for Genome Research has given $50,000 to the National Research Council–National Academy of Sciences study on DNA fingerprinting, which has lawyers and judges advising it. The police want a DNA register of sex offenders; other people may want one of dishonest accountants. People will want DNA fingerprints to prove that a politician's children are really his. At a meeting in Leicester, England, Alec Jeffries showed a slide of a letter from a woman who runs a small hotel in Wales and who wrote that it would be a good idea to have a DNA fingerprint register of bedwetters. Different people will want different information—the possibilities are unlimited. I don't think *anyone* should have access to anyone else's DNA fingerprints.   25

We need to explore the social implications of human genome research and figure out some protection for people's privacy so that these   26 fears do not sabotage the entire project. Deep down, I think that the only thing that could stop our program is fear; if people are afraid of the information we will find, they will keep us from finding it. We have to convince our fellow citizens somehow that there will be more advantages to knowing the human genome than to not knowing it.

## Review Questions

1. Why do some scientific researchers oppose the Human Genome Project, according to Watson?
2. Why does Watson believe that DNA research, including the Human Genome Project, should be of the highest priority?
3. What are the main objectives of the Human Genome Project?
4. According to Watson, what are some of the ethical problems associated with DNA research?

## Discussion and Writing Suggestions

1. Watson concludes, "We have to convince our fellow citizens somehow that there will be more advantages to knowing the human genome than to not knowing it." Has Watson convinced you that the Human Genome Project is both a good thing in itself and a useful expenditure of public funds? If so, which arguments made the greatest impression on you, and why? If not, what are your chief concerns? Should the project be canceled? Should restrictions be placed on genetic research? If so, what kind of restrictions?
2. To what extent, if any, does Watson's own personal stake in the success of the Human Genome Project (and in the success of biotechnology, in general) affect the way that you read this article and accept his arguments? Explain.
3. Watson is a scientist trying to persuade people (both his fellow scientists and others interested in scientific matters) that the project he heads is a vital one. Setting aside for the moment your own views of the genome project, to what extent do you think Watson has done a good job of explaining this scientific project? In particular, did you find this article difficult to follow because of the language in which Watson explained genetic concepts? If so, how might he have made his explanations easier to understand?
4. Watson argues that information gleaned from the Human Genome Project should be made available to all interested parties and that whatever has been discovered in one country should be made available to an international database. A genetic cure for a particular disease might be discovered more rapidly if more than one group of scientists were attacking the problem. But private companies might argue that they are entitled to the patents and financial profits from their own discoveries—that without such rights and rewards, they have no incentive to invest large amounts of money in research. What are your views on this subject? How can the fruits of genetic

research be made widely available, while the rights of companies to earn reasonable profits from their research are protected?
5. Write either (a) an editorial or (b) a short story concerned with one of the ethical problems of DNA research discussed by Watson at the end of his article. Expand on or dramatize one or more of these potential problem areas.

# Achilles Helix

## ROBERT WRIGHT

*One of the most controversial aspects of recent genetic technology is the testing of pregnant women to determine possible defects in fetuses. (Jaroff briefly alluded to this problem in paragraph 8 of his article.) Very frequently, a positive test leads to the abortion of the fetus. Even without such genetic tests, abortion is a particularly divisive issue in this country. Debates over the 1973 Roe v. Wade Supreme Court ruling (which legalized abortion) and the continuing struggle by pro-life and pro-choice activists regularly fill the front pages of our newspapers. The ever-increasing availability of genetic testing is certain to increase the intensity of this debate.*

*In the following selection, Robert Wright discusses the prospect (reminiscent of Brave New World) of what he calls "homemade eugenics": parents using the new biotechnology to select desirable characteristics in their offspring—and to "de-select" offspring without these characteristics. Such possibilities remind many people of the Nazi eugenics programs. Robert Wright is a senior editor of The New Republic, where this passage first appeared as part of a longer article about James D. Watson.*

The first wave of ethical messiness created by genome research is already taking shape. There is a twenty-eight-year-old woman in Canada who knows that she is almost certain to start going crazy slowly in a couple of decades, a victim of Huntington's disease. There are reports about an American couple who, after finding out that their unborn child would have cystic fibrosis, were told by their health maintenance organization to abort the child or lose coverage. The HMO backed off after hearing the word "lawsuit." But expect insurance companies to take a deeper interest in your genome as it becomes more enlightening—and to try to charge you more for insurance, or deny you insurance altogether, if your genes are inauspicious. Theoretically, if this logic is left

Excerpt from "Achilles Helix" by Robert Wright from *The New Republic*, July 9 and 16, 1990. Reprinted by permission of The New Republic.

to play itself out freely, it could mean the end of health insurance as we know it.[1]

But the coming complication of health insurance isn't even close to winning the award for most haunting specter of the genetic age. That goes to eugenics. Biologists and ethicists have by now expended thousands of words warning about slippery eugenic slopes, reflecting on Nazi Germany, and warning that a government quest for a super race could begin anew if we're not vigilant. But the more likely danger is roughly the opposite; it isn't that the government will get involved in reproductive choices, but that it won't. It is when left to the free market that the fruits of genome research are most assuredly rotten.

It's not surprising that few people have noticed this. . . . Ever since societies came to frown on infanticide, eugenics programs have been public sector initiatives, all the way from the early 20th-century sterilization of "imbeciles" in the United States to Singapore's present financial disincentives for birth among the uneducated. But now we have the capacity for homemade eugenics: individual families deciding what kinds of kids they want to have. In fact, this discretion is already being used—mainly by the upper classes. As Arthur Caplan of the University of Minnesota's Center for Biomedical Ethics has noted, the people who use the relatively few fetal diagnoses now available are, for both financial and cultural reasons, concentrated at the high end of the income scale. So a form of bio-social stratification is already here; children with Down's syndrome, for example, are almost certainly being born disproportionately to the less affluent.

You can pretty well guess the next step in bio-social stratification: once we isolate genes conducive not just to specific pathologies but to, say, lower than average intelligence, we're heading toward a literal caste system. Only two questions stand between us and Brave New World: Will science find such genes? Will parents be so ghoulish as to make use of the information? The answers are: probably and probably.

As for the first question: skeptics note that intelligence, a trait of almost ineffable complexity, consists of many subtraits (memory, language skills, spatial conceptualization, etc.), each of which is influenced by (in addition to the environment) many genes. The idea of an "IQ gene" is plainly illusory. On the other hand, one can imagine a fairly simple link between a single gene and a primary dimension of intelligence. Take sheer mental "quickness," for example: it's entirely possible that the presence or absence of a particular protein in the brain could markedly affect the rate of synaptic firing. And, even aside from such

---

[1]See note at end of article, pages 722–23.

easy to envision single-gene effects, it's not at all unlikely that small numbers of identifiable genes together exert marked influence on various other aspects of intellect. Robert Weinberg, a noted molecular biologist at the Massachusetts Institute of Technology and the White-head Institute, says, "Over the next decade, one may begin to stumble across genes that are surprisingly strong determinants of cognition, affect, and other aspects of human function and appearance." To deny this, he says, would be "hiding one's head in the sand." . . .

Actually, Weinberg's prophecy may already be coming true. This **6** spring two researchers announced the discovery of a gene that predisposes people toward alcoholism. They looked at cells taken from seventy dead people, half alcoholics, and found that the alcoholics were markedly more likely to have the gene than non-alcoholics. The small size of the sample gives some grounds for skepticism, but the point is that such statistical correlations are a perfectly valid way to substantiate a link between a gene and a complex behavior. In fact, although in this case the researchers were guided by prior knowledge of the gene's function (it affects the receptiveness of brain cells to dopamine, a neurotransmitter involved in various addictions), statistical correlation can in principle uncover entirely unsuspected links. As genetic information about various people accumulates in the coming decades, its scientific value could be immensely raised by placing it all in a single data base. . . . The key to making this data base productive would be to pair each person's genetic information with other potentially relevant information—health records, psychiatric records, even scores on standardized personality and intelligence tests. (All names could be expunged to protect privacy.) As the data base grew, a sufficiently powerful computer could sift through it and turn up all sorts of suggestive correlations between genes and traits, which further study might then validate.

Question two: Would parents *use* this sort of knowledge? Would **7** they go beyond merely avoiding things like Down's syndrome and choose to avoid things like "unexceptional intellect"? Maybe not, if this meant abortion. But within the past two years it has become feasible to examine the DNA of eggs fertilized in vitro. Just after fertilization, when the egg has multiplied into four or eight cells, one cell can be removed for testing, and the "pre-embryo" (a morally delicate phrasing) simply replaces it. With present tools, it would be hard to test a single cell for the presence of more than one or two particular genes, but that barrier will undoubtedly fall.

Imagine the situation: six pre-embryos await insertion in the uterus. **8** The doctor explains that one of them carries Down's syndrome, and would probably give the child an IQ in the range of 40 to 70. The parents choose to discard it. And just out of curiosity, they ask, is there anything the doctor can say about the other children? Well, yes: assuming the child would live in a moderately rich educational environment, baby A's IQ has a 90 percent chance of falling in the 80–100 (below-average but normal) range; baby B's 90 percent range is 90–110 (average); baby C: 95–115; baby D: 110–130; baby E: 120–140. Well, um, Doctor, as long as we're being selective, could we toss out A and B, too?

In fact, the choices could be much more radical than this. For in vitro **9** fertilization, women are given hormones that boost their egg production well above the normal one per month—to five, ten, sometimes fifteen eggs. (Of these, three or four are re-implanted after fertilization, since the chances of any one developing into a fetus are small.) So it would be possible to collect, fertilize, and freeze ("cryo-preserve") forty or more eggs in the course of seven or eight months, in preparation for a single re-implantation. Choosing four out of forty would mean skimming off the top 10 percent. With that kind of leverage, parents can afford to insist on higher-than-average IQ and broad shoulders as well.

Would a mother actually *choose* in vitro fertilization—now used to **10** circumvent fertility problems—just for eugenic purposes? Would she spend half a year strung out on hormones just for the opportunity to make an anguished, morally momentous decision? I might have said no before I spent a few years in New York City, the ambition capital of the world. Each year thousands of Manhattan parents work up a cold sweat over whether their four-year-olds will get admitted to the best private kindergartens or merely the very good ones. And, for that matter, similar worries preoccupy parents all across the country. They spend millions prepping their kids for SAT tests, honing their athletic skills, and teaching them to carry a tune. Soon—conceivably within five years, quite possibly within fifteen—there could be an easier way.

In a recent newspaper article, Yury Verlinsky, an embryologist at **11** the Illinois Masonic Medical Center who has developed a way to diagnose *un*fertilized eggs in vitro (a morally less complicated, if practically less powerful, technology than the diagnosis of "pre-embryos"), was quoted as saying that "we now can . . . make sure we give back only good eggs to women." By "good," he just meant free of certain inborn diseases. But the reporter, grasping the implications, intoned, "No one knows better than Verlinsky how such techniques might be perverted by tyrants and fools." Tyrants? Fools? No. Just your typical parent, sitting nervously in the bleachers at a Little League game. It is these plain old mothers and fathers—compelled by their genes to suffer silently with their kids—who are the source of legitimate concern, not the white supremacists in Idaho.

No doubt most mothers and fathers—even most who can afford **12** it—won't try to have superkids. Maybe there won't even be one in ten, or in fifty. But it only takes one in 1,000 or 10,000 to create one of the grossest social issues ever—and, for that matter, to start a trend.

The politics of Brave New World aren't that hard to envision, at least in rough outline. Luddites on both the left and the right (exemplified in their extremes by Rifkinites and the Moral Majority, respectively) will want a fairly thorough ban on the new technologies: either outlaw pre-birth screening altogether (unlikely) or try to draw a line between tolerable and intolerable genetic selection: between, for example, physical and behavioral "pathologies" on the one hand (cystic fibrosis, Down's syndrome, manic-depressive illness) and mere "deficiencies" on the other (disposition toward emphysema, likelihood of a sub-average IQ, or of moodiness). 13

The smart money is never on Luddites; technological history isn't exactly an unbroken string of successes for them. Besides, in this case their laws would be hard to enforce, since the crimes they fear would be committed at the microscopic level, in the privacy of a doctor's office. Still, the alternatives to Luddism may give it a stronger than usual chance of political success. 14

If the Luddite coalition fails, we'll be left with a left-right split: between those on the right who want to let the free market work its magic and those on the left who want the government to provide enough money so that all reproductive choices open to the rich are open to the poor. The ugliness of the right-wing option is obvious: the social pyramid would grow taller and steeper, as some upper-class families added genetic advantage to their children's already formidable cultural advantages. The ugliness of the left-wing option is slightly less apparent but not all that different. This route, too, given enough time, could move the social classes further apart and radically reduce interclass mobility, with the lower socioeconomic regions inhabited by people whose ancestors—originally drawn from all social classes—had chosen not to use the new technology. 15

Some politicians might advocate a third path. There are people who think genes underlying intelligence may already be unevenly distributed across social classes. The theory, articulated by Harvard psychologist Richard Herrnstein in *I.Q. in the Meritocracy*, goes like this: given that (a) genes play an important role in intelligence, (b) intelligence plays an important role in economic success, and (c) people tend to marry people in their own intellectual and socioeconomic range, [then] genes conducive to intelligence should drift toward the top of the pyramid. . . . 16

Has this gotten creepy enough for you yet? Basically, all the non- 17

---

Luddite options are so troubling in their own special ways as to inspire new respect for Luddism. But there is a very large problem with following the Luddite plan: the United States can't, in the real world, do it alone. Just imagine [congressional] floor speeches if Japanese parents are selecting for high IQ. Or if Singapore, say, actually *pays* parents to do so. In the absence of an effective international treaty (one with obvious verification problems) it will be hard for any nation to treat this issue sanely. . . .

Note, by the way, that bizarre as all of this sounds, it is based on **18** simple extrapolation; it assumes only the existence of identifiable genes, or small groups of genes, that influence complex behavioral traits in predictable—*statistically* predictable, not infallibly predictable—fashion. No new technological breakthroughs are needed. Such breakthroughs may, of course, occur. Thus, it could be possible someday to genetically *engineer* the sex cells; take eggs or sperm, or the union of the two, and fiddle with them until they meet your specifications. In fact, it is already theoretically *possible* to amend the human germ line; new genes have been introduced into the germ lines of mice, whose reproduction works basically like ours. It's just that so far no biologist has been sufficiently out of touch with reality to propose trying such experiments on humans. But the day will come when we're confident of our ability to intervene and not only spare a girl from cystic fibrosis, but guarantee that her children are spared. Once we cross that line, and face the possibility of inserting all kinds of genes—even entirely novel genes—into the sex cells, the issues raised will be much the same as those outlined in previous paragraphs, except with a lot of exclamation points.

---

*Note*: The more we know about our genes, the less sense health insurance makes. The whole idea behind insurance is to pool uncertainty; since there's no way of knowing who will be stricken by what, various risk-averse people implicitly agree in advance that the lucky among them will help pay for the unlucky. Even in retrospect, the lucky ones don't mind this, because they realize they could just as easily have been unlucky. But the truth is that they couldn't have; to some extent—the exact extent is yet to be discovered—our future health is in our genes. This is true not just of the relatively few clear-cut, single-gene diseases, such as Huntington's chorea, but also of diseases toward which we're simply predisposed by one or more genes. Genes that incline people toward heart disease and colon cancer, for example, have already been located. As medical "luck" becomes more predictable, the enthusiasm of the lucky for subsidizing the unlucky should begin to subside.

The standard fear is that insurance companies will start using genetic screening to set higher rates for the unlucky or deny them insurance altogether. The standard reply is to postulate a new legal principle: your DNA is private, and no one can look at it without your permission. But a law this simple won't be enough. All insurance companies have to do is offer discounts for people whose genes augur well for their health, and who voluntarily give insurance companies a look. Charging them less means charging everyone else more. It may not even be enough for the government to *forbid* people from showing their genes to an insurance company. If people take a peek

## Review Questions

1. With what two questions is Wright primarily concerned in this article?
2. Why does health insurance make less sense in the new age of biotechnology, according to Wright?
3. How does Wright drive home his point that parents may be quite willing to practice eugenics on their unborn children?
4. What distinction does Wright make in the final paragraph? Why are the issues the same, only "with a lot of exclamation points"?

## Discussion and Writing Suggestions

1. As a prospective parent, would you be inclined to take advantage of the kind of knowledge from biotechnology likely to be available in the near future and to select the kind of characteristics you would desire in your offspring? (For example, put yourself in the place of the parents described by Wright in paragraph 7.) To what extent do you think such parental choices should be legally restricted? You may wish to couch your response in the form of a letter to a friend or relative.
2. In what ways is Wright justified in labeling the kinds of possibilities he discusses as "Brave New World"? Compare and contrast Huxley's vision with Wright's.
3. In paragraph 13, Wright suggests that "Luddites" might draw a line between "tolerable and intolerable genetic selection." Thus, not selecting a child likely to have Down syndrome would be "tolerable," but selecting a child likely to be moody would be "intolerable." To what extent do you agree that having such a line might be acceptable, and, if so, that the "Luddite" example of what is tolerable and what is intolerable is a reasonable one? Again, try to put yourself in the position of a prospective parent.

---

themselves, and the ones with the "best" genes want to buy little or no insurance against the diseases they're least likely to get, insurance companies that oblige by offering à la carte policies will siphon off customers from the ones that don't. And the companies that don't will have to adjust their rates upward to pay for their increasingly unfortunate clientele. In the end, the effect will be the same as if the insurance companies did the genetic screening: the unlucky will pay for their misfortune.

The other main hope for keeping insurance humane is government intervention. One approach would be a ban against discrimination by insurance companies and employers. Perhaps simpler, in the end, would be for the government just to provide nationalized health insurance, which is worthwhile on other grounds anyway.

But this has its scary side. For once the government is paying the medical bills, it—no less than an HMO—has an interest in discouraging the birth of unlucky children. (And should members of Congress somehow forget this, taxpayers who choose not to have unlucky children may well remind them.) Probably this discouragement would at most be slight—say, paying in full for the abortion of "defective" children, whereas the normal rate of reimbursement would be 80 or 90 percent. But even in so subtle a form, such incentives amount to the government exerting systematic influence on the gene pool—in other words, a eugenics program.

**4.** Write a critique of Wright's article, drawing on some of your responses to the previous questions.

# The Genetic Labyrinth*

## DANIEL J. KEVLES AND LEROY HOOD

*In "The Gene Hunt," Leon Jaroff noted that the Human Genome Project has been compared to such other massive recent scientific undertakings as the Manhattan Project and the Apollo moon-landing program. To some critics, however, the genome project also incorporates some of the least attractive features of these two other programs. The Manhattan Project, according to Professor of Health Law George Annas, was about "the inevitability of scientific advance" and "the control of nature," while the Apollo Project "was about military advantage disguised as science and hyped as a peace mission." Kevles and Hood are less negative about the Human Genome Project than Annas, although they do see possible dangers ahead, particularly those involving the misuse of genetic information.*

*Daniel J. Kevles heads the Science, Ethics and Public Policy program at the California Institute of Technology. Leroy Hood has taught at the California Institute of Technology and is now a professor of molecular biotechnology at the University of Washington. As Jaroff notes (paragraph 36), Hood is also a member of the Genome Advisory Committee and has designed a machine to sequence 16,000 base pairs a day. This passage is excerpted from* The Code of Codes: Scientific and Social Issues in the Human Genome Project *(1992), edited by Kevles and Hood.*

What makes us human instead of, say, chimpanzees? What are our  1
physical possibilities and our limits as a species? Can we "perfect" our children? And do we want to? Those questions—as much for philosophers as for scientists—have taken on a greater urgency since the late 1980s, when scientists launched the Human Genome Project—a multibillion-dollar effort to obtain the genetic information hidden in every human cell.

The task is enormous: The human genome contains between 50,000  2
and 100,000 genes. These genes are distributed in varying numbers through the cores of 23 pairs of different chromosomes housed in the

"The Genetic Labyrinth" * For permission to photocopy this selection, please contact Harvard University Press. Reprinted by permission of the publishers from *The Code of Codes: Scientific and Social Issues in the Human Genome Project* by Daniel J. Kevles and Leroy Hood, Cambridge, Mass.: Harvard University Press, Copyright © 1992 by Daniel J. Kevles and Leroy Hood.

nucleus of virtually every human cell. Genes are strands of deoxyribonucleic acid—DNA—that wind in a double helix, a spiraling ladder whose
sides are joined by rungs of chemicals called nucleotides. The order in
which the nucleotides appear determines the information carried by
DNA—the information that translates into the human form and, more
specifically, into blue eyes or tallness or predisposition to a particular
disease. Biologists calculate that the human genome contains about 3
billion nucleotide pairs. The genome project will first determine which
chromosome holds which genes, and then specify where each gene is
located on its home chromosome. Scientists will then figure out the
sequence, the order of occurrence, of all the nucleotides in human DNA.

In the United States, the genome project is funded—with a total of    3
$164 million in 1992—by two federal agencies, the National Institutes
of Health and the Department of Energy. With work proceeding at
dozens of laboratories across the country and in Japan and Europe,
researchers hope to complete their basic task by 2005. Although some
critics consider that timetable overly optimistic, innovations in genome
mapping and sequencing are occurring rapidly enough to expect an
enormous amount of information about the human genome by the early
21st Century.

But such information can be gravely misused, with far-reaching and    4
costly implications for consumers, employers and insurers. And research
will undoubtedly continue to yield interpretations that may be wrong,
misapplied, socially volatile or, if the history of eugenics is any guide,
all three.

The basic idea of eugenics was to improve human stock by increas-    5
ing the number of supposedly desirable human beings ("positive" eugenics) and getting rid of "undesirable" ones ("negative" eugenics). In
Nazi Germany, the eugenics movement prompted the state to sterilize
several hundred thousand people and helped lead, by equating undesira-
bility with the ethnicity and religion of Jews and others, to the death
camps. In the United States, a 1926 American Eugenics Society exhibit
included a board on which a light flashed every 15 seconds. With every
flash, it explained, $100 of the observers' money went for the care of
people with "bad heredity." The presentation implied that sterilizing
people with deleterious genes would not only benefit the gene pool but
reduce governments spending on institutions for the mentally deficient
and physically disabled or diseased. The reasoning took hold. Many
states enacted sterilization laws, most notably California, where 6,255
people had been sterilized by 1929—twice the number in all other
states combined. (A 1942 Supreme Court ruling overturned most such
laws, including California's.)

The shadow of eugenics hangs over the Human Genome Project.    6
Some commentators have suggested that the project may stimulate

governments to try positive eugenics—to use genetic engineering to foster or enhance skills in science, math, music, even athletics. Others have warned that the project will more likely spark a revival of negative eugenics.

Economics could easily prompt us to develop such programs, they 7 fear. Today, as health care becomes a public responsibility, funded through taxes, and as the cost escalates, taxpayers may ultimately rebel against paying for the care of those whose genes doom them to severe disease or disability. Governments and institutions may feel pressure to encourage, or even to compel, people not to bring genetically disadvantaged children into the world—not for the sake of the gene pool but in the interest of keeping public health costs down.

In recent years, several governments have developed crude eugen- 8 ics policies. In 1988, China's Gansu province adopted a eugenics law, since enacted more widely, aimed at improving "population quality" by banning the marriages of mentally retarded people unless they first submitted to sterilization. As the official newspaper *Peasants Daily* explained: "Idiots produce idiots."

But genetic scientists know that "idiots" do not necessarily give 9 birth to "idiots" and that mental retardation may arise for reasons not connected to genetics. And political scientists know that reproductive freedom is much more easily curtailed in dictatorships than in democracies. The institutions of political democracy may not have been robust enough to stop the early eugenics movement's attempts to violate civil liberties, but they did contest them effectively in many places. Britain refused to pass eugenic sterilization laws. So did many U.S. states, and in a number where such laws were enacted, they often were not enforced.

Contemporary democracies are unlikely to embrace eugenics be- 10 cause they contain powerful anti-eugenics constituencies. Most geneticists, and the public, aware of the cruelties of past state-sponsored eugenics, tend to oppose such programs. And although prejudice continues against the ailing and the disabled, today they are politically empowered to a degree that they were not in the early 20th Century. They may not have enough power to counter all quasi-eugenic threats, but with allies in the media, the medical profession and in such quarters as the Roman Catholic Church (long a foe of eugenics), they are politically positioned to block or at least hinder eugenic proposals that might affect them.

With the advance of human genetics and biotechnology, we can try 11 a kind of "homemade eugenics," to use the insightful term of *New Republic* commentator Robert Wright—"individual families deciding what kinds of kids they want to have." Parents can now choose not to have children with certain disabilities or diseases, such as Down's syndrome or Tay-Sachs. And in the future, they might, via genetic analysis of eggs fertilized in a test tube, choose to have babies that are superior in some sense to those they might have conceived without scientific intervention. If, for example, a cluster of genes for tallness is identified, scientists could check each of the growing eggs for the cluster and implant one that possesses it into the womb of a mother who wants a child with a better chance of becoming a basketball star.

It is quite possible that people will exploit such possibilities, given the interest that some parents have shown in choosing the sex of their child. Further, a 1989 report to the European Parliament on a proposal for a genome project there noted widespread pressure from families for "individual eugenic choice in order to give one's own child the best possible start." 12

Genetic enhancement would inevitably involve manipulating human embryos, and for better or for worse, human-embryo research is restricted in federally funded research programs and powerfully opposed in virtually all the major Western democracies, especially by Roman Catholics. In an effort to frame debate on the issue, a committee of the European Parliament urged in 1989 that genetic analysis "must on no account be used for the scientifically dubious and politically unacceptable purpose of 'positively improving' the population's gene pool," and called for "an absolute ban on all experiments designed to reorganize on an arbitrary basis the genetic makeup of humans." 13

But genetic improvement is not likely to yield to human effort for some time. While the Human Genome Project will undoubtedly make it easier to identify genes for physical and medically related traits, it will not soon reveal how genes contribute to forming the qualities—particularly talent, creativity, behavior, appearance—that the world so much wants and admires. It's preposterous to think that genetic knowledge will soon permit us to engineer Einsteins. 14

The prospect and possibilities of human genetic engineering tantalize us, of course, even if they are still the stuff of science fiction. But the near-term ethical challenges of the Human Genome Project come not from private forays into genetic improvement or state eugenics programs, but from something the project will produce in abundance: genetic information. How will we control the spread and use of that information in a market economy? The prospects are deeply troubling. 15

Many individuals and families already seek genetic counseling before deciding to conceive, but what happens if post-conception tests show that the fetus has lost the roll of the genetic dice? The pregnant couple then faces the only therapeutic choice available at the moment—to abort or not abort. And these tests can be faulty. In 1991, the test for whether an individual is a carrier of the recessive cystic fibrosis gene, for example, was only 75% reliable—it detected the gene in only three out 16 of four of the people who carried it. So, it revealed only 56% (that's 75% of 75%) of the couples who were truly at risk for bearing a child with the disease.

As technology allows us to pinpoint the genetic causes of more    17
diseases, more people will be drawn, often involuntarily, into the testing network. The potential market for genetic carrier screening and prenatal testing is enormous, said Benjamin S. Wilfond and Norman Fost, both physicians and medical ethicists, in a 1990 article in the *Journal of the American Medical Assn.* As many as 2.8 million people may be tested each year to learn if they carry recessive genes for cystic fibrosis, they estimated. Many more could be tested for such disorders as sickle-cell anemia, hemophilia and muscular dystrophy. Genetic testing can also let people know that they or their newly conceived children are safe from some specific genetic doom, and in that sense it can be liberating. After tests revealed that she did not carry the Huntington's gene, one young woman told Joseph Bishop and Michael Waldholz in their book *Genome* that, "after 28 years of not knowing, it's like being released from prison. ... To have hope for the future ... to be able to see my grandchildren." (Huntington's usually begins to afflict people in their late 30s, causing mental and physical deterioration and death within 15 to 25 years.)

The torrent of new human genetic information will undoubtedly    18
challenge many socioeconomic values and practices. Employers and medical or life insurers may request the genetic profiles of prospective employees or clients. Employers might wish to identify workers likely to contract disorders that affect job performance or that might be brought on by workplace conditions. Both employers and insurers might want to identify likely victims of diseases that result in costly medical or disability payouts. Employers could use the information to assign susceptible people to risk-free duties or environments—but they might also use it to deny them jobs, just as medical or life insurers might exploit it to exclude them from coverage. Whatever the purpose, genetic identification would brand people with what one American labor union official has called a "genetic scarlet letter" or what some Europeans term a "genetic passport."

We've already seen abuses of genetic information. Around 1970, a    19
fear spread that people with sickle-cell trait—those who possess one of the recessive genes for the disease—might suffer damage to their red blood cells in the reduced oxygen of high altitudes. Such people, the overwhelming majority of whom are black, were prohibited from entering the Air Force Academy, restricted to ground jobs by several major commercial air carriers and often charged higher insurance premiums. More recently, a couple whose first child suffers from cystic fibrosis conceived again and sought to have their fetus tested for the disease.

Their insurer agreed to pay for the test—so long as the mother would abort the child if the results were positive. Otherwise, the company would cancel the family's health plan. (The firm relented—after being threatened with a lawsuit.)

A good deal of the genetic discrimination so far has been arbitrary, callous and, especially on the job, a product of ignorance. A recent Harvard Medical School survey turned up about 30 instances of genetic discrimination. People with inherited biochemical disorders were denied insurance even though they had been successfully treated and were not ill. An auto insurer refused to cover a man with a genetically based neuromuscular disorder who suffered no disability, and an employer declined to hire a woman after she revealed that she had the same disorder. The study was not designed to determine whether these agencies "have active policies of genetic discrimination," noted Paul Billings, one of the survey authors and a medical geneticist now at the California Pacific Medical Center in San Francisco, but, he added, the findings "suggest that such policies exist." 20

Perhaps, say some commentators, employers and insurers ought to be barred from nosing into anybody's genome passport. [Recently,] the California Legislature passed a bill banning employers, health service agencies and disability insurers from withholding jobs or protection simply because a person is at genetic risk for a given disease or disability. Gov. Pete Wilson vetoed the measure, but even if similar laws are enacted in California or elsewhere, insurers could sidestep their prohibitions by setting high common rates and offering discounts to clients with healthy genetic profiles, which such clients would, of course, submit voluntarily. Insurers have a natural interest in information that bears on risk. To them, rate discrimination based on genuine knowledge of risk is neither arbitrary nor illegitimate: It is sound business practice. 21

The insurance industry's position is made clear in a 1989 study circulated by the American Council of Life Insurance. If insurers were unable to use genetic tests because of laws requiring that risks be classified on the basis of factors that people can control, wrote Robert Pokorski, one of the study's contributors, "then *equity* would give way to *equality* [equal premiums regardless of risk] and private insurance as it is known today might well cease to exist." 22

Industry representatives say that equalizing premiums would hurt not only insurance providers but also their customers. If a client has a high genetic medical risk not reflected in her premiums, then she would receive a high payout at low cost to herself but a high cost to the company. The company would have to pass its increased costs along to other customers, thus forcing low-risk policyholders to subsidize high-risk ones. 23

To prevent that, insurance companies want to know as much about 24 their clients as their clients know about themselves. They may also decide to go further and require genetic testing so they can tailor rates to risk. The industry expects consumers to resist. "It seems unavoidable that there will be lots of legal battles as this technology unfolds," says Rob Bier, the managing director of communications for the American Council of Life Insurance. "The insurance industry actually wishes genetic testing had never been developed."

The legal battles could grow more heated as the Human Genome 25 Project accumulates more data. As we better understand the links between genetics and disease, companies may be able to determine an individual's risk to the point where risk becomes certainty and lifetime medical costs can be exactly calculated. In those cases, medical insurance premiums would amount to payment for lifetime medical care on the layaway plan.

Alternatively, the more we learn about the human genome, the 26 more will it become obvious that everyone is susceptible to some kind of genetic disease or disability; everyone carries some genetic load and is likely to fall ill in one way or another. Of course, the cost and severity of the illnesses will vary, but if everybody were aware of their genetic jeopardy, we might well see more interest in a risk-rating system that expresses what the Europeans call solidarity. In Europe, according to G. W. de Wit, a professor of insurance economics at Erasmus University in the Netherlands, if parents with a genetically diseased fetus choose to have the child, "all medical expenses for that child will be borne by the insurer. It seems fully justified to have the other policyholders contribute (solidarity)," he said in a paper delivered at a human genome meeting in 1990, "because otherwise the free choice of the parents is jeopardized." De Wit doubts that European insurers will demand genetic information.

Suggesting that it costs too much to provide care or coverage for 27 those with genetically based disorders casts a shadow over people who suffer from them. Already, those who would abort a fetus with such afflictions have been attacked as stigmatizing the living who have those ailments. Barbara Faye Waxman, an activist for the disabled who herself has a neuromuscular impairment, was quoted in a *New York Times* article as criticizing her fellow workers in a Los Angeles Planned Parenthood clinic for displaying "a strong eugenics mentality that exhibited disdain, discomfort and ignorance toward disabled babies."

Some advocates for the disabled have joined the anti-abortion 28 movement. But it seems to make little sense to try to preserve the dignity of one group by limiting the reproductive freedom of another. We'd do better to recognize that values of social decency compel us to live with conflicting principles: We can endorse using genetic information in personal reproductive choices while upholding the rights and dignity of the diseased and disabled.

There are many ways people with purported genetic disorders have **29** been demeaned, but the most reckless have involved claims linking genes and behavior. The early eugenics movement declared immigrant groups from eastern and southern Europe to be biologically inferior in intelligence and inclined to criminality, alcoholism, prostitution and the like. Eugenic science then was obviously riddled with social prejudice, but even purified of bias and vagueness, behavioral genetics poses difficult problems. Not only must we distinguish between nurture and nature but, equally important, we need to define behavioral traits, measure them, and recognize spurious correlations. Typical of dubious behavioral genetics is a 1990 study co-authored by the Harvard psychologist Jerome Kagan, who reported that among a group of 379 students, those who suffered hay fever also scored high on a shyness index. "We think there is a small group of people who inherit a set of genes that predispose them to hay fever and shyness," Kagan said.

Finding the genetic origins of human behavior is a legitimate goal, **30** but it is also socially and scientifically treacherous. In recent years, for example, several family studies reported the discovery of specific genetic susceptibilities to manic depression and schizophrenia, but followup studies failed to confirm the findings.

Personality traits are so hard to specify and explain that we need to **31** use considerable caution in spreading the claims of behavioral genetics, yet such caution has tended to be lacking in the media. It was Page 1 news in April, 1990, when researchers at UCLA and in Texas jointly announced that, having examined the brains of only 70 corpses—half of them severe alcoholics, half of them not—they had detected a gene for alcoholism. But it was Page 10 news in the *New York Times* when, eight months later, scientists at the National Institutes of Health reported that they could not confirm the UCLA/Texas results. Reporters often take as firm conclusions what scientists announce as tentative conclusions, and scientists encourage the process when they hold press conferences to proclaim attention-getting findings—however fragile they may be—linking genes to behavior.

The fears that the genome project will foster a drive to produce **32** superbabies or to callously eliminate the unfit are grossly exaggerated. They also divert attention from the scientific and social issues that the project actually raises—particularly how human genetic information should be used by geneticists, the media, insurers, employers and government. Clearly, we can use our new knowledge to help reduce human suffering, but one thing is equally clear: We cannot allow ourselves, as West Virginia Rep. Bob Wise noted at a 1991 hearing on the issue, "to create a new genetic underclass."

## Review Questions

1. Explain the purpose and nature of the Human Genome Project.
2. What is meant by "positive eugenics" and "negative eugenics"? Why are these programs regarded by many with such horror? What is the connection of eugenics with the Human Genome Project?
3. Why has the Human Genome Project become associated with the issue of abortion?
4. What is genetic discrimination?
5. Define "behavioral genetics." Why, according to Kevles and Hood, is it "socially and scientifically treacherous"?

## Discussion and Writing Suggestions

1. Of the ethical issues associated with the Human Genome Project, which (if any) do you find the most disturbing? Why?
2. Do you agree that eugenics programs may be among the consequences of the Human Genome Project? To what extent would you oppose such programs? To what extent would you support them? (Consider that you may be a parent one day.) In what area(s) are positive and negative eugenics decisions morally acceptable? In what area(s) are they unacceptable?
3. In general, do you favor or oppose genetic screening? Cite your reasons, indicating, if appropriate, under what conditions you believe such testing justifiable.
4. Draft a law that you believe is necessary to regulate the development of the biotechnology that results from the Human Genome Project. Focus on the rights and responsibilities of employers and insurers. Don't worry about drafting legal language; just explain what is and is not permissible and specify the penalties for noncompliance with the law. (For an example of legal language, see the extract from the law on bilingual education on pages 31–32 [under "Paraphrase"].) In a separate, multiparagraph essay, justify the provisions of this law. *Or* write a letter to your congressional representative, recommending such a law.
5. Write a future newspaper or magazine report detailing some new development, either promising or threatening, in genetic technology.

## SYNTHESIS ACTIVITIES

1. Suppose you are writing a survey article on biotechnology for a general audience magazine, such as *Time* or *Atlantic Monthly*. You want to introduce your readers to the subject, tell them what it is and what it may become, and you want to focus, in particular, on the advantages and disadvantages of biotechnology. Drawing on the sources you have read in this chapter, write such an article (i.e., an explanatory synthesis).

For background information on the subject, you can draw on sources like Vickery and the introduction to the chapter. Other sources, like Chamberland, Greenough, Jaroff, Watson, and Kevles and Hood offer many case studies illustrating advantages and disadvantages. And, of course, Huxley serves as a dark example of the kind of thing that *could* happen if bioengineering goes too far.

2. Write an editorial (i.e., an argument synthesis) arguing that additional regulations need to be placed on biotechnology. Specify the chief problem areas, as you see them, and indicate the regulations needed in order to deal with these problems.

    You may want to begin with a survey of biotechnology (in which you acknowledge its advantages) but then narrow your focus to the problem areas. Categorize the problem areas (e.g., problems for prospective parents, for the workplace, for the battlefield, for the commercial applications of biotechnology). The suggested regulations—and explanations of why they are necessary—might be discussed throughout the editorial or saved for the end.

3. *Brave New World* represents one artist's view of how scientific knowledge might be abused to ensure social stability and conformity. Huxley focused on the possibility of dividing fertilized human ova into identical parts and then conditioning the ova before "birth." Write a short story (or a play or screenplay) that represents your own nightmare vision. You may want to focus on other aspects of genetic engineering: the problem of forced genetic testing, of eugenics (creating "perfect" people or eliminating "imperfect" ones), of fostering uniformity among the population, of some fantastic commercial application of bioengineering, or even of some aspect of cloning (among the films dealing with cloning are Ira Levin's *The Boys from Brazil*, Woody Allen's *Sleeper*, and Steven Speilberg's *Jurassic Park*).

    Decide whether the story is to be essentially serious or comic (satirical)—or something in between. Create characters (try to avoid caricatures) who will enact the various aspects of the problem, as you see it. And create a social and physical setting appropriate to the story you want to tell.

4. Write an article for a magazine like *Newsweek* or *Time* or *U.S. News & World Report* on the current status of biotechnology—as of August 2050. Try to make the article generally upbeat (unlike the nightmare vision called for in the previous question), but be frank also about the problems that have been encountered, as well as the problems that remain. Refer, at some point in your article, to views of biotechnology from the late 1980s to establish some basis for comparison between what they thought "then" and what they think "now." You might model your article on the piece by Kevles and Hood or on any contemporary news magazine article of comparable scope. The language should be lively and vivid, and you should include as many "facts" as you can think of. Study your model articles for ideas about how to organize your material.

5. Write a paper on Jeremy Rifkin and the critical reaction to his activities and

his books. Begin by rereading the material on Rifkin (and his critic, Gould) in this chapter. Then go to the *Reader's Guide to Periodical Literature* and locate important articles by and about Rifkin during the past decade or so. Locate Rifkin's books and survey them. Most important, look up reviews of Rifkin's books, starting with the listings in *Book Review Digest.* (This is an annual index that lists reviews during a given year and provides brief excerpts from the most important reviews.)

Begin your paper by summarizing Rifkin's life and work thus far. (Your introductory paragraphs should probably focus on the controversy surrounding Rifkin.) Then focus on the reaction to his work. You may want to divide your paper into sections on positive and negative reactions; or you may want to organize by critical reviews of his various books and activities. At the conclusion, develop an overall assessment of the significance and value of Rifkin's work.

6. Compare and contrast Jeremy Rifkin's position on genetic engineering with Linda Bullard's. To what extent are their views similar? To what extent do they differ? As in the previous question, determine the particular subtopics each writer discusses, find similarities and differences in their treatment of these subtopics, and develop an organizational plan based on your findings.

7. Write a newsmagazine article on the Human Genome Project, focusing on what is being done and how, as well as on expected benefits and potential problems arising from the project. Draw on Jaroff, Watson, Wright, and Kevles and Hood.

---

## RESEARCH ACTIVITIES

1. The main focal points of the debate over genetic engineering and testing have been (1) whether or not the new biotechnologies are safe and ethical; (2) whether or not they will benefit agriculture; (3) whether or not they need stricter regulation (and, if so, what kind); (4) whether or not genetic testing by employers and insurance companies is ethical or should be legal; (5) whether or not genetic testing of fetuses is ethical; (6) whether or not geneticists should do work in biological weapons. Select one of these areas and research the current status of the debate.

In addition to relevant articles, see Jeremy Rifkin, *Algeny* (1983) and *Declaration of a Heretic* (1985); Jack Doyle, *Altered Harvest* (1985); Brian Stableford, *Future Man* (1984); Steve Olson, *Biotechnology: An Industry Comes of Age* (1986); Richard Noel Re, *Bioburst* (1986); Edward J. Sylvester and Lynn C. Klotz, *The Gene Age* (1987); Joseph Fletcher, *Ethics of Genetic Control* (1988); Gerald R. Campbell, *Biotechnology: An Introduction* (1988); Charles Pilar and Keith R. Yamamoto, *Gene Wars* (1988); David Suzuki and Peter Knudtson, *Genethics* (1989); Andrew Linzey, *Slavery: Human and Animal* (1988); Monsanto Company, *Agriculture and the New Biology* (1989);

and Kevles and Hood, *The Code of Codes: Scientific and Social Issues in the Human Genome Project* (1992).

2. Investigate the latest developments in DNA "fingerprint" technology. How has such technology been employed in recent criminal cases? What is the legal status of such technology at both the federal and the local levels? What ethical issues are at stake, according to proponents and opponents of DNA fingerprinting?

3. In August 1992, researchers announced that they had managed through genetic engineering to produce mice that developed cystic fibrosis. Scientists believed that by studying the course of this disease in mice, they would be able to devise new therapies for the treatment of this usually fatal disease in humans. Follow up on either this development or some other development involving the genetic engineering of laboratory animals to further medical research. Describe what is involved in the procedure, how it was developed, and the ethical debate that may have ensued about its practice.

4. Research and discuss some aspect of the early history of genetic engineering as it developed in the 1970s. Begin with a survey of Watson and Crick's work with DNA in the early 1950s, describe some of the early experiments in this area, discuss some of the concerns expressed both by scientists and laypersons, and cover in some detail the Asilomar (California) Conference of 1975 at which scientists worked out guidelines for future research.

5. Research some of the most significant recent advances in biotechnology, categorize them, and report on your findings. You may also wish to consider the Human Genome Project. Use some of the same categories suggested in Research Activity 1, but focus here less on the debate (which you need not ignore) than on what is currently being done, on who is doing it, on the obstacles yet to be overcome, and on the anticipated benefits on the research and development.

6. In 1989 James D. Watson was appointed to head NIH's Human Genome Project. Watson's appointment and his subsequent work as director of the project generated some controversy. Research Watson's professional activities since his discovery with Francis Crick of the structure of DNA, focusing on his more recent activities. See especially, the *full* article on Watson, "The Double Helix," which appeared in *The New Republic,* July 9 and 16, 1990. How do Watson's professional colleagues—and others—assess his more recent work?

7. Since the mid-1970s, genetic technology has been regulated not only by scientists themselves, working as a body, but also by federal agencies, such as the White House Office of Science and Technology Policy; the U.S. Department of Agriculture (USDA: overseeing genetically engineered plants); the NIH's Recombinant DNA Advisory Committee (RAC: overseeing laboratory research); the Environmental Protection Agency (EPA: approving field testing of commercial products affecting the environment); and the Food and Drug Administration (FDA: approving animal and human pharmaceuticals). Research and report on some of the most significant regulations imposed on

the biotechnology industry, consider the views of critics and of scientists themselves, and indicate your own position (and possibly some of your own proposals) on existing and additional regulations.

8. If your college or university has scientists on its faculty who are working on DNA research, interview them to find out what they are doing. Ask them how they feel about some of the ethical issues covered in this chapter. For example, how would they respond to the arguments of Jeremy Rifkin and Linda Bullard? Ask them to recommend references in the professional literature that will enable you to understand more fully the aims of their research; then consult some of these references and use them to provide context for your discussion of this research.

9. Conduct a survey of student attitudes on biotechnology and write a report based on this survey. Devise questions that focus on the main areas of controversy (see Research Activity 1). Phrase your questions in a way that allows a range of responses (perhaps on a scale of 1 to 5, or using modifiers like "strongly agree," "agree somewhat," "disagree somewhat," "strongly disagree"); don't ask for responses that require a yes/no or approve/disapprove response. (See pages 162–63 of Chapter 5.) Correlate the responses to such variables as academic major, student status (lower division, upper division, graduate), gender, ethnic background, geographical area of origin (urban, suburban, rural). Determine also whether respondents personally know someone with a disease for which a genetic cure is either possible or under consideration.

# 13

# BUSINESS ETHICS

Business ethics—both as an academic discipline and as an evolving set of principles used to guide decision making in large and small companies—is a relatively new concept in American life. Before the 1960s and 1970s, the proper role of business was understood as providing goods and services to a consuming public, for profit. Most Americans might have agreed with the sentiment that "What's good for General Motors is good for the country" and trusted General Motors to define "good" on its own terms. No longer. Scandals in business saw corporations dumping toxic chemicals and withholding information about product defects from the public; with the increasing tendency of large companies to gobble up smaller ones came a general wariness of corporations. In response to this wariness, businesses began to consider their social responsibilities. More and more, confronted with the reality of government regulation, managers and executives felt compelled to provide the public with an account of hazards in the workplace or in the environment, of questionable labor or management practices, or of economic decisions that might disrupt entire communities. Business also began to take into consideration public concern over corporate policy *before* decisions were made.

By the 1970s, corporations around the country began accepting the view that they had responsibilities to stakeholders as well as to shareholders—to all who were affected by the conduct of business, be that effect monetary, physical, psychological, or environmental. Money was no longer the only concern. Writing in 1971, the Committee for Economic Development noted:

> Today it is clear that the terms of the contract between society and business are, in fact, changing in substantial and important ways. Business is being asked to assume broader responsibilities to society than ever before and to serve a wider range of human values. Business enterprises, in effect, are being asked to

contribute more to the quality of American life than just supplying quantities of goods and services.[1]

The acknowledgment of corporate America's social responsibilities came just in time, apparently, as Americans began showing their impatience with "business as usual." In a survey conducted in 1968, 70 percent of respondents felt that businesses were managing to earn profits while at the same time showing decent concern for the public's welfare. In 1978, only 15 percent of respondents felt the same way. By 1985, more than half of the respondents to selected surveys claimed that corporate executives are dishonest, that businesses show little regard for the society in which they operate, and that executives violate the public trust whenever money is to be made. Internal studies of business bear out this growing pessimism. In 1992, a leading ethicist who consults with some of America's largest companies reported that, based on in-house surveys, "between 20% and 30% of middle managers have written deceptive internal reports." That is to say, one-fifth to one-third of the managers surveyed admit to lying.

The news is rife with examples of ethical misconduct. Recall the space shuttle *Challenger* disaster, in which the decision to launch was made over the protest of engineers who warned of potentially disastrous defects in the very parts that failed. Recall the Exxon *Valdez* fiasco that saw hundreds of miles of pristine Alaskan coastal waters despoiled by crude oil: The oil leaked from the ruptured hold of a tanker whose captain had left the bridge command to a subordinate unqualified to navigate the vessel in Prince William Sound; setting the causes of the accident aside, Exxon representatives argued with Alaskan and federal officials over the limits of corporate liability in cleaning up the mess. The corporate impulse was to limit corporate cost, whatever the larger environmental cost to the people of Alaska. And recall the spate of mergers in recent years that have left newly acquired companies too heavily in debt to deal flexibly with employees. Other examples of ethical misconduct or ethically questionable practices fill the nightly news and the morning headlines. In early 1992, Sears, one of America's largest retailers, was rocked by scandal when an investigation by a California consumer agency revealed that the company's auto service centers had been systematically overcharging customers and performing unnecessary repairs. Threatened with the shutdown of all its service centers in the state, Sears agreed to a costly settlement. More pervasive than these high-profile stories, and perhaps more damaging, are the "little" violations of ethical standards forced on managers or other employees

---

[1]From pp. 29–30 in *Social Responsibilities of Business Corporations* by the Committee for Economic Development (New York: CED, 1971).

who are asked, or forced, everyday to sacrifice personal values for company gain.

The study of ethics, of course, is not new. From the time of Aristotle (384–322 B.C.), philosophers have debated the standards by which we judge right or good behavior. The systematic study of ethics as applied to business, however, *is* new, and we see in it (according to the current president of the Society for Business Ethics) "an attempt . . . to revive the importance and legitimacy of making moral claims in the world of practical affairs."[2] Two associated developments have accompanied the rise of business ethics. First, corporations have begun drafting codes of ethics for their employees. Second, courses in business ethics are being taught at the graduate and undergraduate levels in schools around the country. The thrust of these courses has been both to justify the need for ethics in business and to provide a model by which students, future business leaders, can make ethical judgments in the world of work.

It is likely that in your life as a person who conducts business of one sort or another you will face an ethical dilemma: You could act one way and maintain your principles—but, perhaps, lose a job or an important account; you could act another way and help to secure your fortune—but, perhaps, at the expense of your integrity. The pressures on people in business to make money, on the one hand, but to do the "right" thing, on the other, are real and often painfully difficult. It is these pressures—clearly defining them and responding to them—that form the subject matter of this chapter. First, writing on "The Case of the Collapsed Mine," Richard T. De George poses a series of questions that effectively surveys the field of business ethics. We might call this an introduction by query. Next, a team of researchers from Baylor University reports on "The Generation Gap in Business Ethics." The authors designed a study to answer this question: Do younger people in business differ from their older colleagues in their tolerance for ethically questionable behavior? Assuming you accept the authors' methodology, the results are not heartening. Albert Carr follows with a highly controversial piece, "Is Business Bluffing Ethical?"—the thesis being that the ethics of business is like the ethics of poker: a certain amount of bluffing is expected. Then, in his "Ethics in Business," philosopher Gerald F. Cavanagh presents a strategy for analyzing ethical dilemmas and defining courses of action. Given these initial selections, you will have the tools to read, analyze, and respond to several case studies that raise questions about ethical behavior in business: "Peter Green's First Day," "Matt Goldspan's Trilogy," and "Why Should My Conscience Bother Me?"

---

[2]W. Michael Hoffman, "Business Ethics in the United States: Its Past Decade and Its Future," *Business Insights* 5, No. 1 (Spring/Summer, 1989): 8.

The chapter concludes with an excerpt from the novel *Babbitt,* by Nobel laureate Sinclair Lewis.

## The Case of the Collapsed Mine

RICHARD T. DE GEORGE

*Studying business ethics can make one sensitive to issues and questions that might otherwise have escaped notice, had no formal training been available. A business situation fraught with dilemmas for one person might for another simply be business as usual, and this is the problem: one person sees conflict; another person sees none. So we begin the chapter with a selection that demonstrates how someone who is sensitive to ethical dilemmas would approach a particular incident. In "The Case of the Collapsed Mine," Richard T. De George presents a case study and then raises a series of questions that, in effect, provides an overview of business ethics. For instance, De George takes up questions of the value of human life as measured against the cost of designing very safe, or relatively safe, products; and the need to restructure systems that reward loyalty at the expense of morality. These are questions you will read more about in the selections to follow. You may be surprised (as we were) by the number of questions De George can draw from the case.*

   *Richard T. De George is University Distinguished Professor of Philosophy and Courtesy Professor of Management at the University of Kansas. He is the author or editor of over fifteen books and more than one hundred scholarly articles concerning business ethics. De George has traveled worldwide in discussing issues of applied ethics; he is president of the American Philosophical Association (Central Division) and at the University of Kansas has won awards for his teaching and scholarship. De George was educated at Fordham University (B.A.), University of Louvain, Belgium (Ph.B.), and Yale (M.A. and Ph.D.).*

The following case illustrates the sorts of questions that might arise in   1
business ethics and various ways to approach them. Consider the case
of the collapsed mine shaft. In a coal mining town of West Virginia,

some miners were digging coal in a tunnel thousands of feet below the surface. Some gas buildup had been detected during the two preceding days. This had been reported by the director of safety to the mine manager. The buildup was sufficiently serious to have closed down operations until it was cleared. The owner of the mine decided that the buildup was only marginally dangerous, that he had coal orders to fill, that he could not afford to close down the mine, and that he would take the chance that the gas would dissipate before it exploded. He told the director of safety not to say anything about the danger. On May 2nd, the gas exploded. One section of the tunnel collapsed, killing three miners and trapping eight others in a pocket. The rest managed to escape.

The explosion was one of great force and the extent of the tunnel's 2 collapse was considerable. The cost of reaching the men in time to save their lives would amount to several million dollars. The problem facing the manager was whether the expenditure of such a large sum of money was worth it. What, after all, was a human life worth? Whose decision was it and how should it be made? Did the manager owe more to the stockholders of the corporation or to the trapped workers? Should he use the slower, safer, and cheaper way of reaching them and save a large sum of money or the faster, more dangerous, and more expensive way and possibly save their lives?

He decided on the latter and asked for volunteers. Two dozen men 3 volunteered. After three days, the operation proved to be more difficult than anyone had anticipated. There had been two more explosions and three of those involved in the rescue operation had already been killed. In the meantime, telephone contact had been made with the trapped men who had been fortunate enough to find a telephone line that was still functioning. They were starving. Having previously read about a similar case, they decided that the only way for any of them to survive long enough was to draw lots, and then kill and eat the one who drew the shortest straw. They felt that it was their duty that at least some of them should be found alive; otherwise, the three volunteers who had died rescuing them would have died in vain.

After twenty days the seven men were finally rescued alive; they 4 had cannibalized their fellow miner. The director of safety who had detected the gas before the explosion informed the newspapers of his report. The manager was charged with criminal negligence; but before giving up his position, he fired the director of safety. The mine eventually resumed operation.

There are a large number of issues in the above account. . . . 5

The director of safety is in some sense the hero of the story. But did 6 he fulfill his moral obligation before the accident in obeying the manager and in not making known either to the miners, the manager's superior, or to the public the fact that the mine was unsafe? Did he have a moral obligation after the explosion and rescue to make known the fact that the manager knew the mine was unsafe? Should he have gone to the board of directors of the company with the story or to someone else within the company rather than to the newspapers? All these questions are part of the phenomenon of worker responsibility. To whom is a worker responsible and for what? Does his moral obligation end when he does what he is told? Going public with inside information such as the director of safety had is commonly known as "blowing the whistle" on the company. Frequently those who blow the whistle are fired, just as the director of safety was. The whole phenomenon of whistle blowing raises serious questions about the structure of companies in which employees find it necessary to take such drastic action and possibly suffer the loss of their jobs. Was the manager justified in firing the director of safety?

The manager is, of course, the villain of the story. He sent the    7
miners into a situation which he knew was dangerous. But, he might argue, he did it for the good of the company. He had contracts to fulfill and obligations to the owners of the company to show a profit. He had made a bad decision. Every manager has to take risks. It just turned out that he was unlucky. Does such a defense sound plausible? Does a manager have an obligation to his workers as well as to the owners of a company? Who should take precedence and under what conditions does one group or the other become more important? Who is to decide and how?

The manager decided to try to save the trapped miners even    8
though it would cost the company more than taking the slower route. Did he have the right to spend more of the company's money in this way? How does one evaluate human life in comparison with expenditure of money? It sounds moral to say that human life is beyond all monetary value. In a sense it is. However, there are limits which society and people in it can place on the amount they will, can, and should spend to save lives. The way to decide, however, does not seem to be to equate the value of a person's life with the amount of income he would produce in his remaining years, if he lives to a statistically average age, minus the resources he would use up in that period. How does one decide? How do and should people weigh human lives against monetary expenditure? In designing automobiles, in building roads, in making many products, there is a trade-off between the maximum safety that one can build into the product and the cost of the product. Extremely safe cars cost more to build than relatively safe cars. We can express the difference in terms of the number

of people likely to die driving the relatively safe ones as opposed to the extremely safe ones. Should such decisions be made by manufacturers, consumers, government, or in some other way?

The manager asked for volunteers for the rescue work. Three of these volunteers died. Was the manager responsible for their deaths in the same way that he was responsible for the deaths of the three miners who had died in the first mine explosion? Was the company responsible for the deaths in either case? Do companies have obligations to their employees and the employees' families in circumstances such as these, or are the obligations only those of the managers? If the manager had warned the miners that the level of gas was dangerous, and they had decided that they wanted their pay for that day and would work anyway, would the manager have been responsible for their deaths? Is it moral for people to take dangerous jobs simply to earn money? Is a system that impels people to take such jobs for money a moral system? To what extent is a company morally obliged to protect its workers and to prevent them from taking chances? 9

The manager was charged with criminal negligence under the law. Was the company responsible for anything? Should the company have been sued by the family of the dead workers? If the company were sued and paid damages to the families, the money would come from company profits and hence from the profits of the shareholders. Is it fair that the shareholders be penalized for an incident they had nothing to do with? How is responsibility shared and/or distributed in a company, and can companies be morally responsible for what is done in their name? Are only human beings moral agents and is it a mistake to use moral language with respect to companies, corporations, and businesses? 10

The decision of the trapped miners to cast lots to determine who would be killed and eaten also raises a number of moral issues. Our moral intuitions can provide in this case no ready answer as to whether their decision was morally justifiable, since the case is not an ordinary one. How to think about such an issue raises the question of how moral problems are to be resolved and underscores the need for some moral theory as guidelines by which we can decide unusual cases. A number of principles seem to conflict—the obligation not to kill, the consideration that it is better for one person to die rather than eight, the fact noted by the miners that three persons had already died trying to rescue them, and so on. The issue here is not one peculiar to business ethics, but it is rather a moral dilemma that requires some technique of moral argument to solve. 11

The case does not tell us what happened to either the manager or the director of safety. Frequently the sequel to such cases is surprising. The managers come off free and are ultimately rewarded for their 12

743

concern for the company's interest, while the whistle blower is black-balled throughout the industry. The morality of such an outcome seems obvious—justice does not always triumph. What can be done to see that it triumphs more often is a question that involves restructuring the system.

Business ethics is sometimes seen as conservative and is also used as a defense of the status quo. Sometimes it is seen as an attack on the status quo and hence viewed as radical. Ideally it should be neither. It should strive for objectivity. When there are immoral practices, structures, and actions occurring, business ethics should be able to show that these actions are immoral and why. But it should also be able to supply the techniques with which the practices and structures that are moral can be defended as such. The aim of business ethics is neither defense of the status quo nor its radical change. Rather it should serve to remedy those aspects or structures that need change and protect those that are moral. It is not a panacea. It can secure change only if those in power take the appropriate action. But unless some attention is paid to business ethics, the moral debate about practices and principles central to our society will be more poorly and probably more immorally handled than otherwise. 13

## Discussion and Writing Suggestions

1. Of the many questions that De George poses regarding "The Case of the Collapsed Mine," which question or set of questions seems most likely to get at the heart of the case? Explain your choice.

2. De George writes: "When there are immoral practices, structures, and actions occurring, business ethics should be able to show that these actions are immoral and why. But it should also be able to supply the techniques with which the practices and structures that are moral can be defended as such." Based on what you've read and seen on news reports, and based on your own experience, perhaps, to what extent are people in business amenable to discussing reasons that an action may or may not be ethical?

3. In paragraph 6, De George poses several questions and then writes: "All these questions are part of the phenomenon of worker responsibility." *Worker responsibility*, then, becomes a category of questions. Reread the selection and create categories for the other questions that De George asks. For instance, some questions concern corporate responsibility, some concern the prohibition against killing, and so on. Compare your categories with a classmate's. (These categories will provide something of an index to the issues addressed in this chapter and, more generally, an index to the concerns of business ethicists.)

4. Summarize the significant details of an event in your own work experience and draw out those elements that raised ethical dilemmas for you or someone you know. In the fashion of De George, write a brief essay in which you

pose a series of questions about the event and the behaviors of the people involved.

# The Generation Gap in Business Ethics

JUSTIN G. LONGENECKER
JOSEPH A. MCKINNEY
CARLOS W. MOORE

*Do today's young people in business differ from their older colleagues in their ethical standards? The authors of the selection that follows, teachers and researchers at Baylor University, designed a study to answer this question. This article first appeared in the journal* Business Horizons *in 1989.*

News reports of the insider trading scandal in 1986 drew attention to brilliant young professionals whose tactics brought them into conflict with the law. They were talented and well compensated, but they broke the rules of their profession. One writer described them as "young men of advantage busily turning opportunity into misfortune." Although some older traders were similarly caught, the plight of young professionals branded as criminals seemed especially poignant.     1

Such episodes raise the question as to whether young people, particularly those on the "fast track," may operate with a less stringent set of ethical guidelines. Do younger managers and professionals differ from the older generation in their views concerning such practices as insider trading, misleading reports to investors, income tax evasion, and exaggerated claims in advertising? If younger organization members play by different rules, they deserve the special attention of leaders concerned with issues of corporate responsibility and ethical behavior. The study reported here explores similarities and differences in attitudes of younger and older generations in business. The findings? Younger managers and professionals are indeed more permissive in what they accept as ethical behavior.     2

**THE SURVEY RESPONDENTS**

To explore the ethical attitudes of business leaders, we conducted a nationwide survey of managerial and professional business personnel. Of the 10,000 questionnaires mailed, 2,156 usable questionnaires were returned. These form the basis for this analysis.     3

## Vignettes

The following are the 16 vignettes used in this study. Those on which the results across age groups were statistically significant are marked with an asterisk.

**A.*** An executive earning $50,000 a year padded his expense account about $1,500 a year.

**B.** In order to increase profits, a general manager used a production process which exceeded legal limits for environmental pollution.

**C.*** Because of pressure from his brokerage firm, a stockbroker recommended a type of bond which he did not consider to be a good investment.

**D.*** A small business received one-fourth of its gross revenue in the form of cash. The owner reported only one-half of the cash receipts for income tax purposes.

**E.** A company paid a $350,000 "consulting" fee to an official of a foreign country. In return, the official promised assistance in obtaining a contract which should produce $10 million profit for the contracting company.

**F.*** A company president found that a competitor had made an important scientific discovery which would sharply reduce the profits of his own company. He then hired a key employee of the competitor in an attempt to learn the details of the discovery.

**G.*** A highway building contractor deplored the chaotic bidding situation and cutthroat competition. He, therefore, reached an understanding with other major contractors to permit bidding which would provide a reasonable profit.

**H.*** A company president recognized that sending expensive Christmas gifts to purchasing agents might compromise their positions. However, he continued the policy since it was common practice and changing it might result in loss of business.

**I.*** A corporate director learned that his company intended to announce a stock split and increase its dividend. On the basis of this information, he bought additional shares and sold them at a gain following the announcement.

**J.** A corporate executive promoted a loyal friend and competent manager to the position of divisional vice president in preference to a better-qualified manager with whom he had no close ties.

**K.** An engineer discovered what he perceived to be a product design flaw which constituted a safety hazard. His company declined to correct the flaw. The engineer decided to keep quiet, rather than taking his complaint outside the company.

**L.*** A comptroller selected a legal method of financial reporting which concealed some embarrassing financial facts which would otherwise have become public knowledge.

**M.** An employer received applications for a supervisor's position from two equally qualified applicants but hired the male applicant because he thought that some employees might resent being supervised by a female.

**N.** As part of the marketing strategy for a product, the producer changed its color and marketed it as "new and improved," even though its other characteristics were unchanged.

**O.*** A cigarette manufacturer launched a publicity campaign challenging new evidence from the Surgeon General's office that cigarette smoking is harmful to the smoker's health.

**P.*** An owner of a small firm obtained a free copy of a copyrighted computer software program from a business friend rather than spending $500 to obtain his own program from the software dealer.

**TABLE 1** *Respondents According to Age*

| AGE GROUP | NUMBER OF RESPONDENTS |
|-----------|------------------------|
| 21–30 | 199 |
| 31–40 | 678 |
| 41–50 | 614 |
| 51–60 | 482 |
| 61–70 | 183 |

**TABLE 2**   *Profile of 21–40 and 51–70 Age Groups*

|  | AGE GROUPS | |
|---|---|---|
|  | 21–40 (%) | 51–70 (%) |
| **Industry** | | |
| Manufacturing | 41.2 | 45.4 |
| Construction | 6.4 | 7.1 |
| Retail/Wholesale | 4.0 | 4.6 |
| Services | 9.1 | 7.3 |
| Finance/Insurance | 5.8 | 4.0 |
| Government | 2.8 | 2.9 |
| Transportation/Communication/Public Utilities | 13.1 | 12.4 |
| Other | 17.7 | 16.2 |
| **Position** | | |
| Top Management | 17.7 | 34.8 |
| Middle Management | 26.7 | 20.6 |
| Finance | 6.6 | 2.3 |
| Marketing/Sales | 8.2 | 6.0 |
| Engineer/Technical | 29.3 | 24.8 |
| Self-Employed | 7.9 | 9.0 |
| Other | 3.7 | 2.5 |
| **Size of Firm** | | |
| **(Number of Employees)** | | |
| Under 20 | 18.2 | 21.0 |
| 20–99 | 15.7 | 18.8 |
| 100–249 | 10.2 | 11.5 |
| 250–999 | 14.3 | 12.6 |
| 1,000–10,000 | 23.9 | 17.0 |
| Over 10,000 | 17.7 | 19.1 |
| **Religion** | | |
| Catholic | 27.6 | 24.8 |
| Protestant | 47.9 | 60.0 |
| Jewish | 3.1 | 4.8 |
| Other Religions | 8.4 | 4.0 |
| No Religion | 13.0 | 6.3 |
| **Importance of Religious Beliefs** | | |
| High | 35.7 | 43.6 |
| Moderate | 41.2 | 41.5 |
| Low | 19.0 | 10.7 |
| No Importance | 4.2 | 4.3 |

Younger and older respondents shared many personal characteristics and a few differences. **Tables 1** and **2** present profiles of the respondents. To simplify our analysis, we have grouped those aged 21–40 and compared them with those aged 51–70. Perhaps the more notable differences between younger and older respondents exist in terms of management level and religious background. As might be expected, a larger percentage of the older group fills top management positions. Younger respondents have larger percentages in middle management and non-managerial professional positions. Also, the older respondents appear to be more religious. For example, 13 percent of the younger group have no religion, compared to 6.3 percent of the older group. Similarly, 19 percent of the younger group attach low importance to religious beliefs, compared to 10.7 percent of the older group.

## CONTRASTING ATTITUDES TOWARD ETHICAL ISSUES

Respondents were presented with a series of 16 vignettes, each involving an ethical issue. Following is an example of one such vignette:

> A company president recognized that sending expensive Christmas gifts to purchasing agents might compromise their positions. However, he continued the policy since it was common practice and changing it might result in loss of business.

They were asked to evaluate, on the basis of their own personal values, the behavior described in the vignettes by selecting one point on a seven-point scale, ranging from 1, "never acceptable," to 4, "sometimes acceptable," to 7, "always acceptable." In their responses to the question about gifts to purchasing agents, younger (21 to 40) respondents were more inclined to condone the practice than were older (51 to 70) respondents. Their average score was 3.37 (on the scale of 1, "never acceptable," to 7, "always acceptable"), whereas the average score for older respondents was only 2.71.

The box [on pages 746–47] presents all 16 vignettes. . . . On 14 of the 16 vignettes, younger respondents showed greater tolerance of ethically questionable behavior by choosing answers farther from the "never acceptable" end of the response scale. On ten of the 16 vignettes, younger respondents differed significantly (in a statistical sense) from those who were older.

Younger respondents were significantly more permissive in their views regarding the ethics in a wide variety of situations. These included cases of padding expense accounts, giving faulty investment advice, evading taxes, hiring a key employee of a competitor to get proprietary information, colluding in bidding, making gifts to purchasing agents, using insider information, engaging in misleading financial reporting, contending with the surgeon general's findings regarding cigarettes, and copying copyrighted computer software. In each case, differences in responses were highly significant.

We also examined the age dimension in greater detail by analyzing responses according to the age groupings of 21–30, 31–40, 41–50, 51–60, and 61–70. Although differences were most marked between respondents in their twenties and those in their sixties, differences also appeared when comparing those in their thirties and forties with older respondents. For example, the 41–50 age group differed significantly from older respondents on five vignettes, the 31–40 age group differed significantly on eight vignettes, and the 21–30 age group differed significantly on nine vignettes. In each instance, the older age groups displayed a less permissive ethical view. [8]

In general, therefore, we find a more demanding ethical judgment on the part of older respondents. There were no vignettes in which younger respondents in any age bracket were significantly more critical of behavior described in the vignettes than were their elders. On the surface, at least, younger respondents appear less exacting in their moral judgments on a broad range of issues. [9]

## What Is Never Acceptable?

Strong ethical views are evident in the selection of "never acceptable" (number 1 on the scale) as a response to vignettes. In most cases, and in every case where differences were significant, a larger percentage of older respondents chose this answer (that is, "never acceptable") as reflecting their personal values. **Figure 1** shows the percentage of the two age groups selecting a "never acceptable" answer for each vignette. [10]

Differences are striking in responses to several vignettes. In Vignette H, involving gifts to purchasing agents, 38.8 percent of the older respondents regarded it as "never acceptable" in contrast to 21.6 percent of the younger respondents. In Vignette L, involving misleading financial reporting, 25.5 percent of the older group as compared to 10.9 percent of the younger group regarded the practice as "never acceptable." [11]

. . .

In his recent best-seller *The Closing of the American Mind*, Allan Bloom decried what he perceives as a societal trend away from firm values based on natural rights. As he sees it, relativism has been increasingly taught, under the guise of tolerance, to recent generations of students. The choice of "never acceptable" in this survey reflects a degree of moral certainty and an absence of doubt about mitigating [12]

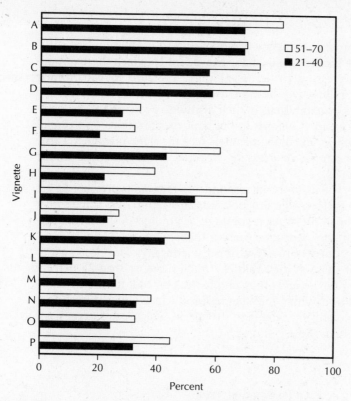

**FIGURE 1.** *"Never Acceptable" responses by age group.*

circumstances that are akin to this idea of well-defined values. The greater acceptance of "never acceptable" as an answer by older respondents thus seems to indicate that older respondents tend more toward moral absolutism and that younger respondents tend more toward moral relativism in their reasoning about ethical issues.

**TABLE 3**  *Degree of Perceived Pressure to Engage in Unethical Behavior*

| | AGE GROUPS | | | | |
|---|---|---|---|---|---|
| | 21–30 (%) | 31–40 (%) | 41–50 (%) | 51–60 (%) | 61–70 (%) |
| **Degree of Pressure** | | | | | |
| None | 65.3 | 69.7 | 75.6 | 75.5 | 77.8 |
| Slight Pressure | 30.7 | 27.7 | 19.9 | 19.6 | 17.6 |
| Extreme Pressure | 4.0 | 2.6 | 4.4 | 4.9 | 4.5 |

## PRESSURE TO ACT UNETHICALLY

In view of the greater tendency of younger respondents toward situa-    13
tional ethics, we should also examine the extent to which these respondents perceive pressure to act unethically. Pressure to compromise
personal standards may well be more destructive for individuals who are
more permissive or ambivalent in their attitudes. Pressure to act unethically is not necessarily uniform throughout organizations. We cannot
assume that younger and older members face the same pressures. **Table
3** indicates the degree of pressure reported by respondents in the
various age groups.

Fortunately, the majority of respondents report no pressure to act    14
unethically, a more favorable situation than that reported in some earlier
studies. Nevertheless, a larger percentage of younger respondents perceive some degree of pressure. Among those who are 21 to 30, 34.7
percent report a sense of pressure to act unethically. This decreases to
30.3 percent for those in their thirties, to a little more than 24 percent
for those in their forties and fifties, and to 22.1 percent for the 61-to-70
group. It is noteworthy that the age groups in which ethical perceptions
are more flexible are the same age groups in which pressure is most
frequently reported.

## THE GENERATION GAP IN PERSPECTIVE

Such differences in ethical attitudes based on age call for explanation.    15
Considering these survey results in the light of more general value
differences among generations may yield some insight into this matter.

An annual survey of college freshmen conducted by the American    16
Council on Education and the University of California, Los Angeles, has
presented a picture of students who are becoming more interested in
material wealth than those of a decade or two earlier. The 1987 survey
found that "being very well off financially" was one of the top personal
goals of 75.6 percent of those polled, nearly twice the 1970 figure of
39.1 percent. In contrast, the percentage of students who called "developing a meaningful philosophy of life" an important goal dropped from
82.9 percent in 1967 to 39.4 percent in 1987.

Whatever the reason, attitudes of college students have shifted    17
dramatically in two decades. Such a changing orientation toward money
and away from a meaningful philosophy of life may be connected in
some way to distinctive views regarding ethical issues.

Gallup polls have also identified age differences regarding accept-    18
ance of religious values. In 1987, for example, respondents were asked
how much confidence they had in the church or organized religion. Of

respondents in the 50-and-older category, 70 percent expressed "a great deal" or "quite a lot" of confidence. In contrast, only 55 percent of those in the 18–29 group expressed similar confidence.

On important moral issues of our day, significant differences have 19 also been detected in the attitudes of older and younger generations. According to a Gallup poll, for example, 65 percent of those over 50 years of age viewed premarital sex as wrong, whereas only 27 percent of those in the 19–29 age category held a similar view.

Young people thus seem to differ in their value systems when 20 compared with those older and with young people of earlier years. Our survey findings of significantly different ethical standards on the basis of age are thus consistent with these more general differences in value systems.

For managers concerned with ethical performance, our survey re- 21 veals an area of concern and possible danger. For whatever reason, there appears to be a greater ethical laxity among younger managers and professionals in business. Senior managers can no longer assume that younger managers and professionals are similar in their ethical views to the cadre of middle-aged or older managers with whom they have most contact.

These findings apply to all managerial processes related to the 22 establishment of values and the maintenance of ethical standards in organizational life. Successful attainment of high ethical performance is a challenging task for the management of any organization. This study draws attention to a soft spot that deserves special attention in any attempt to build or maintain such a corporate culture.

The importance of identifying and clarifying values during recruit- 23 ment, selection, and promotion is highlighted by the results of this study. If there is a conflict between corporate standards and those of individual employees, the potential for future discord and disappoint- ment is increased. Early determination of the fit between individual values and organizational values may thus be important both to the individual and the organization.

Efforts to promulgate and enforce ethical values may likewise re- 24 quire targeting of younger members for special attention. Inculcation of values is obviously difficult, requiring a high degree of managerial skill. A recent study of ethical concerns of practicing managers by Waters and Bird revealed an ambiguity regarding expected ethical behavior. As individuals, the managers often shared similar views regarding morally appropriate standards, but these views were held privately and tacitly, not collectively and publicly. Molding such privately held beliefs into a publicly acknowledged set of values, according to Waters and Bird, requires thorough discussion by corporate leaders, a discussion that moves beyond a statement of abstract principles, that deals with specific issues, and that involves extensive give-and-take on the part of those whose decisions are affected.

There is no simple prescription for resolving intergenerational dif- 25 ferences in ethical attitudes. If anything, the findings of this study complicate the managerial task by exposing an area of danger, the apparently greater tendency of younger professionals to "bend the rules."

These findings also have serious long-term implications for business 26 and society. Younger managers and professionals will obviously move into positions of future corporate leadership. Strengthening the ethical standards of younger organizational members, therefore, is crucially important because of its impact on the future of corporate morality.

## REFERENCES

Allan Bloom, *The Closing of the American Mind* (New York: Simon and Schuster, 1987).

Steven N. Brenner and Earl A. Molander, "Is the Ethics of Business Changing?" *Harvard Business Review*, January–February 1977, pp. 57–71.

*The American Freshman: National Norms for Fall 1987* (Los Angeles: Graduate School of Education, UCLA, 1987).

Gallup Report, August, 1987.

Gallup Report, May, 1987.

James A. Waters and Frederick Bird, "The Moral Dimensions of Organizational Culture," *Journal of Business Ethics*, January 1987, pp. 15–22.

## Review Questions

1. How did the authors set up this study? What was their methodology?
2. What is the general finding of this study?
3. How do the results of this study compare with more general studies on changing values?
4. According to the authors, why should an organization understand and, if necessary, try to change the ethics of individual employees?

## Discussion and Writing Suggestions

1. Reread the sixteen vignettes and respond to them in the same way that the subjects of this study were asked to respond. That is, evaluate each vignette by using "a seven-point scale, ranging from 1, 'never acceptable,' to 4, 'sometimes acceptable,' to 7, 'always acceptable.' " Then compare your answers to those of the respondents (see Figure 1). How do you rate? And how do you react to how you rate?

2. Underlying this study is an assumed definition of appropriate behavior, an assumed value system. That is, the authors themselves are not ethically neutral when reacting to the vignettes. (You will find evidence of their views in paragraphs 12 and 21.) To what extent do you sense in this article a moralizing tone? Do you share the authors' values? If not, how does this affect your response to the article?

3. To what extent is the "never acceptable" response a sign of moral rectitude and solid citizenship (as the authors suggest in paragraph 12), and to what extent is the response a sign of moral rigidity? Cast your answer in light of any one or two of the vignettes.

4. Assuming that you do not dispute the manner in which the study was designed and carried out or the authors' ethical assumptions, how do you account for the results? Are you surprised by the findings of this study? Write out your response in two or three paragraphs, which you then can exchange with a colleague in class. Discuss with one another your reactions to the study.

5. The authors report, "On the surface, at least, younger respondents appear less exacting in their moral judgments [than older respondents] on a broad range of issues." Is this your experience when you have observed people in situations calling for ethical judgment?

# Is Business Bluffing Ethical?

## ALBERT CARR

*"Business ethics? It's a contradiction in terms." Some version of this joke often begins introductions to books on business ethics, whose authors are quick to argue that we must carefully examine the perception that business and ethics don't mix. For if they don't, we're obliged to accept all manner of abuses as legitimate or defensible (in which case we wouldn't call them abuses) so long as businessmen and -women operate within the bounds of law. Recall the Ford Pinto case: An automobile manufacturer rushes a car to market, knowing that in some circumstances the car will prove dangerous to occupants. That car, nonetheless, meets existing federal safety standards. Is the manufacturer behaving unethically by not redesigning the car to reduce a known threat to consumers?*

*A classic in the literature of business ethics calls attention to questions such as this. On publication in the January–February 1968 issue of the* Harvard

Business Review, *Albert Carr's "Is Business Bluffing Ethical?" generated heated debate. Carr claimed that business operates according to its own set of ethical principles, separate and distinct from those of religion. It is confusing and misplaced, he said, to apply standards of religious ethics to business. Many disagreed. Perhaps you will, too.*

A respected businessman with whom I discussed the theme of this 1 article remarked with some heat, "You mean to say you're going to encourage men to bluff? Why, bluffing is nothing more than a form of lying! You're advising them to lie!"

I agreed that the basis of private morality is a respect for truth and 2 that the closer a businessman comes to truth, the more he deserves respect. At the same time, I suggested that most bluffing in business might be regarded simply as game strategy—much like bluffing in poker which does not reflect on the morality of the bluffer.

I quoted Henry Taylor, the British statesman who pointed out that 3 "falsehood ceases to be falsehood when it is understood on all sides that the truth is not expected to be spoken"—an exact description of bluffing in poker, diplomacy, and business. I cited the analogy of the criminal court, where the criminal is not expected to tell the truth when he pleads "not guilty." Everyone from the judge down takes it for granted that the job of the defendant's attorney is to get his client off, not to reveal the truth; and this is considered ethical practice. I mentioned Representative Omar Burleson, the Democrat from Texas, who was quoted as saying, in regard to the ethics of Congress, "Ethics is a barrel of worms"—a pungent summing-up of the problem of deciding who is ethical in politics. I reminded my friend that millions of businessmen feel constrained every day to say *yes* to their bosses when they secretly believe *no* and that this is generally accepted as permissible strategy when the alternative might be the loss of a job. The essential point, I said, is that the ethics of business are game ethics, different from the ethics of religion.

He remained unconvinced. Referring to the company of which he is 4 president, he declared: "Maybe that's good enough for some businessmen, but I can tell you that we pride ourselves on our ethics. In 30 years not one customer has ever questioned my word or asked to check our figures. We're loyal to our customers and fair to our suppliers. I regard my handshake on a deal as a contract. I've never entered into price-fixing schemes with my competitors. I've never allowed my salesmen to spread injurious rumors about other companies. Our union contract is the best in our industry. And, if I do say so myself, our ethical standards are of the highest!"

He really was saying, without saying it, that he was living up to the $\quad$ 5
ethical standards of the business game—which are a far cry from those
of private life. Like a gentlemanly poker player, he did not play in
cahoots with others at the table, try to smear their reputations, or hold
back chips he owed them.

But this same fine man, at the very time, was allowing one of his $\quad$ 6
products to be advertised in a way that made it sound a great deal better
than it actually was. Another item in his product line was notorious
among dealers for its "built-in obsolescence." He was holding back from
the market a much-improved product because he did not want it to
interfere with sales of the inferior item it would have replaced. He had
joined with certain of his competitors in hiring a lobbyist to push a state
legislature, by methods that he preferred not to know too much about,
into amending a bill then being enacted.

In his view these things had nothing to do with ethics; they were $\quad$ 7
merely normal business practice. He himself undoubtedly avoided outright falsehood—never lied in so many words. But the entire organization that he ruled was deeply involved in numerous strategies of deception.

## PRESSURE TO DECEIVE

Most executives from time to time are almost compelled, in the inter- $\quad$ 8
ests of their companies or themselves, to practice some form of deception when negotiating with customers, dealers, labor unions, government officials, or even other departments of their companies. By
conscious misstatements, concealment of pertinent facts, or exaggeration—in short, by bluffing—they seek to persuade others to agree
with them. I think it is fair to say that if the individual executive
refuses to bluff from time to time—if he feels obligated to tell the
truth, the whole truth, and nothing but the truth—he is ignoring
opportunities permitted under the rules and is at a heavy disadvantage
in his business dealings.

But here and there a businessman is unable to reconcile himself to $\quad$ 9
the bluff in which he plays a part. His conscience, perhaps spurred by
religious idealism, troubles him. He feels guilty; he may develop an ulcer
or a nervous tic. Before any executive can make profitable use of the
strategy of the bluff, he needs to make sure that in bluffing he will not
lose self-respect or become emotionally disturbed. If he is to reconcile
personal integrity and high standards of honesty with the practical

requirements of business, he must feel that his bluffs are ethically justified. The justification rests on the fact that business, as practiced by individuals as well as by corporations, has the impersonal character of a game—a game that demands both special strategy and an understanding of its special ethics.

The game is played at all levels of corporate life, from the highest    10
to the lowest. At the very instant that a man decides to enter business, he may be forced into a game situation, as is shown by the recent experience of a Cornell honor graduate who applied for a job with a large company:

> This applicant was given a psychological test which included the statement, "Of the following magazines, check any that you have read either regularly or from time to time, and double-check those which interest you most. *Reader's Digest, Time, Fortune, Saturday Evening Post, The New Republic, Life, Look, Ramparts, Newsweek, Business Week, U.S. News & World Report, The Nation, Playboy, Esquire, Harper's, Sports Illustrated.*"
>
> His tastes in reading were broad, and at one time or another he had read almost all of these magazines. He was a subscriber to *The New Republic*, an enthusiast for *Ramparts*, and an avid student of the pictures in *Playboy*. He was not sure whether his interest in *Playboy* would be held against him, but he had a shrewd suspicion that if he confessed to an interest in *Ramparts* and *The New Republic*, he would be thought a liberal, a radical, or at least an intellectual, and his chances of getting the job, which he needed, would greatly diminish. He therefore checked five of the more conservative magazines. Apparently it was a sound decision, for he got the job.

He had made a game player's decision, consistent with business    11
ethics.

A similar case is that of a magazine space salesman who, owing to    12
a merger, suddenly found himself out of a job:

> This man was 58, and, in spite of a good record, his chance of getting a job elsewhere in a business where youth is favored in hiring practice was not good. He was a vigorous, healthy man, and only a considerable amount of gray in his hair suggested his age. Before beginning his job search he touched up his hair with a black dye to confine the gray to his temples. He knew that the truth about his age might well come out in time, but he calculated that he could deal with that situation when it arose. He and his wife decided that he could easily pass for 45, and he so stated his age on his resume.

This was a lie; yet within the accepted rules of the business game,    13
no moral culpability attaches to it.

## THE POKER ANALOGY

We can learn a good deal about the nature of business by comparing it   14
with poker. While both have a large element of chance, in the long run
the winner is the man who plays with steady skill. In both games
ultimate victory requires intimate knowledge of the rules, insights into
the psychology of the other players, a bold front, a considerable amount
of self-discipline, and the ability to respond swiftly and effectively to
opportunities provided by chance.

No one expects poker to be played on the ethical principles   15
preached in churches. In poker it is right and proper to bluff a friend out
of the rewards of being dealt a good hand. A player feels no more than
a slight twinge of sympathy, if that, when—with nothing better than
a single ace in his hand—he strips a heavy loser, who holds a pair, of
the rest of his chips. It was up to the other fellow to protect himself. In
the words of an excellent poker player, former President Harry Truman,
"If you can't stand the heat, get out of the kitchen." If one shows mercy
to a loser in poker, it is a personal gesture, divorced from the rules of
the game.

Poker has its special ethics, and here I am not referring to rules   16
against cheating. The man who keeps an ace up his sleeve or who marks
the cards is more than unethical; he is a crook, and can be punished as
such—kicked out of the game or, in the Old West, shot.

In contrast to the cheat, the unethical poker player is one who, while   17
abiding by the letter of the rules, finds ways to put the other players at
an unfair disadvantage. Perhaps he unnerves them with loud talk. Or he
tries to get them drunk. Or he plays in cahoots with someone else at the
table. Ethical poker players frown on such tactics.

Poker's own brand of ethics is different from the ethical ideals of   18
civilized human relationships. The game calls for distrust of the other
fellow. It ignores the claim of friendship. Cunning deception and concealment of one's strength and intentions, not kindness and openheartedness, are vital in poker. No one thinks any worse of poker on that
account. And no one should think any worse of the game of business
because its standards of right and wrong differ from the prevailing
traditions of morality in our society.

## DISCARD THE GOLDEN RULE

This view of business is especially worrisome to people without much   19
business experience. A minister of my acquaintance once protested that
business cannot possibly function in our society unless it is based on the
Judeo-Christian system of ethics. He told me:

I know some businessmen have supplied call girls to customers, but there are always a few rotten apples in every barrel. That doesn't mean the rest of the fruit isn't sound. Surely the vast majority of businessmen are ethical. I myself am acquainted with many who adhere to strict codes of ethics based fundamentally on religious teachings. They contribute to good causes. They participate in community activities. They cooperate with other companies to improve working conditions in their industries. Certainly they are not indifferent to ethics.

That most businessmen are not indifferent to ethics in their private lives, everyone will agree. My point is that in their office lives they cease to be private citizens; they become game players who must be guided by a somewhat different set of ethical standards.

The point was forcefully made to me by a Midwestern executive   **20** who has given a good deal of thought to the question:

> So long as a businessman complies with the laws of the land and avoids telling malicious lies, he's ethical. If the law as written gives a man a wide-open chance to make a killing, he'd be a fool not to take advantage of it. If he doesn't, somebody else will. There's no obligation on him to stop and consider who is going to get hurt. If the law says he can do it, that's all the justification he needs. There's nothing unethical about that. It's just plain business sense.

This executive (call him Robbins) took the stand that even industrial   **21** espionage, which is frowned on by some businessmen, ought not to be considered unethical. He recalled a recent meeting of the National Industrial Conference Board where an authority on marketing made a speech in which he deplored the employment of spies by business organizations. More and more companies, he pointed out, find it cheaper to penetrate the secrets of competitors with concealed cameras and microphones or by bribing employees than to set up costly research and design departments of their own. A whole branch of the electronics industry has grown up with this trend, he continued, providing equipment to make industrial espionage easier.

Disturbing? The marketing expert found it so. But when it came to   **22** a remedy, he could only appeal to "respect for the golden rule." Robbins thought this a confession of defeat, believing that the golden rule, for all its value as an ideal for society, is simply not feasible as a guide for business. A good part of the time the businessman is trying to do unto others as he hopes others will *not* do unto him. Robbins continued:

> Espionage of one kind or another has become so common in business that it's like taking a drink during Prohibition—it's not considered sinful. And we don't even have Prohibition where espionage is concerned; the law is very tolerant in this area. There's no more shame for a business that uses secret agents than there is for a nation. Bear in mind that there already is at least one

large corporation—you can buy its stock over the counter—that makes millions by providing counterespionage service to industrial firms. Espionage in business is not an ethical problem; it's an established technique of business competition.

## "WE DON'T MAKE THE LAWS"

Wherever we turn in business, we can perceive the sharp distinction    23
between its ethical standards and those of the churches. Newspapers abound with sensational stories growing out of this distinction:

> We read one day that Senator Philip A. Hart of Michigan has attacked food processors for deceptive packaging of numerous products.
> The next day there is a Congressional to-do over Ralph Nader's book, *Unsafe at Any Speed*, which demonstrates that automobile companies for years have neglected the safety of car-owning families.
> Then another Senator, Lee Metcalf of Montana, and journalist Vic Reinemer show in their book, *Overcharge*, the methods by which utility companies elude regulating government bodies to extract unduly large payments from users of electricity.

These are merely dramatic instances of a prevailing condition; there    24
is hardly a major industry at which a similar attack could not be aimed. Critics of business regard such behavior as unethical, but the companies concerned know that they are merely playing the business game.

Among the most respected of our business institutions are the    25
insurance companies. A group of insurance executives meeting recently in New England was startled when their guest speaker, social critic [now Senator from New York] Daniel Patrick Moynihan, roundly berated them for "unethical" practices. They had been guilty, Moynihan alleged, of using outdated actuarial tables to obtain unfairly high premiums. They habitually delayed the hearings of lawsuits against them in order to tire out the plaintiffs and win cheap settlements. In their employment policies they used ingenious devices to discriminate against certain minority groups.

It was difficult for the audience to deny the validity of these    26
charges. But these men were business game players. Their reaction to Moynihan's attack was much the same as that of the automobile manu-facturers to Nader, of the utilities to Senator Metcalf, and of the food processors to Senator Hart. If the laws governing their businesses change, or if public opinion becomes clamorous, they will make the necessary adjustments. But morally they have in their view done noth-ing wrong. As long as they comply with the letter of the law, they are within their rights to operate their businesses as they see fit.

The small business is in the same position as the great corporation  27
in this respect. For example:

> In 1967 a key manufacturer was accused of providing master keys for au-
> tomobiles to mail-order customers, although it was obvious that some of the
> purchasers might be automobile thieves. His defense was plain and straight-
> forward. If there was nothing in the law to prevent him from selling his
> keys to anyone who ordered them, it was not up to him to inquire as to his
> customers' motives. Why was it any worse, he insisted, for him to sell car
> keys by mail, than for mail-order houses to sell guns that might be used for
> murder? Until the law was changed, the key manufacturer could regard him-
> self as being just as ethical as any other businessman by the rules of the
> business game.

Violations of the ethical ideals of society are common in business,  28
but they are not necessarily violations of business principles. Each year
the Federal Trade Commission orders hundreds of companies, many of
them of the first magnitude, to "cease and desist" from practices which,
judged by ordinary standards, are of questionable morality but which
are stoutly defended by the companies concerned.

In one case, a firm manufacturing a well-known mouthwash was  29
accused of using a cheap form of alcohol possibly deleterious to health.
The company's chief executive, after testifying in Washington, made
this comment privately:

> We broke no law. We're in a highly competitive industry. If we're going to
> stay in business, we have to look for profit wherever the law permits. We
> don't make the laws. We obey them. Then why do we have to put up with
> this "holier than thou" talk about ethics? It's sheer hypocrisy. We're not in
> business to promote ethics. Look at the cigarette companies, for God's sake!
> If the ethics aren't embodied in the laws by the men who made them, you
> can't expect businessmen to fill the lack. Why, a sudden submission to
> Christian ethics by businessmen would bring about the greatest economic
> upheaval in history!

It may be noted that the government failed to prove its case against  30
him.

## CAST ILLUSIONS ASIDE

Talking about ethics by businessmen is often a thin decorative coating  31
over the hard realities of the game:

> Once I listened to a speech by a young executive who pointed to a new
> industry code as proof that his company and its competitors were deeply

aware of their responsibilities to society. It was a code of ethics, he said. The industry was going to police itself, to dissuade constituent companies from wrongdoing. His eyes shone with conviction and enthusiasm.

The same day there was a meeting in a hotel room where the industry's top executives met with the "czar" who was to administer the new code, a man of high repute. No one who was present could doubt their common attitude. In their eyes the code was designed primarily to forestall a move by the federal government to impose stern restrictions on the industry. They felt that the code would hamper them a good deal less than new federal laws would. It was, in other words, conceived as a protection for the industry, not for the public.

The young executive accepted the surface explanation of the code; these leaders, all experienced game players, did not deceive themselves for a moment about its purpose.

The illusion that business can afford to be guided by ethics as 32 conceived in private life is often fostered by speeches and articles containing such phrases as, "It pays to be ethical," or, "Sound ethics is good business." Actually this is not an ethical position at all; it is a self-serving calculation in disguise. The speaker is really saying that in the long run a company can make more money if it does not antagonize competitors, suppliers, employees, and customers by squeezing them too hard. He is saying that oversharp policies reduce ultimate gains. That is true, but it has nothing to do with ethics. The underlying attitude is much like that in the familiar story of the shopkeeper who finds an extra $20 bill in the cash register, debates with himself the ethical problem—should he tell his partner?—and finally decides to share the money because the gesture will give him an edge over the s.o.b. the next time they quarrel.

I think it is fair to sum up the prevailing attitude of businessmen on 33 ethics as follows:

We live in what is probably the most competitive of the world's 34 civilized societies. Our customs encourage a high degree of aggression in the individual's striving for success. Business is our main area of competition, and it has been ritualized into a game of strategy. The basic rules of the game have been set by the government, which attempts to detect and punish business frauds. But as long as a company does not transgress the rules of the game set by law, it has the legal right to shape its strategy without reference to anything but its profits. If it takes a long-term view of its profits, it will preserve amicable relations, so far as possible, with those with whom it deals. A wise businessman will not seek advantage to the point where he generates dangerous hostility among employees, competitors, customers, government, or the public at large. But decisions in this area are, in the final test, decisions of strategy, not of ethics.

## THE INDIVIDUAL AND THE GAME

An individual within a company often finds it difficult to adjust to the    35
requirements of the business game. He tries to preserve his private
ethical standards in situations that call for game strategy. When he is
obliged to carry out the company policies that challenge his conception
of himself as an ethical man, he suffers.

It disturbs him when he is ordered, for instance, to deny a raise to    36
a man who deserves it, to fire an employee of long standing, to prepare
advertising that he believes to be misleading, to conceal facts that he
feels customers are entitled to know, to cheapen the quality of materials
used in the manufacture of an established product, to sell as new a
product that he knows to be rebuilt, to exaggerate the curative powers
of a medicinal preparation, or to coerce dealers.

There are some fortunate executives, who, by the nature of their    37
work and circumstances, never have to face problems of this kind. But
in one form or another the ethical dilemma is felt sooner or later by most
businessmen. Possibly the dilemma is most painful not when the company forces the action on the executive but when he originates it
himself—that is, when he has taken or is contemplating a step which is
in his own interest but which runs counter to his early moral conditioning. To illustrate:

> The manager of an export department, eager to show rising sales, is pressed
> by a big customer to provide invoices, which, while containing no overt
> falsehood that would violate a U.S. law, are so worded that the customer may
> be able to evade certain taxes in his homeland.
>
> A company president finds that an aging executive, within a few years of
> retirement and his pension, is not as productive as formerly. Should he be kept
> on?
>
> The produce manager of a supermarket debates with himself whether to get
> rid of a lot of half-rotten tomatoes by including one, with its good side
> exposed, in every tomato sixpack.
>
> An accountant discovers that he has taken an improper deduction on his
> company's tax return and fears the consequences if he calls the matter to the
> president's attention, though he himself has done nothing illegal. Perhaps if he
> says nothing, no one will notice the error.
>
> A chief executive officer is asked by his directors to comment on a rumor
> that he owns stock in another company with which he has placed large orders.
> He could deny it, for the stock is in the name of his son-in-law and he has
> earlier formally instructed his son-in-law to sell the holding.

Temptations of this kind constantly arise in business. If an executive    38
allows himself to be torn between a decision based on business considerations and one based on his private ethical code, he exposes himself to
a grave psychological strain.

This is not to say that sound business strategy necessarily runs   39
counter to ethical ideals. They may frequently coincide; and when
they do, everyone is gratified. But the major tests of every move in
business, as in all games of strategy, are legality and profit. A man
who intends to be a winner in the business game must have a game
player's attitude.

The business strategist's decisions must be as impersonal as those   40
of a surgeon performing an operation—concentrating on objective and
technique, and subordinating personal feelings. If the chief executive
admits that his son-in-law owns the stock, it is because he stands to lose
more if the fact comes out later than if he states it boldly and at once.
If the supermarket manager orders the rotten tomatoes to be discarded,
he does so to avoid an increase in consumer complaints and a loss of
good will. The company president decides not to fire the elderly executive in the belief that the negative reaction of other employees would
in the long run cost the company more than it would lose in keeping
him and paying his pension.

All sensible businessmen prefer to be truthful, but they seldom feel   41
inclined to tell the *whole* truth. In the business game truth-telling usually
has to be kept within narrow limits if trouble is to be avoided. The point
was neatly made a long time ago (in 1888) by one of John D. Rockefel-
ler's associates, Paul Babcock, to Standard Oil Company executives who
were about to testify before a government investigating committee:
"Parry every question with answers which, while perfectly truthful, are
evasive of *bottom* facts." This was, is, and probably always will be
regarded as wise and permissible business strategy.

## FOR OFFICE USE ONLY

An executive's family life can easily be dislocated if he fails to make a   42
sharp distinction between the ethical systems of the home and the
office—or if his wife does not grasp that distinction. Many a businessman who has remarked to his wife "I had to let Jones go today" or "I
had to admit to the boss that Jim has been goofing off lately," has been
met with an indignant protest. "How could you do a thing like that? You
know Jones is over 50 and will have a lot of trouble getting another
job." Or, "You did that to Jim? With his wife ill and all the worry she's
been having with the kids?"

If the executive insists that he had no choice because the profits of   43
the company and his own security were involved, he may see a certain
cool and ominous reappraisal in his wife's eyes. Many wives are not
prepared to accept the fact that business operates with a special code of

ethics. An illuminating illustration of this comes from a Southern sales executive who related a conversation he had had with his wife at a time when a hotly contested political campaign was being waged in their state:

I made the mistake of telling her that I had had lunch with Colby, who gives me about half my business. Colby mentioned that his company had a stake in the election. Then he said, "By the way, I'm treasurer of the citizens' committee for Lang. I'm collecting contributions. Can I count on you for a hundred dollars?"

Well, there I was. I was opposed to Lang, but I knew Colby. If he withdrew his business I could be in a bad spot. So I just smiled and wrote out a check then and there. He thanked me, and we started to talk about his next order. Maybe he thought I shared his political views. I wasn't going to lose any sleep over it.

I should have had sense enough not to tell Mary about it. She hit the ceiling. She said she was disappointed in me. She said I hadn't acted like a man, that I should have stood up to Colby.

I said, "Look, it was an either-or situation. I had to do it or risk losing the business."

She came back at me with, "I don't believe it. You could have been honest with him. You could have said that you didn't feel you ought to contribute to a campaign for a man you weren't going to vote for. I'm sure he would have understood."

I said, "Mary, you're a wonderful woman, but you're way off the track. Do you know what would have happened if I had said that? Colby would have smiled and said, 'Oh, I didn't realize. Forget it.' But in his eyes from that moment I would be an oddball, maybe a bit of a radical. He would have listened to me talk about his order and would have promised to give it consideration. After that I wouldn't hear from him for a week. Then I would telephone and learn from his secretary that he wasn't yet ready to place the order. And in about a month I would hear through the grapevine that he was giving his business to another company. A month after that I'd be out of a job."

She was silent for a while. Then she said, "Tom, something is wrong with business when a man is forced to choose between his family's security and his moral obligation to himself. It's easy for me to say you should have stood up to him—but if you had, you might have felt you were betraying me and the kids. I'm sorry that you did it, Tom, but I can't blame you. Something is wrong with business!"

This wife saw the problem in terms of moral obligation as con- [44] ceived in private life; her husband saw it as a matter of game strategy. As a player in a weak position, he felt that he could not afford to indulge an ethical sentiment that might have cost him his seat at the table.

## PLAYING TO WIN

Some men might challenge the Colbys of business—might accept seri-  45
ous setbacks to their business careers rather than risk a feeling of moral
cowardice. They merit our respect—but as private individuals, not
businessmen. When the skillful player of the business game is compelled
to submit to unfair pressure, he does not castigate himself for moral
weakness. Instead, he strives to put himself into a strong position where
he can defend himself against such pressures in the future without loss.

If a man plans to take a seat in the business game, he owes it to  46
himself to master the principles by which the game is played, including its special ethical outlook. He can then hardly fail to recognize that
an occasional bluff may well be justified in terms of the game's ethics
and warranted in terms of economic necessity. Once he clears his
mind on this point, he is in a good position to match his strategy
against that of the other players. He can then determine objectively
whether a bluff in a given situation has a good chance of succeeding
and can decide when and how to bluff, without a feeling of ethical
transgression.

To be a winner, a man must play to win. This does not mean that  47
he must be ruthless, cruel, harsh, or treacherous. On the contrary, the
better his reputation for integrity, honesty, and decency, the better his
chances of victory will be in the long run. But from time to time every
businessman, like every poker player, is offered a choice between certain
loss or bluffing within the legal rules of the game. If he is not resigned
to losing, if he wants to rise in his company and industry, then in such
a crisis he will bluff—and bluff hard.

Every now and then one meets a successful businessman who has  48
conveniently forgotten the small or large deceptions that he practiced
on his way to fortune. "God gave me my money," old John D. Rockefel-
ler once piously told a Sunday school class. It would be a rare tycoon
in our time who would risk the horse laugh with which such a remark
would be greeted.

In the last third of the twentieth century even children are aware  49
that if a man has become prosperous in business, he has sometimes
departed from the strict truth in order to overcome obstacles or has
practiced the more subtle deceptions of the half-truth or the misleading
omission. Whatever the form of the bluff, it is an integral part of the

game, and the executive who does not master its techniques is not likely
to accumulate much money or power.

## Review Questions

1. Albert Carr's definition of the term "business ethics" is inconsistent with the
   term as defined by others in this chapter. How so?
2. Much of Carr's argument derives from what he calls "the poker analogy."
   Summarize this analogy.
3. According to Carr, decisions in business are governed by strategy, not ethics.
   Why are the two sometimes confused?
4. What are the consequences of an individual's being caught between a
   personal code of ethics and "a decision based on business considerations"?

## Discussion and Writing Suggestions

1. By the third paragraph of the article, Carr directly states his essential point:
   ". . . the ethics of business are game ethics, different from the ethics of
   religion." This is to say, the ethical considerations that help you to make
   decisions in your private life are different from the ones that guide business
   people in making decisions. Business has its own rules. Do you agree?
   Develop your answer into a brief essay.
2. Carr presents several examples of playing "within the accepted rules of the
   business game": lying about one's age in a job application; conducting
   industrial espionage; taking any action, even at the expense of others, if the
   law allows it. If you were running a business, to what extent would you
   endorse these behaviors?
3. "Cunning deception and concealment of one's strength and intentions,
   not kindness and openheartedness, are vital in poker"—and to the success
   of a business enterprise, implies Carr through his analogy. What's your response?
4. Do you accept Carr's final assertion that "whatever the form of the bluff, it
   is an integral part of the game, and the executive who does not master its
   techniques is not likely to accumulate much money or power"?
5. Carr states that "most executives from time to time are almost compelled, in
   the interests of their companies or themselves, to practice some sort of
   deception when negotiating with customers, dealers, labor unions, government officials, or even other departments of their companies." Check the
   accuracy of this assertion by interviewing one or more men or women
   involved in business life. Summarize Carr's thesis for them and ask for their
   reactions. Report on your findings.
6. In an analysis attempting to refute Carr's thesis and prove that business does
   *not* operate according to its own code of ethics, writers Joseph R. Desjardins
   and John J. McCall offer the following argument:

Think of the Mafia and the elaborate code of conduct that guides behavior within this group. Following Carr's use of "ethics," we can call such rules "Mafia ethics." Now, could an argument similar to Carr's be constructed to show that Mafia hit squads are ethical? We might write a paper on the topic and call it "Is Mafia Murder Ethical?" Within the ethics of organized crime, such activity is accepted, is well-known by the participants, and is necessary for the successful operation of organized crime. Murder is, after all, part of the "rules of the game." To paraphrase the final sentence in Carr's final section on poker, "No one should think any the worse of the Mafia game because its standards of right and wrong differ from the prevailing traditions of morality in our society."

Presumably, however, we all want to say that murder is morally wrong regardless of its role in the rules of the Mafia game. In fact, we would say that the entire game is immoral. We would, in other words, insist that the standards of morality be applied to the activities of organized crime and conclude that morality overrides the rules of the game.

This example demonstrates what should happen when we remain clear about the two uses of "ethics." When "ethics" is taken to mean just any rules of conduct, it is easy to think that all "ethics" are equally valid when applied to their own activities and equally invalid when imported into other fields. However, when ethics is understood as "morality," we normally do not hesitate to make ethical (moral) judgments about any serious human activity. (11–12)[1]

Discuss your reactions to this argument against Carr's thesis.


# Ethics in Business

## GERALD F. CAVANAGH

*The case method is used as an instructional strategy in schools of business and departments of business ethics in colleges and universities around the country. Students read varied accounts (real or hypothetical) of life in the world of business and then are asked to analyze a case and advise the principals what to do. For instance, students of business might read about specific business transactions (or the preliminaries leading up to such transactions); accounts of interpersonal behaviors within organizations that call for management to take action; or accounts of organizational structures and how these impede or promote productivity. One class of cases that students*

---

[1]From *Contemporary Issues in Business Ethics* by Joseph R. Desjardins and John J. McCall. © 1985 by Wadsworth, Inc. Reprinted by permission of the publisher.

Gerald F. Cavanagh, *American Business Values*, second edition © 1984, pp. 126–150. Reprinted by permission of Prentice-Hall, Inc., Englewood Cliffs, New Jersey. The material in this chapter owes much to several years of work with Manuel Velasquez, S.J., and Dennis Moberg of the University of Santa Clara, Santa Clara, California.

---

are increasingly being asked to read involves ethical dilemmas faced by corporate executives, managers, and individual contributors. In all these cases, students are expected to conduct a systematic analysis and make specific, defensible recommendations.

In cases concerning financial analysis, you would perhaps be asked to use spreadsheets in arriving at your recommendations. In cases concerning ethical analysis, you would be expected to use one or another model—a set of well-defined criteria—in arriving at your recommendations. Gerald Cava-nagh offers such a model in his "Ethics in Business," which appeared origi-nally in his American Business Values (1984), a text written for college course work. You'll find Cavanagh's discussion clearly written and organized (divided into sections and subsections), but you may also find the discussion somewhat difficult, for Cavanagh must define three ethical theories in order to establish his model for decision making. Read slowly, take notes, and respond to all the review questions on pages 786–87 as you read, and you will find the discussion in your grasp—which is important, because you'll be asked to apply Cavanagh's model to several cases.

Gerald Cavanagh is professor of management, associate dean, and director of Graduate Programs in the University of Detroit's College of Business and Administration. Cavanagh holds a B.S. in engineering, has graduate degrees in philosophy, theology, and management (Ph.D., Michigan State Univer-sity), and was ordained a Jesuit priest in 1964. He has served on boards of trustees of several universities, and he referees papers for several scholarly journals and for national meetings of the Academy of Management. He has also given ethics workshops at universities throughout the country.

Freedom is expendable, stability is indispensable.

—Arnold Toynbee

No human institution can long exist without some consensus on what is right and what is wrong. Managers recognize the need for ethical norms in their daily dealings. Decisions made at every level of the firm are influenced by ethics, whether these be decisions which affect quality of work, employment opportunity, safety of worker or product, truth in advertising, use of toxic materials, or operations in third world countries. An increasing sense of the importance of ethical norms among execu-tives is demonstrated by the facts that

1. Almost three-quarters of U.S. firms now have a code of ethics.[1]

---

[1] According to a survey by Opinion Research Corporation, 73 percent of the larger corporations in the United States now have a written code of ethics. See Chronicle of Higher Education, August 6, 1979, p. 2. [All footnotes by Cavanagh unless otherwise noted.]

2. More than 100 boards of directors of large firms have established an ethics, social responsibility, or public policy committee of the board.[2]

3. Speeches of chief executive officers and annual reports more often allude to the importance of ethics in business decisions.[3]

Managers understand that without ethics the only restraint is the law. Without ethics, any business transaction that was not witnessed and recorded could not be trusted. If government regulation and legislation are perceived to be unneeded and burdensome, then each manager must possess a set of internalized and operative ethical criteria for decision making. Or, as some have put it: "Shall we be honest and free, or dishonest and policed?" 2

## NEED FOR ETHICS IN BUSINESS

A significant minority of large American firms have been involved not only in unethical activities but also in illegal activities. During the 1970s, 11 percent of the largest U.S. firms were convicted of bribery, criminal fraud, illegal campaign contributions, tax evasion, or some sort of price fixing. Firms with two or more convictions include Allied, American Airlines, Bethlehem Steel, Diamond International, Firestone, Goodyear, International Paper, J. Ray McDermott, National Distillers, Northrop, Occidental Petroleum, Pepsico, Phillips Petroleum, Rapid-American, R. J. Reynolds, Schlitz, Seagram, Tenneco, and United Brands. Those that lead the list with at least four convictions each are Braniff International, Gulf Oil, and Ashland Oil.[4] Perhaps Gulf and Ashland will suffer the same punishment meted out to [now bankrupt] Braniff! 3

Most of the major petroleum firms illegally contributed to Richard Nixon's reelection committee in the mid-1970s: Gulf, Getty, Standard 4

---

[2]"Business Strategies for the 1980's," in *Business and Society: Strategies for the 1980's* (Washington, D.C.: U.S. Department of Commerce, 1980), pp. 33–34.

[3]For example, Reginald Jones of General Electric, who was selected by his fellow CEOs as the best CEO, has often made a strong case for ethics. See, for example, Reginald Jones, "Managing in the 1980's," address at Wharton School, February 4, 1980, p. 5. See also Richard J. Bennett, chairman of Schering-Plough, "A New Compact in the Age of Limits," address at Fordham University, November 5, 1981.

[4]Irwin Ross, "How Lawless Are Big Companies?" *Fortune*, December 1, 1980, pp. 56–64. See also Robert K. Elliott and John J. Willingham, *Management Fraud: Detection and Deterrence* (New York: Petrocelli Books, 1980).

---

of California, Phillips, Sun, Exxon, and Ashland. The chairman of Phillips personally handed Richard Nixon $50,000 in Nixon's own apartment. Many firms were also involved in multimillion-dollar foreign payments: Exxon, Lockheed, Gulf, Phillips, McDonnell Douglas, United Brands, and Mobil.[5] The presidents of Gulf, American Airlines, and Lockheed lost their jobs because of the unethical payments. Other presidents just as guilty—Northrop, Phillips, and Exxon—were excused by their boards. Firms based in the United States are, of course, not alone in engaging in unethical behavior. Sixteen executives of two large Japanese electronics firms, Hitachi and Mitsubishi, were indicted for stealing trade secrets from IBM.[6]

## Corporate Pressure and Fraud

Embezzlement, fraud, and political backbiting are most often due to personal greed. Bribery, price fixing, and compromising product and worker safety generally stem from the pressure for bottom line results. In a study of managers at several firms, 59 to 70 percent "feel pressured to compromise personal ethics to achieve corporate goals."[7] This perception increases among lower level managers. A majority felt that most managers would not refuse to market off-standard and possibly dangerous products. On the more encouraging side, 90 percent supported a code of ethics for business and the teaching of ethics in business schools.

This pressure and organizational climate can influence the ethical judgments of individual managers. What the manager finds unethical in another setting or before taking this job is more readily considered acceptable behavior once the job is taken. Two recent research studies question whether American executives have a sufficient sensitivity to ethical issues, and whether their work environment works against such a sensitivity. Public affairs officers in firms have the direct responsibility for dealing with a wide variety of stakeholders: customers, suppliers, local community, and shareholders. These officers are a principal

5

6

---

[5]Marshall B. Clinard and Peter C. Yeager, *Corporate Crime* (New York: Free Press, 1980); and "Drive to Curb Kickbacks and Bribes by Business," *U.S. News & World Report*, September 4, 1978, pp. 41–44.

[6]"IBM Data Plot Tied to Hitachi and Mitsubishi," *Wall Street Journal*, June 23, 1982, p. 4.

[7]Archie Carroll, "Managerial Ethics: A Post-Watergate View," *Business Horizons*, April 1975, pp. 75–80; and "The Pressure to Compromise Personal Ethics," *Business Week*, January 31, 1977, p. 107. See also "Some Middle Managers Cut Corners to Achieve High Corporate Goals," *Wall Street Journal*. November 8, 1979, pp. 1, 19.

conduit through which the firm is informed of new social concerns. Evidence shows that even though these public affairs officers spend more time with these various stakeholders, they tend to be poor listeners. In fact, according to this study, the more contact company officers have with external publics, the less sensitive they become to their concerns.[8]

Another study was in an ethically sensitive area: corporate political activities. It was found that the more involvement a company officer had in these activities, the less likely he or she would be alert to ethical issues. The more involved the manager was, the more dulled became her or his conscience. There are many ethically debatable areas with regard to a firm's political activities, and this evidence shows that those who are most involved in these activities are precisely those who are less sensitive to the moral and ethical issues involved. The more involved manager is more likely to declare a debatable activity to be ethically acceptable and is also more likely to declare as gray an activity that fellow managers would declare ethically unacceptable.[9]

Laboratory research has shown that unethical behavior tends to rise as the climate becomes more competitive, and it increases even more if such behavior is rewarded. However, a threat of punishment tends to deter unethical behavior. Whether a person acts ethically or unethically is also very strongly influenced by the individual's personal ethical values and by informal organizational policy.[10]

These instances of unethical behavior of managers point to the need for (1) a sensitive and informed conscience, (2) the ability to make ethical judgments, and (3) a corporate climate that rewards ethical behavior and punishes unethical behavior. Technical education does not bring with it better ethics, as we have seen, for example in Nazi Germany. In fact, as society becomes more technical, complex, and interdependent, the need for ethics increases dramatically. When encounters are person to person, there exists the built-in sanction of having to live with the people one has lied to. In the large, complex organization, or when one deals with people over the telephone or via a computer, ethical sensitivities and decision-making abilities are far more important.

. . .

---

[8]Jeffery Sonnenfeld, "Executive Differences in Public Affairs Information Gathering," *Academy of Management Proceedings,* 1981, ed. Kae H. Chung, p. 353.

[9]Steven N. Brenner, "Corporate Political Actions and Attitudes," *Academy of Management Proceedings,* 1981, pp. 361–362.

[10]W. Harvey Hegarty and Henry P. Sims Jr., "Unethical Decision Behavior: An Overview of Three Experiments," *Academy of Management Proceedings,* 1979, p. 9.

---

## Ethical Theories

Ethical criteria and ethical models have been the subject of consider-   10
able thinking over the centuries. Of all the ethical systems, businesspeople feel most at home with utilitarian theory—and not surprisingly, as it traces its origins to Adam Smith, the father of both modern
economics and utilitarian ethics. Jeremy Bentham[11] and John Stuart
Mill[12] more precisely formulated utilitarianism a bit later. Utilitarianism evaluates behavior in terms of its consequences. That action
which results in the greatest net gain for all parties is considered
moral.

Rights theories focus on the entitlements of individual persons.   11
Immanuel Kant[13] (personal rights) and John Locke[14] (property rights)
were the first to present developed theories of rights. Justice theories have a longer tradition, going back to Plato and Aristotle in the
fifth century B.C.[15] Theoretical work in each of these traditions has
continued to the present.[16] For an overview of these three theories—history, strengths and weaknesses, and when most useful—see
Table A.

## Utilitarianism

Utilitarianism judges that an action is right if it produces the greatest   12
utility, "the greatest good for the greatest number." It is very much like
a cost-benefit analysis applied to all parties who would be touched by
a particular decision: That action is right that produces the greatest net
benefit, when all the costs and benefits to all the affected parties are
taken into consideration. Although it would be convenient if these costs
and benefits could be measured in some comparable unit, this is not
always possible. Many important values (for example, human life and
liberty) cannot be quantified. So it is sufficient to state the number and

---

[11]Jeremy Bentham, *An Introduction to the Principles of Morals and Legislation* (1789) (New York: Hafner, 1948).

[12]John Stuart Mill, *Utilitarianism* (1863) (Indianapolis, Ind.: Bobbs-Merrill, 1957).

[13]Immanuel Kant, *The Metaphysical Elements of Justice* (1797), tr. J. Ladd (New York: Library of Liberal Arts, 1965).

[14]John Locke, *The Second Treatise of Government* (1690) (New York: Liberal Arts Press, 1952).

[15]Aristotle, *Ethics*, tr. J. A. K. Thomson (London: Penguin, 1953).

[16]For example, John Rawls, *A Theory of Justice* (Cambridge, Mass.: Belknap, 1971). See two books of readings: Thomas Donaldson and Patricia Werhane, *Ethical Issues in Business* (Englewood Cliffs, N.J.: Prentice-Hall, 1979); and Tom Beauchamp and Norman Bowie, *Ethical Theory and Business* (Englewood Cliffs, N.J.: Prentice-Hall, 1979).

---

**TABLE A.** *Ethical Models for Business Decisions*

| DEFINITION AND ORIGIN | STRENGTHS | WEAKNESSES | WHEN USED |
|---|---|---|---|
| **Utilitarianism** "The greatest good for the greatest number: Bentham (1748–1832), Adam Smith (1723–1790), David Ricardo (1772–1823) | 1. Concepts, terminology, methods are easiest for businesspersons to work with; justifies a profit maximization system. 2. Promotes view of entire system of exchange beyond "this firm." 3. Encourages entrepreneurship, innovation, productivity. | 1. Impossible to measure or quantify all important elements. 2. "Greatest good" can degenerate into self-interest. 3. Can result in abridging person's rights. 4. Can result in neglecting less powerful segments of society. | 1. Use in all business decisions, and will be dominant criteria in 90%. 2. Version of model is implicitly used already, although scope is generally limited to "this firm." |
| **Theory of Justice** Equitable distribution of society's benefits and burdens: Aristotle (384–322 B.C.), Rawls (1921–  ) | 1. The "democratic" principle. 2. Does not allow a society to become status- or class-dominated. 3. Ensures that minorities, poor, handicapped receive opportunities and a fair share of output. | 1. Can result in less risk, incentive, and innovation. 2. Encourages sense of "entitlement." | 1. In product decisions usefulness to *all* in society. 2. In setting salaries for unskilled workers, executives. 3. In public policy decisions: to maintain a floor of living standards for all. 4. Use with, for example, performance appraisal, due process, distribution of rewards and punishments. |
| **Theory of Rights** Individual's freedom is not to be violated: Locke (1635–1701)— property; Kant (1724–1804)— personal rights | 1. Ensures respect for individual's property and personal freedom. 2. Parallels political "Bill of Rights." | 1. Can encourage individualistic, selfish behavior. | 1. Where individual's property or personal rights are in question. 2. Use with, for example, employee privacy, job tenure, work dangerous to person's health. |

the magnitude of the costs and benefits as clearly and accurately as possible.

The utilitarian principle says that the right action is that which 13 produces the greatest net benefit over any other possible action. However, this does not mean that the best act is that which produces the greatest good for the person performing the action. Rather, it is the action that produces the greatest summed net good for all those who are affected by the action. Utilitarianism can handle some ethical cases quite well, especially those that are complex and affect many parties. Although the model and the methodology are clear, carrying out the calculations is often difficult. Taking into account so many affected parties, along with the extent to which the action touches them, can be a calculation nightmare.

Hence several shortcuts have been proposed that can reduce the 14 complexity of utilitarian calculations. Each shortcut involves a sacrifice of accuracy for ease of calculation. Among these shortcuts are (1) adherence to a simplified rule (for example, the Golden Rule, "Do unto others as you would have them do unto you"); (2) for ease of comparison, calculate costs and benefits in dollar terms; and (3) take into account only those directly affected by the action, putting aside indirect effects. In using the above decision-making strategies, an individual should be aware that they are simplifications and that some interests may not be sufficiently taken into consideration.

A noteworthy weakness of utilitarianism as an ethical norm is that 15 it can advocate, for example, abridging an individual's right to a job or even life, for the sake of the greater good of a larger number of people. This, and other difficulties, are discussed elsewhere.[17] One additional caution in using utilitarian rules is in order: It is considered unethical to opt for the benefit of narrower goals (for example, personal goals, career, or money) at the expense of the good of a larger number, such as a nation or a society. Utilitarian norms emphasize the good of the group; it is a large-scale ethical model. In this sort of calculation, an individual and what is due that individual may be underemphasized. Rights theory has been developed to give appropriate emphasis to the individual and the standing of that individual with peers and within society.

---

[17]Gerald F. Cavanagh, Dennis J. Moberg, and Manuel Velasquez, "The Ethics of Organizational Politics," *Academy of Management Review*, 6 (July 1981), 363–374; and the more complete treatments in Manuel Velasquez, *Business Ethics: Concepts and Cases* (Englewood Cliffs, N.J.: Prentice-Hall, 1982), pp. 46–58; and Richard T. De George, *Business Ethics* (New York: Macmillan, 1982), pp. 47–54.

## Rights of the Individual

A right is a person's entitlement to something.[18] Rights may flow from    16
the legal system, such as the U.S. constitutional rights of freedom of
conscience or freedom of speech. The U.S. Bill of Rights and the United
Nations Universal Declaration of Human Rights are classical examples
of individual rights spelled out in some detail in documents. Legal rights,
as well as others which may not be written into law, stem from the
human dignity of the person. Moral rights have these characteristics: (1)
They enable individuals to pursue their own interests, and (2) they
impose correlative prohibitions and/or requirements on others. That is,
every right has a corresponding duty. My right to freedom of conscience is supported by the prohibition of other individuals from unnecessarily limiting that freedom of conscience. From another perspective, my right to be paid for my work corresponds to a duty of mine
to perform "a fair day's work for a fair day's pay." In the latter case, both
the right and duty stem from the right to private property, which is a
traditional pillar of American life and law. However, the right to private
property is not absolute. A factory owner may be forced by law, as well
as by morality, to spend money on pollution control or safety equipment. For a listing of selected rights and other ethical norms, see
Table B.

Judging morality by reference to individual rights is quite different    17
from using utilitarian standards. Rights express the requirements of
morality from the standpoint of the individual; rights protect the individual from the encroachment and demands of society or the state.
Utilitarian standards promote society's benefit and are relatively insensitive to a single individual, except insofar as that individual's welfare
affects the overall good of society.

A business contract establishes rights and duties that were not there    18
before: The right of the purchaser to receive what was agreed upon, and
the right of the seller to be paid what was agreed. Formal written
contracts and informal verbal agreements are essential to business transactions.

Immanuel Kant recognized that an emphasis on rights can lead    19
one to focus largely on what is due oneself. So he formulated what he
called his "categorical imperatives." As the first of these, Kant said, "I
ought never to act except in such a way that I can also will that my
maxim should become a universal law." Another way of putting this
is: "An action is morally right for a person in a certain situation if and
only if the person's reason for carrying out the action is a reason that

---

[18]Velasquez, *Business Ethics*, p. 29. See also Thomas Donaldson, *Corporations and Morality* (Englewood Cliffs, N.J.: Prentice-Hall, 1982).

## TABLE B.   *Some Selected Ethical Norms*

**Utilitarian**

1. *Organizational goals* should aim at *maximizing the satisfactions* of the organization's constituencies.
2. The members of an organization should attempt to attain its goals as *efficiently* as possible by consuming as few inputs as possible and by minimizing the external costs which organizational activities impose on others.
3. The employee should use *every effective means* to achieve the goals of the organization, and should neither jeopardize those goals nor enter situations in which personal interests conflict significantly with the goals.

**Rights**

1. *Life and safety:* The individual has the right not to have her or his life or safety unknowingly and unnecessarily endangered.
2. *Truthfulness:* The individual has a right not to be intentionally deceived by another, especially on matters about which the individual has the right to know.
3. *Privacy:* The individual has the right to do whatever he or she chooses to do outside working hours and to control information about his or her private life.
4. *Freedom of conscience:* The individual has the right to refrain from carrying out any order that violates those commonly accepted moral or religious norms to which the person adheres.
5. *Free speech:* The individual has the right to criticize conscientiously and truthfully the ethics or legality of corporate actions so long as the criticism does not violate the rights of other individuals within the organization.
6. *Private property:* The individual has a right to hold private property, especially insofar as this right enables the individual and his or her family to be sheltered and to have the basic necessities of life.

**Justice**

1. *Fair treatment:* Persons who are similar to each other in the relevant respects should be treated similarly; persons who differ in some respect relevant to the job they perform should be treated differently in proportion to the difference between them.
2. *Fair administration of rules:* Rules should be administered consistently, fairly, and impartially.
3. *Fair compensation:* Individuals should be compensated for the cost of their injuries by the party that is responsible for those injuries.
4. *Fair blame:* Individuals should not be held responsible for matters over which they have no control.
5. *Due process:* The individual has a right to a fair and impartial hearing when he or she believes that personal rights are being violated.

*Source:* Reprinted by permission of American Management Association from *Organizational Dynamics,* Autumn 1983. © 1983. American Management Association, New York. All rights reserved.

he would be willing to have every person act on, in any similar situation."[19] As a measure of a difficult judgment, Kant asks if our reason for taking this action is the same reason that would allow others to do the same thing. Note that Kant is focusing on a person's motivation or

---

[19]Immanuel Kant, *Groundwork of the Metaphysics of Morals,* tr. H. J. Paton (New York: Harper & Row, 1964), pp. 62–90. See also Velasquez, *Business Ethics,* pp. 66–69.

intention, and not on the consequences of the action, as is true of utilitarianism.

Kant's second categorical imperative cautions us against using other 20 people as a means to our own ends: "Never treat humanity simply as a means, but always also as an end." An interpretation of the second imperative is: "An action is morally right for a person if and only if in performing the action the person does not use others merely as a means for advancing his or her own interests, but also both respects and develops their capacity to choose for themselves."[20] Capital, plant, and machines are all to be used to serve men and women's purposes. On the other hand, individual persons are not to be used merely as instruments for achieving one's interests. This rules out deception, manipulation, and exploitation of other people.

## Justice

Justice requires all persons, and thus managers too, to be guided by 21 fairness, equity, and impartiality. Justice calls for evenhanded treatment of groups and individuals (1) in the distribution of the benefits and burdens of society, (2) in the administration of laws and regulations, and (3) in the imposition of sanctions and means of compensation for wrongs a person has suffered. An action or policy is just in comparison with the treatment accorded to others.

Standards of justice are generally considered to be more important 22 than utilitarian consideration of consequences. If a society is unjust to some group of its members (for example, apartheid treatment of blacks in South Africa), we generally consider that society unjust and condemn it, even if the results of the injustices bring about greater productivity. On the other hand, we seem to be willing to trade off some equity, if the results will bring about greater benefits for all.

Standards of justice are not as often in conflict with individual rights 23 as are utilitarian norms. This is not surprising, since justice is largely based on the moral rights of individuals. The moral right to be treated as a free and equal person, for example, undergirds the notion that benefits and burdens should be distributed equitably. Personal moral rights are so basic that they generally may not be traded off (for example, free consent, right to privacy, freedom of conscience, right to due process) to bring about a better distribution of benefits in a society. On the other hand, property rights may be abridged (for example,

---

[20]Kant, *Groundwork*; Velasquez, *Business Ethics*, p. 68.

graduated income tax, tax on pollution) for the sake of a more fair distribution of benefits and burdens.

Distributive justice becomes important when there are not enough 24 of society's goods to satisfy all needs or not enough people to bear the burdens. The question then becomes: What is a just distribution? The fundamental principle is that equals should be treated equally, and unequals treated in accord with their inequality. For example, few would argue that a new person who is hired for the same job as a senior worker with twenty years' experience should receive the same pay as the experienced worker. People performing work of greater responsibility or working more difficult hours would be eligible for greater pay. However, it is clear that pay differentials should be related to the work itself, not on some arbitrary bias of the employer.

Having said all of the above does not determine what is a fair 25 distribution of society's benefits and burdens. In fact quite different notions of equity are generally proposed. A classic difference is the capitalist model (justice based on contribution) versus the socialist ("from each according to abilities, to each according to needs"). A more recent contribution to justice theory has been the work of John Rawls.[21] Rawls would have us construct the rules and laws of society as if we did not know what role we were to play in that society. We do not know if we would be rich or poor, male or female, African or European, manager or slave, handicapped or physically and mentally fit. He calls this the "veil of ignorance." The exercise is intended to try to rid ourselves of our status, national, and sexist biases. Under such circumstances each of us would try to design the rules of society to be of the greatest benefit to all, and not to undermine the position of any group. Thus Rawls proposes that people generally develop two principles:

1. Each person is to have an equal right to the most extensive liberty compatible with similar liberty for others.
2. Social and economic inequalities are to be arranged so that they are both reasonably expected to be to everyone's advantage and attached to positions and offices open to all.

The first principle is consonant with the American sense of liberty and thus is not controversial in the United States. The second principle is more egalitarian, and also more controversial. However, Rawls maintains that if people are honest behind the "veil of ignorance" they will opt for a system of justice that is most fair to all members of that society.

---

[21]Rawls, *A Theory of Justice.*

## SOLVING ETHICAL DILEMMAS

Any human judgment is preceded by two steps: gathering data and **26** analyzing the data. Before any ethically sensitive situation can be assessed, it is essential that all the relevant data be at hand. As an aid to analysis, the three classical norms—utility, rights, and justice—have been offered. For a schematic diagram of how ethical decision making can proceed, see Figure A. The diagram is simplified, but nevertheless it can be an aid in our handling of ethical problems.

Let us apply our scheme to the case of an executive padding her **27** expense account.[22] For our purposes, we will accept the limited data as provided in the case. Applying the utility criteria, we would judge that although padding the expense account satisfies the interests of the executive doing it, it does not optimize the concerns of others: shareholders, customers, more honest executives, and people in other firms in similar situations. It also adds to the expense of doing business. Hence, it seems that utility would not allow for such padding. The rights of individuals are not so involved here: The executive has no right to the extra money, although we might make the case that the shareholders' and customers' right to private property is being violated. With regard to justice, salary and commissions are the ordinary compensation for individuals. Expense accounts have a quite different purpose.

In this instance, most managers responding to the case held that it **28** was unethical for the executive to pad her expense account. John Rawls would maintain that any one of us would set the rules in this fashion, given the fact that we would not know what role we ourselves would have in the society. Hence, we conclude that padding one's expense account is judged unethical on all three ethical norms, so it is clearly wrong. Notice that this agrees with the judgment of 73 percent of the executives who were asked.

On the other hand, the *Wall Street Journal* recently described an **29** entrepreneur who sells blank official-looking receipts of fifty different plausible but fictitious restaurants. The individual can then fill out the receipts as he likes and can submit them to his firm for reimbursement. And he has the receipts to prove the purchase of the meal! What would we say of the ethics of selling such receipts? Of purchasing them and using them?

---

[22]Cavanagh, here, is referring to a case in which "an executive earning $30,000 a year has been padding his/her expense account by about $1,500 a year." In a survey of 1,700 "business executive readers of *Harvard Business Review*," 85 percent thought that the padding—or false reporting of expenses—was unethical. [Behrens and Rosen]

---

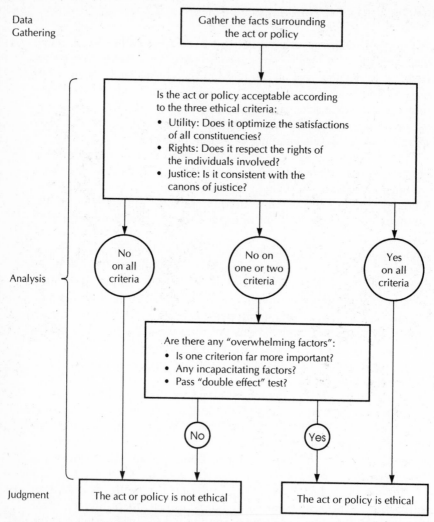

Data
Gathering

Gather the facts surrounding
the act or policy

Is the act or policy acceptable according
to the three ethical criteria:
- Utility: Does it optimize the satisfactions
  of all constituencies?
- Rights: Does it respect the rights of
  the individuals involved?
- Justice: Is it consistent with the
  canons of justice?

No
on all
criteria

No on
one or two
criteria

Yes
on all
criteria

Analysis

Are there any "overwhelming factors":
- Is one criterion far more important?
- Any incapacitating factors?
- Pass "double effect" test?

No

Yes

Judgment

The act or policy is not ethical

The act or policy is ethical

**FIGURE A.** *Flow diagram of ethical decision making.*

## Model Aids Solution

Let us examine another case:

30

Brian Curry, financial vice president of Digital Robotics Corporation, is about
to retire and has been asked to recommend one of his two assistants for
promotion to vice president. Curry knows that his recommendations will be

acted upon. He also knows that, since both assistants are about the same age, the one not chosen will find future promotions unlikely. Debra Butler is the most qualified for the position. She is bright and outgoing and has better leadership ability. Moreover, her father is president of the largest customer of Digital, and Curry correctly reasons that they will more likely keep this business with Butler as an officer of Digital. On the other hand, Charles McNichols has been with the company longer, has worked seventy-hour weeks, and has pulled the company through some very difficult situations. He did this because he was told he was in line for the vice presidency. Nevertheless, Curry recommends Butler for the job.

Using our schema to examine this case, utility would conclude that 31 the selection of Debra Butler would optimize the satisfaction of top management, most of the workers, because she is a better leader, and shareholders and customers, for the same reason. The only cost is that to McNichols. Justice would conclude that because the promotional decision was made on relevant capabilities, it did not violate fair treatment. On the other hand, McNichols had been told that he would get the job, and worked extra hours because he thought the job would be his. He is being used in a fashion to which he did not consent. His rights are violated. Moreover, in being promised the job, and then having the promise broken, he is not being treated with fairness and equity.

Thus utility accepts the appointment of Butler as morally accept- 32 able, since there will be a net gain in satisfaction. However, because of the promise made earlier to McNichols and his resultant extended work weeks, his rights are being violated. We can then ask if there are any "overwhelming factors" that ought to be taken into consideration (see Figure A, p. 782).

## Overwhelming Factors

"Overwhelming factors" are data from the situation which may, in a 33 given case, justify overriding one of the three ethical criteria: utility, rights, or justice. Overwhelming factors can be examined when there is a conflict in the conclusions drawn from the ethical norms. The first of the overwhelming factors are incapacitating factors. That is, if there are any elements that coerce an individual into a certain posture, then that individual is not held to be fully responsible. Managers at an H. J. Heinz plant felt great pressure from top management to show a profit. They could not do as well as was expected, so they began to juggle the books. While this meant cumulative overstatement of profits of $8.5 million, the managers who did the falsification would probably be judged less unethical than the top management that brought the unrelenting pressure to bear. Even though the act of falsifying the books was objectively unethical, the plant manager did not bear full responsibility because he was pressured by superiors.[23]

Second, the manager might not be able to utilize the criteria because she does not possess full information. She might think that another employee is embezzling from the bank. However, to report the employee to superiors might ruin the individual's reputation. So, even though stealing is a violation of justice, in this case there is not yet sufficient information to utilize the criteria. Finally, the manager may be sincerely uncertain of the criteria or their applicability in this particular case. 34

To return to the appointment of a financial vice president case: While utility would clearly call for recommending Debra Butler for the vice president's position, justice would call for considering McNichols' claim on the position more strongly. McNichols has worked harder, having considered this to be proportionate to the future promised reward. Moreover, since the position has been promised to him, fair treatment would call for some special consideration. Justice would probably say that, under these special circumstances, McNichols should get the position. 35

Because there is now a conflict between these two norms, it is necessary to see if any overwhelming factors should be taken into account. There seems to be little coercion involved, certainly no physical coercion. Curry made his decision freely. There might have been psychological coercion, however, if Debra Butler's father had mentioned the possible promotion to top management at Digital. Even without his mentioning it, the situation may still have caused psychological pressure for Curry. 36

The ultimate solution of this case would depend on a number of factors: How much better a manager would Butler be than McNichols, and how would this affect the firm's performance and the jobs of others at Digital? Exactly what sort of promise was made to McNichols? Was it clear and unequivocal? If the promise was more in McNichols' mind, and if Butler's performance would be judged to be significantly better than McNichols', then Curry could ethically recommend Butler. However, some sort of compensation should be made to McNichols. 37

Another kind of overwhelming factor occurs when criteria come to differing conclusions on the same case. The so-called "principle of double effect" can be useful here. When an act has both a good effect 38

[23]"Some Middle Managers Cut Corners to Achieve High Corporate Goals," *Wall Street Journal*, November 8, 1979, pp. 1, 19.

and a bad effect (for example, appointing Butler and not appointing McNichols), one may morally perform the act under three conditions: (1) One does not directly intend the bad effect (Curry is not trying to backstab or get back at McNichols); (2) the bad effect is not a means to the good end but is simply a side effect (the nonappointment of McNichols is not a means to Butler being appointed); and (3) the good effect sufficiently outweighs the bad (Butler's performance would be significantly superior to McNichols'). So this case passes the test of the double effect. Hence, in sum, Curry may ethically recommend Butler for the vice presidency.

### Case of the Flammable Crib

Let us examine another case, this one on the issue of product safety and quality:    39

> Assume you are president of a firm which manufactures baby cribs. You have the option of installing either of two pads: a less expensive one which meets what you feel to be too lenient federal safety requirements regarding flammability (a requirement which you are quite sure was established as a result of pressure from your industry) and one which is safe but somewhat more expensive. Assume that the safe pad will not bring a higher price for the crib.

Would using the flammable pad be unjust to purchasers? Initially,    40
it would seem that there is no injustice here—all purchasers of baby cribs are being treated the same. A possible source of injustice, however, would be to the consumer, who is presuming that he is purchasing a safe and not flammable baby crib. When examining rights, this becomes even clearer: The consumer presumes that his baby will be safe and that the product being sold has sufficient safeguards. The fact that the firm meets federal safety requirements does not settle the question, since the president is convinced that these are too lenient and were only set because of pressure from the industry. At stake are the lives of infants who might be burned. In fact, statistics tell us that some infants will be burned needlessly. As with sleepwear and toys, special precautions must be taken with infants and young children, since they cannot protect themselves. Although they don't smoke in bed, they nevertheless cannot put out a fire once it has begun from whatever source.

Applying the utilitarian norm demands weighing the costs and    41 benefits of the two pads to all parties. The cheaper pad would result in lower cost to the consumer and probably better enable the firm to meet the lower price of its competitors. The cost of the lower priced pad would be the cost of the infants who would be burned because the cheaper pad was used. On the other hand, the safer pad could be advertised as such, and it might establish the firm as a manufacturer of safe children's goods. Presuming that there is a significant difference in the flammability, and thus the number of children's lives saved, utility would probably call for installing the safer pad. Since there are no ethical criteria that would call for the installation of the cheaper pad, we can then judge that ethics would ask the president to call for the safer, even though more expensive, pad.

This judgment is also the judgment of corporate executives. In a 42 survey of chief executive officers, 94 percent would use the safe pad, even though it is more expensive.[24] Perhaps these executives are using a shortcut ethical test of a possible action: Would I do it if I knew that the decision was to be featured on this evening's TV news? Can my decision bear the sharp scrutiny of a probing reporter?

. . .

Ethics is a system of moral principles and the methods for applying 43 them; ethics thus provides the tools to make moral judgments. It encompasses the language, concepts, and models that enable an individual to effect moral decisions.

Mature ethical judgments are not always easy to make. The facts 44 of the case are not always clear-cut; the ethical criteria or principles to be used are not always agreed upon even by the experts themselves. Hence, ethics seems to most businesspeople, indeed to most Americans, to be subjective, amorphous, and ill-defined and thus not very useful. Just as with politics and religion, there is often more heat than light in discussion. This lack of confidence in ethics is unfortunate, since without some commonly agreed-upon ethical principles, it is everyone for him- or herself, and trust, which is basic to all business dealings, is undermined.

## Review Questions

1. Why, in order to prevent the intrusion of government into business, must "each manager . . . possess a set of internalized and operative ethical criteria for decision making"?
2. Briefly define the ethical theories of utility, justice, and rights.
3. What is an "overwhelming factor" in the context of making a decision about ethics?

---

[24]"Business Executives and Moral Dilemmas," *Business and Society Review* (Spring 1975), p. 55.

**4.** "What is the principle of "double effect," and how is it applied in the context of making a decision about ethics?

## Discussion and Writing Suggestions

**1.** According to Cavanagh, between 59 and 70 percent of managers surveyed "feel pressured to compromise personal ethics to achieve corporate goals." Are you surprised? Why or why not? Develop your response into a brief essay.

**2.** Do you agree with Cavanagh's analysis of the Digital Robotics case, in which Debra Butler was recommended for vice president over Charles McNichols? Why? If you disagree, provide a rationale for your decision, as Cavanagh does for his.

**3.** How practical is it, in your view, to apply Cavanagh's flow diagram for making ethical decisions? How important is it for the conduct of ethical business that managers use *some* systematic model for making difficult decisions?

# Cases for Analysis and Discussion

*Following, you'll find three cases for analysis and discussion, each of which will raise certain ethical dilemmas. In business schools around the country, the "case method" is an instructional technique of long standing. Whether the course be in finance, business law, management training, investment strategies, or business ethics, the rationale for presenting cases is the same. The "case," usually a narrative account, re-creates a problem or a particular challenge in a business context. The case amounts to raw data that the student reviews in light of principles learned in class. The student then is asked to define problems and to recommend or evaluate courses of action, based on a clear method of analysis.*

*The cases that follow present ethical dilemmas that resulted from business dealings. As we've suggested, your job will be to read the cases, to define the problems, and to evaluate or recommend courses of action. What would you do in similar circumstances or if you were asked to advise those involved? What business decisions would follow from your recommendations? What would be the consequences of those decisions? These among other questions are fundamental to case-method instruction.*

*As you read, keep in mind the remarks of Gerald Cavanagh, who provides criteria that you can apply in defining problems and developing responses.*

# Case 1: Peter Green's First Day

Peter Green came home to his wife and new baby a dejected man. What    1
a contrast to the morning, when he had left the apartment full of
enthusiasm to tackle his first customer in his new job at Scott Carpets.
And what a customer! Peabody Rug was the largest carpet retailer in the
area and accounted for 15% of the entire volume of Peter's territory.
When Peabody introduced a Scott product, other retailers were quick to
follow with orders. So when Bob Franklin, the owner of Peabody Rug,
had called District Manager John Murphy expressing interest in "Carpet
Supreme," Scott's newest commercial-duty home carpet, Peter knew that
a $15,000–$20,000 order was a real probability, and no small show for
his first sale. And it was important to do well at the start, for John
Murphy had made no bones about his scorn for the new breed of
salespeople at Scott Carpet.

Murphy was of the old school: in the business since his graduation    2
from a local high school, he had fought his way through the stiffest retail
competition in the nation to be District Manager of the area at age
fifty-eight. Murphy knew his textiles, and he knew his competitors'
textiles. He knew his customers, and he knew how well his competitors
knew his customers. Formerly, when Scott Carpet had needed to fill sales
positions, it had generally raided the competition for experienced personnel, put them on a straight commission, and thereby managed to
increase sales and maintain its good reputation for service at the same
time. When Murphy had been promoted eight years ago to the position
of District Manager, he had passed on his sales territory to Harvey
Katchorian, a sixty-year-old mill rep and son of an immigrant who had
also spent his life in the carpet trade. Harvey had had no trouble keeping
up his sales and had retired from the company the previous spring after
forty-five years of successful service in the industry. Peter, in turn, was
to take over Harvey's accounts, and Peter knew that John Murphy was
not sure that his original legacy to Harvey was being passed on to the
best salesperson.

Peter was one of the new force of salespeople from Scott's Sales    3
Management Program. In 1976 top management had created a training
program to compensate for the industry's dearth of younger salespeople
with long-term management potential. Peter, a college graduate, had

entered Scott's five-month training program immediately after college and was the first graduate of the program to be assigned to John Murphy's district. Murphy had made it known to top management from the start that he did not think the training program could compensate for on-the-job experience, and he was clearly withholding optimism about Peter's prospects as a salesperson despite Peter's fine performance during the training program.

Peter had been surprised, therefore, when Murphy volunteered to 4 accompany him on his first week of sales "to ease your transition into the territory." As they entered the office at Peabody Rug, Murphy had even seemed friendly and said reassuringly, "I think you'll get along with Bob. He's a great guy—knows the business and has been a good friend of mine for years."

Everything went smoothly. Bob liked the new line and appeared 5 ready to place a large order with Peter the following week, but he indicated that he would require some "help on the freight costs" before committing himself definitely. Peter was puzzled and unfamiliar with the procedure, but Murphy quickly stepped in and assured Bob that Peter would be able to work something out.

After the meeting, on their way back to Scott Carpets' district office, 6 Peter asked Murphy about freight costs. Murphy sarcastically explained the procedure: Because of its large volume, Peabody regularly "asked for a little help to cover shipping costs," and got it from all or most suppliers. Bob Franklin was simply issued a credit for defective merchandise. By claiming he had received second-quality goods, Bob was entitled to a 10%–25% discount. The discount on defective merchandise had been calculated by the company to equal roughly the cost of shipping the 500-lb. rolls back to the mill, and so it just about covered Bob's own freight costs. The practice had been going on so long that Bob demanded "freight assistance" as a matter of course before placing a large order. Obviously, the merchandise was not defective, but by making an official claim, the sales representative could set in gear the defective-merchandise compensation system. Murphy reiterated, as if to a two-year-old, the importance of a Peabody account to any sales rep, and shrugged off the freight assistance as part of doing business with such an influential firm.

Peter stared at Murphy. "Basically, what you're asking me to do, 7 Mr. Murphy, is to lie to the front office."

Murphy angrily replied, "Look, do you want to make it here or not? 8 If you do, you ought to know you need Peabody's business. I don't know what kind of fancy think they taught you at college, but where I come from you don't call your boss a liar."

From the time he was a child, Peter Green had been taught not to 9 lie or steal. He believed these principles were absolute and that one should support one's beliefs at whatever personal cost. But during college the only even remote test of his principles was his strict adherence to the honor system in taking exams.

As he reviewed the conversation with Murphy, it seemed to Peter 10 that there was no way to avoid losing the Peabody account, which would look bad on his own record as well as Murphy's—not to mention the loss in commissions for them both. He felt badly about getting into a tiff with Murphy on his first day out in the territory, and knew Murphy would feel betrayed if one of his salespeople purposely lost a major account.

The only out he could see, aside from quitting, was to play down 11 the whole episode. Murphy had not actually *ordered* Peter to submit a claim for damaged goods (was he covering himself legally?), so Peter could technically ignore the conversation and simply not authorize a discount. He knew very well, however, that such a course was only superficially passive, and that in Murphy's opinion he would have lost the account on purpose. As Peter sipped halfheartedly at a martini, he thought bitterly to himself, "Boy, they sure didn't prepare me for this in Management Training. And I don't even know if this kind of thing goes on in the rest of Murphy's district, let alone in Scott's eleven other districts."

## Review Questions

1. Why was John Murphy skeptical about Peter Green's abilities as a salesperson?
2. What are "freight costs," and how do they tie in to the general question of business ethics?

## Discussion and Writing Suggestions

1. What would you do if you were Peter Green? Which considerations would take priority, and why?
2. If Green decides to "lie to the front office," who will be hurt? Is it in the best interest of Scott Carpets (as well as of Bob Franklin, John Murphy, and Peter himself) to go along with the lie that Peabody Rug had received defective merchandise and so was entitled to a credit?
3. Murphy is an experienced, successful salesman, and Scott Carpets is a successful company. Yet the way they do business is being questioned by a young man fresh out of college, with little or no practical experience—a young man who relies primarily on the "absolute" principles of honor and integrity that he had been taught as a child. To what extent do you think (as Carr, above, suggests) that there is an inherent conflict or incompatibility between basic ethical principles and the path to business success?

4. Assume for the moment that a sales representative from a competing carpeting manufacturer was willing and eager to issue a defective merchandise credit to Peabody Rug. If you were Peter Green, would this knowledge make it easier for you to issue the credit?

# Case 2: Matt Goldspan's Trilogy

## JAY A. HALFOND

Matt Goldspan was a valued member of a thriving financial services 1 company, where he had worked for the decade since completing college. To recognize his performance, his company paid for his MBA program, provided ample financial rewards, and, within the last three years, elevated him to manager of one of the major branch offices. As a 32-year-old branch manager, Matt was now the supervisor of thirty-five employees.

Even though his enterprise was financial, he ultimately believed his 2 skills and priorities were in how well he handled people. He particularly relished the interactions with both staff and clients. He felt he had the best of both worlds: autonomy as the manager of a small business, with the security and mentorship of a larger company. His staff respected his poise and dynamism, as well as his ability to encourage cooperation and finesse any interpersonal differences. He invested much of his time in motivating and overseeing the work of his employees. He was careful not to become too remote as he tried to develop several of his key staff into intermediate positions of authority.

The parent company played a hands-off role: because Matt had 3 justified autonomy and trust, the executives in corporate headquarters have tried to support, without infringing upon, the activities of the branch office.

### I: SALARY INEQUITIES

Denise Contra reported directly to Matt as his executive assistant. 4 Among other responsibilities, Denise maintained the office's personnel records. She had worked in the office for fifteen years. Denise was somewhat of a fixture in the operation: even though she had received

"Matt Goldspan's Trilogy" by Jay A. Halfond from *Journal of Business Ethics* 10 (1991), pp. 317–321. Reprinted by permission of Kluwer Academic Publishers.

a few promotions, she had not been particularly ambitious or restive. She had always viewed her work as supplemental to her family responsibilities yet an important source of income.

Since her recent divorce, Denise had shared some of her anxieties 5 about money with Matt. She was now the sole supporter of her three children, and had found the financial and emotional strains very difficult to bear. Denise had always been a steady, reliable employee, though not much beyond satisfactory in her performance. Matt's ability to help her was limited to expressions of his sympathy.

One afternoon, Denise timidly confronted Matt with the results of 6 a study she had conducted:

> Matt, I know you didn't ask me to look into this, but I knew the company 7 would find this information important. What I have discovered is that the women in our office are not being paid fairly compared to the men—based on their positions and years of service.
>
> Most of our employees are women, and, like me, many have been in their 8 jobs for a long time. I've seen men brought in at higher salaries, and, in some cases, promoted more quickly than the women. So when I began to look at current salaries, I wasn't surprised to see a pattern emerge.
>
> I am not blaming you, since many of these inequities began long before you 9 became a supervisor. But I would like you to do something, if you can, to fix the situation. If you're not able to, maybe it should be referred to corporate to resolve. Since merit review time is approaching, you could use the raise pool to address this problem. Men wouldn't like it, but it's as if they've had access to our money for all these years. And it would straighten things out, quickly, once and for all.
>
> Regardless, I would appreciate your reactions to my numbers. You'll see 10 that *I*, in particular, deserve to be paid more.

## II: AFFIRMATIVE ACTION

Within the past two years, Matt's corporation had centralized hiring 11 procedures to promote more aggressive hiring of minorities in all ranks of the company. Matt himself was a firm believer in providing opportunities to those disadvantaged, and took pride in the success he had had, without corporate intervention, to create an integrated workplace. Since his clientele were heterogeneous, he believed that affirmative action was not only morally desirable but contributed to the success of his business. Matt did, however, resent this one intrusion into his autonomy. He believed that corporate controls only added bureaucracy, not better hiring practices—at least within his operation. He prided himself on the outreach efforts he would normally make, the democratic and comprehensive means he used to screen applicants, and the open-mindedness he conveyed to his staff about increasing the diversity of the office personnel.

Celina Longstreet, Vice-President for Affirmative Action, mandated 12 a procedure, endorsed by the Board of Directors, that required that she approve all letters of employment *before* the candidate is offered the position officially. Logistically, this added about a week to the process; under the rare instance when a question was raised, the delay could be longer.

Matt had a critical opening in the data processing section of his 13 office. The previous employee had left abruptly, and, to the dismay of the office, had poorly documented the intricacies of her systems. It had become impossible to produce routine correspondence to customers on the status of their accounts. While Matt frantically attempted to recruit someone who would be a "quick start," he had a temporary programmer try to generate the reports. Subtle but embarrassing errors only led to further customer questions and complaints.

Fortunately, one candidate surfaced who seemed perfect. Alicia 14 Verango was referred by a friend of one of Matt's staff. Matt was able to get honest and substantial references, as well as verify that the candidate had previously worked in a remarkably similar environment. Because she was returning to the workplace after a maternity absence, she was available immediately. Others who interviewed the candidates concurred enthusiastically that Alicia was also their first choice.

Once he had satisfied himself that Alicia was the ideal candidate for 15 the position, Matt called her:

Alicia, you'll be pleased to hear that we were all very impressed with you here, 16 and would like you to start as soon as possible. I'm even confident we can pay the salary we had discussed.

If you can begin as soon as next Monday, you should come directly to my 17 office and I'll introduce you and help get you situated. Our corporate headquarters requires some paperwork, but we'll try to get you on the payroll as soon as possible. They'll technically need to make the "offer" to you, and explain benefits, and so on. The important thing is that we need you a.s.a.p.! I'm certain you'll be a real asset to our operation.

Alicia was thrilled with this challenging opportunity and agreed to 18 begin work that following week. Several days later, Matt received a call from Celina Longstreet:

Matt, I just received the paperwork on an Alicia Verango. She seems ade- 19 quately qualified for the requirements of the position. But, before I approve an offer to her, I need to be assured that you did not overlook a qualified minority candidate. I see you had a black applicant from another branch office. He's clearly not as good as Verango, but he still seems to meet the minimal qualifications. And this would be an opportunity to promote a minority employee. I'd like to sit down with you next week to see if he can do the job. Maybe I'll invite his supervisor to attend.

I know you're anxious to fill this position. I also appreciate that you've been **20** through an exhaustive process. But I'm responsible for seeing that our broader, more longterm objectives are also met. I'll work hard to ensure that we reach a resolution within a few weeks.

## III: EMPLOYEE THEFT

Harriet Wearington was a black employee who was a model for the **21** efforts Matt had tried to make in promoting minority employees. Harriet was a single mother who had begun working part-time five years prior in the lowest clerical position in the office. When her son entered his teens and Harriet was able to work more hours, Matt promoted her steadily to where she was now office manager for customer services. She was an exemplary, hard-working employee, well-regarded by the five employees who reported to her.

Each summer, Harriet's son, Jason, would help out in the office. He **22** would run errands, maintain office supplies and inventory, and file customer correspondence. Matt had indicated to Harriet that Jason should not work directly for his mother, but be available to help others throughout the branch office. But, in fact, Harriet tended to supervise Jason and ensure he was kept busy. Some staff resented that Harriet seemed to have a personal assistant in Jason, but most felt assured that Harriet, in particular, would be both fair and demanding in how she utilized her son.

Late one July, Denise Contra came in Matt's office and closed his **23** door.

Matt, you're not going to believe the call I just received from the office supply **24** place down the street. It seems Jason Wearington tried to use *our* charge account there to buy over a hundred dollars of video supplies for himself and his friends.

The manager called us and I told Harriet. She's furious—and mortified! I **25** told her I'd let you know. She probably knows you'll have to let Jason go. That store manager certainly won't want to see Jason again. When I told some of the others in the office they felt just terrible for Harriet—and bad for you that you'd have to fire her son.

Matt knew Denise was right, even though he was somewhat annoyed at her lack of discretion. He did not want to embarrass Harriet by summoning her into his office, so at lunch time he stopped by her desk to ask her if she wanted to go for a walk to the park across the street. Harriet was very grateful for the opportunity to vent her frustrations:

> Matt, I'm so ashamed. I can't believe he'd do such a stupid, dishonest thing. **26** And can you believe he tried to deny it! Then when I told him how embarrassing this was for me, he broke down and cried. He cried, can you believe it? He said he didn't think about how it would hurt me, or that it was stealing. Some of his so-called friends, it seems, goaded him into doing it.
>
> We've agreed to a punishment. This was such an important lesson for him, **27** Matt. It's hard raising a teenager alone, but in a strange way, I'm almost glad this happened here. I'm glad he was caught and that he was confronted by what he did wrong. He returned the merchandise and apologized to the store manager. I'm going to stop by the store also. It's so hard to face the others, though.
>
> I told him I'm going to watch him like a hawk! And I'll fire him if anything **28** ever happens again. Even if he's my son, I can't tolerate dishonesty and theft. I think he'll be okay now. He's a good kid, really he is, but this is a tough period in a child's life.

## Review Questions[1]

### Salary Inequities

1. What is Matt Goldspan's immediate dilemma?
2. Matt has an interpersonal problem and, perhaps, a problem with the system in which he works. Identify these problems.

### Affirmative Action

3. In what way did Matt act prematurely and precipitously?
4. What were Matt's motives in taking this action?

### Employment Theft

5. Summarize the case.
6. What political and ethical dilemmas does Matt face?

## Discussion and Writing Suggestions

### Salary Inequities

1. How should Matt determine the validity of Denise's data?
2. Even if Matt determines that salary differences are inherently unfair, how should he respond?

---

[1]The questions for this case are taken directly from Jay Halfond's "Teaching Notes" for the Matt Goldspan trilogy. Phrasings have been altered to fit the format of *Writing and Reading Across the Curriculum*.

### Affirmative Action

**3.** Do you believe that affirmative action is a justified approach to integrating the workplace, even when it results in a less qualified applicant being hired?

**4.** Is Matt's well-intended hiring approach more justified than the external control system that monitors affirmative action? Is Matt being constrained by excessive bureaucracy or by legitimate corporate concern?

**5.** Matt is clearly making a choice between the immediate needs of his office and the more long-term interests of his parent company. Is this Matt's decision to make?

### Employment Theft

**6.** What is nepotism, and is Jason's situation an example?

**7.** Was Harriet's response to Jason reasonable and fair?

**8.** How should Matt now respond? Whose expectations should now prevail— Denise's or Harriet's?

## Case 3: Why Should My Conscience Bother Me?

KERMIT VANDIVIER[1]

The B. F. Goodrich Co. is what business magazines like to speak of as "a major American corporation." It has operations in a dozen states and as many foreign countries, and of these far-flung facilities, the Goodrich plant at Troy, Ohio, is not the most imposing. It is a small, one-story building, once used to manufacture airplanes. Set in the grassy flatlands of west-central Ohio, it employs only about six hundred people. Nevertheless, it is one of the three largest manufacturers of aircraft wheels and brakes, a leader in a most profitable industry. Goodrich wheels and brakes support such well-known planes as the F111, the C5A, the Boeing 727, the XB70 and many others. Its customers include almost every aircraft manufacturer in the world.

Contracts for aircraft wheels and brakes often run into millions of dollars, and ordinarily a contract with a total value of less than $70,000, though welcome, would not create any special stir of joy in the hearts of Goodrich sales personnel. But purchase order P-23718, issued on June 18, 1967, by the LTV Aerospace Corporation, and ordering 202 brake assemblies for a new Air Force plane at a total price of $69,417, was received by Goodrich with considerable glee. And there was good reason. Some ten years previously, Goodrich had built a brake for LTV

"Why Should My Conscience Bother Me?" by Kermit Vandivier from *In the Name of Profit*, by Robert Heilbroner, © 1972 by Doubleday, a division of Bantam, Doubleday, Dell Publishing Group, Inc. Reprinted by permission of the publisher.

[1]Reporter, *Daily News*, in Troy, Ohio.

that was, to say the least, considerably less than a rousing success. The brake had not lived up to Goodrich's promises, and after experiencing considerable difficulty, LTV had written off Goodrich as a source of brakes. Since that time, Goodrich salesmen had been unable to sell so much as a shot of brake fluid to LTV. So in 1967, when LTV requested bids on wheels and brakes for the new A7D light attack aircraft it proposed to build for the Air Force, Goodrich submitted a bid that was absurdly low, so low that LTV could not, in all prudence, turn it down.

Goodrich had, in industry parlance, "bought into the business." Not      3
only did the company not expect to make a profit on the deal; it was prepared, if necessary, to lose money. For aircraft brakes are not something that can be ordered off the shelf. They are designed for a particular aircraft, and once an aircraft manufacturer buys a brake, he is forced to purchase all replacement parts from the brake manufacturer. The $70,000 that Goodrich would get for making the brake would be a drop in the bucket when compared with the cost of the linings and other parts the Air Force would have to buy from Goodrich during the lifetime of the aircraft. Furthermore, the company which manufactures brakes for one particular model of an aircraft quite naturally has the inside track to supply other brakes when the planes are updated and improved.

Thus, that first contract, regardless of the money involved, is very      4
important, and Goodrich, when it learned that it had been awarded the A7D contract, was determined that while it may have slammed the door on its own foot ten years before, this time, the second time around, things would be different. The word was soon circulated throughout the plant: "We can't bungle it this time. We've got to give them a good brake, regardless of the cost."

There was another factor which had undoubtedly influenced LTV.      5
All aircraft brakes made today are of the disk type, and the bid submitted by Goodrich called for a relatively small brake, one containing four disks and weighing only 106 pounds. The weight of any aircraft part is extremely important. The lighter a part is, the heavier the plane's payload can be. The four-rotor, 106-pound brake promised by Goodrich was about as light as could be expected, and this undoubtedly had helped move LTV to award the contract to Goodrich.

The brake was designed by one of Goodrich's most capable engi-      6
neers, John Warren. A tall, lanky blond and a graduate of Purdue, Warren had come from the Chrysler Corporation seven years before and had become adept at aircraft brake design. The happy-go-lucky manner he usually maintained belied a temper which exploded whenever anyone ventured to offer any criticism of his work, no matter how small. On these occasions, Warren would turn red in the face, often throwing or slamming something and then stalking from the scene. As his coworkers learned the consequences of criticizing him, they did so less and less

readily, and when he submitted his preliminary design for the A7D brake, it was accepted without question.

Warren was named project engineer for the A7D, and he, in turn, assigned the task of producing the final production design to a new-comer to the Goodrich engineering stable, Searle Lawson. Just turned twenty-six, Lawson had been out of the Northrup Institute of Technology only one year when he came to Goodrich in January 1967. Like Warren, he had worked for a while in the automotive industry, but his engineering degree was in aeronautical and astronautical sciences, and when the opportunity came to enter his special field, via Goodrich, he took it. At the Troy plant, Lawson had been assigned to various "paper projects" to break him in, and after several months spent reviewing statistics and old brake designs, he was beginning to fret at the lack of challenge. When told he was being assigned to his first "real" project, he was elated and immediately plunged into his work.

The major portion of the design had already been completed by Warren, and major assemblies for the brake had already been ordered from Goodrich suppliers. Naturally, however, before Goodrich could start making the brakes on a production basis, much testing would have to be done. Lawson would have to determine the best materials to use for the linings and discover what minor adjustments in the design would have to be made.

Then, after the preliminary testing and after the brake was judged ready for production, one whole brake assembly would undergo a series of grueling, simulated braking stops and other severe trials called qualification tests. These tests are required by the military, which gives very detailed specifications on how they are to be conducted, the criteria for failure, and so on. They are performed in the Goodrich plant's test laboratory, where huge machines called dynamometers can simulate the weight and speed of almost any aircraft. After the brakes pass the laboratory tests, they are approved for production, but before the brakes are accepted for use in military service, they must undergo further extensive flight tests.

Searle Lawson was well aware that much work had to be done before the A7D brake could go into production, and he knew that LTV had set the last two weeks in June, 1968, as the starting dates for flight tests. So he decided to begin testing immediately. Goodrich's suppliers had not yet delivered the brake housing and other parts, but the brake disks had arrived, and using the housing from a brake similar in size and weight to the A7D brake, Lawson built a prototype. The prototype was installed in a test wheel and placed on one of the big dynamometers in the plant's test laboratory. The dynamometer was adjusted to simulate the weight of the A7D and Lawson began a series of tests, "landing" the wheel and brake at the A7D's landing speed, and braking it to a stop.

7

8

9

10

The main purpose of these preliminary tests was to learn what temperatures would develop within the brake during the simulated stops and to evaluate the lining materials tentatively selected for use.

During a normal aircraft landing the temperatures inside the brake    11
may reach 1000 degrees, and occasionally a bit higher. During Lawson's first simulated landings, the temperature of his prototype brake reached 1500 degrees. The brake glowed a bright cherry-red and threw off incandescent particles of metal and lining material as the temperature reached its peak. After a few such stops, the brake was dismantled and the linings were found to be almost completely disintegrated. Lawson chalked this first failure up to chance and, ordering new lining materials, tried again.

The second attempt was a repeat of the first. The brake became    12
extremely hot, causing the lining materials to crumble into dust.

After the third such failure, Lawson, inexperienced though he was,    13
knew that the fault lay not in defective parts or unsuitable lining material but in the basic design of the brake itself. Ignoring Warren's original computations, Lawson made his own, and it didn't take him long to discover where the trouble lay—the brake was too small. There simply was not enough surface area on the disks to stop the aircraft without generating the excessive heat that caused the linings to fail.

The answer to the problem was obvious but far from simple—the    14
four-disk brake would have to be scrapped, and a new design, using five disks, would have to be developed. The implications were not lost on Lawson. Such a step would require the junking of all the four-disk-brake subassemblies, many of which had now begun to arrive from the various suppliers. It would also mean several weeks of preliminary design and testing and many more weeks of waiting while the suppliers made and delivered the new subassemblies.

Yet, several weeks had already gone by since LTV's order had    15
arrived, and the date for delivery of the first production brakes for flight testing was only a few months away.

Although project engineer John Warren had more or less turned the    16
A7D over to Lawson, he knew of the difficulties Lawson had been experiencing. He had assured the young engineer that the problem revolved around getting the right kind of lining material. Once that was found, he said, the difficulties would end.

Despite the evidence of the abortive tests and Lawson's careful    17
computations, Warren rejected the suggestion that the four-disk brake was too light for the job. Warren knew that his superior had already told LTV, in rather glowing terms, that the preliminary tests on the A7D brake were very successful. Indeed, Warren's superiors weren't aware at this time of the troubles on the brake. It would have been difficult for Warren to admit not only that he had made a serious error in his

calculations and original design but that his mistakes had been caught by a green kid, barely out of college.

Warren's reaction to a five-disk brake was not unexpected by Lawson, and, seeing that the four-disk brake was not to be abandoned so easily, he took his calculations and dismal test results one step up the corporate ladder. · 18

At Goodrich, the man who supervises the engineers working on 19 projects slated for production is called, predictably, the projects manager. The job was held by a short, chubby and bald man named Robert Sink. A man truly devoted to his work, Sink was as likely to be found at his desk at ten o'clock on Sunday night as ten o'clock on Monday morning. His outside interests consisted mainly of tinkering on a Model-A Ford and an occasional game of golf. Some fifteen years before, Sink had begun working at Goodrich as a lowly draftsman. Slowly, he worked his way up. Despite his geniality, Sink was neither respected nor liked by the majority of the engineers, and his appointment as their supervisor did not improve their feelings about him. They thought he had only gone to high school. It quite naturally rankled those who had gone through years of college and acquired impressive specialities such as thermodynamics and astronautics to be commanded by a man whom they considered their intellectual inferior. But, though Sink had no college training, he had something even more useful: a fine working knowledge of company politics.

Puffing upon a Meerschaum pipe, Sink listened gravely as young 20 Lawson confided his fears about the four-disk brake. Then he examined Lawson's calculations and the results of the abortive tests. Despite the fact that he was not a qualified engineer, in the strictest sense of the word, it must certainly have been obvious to Sink that Lawson's calculations were correct and that a four-disk brake would never have worked on the A7D.

But other things of equal importance were also obvious. First, to 21 concede that Lawson's calculations were correct would also mean conceding that Warren's calculations were incorrect. As projects manager, he not only was responsible for Warren's activities, but, in admitting that Warren had erred, he would have to admit that he had erred in trusting Warren's judgment. It also meant that, as projects manager, it would be he who would have to explain the whole messy situation to the Goodrich hierarchy, not only at Troy but possibly on the corporate level at Goodrich's Akron offices. And, having taken Warren's judgment of the four-disk brake at face value (he was forced to do this since, not being an engineer, he was unable to exercise any engineering judgment of his own), he had assured LTV, not once but several times, that about all there was left to do on the brake was pack it in a crate and ship it out the back door.

There's really no problem at all, he told Lawson. After all, Warren    **22**
was an experienced engineer, and if he said the brake would work, it
would work. Just keep on testing and probably, maybe even on the very
next try, it'll work out just fine.

Lawson was far from convinced, but without the support of his    **23**
superiors there was little he could do except keep on testing. By now,
housings for the four-disk brake had begun to arrive at the plant, and
Lawson was able to build up a production model of the brake and
begin the formal qualification tests demanded by the military.

The first qualification attempts went exactly as the tests on the    **24**
prototype had. Terrific heat developed within the brakes and, after a
few, short, simulated stops, the linings crumbled. A new type of lining
material was ordered and once again an attempt to qualify the brake was
made. Again, failure.

On April 11, the day the thirteenth test was completed, I became    **25**
personally involved in the A7D situation.

I had worked in the Goodrich test laboratory for five years, starting    **26**
first as an instrumentation engineer, then later becoming a data analyst
and technical writer. As part of my duties, I analyzed the reams and
reams of instrumentation data that came from the many testing machines in the laboratory, then transcribed it to a more usable form for
the engineering department. And when a new-type brake had successfully completed the required qualification tests, I would issue a formal
qualification report.

Qualification reports were an accumulation of all the data and test    **27**
logs compiled by the test technicians during the qualification tests, and
were documentary proof that a brake had met all the requirements
established by the military specifications and was therefore presumed
safe for flight testing. Before actual flight tests were conducted on a
brake, qualification reports had to be delivered to the customer and to
various government officials.

On April 11, I was looking over the data from the latest A7D test,    **28**
and I noticed that many irregularities in testing methods had been noted
on the test logs.

Technically, of course, there was nothing wrong with conducting    **29**
tests in any manner desired, so long as the test was for research purposes only. But qualification test methods are clearly delineated by the
military, and I knew that this test had been a formal qualification attempt. One particular notation on the test logs caught my eye. For
some of the stops, the instrument which recorded the brake pressure
had been deliberately miscalibrated so that, while the brake pressure
used during the stops was recorded as 1000 psi (the maximum pressure that would be available on the A7D aircraft), the pressure had
actually been 1100 psi!

I showed the test logs to the test lab supervisor, Ralph Gretzinger, **30** who said he had learned from the technician who had miscalibrated the instrument that he had been asked to do so by Lawson. Lawson, said Gretzinger, readily admitted asking for the miscalibration, saying he had been told to do so by Sink.

I asked Gretzinger why anyone would want to miscalibrate the **31** data-recording instruments.

"Why? I'll tell you why," he snorted. "That brake is a failure. It's way **32** too small for the job, and they're not ever going to get it to work. They're getting desperate, and instead of scrapping the damned thing and starting over, they figure they can horse around down here in the lab and qualify it that way."

An expert engineer, Gretzinger had been responsible for several **33** innovations in brake design. It was he who had invented the unique brake system used on the famous XB70. A graduate of Georgia Tech, he was a stickler for detail and he had some very firm ideas about honesty and ethics. "If you want to find out what's going on," said Gretzinger, "ask Lawson, he'll tell you."

Curious, I did ask Lawson the next time he came into the lab. He **34** seemed eager to discuss the A7D and gave me the history of his months of frustrating efforts to get Warren and Sink to change the brake design. "I just can't believe this is really happening," said Lawson, shaking his head slowly. "This isn't engineering, at least not what I thought it would be. Back in school, I thought that when you were an engineer, you tried to do your best, no matter what it cost. But this is something else."

He sat across the desk from me, his chin propped in his hand. "Just **35** wait," he warned. "You'll get a chance to see what I'm talking about. You're going to get in the act, too, because I've already had the word that we're going to make one more attempt to qualify the brake, and that's it. Win or lose, we're going to issue a qualification report!"

I reminded him that a qualification report could only be issued after **36** a brake had successfully met all military requirements, and therefore, unless the next qualification attempt was a success, no report would be issued.

"You'll find out," retorted Lawson. "I was already told that regard- **37** less of what the brake does on test, it's going to be qualified." He said he had been told in those exact words at a conference with Sink and Russell Van Horn.

This was the first indication that Sink had brought his boss, Van **38** Horn, into the mess. Although Van Horn, as manager of the design engineering section, was responsible for the entire department, he was not necessarily familiar with all phases of every project, and it was not uncommon for those under him to exercise the what-he-doesn't-know-won't-hurt-him philosophy. If he was aware of the full extent of the

A7D situation, it meant that matters had truly reached a desperate stage—that Sink had decided not only to call for help but was looking toward that moment when blame must be borne and, if possible, shared.

Also, if Van Horn had said, "Regardless what the brake does on test, it's going to be qualified," then it could only mean that, if necessary, a false qualification report would be issued! I discussed this possibility with Gretzinger, and he assured me that under no circumstances would such a report ever be issued. 39

"If they want a qualification report, we'll write them one, but we'll tell it just like it is," he declared emphatically. "No false data or false reports are going to come out of this lab." 40

On May 2, 1968, the fourteenth and final attempt to qualify the brake was begun. Although the same improper methods used to nurse the brake through the previous tests were employed, it soon became obvious that this too would end in failure. 41

When the tests were about half completed, Lawson asked if I would start preparing the various engineering curves and graphic displays which were normally incorporated in a qualification report. "It looks as though you'll be writing a qualification report shortly," he said. 42

I flatly refused to have anything to do with the matter and immediately told Gretzinger what I had been asked to do. He was furious and repeated his previous declaration that under no circumstances would any false data or other matter be issued from the lab. 43

"I'm going to get this settled right now, once and for all," he declared. "I'm going to see Line [Russell Line, manager of the Goodrich Technical Services Section, of which the test lab was a part] and find out just how far this thing is going to go!" He stormed out of the room. 44

In about an hour, he returned and called me to his desk. He sat silently for a few moments, then muttered, half to himself, "I wonder what the hell they'd do if I just quit?" I didn't answer and I didn't ask him what he meant. I knew. He had been beaten down. He had reached the point when the decision had to be made. Defy them now while there was still time—or knuckle under, sell out. 45

"You know," he went on uncertainly, looking down at his desk, "I've been an engineer for a long time, and I've always believed that ethics and integrity were every bit as important as theorems and formulas, and never once has anything happened to change my beliefs. Now this. . . . Hell, I've got two sons I've got to put through school and I just. . . ." His voice trailed off. 46

He sat for a few more minutes, then, looking over the top of his glasses, said hoarsely, "Well, it looks like we're licked. The way it stands now, we're to go ahead and prepare the data and other things for the graphic presentation in the report, and when we're finished, someone upstairs will actually write the report. 47

"After all," he continued, "we're just drawing some curves, and what **48** happens to them after they leave here, well, we're not responsible for that."

He was trying to persuade himself that as long as we were con-**49** cerned with only one part of the puzzle and didn't see the completed picture, we really weren't doing anything wrong. He didn't believe what he was saying, and he knew I didn't believe it either. It was an embarrassing and shameful moment for both of us.

I wasn't at all satisfied with the situation and decided that I too **50** would discuss the matter with Russell Line, the senior executive in our section.

Tall, powerfully built, his teeth flashing white, his face tanned to a **51** coffee-brown by a daily stint with a sun lamp, Line looked and acted every inch the executive. He was a crossword-puzzle enthusiast and an ardent golfer, and though he had lived in Troy only a short time, he had been accepted into the Troy Country Club and made an official of the golf committee. He commanded great respect and had come to be well liked by those of us who worked under him.

He listened sympathetically while I explained how I felt about the **52** A7D situation, and when I had finished, he asked me what I wanted him to do about it. I said that as employees of the Goodrich Company we had a responsibility to protect the company and its reputation if at all possible. I said I was certain that officers on the corporate level would never knowingly allow such tactics as had been employed on the A7D.

"I agree with you," he remarked, "but I still want to know what you **53** want me to do about it."

I suggested that in all probability the chief engineer at the Troy **54** plant, H. C. "Bud" Sunderman, was unaware of the A7D problem and that he, Line, should tell him what was going on.

Line laughed, good-humoredly. "Sure, I could, but I'm not going to. **55** Bud probably already knows about this thing anyway, and if he doesn't, I'm sure not going to be the one to tell him."

"But why?" **56**

"Because it's none of my business, and it's none of yours. I learned **57** a long time ago not to worry about things over which I had no control. I have no control over this."

I wasn't satisfied with this answer, and I asked him if his conscience **58** wouldn't bother him if, say, during flight tests on the brake, something should happen resulting in death or injury to the test pilot.

"Look," he said, becoming somewhat exasperated, "I just told you **59** I have no control over this thing. Why should my conscience bother me?"

His voice took on a quiet, soothing tone as he continued. "You're 60 just getting all upset over this thing for nothing. I just do as I'm told, and I'd advise you to do the same."

He had made his decision, and now I had to make mine.      61

I made no attempt to rationalize what I had been asked to do. It 62 made no difference who would falsify which part of the report or whether the actual falsification would be by misleading numbers or misleading words. Whether by acts of commission or omission, all of us who contributed to the fraud would be guilty. The only question left for me to decide was whether or not I would become a party to the fraud.

Before coming to Goodrich in 1963, I had held a variety of jobs, 63 each a little more pleasant, a little more rewarding than the last. At forty-two, with seven children, I had decided that the Goodrich Company would probably be my "home" for the rest of my working life. The job paid well, it was pleasant and challenging, and the future looked reasonably bright. My wife and I had bought a home and we were ready to settle down into a comfortable, middle-age, middle-class rut. If I refused to take part in the A7D fraud, I would have to either resign or be fired. The report would be written by someone anyway, but I would have the satisfaction of knowing I had had no part in the matter. But bills aren't paid with personal satisfaction, nor house payments with ethical principles. I made my decision.[2]

## Review Questions

1. Why did Lawson conclude that Warren's design was flawed?
2. Why did Warren not consider redesigning the brakes? Why did Sink choose to support Warren, instead of Lawson, when he must have realized that Lawson was right about the brakes?
3. Both Ralph Gretzinger and Vandivier at first refused to go along with the demand that they falsify test data. Why did both men eventually cave in to their superiors?
4. At what point did Vandivier consult a lawyer? Why then—and not earlier?

## Discussion and Writing Suggestions

1. If you were Vandivier, would you have acted as he did? (Consider especially the personal dilemma he describes in paragraph 62.) Do you believe that he acted responsibly at all stages of this case? Explain.
2. In paragraph 71 on page 818, Vandivier says that he and Lawson "discussed

---

[2]Turn to page 817 for the author's concluding discussion on what happened in this case. Before reading that discussion, however, try to anticipate Vandivier's decision.

such things as the Nuremberg trials [the post World War II tribunals at which Nazi officials were found guilty of war crimes] and how they related to our guilt and complicity in the A7D situation." To what extent to you see parallels between these two situations?

3. Apply Cavanagh's ethical decision-making model to this case. To what extent do the principles of utilitarianism, rights, and justice apply? Are there any "overwhelming factors" that could help determine which principles are more important in this case?

4. Assume that you are a member of a commission charged with investigating the Goodrich case. Assume also that you found Vandivier's account of the matter to be credible. Consider all of the things that went wrong, and try to devise safeguards—in the form of a series of recommendations—to prevent such mishaps in the future.

5. Ethically, what similarities do you find between this case and the Peter Green case? (Consider, for example, the similarities between Peter Green and Searle Lawson.) What differences do you find?

# Babbitt

## SINCLAIR LEWIS

*Henry Sinclair Lewis—writer of poetry, plays, and more than twenty novels—was the first American to receive the Nobel Prize for literature. He is known for taking large themes important to the emerging, urban identity in America after World War I and, with sharp satirical treatment, exposing hypocrisies. In* Main Street *(1920), Lewis explored the "virus" of village and small-town life that bred boredom and spiritual death; in* Arrowsmith *(1925), he probed conflicts between science and profit; in* Elmer Gantry *(1927), he savaged the pretensions of fundamentalist preachers; and in* Babbitt *(1922), Lewis exposed the petty, materialistic, conforming ways of the new business class. The novel is set in the fictional city of Zenith—the great, shining representative of American urban life. In George Babbitt, Sinclair Lewis gave the English language a new word. The* Random House Dictionary *defines a "babbitt" as "a self-satisfied person who conforms readily to conventional, middle-class ideas and ideals, especially of business and material success." Earlier novels on American business celebrated the tycoon spirit of railway magnates and industrial giants. In* Babbitt, *Lewis examined the life of one middle-class realtor who embraced the politics, the mores, and the country-club life that his culture had taught him to value and yet still found himself unhappy. The novel documents the growth and causes of George Babbitt's discontent.*

*Sinclair Lewis was born in 1885 in the small town of Sauk Center, Minnesota (population 2,500). His mother, a schoolteacher, died when he was three; his father, a teacher-turned-country-doctor, soon remarried. The young Lewis showed more interest in reading and creative writing than in sports. He graduated from Yale in 1908 (having taken time off in his senior year to work on the Panama Canal). Lewis's first novel,* Our Mister Wren, *was published in 1914. A year later, the* Saturday Evening Post *published the first of what was to be many of his short stories. Five unsuccessful novels followed before the writing of* Main Street *and* Babbitt, *which secured Lewis's fame and fortune. He reached the height of his career in 1930 with the awarding of the Nobel Prize but in the years after suffered a decline, due in part to a recurring drinking problem. Lewis died in Rome, Italy, in 1951.*

*In the excerpt to follow, you will read of a real estate transaction in George Babbitt's office. Consider the ethics as well as the legality of the transaction. Is Babbitt doing anything wrong by trying to maximize his and his client's profits?*

His name was George F. Babbitt. He was forty-six years old now, in April, 1920, and he made nothing in particular, neither butter nor shoes nor poetry, but he was nimble in the calling of selling houses for more than people could afford to pay. 1

His large head was pink, his brown hair thin and dry. His face was babyish in slumber, despite his wrinkles and the red spectacle-dents on the slopes of his nose. He was not fat but he was exceedingly well fed; his cheeks were pads, and the unroughened hand which lay helpless upon the khaki-colored blanket was slightly puffy. He seemed prosperous, extremely married and unromantic; and altogether unromantic appeared this sleeping-porch, which looked on one sizable elm, two respectable grass-plots, a cement driveway, and a corrugated iron garage. Yet Babbitt was again dreaming of the fairy child, a dream more romantic than scarlet pagodas by a silver sea. 2

For years the fairy child had come to him. Where others saw but Georgie Babbitt, she discerned gallant youth. She waited for him, in the darkness beyond mysterious groves. When at last he could slip away from the crowded house he darted to her. His wife, his clamoring friends, sought to follow, but he escaped, the girl fleet beside him, and they crouched together on a shadowy hillside. She was so slim, so white, so eager! She cried that he was gay[1] and valiant, that she would wait for him, that they would sail— 3

---

[1]In 1922, the sense of the word "gay" is "merry."

Rumble and bang of the milk-truck.　　　　　　　　　　　　4

Babbitt moaned, turned over, struggled back toward his dream. He　5
could see only her face now, beyond misty waters. The furnace-man
slammed the basement door. A dog barked in the next yard. As Babbitt
sank blissfully into a dim warm tide, the paper-carrier went by whistling,
and the rolled-up *Advocate* thumped the front door. Babbitt roused, his
stomach constricted with alarm. As he relaxed, he was pierced by the
familiar and irritating rattle of some one cranking a Ford: snap-ah-ah,
snap-ah-ah, snap-ah-ah. Himself a pious motorist, Babbitt cranked with
the unseen driver, with him waited through taut hours for the roar of
the starting engine, with him agonized as the roar ceased and again
began the infernal patient snap-ah-ah—a round, flat sound, a shivering
cold-morning sound, a sound infuriating and inescapable. Not till the
rising voice of the motor told him that the Ford was moving was he
released from the panting tension. He glanced once at his favorite tree,
elm twigs against the gold patina of sky, and fumbled for sleep as for
a drug. He who had been a boy very credulous of life was no longer
greatly interested in the possible and improbable adventures of each
new day.

He escaped from reality till the alarm-clock rang, at seven-twenty.　6

. . .

His morning was not sharply marked into divisions. Interwoven　7
with correspondence and advertisement-writing were a thousand nervous details: calls from clerks who were incessantly and hopefully
seeking five furnished rooms and bath at sixty dollars a month; advice
to Mat Penniman on getting money out of tenants who had no money.

Babbitt's virtues as a real-estate broker—as the servant of society　8
in the department of finding homes for families and shops for distribu-
tors of food—were steadiness and diligence. He was conventionally
honest, he kept his records of buyers and sellers complete, he had
experience with leases and titles and an excellent memory for prices. His
shoulders were broad enough, his voice deep enough, his relish of
hearty humor strong enough, to establish him as one of the ruling caste
of Good Fellows. Yet his eventual importance to mankind was perhaps
lessened by his large and complacent ignorance of all architecture save
the types of houses turned out by speculative builders; all landscape
gardening save the use of curving roads, grass, and six ordinary shrubs;
and all the commonest axioms of economics. He serenely believed that
the one purpose of the real-estate business was to make money for
George F. Babbitt. True, it was a good advertisement at Booster Club
lunches, and all the varieties of Annual Banquets to which Good Fellows
were invited, to speak sonorously of Unselfish Public Service, the Broker's Obligation to Keep Inviolate the Trust of His Clients, and a thing
called Ethics, whose nature was confusing but if you had it you were a

High-class Realtor and if you hadn't you were a shyster, a piker, and a fly-by-night. These virtues awakened Confidence, and enabled you to handle Bigger Propositions. But they didn't imply that you were to be impractical and refuse to take twice the value of a house if a buyer was such an idiot that he didn't jew you down on the asking-price.

Babbitt spoke well—and often—at these orgies of commercial    9
righteousness about the "realtor's function as a seer of the future devel-
opment of the community, and as a prophetic engineer clearing the pathway for inevitable changes"—which meant that a real-estate broker could make money by guessing which way the town would grow. This guessing he called Vision.

In an address at the Boosters' Club he had admitted, "It is at once   10
the duty and the privilege of the realtor to know everything about his own city and its environs. Where a surgeon is a specialist on every vein and mysterious cell of the human body, and the engineer upon electric-ity in all its phases, or every bolt of some great bridge majestically arching o'er a mighty flood, the realtor must know his city, inch by inch, and all its faults and virtues."

Though he did know the market-price, inch by inch, of certain   11
districts of Zenith, he did not know whether the police force was too large or too small, or whether it was in alliance with gambling and prostitution. He knew the means of fire-proofing buildings and the relation of insurance-rates to fire-proofing, but he did not know how many firemen there were in the city, how they were trained and paid, or how complete their apparatus. He sang eloquently the advantages of proximity of school-buildings to rentable homes, but he did not know—he did not know that it was worth while to know—whether the city schoolrooms were properly heated, lighted, ventilated, furnished; he did not know how the teachers were chosen; and though he chanted "One of the boasts of Zenith is that we pay our teachers adequately," that was because he had read the statement in the *Advocate-Times*. Himself, he could not have given the average salary of teachers in Zenith or anywhere else.

He had heard it said that "conditions" in the County Jail and the   12
Zenith City Prison were not very "scientific"; he had, with indignation at the criticism of Zenith, skimmed through a report in which the notorious pessimist Seneca Doane, the radical lawyer, asserted that to throw boys and young girls into a bull-pen crammed with men suffering from syphilis, delirium tremens, and insanity was not the perfect way of educating them. He had controverted the report by growling, "Folks that think a jail ought to be a bloomin' Hotel Thornleigh make me sick. If people don't like a jail, let 'em behave 'emselves and keep out of it. Besides, these reform cranks always exaggerate." That was the begin-ning and quite completely the end of his investigations into Zenith's

charities and corrections; and as to the "vice districts" he brightly expressed it, "Those are things that no decent man monkeys with. Besides, smatter fact, I'll tell you confidentially: it's a protection to our daughters and to decent women to have a district where tough nuts can raise cain. Keeps 'em away from our own homes."

As to industrial conditions, however, Babbitt had thought a great 13 deal, and his opinions may be coördinated as follows:

"A good labor union is of value because it keeps out radical unions, 14 which would destroy property. No one ought to be forced to belong to a union, however. All labor agitators who try to force men to join a union should be hanged. In fact, just between ourselves, there oughtn't to be any unions allowed at all; and as it's the best way of fighting the unions, every business man ought to belong to an employers'-association and to the Chamber of Commerce. In union there is strength. So any selfish hog who doesn't join the Chamber of Commerce ought to be forced to."

In nothing—as the expert on whose advice families moved to new 15 neighborhoods to live there for a generation—was Babbitt more splendidly innocent than in the science of sanitation. He did not know a malaria-bearing mosquito from a bat; he knew nothing about tests of drinking water; and in the matters of plumbing and sewage he was as unlearned as he was voluble. He often referred to the excellence of the bathrooms in the houses he sold. He was fond of explaining why it was that no European ever bathed. Some one had told him, when he was twenty-two, that all cesspools were unhealthy, and he still denounced them. If a client impertinently wanted him to sell a house which had a cesspool, Babbitt always spoke about it—before accepting the house and selling it.

When he laid out the Glen Oriole acreage development, when he 16 ironed woodland and dipping meadow into a glenless, orioleless, sunburnt flat prickly with small boards displaying the names of imaginary streets, he righteously put in a complete sewage-system. It made him feel superior; it enabled him to sneer privily at the Martin Lumsen development, Avonlea, which had a cesspool; and it provided a chorus for the full-page advertisements in which he announced the beauty, convenience, cheapness, and supererogatory healthfulness of Glen Oriole. The only flaw was that the Glen Oriole sewers had insufficient outlet, so that waste remained in them, not very agreeably, while the Avonlea cesspool was a Waring septic tank.

The whole of the Glen Oriole project was a suggestion that Babbitt, 17 though he really did hate men recognized as swindlers, was not too unreasonably honest. Operators and buyers prefer that brokers should not be in competition with them as operators and buyers themselves, but attend to their clients' interests only. It was supposed that the

Babbitt-Thompson Company were merely agents for Glen Oriole, serving the real owner, Jake Offutt, but the fact was that Babbitt and Thompson owned sixty-two per cent. of the Glen, the president and purchasing agent of the Zenith Street Traction Company owned twenty-eight per cent., and Jake Offutt (a gang-politician, a small manufacturer, a tobacco-chewing old farceur who enjoyed dirty politics, business diplomacy, and cheating at poker) had only ten per cent., which Babbitt and the Traction officials had given to him for "fixing" health inspectors and fire inspectors and a member of the State Transportation Commission.

But Babbitt was virtuous. He advocated, though he did not practise, 18 the prohibition of alcohol; he praised, though he did not obey, the laws against motor-speeding; he paid his debts; he contributed to the church, the Red Cross, and the Y.M.C.A.; he followed the custom of his clan and cheated only as it was sanctified by precedent; and he never descended to trickery—though, as he explained to Paul Riesling:

"Course I don't mean to say that every ad I write is literally true 19 or that I always believe everything I say when I give some buyer a good strong selling-spiel. You see—you see it's like this: In the first place, maybe the owner of the property exaggerated when he put it into my hands, and it certainly isn't my place to go proving my principal a liar! And then most folks are so darn crooked themselves that they expect a fellow to do a little lying, so if I was fool enough to never whoop the ante I'd get the credit for lying anyway! In self-defense I got to toot my own horn, like a lawyer defending a client—his bounden duty, ain't it, to bring out the poor dub's good points? Why, the Judge himself would bawl out a lawyer that didn't, even if they both knew the guy was guilty! But even so, I don't pad out the truth like Cecil Rountree or Thayer or the rest of these realtors. Fact, I think a fellow that's willing to deliberately up and profit by lying ought to be shot!"

Babbitt's value to his clients was rarely better shown than this 20 morning, in the conference at eleven-thirty between himself, Conrad Lyte, and Archibald Purdy.

Conrad Lyte was a real-estate speculator. He was a nervous specula- 21 tor. Before he gambled he consulted bankers, lawyers, architects, contracting builders, and all of their clerks and stenographers who were willing to be cornered and give him advice. He was a bold entrepreneur, and he desired nothing more than complete safety in his investments, freedom from attention to details, and the thirty or forty per cent profit which, according to all authorities, a pioneer deserves for his risks and foresight. He was a stubby man with a cap-like mass of short gray curls and clothes which, no matter how well cut, seemed shaggy. Below his eyes were semicircular hollows, as though silver dollars had been pressed against them and had left an imprint.

Particularly and always Lyte consulted Babbitt, and trusted in his slow cautiousness. 22

Six months ago Babbitt had learned that one Archibald Purdy, a grocer in the indecisive residential district known as Linton, was talking of opening a butcher shop beside his grocery. Looking up the ownership of adjoining parcels of land, Babbitt found that Purdy owned his present shop but did not own the one available lot adjoining. He advised Conrad Lyte to purchase this lot, for eleven thousand dollars, though an appraisal on a basis of rents did not indicate its value as above nine thousand. The rents, declared Babbitt, were too low; and by waiting they could make Purdy come to their price. (This was Vision.) He had to bully Lyte into buying. His first act as agent for Lyte was to increase the rent of the battered store-building on the lot. The tenant said a number of rude things, but he paid. 23

Now, Purdy seemed ready to buy, and his delay was going to cost him ten thousand extra dollars—the reward paid by the community to Mr. Conrad Lyte for the virtue of employing a broker who had Vision and who understood Talking Points, Strategic Values, Key Situations, Underappraisals, and the Psychology of Salesmanship. 24

Lyte came to the conference exultantly. He was fond of Babbitt, this morning, and called him "old hoss." Purdy, the grocer, a long-nosed man and solemn, seemed to care less for Babbitt and for Vision, but Babbitt met him at the street door of the office and guided him toward the private room with affectionate little cries of "This way, Brother Purdy!" He took from the correspondence-file the entire box of cigars and forced them on his guests. He pushed their chairs two inches forward and three inches back, which gave an hospitable note, then leaned back in his desk-chair and looked plump and jolly. But he spoke to the weakling grocer with firmness. 25

"Well, Brother Purdy, we been having some pretty tempting offers from butchers and a slew of other folks for that lot next to your store, but I persuaded Brother Lyte that we ought to give you a shot at the property first. I said to Lyte, 'It'd be a rotten shame,' I said, 'if somebody went and opened a combination grocery and meat market right next door and ruined Purdy's nice little business.' Especially—" Babbitt leaned forward, and his voice was harsh, "—it would be hard luck if one of these cash-and-carry chain-stores got in there and started cutting prices below cost till they got rid of competition and forced you to the wall!" 26

Purdy snatched his thin hands from his pockets, pulled up his trousers, thrust his hands back into his pockets, tilted in the heavy oak chair, and tried to look amused, as he struggled: 27

"Yes, they're bad competition. But I guess you don't realize the 28 Pulling Power that Personality has in a neighborhood business."

The great Babbitt smiled. "That's so. Just as you feel, old man. We 29 thought we'd give you first chance. All right then—"

"Now look here!" Purdy wailed. "I know f'r a fact that a piece of 30 property 'bout same size, right near, sold for less 'n eighty-five hundred, 'twa'n't two years ago, and here you fellows are asking me twenty-four thousand dollars! Why, I'd have to mortgage—I wouldn't mind so much paying twelve thousand but—Why good God, Mr. Babbitt, you're asking more 'n twice its value! And threatening to ruin me if I don't take it!"

"Purdy, I don't like your way of talking! I don't like it one little bit! 31 Supposing Lyte and I were stinking enough to want to ruin any fellow human, don't you suppose we know it's to our own selfish interest to have everybody in Zenith prosperous? But all this is beside the point. Tell you what we'll do: We'll come down to twenty-three thousand— five thousand down and the rest on mortgage—and if you want to wreck the old shack and rebuild, I guess I can get Lyte here to loosen up for a building-mortgage on good liberal terms. Heavens, man, we'd be glad to oblige you! We don't like these foreign grocery trusts any better 'n you do! But it isn't reasonable to expect us to sacrifice eleven thousand or more just for neighborliness, is it! How about it, Lyte? You willing to come down?"

By warmly taking Purdy's part, Babbitt persuaded the benevolent 32 Mr. Lyte to reduce his price to twenty-one thousand dollars. At the right moment Babbitt snatched from a drawer the agreement he had had Miss McGoun type out a week ago and thrust it into Purdy's hands. He genially shook his fountain pen to make certain that it was flowing, handed it to Purdy, and approvingly watched him sign.

The work of the world was being done. Lyte had made something 33 over nine thousand dollars, Babbitt had made a four-hundred-and-fifty dollar commission, Purdy had, by the sensitive mechanism of modern finance, been provided with a business-building, and soon the happy inhabitants of Linton would have meat lavished upon them at prices only a little higher than those down-town.

It had been a manly battle, but after it Babbitt drooped. This was the 34 only really amusing contest he had been planning. There was nothing ahead save details of leases, appraisals, mortgages.

He muttered, "Makes me sick to think of Lyte carrying off most of 35 the profit when I did all the work, the old skinflint! And—What else have I got to do to-day? . . . Like to take a good long vacation. Motor trip. Something."

## Discussion and Writing Suggestions

1. [I]t was a good advertisement . . . to speak sonorously of . . . a thing called Ethics, whose nature was confusing but if you had it you were a High-class Realtor and if you hadn't you were a shyster, a piker, and a fly-by-night. These virtues awakened Confidence, and enabled you to handle Bigger Propositions. But they didn't imply that you were to be impractical and refuse to take twice the value of a house if a buyer was such an idiot that he didn't [work] you down on the asking price.

   Do you agree with Babbitt's code of ethics? That is, is it reasonable to you that a realtor would accept twice the value of a property if a buyer were foolish enough to offer it? How does Babbitt exemplify Albert Carr's "bluffing principles"?

2. The grocer, Purdy, is an example of "an idiot" that doesn't work a realtor down on the asking price. (See the preceding question.) Accordingly, Babbitt and his client Conrad Lyte succeed in making a handsome profit—legally. What is your reaction to this "work of the world," as Lewis calls it?

3. In your experience, have you seen or heard of any business conducted in the manner of the Conrad Lyte–Purdy affair? Describe the important "players" in this transaction and then, either in narrative form or as lines in a miniplay, recount what happened.

4. Lewis presents a series of apparent contradictions in Babbitt's character, to which Babbitt seems oblivious. For instance, while Babbitt believes realtors should know every inch of their city so that they may then communicate valuable information to customers, he does not himself know much about the adequacy of the police or fire departments, or whether teachers are paid well. Cite other apparent contradictions in Babbitt's character.

5. *Babbitt* was written in 1922. To what extent do the subjects taken up here remain current in the discussion of business ethics seventy years later? Develop your answer into an essay.

6. Characterize the tone of Lewis's portrait of George Babbitt. What attitude does the narrator adopt toward the character? In answering this question, cite particular sentences in the excerpt and discuss the tone of each.

## SYNTHESIS ACTIVITIES

1. Analyze an action taken or contemplated by a protagonist in any of the cases you've read in this chapter (or in the excerpt from *Babbitt*). Consider the case in two ways:

- ◆ Analyze the actions taken or contemplated based on Gerald Cavanagh's strategy for making ethical business decisions.
- ◆ Analyze the case following principles set out in Albert Carr's article.

Having conducted your two analyses, explain which one seems more satisfying—and why.

2. Devise your own criteria for making ethical business decisions. As you devise these criteria, bear in mind that a decision maker in business must seek to balance financial needs with the rights of employees, consumers, and the community. Then, using your criteria, analyze one of the cases presented in this chapter.

3. Albert Carr argues that we should free decisions in business from the moral considerations that govern behavior in private life. Write a critique of Carr's position. At some point in the critique, you will need to articulate *your* views on the role of ethics in business. You may find it helpful in the critique to refer to one or more of the ethical predicaments illustrated in the chapter's cases.

4. Prepare summaries of Gerald Cavanagh's method for making ethical decisions in business and Albert Carr's position on the use of deception in business. Then present these summaries to a businessman or -woman. Interview this person after he or she has read the summaries and ask which of the views seems the more appealing—or more realistic—and why. In a paper, introduce the interview and the occasion for holding it; provide a partial transcript of the interview; and conclude with an analysis of the interviewee's remarks. What have you learned about ethics and business both from summarizing the articles and from conducting the interview?

5. Conduct your own version of the Longenecker/McKinney/Moore study in which you present sixteen vignettes (see box, pages 746–47) to eight or ten people who work in a business setting. Half of the respondents should be your age; half should be the age of your parents. Provide respondents with a rating sheet and ask them to "evaluate, on the basis of their own personal values, the behavior described in the vignettes by selecting one point on a seven-point scale, ranging from 1, 'never acceptable,' to 4, 'sometimes acceptable,' to 7, 'always acceptable.'" Compare your results to those of Longenecker and his colleagues, and reach some conclusion about the value of both your study and theirs.

6. How effective is studying and discussing hypothetical dilemmas (i.e., studying cases) in preparing you for the pressures of actual dilemmas in the workplace? Develop your answer into an argument synthesis that draws on three or more cases in this chapter. If possible, refer to actual ethical dilemmas with which you've struggled in your own work.

## RESEARCH ACTIVITIES

1. Research the practice of intelligence gathering in business. A business professional must pay close attention to competitors, but how close? Is espionage permissible? In looking for sources, consult the cumulative indexes of two journals: *Business Ethics* and *Business Horizons.* The following books should be of use: Ian Gordon, *Beat the Competition: How to Use Competitive Intelligence to Develop Winning Business Strategies;* Howard Sutton, *Competitive Intelligence* (1988); William L. Sammon, ed., *Business Competitor Intelligence: Methods for Collecting, Organizing, and Using Information* (1984); Richard M. Greene, Jr., *Business Intelligence and Espionage* (1966).

2. Research the history of business ethics in America, and address this question: To what extent have Americans, over their history, been careful to observe standards of ethical behavior in their business dealings? The following study will be especially helpful: Peter Baida, *Poor Richard's Legacy: American Business Values from Benjamin Franklin to Donald Trump* (1990).

3. Locate as many books as you can on the topic of "climbing-the-ladder-to-corporate-success." Make a study of the advice in these books and report on the ethical values implicit in them. Can you classify varieties of advice? Do you find yourself agreeing with any particular strategies? What does your agreement reveal about *you?*

4. Investigate the topic of whistleblowing, the action a lone employee takes when he or she feels that a company's unethical behavior may harm the public. Under what conditions should an employee blow the whistle? What are the personal ramifications of blowing the whistle? How do companies and fellow employees respond to whistleblowers? What are the laws that protect whistleblowers? One possible source: Sissela Bok, *On the Ethics of Concealment and Revelation* (1982). Many books on the general topic of business ethics have chapters devoted to whistleblowing.

5. Choose some company that interests you, and to which you have at least limited access. Investigate the extent to which the topic of business ethics is on people's minds and on the company's agenda. Does the company have a formal code of ethics? Does the company have in place a procedure for employees who wish to raise questions about the ethics of particular practices? Has the company asked any of its employees to attend workshops on business ethics? Does the company feel the need to address any of these questions?

6. Obtain a copy of the May/June 1968 *Harvard Business Review* and read "Showdown on 'Business Bluffing.'" In this piece, Timothy Blodgett (then editor of the *Review*) summarizes and presents excerpts from volumes of letters that were sent in response to Albert Carr's article "Is Business Bluffing Ethical?" Read Carr's article (pages 755–69), and then read the letters that Blodgett collected. Write a paper in which you synthesize this material. Be

sure to develop your own views of Carr. In addition, comment on how timely the 1968 debate is in today's business environment.

7. Investigate and report on any of the insider trading scandals of the 1980s. You might begin by doing a literature search on two names: Ivan Boesky and Michael Milken. In your paper, explain how insider trading works and why it is both ethically problematic and illegal.

Following are the concluding paragraphs to the Vandivier case, presented earlier.

## Conclusion to "Why Should My Conscience Bother Me?"

. . . The next morning, I telephoned Lawson and told him I was ready    64
to begin on the qualification report.

In a few minutes, he was at my desk, ready to begin. Before we    65
started, I asked him, "Do you realize what we are going to do?"

"Yeah," he replied bitterly, "we're going to screw LTV. And speak-    66
ing of screwing," he continued, "I know now how a whore feels, because
that's exactly what I've become, an engineering whore. I've sold myself.
It's all I can do to look at myself in the mirror when I shave. I make me
sick."

I was surprised at his vehemence. It was obvious that he too had    67
done his share of soul-searching and didn't like what he had found.
Somehow, though, the air seemed clearer after his outburst, and we
began working on the report.

I had written dozens of qualification reports, and I knew what a    68
"good" one looked like. Resorting to the actual test data only on
occasion, Lawson and I proceeded to prepare page after page of elaborate, detailed engineering curves, charts, and test logs, which purported
to show what had happened during the formal qualification tests. Where
temperatures were too high, we deliberately chopped them down a few
hundred degrees, and where they were too low, we raised them to a
value that would appear reasonable to the LTV and military engineers.
Brake pressure, torque values, distances, times—everything of consequence was tailored to fit the occasion.

Occasionally, we would find that some test either hadn't been    69
performed at all or had been conducted improperly. On those occasions,
we "conducted" the test—successfully, of course—on paper.

For nearly a month we worked on the graphic presentation that    70
would be a part of the report. Meanwhile, the fourteenth and final
qualification attempt had been completed, and the brake, not unexpect-
edly, had failed again.

During that month, Lawson and I talked of little else except the    71
enormity of what we were doing. The more involved we became in our
work, the more apparent became our own culpability. We discussed such
things as the Nuremberg trials and how they related to our guilt and
complicity in the A7D situation. Lawson often expressed his opinion
that the brake was downright dangerous and that, once on flight tests,
"anything is liable to happen."

I saw his boss, John Warren, at least twice during that month and    72
needled him about what we were doing. He didn't take the jibes too
kindly but managed to laugh the situation off as "one of those things."
One day I remarked that what we were doing amounted to fraud, and
he pulled out an engineering handbook and turned to a section on laws
as they related to the engineering profession.

He read the definition of fraud aloud, then said, "Well, technically    73
I don't think what we're doing can be called fraud. I'll admit it's not right,
but it's just one of those things. We're just kinda caught in the middle.
About all I can tell you is, do like I'm doing. Make copies of everything
and put them in your SYA file."

"What's an 'SYA' file?" I asked.    74

"That's a 'save your ass' file." He laughed.    75

On June 5, 1968, the report was officially published and copies were    76
delivered in person to the Air Force and LTV. Within a week, flight tests
were begun at Edwards Air Force Base in California. Searle Lawson was
sent to California as Goodrich's representative. Within approximately
two weeks, he returned because some rather unusual incidents during
the tests had caused them to be canceled.

His face was grim as he related stories of several near crashes during    77
landings—caused by brake troubles. He told me about one incident in
which, upon landing, one brake was literally welded together by the
intense heat developed during the test stop. The wheel locked, and the
plane skidded for nearly 1500 feet before coming to a halt. The plane
was jacked up and the wheel removed. The fused parts within the brake
had to be pried apart.

Lawson had returned to Troy from California that same day, and    78
that evening, he and others of the Goodrich engineering department left
for Dallas for a high-level conference with LTV.

That evening I left work early and went to see my attorney. After    79
I told him the story, he advised that, while I was probably not actually
guilty of fraud, I was certainly part of a conspiracy to defraud. He
advised me to go to the Federal Bureau of Investigation and offered to
arrange an appointment. The following week he took me to the Dayton

office of the FBI, and after I had been warned that I would not be immune from prosecution, I disclosed the A7D matter to one of the agents. The agent told me to say nothing about the episode to anyone and to report any further incident to him. He said he would forward the story to his superiors in Washington.

A few days later, Lawson returned from the conference in Dallas and said that the Air Force, which had previously approved the qualification report, had suddenly rescinded that approval and was demanding to see some of the raw test data taken during the tests. I gathered that the FBI had passed the word.  **80**

Finally, early in October 1968, Lawson submitted his resignation, to take effect on October 25. On October 18, I submitted my own resignation, to take effect on November 1. In my resignation, addressed to Russell Line, I cited the A7D report and stated: "As you are aware, this report contained numerous deliberate and willful misrepresentations which, according to legal counsel, constitute fraud and expose both myself and others to criminal charges of conspiracy to defraud. . . . The events of the past seven months have created an atmosphere of deceit and distrust in which it is impossible to work. . . ."  **81**

On October 25, I received a sharp summons to the office of Bud Sunderman. As chief engineer at the Troy plant, Sunderman was responsible for the entire engineering division. Tall and graying, impeccably dressed at all times, he was capable of producing a dazzling smile or a hearty chuckle or immobilizing his face into marble hardness, as the occasion required.  **82**

I faced the marble hardness when I reached his office. He motioned me to a chair. "I have your resignation here," he snapped, "and I must say you have made some rather shocking, I might even say irresponsible, charges. This is very serious."  **83**

Before I could reply, he was demanding an explanation. "I want to know exactly what the fraud is in connection with the A7D and how you can dare accuse this company of such a thing!"  **84**

I started to tell some of the things that had happened during the testing, but he shut me off saying, "There's nothing wrong with anything we've done here. You aren't aware of all the things that have been going on behind the scenes. If you had known the true situation, you would never have made these charges." He said that in view of my apparent "disloyalty" he had decided to accept my resignation "right now," and said it would be better for all concerned if I left the plant immediately. As I got up to leave he asked me if I intended to "carry this thing further."  **85**

I answered simply, "Yes," to which he replied, "Suit yourself."  **86**

Within twenty minutes, I had cleaned out my desk and left. Forty-eight hours later, the B. F. Goodrich Company recalled the qualification report and the four-disk brake, announcing that it would replace the brake with a new, improved, five-disk brake at no cost to LTV.

Ten months later, on August 13, 1969, I was the chief government witness at a hearing conducted before Senator William Proxmire's Economy in Government Subcommittee of the Congress's Joint Economic Committee. I related the A7D story to the committee, and my testimony was supported by Searle Lawson, who followed me to the witness stand. Air Force officers also testified, as well as a four-man team from the General Accounting Office, which had conducted an investigation of the A7D brake at the request of Senator Proxmire. Both Air Force and GAO investigators declared that the brake was dangerous and had not been tested properly. 87

Testifying for Goodrich was R. G. Jeter, vice-president and general counsel of the company, from the Akron headquarters. Representing the Troy plant was Robert Sink. These two denied any wrongdoing on the part of the Goodrich Company, despite expert testimony to the contrary by Air Force and GAO officials. Sink was quick to deny any connection with the writing of the report or of directing any falsifications, claiming to be on the West Coast at the time. John Warren was the man who supervised its writing, said Sink. 88

As for me, I was dismissed as a high-school graduate with no technical training, while Sink testified that Lawson was a young, inexperienced engineer. "We tried to give him guidance," Sink testified, "but he preferred to have his own convictions." 89

About changing the data and figures in the report, Sink said: "When you take data from several different sources, you have to rationalize among those data what is the true story. This is part of your engineering know-how." He admitted that changes had been made in the data, "but only to make them more consistent with the overall picture of the data that is available." 90

Jeter pooh-poohed the suggestion that anything improper occurred, saying: "We have thirty-odd engineers at this plant . . . and I say to you that it is incredible that these men would stand idly by and see reports changed or falsified. . . . I mean you just do not have to do that working for anybody. . . . Just nobody does that." 91

The four-hour hearing adjourned with no real conclusion reached by the committee. But, the following day the Department of Defense made sweeping changes in its inspection, testing and reporting procedures. A spokesman for the DOD said the changes were a result of the Goodrich episode. 92

The A7D is now in service, sporting a Goodrich-made five-disk  93
brake, a brake that works very well, I'm told. Business at the Goodrich
plant is good. Lawson is now an engineer for LTV and has been assigned
to the A7D project. And I am now a newspaper reporter.

At this writing, those remaining at Goodrich are still secure in the  94
same positions, all except Russell Line and Robert Sink. Line has been
rewarded with a promotion to production superintendent, a large step
upward on the corporate ladder. As for Sink, he moved up into Line's
old job.

INSTRUCTOR'S MANUAL
TO ACCOMPANY

# WRITING AND READING ACROSS THE CURRICULUM

FIFTH EDITION

## LAURENCE BEHRENS
*University of California, Santa Barbara*

## LEONARD J. ROSEN
*The Expository Writing Program, Harvard University*

HarperCollins*CollegePublishers*

# CONTENTS

## 7

## THE CASE OF CHRISTOPHER COLUMBUS   9

Contents

# 8

## OBEDIENCE TO AUTHORITY    20

# Contents

# 11
# GENDER STEREOTYPING AND THE MEDIA   *47*

Contents

# 12

## THE BRAVE NEW WORLD OF BIOTECHNOLOGY   57

# 13

## BUSINESS ETHICS   71

# Contents

## A NOTE ON THE QUESTIONS

Students should be advised to read the *headnotes,* to master information about the author and the work that should be incorporated in some form into their syntheses and critiques.

There are two sets of *questions* in each chapter. One set (Review Questions, Discussion and Writing Suggestions) follows each reading selection. Another set (Synthesis Activities) follows the last set of Discussion and Writing Suggestions in each chapter.

The *Review Questions* are factual. Someone who has carefully read the preceding selection should be able to correctly answer these questions in a few sentences. The Review Questions are designed simply to facilitate recall and not to delve into the broader implications of the reading; they may be viewed as a helpful and necessary step in preparing a summary. The *Discussion and Writing Suggestions* are designed to stimulate further thought about the issues discussed in the reading selections; there are no "correct" answers, and answers are not necessarily confined within the boundaries of the reading selection itself. The Discussion and Writing Suggestions, therefore, should be helpful in preparing students to write syntheses or critiques. Or they may serve as alternate writing assignments to the Synthesis Activities. Either used exclusively or in combination with the synthesis activities, they allow the student to develop imaginative, personal, or simply less structured essays.

The *Synthesis Activities* following each unit are designed to give the student practice in the skills that are the focus of Part I.

## SAMPLE SYLLABI FOR *WRITING AND READING ACROSS THE CURRICULUM,* FIFTH EDITION

In these sample syllabi we suggest two of the possible classroom approaches to the material in *Writing and Reading Across the Curriculum,* Fifth Edition. For each week, we offer reading and writing suggestions; instructors will want to modify these to suit the needs of their own classes. In both syllabi, the preliminary material from Part I (summary, critique, synthesis, introductions, conclusions, thesis statements, and quoting and citing sources) has been integrated into the subject units of the anthology (Part II) so that students may reinforce their writing and reading skills as they work on the anthology material. Teachers who wish to loosen some of the rigor of the synthesis approach (based on the questions at the end of each chapter) may want to assign the less academic Discussion and Writing Suggestions following the individual selections.

## Syllabus 1

This syllabus assumes a ten-week course that meets three times per week. Students read the chapters in Part I and complete reading and writing assignments for three chapters in Part II.

### Week 1
A. Read "A Note to the Student." Read pages 3–35, Summary and Paraphrase.
B. Complete the summary assignment on page 229 in Chapter 6. Small group exercise: students compare summaries to determine essential information.
C. Complete the summary assignment on page 230 in Chapter 6. Small group exercise: students compare summaries to determine essential information.

### Week 2
A. Read Chapter 4, Synthesis.
B. Complete the comparison and contrast assignment on page 233 in Chapter 6.
C. Read the selection by Shelby Steele on pages 222–29 in Chapter 6.

### Week 3
A. Read pages 36–43 on writing thesis statements. Draft three theses based on your reading in Chapter 6. Each thesis should be written at a different level of difficulty. Write three outline sketches of the papers that would follow from these working theses. Choose one outline and working thesis and begin the rough draft of a paper.
B. Read pages 43–52 on quoting sources. Scan the readings in Chapter 6 and choose five or six quotations that you feel would reinforce points made in your paper.
C. Rough draft due.

### Week 4
A. Read Newman, "American Nightmares" (Chapter 9, pages 400-409), and write a summary. Small group exercise: students compare summaries to determine essential information.
B. Read Gandhi, "Still the Promised Land," and Derber, "The Good Man Fills His Own Stomach." Write a summary of one article. Small group exercise: students compare summaries to determine essential information.
C. Conference on paper 1, in lieu of class.

### Week 5
A. Read the discussion on critique, pages 73–85. Read Jimmy Carter, "Energy and National Goals" (396–99), and Bill Clinton, "Inaugural Address" (445–49). For each, make notes toward writing a critique.

B. Draft a critique of Derber, Carter, or Clinton.

C. Read Robert Reich (389–95). Read James Q. Wilson (430–38) or Gertrude Himmelfarb (439–44).

## Week 6

A. Final draft of paper 1, due. Read P. J. O'Rourke (419–26), Jerry Sterner (450–58), and Maya Angelou (459–62).

B. Draft three theses based on your reading in Chapter 9. Each thesis should be written at a different level of difficulty. Write three outline sketches of the papers that would follow from these working theses. In each outline, draw on four sources.

C. Choose one outline and working thesis and begin the rough draft of a paper.

## Week 7

A. Conference on paper 2, in lieu of class.

B. Draft of paper 2, due. Copies of paper are due to peer editors *before* class. Peer editors exchange their editing reports in class—and discuss potential revisions.

C. Read Tanith Lee, "When the Clock Strikes" (485–98), and Charles Perrault, "Cinderella" (474–79).

## Week 8

A. Read Jakob and Wilhelm Grimm, "Ashputtle" (479–84); "A Native American 'Cinderella'" (505–507); and "An African 'Cinderella'" (500–505). Assignment for class discussion: select a version of "Cinderella" you would read to your children, and be prepared to defend your selection.

B. Read Bruno Bettelheim, "'Cinderella': A Story of Sibling Rivalry and Oedipal Conflicts" (513–21).

C. Read Madonna Kolbenschlag, "A Feminist's View of 'Cinderella'" (522–28), and Jane Yolen, "America's 'Cinderella'" (528–35). Write a critique of Bettelheim, Kolbenschlag, *or* Yolen.

## Week 9

A. Final draft of paper 2, due.

B. Draft three theses based on your reading in Chapter 10. Each thesis should be written at a different level of difficulty. Write three outline sketches of the papers that would follow from these working theses. In each outline, draw on four sources.

C. Choose one outline and working thesis and begin the rough draft of a paper.

## Week 10

A. Conference on paper 3, in lieu of class.

B. Draft of paper 3, due. Copies of paper are due to peer editors *before* class. Peer editors exchange their editing reports in class—and discuss potential revisions.

C. Semester review. Final draft of paper 3 due during exam period.

## Syllabus 2

This syllabus provides for more reading and writing assignments than Syllabus 1. Naturally, the number of reading and writing assignments may be reduced to suit the needs of the particular class. In any case, we recommend no more than six or seven formal writing assignments during the course of a fifteen-week term. (Even if your students can handle more, you probably can't!) Other assignments may be informal, ungraded writing done in notebooks. These may include journal entries and other pre-writing activities, responses to the readings, or responses to Review Questions and Discussion and Writing Suggestions following the readings. You may wish to schedule regular peer review sessions during which students evaluate each other's rough drafts.

### Week 1
*Reading Assignments*
A Note to the Student
Chapter 1: Summary and Paraphrase

*Writing Assignment*
Summary of Porter, "Perils in the Demand for Biculturalism" (Chapter 1) *or* Kevles and Hood, "The Genetic Labyrinth" (Chapter 12)

### Week 2
*Reading Assignments*
Chapter 2: Thesis, Quotations, Introductions, and Conclusions
Chapter 7: The Case of Christopher Columbus
    Irving and others, "A Man of Great and Inventive Genius"
    Davidson, Sherwood, "Columbus and the Discovery of America"

*Writing Assignments*
Writing suggestions following the readings

### Week 3
*Reading Assignments*
Chapter 3: Critical Reading and Critique
Chapter 7: The Case of Christopher Columbus (cont.)
    Bigelow, "Columbus in the Classroom"
    Columbus, "I Take Possession for the King and Queen"
    Las Casas, "The Destruction of the Indians"

*Writing Assignment*
Critique of Bigelow (or other reading in Columbus chapter)

## Week 4
*Reading Assignments*
Chapter 4: Synthesis ("The Explanatory Synthesis")
  "Citing Sources" section of Chapter 5
Chapter 7: The Case of Christopher Columbus (cont.)
  "Resolution of the National Council of Churches"
  Muldoon, "Should Christians Celebrate the Columbus
  Quincentennial?"
  Sale, "What Columbus Discovered"

*Writing Assignment*
Explanatory synthesis of selected articles in Chapter 7

## Week 5
*Reading Assignments*
Chapter 4: Synthesis ("The Argument Synthesis")
Chapter 7: The Case of Christopher Columbus (cont.)
  Schlesinger, "Was America a Mistake?"
  Harjo, "I Won't Be Celebrating Columbus Day"
  Vargas Llosa, "Questions of Conquest"
  Erdrich and Dorris, "The Indians Encounter Columbus"

*Writing Assignment*
Argument synthesis of selected articles in Chapter 7

## Week 6
*Reading Assignments*
Chapter 8: Obedience to Authority
  Lessing, "Group Minds"
  Milgram, "The Perils of Obedience"
  Reviews of Milgram's experiments by Herrnstein, Baumrind, Meyer

*Writing Assignments*
Explanatory *or* argument synthesis on Milgram experiment
*or* Writing Suggestion following one or two of the readings

## Week 7
*Reading Assignments*
Chapter 5: Research (first half)
Chapter 8: Obedience to Authority (cont.)
  Fromm, "Disobedience as a Psychological and Moral Problem"
  Janis, "Groupthink"

*Writing Assignments*
Begin selecting research topic.
Critique of one article in Chapter 9
*or* Writing Suggestion following one or two of the readings

## Week 8
*Reading Assignments*
Chapter 5: Research  (second half)
Chapter 9: America's Crisis of Confidence
   Reich, "An American Morality Tale"
   Carter, "Energy and National Goals"
   Newman, "American Nightmares"
   Derber, "The Good Man Fills His Own Stomach"

*Writing Assignments*
Select research topic
Critique on one article in Chapter 9
*or* Writing Suggestion following one or two of the readings
*or* Synthesis Activity at the end of the chapter

## Week 9
*Reading Assignments*
Chapter 9: America's Crisis of Confidence (cont.)
   O'Rourke, "Slamming and Jamming"
   Gandhi, "Still the Promised Land"
   Wilson, "The Contradictions of an Advanced Capitalist State"
   Himmelfarb, "A De-moralized Society?"

*Writing Assignments*
Conduct preliminary research for research paper. Critique of one article in Chapter 9
*or* Writing Suggestion following one or two of the readings
*or* Synthesis Activity at the end of the chapter

## Week 10
*Reading Assignments*
Chapter 9: America's Crisis of Confidence (cont.)
   Clinton, "Inaugural Address"
   Sterner, "Other People's Money"
   Angelou, "On the Pulse of Morning"

*Writing Assignments*
Conduct focused research for research paper. Critique of one article in Chapter 9
*or* Writing Suggestion following one or two of the readings
*or* Synthesis Activity at the end of the chapter

## Week 11
*Reading Assignments*
Chapter 12: The Brave New World of Biotechnology
   Huxley, "Brave New World"
   Rifkin, "A Heretic's View on the New Bioethics"
   Gould, "On the Origin of Specious Critics"

*Writing Assignments*
Conduct focused research for research paper. Critique of one article in Chapter 12
*or* Writing Suggestion following one or two of the readings
*or* Synthesis Activity at the end of the chapter

## Week 12
*Reading Assignments*
Chapter 12: The Brave New World of Biotechnology (cont.)
   Bullard, "Killing Us Softly: Toward a Feminist Analysis of Genetic Engineering"
   Jaroff, "The Gene Hunt"
   Watson, "The Human Genome Project: A Personal View"

*Writing Assignments*
Conduct focused research for research paper; develop outline for paper. Critique of one article in Chapter 12
*or* Writing Suggestion following one or two of the readings
*or* Synthesis Activity at the end of the chapter

## Week 13
*Reading Assignments*
Chapter 12: The Brave New World of Biotechnology (cont.)
   Wright, "Achilles Helix"
   Kevles and Hood, "The Genetic Labyrinth"

*Writing Assignments*
Begin drafting research paper.
Writing Suggestion following one or two of the readings
*or* Synthesis Activity at the end of the chapter

## Weeks 14 and 15
*Writing Assignments*
Conferences on research paper
Oral reports/peer reviews for research paper

# 7

# THE CASE OF
# CHRISTOPHER COLUMBUS

The Columbus Quincentennial has come and gone, but the underlying issue of historical re-interpretation remains. This chapter provides students an opportunity to see how historical events and figures undergo reassessment over the centuries and as the temper of the times changes. An adage informs us that history is written by the winners; but in time, the losers (or their descendants) and various interested observers may also get their turn. The demonization of the Yorkist Richard III began with his bloodied corpse on Bosworth Field (and was greatly reinforced and prolonged by Shakespeare's Tudor interpretation); eventually, however, a more balanced interpretation of Richard became possible. In our own country, images of savage "Indians" and peace-loving "pioneers" have pervaded the collective consciousness of several generations of white Americans. Today, in accordance with new perspectives—and newly researched historical information—that view has been turned on its head. Such new perspectives are sometimes derisively labeled "politically correct" by those who charge that the stereotypical heroes and villains have merely traded places. Now, they claim, whites can do no right; people of color can do no wrong. That's not the point, goes the rejoinder: it is, rather, a long history of oppression and brutality by Europeans and their descendants against Native Americans, Africans, and African-Americans.

Is Columbus a hero or a villain? The question itself is simplistic, and finding an answer to it should not be the end product of students' study of this chapter. Rather, we hope that they will gain a greater understanding of how Columbus and his heritage have been viewed by people of various centuries, and by extension, the implications for historical interpretation of these various viewpoints. These articles should provide a rich source of material for synthesis and for critique. The chapter contains a number of primary sources, including selections by Columbus himself and by Bartolomé de Las Casas, a younger contemporary who excoriated the Spanish heritage in the Americas. The two opening selections, accounts of Columbus by Washington Irving and others and a couple of textbook extracts, serve both as secondary sources for their interpretation of Columbus and as primary sources for their exemplification of the uncritical, even adulatory view of Columbus common until very recently. A contemporary high school teacher, Bill Bigelow, reviews the older textbook accounts in "Columbus in the Classroom," explains how they are—in effect—lies, and suggests ways of teaching students the truth. The bulk of the chapter is taken up with opposing views of Columbus and his heritage—an argument occasioned by the five hundredth anniversary of Columbus's landfall on Samana Cay island.

In conjunction with this chapter, you may want to consider asking students to view portions of one or two of the Columbus feature films that were released in 1992: John Glen's *Christopher Columbus: The Discovery* (with George Corraface as Columbus, Tom Selleck as King Ferdinand, and Marlon Brando as the Inquisitor Torquemada) and Ridley Scott's *1492* (with Gerard Depardieu as Columbus, Sigourney Weaver as Queen Isabella, and Armand Assante as Sanchez, one of Columbus's captains). Neither film was particularly well reviewed or commercially successful (though *1492* was praised for its visual qualities), but the two serve to exemplify alternative ways of viewing Columbus. More historically accurate—and arguably more entertaining—is the seven-part PBS series, *Columbus and the Age of Discovery*, available on videotape from PBS and from some rental outlets.

# A Man of Great and Inventive Genius (p. 241)

## WASHINGTON IRVING AND OTHERS

The purpose of this first set of pieces, of course, is to introduce students at the outset of the chapter to the "pre-revisionist" view of Columbus, as it existed until quite recently, particularly at the school (and Columbus Day) level—a view of virtually unvarnished adulation. Students need to understand that the sentiments expressed in these panegyrics were the rule, rather than the exception; only then can they begin to appreciate the depths and vehemence of the anti-Columbus (and anti-European) reaction that swelled to a crescendo before and during the quincentennial.

### Review Questions

1. According to Irving, Columbus was concerned with wealth not because he wanted to become rich, but because he wanted to put the proceeds from his voyages to good use: alleviating the plight of the poor, building churches, and supporting religious crusades.

2. Irving believes that Columbus was unsuccessful as an administrator because it was his misfortune to command "a dissolute rabble" (referring to his crew, rather than the natives) who resented having to submit to law and order.
3. Irving acknowledges that Columbus's practice of enslaving the natives and harshly punishing them for disobedience was a character flaw. However, for Irving this flaw is at least partially excused because such behavior was sanctioned by the custom of the time. Columbus was also driven to such practices because of his enemies and royal greed.

# Columbus and the Discovery of America: The Textbook Version (p. 248)

## WILLIAM M. DAVIDSON
## HENRY NOBLE SHERWOOD

These two passages are typical of the uncritical praise lavished upon Columbus and his expeditions in textbooks until recently. Sherwood's characterization of the Indians is also typical of the tendency to treat the native populations as somewhat less than human, and whose fate at the hands of the Europeans is either unmentioned or (because of their perceived barbarism) tacitly justified. In striving to heroicize Columbus, Davidson neglects to mention that the sailor who first saw San Salvador was cheated out of his promised reward money by Columbus, who later took both the reward and the credit entirely for himself (see paragraphs 2–5 of Columbus's log, later in the chapter).

### Review Questions

1. During his four voyages, Columbus sailed to various islands in the Bahamas, to parts of Central America, and (on his final voyage) to the mouth of the Orinoco, in what is now Venezuela.
2. In Sherwood's account, the Indians are characterized as primitive, superstitious, bloodthirsty (cutting off people's heads and drinking their blood), although awestruck by the Europeans and eager to follow them.

# Columbus in the Classroom (p. 254)

## BILL BIGELOW

This is a highly accessible piece that both responds to the passages that precede it and serves as a good introduction to the "revisionist" articles on

Columbus to follow. Of course, Bigelow is specifically concerned with the case of Columbus; but underlying his article is a set of assumptions about the purpose of teaching that some will agree with and others disagree. Bigelow briefly discusses Paolo Freire, who scorns the "banking method" of education, which treats students as empty vessels to be filled with received wisdom, as opposed to "active participants in their own learning." Only the latter type of education, claim Freire and Bigelow, adequately prepares students to be responsible citizens of a democracy. Others feel that younger students are not yet wise or experienced enough to question authority and must learn the received version of history (or society) before they can question it. Is it worse to grow up learning lies or to grow up not trusting anything or not knowing *what* is true? Bigelow, of course, would reject both alternatives, claiming that the latter was a manifestation of *cynicism*, not *skepticism*. But how, in the classroom, does one establish the difference between skepticism and cynicism—or convince skeptical others that there is a difference?

## Review Questions

1. Bigelow has devised his purse-snatching lesson to dramatize to students the immorality and illegality of taking something from its rightful owner (ownership being established by the fact that labor was required to earn the money to purchase the item) and claiming to own it (or to have "discovered" it) because it has been acquired by force. He has no more right to call the purse his own than Columbus had to claim any part of the Americas for the Spanish crown.

2. Unlike the authors of the "official" textbooks, Koning points out that Columbus and those who followed him enslaved the Native Americans, mutilated and killed them when they didn't bring sufficient gold, and brought about the extermination of much of the indigenous population.

3. In urging his students to question everything in their textbook, Bigelow hopes to encourage them to actively participate in their own learning (rather than to act simply as passive receptacles of information) and, by questioning all authority, to become responsible citizens of a democratic society.

# I Take Possession for the King and Queen (p. 265)

## CHRISTOPHER COLUMBUS

These passages provide Columbus's own account of his expedition (or at least his own account, as transcribed by Bartolomé de Las Casas) and so allow students to begin to make their own judgment about Columbus and his explorations, without the intercession of historians and critics. Note that Columbus combines a fine eye for detail with a mixture of impulses: resourcefulness, calculation, benevolence (when it suits his purposes), arrogance, avariciousness. Since these two selections immediately follow Bigelow, you might ask students whether Columbus's account of his expedition shares the same faults as the textbooks that Bigelow condemns.

## Review Questions

1. Columbus asks certain of his officers (and for good measure, the rest of the fleet) to witness the ceremony in which he formally declares that he is taking possession of the land in the name of the King and Queen of Spain, and in which he displays the royal banner. These testimonies are then set down in writing.
2. Columbus was favorably impressed with the appearance and the gentle disposition of the natives, and his first impulses were of kindness and generosity. He warned his men, for example, not to take anything from the natives without giving something in return. On the other hand, his primary motive for treating them kindly was to more easily facilitate their conversion to Christianity. And, of course, he immediately recognized the potential for using the natives as servants and for selling them as slaves.
3. During his first voyage Columbus was primarily seeking China and Japan and access to their great wealth. He believed he was in the vicinity of China (Cathay) and Japan (Cipango), but was frustrated by his inability to discover large cities or native kings. He was able, however, to find gold and other minerals, numerous spices, fruits, cotton, and, of course, slaves.

# The Destruction of the Indians (p. 274)

## BARTOLOMÉ DE LAS CASAS

Las Casas was the first "revisionist" historian of the Spanish experience in the Americas. This passage serves as the introduction to the rest of his book, which proceeds to give detail after gruesome detail of the atrocities inflicted by the Spaniards on the native peoples they encountered. Las Casas's book prevents critics of the modern revisionists from claiming that they are judging Columbus by contemporary standards that did not apply at the time. Las Casas, a younger contemporary of Columbus, makes the strongest possible case that judged by any standard—including the standards of decent people in the fifteenth century—the actions of the Spanish conquistadors were barbaric and inexcusable. The question remains open as to the extent to which Columbus, an explorer, rather than a conquistador, should share in the condemnation.

## Review Questions

1. According to Las Casas, the inhabitants of the West Indies were a docile, trusting, unavaricious, and generous people. Physically unsuited to hard labor, they lived ascetically.
2. The Spaniards' depredations were motivated by the lust for gold, according to de Las Casas.

# Resolution of the National Council of Churches (p. 278)

This selection is the first of the contemporary broadsides reprinted here against the celebration of the Columbus Quincentary. Obviously, the N.C.C. Resolution harks back to the condemnations of Bartolomé de Las Casas (on which its draws), echoing its themes; but the recent document is more systematic and broadly based, if no more impassioned. This was not the first time that a major Church organization had spoken out on a political and social issue; in 1981, for example, the National Conference of Catholic bishops drafted a much discussed pastoral letter on nuclear war. In both cases, some people felt that Church bodies should confine themselves to religious matters; others felt that it was the Church's duty to speak out on issues of wide public interest. Note the systematic organization of the resolution: following an introductory paragraph the document details the exploitation and destruction of particular peoples; acknowledges the Church's complicity in these crimes; calls on the Church to take general and specific measures both to atone for past sins and to urge new ways of thinking, teaching, and acting, thus moving "forward together as God's creatures honoring the plurality of our cultural heritage."

## Review Questions

1. The authors of the resolution claim that the arrival of Columbus was the beginning of a period of genocide, slavery (of both indigenous people and, later, Africans), theft of natural and mineral resources, "ecocide," and the destruction of native civilizations. The legacy varied, depending upon the geographical area and the peoples affected.
2. The Church bears a large part of the blame for this legacy of destruction because its representatives accompanied the explorers and the conquistadors, implicitly or explicitly sanctioning their activities in the name of the Church. More directly, by insisting on the conversion of "infidels," the Church helped destroy native religions.
3. The resolution proposes that the Church: encourage meditation, prayer, and repentance; use the media to influence its constituency; influence the

treatment of this period in textbooks and other materials; and attempt to strengthen Indian ministries.

# Should Christians Celebrate the Columbus Quincentennial? (p. 283)

## JAMES MULDOON

Obviously, Muldoon's article serves as a counterpoint to the N.C.C. resolution that precedes it. Muldoon analyzes the assumptions behind the resolution and systematically refutes them. (Whether or not he effectively refutes them readers must decide for themselves.) It may be interesting to sound out students on the extent to which they agree with the N.C.C. resolution both before and after reading Muldoon. Caution them not to make up their minds too definitely, however, since further arguments on both sides follow.

## Review Questions

1. Some Hispanic Catholics (and perhaps others) consider the N.C.C. resolution racist because it appears to single out the Spanish for condemnation while lightly passing over the heritage of other nationalities—English, French, Dutch, etc.—who colonized North America.
2. Muldoon believes that the N.C.C.'s treatment of Native Americans is patronizing because it assumes that they lived lives of natural virtue—an odd assumption for a Church founded on the concept of original sin. Muldoon also asserts that even before the Europeans arrived, many non-native peoples kept and traded slaves, and that they engaged in brutal wars against their neighbors.
3. In addition to ignoring the points mentioned above, the resolution understates the attempts of many Catholic missionaries to understand native culture and religion and the attempts of people like Las Casas (who once advocated using black African slaves instead of Native Americans) to help foster peaceful coexistence between natives and Europeans and to publicize the atrocities of the Spanish.
4. The underlying purpose of the N.C.C. resolution, according to Muldoon, is less to criticize the heritage of Columbus than to lay a moral basis for present and future relationships between the largely white First World and the largely non-white Third World. Muldoon has no quarrel with this goal but strongly believes that such moral theories must be grounded upon historical fact.

# What Columbus Discovered (p. 289)

## KIRKPATRICK SALE

Sale's article is a powerful indictment of Columbus and his legacy. He begins with a telling account of exactly how Columbus "discovered" the New World. This negative interpretation has not been disputed by many Columbus scholars; but Sale's next set of arguments—that Columbus was a rootless man, a perfect representative of a rootless society—is unusual, as is the lesson he draws for contemporary civilization. Whether readers agree with Sale's attempt to deconstruct Columbus will depend on their prior political attitudes (and, possibly, their ethnic backgrounds). For some readers, Sale's arguments overreach. Gary Wills, reviewing *Conquest of Paradise* for the *New York Times,* writes:

> . . . in pursuit of this dead-male white whale, Sale has developed fixations of an Arab dimension. It is not enough to say that Columbus initiated genocide for Tainos and Aztecs and Incas; he infected the entire world. . . . He raped the globe. He brought to the idyllic world outside Europe's dread itch for control "an ancient phobia against the forces of nature and the earth goddesses." He had an "ecohybris" to which we can trace all the disturbances of our time. Like all Europeans, he hated forests and mountains. He is the best example of European man's "obsessive will to try 'subduing nature'."

### Review Questions

1. The fact that Columbus claimed the reward money that rightfully belonged to another is for Sale emblematic of the deceit and treachery that marked the initiation of the European incursion into the Americas.
2. For Sale, Columbus was a rootless man "without place"—a man connected not to land, but rather to the sea, to the wooden deck of a moving vessel. The native peoples like the Taino, conversely, were strongly rooted in their local place, and lived in harmony with the land.
3. The pathway to salvation, for Sale, is a deep commitment to, and a resacralization of, *place.*

# Was America a Mistake? (p. 295)

## ARTHUR SCHLESINGER

Schlesinger's article serves as a counterpoint to those by the authors of the N.C.C. resolution, Sale, and Harjo. Without denying the brutality of the

European invasion of the Americas, Schlesinger concludes that the benefits of the European legacy outweigh its crimes. Students might be asked whether one's position on Columbus and his followers depends only on one's point of view (clearly, Harjo would not agree with Schlesinger), or whether it is possible to objectively assess the question. One's assessment may also depend on the language in which the argument is couched: for example, students may wish to compare Schlesinger's tone with that of Michael Berliner (quoted in Discussion and Writing Suggestion #4).

## Review Questions

1. Schlesinger believes that it makes no sense to blame Columbus for the Europeans' often bloody legacy in the New World because had Columbus not made his voyages, others would have within a very short time.
2. While Schlesinger condemns the Europeans for their frequently brutal deeds in the New World, he points out that the extent of their brutality may have been exaggerated by Protestants eager to blacken the Catholics, that Europeans generally behaved no better to their enemies at home, and that the migration of peoples (including Amerindians) and their customs and habits has been a constant of history.
3. Among the benefits of the European legacy, for Schlesinger, are both material and spiritual gains, including "individual dignity, political democracy, equality before the law, religious tolerance, cultural pluralism, [and] artistic freedom."

# I Won't Be Celebrating Columbus Day (p. 299)

## SUZAN SHOWN HARJO

Suzan Shown Harjo offers a Native American perspective on the Columbus dispute, although it ought to be added that she does not necessarily offer *the* Native American perspective. As she notes, the "participation of some Native people [in the Columbus festivities] will be its own best evidence of the effectiveness of 500 years of colonization . . ."; on the other hand, there are those, more militant than she, who would "mark the occasion by splashing blood-red paint on a Columbus statue here or there." Harjo scornfully rejects the suggestion (advanced by Muldoon and others) that the fruits of Western civilization ("pickup trucks and microwave ovens") make up for centuries of oppression. In the second half of her article she suggests ways in which the United States, the Church, and individuals *can* begin to make concrete restitution for the injustices in the past.

## Review Questions

1. For Harjo and many other Native Americans, Columbus means "genocide and ecocide," a brutal system of colonization, the violation of treaties, the destruction of religious freedom, the desecration of holy places, the creation and perpetuation of demeaning stereotypes of Native Americans, and a heritage of poverty.
2. To partially atone for the injustices of the past, Harjo suggests that government and church officials first acknowledge their responsibility for the crimes of their ancestors and then take steps to alter present-day policies that keep Native Americans at the poverty level. This latter step would involve direct financial assistance, particularly to combat disease. Officials should also ensure that treaties are honored. They should take steps to ban demeaning stereotypes (such as Native American names for sports teams and recreational vehicles) and should ensure that teachers tell the truth about the interaction between the colonizers and Native Americans since 1492.

# Questions of Conquest (p. 302)

## MARIO VARGAS LLOSA

Vargas Llosa chooses not to enter into the debate of whether or not the Columbian legacy was a good thing, concentrating instead on a carefully reasoned analysis of why he believes the huge Inca empire collapsed as quickly as it did in the face of a handful of Spaniards. He attributes the Inca defeat to their "beehive" social structure in which all individuals were subordinated to the will of the ruler. The Europeans, on the other hand, represented the civilization in which individual sovereignty was to reign supreme; and it is this freedom of will, Varga Llosa believes, that is most responsible for the great scientific, political, and cultural achievements of Western civilization.

## Review Questions

1. In this article Vargas Llosa is not concerned with the question of whether or not the European conquest of the Americas was a crime; rather, he is concerned with how the mighty empires of the Mexicans and Peruvians could have been defeated by a relatively small band of Spaniards, however well armed.
2. According to Vargas Llosa, the Inca empire was organized like a beehive. Its "vertical and totalitarian structure" prohibited individuals from acting

according to their own independent will. Once the Emperor had been captured, the Incas were left with no source of authority, and so were immobilized and allowed themselves to be slaughtered and conquered. Subsequently, the Incas transferred their absolute loyalty to their new Spanish masters.

3. For Vargas Llosa, European civilization contributed the vital idea of individual sovereignty—the idea that the individual was not simply an insignificant part of a vast social organism, but a separate being from the state, with a legitimate free will. It contributed the idea that state authority derived from the people and not from the ruler. This idea of individual sovereignty also made it possible for individuals (like Las Casas) to question the policies of the state, for individuals to raise questions about (for instance) the brutality of the Spaniards in the New World, questions of a type inconceivable in "antlike societies."

# The Indians Encounter Columbus: "Another Set of Weirdos in an Unpredictable World" (p. 309)

## LOUISE ERDRICH
## MICHAEL DORRIS

Erdrich and Dorris offer a sardonic alternate view to Vargas Llosa's theory about why the Indians succumbed to the Europeans. The novelists postulate that the Native Americans were the sophisticates, the Europeans the barbarians; but the Indians were unable to counter a lethal combination of Spanish high technology, "chutzpah and positive thinking," and germs. The humor and irony through which the dramatic scene (of somewhat jaded instructor and naive students) is rendered serve as a refreshing counterpoint to the moral outrage (on the one hand) or defensiveness (on the other) with which the encounter is frequently described.

# 8

# OBEDIENCE TO AUTHORITY

As with the four earlier editions of *Writing and Reading Across the Curriculum,* this edition includes a chapter on obedience to authority, the central feature of which is the Milgram experiment. New to this edition are selections by Erich Fromm and Irving Janis. The Janis essay, on "groupthink," appeared in the third edition of the text. We reprint it here both because it provides an especially useful way of thinking about Shirley Jackson's "The Lottery" and because it can help students understand the pressures of concurrence-seeking behavior in their own lives. Deleted from this edition is the essay by Larry Crockett.

As in the other editions of WRAC, this chapter asks how much obedience to figures of authority is necessary to ensure social well-being? When individuals refuse to relinquish any of their own autonomy for the welfare of the larger group, anarchy may result. When the state refuses individuals the right to exercise personal freedoms, totalitarianism follows. The balance civilized people try to strike between these extremes is the territory addressed in the selections here. The chapter begins with an essay by novelist Doris Lessing, who sets the issue of obedience in the context of Western civilization's greatly prized individualism. Lessing values individual effort, but she believes us to be "group animals," a characterization that students might find offensive. Lessing cites examples to defend her claim, and she wonders why we do not accept and teach our children to be wary of the obedient streak in our natures. Following Lessing is the chapter's key selection, by Stanley Milgram, a psychologist who in the 1960s conducted experiments to determine the conditions under which people can be expected to obey immoral orders—orders that appear to result in the injury of persons for no justifiable reason. These experiments raised a furor, and we include three reactions of Milgram's work—one clearly favorable (Herrnstein), one unfavorable (Baumrind), and one ambiguous (Meyer). Milgram's account of his experiments, followed by these three reviews, can form a sub-unit on the ethics of experimenting on humans.

Four selections follow those devoted to the Milgram experiment, the first of which, by Gibson and Haritos-Fatouros ("Education of a Torturer"), examines the training of torturers in Greece—a subject safely removed from the lives of students. But then the authors draw a disturbing parallel to rituals of fraternity initiation. Next, Erich Fromm sets the problem of obedience in a psychological and moral context. Fromm is especially good in alerting students to the seductive comforts of obedience. His categorization of some forms of obedience as destructive and others as life affirming can challenge students to make distinctions about forms of obedient behavior in their own lives. A second sub-unit in the chapter would focus on obedience in the lives of students. Readings would include Lessing, Milgram, Fromm, and Gibson and Haritos-Fatouros.

Two selections remain: the essay by Irving Janis, describing his theory of "groupthink," and Shirley Jackson's "The Lottery." Many students will have read Jackson's story, but likely not in the context of the observations by Milgram, Janis, and Lessing. Students may be able to recognize in Jackson's fiction our common and necessary need to obey, taken to hideous ends. Obliquely, disobedience is considered by characters in the story but then is quickly discounted. You might want to ask students how Jackson raises the issues discussed in Milgram, Janis, and Lessing—selections that can form a third sub-unit in the chapter. As in other chapters, literature can serve as a counterpoint to other (more academic) ways of knowing.

# Group Minds (p. 318)

## DORIS LESSING

Lessing provides a good opportunity for students to challenge their own views about individuality. Though we may be "group animals," according to Lessing, when we (Westerners) look in the mirror we see rugged individualists staring back. Students may style themselves as individualists—and if they do, Lessing will raise questions for them. The selection provides a good entry into the discussion of obedience. Lessing sets the stage for the discussion by Milgram.

### Review Questions

1. The flattering portrait: that we, as citizens of a free society, are free to express our opinions and to make individual choices.
2. We in the West are "helpless against all kinds of pressures . . . to conform in many kinds of ways" because we are group-oriented people who would rather betray our own view of the world than risk ostracism. Lessing claims that it is the "hardest thing in the world to maintain an individual dissident opinion" and remain a member of a group.

3. Lessing refers to a group of experiments designed to test the extent to which individuals can stand against group opinion or the opinion of an authority figure.

# The Perils of Obedience (p. 322)

## STANLEY MILGRAM

Milgram's popularized account of his experiments appeared in *Harper's* in 1973. In this piece, Milgram summarizes his experimental findings in what some might term perversely dispassionate detail. Subjects are seen anguishing over the course of action they should take; their moral dilemmas can be quite painful for readers, some of whom will—like Diana Baumrind—question the ethics of an experiment that causes such emotional distress. On finishing the selection, students should be clear on Milgram's principal experimental design and its significant variations.

### Review Questions

1. Obedience is a basic structure of social life. Systems of authority are required by all communal living. Where authority is established, commands must be respected or anarchy will ensue. Social order is premised on a given amount of obedience.
2. The dilemma inherent in the issue of obedience is an ethical one: Why should a person obey a command that conflicts with personal conscience?
3. A summary of the obedience experiments will be based on paragraphs 4–24. Writing a summary will be tricky in that students often have difficulty articulating the difference between the experimenter's confederate—the "learner"—and the actual subject—the "teacher." We suggest that each student write a summary and then work in groups to agree on essential information. Various groups can then share their collective summaries—which, if accurate, will cover the same territory.
4. Experts predicted that virtually all subjects would refuse to continue shocking victims beyond 150 volts. Only 4 percent would continue to 300 volts, and only 0.1 percent would continue to the end of the shock board. As Milgram states, "These predictions were unequivocally wrong. Both college students at Yale and adults from the general population in New Haven were fully obedient roughly 60 percent of the time."
5. Milgram refutes these assumptions, based on an experimental design in which subjects could choose their own levels of shock (as opposed to being ordered to increase shocks incrementally). In this design, subjects overwhelmingly selected lower levels of shock, disproving (according to Milgram) the theory about innate aggressiveness. The second assumption,

that only a lunatic fringe would shock learners with the maximum voltage, is undetermined by Milgram's finding that nearly two-thirds of all subjects administered the maximum shock. See paragraphs 82–86.

6. Arendt contended that the portrayal of Eichmann as a sadistic monster was incorrect—that he was, rather, an uninspired, middle-level bureaucrat simply doing his job. Milgram's conclusions, that nearly two-thirds of his subjects became agents in a destructive process, seem to corroborate Arendt's thesis.

7. See paragraph 108: The essence of obedience is "that a person comes to view himself as the instrument of carrying out another person's wishes, and he therefore no longer regards himself as responsible for his actions." All essential features of obedience follow once this shift has occurred: The "agent" feels responsibility to a figure of authority, not to the victim.

8. When subjects did not need to take direct responsibility for inflicting painful shocks, thirty-six of forty proceeded in their roles—resulting in the learners being shocked at the maximum level.

9. It was a fragmentation of the total human act that led to the atrocities of the concentration camps in World War II. Eichmann shuffled papers and gave orders that he did not have to see carried out; thus he did not face the direct effects of his actions. Persons at the other end of the chain of command, those who actually gassed victims, could claim that they were merely following orders, thus relieving themselves of the responsibility for their acts. With no one person responsible for the total act (i.e., designing and implementing the Final Solution), no one person was forced to live with the ramifications of that act. Every person in the chain had a convenient means of absolving him- or herself of guilt.

# Review of Stanley Milgram's Experiments on Obedience (p. 337)

## RICHARD HERRNSTEIN

Herrnstein discusses the various criticisms of the experiment, especially emphasizing the question of ethics. He argues his position well, and students may want to study how he accepts the reasonableness of opposing views, only to discount them later.

### Review Questions

1. Individuals must relinquish some control in order for the community to function smoothly. "A degree of obedience is the given in human society," says Herrnstein.

**2,3.** The "critical dilemma" is the balance between excessive and reasonable individualism. Americans value a society in which personal conscience is a vital determiner of behavior. But individualism carried to excess ends in anarchy.

**4.** The experiment received mixed reviews because it was so controversial. Some objected because they didn't want to acknowledge new and awful truths about human nature. Others, whom Herrnstein accuses of not wanting to admit their surprise at the experiment's findings, complained that social scientists never discover anything we don't already know. Still others objected to the level of deception practiced in the experiment.

**5.** Herrnstein believes that some deception is unavoidable in social scientific research. Short of placing subjects in hazardous conditions, which would be criminal, researchers can do little but manipulate ordinary experience (by deceiving subjects) in order to observe how human beings behave under stress.

# Review of Stanley Milgram's Experiments on Obedience (p. 342)

## DIANA BAUMRIND

Baumrind's criticism of Milgram's experiment contrasts sharply with Herrnstein's praise. Students should be able to distinguish the two lines of Baumrind's attack—the procedural and the ethical.

### Review Questions

**1.** Subjects might volunteer for an experiment for public reasons: to have a stimulating experience, to acquire knowledge, to make a contribution to science. Subjects might volunteer for a private reason: to be in contact with someone who has psychological training. The subject's characteristic dependent attitude is due to private needs and the experimental condition, which requires following directions.

**2.** A laboratory is not a suitable setting for an experiment in obedience because subjects are inclined to be obedient in unfamiliar surroundings. The subject is also highly suggestable—a function of his or her volunteering. Baumrind claims that the baseline for obedience or suggestability is probably higher in a lab than elsewhere.

**3.** Baumrind gives four reasons why the Milgram experiment was potentially harmful: (a) The experiment could affect the subject's self-image or ability to trust adult authorities in the future. (b) The subject's feeling of personal responsibility for acts committed might not be completely erased after experimentor explains the procedure. (c) The subject might feel as though he's made a fool of himself. (d) The subject might find it difficult to express anger at the hoax.

4. (a) When following orders, subordinates in Nazi Germany had no reason to believe that officers were kindly disposed to them or to their victims. (b) The subordinates followed orders in a social context in which it was acceptable to brutalize others. (c) In Germany, the victims were regarded as subhuman. None of these conditions applied to Milgram's experimental setting.

# Review of Stanley Milgram's Experiments on Obedience (p. 349)

## PHILIP MEYER

Meyer takes issue with Milgram's implied assertation that what the world needs is a more defiant citizenry. One value of having a civil order is to relieve people of agonizing over the many decisions they make daily. Another value is that chains of authority work. A society in which everyone stopped to weigh ethical dilemmas would not function. Meyer touches on a distinction raised by others in the chapter, between code ethics and situation ethics. Students would do well to learn this distinction and then to apply it in their discussions of obedience.

### Review Questions

1. Powers said that as a soldier his job was to follow orders—that superiors were the ones who should concentrate on the larger implications of a military operation.
2. Code ethics: one's system of belief that attempts to resolve all dilemmas before one ever confronts them in fact. A rigid set of ethical rules cannot solve the obedience dilemma because compliance is a situational behavior. The decision to obey or disobey depends (for Meyer) on the nature of the authority requesting the obedience.

# The Education of a Torturer (p. 353)

## JANICE T. GIBSON
## MIKA HARITOS-FATOUROS

Students know about the Holocaust—they know that millions of innocent people died in gas chambers. So widely publicized are these horrors that students may think they have no bearing on the ways people behave today. But as this article shows, obedience to malevolent authority is a problem in more recent times as well, not in only in Greece but potentially everywhere. The conditions that give rise to damaging obedience can be found across the globe—even on college campuses.

## Review Questions

1. Sixteen Rorschach ink blot tests reports were submitted to fifteen experts for analysis to determine whether the experts could distinguish "normal" from "aberrant" traits. Half of the reports were taken from psychological profiles of Nazi officials while the other reports were taken from the profiles of both well-adjusted and severely disturbed Americans. The experts were unable to distinguish the reports of the Nazis from those of the Americans and judged an equal number of both to be well adjusted. The psychologists conclude that torturers are not "freaks"; they are "ordinary people."

2. There are three reasons for obeying or disobeying a figure of authority: First, the person whose family and school lives encouraged obedience will likely be responsive to an authority figure. Second and third—if "binding" experiences (those that made a person feel comfortable when he or she obeyed authority) are more prevalent and more compelling than experiences of "strain" (unpleasant associations with obedience), individuals are more likely to obey an authority figure. The authors expand Milgram's theories to explain how torture can occur over an extended period of time when *no* authority figure exists. The authors believe that "torture can be taught" through techniques that reduce strain and increase binding.

3. Five attributes were sought when recruiting potential torturers: First, hostile attitudes toward potential victims (because of differences in politics, religion, etc.); second, the ability to "keep your mouth shut"; third, the tendency to show aggression; fourth, intelligence and strength; fifth, being "their man"—demonstrating an ability to report on peers and to follow orders blindly.

4. The "Third Wave" was an experiment conducted by a high-school teacher to demonstrate the process by which people might have become Nazis in World War II. Conducted over five days, the experiment enlisted students through binding rituals such as membership cards, chants, slogans, etc.

5. The Stanford prison experiment was a six-day experiment similar in nature to the "Third Wave." College students were divided into two groups, guards and prisoners, and were told to act their respective roles. Though there was no specialized training, "guards" began to exhibit traits—aggression, the will to be powerful—similar to those exhibited by Greek military recruits.

# Disobedience as a Psychological and Moral Problem (p. 361)

## ERICH FROMM

Erich Fromm brings a philosophical and psychological perspective to bear on the question of obedience. Of special importance are paragraphs 13–16, in which Fromm discusses the comforts of obedience and the necessary *discomfort* one must endure in order to disobey. Through acts of disobedience, Fromm suggests, one can become free. The concept may be difficult for students and may be worth class discussion. You might also devote time to clarifying the distinctions Fromm makes among types of obedience, the point of these being that any act ending in submission of one person's will to another's or to a group's is cowardly and destructive; that any act affirming individual will and autonomy (even if this be an act of obedience, though to reason) is an act of freedom. In equating obedience and cowardice, Fromm works especially well in tandem with Lessing, who observes that "among our most shameful memories is this, how often we said black was white because other people were saying it"; and Fromm works well with Shirley Jackson, in whose short story obedience is indeed cowardly and leads to murder.

### Review Questions

1. Civilization begins, according to both the Greek and Hebrew traditions, with an act of disobedience: Adam and Eve eat the forbidden fruit; Prometheus steals the gods' sacred fire and gives it to humans. These first acts of disobedience liberated humans by forcing them to rely on, and discover, their own human powers. Not to have disobeyed would have meant that humans would be in nature as animals are. With no consciousness of their separateness from nature, humans would lose what makes them human.

2. Fromm refers to the disobedience of Adam and Eve (and Prometheus) as the beginning of human history (see above); the end of history may come when some military subordinate obeys orders and pushes a button that will launch a nuclear missile and precipitate a nuclear war.

3. Heteronomous obedience is the subordination of one person's will and authority to another's (or to the state's) and involves an act of submission; autonomous disobedience is the following of one's own judgment and does *not* involve submission but, rather, is an affirmation of the person's moral and logical authority.

4. Authoritarian conscience is the inner voice of paternal or state authority which, through fear and intimidation, demands compliance; humanistic conscience is based on an intuitive sense of what is humane and life sus-

taining (as opposed to that which is inhumane and destructive). Obedience to authoritarian conscience involves submission, since the outer authority has been internalized; obedience to humanistic conscience is, by contrast, an affirmation.

5. Obedience to another person is *not* submission—that is, a negation of personal authority—if the other person is acting in the name of reason and without coercion.

6. See paragraph 13. Fromm's answer to this question is lengthy but can be summarized as follows: Obedience is, psychologically, a pleasant state since the obedient one feels protected by and can identify with the larger power or group. Authorities require obedience for economic reasons: there exist only enough treasures for the few; the desires of the many must therefore be checked, and the mechanism for so checking is obedience—not obedience based on fear (an obedience that can turn at any moment) but on desire. People obey because they wish to gain the psychological comfort of being part of a protected, and sanctioned, group.

# Groupthink (p. 368)

## IRVING L. JANIS

We included this essay in the third edition of *Writing and Reading Across the Curriculum* and reintroduce it here for two reasons: First, Janis provides an unusually effective way of thinking about Shirley Jackson's "The Lottery." Janis also extends the work of Milgram, who studied the concurrence-seeking behavior of individuals, to include such behavior among groups. Students are bound to find themselves in situations in which peers or colleagues generate group momentum for making decisions, perhaps poor ones. In this essay, students may find principles that help them to remain independent, moral thinkers while they function as effective members of groups.

### Review Questions

1. Groupthink is a pattern of conformist thinking among groups that lead to poor, sometimes disastrous, decisions. In paragraphs 11–12, Janis examines "six major defects in decision-making" that contribute to groupthink. (See question 3.)

2. Dissenting opinion, openly expressed, can help group members fight the tendency to reach quick agreement on a potentially poor decision. Without dissension, group members may convince themselves, erroneously, that their decisions are the only reasonable ones.

3. Janis purposefully gave the term *groupthink* a troubling, Orwellian con-notation. He writes that "groupthink refers to a deterioration of mental efficiency, reality testing and moral judgement"—insidious qualities that characterized Orwell's fictional world.

4. In paragraphs 11–12, Janis reviews six defects of thinking that can lead to groupthink: (1) group members do not consider a full range of solutions; (2) once a decision is reached, members do not re-evaluate its efficacy; (3) members do not re-visit earlier, rejected solutions, elements of which might still prove helpful; (4) members do not seek the advice of indepen-dent experts; (5) members respond favorably only to information that agrees with them and reject contrary point of view; and (6) members fail to anticipate problems and set contingency plans.

5. Janis writes that when self-esteem is endangered, particularly by morally questionable decisions, members of a group will bond. They will look to each other, and to their joint decision, as proof that they've made a moral and humane decision.

# The Lottery (p. 373)

## SHIRLEY JACKSON

Shirley Jackson's famous story has both the advantage and disadvantage of being widely known. Students familiar with it will not be shocked, as they were on a first reading, by the violence—and much of the effect of the story will be lost the second time around. Just the same, as they contemplate another reading students can bear in mind Milgram's and Lessing's views on obedience to authority. Why do the people in this town follow through with the ritual year after year? What is the power of ritual in people's lives? What is the force of a community's pressure to conform? Students who have read the story may not have seen any of the reactions it generated on publication. For a sample of these, see the Discussion and Writing Questions.

# 9

# AMERICA'S CRISIS OF CONFIDENCE

This chapter, a total reworking of "Is America in Decline?" from the fourth edition, takes its title from the famous "malaise" speech of 1979, in which President Jimmy Carter asserted that the nation was suffering a crisis of confidence. The Reagan revolution refuted Carter's dour assessment of "our national will." But that same assessment crept back into the nation's consciousness during the 1992 presidential race, which turned partly on the question of whether Americans believed any longer in the American Dream. Working on the belief that the Dream had been lost for many, independent candidate Ross Perot vowed to make it possible for every American to once again achieve and grow prosperous. The theme had appeal, presumably because so many people had lost confidence in their country. In his presidential campaign and inaugural address, Bill Clinton acknowledged these same concerns, leaning heavily on the word *hope* (the name of his hometown in Arkansas). Carter appears to have been ahead of his time in sensing America's crisis of confidence. These days, the crisis is acknowledged openly—and we have taken it as the subject of this chapter.

We begin with Robert Reich's "An American Morality Tale." Though students may not have read this before, the story will nonetheless be familiar, for it is the American success story: modest but dedicated and principled man makes good on his talents, secures his fortune, and becomes a pillar of the community. Students may know the story through adults who overcame hardship and were successful; students may also be striving to achieve for themselves the story's conclusion, and so find themselves in college. In either event, Reich's tale provides a point of reference for the chapter—the idealized version of what America and Americans can be.

If the story of Reich's character, George, embodies important themes in American life, then writers like Katherine Newman, Charles Derber, P. J. O'Rourke, Jerry Sterner, James Q. Wilson, and Gertrude Himmelfarb offer counter themes. Katherine Newman is an anthropologist who has studied the phenomenon of "downward mobility," the disquieting and re-occurring movement of schooled and well-paid professionals *down* the socio-economic ladder, through no fault of their own. Derber and O'Rourke are, perhaps, the most damning in their criticisms of the country: Derber terms America a "wilding" society; O'Rourke, alternately brutal and humorous, describes in vivid, concrete language a raid on a crack house. Himmelfarb believes that with our scrupulous neutrality concerning personal lifestyles we have "de-moralized" the country. She argues that we must take the politically unpopular action of defining—and rewarding—values "implicit in the very idea of a social, a legal and a moral 'order.'" James Q. Wilson, not nearly as alarmed as O'Rourke, Derber, or Himmelfarb, suggests that a certain amount of chaos is to be expected in a system that promotes personal freedoms and democracy. Jerry Sterner takes on many of these issues in his wickedly cynical and funny play, *Other People's Money.*

Offsetting the views of those who dwell on America's troubles are writers who point us back to long-cherished values that we may have violated but that, embraced again, can restore a sense of national purpose. Natwar Gandhi, an immigrant, finds flaws in the pessimism about America's future. He looks to the country's social and political resources and concludes that America is still a "promised land." Bill Clinton's inaugural address is a paean to hope, hard work, and shared sacrifice. Maya Angelou's poem, delivered at Clinton's inaugural, looks to unity and harmony.

The readings in this chapter can help students to examine and articulate their own sense of what it means to be an American. Students themselves are a good barometer of the nation's mood. Are your students confident they will find a job upon graduation? Do they believe this nation's racial problems are intractable? Do they see their fellows, perhaps even themselves, worshipping the "self-indulgence and consumption" that so troubled Jimmy Carter? On completing their reading in this chapter, students might write Carter a letter responding to his speech. (They could send letters care of the Jimmy Carter Library, Atlanta, Georgia 30307-1498.) Carter is a busy man who nonetheless finds time for many things. Perhaps he might reply.

# An American Morality Tale (p. 389)

## ROBERT REICH

Before students read Reich's morality tale, have them write their own parable describing a successful life in America. Students can compare efforts and then read Reich's selection. Rich comparisons can be made that call attention to the assumptions students have about hard work's eventual payoffs. The readings that follow Reich will prove more of a counterpoint if it is the student's own idealized version of America being challenged.

## Review Questions

1. The four themes that emerge from the morality tale are, essentially, the core traits to which Americans aspire—traits perceived both as great strengths and as qualities that set Americans apart from people of other nations: humility, generosity, honesty, and industry.
2. Four American parables are embodied in George's story: "the flight from older cultures"; the "rejection of central authority and aristocratic privilege"; "the lure of the unspoiled frontier"; and "the struggle for harmony and justice."
3. As the four cultural parables illustrate, the aspirations of Americans are more utopian than objective. As such, they are too "vast and vague" to be realistically achieved. The principle that underlies American idealism is that we are, in the absence of "common history," bound together by "common hope."

# Energy and National Goals (p. 396)

## JIMMY CARTER

Jimmy Carter's "malaise" speech provides a thematic backbone for the selections in this chapter. Carter was generally reviled for having attributed blame to others that he should have taken on himself. In effect, he blamed the American people. But just as Carter's reputation has been restored—he is the most respected of our living former presidents—so, too, has his analysis that America is suffering from a crisis of confidence. The fifteen years since Carter delivered the speech seem only to have made more plain the reasons for his lament. For background information on the speech, students should read the general introduction to the chapter.

## Review Questions

1. In paragraphs 4–7, Carter speaks of America's loss of faith in the future. That faith, he suggests, is key to the country's well-being: faith in the future, in the progress of society, "was the idea which founded our nation" and is key to sustaining just about everything Americans accomplish.
2. Carter asks Americans to remember and to recommit themselves to the traditional values associated with family, community, hard work, and democracy. In paragraph 21, Carter speaks of our fathers and mothers who reclaimed the country from Depression, fought and won wars, and forged a new world peace. In the place of traditional values and commitments, Carter saw a worshipping of "self-indulgence and consumption."

3. In paragraph 9 Carter bemoans a statistic that continues to suggest that Americans feel they have no role to play in government: two-thirds of the people do not vote.

4. Political assassinations, the war in Vietnam, and Watergate were three of the main assaults on the confidence that Americans had in their government. (See paragraph 11.)

5. Carter's two paths: self-interest, which will lead to conflict, and "the path of common purpose and the restoration of American values." (See paragraphs 23–24.)

# American Nightmares (p. 400)

## KATHERINE S. NEWMAN

Newman's anthropological study is disturbing precisely because it describes a world in which people play by the rules of hard work and self-sacrifice— and still lose. The implications of this selection are enormous. As Newman shows, it is a myth that one's fortunes are tied exclusively to one's efforts, as the America success story suggests. If larger forces are at work shaping the lives of individuals, then individual commitment and dedication may not— in the end—count for much. Why should individuals sacrifice at all? One way of engaging students in this selection is to ask if they believe David's fate could befall them—or their parents.

### Review Questions

1. David felt isolated and abandoned by his friends with whom he no longer shared common experiences and with whom he could no longer afford to socialize. He felt guilty for having uprooted and disappointed his children, yet frustrated by their resentment since he had made career moves with their welfare in mind. His relationship with his wife became strained, and he became resentful of her accusatory attitude at his continued failure to work.

2. Downward mobility occurs when skilled and well-educated individuals who have attained occupational and financial success suddenly experience a sharp reversal in their fortunes. The phenomenon is an ongoing, rather than an unusual, occurrence that affects over 20% of the American population.

3. The poor tend to originate and to remain at the bottom of the social and economic hierarchy. The downwardly mobile, by contrast, possess the skills, educations, and career experience that once enabled them to achieve (at least) a middle-class life style.

**4.** American culture, which values success and firmly believes in the ability of the individual to control his or her own destiny, is embarrassed by and fears the downwardly mobile. The downwardly mobile are therefore ignored, a tendency reinforced by both research groups and the media, who don't feel the problem is worthy of notice. The public remains uninformed of the problem and believes that individuals who slide *down* the ladder of success are somehow flawed and deserving of their misfortune.

# The Good Man Fills His Own Stomach (p. 410)

## CHARLES DERBER

Derber offers an arresting thesis: that America has become a wilding society and that pursuit of the American Dream, long respected as an agent of progress, has turned pathological. Students may well resist this conclusion and label Derber a cynic. If this is the reaction, you might call for proof that Derber is wrong. For those students who embrace Derber's concept of wilding, you might ask what one does with such disturbing information. (Do we, for instance, give up on America and each turn our separate ways?) You might also ask students to explore the connections between what Derber says we have become and what Jimmy Carter warned we were becoming in his "malaise" speech.

## Review Questions

**1.** The term "wilding" was coined in 1989 after the brutal beating and rape of a woman jogger in Central Park. A group of adolescents viciously attacked the woman; when caught, the youths not only showed no signs of remorse but apparently felt smug satisfaction with their deed.
**2.** According to Derber, wilding—vicious, sociopathic behavior by poor young urban men of color—played directly to the fears of middle-class whites who feared the lawlessness of America's urban centers. The cities were jungles; the youths who roamed the streets, predators. This racial and class view of wilding needed to be expanded, says Derber, after white, middle-class Charles Stuart murdered his pregnant wife for insurance money to open a restaurant. The thread connecting the Central Park attack and the Stuart murder was an all-encompassing self-interest that could justify the most brutal acts of violence. America is becoming a wilding society, suggests Derber. The attitude responsible for wilding cuts across lines of class and race.
**3.** Derber believes that the logic of wilding and the American Dream are connected. He suggests that those who attacked the jogger in Central

Park were locked out of the American Dream, whereas Charles Stuart, in an attempt to realize his American Dream, murdered his wife. Both actions were prompted by self-interest. In "unsentimental" terms, says Derber (who quotes anthropologist Colin Turnbull), the logical extension of the American Dream ends in a "a conglomeration of individuals of all ages, each going his own way" (see paragraph 19). The Dream has prompted in Americans an insatiable appetite for success. An "inability to satisfy [such a] chronic gnawing hunger is fertile breeding ground for a culture of wilding." (See paragraph 26.)

4. The Ik, a dispossessed people living in Uganda, are according to anthropologist Colin Turnbull "a loveless people" who fend only for themselves, without one thought for communal welfare. Derber uses Turnbull's work and sociologist Ashley Montegue's commentary on that work to illustrate a wilding society that is "dying because [the people] have abandoned their own humanity." Derber points to the Ik in a cautionary way, using the sociopathic mechanisms that are undermining that culture to analyze our own. The title of Derber's chapter comes from the "Ik concept of goodness [marangik], which means filling one's own stomach."

5. See paragraphs 25–27. Derber, citing Christopher Lasch, suggests that narcissism in the 1970s was a "mushrooming psychic cancer" that predisposed Americans to thinking of themselves to the exclusion of others. The Reagan and Bush administrations promoted the ideological line that individual initiative and self-interest (read selfishness) was good and ultimately productive for the country. These converging attitudes, one personal and psychological and the other national and ideological, helped to create a climate in which wilding could exist.

# Slamming and Jamming (p. 419)

## P. J. O'ROURKE

P. J. O'Rourke takes an irreverent, caustic, and frequently humorous view of American government in his best selling *Parliament of Whores*. Running through much of his humor is an impatience with government bureaucracy and Washington's inability to deal with the crippling problems of our times. In this selection, excerpted from his chapter entitled "Poverty Policy: How to End Privation," O'Rourke describes a raid on a South Bronx crack house.

To O'Rourke, the Guardian Angels are fighting to keep hope alive and drug-related misery away from depressed neighborhoods in America's urban centers. O'Rourke favors such action, even if he does find considerable irony in it. Students should find the descriptions vivid—and quick—reading, and they will be inclined to discuss the crack raid as a raid, in all its dramatic detail. Having discussed the raid, you might try to work the discussion back to the crisis of confidence that is the focus of this chapter. Questions like the following might help: "Is vigilantism a good thing for this country?" and "What does vigilantism suggest about people's confidence in their government?"

O'Rourke, who spends part of his time chronicling the despair among the poorest of Americans, follows Newman, who investigates despair among the middle class. Both of these readings can be played off Carter's "malaise" speech and contrasted to the hopefulness implicit in Reich's morality tale of George.

# Still the Promised Land (p. 427)

## NATWAR M. GANDHI

Robert Reich wrote that the aspirations of Americans were more utopian than objective. Natwar Gandhi would agree, and he believes the pessimism of American commentators is a function of their idealism. Compared to an ideal, the real world always suffers. As an immigrant, Gandhi does not take freedom or national achievement for granted. His appreciation for this country implicitly challenges native-born naysayers to re-examine the basis of their pessimism. Why should it take a relatively new arrival to America to appreciate its political system and economic prosperity?

### Review Questions

1. Keenan and Wilson are pessimistic because the real America falls short of the country they grew up believing in. We are not living up to our ideals. Keenan and Wilson focus on how far the U.S. has to go, rather than on how far it has come.
2. Gandhi measures America's accomplishments with such yardsticks as race relations—and in these terms he does not see America in decline.
3. Given the current rates of immigration and current U.S. birth trends, the U.S. population will no longer be represented by a white majority in fifty years. White birth rates have declined relative to that of other racial groups. Asians have replaced Europeans as the most common U.S. immigrants.
4. As an immigrant from a country whose citizens do not enjoy privileges common in the U.S., Gandhi can appreciate the American dream—however unrealistic it may have become. Americans, who have always known these privileges, are more apt to complain.

# The Contradictions of an Advanced Capitalist State (p. 430)

## JAMES Q. WILSON

While acknowledging that serious problems exist in this country and that Americans have good cause to be grumpy, James Q. Wilson advises us to "cheer up." His reason: messy as our system of government is, no other system could do a better job. Students might be willing to debate whether Wilson's position, extended, becomes an argument for complacency. That is, if this (i.e., our present messy system) is as good as we're likely to get, we should not try to reform the system even if it is confused, petty, incompetent, and gridlocked. In his conclusion, Wilson sets America's present grumpiness in an international, political context that is calculated to make people feel happier about living in America. Finally, students reading this article should be able to restate the "contradiction" that Wilson refers to in his title. Reading carefully, students should be able to see that the contradiction is implied in how Wilson sets up his discussion of prosperity, freedom, and democracy.

### Review Questions

1. See paragraph 14. Prosperity enabled middle-class Americans to leave the city for small towns; when the middle class left, so did "the system of informal social controls" that helped to maintain order, and so did the jobs. Companies moved to where the work force was, and the city eventually was left impoverished. Also, criminals had, through drug money, become prosperous enough to lose interest in earning a livelihood through legitimate work and thus were deprived of exposure to normalizing social influences.
2. See paragraphs 23–25. Restraints on the behavior of police and teachers have limited their ability to deal (as once was possible) swiftly and authoritatively with disorderly people.
3. According to polls, says Wilson, Americans want the government to spend more but tax less—without deficit financing. The contradiction of this stance is avoided when we say: "Cut waste and fraud." In fact, Wilson says, we are not particularly well equipped to make tough choices about spending because of the Constitution, which is designed to put up barriers to quick (and authoritarian) decision making. The electoral process in America and the federal government is, by design, messy and open and contentious.
4. Participatory democracy results in a highly visible, and much detested, "confusion, pettiness, incompetence, and gridlock." That the causes

and effects of these problems are the same—prosperity, freedom, and democracy——account for the "contradiction" of advanced capitalism that Wilson refers to in his title.

5. Wilson says that we have a right to be grumpy, given the inherent messiness of American participatory government. But Americans should cheer up, since "there is no system for governing a large, free and complex society such as ours that is likely to do much better or make you less grumpy."

# A De-moralized Society? (p. 439)

## GERTRUDE HIMMELFARB

Gertrude Himmelfarb provides a moral perspective on America's crisis of confidence, in contrast to Wilson's political perspective. In this article, Himmelfarb develops an argument that liberals abhor: the moral content of our culture *is* a matter for public discourse and should explicitly be an element of public policy. Students may have a difficult time understanding the liberal position on morality; it is probably worth giving some attention in class to paragraphs 9–14 so that students can understand—and respond to—the position that Himmelfarb is rejecting. One hopes that students will want to debate the extent to which morality should be a part of public discourse and public policy. The problem of deciding what constitutes morally acceptable behavior is difficult at best; you might set up a debate in class or have students take opposing sides in written arguments.

### Review Questions

1. By "de-moralized," Himmelfarb means that we have been so scrupulously neutral in matters of morality, refusing to condemn lifestyles that are out of the mainstream, that we have created a society that lacks a moral base, a condition in which citizens (and one would suppose youths, especially) do not know right from wrong. Intractable social problems, like poverty, have a moral component, says Himmelfarb; by ignoring this component in the name of value-free government, we have harmed the very people we had hoped to help.

2. Himmelfarb wants to distinguish between events that are cause for real alarm and what she terms the sentimental, emotional discontent expressed by Carter and others. In paragraph 13, Himmelfarb claims that the current malaise is not a product of mere irritation or trendy longing for fulfillment but rather a product of a legitimate concern that our society is now "de-moralized"; our legal system, ineffective; our social order, "disordered."

3. In accepting the depressing social statistics that Himmelfarb points to in paragraph 7, liberals would have to contradict a cherished belief ("the prevailing American ethos") that "material and moral progress are the necessary by-products of a free society" (paragraph 9).

4. In Victorian England and nineteenth-century America, morality was both a "natural part of social discourse" and a "conscious part of social policy" (paragraph 10). A century ago, on both sides of the Atlantic, people *expected* conversations and public policies to deal with moral matters. Himmelfarb attributes many of our nation's problems to the fact that, with our liberal leanings, we have severed the moral element from our national life.

5. Today, liberals are loathe to assume that their value system is inherently better than anyone else's; accordingly, they are inclined to morally neutral statements like "That behavior is different from ours," as opposed to "That behavior is wrong." The consequence of rejecting morality, says Himmelfarb, is today's moral relativism (the belief that all values are equally legitimate) and a refusal to attach any moral preconditions to a beneficiary's accepting federal money. This, says Himmelfarb, damages the very people the government wants to help.

# Bill Clinton's Inaugural Address (p. 445)

Because it was delivered so recently, Bill Clinton's inaugural address will be fresh in the minds of many students, who will have watched the inaugural ceremonies. The speech, here, may prove the first time students have seen it in print and the first time they will have the opportunity to read it closely. Certainly Clinton's inaugural address is the most optimistic selection in this chapter. Along with Natwar Gandhi and Maya Angelou, Clinton counterbalances the cynical and despairing tones of Himmelfarb, Derber, O'Rourke, and Sterner and converts the chapter's coverage of America's crisis of confidence from a dirge into a real debate. No less than others, Clinton acknowledges the problems facing this country; but unlike others, he will not give in to despair. Clinton certainly suffers from no crisis of confidence; and if he has his way, neither will America. Throughout the presidential campaign he made metaphorical use of his hometown—Hope, Arkansas. The theme of hope, mixed with hard work and shared sacrifice, runs strong in Clinton's inaugural address. The predictive power of his optimism will be measured, at least in part, by its reception among college students—who upon graduation face the immediate challenge of finding meaningful, well-paying work. It should be illuminating to have students compare their reactions to the inaugural address with their reactions to the bleaker, more cynical views of writers like O'Rourke and Himmelfarb.

# Other People's Money (p. 450)

## JERRY STERNER

Students will enjoy reading this excerpt from Jerry Sterner's long-running play, *Other People's Money*. (The movie based on the play, in which Danny DeVito and Gregory Peck play the parts of Garfinkle and Jorgenson, can be rented at most video stores.) We include this particular excerpt from Sterner's play because we think the speeches by Garfinkle and Jorgenson lay bare competing values that underlie the discussion in this chapter. If Americans have fallen from grace, if we have lost our sense of moral and political direction, from what prior state have we fallen? What values were implicit in that prior state? To what extent were those values part of a mythology that should, at the end of the twentieth century, be abandoned? It is to Sterner's credit that the speeches by Jorgenson and Garfinkle are treated evenly. As readers (and as viewers of the movie), we were convinced by each speaker in turn: we enjoyed having the stockholders' decision placed in our lap, and we hope students will find the speeches similarly engaging. These are some of the questions that occurred to us: What responsibilities does a company have beyond making a profit? What do the values that Jorgenson espouses—the values of production, community, and hard work—have to do with the values that Carter calls our attention to in the "malaise" speech? If Jorgenson's company is losing money, and if it is being kept afloat by subsidiaries, should (must) the company be closed? With what action is the greater good served? Jimmy Carter warned of a nation in which people would selfishly guard their own interests. Does Lawrence Garfinkle represent the epitome of that selfishness, pitting as he does the scruples of stockholders against their pocketbooks?

# On the Pulse of Morning (p. 459)

## MAYA ANGELOU

Angelou composed "On the Pulse of Morning" at the invitation of President Clinton, and read the poem immediately after Clinton delivered his inaugural address. Given the occasion of its writing and delivery, "On the Pulse of Morning" is a poem *about* America and the crisis of confidence taken up by the various writers in this chapter. It is also a poem about the survival of our species and of the planet. Angelou does a marvelous job of acknowledging the trouble of these times and setting them in the sweeping context of life itself on Earth. We humans are a species, she says, as the mastodon was a species; and we, like it, could become extinct. Unlike the mastodon, however, we have some choice in the matter. By embracing change (a word important to Bill Clinton), by learning from the past, we can unify ourselves and live harmoniously. You might ask students to compare and contrast the poem and Clinton's inaugural address. Both writers point to better times. Finding a way from a troubled present to a happier future is the business at hand, and Clinton in his pragmatic way and Angelou in her metaphorical way both point a course.

Along with Natwar Gandhi and Bill Clinton, Angelou counterbalances the darker, more cynical views of America that students have read in this chapter. Working with these three pieces, students can mount a strong argument against cynicism, if they choose.

# 10

# FAIRY TALES: A CLOSER LOOK AT "CINDERELLA"

Many feel that fairy tale literature should be off limits to aggressive, critical inquiry. "A Closer Look at 'Cinderella'" presents students with the opportunity to challenge this view. The readings here raise several questions: to what extent does critical inquiry illuminate? obscure? make something of nothing? In attempting to answer these questions, students will themselves invoke critical distinctions—perhaps similar to those we've included here: "Cinderella" may be approached as literature (Thompson and Yolen), as an occasion for psychological inquiry (Bettelheim), and as an example of gender-role typing (Kolbenschlag). By first reading the eight variants of "Cinderella," students will be able to make their own critical observations of the tale and then compare these with the observations made by professionals.

This chapter is a slightly revised version of that appearing in the fourth edition of *Writing and Reading Across the Curriculum*. The revisions have been limited to the variants of "Cinderella" that students will read. Gone are the versions by Basile and Gardner. New to this edition are "A Native American 'Cinderella,'" "An African 'Cinderella,'" and a most unusual literary reworking of the tale that retains important structural elements of earlier versions: Tanith Lee's "When the Clock Strikes," in which the story's main character is a witch. We begin with a general introduction to fairy tale literature by Stith Thompson. The variants of "Cinderella" follow—the modern variants (which can be read as a subunit) being Disney, Sexton, and Lee. The chapter ends with appraisals of the story by Bettelheim, Kolbenschlag, and Yolen.

The selections by Bettelheim, Kolbenschlag, and Yolen are each complex enough to make summaries worthwhile. The variants of the story lend themselves quite naturally to comparison and contrast. Opportunities for critique and argument abound, as students respond to the three critiques of "Cinderella."

# Universality of the Folktale (p. 469)

## STITH THOMPSON

This selection introduces Thompson's book *The Folktale*. Thompson is a much-acclaimed folklorist and author of a six-volume *Motif-Index of Folk Literature* (1932–37, 1955–58, 2nd ed.). He concentrates here on the definition and history of the folktale, so the piece serves as an excellent overview to the chapter. We recommend that students read it directly before or after the variants of "Cinderella," and certainly before any of the critical examinations (namely, Bettelheim on "Oedipal Conflicts," Kolbenschlag, and Yolen). The final paragraph, and especially the final sentence, of Thompson's selection may be of special interest in establishing a mood of acceptance, or at least tolerance, of the various analyses of "Cinderella."

### Review Questions

1. The storyteller is treasured by societies for providing information and amusement; inspiration (both secular and religious); and stimulation, as well as escape from routine.
2. Thompson claims that the most significant difference between the folktale and modern fiction is the traditional nature of folk material—tales that are not original in our sense of the word but that are passed along skillfully, bearing the authority of great age and constituting an act of conservation and reverence. Moreover, a folktale is meant to be listened to, not read. See paragraph 9.
3. Religion involves an attempt to understand personal, tribal, and cosmic origins; folktales are concerned generally with the "olden days." Their own origins are prehistoric, as are religion's.
4. The same tale is often dispersed widely throughout different parts of the world.

# Eight Variants of "Cinderella" (p. 473)

We have placed the Perrault and Grimm versions of "Cinderella" first (not in chronological order), since these will be the most familiar to students. Five variants of the tale—Perrault, Grimm, the Native American and African versions, and Tuan Ch'êng-shih—can be compared and contrasted as the so-called "traditional" renderings of "Cinderella." The three explicitly literary versions, by Disney, Sexton, and Lee, might be compared as modern renderings. Comparisons and contrasts can obviously be drawn between the traditional and modern versions, with students arguing their preferences.

This chapter presents students with an excellent opportunity to practice their own analysis of primary material before reading the analyses of professional commentators.

# "Cinderella": A Story of Sibling Rivalry and Oedipal Conflicts (p. 513)

## BRUNO BETTELHEIM

Bettelheim's analysis of "Cinderella," excerpted from *The Uses of Enchantment,* is one of the longer and more complex selections in the text. The author's psychoanalytic premise is summarized in Discussion Question 2, and students may profit by reading this question as they prepare for summaries or class discussions. The principal assumption—that complex unconscious and subconscious mechanisms explain human behavior—may be unacceptable to some students, especially as it is applied to the apparently innocent "Cinderella." Bettelheim's intricate analysis can demonstrate how arguments follow from their premises and how, if students want to object, they should examine premises and the consistency of their application.

### Review Questions

1. Living among the ashes symbolizes sibling rivalry and Cinderella's debased condition.
2. The stepsisters in "Cinderella" may be a device "to explain and make acceptable an animosity which one wishes would not exist among true siblings."
3. A child experiencing sibling rivalry may feel that a parent is overlooking his or her welfare for the welfare of another child; the child may also feel persecuted at the hands of a sibling and believe that the parent is indifferent to this persecution.
4. Through Cinderella's triumph, the child gains "exaggerated hopes for his future which he needs to counteract the extreme misery" of sibling rivalry.
5. The fantasy solution to "Cinderella" is appropriate for children in that children do not believe they can actually reverse their fortunes; children also gain relief through fantasies of glory and domination over their siblings.
6. The child who identifies with Cinderella reasons that since Cinderella's goodness is eventually acknowledged by all—so too, one day, will his or her goodness be acknowledged.

7. By comparison with the vileness of the stepmother and stepsisters, the child feels his inadequacies and wrongdoings are minor. The vileness of these characters also justifies whatever harm is done to them in the story.

8. Cinderella's paradox is that she believes herself to be superior to her step-mother and stepsisters but at the same time feels that she deserves her degraded state.

# A Feminist's View of "Cinderella" (p. 522)

## MADONNA KOLBENSCHLAG

This feminist critique of "Cinderella" should stir discussion. Kolbenschlag is interested in the sociological effects of fairy tales and the ways in which they transmit cultural values. Those who accept a subservient role for women will doubtless disagree with the analysis—perhaps on the grounds that, yes, fairy tales do transmit cultural values and, in this case, correct ones; perhaps on the grounds that all intricate analyses of fairy tales lack validity (i.e., the argument that fairy tales are entertainment, nothing more). (On granting permission to use her essay, Kolbenschlag stipulated that there be no Review or Discussion and Writing Questions.)

# America's "Cinderella" (p. 528)

## JANE YOLEN

In this article, Yolen distances herself from the views of feminists such as Kolbenschlag, and students should be able to say how. The author's condemnation of Disney's "Cinderella" may throw down a challenge to students who are fond of this variant. One hopes a discussion will ensue in which students reread the variants and argue for or against Yolen's analysis.

### Review Questions

1. Yolen contends that "Cinderella" is a story not of rags to riches, but of riches recovered and a stripping away of disguises. Cinderella is rich in spirit, deserving of praise all along.

2. Yolen believes that the feminist attack on "Cinderella" should be aimed at the American, candied versions of the tale. Older European and Oriental versions, she feels, feature a more resilient, resourceful heroine.

3. In Walt Disney's version of "Cinderella," the heroine is denied her "birthright of shrewdness, inventiveness, and grace under pressure."
4. We each have been Cinderella in that as children we have felt mistreated and forsaken. We have realized that action and intelligent decisions were needed to solve difficult problems.

# 11

# GENDER STEREOTYPING AND THE MEDIA

The present chapter on gender and the media is much changed from its earlier incarnations in the first, third, and fourth editions of *Writing and Reading Across the Curriculum*. This chapter has a two-part organization, reflecting the two parts of its title. The first four selections are devoted to the consequences of gender stereotyping. The second five readings focus on the ways in which gender roles are portrayed in the media. Subunits of the chapter could be based on either set of readings.

At the age of eighteen, first-year college students are making the transition from late adolescence to young adulthood, a transition fraught with questions of gender: Now that they are preparing to enter the working world of adults, how will students identify themselves as adult men and women? How will gender roles explored in dating relationships carry over into marriage? How readily will students acknowledge that their images of masculine and feminine are culturally determined?

Masters and Johnson (with Kolodny), the lone holdover from the fourth edition, open the chapter with an overview of gender-role socialization, birth through adulthood. Students might be tempted to think of Masters and Johnson as an "objective" view on gender identity. The tone may be social scientific and therefore may sound impartial and authoritative. Yet social science has its own assumptions, of course, and the chapter provides occasions for playing the "truths" of science off against the truths of fiction and reflection-by-essay. You may want to ask students, for instance, what they learn from Masters and Johnson, as compared to what they learn from the first-person accounts of gender stereotyping found in Friedan and Farrell or from the journalistic investigations of Faludi.

Implicitly, the chapter asks students to do something quite difficult: to step back from the routine of everyday life and to observe what it means to be a young man or woman—and to understand how these meanings can be influenced by the media: Katha Pollitt, Ian Harris, Matthew Gilbert and Vito

Russo investigate and comment on media depictions of masculinity and femininity. R. Stephen Craig shows students how a sociologist examines the ways in which gender is constructed in television commercials. His article suggests criteria that students can use in analyzing gender stereotypes in commercials. And the short-story writer Sandra Cisneros explores how one particular media myth, the Marlboro Man, embodies certain expectations of masculinity that no one man could fulfill.

The chapter is meant to engage students, but in order for them to become engaged they must be willing to debate themselves, the authors of these selections, and their fellow students. In the classroom, discussions on gender often degenerate into a series of unexamined assertions about the way men and women are or should be. The chapter offers an opportunity to test these assertions, to push students into examining the beliefs that underlie traditional views of gender-role typing.

# Gender Roles (p. 543)

## WILLIAM H. MASTERS
## VIRGINIA E. JOHNSON
## ROBERT C. KOLODNY

The selection that opens this chapter reviews patterns of gender-role stereotyping from birth through adulthood. As would be expected from sex researchers Masters, Johnson, and Kolodny, the tone and method of this selection is social scientific. The authors carefully cite research whenever they make broad claims. You might want to ask students to compare the tone of this piece with that of other selections in the chapter that are based on personal reflection.

## Review Questions

1. Traditionally, American men are seen as "strong, courageous, self-reliant, competitive, objective, and aggressive." Women are seen as "intuitive, gentle, dependent, emotional, sensitive, talkative, and loving."
2. Earlier assumptions underlying psychological testing of gender role characteristics tended to view masculine and feminine traits on a single scale: one was judged either more or less masculine or feminine. A male who tested out of the masculine range or female out of the feminine were seen as "less emotionally adapted" than others. More recent tests assume that the classically gender specific traits (see Review Question 1) coexist within the same individual, who may exhibit masculine attributes such as aggressiveness in one sphere of activity but feminine ones (e.g., tenderness) in another.

3. The student will need to write a summary of the authors' sections on patterns of gender-role socialization at birth and infancy, in early childhood, in the school-age years, in adolescence, and in adulthood. The point of the summary should be that patterns of gender-role socialization are laid down at the earliest stages of development. Through toys, television, dress, behavior of parents, choice of appropriate sports, and more, gender-appropriate behavior is clearly communicated in our culture.

4. The authors cite a variety of evidence to suggest that women are discriminated against: intellectually, with expectations that attractive women cannot be bright as well; financially, with women being paid less than men for comparable work; professionally, with women having greater difficulty than men reaching senior executive positions; and sexually, with women being touched, spoken to, or joked about in offensive ways. The authors do feel that times are changing; they cite examples of women entering traditionally male jobs and seeking or having achieved high public office or high-status occupations.

# The Problem That Has No Name (p. 559)

## BETTY FRIEDAN

Students reading from this famous opening to *The Feminine Mystique* will discover something of Friedan's rhetorical powers. Her book had a monumental impact on feminism in the 1960s and beyond, and we include an excerpt here both to introduce students to what has become an important document and to establish a baseline of stereotyped gender roles. (Warren Farrell's "Ralph's Story" establishes this baseline for men.) Later in this chapter, Susan Faludi, Katha Pollitt, R. Stephen Craig, and Ian Harris will argue that these traditional roles are very much with us and exert a great deal of influence.

### Review Questions

1. Friedan devotes the first eleven paragraphs of her essay to defining the mystique of feminine fulfillment. The mystique is an assumption that women should have no higher aim in life than to be good homemakers, good mothers, and good wives. Happiness for a woman comes through fulfillment of a culturally defined role, not through a woman's individual efforts to seek happiness in the professions, the academy, or the arts.

2. The "problem that has no name" was the psychological and spiritual emptiness many women felt at having yearnings that could not be satisfied in their roles as homemakers and wives.

3. As Friedan explains it, "the problem" is the psychologically damaging corollary to the feminine mystique. If the culture teaches that women should be satisfied by their traditional role, then women who are *dis*satisfied are afraid to speak, thinking their unhappiness is a personal problem, a neurosis. Friedan was largely responsible for naming the growing discontent among women and suggesting that the problem was not personal but cultural.

4. Friedan uses these first-person narratives both to help define the problem with no name and to bolster her case that the problem is real and a corollary to the mystique of feminine fulfillment. Friedan's two rhetorical strategies—her third-person overview of the problem and her use of first-person narratives—combine to create a forceful document. The desperation that Friedan describes is not abstract; it is real, and it is in many cases devastating.

# Ralph's Story (p. 567)

## WARREN FARRELL

Warren Farrell, a widely read writer about the men's liberation movement, recounts the story of man he calls "Ralph," who at his wife's insistence attends a men's group headed by Farrell. An unwilling participant at first, Ralph finally speaks—to share the discovery that the masculine role he has played so adroitly as a high-powered lawyer has left him a stranger to himself, his wife, and his children. The discovery that he had let stereotyped roles of masculinity so define him is devastating to Ralph. Significantly, Farrell has re-created this recollected story in the first person and has told it from Ralph's point of view. We include the piece in the chapter to offer a baseline of male stereotyping—a male counterpart to Friedan's problem that has no name. As a lawyer, Ralph is empowered in a way that the women Friedan writes of are not; but it is also true (and this is Farrell's reason for telling Ralph's story) that men suffer the consequences of stereotyping as surely as women do.

## Review Questions

1. The problem is best expressed in two paragraphs, 27 and 33. First, Ralph says that he worked as hard as he could and became somebody he didn't like. And then he remarks that all his life he *succeeded,* he played by the rules—did everything that was expected of a man. As a reward for his efforts, he alienated his wife and sons. Ralph is angry and embittered as he makes this discovery.

2. Initially, Ralph gave up his love of baseball in order to secure the fortunes of his future family. In college, he realized that to "really stand out" he would need to get good grades and enter a well-respected graduate school, which he did. He decided on "missionary law" but then practiced corporate law instead, promising himself that this experience would make him a better social-work lawyer. Rather than leave corporate law after two years to pursue his original legal interests, Ralph stayed and set his sights on a junior partnership—and then a senior partnership, and with each passing year retreated from his original intention of helping "people who most needed it."

3. Ralph showed love to his wife through working relentlessly at his profession in order to secure promotions. His wife, however, wanted Ralph's time and more direct involvement with her and with their children. See paragraphs 16–22.

# Blame It on Feminism (p. 572)

## SUSAN FALUDI

Susan Faludi directly challenges the argument that feminism has been bad for women. In this first chapter from her widely read *Backlash: The Undeclared War Against American Women,* Faludi claims that whatever partial gains were won during the sexual revolution are now under assault from the government, industry, and media—forces whose backlash against feminism is based on the fear that equal status for women severely threatens the status quo. As other articles in this chapter will suggest, our culture boasts of changed gender role assignments and talks of liberation, but a great many of our assumptions about gender are the same ones Friedan targeted thirty years ago in *The Feminine Mystique.* These same assumptions concerning the proper roles of men and women fuel what Faludi sees as the current backlash against feminism.

### Review Questions

1. Over the past decade, critics have claimed that women "are unhappy precisely *because* they are free. Women are enslaved by their own liberation" (paragraph 6).

2. Despite the "good fortune" American women are supposed to enjoy at the end of the twentieth century, thanks to the advances made possible by the women's movement, women are despairing. Critics argue that "equality is to blame." Faludi challenges the critics and says that, in fact, women have not achieved equal status in pay, job possibilities, family leave, reproductive rights, or education. *Inequality* is the problem (see

paragraphs 24–29). Despite some high-profile gains, most women are irritated that men resist changes in traditional gender roles.

3. See paragraphs 8–13. Newspaper and magazine writers, psychologists, politicians, academics, and some feminists have indicted feminism for the parade of problems besetting women: lack of men, depression, declining fertility rate, family upheaval, and identity crises. These critics blame the women's movement for helping to create a culture in which self-reliant and high-powered women feel alienated.

4. See paragraphs 14–23. According to Faludi, women have failed to gain equality with men in numerous respects: women's salaries do not match men's; women still tend to fill secretarial and related jobs; women do not enjoy liberal family leave policies; women do not control their reproductive rights; women suffer discrimination in schools; and women continue to do most of the traditional household chores.

5. Faludi sees a cultural backlash against women's liberation. She defines backlash as "an attempt to retract the handful of small and hard-won victories that the feminist movement did manage to win for women."

# The Smurfette Principle (p. 582)

## KATHA POLLITT

In this essay, which first appeared in the "Hers" column of the *New York Times* (April 7, 1991), Katha Pollitt attaches a playful name to a debilitating pattern. "The sexism in preschool culture deforms both boys and girls," she writes, dismayed that twenty-five years of feminist protest have not in the least bit changed the gender content of children's books and programming. You might ask students: if this is so (invite them to make their own surveys), to what extent are the changes wrought by feminism illusory? If the changes are real, why have they not affected preschool culture? Pollitt's essay begins the second part of the chapter, on gender portrayals in the media.

### Review Questions

1. Pollitt playfully borrows the title from the cartoon "Smurfs" to make a serious point about gender role stereotypes on children's television. The "Smurfette" principle is as follows: in hastily made shows as well as in more carefully made ones, the main characters are boys or men, while subordinate characters are girls or women.

2. The gender message underlying the Smurfette principle "is clear," says Pollitt. "Boys are the norm, girls the variation; boys are central, girls peripheral; boys are individuals, girls types. Boys define the group,

its story and its code of values. Girls exist only in relation to boys" (paragraph 4).

3. Pollitt's inventory of *Sesame Street* reveals that although the human cast is gender balanced, most of the muppets, the show's main characters and main interest, are male. *Mr. Roger's Neighborhood* fares no better.

4. Books for children exhibit the same gender stereotyping. Only in a relatively small selection of books for children is the main character a girl. As evidence, Pollitt cites Christmas books honorably mentioned in *Newsweek:* all but two of the fourteen books praised had a boy as a central character.

5. Gender stereotypes "deform" children, says Pollitt. Kids watching television, reading books, seeing movies are fed a steady message that girls, and later women, are subordinate to boys and men. At home, Pollitt and her husband try to counteract these gender images.

# Media Myths and the Reality of Men's Work (p. 585)

## IAN HARRIS

Ian Harris, long active in the men's liberation movement, believes that gender stereotyping has limited men's behavior just as it has women's. Harris effectively uses statistics when comparing the actual number of male white-collar workers with the prevailing image of white-collar success on television. Relatively few men earn enough to achieve white-collar status, yet this status is the only one paraded on television as worth striving for. Harris casts a critical eye. His article is a good candidate for critique and offers students several opportunities to both agree and disagree. For instance, Harris views most labor as alienating; he views most white-collar jobs as stress inducing and dehumanizing. Students may disagree.

### Review Questions

1. Advertisers generally portray the American male as an affluent white-collar worker living in the suburbs. In fact, as of 1981 the vast majority of employed American men (85%) did not work in white-collar occupations. As of 1984, 71% of American men earned less than $25,000 a year—a figure that does not allow the levels of comfort and travel available to the successful male in television advertisements.

2. See paragraph 5. Forty-five percent of employed men work in blue-collar jobs, many of which are "dull, repetitive, and dangerous" and lack opportunities for advancement. These jobs belie the Horatio Alger myth that hard work and a vision of a better life will advance one in life.

3. Harris claims that the white-collar life idealized on television is highly stressful and predisposes men to health problems.

4. The underclass consists principally (70%) of minority males who have been shut out of mainstream economic life. The images of male success advertised on television are even more out of reach for underclass men than for blue-collar men. As a result, many of the underclass resent the entire economic system for exciting their desires but excluding them from any realistic hope of achieving those desires.

5. According to Harris (paragraph 12), the leaders of the men's movement, largely white (and white-collar) males, do not understand the conditions of the unemployed underclass or of blue-collar workers. One reason for this misunderstanding is that the leaders never see representations on television of men significantly different from themselves.

6. Harris says that the media have helped to create the myth of male success and should, therefore, help to promote a solution: namely, to foster an image of men as caring stewards of the planet.

# A Gender Analysis of TV Commercials (p. 589)

## R. STEPHEN CRAIG

Craig's content analysis of television commercials may prove a difficult selection for students, but his analysis is worth the effort, if for no other reason than to demonstrate different methods of proof in different disciplines. Craig reaches much the same conclusion as Pollitt does about gender portrayals. Pollitt's analysis is anecdotal and informal; Craig's is rigorous and highly formal. You might ask students which analysis has more authority—and then use the idea of varying standards of authority as a way of discussing how arguments are conducted in differing academic disciplines.

### Review Questions

1. According to Craig (in his literature review, paragraphs 1–8), earlier content analyses failed to consider stereotyped portrayals of both women *and* men, and failed to consider the ways in which the time a commercial is aired affects the gender portrayals in the commercials. See paragraph 8, especially.

2. Advertisers aim their commercials at particular groupings of people. This is "demographic targeting." The term "day part" is used by the television industry and by advertisers to denote periods of the broadcast day in which the viewing public is "relatively stable demographically." Advertisers target specific commercials to specific populations of viewers. When the "day part" suggests that mostly women homemakers are watch-

ing, advertisers air one type of commercial; when the day part suggests that mostly men are watching, advertisers air another type of commercial.

3. By not telling coders the day part during which commercials were aired, Craig wanted to reduce the possibility of coder bias. Craig did not want a coder's knowledge (say, that the commercial was aired during a football game) to affect the coding of a commercial.

4. In paragraph 36, Craig writes the following: "The results of this study support the hypothesis that television commercials targeted to one sex tend to portray gender differently than ads targeted to the other sex."

5. Because more working women watch television during prime-time hours, advertisers are careful to show women in positions of authority away from the home; men are more frequently shown at home, with family or spouse, in prime time as opposed to weekends, when men are shown in rugged, physically demanding settings away from home. On the weekends, during sports broadcasts, women are portrayed as subservient to men. During daytime commercials, women predominate as homemakers selling food or body products. Men in daytime commercials are shown in stereotypical positions of authority over women. See paragraphs 36–40.

# Homosexuality in the Movies: Beyond Villains and Buffoons (p. 606)

## MATTHEW GILBERT
## VITO RUSSO

This selection consists of two pieces from separate sources: Matthew Gilbert's overview of Hollywood's portrayals of gays and lesbians in the movies, and Vito Russo's analysis of the gay sub-texts in several films. These discussions should establish for students the prevalence of homosexual stereotyping in the film industry. The authors mention many films with a gay or lesbian sub-text, and students might find it illuminating to view the films in light of the ways in which gays and lesbians are stereotyped just as relentlessly as heterosexuals are in commercials (see Stephen Craig) or in children's programming (see Katha Pollitt).

## Review Questions

1. Activists have found the portrayals of three lesbian and bisexual characters in *Basic Instinct* to be offensive and inaccurate. "The characters' villainy largely arises from their sexual orientations," which suggests that homosexuality is a sickness. Beyond protesting the single film, activists were calling attention to historical representations of homosexuals in the

movies. Today, as in the 1930s and earlier, homosexuality continues to be shown as deviant—or not shown at all.

2. Disagreement exists among gay and lesbian communities regarding portrayals of homosexuality on-screen. Some activists insist that movies do a disservice unless gay and lesbian relationships are depicted openly. Other activists see the character of the relationship, regardless of whether it is tacitly or openly homosexual, as the more important consideration.

3. Portrayals of homosexuals on-screen receive close scrutiny because the quantity of such portrayals is so limited. Quality of portrayal, therefore, receives careful attention.

4. Television regularly includes gay and lesbian characters on-screen. Portrayals are more sympathetic and actors and producers are more willing to exert influence to include gay and lesbian elements into the story lines. One reason: so few jobs exist in the film industry that few people are willing to typecast themselves as a "gay actor," which in their view might limit their marketability in future films.

5. Early filmmakers and filmgoers were busy creating an American myth of rugged, manly individualism in which strong male characters subdued a dangerous wilderness. The myth left little room for men as anything other than heroic.

6. In his horror classics *Frankenstein* and *The Bride of Frankenstein,* James Whales uses the monster as a metaphor for the ostracism Whales felt as a homosexual. The "monster" prevents the natural union of Dr. Frankenstein and his wife. The monster believes that he, and those like him, are better off dead.


# The Marlboro Man (p. 622)

## SANDRA CISNEROS

This humorous story is structured as a conversation between two girls who are trying to sort out the Marlboro Man in fact and in myth—and who don't get very far. The conversation might remind some students of Vito Russo's line that "in bed, Clark Gable was no Clark Gable." When real men give physical form to myths of masculinity, the men themselves can hardly live up to the masculine ideal they portray: this contrast, between the masculine ideal and the life of actual men, underlies much of the humor in Cisneros's short story. The exchange between the two girls calls to mind Russo's analysis of *Midnight Cowboy* (see the end of the previous selection): "If there is no real difference between the cowboy hero and the faggot on Forty-second Street, then what remains of American masculinity?" You might put this question to your students.

# 12

## THE BRAVE NEW WORLD OF BIOTECHNOLOGY

At first glance this science-based unit may appear somewhat daunting to non–science-oriented students. But the chapter is focused less on the scientific aspects of genetic engineering (though we do make some attempt to explain the process in the introduction and in the second selection) than on the social and moral dimensions of this new technology. As such, the premise underlying the chapter is a familiar one in our modern age. Our scientific and technological achievements have outstripped our social and moral development. This has been particularly true of weapons development, even prior to the nuclear age—and certainly since Hiroshima. But it is true of other areas, as well. Modern computers make it possible for us to store and retrieve vast quantities of information on everything and everybody. This is just the kind of technology that a police state would find essential. In another area, consider the moral (and legal) dilemmas that have been created by dramatic advances in medical technology. It is now possible to keep some dying patients alive almost indefinitely, as long as they are hooked up to a battery of medical equipment. Does this mean that they *should* be kept alive? The century's two most famous dystopias, *1984* and *Brave New World,* are premised on technological developments: the former on ubiquitous television screens that can transmit as well as receive, making possible total surveillance of the citizenry; the latter on genetic developments that make possible birth without motherhood, and thus, the abolition of the family.

This chapter considers some of the dilemmas created by the new science of biotechnology. We begin with Huxley's *Brave New World* because this novel has come to represent a peculiarly modern nightmare of what happens when we abuse biological technology (indeed, from Shakespeare's time to the present, the title itself has come to indicate an ironic denial of the benefits of modernity). The next selection by Ann C. Vickery offers a somewhat technical discussion of the hows and wherefores of genetic engineering, but one that should not prove overly daunting to students. We chose Dennis Chamberland's "Genetic Engineering: Promise and Threat" to follow because it offers a clear survey of the history and some of the main ethical issues involved in the controversy over genetic engineering. The next two articles on the ethics of genetic engineering were selected to be read against one another: Jeremy Rifkin, the chief critic of genetic engineering experiments, argues against this technology; biologist Stephen Jay Gould responds to Rifkin's arguments. Linda Bullard's feminist critique of genetic engineering should provoke some lively discussions. Next, Beverly Sills Greenough offers a strong defense of gene therapy. The remainder of the chapter moves away from genetic engineering and into the areas of the Human Genome Project and the ethical dilemmas raised by the possible misuse of genetic information. Leon Jaroff ("The Gene Hunt") and James D. Watson ("The Human Genome Project: A Personal View") focus on the Genome Project: the former serving as a relatively neutral secondary source; the latter (by one of the co-discovers of DNA structure and the director of the Genome Project) offering a spirited defense of the project. The final two articles consider two types of problems arising from our expanding genetic knowledge: Robert Wright's "Achilles Helix" considers the possibility of "homemade eugenics"—accepting or rejecting fetuses on the basis of their genetic makeup; Daniel J. Kevles and Leroy Hood, in "The Genetic Labyrinth," explore the prospects of genetic discrimination by employers and insurance companies.

# Brave New World (p. 632)

## ALDOUS HUXLEY

As we've suggested, the very phrase "brave new world" has become a part of the modern vocabulary, connotating an ironic attitude toward the value of supposedly modern improvements over more traditional ways of life. But how valid is Huxley's nightmare vision of the future? On a literal level, there seems little danger of the kind of world Huxley envisions coming to pass in the near future. No one (at least in our own country) is suggesting the mass production of human beings outside of the womb, nor the physical manipulation of human embryos to conform to the requirements of a rigid intellectual caste system. On a less literal level, there is considerably more room for debate as to whether or not we are now living (or are soon about to live) in a brave new world. You might ask your students how society encourages, perhaps even demands, an intellectual caste system. To what extent does society value uniformity, predictability, stability? What other values are sacrificed in the process? You may also wish to tell them something about the rest of the novel, particularly its emphasis on a hedonistic society. To what extent is our own society based on instant gratification? On sexual promiscuity? (Of course, Huxley wrote long before AIDS.) On the need for narcotics to evade unpleasant realities? On the contempt for all things "primitive" and ritualistic?

## Review Questions

1. The Bokanovsky process, by splitting fertilized human ova into up to 96 identical eggs (resulting eventually in identical people) encourages social stability, because it suppresses individuality.
2. After boasting of the great number of adult individuals the London Center had derived from a single egg, Foster remarks somewhat ruefully that "the tropical Centres" had "unfair advantages." "You should see the way a negro ovary responds to a pituitary!" he remarks. "It's quite astonishing when you're used to working with European material." Foster thus perpetuates the racial stereotype that in some respects blacks are physically superior to whites, though, of course, whites do all of the thinking and managing.
3. Alphas, Betas, Deltas, Gammas, and Epsilons, labels for the major castes in the brave new world, are born (or "decanted"), respectively, in increasing numbers, but also, respectively, with declining levels of intelligence. The controllers of brave new world have determined that there must be a limited number of highly intelligent people (Alphas, the administrators and managers) to run society, a somewhat greater number of somewhat less intelligent people (Betas, who are generally technicians), and so on, through relatively large numbers of workers (Deltas and below). Such an organized society assures a high level of social stability and a low level of dissatisfaction, since it is assumed that less intelligent people are more likely to be contented with their relatively menial jobs.
4. Scientists in Huxley's *Brave New World* had still not solved the problem of making humans mature as fast as animals, such as dogs or horses, so that they could do productive work at, say, six years old.

# Gene Science (p.644)

## ANN C. VICKERY

Vickery's article will probably present some comprehension difficulties for students; it is less easy to understand than, say, Jaroff's discussion of the Genome Project later in the chapter. This is due largely to its relatively dry scientific tone, its generally lengthy sentences, and its often unfamiliar vocabulary of genetic terms. (At the same time, most students who need to fulfill their general education requirement in science will be faced with text-books that are frequently more difficult to comprehend than this passage.) Careful reading—and a good desk dictionary—should reveal most of its essential meaning. In any case, it is less important to students to understand every sentence (many of the most important concepts will be discussed in more readable terms later in the chapter) than to understand the general concepts under discussion.

## Review Questions

1. Essentially, the process of genetic recombination involves splicing a section of DNA (cut by means of a *restriction enzyme*) and inserting it into another DNA molecule. The "sticky ends" of the cut DNA adhere to the ends of the cut DNA molecule (frequently a circular molecule called a *plasmid*) into which it is inserted. This hybrid molecule is capable of quick self-replication.
2. According to Vickery, the main areas of research in DNA science are the establishment of genetic databases (not only of humans, but also of plants and animals) and the Human Genome Project, whose goal is to precisely map the estimated three billion base pairs in the 300,000 genes making up human chromosomes. Research is also being conducted into the treatment of genetic diseases in humans, into the improvement of agricultural yields and the genetic alleviation of famine, and into the improvement of certain industrial processes through the genetic engineering of micro-organisms.
3. While both mutations and gene splicing involve genetic changes to organisms, mutation is a natural process that occurs infrequently (often as a result of environmental conditions) and whose evolutionary effects are generally slow. Gene splicing is a process induced in laboratories (see question 1 above), whose evolutionary effects are much more rapid.
4. To avoid unwanted consequences of gene splicing, scientists have developed containment procedures for genetically recombined organisms and have frequently altered their genetic structure so that they cannot survive outside the laboratory.

# Genetic Engineering: Promise and Threat (p. 652)

## DENNIS CHAMBERLAND

Chamberland's article provides an excellent survey of genetic engineering: its origins, its achievements, its prospects, its dangers. As such, it provides a good introduction to the articles that follow. Some of the topics simply raised by Chamberland here (such as patenting genetically engineered organisms, or genetically screening employees) are treated in greater detail elsewhere in the chapter. Since this article was first published in *Christianity Today,* its perspective is generally religious, but it is neither dogmatic nor sectarian in tone. The reservations expressed about genetic engineering are, in fact, the same reservations as might arise in any ethically focused discussion of the subject. As Chamberland observes (in paragraph 52), "The abuse of genetic engineering will come from two familiar directions: (1) ill-defined or nonexistent norms of acceptable social direction and (2) disguised social principles of accomplishing one goal by way of another."

## Review Questions

1. James Watson (an American) and Francis Crick (a Briton) were the first to discover the structure of the DNA molecule, the basic building block of all life and the means by which hereditary information is passed from one generation to another. They first published the results of their studies in 1953. For their achievement—the basis of all subsequent work in genetic engineering—they were awarded the Nobel Prize.

2. *E. Coli* is a single cell bacterium. Its biological simplicity (as opposed to the complexity of a human cell) assured that experiments were able to study the effects of mutating and recombining (splicing) its genetic material.

3. Soon after their formation, genetic engineering companies were able to produce—for a fraction of their former cost—*interferon,* a cancer-fighting agent; *human growth hormone,* to correct pituitary deficiencies; and *human insulin,* to treat diabetes. Scientists envisage using recombinant DNA technology to treat thousands of other genetic disorders. In addition to such medical applications, genetic engineering can be (or will be) used to improve agricultural yields, to fight oil spills, to retard aging, and even to reconstruct species on the verge of extinction.

4. Possible abuses of genetic engineering: creating new agents of biological warfare, using genetic screening as part of the employment application process, engineering "perfect" human beings (somewhat like the Central London Hatchery in *Brave New World*), and cloning human beings.

5. Chamberland sees the threat in genetic engineering less in the technology itself than in the principles by which it is applied. Just as nuclear technology can be used to improve life or to destroy it, genetic engineering holds both promise and threat. Chamberland acknowledges the complexity of the moral issues involved, argues against simplistic solutions "that try to capture vague fears," and maintains that Christians (among others) should try to exert influence by emphasizing values, as well as technology.

# A Heretic's View on the New Bioethics (p. 662)

JEREMY RIFKIN

This selection is a combination of two separate sources: a portion of Rifkin's book, *Algeny,* and an interview with Rifkin by a *Science Digest* writer. To many scientists, Rifkin must seem like a crazy man—someone who, in effect, wanders wild-eyed through the streets carrying a sign warning of the world's approaching end. Actually, as these selections show, Rifkin is quite articulate and rational. The gap between the myth and the man is amusingly crystallized in the first sentence of "Jeremy Rifkin Just Says No," a *New York Times Magazine* article by Edward Tivnan (16 Oct. 1988): "Giant Killer Tomatoes . . . With a frustrated shake of his head, Jeremy Rifkin says the three words most likely to find a place in his obituary; then he laughs and proceeds to polish off a dish of apple pie and ice cream."

Actually, Rifkin's objections to genetic engineering may sound a familiar note to anyone who has studied the attacks on science and technology from the time (perhaps around the time of Copernicus and Galileo) when they began to threaten the established order—or the way that people viewed the established order. This is not to argue that Rifkin is merely a hidebound conservative, afraid of innovation because it threatens his own worldview. Indeed, the kinds of general reservations he expresses (as opposed to the specific analogies he draws between genetic engineering and the Nazis' eugenics programs) are not unlike the reservations expressed by satirists like Huxley in *Brave New World.* Rifkin sees a brave new world, indeed, and he doesn't like it. Such skepticism is deeply permeated into our arts and popular culture. In the nineteenth century it was expressed by (among others) Mary Shelley (in *Frankenstein*), Whitman ("The Learned Astronomer"), and Hawthorne ("The Birthmark"). And the theme of more than a few science-fiction films of the 1950s was that science was interfering with the natural order of things or creating more problems than it solved ("Them," "The Beast from 20,000 Fathoms," "The Day the Earth Stood Still"). Still, it is one thing to sincerely express skepticism; it is another to become a "Luddite" (as Rifkin's critics have charged) and to try to smash the machinery—or in Rifkin's case, to try to legally block certain types of genetic experimentation. Rifkin would probably be considerably less controversial had he confined his objections to his writings and his speeches and not taken up an activist role. Nonetheless, it may be possible to dispassionately study his ideas, as expressed in the two passages that make up this selection, and to draw some conclusions about both the validity and the value of his ideas on genetic engineering—and how genetic engineering exemplifies the problems with modern science and technology.

## Review Questions

1. By "desacralization" of life or of nature, Rifkin means that modern scientists, and particularly bio-engineers, no longer consider living organisms as discrete structural or biological entities (dog, human, etc.), but rather as patterns of information—represented by their distinctive genetic codes—that can be manipulated at will by genetic engineers. According to Rifkin, Darwin began this process of desacralization by postulating Nature as "an aggregate of standardized, interchangeable parts assembled into various functional combinations."

2. Eugenics is concerned (in its negative form) with the elimination of unfavorable physical and mental characteristics and (in its positive form) with the preservation or reinforcement of favorable characteristics. In the 1920s certain U.S. immigration laws were designed with eugenic purposes in mind. Far more catastrophic was the infamous Nazi eugenics program which resulted not only in the selective breeding of superior Aryan specimens, but also in the extermination of millions of "inferior" people. Since genetic engineering involves the manipulation of genetic strings in organisms in order to eliminate undesirable characteristics and to create or reinforce favorable characteristics, it carries about it an aura of eugenics. But while the old eugenics was grounded in social doctrine and ideology, the new eugenics is grounded in economic and utilitarian considerations.

3. Rifkin is opposed to the kind of scientific application—technology—that seeks to change or control nature through the use of "inordinate power." He believes, for instance, of nuclear power, as of genetic engineering, that the "inherent power of the technology was so inordinate that its mere use—regardless of the intentions of those using it—was irresponsible." Rifkin is not opposed to scientific research that seeks an empathetic understanding of the environment.

# On the Origin of Specious Critics (p. 675)

## STEPHEN JAY GOULD

Gould's withering attack on Rifkin may at first strike students as a somewhat arcane disagreement between two scientists on such musty matters as Darwinian theory. They should be reminded, first, that Rifkin is not a scientist—though Gould does not attack him so much for his lack of scientific credentials as for what he considers Rifkin's "shoddy" and "anti-intellectual arguments masquerading as scholarship." Second, they should understand that the significance of the debate is broader than a simple disagreement between two individuals on the interpretation of particular texts. The disagreement is symptomatic of the dichotomy between those who are suspicious about science and technology, considering them as fundamentally antihumanistic enterprises (frequently placed in the service of an oppressive state), and those who defend these endeavors as promising humankind a healthier and happier future. Gould also attacks Rifkin for what he perceives as his misunderstanding of science and scientific procedure, as well as for his faulty argumentation. However, it is just as unlikely that Rifkin would be converted by Gould's arguments as that Gould would be persuaded by Rifkin's. Students may enjoy deciding who comes off better in the debate—and explaining why.

## Review Questions

1. Gould offers his overall critical reaction to *Algeny* in paragraph 4 of his article.
2. Gould maintains that in *Algeny* Rifkin: (1) misunderstands Darwin's theories; (2) misunderstands the norms and procedures of science; (3) does not respect the procedures of fair argument; (4) ignores several basic procedures of scholarship; and (5) commits many factual errors.
3. Gould agrees with Rifkin's argument that the integrity of the species should be respected; but he rejects Rifkin's contention that most other biological scientists feel otherwise, and he also rejects Rifkin's contention that we should halt experiments and applications in genetic engineering because one day someone may abuse the technology.

# Killing Us Softly: Toward a Feminist Analysis of Genetic Engineering (p. 685)

## LINDA BULLARD

This article should be provocative for students who may have problems viewing genetic engineering as a particularly feminist issue. Clearly, feminists should have an interest in the new reproductive technologies; but as for human health products, agriculture, and so on, why is a feminist analysis relevant? To accept the premises of the article, students need to at least understand, if not agree with the assessment, that genetic engineering (and perhaps science, in general) can be viewed as a patriarchal endeavor—related, let's say, to the kind of social order in which women have historically been prevented from enjoying the same rights as men. This article should generate heated debate on both sides and, perhaps, a heightened understanding of both feminism and the implications of genetic engineering.

## Review Questions

1. Bullard discusses recent developments in genetic engineering in the areas of reproductive technology, health-related products, animal husbandry, agriculture, information technology, environmental engineering, and biological warfare.

2. Genetic engineering might be perceived as a safer way of dealing with the environment than toxic pesticides and as a benign way of increasing agricultural yields through "organic" methods. Thus, the products of biotechnology may have eliminated the kind of objections that feminists and environmentalists had to chemicals. But Bullard and others have strong objections to genetic engineering on other grounds.

3. Bullard considers genetic engineering reflective of the "old patriarchal fears [of female power to create life] and dreams [of destroying life]." More specifically, she believes that genetic engineering will result in "erosion of the genetic diversity of the planet, further concentration of power and capital, wiping out the small farmer, reinforcing the dependency of Third World countries, and contamination of the environment . . ." (paragraph 19).

# Why I Support Gene Therapy (p. 692)

## BEVERLY SILLS GREENOUGH

Beverly Sills Greenough is, of course, most well known as an opera singer, and so some might question her credentials and credibility as an advocate of gene therapy. But as she points out, both her role as national chair of the March of Dimes Birth Defects Foundation and as the mother of disabled children give her a claim on public attention.

## Review Questions

1. Greenough explains how doctors remove defective cells (i.e., those missing a particular gene) from the body, restore the missing gene, and reintroduce the cells into the body, where they reproduce, enabling the body to restore some measure of immunity. She cites the example of the girl with an immune system so disabled that until being treated with gene therapy, she had to live in virtual isolation, a prisoner in her own home.

2. Greenough acknowledges that the public often fears new therapies (she cites the anxieties generated by the polio vaccine) and gene therapies in particular (the creation of "super" humans, invasion of privacy). But she contends that such fears are based largely on ignorance and that "we *cannot* let our fears destroy our hopes." The benefits of gene therapy, she contends, far outweigh the dangers.

# The Gene Hunt (p. 695)

## LEON JAROFF

This article offers a readable and informative survey of the Human Genome Project. It is largely positive (reservations about the Human Genome Project and our increased knowledge of genes are more fully explored in the subsequent articles by Wright and Kevles and Hood), although it is less potentially self-serving than the following article by Human Genome Project Director James Watson. Students may have some difficulty following the technical discussion in paragraphs 17ff and in the diagram; but on the whole, Jaroff does a good job rendering the scientific complexities of the Human Genome Project accessible to the intelligent lay reader. (The article originally appeared in a mass circulation newsmagazine.) And most students taking required or elective science courses will be well aware that this article is considerably easier to follow than their standard reading in those courses; some science majors may even find it simplistic!

## Review Questions

1. Supporters of the Human Genome Project believe that it will lead to a better understanding of inherited diseases, such as cystic fibrosis, and new techniques to treat or prevent such diseases, either indirectly by the creation and application of new drugs or directly by means of gene therapy (i.e., altering particular genes).
2. A genetic marker is a "signpost" on a chromosome that indicates the proximity (though not the exact location) of a particular gene. Specifically, markers are differences in the genetic sequences in the corresponding sections of a pair of chromosomes. These differences originate when genetic material in a matching pair of chromosomes is exchanged just before the chromosomes separate to form sex (sperm or egg) cells. If the trait—one that leads to a disease or disorder—determined by the newly constituted chromosome is transmitted through succeeding generations, then the existence of this particular marker indicates that the gene determining the trait is nearby.
3. Scientists attempting to map the human genome face numerous difficulties: (1) the sheer number of genes (about 100,000) in the genome and in the number of code letters (between 10,000 and 150,000 in each gene); (2) the fact that many of the code letters seem to be nothing but nonfunctional "genetic gibberish"; (3) the difficulty of learning the nature of the machinery by which genetic information is sequenced; (4) the difficulty of determining which genes belong to which chromosomes; (5) the difficulty of finding the precise location of particular genes on the chromosome; (6) once a gene has been located, the tedious work involved in

determining the sequence of base pairs (i.e., pairs of A-T and C-G) in the DNA chain (automation has helped here).

4. Mendel was an Austrian monk whose experiments in cross-breeding in the mid-nineteenth century led him to formulate the first scientifically sound theory of heredity. Mendel did not actually discover or name genes, but he correctly identified their function.

5. Once the genetic basis of a disease or genetic disorder is determined, scientists argue, then people susceptible to the disease could adopt a lifestyle that could minimize the effects of the disease or disorder. This might involve adjustments in diet or environment or it could involve taking drugs (or some combination).

# The Human Genome Project: A Personal View (p. 708)

## JAMES D. WATSON

As co-discoverer of the double-helix structure of the DNA molecule, and as Director of the Human Genome Project, James D. Watson carries considerable credibility. Still, our response to his "personal view" and of his defense of the project depends less on his scientific expertise than on our agreement with his priorities. One of Watson's first tasks is to defend the huge appropriations of money for the genome project (money that is not going to other projects). Scientists working on AIDS-related research have faced similar criticism: that the publicity over AIDS has influenced politicians to spend so much money on finding a cure for AIDS that research on other diseases, such as cancer and heart disease, is now underfunded. Watson next discusses his priorities for the genome project during its first five years. Most laypersons will find themselves unqualified to assess these priorities but may be interested in the scientific problems he describes. Finally, Watson turns to the ethical problems of DNA research, a discussion that will serve as an introduction to some of the matters discussed more fully later in the chapter.

## Review Questions

1. According to Watson, some scientific researchers oppose the Human Genome Project because they fear it will divert funding from their own areas of (non-genetic) research. Thus, they are competing with genetic researchers for the same limited appropriations.

2. Watson believes that many diseases, including cancer, Alzheimer's disease, and schizophrenia, are genetic in origin, and that we cannot find

effective cures for such diseases unless we better understand the human gene—primarily through the Human Genome Project. As he writes, "Ignoring genes is like trying to solve a murder without finding the murderer."

3. The overall objective of the Human Genome Project, according to Watson, is to "learn the nucleotide sequence of human DNA." In the first five years of the project, he identifies three subsidiary goals: (1) to get good genetic maps, identifying key genetic markers, if not the genes themselves; (2) to set up a bank of overlapping fragments of DNA, so that researchers can draw on this bank and identify particular genetic sequences; and (3) to support scientists who are working on efficient and relatively inexpensive techniques of "megabase sequencing."

4. Watson concedes that DNA research is fraught with ethical dilemmas. It is important that people know if they or their babies have genetic problems; but it is also vital that people be protected from genetic discrimination. He thinks that genetic "fingerprinting" techniques should be useful to law enforcement agencies, but he is concerned that such techniques not be used for frivolous purposes (like identifying potential bedwetters to hotelkeepers).

# Achilles Helix (p. 717)

## ROBERT WRIGHT

This article raises disturbing ethical dilemmas. The underlying question is a central one in our technological age: now that we have this new capability, this new knowledge, what do we do with it? More specifically, now that we are able to detect genetic defects before birth, what—if anything—do we do when we discover them? Wright appears to be opposed to parents making use of such knowledge, and this may be most students' first inclination, also. But you may want to ask them if their opposition would hold up were they prospective parents actually faced with the kind of choices available to the parents described in paragraph 8. To what extent, if at all, do they think legal restrictions should be placed on the way that we make use of the new biotechnology in decisions about human birth? And where do we draw the line?

## Review Questions

1. Wright is primarily concerned with two questions: (1) Will science be able to locate genes that correlate to specific pathologies and behavioral traits? (2) Will parents make use of such information in deciding whether

or not to have offspring with certain characteristics? (The answer to both questions, according to Wright, is "probably.")

2. If people have advance knowledge of adverse health conditions in themselves or in their unborn children, and if insurance companies also have access to this information (whether or not people supply it voluntarily), then these companies are unlikely to provide insurance at reasonable prices. Thus, financial pressure exerted by insurance companies (or even a government-run insurance program) could lead to a de facto eugenics program: i.e., a program that encourages the breeding of "normal" babies and discourages the breeding and birth of "abnormal" babies.

3. To demonstrate that many parents are capable of practicing eugenics on their unborn children, Wright points to the intense competitiveness of American parents about their kids in everything from private schools to SATs to Little League games. Parents are so anxious for their kids to do well, he suggests, that they will do almost anything to assure success. If this means selecting one "pre-embryo" in preference to others, they will do it.

4. In the final paragraph Wright discusses the possibility of genetically engineering germ or sex cells. Previously, he has discussed only the possibility of selecting or altering the behavioral characteristics of a single organism. But altering the sex cells would represent a quantum eugenics leap: it would affect not only that organism, but all the offspring of that organism and all subsequent generations.

# The Genetic Labyrinth (p. 724)

DANIEL J. KEVLES
LEROY HOOD

In a survey article Kevles and Hood describe the purpose of the Human Genome Project and go on to discuss some of its implications. They focus on the issues of eugenics and the use of genetic information by insurers and employers. Less polemical than Rifkin's article, this piece should provoke students into a discussion of both the promising possibilities and the dangers of our increasing genetic knowledge. In particular, you may want to ask students what is *wrong* with wanting to have a baby with as many desirable and as few undesirable qualities as possible?

## Review Questions

1. The purpose of the Human Genome Project is to map the complete genetic information contained in the nucleus of almost every human cell.

Each nucleus contain twenty-three pairs of chromosomes, in which are distributed thousands of genes—strands of DNA. Connecting the sides of the double helix of each strand of DNA are nucleotides. Scientists working on the project are attempting to determine first, which chromosomes hold which genes, and then, the sequence of nucleotides on each chromosome. They hope to complete the work by the year 2005.

2. Positive eugenics aims to increase the (supposedly) desirable qualities of human beings. Negative eugenics aims to reduce or eliminate the (supposedly) undesirable qualities—sometimes by eliminating "undesirable" human beings. Past attempts at eugenics—most notably the Nazis' efforts to breed a "superior" race and to eliminate "inferior" races, such as Jews—have cast disrepute upon eugenics and have made it impossible for democracies to implement such policies. Some fear that once the human genome has been mapped through the Human Genome Project, the knowledge gained may be used for eugenics programs and policies.

3. The knowledge gained from mapping the human genome will provide parents with the knowledge that a fetus may have one or more "undesirable" characteristics (cystic fibrosis, for example, or other diseases). Armed with such knowledge, the parents may decide to abort the fetus.

4. Genetic discrimination is the use of genetic information by insurers to deny insurance or by employers to deny employment to those they have determined to be poor risks for insurance or employment.

5. Behavioral genetics is the attempt to link particular behavior (for example, shyness, criminality, alcoholism) with particular genes. At present there is little hard evidence to support such links, which often reflect social prejudices rather than hard scientific evidence. This fact has not prevented some scientists from prematurely announcing preliminary findings of linkages between genes and behavior—findings that have been reported by the press as definitive conclusions.

# 13

# BUSINESS ETHICS

Aside from being an occasion for student writing, this chapter seeks to introduce freshmen to the subject of ethics and to business ethics in particular; to offer models for making ethical decisions; to provide cases upon which students can test those models; and to raise difficult, debatable questions about values in business life and the extent to which these differ from values in personal and family life. The reading selections in the chapter were chosen to match these pedagogical aims. Richard De George and Gerald Cavanagh introduce students to the subject of ethics and business ethics. Cavanagh provides methods of analysis for puzzling through difficult ethical decisions, models that can then be applied to several cases in the chapter, including a scene from Sinclair Lewis's *Babbitt*. Students will likely debate points throughout the chapter, especially when discussing the cases. The possibilities of debate will be heightened when students read Carr's "Is Business Bluffing Ethical?" Here, Carr maintains that a separate code of ethics applies to business, a code that is dirtier than the one governing personal relations. Students will want to read the critique of his argument quoted in Discussion and Writing Suggestion #6, following the article itself.

Soon enough, many students will find themselves in the working world, and it is all but inevitable that at some point they'll encounter situations where they are asked (or are required) to behave one way when conscience dictates that they behave another. Many students, working their way through school, have already encountered such predicaments, and for these young men and women the cases and models for analysis offered here will be pertinent, indeed. The largest goal of the unit is to inform students that strategies exist for making difficult ethical decisions. Students need not rely on instincts alone in ethically troubling circumstances; indeed, they *should* not, according to several writers in this chapter who believe that *analyses* must be brought to bear so that one can explain the reasons for choosing one course of action over another.

# The Case of the Collapsed Mine (p. 740)

## RICHARD T. DE GEORGE

In this hypothetical case of a mining accident, with a style of posing questions but providing no answers, Richard T. De George does an admirable job of surveying the territory of business ethics. Those who read this piece will know something of the variety of issues important to the business ethicist—and to any business person committed to making "right" decisions. No student who reads the case can fail to be impressed with how one who is sensitive to ethical concerns can draw out ambiguities—can see many problems where, to the uninitiated, there are few. Students may be overwhelmed by De George's success at problematizing the case of the collapsed mine; if so, ask them to choose a single one of his categories of questioning and to reflect on that. You might also tell students that in a later reading, Gerald Cavanagh offers a model for answering many of the questions that De George raises.

# The Generation Gap in Business Ethics (p. 745)

## JUSTIN G. LONGENECKER
## JOSEPH A. MCKINNEY
## CARLOS W. MOORE

Here is a study that lays the questions of ethics squarely in the lap of students. The findings are unambiguous: the younger a person in the business world, the less ethically rigorous is that person. Students should find much to discuss here. Perhaps they will feel their characters have been impugned. Righteous rejection of the findings, by at least some members of the class, will ensure hearty debate. Once the first wave of response has passed, try getting students to ferret out the value system underlying the study. The authors are certainly *not* moral relativists. They have clear views concerning acceptable behavior, and many people would endorse their ethical standards. We do. Nonetheless, they have engineered a study and written an article that implies a certain set of beliefs, which students should understand. To begin this part of the inquiry, you might point the class to paragraphs 12 and 22. You might help define for students the concept of *ethical relativism*. On this point, see the selection by Gertrude Himmelfarb, "A Demoralized Society?" (pages 439–44). Also, you might want to investigate with students the following issue: the authors assume that young people in business are less ethical than older people. The authors do not consider that as young people age, they may as a natural part of the maturation process become more ethical. Does ethical awareness increase in the process of aging?

For those students who thrive on the philosophical, you might suggest Philip Meyer's critique of Stanley Milgram's research (pages 349–52, especially paragraphs 6 and 7). The present Generation Gap study suggests that the situation ethics of young people in business leads to an alarming ethical permissiveness. Meyer points out some clear advantages to situation, as opposed to code (or rigid), ethics. Students may want to investigate the issue.

## Review Questions

1. The authors mailed questionnaires to 10,000 possible respondents and received 2,165 usable responses. Each respondent rated on a scale of 1 to 7, from "never acceptable" to "always acceptable", a series of ethically questionable behaviors. The authors grouped respondents according to age and then compared the ratings of different age groups.

2. The authors found that the older the respondent to the questionnaire, the more ethically demanding was that person's judgment. That is, older respondents more frequently had answers closer to the "never acceptable" end of the scale. The authors conclude: "Younger managers and professionals are indeed more permissive in what they view as ethical behavior."

3. See paragraphs 16–20. For (at least) twenty-five years, the American Council on Education and UCLA have conducted annual studies of college freshmen to determine their attitudes on a variety of issues. The Gallup organization has conducted surveys of the general population. Analysis of results over the years shows that young people are becoming more material in their outlook, interested in money more than in a "meaningful philosophy of life." Young people today differ in their attitudes both with respect to older people today and to young people ten and twenty years ago. Based on these general surveys, the authors conclude that their results are consistent with trends noted elsewhere.

4. In these times, corporations are expected to hold high ethical standards. The findings of this survey indicate that younger employees of an organization may not endorse the same standards as managers or senior executives. Such differences can create tension within an organization and may lead to violations of corporate—or legal—codes. These differences therefore must be addressed—both to avoid immediate lapses and to ensure that future leaders (who are now the younger and more ethically permissive members of the organization) will set the highest ethical standards for their organizations when they assume positions of influence.

# Is Business Bluffing Ethical? (p. 755)

## ALBERT CARR

Albert Carr's article in the *Harvard Business Review* (HBR) caused an immediate firestorm of reaction. Carr's thesis is that different standards of morality apply to the world of commerce than they do to one's private world of family and social relations. Some students may vigorously denounce Carr's philosophy as cynical, others may accept Carr's thesis grudgingly and wish the world were otherwise. As with the three cases for discussion, the issues here are highly charged, and students should be encouraged to respond with an *analysis* based either on the models offered by Cavanagh or on other criteria that students clearly define. (Note: In Discussion and Writing Suggestion #6, students will find a critique of the key assumption in Carr's argument.)

### Review Question

1. Unlike other authors, Carr makes a distinction between standards of business ethics and standards of personal or religious ethics. Carr describes a situation in which personal or religious ethics has no place in business, which is governed by a "game ethics" similar to that of poker. If businessmen or women want to survive in the world of business, they had better become adept at the "game."

2. In comparing business ethics to the ethics of poker, Carr notes several similarities, such as the "element of chance," the importance of "steady skill," and knowledge of both the rules and the opponent's strengths and weaknesses. He goes on to assert that no one expects the poker player to be motivated by personal or religious morals. The skillful player is expected to bluff and, most importantly, to win. In poker, the unfair player is the one who, "while abiding by the letter of the rules, finds ways to put other players at an unfair disadvantage." Unlike personal ethics, the ethics of poker calls for distrust, ignores friendships, and encourages deception.

3. According to Carr, strategy and ethics are sometimes confused because "non-players" assume that business ethics are synonymous with personal ethics. The confusion is compounded when a "player" does act in a moral way. The public assumes the player acted out of ethical responsibility when in fact he or she was simply using a business strategy.

4. In addition to the psychological strain that results when personal ethics collide with business ethics, the individual may suffer criticism from "non-players" such as family members or friends who are unaware of the distinctions between personal and business ethics. Conversely, the player who chooses the "moral route" risks being labeled by associates as an "oddball or radical."

# Ethics in Business (p. 769)

## GERALD F. CAVANAGH

Cavanagh provides an important overview of business ethics. He justifies the need for corporate ethics, reviews ethical theories (thereby setting the discussion of business ethics in a broader philosophical context), and then offers a model for making ethical decisions in business. This model (in the form of a flow chart) can be used by students in thinking about the several case studies in the chapter. Students may find it difficult to keep the defining strands of the ethical theories separate. Cavanagh conveniently provides two tables to help students with the definitions. Students should be urged to read and use the tables, not to memorize definitions.

### Review Questions

1. "Each manager [must] possess a set of internalized and operative ethical criteria for decision making" because the alternative is an unacceptable level of government intervention to maintain an orderly and well-functioning world of business. Aside from adversely affecting efficiency and productivity, excessive government intervention would foster an atmosphere where "any transaction that was not witnessed and recorded could not be trusted." According to Cavanagh, maintaining an ethical society is the best way to ensure a free society.
2. The utilitarian theory of ethics, first proposed by economist Adam Smith, defines a moral act as that which benefits the greatest number of people. Conversely, the rights theory places highest value on the individual's personal and property rights. The justice theory of ethics stresses that any act or policy should be democratic and equitable to the interests of all persons, including minorities.
3. Cavanagh defines overwhelming factors as "data from the situation which may in a given case justify overriding one of the three ethical criteria: utility, rights, or justice." In other words, there will be times when the criteria cannot be easily applied to a situation because of extenuating circumstances. Two examples are offered in the reading: "incapacitating factors" that "coerce" individuals to behave in a manner they ordinarily wouldn't; and "incomplete information" that prevents individuals from making ethical decisions.
4. A third overwhelming factor is the "principle of double effect," which comes into play when an "act has both a good and a bad effect." In deciding whether or not to go forward with the act, a person should pose three questions: First, is the act intended to result in a bad effect? Second, is the bad effect intended as a means to a good end? Third, does the good end sufficiently justify the bad effect?

# Cases for Analysis and Discussion (p. 787)

The three cases for analysis and discussion offer students an opportunity to analyze and take a stand on one hypothetical and two actual situations in which individuals are compelled to act in ways that compromise them ethically. You might point out to students that these cases lend themselves to rich and complex investigations, provided students are alert to ethical concerns. (Recall how De George was able to draw out dozens of questions from the case of the collapsed mine.) Students should remain open to ambiguity here. They should base responses to the cases on *explicit* criteria, or guiding questions, such as the ones offered by Cavanagh.

# Peter Green's First Day (p. 788)

## Review Questions

1. John Murphy, an old hand in the carpet business, thought Peter Green was a greenhorn. Fresh out of college, the young man's only "experience" as a salesman was through the company's five-month training program—something that did not substitute for on-the-job experience, as far as Murphy was concerned.
2. "Freight costs" were intended to reimburse the purchaser for shipping defective carpets back to the mill. The carpets (which in this and similar cases were *not* defective) were not actually shipped back to the mill; but "freight costs" were issued as a credit against future purchases. Thus, "freight costs" actually were a 10–25% discount on large purchases. Green thought the long-established practice unethical because both he (the salesman) and the purchaser were, in effect, lying to the manufacturer that the carpets were defective.

# Matt Goldspan's Trilogy (p. 791)

JAY A. HALFOND[1]

"Matt Goldspan's Trilogy" consists of three discrete cases—all involving one manager. By sharing one company context, students not only can relate

[1]The introduction to this entry in the Instructor's Manual, as well as all answers to the Review Questions, are taken directly from Jay Halfond's "Teaching Notes" for this case. Phrasings have been altered to fit the format of *Writing and Reading Across the Curriculum*.

details and characteristics from one case to another, but might in fact find interrelationships in their analysis of the issues.

These cases can be used in a business ethics class, or, even more preferably, in a course on human resource management. Each case could occupy an hour of class discussion, perhaps coupled with appropriate readings and lectures on comparable worth, affirmative action, preferential hiring, employee theft, and nepotism. Alternatively, the instructor could integrate all three cases, over a two-hour class, to focus on the ethical issues that managers can face in the course of supervising others.

Often, cases written for ethics discussion deal with lofty issues that might be remote from the world most college graduates can expect. In addition, as allegories or examples of the consequences of top-level corporate behavior, they often lack a particular empathetic managerial focus or issue to address. This trilogy attempts to address these deficiencies by providing a realistic, almost mundane set of dilemmas that one, very well-meaning manager must face.

## Review Questions

*Salary Inequities*
1. Matt's immediate dilemma is whether to respond negatively to the *idea* of the study or to address the content of Denise Contra's analysis.
2. Matt's interpersonal problem is how to deal with Denise. His possible problem with the system in which he works is whether or not salary inequities exist.

*Affirmative Action*
3. Matt acted prematurely and precipitously by offering a key position in his office before he had the approval of corporate headquarters.
4. His overt motive was to remedy a critical problem. His more subtle objective may have been to circumvent what he perceived to be the needless and offensive interference of the corporate office.

*Employment Theft*
5. The son of a valued employee, who works temporarily in the office, purchased personal goods at company expense. Normally, we are told, such behavior leads to termination. In fact, other employees expect that consequence. However, Matt is presented with another *fait accompli:* the employee's mother-supervisor has decided on her own, more forgiving reply. Jason will be punished privately as her son, and not as an employee.
6. Matt's political dilemma is to satisfy both Harriet, who expects that the matter has been settled (privately), and the other employees, who expect that Jason be fired. Matt's ethical dilemma is to decide what is fairest for

all concerned. Whose interests and needs are paramount in this decision? Has Harriet sufficiently levied "justice"?

# Why Should My Conscience Bother Me? (p. 796)

## KERMIT VANDIVIER

### Review Questions

1. After a number of test failures, Lawson realized that the four-disk brakes did not have enough surface area to stop the aircraft without generating enough heat to destroy the brake linings.
2. Warren refused to consider redesigning the brakes because he was a proud and arrogant man who could not admit that he had made a mistake, especially one so crucial as this. Robert Sink, the projects manager who supervised the engineers, was reluctant to support Lawson over Warren because the latter's failure would reflect badly on his own judgment. And since Sink lacked training as an engineer, he could not rely on his own technical assessment. Finally, Sink had already assured the contractor, LTV, that the brakes were proceeding satisfactorily and on schedule.
3. Gretzinger was determined to tell management that he would have no part in falsifying test data; but after a session with Russell Line, manager of the Goodrich Technical Services division, he was browbeaten into changing his mind. Vandivier initially felt the same way as Gretzinger, but then he considered that if he refused to go along, he would either have to resign or be fired. At forty-two, with a good job, a new home, and a wife and seven children to support, he felt that he could not afford to do the ethical thing.
4. Vandivier has been reluctantly willing to falsify test data as long as the deception was confined to paper. As Gretzinger remarked, "We're just drawing some curves, and what happens to them after they leave here, well, we're not responsible for that." But after a few near plane crashes during the Air Force flight tests, Vandivier realized that he could be held legally responsible for the falsifications. And, in fact, his lawyer told him that he was "certainly part of a conspiracy to defraud."

# Babbitt (p. 806)

## SINCLAIR LEWIS

Sinclair Lewis's story of George Babbitt appears as the final "case" in this chapter—but, as a work of literature, it is more. Because of Lewis's talents, readers gain access to the motivations of characters in ways not possible in the other cases. Motivations here are complex: actions follow from motivations, and descriptions of actors are piquant and memorable. As with the other cases, student reactions can be expected to split—in this instance on the question of whether or not Babbitt has done anything wrong by "buying low and selling high." Students will likely debate differences between what is legal and what is right. As with their responses to other cases in the chapter, students should be encouraged to be analytical here. If Babbitt is justified in conducting the real estate transaction as he does, *why* is he justified? If he is wrong, students should be able to offer their reasons—once again drawing on Cavanagh's model or on Carr's logic to do so.